Disorders of Childhood: Development and Psychopathology

Disorders of Childhood: Development and Psychopathology

Robin Hornik Parritz
Hamline University

Michael F. Troy
Children's Hospitals and Clinics of Minnesota

WADSWORTH
CENGAGE Learning™

Australia • Brazil • Japan • Korea • Mexico • Singapore • Spain • United Kingdom • United States

Library of Congress Control Number: 2009930586

ISBN-13: 978-0-534-59274-5

ISBN-10: 0-534-59274-0

Wadsworth
20 Davis Drive
Belmont, CA 94002-3098
USA

Cengage Learning is a leading provider of customized learning solutions with office locations around the globe, including Singapore, the United Kingdom, Australia, Mexico, Brazil, and Japan. Locate your local office at **www.cengage.com/global.**

Cengage Learning products are represented in Canada by Nelson Education, Ltd.

To learn more about Wadsworth, visit **www.cengage.com/wadsworth**

Purchase any of our products at your local college store or at our preferred online store **www.ichapters.com**.

Printed in Canada
1 2 3 4 5 6 7 13 12 11 10 09

Dedication

Robin dedicates this book to her parents, Linda and Peter Hornik, who sent her into the world thinking that she could do anything. Thank you for a lifetime of love and support.

Mike dedicates this book to the memory of his parents, Carmen and Bill Troy, who taught him the fundamental lesson that a parent's love is the bedrock of development.

Brief Contents

Detailed Contents

About the Authors

Robin Hornik Parritz, PhD, is a Professor of Psychology at Hamline University in St. Paul, Minnesota. Robin received her undergraduate degree in psychology from Brandeis University in 1983, and her PhD in Clinical Psychology from the University of Minnesota in 1989. Her research and clinical areas of interest include emotional development, developmental psychopathology, and programs designed to increase knowledge and decrease stigma related to children's psychological disorders. Robin teaches Disorders of Childhood, Abnormal Psychology, Theories of Psychotherapy, Psychology of Emotion, Positive Psychology, and Clinical Psychology. Robin is married to Jon Parritz and has three sons, Ari, Adam, and Jesse.

Michael Troy, PhD, is a clinical psychologist and Manager of Behavioral Health Services at Children's Hospitals and Clinics of Minnesota. Michael received his undergraduate degree from Lawrence University in Appleton, Wisconsin, and his PhD in Clinical Psychology from the University of Minnesota in 1988. He completed his internship and fellowship at Hennepin County Medical Center in Minneapolis and has been on staff at Children's of Minnesota since 1988. He has also been an instructor in the psychology departments of the University of Minnesota and Hamline University, and is the past president of Minnesota Child Psychologists. Michael is married to Cynthia Koehler Troy and has two sons, Kevin and Brendan.

Preface

Writing a textbook on the psychological disorders of infants, children, and adolescents involves multiple decisions about content, emphasis, and organization. These decisions reinforce and extend the knowledge base of the field and determine what is distinctive about the authors' approach. The decisions we made while writing this book were influenced by our academic and clinical experiences involving both typical and atypical development. When we made the decision to write this book, we were particularly interested in providing a text that was both relevant and compelling. We believed that many of the available textbooks required students to create meaningful frameworks and make important connections *on their own*; in our text, we wanted to provide those frameworks and highlight those connections to ensure that students would learn as much as possible. We also wanted to offer teachers a more practical and more true-to-life approach to organizing their courses.

Four themes recur throughout the text; together they distinguish our clinical and teaching emphases. Each of these themes is informed by the principles and practices of *developmental psychopathology*, an interdisciplinary approach that asserts that maladaptive patterns of emotion, cognition, and behavior occur in the context of normal development. The first theme emphasizes multi-factor explanations. *Multi-factor explanations* of disorders encompass biological, psychological, and sociocultural factors. These factors are examined in detailed analyses of etiologies, assessments, diagnoses, developmental pathways, and interventions. Especially distinctive is the way we make sure to discuss the multiple ways that factors at every level of analysis need to be explored for both typically developing and atypically developing children.

The second theme is focused on *developmental frameworks* and *developmental pathways*, and is reflected in the sequencing of chapters, unique chapter sections summarizing key developmental tasks and challenges, and our descriptions of disorders over time. Disorders that emerge or are diagnosed early in development are presented first, followed by disorders that emerge or are diagnosed in the elementary-school years, followed by those that emerge or are diagnosed in adolescence. This sequencing serves several purposes. First, it allows students to consider specific disorders and sets of disorders that occur in a particular developmental period in proximity and relation to one another. Second, this sequencing allows for an ongoing focus on the constructs of risk and resilience, and provides a basis for coherent discussions of early-occurring disorders as risk factors for later-occurring disorders. For example, the chapter on disorders of attachment focuses first on understanding the nature and course of these disorders in and of themselves; it also previews the multiple connections that will be made in subsequent chapters between attachment difficulties and later forms of psychopathology. Third, this sequencing emphasizes a more complex understanding of disorders: we think differently, for example, about depression that is identified early and on its own than we do about depression that follows and may be related to an anxiety disorder or attention-deficit hyperactivity disorder.

Unique sections at the beginning of chapters summarize the developmental tasks and challenges experienced by typically developing children that are especially relevant given the disorders discussed in the chapter. For instance, a detailed summary of the development of executive functions and self-regulation is presented before a clinical presentation of attention-deficit hyperactivity disorder; an overview of the development of self is presented at the beginning of the section focused on adolescent disorders. These introductory sections allow students to appreciate the developmental contexts of disorders and their core symptoms; to make distinctions among the everyday issues that most children experience, more difficult types of problems, and clinically meaningful psychopathology; and to make comparisons between the factors that influence the multiple pathways of normal development and the multiple pathways of psychopathology. These developmental pathways, or descriptions of disorders over time, accurately reflect how each child's psychopathology unfolds over time in real life. This pathway model also emphasizes opportunities for growth and change. For example, we describe age-related experiences, such as the transition to middle school, that are associated with some struggling children getting back on track, and certain well-functioning children experiencing distress.

The third theme takes into account the *child in context*, and calls attention to the multiple settings in which the child is embedded. Discussions throughout the text are intended to highlight the many ways in which children and their disorders are understood in larger social contexts (e.g., families, schools and communities, cultures, and historical eras).

The fourth theme involves a *broad focus on the whole child*, rather than a narrow focus on disorder, developmental delay, or deviance. This holistic appreciation of the child emphasizes patterns of interests, abilities, and strengths. We make sure that our case studies include this kind of information, to remind students as often as possible that the diagnosis of a particular disorder does not provide all of the important information about a child. We need to appreciate the everyday joys and special accomplishments that are part of all children's lives. In addition, we believe this holistic focus provides a number of opportunities to talk about the stigma associated with psychopathology, and to encourage awareness, tolerance, respect, and compassion for children and adolescents who struggle with disorders.

Our hope is that this book will enable students to think about disorders in the same way that caring adults think about disorders they encounter every day—in terms of an individual child who is coping with distress and dysfunction: a boy or a girl of a certain age with a specific temperament, characteristic strengths, and personal history, with a family and a network of friends, embedded in a community and culture. We believe that we have written a textbook that places the child at the center of comprehensive and meaningful information, reflecting the most up-to-date understandings of child and adolescent psychopathology, in a format designed to support learning and understanding.

Key Features

In addition to the previously discussed case studies woven throughout, our textbook offers a variety of feature boxes that highlight important topics of interest for students. The themes covered in these boxes are (1) The Child in Context, (2) Clinical Perspectives, (3) Risk and Resilience, and (4) Emerging Science. For study and review, each chapter includes a chapter summary and list of key terms that appear in boldface in the text.

Supporting Resources:

Along with this textbook, Cengage Learning offers the following companion resources.

For Instructors

- Instructor's Manual with Test Bank. This supplement contains valuable resources for preparing for class, including chapter outlines, lecture topics, class activities, and testing materials.
- PowerPoint Lecture Outlines on eBank. Prepared by the authors, these lecture outlines are a great starting point to help you prepare for class.

For Instructors and Students

- Companion website. The book's companion website contains resources for both students and instructors, helping the professor to prepare for class and enhancing the students' learning experience.

Acknowledgments

As this years-long project is completed, we wish to thank the many individuals who have inspired, challenged, encouraged, and supported us. Although our two names are on the cover, we are deeply aware that our text reflects the work of countless others whose research studies and clinical insights we have cited and summarized. We thank them for their contributions to this text and to the field of developmental psychopathology.

We are grateful for the exceptional educational, research, and clinical experiences that have motivated us to write this book. We are grateful to teachers and colleagues who have shared their knowledge of child development and psychopathology, along with their vision of sound, compassionate intervention. We especially acknowledge our undergraduate, graduate, and clinical mentors, who exemplify professional accomplishment and generosity, and who model passionate commitment to children's well-being: Joseph Cunningham of Brandeis University (who has never read anything Robin wrote without scrutinizing, praising, and then improving it), Megan Gunnar and Alan Sroufe of the University of Minnesota, and Ada Hegion and Vivian Pearlman of the Hennepin County Medical Center. We could not be prouder to be their students.

We thank our own students and clients who have challenged us to be better explainers of theory and more thoughtful models of practice. We also thank our colleagues at Hamline University (in particular Matthew Olson, Chair of the Department of Psychology) and at Children's Hospitals and Clinics of Minnesota (especially Regina Driscoll) for their ongoing encouragement and support. Thanks also to Holly Bell and Wendy Werdin, wonderfully obliging administrative assistants at Hamline University, for typing thousands of references.

This is our first book. Apart from writing at our computers, we had no real idea what publishing a book entailed. Now we do, and we also know that first-time authors require even more than the usual time and effort. We have many people to thank at Cengage: Marianne Taflinger, who saw the promise in our proposal and stifled her laughter at our original 18-month timeline; Michele Sordi, Jamie Perkins, and Michelle Julet, who provided much-appreciated editing and publication assistance; Dan Moneypenny (Associate Development Editor), whose meticulous review has improved this text in so many ways; and Jon-David Hague (Executive Editor, Psychology) who provided invaluable advocacy, enthusiasm, know-how, and experience. We also thank all the individuals on the production team, including Bob Kauser (Permissions Editor), Rebecca Rosenberg (Assistant Editor, supplements), Liz Rhoden (Marketing Manager), and Charlene Carpentier (Content Project Manager) at Cengage, and Lynn Lustberg at MPS Content Services.

This text has benefited greatly from the comments and suggestions of many reviewers. They include:

Bethann Bierer, *Metropolitan State College of Denver*
Mia Smith Bynum, *Purdue University*
Richard Cavasina, *California State University*
Lindsey L. Cohen, *Georgia State University*
Arin M. Connell, *Case Western Reserve University*
David Crystal, *Georgetown University*
Tanya L. Eckert, *Syracuse University*
Wendy Hart, *Arizona State University*
Gregory P. Hickman, *Arizona State University*
Melissa Hunter, *Pennsylvania State University*
Louise H. Jackson, *Bemidji State University*
Sheelagh Jamieson, *St. Lawrence College*
Shari Kidwell, *Morehead State University*
Jannette McMenamy, *Fitchburg State College*
Kerri Modry-Mandell, *Tufts University*
Suzanne Morrow, *Old Dominion University*
Claire Novosad, *Southern Connecticut State University*
Irene Ozbek, *University of Tennessee— Chattanooga*
Kimberly Renk, *University of Central Florida*
Sharon E. Stein, *Ferrum College*
Tami Sullivan, *State University of New York—Brockport*
Kim Trudeau-Craig, *St. Lawrence College*
Rob Weisskirch, *California State University— Monterey Bay*
Marilyn Welsh, *University of Northern Colorado*
Keith M. Wismar, *Louisiana State University— Baton Rouge*
Britt Zampano, *Casenovia College*

Robin Parritz especially thanks Mike Troy, a co-author whose intellect and passion have made all aspects of this collaboration rewarding. Robin thanks her friends for offering themselves and their children as case examples, and for celebrating every single announcement of the book's completion. Robin also thanks Steven and Todd, both brothers and friends, and their families, for love from coast to coast. Robin is grateful to her sons, Ari, Adam, and Jesse for their own case-worthy examples of challenge and growth, and for every kind of happiness, and to her husband, Jon Parritz, for enormous amounts of love, counsel, and support.

Mike Troy thanks, first and foremost, Robin Parritz. Her vision, knowledge, and commitment have made this book possible, while her patience and faith have allowed him to share the journey. Mike thanks his friends, especially Paul, Tom, and Brian, for being, well, friends, through it all. Mike also thanks his six siblings; each has played an irreplaceable and treasured role throughout his life. Mike is grateful to his sons, Kevin and Brendan, for bringing wonder, joy, and pride to his life as a parent, and to his wife, Cynthia Koehler Troy, whose wisdom, endless support, and inexhaustible love sustain him always.

CHAPTER 1

Introduction

WHEN WE THINK ABOUT childhood and about growing up, images of wonder, energy, excitement, and joy are common. Babies sharing first smiles and taking first steps. Kindergarteners singing loud songs and looking forward to family vacations. Children reading books, riding bikes, sleeping over with friends. Teens studying for exams, learning to drive, and falling in love. In the midst of all of this growth and change, however, we notice children who are almost always sad, worried, afraid, or angry. We meet children who believe that they are bad, that they have no control over their lives, that the world is an awful place. There are children who lash out at others, and others who withdraw from relationships. Some children exhibit patterns of feelings, thoughts, and behaviors that are best understood as specific kinds of psychological disorders.

The goal of this textbook is to provide a basic understanding of these children and their disorders, and of the theories, methodologies, and findings of developmental psychopathology. We need to understand so that we may meaningfully describe the psychological disorders of infancy, childhood, and adolescence. We need to understand so that we can design appropriate interventions for struggling children. We need to understand so that we can increase awareness and empathy for children who deserve to be treated with dignity and respect. We need to understand so that we can provide the necessary support and resources to families, schools, and communities. And we need to understand so that we can identify the numerous factors that increase the vulnerability of individuals to psychopathology. Such understanding helps us to prevent some disorders and delay the emergence of others, as well as to intervene early with distressed children.

Our approach in writing and organizing this textbook is based on the central premise of **developmental psychopathology**, which suggests that we gain a better understanding of children's disorders when we think about those disorders *within the context of normal development.* We believe that infant, child, and adolescent psychopathology can only be understood by placing descriptions of disorders against the background of typical emotional, cognitive, and behavioral development. We also believe that it is necessary to acknowledge the everyday problems and difficult phases that characterize normal child development, and to make clear both the connections and the distinctions between adaptation and maladaptation. We feel it is most helpful, then, to present children's disorders in developmental sequence, following the child's own growth from birth through early adulthood.

Defining Disorders of Infancy, Childhood, and Adolescence

Emma is a 5 ½-year-old girl whose parents are becoming increasingly concerned about her. Emma has always been somewhat quiet and reserved, taking her time to check out unknown situations and new children, but usually warming up to join activities and play. As the time for kindergarten approaches, Emma is exhibiting more anxiety around others, preferring to stay home, close by her mother. She is displaying new fears about the dark, about strangers, and about getting lost in the new school building. Emma is also crying more frequently and seems almost constantly on edge.

Should Emma's parents call the pediatrician? The kindergarten teacher? A child psychologist? Should they wait a few months to see if Emma grows out of this phase and hope that waiting doesn't make things worse?

Understanding psychopathology is complicated. Parents, teachers, and children themselves are often confused about whether a particular pattern of feelings, thoughts, and behaviors reflects an actual disorder, and if so, whether that disorder involves minor, moderate, or major maladjustment. One of the first steps leading to accurate and useful conceptualizations of psychopathology is to recognize the many connections between "normal" and "abnormal" development. In Emma's case, it is important to consider other children's normal experiences of wariness and fear, differences among children's temperaments, and whether and how her distress interferes with daily life.

Before making decisions about Emma by examining the many theoretical and research approaches to the field of psychopathology, we need to review some of the many approaches to the field of child development itself. Models of childhood and child development have been influenced by changing historical notions of children as miniature adults, blank slates, savages, and innocent beings, as well as more recent images of children as innately and surprisingly competent individuals (Elkind, 1994; Hwang, Lamb, & Sigel, 1996; Mintz, 2006; White, 1996). Depending on the model, our understanding of childhood may lead us to expect that almost all normally developing children will engage in idyllic play, or skill learning and practice, or avoidance of danger. We need to think realistically about whether most children amuse themselves for hours on end, or practice piano or take swimming lessons without complaint, or never run into the street without looking for cars.

Most contemporary theorists, researchers, and clinicians emphasize that a useful model of normal development requires a dynamic appreciation of children's strengths and weaknesses, advances and retreats, and resolved problems and new challenges. A model like this takes into account the complexities of individual, familial, ethnic, cultural, and societal beliefs about desirable and undesirable outcomes for children and adolescents. Against this multilayered background of normal child development, we identify children whose distress and dysfunction are exceptional. Empirically sound and clinically appropriate definitions of disorder can be provided only if we carefully examine various beliefs, as well as the data, about what is normal.

What is Normal?

Common descriptions of normality and psychopathology often focus on (1) **statistical deviance**—the infrequency of certain emotions, cognitions, and/or behaviors; (2) **sociocultural norms**—the beliefs and expectations of certain groups about what kinds of emotions, cognitions, and/or behaviors are undesirable or unacceptable; and (3) **mental health definitions**—theoretical or clinically based notions of distress and dysfunction.

Statistical Deviance

From a statistical deviance perspective, a child who displays too much or too little of any age-expected behavior (such as dependency or assertiveness) might have a disorder. Children of a certain age above the "high number" cutoff, or below the "low number" cutoff would meet the criterion for disorder (see Figure 1.1). Thinking again about Emma, we will be more concerned about a possible disorder if she is much more anxious and fearful than her peers, and less concerned if her peers are also experiencing these difficulties.

Sociocultural Norms

From a sociocultural norm perspective, children who fail to conform to expectations that they adopt age- or gender-specific beliefs about themselves, or who insist that displaying expected age- or gender-based behaviors is upsetting, might have a disorder. Pressure in a particular neighborhood or peer group to prove oneself with belligerent or aggressive behavior, for instance, may contribute to the diagnosis of psychopathology

FIGURE 1:1 Statistical Deviance Model of Disorder

by others outside of that neighborhood or peer group. This time when we consider Emma's fears and anxieties, we are focused on specific social and cultural expectations for a young girl's independence. Are her feelings and behaviors within a generally acceptable range? Depending on the particular social and cultural settings, norms will vary, but there will always be certain patterns of emotion, cognition, and behavior that are considered evidence of psychopathology.

Mental Health Definitions

From a mental health perspective, a child's psychological well-being is the key consideration. The 1999 landmark report of the United States' Surgeon General (U.S. Department of Health and Human Services, 1999) states that "Mentally healthy children and adolescents enjoy a positive quality of life; function well at home, in school, and in their communities; and are free of disabling symptoms of psychopathology" (p. 123). Using this criterion, children who have a negative quality of life, or who function poorly, or who exhibit certain kinds of symptoms, might have a disorder. Again, we think of Emma. From this perspective, what matters most is how Emma's fears and anxieties make the transition to kindergarten painful, and whether she is able to comfortably participate in various academic and social tasks. Other definitions of disorders combine aspects of two or more perspectives (e.g., Wakefield, 1997).

The Role of Values

Closer examination of these definitions and examples of disorder reveals that each raises questions about the **role of values** in conceptualizations of mental health and psychopathology. Box 1.1 provides one example of a value-informed set of children's needs for psychological well-being. Whether the definitions of psychopathology and disorder focus on statistical deviance, sociocultural norms, or mental health evaluations, definitions require several types of value judgments (Sonuga-Barke, 1998; Wakefield, 2002). One important judgment involves personal or group standards of *adequate or average* adaptation, or *optimal* adaptation (Offer, 1999). **Adequate adaptation** has to do with what is considered okay, acceptable, or good enough. **Optimal adaptation** has to do with what is excellent, superior, or "the best of what is possible." The following cases illustrate the difference between the adequate and optimal approaches.

The Irreducible Needs of Children

As noted, our understanding of children's psychological disorders is continuously informed by our understanding of children's usual development. When we think about what happens differently in some children's lives, or goes wrong in other children's lives, we need to remember not only the range and variety of hoped-for outcomes but the basic, bottom-line components of "what every child must have to grow, learn, and flourish." Two prominent children's advocates, T. Berry Brazelton and Stanley Greenspan, have described these essential needs (Brazelton & Greenspan, 2000). They include:

- the need for ongoing nurturing relationships
- the need for physical protection, safety, and regulation

- the need for experiences tailored to individual differences
- the need for developmentally appropriate experiences
- the need for limit-setting, structure, and expectations, and
- the need for stable, supportive communities and cultural continuity.

In our descriptions and discussions of children's disorders, we will repeatedly refer to prevention and intervention strategies that are based on these needs. Satisfaction of these needs—from birth through adulthood—is an index of our concern, compassion, and commitment to children's well-being.

Adequate Adaptation

The Case of Thomas

Thomas is a 6-year-old boy who is currently in his third foster home. Thomas was severely neglected early in his life and was removed from his biological mother's home when he was 9 months old by the county's child protection services. After two brief foster placements, Thomas has been in a stable and nurturing foster home for two years.

Although his teachers have no concerns about his basic academic skills, they note that Thomas does have difficulty paying attention and that he is frequently impulsive. Thomas has several friends who he likes to play with, but he is seldom sought out as a playmate by other children. His feelings are hurt easily and he sometimes misinterprets the intentions of others, feeling that they are out to get him. Consequently, he is quicker than other children to resort to name-calling or shoving when he is upset.

Thomas is more comfortable and relaxed at home with his foster parents, but asks often if he will have to move away from them. While being as reassuring as possible, his foster parents have acknowledged that they do not know how long Thomas will be with them. Thomas clearly worries about leaving his current home, but is adamant that he does not want to talk about this. ■

Optimal Adaptation

The Case of Jenny

Jenny is a 6-year-old girl who also suffered an early loss. Jenny's mother was a single parent who died in an automobile accident when Jenny was two. Following her mother's death, Jenny went to live with her maternal grandparents. Although distraught at the loss of their daughter, they dedicated themselves to caring for Jenny to the best of their ability.

In addition to her grandparents, Jenny is also involved with and supported by her many relatives who live nearby and include Jenny in their lives. Jenny's teachers describe her as bright and enthusiastic in the classroom. She is enjoying her developing ability to read and seems to have a special aptitude for math. Jenny is well-liked by both the girls and the boys in her class, and is often invited to play dates and birthday parties.

At home, Jenny enjoys hearing stories about her mother, and thinking of how loving and proud her mother would be. There are times, of course, when Jenny and her grandparents cry for her mother, but they are able to take comfort in each other, and in the warm and secure home they have created together. ■

Cultural norms influence developmental expectations.

Digital Vision/Getty Images

Even with the traumatic beginnings of their childhoods, both Thomas and Jenny are moving in a positive developmental direction. Still, Thomas' adequate adaptation is different from Jenny's optimal adaptation in the degree to which each successfully manages past trauma and current challenges, the quality of caregiving and friendship, and the potential for growth in coming years. Neither adequate nor optimal adaptation assumes smooth sailing throughout development. Challenges are inevitable, and struggles themselves are not evidence of disorder. Indeed, challenge and struggle are viewed by most developmental psychologists as forces of growth. Sameroff (1993), in fact, suggests that "all life is characterized by disturbance that is overcome, and that only through disturbance can we advance and grow …. In this view, it is the overcoming of challenge that furnishes the social, emotional, and intellectual skills that produce all forms of growth, both healthy and unhealthy" (p. 3).

The Impact of Values on Definitions of Disorder

Other important judgments involving values are tied to specific definitions of disorder. With statistical deviance definitions, it sometimes makes sense to examine *both* extremes of the continuum (e.g., too

much intense emotion as well as too little intense emotion), because we have made a judgment that there is a desirable middle course related to emotional intensity (again, see Figure 1.1). At other times, it makes sense to focus only on the "bad" end of the continuum and ignore the "good" end (e.g., too little empathy, but not too much empathy; too little intelligence, but not too much intelligence). In these specific cases, we have made judgments that some types of extreme characteristics are to be accepted or prized.

With sociocultural definitions, value judgments are the very basis of different definitions of disorder. Whether casual use of mind-altering substances is tolerated or condemned by a particular sociocultural group influences evaluations of pathological addiction. Whether independence or connectedness is more valued influences evaluations of pathological dependency. For example, among traditional Hmong families living in the United States after emigrating from Southeast Asia, it would be considered inappropriate or disrespectful for an unmarried child to leave home. So, while graduation from high school may be seen as a transition to more independent functioning in traditional Western culture, with young adults going away to college, such behavior would not be viewed as developmentally appropriate or healthy in many Hmong families.

With mental health definitions, the values of psychologists, psychiatrists, and clinical social workers are embedded in both scientific and lay community decision-making. Returning to the Surgeon General's description of psychological well-being, clinicians must evaluate whether a young person's life is characterized by a positive quality, adequate functioning, and few symptoms. Whether these particular benchmarks represent the least we can do for children and adolescents, or the best we can hope for, is yet another value judgment.

Definitions of Psychopathology and Developmental Psychopathology

For the purposes of this textbook, we will work within the framework provided by the following definitions of disorder. *Psychopathology refers to intense, frequent, and/or persistent maladaptive patterns of emotion, cognition, and behavior. Developmental psychopathology extends this description to emphasize that these maladaptive patterns occur in the context of normal development, and result in the current and potential impairment of infants, children, and adolescents.*

Rates of Disorders in Infancy, Childhood, and Adolescence

If definitions of disorder are problematic, estimates of rates of disorder are even more so. The multipart task of estimating rates of disorder includes (1) identifying children with clinically significant distress and dysfunction, whether or not they are in treatment (and most of them are not); (2) calculating levels of general and specific psychopathologies, and the impairments associated with various disorders; and (3) tracking changing trends in the identification and diagnosis of specific categories of disorder (e.g., autism, attention deficit hyperactivity disorder, and depression) (Maughan, Iervolino, & Collishaw, 2005; Prosser & McArdle, 1996; Roberts, Attkisson, & Rosenblatt, 1998; Rutter & Smith, 1995). Personal, clinical, and public policy implications must be considered when collecting these data. For instance, specific diagnoses may or may not qualify for insurance coverage. Or increases or decreases in the diagnosis of certain disorders may have an impact on the staffing of special education programs in schools.

The prevalence of disorders in infants, children, and adolescents can be estimated with varied methodologies and within varied groups (Bird, 1996; Hackett & Hackett, 1999; Lahey et al., 1996; Roberts, Attkisson, & Rosenblatt, 1998). Prevalence and incidence rates are both measures of psychopathology cases in a population. **Prevalence** refers to all current cases; **incidence** refers to new cases in a given time period. Random sampling of a general population is one option for estimating prevalence (e.g., using surveys, phone questionnaires, and/or detailed psychopathology screening instruments). For example, the investigators in the Great Smoky Mountains Study interviewed 9-, 11-, and 13-year-olds from the southern Appalachian mountain region of the United States in order to compare rates of disorders in rural versus urban settings (Costello, Angold, et al., 1996). Sampling in schools, using teachers' assessments, is another option. Or samples can focus on types of disorders that are seen in children's primary care and mental health clinics.

Whatever method is selected, there can be no doubt that many children struggle with clinically significant disorders. In a recent Surgeon General's report (2001), 21% of children between the ages of 9 and 17 met diagnostic criteria for a disorder associated with at least minimum impairment; 11% met diagnostic criteria for disorders associated with significant impairment; and 5% met the diagnostic criteria for disorders associated with extreme impairment. Using somewhat different developmental information, Roberts et al. (1998) estimated that 8% of preschoolers, 12% of preadolescents, and 15% of adolescents struggle with some form of psychopathology. These rates are comparable to those observed in other studies conducted in the United States (Angold et al., 2002; Costello, Mustillo, Erkanli, Keeler, & Angold, 2003; Jaffee, Harrington, Cohen, & Moffitt, 2005; Newman et al., 1996) and other countries, including Australia, Britain, China, Germany, Greece, Israel, Kenya, the Netherlands, Thailand, and Puerto Rico (Canino et al., 2004; Crijnen, Achenbach, & Verhulst, 1997; Ford, Goodman, & Meltzer, 2003; Kroes et al., 2001; Sawyer et al., 2001; Weisz, Sigman, Weiss, & Mosk, 1993).

Selected Critical Issues

Allocation of Resources, Availability and Accessibility of Care

Although it is always the case that children's psychopathology deserves our attention, our compassion, and our best clinical responses, a number of critical issues demand renewed and innovative effort. Even with research-based knowledge about ways to promote children's physical and mental well-being that has been available for years (e.g., Achenbach, 1997; Weisz, Sandler, Durlak, & Anton, 2005; Zigler & Valentine, 1979), parents, schools, communities, and policy makers have struggled to allocate often-scarce emotional, social, and financial resources (Cook et al., 2004; Flisher et al., 1997; Leaf et al., 1996; Levant, Tolan, & Dodgen, 2002). One continuing difficulty involves access to care. Recent investigations suggest that at least 10% of children and adolescents need mental health interventions, but fewer than half receive them (Power, Eiraldi, Clarke, Mazzuca & Krain, 2005; U.S. Department of Health and Human Services, 1999). Indeed, "the current state of affairs not only fails to take responsibility for the health and welfare of children, it also fails to recognize the costs and waste in economic and human potential" (Tolan & Dodge, 2005, p. 602).

Barriers to care are widespread and have been extensively summarized by Owens et al. (2002). Structural barriers include lack of provider availability, long waiting lists, inconveniently located services, transportation difficulties, inability to pay and/or inadequate insurance coverage. Barriers related to perceptions about mental health difficulties include the inability to acknowledge a disorder, denial of problem severity, and beliefs that difficulties will resolve over time or will improve without formal treatment. Barriers related to perceptions about mental health services involve a lack of trust in the system, previous negative experiences, and the stigma related to seeking help.

When children do receive psychological care, the cost of appropriate intervention, whether oriented to the individual, the family, or the school, is often prohibitive, and insurance coverage varies widely. Until recently, most health insurance policies placed restrictive limits on reimbursement of mental health coverage (e.g., $500 per year). State and federal legislation to eliminate these kinds of restrictions has made progress of late, but many families still face such coverage limits. That there are effective therapies and treatments for a variety of psychological disorders is significant only if infants, children, and adolescents are able to take advantage of them (Hofferth, Phillips, & Cabrera, 2001; Tolan & Dodge, 2005).

Inadequate money for prevention efforts is also a public policy dilemma, especially given recent estimates that the economic burden of treatment of child and adolescent mental illness surpasses 10 billion dollars (Edwards & Thalanany, 2001; National Institute of Mental Health, 2004). There is abundant research, for example, documenting the positive psychosocial impact of early educational programs (Woodhead, 1988), but full funding and increased access remain difficult. And for children from minority and disadvantaged backgrounds, access to treatment and prevention programs is even more problematic (Garcia Coll, Akerman, & Cicchetti, 2000; Garland et al., 2005; Kerkorian, McKay, & Bannon, 2006; Thompson & May, 2006).

Tolan and Dodge (2005) propose a four-part model for a comprehensive system that "simultaneously promotes mental health within normal developmental settings, provides aid for emerging mental health issues for children, targets high-risk youth with prevention, and provides effective treatment for disorders: (1) Children and their families should be able to access appropriate and effective mental health services directly; (2) Child mental health should be a major component of healthy development promotion and attention in primary care settings such as schools, pediatric care, community programs, and other systems central to child development; (3) Efforts should emphasize preventive care for high-risk children and families; (4) More attention must be paid to cultural context and cultural competence" (pp. 607-608). These kinds of proposals lay the groundwork for resource allocation and policy implementation that will have longstanding consequences for the well-being of countless children.

The Role of The Media

The role of the media in setting research and clinical agendas is another area of concern. The media certainly provide important information to the general public; however, at times, this information is dramatized and oversimplified. As one example, the recent flurry of reports on the all-important nature of early experiences (e.g., brain development during the first three years of life) requires careful study to fully appreciate many of the individual and public policy implications. For instance, the data suggest that "the first few years of life are important, but so are the next few years and the next few years after that" (Nelson, 1999, p. 235; see also Dawson, Ashman, & Carver, 2000; Thompson & Nelson, 2001) (see Box 1.2).

Science and the Media

Contemporary models of child development, psychopathology, and treatment benefit in both theoretical and practical ways from advances in the neurosciences. These advances have been associated with both well-deserved excitement in scientific communities and, sometimes, not so well-reported stories in the media. Media reports often exaggerate or sensationalize preliminary findings, or do not provide important information that would more accurately explain complex psychological phenomena (Nelson, 1999; Thompson & Nelson, 2001).

For example, much has been made of early reports on the many benefits of exposing young children to classical music (i.e., "the Mozart effect") (Rauscher, Shaw, & Ky, 1993; Campbell, 2000), with benefits presumably tied to changes in neuropsychological structure and function. Parents have bought CDs and videos (and played them over and over again), hoping to provide their children with an intellectual advantage. Repeated failures to replicate the initial positive findings

have not been well publicized (e.g., Chabris, 1999; Steele, Bass, & Crook, 1999; Thompson, Schellenberg, & Husain, 2001).

Another example of incomplete journalistic coverage involves recent reports about important brain development in the first three years of life. While highlighting the impact of early experiences on brain structure and function, these reports often ignore data suggesting that equally impressive brain development occurs in the prenatal period, and throughout the later years of childhood, adolescence, and adulthood (Nelson, 1999; Thompson & Nelson, 2001).

Better science-media communication and cooperation have several benefits. These include (1) providing interesting, accurate, and practical information to the general public; (2) focusing the attention of policy makers and advocacy groups on significant issues of child welfare; and (3) enhancing public trust and respect for complex scientific endeavors (Shonkoff & Phillips, 2000; Thompson & Nelson, 2001).

As another example, media accounts of shootings in middle schools, high schools, and universities have focused public attention on the prevalence of violence in contemporary society; children's exposure to violent images in movies, television, and video games; and the complicated social worlds of adolescents. Questions are often raised about the contributions of parents and peers to the adolescents' breakdowns and mental health professionals' inability to predict why some children resort to violence, without enough television time (or newspaper space) to explore psychological, legal, and ethical concerns. Useful discussion of these questions in the media is difficult when research data, clinical hunches, and public fears become entangled.

The Stigma of Psychopathology

A final issue concerns the continued and painfully unnecessary stigmatization of individuals with psychopathology (Adler & Wahl, 1998; Corrigan, 2005; Hinshaw, 2005; Hinshaw & Cicchetti, 2000; Pescosolido, 2007). For parents concerned about their children's distress or dysfunction, there is almost always shame, fear, and/or blame. For

children, experiences of secrecy and rejection are commonplace. Lack of respect and lack of access to care (again) are often the results of personal, familial, and social stigma (Hinshaw, 2005; Wahl, 1999). A clinician seeking parental permission to obtain information from a child's teacher is not surprised when a father says: "You know, doctor, we'd prefer that the school not know anything about this. We haven't told his brothers or his grandparents. No one else needs to know." Or a teacher, preparing a child to begin attending a social skills group the following week, is asked: "Why do I have to leave your room, Mrs. Stern? I don't want to go with those kids. They're weird. I'm not weird. I'm not crazy."

Box 1.3 provides additional perspective on this kind of stigma. To understand the development, course, and treatment of psychopathology in infants, children, and adolescents represents only half the battle. To increase our tolerance and compassion for the diverse group of those who are diagnosed with psychopathology and to believe in the inherent worth of each struggling infant, child, and adolescent makes up the other, far more difficult, half.

BOX 1:3   THE CHILD IN CONTEXT

The Stigma of Mental Illness

Ignorance and intolerance have long been identified as critical issues for those struggling with mental illness. Much of the available research focuses on adults' limited and inaccurate knowledge and negative attitudes toward other adults with mental illness. In study after study, the data suggest that most adults tend to think primarily in terms of serious psychopathology (such as schizophrenia and bipolar disorder), believe that individuals are responsible for their disorders, and overestimate the likelihood of aggression and violence in adults with mental illness; stigmatization, in terms of ridicule, avoidance, and rejection, is rampant (Corrigan, 2005; Hinshaw, 2005; Wahl, 2002).

Adults also exhibit distorted beliefs and harmful attitudes toward children who are struggling with mental illness and their families. Adults both trivialize the reality of children's distress and dysfunction by suggesting that children are overdiagnosed, overmedicated, and poorly parented, and exaggerate the extent to which these same children are unpredictable, dangerous, and deviant (Giummarra & Haslam, 2005; Hinshaw, 2005; Pescosolido, Fettes, Martin, Monahan, & McLeod, 2007).

How do children and adolescents compare to their adult counterparts?

Sadly, their beliefs and attitudes are all too similar. Surveys of children's labels for those dealing with mental illness—including *crazy, nuts, retarded, psycho,* and *lunatic*—reveal their aversion (Bailey, 1999; Woolfolk, 2001). Although children do display increasing knowledge about the causes of mental illness as they age, their attitudes reflect ongoing stigmatization related to views of those struggling with mental illnesses as violent, unpredictable, blameworthy, and hopeless (Adler & Wahl, 1998; Corrigan et al., 2007; Wahl, 2002; Watson, Miller & Lyons, 2005). It is not surprising, then, to find that children with disorders "self-stigmatize"; that is, they internalize these negative beliefs and attitudes and exhibit low levels of self-esteem and self-efficacy (Corrigan, Watson, & Barr, 2006).

Given that children are exposed to multiple sources of information and attitudes, including parents, peers, and the media, how can stigmatization be prevented or minimized? Many types of programs, from those designed for single classrooms to those intended as national demonstration projects, have shown improvements in knowledge and attitudes (e.g., Corrigan, 2005; Crisp, Cowan, & Hart, 2004; Pitre, Stewart, Adams, Bedard, & Landry, 2007; Watson et al., 2004). Several themes about interventions emerge from successful programs. They must begin early; target multiple dimensions of knowledge and attitudes; be developmentally appropriate; and include individuals, families, and communities. Children can learn lies or they can learn facts; they can display ugly attitudes or they can display compassion. The choices are theirs, and ours.

■ Key Terms

Developmental psychopathology (pg. 2)
Models of childhood and child development (pg. 2)
Statistical deviance (pg. 3)
Sociocultural norms (pg. 3)
Mental health definitions (pg. 3)
Role of values (pg. 3)
Adequate adaptation (pg. 3)
Optimal adaptation (pg. 3)
Psychopathology (pg. 6)
Prevalence (pg. 6)
Incidence (pg. 6)
Barriers to care (pg. 7)
Stigmatization (pg. 8)

■ Chapter Summary

- Developmental psychopathology refers to intense, frequent, and/or persistent maladaptive patterns of emotion, cognition, and behavior, considered within the context of normal development, resulting in the current and potential impairment of infants, children, and adolescents.
- Prevalence refers to all current cases of a set of disorders, while incidence refers to new cases in a given time period. Although specific study results vary, government estimates suggest that over 20% of children and teens meet at least minimal diagnostic criteria for a mental health disorder; over 10% meet criteria for disorders with significant

impairment; and approximately 5% meet criteria for disorders with extreme impairment.

- There are a number of critical issues currently facing the field of developmental psychopathology. For example, less than one-quarter of children who need mental health care have access to that care. Another important issue is the ongoing challenge of overcoming the stigmatization of individuals and families dealing with psychopathology.

CHAPTER 2

Models of Child Development, Psychopathology, and Treatment

The Case of Max

Max is 8 years old. He can often be found squirming at his second grade desk, looking out the window, rearranging his pencils, knocking papers on the floor, poking the girl in front of him. From his teacher's perspective, Max's situation is becoming more and more problematic, and she has referred him for evaluation.

Max's parents describe a normal development for him, although they say that he has always been "on the go." Max lives with his father and mother, both of whom graduated from high school, and his siblings. The family lives in a duplex home; Max's maternal grandparents, who emigrated from Honduras, live in the other half.

In kindergarten, Max was described as active and energetic, but his teacher had no significant concerns. In first grade, his difficulties increased over the course of the year. Concerns noted at that time included problems completing classwork and instances of bothering other children. Max's school problems have continued in second grade, where his teacher describes him as generally disorganized and as falling behind in reading and math.

Max's parents provided other information that also suggested that Max's struggles were not typical. Beginning in first grade, they noticed some problems at home including irritability and impulsivity. His parents remembered that these negative emotions and behaviors were more pronounced after the school day. Also, Max began to argue and fight more frequently with his 10-year-old brother and especially his 4-year-old sister. His parents report that Max still enjoys playing with friends in the neighborhood, but is becoming increasingly resistant, discouraged, and pessimistic about school. The more stressful family problems coincided with Max's father being laid off from his job as a master electrician. Max's father has spent increasing amounts of time at home, with escalating conflicts between Max's mother (who does not work outside the home) and himself about child care and discipline. ■

The Case of Maggie

Maggie is 14. She spends a lot of her free time alone in her room, feeling blue, not doing much of anything. She rarely gets together with other kids, who have mostly stopped asking her to join them. Maggie's mother is worried about her sadness and withdrawal, and has called her family physician for a referral.

Maggie's mother has been a single parent since Maggie's birth, and is employed as a customer service representative for a health care company. Maggie's father has a long history of hospitalizations for both major depression and alcohol abuse.

Maggie's mother describes her infancy and childhood as normal. Throughout elementary school, Maggie was generally quiet and cooperative and received average grades. Although not especially social, she always had a few good friends, and was active in sports and with her church youth group. Looking back, Maggie's mother notes that she seemed to worry more than most other children, but not to the point where it interfered with her schoolwork or social activities. The transition to middle school was difficult. Maggie's mother reports that Maggie seemed somewhat overwhelmed by the size of the school and had difficulty adjusting to changing classes and increased homework. Further, she had less contact with her elementary school friends and had trouble making new friendships.

Although Maggie does not talk much about her situation, her increasing withdrawal, apathy, and occasional irritability are apparent. Maggie no longer participates in athletics, has dropped out of her church youth group, and spends most of her time at home alone. She is increasingly behind in her schoolwork, and her grades have dropped significantly. ■

The Role of Theory in Developmental Psychopathology

Models of development, psychopathology, and treatment allow us to organize our clinical observations of children and our research findings into coherent, informative accounts. In this chapter, the cases of Max and Maggie will illustrate key concepts related to normal developmental processes, the emergence of disorder, and intervention goals and strategies. For introductory purposes, the sections on Max and Maggie present somewhat simplified examples; by the end of this chapter and throughout the next chapter, the models will be increasingly complex, integrated, and realistic.

Dishion and Patterson (1999) describe the construction of models as an ongoing process, such that an initial theory is described, followed by observation, definitions, measurements, and experiments, which

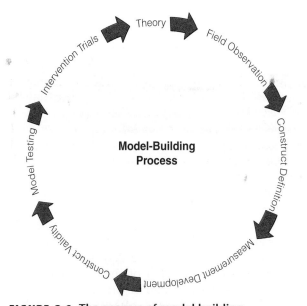

FIGURE 2:1 The process of model building.
Source: From Dishion & Patterson (1999), "Model building in developmental psychopathology: A programmatic approach to understanding and intervention", 'Journal of Clinical Child Psychology', 28, 502-512. Reprinted by permission.

lead to theory revision, and the process begins again (see Figure 2.1). Such an ongoing process of construction, reflection, and revision is characteristic of both adult and child models of development and psychopathology; it is important to keep in mind our changing understandings through time. Before the practices and principles of developmental psychopathology are described in Chapter 3, we will summarize the historical models—the "big theories" (Damon & Lerner, 1998)—that have contributed valuable ideas to our contemporary understanding. Although these models are presented separately and are most often conceptualized as complete and comprehensive in and of themselves, *they are not mutually exclusive.* It is more useful to think of these models as providing different and complementary perspectives on the complicated phenomena of development, psychopathology, and treatment (Damon & Lerner, 1998).

Continuous and Discontinuous Models

To provide some additional background for the upcoming summaries, it is useful to consider how various definitions of disorder correspond with continuous versus discontinuous models of psychopathology. **Continuous models of psychopathology** emphasize the

ways in which normal feelings, thoughts, and behaviors gradually become more serious problems, which may then intensify and become clinically diagnosable disorders. With continuous models, there are no sharp distinctions between adjustment and maladjustment. **Discontinuous models of psychopathology,** in contrast, emphasize discrete and qualitative differences in individual patterns of emotion, cognition, and behavior. With discontinuous models, there are clear distinctions between what is normal and what is not.

The cases of Max and Maggie provide one way to think about continuous and discontinuous models. For instance, are the difficulties experienced by these children extremes of normal difficulties (continuous examples) or are they problems of a different sort altogether (discontinuous examples)? What do parents, teachers, and clinicians gain from a perspective that emphasizes the connections between kids who are struggling and kids who are not? And what is gained from a perspective that instead emphasizes the unique patterns of problematic emotions, thoughts, and behaviors that give rise to significant maladjustment?

Physiological Models

Historical and Current Conceptualizations

At their most basic, **physiological models** propose that there is a physiological (i.e., structural, biological, or chemical) basis for all psychological processes and events. These physiological bases must be accounted for when we are talking about theories of normal development, theories of abnormal development, or intervention possibilities. Advances in neuroscience have resulted in new research and clinical opportunities that expand our understanding of normal child development (Nelson & Bloom, 1997) and brain development from birth through young adulthood (Diamond, 2002; Giedd et al., 2004; Spelke, 2002). Infants, children, and adolescents have had their working brains pictured using magnetic resonance imaging (MRI), their brain waves traced by electroencephalograms (EEG), and their blood and saliva collected and evaluated. Using newer technologies that either directly or indirectly image the structure, function, or pharmacology of the brain (see Table 2.1), we are becoming more knowledgeable about "how a child builds a brain" (Cicchetti, 2002).

What we know about psychopathology is also influenced by these physiological models (Cicchetti & Walker, 2003). For some disorders, psychopathology

---

TABLE 2:1 NEUROIMAGING TECHNOLOGIES: METHODS AND DATA

CT

Computed Tomography (CT) is a common diagnostic imaging technique that uses x-rays to generate images of brain anatomy. CT is most frequently used in emergency circumstances to evaluate the effects of trauma; it is also used to guide treatment decisions and monitor treatment effects.

EEG

The electroencephalogram (EEG) is a noninvasive technique that measures patterns of electrical impulses in the brain. Electrodes are attached to the scalp, and the electrical activity is measured and recorded as wave patterns. Variations in brain wave activity are associated with neurological conditions (such as seizure disorders) and psychological states (such as levels of consciousness).

MRI

Magnetic Resonance Imaging (MRI) is a noninvasive type of imaging scan that uses magnetic fields to produce images of internal body structures, including the brain. A single MRI exposure produces a two-dimensional image; a series of MRI exposures provides a virtual three-dimensional view.

fMRI

Functional Magnetic Resonance Imaging (fMRI) is a type of MRI that measures changes in the flow of blood and blood oxygenation in different parts of the brain. In addition to an anatomical view of the brain, this allows researchers to see functional changes in brain activity by highlighting the particular structures that are active during specific mental processes (such as cognitive or emotional tasks).

PET

Positron Emission Tomography (PET) is a form of x-ray that uses short-lived radioactive substances to measure metabolic activity by monitoring the use of glucose in various brain regions. Because healthy and nonhealthy cells metabolize glucose at different rates, PET scans are able to provide data on diseased or damaged regions.

---

unfolds according to a "maturational blueprint," with deviance innately and inevitably related to damage or dysfunction (Sameroff, 1993). Certain severe forms of mental retardation are examples of this type of psychopathology. For most disorders of childhood and adolescence, this too-simple model of physical cause and psychopathological effect can be dismissed (Courchesne, Townsend, & Chase, 1995; Mash & Dozois, 1996; Sameroff, 1993).

More complicated models suggest that there are inborn or acquired vulnerabilities to disorders—including genetic abnormalities, structural pathologies, and biochemical disturbances—which *may* lead to psychological distress and dysfunction (Hooper & Tramontana, 1997; Schore, 1996, 1997). According to this physiological **diathesis-stress model**, minor structural damage or chemical imbalance does not *by itself* lead to disorder. Rather, diatheses (or predispositions) such as neurological damage at birth or genetic risk for disorder, *in combination with* additional stress (either physiological or environmental), can result in the development of a disorder.

Finding the genes responsible for increasing the risk of psychopathology depends on the talent and dedication of many investigators and the availability of significant technological, methodological, and financial resources (see Table 2.2). Gene research also requires consideration of the complementary roles of genes (nature) and environment (nurture) across development. Indeed, after years of emphasizing the impact of genes on psychopathology, we are now re-emphasizing the role of the environment; "*environment* in genetic research really means *nongenetic*, which is a much broader definition of environment than is usually encountered in psychology. That is, environment denotes all nonheritable factors, including possible biological events such as prenatal and postnatal illnesses, not just psychological factors" (Plomin, 2004, p. 343). Some of the numerous contributions of the Human Genome Project and related investigations are described in Box 2.1.

Two variations of the diathesis-stress model are illustrated in the following cases. In the first case, a child with phenylketonuria (PKU) is born with a particular metabolic dysfunction, an inactive liver enzyme (a physiological diathesis of genetic origin). The presence of phenylalanine (a physiological stressor) in the child's diet and the subsequent metabolic abnormalities result in severe mental retardation. Treatment of this condition involves a diet low in phenylalanine, beginning shortly after birth; this treatment is associated with normal intellectual development. In the second case, a child's physical and psychological well-being may be adversely affected by maternal drug abuse during pregnancy (again, a physiological diathesis, but this one of nongenetic origin). After birth, poor parenting (a psychosocial stressor) may lead to a number of clinical syndromes. High-quality parenting, in contrast, may buffer or protect the child from particular negative outcomes. Somewhat beyond the scope of this

TABLE 2:2 CURRENT UNDERSTANDING OF THE GENETIC BASIS OF SELECTED DISORDERS

DISORDER	PATTERN OF INHERITANCE	GENE MAPPING
Fragile X mental retardation	Nonstandard X-linked dynamic mutation	Two genes identified (*FMR1* and *FMR2*), both with unstable trinucleotide repeats.
Attention Deficit Hyperactivity Disorder	Common complex	Three contributory loci in the dopamine system, *DRD4*, *DAT1*, and *DRD5*. *DRD4* best replicated, others less certain.
Dyslexia	Common complex	Two contributory loci suggested on chromosomes 6 and 15; findings replicated.
Schizophrenia	Common complex	Numerous reported linkages including chromosomes 1, 5, 6, 10, 13, 15, and 22, but no consensus.

text, even more complex models detail the myriad ways in which diatheses and stressors, or genetic and environmental factors, interact (Gottlieb, 2003; Rutter & Silberg, 2002).

Although the role of physiological factors seems obvious, the design of research, the collection of data, and the interpretation of findings are often problematic. Work on the construct of **neural plasticity,** or the ability of the brain to flexibly respond to physiological and environmental challenges and insults, illustrates the difficulty of pursuing cutting-edge questions and disseminating complex psychophysiological findings (Benes, 1994; Davidson, 1994; Greenough & Black, 1992; Nelson, 2000). First, neuroscientists design increasingly sophisticated studies, moving beyond "molecules, membranes, and single

BOX 2:1 EMERGING SCIENCE

Genomics and Developmental Psychopathology

Remarkable advances in scientific knowledge and technology have enabled investigators from many disciplines to ask, and begin to answer, questions about the biopsychosocial nature of human experience. The most comprehensive set of questions and data are provided by the **Human Genome Project,** a collaborative effort by the Department of Energy and the National Institutes of Health to identify the approximately 30,000 genes in human DNA and determine the sequences of the 3 billion chemical base pairs that make up human DNA (genomics.energy.gov). The goals of the project include basic science data on the mapping, sequencing, and analysis of genes, or **genomics** (a term used by Thomas Roderick in 1986), and the application of this data for medical, educational, and technological benefit.

The bottom-up process of understanding, in terms of molecular biology, how individual genes work is called **functional genomics**. The top-down process of understanding the impact of genes at the psychological level is called **behavioral genomics**. According to Plomin (2002), the meeting of the bottom-up and top-down approaches occurs in the brain. And the linking of genes, brain, and behavior, with a focus on how genes influence the heritability of disorder, is at the heart of developmental psychopathology (McGuffin, 2004; Plomin, DeFries, Craig, & McGuffin, 2003; Plomin & McGuffin, 2003).

Almost all of the information to date suggests that multiple gene systems, rather than single genes, are responsible for the heritable component of both normal and abnormal psychological characteristics. Variations in patterns of DNA, then, provide explanations for the neurological basis of individual differences. Interacting with a variety of environmental factors, these DNA variations bring us one step closer to understanding the emergence of psychopathology (see Table 2.2). Even with these exciting data, we need to be cautious about overstating our hypotheses and findings. Kendler (2005) argues that the phrase "X is a gene for Y" is widely used, yet inappropriate for psychiatry and psychology. Kendler states that there are clear criteria for being able to claim that a gene for some psychopathology has been identified. So far, these criteria have not been met; given the nature of individuals and disorders, they are not likely to ever be met. Still, genomics provides a valuable framework for developmental psychopathology; its impact will be felt for decades to come.

neurons…to examining complex neural systems" (Cicchetti, 2002, p. 27), involving anatomical, chemical, and/or metabolic processes in the brain.

These types of studies often depend on research with animals (Gottlieb, Wahlsten, & Lickliter, 1998; Nelson & Bloom, 1997), and there are obvious theoretical and practical difficulties involved in making comparisons between, for example, mice and babies. We need to be careful generalizing from animals to children when we observe, for example, that early nutrition may have long-term effects on brain structure and function (Rao & Georgieff, 2000) or that "[s]ufficiently rich experience" in rats is related to a "cascade of neurochemical events causing plastic changes in the brain," including increases in cortical thickness, dendritic length and branching, and the size of synaptic contacts (Rosenzweig & Bennett, 1996). These animal data become more compelling when we examine similarly complex studies and similarly intriguing results in human infants (Rao & Georgieff, 2000). Using neuroimaging techniques, Huttenlocher (1994, 1999) demonstrated the plasticity of the developing cerebral cortex, observing quantitative changes in dendrites and synapses (e.g., length of dendritic branches, complexity of branching, and number and density of synapses).

In other work on plasticity, Bell and Fox (1996) documented different patterns of physiological and EEG activity in groups of 8-month-olds with various crawling histories. Comparisons of infants who have not yet started to crawl, beginning crawlers, and experienced crawlers provide evidence that brain development specific to crawling involves an initial overproduction of cortical connections that are then "pruned" with additional crawling experience. This pattern of production and pruning illustrates how the brain's development reflects an ongoing transaction between nature (e.g., the genetically timed creation of neurons) and nurture (e.g., the environmentally influenced selection of neurons to maintain).

Another compelling example of the impact of experience on the developing brain comes from research with maltreated children. Cicchetti and his colleagues (Cicchetti, 2002) have found that the experience of neglect and/or abuse may result in actual changes in brain structure and function (in addition to the more frequently described psychological and social impairments). Specifically, physiological responses to emotional stimuli are

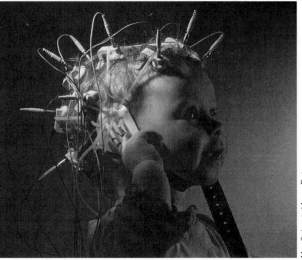

Advances in neuroimaging techniques are crucial to research into how genetics and environment influence the developing brain.

processed differently in children with histories of maltreatment (Cicchetti & Rogosch, 2001a, 2001b; Pollak, Klorman, Thatcher, & Cicchetti, 2001).

Neural plasticity has both beneficial and detrimental effects. Whereas some neuroscientists once believed that brain development was relatively complete by age 3, and that any damage was permanent and irreversible, we now accept that plasticity is associated with important growth after the age of 3, as well as the recovery and reorganization of functioning following damage (Dennis, 2000; Nelson, 1999). There are, of course, limits on plasticity, and increased localization of function occurs within the cerebral cortex as a result of both maturation and experience (Bell & Fox, 1996; Depue, Collins, & Luciana, 1996; Johnson, 1999; Nelson, 2000). There is also evidence of immediate and continuing neuropsychological impairments in many children with early brain disease or injury (Dennis, 2000; Taylor & Alden, 1997). In contrast to earlier, direct models of disease, damage, or dysfunction, current physiological models of psychopathology seek to explain the interplay of physical and biological factors, neurological processes, development, and life experiences in order to understand the emergence, the course, and the treatment of psychopathology (Cicchetti, 2002; Cicchetti & Cannon, 1999; Davidson, 1994; Kandel, 1999; Merikangas, 2000; Nelson, Bloom, Cameron, Amaral, Dahl, & Pine, 2002; Pennington, 2002).

Thinking About Max

From a physiological perspective, we emphasize the role of brain structure and function, and consider the likelihood of abnormal biochemical processes in the development of disorder. Specifically, physiologically oriented clinicians conceptualize Max's difficulties as primarily due to underarousal of key parts of Max's brain; because of this, he lacks sufficient focus and sustained engagement with the environment, resulting in inattentive and impulsive behavior. These difficulties, consistent with a diagnosis of attention-deficit hyperactivity disorder (ADHD), are not typical of other similar-age children.

Because the disorder is physiologically based, the first choice for intervention is physiological in nature. As the clinical literature suggests that stimulant drugs such as Ritalin are effective in treating children with ADHD, a trial of stimulant medication would be prescribed. In addition, although pharmacological treatment is the primary intervention, behaviorally influenced strategies would be routinely included in both the school and home settings.

Thinking About Maggie

Again, from a physiological perspective, we note with special interest Maggie's family history that includes her father's episodes of clinical depression, and consider the possibility of a genetic vulnerability to depression. Maggie's various problems, then, might be usefully conceptualized as the psychological expression of a biochemical imbalance. For example, Maggie's symptoms may be a result of low levels of the neurotransmitter serotonin.

Although treatment recommendations may include suggestions that Maggie participate in structured social activities in school as a way of helping her to be more active and successful in friendships, the first-step intervention is the initiation of a trial of antidepressant medication designed to correct the biochemical imbalance.

Psychodynamic Models

Historical and Current Conceptualizations

Psychodynamic models have a rich past and a recently revived future (Fonagy & Target, 2000), and include the classic psychoanalytic explanations set forth by Sigmund Freud, the socially oriented explanations

of Erik Erikson and Harry Stack Sullivan, the more recent work of object-relations theorists such as Mahler and Winnicott, and the contemporary perspectives provided by Emde, Stern, and others. Psychodynamic models have historically focused on several themes, including (1) the impact of unconscious processes on normal and abnormal personality development; (2) conflicts among processes and structures of the mind (e.g., id, ego, and superego); (3) stages of development, with different ages associated with distinctive emotional, intellectual, and social challenges; and (4) the lasting impact of more (or less) successful resolutions of stage-related challenges on later outcomes. Indeed, these themes were well appreciated by the novelist and astute observer of human nature, William Faulkner, who wrote: "The past is never dead. It's not even past."

Psychodynamic theorists and clinicians usually emphasized a fixation-regression model of psychopathology, which suggested that individuals who failed to work through developmental issues become "stuck" in the past. Disorders themselves were rooted in traumas or conflicts experienced during early childhood (e.g., the oral, anal, and phallic stages). From a treatment perspective, psychodynamic models rejected the idea that childhood trauma inevitably led to disorder (Costello & Angold, 1996), and focused on the possibility of better functioning through insight-oriented therapy. Psychoanalytic interventions for children, such as those of Anna Freud and Melanie Klein, made special use of play (using toys and games) and art to bring repressed traumas and unconscious conflicts into therapeutic awareness.

Even setting aside some of the more scientifically suspicious claims of early psychodynamic models, we are left with much to consider. Contemporary psychodynamic approaches continue to emphasize (1) unconscious cognitive, affective, and motivational processes; (2) mental representations of self, other, and relationships; (3) the meaningfulness of individual (i.e., subjective) experiences; and (4) a developmental perspective, focused on the origins of normal and abnormal personality in early childhood, and the constantly changing psychological challenges faced by children as they age (Emde, 1992; Fonagy & Target, 2000; Surgeon General's Report, 2001; Westen,1998). These emphases are evident in some of today's most significant psychodynamically informed research, such as work on parent-child attachment (Emde & Hewitt, 2001), and attachment's enduring effects on personality and interpersonal functioning (Grossman & Grossman, 2005).

Although recent psychodynamic models certainly take into account neurophysiology and neurochemistry (Davidson & Sutton, 1995; Davidson, 1998; Kandel, 1998, 1999; Schore, 2001), there is still an emphasis on the importance of psychological contexts, such as relationships, when explaining the development of personality and psychopathology (Zeanah, Anders, Seifer, & Stern, 1989). Also, rather than a belief that an individual is fixated in the past, there is a "continuous construction model," which suggests that early problems are carried forward, with ongoing contributions to maladjustment (Zeanah et al., 1989). Today's psychodynamic assessments and treatments continue to rely on play to make connections with troubled children, to identify the specific pathology, and to effect change.

Thinking About Max

From a psychodynamic perspective, we are concerned that the management of early developmental challenges may have compromised Max's current adjustment. For example, do Max's inattentive and distractible activity, and lack of school success, reflect unconscious conflicts about autonomy that he failed to resolve during his preschool years? Or has a somewhat older Max encountered a more troubling set of issues related to competence and achievement? Should we consider the possibility of an underlying identification with his recently unemployed father? And are there connections between problems with family relationships and problems with peer relationships?

With these types of dynamic issues to explore, it will take some time to formulate a clear clinical understanding of Max and a focused intervention plan. Treatment strategies may include the exploration of such dynamic issues through art, games, and imaginative play, with less specific, more open-ended treatment goals.

Thinking About Maggie

From a classic psychodynamic perspective, we wonder about whether the physical and emotional changes associated with early adolescence have stirred up long-dormant conflicts about intimacy and sexuality. Within a more general attachment framework, Maggie may be struggling with a basic sense of insecurity. Early and ongoing experiences with her father's inconsistent emotional availability

may contribute to her wariness in relationships and increasingly negative expectations about her ability to manage demanding school and social challenges. In addition, Maggie's mother's insistence on close supervision of her friendships and restrictions on school activities may be making it difficult to express age-appropriate individuality or independence.

Given her age, Maggie's assessment and treatment are more likely to include therapeutic dialogue and discussion, with an emphasis on dynamic strategies of interpretation and clarification. Treatment goals will be focused on intellectual and emotional insight, based on the idea that insight will lead to improved functioning in Maggie's everyday life.

Behavioral and Cognitive Models

Historical and Current Conceptualizations

In contrast to the inward orientation of the physiological and psychodynamic models, the behavioral models have an outward orientation, focusing on the individual's *observable behavior within a specific environment*. According to behavioral models, environmental variables have powerful effects on the development of personality and psychopathology, and these effects have been described by major theorists such as Skinner, Mischel, and Bandura.

Behavioral models are based on core concepts and principles of learning theories, and share a strong empirical foundation with them. These theories propose that both normal and abnormal behaviors are gradually acquired via processes of learning, including the classical conditioning processes described by Pavlov, the operant conditioning processes described by Skinner, and the observational learning processes described by Bandura. The construct of reinforcement (i.e., the idea that positive and negative consequences lead to changes in behavior) is a critical component of all of these learning processes.

According to Thomas's (2001) summary of Skinner's behaviorism, "As a child grows up, two things develop: (a) the variety of behavior options (potential ways of acting) that the child acquires and (b) the child's preferences among those options. As children interact with their environments, they learn to prefer rewarding over nonrewarding actions" (p. 14). Psychopathology, within the behavioral framework, is understood as the result of learning gone awry:

the acquisition and reinforcement of maladaptive or undesirable behaviors, the lack of opportunity to learn adaptive or appropriate behaviors, and/or unavailable or inadequate reinforcement of those adaptive or appropriate behaviors. Behaviorally oriented treatments, then and now, focus on unlearning, relearning, and new learning.

Newer cognitive-behavioral and cognitive approaches correspond to the cognitive revolution of the 1960s, 70s, and 80s (Morrison & Ornstein, 1996; Thomas, 2001). With respect to cognitive and behavioral integration, these approaches increasingly emphasize the ways in which children's thinking influences the many varieties of learning (Fischer & Pare-Blagoev, 2000; Keil, 1999; Kendall & Dobson, 1993; Meichenbaum, 1977).

With respect to more theoretically "pure" **cognitive models**, the focus is on the components and processes of the mind and mental development (Flavell 1982; Thomas, 2001). We consider Piaget's landmark studies on stages of cognitive development, as well as later information-processing and interactionist models, with contemporary revisions, elaborations, and innovations (Case, Demetriou, Platsidou, & Kazi, 2001; Newcombe, 2002; Thomas, 2001; Yan & Fischer, 2002). According to these perspectives, both the content of children's thinking (e.g., whether kids see themselves as competent or incompetent), and the developmental level of children's thinking (e.g., preschoolers versus adolescents) must be taken into account during the emergence of a disorder, as well as during its course and treatment. Kendall and his colleagues have described the multiple influences of cognitive structures, contents, processes, and products on psychopathology, with different difficulties such as cognitive deficiencies (e.g., too little thinking) and cognitive distortions (e.g., incorrect appraisals or perceptions) associated with different types of disorders (Kendall & MacDonald, 1993).

Thinking About Max

Within the behavioral and cognitive-behavioral frameworks, Max's difficulties may be understood as a reflection of maladaptive learning and/or cognitive deficits. For example, Max's inappropriate classroom behaviors may result in increased displays of adult concern and adult contact. Although negative in tone, these episodes may be positively reinforcing because of the adult attention and proximity they generate. These interactions may be especially salient given his father's change in employment status, and the change in his family's focus from children's activities to adult worries. Additional focus on Max's on-task behaviors, such as reading quietly in his seat and completing his math problems within the allotted time, and rewards for homework, may be required. Both school performance and peer problems may also be influenced by Max's impulsive decision-making. A cognitive emphasis on more extensive analysis of situational cues and more deliberate examination of the likely consequences of particular actions may be a key part of Max's treatment plan.

Thinking About Maggie

As with Max, Maggie's problems are viewed from a cognitive-behavioral perspective as a result of maladaptive learning and cognitive distortions. Maggie's social difficulties are conceptualized as rooted in her misinterpretations of the intentions and actions of others. This misreading of benign social cues as signifying rejection has had a negative effect on Maggie's self-esteem and on her belief in her ability to positively influence her environment. These cognitive errors, in turn, have led to avoidant behaviors. These avoidant behaviors, which—in the short term—minimize the distress that Maggie feels, are then reinforced and lead to further isolation.

The intervention designed to ameliorate these behavioral and cognitive deficits includes identifying the cognitive errors Maggie makes and teaching Maggie new ways to interpret and think about social situations. In addition, it is necessary to devise a schedule of positive reinforcements and rewards for increasing adaptive and healthy behaviors.

Humanistic Models

Historical and Current Conceptualizations

Humanistic models have also made valuable contributions to our understanding of development, psychopathology, and treatment. These models, including those of Carl Rogers and Abraham Maslow, emphasized personally meaningful experiences, innate motivations for healthy growth, and the child's purposeful creation of a self. Within the humanistic framework, psychopathology is usually linked to interference with or suppression of the child's natural tendencies to develop an integrated (or whole) sense of self, with valued abilities and talents. Parents, teachers, social conventions, and children themselves can hinder healthy development. Intervention, then, involves the discovery or rediscovery of internal resources and provision of external support for self-organization, self-direction, and self-righting capacities.

At times criticized as overly optimistic with respect to the potential for happiness, creativity, and actualization, the humanistic models are thematically related to recent discussions of the self (Constantino & Castonguay, 2003; Rosenfield, Lennon, & White, 2005), wellness (Cicchetti, Rappaport, Sandler, & Weissberg, 2000; Cowen, 1994) and **positive psychology** (Keyes & Lopez, 2002; Seligman & Csikszentmihalyi, 2000), and renewed emphases on the experiential development of children (Csikszentmihalyi & Rathunde, 1998). We see increasing emphasis on "positive subjective experience, positive individual traits, and positive institutions" that seek to promote individual, family, social, and community well-being (Seligman & Csikszentmihalyi, 2000). "Positive youth development" in adolescence, involving identifying opportunities for initiative and engagement, is one application of this model (Larson, 2000). Another application involves the study of wisdom and the pursuit of excellence (Baltes & Staudinger, 2000). Although the focus of this textbook is on psychopathology, thinking about "what makes...life most worth living, most fulfilling, most enjoyable, and most productive" (Seligman & Csikszentmihalyi, 2000) provides us with an essential perspective when considering children's distress and dysfunction.

Thinking About Max

Max has experienced an abrupt shift in educational atmosphere, from activity-centered learning to a teacher-organized approach, with much less time for highly enjoyed art and music. As the classroom expectations for academic achievement become more prominent, Max has struggled to find his place in the classroom setting. It is hard for him to relate what he is expected to learn with what he sees as his abilities and talents. From a humanistic perspective, Max's problems with peers may reflect his dissatisfaction with himself and his feelings of incompetence.

Humanistically oriented treatment will focus on increasing Max's chances for pleasure and mastery in school. In addition, therapeutic work may include numerous opportunities (talk-based, play-based, art-based) for the creation (and re-creation) of a valued sense of self. With a strong belief in the self-righting tendencies of children, we expect that Max will be able to use these resources for academic and social benefit.

Thinking About Maggie

Maggie, too, is faced with a new school setting, and increasing demands from her mother, her peers, and society that she identify special interests and specific goals for her future. Unlike Max, Maggie does not feel that she has any unique gifts which provide personal satisfaction or which make a contribution to others. In fact, over time, Maggie has come to see herself as unintellectual, unartistic, unathletic, and unattractive. These feelings have led to her sadness, irritability, and withdrawal.

Within this framework, psychotherapeutic challenges that require Maggie to take charge of planning, decision-making, and her own happiness will be balanced by clear expressions of support and encouragement that she is capable, competent, and indeed uniquely qualified for this responsibility.

Family Models

Historical and Current Conceptualizations

Tolstoy proposed in *Anna Karenina* that "Happy families are all alike, but every unhappy family is unhappy in its own way," with much insight into the myriad ways that misery and dysfunction may be experienced and expressed by husbands and wives, parents and children, and brothers and sisters. However, Tolstoy's assertion about the uniformity of happy families is inaccurate, for there are also myriad ways in which joy and compassion may be experienced and expressed. Different families have different beliefs about the essential nature of children (Harold, 2000; Hwang et al., 1996). Different families have different dreams for themselves and their children, as well as different fears (Bornstein et al., 1998; Garcia Coll & Meyer, 1993), and these different beliefs, dreams, and fears have impacts on the functioning and adjustment of both happy and unhappy families.

In many individually focused models of disorder, we examine the "identified patient," and his or her unique collection of psychologically healthy and unhealthy traits (including physiological vulnerabilities, psychodynamic demons, and maladaptive learning). In contrast, **family models** propose that the best way to understand the personality and psychopathology of a particular child is to understand the dynamics of a particular family (Bateson, Jackson, Haley, & Weakland, 1956; Emery & Kitzmann, 1995; Haley, 1976; Minuchin, 1974; Repetti, Taylor, & Seeman, 2002). In fact, almost from the beginning of our concern with childhood disorders, there has been some recognition that these disorders may reflect, at least in part, family psychopathology. At times, we have correctly recognized the connections between, for example, child and parent anxieties. At other times, with heartbreaking consequences, we have erroneously linked specific child disorders such as autism with alleged parental shortcomings and maladaptive behaviors (Bettelheim, 1967; Phares, 1996).

Families have a special impact on normal and abnormal development because they are the first context of children's experiences (Goodnow, 1999); the influence of parents is clear and powerful (Collins, Maccoby, Steinberg, Hetherington, & Bornstein, 2000; Maccoby, 2000). Families are challenged to meet a variety of children's needs, including nurturing and socializing, promoting education, and providing financial support, and they can succeed or fail at any or all of these tasks (Emery & Kitzmann, 1995). With respect to both positive and negative outcomes, a number of family characteristics have received theoretical and empirical attention (Parke, 2004a). These include structural variables such as forms of families (e.g., two-parent, single-parent) (Emery & Kitzmann, 1995) and principles of family dynamics such as hierarchies, boundaries, and power (Guerin & Chabot, 1997; Minuchin, 1974). Other process variables such as parenting style (Baumrind, 1967, 1971), marital conflict (Cummings & Davies, 1994), and changes in family relationships over time have also been investigated (Cowan & Cowan, 2003; Dunn, 2004). The impact of religion on family life is an example of more recent psychological inquiry (Parke, 2001). More broadly, the often unstated but still-powerful rules, rituals, and myths, as well as role expectations that bear upon the personalities of all individuals in the family, can be explored (Fiese et al., 2002; Harold, 2000). Whereas almost all of the historical information, and much of the recent data, on families comes with a focus on the mother, the role of the father is increasingly appreciated and investigated (Parke, 2004b; Parke et al., 2005; Phares, 1996).

The family factors that have been discussed so far are examples of **shared environment**, the aspects of family life and function that are shared by all

children in the family. Shared environmental variables are those variables that are often contrasted with genetic variables; that is, what is not explained by genes, or nature, is usually thought to be explained by shared environment, or nurture. In reality, however, **nonshared environment**, the aspects of family life and function that are specific and distinct for each child, has received considerable attention in recent years. Nonshared environmental variables are those that contribute to sibling dissimilarity (Asbury, Dunn, Pike, & Plomin, 2003; Pike & Plomin, 1996; Turkheimer & Waldron, 2000). Siblings are unique, for instance, in terms of gender, age, and temperament, and may elicit different types of parenting, affection, and/or material advantages. Sibling relationships themselves may be the source of nonshared experiences; how one of a pair of siblings views support, conflict, and respective value within the family may differentially influence adjustment (Brody, 2004; Deater-Deckard, Dunn, & Lussier, 2002).

With family models, assessment and treatment of psychopathology addresses the child in the family unit. Interventions include parents and oftentimes siblings. Treatment outcomes are evaluated with respect to both individual and family-wide changes.

Thinking About Max

Within the family framework, Max's difficulties are viewed as an expression of family distress and disorganization. In part, Max's school struggles and sibling conflicts may serve as a less-threatening distraction for his parents than their marriage and financial concerns. Even if Max is the identified patient, we cannot ignore the context in which his disorder developed and in which it is maintained.

Other family variables may also contribute to the maladjustment. It may be important that the ideal classroom and school environments for Max are less hierarchical and more egalitarian than his close-knit but highly autocratic family environment. It may also be useful to closely examine Max's parents' beliefs about children's growing-up years, their expectations about his academic success and dreams for his future. How do these beliefs support or interfere with his ongoing developmental challenges?

A family-oriented intervention for Max addresses these many variables and capitalizes on his affectionate family bonds. In addition to techniques designed to enhance his sense of self as a valued family member, Max and his parents are likely to be taught specific cognitive and behavioral strategies for his use in school and at home (e.g., keeping records of school assignments, specific folders for completed homework, and schedules of chores posted on the refrigerator). Family sessions will be employed with goals to foster emotional and problem-solving communication skills, to strengthen the parents' alliance, and to diffuse sibling tension. Meetings alone with the parents may also address some parenting and marital issues.

Thinking About Maggie

Family-oriented theorists may closely examine Maggie's mother's family values, beliefs, and practices. Perhaps Maggie and her mother are close in unhealthy ways, with Maggie's mother overinvolved in her everyday decisions and Maggie overly responsible for her mother's welfare and happiness. Or perhaps Maggie's mother signals ambivalence or discouragement in response to any signs of Maggie's interest in dating, to the extent that it reminds her of her own romantic unhappiness. As Maggie grows older and begins to explore dating, previous disappointments and current struggles may lead to her symptoms of depression.

Identifying the family variables that contribute to Maggie's difficulties will lead to specific hypotheses about the kinds of therapeutic discussions that may be effective; these therapeutic opportunities will include joint mother-daughter sessions as well as individual sessions for both Maggie and her mother.

Beyond Family Relationships: The Role of Peers

Just as relationships within nuclear families are associated with better and worse psychological outcomes, relationship networks outside of families are also related to immediate and long-term consequences (Sroufe, Egeland, & Carlson, 1999). For example, many children derive great pleasure from close relationships with extended family members, neighbors, and peers. In addition to pleasure, these relationships serve as rich settings for socioemotional learning (Hartup & Laursen, 1999). **Peer relationships,** and friendships in particular, provide opportunities for companionship, acceptance, and intimacy (Hartup, 1980; Rudolph & Asher, 2000). An absence of friendships, because of rejection, conflict, or withdrawal, is associated with maladajustment (Kupersmidt & DeRosier, 2004).

Sociocultural Models

Historical and Current Conceptualizations

Many early revisions of classic psychoanalytic theory attempted to take into account relevant cultural factors. For instance, Karen Horney, following Freud, argued that his understanding of "penis envy" was mistaken. Rather than girls being envious of the physical fact of maleness, she suggested that they were, instead, envious of the social and cultural rewards associated with being a boy. Decades later, feminist theorists continued to make the case that the identification of disorders and particular interventions was very much influenced by gender-based norms and expectations about desirable personality outcomes.

More recently, **sociocultural models** of development, personality, and psychopathology have undergone a *paradigm shift*, in which cultural considerations have moved from the periphery of inquiry to the core (Garcia Coll, 2001; Garcia Coll & Magnuson, 1999). Specifically, researchers, theorists, and clinicians are thinking about culture in a very different way. Culture is not only the background for development. Rather, it is a major influence on development itself (Bornstein, 2002; Shweder et al., 1998; Sternberg & Grigorenko, 2004).

When we think about culture in this way, we need to account for a variety of variables that have meaningful impacts. Wicker (1992; see also Thompson, 2001) has described the immediate environments, or "behavior settings," in which children grow and make sense of their lives. These kinds of behavior settings, components of **ecological models,** include homes, classrooms, and neighborhood playgrounds

The quality of friendships in childhood is associated with a variety of developmental outcomes.

Radius Images/PhotoLibrary

(Bronfenbrenner, 1986; Bronfenbrenner & Morris, 1998; Weisz, 2004; see Figure 2.2). These behavior settings are, in turn, influenced by broader variables, such as current societal values and norms, political conditions, economic events, technological changes, demographic conditions, and geographic conditions (Rose et al., 2003; Wicker, 1992).

Glen Elder and his colleagues have emphasized an even broader perspective, attending to the influence of time and history on children's development. In Elder's model, there are four key assumptions:

1. *Children develop within the social arrangements of a given moment.*
2. *These arrangements are changed by events and trends.*
3. *Developing individuals change history.*
4. *Cultures make sense of the ways of development. (Modell & Elder, 2002, p. 174)*

The construct of **birth cohort** illustrates Elder's approach. A birth cohort includes individuals born in a particular historical period who share key experiences and events. Kids growing up during the Great Depression in the United States belong to a cohort group. Baby boomers are another cohort. So are Generation X and Generation Y (see Figure 2.3). According to Thomas (2001), "not only are societal trends reflected in the lives of children who constitute a given birth cohort, but the lives of individuals from different cohorts are linked in ways that also influence development, particularly when the values and lifestyles of one cohort conflict with those of another, thereby resulting in disagreements between parents and their children as well as among grandparents, parents, and the young" (pp. 98–99).

Developmental psychologists have frequently paid attention to "socially transmitted patterns" of thinking, feeling, and behaving (Garcia Coll et al., 2000); however, discussion of these patterns has too often focused on the ways in which differences are conceptualized as "deviation, maladaptation, or pathology" (Garcia Coll et al., 2000, p. 338). This **deficit approach** to cultural variation may be compared to the **difference approach,** where "cultural differences can be seen as legitimate, appropriate, and even desirable. . . ." (p. 338). The deficit/ difference distinction provides additional perspective on the discussion in Chapter 1 of cultural norms and cultural values in definitions of abnormality. As theorists, researchers, and clinicians increasingly acknowledge and appreciate the diversity that exists among countries and cultures outside the United States, as well as within the United States (Garcia Coll & Meyer, 1993; Lopez & Guarnaccia, 2000; McLoyd, 1999), our models must take into account both the advantages and the disadvantages of culturally diverse experiences.

Culture-specific investigations provide examples of the complex role of culture, identifying both straightforward and mixed results. For instance, although adolescents from Asian, Latin American, and European backgrounds report different levels of family obligation, parental authority, and autonomy, levels of family conflict and family cohesion, as well as individual adjustment and academic achievement, are similar (Fuligni, 1998b; Fuligni, Tseng, & Lam, 1999; Fuligni, Witkow, & Garcia, 2005). A more mixed set of findings comes from data comparing the adjustments of children and adolescents from immigrant backgrounds. Fuligni (1997, 1998a) reported that children who moved to the United States from Asian and Latin American countries displayed "remarkable" adjustments, and suggested that strong family values related to cultural identification, family obligations, and education contributed to their success. In contrast, Mirsky (1997) and Birman, Trickett, and Buchanan (2005) observed increased psychological distress and dysfunction in samples of immigrants from the former Soviet Union to Israel and the USA. Various hypotheses have been suggested to explain the disparate findings, including the stressful qualities of migration, the influences of ethnic identity and the role of language (Slonim-Nevo, Sharaga,

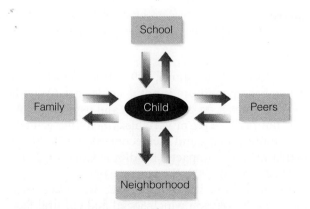

FIGURE 2:2 An ecological model of child development and psychopathology.
Source: From J.R. Weisz, "Psychopathology for Children and Adolescents", p. 415 (New York, NY: Cambridge University Press, 1986). Copyright © 1986 Cambridge University Press. Reprinted with the permission of Cambridge University Press.

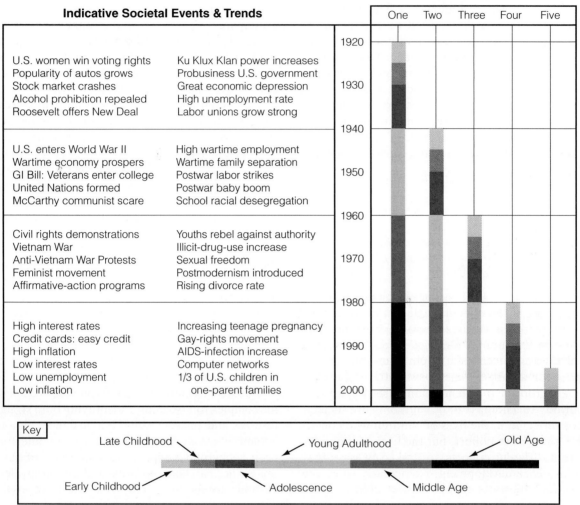

FIGURE 2:3 Relationship of societal conditions and birth cohorts.
Source: From R.M. Thomas (2001), "Recent Theories of Human Development", p.99 (Sage Publications, Inc.). Reprinted by permission.

Mirsky, Petrovsky, & Borodenko, 2006; Vedder & Virta, 2005).

With these models of development and psychopathology, we recognize the powerful impact of social context (Boyce et al., 1998; Harkness & Super, 2000; Lochman, 2004; Rogoff & Morelli, 1989; Taylor, Repetti, & Seeman, 1997; Weisz, McCarty, Eastman, Chaiyasit, & Suwanlert, 1997). We go beyond the behavioral emphasis on the specifics of environmental rewards and punishments to a broad emphasis on the social and cultural norms and expectations that influence much (if not most) of what we think, feel, and do (Bukowski & Sippola,

1998; Rubin, 1998; Saarni, 1998). It is important to remember that culture is not a single variable with a simple impact on development and psychopathology, but rather a set of variables (including gender, race, and ethnicity, and socioeconomic status [SES]) with a variety of impacts (Bradley & Corwyn, 2002; Emde & Spicer, 2000; Weisz et al., 1997).

From a historical perspective, we necessarily focus on the ways in which social and cultural factors uniquely disadvantage certain groups in society (e.g., girls, minorities, lower SES families) and increase vulnerability to disorders in these groups (e.g., Fisher, Jackson, & Villarruel, 1998; Gallay &

Flanagan, 2000; Rutter, 1999; Spencer, 1990). For example, Garcia Coll & Meyer (1993) report that minority individuals have different "resource environments," with respect to employment status, education, housing, and access to medical care. Luthar (2000) notes that "among inner-city teenagers, successful negotiation of one developmental task (e.g., peer acceptance) might be a proxy for *failure* on another stage-specific task (academic success)" (p. 467), and this may necessitate modifying mainstream developmental theories. Both the conceptualization and the treatment of psychopathology, then, must address the social and cultural inequities that make it difficult to ameliorate distress and dysfunction.

One sociocultural inequity that has been intensively researched is poverty. Poverty's deleterious impact on the physical and mental health of children and adolescents is well documented (Caspi, Taylor, Moffitt, & Plomin, 2000; Chen, Matthews, & Boyce, 2002; Duncan & Brooks-Gunn, 2000; Lerner, 2003). A natural experiment contrasted American Indian children before and after a casino opening that resulted in differential levels of increased income and changes in poverty status; children who were no longer poor displayed fewer psychiatric symptoms compared to those who remained poor (Costello, Compton, Keeler, & Angold, 2003).

Thinking About Max

Within a sociocultural framework, the assessment of Max will include identification of, for example, the impact of his family's socioeconomic status (previously solidly middle class, now less secure), the balance between assimilation and preservation of Honduran traditions, the embedding of the family in the Honduran/Latino community, and the possibility of faith-based resources. The details, significance, and likely outcome of Max's situation will be interpreted in light of a set of particular cultural values and expectations. A culturally informed intervention will take into account the concern and availability of Max's immediate and extended family, and may provide culturally accessible conceptualizations of disorder and intervention.

Thinking About Maggie

Contributions from a sociocultural perspective will also help us understand Maggie's situation. There may be fewer financial resources for Maggie and her mother, but their participation in church-related activities may provide additional support. Perhaps Maggie will become more interested in developing connections to her religious community, or will become more aware of her personal concerns related to gender or politics. In all instances, we expect this perspective to lead to a fuller, more nuanced approach to disorder and intervention.

Over the course of this chapter, it has become abundantly clear that a single model of development, psychopathology, and treatment, no matter how comprehensive, cannot provide all of the necessary information. Depending on the particular child, different aspects of various models, taken together, contribute to better understanding and a greater number of specific options for support and intervention. This emphasis on complexity and integration will naturally lead us, in the next chapter, to consideration of contemporary principles and practices of developmental psychopathology.

■ Key Terms

Continuous models of psychopathology (pg. 13)
Discontinuous models of psychopathology (pg. 13)
Physiological models (pg. 13)
Diathesis-stress model (pg. 14)
Neural plasticity (pg. 15)
Human Genome Project (pg. 15)
Genomics (pg. 15)
Functional genomics (pg. 15)
Behavioral genomics (pg. 15)
Psychodynamic models (pg. 17)
Fixation-regression model (pg. 17)
Behavioral models (pg. 18)
Classical conditioning (pg. 18)
Operant conditioning (pg. 18)
Observational learning (pg. 18)
Reinforcement (pg. 18)
Cognitive models (pg. 19)
Humanistic models (pg. 19)
Positive psychology (pg. 20)
Family models (pg. 20)
Shared environment (pg. 21)
Nonshared environment (pg. 21)
Peer relationships (pg. 22)
Sociocultural models (pg. 22)
Ecological models (pg. 22)
Birth cohort (pg. 23)
Deficit approach (pg. 23)
Difference approach (pg. 23)

■ Chapter Summary

- Theoretical models of development, psychopathology, and treatment help to organize clinical observations, direct research efforts, and design treatment programs.
- Continuous models of psychopathology emphasize the gradual transition from the normal range of feelings, thoughts, and behaviors to clinically significant problems.
- Discontinuous models of psychopathology emphasize differences between distinct patterns of emotion, cognition, and behavior that are within the normal range and those that define clinical disorders.
- Physiological models emphasize biological processes, such as genes and neurological systems, as being at the core of human development and experiences, including the development of psychopathology.
- Current physiological models, such as the diathesis-stress model, emphasize the interplay of various physiological factors and stress in order to understand the emergence, course, and treatment of psychopathology.
- Psychological models, such as the psychodynamic, cognitive-behavioral, humanistic, and family models, emphasize intrapersonal or interpersonal factors in the development, course, and treatment of psychopathology.
- Sociocultural models emphasize the importance of the social context, including gender, race, ethnicity, and socioeconomic status, in the development, course, and treatment of psychopathology.

CHAPTER 3

Principles and Practices of Developmental Psychopathology

AS WE EXAMINE THE PRINCIPLES and practices of developmental psychopathology, keep in mind the definitions provided in Chapter 1's introduction: **Psychopathology** refers to intense, frequent, and/or persistent maladaptive patterns of emotion, cognition, and behavior; and **developmental psychopathology** extends this description to emphasize that these maladaptive patterns occur in the context of normal development, and result in the current and potential impairment of infants, children, and adolescents. We will use these definitions as our cornerstones, building upon them to explore related concepts of distress and dysfunction. This chapter has three sections. The first section is primarily focused on development; the concept of developmental pathways and notions of child competence and incompetence are summarized. The second section reviews the key constructs of risk and resilience; examples from studies of child maltreatment make explicit the connections between theoretical constructs and real-life children. The third section provides an overview of research strategies in developmental psychopathology.

The Framework of Developmental Psychopathology

Investigators working to accurately place developmental psychopathology within the broad framework of psychology have variously conceptualized it as a "field" of psychology, a "subfield," a "domain," a "discipline," and a "macroparadigm" (Cummings, Davies, & Campbell, 2000). For our purposes, however, what matters more than terminology is whether developmental psychopathology provides a useful approach for understanding how specific disorders develop, what happens over time to children who develop disorders, and what we can do to help these children.

From a theoretical perspective, developmental psychopathology is *not* associated with a single point of view. Rather, as noted in Chapter 2, developmental psychopathology "integrates and coordinates a wide range of theories (e.g., psychodynamic, behavioral, cognitive, biological, family systems, and sociological)" (Mash & Dozois, 1996, p. 35). From a clinical perspective, developmental psychopathologists assume that a variety of assessment, prevention, and intervention techniques will prove useful. In addition to appreciating multiple psychological perspectives, the contributions of other disciplines are explicitly acknowledged. Numerous researchers and clinicians in psychiatry, social work, education, and public policy provide important hypotheses, data and interpretive insight, and mental health care.

As we review the principles and practices of developmental psychopathology, remember that, like the evolution of general scientific models, understandings of developmental psychopathology also evolve (Dishion & Patterson, 1999). Many individuals have contributed to the growth of the field; their seminal reviews have focused the organization and content of this chapter (Achenbach, 1982, 1990, 1997; Cicchetti, 1984, 1990a, 1990b; Cicchetti & Sroufe, 2000; Garmezy & Rutter, 1983; Hobson, 1999; Mash & Dozois, 1996; Rutter & Sroufe, 2000; Sameroff, 2000; Sroufe, 1997; Sroufe & Rutter, 1984).

In 1984, a special issue of the journal *Child Development* reviewed the history, theory, research methodologies, and practical applications of developmental psychopathology. At that time, Sroufe and Rutter (1984) defined the domain of developmental psychopathology as "*the study of the origins and course of individual patterns of behavioral maladaptation, whatever the age of onset, whatever the causes, whatever the transformations in behavioral manifestation, and however complex the course of the developmental pattern may be*" (p. 18, italics in original). This broad description takes into account the development of both normal functioning and psychopathology, as well as the relations between patterns of adjustment and maladjustment (Cicchetti, 1984; see Figure 3.1).

Psychopathology, then, might be understood as a developmental distortion, or a form of unsuccessful adaptation. More specifically, Mash and Dozois (1996) characterize psychopathology in children as an adaptational failure that "may involve deviation from age-appropriate norms, exaggeration or diminishment of normal developmental expressions, interference in normal developmental progress, failure to master age-salient developmental tasks, and/or failure to develop a specific function or regulatory mechanism" (p. 5). These types of adaptational failures have, for years, been viewed as either delay (e.g., the child acquires language more slowly than other children), fixation (e.g., the child continues to suck her thumb long after other children have stopped), or deviance (e.g., the child behaves strangely, unlike other children) (Fischer et al., 1997). Understanding children's disorders as delay, fixation, or deviance highlights the difficulties of *a particular child at a particular point in time,* and provides us with one way of thinking about the connection between normal and abnormal development.

Another way of thinking about the connection between normal and abnormal development is to examine the notion of process. Sroufe and Rutter's (1984) original definition of developmental psychopathology suggests that adaptation (or maladaptation) is an ongoing activity, with transformations of patterns of thinking, feeling, and behaving at various developmental stages. With respect to process, we can think about disorders as "successions of deviations over time," with small problems leading to larger problems, or different problems, and so on (Cummings et al., 2000); children's psychopathology, then, does not emerge all of a sudden or out of the blue, but rather unfolds over time. Shirk, Talmi, and Olds (2000) identify three related types of processes that affect children's development. Dynamic systems processes have to do with the idea that dysfunction involves many

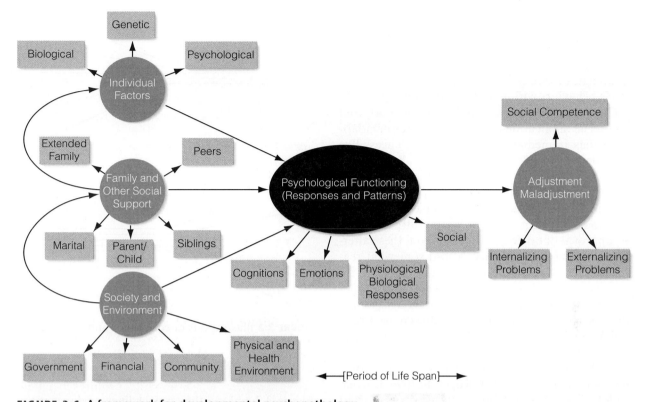

FIGURE 3:1 **A framework for developmental psychopathology.**
Source: From E.M. Cummings, 1999, in T.L. Whitman et al (Eds.), "Life-Span perspectives on health and illness", pp. 277-294 (Lawrence Erlbaum & Associates). Reproduced with permission of Lawrence Erlbaum & Associates in the format Textbook and in the format Internet posting via Copyright Clearance Center.

different individual factors (e.g., biological and psychological stressors). Transactional processes refer to the notion that children are embedded in environments that have an impact on dysfunction (similar to some of the sociocultural models discussed in the previous chapter). And longitudinal processes involve consideration of the child over time, including what factors serve to maintain disorders once they are present.

To make these descriptions somewhat less abstract, we can think metaphorically of developmental psychopathologists making difficult choices between taking photographs or videos of troubled children. Single photographs can be compelling, but are time-bound. Videos provide more fluid perspective, but wide-angle views may miss some detail. We will have to be creative in our use of camera lenses and films as we try to capture the essence of children's psychopathology. Acknowledging the ways that the "active, changing" child is embedded in "a dynamic, changing context" makes our understandings of disorders more complicated, but more real (Cummings et al., 2000, p. 24).

Developmental Pathways, Stability, and Change

The concept of developmental pathways illustrates the belief that adjustment and maladjustment are points or places along a lifelong map. Considering the stage-salient (age-related) issues that challenge young children (such as the development of trust, or independence, or friendship), we understand that there are a great variety of adaptational efforts and outcomes, which can be grouped according to shared features (what Fischer et al., 1997, refer to as "families" or sets of pathways). There are diverse positive developmental pathways; many different ways for children to grow up safe, happy, and capable. Less happy, less adept children also follow multiple problematic developmental pathways, but these are distinct, different roads.

The 2001 Surgeon General's report on children's mental health and mental illness makes essentially the same point about both normal and abnormal individual development. The report highlights children's active self-organizing and self-righting tendencies, asserting that "a child within a given context naturally adapts (as much as possible) to a particular ecological niche . . . . When environments themselves are highly disordered or pathological, children's adaptations to such settings may also be pathological, especially when compared with children's behaviors within more healthy settings."

Children's maladaptations have both short- and long-term implications. Sometimes, the maladaptation has immediate negative consequences. For example, one child who is physically abused may, in an effort to prevent additional pain, become aggressive toward other adults or peers. Another child in the same situation may exhibit overly solicitous and compliant behavior in an effort to ensure the approval of others. In the short run, these alternative coping strategies may afford somewhat reasonable (and somewhat useful) accommodations. However, over time, such entrenched patterns of preemptory aggression or compliance may lead to a diminished sense of self and difficulties in peer relationships (Fischer et al., 1997).

Equifinality and multifinality refer to similarities and differences in individual pathways to a disordered outcome (Cicchetti & Rogosch, 1996; Loeber, 1991; Sroufe, 1997; see Figure 3.2). **Equifinality** is best understood as sets of differing circumstances that lead to the same diagnosis. For example, one child may fall behind in school. Another may be part of a family that is disengaged and hostile. Still another may have a genetic vulnerability to mood disorder. Equifinality describes the process whereby all three of these children go on to develop major depression in adolescence. With equifinality, different beginnings result in similar outcomes.

Multifinality is best understood as sets of similar beginnings that lead to different outcomes. Here, three children all begin with the same set of circumstances, perhaps involving maternal psychopathology and severe economic disadvantage. One child may struggle and manage to just get by. Another may surpass all expectations. And the last may fail in school, in relationships, and in the job market. With multifinality, similar beginnings result in different outcomes. For both equifinality and multifinality, we are concerned with the kinds of individual, familial, and social variables that influence children's developmental pathways both toward and away from disorder.

So far, our discussion of developmental pathways emphasizes stability, the ways in which maladaptation continues over time and place. We can look at

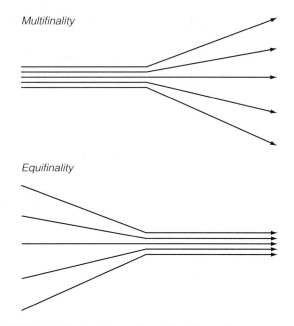

Multifinality

Equifinality

FIGURE 3:2 Illustrations of *equifinality* and *multifinality*.

Figure 3.2 and see the straight lines or direct paths of development, and the apparent inevitability of certain outcomes. But developmental pathways also encompass change. The Surgeon General's report (2001) emphasizes this possibility, suggesting that while early maladaptation often leads to later maladaptation, developmental discontinuities also occur, and "may reflect the emergence of new capacities (or incapacities) as the child's psychological self, brain, and social environment undergo significant reorganization." The "emergence of new capacities" in a child may lead to numerous instances of change for the better, with difficulties outgrown over time, or successfully managed by parents, teachers, and children themselves. There are also, unfortunately, numerous instances of change for the worse, with well-adjusted youngsters developing psychopathologies in later years. The developmental pathways model will need to account for both these types of trajectories. Figure 3.3 provides additional examples of zigzag, curving, or indirect developmental paths.

Two of the most important things to remember in thinking about the pathways model are that (1) change is possible at many points; however, (2) change is constrained or enabled by previous adaptations. For example, the transition to middle school is often associated with a larger group of

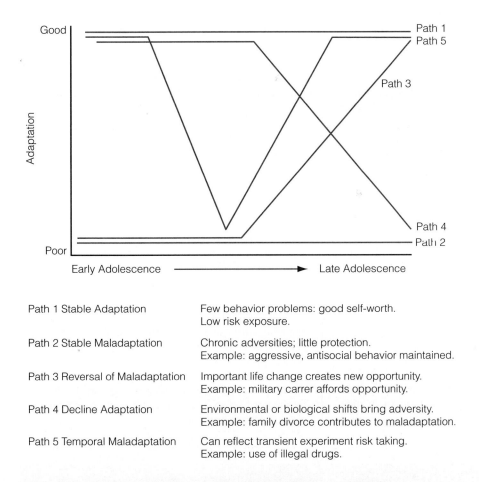

FIGURE 3:3 Zigzag and indirect pathways.
Source: From Compas, B.E, et al (1995), "Adolescent development: Pathways and processes of risk and resilience", 'Annual Review of Psychology', 46, 265-293. Reproduced with permission in the format Textbook and in the format Internet posting via Copyright Clearance Center.

Path 1 Stable Adaptation — Few behavior problems: good self-worth. Low risk exposure.

Path 2 Stable Maladaptation — Chronic adversities; little protection. Example: aggressive, antisocial behavior maintained.

Path 3 Reversal of Maladaptation — Important life change creates new opportunity. Example: military carrer affords opportunity.

Path 4 Decline Adaptation — Environmental or biological shifts bring adversity. Example: family divorce contributes to maladaptation.

Path 5 Temporal Maladaptation — Can reflect transient experiment risk taking. Example: use of illegal drugs.

peers from which a child may choose new friends; whether a child is able to develop new friendships may depend on his or her self-image, social skills, and earlier successful (or unsuccessful) experiences in elementary school. Depending on a collection of unique factors for any given child—the timing of diagnosis, the specific disorder, the kind of intervention, specific familial and environmental variables—we expect differences in the likely types of change or rates of change.

Rutter (1996) has explored the "transitions and turning points" of developmental pathways, examining the kinds of variables that are associated with change. He identifies both internal, intrinsic factors (such as the acquisition of language or the onset of puberty) as well as external factors (such as a move to a new home or a divorce). Rutter ties these transitions to the shutting down or opening up of opportunities. For example, the decision by an academically struggling adolescent to drop out of school may result in the shutting down of a number of employment options, or the closing off of certain

aspects of a positive self-image. Or following a move to a new neighborhood, a child with a difficult reputation among peers may be able to develop new and more successful friendships.

Time-related aspects of change also need to take into account the **plasticity** (i.e., the relatively changeable nature) of the individual and the individual's environment (Sameroff, 1993). Lerner (1998) suggests that some children are more plastic, more changeable than others. Likewise, some environments (families, for example) are more plastic, more open to change. Effective interventions, then, must take into account both the child's and his or her environment's changeable nature.

Whether we describe stable or changing patterns in development, it is important to understand that "the course of development is lawful" (Sroufe & Rutter, 1984). Lawful, or coherent, development is different from stability. Sroufe and Rutter argue that we need to look for connections that make developmental sense. For example, a child's approach to calming herself may look different when she is

8 years old (e.g., talking quietly to herself, breathing deeply) than it did when she was 4 years old (e.g., curling up with a favorite blanket), but her later efforts are meaningfully related to her earlier approach. As another example, some children who are bullied by older siblings at home go on to bully children in younger grades in elementary school. Being maltreated and maltreating others are *not* identical forms of behavior, but they are sometimes connected in terms of ideas about the self, relationships, and power. This notion of coherence is the final component of our understanding of both direct and indirect developmental pathways. Coherence reflects our belief that beginnings may be logically linked to outcomes if we carefully evaluate the variables that lead to stability as well as the variables that lead to change.

Competence and Incompetence

Up to this point, we have assumed that children either do well or do poorly. We have assumed that psychological well-being is characteristic of some children, but not others. In reality, of course, well-being is not an all-or-none phenomenon. Most normally developing children do better, or are more competent, in some areas than in others. Competence, within the framework of developmental psychopathology, reflects "effective functioning in important environments" (Masten, Morison, Pellegrini, & Tellegen, 1990, p. 239). Competence involves multiple components, including a child's skills and talents, beliefs about his or her effectiveness, personality characteristics, and accomplishments (Harter, 1993; Harter, Whitesell, & Junkin, 1998; Masten & Coatsworth, 1995).

The Case of Ryan

Ryan is in seventh grade. While his childhood to date has been relatively happy and uneventful, tensions in the home have increased in the year since his father was laid off from his job. Initially supportive of her husband, Ryan's mother has begun to resent Ryan's father's rejection of several job opportunities that he felt were less than what he deserved. Money has become tight and the family has had to restrict purchases such as new school clothes and supplies.

BOX 3:1   THE CHILD IN CONTEXT

Parental Views of Child Competence in a Village Community

All parents in all cultures have ideas about what characteristics make a child successful and well-adjusted. As you might expect, many of the hoped-for characteristics are similar across settings and circumstances, such as being well-behaved, getting along with friends, and doing well in school (Durbrow et al., 2001). Other characteristics appear more culture-specific. In a study of child competence in the Caribbean, Durbrow (1999) collected data using parent interviews. Parents described less competent children using a variety of mild to moderately negative terms, including *troublesome, miserable, greedy, hardened, lazy* and *wicked*. In this study, children were viewed as competent if they were respectful and obedient, completed their chores, were satisfactory students, were friendly with peers, and were involved in positive activities outside of home and school. Less salient, but still useful, indicators of competence included attending church, practicing good health habits, and having a content personality. These adult criteria for competence were similar for younger girls, adolescent girls, and younger boys. Adolescent boys were less likely to be seen as doing well in school, and that criterion was mentioned less frequently for them. For adolescent boys, doing chores well was a more influential indication of competence.

Parents provided a number of explanations for child competence. About half of the parents referred to the extent of firm and responsible caregiving as a factor contributing to child behavior or misbehavior. Other factors included the child's innate characteristics, adequate nutrition and health, and neighborhood characteristics. Some of the differences in parental conceptions of competence likely reflect specific demands of communities and socioeconomic concerns. Multicultural investigations of competence across development will need to continue to address these factors as they explore competence within and across diverse populations.

Ryan, a rather shy individual, is self-conscious and generally uncomfortable around his classmates. He had difficulty making the transition to middle school in sixth grade, and felt overwhelmed by the large and bustling setting. Ryan is a talented student with an especially strong aptitude in math and science. In fact, his science teacher, Mr. Gordon, invited him to join the middle school math team. Ryan has made a significant contribution there, and was asked by several other team members to join them in developing and entering a project for a science competition. Within these more structured social settings, Ryan has begun to relax and develop some genuine friendships. Mr. Gordon has continued to mentor Ryan and has told Ryan's parents that Ryan is his hardest working student, and that he is recommending that Ryan switch to the school's accelerated academic track for the following semester. Even with these school achievements, Ryan has become increasingly withdrawn and irritable at home, where the arguments between his parents have become more frequent. ■

The Case of Jasmine

Jasmine is in the seventh grade. When she was 8 years old, her parents divorced after several turbulent years during which each developed serious chemical dependency problems. Jasmine was sent to live with her grandmother for a year. During that time, Jasmine struggled with a number of anxiety symptoms and sleep disturbances, and experienced many problems at school. Her grandmother, however, was patient and supportive of both her granddaughter and her daughter while Jasmine's mother completed a successful course of treatment, found work and an apartment close by. After rejoining her mother, Jasmine gradually came to trust the stability of her new home and continued to be very involved with her grandmother.

After several failed attempts to overcome his addictions, Jasmine's father recently found a treatment program that has helped him to make real progress. While his contact with Jasmine has been limited, he has slowly reentered her life with the approval and encouragement of Jasmine's mother. In particular, he has taken a strong interest in Jasmine's soccer and basketball teams, attending as many games as possible. Like her father, Jasmine is an outstanding athlete. She has great natural ability, works hard at practice, and

loves to compete. All of her close friendships have developed from time spent with teammates. She often says that she is far happier on the soccer field and basketball court than in the classroom.

In fact, school is an increasing challenge for Jasmine. Although her pleasant personality and diligence served her well in elementary school, these qualities have not been enough to make up for her poor reading skills and difficulty comprehending the more abstract and complex content of her middle school courses. She is always behind in her assignments, and her resistance to spending time on her homework is the one major area of conflict between Jasmine and her mother. ■

Thinking about Ryan and Jasmine, it becomes clear that children's developmental pathways cannot be described as altogether good or altogether bad. And children's developmental outcomes are not altogether competent or altogether incompetent. Ryan displays academic strengths, but struggles to feel comfortable with his family. Jasmine is well-liked by peers and is a gifted athlete, but functions poorly in the school setting. As an adult, Ryan may eventually derive great satisfaction from a career as an engineer, but may always feel some discomfort with intimate relationships. Jasmine may believe that her low-paying service job reflects negatively on her overall worth as a person, but feel more accomplished when she thinks about her close-knit family and her several awards for volunteer work in her community. Like Ryan and Jasmine, all children display various **domains of competence,** involving particular skills and achievements, combined with domains (or areas or types) of incompetence, involving lack of skill or lack of achievement. Other researchers have referred to similar constructs as **arenas of comfort**, or spaces of relative calm (Simmons & Blyth, 1987): "An arena of comfort provides a context for the individual to relax and rejuvenate so that potentially stressful changes and experiences in another area can be endured or mastered" (Call & Mortimer, 2001, p. 2). Combinations of competencies and incompetencies are as true of children *with* disorders as they are of children *without* disorders. As we present specific psychopathologies in following chapters, it will be essential to remember that *children's disorders coexist with their talents and successes.* We will emphasize the need to take into account children's strengths during assessment and diagnosis, as well as the need to draw upon those strengths in designing effective treatment plans.

Garmezy, Masten, and Tellegen (1984) described three domains of competence in younger school-aged children: academic achievement, behavioral competence, and social competence. Two additional domains appear in adolescence: romantic competence and job competence (Masten et al., 1995). These domains are conceptually distinct, but there is some overlap. Generally, children who are competent in one area are somewhat more likely to be competent in other areas. Even so, competence in one area by no means assures competence in another. By adolescence, there is less overlap than in childhood, with social competence no longer related to academic achievement or behavioral competence (Masten et al., 1995). For instance, many adolescents make increasingly specific decisions about high school coursework (e.g., enrolling in science or language courses that are college prerequisites) and extracurricular activities (e.g., vacations with families or employment opportunities) that lead to increases or decreases in domain-specific skills. Competence in any domain does not emerge full-blown, and there are many factors that contribute to the development and maintenance of competence in children. Parents, in particular, may have a variety of views on the personal characteristics used to describe competent children, and a variety of views on the family and social factors linked to children's competence (Durbrow, 1999; Durbrow, Pena, Masten, Sesma, & Williamson, 2001; see Box 3.1).

Risk and Resilience

We turn now to discussions of some of the multiple factors that enhance or complicate children's development and functioning, and focus first on risk and resilience (Cicchetti & Garmezy, 1993; Garmezy & Rutter, 1983; Haggerty, Sherrod, Garmezy, & Rutter, 1994). The constructs of risk and resilience have been investigated for several decades, with much of the early work focused on the developmental outcomes of children of parents with schizophrenia (Garmezy, 1974; Mednick & Schulsinger, 1968). Key observations regarding this group of children were (1) significantly more of them developed psychopathologies compared to children whose parents were not diagnosed with schizophrenia, and (2) many of these children, despite their difficult family circumstances, had adequate and even excellent

outcomes. Why some children struggle, and why others prevail, are the questions at the heart of risk and resilience research.

Risk is defined as *increased vulnerability to disorder*. Risk factors are the individual, family, and social characteristics that are associated with this increased vulnerability. Resilience is defined as *adaptation (or competence) despite adversity*. Protective factors are the individual, family, and social characteristics that are associated with this positive adaptation.

Risk and Risk Factors

As noted, risk has to do with increased vulnerability to disorder. This vulnerability takes two forms: (1) nonspecific risk, which involves increased vulnerability to any, or many, kinds of disorders; and (2) specific risk, which involves increased vulnerability to one particular disorder. As an example of specific risk, the inactive liver enzyme that interferes with the metabolism of phenylalanine is associated with a specific type of mental retardation. As an example of nonspecific risk, poverty is associated with a variety of negative outcomes. And just to make things interesting, there are factors that are both somewhat specific and somewhat nonspecific. For example, children whose parents are diagnosed with schizophrenia display increased vulnerability to schizophrenia itself, as well as increased vulnerability to a number of other psychological disorders.

Types of Risk Factors

The most common distinctions made among types of risk factors involve individual, family, and social examples. Individual risk factors are child-oriented and include things like gender, temperament, and intelligence. As we will see in upcoming chapters, being a boy or a girl makes one more or less vulnerable to certain psychopathologies (Crick & Zahn-Waxler, 2003). Being very intense, or easily aroused, or difficult to soothe, also makes a child more vulnerable to disorder. And being less intelligent is associated with more frequent negative outcomes.

Family risk factors are those associated with the child's immediate caretaking environment, and include parent characteristics such as the presence of psychopathology or harsh, punitive styles of parenting, as well as family characteristics such as unusual discord among siblings (e.g., Lerner, 2001). Maternal psychopathology is often cited as a nonspecific risk factor (Connell & Goodman, 2002; Cummings

Nathan Benn/Corbis

Social risk factors, including socioeconomic disadvantage, are associated with academic and health struggles.

& Davies, 1994; Seifer, 1995). That is, having a mother with a serious psychological disorder is related to children developing disorders; these disorders are sometimes similar to the mother's, but they are also often different. Depressed moms can have depressed kids, but depressed moms have anxious kids and kids with conduct problems too.

Social risk factors include those associated with the child's larger environment, including neighborhood and socioeconomic niche, school system, and racial, ethnic, and cultural characteristics. Specifically, we want to know if membership in any particular group is associated with increased vulnerability to disorder (Sameroff, Seifer, & Bartko, 1997), and whether poverty or ethnicity makes a child more likely to develop disorders (Apfel & Seitz, 1997; Katz & Kofkin, 1997; Luthar, 1997). To further illustrate this idea of social risk, we can think about the connection between neighborhoods and academic performance, and evidence that disadvantaged neighborhoods are associated with children's academic struggles in the elementary school years (Shumow, Vandell, & Posner, 1999).

Certain kinds of family and social risk factors are frequently conceptualized as stressful or adverse life events (e.g., divorce, parental unemployment). Stressful life events also include experiencing natural disasters such as floods or tornadoes. With respect to nonspecific and specific effects of stressful life events, there are recent data that suggest that we look more closely at some particular associations. For example, depression and conduct disorders appear to be more reliably correlated with stressful life events than attention-deficit hyperactivity disorder and phobias are (Tiet et al., 2001).

Another aspect of risk that should be noted is whether the risk is transient or enduring. Transient risk factors are temporary or short-lived, such as months-long financial difficulties when a parent is laid off that improve when that parent is rehired. Enduring risk factors are more permanent, such as a child's diminished intellectual ability or marital conflict that lasts for years.

Numbers of Risk Factors

Many researchers have observed that the total number of risk factors that children experience is even more important than the particular type of risk factors. Rutter (1979), Simmons and Blyth (1987), and others have provided convincing data that the more risk factors to which children were exposed, the more negative the developmental outcome. So, even though any risk is unfortunate, we need to be especially watchful over children who experience risk on top of additional risk.

Timing of Risk Factors

Understanding the role of timing is more complicated than understanding the type or the total number of risk factors. Stressors may have no impact, little impact, or profound impact, *depending on the age at which they occur* and whether they occur alone or with other stressors and risk factors. For example, in the disadvantaged neighborhood study mentioned above, the academic struggles of children were observed in the later elementary grades and not the earlier ones (Shumow et al., 1999). If we had only looked at the early grades, we might have missed the later connection and erroneously concluded that poor neighborhoods had little impact on academics. Another example of this differential impact involves divorce, where children's age-related skills and resources interact with the stressful events to produce different outcomes at different ages (Hetherington, Bridges, & Insabella, 1998; Zill, Morrison, & Coiro, 1993).

Patterns of Risk Factors

Negative outcomes are also related to whether certain risk factors occur alone or with others; that is, we look to see whether a particular pattern of risk is in place. Some combinations of risk factors may be more problematic than others. For instance, Rutter (1987) observes that boys are more likely than girls to develop particular disorders in the presence of similar risk factors. He hypothesizes that this greater risk may be related to individual risk factors (such as neurophysiological vulnerability), parental risk factors (such as parents arguing more in front of boys than girls), and boys' increasingly negative chain reactions to initial difficulties. Understanding the complexities of patterns of risk may help us understand why there are different developmental outcomes for children in the same family, or among children from similar backgrounds (Kohen, Leventhal, Dahinten, & McIntosh, 2008; Morales & Guerra, 2006).

Overall, when we think about risk and risk factors, we are concerned with both immediate and eventual outcomes. The decades-long Kauai study, involving multiethnic children from the Hawaiian island of Kauai, suggests that two-thirds of the children who experience multiple risks, including perinatal stress (an individual factor), dysfunctional families (a family factor), and poverty (a social factor) struggle to adapt, with many of them developing clinically significant disorders (Werner, 1993; Werner & Smith, 1982). These kinds of findings illustrate previously discussed notions of developmental pathways, along with continuities and discontinuities in development. Taken together, these data demonstrate that the construct of risk is complex, and that risk type, number, timing, and pattern all interact to influence children's capacity for weathering the difficulties they encounter.

The Example of Child Maltreatment

Because the construct of risk is so central to the field of developmental psychopathology, we want to take additional time to consolidate our understanding using the example of child maltreatment. Child maltreatment is a broad category including physical abuse, sexual abuse, psychological abuse and neglect, reflecting the "gross violation of the rights of a vulnerable and dependent child" (Cicchetti & Toth, 1995, p. 541). *Child maltreatment is not a diagnosis* that is assigned to a child. Rather, it is a risk factor that affects hundreds of thousands of children each year, costing billions of dollars, and resulting in 1500 preventable deaths in the United States (U.S. Department of Health and Human Services [DHHS], 2007).

The Department of Health and Human Services (2007) identified the primary form of maltreatment in individual cases and reported that 61% of maltreated children were victims of neglect, with a parent or primary caregiver failing to provide basic shelter, nutrition, medical care, and/or supervision. Nineteen percent of maltreated children were physically abused. Ten percent of maltreated children were sexually abused. Five percent of maltreated children were emotionally abused. Most cases of maltreatment involved combinations of abuse and neglect, an awful example of multiple risks. With respect to age, DHHS reported that infants and toddlers had the highest rates of victimization and the highest fatality rates. With respect to race and ethnicity, African-American children, Pacific Islander children, and Native American children exhibited the highest maltreatment rates. Low socioeconomic status and social isolation were frequently correlated with maltreatment. Most maltreatment (79%) was perpetrated by parents, with neglect as the most common form.

Child maltreatment is a nonspecific risk factor, with increased likelihood of immediate, short-term, and long-term negative developmental outcomes (Belsky, 1980, 1993; Cicchetti & Toth, 1995, 2003). There is widespread evidence of neurophysiological impact, including negative effects on the hypothalamic-pituitary-adrenal axis, the dysregulation of the stress response, and other neuroanatomical changes that lead to later psychopathology (De Bellis, 2002; Gunnar, 2000; Heim, Meinlschmidt, & Nemeroff, 2003; Putnam, 2003). There are also abundant data that document the psychological consequences of maltreatment, including deviant emotional and social development, disrupted family relationships (e.g., Howes, Cicchetti, Toth, & Rogosch, 2000), poor school performance, and psychopathology involving antisocial and aggressive behavior, depression, and substance abuse (e.g., Cicchetti & Toth, 2003; Jaffee, Caspi, Moffitt, & Taylor, 2004). Indeed, "although the thought of a maltreated child conjures up images of head trauma, bruises, broken bones, malnutrition, and the like, it appears that emotional damage, not physical damage, may exert the most long-term harmful effect" (Cicchetti & Toth, 2003, p. 190).

Advocates for children need to think about maltreatment in multiple ways: as its own risk factor, as one of several co-occurring risk factors, and as a marker of other risk factors. Maltreatment cannot be traced to a single source, such as parent psychopathology, a parent's own history of being maltreated, poverty, or some constellation of difficult characteristics in a child; instead, it is a multiply determined risk, with equal emphasis on family and environmental factors (Belsky, 1993; Cicchetti & Toth, 2003). Although child maltreatment clearly illustrates the construct of risk as involving increased vulnerability to a range of distress and dysfunction, many instances of maltreatment do not inevitably lead to tragic outcomes. That some children manage to stay on track developmentally, and that some children exceed all expectations, leads to our discussion of resilience.

Resilience and Protective Factors

Remember that resilience is a special instance of adaptation; it is *competence in the face of adversity.* Specifically, "*Resilience* refers to the process of, capacity for, or outcome of successful adaptation despite challenging or threatening circumstances" (Masten, Best, & Garmezy, 1990, p. 426). Children who have all of the advantages of life—good health, supportive parents, safe neighborhoods, and effective social institutions—and thrive are not "resilient"; they are skillful, blessed, or lucky, or some combination of those. Resilient children do well *despite* their individual, family, or social circumstances. These are children of adversity who "worked well, played

well, loved well, and expected well" (Werner & Smith, 1982). Three types of resilient children have been described: (1) children with many risk factors who have good outcomes; (2) children who continue to display competence when they are experiencing stress; and (3) children who display good recoveries following stress or trauma.

Developmental psychopathologists have argued that resilience is not a trait or characteristic that certain children have and others do not. Instead, they see resilience as a process, a capacity that develops over time (Egeland, Carlson, & Sroufe, 1993; Freitas & Downey, 1998; Luthar, Cicchetti, & Becker, 2000b; Masten, 2001; Masten & Reed, 2002). Thus some children display certain types of resilience but not others (e.g., keeping up grades while continuing to struggle emotionally) or resilience that is built up over years (e.g., keeping up grades, then mending friendships, then repairing self-image) (see Box 3.2).

Definitions must also take into account the positive developmental outcomes that are the basis of resilience. In Chapter 1, we discussed whether definitions of abnormality should focus on adequate or optimal adaptations; we now consider whether good outcomes are simply the absence of clinically significant disorder, or whether the presence of joy and accomplishment is also important (Benard, 1999; Cowen, Work, & Wyman, 1997; Masten & Reed, 2002). Connections between the study of resilience and the study of positive psychology described in Chapter 2 are also important (Yates & Masten, 2004). From staying out of trouble with the law to achieving award-winning success, we need to acknowledge the range of resilient outcomes we are likely to observe. With these ideas about resilience in mind, we now turn to descriptions of specific protective factors. According to Masten, Morison, et al., (1990), *given the presence of risk*, these protective factors make negative outcomes *less likely.* Similar to investigations of risk factors, investigations of protective factors also focus on the various characteristics associated with better outcomes, with most of the research examining types and patterns of factors.

Types of Protective Factors

As with risk, we need to consider individual, family, and social types of protective factors (see Table 3.1). The most frequently noted individual factors have to do with children's personality characteristics. Children who have sunny dispositions, engaging manners, and who are more intelligent fare better

BOX 3:2 RISK AND RESILIENCE

"Ordinary Magic"

The study of risk and resilience is one of the foundations of the field of developmental psychopathology (Anthony, 1974; Garmezy, 1974; Rutter, 1979). The critical issue behind this important area of research is the investigation of the circumstances and mechanisms by which some children thrive and other children falter under conditions of stress and challenge. This has been a rich research vein, mined by many innovative and talented clinical researchers over the decades (Masten & Coatsworth, 1998; Rutter, 1990; Sroufe, 1997). In her seminal article, "Ordinary Magic," Ann Masten (2001) highlights several important lessons learned from resilience research. Most important is the somewhat unexpected finding that resilience turns out to be the rule in development, rather than the exception.

There is now abundant evidence of how resilience "arises from the normative functions of human adaptational systems" (Masten, 2001, p. 227), and this resilience

is an example of children's self-righting tendencies. Consequently, even under circumstances of extreme stress, resilience is the likely outcome if basic systems are in place and basic needs are met. These needs include consistent caregiving, and cognitive, emotional, and social nurturing. Resilience is observed in many children who experience poverty, in many children who struggle with physical illnesses, and in many children who are victims of natural disasters. Of course, if children's needs are compromised, even conditions of very low stress may result in problematic development and psychopathology. Masten concludes: "What began as a quest to understand the extraordinary has revealed the power of the ordinary" (p. 235). As Masten emphasizes, we are finding new reasons to be optimistic about the effectiveness of early interventions and current efforts to strengthen coping and minimize risk for all children and families.

(Masten, Morison et al., 1990). Particular kinds of psychological resources also matter. For example, children who have several coping strategies for dealing with stress (e.g., reframing their cognitive explanations for events, or talking about distress with a loving adult) experience more positive adaptations (Murphy & Moriarty, 1976; Rothbaum, Weisz, & Snyder, 1982).

Protective factors, such as positive temperament and a supportive family, promote resilience in the face of stress.

Christopher Futcher/Shutterstock.com

TABLE 3:1 CHILD, FAMILY, AND COMMUNITY PROTECTIVE FACTORS

Within the Child
Good cognitive abilities, including problem-solving and attentional skills
Easy temperament in infancy; adaptable personality later in development
Positive self-perceptions; self-efficacy
Faith and a sense of meaning in life
A positive outlook on life
Good self-regulation of emotional arousal and impulses
Talents valued by self and society
Good sense of humor
General appeal or attractiveness to others

Within the Family
Close relationships with caregiving adults
Authoritative parenting (high on warmth, structure/monitoring, expectations)
Positive family climate with low discord between parents
Organized home environment
Postsecondary education of parents
Parents with qualities listed as child protective factors (above)
Parents involved with child's education
Socioeconomic advantages

Within Other Relationships
Close relationships with competent, prosocial, and supportive adults
Connections to prosocial and rule-abiding peers

Within the Community
Effective schools
Ties to prosocial organizations (e.g., schools, clubs)
Neighborhoods with high "collective efficacy"
High levels of public safety
Good emergency social services (e.g., 911 or crisis nursery services)
Good public health and health care availability

Source: Masten & Reed (2002).

Family factors also serve to protect children in difficult situations, such as children living in impoverished circumstances. Characteristics such as family cohesion and warmth are helpful. Having supportive, emotionally available, and determined parents makes it more likely that at-risk children are able to avoid an ever-increasing string of negative events than children with less capable parents. Recent research on children living in poverty suggests that resilience is not uncommon and is associated with both genetic and environmental factors (Buckner, Mezzacappa, & Beardslee, 2003; Kim-Cohen, Moffitt, Caspi, & Taylor, 2004).

Social factors are also important (Garmezy, 1985; Rickel & Becker, 1997). Children whose lives

are embedded in ethnic and cultural and religious groups where their well-being is a communal responsibility may have access to support and resources which other children do not. From both theoretical and clinical perspectives, at-risk children with access to economic and political advantages, such as psychological counseling or school-based services, have better outcomes.

Patterns of Protective Factors

Again, to appreciate the complexities of patterns of protection, we can look at children in the same family who have similar risks but different outcomes. We expect that, even with siblings, different temperaments will have an impact on functioning, as will different teachers in school, and differences in the timing and number of stressful events (Smith & Prior, 1995). We can also look at the factors that promote better outcomes given particular psychopathologies (Kilmer, Cowen, & Wyman, 2001). How do these protective factors exert their beneficial effects? What are the mechanisms by which they influence the course and direction of children's developmental pathways? Rutter (1987, 1990) suggests that protective factors influence children's outcomes by (1) reducing the impact of risk, (2) reducing the negative chain reactions that follow exposure to risk, (3) serving to establish or maintain self-esteem and self-efficacy, and/or (4) opening up opportunities for improvement or growth.

Reducing the impact of risk involves exposing children to fewer negative events. Reducing the impact may also involve altering the meaning of exposure, so that children think about risk factors in less harmful ways. For example, a child who has experienced physical or sexual abuse can be encouraged to see him- or herself as heroic for reporting the abuse and saving other children from being victimized.

Reducing negative chain reactions has to do with intervening before a series of negative responses or additional negative events occur. For example, a child who experiences separation anxiety and misses school may be quickly referred for therapy, and a plan put into place to return the child to the classroom. With this plan, the consequence of avoiding anxiety by staying home is not reinforced, and academic difficulties resulting from missed class assignments are avoided. As another example, children at risk because they or their siblings have a chronic illness such as diabetes may be helped to recognize the range of emotional reactions connected to the waxing and waning of symptoms. Family members or friends may provide support before children become overwhelmed by frustration or panic.

Developing and maintaining self-esteem and self-efficacy is clearly related to our understanding of the role of personality characteristics in moderating distress and dysfunction. As an example, a student with dyslexia who is given the opportunity to meet other students with dyslexia is less likely to view information-processing problems as evidence of personal inferiority, lack of intelligence, or insufficient effort.

As to Rutter's final way that protective factors influence children's outcomes, opening up opportunities for improvement and growth involves the appreciation of turning points in children's lives. Recognizing the particular developmental challenges that children face, and then taking advantage of both expected and unexpected bumps in the road of development, may have noticeable effects. For a straightforward example, we can consider that a move to a new neighborhood may allow a child to develop other friends. For a more paradoxical example, we can think about Parmelee's (1986) discussion of the beneficial effects of illnesses in children. In his view, relatively minor illnesses such as chicken pox or a broken bone allow children to experience small frustrations that involve coping efforts. This practice sets the stage for later successful coping with more serious or difficult stressors. A child who never experiences frustration or disappointment, then, is actually at a disadvantage; he or she will be easily upset and without well-practiced strategies when the inevitable stressor occurs. As you can see, the possible relations between the experience of stress and the capacity to cope can be very complicated.

The Example of Child Maltreatment

Returning to the example of child maltreatment, concerned adults must focus on ways to promote psychological wellness in at-risk children (Cicchetti et al., 2000). There is both theory and research to guide adults in their efforts. Data suggest that many children and adolescents who experience physical or sexual abuse display resilience throughout their lives (Perkins & Jones, 2004; Rind, Tromovitch, & Bauserman, 1998). *This resilience, of course, in no way minimizes the moral or legal wrongfulness of maltreatment.* Rather, it shows us that parents, teachers, and mental health professionals must work together to identify protective factors at individual, familial, and social levels: resources such as self-esteem, family and peer

support, a positive school climate, the presence of other caring adults, and access to both short- and long-term treatments (Cicchetti & Rogosch, 1997; Perkins & Jones, 2004).

Resilience, then, reflects the combined contributions of protective factors from individual, family, and social levels. So a child judged to be resilient in the face of early maltreatment, despite a chaotic and inconsistent home, may have exceptional personal strengths such as an easy temperament, strong intellectual abilities, and a warmth that draws adults and peers close. In addition, factors such as the type, duration, and timing of maltreatment influence resilience as well. Looked at in this way, the construct of resilience is better understood as the probabilistic outcome of multiple dynamic variables rather than as a static condition of the child or the environment (Yates, Egeland, & Sroufe, 2003). With this understanding, researchers are beginning to study, in much greater detail, the interactive influence of biological factors (such as stress-related hormones) and personality characteristics (such as emotional reactivity and self-control) (Cicchetti & Rogosch, 2007). The quality of relationships, from childhood through adolescence and into adulthood, has also been found to mediate the development of psychopathology for individuals maltreated during childhood (Collishaw et al., 2007).

Multicultural Research on Risk and Resilience

Given the concern with the social and cultural variables identified as either risk or protective factors, and with data about differing rates of disorder in various groups of children, we must take additional time to consider research findings that ask very specific questions about race and ethnicity. We must also pay special attention to ethical concerns in mental health research focused on minority children (Fisher et al., 2002). For example, do we observe the same kinds, and similar total numbers, of risk and protective factors in diverse groups of children? Are there differences in patterns and outcomes?

There are increasing numbers of both multicultural comparisons (across different cultures) and within-culture investigations of individual, family, and social risk factors. For example, Kilmer, Cowen, Wyman, Work, and Magnus (1998) sampled Hispanic, African American, and European American children from poor neighborhoods and found differences in the kinds of risks experienced. African American and Hispanic children more frequently had a family member arrested or in jail. More African American children were in foster care, or living with relatives or friends. Hispanic children struggled more often with parental separations and divorce. European American children encountered family dysfunction more often, and were diagnosed more frequently with medical problems.

Although the Kilmer et al. (1998) study reported that different groups of children encountered similar numbers of risks, other studies suggest that differences in numbers may require close attention. Jose et al. (1998) found similar numbers of major stressors among 10- to 14-year-old Russian and American children, but more daily hassles in the Russian group. This is important because ongoing hassles or small frustrations of everyday life like frequent family arguments, as well as school difficulties such as frequent teacher turnover, are often more strongly associated with poor outcomes than major events are (Lazarus & Folkman, 1984). We also need to think about the possibility that similar risks may lead to different outcomes for various groups of children. Latino children who are maltreated, for example, may fare worse than non-Latino children (Flores, Cicchetti, & Rogosch, 2005).

With respect to resilience and protective factors, research suggests that similar kinds of protective factors are in play for various racial, ethnic, and cultural groups. These include individual factors such as a positive self-image, empathy, a sense of competence, and realistic perceptions of control, and family factors such as close relationships with a caregiver (Magnus, Cowen, Wyman, Fagen, & Work, 1999). In their recent study of maltreated Latino children, Flores et al. (2005) reported that some of the same personality characteristics that protect non-Latino children also serve to enhance Latino children's resilience. However, there may also be some specific differences. Conceptualizing sociocultural approaches as focused on differences rather than deficits, researchers have explored resilience in African-American youth (e.g., Apfel & Seitz, 1997; Taylor et al., 2000), Latino youth (e.g., Reese, Kroesen, & Gallimore, 2000; Taylor et al., 2000), and Asian-American youth (e.g., Chao, 2000; McCarty et al., 1999). Overall, resilient outcomes may "transcend racial boundaries" (Magnus et al., 1999, p. 482), but there is still much work to be done on understanding protective factors related to race, ethnicity, and culture.

A Life-Span Approach to Risk and Resilience

Our discussion of risk and resilience has provided numerous examples of both difficult and encouraging outcomes during the developmental periods of childhood and adolescence. However, we continue to be affected by previous and ongoing challenges throughout our lifetimes. We must, again, emphasize the notion of process as we think about the impact of risk and protective factors on adult development and psychopathology (Staudinger, Marsiske, & Baltes, 1993; Zigler & Glick, 1986).

According to Staudinger et al. (1993), children continue on developmental pathways into adulthood and throughout their lives. Over time, though, we can expect that relatively more of our resources are spent trying to stay on track, and fewer are expended on forging new trails. Some individuals do encounter new risks in their adult years, or discover that adaptations that were effective in childhood no longer work for them as adults. These individuals may, in fact, exhibit novel responses and create new opportunities for growth. Overall, the course of risk and resilience is complex and subject to change, and must be considered across the full breadth of our lives.

Research Strategies in Developmental Psychopathology

As in developmental psychology and psychology in general, research in developmental psychopathology takes advantage of all of the core research methodologies, including case studies, correlational approaches, and experimental and quasi-experimental designs. In addition, there are a number of distinctive research methodologies with special importance for investigators in developmental psychopathology. We will focus on three especially relevant issues related to these methodologies: cross-sectional versus longitudinal approaches; complex hypotheses and complex models; and research in real-world settings with practical applications.

Cross-Sectional and Longitudinal Approaches

Cross-sectional research involves the collection of data at a single point in time, with comparisons made among groups of participants. For example, we might ask children in first, fourth, and seventh grades, in the middle of the school year, about their daily hassles. We might compare the children's replies, looking for age-related differences among the younger and older children (e.g., how are the first graders different from the fourth graders; are either or both groups different from the seventh graders?). Longitudinal research, in contrast, involves the ongoing collection of data from the same group of participants, or the study of individuals over time. With this approach, we also recruit first graders in the middle of their school year and talk with them about their hassles. But we wait until this same group is in the fourth grade before we collect more data. And then we wait again until the group is in the seventh grade. The longitudinal approach allows us to interpret and discuss data with respect to age (e.g., first versus fourth versus seventh graders) *and* individual differences (i.e., specific children whose hassles increase or decrease over the course of their school years). The research goals for the two types of studies are different. The cross-sectional study focuses on identifying age-related differences (or outcomes at a particular point in childhood). Cross-sectional research has the advantage of providing answers quickly, but the disadvantage of sampling different individuals at different ages. The longitudinal study provides additional data, and highlights

the developmental processes that occur for the same children across a significant span of time.

Although longitudinal research in developmental psychopathology has occurred for decades, it has become an increasingly common research methodology. Murphy's groundbreaking studies of children's coping (Murphy, 1962, 1974; Murphy & Moriarty, 1976) and Robins's work on deviant children (Robins, 1966) are important early examples of longitudinal investigations of adaptive and maladaptive developmental pathways. Werner's studies of Hawaiian children (Werner, 1993; Werner & Smith, 1977, 1982, 1989; see Box 3.3) and Masten's ongoing investigations of resilience (Masten et al., 1999) provide more contemporary illustrations.

These more recent longitudinal studies are also increasingly complex (Cicchetti & Toth, 1995; Rutter & Sroufe, 2000), given their attempts to address larger developmental questions. Sroufe and Rutter (1984), for example, describe the goals of prospective risk research (i.e., research done over the years *before* psychopathology is evident) as providing valuable data about "not only the different developmental course of at-risk subjects and controls but, especially, the development of those at-risk subjects who do and do not ultimately develop

---

BOX 3:3 RISK AND RESILIENCE

The Kauai Longitudinal Studies

An important example of a longitudinal study of a high-risk population is the Kauai Longitudinal Study (Werner, 1993; Werner & Smith, 1982). Begun in 1955 on the Hawaiian island of Kauai, a group of mental health and medical professionals undertook a prospective study of 201 infants who experienced moderate to significant perinatal distress, lived in poverty, and experienced significant psychosocial stress. Comprehensive data were gathered following the birth of these babies, and their overall developmental progress was tracked at the ages of 1, 2, 10, 18, and 32 years. Although the study began with an emphasis on the effects of vulnerability, over time it became equally focused on issues related to resilience. Much of the study's focus was on a group of 72 children who, despite the early and pervasive challenges they faced, grew into "competent, confident, and caring young adults" (Werner, 1993, p. 504).

Many of the findings point to the fact that, within broad parameters, quality of childrearing appeared to be a more powerful determinant of outcome than biological risk factors. A related finding was that, in general, the impact of reproductive stress diminished over time, presumably as the importance of the child's social world exerted increasing influence. This is not to suggest, however, that the developing children in this study were merely passive recipients of either a negative or positive environment. Indeed, the investigators note that from a very early age, the most resilient children elicited positive attention from both family members and strangers. They were seen as active, alert, bright and confident. Their sense of self-efficacy both created and elicited a more supportive social context within which to develop. It is the unique perspective of a longitudinal study such as this one that allows for complex and comprehensive hypotheses to be both designed and answered.

the disorder" (p. 19). Sroufe (1997) has discussed the need for longitudinal data on the factors that are associated with change and continuity once disorder is observed. Of course, we need to remember that, even with the numerous benefits associated with longitudinal research, there are many instances when longitudinal research is not feasible, and many other instances when the design of choice would be cross-sectional.

Complex Hypotheses and Complex Models

It is very clear that our research designs are becoming ever more complicated (again, see Figure 3.1). With respect to our hypotheses and models, Garcia Coll and Magnuson (1999) summarize: "we begin to ask *new* questions in our research or *old* questions in different ways" (p. 3). We not only stretch our data collection over months, years, and decades, we examine multiple variables at each particular point in time. In keeping with the interdisciplinary model of developmental psychopathology, researchers are including biological, psychological, and social variables in their studies. Whereas we once focused our investigations on children and their immediate environments, we now broaden our approaches to include macro-systems such as culture (Boyce et al., 1998). Always, we expect to encounter complex models of causality (Cicchetti & Dawson, 2002), with a "larger number of reciprocally related variables, and the emergence of statistical techniques that permit the analysis of such complex processes" (Mash & Dozois, 1996, p. 35).

Current research on child maltreatment provides numerous examples of complexity. Instead of examining a single variable (such as maltreatment versus no maltreatment) and its association with outcome, investigators account for multiple characteristics of that variable (type of maltreatment, frequency of maltreatment, source of maltreatment), leading to a better understanding of risk and resilience. Danielson, de Arellano, Kilpatrick, Saunders, and Resnick (2005) found that adolescents who had experienced both physical and sexual abuse reported more symptoms of depression than adolescents who had experienced only physical abuse (and adolescents who had no history of abuse). Adolescents who experienced chronic abuse were more depressed than those who experienced single abusive episodes. And girls who were maltreated were more depressed than boys who were maltreated. Another research example involves the impact of childhood trauma

on neuroanatomy and neurobiology, the subsequent development of depression, and response to antidepressant treatment in adult women (Heim & Nemeroff, 2001; Kaufman, Plotsky, Nemeroff, & Charney, 2000; Vythilingam et al., 2002). Early maltreatment is hypothesized to sensitize the stress-response system; both genetic factors and subsequent caregiving may ameliorate some of the negative consequences of maltreatment (Kaufman et al., 2000).

In addition to the emphasis on complex hypotheses and complex models, we also pay more attention to the variety of available methods for collecting data. Quantitative methods have been the standard for years, but there is renewed interest in qualitative methods such as diaries, narratives, and holistic observations (Sullivan, 1998).

Research in Real-World Settings with Practical Applications

One of the more compelling aspects of research in developmental psychopathology is its concern with practical applications and its focus on child advocacy (Garrett, Thorp, Behrmann, & Denham, 1998; Lerner, 1998; Marcell & Falls, 2001; Zigler & Finn-Stevenson, 1992). Primary prevention research, or investigations of how to avoid or reduce psychopathology in children, provides numerous illustrations of principles and practices in action (Power, Shapiro, & DuPaul, 2003).

Early intervention foster care programs for high-risk preschoolers identify sets of factors which are associated with poor outcomes, and then provide foster families with resources to offset those risks (Fisher, Gunnar, Chamberlain, & Reid, 2000). These types of programs have been successful in promoting better functioning. The Fast Track prevention program is focused on children at risk for the development of conduct problems and antisocial behavior (Conduct Problems Prevention Research Group, 1992, 1999a, 1999b, 2002). Specific assistance is offered to the children, their families, and their teachers, designed to reduce current negative behaviors and forestall future difficulties.

And, as just described, we can target our interventions in a variety of ways. The most common involve children and families, but schools are another important setting for prevention efforts. The Consortium on the School-Based Promotion of Social Competence (1994) has summarized research focused on risk reduction and the enhancement of protective factors in schools, with clear support for the effectiveness of school-based interventions. In all of these illustrations, we see the thoughtful integration of developmental theory into prevention work. In the best circumstances, this type of research serves both to avoid the development of disorder and to promote the well-being of young persons (Izard, 2002; Jensen, 1999; Schulenberg & Maggs, 2001).

■ Key Terms

Psychopathology (pg. 27)
Developmental psychopathology (pg. 27)
Adaptational failure (pg. 28)
Delay (pg. 28)
Fixation (pg. 28)
Deviance (pg. 28)
Process (pg. 28)
Dynamic systems processes (pg. 28)
Transactional processes (pg. 29)
Longitudinal processes (pg. 29)
Developmental pathways (pg. 29)
Equifinality (pg. 30)
Multifinality (pg. 30)
Plasticity (pg. 31)
Coherence (pg. 32)
Competence (pg. 32)
Domains of competence (pg. 33)
Arenas of comfort (pg. 33)
Risk (pg. 34)
Risk factors (pg. 34)
Resilience (pg. 34)
Protective factors (pg. 34)
Nonspecific risk (pg. 34)
Specific risk (pg. 34)
Child maltreatment (pg. 36)
Physical abuse (pg. 36)
Sexual abuse (pg. 36)
Psychological abuse (pg. 36)
Neglect (pg. 36)
Cross-sectional research (pg. 41)
Longitudinal research (pg. 42)

■ Chapter Summary

- Developmental psychopathology focuses on the developmental context within which maladaptive patterns of emotion, cognition, and behavior occur.
- By studying developmental pathways, we are able to consider patterns of adjustment and maladjustment over time.
- Equifinality refers to developmental pathways in which differing circumstances lead to the same diagnosis.
- Multifinality refers to developmental pathways in which similar beginnings lead to different outcomes.
- The pathways model emphasizes that change is possible at many points, although change is always influenced by previous adaptations.
- Coherence in development reflects the logical links between early developmental variables and later outcomes. Continuity is found in understanding the relationship between outcomes and the variables that lead to stability or change.
- Competence, from a developmental perspective, reflects effective functioning in relation to relevant developmental tasks and issues; evaluations of competence are embedded in the environment within which development is occurring.
- Risk is defined as *increased vulnerability to disorder*, while risk factors are the individual, family, and social characteristics that are associated with this increased vulnerability.
- Resilience is defined as *adaptation (or competence) despite adversity*, and protective factors are the individual, family, and social characteristics that are associated with this positive adaptation.
- Cross-sectional research involves the collection of data at a single point in time, with comparisons made among groups of participants, whereas longitudinal approaches involve the ongoing collection of data from the same group of participants, or the study of individuals over time.

CHAPTER 4

Classification, Assessment and Diagnosis, and Intervention

ON THE ONE HAND, we have infants, children, and adolescents who are struggling, who are distressed, who are deeply pained. On the other hand, we have theories about normal and abnormal development, proposals about risk and resilience, and beliefs about psychotherapy. In this chapter, we are going to make specific and practical connections between the children and the theories. The most basic questions are addressed: What kinds of disorders do children experience? Which disorder best describes a particular child's distress and dysfunction? And what can be done to help?

Classification

Given that it is useful to conceptualize some forms of children's struggle, distress, and pain in terms of disorder, we need to have some reasonably organized way to think about the different kinds of disorders we encounter. We need classification. **Classification** is defined as a system for describing the important categories, groups, or dimensions of disorder. Classification is differentiated from **diagnosis,** which is the method of assigning children to specific classification categories.

A good classification system serves several clinical, research, and theoretical purposes (Clark, Watson, & Reynolds, 1995; Sonuga-Barke, 1998). It enhances clinical utility; that is, it helps clarify thinking about the emergence of particular disorders, and about prognosis and treatment decisions. For example, if we know that a child's pattern of cognitive, emotional, and behavioral difficulties is consistent with the clinical presentation of autism, then we know something important about the cause and course of the disorder, and we know something useful about effective interventions. Classification also allows mental health professionals to communicate effectively about their clients and various psychopathologies. If we are working with a child with autism, then, we can discuss the relevant options for treatment with other clinicians, or school personnel, or representatives from insurance companies.

Classification also improves research efforts. Different investigators with similar understandings of disorders are better able to develop theories about the nature of specific psychopathologies, explain hypotheses, recruit participants, and talk about data. As a result, there are many specialized journals, conferences, and institutes focused on single disorders. Finally, efforts to improve classification contribute to the ongoing revisions of the principles and practices of developmental psychopathology discussed in the previous chapter. Across all of these classification purposes, we want to create and/or increase order and organization.

As we consider various classification schemes, it is important to keep in mind that any classification results in the loss of individual information. Classification in developmental psychopathology is focused on the many ways in which children with particular disorders are *alike*. But we know, of course, that each child is unique in his or her pattern of difficulties (and strengths). Knowing, for instance, that a child

displays the distress and dysfunction associated with depression (in contrast to anxiety) is one significant source of information, but it is also important to evaluate each depressed child's unique circumstances.

Clinical (Categorical) Classification

Clinical, categorical classification depends on identifying sets of symptoms that co-occur (or hang together), and that collectively are best understood as distinct, different disorders (similar to the idea of discontinuous models discussed in Chapter 2). Clinical, categorical classification assumes that there are groups of individuals with relatively similar patterns of disorder. With an ideal categorical scheme, each of the disorders would have its own specific etiology, course, and treatments.

The Diagnostic and Statistical Manual

The best known—although far from ideal—example of such classification is the **Diagnostic and Statistical Manual** (the **DSM**) of the American Psychiatric Association. Introduced in 1952, the DSM was designed as a practical tool for clinicians. Despite that era's pervasive psychoanalytic influence, the DSM was intended to be atheoretical and primarily descriptive, providing useful information about the clinical picture and the course of psychopathology. The 1952 DSM included only one separate childhood disorder, adjustment reaction of childhood and adolescence, listed in the section of "transient situational disorders." All other classifications of children's disorders were understood as identical to adult disorders, with the same clinical presentation and prognosis.

DSM-II, published in 1968, included nine different disorders observed in children, with two of them, mental retardation and childhood schizophrenia, in a separate childhood section. By 1980, with DSM-III (and 1987, with DSM-III-Revised), 44 child and adolescent disorders were described, with a much larger section specifically focused on disorders diagnosed in early development. DSM-III introduced the system of multiple axes, in which individuals were evaluated with respect to clinical symptoms as well as important contextual factors such as physical disease and level of stress (see Table 4.1). Following extensive literature reviews, data analyses, and field trials, DSM-IV was presented in 1994, with over 350 different categories of adult and child disorders. DSM-IV again increased the number of classification categories for children, and made special efforts to incorporate more developmental data (see Table 4.2). The process of revision for the DSM continues, with the publication of DSM-IV-TR (Text Revision) in 2000 (with additional information provided about many disorders, but with few changes to diagnostic categories or criteria). The latest manual, with selected changes and corrections, serves as a bridge between the fourth and upcoming fifth edition of the DSM.

The Medical Model

The DSM is tied, in large part, to the medical model of psychopathology. Key assumptions of the medical model are that (1) disorders are categorical (i.e., reflecting clear distinctions between healthy and disordered adjustments); (2) disorders are associated with "constitutional dysfunction" (i.e., the idea that the child somehow fails to display his/her natural function) (Wakefield, 1992, 1997); and (3) disorders are endogenous (i.e., characteristic of the individual, rather than an individual-environment transaction) (Sonuga-Barke, 1998).

With any system of classification, we are concerned with indices of reliability and validity. Reliability has to do with whether different clinicians, using the same set of criteria, classify children into the same clearly defined categories. Inter-rater reliability is noted when, for example, two or more clinical psychologists, gathering information about

> **TABLE 4:2 CATEGORIES OF DISORDERS LISTED IN DSM-IV AS USUALLY FIRST DIAGNOSED IN INFANCY, CHILDHOOD, OR ADOLESCENCE**
>
> Mental Retardation (diagnosed on Axis II)
>
> Learning Disorders
>
> Motor Skills Disorders
>
> Pervasive Developmental Disorders
>
> Attention-Deficit and Disruptive Behavior Disorders
>
> Feeding and Eating Disorders
>
> Tic Disorders
>
> Elimination Disorders
>
> Other disorders, including separation anxiety disorder, selective mutism, and reactive attachment disorder
>
> Note: Diagnoses such as major depression or generalized anxiety disorder are made using criteria similar to those used for adult diagnoses.

one child's developmental history and current difficulties, come to the same decision about the type of disorder. Cross-time reliability is noted when a child is similarly classified by the same clinician at two different points in time. Especially for disorders that are understood as chronic, such as mental retardation, a classification system that includes descriptions of both continuity and change is important. With a reliable classification system, a child with mental retardation would be similarly classified at age 3 and at age 10, even though there would be somewhat different patterns of symptoms and adjustments.

How reliable is the DSM-IV? Given the complexity of the construct of reliability, it is difficult to provide a clear and convincing response. Still, with each successive edition of the DSM, reliability has increased (Lahey, Applegate, Barkley, et al., 1994; Rapaport & Ismond, 1996; Volkmar et al., 1994). With increasingly specific criteria for classification, inter-rater reliability has improved. With more developmental data, cross-time reliability has also improved. But, as always, clinical efforts continue to focus on better applications of the categorical system.

Validity has to do with whether the classification gives us true-to-life, meaningful information. Specifically, internal validity tells us something important about the etiology of a disorder, or the core patterns of symptoms or difficulties experienced by children with a particular type or subtype of

> **TABLE 4:1 DSM-IV AND DESCRIPTION OF AXES**
>
> The Diagnostic and Statistical Manual of Mental Disorders (DSM-IV) is the diagnostic system currently used in the United States, as well as in many other countries, to describe types of mental illness. Objective criteria are used to define both broad and specific domains of psychopathology. A full DSM-IV diagnosis includes the assignment of a formal diagnostic label on one or both of the two clinical axes (Axis I and Axis II), along with notations of medical symptoms and syndromes (Axis III), and more subjective judgments on two other axes (Axis IV and Axis V).
>
> Axis I: Clinical Syndromes
>
> Axis II: Personality Disorders and Mental Retardation
>
> Axis III: General Medical Conditions
>
> Axis IV: Psychosocial and Environmental Problems
>
> Axis V: Global Assessment of Functioning

disorder. External validity tells us something important about the implications of the disorder (Szatmari, 2000). For example, children with specific disorders might be expected to respond favorably to certain interventions.

How valid is the DSM-IV? Validity, like reliability, is a difficult construct to evaluate. Some categories, such as schizophrenia, have long been presented as types of dysfunction and distress. Other categories, such as disorders of attachment, reflect newer conceptualizations of maladjustment. Ongoing research on some disorders, such as autism spectrum disorders, has led to frequent revision of the general category of disorder as well as the specific diagnostic criteria. Thus, we cannot make definitively positive statements about the internal and external validity of the whole DSM system, although there are categories with better validity support than others. For our purposes, we emphasize the valuable work that continues to address the increasing validity of various child classifications (Beauchaine, 2003; Cantwell, 1996; Hartman et al., 2001; Kagan, 1997; Lahey et al., 2004; Ollendick & Vasey, 1999; Sonuga-Barke, 1998).

Empirical (Dimensional) Classification

The DSM approach initially grew out of the subjective impressions and descriptions of experienced clinicians. Over the years, a more objective strategy for conceptualizing disorder has emerged. Achenbach (1997) characterizes this empirical approach to classification as a bottom-up process involving (1) the collection of data from children with normal and abnormal adjustments followed by (2) attempts to statistically group the many distresses and dysfunctions into meaningful dimensions (or important characteristics) of disorder. This process contrasts with the top-down approach of clinical classification, involving (1) the identification of types of disorder and then (2) the specification of symptoms of the disorders. Owing much to Achenbach's decades-long work, this type of classification is based on statistical techniques that identify key dimensions of children's functioning and dysfunction, with the assumption that all children can be usefully described along these dimensions (see also Weiss, Susser, & Catron, 1998). Differences among children, then, reflect *differences in degree* (or quantity) of a dimension, rather than *differences in kinds* of dimensions. Benefits of this type of classification include reduction of the large

number of categories of disorder to fewer dimensions (Clark et al., 1995), and a better reflection of the reality of continuous models of adjustment/maladjustment (Sonuga-Barke, 1998).

The two most commonly cited broad dimensions of disorder include (1) an externalizing dimension, with undercontrolled behaviors such as oppositional or aggressive behaviors that are often directed at others; and (2) an internalizing dimension, with overcontrolled behaviors such as anxiety or social isolation that are often directed toward the self. A child would be diagnosed with a disorder when he or she exceeded a certain number of symptoms. In addition to the basic internalizing versus externalizing distinction, more recent descriptions of important narrow dimensions include: *withdrawal, somatic complaints, social problems, thought problems, aggressive behavior, delinquent behavior, attention problems*, and *anxious/depressed problems*.

Analyses of these more specific dimensions also take into account age and gender differences in the experience and expression of difficulties. Children may display distress and dysfunction that reflects mostly internalizing difficulties (e.g., a combination of anxious/depressed problems and somatic complaints), mostly externalizing difficulties (e.g., a combination of social problems and aggressive behavior), or a mixture of both (e.g., attention problems, aggressive behavior, and anxious/depressed problems). Figure 4.1 illustrates one way that internalizing and externalizing dimensions might be mapped. Children low on both internalizing and externalizing dimensions would include a variety of typically developing children. Children with moderate scores on either or both internalizing or externalizing dimensions might warrant extra attention, but would not necessarily meet clinical or statistical criteria for actual psychopathology. Only those children with significantly deviant scores on either or both dimensions would be diagnosed with a disorder.

Cultural Contributions to Classification Systems

In Chapter 2, sociocultural models of child development, psychopathology, and treatment were described. Culture also influences systems of classification. There are many reviews of the impact of culture on adult disorder, but our emphasis is on the current work related to child and adolescent classification (Harkness & Super, 2000; Thakker & Ward, 1998; Weisz, McCarty, Eastman, Chaiyasit, & Suwanlert, 1997). The major

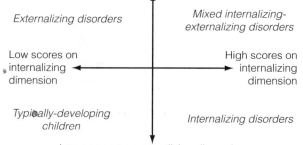

High scores on externalizing dimension

Externalizing disorders

Mixed internalizing-externalizing disorders

Low scores on internalizing dimension ←→ High scores on internalizing dimension

Typically-developing children

Internalizing disorders

Low scores on externalizing dimension

FIGURE 4:1 Children's psychopathology along internalizing and externalizing dimensions.

concern is how well the classification categories or dimensions of disorder account for children's distress and dysfunction in different cultures or subcultures. A review by Verhulst and Achenbach (1995) suggests that current classifications are, in fact, both relevant and robust across different cultures. Verhulst and Achenbach conclude that, with respect to a variety of cultures, there are only small differences in both the estimates of disorder and the underlying dimensions of disorder in children, and there is overall similarity associated with gender and SES factors. Still, we need to be aware of ongoing research in the area of cultural variations, and make refinements in classifications as necessary (Alarcon et al., 2002; Pine et al., 2002).

Developmental Contributions to Classification Systems

Beginning with initial attempts to devise useful descriptions of psychopathology, the focus has been on the classification of adult disorders. For accurate classification of child disorders, it is necessary to integrate a developmental perspective into classification systems, emphasizing salient age- and stage-related concerns as well as continuity and change in clinical difficulties (Achenbach, 1997; Garber, 1984; Ollendick & Vasey, 1999; Sroufe & Rutter, 1984). This developmental perspective is most frequently observed when, as described in the previous chapter, clinicians conceptualize children's disorders as delay, fixation, or deviance (Fischer et al., 1997). These kinds of conceptualizations depend upon a clear understanding of what is normal during particular periods of development, and provide one important way to describe development that is off track. But there are other frameworks for examining the way in which

children's disorders are embedded in a developmental context.

Examples of Developmental Classification

One example of a classification scheme that illustrates the connections between normal and abnormal development is the Diagnostic Classification of Mental Health and Developmental Disorders of Infancy and Early Childhood, published by the Zero to Three Association (1994, 2005). Like the DSM, Zero to Three's system is categorical, and also makes use of multiple descriptive axes (see Table 4.3). But the Zero to Three system, focused exclusively on the earliest manifestations of psychopathology, is much more explicit in its developmental orientation. For example, the child-caregiver relationship is understood as a possible locus of disorder. The clinician considers (a) the behavioral quality of the relationship between the child and caregiver, (b) the emotional tone of the relationship, and (c) the degree of psychological involvement. This information is used to assess the

TABLE 4:3 AXES OF THE ZERO TO THREE CLASSIFICATION SYSTEM	
AXIS I	Primary Diagnosis
	Traumatic Stress Disorder
	Disorders of Affect
	Adjustment Disorder
	Regulatory Disorders
	Sleep Behavior Disorder
	Eating Behavior Disorder
	Disorders of Relating and Communicating
AXIS II	Relationship Disorder Classification
	Overinvolved
	Underinvolved
	Anxious/tense
	Angry/hostile
	Mixed
	Abusive
AXIS III	Medical and Developmental Disorders and Conditions
AXIS IV	Psychosocial Stressors
AXIS V	Functional Emotional Developmental Level

The Zero to Three diagnostic classification system focuses on early signs of psychopathology, including those found in the child-caregiver relationship.

Gary Buss/Taxi/Getty Images

severity of relationship difficulties, and whether they are best characterized as a "perturbation," a "disturbance," or a "disorder." This approach recognizes that very young children's "sense of self and of their place in the world is shaped at its very core by the interactions with those who have major responsibility for their care" (Lieberman, Wieder, & Fenichel, 1997, p. 11).

Another innovative example of the developmental perspective can be found in the work of Benjamin Lahey and his colleagues (e.g., Lahey et al., 2004; Lahey & Waldman, 2003). In Lahey's classification model, the structure of psychopathology is anchored in empirically derived clusters of symptoms. Although similar to the categorical approach of DSM-IV, the disorders are organized primarily on the basis of statistical analyses, rather than being grouped on the basis of clinical observation and tradition (see Figure 4.2).

The Lahey model goes further in its attempts to explore connections between normal and abnormal development, and between categorical and dimensional approaches, because the structural model of psychopathology is tied to a structural model of temperament. Statistical methods (such as multivariate analysis) are used to reveal three genetically influenced dimensions of temperament. Each of these temperament dimensions, interacting with other genetic and environmental factors, confers

certain risks and protections with regard to specific disorders (see Figure 4.3). For instance, a certain temperament may predispose a child to an externalizing disorder such as ADHD or conduct disorder. Lahey is quick to point out, however, that temperament is not destiny. Environmental factors like parenting skills, community support, education, and other individual attributes such as academic or athletic skills, all have a role to play. Consequently, although genetic factors may very well create greater risk for certain types of problems, individual differences and life context will always influence whether actual psychopathology is present.

Ongoing Work in Classification

Each classification system has advantages and drawbacks. Given the multiple goals of classification, there is no single right or best approach. However, there is increasing appreciation for multiple perspectives on classification, and increasing convergence of categorical and dimensional approaches (Kasius, Ferdinand, van den Berg, & Verhulst, 1997; Lahey et al., 2004). In addition, the revisions of well-used manuals and the designs of new schemes explicitly include important data on development and individual differences. Reflecting new research data on childhood disorders and theoretical shifts that inform the field's interpretations of disorders, these are positive steps toward better classification.

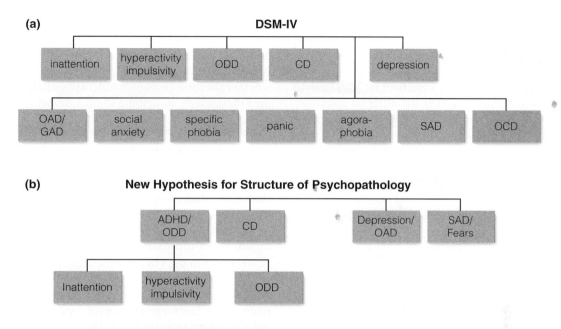

FIGURE 4:2 A comparison of the categories of the Diagnostic and Statistical Manual with those of the Lahey model.
Source: From B.B. Lahey, et al (eds.), "Causes of Conduct Disorder and Juvenile Delinquency", pp. 76-117 (New York: Guilford Press). Copyright © 2003. Reproduced with permission of Guilford Press in the format Textbook and in the format Internet posting via Copyright Clearance Center.

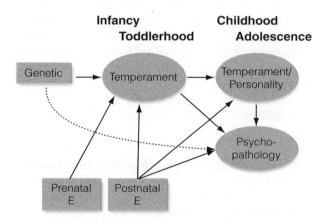

FIGURE 4:3 General working model of development of psychopathology; *E* stands for "environment."
Source: From B.B. Lahey, et al (eds.), "Causes of Conduct Disorder and Juvenile Delinquency", pp. 76-117 (New York: Guilford Press). Copyright © 2003. Reproduced with permission of Guilford Press in the format Textbook and in the format Internet posting via Copyright Clearance Center.

The Phenomenon of Comorbidity

So far, our discussion has implicitly assumed that a classification system involves such distinctive categories that any particular child at a particular point in time can be reliably and validly described as having one—and only one—disorder. But the reality is

otherwise. For multiple reasons, we must consider comorbidity. Comorbidity, a phenomenon that has received much attention in recent years, can be defined in several related ways. The simplest, most straightforward definition of comorbidity involves the co-occurrence of two or more disorders in one individual. Here, a child might be struggling with *any* two disorders: a mood disorder *and* a substance abuse disorder, or an anxiety disorder *and* an eating disorder.

Another way that researchers and clinicians have defined comorbidity involves the co-occurrence of two or more disorders, where the co-occurrence is greater than chance (Caron & Rutter, 1991; Clark et al., 1995; Lilienfeld, Waldman, & Israel, 1994). That is, we are not looking for *any* two disorders, but rather two disorders that are frequently observed together. This definition makes explicit the idea that comorbid conditions are not random. In fact, there are many "systematic comorbidities." Common, nonrandom pairings in children include attention-deficit hyperactivity disorder and conduct disorder, autism and mental retardation, and depression and anxiety.

Just to make the definitional issues as interesting (or as complicated) as possible, there are a few other variations on the basic definitions (Angold, Costello, & Erkanli, 1999). The first variation takes into account whether there is homotypic comorbidity, or two or more diagnoses within a classification group (for example, two different anxiety disorders), or **heterotypic comorbidity,** or diagnoses from different classification groups (for instance, depression and conduct disorder). Another variation, **familial comorbidity,** has to do with whether the different disorders are understood as theoretically or clinically related to one another (such as some combinations of substance abuse, depression, and personality disorders). Finally, we might consider whether disorders are experienced at the same time, as with **concurrent comorbidity,** or whether disorders are experienced sequentially, one after the other, as with **successive comorbidity.**

No matter what definition we use, "Comorbidity is the rule, not the exception" (Sroufe, 1997, p. 257). In community samples of adults, half of persons with one disorder also have another disorder (Clark et al., 1995). And the picture is similar for children and adolescents. Pure, unmixed cases are infrequent occurrences. Given this situation, we need to look closely at the factors that are related to decisions about comorbidity.

Inaccurate Decisions about Comorbidity

Comorbidity is affected by a number of factors related to classification issues, methodological considerations, and developmental concerns. These factors can be sources of error, or they can be sources of valid information. Childhood disorders may be difficult to differentiate because of the imperfections of all classification schemes (Clark et al., 1995). That is, given that all classification emphasizes group similarities rather than unique variations, some children are not going to match up well with strictly defined categories. The clinical picture for these children may include a mix of symptoms from different disorders. Clinicians may then diagnose two disorders, neither of which is quite right (or quite wrong). These kinds of errors occur because of categories that do not allow for much individual variation. Alternatively, categories that are too loosely or vaguely defined, with lots of symptom overlap among categories, also contribute to the appearance of comorbidity (Clark et al., 1995). So some children may meet multiple sets of criteria. These errors occur because there is not enough detail or specification.

For methodological considerations, we are chiefly concerned with the people who are filling out forms (i.e., informant-related factors) and the forms themselves (i.e., instrument-related factors). Informant-related factors have to do with whether individuals (children, parents, or teachers) who report particular patterns of symptoms are more likely to also report

other negative symptoms. The tendency to report any and all negative symptoms may lead to many additional—and inaccurate—instances of comorbidity. Instrument-related factors have to do with whether the tools of assessment, rather than the disorders themselves, contribute to the number of cases.

Accurate Decisions about Comorbidity

In contrast to factors related to error, there are factors that influence valid instances of comorbidity. Krueger, Silva, Caspi, and Moffitt (1998) suggest that comorbidity may reflect "core psychopathological processes." In other words, the same underlying vulnerability may be a general risk factor for a number of disorders. For example, a child might be deficient in the ability to interpret emotional signals from other people. This deficiency may hinder the child's early relationships with parents and with peers. The later emergence of oppositional defiant disorder, depression, and/or conduct problems directed at peers might all relate back to the initial psychopathological process.

Nottelmann and Jensen (1995) present a different set of hypotheses related to comorbidity. They first propose that comorbid disorders "may reflect amorphous, nonspecific expressions of psychopathology in younger children" (p. 110). That is, younger children appear to have multiple difficulties because they are observed at a point in time when particular patterns of symptoms have not yet coalesced. In these cases, we expect that specific problems will become more differentiated with age. So a 6-year-old child exhibiting angry, defiant behavior, numerous fears, and problems with friends may become the 10-year-old child whose presenting symptoms are organized more coherently and consistently as generalized anxiety disorder.

Nottelmann and Jensen also suggest that comorbid disorders "could be a developmentally influenced, transient phenomenon. . . . Thus, one disorder may be the early manifestation of another" (pp. 110–111). For example, some adolescent girls with conduct disorder eventually are diagnosed with depression in adulthood. Many investigators have hypothesized that these women are still dealing with the same underlying difficulties with which they struggled in adolescence, but that time and experience may alter the "surface variation" of the disorder (Waldman & Lilienfeld, 2001).

Nottelmann and Jensen provide one additional possibility, that comorbid disorders may come about because one disorder compromises functioning in such a way that a second disorder also develops (successive comorbidity). For instance, disorders of attachment in the early years increase the likelihood that other types of psychopathology will emerge in later years, including conduct disorders, personality disorders, and depression. Given that the long-term effects of comorbidity include greater severity of disorder, more complicated courses, and more negative outcomes, it is encouraging that ongoing research continues to refine the methods and systems of classification.

Assessment and Diagnosis

Definitions of Assessment and Diagnosis

In order to evaluate a child, we need some orderly way of gathering information. Assessment involves the systematic collection of relevant information, and is used to solve two kinds of practical problems described by Costello and Angold (1996): (1) differentiating everyday problems or transient difficulties from clinically significant psychopathology, and (2) classifying and caring for those who have been identified as having disorders.

The first practical problem for assessment involves a decision about whether diagnosis is necessary or appropriate, and necessitates thinking about disorder within a developmental framework (Emde, Bingham, & Harmon, 1993). After collecting information about a child's various difficulties (and strengths), current distress and dysfunction (and achievements), and likely outcomes, a clinician may conclude that a child is functioning within the normal range, or is experiencing a "bump-in-the-road" kind of problem. In these cases, although advice or support may be provided, a diagnosis might not be made. In other cases, a clinician may become convinced that the child displays more serious maladaptation. Assessment, then, would likely result in a specific diagnosis.

The second practical problem involves the method of assigning individuals to specific classification categories, or diagnosis. Diagnosis becomes particularly important when psychologists talk to parents about the nature of their child's disorder, when clinical decisions about treatments have to be made, or when insurance companies require verification of a disorder in order to approve reimbursements for the cost of care. With respect to these practical issues, assessment certainly depends on gathering information about the specific distress and dysfunction experienced by a child, but it also

must include information about a child's strengths and accomplishments. We need to know what a child does well, not only to help with accurate diagnosis, but also to provide valuable insights about more effective plans for treatment.

After evaluating the intensity, frequency, duration, and pattern of difficulties in a developmental context, we need to decide what the best fit is between the clinical presentation and available classification categories. When choosing the correct category, it is also important to consider whether a child's clinical presentation reflects a single, pure case of disorder, an a typical or mixed symptom case, or a combination of comorbid conditions. At times, DSM-IV classification requires clinicians to make **differential diagnoses:** decisions about mutually exclusive categories of disorder. For example, a child would not receive diagnoses of both oppositional defiant disorder *and* conduct disorder, because the former is usually conceptualized as a precursor or a mild form of the latter. Overall, researchers and clinicians are concerned with **diagnostic efficiency,** the degree to which clinicians maximize diagnostic hits and minimize diagnostic misses.

With all of these diagnostic issues in mind, it is important to remember that we will always have more children with more kinds of problems than we have categories in which to place them. But as we continue to try to improve classification and diagnosis, we must emphasize that naming a disorder, or diagnosing a child, is not the same thing as understanding the disorder or the child. Naming is the first step, not the only step. In addition, we need to remember that assigning a particular child's disorder to a classification category is accomplished at *a moment in time*. Because children change and continue to develop after a diagnosis is made, diagnoses must be periodically reviewed and reevaluated.

A final concern about diagnosis relates to the effects of labeling. As discussed at the end of Chapter 1, the stigmatization of mental illness is difficult for children and their families to manage. According to Lieberman et al. (1997, p. 12), "It is essential to remember that people are not defined by their psychiatric diagnoses. Individuals may have a disorder, but they also possess a core human dignity as well as areas of experiences where they function flexibly, competently, and creatively." The effects of labeling are often viewed as damaging. For example, we are concerned with the self-fulfilling prophecy of children who internalize adult expectations for struggle or failure given a particular diagnosis (such as pervasive developmental disorder or attention-deficit hyperactivity disorder), or with the potential for adults to mischaracterize them as "alphabet children" who receive diagnosis (ADHD) after diagnosis (LD) after diagnosis (ODD) (Baum & Olenchak, 2002).

We must also recognize, however, that labels may have some positive impact. Parents who have been confused and upset by their children's behavior, who have questioned their own competence, and who have despaired over their children's futures may view labels as providing "validation and legitimation of their experience" (Klasen, 2000). Labels may also provide both parents and children with knowledge about ways to deal with the difficulties of disorders. Given these multiple perspectives, negotiation among professionals, parents, and children for particular labels with particular meanings is an ever-present issue (Abrams & Goodman, 1998).

Methods and Processes of Assessment

The Case of Alicia

Alicia is a 9-year-old fourth grader referred for a psychological evaluation by her parents at the suggestion of her teacher. Alicia began to experience school difficulties in third grade that continued into fourth grade, and which have gotten considerably worse as the school year goes on. She has difficulties with work completion, especially on long-term projects, and often fails to turn in assignments; her grades are consistently lower than what either her parents or her teachers believe she is capable of. ■

The Case of David

David is a 12-year-old sixth grader referred by his parents for evaluation and therapy at the suggestion of David's pediatrician. David currently resists going to school in the mornings due to his extreme and disabling anxiety. He also experiences severe headaches before leaving home. Socially, David has become increasingly isolated from his classmates, and generally plays alone or with a neighbor two years younger. ■

The Case of Tyler

Tyler is a 3½-year-old boy referred for assessment and therapy by his pediatrician after noting that Tyler and his mother's interactions in the office were characterized by frustration and conflict. Additional concerns expressed by Tyler's mother and his day care provider included oppositionality, frequent temper tantrums, and occasional physical aggression. There have been several instances when Tyler has kicked and bitten others at preschool and at home. ■

In the real world, clinical assessments begin with a specific concern, question, or problem. In the above cases, we think about whether Alicia's school difficulties are the result of anxiety, attention-deficit hyperactivity disorder, or specific learning disabilities. We think about whether David's distress is best characterized as anxiety or depression, whether it is going to resolve on its own, and available options for treatment. We think about whether Tyler's dysfunction reflects the emergence of a severe psychopathology such as pervasive developmental disorder, which requires intensive intervention, or whether we are dealing with less dramatic difficulties that call for a supportive educational treatment focused on temperament and parenting issues.

These specific concerns influence the assessment strategy that is devised, but most assessments also include a more general overview of the child's circumstances. Clinicians should, of course, respond to the presenting concern, but need to remain alert to many kinds of contextual information, other possible problems, and the child's positive characteristics. A narrow focus early on in the assessment process may lead to diagnostic error, with a quick confirmation of the initial hypothesis without consideration of alternatives.

Assessment Technique: The Interview

Assessments usually begin with **interviews**. Initial interviews allow parents and children to explain their concerns, and more broadly, to tell their stories. Interviews also provide opportunities to start to build the helping relationship, an especially important consideration when a clinician knows that he or she will be working closely with various family members (Seligman, 2000). There are many potential informants for interviews, with different perspectives and agendas. Each informant provides "unique and indispensable" information (Verhulst, Dekker, & van der Ende, 1997), even when the information varies somewhat from person to person. Clinicians are interested in the areas of agreement among informants as well as areas of disagreement; both kinds of information can be useful.

Whenever possible, interviews are conducted with both parents. Parents are able to provide helpful data about their children, and in many cases, are the ones most likely to detect problems in their early stages (Glascoe, 1995, 2000). Parental and family characteristics, such as psychopathology and life events, are important to keep in mind, however, because these kinds of characteristics appear to affect their ratings of their children's functioning. Parents who struggle with their own mental illnesses or with economic hardship, for instance, have lower thresholds for identifying behavior as problematic (Verhulst & van der Ende, 1997; Youngstrom, Loeber, & Stouthamer-Loeber, 2000). And again, clinicians would do well to attend to the parents' and families' strengths as well as their limitations, because they may have important implications for diagnosis and treatment.

Research suggests that mothers and fathers provide somewhat different data. For example, Achenbach, Howell, Quay, and Conners (1991) found that mothers report more problems than do fathers. More recently, it has been suggested that mothers and fathers report similar numbers of problems, but that they report different types of problems, with fathers more concerned with cognitive difficulties (Hay et al., 1999). In the Hay et al. study, mothers' and fathers' reports were associated with different kinds of adjustments years later, with fathers' reports correlated with school problems and mothers' reports correlated with difficult parental and family relationships.

Accurate assessment of children may also need to take into account the cultural background of parents and families (Cohen & Kasen, 1999; Garcia Coll & Meyer, 1993; Hoagwood & Jensen, 1997; Schwab-Stone, Ruchkin, Vermeiren, & Leckman, 2001). Parents from certain cultures may be more sensitive to internalizing or externalizing kinds of problems in children (Lambert et al., 1992; Weisz, Sigman, Weiss, & Mosk, 1993). Parents may also differ with respect to the levels of concern they display, with some parents more likely to believe that their children will improve over time (Schneider, Attili, Vermigli, & Younger, 1997; Weisz et al., 1988, 1991).

In the interview with Alicia's parents, they emphasized that school is becoming increasingly stressful for both Alicia and for them, with much more time spent closely monitoring assignments, homework, and teacher concerns. In addition, Alicia has begun to complain about stomachaches and has missed

school as a result. Alicia's mother and father are particularly upset about the fact that Alicia has lied to them about schoolwork because they have always felt that they could trust their daughter. Alicia's parents also provided information about the extended family, noting that two of Alicia's cousins have been diagnosed with attention-deficit hyperactivity disorder. They believe that Alicia does not display the increased activity or impulsiveness observed in these other children. In contrast to these recent difficulties, her parents report that Alicia seemed relaxed and happy during the summer and enjoys playing with her younger sister and in community sports programs. When the focus is not on school, Alicia can be very pleasant and is able to entertain herself for long periods of time coloring and doing crafts.

David's parents noted that, in addition to seeming anxious, he has become increasingly irritable at home, and often becomes angry and aggressive when frustrated. They described David as having a "short fuse" and as being both oppositional and inflexible. The also reported that the summer prior to this school year, David seemed to lose interest and enjoyment in his usual activities.

Tyler's mother reported that he had been a difficult infant, easily upset and difficult to comfort. His infancy was a challenging time for her as she was in the middle of ending an abusive relationship. She reported that by the age of 2, Tyler was consistently aggressive with others and seemed especially stressed in social situations. She talked about feeling very guilty about her current anger and resentment toward Tyler. She said that while she does love Tyler, she no longer expects to have a pleasant and easy time with him, and is resigned to the belief that each day with him will be a struggle. She also acknowledged that she feels exhausted and impatient, and despairs of finding anything helpful in dealing with her son.

Interviews with children are also critical sources of information, although the types of interviews conducted with David, Alicia, and Tyler are going to be very different. The format of child interviews ranges from structured play to highly planned sets of questions to open-ended conversations, and takes into account characteristics such as age and whether the child is comfortable interacting with a clinician apart from parents (Angold & Fisher, 1999). Even the youngest children with limited verbal skills can be expected to provide unique assessment data through, for example, their behavioral and play patterns (Sessa, Avenevoli, Steinberg, & Morris, 2001).

And, again, areas of agreement and disagreement between parents and their children provide an important perspective (Hope et al., 1999; Jensen et al., 1999; see Box 4.1).

In the interview with 9-year-old Alicia, she was subdued and reluctant to talk at first, but was easily reassured and quickly became more open and communicative. Alicia is very aware of her current school difficulties, and said she thinks she needs to try harder. Alicia said that she tries to pay attention in class, but when she later tries to complete assignments at home, she has forgotten what the teacher talked about. She acknowledges that she has sometimes told her parents that she does not have homework because the work is too hard and she wants to have more free time at home. Alicia was able to describe a number of activities she enjoys, including time spent with a best friend, and talked excitedly about a planned trip with her family. Alicia did describe trouble falling asleep at night because she is worried about things such as upcoming tests and about someone breaking into the house. When this happens, she leaves her room and crawls into bed with her parents.

In the interview with 12-year-old David, he acknowledges that he does not like to go to school,

---

BOX 4:1   THE CHILD IN CONTEXT

Agreement and Disagreement between Parents and Children

When thinking about the assessment of a child or adolescent, it makes sense that gathering data from multiple sources provides a more accurate clinical picture than gathering data from a single source. That is, the pieces of information provided by a child, coupled with those provided by a parent, accompanied by additional pieces from a teacher, should—like a puzzle—result in a meaningful, interlocking whole. Unfortunately, this is not a common outcome. Indeed, one of the most consistent research findings related to assessment is that individuals who provide information seldom agree with one another about the type, scope, or cause of the difficulties (Achenbach, McConaughy, & Howell, 1987; De Los Reyes & Kazdin, 2005; Hawley & Weisz, 2003; Youngstrom, Findling, & Calabrese, 2003). Parents disagree with children, mothers disagree with fathers, and teachers disagree with students.

Given the fact that few children and adolescents refer themselves for psychotherapy, it is hardly surprising that when they find themselves in the office of a mental health professional they rarely agree with adult perceptions of themselves or their difficulties. We might hope that, once more formal assessment takes place, some of the disagreements might be resolved. However, at this time, "there is no single measure or method of assessing psychopathology in children that provides a definitive or 'gold standard' to gauge which children are experiencing a given set of problems" (De Los Reyes & Kazdin, 2005, p. 483). These circumstances contribute to a pervasive clinical dilemma: *over three-quarters of parent-child-therapist triads fail to agree about a single target problem* (Hawley & Weisz, 2003). Disagreements must be acknowledged and addressed because failure to agree about the nature of the problems or the goals of treatment is likely associated with poor outcomes (Ferdinand, van der Ende, & Verhulst, 2004).

Both child and parent factors influencing lack of agreement have been investigated. Lack of agreement is *not* reliably associated with either child age or gender; and although there is some evidence that children and adolescents attempt to portray themselves and their adjustments in the most positive light, these data are also not always replicated (De Los Reyes & Kazdin, 2005). The Attribution Bias Context (ABC) Model detailed by De Los Reyes and Kazdin hypothesizes that parents, in general, focus more on child dispositions, whereas children focus more on external explanations for current difficulties. Other parent factors are associated with additional complications. Parental psychopathology (such as depression), for example, may lead to more negative ratings of children and their struggles (Chi & Hinshaw, 2002). The type of disorder also plays a part. Better rates of agreement between parents and children, and between mothers and fathers, are documented for observable, externalizing problems (De Los Reyes & Kazdin, 2005; Duhig, Renk, Epstein, & Phares, 2000; Yeh & Weisz, 2001).

Clinicians tend to agree with parents more often than with children or adolescents (De Los Reyes & Kazdin, 2005; Hawley & Weisz, 2003). Even so, they must actively reconcile conflicting information, perspectives, and motives. This reconciliation must occur during the initial phases of the assessment and treatment process in order to facilitate engagement and cooperation from all participants, and to prepare for the development of the therapeutic alliance.

which he describes as "mostly boring." He says he used to do well in school, but does not talk about his accomplishments with any sense of pride or joy. He disputes his parents' description of his behavior at home, saying that he would prefer to be left alone, but that his parents are "always bugging me about everything" and that he gets upset. David said that he frequently worries that he will get sick in school and throw up in the classroom. This worry has led him to go to the school nurse almost every day, and to resist going to school at all if he thinks he might be feeling ill. In response to questions about his interests, David said that he used to like playing baseball and practicing piano. Now, however, he describes these as "boring and dumb," and has dropped both activities.

In the interview with 3½-year-old Tyler, he was briefly seen alone, and then with his mother. Tyler had no difficulty separating from his mother and played enthusiastically but impulsively with various toys in the office. He generally ignored the clinician and rebuffed attempts to engage in shared play activities. When joined by his mother, Tyler became somewhat more active, impulsive, and aggressive. At one point, he hit his mother with a toy car and laughed. Tyler's mother told him that he had hurt her, and that if he did it again, she would not allow him to watch television when they got home.

Assessment Technique: The Standardized Test

In addition to the rich information that can be gathered from interviews, data from standardized tests are almost always part of an assessment. Standardized tests are assessments in which the data from a particular child can be compared to data gathered

Psychological assessments of children often include standardized tests.

Laura Dwight / PhotoEdit

from large samples of children, including normally developing children and children with a variety of diagnoses. Results from standardized tests are often evaluated with respect to specific age and gender characteristics. That is, a result from a 5-year-old girl is compared to the results of other young girls, and a result from a 14-year-old boy is compared to the results of other adolescent boys. The most common standardized tests are rating scales, checklists, and basic questionnaires completed by parents and adolescents (Hart & Lahey, 1999). These are global measures of personality functioning and problem areas, such as the widely used Child Behavior Check List (Achenbach & Edelbrock, 1983; Achenbach, 1991), which has many forms and numerous translations (see Box 4.2).

Other common standardized tests include measures of general cognitive or intellectual functioning such as the Wechler Intelligence Scales for Children or the Stanford-Binet. Neurological and neuropsychological evaluations are sometimes part of the standardized assessment plan (Korkman, Kemp, & Kirk, 2001). There are also tests that are domain-specific, focusing on a particular disorder such as depression or anxiety. The Reynolds Child Depression Scale and the Reynolds Adolescent Depression Scale are examples of self-report tests that take the age of the child into account when asking particular types of questions and in the way in which questions are phrased.

Other traditional measures of personality and clinical symptoms would include projective measures such as the Rorschach inkblots and the Thematic Apperception Test, a story-telling task. Projective measures are based on the assumption that, given an ambiguous stimulus, individuals' responses will reflect the *projection* of unconscious conflicts. Although academic researchers frequently decry the continued use of projective measures, given the relatively poor data on their reliability and validity (Garb, Wood, Lilienfeld, & Nezworski, 2002), clinicians counter that these measures often allow us to engage children in ways that enable them to talk about difficult feelings or experiences indirectly, and in ways that are developmentally more familiar and appropriate.

Assessment Technique: Observation

Another source of valuable information comes from observations made by the clinician. Clinicians usually observe children in clinical settings such as offices, but may also observe children in naturalistic

---

BOX 4:2 CLINICAL PERSPECTIVES

Summary of Information Provided by the CBCL

The Child Behavior Checklist (CBCL) (Achenbach, 1991) is a common measurement instrument used to assess the clinical significance of a wide range of potentially problematic behaviors. The 112 items on the CBCL were factor analyzed to empirically generate scales representing a variety of clinical problems. These scales are organized into two larger dimensions: Internalizing and Externalizing problems. The table below shows these two broad dimensions and the specific scales that contibute to each of them.

It is important to note that the names of the specific scales are simply descriptive labels for the group of items that clustered together in the factor analysis. They are not diagnostic labels for underlying psychopathology. For each scale, both a raw score and a T-score are generated. The T-score provides a way of considering the extent of a problem as a point on a continuous scale, while cutoff points (reflecting normal, borderline, and clinical scores) allow for more discrete judgements to be made.

In addition to the CBCL, which is typically completed by a parent, there are teacher report (TRF) and youth self-report (YSR) forms of the checklist as well. These different forms allow for the consideration of various perspectives on the youth's functioning.

INTERNALIZING	EXTERNALIZING	TOTAL SCORE
Withdrawn	Delinquent	Composite of all scales
Somatic Complaints	Aggressive Behavior	
Anxious/Depressed		

---

settings such as the home or school. These behavioral observations can provide specific sorts of contextual data, including analyses of what comes before, and what follows, a child's dysfunctional behavior. Observations may also be more encompassing. For example, a clinician might focus on evaluating children's relationships to determine whether the relationship is itself the cause of disorder, or how it plays a part in the maintenance of a child's disturbance.

Because many of the initial concerns about children are related to school functioning, teachers and schools can be important sources of clinical data (Glascoe, 2001). In some cases, teachers complete parallel forms of parent questionnaires. Many times, teachers' information is consistent with that provided by parents and children; other times, different information becomes available. Youngstrom et al. (2000) report that teachers identify fewer and somewhat different problems than do parents (see also Offord et al., 1996). Teacher characteristics may influence the information provided about children. Mash and Dozois (1996) suggest that these influences may reflect bias or error on the part of the teacher. For instance, both Sbarra and

Pianta (2001) and Youngstrom et al. (2000) report that teacher ratings of students can be influenced by the students' racial backgrounds, with African American children rated as having more difficulties compared to similar European American children. Other differences in teacher ratings may be tied to actual differences in children's behaviors in various settings (at home versus in school). In addition to teacher ratings and school records, a large armamentarium of possible tests is available, designed to examine many different aspects of ability and achievement, as well as to measure cognitive functioning such as inattention and memory that might affect learning.

For Alicia, the set of tests included the parent version of the CBCL; the teacher version of the CBCL; two self-report questionnaires, including the Depression Self-Rating Scale and the Children's Manifest Anxiety Scale; the Wechsler Intelligence Scale for Children; the Woodcock-Johnson III Tests of Achievement, and the Integrated Visual and Auditory Continuous Performance Test, designed to measure one's ability to inhibit response, remain vigilant, demonstrate consistency of attentional focus, and respond quickly.

Alicia's diagnostic summary: Alicia's current difficulties are most consistent with a DSM-IV diagnosis of attention-deficit hyperactivity disorder, inattentive type. Because externalizing problems such as hyperactivity are not characteristic of this subtype, the diagnosis is often made later when demands for organization and independent functioning in school begin to increase. Alicia's academic achievement is generally consistent with her intellectual functioning, so there is no strong case to be made for a specific learning disability. Clearly, Alicia is a somewhat anxious child, and the school problems she is experiencing have exacerbated this vulnerability. While a case can be made for also diagnosing an anxiety disorder, it may be most reasonable to monitor the anxiety symptoms as the ADHD is addressed.

For David, a set of tests similar to Alicia's was used. However, because there were no concerns about academic problems, the cognitive and attentional measures were not administered. As the underlying emotional state was problematic, along with social adjustment and his perception of these areas, some projective techniques were used during the assessment. The Rorschach and the TAT provided additional ways to understand David's subjective experience of the world around him. In completing the self-report measures of emotional functioning, David denied most of the obvious symptoms of depression and anxiety, with the exception of anxiety related to being physically ill. Projective data (e.g., repeated sad and discouraging themes in David's TAT stories), however, suggested depressed mood, relative developmental immaturity, and a poor sense of self-efficacy. David's parents independently completed the CBCL. There were striking consistencies in their reports, with highly significant elevations on the three internalizing scales reflecting symptoms of social withdrawal, anxiety, and depression.

David's diagnostic summary: Taken together, the data provided suggest that David is experiencing both an anxiety disorder and a depressive disorder. His symptoms meet the DSM-IV criteria for both classification categories, both disorders contribute to current distress and dysfunction, and both disorders appear to require immediate intervention.

For Tyler, age and presenting concerns influence a different selection of tests. Because of his age, Tyler did not complete any assessment measures himself. His mother did complete the CBCL. The

resulting profile had extremely high scores on all of the externalizing scales, indicating that aggression, impulsivity, and hyperactivity were all significant problems. Because some of the initial concerns reflected a high level of discomfort in social situations and some other atypical behaviors and developmental patterns, the Children's Autism Rating Scale (CARS) was completed by the psychologist. The score on the CARS was not in the clinically significant range.

Tyler's diagnostic summary: Although ADHD is a reasonable diagnosis given the clinical presentation, it is a difficult diagnosis to make confidently given Tyler's very young age, the high level of stress he and his mother have experienced, and their relative lack of social support. A diagnosis of oppositional defiant disorder was made as a way of capturing the most important concern at this time, which centers on Tyler's difficulty internalizing developmentally appropriate self-control and his mother's difficulty managing day-to-day routines and interactions with him.

Intervention

Classification, assessment, and diagnosis are most practical when they provide information about what can be done to help children who are distressed and dysfunctional. This section provides a general introduction to the topic of psychological interventions for children and adolescents, with an emphasis on the progress that has been made in mental health-related responses to children with disorders, extending from years ago when policies of isolation were recommended to a more contemporary approach in which policies of preventive interventions are advocated (Costello & Angold, 2000; Domitrovich & Greenberg, 2004; Ripple & Zigler, 2003; Weissberg, Kumpfer, & Seligman, 2003).

The contributions of a developmental psychopathology framework to intervention efforts are noteworthy, including the basic notion that age-related norms and expectations must be taken into account when designing any intervention strategy (Masten & Braswell, 1991; Weisz & Hawley, 2002). This background informs decisions about whether and when to intervene, the goals of intervention, and simple versus more complex treatments and techniques. The developmental background emphasizes the unique context of treatment for each child, with respect to the family factors that have contrib-

In order to be effective, therapeutic interventions must reflect developmentally appropriate norms and expectations.

uted to the child's disorder, the family factors that contribute to the child's improvement, factors related to the network of peers and friends, factors related to the school setting, and cultural contributions (Kratochwill & Stoiber, 2000; Lerner, Ostrom, & Freel, 1997; Lochman, 2004; Ringeisen, Henderson, & Hoagwood, 2003).

The Efficacy of Psychotherapy in Children and Adolescents

Research on psychotherapy can be generally sorted by whether it is focused on outcome or process. Outcome research has to do with whether children and adolescents have improved at the end of treatment relative to their pre-treatment status, and compared to others who have not received treatment. Results of numerous meta-analytic studies confirm that psychotherapy works, with statistically significant and clinically meaningful effects for infants, toddlers, children, and adolescents (Casey & Berman, 1985; Kazdin, 2003; Shonkoff & Meisels, 2000; Weisz, Weiss, Alicke, & Klotz, 1987; Weisz, Doss, & Hawley, 2005; Zeanah, 2000). Therapies that focus on helping children by working with their parents and families have also received much research support (Cummings, Davies, & Campbell, 2000; Dunst, Trivette, & Deal, 1994). Process research deals with the specific mechanisms and common factors which account for therapeutic change (Kazdin, 2000; Kazdin & Nock,

2003; Russell & Shirk, 1998). Process-related discussions have focused on shifts from a one-size-fits-all model of treatment to models that emphasize specific pairings (or matching) of disorders and treatments (Shirk, Talmi, & Olds, 2000), and the realities of "clinic therapy" (i.e., what happens every day in the real world of children, families, and schools), in contrast to the very regularized therapy of research studies (Shirk, 2001; Weisz, Weiss, & Donenberg, 1992).

Primary, Secondary, and Tertiary Interventions

Interventions can be characterized in a variety of ways, from the target of intervention (child, parent, or school) to the timing of intervention. Differences in primary, secondary, and tertiary interventions are related to timing. Primary prevention involves reducing or eliminating risks, as well as reducing the incidence of disorder in children. Cowen (1994, 1996; Cowen & Durlak, 2000) identifies two types of primary prevention strategies. The first involves the identification of risk factors plus early treatments intended to minimize their impact. The second is a more inclusive approach, emphasizing the enhancement of psychological wellness as a general protective factor, as illustrated in Figure 4.4.

Following Gordon's (1983, 1987) work, Fonagy (1998) distinguishes three types of preventive measures: (1) universal preventive measures, which are provided for entire populations (e.g., mandatory

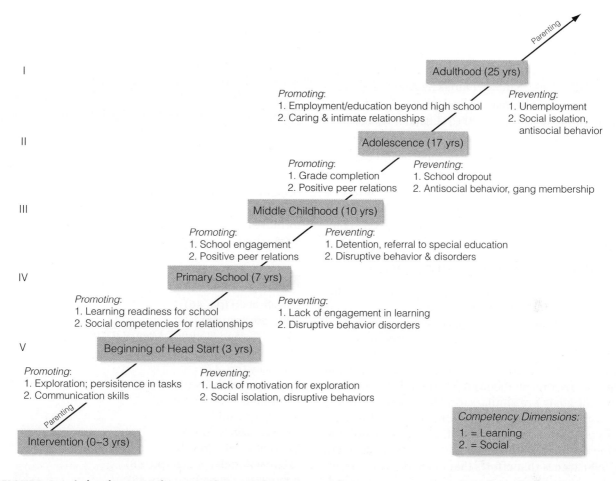

FIGURE 4:4 A developmental perspective on primary prevention.
Source: From J.P. Shonkoff and S.J. Meisels (Eds.), "Handbook of Early Childhood Intervention", 2/e, p. 160. Copyright © 2000 Cambridge University Press. Reprinted with the permission of Cambridge University Press.

immunizations for children); (2) **selective preventive measures,** provided for groups at above-average risk (e.g., Head Start programs for preschoolers from disadvantaged backgrounds); and (3) **indicated preventive measures,** provided for groups with specific risk factors that include more extensive interventions (e.g., packages of services for families with prematurely born infants). The principles of prevention associated with the most positive results have been summarized by Cummings et al. (2000): Primary interventions that begin early, last longer, and are more intensive are more likely to be effective. More effective programs target the child. And the initial positive effects of comprehensive and multifaceted intervention programs require continued environmental support.

Secondary prevention has to do with interventions that are implemented following the early signs of distress and dysfunction, before the disorder is clearly established in the child. **Tertiary prevention** has to do

with responding to already present and clinically significant disorders. The goals of secondary and tertiary prevention include restoring healthy functioning and minimizing future impairments. Most of what clinicians do when working with children and adolescents involves secondary and tertiary prevention. As with primary prevention, research and clinical data suggest that these are effective interventions (Durlak & Wells, 1997, 1998).

Working with Children

Several key influences on current services for children can be identified, including the mental hygiene movement of the early twentieth century, primarily related to concerns about the poor treatment of adults in state mental hospitals; the child guidance clinics, focused on the reform and rehabilitation of juvenile offenders; and the emergence of psychoanalysis, emphasizing the etiology of psychopathology during childhood (Morris & Kratochwill, 1998). Noteworthy recent trends include the strengthening of connections between research and clinical practice (Chorpita, Barlow, Albano, & Daleiden, 1998; Weisz, Sandler, Durlak, & Anton, 2005); the introduction of pharmacological interventions for children (Brown & Sammons, 2002; Galanter, Wasserman, Sloan, & Pine, 1999; Greenhill et al., 2003); the implications of social policies such as mental health parity in insurance coverage; and intervention guidelines that emphasize short-term and evidence-based therapies (Burns & Hoagwood, 2004; Chambers, Ringeisen & Hickman, 2005; Christopherson & Mortweet, 2001; Jensen, 1999; Mash & Hunsley, 2005).

Working with Parents and Families

Svanberg (1998) advises that different parents require different helping strategies and/or different combinations of strategies. Some parents need educational information about children and development. Some parents need social and/or emotional support. And there are parents who need psychological treatment themselves. For all parents, the overall goals are similar: to help caregivers create and provide environments conducive to children's physical, emotional, intellectual, and social growth. One key issue is the timing of intervention. Svanberg (1998) argues that efforts that coincide with parent-related transitions (e.g., pre-birth, entrance to toddlerhood) are particularly efficacious.

Because parents are usually responsible for recognizing the need for intervention and following through on intervention efforts, the relationship between the therapist and the parent or parents is critical. General agreement about the goals of therapy, the expectations for the child and his or her family, and financial considerations will all play important roles in children's access to mental health care. Numerous actual and perceived barriers to treatment, such as economic hardship, the belief that therapy is irrelevant, or the therapist blaming the parent for the child's difficulties, are related to dropping out of the treatment process (Farmer, Burns, Phillips, Angold, & Costello, 2003; Kazdin, Holland, & Crowley, 1997; Owens et al., 2002).

Working with Schools and Communities

Because teachers frequently refer children and adolescents for assessment and treatment, and because difficulties are often displayed in the school setting, it makes sense that many interventions are attempted in schools with the cooperation of school personnel. For these interventions to be successful, it is important for therapists to pay attention to the ecological context of schools and the central role of teachers (Hoagwood & Erwin, 1997; Kratochwill & Stoiber, 2000). Finally, therapists must also be well versed in relevant legislation, with the many federal and state laws, regulations, and requirements related to access to school services for children with various kinds of disabilities. For example, therapists are often consulted by school personnel during the design of an Individualized Education Plan (IEP), which the school is required to formulate whenever a child's academic performance is impaired by an identified disability.

■ Key Terms

Classification (pg. 46)
Diagnosis (pg. 46)
Diagnostic and Statistical Manual (DSM) (pg. 46)
Medical model (pg. 47)
Reliability (pg. 47)
Inter-rater reliability (pg. 47)
Cross-time reliability (pg. 47)
Validity (pg. 47)
Internal validity (pg. 47)
External validity (pg. 48)
Externalizing dimension (pg. 48)
Internalizing dimension (pg. 48)
Comorbidity (pg. 51)
Homotypic comorbidity (pg. 51)
Heterotypic comorbidity (pg. 51)
Familial comorbidity (pg. 51)
Concurrent comorbidity (pg. 52)
Successive comorbidity (pg. 52)
Assessment (pg. 53)
Differential diagnosis (pg. 53)
Diagnostic efficiency (pg. 53)
Interviews (pg. 54)
Standardized tests (pg. 57)
Projective measures (pg. 57)
Observations (pg. 57)
Outcome research (pg. 60)
Process research (pg. 60)
Primary prevention (pg. 60)
Universal preventive measures (pg. 60)
Selective preventive measures (pg. 61)
Indicated preventive measures (pg. 61)
Secondary prevention (pg. 61)
Tertiary prevention (pg. 61)

■ Chapter Summary

- Diagnostic classification systems group individuals with similar patterns of disorder. Effective classification systems help to organize symptom patterns into meaningful groups, facilitate communication among professionals, and inform research and treatment efforts.
- The most commonly used clinical classification system with adults and children is the Diagnostic and Statistical Manual (the DSM-IV-TR) of the American Psychiatric Association. This type of classification identifies types of disorders and then specifies the defining symptoms of the disorders.
- Empirically based classification systems have been an especially useful way to consider the development of psychopathology. This approach is based on statistical techniques that identify key dimensions of children's functioning and dysfunction, with the assumption that all children can be meaningfully described along these dimensions.
- The two clinically useful and well researched clinical dimensions are the externalizing dimension, with undercontrolled behaviors such as oppositional or aggressive behaviors, and the internalizing dimension, with overcontrolled behaviors such as anxiety or depression.
- Comorbidity is the co-occurrence of two or more disorders in one individual. Systematic comorbidities reflect the fact that certain disorders are likely to often occur together (e.g., ADHD and oppositional defiant disorder).
- Psychological assessment involves the systematic collection of relevant information in order to differentiate everyday problems from psychopathology, and to accurately diagnose disorders.
- Assessment methods, including interviews, standardized tests, and projective measures, all contribute to a diagnosis; making a decision about which of several diagnoses best describes an individual is called differential diagnosis.
- Research on psychotherapy generally focuses on either outcome or process. Outcome research has to do with whether, at the end of treatment, children and adolescents have improved relative to their pre-treatment status, and compared to others who have not received treatment. Process research has to do with the specific mechanisms and common factors that account for therapeutic change.

Disorders of Early Development

FOR MANY DECADES, the mental health and psychopathology of infants were discussed almost exclusively by psychodynamically oriented clinicians who focused their atention on problems in the caregiving relationship. Conceptualizations of infant disorders within a broader biopsychosocial framework are fairly recent, owing much to theory and research focused on neurobiological development, temperament, and attachment (Emde & Spicer, 2000; Seifer, 2001). Taking the pioneering work of the psychiatrist Stanley Greenspan and the longitudinal studies of Stella Chess and Alexander Thomas as a point of departure, most clinicians and researchers now accept the need to identify and respond to infant distress and dysfunction (Gelfand, 2001, Shonkoff & Phillips, 2000), and to increase the numbers of programs devoted to infant mental health (Bornstein, Davidson, Keyes, & Moore, 2003; Harmon, 2002; Harmon & Frankel, 1997; Zeanah, Boris, & Larrieu, 1997).

In this chapter, we examine the earliest manifestations of adjustment and maladjustment. We describe several clinical presentations that many mental health professionals believe reflect distinct disorders. We also present evidence that certain early patterns of development are risk factors for many different kinds of later psychopathology.

Developmental Tasks and Challenges Related to Physiological and Emotional Functioning

From birth onward, infants interact with their interpersonal and material worlds in ways that promote physical, emotional, intellectual, and social development. This growth is marked by three *biobehavioral shifts* that signal important intra- and interpersonal changes (Emde, 1985); Brazelton (1994, 2006) has referred to these periods as "touchpoints." The first of these biobehavioral shifts occurs between 2 and 3 months of age, after infants and caregivers have negotiated the transition from intrauterine to extrauterine experience through their rhythmic routines of feeding, dressing, and comforting (Hofacker & Papoušek, 1998; Mirmiran & Lunshof, 1996). Later in the first year, between 7 and 9 months, another shift takes place. By this time, most babies communicate their feelings and intentions through gestures and vocalizations, play with toys, and have a number of daily and nightly schedules. The third shift occurs between 18 and 20 months. By then, toddlers are walking and talking, and are increasingly independent explorers of their many

environments (Crockenberg & Leerkes, 2000; Hofacker & Papoušek, 1998; Shonkoff & Phillips, 2000). These accomplishments—involving new, challenging, and sometimes stressful events—are no less astounding because they are common outcomes. Indeed, these achievements reflect the remarkable capacities and motivations for learning of the average newborn.

Temperament

In addition to these normative developments, there are important individual differences that are quickly noted by parents and others. Mary Rothbart and her colleagues have described variations in newborns' styles of attention, activity, and distress. These "constitutionally based individual differences in reactivity and self-regulation" make up the construct of **temperament** (Rothbart, 1991). **Reactivity** involves the infant's excitability and responsiveness. For instance, some infants may become quite agitated while being passed from relative to relative during a family reunion. Other infants may accept strangers' kisses, hugs, and peek-a-boo games in stride. **Regulation** involves what the infant does to control his or her reactivity. Some upset infants seek and receive comfort from a parent and quickly settle down; others may wail and thrash about and take a much longer time to recover. Infant temperament has been and continues to be the focus of many scientists and clinicians; this brief overview is intended to introduce important ideas and findings, especially those that are relevant to the upcoming discussion of disorders of regulation.

The nature of temperamental reactivity and regulation has been widely discussed, with proposals

Temperamental characteristics, such as negative affectivity, are significant factors in later child and adult personality.

for both categorical and continuous models. Kagan and his colleagues have identified two general categories or types of temperament that distinguish some babies from others (Kagan & Snidman, 1991; Kagan, Snidman, Arcus, & Reznick, 1994; Woodward, Lenzenweger, Kagan, Snidman, & Arcus, 2000). The first type is highly reactive and inhibited, and the second type is less reactive and uninhibited (see also Schmidt & Fox, 2002).

Current continuous, or dimensional, models of temperament emphasize **surgency** (i.e., extraversion), **negative affectivity** (i.e., predispositions to experience fear and frustration/anger), and **effortful control** (i.e., infant attempts to regulate stimulation and response) (Rothbart & Putnam, 2002). Each of these dimensions reflects, in part, **infant emotionality**, including the latency to respond to emotional stimuli, and the average and peak intensities of emotional response (Davidson, 1998; Kochanska, Coy, Tjebkes, & Husarek, 1998; Stifter, 2002). Individual infants possess varying amounts of each characteristic, leading to many different combinations. Other researchers have combined aspects of the categorical and continuous approaches. For example, Fox and Henderson (1999) have differentiated

very reactive children who are also highly negative in their emotional responses (the inhibited group), from very reactive children who are highly positive in their responses (the exuberant group) (see also Polak-Toste & Gunnar, 2006).

Research on gender and temperament is plentiful. Data suggest that boys are more likely to score higher on scales measuring surgency, whereas girls score higher on measures of effortful control; there are few differences related to negative affectivity (Else-Quest, Hyde, Goldsmith, & Van Ulle, 2006). Research on culture and temperament is relatively scarce, although there are data suggesting some differences in Eastern versus Western cultures and among various Western cultures (Arbiter, Sato-Tanaka, Kolvin, & Leitch, 1999; Gartstein et al., 2006; Kerr, 2001; Pomerleau, Sabatier, & Malcuit, 1998).

Overall, however, there is agreement that it is helpful to think about temperament as the foundation of later child and adult personality (Eder & Mangelsdorf, 1997; Goldsmith, Lemery, Aksan, & Buss, 2000; McCrae et al., 2000; Rothbart, 2007). Consistent with this idea, Graziano, Jensen-Cambell, and Sullivan-Logan (1998) have creatively described temperament as a "hard ice ball, around which the softer snowball of personality" develops (p. 1267).

Newborn Characteristics

Looking more closely at the origins of temperament, we must first take into account the biology-behavior links, including contributions of neuroanatomy and the maturation and increasing coordination of physiological systems (Davidson, 1998; Fox, Henderson, Marshall, Nichols, & Ghera, 2005; Gunnar, 2000; Henderson & Wachs, 2007; Nelson & Bosquet, 2000; Posner, Rothbart, Sheese, & Tang, 2007; Schore, 1996). More specifically, researchers have linked individual differences in temperament to adrenocortical activity (Gunnar, Brodersen, Krueger, & Rigatuso, 1996; Gunnar, Bruce, & Donzella, 2001), cardiac function and vagal tone (Beauchaine, 2001; Bornstein & Suess, 2000; Calkins & Keane, 2004; Porges, 2003; Porges & Doussard-Roosevelt, 1994; Porter, 2001), and the organization of the brain's right hemisphere and frontal EEG asymmetry (Fox, 1991; McManis, Kagan, Snidman, & Woodward, 2002; Schore, 2000).

Individual differences in effortful control are also important, with developments in neurophysiology and other physical domains related to changes in the infant's ability to attend and respond to incoming stimuli (Bornstein, Brown, & Slater, 1996; Mangelsdorf, Shapiro, & Marzolf, 1995; Rueda, Posner & Rothbart, 2005). Differences in effortful control are frequently discussed in the context of arousal and emotion (Cole, Martin, & Dennis, 2004; Stifter, 2002). Arousal is an adaptive phenomenon, alerting individuals to potential threats as well as potentially rewarding stimuli. But some infants and children experience too much arousal, or too frequent arousal, or arousal without purpose; many of these experiences are related to the management of fear and anger (Bridges & Grolnick, 1995; Buss & Goldsmith, 1998; Derryberry & Rothbart, 1997; Kopp, 1989). Although negative emotions are central to the construct of temperament, we cannot overlook the part that positive emotions play. Well-adjusted children have access to the full range of positive

and negative emotions, as well as mild, moderate, and strong intensities of experience (Cicchetti, Ackerman, & Izard, 1995; Cole, Michel, & Teti, 1994). Developmental psychopathologists emphasize the variety of normal positive and negative emotional responses and the "strong, self-righting properties of the healthy newborn" (Gunnar, Porter, Wolf, & Rigatuso, 1995, p. 1), and then make connections to the difficulties experienced by some high risk infants (see Box 5.1).

Caregiver Characteristics

Even as theorists and researchers focus primarily on the role of nature (genetic predispositions or inborn tendencies), there is also a place for nurture (parents and families) in almost all temperament models (Goldsmith, Buss, & Lemery, 1997; Jahromi, Putnam, & Stifter, 2004). The influence of the

BOX 5:1 RISK AND RESILIENCE

The Early Development of At-Risk Infants

With estimates of 45,000 cocaine-exposed infants born each year in the United States (Lester, Boukydis, & Twomey, 2000), it is imperative that we understand the physiological and psychological impact of drug use by pregnant women. There have been numerous investigations of the short-term and long-term consequences of prenatal drug exposure. Studies of infants exposed to cocaine in utero provide an illustration of the many challenges faced by these babies as well as the challenges faced by researchers working with multi-problem populations.

Multiple forms of subtle, moderate, and severe neurobehavioral dysfunction have been documented in a variety of developmental domains (Dow-Edwards, Mayes, Spear, & Hurd, 1999; Lester et al., 2000). For example, "cocaine babies" show atypical responses, including high stress reactivity, to both internal and external stimulation (Mayes, 2002), and physiological differences that have direct and indirect influences on the developing brain (Shonkoff & Marshall, 2000). These disruptions in arousal regulation have adverse effects on attention, memory and learning, behavior, and social systems (Mayes, 2002; Lewis, Misra, Johnson, & Rosen, 2004; Mayes, Grillon, Granger, & Schottenfeld, 1998; Singer et al., 2004; Warren, Malik, Lindahl, & Claussen, 2006).

As well as immediate physical and physiological dysfunction, we need to take into account the dynamic interplay between prenatal drug exposure and "postnatal environments also shaped by ongoing parental substance abuse" (Mayes & Bornstein, 1996). In other words, cocaine babies often come into the world with two strikes: neurobehavioral difficulties and parents poorly equipped to support their special needs (Lester et al., 2000; Mayes et al., 1998; Mayes & Bornstein, 1997a, 1997b; Schuler, Nair, & Black, 2002). Both neglect and abuse are more frequently observed in these at-risk families (Mayes & Bornstein, 1997b). For those infants with less compromised developmental outcomes, there remains an ongoing negative impact on infant-mother interactions and relationships (Minnes, Singer, Arendt, & Satayathum, 2005; Sheinkopf et al., 2006; Tronick et al., 2005).

Four particularly problematic developmental pathways have been described by Mayes and Bornstein (1996). These include (1) continued exposure to cocaine through the passive absorption of crack smoke; (2) increased genetic risk related to parental addictions and other psychopathologies; (3) continuing negative effects on neuropsychological functions; and (4) growing up in a generally negative atmosphere. Because intervention improves a range of developmental outcomes (Claussen, Scott, Mundy, & Katz, 2004), our efforts on behalf of these needy babies and their parents must be ethically responsible and medically, psychologically, and socially comprehensive.

caregiver on measures of both infant reactivity and infant regulation is frequently observed. For example, there is evidence that sensitive caregiving, in both everyday and adverse circumstances, is associated with positive changes in infants' stress-reactive hormones (Calkins & Hill, 2007; Gunnar, 1998, 2000; Gunnar & Donzella, 2002). The beneficial impact of touch (and massage) has also been discussed in this context (Feldman, Weller, Sirota, & Eidelman, 2002; Field, 2002).

But most of the attention has been on how caregivers influence regulation, including the ways that infants depend on active regulation by others and the ways that caregivers support infants' own attempts at self-regulation (Bell & Calkins, 2000; Calkins & Hill, 2007; Eisenberg, 2002; Grolnick, McMenamy, & Kurowski, 1999). Caregivers regulate their infants by responding to their signals of discomfort, such as changing wet diapers or rocking tired babies to sleep. Mothers and fathers help babies by providing the shoulders to cry on, the blankets to cuddle in, and the soothing lullabies at bedtime. In each of these instances, infants, caregivers, and their relationships benefit from successful regulation.

In addition to actual caregiving behaviors, parental beliefs about temperament also influence the infant's emerging personality (Graziano et al., 1998). Cultural variability in such beliefs leads to cultural differences in parental responses (Pomerleau et al., 1998; Shonkoff & Phillips, 2000). For example, parents who believe that babies should be able to control their emotions and behaviors quickly and quietly are likely to respond differently than parents who believe that babies should be allowed to be loud and active at all times in all places. Also, particular behaviors

associated with temperament may be consequential for some caregivers but not others, again eliciting different responses; certain parents, for instance, might be more accepting of less active girls than less active boys (Graziano et al., 1998).

Goodness of Fit

Thomas and Chess (1977; Chess & Thomas, 1984) describe **goodness of fit** as the interplay between infant temperament and parenting (see also Putnam, Sanson, & Rothbart, 2002; Seifer, 2000). Some of the more frequently mentioned combinations include the well-matched pairs (e.g., easygoing babies with easygoing parents and exuberant babies with exuberant parents), and the less well-matched pairs (e.g., easygoing babies with exuberant parents and exuberant babies with easygoing parents). But, it is important to understand that the goodness of fit between infants and their caregivers is not an all-or-nothing situation. Within any infant-caregiver pair, there are both matches and mismatches, with some mismatches associated with growth and the broadening of the infant's set of experiences (Stern, 1985). For example, a parent might offer an encouraging smile to a wary baby as she struggles to approach a lamb at the petting zoo. More problematic are the infant-caregiver pairs with more frequent or more extreme mismatches (Cole et al., 1994; Seifer & Dickstein, 2000). For instance, we expect frequent or ongoing conflict to occur if a very gregarious parent is regularly insisting that a behaviorally inhibited child approach unfamiliar children and adults with enthusiasm.

When discussing goodness of fit, "difficult" temperaments are often discussed, with descriptions of babies who are quickly aroused, emotionally intense, and hard to soothe (Chess & Thomas, 1984). While overlapping in some ways, difficult temperament is not the same thing as colic (see Box 5.2). The assumption is that temperamentally difficult, demanding babies are challenging for any kind of parent, and that is almost certainly so (Calkins, Hungerford, & Dedmon, 2004; Crockenberg, 1986; Williford, Calkins, & Keane, 2007). Infants with difficult temperaments, for example, influence trajectories of parenting over time. There are data that suggest that, for parents of varied backgrounds, infant irritability is associated with negative perceptions of infant temperament, increases in parenting stress, and decreases in parent responsivity (Owens, Shaw, & Vondra, 1998; Sheinkopf et al., 2006; Wachs & Kohnstamm, 2001).

Somos/Veer/Jupiter Images

Goodness of fit refers to the complementary relationship between infant temperament and parenting.

A Current Conceptualization of Colic

One of the key distinctions that pediatricians and mental health professionals need to make is between problems and psychopathology. Colic, defined as crying or fussing for more than 3 hours a day for at least 3 days, provides a useful illustration of this distinction. Many worried parents call their pediatricians (or their mothers!) to ask about their inconsolable babies. Are their babies hungry? Or tired? Or sick? For most of these parents, reassurance comes quickly. Excessive crying usually resolves on its own within the first few months (Barr, Paterson, MacMartin, Lehtonen, & Young, 2005). And parent massage of the baby may provide some helpful relief as families wait out this phase (Field, 1998; Field & Liepack, 1999).

But what explains the crying in the first place? Gunnar and her colleagues hypothesize that time-limited overreactivity is the underlying cause of colic (Barr & Gunnar, 2000; Gunnar & Donzella, 1999; Prudhomme White, Gunnar, Larson, Donzella, & Barr, 2000). Rather than viewing colic as an early indicator of

a difficult temperament, Gunnar et al. focus on the inconsistencies between behavioral indices of stress and discomfort (such as crying and fussing) and physiological measures (such as activity of the HPA axis) (Barr & Gunnar, 2000; Gunnar & Donzella, 1999; Prudhomme White et al., 2000).

How early colic relates to later development has also been a concern. Most investigations have emphasized that colic is not associated with later problems, although there is some recent data suggesting that excessive crying and/or hours of fussing may be tied to later difficulties in regulating emotion and behavior (Desantis, Coster, Bigsby, & Lester, 2004; Stifter & Spinrad, 2002). Other data examine the hypothesis that many instances of colic are better understood as early instances of esophageal reflux disorder (Orenstein, Izadnia, & Kahn, 1999; Heine, Jordan, Lubitz, Meehan, & Catto-Smith, 2006). Overall, we can be reasonably confident that colic reflects a "bump in the road" rather than early psychopathology.

Temperament Over Time

At about 3 or 4 months of age (following that first biobehavioral shift), various aspects of temperament appear to come together in meaningful ways (Shonkoff & Phillips, 2000). With the idea that temperament characteristics provide many of the building blocks of personality, we would then expect to see evidence of temperamental **consistency** across a variety of situations and **stability** across time. Within the categorical framework, several longitudinal studies provide this evidence, suggesting modest but clear associations between early temperament and later toddler and preschooler personality (Fox, Henderson, Rubin, Calkins, & Schmidt, 2001; Kagan & Snidman, 1991; Kagan, Snidman, & Arcus, 1998; Schmidt & Fox, 2002).

From the perspective of continuous dimensions of temperament, there is also research that supports both continuity and stability. Most important for our purposes are studies focused on the dimension of effortful control (Kochanska, Murray, & Harlan, 2000; Murray & Kochanska, 2002). Whether young children come into the world with predispositions toward inhibition or exuberance, all children must

learn ways to manage their emotions, moods, and behaviors. Acquiring self regulation is one of the central tasks of early development (Bronson, 2000; Calkins & Hill, 2007; Kochanska, Coy, & Murray, 2001; Kopp, 1982, 1989), and one which will have continuing impact throughout children's lives.

Temperament and Psychopathology

For some infants and children, temperament characteristics are not the source of interesting variations in personality, but the roots of later child and adult psychopathology (Clark, 2005; Watson, Kotov, & Gamez, 2006). As discussed in Chapter 3, **risk** is conceptualized as one or more factors that make it more likely that a child will develop or experience psychopathology. A **general risk factor** is associated with increased vulnerability to any, or many, possible disorders. A **specific risk factor** is associated with increased vulnerability to a particular disorder. Much of the work on temperament as a general risk factor has focused on children with difficult temperaments and problems with either under- or overregulation (Cole et al., 1994; Keenan, 2000; Nigg, 2006; Rothbart, Posner, & Hershey, 1995; Zeanah et al., 1997), as well as the specific combination of high levels of negative affectivity and low levels of effortful control (Calkins & Fox, 2002; Muris & Ollendick, 2005; Oldehinkel, Hartman, Ferdinand, Verhulst, & Ormel, 2007).

Discussions of specific risks have focused on connections between highly reactive, inhibited children and later internalizing disorders such as anxiety, and between less reactive, uninhibited children and later externalizing disorders such as conduct disorder (Aksan et al., 1999; Frick & Morris, 2004; Goldsmith & Lemery, 2000; Kagan, Snidman, Zentner, & Peterson, 1999; Keenan, Shaw, Delliquadri, Giovanelli, & Walsh, 1998; Schwartz, Snidman, & Kagan, 1996). Lahey's model, discussed previously, also maps out possible relations between the temperamental characteristics of emotionality, sociability, and impulsivity and later specific psychopathologies (Lahey & Waldman, 2003).

In order to better explain the connection between early temperament type and specific disorder, a number of researchers have examined the role of caregivers' responses to their inhibited children. These researchers report poorer outcomes—meaning more consistent and more extreme inhibition and anxiety—for children who have parents who are overinvolved, controlling, or intrusive (Calkins et al., 2004; Feldman, 2007; Ispa et al., 2004; Nachmias, Gunnar, Mangelsdorf, Parritz, & Buss, 1996; Rubin et al., 1997). Of course, not all shy or exuberant children go on to struggle with anxiety or conduct disorders, and not all adults with anxiety or conduct disorders were shy or exuberant as children (Prior, Smart, Sanson, & Oberklaid, 2000); there are multiple developmental pathways to both adjustment and maladjustment. The pathways to early instances of maladjustment are the focus of the rest of the chapter.

Disorders of Early Development

The organization of the following sections is similar to discussions of psychopathology in all subsequent chapters. The clinical characteristics and course of various disorders are presented, followed by discussions of developmental course, etiology, assessment and diagnosis, and treatments. The focus in this chapter is on disorders involving basic physiological functioning and patterns of dysregulation. Problems

with feeding and sleeping can be very distressing, for caregivers as well as their children. Two types of diagnostic categories are fairly dramatic, but infrequently observed (Benoit, 2000): **pica**, or the ingestion of non-food substances such as paint, pebbles, or dirt, and **rumination**, or the repeated regurgitation of food (DSM-IV-TR, 2000). More common are feeding disturbances related to not eating enough for normal growth and development. A brief overview of this kind of problem, feeding disorder of infancy or early childhood, is presented below. **Sleep disorders** are also disruptions of basic functioning. Both DSM-IV and the Zero to Three classification systems describe several kinds of these disorders observed in infancy.

Regarding dysregulation, we attempt to understand patterns of atypical development characterized by difficulties in sensory, sensorimotor, or organizational processing, and problems achieving and maintaining calm, alert, emotionally pleasant moods (Zero to Three, 1994, 2005). These early patterns of distress and dysfunction, including **hypersensitivity, underreactivity,** and **motor disorganization,** have been the subject of much theoretical speculation by Greenspan and DeGangi and their colleagues (DeGangi et al., 2000; Greenspan & Weider, 1993) and by Dunn (1997). Whether these patterns are best characterized as actual clinical syndromes relates to the validity of (a) diagnosing disorders in very young infants, and (b) diagnosing disorders in infants rather than infant-caregiver pairs (Barton & Robins, 2000; Eppright, Bradley, & Sanfacon, 1998; Hofacker & Papoušek, 1998). In fact, although these specific syndromes are described in detail in the Zero to Three classification system, they are *not* included in the DSM-IV-TR (2000). However, with the developmental framework of this textbook, and the emphasis on risk in developmental psychopathology, it is important to become familiar with these early unusual and/or extreme presentations.

Feeding Disorders

Although the organization of efficient and effective feeding is an especially salient developmental task in infancy and early childhood, there are few uniformly accepted categories of **feeding disorders**. In part, this is because it is not easy to determine when feeding quirks become feeding problems, and when feeding problems become disorders (Benoit, 2000). Current research and clinical efforts attempt to identify subtypes that differentiate difficulties on the basis of cause, course, and treatment, including feeding disorder of state regulation, feeding disorder associated with lack of parent-infant reciprocity, and posttraumatic feeding disorder (Chatoor, 2002; Chatoor & Ammaniti, 2007). The following cases provide some perspective.

The Case of Alex

Alex is a 6-month-old infant referred by his pediatrician to a feeding clinic in a children's hospital. Alex recently experienced a severe gastrointestinal illness that led to decreased appetite and repeated refusal to drink from his bottle. After growing concerned about possible weight loss, Alex's parents began to feed him by bottle while he was sleeping. Consequently, even as Alex recovered from his illness, he lost interest in feeding when awake. From the behavioral viewpoint, Alex has lost the positive connection between the act of sucking and relief from hunger. From a psychodynamic perspective, the cuddling and play that often accompanied feeding have been replaced by tension. In this case, the feeding clinic provided both reassurance and education to the parents regarding the problematic pattern that has been established, as well as the steps necessary to change the behavioral patterns and emotionally unpleasant interactions. Specifically, the staff worked with the parents to set up a feeding schedule designed to heighten Alex's experience of hunger when he is awake, and to foster an appreciation of the feeding interaction's positive emotional and social consequences. ∎

The Case of Jessica

Jessica is a 3-year-old girl who experienced in-utero drug and alcohol exposure. She was born prematurely and suffered extensive neglect in her first year before being removed from her home and placed in foster care. Significant developmental delays, particularly in the areas of cognition and speech, have been documented. Although always a fussy eater, Jessica's diet has become progressively more restricted and she is now at the point of subsisting almost entirely on apple juice and french fries. Intervention efforts involving Jessica's foster parents and early childhood special education services centered on gradually introducing new foods and reinforcing Jessica for tasting them.

Providing more structured mealtimes, with social stimulation and clear reinforcement, was also helpful in expanding the range of Jessica's food options. Equally important was the focus on promoting reciprocity and decreasing conflict within the caregiver relationship. ∎

Developmental Course

From the start, feeding involves the integration and coordination of internal processes (such as orienting, sucking, and swallowing) and relational processes (such as communication and reciprocity). By the time infants make the transition to solid foods, typically between 4 and 6 months of age, pleasant patterns of interactions between most infants and their parents have evolved. Benoit (2000) summarizes the infant characteristics that underlie this process, including the ability to experience hunger and satiety, oral-sensory and oral-motor functioning, developmental readiness, and past feeding experiences. Over the early years, many young children display peculiar food behaviors: eating macaroni and cheese every meal, making sure that different foods do not touch, or refusing previous favorites. Almost always, these are temporary situations and are not cause for alarm (Benoit, 2000; Black, Cureton & Berenson-Howard, 1999).

Sometimes, however, as with Alex and Jessica, the process goes awry. When it does, the responses of caregivers may exacerbate the situation. Even though Alex's parents were well-intentioned, feeding Alex while he was sleeping made daytime feeding more difficult. Because being able to successfully nourish infants is a notable early parenting achievement, ongoing feeding problems may also have an increasingly negative impact on the caregiver (Benoit, 2000; Black et al., 1999). Feelings of personal incompetence, and anger toward the child, may create additional distress and dysfunction, with increasing difficulties related to amounts of food, choices of food, and mealtime behavior. More serious situations may be associated with poor growth and compromised development (Benoit, 2000).

Etiology

In developmental psychopathology, the causes of disorder are usually complex and interacting. In all the upcoming chapters, we will review individual, family, and social factors that contribute to the development and maintenance of disorders.

We examine physiological, emotional, cognitive, and behavioral characteristics of the child. We consider parents, siblings, and other related factors. We include socioeconomic or cultural variables. In this chapter, given the emergence of infant disorder in a relatively short time frame, we focus primarily on individual and parent factors.

Feeding difficulties may be the result of developmental delays, genetic conditions, or abnormalities of oral anatomy. Some infants may be less sensitive to feelings of hunger, or may present signals that are unclear or difficult to read by their caregivers. Temperamental differences may also come into play, with children who are highly reactive to new stimuli responding more negatively to the introduction of new tastes and textures. Infants who, for a variety of reasons, may be "too sleepy, excited or distressed to feed are at risk" (Chatoor, 2002, p. 166). For certain children, including Jessica, the issue of control may be important. For other children, such as Alex, a traumatic event like serious illness, with associated physical discomfort and stomach pain, may interfere with normal development patterns.

Parents who are insecure, anxious, and/or controlling, or parents with unresolved issues related to food, may also contribute to the emergence of feeding disorders (Chatoor, 2002). Infant-parent relationship factors such as reciprocity are essential to explore. Reciprocity involves the back-and-forth emotional engagement of the infant and caregiver, displayed in mutually satisfying exchanges of eye contact, vocalizations, and touch. "If caregiver and infant are not successfully engaged with each other, feeding and growth of the infant suffer" (Chatoor, 2002, p. 167). Touch appears to be especially disturbed, with caregivers displaying more problematic types of contact and infants displaying more aversion to touch (Feldman, Keren, Gross-Rozval, & Tyano, 2004). Parenting decisions related to the routine and timing of feeding may also have an impact. If parents introduce solid foods earlier than the usual 4–6 month period, for example, or if parents offer food inconsistently or insensitively, feeding difficulties are more likely.

Assessment and Diagnosis

For all of the disorders of early development, useful assessments depend on establishing a therapeutic alliance with the child's caregiver (Lieberman, Van Horn, Grandison, & Pekarsky, 1997; Meisels & Atkins-Burnett, 2000). Parents whose infants are

Jose Luis Pelaez, Inc./Corbis Edge/Corbis

Effective infant feeding involves the coordination of physiological skills of the infant and relational processes between the infant and caregiver.

struggling with basic developmental tasks often feel confused and guilty. Recognizing the role of parental factors in the etiology and/or maintenance of disorder does not equate with focusing blame on parents. Given the primary goal of improving the child's well-being, mental health professionals and parents will need to work together.

Basic assessments involve multiple sources and multiple types of data (Meisels & Atkins-Burnett, 2000). The first step is usually focused on gathering data about children's overall health and development, including prenatal care, birth complications, and early experiences. With feeding disorders, detailed feeding histories are obtained, and diagnostic tests of physiological functioning such as swallowing are common. Specific rating scales may be completed by parents, nurses, or therapists. Actual observation of parent-child feeding interactions may be most helpful (Benoit, 2000).

Intervention

Intervention is always focused on the interplay of physiological, behavioral, and environmental factors, and is tied to the alliance developed during the assessment process (Lieberman et al., 1997; Meisels & Atkins-Burnett, 2000). Depending on the particular constellation of symptoms and infant-caregiver pairs, treatments range from empirically supported behavioral interventions (Kerwin, 1999) to more psychodynamically informed approaches focused on relationships, vulnerability, and conflict (Chatoor, 2002). Benoit and Coolbear (1998) describe a three-part treatment designed for children who struggle with feeding following a trauma. They suggest that physiological and environmental changes be made to address the dysfunction in cycles of hunger and satiety. In Alex's case, the parents needed to stop feeding Alex while he was sleeping, so he could re-experience hunger when awake. The second part of treatment involves nutritional monitoring. In Alex's case, careful measurement of intake and weight gain is required. The third part of treatment focuses on behavioral techniques. For Alex, this involved emphasizing the positive social and emotional aspects of feeding situations, in order to make these interactions more rewarding.

Sleep Disorders

Four types of sleep disorders diagnosed in both adults and children are described in the DSM-IV-TR, including primary sleep disorders, sleep disorders related to other mental disorders, sleep disorders associated with a medical condition, and substance-induced sleep disorders. The **primary sleep disorders** are divided into two groups: the **dyssomnias** (i.e., disturbances in the normal rhythms or patterns of sleep), and the **parasomnias** (i.e., disorders involving sleep dysfunctions, such as night terrors, nightmare disorder, or sleepwalking). The Zero to Three classification system also includes a category for "sleep behavior disorder," reflecting atypical difficulties falling and/or staying asleep. Anders, Goodlin-Jones, and Sadeh (2000) suggest a more differentiated set of categories that takes into account severity of disorder, relationship factors, infant factors, and contextual factors (see Table 5.1). In the early years of life, difficulties going to sleep and difficulties staying asleep are the most commonly observed, with estimates of incidence ranging from 10% to 30% in families with young children (Anders & Dahl, 2007; Gaylor, Burnham, Goodlin-Jones, & Anders, 2005). The following case, summarized from Dahl (1996), provides a more personal view.

TABLE 5:1 FOUR-AXIS APPROACH TO THE DIAGNOSIS OF SLEEP DISORDERS	
AXIS I:	Perturbation/Disturbance/Disorder
	Night waking protodysomnia
	Sleep-onset protodysomnia
	Schedule disruption protodysomnia
AXIS II:	Parent-child interaction styles
	Balanced/synchronous
	Overregulating/controlling
	Underregulating/distant
	Inconsistent/unpredictable
AXIS III:	Infant factors
	Temperament
	Developmental quotient
	Medical illnesses
AXIS IV:	Context factors
	Family/marital stress
	Parenting stress/hassle
	Family psychopathology
	Family trauma/violence
From Anders, Goodlin-Jones, & Sadeh (2000).	

The Case of Cassandra

Cassandra was a 16-month-old girl brought in by her mother for chronic difficulties with night waking. For months, Cassandra would awaken several times each night and would often require hours of interaction with her parents to get back to sleep. She was also resistant to daytime naps (except when falling asleep during car rides). Other aspects of her health, growth, and development were completely normal. Cassandra's behavior during the day, however, showed extreme irritability, fussiness, and very low frustration tolerance. She cried frequently, and was difficult to console when upset. Also, her attention span was very short and she changed activities rapidly. Her parents, equally fatigued and frustrated at their inability to get Cassandra to sleep, dreaded the nighttime hours. Cassandra's sleep problems responded well to a behavioral program focused on self-comforting and cessation of parental involvement at sleep onset. The change in daytime behavior was equally positive, with decreases in negative emotions and improved attention. Cassandra is now a more pleasant, happy child with much better relationships. ■

Cassandra's situation is appropriately characterized as a disorder because it reflects marked and persistent difficulties settling down and falling asleep as well as maintaining sleep through the night. These ongoing difficulties are associated with impaired daily functioning and increasingly distressed relationships with her caregivers.

Developmental Course

Although many sleep difficulties and disorders resolve over time, many persist. Night waking problems tend to decrease over time, whereas sleep onset problems such as bedtime resistance and bedtime struggles remain stable or increase in frequency or severity (Gaylor et al., 2005). It is important to understand that the course of infant and toddler sleep disorders is superimposed on the changing course of sleeping during the first three years of life. Observing that over half of these years are spent sleeping, Dahl (1996) states that sleep is the "*primary* activity of the brain" during infancy (p. 3), and that understanding sleep is the key to understanding early brain development. With respect to time spent sleeping, kinds of sleep, and physiological and interpersonal regulation of sleep, these years involve great changes in the patterns of sleep-wake organization and the varieties of sleep rhythms (stages of sleep) (Anders et al., 2000; Benhamou, 2000; Goodlin-Jones, Burnham, & Anders, 2000; Meltzer & Mindell, 2006). Throughout these years, adequate sleep is essential for cognitive, emotional, and social development (Anders & Dahl, 2007).

Although most people, including parents, believe that infants sleep through the night by the second half of the first year, all infants continue to awake during nighttime (Anders & Dahl, 2007; Keener, Zeanah, & Anders, 1989). The key difference is that some infants soothe themselves back to sleep, whereas others signal their caregivers ("non-self-soothers") (Keener et al., 1989). The issue is not that the infant wakes up, it is that the infant signals the caregiver (as Cassandra did), demanding repeated attention and assistance before falling asleep again (Anders et al., 2000).

The immediate consequences of sleep disorders are observed in both children and their families. Children's daytime emotions and moods, attention and cognitive activities, and social relationships are all likely to be negatively affected. Tired and distressed children are also likely to have tired and distressed parents. Investigators have documented negative impacts on parents' self-efficacy, parents' marital satisfaction, and overall family climate (Anders & Dahl, 2007; Fiese, Winter, Sliwinski, & Anbar, 2007; Meijer & van den Wittenboer, 2007; Meltzer & Mindell, 2007). Long-range consequences

have also been described, including behavioral difficulties such as acting out, academic difficulties, and ongoing family conflict (El-Sheikh, Buckhalt, Cummings, & Keller, 2007; Hall, Zubrick, Silburn, Parsons, & Kurinczuk, 2007).

Etiology

Individual variations in the ability to self-regulate and self-soothe are frequently mentioned as contributing to sleep difficulties, tied to underlying differences in the neurophysiological systems related to arousal and attention (Anders et al., 2000; Gaylor et al., 2005). The constellation of characteristics called "difficult temperament" has also been cited as a risk factor (Anders & Dahl, 2007); the temperamental characteristic of resistance to control seems particularly important (Goodnight, Bates, Staples, Pettit, & Dodge, 2007).

Parent factors such as problematic cognitions related to setting limits (e.g., thinking that enforcing a bedtime reflects controlling or mean parenting) and anxiety and/or depression increase the likelihood of sleep disorders (Anders et al., 2000; Morrell & Steele, 2003; Sadeh, Flint-Ofir, Tirosh, & Tikotzky, 2007). Relationship factors such as inconsistent or insensitive caregiving are also risk factors (Morrell & Steele, 2003). Racial, ethnic, and cultural values and practices are also important to take into account (Anders & Dahl, 2007; Milan, Snow, & Belay, 2007). Co-sleeping provides one example. Whether co-sleeping is viewed by the family and/or by the clinician as a negative consequence of child awakening or as a positive family experience is a clinically relevant factor.

Many investigators emphasize the distinction between factors that influence the *emergence of sleep disorders* and factors that influence the *maintenance of disorders* (Minde, 2002). For instance, transient disturbances such as ear infections or teething may lead to parents offering high levels of physical comforting during bedtime; continuing these bedtime interactions may reinforce maladaptive patterns for non-self-soothing infants and toddlers and may exacerbate already-observable sleep difficulties (Burnham, Goodlin-Jones, Gaylor, & Anders, 2002; Morrell & Steele, 2003).

Assessment and Diagnosis

Because we expect to see many changes in patterns of infant sleep, it is difficult to know exactly when to diagnose a sleep disorder. In addition to general overviews of health and development, sleep diaries are often requested from parents (Meltzer & Mindell, 2006). Sleep diaries provide quantitative data related to the frequency and intensity of symptoms. Using these criteria, we can distinguish among perturbations (i.e., one episode per week for at least 1 month), disturbances (i.e., two to four episodes per week for at least 1 month), and disorders (i.e., five to seven episodes per week for at least 1 month) (Anders & Dahl, 2007). Additional issues in this kind of assessment include: "Does an infant's schedule conform to the family's schedule in a socially appropriate way, and does it meet the infant's need for sleep?" (Anders et al., 2000, p. 332). Here, the degree of parent tolerance for sleep disruptions may influence whether and when parent concerns lead to seeking help. Sometimes lab assessments, in which babies are directly observed and physically monitored while they sleep in the hospital, are necessary to rule out physiological complications, such as sleep apnea (Anders et al., 2000).

Intervention

Behavior therapies and other dynamically oriented approaches (focused on relationships and parental adjustments) have all been used to treat infants with sleep disorders, although drug treatments are sometimes included. These approaches are associated with significant improvements (Anders et al., 2000; Mindell, Kuhn, Lewin, Meltzer, & Sadeh, 2006; Robert-Tissot et al., 1996).

Night Terrors and Nightmare Disorder

In addition to the basic disturbances of sleep already described, **night terrors** and **nightmare disorder** are two other relatively common problems experienced by young children. These two types of parasomnias involve "activation of the autonomic nervous system, motor system, or cognitive processes during sleep or sleep-wake transitions" (DSM-IV-TR, 2000). Table 5.2

provides a useful comparison. Although nightmares and night terrors are usually transient and outgrown without specific interventions, children often appreciate reassurance and comfort following a nightmare (Anders et al., 2000).

Disorders of Regulation

Keeping in mind the need for much more empirical work to help us understand both how effective regulation unfolds and how dysregulation develops, the following sections make use of the hypersensitive, underreactive and disorganized classifications of the Zero to Three diagnostic system, and are summarized and adapted from the cases presented by Black (1997), Kalmanson (1997), and Ahrano (1997) in the Zero to Three casebook (Lieberman, Wieder, & Fenichel, 1997).

The Case of Sara

Sara is a first-born 1-year-old girl who was referred for evaluation by her parents following several months of waiting for Sara to "grow out of a difficult phase." Sara's parents describe her as extremely reactive to both sounds and lights, and they contrast her overly negative responses to other babies they know. Sara's mother reports that she cannot turn on the television or the radio without Sara starting to cry. Switching on lights also results in loud and prolonged protests. So far, Sara's parents have managed to keep their home relatively quiet and dark, but it is getting more and more difficult to anticipate Sara's reactions when they visit a friend or go on errands where she displays wary and fearful behaviors. In addition, Sara's parents say that she has always had a hard time feeding, often gagging, with the transition to solid food especially problematic. Sara also has a history of sleep problems. She continues to wake

TABLE 5:2 COMPARISON OF NIGHTMARES AND NIGHT TERRORS		
	NIGHT TERRORS	NIGHTMARES
Peak age	3 to 5 years	7 to 10 years
Signs of physiological anxiety	Dramatic	Less dramatic
Sleep cycle	Deep (stage 4)	REM stage
Frightening dream content	No	Yes
Memory the following morning	No	Yes

several times each night, and fusses whenever she is laid down for a nap. At this point, Sara's parents are increasingly concerned about their daughter's overall development, wondering whether they waited too long to seek professional help, and whether Sara will ever be happy. ∎

The characteristics of this type of **hypersensitive regulatory disorder** consist of heightened or exaggerated sensitivity to both auditory and visual stimulation. When aroused, Sara is very difficult to soothe, and what works at one time does not necessarily work at another. Sara's parents also describe feeding and sleeping irregularities, and note that this pattern of discomfort has been evident since birth. Of the two common subtypes of this regulatory disorder, Sara's clinical presentation is more consistent with the highly inhibited and fearful subtype, although she does display some features of the negativistic and defiant subtype.

The Case of Jerry

Jerry is a 32-month-old boy whose parents are concerned about his combination of unusual physiological and behavioral responses. Jerry prefers to play alone, is physically awkward, and displays peculiar patterns of attention and language. Jerry's parents described him as an easy baby, although somewhat "floppy," who was often content to lie alone and look around. They did report some sound sensitivities, and fears connected to, for example, the noise of the vacuum. As a toddler, Jerry appears to respond slowly to requests and demands, whether the tone is positive or negative. Both at home and at preschool, Jerry is often distracted and disengaged from other children and group activities. ∎

Jerry's history and presentation are characteristic of **underreactive regulatory disorder**, with poor motor tone and coordination, self-absorption, and lagging skills in organizational processing. Although reminiscent in some ways of other developmental disorders such as Asperger's syndrome (discussed in Chapter 8), Jerry's social and emotional interactions with his mother and father are more positive and more animated than the kinds of interactions usually observed in children with Asperger's syndrome.

The Case of Amanda

Amanda is a loud, high-spirited 2-year-old girl, adopted at birth, who demonstrates irregular attention, delayed language, and impulsive—often reckless—behavior. Amanda previously received speech and language therapy, but remains highly active, intrusive, and undercontrolled. Amanda is frequently nonresponsive to attempts to direct or control her. Amanda's parents are most worried about increases in negative behaviors such as hitting others and engaging in dangerous activities such as climbing and jumping from heights. Her parents are inconsistent in their interactions with Amanda, with her mother sometimes able to help Amanda organize herself and her behaviors, and her father often distant or angry in his responses. They are seeking psychological advice to better understand and help their daughter. ∎

Amanda's experiences are best categorized as a **motorically disorganized, impulsive regulatory disorder,** with displays of significant disruptive activity and frequent sensation-seeking behavior. Similar to Sara and Jerry, Amanda is usually unable to soothe or control herself when she becomes aroused; others' attempts to manage her difficult moods and behaviors are unpredictable.

At this point, we want to emphasize that these subtypes are based mainly on theoretical assumptions, although there are data providing initial support for these constructs (Tirosh, Bendrian, Golan, Tamir, & Dar, 2003). That is, it makes sense that different patterns of reactive and regulatory dysfunction are extreme examples of different types of normal variations. However, there is not much empirical data that support these particular subtypes; indeed, the **mixed category of regulatory disorder** in the Zero to Three classification scheme suggests the current lack of clinical consensus in this area.

Developmental Course

Given the rocky start of infants and toddlers with regulatory disorders, we expect to see evidence of ongoing problems related to reactivity and regulation. And, in fact, we do. In two longitudinal studies, DeGangi and colleagues observed poorer developmental outcomes for infants who displayed early dysregulation (DeGangi et al., 2000; DeGangi, Porges, Sickel, & Greenspan, 1993). In the later study, 40% of 4-year-olds diagnosed with a mild regulatory disorder in infancy and 95% with a history of moderate to severe regulatory disorder experienced later developmental delays and/or parent-child difficulties. The persistent nature of this disorder is summarized well by Hofacker and Papoušek (1998) who state that "the longer dysfunctional reciprocities are maintained in a kind of a vicious cycle the more likely they become automated, ritualized, and rigid" (p. 185). In addition to the stability of specific symptoms related to reactivity and regulation, other theoretical and empirical links have been made between early effortful control and later conscience development (Kochanska et al., 2000), as well as between effortful control and internalizing and externalizing behaviors (Murray & Kochanska, 2002). From a more psychodynamic perspective, the ways in which infants come to regulate themselves and their emotions are understood to have a profound impact on the emergence of a sense of self (Schore, 1994).

Etiology

The characteristic disturbances in sleep, feeding, self-calming, and the self-regulation of emotion that appear very early in life suggest a neurophysiological basis to disorder. Data that support the notion of physiological risk come from numerous studies of infants with histories of prematurity and low birth weight, maternal substance abuse, and early adverse experiences; these types of infant difficulties are associated with many disruptions in early regulation (Gunnar, 2000; Lester et al., 2000; Lester & Tronick, 1994; Minde, 2000; Nelson & Bosquet, 2000). Infant arousability, intensity, and soothability—taken together, the "difficult temperament"—all appear to be involved. Additional support for this hypothesis comes from genetic and biologically based investigations of temperament, with an emphasis on the far ends of normally distributed characteristics. There are many hypotheses about one or more underlying vulnerabilities, including autonomic hyper-irritability (DeGangi, DiPietro, Greenspan, & Porges, 1991).

We have already summarized studies of normal temperament and developmental outcome where, for all babies, parental beliefs, parental behaviors, and goodness of fit are important. These parent and caregiving factors are even more salient for the baby who struggles with extremes of reactivity and regulation. To the extent that caregivers recognize and respond to the special needs of certain infants, the emergence of disorder may be prevented or delayed. Once the disorder is present, caregivers' behaviors may either aggravate or improve symptoms.

Assessment and Diagnosis

For the most part, the assessment of regulatory disorders depends on interviews and observations. Given that parental concerns about infant and toddler development are the reason for most early referrals to clinics (Keren, Feldman, & Tyano, 2001), developmental and medical histories are key sources of information. New interview instruments designed to assess regulatory disorders can also be used (Eppright et al., 1998; Dunn & Westman, 1997). In addition to parents, other informants such as day care providers, preschool teachers, and pediatricians may provide valuable data (DeGangi, Poisson, Sickel, & Weiner, 1998). Observations by clinicians can be done in the office or during home visits. These multiple perspectives on child functioning are evident in the assessments of Sara, Jerry, and Amanda, where parents identify, and other adults confirm, abnormal patterns early on.

Depending on the age of the child, different rating forms for temperament are available, with numerous reviews of the reliability and validity of such data (Mangelsdorf, Schoppe, & Buur, 2000; Rothbart & Hwang, 2002). And for some children, various neuropsychological tests might be appropriate. In addition to information about distress and dysfunction, descriptions of the infant's strengths and competencies should also be included (Meisels & Atkins-Burnett, 2000).

Intervention

Many different successful interventions have been documented for regulatory disorders, with the majority of families reporting significant improvement after three sessions (Cohen et al., 1999; Robert-Tissot et al., 1996). Stern (1995) suggests that serial brief therapy might be especially useful, with sets of treatment sessions offered at several times during the first few years for infants and caregivers to deal with continuing development and change.

The meaningful impact of sensitive parenting has been emphasized throughout this chapter, and it has been a major focus of treatment efforts (Barton & Robins, 2000; Maldonado-Duran & Sauceda-Garcia, 1996; VanFleet, Ryan, & Smith, 2005). As always, parent-centered interventions depend on the alliance established during the assessment process.

Hofacker and Papoušek's (1998) interaction-centered infant-parent psychotherapy and VanFleet et al.'s (2005) filial therapy are two approaches that include treatment tasks geared to the infant, the mother (regular relief from stress, distress), and the father (increasing involvement and support; see also Barrows, 1999), with the intention of increasing positive interactions between parents and babies. Other parent-oriented treatments focus on psychodynamic therapy for the parents (Baradon, 2002).

Another common intervention involves occupational therapy, with the primary goal of increasing infants' and toddlers' sensory adaptation (Barton & Robins, 2000). Examples of these occupational techniques include rubbing fuzzy blankets, water play, and listening to loud and soft music. Another close look at the intervention plans for Sara (Black, 1997), Jerry (Kalmanson, 1997), and Amanda (Ahrano, 1997) provides additional detail.

Some Cases Revisited
The Case of Sara
A better understanding of Sara's deficits and abilities allows the clinician and her parents opportunities to compensate for her weaknesses and play to her strengths. Sara's parents, like many parents of poorly regulated children, felt responsible and incompetent. They needed education, support, and specific intervention techniques such as increasing predictability and structure, and anticipating difficult events. Learning to follow Sara's lead was accomplished by having mom and dad spend "floor time" with her, a structured form of play in which parents align their responses to those of the child (Greenspan, 1992). Musical instruments were also found to be calming for Sara, who enjoyed both listening and playing.

The Case of Jerry
A parent and family approach to treatment was planned, in coordination with speech and language specialists. For Jerry's parents, reciprocity in play was emphasized, so that Jerry might experience positive, self-directed activity. In addition, the clinician suggested that increased involvement on the part of Jerry's father would benefit both Jerry and the family.

The Case of Amanda
A more comprehensive intervention was indicated for Amanda. The first step was enrolling Amanda in a therapeutic day treatment program for young children, where a more structured, calmer setting proved beneficial. In addition, Amanda began swimming and dancing lessons designed to improve her sensorimotor integration. Finally, Amanda's parents received education and support to boost their confidence and skills in dealing with their daughter's development.

■ Key Terms
Temperament (pg. 66)
Reactivity (pg. 66)
Regulation (pg. 66)
Surgency (pg. 67)
Negative affectivity (pg. 67)
Effortful control (pg. 67)
Infant emotionality (pg. 67)
Goodness of fit (pg. 69)
Consistency (pg. 70)
Stability (pg. 70)
Risk (pg. 70)
General risk factor (pg. 70)
Specific risk factor (pg. 70)
Pica (pg. 71)
Rumination (pg. 71)
Sleep disorders (pg. 71)
Hypersensitivity (pg. 71)
Underreactivity (pg. 71)
Motor disorganization (pg. 71)
Feeding disorders (pg. 71)
Primary sleep disorders (pg. 74)
Dyssomnias (pg. 74)
Parasomnias (pg. 74)
Night terrors (pg. 76)
Nightmare disorder (pg. 76)
Hypersensitive regulatory disorder (pg. 77)
Underreactive regulatory disorder (pg. 77)
Motorically disorganized, impulsive regulatory disorder (pg. 77)
Mixed category of regulatory disorder (pg. 77)

■ Chapter Summary
● There is widespread acceptance of the need to identify and respond to infant and toddler distress and dysfunction.
● The interaction of infant temperament with the caregiver's response to that temperament is related to both adjustment and maladjustment in later development.

- Recent research in areas such as neurobiological development, temperament, and attachment are all contributing to the emerging field of infant mental health.
- Disorders of sleeping and feeding represent problems with basic physiological functioning.
- Feeding disorders represent an impairment of efficient and effective feeding—an especially salient developmental task in infancy and early childhood. Feeding disorders may be the result of developmental delays, genetic conditions, abnormalities of oral anatomy, caregiver difficulties, or combinations of those factors.
- The sleep disorders most common in early development are those that involve significant difficulties falling or staying asleep. Other common problems are night terrors and nightmare disorder.
- The assessment of both feeding and sleep disorders requires careful consideration of general health and developmental history, as well as current behavioral and relationship patterns.
- Disorders of regulation include several patterns of dysregulation that interfere with the measured and efficient processing of sensory stimuli in early childhood.

THE HISTORICAL CONTEXT for current conceptualizations of disorders of attachment is provided, in large part, by Rene Spitz's (1945, 1946) compelling studies of institutionalized infants, by John Bowlby's (1953, 1961) reviews of maternal deprivation and infant mourning, and by Tizard's reports on children in residential nurseries (Tizard & Hodges, 1978; Tizard & Rees, 1975; see Box 6.1). Indeed, as models of developmental psychopathology would suggest, much of what we know about attachment in clinical samples of children is based on what we know about attachment in normally developing children. With this back-and-forth exchange between developmental constructs and clinical applications in mind, we first review information on the normative processes of attachment in order to provide a framework for understanding disorders of attachment in the early years.

BOX 6:1 RISK AND RESILIENCE

Institutionalized Infants, Then and Now

Concerns over breakdowns in early caregiving predated research on the attachment process. In their psychiatric work, Rene Spitz, John Bowlby, and others called attention to the devastating developmental impact of early psychological deprivation. In orphanages, hospitals, and residential nurseries, clinicians observed infants and young children whose basic physical requirements were met, but whose emotional and social needs went unrecognized and unfulfilled. Whereas some orphanages, for example, provided babies with both nutrition and nurturance, others—because of overcrowding, lack of resources, and lack of knowledge—provided only the barest essentials: a crib, bottles of milk, and rigid feeding and changing schedules. Caregivers changed from morning to evening; intimate and enduring relationships were impossible.

We know now that a cheerful, stimulating environment, with warm and consistent caregiving, is the foundation for psychological growth. But our knowledge has not eliminated the poor institutional care that was blamed for the intellectual, emotional, and social struggles of so many deprived children during and following World War II. We have only to look at the more recent experiences of children in Romanian and other Eastern European orphanages to see that—for multiple reasons—basic needs for contact, care, and comfort from a familiar adult are too often unmet.

The experiences of Romanian babies abandoned to poor quality institutions and later adopted (or fostered) by well-functioning families have been described by at least three major longitudinal research programs in the United States (the Bucharest Early Intervention

Program), the United Kingdom (English and Romanian Adoptees (ERA) study), and Canada; these research programs provide data about wide-ranging developmental delays and patterns of maladjustment, as well as frequent instances of resilience and the possibility of remarkable recovery. All of these longitudinal studies have documented the powerfully negative impact of early deprivation on physical, cognitive, emotional, social, and behavioral development (Morison, Ames, & Chisholm, 1995; Nelson, 2007; Nelson, Zeanah, & Fox, 2007; Rutter & the ERA Study Team, 1998), with worse outcomes for babies adopted or fostered at older ages (with longer times in institutional settings) (Fisher, Ames, Chisholm, & Savoie, 1997; MacLean, 2003; Morison & Ellwood, 2000). Many studies have identified attachment difficulties and parenting stress as special areas of concern (Ames & Chisholm, 2001; Mainemer, Gilman, & Ames, 1998; Roy, Rutter, & Pickles, 2004; Zeanah, Smyke, Koga, & Carlson, 2005).

As salient as these negative consequences of early deprivation are, it is equally impressive to note the dramatic turnarounds that may occur with family placements. Improvements have been described for all types of functioning, with normalization of some domains and the diminishment of severity of disorder in others (Nelson et al., 2007; Nelson, Zeanah, & Fox, 2007; Rutter et al., 1998; Rutter et al., 2004). Even with these positive outcomes, we need to keep in mind that a significant minority of children continue to struggle; appropriate interventions for all of the children remain the focus of ongoing study.

Developmental Tasks and Challenges Related to Attachment

We already know that there are all kinds of babies. Affable, cuddly babies. Cranky, demanding babies. Babies who are into everything. Babies who are content to observe. Some babies are temperamentally difficult, and some babies are temperamentally easy. For all of these babies, there are also many kinds of caregivers and many kinds of caregiving relationships. By the end of the first year, most infants—together with their caregivers—have accomplished several key tasks and challenges. These include the development of an **attachment relationship**, a rudimentary **sense of self**, and a basic **understanding of others and the world**. Attachment relationships include caregivers and infants, and reflect the degree to which infants experience safety, comfort, and affection. Sense of self involves the earliest set of cognitions and emotions focused on the infant as a separate being (e.g., Who am I? Am I likeable? Am I good?). An understanding of others and the world involves early beliefs about unfamiliar adults and children, along with the new situations in which infants so often find themselves. For most infants, whose early caregiving is characterized by sensitivity, consistency, and warmth, these early challenges are positively resolved.

As described in the previous chapter, much of the first year of life is devoted to the establishment of routines that promote physical, intellectual, emotional, and social growth. During this year, most infants thrive in homes that provide for their needs and desires in ways that are *mostly* sensitive, *reasonably* consistent, and *usually* warm. Over time, most infants come to understand, in a fundamental way, that they will be cared for, that they are worthy of care, and that the world around them is a pleasant place with interesting people, objects, and activities. This understanding—experienced and expressed emotionally, cognitively, and behaviorally—is the basis of attachment. According to attachment theorists (Ainsworth, 1969, 1979; Bowlby, 1969/1982; Main, Kaplan, & Cassidy, 1985; Sroufe & Waters, 1977), the development of an attachment relationship is *the significant psychological achievement* of late infancy.

Most infants and toddlers are able to use the caregiver for several important purposes, in everyday settings as well as difficult circumstances. The most critical advantage of attachment, from an evolutionary perspective, is to ensure the protection and the survival of the young infant (Bowlby, 1969/1982; Bretherton, 1992). Protection and survival are linked by Bowlby to several defining features of caregivers: (1) providing a **safe haven**, a person to whom the infant can turn to for comfort and support; (2) allowing for **proximity maintenance**, for an infant who seeks closeness and resists separation; and (3) establishing a **secure base**, a person whose presence serves as a source of security from which a child ventures out to explore the world, and to which he or she can reliably return.

In their daily interactions with caregivers, infants and toddlers process and express a variety of positive and negative experiences, and exchange relevant emotions and appraisals (e.g., moving closer to a parent for comfort during a thunderstorm, or sharing surprise when a jack-in-the-box pops up). Infants and toddlers also balance their wishes to explore with their ongoing concerns for maintaining interpersonal connections. For example, very young children may play with other children and toys in an unfamiliar home as long as a parent is nearby. When a parent moves farther away or leaves the room, keeping the parent within view or reestablishing closeness may become more important than exploration. In more challenging or stressful circumstances, such as the birth of a sibling, a difficult illness, or parental stress after losing a job, attachments provide a deeply rooted sense of safety and security. Although a young child may struggle (and struggle mightily) with adults who fuss over a new brother or sister, with painful medical procedures, or with a move to a different apartment, attachment relationships are instrumental in terms of children's abilities to keep hold of feelings of worth and love.

Individual Differences in Attachment

Whereas the normative processes of attachment can be described as they unfold over months of caregiving (Ainsworth, Blehar, Waters, & Wall, 1978; Bowlby, 1969/1982; Weinfield, Sroufe, Egeland, & Carlson, 1999), there are also distinctive patterns in the attachments of particular children. Individual differences emerge from particular caregiving and relationship histories that become internalized early in development; very similar patterns are observed in all countries and cultures (see Box 6.2). Caregiver availability and responsiveness—or

---

BOX 6:2 THE CHILD IN CONTEXT

Attachment across Cultures

There are several approaches to the classification of attachment. Much of the work has been accomplished in the laboratory. Mary Ainsworth's development of the **Strange Situation Procedure** is an example of the way in which a carefully designed lab assessment provides rich data about life outside the lab. In this procedure, the child and caregiver are observed in a playroom as they engage in a series of brief but increasingly upsetting separations and reunions. In these episodes, infants and toddlers are challenged to regulate themselves and use their caregivers or an unfamiliar adult for assistance and support. Young children's patterns of emotions and behaviors are interpreted to reflect attachments that are classified as secure, insecure-avoidant, insecure-resistant, and insecure-disorganized.

Keeping in mind that Ainsworth's original investigations were conducted in Uganda and then replicated in Baltimore, Maryland, continuing cross-cultural research suggests that babies around the world exhibit very similar kinds of attachment. In the United States, using the Strange Situation Procedure, approximately two-thirds of babies are classified as having a secure attachment. Similar percentages are observed in Northern European countries, in Japan, in China, in parts of Africa, and in Israel. The relative percentages of insecure-avoidant and insecure-resistant attachments appear to vary more relative to cultural context. For example, avoidant attachments are more frequent in the United States and Europe, whereas resistant attachments are more frequent in Japan and Israel (Van IJzendoorn, 1995). Similarities in attachment processes and behaviors are thought to reflect evolutionary (i.e., functional) adaptations (Grossmann, Grossmann, & Keppler, 2005; Posada, Carbonell, Alzate, & Plata, 2004; Posada & Jacobs, 2001).

Even with abundant data supporting many aspects of similarity across cultures, a number of investigators have begun to focus more specifically on cultural relativism related to the development and consequences of attachment. These investigators have described multiple instances of culturally specific caregiving practices and attachment behaviors, with a focus on differences in Western and Japanese samples (Rothbaum, Kakinuma, Nagaoka, & Azuma, 2007; Rothbaum & Morelli, 2005; Rothbaum, Weisz, Pott, Miyake, & Morelli, 2000; Weisner, 2005). Ongoing research will undoubtedly provide additional examples of the impact of culture; whether these examples lead to subtle refinements or more significant revisions remains to be seen.

---

unavailability or unpredictability—contribute to infants' and toddlers' emotionally salient beliefs and expectations related to self ("I am worthy/not worthy of care," "I am/am not lovable"), significant others ("I can/cannot trust that you will respond to me in appropriate ways"), and the world ("The world is/is not safe and pleasant"). These specific patterns of attachment can be broadly characterized as **secure** or **insecure.**

Patterns of secure attachment, in general, reflect caregiving histories in which the caregiver responds consistently, appropriately, and sensitively to an infant's physical, emotional, and social needs. In contrast, patterns of insecure attachment develop over time as a result of inconsistent, inadequate, or unavailable care, with such caregiver inadequacies sometimes interacting with difficult infant characteristics and/or contextual stressors. Patterns of infant insecurity are usually interpreted in terms of resistant, avoidant, and disorganized/disoriented attachments (Ainsworth et al., 1978; Cassidy & Shaver, 1999; Main et al., 1985; see Figure 6.1).

Yann Layma/The Image Bank/Getty Images

Although specific child-rearing practices may vary across cultures, the importance of a secure attachment relationship to healthy psychological development is universal.

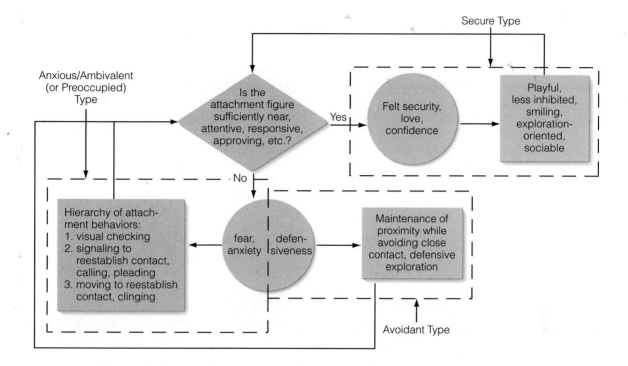

FIGURE 6:1 Patterns of secure, resistant, and avoidant attachments.
Source: From C. Hazan and P.R. Shaver (1994), "Attachment as an organizational framework for research on close relationships", 'Psychological Inquiry', 5(1), 1-22. Reproduced with permission in the format Textbook and in the format Internet posting via Copyright Clearance Center.

Resistant (or **anxious/ambivalent**) **attachment** is generally related to inconsistency or unpredictability. Mothers may respond to an infant's signals for affection on some days and not others. Fathers may feed a hungry baby at certain times, and misread the discomfort of hunger at other times. Scrapes and fears may be sensitively addressed or they may be ignored. These types of on-again, off-again caregiving environments are confusing and frustrating. Depending on the kind and the degree of inconsistent care, very young children with resistant attachments often appear unsure and anxious about themselves, their caregivers, and their situations. These children may or may not feel comfortable enough to explore a new playground. These children may or may not settle down with a familiar babysitter when mom runs a few errands. And these children may or may not happily reconnect with mom when she returns.

Avoidant (or **anxious/avoidant**) **attachment** is generally related to inadequate care. Caregivers who are less competent or overwhelmed or resentful may repeatedly fail to protect or nurture their children. Intrusive, excessively controlling care may also influence the development of an avoidant attachment.

With inadequate care, very young children appear emotionally constricted and distant, with a sense of themselves as less worthy of care and concern. Individuals in the child's immediate and wider social settings may be perceived as unfriendly and without much value. With intrusive care, children may avoid overstimulating interactions, blunt their emotional displays, attempt to care for themselves, and look to persons other than their caregivers for play and comfort.

Disorganized attachment signals a pattern of care in which the caregiver is perceived as frightening, frightened, or malicious (Cassidy & Mohr, 2001; Hazan & Shaver, 1994; Lyons-Ruth, Melnick, Bronfman, Sherry, & Llanas, 2004; Main & Solomon, 1990; Van IJzendoorn, Schuengel, & Bakermans-Kranenburg, 1999). Solomon and George (1999a, 1999b) report that this pattern may also be observed in young children who have experienced long or repeated separations from a caregiver. Recent work has focused on an unusual pattern of behavior and emotion that suggests that the child is distressingly conflicted. Examples of such unusual attachment responses include behavioral "freezing," screaming for the parent during separation but moving away during reunions, multiple and rapid changes in emotion, and bewildered wandering (Lyons-Ruth & Jacobvitz, 1999). The attachment conflict is centered on the caregiver, who is experienced as both a source of comfort and a source of anxiety. Unable to resolve the conflict, the child displays—especially in times of stress—behaviors and emotions that are disorganized with regard to establishing or maintaining a sense of safety or security.

The Case of Sam

"Sam approached his mother with his eyes cast down. When he was about two feet away, he looked up at her, rising suddenly to his toes and making gasping noises with sharp intakes of breath as he did so. He quickly looked down again, bared his teeth in a half-grimace/half-smile, and turned away. Hunching his shoulders and holding his arms and legs stiffly, he tiptoed to the chair on the other side of the room. He sat motionless in the chair for 30 seconds, grasping the armrests and staring straight ahead with a dazed expression" (Jacobvitz & Hazan, 1999, p. 131). ∎

Factors Influencing the Development of Attachment

Numerous factors have been identified that influence the kind of care that infants receive. Briefly, some of the factors receiving theoretical and empirical attention include patterns of sensitive caregiving (De Wolff & Van IJzendoorn, 1997), interactions of infant temperament and parenting variables (Belsky, Fish, & Isabella, 1991; Mangelsdorf, Gunnar, Kestenbaum, & Lang, 1990; Vaughn & Bost, 1999), the role of the father (Jain, Belsky, & Crnic, 1996), non-maternal care (Van IJzendoorn & De Wolff, 1997), the attachment histories of the parents (George & Solomon, 1999; Hesse, 1999; Steele, Steele, & Fonagy, 1996), marital relationships (Cummings & Davies, 1994; Frosch, Mangelsdorf, & McHale, 2000), parents' psychological well-being and/or psychopathology (Belsky & Vondra, 1989; Gelfand & Teti, 1990), and the sociocultural context of childrearing (Belsky & Isabella, 1988; Van IJzendoorn & Sagi, 1999).

It is important to understand that it is not the presence or absence of *any one* particular factor that determines relative security or insecurity. Instead, it is *the additive or cumulative effect* of positive or negative factors—including child variables, parent variables, interaction variables, and contextual variables—that underlies attachment in any particular child (Belsky, 1999; Zeanah, 1996). An even more complex process is suggested by De Wolff and Van IJzendoorn (1997) and Sroufe, Carlson, Levy, and Egeland (1999), who argue that we should consider not only the numbers of positive and negative factors, but the *dynamic interplay* of child, parent, interaction, and contextual factors.

Although stability and coherence over time in attachment-related emotions, cognitions, and behaviors is expected, there is also a real possibility for change (from secure to insecure, or vice versa). Changes in parental expectations or behaviors (Thompson, 1997) and/or changes in social support for the caregiver (Vaughn, Egeland, Sroufe, & Waters, 1979) are associated with changes in infants' attachment classifications (Belsky, Campbell, Cohn, & Moore, 1996; Crittenden, 1995).

Outcomes of Early Attachment

Attachment is a critical challenge and meaningful achievement for several reasons. First, the process of attachment may positively or adversely influence neurological development (Depue & Morrone-Strupinsky, 2005; Greenberg & Snell, 1997; LeDoux, 1995; Schore, 2001; Swain, Lorberbaum, Kose, & Strathearn, 2007). Second, the attachment relationship influences the emergence and organization of emotion regulation, and highlights the central role of emotion in early personality development (Denham, 1998; Eder & Mangelsdorf, 1997; Saarni, 1999; Sroufe, 1995). Third, the attachment relationship provides a relationship prototype, with modeling of how to behave in relationships (Berlin & Cassidy, 1999; Bretherton, 1990; Sroufe & Fleeson, 1986). Finally, by providing children with internalized representations (or "working models") of the self and the world, attachment influences current and later personal and social adaptation (Thompson, 1998, 1999; Weinfield et al., 1999).

Attachment and Psychopathology

It is necessary to emphasize that *not all insecure patterns are, in and of themselves, clinical disorders* (Greenspan & Lieberman, 1988; Sroufe, 1988; Zeanah & Emde, 1994). Remember that in normal, non-clinical samples approximately two-thirds

Taro Yamasaki/Time Life Pictures/Getty Images

The absence of consistent and competent care provided by a reliable attachment figure is a significant risk factor for later psychopathology.

of babies are classified as secure (see Box 6.2); it simply does not make sense that one-third of babies in normal samples have a diagnosable attachment disorder (Belsky & Nezworski, 1988; Rutter, 1995). Toddlers who are not delighted when a parent picks them up at day care are not necessarily insecurely attached, much less disordered; indeed, they may be reluctant to leave because they are also securely attached to their day care providers. Here, again, we need to think about the concept of **risk**. Infants with insecure attachments are at *a higher risk* for the development of certain kinds of difficulties than infants with secure attachments. Insecure babies with disorganized attachments are at *even greater risk* than insecure babies characterized as avoidant or resistant (Solomon & George, 1999b).

It is certainly true that many young children with either relatively transient or subclinical difficulties would benefit from early recognition of their problems and early intervention. Still, just as secure attachments do not always lead to trouble-free childhoods, we *cannot* assume that all insecure attachments lead to inevitably negative outcomes. Instead, it is useful to view early relationship difficulties as a possible "marker of a beginning pathological process," with a focus that shifts from problems within a particular relationship to problems within a particular child (Sroufe et al., 1999). Over time, what was mostly characteristic of a child and his or her primary relationship may become characteristic of that child in multiple relationships, and this shift signals increasing difficulties.

Disorders of Attachment

Some young children exhibit such extreme attachment-related distress and dysfunction that they are best understood as having a clinically significant disorder (Lieberman & Pawl, 1988, 1990; Zeanah & Boris, 2000). However, as with disorders of regulation in early development, there are different approaches to identification and classification of this relatively new category of disorder. DSM-IV-TR describes a single category of attachment disorders, **reactive attachment disorder**, with two subtypes, **inhibited type** and **disinhibited type**, that are diagnosed in children younger than five years of age (see Table 6.1). The diagnostic criteria in DSM-IV-TR include "markedly disturbed and developmentally inappropriate social relatedness in most contexts." There are problems with this criterion, including the requirement that attachment disorders occur *only* in caregiving environments characterized by gross maltreatment (evidenced by persistent disregard for basic physical and/or emotional needs), and that disturbed behavior be evident in *all or almost all social* relationships (rather than a *particular caregiving relationship*) (Greenberg, 1999; Zeanah, 1996).

TABLE 6:1 COMPARISON OF THE DSM-IV-TR AND ZERO TO THREE CLASSIFICATIONS

DSM-IV-TR CLASSIFICATION	ZERO TO THREE CLASSIFICATION
Reactive Attachment: Inhibited Type	Disordered Attachment with Inhibition
Reactive Attachment: Disinhibited Type	Disordered Attachment with Self-Endangerment
	Disordered Attachment with Role Reversal
	Nonattachment with Emotional Withdrawal
	Nonattachment with Indiscriminate Sociability
	Disrupted Attachment

Given ongoing theoretical and empirical work on the nature of disorders of attachment, many theorists and clinicians make use of an alternative approach to classification (see Table 6.1). The Zero to Three (1994, 2005) classification scheme identifies five different patterns of disordered attachment, and one additional attachment disorder based on the loss of a significant caregiver. Reviews of atypical attachments emphasize that it is important to distinguish among various patterns of distress and dysfunction related to (1) the young child's never having formed a specific or special attachment with any caregiver, (2) the young child's experience of inadequate or abusive care, and (3) the young child's loss of an already-established attachment (Bowlby, 1953; Lieberman & Pawl, 1988, 1990; Rutter, 1980). Based on these reviews, as well as data suggesting that these alternative categories demonstrate good reliability (Boris et al., 2004; Boris, Zeanah, Larrieu, Scheeringa, & Heller, 1998), we will use these more differentiated classifications of attachment disorders.

The Case of Andrew: Nonattachment with Emotional Withdrawal

"Andrew, a white, 12-month-old boy, was . . . the product of an unwanted pregnancy of a 29-year-old mother of five. Andrew was described by his mother as a 'happy and pleasant baby.' His birth weight was 2.7 kg [5.9 lbs], and when he was admitted just before his first birthday he weighed 3.7 kg [8.1 lbs] (he placed well below the 5th percentile in weight, height, and head circumference). In the hospital, Andrew was irritable and wary in the presence of his mother and showed no preference for her over various nursing staff. He rarely sought comfort when distressed and did not engage easily with

others. Feeding interactions were marked by gaze aversion. Andrew was minimally responsive to his mother, despite her intermittently sensitive and responsive cues while being observed. Cognitive delays were only mild, and he appeared to have the capacity for social engagement. Home visits revealed that the family was living in 'deplorable' physical conditions" (Boris et al., 1998, p. 297). ■

The Case of Julie: Nonattachment with Indiscriminant Sociability

"Julie, a 35-month-old mixed race child, was referred by Child Protective Services and her pediatrician for evaluation. She had been placed in foster care five months before referral because her mother was known to have a drinking problem and her father was in prison. She had reportedly witnessed violence between her parents before placement, although her biological mother denied this. Her foster mother reported that Julie was preoccupied with being separated from her foster parents and frequently insisted on sleeping in their room. However, she would also seek closeness from adult strangers at the playground and would refuse to be separated from babysitters she had just met. At her initial evaluation, Julie displayed overly bright affect, engaged quickly with the examiner, and then sat in his lap and asked whether he would 'like a little girl like her'" (Boris et al., 1998, p. 297). ■

When very young children exhibit no emotional or behavioral preference for a particular caregiver or attachment figure, a disorder of nonattachment is diagnosed. Most nonattached children have never enjoyed a special connection with a specific caregiver. For disorders of **nonattachment with emotional withdrawal**, children appear unable to make interpersonal connections with others, pulling away from contact and withholding emotional investments. Andrew displays this type of nonattachment. For disorders of **nonattachment with indiscriminate sociability**, children appear to easily and sometimes uncomfortably and inappropriately establish relationships with unfamiliar others. This type of nonattachment is observed with Julie.

The Case of Maria: Disordered Attachment with Inhibition

Maria was a 32-month-old girl who was brought in by her parents after being referred by a day care provider who had been unable to console or comfort the young girl even after weeks of attempts to gradually accustom her to the new day care setting (and her mother's part-time work schedule). In the first evaluation session with the psychotherapist, Maria never left her mother's lap. Even when favorite toys and books were offered, and Maria appeared interested in playing, she did not leave her mother. Maria did not interact with the therapist, often looking away from her after friendly overtures. Maria's mother reported that she had always been shy and somewhat solitary, preferring to play in her own home with her mother nearby. ∎

For young children who have established preferential connections with caregivers, there are three categories of disordered attachment. Children diagnosed with **disordered attachment with inhibition** do not exhibit a well-adjusted balance between security and exploration. These children are withdrawn and clingy, hypervigilant with respect to the caregiver's whereabouts and availability, and unable to venture beyond the immediate vicinity of the attachment figure. The example of Maria emphasizes the excessive clinging associated with one subtype of this disorder. For some children, the inhibition is also associated with "compulsive compliance" and lack of pleasure in the company of the attachment figure, and may reflect past fearful interactions.

The Case of Robert: Disordered Attachment with Self-endangerment

"Robert was referred to an infant mental health clinic when he was 34 months old for evaluation of a variety of behavioral problems, including

frequent tantrums, aggressive behavior, running out of his house and into the street, and willingness to "go with anyone." All of these problems had been apparent since he was about 1½ years old. He had always lived with his mother and a younger sister who was 16 months old. . . . During the intake family interview, which included the three family members and a parent aide, Robert seemed initially to ignore his mother and interacted primarily with the parent aide. . . . Progressively, his behavior became more unruly and disruptive. He could not sustain an activity, and he was quite provocative with his mother. . . . Robert was taken out of the room by the parent aide in order to settle him down. . . . He ran around the waiting room, and two adults could not interest him in toys or activities. Suddenly, he bolted into an adjacent room and began pulling a pot of hot coffee off a warmer. He was stopped before it spilled on him.

"Because of his frenetic, out-of-control, and risk-taking behavior at home, and because neither his mother nor the parent aide felt he could be safely managed at home, Robert was hospitalized for a more intensive assessment. In the hospital, he did not pose the behavior problems that were anticipated. Instead, he was quiet and easily engaged by play with toys. What was striking about his behavior was his active seeking of nurturance from total strangers. He greeted adults he had never seen with open arms and requested hugs and kisses from them. It became clear that only during visits with his mother did the risk taking and recklessness become pronounced" (Zeanah, Mammen, & Lieberman, 1993, pp. 340–341). ∎

Children like Robert, diagnosed with **disordered attachment with self-endangerment,** also display maladjustment related to security and exploration. These children appear unconcerned with maintaining interpersonal connections. They fail to use the attachment figure as a secure base, frequently finding themselves (or placing themselves) in situations that are likely to cause harm.

The Case of Beth: Disordered Attachment with Role Reversal

"Beth was a 24-month-old girl who was referred to an infant mental health clinic for evaluation of a sleep disturbance that had been present for over a year. Her mother reported that she had not slept in her own bed since she was 10 months old, which was about 2 months before she and her husband had separated. The most striking features of the intake session were Beth's mother's depressed mood, frequent crying, and psychomotor retardation. Although toys were available, Beth played with them only in the first 20 minutes of the interview, when her mother seemed more animated. Her mother looked sadder and began to cry as she described her frustration and hopelessness about a number of stressors. Beth walked over to her and signaled to be picked up. She remained in her lap for almost the entire remainder of the session. As her mother continued to tell their story tearfully, Beth began to stroke her mother's hair gently. She continued caressing her mother's hair and back intermittently for about 20 minutes. At times, however, she pulled her mother's hair vigorously and provocatively. . . . History confirmed that Beth's mother had tended to look to her for comfort and support for a long time, and that Beth bore an excessive amount of the psychological burden on the relationship" (Zeanah et al., 1993, p. 344). ∎

Children diagnosed with **disordered attachment with role reversal** appear to have taken, uncomfortably and inappropriately, the parental role. Some children, like Beth, are focused on caregiving, expressing concern and worry for the parent's well-being. Other children are focused on control and coercion with parents and others; these children take the lead in directing and managing interactions, often with anger and derision.

Disrupted Attachment

Disrupted attachment, originally described by Bowlby (1980), occurs in instances involving extended separation, divorce, or death. He identified a sequence including emotional and behavioral protests related to the immediate loss of the attachment figure, followed by despair, and then emotional detachment. Bowlby characterized these as evolutionarily adaptive responses. The child's initial protests were useful because, when possible, the attachment figure often returned. When the attachment figure did not return, despair quieted the now-vulnerable child, protecting him or her from exploitation. Eventual detachment from the absent attachment figure allowed for the resumption of normal activities and the construction of a new emotional relationship. Children who experience the loss of an attachment relationship, through divorce

or death, often grieve. The intensity, duration, and extent of the child's distress and dysfunction is difficult to watch and difficult to manage. Differentiating between pathological and non-pathological grief, and facilitating the healing process, requires much clinical knowledge and empathy.

Developmental Course

Young children diagnosed with disorders of attachment may follow a number of developmental pathways (Belsky & Cassidy, 1994; Rutter, 1995; Thompson, 1999). Keeping in mind that early difficulties are related to a range of possible negative outcomes, we will review data on the sequelae of difficult attachments, including both narrow, attachment-specific behaviors and more broadly defined developmental consequences. It is important to remember that most of the longitudinal research has been done with samples of infants who were classified as insecure, rather than infants diagnosed with clinically significant disorders of attachment.

Child Outcomes

Children with insecure attachments and disorders of attachment exhibit ongoing difficulties in emotional, behavioral, and cognitive domains (Thompson, 1999). Although young children's behavior with their caregivers receives special emphasis, many of these children's other relationships are also impaired. Some of the most salient difficulties are related to emotional experiences, and include problematic patterns of emotional arousal, feelings of security, and emotion regulation (Cicchetti, Ackerman, & Izard, 1995; Cummings & Davies, 1996; Thompson, Flood, & Lundquist, 1995).

With respect to physiological correlates of attachment, there are abundant data that caregiving influences developing stress systems, with a variety of impacts on infant sensitivity to stress, infant arousal, and infant responsivity (Luecken & Lemery, 2004). Increased sensitivity, arousal, and responsivity can be observed in studies of heart rate (Burgess, Marshall, Rubin, & Fox, 2003; Spangler & Grossman, 1993; Sroufe & Waters, 1977), levels of stress hormones (Hertsgaard, Gunnar, Erickson, & Nachmias, 1995; Nachmias, Gunnar, Mangelsdorf, Parritz, & Buss, 1996; Spangler & Grossman, 1993), and asymmetries in brain electrical activity (Fox, Calkins, & Bell, 1994; Fox & Card, 1999). In particular, babies with disorganized attachment display more physiological dysregulation, including higher levels of cortisol and higher cardiac activity, reflecting more intense arousal (Hertsgaard et al., 1995; Lyons-Ruth, Bronfman, & Atwood, 1999; Spangler & Grossman, 1993, 1999).

Intrapersonal experiences and interpersonal expressions of emotions are also problematic. Insecurely attached children frequently exhibit many types of negative emotion (e.g., fear, anger, sadness) in multiple situations (e.g., both in and out of the home) (Erickson, Sroufe, & Egeland 1985; Thompson et al., 1995). Feelings of security are often diminished or absent. In addition, the development of emotional dispositions, including competencies related to the signaling and interpretation of emotion are tied to early attachment patterns (Magai, 1999). The defensive avoidance and inhibition of emotional expression of some babies are interpreted as ways to regulate anxiety, and are associated with the covert (i.e., hidden or unexpressed) experience of anger (Cummings & Davies, 1995).

The most salient effect of disordered attachment is on the parent-child relationship, and the ways in which children and parents play together, learn together, and work together (Thompson, 1999). In many different studies, children with insecure attachments display less agreeable and less competent interactions than children with secure attachments. Avoidant infants display less intense emotional responses to separation, more self-isolation and self-comforting (Braungart & Stifter, 1991; Sroufe, 1983). Resistant infants display more intense emotional responses, more vigilance, and more dependency (Sroufe, 1983). Displays of fear and confusion in babies with disorganized attachments are also noteworthy (Teti, 1999). Disorganized attachment is also associated with controlling-caregiving or controlling-punitive behaviors (i.e., role reversals), and aggressive, withdrawn, and odd behaviors (Lyons-Ruth et al., 2004; Solomon, George, & DeJong, 1995).

The emphasis on cognitive components of attachment, and the development of internal models and mental representations of self, other, and the world, provide a theoretical basis for the association between attachment difficulties and cognitive difficulties. With respect to cognitive content, Greenberg, Speltz, and DeKlyen (1993) have observed that insecure children have cognitive models "in which relationships are . . . characterized by anger, mistrust, chaos and insecurity" (p. 201); these investigators link these negative cognitions to the

aggressive behavior exhibited by insecure children. A 6-year-old child's story of what happens in playing with dolls illustrates this point: "And see, and then, you know what happens? Their whole house blows up. See . . . . They get destroyed and not even their bones are left. Nobody can even get their bones. Look. I'm jumping on a rock. This rock feels rocky. Aahh! Guess what? The hills are alive, the hills are shakin' and shakin'. Because the hills are alive. Uh huh. The hills are alive. Ohh! I fall smack off a hill. And get blowed up in an explosion. And then the rocks tumbled down and smashed everyone. And they all died" (Solomon & George, 1999b, p. 17).

With respect to cognitive skills, Fonagy and Target (1996, 1997) highlight the compromised capacity of insecurely attached children for "mentalizing," or understanding others in terms of their own mental states. Further, Fonagy (1998) suggests that children with insecure attachments have inadequate "mind-reading skills." Children with mind-reading difficulties exhibit, for example, less acceptance of personal responsibility, a lack of appreciation for others, and less concern with distress in others. (Significant difficulties with mind-reading are also evident in children with autism spectrum disorders, discussed in Chapter 8.)

For children with disorganized/disoriented attachments, researchers have observed dysfunctional cognitive processes. Lyons-Ruth and colleagues propose that cognitive difficulties in reconciling conflicting or ambiguous messages related to the caregiver, coupled with physiological dysregulation, lead to numerous difficulties across developmental domains. Main and Hesse (1990) and Liotti (1992) hypothesize that conflicting models of the self and of the caregiver (as both frightening and frightened) may overwhelm immature conscious processing in cognitive systems, resulting in unusual, fragmented thoughts and behaviors. Of course, many children at times daydream or become absorbed in play, but in cases of disorganized attachment, sometimes troubling indications of early dissociation, such as spacing out or being unaware of what just happened, are apparent (Lyons-Ruth & Jacobvitz, 1999; Ogawa, Sroufe, Weinfield, Carlson, & Egeland, 1997; Solomon & George, 1999b). Dissociation is an especially concerning symptom because it reflects disrupted integration of the core functions of consciousness, including memory, identity, and awareness of the environment. Ongoing integration is fundamental to healthy social and emotional development.

After infancy and toddlerhood, the effects of problematic attachments continue. Preschoolers display impairments in the self-system (Cassidy, 1988, 1990; Cicchetti, 1991; Ogawa et al., 1997), including atypical development of conscience (Kochanska, 1995). The understanding of negative emotions and ongoing emotional regulation is also influenced (Labile & Thompson, 1998; Thompson, 1999). Some research suggests that children with insecure attachments score lower on personality indices of ego-resiliency and curiosity (Arend, Gove, & Sroufe, 1979; Grossman & Grossman, 1991; Sroufe, 1983). Peer problems in preschool are also of concern, with social expectations and social skills clearly affected (Thompson, 1999; Thompson & Lamb, 1983). Patterns of withdrawal and victimized children, and patterns of aggression and bullying children, are frequently noted (Lyons-Ruth, Alpern, & Repacholi, 1993; Troy & Sroufe, 1987).

The disorganized/disoriented types of attachment is associated with the highest risk of dysfunction (Carlson, 1998; Speltz, DeKlyen, & Greenberg, 1999). Teti (1999) describes two variants of the controlling behaviors first exhibited in late infancy: solicitous, "overbright" caregiving and punitive, coercive control (see also Cassidy & Marvin, in collaboration with the MacArthur Working Group, 1992; Crittenden, 1992, 1995). Teti points out that some infants who previously displayed incoherent and disorganized behaviors have achieved some degree of behavioral organization at preschool age, although the developmentally inappropriate caregiving and punitive control certainly reflect maladaptive accommodations. In contrast, some preschoolers continue to display a lack of any coherent strategy for any kind of organized relationship with the parent.

Notwithstanding the more or less problematic differences in maladaptive and absent behavioral organization, Teti (1999) assumes that for all of these preschoolers, there is an underlying similarity of attachment disorganization at the representational (i.e., mental) level, and that these deficits can be identified with careful assessments. Difficulties, including a range of dissociative outcomes, depend on ongoing caregiving problems and continuing trauma (Liotti, 1992). From a normative developmental perspective, the dissociation sometimes observed in the preschool years is less problematic than dissociation in the later school years. For example, the capacity of 3- and 4-year-olds to become absorbed in fantasy play is not necessarily associated with distress or dysfunction. Only with age and cognitive advancements are dissociative symptoms associated with psychopathology (Egeland & Susman-Stillman, 1996; Ogawa et al., 1997; Teti, 1999).

In the elementary school years, multiple consequences of insecure attachments remain evident. Difficulties related to the self and self-understanding, "mind-reading" competence, and academic performance (Fonagy, 1998; Moss, St-Laurent, & Parent, 1999) are all concerns. Although results are somewhat mixed, children with insecure attachments appear to have more problems with peers and friends. For many children, externalizing behavior problems continue, which for some coalesce into a conduct disorder (Carlson, 1998; Fonagy, 1998; Speltz et al., 1999). For other children, internalizing symptoms such as depression, anxieties, and fears become more problematic (Bowlby, 1980; Cummings & Cicchetti, 1990; Moss et al., 1999).

Adolescent Outcomes

The attachment tasks of security and independence are revisited, again in an emotionally charged manner, during adolescence. For children who have struggled all along with themselves, with others, and with their environments, difficulties mount, especially in the domain of socioemotional competence (Allen, Houser, & Borman-Spurrell, 1996; Sroufe et al., 1999). For some children, there is a coming together of underlying issues and symptomatology into more clearly identifiable disorders. For example, babies who were classified as resistant in infancy are more likely to be diagnosed with anxiety disorders by age 17 (Warren, Huston, Egeland, & Sroufe, 1997). As noted, we also see a continuation of aggressive and externalizing symptoms readily diagnosed as conduct disorder. Children who were classified as disorganized/disoriented continue to experience difficulties with dissociation, particularly related to amnesia and depersonalization, with additional stress and trauma contributing to the stability of symptomatology (Carlson, 1998; Ogawa et al., 1997). Again, remember that dissociative symptoms have different clinical meanings at different ages. The fantasy play of preschoolers is usually not worrisome; the depersonalization of adolescents is (Egeland & Susman-Stillman, 1996).

Adult Outcomes

Whereas a number of connections between early attachments and later indices of various types of adult attachment have been hypothesized and documented (Crowell, Fraley, & Shaver, 1999; Main, 2000; Waters, Merrick, Treboux, Crowell, & Albersheim, 2000), the clinical implications of young children's insecure and disordered attachments remain somewhat speculative. There are data, however, that suggest that early and ongoing distress and dysfunction in attachment relationships has meaningful impact on adults' personalities, relationships, and parenting. Although much of this data emphasizes the negative impact of early insecurity, researchers do describe the "earned secure" classification in adults (Hesse, 1999; Main, Hesse, & Kaplan, 2005; Roisman, Padron, Sroufe, & Egeland, 2002). The "earned secure" classification refers to adults who have experienced all types of inadequate caregiving, but who can talk about their early trauma and poor care in an emotionally coherent, self-reflective manner. We are reminded again that early inadequate, traumatic, or abusive patterns of care, while truly awful to experience, do not always doom a child to a lifetime of maladjustment. With skilled intervention, or with personal strength and others' support, some individuals display resilience into their adult years. For many individuals, however, the impact of early problems in attachment, in complex interaction with other influential variables, is observed in adult life (Berlin & Cassidy, 1999; Brennan & Shaver, 1998; Dozier, Stovall, & Albus, 1999; Feeney, 1999; Main et al., 2005).

Etiology

Much of what is known about the etiology of disorders of attachment is based on what we know about the development of insecure patterns in normal and at-risk children. We hypothesize that common etiological factors contribute in similar ways to transient problems, more serious attachment struggles, and clinical disorders.

Caregiving Factors

Across all types of clinical disorders of attachment, the causal role of caregiving is primary. Inadequate, inattentive, inconsistent, and intrusive care has been repeatedly associated with insecure attachment in children. Neglectful and abusive parenting leads to insecurity and disorders of attachment, with more neglect and more abuse associated with increasing disorganization. Comparisons of maltreated infants with non-maltreated infants provide a poignant illustration of the impact of caregiving on attachment.

Maltreated infants and toddlers are much less likely to be classified as securely attached, with some evidence suggesting that only 5–10% of poorly treated children are able to balance the developmental demands of security and exploration (Carlson, Cicchetti, Barnett, & Braunwald, 1989; Schneider-Rosen & Cicchetti, 1984; Zeanah et al., 2004).

Solomon and George (1999b) hypothesize that a relevant piece of the caregiving puzzle for attachment disorganization has to do with parents who do not "correct or repair" their own interactional "errors." All caregivers make mistakes, inadvertently misreading, neglecting, or upsetting their infants. Solomon and George point out that what happens *following the mistake* is what distinguishes parents of disorganized infants from parents of organized infants. Parents of organized infants make attempts to correct their mistakes, while parents of disorganized infants fail to notice their errors, fail to appreciate the impact of their error on their child, or fail to adjust their behavior in the future. Also related to understanding the etiology of disorganization/disorientation are efforts to tease apart the influence of negative events that occur very early in development, severely negative events, and ongoing negative circumstances. Early trauma, severe trauma, and chronic trauma, however, are highly correlated with one another, and all are associated with later dissociation in at-risk samples (Ogawa et al., 1997).

Parent Factors

Reviews of parental factors include personality and psychopathology, attachment history, and other contextual variables. Mental illness in parents has received a lot of attention (Seifer & Dickstein, 2000). Maternal depression, bipolar disorder, anxiety, substance abuse, and schizophrenia have all been associated with greater frequency of insecurity in children (Beckwith, Howard, Espinosa, & Tyler, 1999; Manassis, Bradley, Goldberg, Hood, & Swinson, 1994; Teti, Gelfand, Messinger, & Isabella, 1995). There is mixed data specifically related to mental illness and the etiology of disorganization. DeMulder and Radke-Yarrow (1991) have observed higher rates of disorganization in babies of bipolar mothers than babies of mothers diagnosed with unipolar depression. And Lyons-Ruth, Repacholi, McLeod, and Silva (1991) observe higher rates of depressive symptoms and psychiatric hospitalization in mothers of a particular subset of babies classified as disorganized. Carlson (1998), however, did not find an association between psychological problems in the mother, and argues that environmental variables, such as single parenthood, insensitive and intrusive caregiving, and early maltreatment are more strongly associated with the development of disorganization.

The intergenerational transmission of problematic attachments has also received attention. Selma Fraiberg's metaphor of "ghosts in the nursery" (Fraiberg, Adelson, & Shapiro, 1980) aptly describes the often unacknowledged but powerful influence of parents' disturbed attachment histories on their relationships with their own children. In many studies, the attachment status of infants has been reliably predicted from mothers' narratives about their own childhoods and their own attachments (Ainsworth & Eichberg, 1991; Main & Hesse, 1990; Solomon & George, 1999a; Zeanah & Zeanah, 1989).

Parent conflict and domestic violence are key factors influencing the emergence of emotional insecurity (Davies, Winter, & Cicchetti, 2006; see Figure 6.2). Finally, the influence of other parent-related factors has been noted. Repeated observations have emphasized that the availability of social supports and other variables such as family stability, adequate housing, and employment contribute to the abilities of parents to provide nurturant care to their children (Belsky & Isabella, 1988; Halpern, 1993).

Child Factors

Attachment research is primarily focused on caregiving and parental factors. There is evidence, however, that particular infant characteristics do have some effect on attachment variables. For example, for some babies and caregivers, difficult temperament is associated with higher rates of insecure attachment, with more negative, more intense, and more difficult-to-soothe babies making sensitive and consistent caregiving less likely. For the most part, though, many different kinds of babies—easy, demanding, happy, and cranky—are observed in both secure and insecure categories of attachment (Vaughn & Bost, 1999). With respect to other hypothesized neurological or genetic influences, and infant predisposition to disorganized attachments, Main and Solomon (1990) report that only 3 of 35 babies classified with disorganized attachments

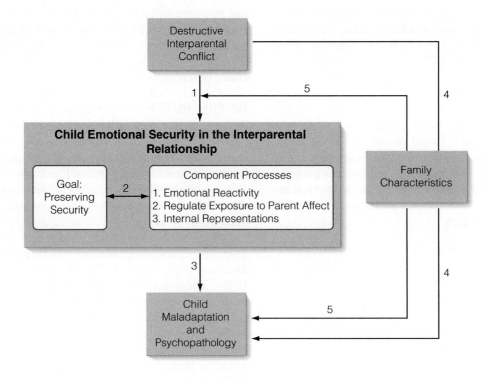

FIGURE 6:2 A model of the impact of parent conflict on emotional security.
Source: From Davies, et al, 'Development and Psychopathology', 18, 705-735. Copyright © 2006 Cambridge University Press. Reprinted with the permission of Cambridge University Press.

with one parent are also classified as disorganized with the other parent. That attachment is relationship-specific, rather than infant-specific, suggests that child variables are *not* the root of attachment classifications.

Atypical populations (i.e., babies with special medical histories or needs) provide additional perspective on the contributions of infants to the development of normal and maladaptive attachment. For example, infant prematurity by itself does not lead to higher rates of insecure attachment (Crnic, Greenberg, & Slough, 1986; Easterbrooks, 1989). But with added stressors and few resources or additional medical complications, there is an increase in insecurity (Plunkett, Meisels, Steifel, & Pasik, 1986; Wille, 1991). Empirical reviews of other atypical developments report somewhat lower rates of security in infants with various congenital or medical conditions compared to normal samples (50% versus 65%) (Van IJzendoorn, Goldberg, Kroonenberg, & Frenkel, 1992; Barnett et al., 1999).

There is also evidence that children with certain neurological difficulties, such as Down syndrome or autism, may display unusual attachments (Capps, Sigman, & Mundy, 1994; Ganiban, Barnett, & Cicchetti, 2000; Vaughn, Goldberg, Atkinson, & Marcovitch, 1994). Babies diagnosed with cystic fibrosis and congenital heart defects are later classified as disorganized/disoriented at higher rates than typically-developing babies (Goldberg, Gotowiec, & Simmons, 1995); this is also the case with babies diagnosed with epilepsy (Marvin & Pianta, 1996). Diagnostic differentiation of overlapping clinical presentations is a difficult task (Barnett et al., 1999; Pipp-Siegel, Siegel, & Dean, 1999). Regarding the development of attachment in atypical infants, it appears that a combination of factors is critical, including parental acceptance and understanding of a child's medical condition and needs, personal and family demands, and child characteristics that present caregiving challenges.

Assessment and Diagnosis

In contrast to much of the research-oriented assessment of attachment in normal and at-risk samples of young children, the clinically oriented assessment of disorders of attachment involves more naturalistic data collection (O'Connor & Zeanah, 2003). Home visits or assessments in home-like settings are preferable, and in some cases may be necessary. Keeping in mind the criterion that the child's distress and/or

dysfunction must be clearly evident in interactions with specific caregivers, Zeanah and Emde (1994) emphasize that the focus of the assessment should be on the child's relationships with his or her primary attachment figures, rather than on the child's general social and emotional behavior. For example, a child may be reasonably appropriate during her infrequent visits to her grandparents' home but, from a diagnostic perspective, her atypical behavior at home with her mother is a more important piece of information.

An assessment of the child's attachment(s) will also depend, in a very significant way, on fostering a therapeutic alliance with the parent (or other primary caregiver). This particular therapeutic alliance may be more problematic than other parent-professional collaborations, because the child's core distress and dysfunction relate to issues of caregiving (Hirshberg, 1993). Managing to collect information that may reflect poorly on actual caregiving attitudes and behaviors of parents or that may exacerbate parental beliefs about incompetency is often difficult. Highlighting shared parental and clinical concerns about improvements in the child's well-being may help smooth the assessment process.

History Taking and Interviews

Basically, the initial assessment must provide relevant data on the attachment struggles of a particular child; what kind of caregiver is involved; and what match there is between this particular baby and this particular caregiver. The characteristics of the child that are most frequently addressed include birth variables (such as prematurity or peri- and postnatal complications), temperament, patterns of early regulation, and timetables for developmental milestones (such as crawling and talking).

The characteristics of parents that are often addressed include general perceptions and specific knowledge about infants and caregiving, available support and resources, personalities, parental attachment histories, and associated family dynamics. If we think about the possibility that parental attachment issues are re-enacted and renegotiated in the new caregiving relationship, it may be especially important to gain perspective on parents' own attachment experiences (George & Solomon, 1999; Hesse, 1999; Steele et al., 1996). This information may be gathered using the Adult Attachment Interview (AAI), a semistructured interview about early childhood experiences and current interpretations of those experiences (George, Kaplan, & Main, 1984,

1996). Individuals' responses to the AAI protocol are judged with respect to consistency, coherence, and collaboration, and are categorized as *secure/autonomous*, *dismissing*, *preoccupied*, or *unresolved/disorganized*. The categories reflecting insecurity have been empirically related to the experience of clinical distress (Crowell, Fraley, & Shaver, 1999; Hesse, 1999).

Still, because parents usually come to therapy because of difficulties with a child, and *not* to explore their own issues, it makes sense to keep the focus of the assessment on "the past as it is active in the present" (Hirshberg, 1993, p. 177). That is, clinicians may need to emphasize the specific ways in which unresolved or intensely experienced parental attachment contributes to the current child or family difficulties. Valuable context for such information might be provided by having parents talk about the ways in which their temperaments, their personalities, and their preferences for activities and goals, do and do not mesh with their child's, and the ways in which particular caregiving attitudes and behaviors may have compromised their child's attachments.

Questionnaires and Structured Tasks

Other sources of assessment data in clinical settings include a variety of instruments and procedures originally designed for use with normal samples of young children. One of the more widely used instruments, developed as an alternative to the Strange Situation Procedure, is the Attachment Q-Sort for children between 1 and 5 years (Waters, 1995). Bretherton, Ridgeway, and Cassidy (1990) developed an attachment-relevant story completion task for preschoolers, using doll play and story situations designed to tap challenging parent-child experiences (e.g., child injury, separation, fear of monsters). Their data suggest that 3-year-olds are capable of producing coherent story narratives in which parents are described as supportive and empathic. For assessments related to disorders of attachment, we would expect less coherent narratives and more descriptions of parents as unable to protect the child, as less warm and more punitive. This assessment hypothesis requires additional research.

Observations

Perhaps the most important contributions to the accurate assessment of disorders of attachment are observations of "the infant in context" (Hirshberg, 1993). Clinical interpretations of real-life parent-child interactions are essential for understanding the dynamics of attachment. In all of the clinical cases presented earlier in the chapter, direct observation of the children contributed to making the correct diagnosis. The rating and analysis of observed parental behaviors in everyday and challenging situations may provide additional perspective. The Parental Acceptance Scoring System reflects individual differences in the extent to which parents are able to appreciate and integrate a child's needs with their own needs in a realistic manner (Schneider-Rosen, 1993).

Assessments in Older Children and Adolescents

Although much of the theoretical and clinical attention currently paid to disorders of attachment is focused on the first few years of life, it is likely that many instances of these disorders will be identified and assessed in older children. As already discussed, in terms of the normative processes of attachment, we expect coherence and stability in the years beyond infancy and preschool, as well as salient differences in the experience and expression of attachment. For example, by the age of 6, there is a new emphasis on language-mediated information (Main et al., 1985). Main and her colleagues suggest that children's more-developed language abilities allow for meaningful assessments of emotional openness in discussions of parent-child separations and/or other aspects of relationships. For adolescents, an alternative to parent-child observations, doll play, or storytelling might be the Adult Attachment Interview, described above.

With increasing age, it becomes more difficult to assess and diagnose specific disorders of attachment. Older children and adolescents often exhibit multiple problems, including aggression, anxiety, and depression, with a number of children meeting the diagnostic criteria for several disorders. Some of these disorders have their etiological roots in disorders of attachment, and some do not. A comprehensive assessment—whether simple and straightforward or messy and complicated—will always keep the child in full view.

Intervention

Within the framework of developmental psychopathology, it is both theoretically and practically easier to prevent the development of disorder than it is to intervene effectively. However, children, parents, and mental health professionals must deal with real-life circumstances. Real life demands that we design and validate therapeutic interventions for disorders of attachment.

Prevention Strategies

Prevention strategies related to disorders of attachment can be usefully categorized as **universal measures** for the general population, **selective measures** for groups at above-average risk, and **indicated measures** for groups with specific risk factors requiring more extensive help (Barnard, Morisset, & Spieker, 1993; Fonagy, 1998; Gordon, 1983, 1987). One example of a universal measure designed to promote infant and parent well-being is the early child education program, delivered before and after the baby is born (Feinberg & Kan, 2008). Another universal measure with mostly anecdotal support is the recommendation to carry young infants in a soft carrier next to the caregiver's body. Carrying babies for several hours a day in this way provides close parent-infant contact, and offers opportunities for caregivers to notice and differentiate infant signals and establish emotional rapport and communication patterns. In an at-risk sample, children whose mothers were given soft carriers and encouraged to use them were later classified as secure more frequently than children whose mothers were not given the carriers (Anisfeld, Casper, Nozyce, & Cunningham, 1990).

Home-based strategies provide illustrations of selected and indicated preventive measures. Overall, it is difficult to enhance parental sensitivity; effective interventions have clear goals and, often, a behavioral emphasis (Bakermans-Kranenburg, Van IJzendoorn, & Juffer, 2003). Clinicians have also been successful in strengthening parent-child relationships using psychodynamically informed filial therapy (VanFleet, Ryan, & Smith, 2005). Home visits with depressed mothers during the child's first year, with education and support provided, were later associated with higher-than-expected rates of secure attachment (Lyons-Ruth, Connell, Gruenbaum, & Botein, 1990). Erickson's Steps Toward Effective, Enjoyable Parenting (STEEP) model (Erickson, Korfmacher, & Egeland, 1992), based on the Minnesota Mother-Child Project, targets at-risk parents. Individual and group sessions during the mother's pregnancy and through the child's first year, exploring the mother's feelings, attitudes, and behaviors related to caregiving, are designed to influence the mother's internal working model of attachment. Changes in the mother's working model positively influence children's security. A similar program at UCLA has also demonstrated significantly positive impact (Heinicke et al., 1999). Another ambitious, multidisciplinary, home-based model was developed by Cicchetti and Toth (1987, 1995) in Rochester, involving social workers, psychologists, psychiatrists, special educators, and other health professionals, and focuses on parent, child, and environmental variables.

Child Treatment

With respect to therapeutic approaches for children already diagnosed with problematic or disordered attachments, meaningful improvement depends on the duration and degree of disorder, particular etiology, age of the child, and the scope of environmental change. And, as discussed previously, therapeutic approaches can be primarily oriented toward the parent, the child or both (Meisels, Dichtelmiller, & Liaw, 1993). Several effective interventions focus on the role of the parents; in all cases, a more nurturing and more consistent caregiver is a priority. In cases of disrupted attachments, or disorders of nonattachment, the ongoing availability of a special caregiver is especially critical.

With attachment figures who are already in place, McDonough (1993) describes "interaction guidance" therapy which builds on the skills and strengths (however fleeting or minimal) that caregivers display. In each therapeutic session, caregivers and their infants are videotaped, with opportunities for immediate processing and feedback. Consider a mother who displayed distant, emotionally constricted care for her young son, saying "I just don't seem to matter to him. No one does" (McDonough, 1993, p. 423). Viewing a just-videotaped interaction of the child's smiling in response to the mother's brief imitation of the child's vocalizations allowed the mother to see her child's actual happiness. Changing the caregiver's perceptions and behaviors, little bit by little bit, leads to changes in the attachment relationship.

Targeting one of the cognitive deficits observed in children with disturbed attachments, Fonagy (1998) focuses on the enhancement of mentalizing, with caregivers paying more attention to moment-by-moment changes in infants' mental states. Over time, with increased parental attunement, the child is able to explore the mental state of the caregiver and find "an image of himself as motivated by beliefs, feelings, and intentions" (p. 141), allowing for development of the self and the self-in-relationships. Speltz (1993) presents a behavioral parent-training approach, with an emphasis on skills training related to conflict reduction in disordered attachment relationships.

A noteworthy example of the repair of attachment relationships is provided by Stovall and Dozier's (2000) case studies of new attachments in very young children placed in foster care. Stovall and Dozier explored the effects of early versus later placement and the attachment status of the foster parent. New, secure attachments developed over the course of two months for those children placed early with autonomously attached foster parents. Children placed later, or those placed with adults with unresolved or dismissive attachments, exhibited insecure patterns of attachment. Foster parents who responded to their children's difficult and often alienating behaviors with nurturant caregiving were more likely to have securely attached children.

Infant-Parent Psychotherapy

In another clinical approach, Lieberman and Pawl (1993) and Cicchetti, Toth, and Rogosch (2004) describe infant-parent psychotherapy, based on Fraiberg's work (Fraiberg, 1980; Fraiberg et al., 1975), for disordered or disrupted attachment relationships. In infant-parent psychotherapy, there is a joint emphasis on what the parent and the child each bring to the difficult relationship, as well as the subjective experiences of both parent and child. This psychotherapy is a collaborative endeavor, with the therapist and parent working together to create agendas, determine goals, and establish procedures for evaluation. Acknowledging complex parent motivations and feelings, including "anger, relief, reluctance, and hope" (Lieberman & Pawl, 1993, p. 429) is important. Lieberman and Zeanah (1999) further note that the therapist's positive regard for the parent(s), and his/her empathy and attention during difficult moments, illustrate adaptive and positive ways of relating, which the parent can— over time—both internalize and express in attachment relationships. Infant-parent psychotherapy has proven useful for varied clinical samples, including infants in maltreating families (Cicchetti, Rogosch, & Toth, 2006; Cohen, Lojkasek, Muir, Muir, & Parker, 2002; Cohen et al., 1999).

The therapist-child relationship, and the ways in which the relationship serves as a template or a substitution for the actual parent-child relationship require special attention. In particular, therapists must be wary of the following situation: "When the parent blames the baby, the therapist blames the parent. In this therapeutically damaging parallel process, parent and therapist both forget that the situation at hand is only the immediate and concrete representation of a tormented emotional landscape where both parent and baby are being victimized. Blame does not help. Only understanding holds hope. . ." (Lieberman & Pawl, 1990, p. 438).

With respect to the efficacy of various interventions, results are mixed. Treatment outcome research provides some support for the infant-parent psychotherapy approach to disorders of attachment (Cicchetti et al., 2006; Lieberman, Weston, & Pawl, 1991). Reviews of the empirical data suggest that strategies designed to improve maternal sensitivity, and thereby attachment status, sometimes do and sometimes do not achieve expected outcomes (Cohen et al., 1999; Van IJzendoorn, Juffer, & Duyvesteyn, 1995), suggesting that additional work on specific and efficacious treatments is clearly needed.

Finally, as repeatedly discussed, it is absolutely critical to understand that there is no clear professional consensus related to the assessment, diagnosis, and treatment of attachment disorders. Theoretical accounts remain speculative, and much empirical work remains to be done before we can achieve a reliable understanding of these phenomena. In the interim, it is important that our working formulations do not lead us to excessively pathologize children. For example, we must take care to ensure that adults do not misperceive children diagnosed with attachment disorders as permanently damaged or impaired. To the contrary, as described in Box 6.1, the evidence to date suggests that the earlier at-risk children are provided with healthy emotional and social support, the better their prospects for reduced developmental delay and recovery of emotional and cognitive well-being (e.g., Nelson et al., 2007).

■ Key Terms

Attachment relationship (pg. 83)
Sense of self (pg. 83)
Understanding of others and the world (pg. 83)
Safe haven (pg. 83)
Proximity maintenance (pg. 83)

■ Chapter Summary

- The development of a secure attachment relationship between infant and caregiver is the critical task in the first year of life.
- Secure attachment relationships are the result of consistent, appropriate responsiveness by the caregiver to the infant's physical, emotional, and social needs.
- Resistant attachment relationships stem from inconsistent caregiving behavior.
- Avoidant attachment relationships result from ineffective or inappropriate caregiving.

- Disorganized attachment relationships occur when the caregiver is associated with frightening or malicious events. They involve a distinctive pattern of both approach and avoidance in infants.
- Early attachment relationships impact neurological and personality development, and provide models for future relationships.
- The DSM-IV-TR diagnostic category for such attachment patterns is reactive attachment disorder. With its focus on early childhood, the Zero to Three classification system identifies several specific patterns of disordered attachment.
- Attachment disorders may compromise a number of developmental domains, including social, cognitive, and emotional development. These outcomes can reverberate throughout childhood, adolescence, and adulthood.
- Caregiving, parental, and some child-based factors influence the etiology of attachment disorders.
- Assessment takes a variety of forms, including clinical and naturalistic observation as well as standardized interviews and questionnaires with parents and children.
- Prevention strategies range from universal measures for the general population to more selective measures, which target more specific risk factors and high-risk groups.
- Child-oriented, parent-oriented, and joint (especially infant-parent psychotherapy) therapeutic approaches have met with mixed empirical success, meriting further study of treatments for attachment disorders.

■ **CHAPTER OUTLINE**

"Adam deals with many things more graciously than I do. Take illness, for example. My first clue that he isn't feeling well is usually a polite knock on my door in the middle of the night. After a pause, just as I'm telling myself that I didn't hear anything and should go back to sleep, a small, gruff voice will rasp, 'Mom, U'm gick.'

"I'll drag myself awake to find him standing by my bed, fraught with some horrific assortment of symptoms: blazing fevers, rashes that turn his usually flat little face into a topographical map of Nepal, chest coughs that sound like gang warfare between two prides of lions. Adam's immune system is weaker than a normal nine-year-old's, and every germ he catches rollicks gaily through his body, holding orgies of self-reproduction and sending enthusiastic invitations to others of its kind. When Adam gets gick, he gets really, really gick.

"Gick, if you haven't figured it out by now, is Adam's word for sick. He has learned to speak fairly well in the last few years, but the muscles of his mouth aren't formed for our language, so he often uses his own. Adamic, we call it. It is a strange dialect, in which syllables are often reversed or replaced with random consonants, sound effects, and gestures. . . .

"Eventually I get out of bed, and we go down the hall together, Adam holding my hand in his small, dry, stubby fingers. We stand in the doorway of his room and assess the damage. This is what always amazes me: if he's thrown up, he will have done his best to clean the room before involving me. 'Bleah,' he will explain, flipping his hand from his mouth outward, as though the smell alone weren't enough to tell me what happened. 'I keen.' 'Yes,' I'll say. 'You cleaned up. Thanks, buddy. Good boy.'

"Then Adam, ill and weary as he is, helps me spray the rug with cleanser, scrub out the stain, and change his sheets. He gamely swallows a dose of Tylenol, says 'Unkoo, Mom'—and flops down on his pillow, already asleep. The genetic weakness of his muscles (hypotonia, the doctors call it) lets his body fall into strange shapes, as though he has been dropped out of a plane to his death; legs twisted under him, undersize head bent too far back, chunky little arms flung wide. His small, slanted eyes flicker beneath their lids as he begins to dream. Watching him, I think he is the most beautiful child I have ever known" (from Martha Beck's *Expecting Adam*, pp. 20–21). ∎

There have always been children like Adam: children with mental retardation who have been the causes of bewilderment, the targets of ridicule and institutionalization, and the focus of parents' love and care. Any historical perspective on mental retardation must include the centuries of mistaken beliefs and woeful attempts at intervention (see Box 7.1); it must also include the longstanding concern expressed for children with mental retardation by parents, teachers, and mental health professionals, and the recent developments related to progress in mapping the human genome (www.genome.gov). With interest and research at an all-time high, mental retardation has gone from the "Cinderella" of child psychiatry to the "belle of the biopsychosocial ball" (State, King, & Dykens, 1997, p. 1664).

Developmental Tasks and Challenges Related to Intelligence and Cognition

"A child's IQ is more closely related to the child's later occupational success than is the socioeconomic status of the family within which the child grows up, the family's income, the school the child attends, or any other variable that has been studied" (Siegler, 2003, p. 314). Siegler's summary of the empirical data underscores the need to understand the complex construct of intelligence and its contribution to normal and pathological aspects of development. Given the many controversies surrounding the nature and assessment of intelligence, the following descriptions are necessarily brief. They are organized around several key issues: (1) What are the underlying components and mechanisms of intelligence? (2) How does cognitive and intellectual development unfold over time? (3) What kinds of individual differences are observed? (4) What are the roles of heredity and the environment in the development of intelligence?

Components and Mechanisms of Intelligence

The most basic question involves the nature of intelligence. Our working definition of intelligence is "cognition comprising sensory, perceptual, associative, and relational knowledge" (Das, 2004). Hypotheses about the components of intelligence range from a single, unitary competence that influences almost all that we do (and that each of us possesses to a greater or lesser degree), to unique collections of particular talents and skills that exhibit little overlap, to hierarchically organized sets of both general and specific abilities. Most theorists agree that intelligence

A Look Back at History—The Eugenics Movement

Over the past two centuries, public attitudes and policies related to the treatment of individuals with mental retardation have undergone dramatic shifts (Baumeister & Baumeister, 1995; Mesibov, 1976; O'Brien, 1999). Mesibov (1976) describes the mid-19th century as a time when individuals with mild or moderate mental retardation probably blended into the mostly unschooled, agrarian American landscape. Over time, physicians and other professionals became increasingly interested in training persons with mental retardation so that they could become active, productive members of a more complex society, with changing forms of labor and sociocultural organization. Intensive training took place primarily in residential settings designed to prepare individuals with mental retardation for their successful adjustment to their communities. These plans were overly optimistic and many became discouraged. Residential programs "slowly became places of refuge for mentally retarded people who were now thought to be unable to live in modern society" (Mesibov, 1976, p. 27).

By the late nineteenth and early twentieth century, attitudes and policies took an alarming turn (Baumeister & Baumeister, 1995; Mesibov, 1976; O'Brien, 1999). With new knowledge about heredity and the development of intelligence tests, scientists, mental health professionals, and government officials accepted the premises of eugenics—that social control of reproduction could and would improve the species—and began to view individuals with mental retardation with scorn and disapprobation. Hysterical concern about the impact of the "feeble-minded," the "morons," and the "degenerates" on crime rates and every other social ill were widespread. Two solutions seemed reasonable to the overwrought citizens: segregation and sterilization. Segregation involved the forced separation of men and women in residential care; sterilization laws were passed in many states. Even the extreme option of euthanasia was discussed, but it did not receive widespread support. With more data, and moral and practical reflection, segregation and sterilization came to be seen as unethical and unnecessary. Recent decades have been characterized as focused on advocacy and support for those who struggle with mental retardation.

involves the performance of basic mental tasks, including perceiving the environment, communication and language, and higher-level tasks such as reasoning, problem-solving, and planning (Birney & Sternberg, 2006; Gardner, 1993; Siegler, 2003). Although traditional models emphasize the components or capacities of intelligence that are related to academic, educational, and occupational outcomes (i.e., verbal and mathematical abilities), these models may also include capacities for music, art, mechanics, and relationships (Siegler, 2003). In addition to these components, mechanisms such as speed (or efficiency) of mental processing and working memory must be accounted for in models of intellectual functioning (Anderson, 2001; Kail, 2003). Motivational aspects such as curiosity and exploration must also be understood (Wentworth & Witryol, 2003).

Development of Cognitive and Intellectual Functioning

To understand the slowed and deviant pathways for children with mental retardation, we must appreciate both cognitive development, or general age-related trends, and intellectual development, or individual differences observed among normally developing children at every age. With respect to cognitive development, it is well-accepted that there is steady, linear progress with increasing age, with occasional reorganizations, or qualitatively distinct "developmental leaps" (Hodapp & Zigler, 1995, McArdle, Ferrer-Caja, Hamagami, & Woodcock, 2002). This progress is reflected in both cognitive content and cognitive processing (Barnett & Ceci, 2005). For example, children learn and remember more information as they age, but they also become faster and more efficient at manipulating that information; the pace of progress is greater through the preschool and elementary school years, and slows somewhat during adolescence (Kail, 2000, 2003).

With respect to intellectual development, there is a general emergence of intellectual functioning, as well as specific patterns of strengths and weaknesses in both components and mechanisms, reflected in individual differences in various intellectual domains (Birney & Sternberg, 2006; Flavell, 1982a, 1982b; Gardner, 1983; Hodapp & Burack,

1990). These patterns of individual differences appear relatively stable from 4 or 5 years of age through adulthood, with both growth and decline observed throughout the lifespan (Bornstein, 1998; McArdle et al., 2002; Siegler, 2003).

Heredity and the Environment

There is overwhelming evidence that both heredity and the environment contribute to children's cognitive and intellectual development (Cherney, Fulker, & Hewitt, 1997; Newcombe, 2002). Data from numerous twin, family, and adoption studies suggest that genes influence about 50% of the variation in intelligence (with overlapping genetic effects on specific cognitive abilities), and that the genetic influence increases with age (Alarcon, Plomin, Fulker, Corely, & DeFries, 1999). That is, "the genetic contribution to intelligence becomes larger, not smaller, as children develop" (Siegler, 2003, p. 314). This is associated with some of the genetic impact expressed after infancy, along with children's increasingly active role in choosing particular tasks and environments for themselves (Petrill et al., 2004; Scarr, 1997, 1998; Siegler, 2003). The Colorado Adoption Project provides support for both increased genetic influence and the role of nonshared environmental factors (Alarcon, Plomin, Fulker, Corley, & DeFries, 1998; Petrill et al., 2004).

The child's immediate and larger environments also have considerable impact (Dickens & Flynn, 2001; Siegler, 2003). From birth, parental stimulation and responsiveness are associated with both specific and indirect effects on intellectual functioning (Bornstein & Tamis-LeMonda, 1997). Factors such as parental education, parental interest in academics, and parental beliefs about children's intelligence have been associated with more positive outcomes (Nevo & Bin Khader, 1995; Roberts, Bornstein, Slater, & Barrett, 1999; Siegler, 2003). Many researchers have also described within-family, nonshared effects on children's intelligence related to siblings' differing expectations, roles, and birth order positions (Siegler, 2003).

The most frequently mentioned influence from the larger environmental milieu is poverty, with damaging effects on intellectual development and achievement. According to Siegler (2003), "Poverty exerts its negative effects on intellectual development through several mechanisms: inadequate diet, lack of timely access to health services, parental preoccupation with other problems, and insufficient

intellectual stimulation and support in the home" (p. 316; see also Lawlor et al., 2005). He continues, "In 1998, 26% of African American and Hispanic children lived in families with incomes below the poverty line versus 8% of European American children (U.S. Census Bureau, 2000). This means that the effects of poverty are not randomly distributed among families in the United States; they are concentrated in African American and Latino families" (p. 316). How our society addresses these inequalities is an ethical issue with far-reaching consequences.

Mental Retardation

Mental retardation (MR) involves two types of deficits that are evident before age 18: deficits in intellectual functioning and deficits in adaptive behavior (American Association on Mental Retardation [AAMR], now the American Association on Intellectual and Developmental Disabilities, 2002; DSM-IV-TR, 2000). For many conceptualizations of MR, including the DSM-IV-TR, the most important symptom is level of intellectual functioning: mild, moderate, severe, and profound mental retardation (see Table 7.1). For the majority of those diagnosed with MR, this deficit represents the low end of the continuous distribution of IQ scores in the general population, but also includes those whose deficits reflect qualitative dysfunction (see Figure 7.1). Adaptive functioning reflects the overall coherence of development as it pertains to living in the everyday world, including cognitive, emotional, and social domains (Whitman et al., 1997). Models of MR require the display of difficulties in various adaptive behaviors including self-care, language and communication, and social skills. Some children with poor adaptive functioning exhibit significant problems with basic activities of daily living such as getting dressed and maintaining hygiene; others do well with basic tasks but struggle with more complex activities such as preparing snacks or performing household chores.

The American Association on Intellectual and Developmental Disabilities (AAIDD) presents a somewhat more holistic perspective (AAMR/ AAIDD, 2002). In this view, MR is not a physical or mental disorder, but "a disability characterized by significant limitations both in intellectual functioning and in adaptive behavior as expressed in conceptual, social, and practical adaptive skills." Each area of dysfunction includes a corresponding

TABLE 7:1   COMPARISON OF DIAGNOSTIC DESCRIPTIONS OF MR FROM DSM-IV-TR AND AAIDD

DSM-IV-TR: Categories based on assessments of intelligence and adaptive functioning

A. Significantly subaverage intellectual functioning
B. Concurrent deficits or impairments in present adaptive functioning in at least two of the following: communication, self-care, home living, social/ interpersonal skills, use of community resources, self-direction, functional academic skills, work, leisure, health, and safety
C. Onset before 18 years

Degree of severity reflecting level of intellectual impairment:

Mild mental retardation:	IQ level 50-55 to 70
Moderate mental retardation:	IQ level 35-40 to 50-55
Severe mental retardation:	IQ level 20-25 to 35-40
Profound mental retardation:	IQ level below 20-25

AAIDD: Categories based on children's needs for supportive services

Intermittent	High or low intensity support only when needed, and often during life transitions
Limited	Consistent support on a time-limited basis. Includes support that lasts for longer periods, although the support is not required for the entire lifetime
Extensive	Consistent support for long periods of time in one or more settings
Pervasive	Consistent long-term support in all settings

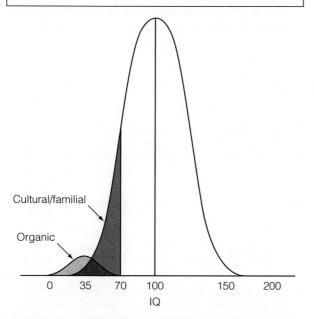

Cultural/familial

Organic

0   35   70   100   150   200
IQ

FIGURE 7:1 Bimodal distribution of IQ scores.
Source: From E. Zigler & R.M. Hodapp, "Understanding Mental Retardation", p. 73 (New York, NY: Cambridge University Press, 1986). Copyright © 1986 Cambridge University Press. Reprinted with the permission of Cambridge University Press.

description of the support necessary for maximizing the individual's well-being: **intermittent, limited, extensive,** or **pervasive support**. Rather than emphasizing the degree of deficit, the AAIDD emphasizes the possibility of adaptation (see Table 7.1). Both the DSM-IV-TR and the AAIDD conceptualizations recognize the interdependent nature of intellectual and adaptive functioning, as well as multiple etiologies and outcomes of MR. Whether the definition of MR emphasizes deficits or supports, we need to acknowledge the impact that the actual name of a disorder or a disability has on individuals who are diagnosed, on family members, and on society (see Box 7.2).

The Case of Caroline

Caroline is 8 years old, the fourth of seven brothers and sisters, but her mother Mary always refers to her as "my baby, because she never fusses." Mary and her family live with her mother in the cramped three-bedroom apartment where Mary grew up. She dropped out of high school when she became pregnant with her first baby at age 15. Caroline's grandmother cleans houses for a living, and Mary cares for the children, who range from 2 to 14 years of age. Caroline's father Philip is a food services worker at the local hospital, but he only sees the children on occasion.

When Caroline neared the end of first grade, Mary was surprised to hear her teacher's concern that Caroline wasn't making adequate progress at school. Caroline's three older brothers had been a handful, each of them experiencing discipline problems ahead of Caroline in the same public school. Mary had noticed that Caroline seemed to lag a little behind her brothers in learning to walk and talk, but she just figured that she would eventually catch up. Mary didn't usually make it to parent nights at school, but she had heard no bad reports on Caroline from the kindergarten teacher, and she was always pleased by how Caroline played so well with her younger sisters. But the teacher told Mary that Caroline wasn't making progress in letter and word recognition, had a hard time following directions, and seemed to be getting more and more anxious and disconnected from the other children as the year went on. It didn't help that some of the other children had started to tease Caroline about her reading struggles.

The school psychologist's assessment of Caroline revealed that she had an IQ of 65 and adaptive skill deficits in the sensorimotor, communication, and self-help areas. Caroline's functioning in all of those areas was more than 2 standard deviations (SD) below the norm for her peers, which led to her diagnosis of mild mental retardation. An Individualized Education Plan (IEP) was developed in which Caroline remains in the regular classroom for about half the day, with the support of a teacher's aide to guide her work more closely. She also leaves the classroom periodically to participate in specialized classes dedicated to more intensive work on her reading, fine motor, and auditory processing abilities. The IEP contains very specific goals in each skill area, along with a timetable for evaluating Caroline's progress toward each of the goals several times a year. Like any child, Caroline has individual strengths and weaknesses in different areas, and the learning goals are continually readjusted over time to reflect her differential rates of progress. Caroline's classroom teacher has also adopted a curriculum unit that addresses disability stereotyping and helps the children to both understand and be more supportive of Caroline.

The school psychologist met with Mary to help her better understand the nature of Caroline's disability and her future expectations. She explained that Caroline's development in many ways follows the same sequence and growth pattern as other children, but progresses more slowly and will not continue as far in terms of her ability to think abstractly and process complex information. As she matures, her caregivers will need to pay increasing attention to the level of support Caroline requires, in line with the standards established by the American Association of Intellectual and Developmental Disabilities (AAMR/AAIDD, 2002). It is likely that Caroline's necessary support level as she moves into adulthood will fall somewhere between Intermittent (e.g., as needed, such as following a job loss or health crisis) and Limited (e.g., consistent support in areas like vocational training and housing assistance that varies in intensity). ∎

BOX 7:2 THE CHILD IN CONTEXT

Changing Names, Changing Stigma?

The names that professionals and lay people use to describe psychopathology provide important information about historical and current attempts to balance scientific knowledge and the social construction of mental illness. Over the years, the terms *moron, idiot, imbecile, changeling,* and *feebleminded* have been used to refer to individuals with particular kinds of intellectual and adaptational limitations. More recently, descriptive concepts such as *mild, moderate, severe,* and *profound mental retardation* are being replaced by the general notion of *developmental disabilities.* Because the language we use depends, in part, on time and context, we must be careful about assumptions related to the similarity of underlying conceptualizations (Gelb, 2002; Goodey, 2001; Smith, 2002; Stainton & McDonagh, 2001). In some important ways, what we identify and understand about mental retardation is the same across generations; in other equally important ways, what we identify and understand is very, very different.

Still, a few general trends emerge. First, with every new name, we see an attempt to clarify the essential nature of a specific psychopathology (Smith, 2002). Each attempt takes place within a specific historical milieu and has a variety of functions. These functions include selecting appropriate interventions and designing prevention programs, as well as assigning the individual some status reflecting moral, legal, and social standards. The powerful roles of religion, class, race, and gender that are associated with these functions remain to be fully explored and insistently challenged (Goodey, 2001; Stainton & McDonagh, 2001).

The second trend involves the rethinking of the typological approach to mental retardation (Gelb, 1997; Smith, 2002). That is, we see a clear shift in our understanding from (1) an emphasis on the distinction between normal and abnormal, with a de-emphasis on differences among individuals with mental retardation to (2) an emphasis on the continuity between normal and abnormal, with a heightened appreciation of "people with very diverse needs and characteristics" (Smith, 2002, p. 64).

The third trend involves the attempt to address the stigma that is quickly attached to terms used for psychopathological diagnosis. Whether we name a disorder in order to segregate, protect, or treat struggling individuals, the names we use often become pejorative words used to mock and ridicule vulnerable persons (Gelb, 2002). Remember how awful it was (and is) to be called a "retard" in school. Many have argued that the label mental retardation should be abandoned and replaced with a more descriptive and more general label (e.g., intellectual disability or developmental disability). The new label would theoretically allow for an increasingly accurate, less stigmatizing approach to understanding and treating the psychopathology. The historical record suggests, unfortunately, that any new term is likely to have limited success in countering misconception and prejudice.

Taking into account various definitions of mental retardation and the difficulties associated with accurate calculations, epidemiological estimates of the prevalence of MR range between 1% and 3% of the population (Baumeister & Baumeister, 1995; Durkin, 2002; Larson et al., 2001; Leonard & Wen, 2002; Roeleveld, Zielhuis, & Gabreels, 1997; State et al., 1997). Most individuals (85%) with mental retardation are diagnosed with mild MR (as described here in the case of Caroline). Approximately 10% are diagnosed with moderate MR, 3–4% with severe MR, and 1–2% with profound MR (Singh, Oswald, & Ellis, 1998). Mental retardation is observed more frequently in boys.

Zigler's Developmental Approach to MR and the Developmental-Difference Debate

Several of the most important and affirming proposals about children with mental retardation were put forth by Edward Zigler (1969, 1971). Zigler proposed that, in many respects, the majority of children with mental retardation are similar to children without mental retardation. Although delayed in their mastery of most motor, cognitive, emotional, and social tasks and stopping short of the eventual achievements of their normal peers, children with mental retardation display the same kinds of sequences and coherent growth that are characteristic of most children. That is, mentally retarded children develop slowly, but in organized ways. Broadening his concern beyond deficits and dysfunctions, Zigler also emphasized a holistic perspective, and the need to understand the motivations and personalities of children with mental retardation (see also Cicchetti & Pogge-Hesse, 1982).

The **developmental-difference debate** focused specifically on the nature of cognitive disability. Zigler and his colleagues suggested that children with mental retardation possess similar cognitive structures and slowly progress in a similar cognitive sequence to that of their non-retarded peers (the developmental side of the debate). Others argued that children with MR think in qualitatively distinct (and deficient) ways (the difference side of the debate); an emphasis on difference is often presented along with data on the genetic etiologies of MR (discussed next). As with most complex issues, there is evidence to support both hypotheses (M. Anderson, 1998; Bennet-Gates & Zigler, 1998; Burack, 1997; Gordon & Saklofske, 1994; Hodapp, 1997; Pennington, 2002).

Genotypes and Behavioral Phenotypes

Alternative classification models have focused on identifying and understanding children with mental retardation by grouping them according to etiology, with much of the attention focused on various **genotypes**—the underlying genetic causes— associated with MR (Baumeister & Baumeister, 1995; Dykens, 1995; Hodapp & Dykens, 2003). These genetic subtypes are medical diagnoses rather than psychiatric or psychological categories; the genotype assumption is that different etiological explanations are reflected in differences in specific dysfunction and disability, differences in the course of MR, and differences in family backgrounds and adjustments (Dykens & Hodapp, 2001). The related construct of **behavioral phenotypes** emphasizes the increased probability that a child will display a particular set of behaviors or symptoms given a particular genetic etiology. In other words, many children—but not all children—with a particular genetic background will display similarities related to physical characteristics, cognitive and linguistic profiles, perceptual skills and deficits, socioemotional patterns, and overall outcomes (Hodapp & Dykens, 2005).

Genetic disorders appear to influence subsequent behaviors in two ways (Hodapp & Dykens, 2005): First, a genetic disorder may be linked to a unique symptom or pattern observed in all children with the diagnosis. This type of link is observed in the extreme eating behaviors observed in individuals with Prader-Willi syndrome, and is relatively rare. A second, more commonly observed link is when two or more genetic disorders lead to shared outcomes. This type of link is confirmed by findings that, for example, many forms of MR are associated with similar attention and/or hyperactivity difficulties.

Down Syndrome

Three brief descriptions of behavioral phenotypes associated with specific genotypes illustrate this classification approach to MR. **Down syndrome**, caused by an extra chromosome 21 (i.e., trisomy 21), is among the most widely known genetically influenced forms of MR. As with many forms of MR, there are accompanying physical characteristics, including distinctive facial features, heart problems, and poor muscle tone. Intellectual challenges almost always involve language difficulties, with expressive speech more problematic than receptive speech

(Abbeduto, Warren, & Conners, 2007; Chapman, Seung,Schwartz,&Kay-RainingBird,1998;Chapman, Schwartz, & Kay- Raining Bird, 1991). Visual short-term memory is often a relative strength. Intelligence estimates range from mild to severe. With respect to personality and psychopathology, parents often report that their children with Down syndrome are happy and outgoing; indeed, Down syndrome is sometimes referred to as "Prince Charming" syndrome (Dykens, 2000). Compared to others with MR, children with Down syndrome display relatively few maladaptive behaviors during childhood (Dykens & Kasari, 1997), although both internalizing and externalizing symptoms occur in some children (Dykens, Shah, Sagun, Beck, & King, 2002; Fidler, 2006; Fidler, Most, Booth-LaForce, & Kelly, 2006).

Williams Syndrome

Williams syndrome, caused by a microdeletion on chromosome 7, is associated with its own distinctive pattern of MR (Braden & Obrzut, 2002; Semel & Rosner, 2003; Stromme, Bjornstad, & Ramstad, 2002). The syndrome is characterized by deficits in general cognitive function and visual-spatial skills, and relative strengths in language and music domains (Bellugi, Lichtenberger, Jones, Lai, & George, 2000; Mervis et al., 2000; Semel & Rosner, 2003). Even though the language of children with Williams syndrome seems relatively unaffected in comparison with children with other types of MR, many studies provide data suggesting that there are specific language difficulties that have an impact on reading and require educational interventions (Clahsen & Temple, 2003; Laing, 2002; Temple, Almazan, & Sherwood, 2002; Vicari, Caselli, Gaglirdi, Tonucci, & Volterra, 2002). Children with Williams syndrome exhibit "sparkling dispositions" and "a remarkable and contagious zest for life" (Dykens, 2006, p. 190). That said, social disinhibition is a frequent concern for children with Williams syndrome, who "crave attention and interaction" and who frequently display overly friendly and talkative behaviors (Dykens, 2006). Children with Williams syndrome usually demonstrate a special facility for facial and emotion recognition, and are known for their displays of empathy (Garfield & Perry, 2001; Pearlman-Avnion & Eviatar, 2002; Tager-Flusberg, Boshart, & Baron-Cohen, 1998). The most common psychopathological symptoms include numerous fears and anxieties (Dykens, 2003; van Lieshout, De Meyer, Curfs, & Fryns, 1998).

Fragile X Syndrome

Fragile X syndrome, caused by a mutation on the FMR1 gene, is the most common type of inherited MR in boys, affecting 1 in 4,000 boys and 1 in 8,000 girls; it is seen in all racial and ethnic groups. Boys, who have only a single fragile X gene, are likely to be more severely affected, and are more frequently diagnosed with moderate MR. Girls usually are diagnosed with mild MR. There are fewer physical characteristics of fragile X syndrome, although some babies do have large head circumferences, somewhat unusual facial features, and loose joints (Koukoui & Chaudhuri, 2007; Schwarte, 2008). Speech and communication difficulties underlie the fragile X cognitive profile (Abbeduto, Brady, & Kover, 2007; Abbeduto & Hagerman, 1997). Psychopathological symptoms associated with fragile X syndrome range from difficulties relating to others to autism; boys are more likely to experience severe behavioral difficulties such as high activity, poor attention, and low adaptability (Bailey, Hatton, & Skinner, 1998; Dykens, 2000; Roberts, Boccia, Hatton, Skinner, & Sideris, 2006; van Lieshout et al., 1998).

Researchers describe several benefits to an approach emphasizing genetic etiology. The most important of these benefits include the potential for prevention and early diagnosis (Huang, Sadler, O'Riordan, & Robin, 2002). Taking into account different patterns of strengths and weaknesses, treatments might be able to be more effectively specialized (Fidler, Hodapp, & Dykens, 2002; Hodapp & DesJardin, 2002). Others note the drawbacks to this kind of approach. These include the possibility that with increasing numbers of subtype classifications (numbering now in the hundreds), clinicians and others may overlook key similarities among children with MR, with negative implications for both diagnosis and intervention (Burack, 1997). Given the current variety of outcomes for individuals with the same etiologies, Pennington (2002) suggests that for "any psychopathology, there is no doubt that etiological definitions will help focus medical interventions, but short of a medical cure, we will also need behavioral definitions to guide treatments" (p. 250).

So far, our emphasis has been on describing several genotypes associated with MR, each of which is usually associated with a diagnosis of moderate to severe MR. We must keep in mind that the majority of cases of children diagnosed with MR are, in fact, diagnosed with mild MR, as the case of Caroline illustrates. Children with mild MR are not readily identified by genetic assays, physical characteristics, unique language or social presentations, or other sets of difficulties. These children must not be overlooked; indeed, efforts to identify and support these children must be renewed and reinvigorated.

Comorbid Conditions

Depending on the etiology and severity of MR, estimates of comorbid conditions range widely, from 10% to 70% (Dykens, 2000; State et al., 1997). Common medical conditions include epilepsy, heart problems, sensory disorders, deafness, and physical abnormalities (Baumeister & Baumeister, 1995; Hurley, 2001; Levitas & Silka, 2001; Reiss & Valenti-Hein, 1994; Sturmey, 1998). Psychopathological complications are also frequent (Baumeister & Baumeister, 1995; Dosen & Day, 2001; Rojahn & Tasse, 1996; Sachs & Barrett, 2000). For children diagnosed with mild MR, internalizing symptoms (such as anxiety and mood disturbances) and externalizing problems (such as oppositional defiant disorder and attention deficit hyperactivity disorder) are frequently observed (Baker, Blacher, Crnic, & Edelbrock, 2002; Burack, Evans, Klaiman, & Iarocci, 2001; Dykens, 2000; Hardan & Sahl, 1997). For children diagnosed with more severe forms of MR, autistic symptoms and self-injurious behaviors are frequently reported (Dykens, 2000).

Etiology

The most common distinction in discussions of etiology is between **organic** and **nonorganic causes**. Organic causes of MR are associated with a specific physiological or physical origin; organic causes are usually associated with more severe forms of MR, and are observed across all family and socioeconomic status backgrounds. Organic explanations may be either genetic or environmental (see Table 7.2), and there are hundreds of possibilities. Genetic causes, such as those just described, include relatively rare dominant gene disorders, recessive gene disorders resulting in errors in metabolism (e.g., treatable PKU and non-treatable Tay-Sachs), X-linked disorders, and chromosomal abnormalities (Winnepenninckx, Rooms, & Kooy, 2003; Simonoff, Bolton, & Rutter 1996). Figure 7.2 provides information about the relative incidence of

Joseph Sohm/Visions of America/Corbis

For most children with developmental delays, feelings of individual competence and social connection are key to a positive and resilient developmental trajectory.

various genetic causes. Environmental causes include infectious diseases (such as in-utero exposure to rubella, cytomegalovirus, and HIV/AIDS), prenatal

TABLE 7:2 SELECTED ETIOLOGICAL EXPLANATIONS FOR MENTAL RETARDATION

1. Prenatal causes
   a. Chromosome disorders (e.g., Down syndrome)
   b. Syndrome disorders (e.g., Tuberous sclerosis)
   c. Inborn error of metabolism (e.g., Phenylketonuria)
   d. Developmental disorders (e.g., spina bifida)
   e. Intrauterine malnutrition (e.g., fetal alcohol syndrome and other prenatal toxicants)
   f. Unknown

2. Perinatal causes
   a. Intrauterine disorders (e.g., prematurity)
   b. Neonatal disorders (e.g., intracranial hemorrhage)

3. Postnatal causes
   a. Head injuries (e.g., cerebral concussion)
   b. Infections (e.g., pediatric HIV)
   c. Demyelinating disorders (e.g., Schilder disease)
   d. Degenerative disorders (e.g., Rett syndrome)
   e. Seizure disorders (e.g., myoclonic epilepsy)
   f. Toxic metabolic disorders (e.g., lead exposure)
   g. Malnutrition (e.g., protein caloric deficiency)
   h. Environmental deprivations (e.g., psychosocial disadvantage)

SOURCE: Pennington (2002).

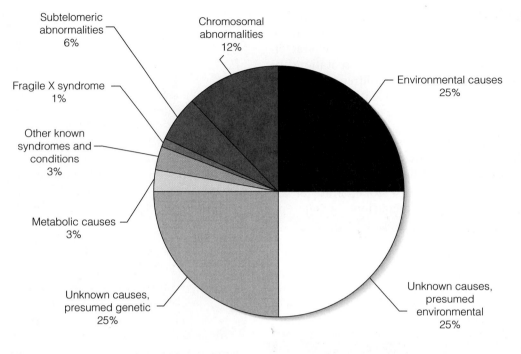

FIGURE 7:2 Overview of causes of mental retardation.
SOURCE: From Winnepenninckx Birgitta, Rooms Liesbeth, Kooy Frank, "Mental retardation: A review of the genetic causes", 'The British Journal of Developmental Disabilities, 49 (2003), pp. 29-44. Reprinted by permission of Wiley-Blackwell.

exposure to toxic substances (such as alcohol or other drugs that may lead to fetal alcohol syndrome), or neurotoxins following birth (such as lead and methylmercury) (Mendola, Selevan, Gutter, & Rice, 2002), and physical trauma (such as birth complications, encephalitis, or head injury) (Baumeister & Baumeister, 1995; Dammann & Leviton, 1997; Ornoy, 2002).

Nonorganic causes of MR are also referred to as familial or cultural-familial, and are generally understood to reflect "an expression of both polygenetically inherited low intelligence that is within the normal range of human variability and environmental circumstances that are not conducive to optimal cognitive development" (Baumeister & Baumeister, 1995, p. 290). In other words, the mental retardation observed in some children is predicted by multiple risks, including the normal variability of intelligence in the general population (i.e., there are always going to be some children at the very far ends of the distribution) coupled with adverse life situations (such as poverty and economic deprivation). Unlike MR associated with organic causes, this type of mental retardation is observed more often in groups of individuals with disadvantaged backgrounds (Baumeister & Baumeister, 1995; Siegler, 2003; Simonoff, 1996).

This type of MR also runs in families. To the extent that the components and processes of intelligence are genetically transmitted, we expect that a family's other children, who share some of the same genes as their parents and their sibling with MR, display below average intelligence, and they do (Pennington, 2002; Plomin & Kovas, 2005). This family pattern can be compared to organic forms of MR where, for example, a genetic error is a one-time mutation and not part of a parent's genetic makeup passed on to other children; in these families, the siblings of the affected child display near average intelligence (Pennington, 2002). The organic-nonorganic distinction is also explored in connection with Zigler's developmental-difference hypothesis; there, nonorganic etiologies are associated with slowed or delayed intellectual functioning that reflects the similar sequences and coherent growth observed in typically developing children.

Developmental Course

Given the number and range of etiologies, marked differences in children's developmental trajectories are expected and observed (Dykens & Hodapp, 1999; Hodapp & DesJardin, 2002; Hodapp & Zigler, 1995). In general, poorer prognoses are associated with organic etiologies. Not only are the organic etiologies related to more severe mental retardation, but many are also associated with life-threatening physical disease and dysfunction. For the most impaired children, outcomes may include institutionalization, total dependence on others for care, and briefer lives. More positive outcomes tend to be observed in children with mild or moderate degrees of mental retardation, with organic, nonorganic, mixed, or unclear etiologies. For all of these children, keeping in mind the holistic approach favored by Zigler and others, we can examine the course of disorder as it plays out in various domains of development.

Physical and Neurological Domains

As already described, for many types of mental retardation, there are physical abnormalities associated with the disorder. Although both immediate and long-term growth and health are often compromised, medical advances have made a life span approach to MR essential (Hodapp & Burack, 2006). In fact, longevity has increased so dramatically that researchers are now focused on identification, assessment, and treatment for a variety of specific complications, such as Alzheimer's disease in individuals with Down syndrome emerging in middle to later years (Zigman et al., 2004).

With respect to neurological development, brain structure and brain development have been the focus of much recent attention. Researchers have

described microcephaly and reduced volumes in the frontal lobes and cerebellum in adults with Down syndrome, microcephaly in Williams syndrome, and structural abnormalities in individuals with fragile X syndrome (Nadel, 1999; Pennington, 2002). The various functions of the prefrontal cortex and the hippocampus have also been examined (Pennington, Moon, Edgin, Stedron, & Nadel, 2003). In addition, abnormalities in the genetic regulation of dendritic and synaptic growth and neuronal pruning have been identified (Harum & Johnston, 1998; Dierssen & Ramakers, 2006; Huttenlocher, 1999; Pennington, 2002). These types of defects have direct and indirect, and short- and long-term consequences for the overall development of the child. These investigations of brain development and function reflect contemporary trends involving longitudinal perspectives and provide essential data illustrating the brain pathways that underlie the many patterns of deficits, dysfunctions, and relative strengths observed in various forms of MR.

Intelligence, Language, and Communication

Although issues remain with the conceptualization of intelligence as a general competence or as multiple abilities, and the understanding of the deficits in mental retardation as delays or differences, we still must describe the paths and outcomes related to the cognitive domain of functioning. As Pennington (2002) states, "there is the fact that individuals with

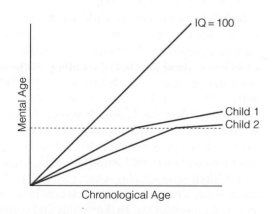

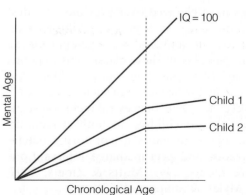

FIGURE 7:3A Task-related slowing of development.
Source: From MENTAL RETARDATION by Hodapp. Copyright 1993 by American Association on Intellectual Developmental Disabilities. Reproduced with permission of American Association on Intellectual Developmental Disabilities in the format Textbook and in the format Internet posting via Copyright Clearance Center.

FIGURE 7:3B Age-related slowing of development.
Source: From MENTAL RETARDATION by Hodapp. Copyright 1993 by American Association on Intellectual Developmental Disabilities. Reproduced with permission of American Association on Intellectual Developmental Disabilities in the format Textbook and in the format Internet posting via Copyright Clearance Center.

MR do develop, that they follow a normal sequence of developmental acquisitions much more often than not, and that their performance on most, but not all tasks is well predicted by mental age" (p. 264). Against this changing background, there are various cognitive and intellectual impairments displayed by children with mental retardation, with specific etiological patterns of relative strengths and weaknesses in language, memory, and information-processing (M. Anderson, 1998; Kail, 1992; Pennington, 2002).

Children with mental retardation exhibit different trajectories of intellectual development relative to the rate and timing of growth for normally developing children (Hodapp & Zigler, 1995; Pennington, 2002; see Figures 7.3a and 7.3b). In addition, children with MR show "less solid, more 'fragile' developments of their highest stages" (Hodapp & Zigler, 1995, p. 311). These changes are likely tied to innate characteristics, but are also influenced by the interaction of the child's abilities and environmental factors (Abbeduto, Evans, & Dolan, 2001; Nadel, 1999). For many children with MR, cognitive and linguistic profiles of strengths and weaknesses also change over time, with strengths becoming stronger and weaknesses becoming weaker (Hodapp & Burack, 2006).

One particularly relevant environmental variable is education. In the United States, the Individuals with Disabilities Education Act mandates diagnostic, educational, and support services from birth to age 21, with individual education plans developed with input from parents, teachers, and mental health professionals. Educational approaches have changed over previous decades, and now emphasize inclusion of children with developmental disabilities in age-appropriate classrooms. Success in these classrooms depends on many variables, and "behavioral problems are the chief reason for the failure of such placements" (Szymanski et al., 1999). Successful inclusion strategies described for children in both elementary and middle schools include self-monitoring, behavioral contracts, and peer-mediated interventions (Gildner & Zionts, 1997; Matts & Zionts, 1997; Simpson, Myles, & Simpson, 1997).

Because the mild forms of MR are often identified in the early school years, with increasing demands for academic performance in each successive year (State et al., 1997), it is not surprising that eventual educational accomplishments are, in part, related to

teachers' attitudes toward inclusion (Avramidis & Norwich, 2002; Balboni & Pedrabissi, 2000; Gilmore, Campbell, & Cuskelly, 2003; Hastings & Oakford, 2003; Heiman, 2001; Villa, Thousand, Meyers, & Nevin, 1996; see Box 7.3). The school milieu also includes other children, and their beliefs and behaviors are also important (Heiman, 2000; Heiman & Margalit, 1998). Although some negative biases are common (Nowicki & Sandieson, 2002), we can be encouraged by the slightly more positive attitudes of high school students toward their peers with MR over the last several decades (Krajewski, Hyde, & O'Keefe, 2002).

Social, Emotional, and Personality Development

The general course of adaptive functioning is variable. Some groups of children with MR show improvements over time, others display up-and-down patterns of adjustment, and still others exhibit declines (Hodapp & Burack, 2006; Pennington, 2002; State et al., 1997). For all groups, however, the emphasis remains on supporting personality development and functioning (Keith, Heal, & Schalock, 1996; Zigler, 1999; Zigler & Bennet-Gates, 1999), and achieving a positive quality of life (Dykens, 2006; Schalock, 1996, 1997, 2000). As we have already discussed, Zigler's "approach was aimed at understanding the 'whole child' with mental retardation, in all of that child's psychological complexity" (Hodapp & Zigler, 1995, p. 316). And many investigators since Zigler have focused on identifying essential similarities and differences in children with and without mental retardation. Research on emotion, attachment, and play in children with Down syndrome, for example, supports Zigler's position that children with MR exhibit basic emotion skills, appreciate humor, and experience complex emotional relationships (Cicchetti & Serafica, 1981; Marcell & Jett, 1985; Motti, Cicchetti, & Sroufe, 1983; Reddy, Williams, & Vaughan, 2001; Whitman, O'Callaghan, & Sommer, 1997). With increasing age, however, children with Down syndrome also exhibit fewer positive emotions and increased withdrawal (Dykens, 2006).

Children also display characteristic patterns of social competence and peer relationships, depending on their etiological backgrounds and surrounding environments (Rosner, Hodapp, Fidler, Sagun, & Dykens, 2004; Sigman & Ruskin, 1999). Compared to typically developing children, for instance, children with mental retardation appear more motivated to

BOX 7:3   THE CHILD IN CONTEXT

Teachers' Attitudes toward Inclusion

There is a complicated historical and legal background to the discussion of inclusion of children with special needs into regular classroom settings. In general, we see a move from demands for the "least restrictive environments" for children with MR to more recent efforts that emphasize both inclusion and integration for children and educational curricula (Farrell, 1997; Kavale, 2002; Kavale & Forness, 2000; Lowenthal, 1999; Miller, Fullmer, & Walls, 1996). With a diversity of parent and teacher beliefs and attitudes about inclusion (Palmer, Borthwick-Duffy, Widaman, & Best, 1998), research evidence is necessary to make informed and valued policy decisions (Farrell, 1997; Kavale, 2002; Kavale & Forness, 2000; Lowenthal, 1999; Miller, Fullmer, & Walls, 1996).

Many discussions of inclusion presume that successful outcomes depend, in part, on teacher attitudes (Avramidis & Norwich, 2002; Heiman, 2001), and reviews of the literature suggest that teachers have positive attitudes about inclusion and integration. However, their attitudes and beliefs are influenced by the nature and severity of children's special needs, as well as their own needs for personal and educational support for their work (Avramidis & Norwich, 2002; Heiman, 2001).

Teachers' positive attitudes are countered by their lack of confidence in their abilities to manage classrooms with special needs children (Avramidis, Bayliss, & Burden, 2000; Buell, Gamel-McCormick, & Hallam, 1999; Center & Ward, 1987). This lack of confidence may underlie their reluctance to fully embrace the notion of inclusion. Many investigators have observed that knowledge about specific disabilities, along with training, experience and collaborative work with other teachers, has an impact on teachers' perceived competence (Avramidis et al., 2000; Buell, Hallam, Gamel-McCormick, & Scheer, 1999; Minke, Bear, Deemer, & Griffin, 1996; Snell & Janney, 2000), although there are some data suggesting that experience may be related to some teachers' greater hostility toward inclusion (Soodak, Podell, & Lehman, 1998).

It seems clear that additional work remains to document both the benefits and costs related to inclusion for both children and teachers (Janney, Snell, Beers, & Raynes, 1995), and that the acceptance and translation of policy into practice is ongoing (Carrington & Elkins, 2002).

seek and obtain approval and positive reinforcement from others, and to look more frequently to others for information and guidance (Hodapp & Zigler, 1995). With respect to leisure activities, etiology-associated patterns are again observed, with differences in the selection and practice of social activities, visual tasks, musical activities, and physical activities (Sellinger, Hodapp, & Dykens, 2006). With age, individuals with Down, Williams, and Prader-Willi syndromes all increased social activities; other increases and decreases in specific activities were also observed (Sellinger et al., 2006).

It is important to understand that children with MR are not just occupying themselves or following others' directives related to various activities. In many cases, selection and pursuit of specific activities appear related to a number of positive internal strengths (Dykens, 2006). Individuals with Williams syndrome, for instance, may be assisted in their drive for relationships to make safe, appropriate, and reciprocated overtures to others. Given their pleasure, skill, and deep engagement in music,

they may also be encouraged, challenged, and supported in their musical journeys (Dykens, 2006).

Maladaptive Behavior and Psychopathology

The prevalence and types of comorbid symptoms and disorders were already summarized. In this section, we explore why children with MR are at increased risk for various psychopathologies and how these psychopathologies play out over time (Hodapp & Dykens, 2005). Certainly shared genetic and physiological vulnerabilities contribute to overlapping psychopathologies (Dykens, 2000). But Dykens (2000) suggests that another reason that children with MR struggle in multiple ways is related to the nature of lower intellectual functioning. That is, children with MR generate fewer problem-solving strategies and have fewer cognitive resources, leading to unrealistic appraisals of tasks and abilities, and less successful outcomes for a variety of intellectual and social challenges. Distress is likely, along with increasingly negative self-evaluations.

Over time, particularly for children and adolescents with mild MR, anxiety, mood, and behavioral symptoms may exacerbate intellectual and adaptive functioning. Another example of developmental complications involves the consequences of problematic peer relationships. According to Dykens (2000), many individuals with MR are at increased risk for physical abuse and sexual exploitation, given histories of sociability and failed social overtures. Additional research investigating the emergence and maintenance of additional maladaptation is essential in order to decrease poor outcomes and increase the likelihood of physical and mental well-being.

Adult Outcomes

With emphases on quality of life and appropriate support for individuals with MR, we look to the future with hope. For some individuals with mild mental retardation, leaving the school system, with its focus on academic skills and achievement, leads to improvements in adaptation. State et al. (1997) and others have documented many instances of persons with a diagnosis of intellectual disability who essentially disappear into society and function well enough that they no longer meet the diagnostic criteria for mental retardation. Most, however, continue to struggle with many of the tasks of daily living. As these individuals move into early adulthood, they and their families may look for community activities or employment opportunities. Interest and success in these endeavors is likely related to the productive and/or dysfunctional career beliefs observed in adults with disabilities (Lustig & Strauser, 2002).

Other predictable developmental challenges are also observed (Levitas & Gilson, 2001). One of the most difficult challenges involves adult sexuality. Historically, both mental health professionals and the general public exhibited strong negative attitudes about sexual behavior in adults with MR; sexual freedom was rarely permitted (Kempton & Kahn, 1991; Lumley & Scotti, 2001; Rhodes, 1993). Although recent surveys continue to reveal negative perceptions (Lunsky & Konstantareas, 1998), sexuality is increasingly understood as an important aspect of life satisfaction for persons with mental retardation. Sex education, therefore, is essential (Held, 1993; Lumley & Scotti, 2001; McConkey & Ryan, 2001; Valenti-Hein & Dura, 1996; Zuker-Weiss, 1994). Of course, specific concerns about the sexual abuse of vulnerable adults and unwanted pregnancies must also be addressed (Held, 1993; Sundram & Stavis, 1994).

Adults with mental retardation live in a variety of environments, from family homes to group settings (Braddock, Emerson, Felce, & Stancliffe, 2001). Very few adults (and even fewer children) reside in institutions; those who do are likely to exhibit comorbid psychopathology (Szymanski et al., 1999). Reviews of studies published following deinstitutionalization suggest that long-term community placements are associated with increases in overall adaptive behavior (Kim, Larson, & Lakin, 2001), with more positive outcomes in smaller, less restrictive settings (Gardner, Carran, & Nudler, 2001).

The Role of the Family

As children with mental retardation develop, so do their families. Many patterns of emotional response and eventual adjustment to babies with disabilities have been described, with differences depending on family characteristics, the perception and meaning of the individual child, and the type of mental retardation; the particular maladaptive behaviors associated with specific etiologies are especially important to consider in this respect (Fidler, Hodapp, & Dykens, 2000; Glidden, 2002; Hodapp, 2002). These factors may underlie what has been described as the "Down syndrome advantage," the tendency for families of children with Down syndrome to cope better than families of children with other forms of MR (Hodapp, 2007). Despite the financial and social difficulties of raising a child with MR in the home, parents want to be responsible for their children's care (Hadadian & Merbler, 1995b; Hodapp & Zigler, 1993). Effective care depends, in part, on the information provided to families. Information that includes both general overviews of disorder, specific descriptions of a child's weaknesses and strengths, and concrete, life-span support strategies is essential (Fidler, Hodapp, & Dykens, 2002; Hodapp & Burack, 2006; Hodapp, 2007). There are many different types of informal and professional support available; this may vary by culture or country (Shin, 2002).

Early on, different roles for mothers and fathers are often observed, with mothers taking a more active role in caregiving, and fathers more preoccupied with financial and practical concerns (Hadadian & Merbler, 1995a). Outcomes for children and their families are related to individual and parent variables. For example, young children with mothers who are both highly sensitive and highly directive have better prognoses (Hodapp & Zigler, 1995). Family well-being is associated with the extent of help and cooperation achieved by parents (Simmerman & Baker, 2001).

Considering the many unique family contexts, many stress-and-coping models of ongoing family adjustment discuss both positive and negative aspects of having a child with MR (Crnic, Friedrich, & Greenberg, 1983; Floyd, Singer, Powers, & Costigan, 1996; Hodapp & Zigler, 1995; Minnes, 1988; Scorgie & Sobsey, 2000). With respect to stress, for instance, there are difficulties associated with children's transitions and milestones (Harris, Glasberg, & Delmolino, 1998; Wikler, 1986). According to Hodapp and Burack (2006), families of children with MR attend to developmental issues (such as the first smile), chronological issues (such as entrance into school), and familial issues (such as a younger child passing the first) that may all be problematic; each event may lead to parents reexperiencing sadness. With respect to coping and resilience, many researchers have documented effective personal, familial, and environmental strategies (Heiman, 2002; Lustig, 2002; Minnes, 1988; Scorgie, Wilgosh, & McDonald, 1998). Some of the most positive rewards of having a child with MR families describe include the joy that the child brings to the family, a sense of purpose, expanded personal and social networks, personal growth, and increased tolerance (Stainton & Besser, 1998). Overall, our understanding of parents has shifted to "a more positive, coping perspective" (Hodapp & Zigler, 1995, p. 314).

Assessment and Diagnosis

The American Association on Intellectual and Developmental Disabilities (AAMR/AAIDD, 2002) sets forth a number of assumptions that must be considered before a diagnosis of mental retardation is made: "(1) limitations in present functioning must be considered within the context of community environments typical of the individual's age, peers, and culture; (2) valid assessment considers cultural and linguistic diversity as well as differences in communication, sensory, motor, and behavioral factors; (3) within an individual, limitations often coexist with strengths; (4) an important purpose of describing limitations is to develop a profile of needed supports; (5) with appropriate personalized supports over a sustained period, the life functioning of the person with mental retardation generally will improve." With these assumptions in mind, we can examine the ways in which assessments and diagnoses are made.

Background Information

Medical and developmental histories are a key component of the assessment of mental retardation. Almost always, clinicians rely on parents and others for these types of reports and observations, although there is evidence that interviews and self-reports may also be useful with some individuals with MR (Finlay & Lyons, 2001; Levitas, Hurley, & Pary, 2001). For less severe clinical presentations, clinicians must evaluate whether the presence of more specific developmental delays in speech, language, and reading account for intellectual and adaptive delays. Physical concerns such as hearing difficulties or hearing loss may also have an impact on cognitive and language development.

Assessment of Intellectual Functioning

Standardized tests of intelligence, such as the Stanford-Binet (Roid, 2003) or one of the Wechsler tests (Wechsler, 2003), are administered individually. In addition to a general evaluation of intellectual functioning, evaluations of particular cognitive processes may also be included. It is important to note that these types of tests have both technical and nontechnical concerns. With respect to technical issues, there is one clear advantage to current instruments: "A score of 130 at age 5 means that a child's performance exceeds that of 98% of age peers; a score of 130 at age 10 means exactly the same thing" (Siegler, 2003, p. 313). And, although "measured intelligence tells us nothing about how these deviations in development occur, whether they are endogenous or exogenous, whether they present different medical complications, whether the basic underlying condition is alterable, how individual growth and development are likely to proceed, how generalized the disabilities are, or how to evaluate prognosis" (Baumeister & Baumeister, 1995, p. 285), scores on intelligence tests do allow comparisons among groups of children with MR. Other assessment concerns involve the focus on formal academic skills and predicting school achievement in standardized tests, and the comparability of scores for children of different ethnic and racial backgrounds on traditional and nontraditional intelligence tests (Figueroa & Sassenrath, 1989; Heflinger, Cook, & Thackrey, 1987).

A final issue is raised by differing definitions. The DSM-IV identifies the cutoff score for diagnosis at

2 SD below the norm. For a test with a mean of 100, that is a score of 70. The AAIDD (2002) has recently advocated that the cutoff be raised to 75 (reflecting scores at 1.66 SD below the norm). Given the distribution of IQ scores in the general population, this doubles the number of individuals who would be eligible for a diagnosis of MR, with multiple consequences, both positive and negative (Kanaya, Scullin, & Ceci, 2003; Pennington, 2002). These types of recommendations need to be understood in the context of the "Flynn effect," the gradual increase in IQ scores over the past several decades (Flynn, 1987, 2007). Fluctuations in IQ scores, coupled with restrictive notions of low intellectual functioning, may have serious impacts on children and adolescents who are repeatedly tested throughout their school lives (Kanaya & Ceci, 2007).

Assessment of Adaptive Functioning

Of the various standardized scales for assessment of adaptive functioning, the most common are the Vineland Social Maturity Scale and the AAIDD Adaptive Behavior Scale (Sparrow, Cicchetti, & Balla, 2005). These instruments are designed to measure basic skills in different developmental domains, including communication, self-care and health, social skills, and leisure and work, at various ages. They are usually completed by adults who know the child well. Although most often conceptualized as tapping separate areas of functioning, there are data to support the notion of an underlying, general factor of adaptation (Hodapp & Dykens, 1996; Pennington, 2002). Given the somewhat variable course of intellectual and adaptive functioning for different groups of children with mental retardation (Widaman & McGrew, 1996), repeat assessments throughout the growing years are important.

Following the collection of information on significant deviations in intellectual and adaptive functioning, and after the diagnosis of mental retardation, additional assessment may be especially valuable. Information about maladaptive behaviors and psychopathology must be included (Dykens, 2000). Specific behavioral assessments (Linscheid, Iwata, & Foxx, 1996), socially oriented assessments (Matson & Hammer, 1996; Nanson & Gordon, 1999), and personality measures such as happiness (Dillon & Carr, 2007; Simeonsson & Short, 1996; Zigler, Bennett-Gates, Hodapp, & Heinrich, 2002) may provide a more complete picture of a whole child. Plans for supporting physical and psychological

well-being depend on this more comprehensive approach (Schalock, Stark, Snell, & Coulter, 1994).

Intervention

When considering intervention for children and adolescents with mental retardation, two points are worth emphasizing. First, in general, we are not trying to treat the condition as we would most episodes of psychopathology. Rather, we are attempting to maximize the potential of the individual to meet developmental demands, while at the same time modifying the environment to better match the individual's deficits and strengths. Consequently, the majority of mental health professionals, educators, and advocacy groups stress the importance of intervention plans that target multiple points along the developmental continuum, as well as a range of relevant social and educational systems within which the child functions. These include, for example, early screening and identification, early intervention for the child and the family, appropriate school programming, and coordination of the various persons and agencies involved in the child's care.

The second point to emphasize in the context of this textbook is that mental health is an important issue for everyone, regardless of level of intellectual functioning. We must be careful not to define a person by a single, if salient, attribute like mental retardation (or, for that matter, being intellectually gifted or a star athlete). Psychological variables such as emotion, social relationships, and impulse control are every bit as relevant for individuals diagnosed as mentally retarded as for those who are not. Intervention strategies, then, must be designed to address all relevant problem areas. Finally, while exceptional progress in the treatment of mental illness has been made in recent years, these advances are often delayed in their applications to special needs populations such as children and adolescents with mental retardation. The mental health field has a clear obligation to improve its efforts to apply emerging treatment approaches to all groups, including the mentally retarded.

Genetic Screening and Prevention Strategies

Genetic screening of parents, prenatal testing, and **genetic counseling** afford many specific intervention opportunities (Durand, 2001; Simonoff, 1996; Stainton, 2003). However, with "technology… advancing more rapidly than the ethical and practical guidelines for its use" (Simonoff, 1996, p. 273), we must be careful to respect many different perspectives (see Box 7.4). Broad-based prevention approaches, such as public information campaigns discouraging drinking while pregnant, are also possible (see Box 7.5). In addition, measures including supplementing women's diets with folic acid to reduce neural tube defects and removing lead from the environment reduce rates of MR (Szymanski et al., 1999).

Pharmacological Treatment

Once mental retardation has been diagnosed, there are a variety of treatment options sharing similar goals: to develop and maintain skills, increase positive attributes, and decrease negative characteristics of MR. Pharmacological treatments of associated maladaptive behaviors are common, with the majority of individuals with mental retardation who

reside in institutions on some sort of psychotropic medication, with multiple medications increasingly prescribed (Howerton et al., 2002; State et al., 1997). Available data on outcome are mixed, but the most frequently used drugs associated with behavioral improvements are methylphenidate (Ritalin), antipsychotics, and mood-related medications (Dosen, 2001; Matson et al., 2000; State et al., 1997; Tyrer & Hill, 2001). There is also interest in nutritional and hormonal treatments to support better outcomes (Ellis, Singh, & Ruane, 1999). The evaluation of side effects and adverse drug reactions is especially important to consider in a population of children and adolescents who may have difficulty communicating (Dosen, 2001; Kalachnik, 1999). Indeed, accepted practice parameters suggest that individuals with MR be prescribed psychotropic medications cautiously, given difficulties related to informed consent, enhanced sensitivity to drugs

BOX 7:4 EMERGING SCIENCE

Ethical Issues in Prenatal Genetic Counseling

Advances in our abilities to detect abnormalities during prenatal development are associated with a host of pragmatic and ethical issues for parents, medical and mental health providers, and society (Bower, Veach, Bartels, & LeRoy, 2002; Okasha, 2002; Tangri & Kahn, 1993; Veach, Bartels, & LeRoy, 2001, 2002). For parents, prenatal decision-making is a multipart process. For some parents, genetic screening is routine; for others, it involves the first of many practical and moral decisions (Rice, 2001; Santalahti, Hemminki, Latikka, & Ryynaenen, 1998). Deciding what to do with available information, especially given the high false positive rates of some genetic screening techniques, is the next difficult step, and diverse parental values and beliefs are among the most important factors that have an impact on these decisions (G. Anderson, 1998; Copel & Bahado-Singh, 1999; Rice, 2001). Parents who are making these kinds of multiple eventful decisions require accurate information and support (Santalahti et al., 1998; Williams, Alderson, & Farsides, 2002).

Medical and mental health providers also encounter many ethical and professional challenges. Determining what conditions to screen for, and when and how to screen for them, are among the immediate decisions to be made (Copel & Bahado-Singh, 1999; Williams et al., 2002). Veach et al. (2001, 2002) and

Bower et al. (2002) describe a number of other challenges that underlie and follow these first ones. Among the most demanding include: informed consent, withholding information, facing uncertainty, value conflicts, resource allocation, professional identity, and proficiency. The extent to which a genetic counselor is directive or nondirective may require special ethical attention (Bower et al., 2002; Veach et al., 2001, 2002; Weil, 2003).

From a societal standpoint, there is much to be addressed. First, we need to recognize that there are many perspectives in this multidisciplinary field (Pelletier & Dorval, 2004). There are parents, physicians, psychologists, bioethicists, advocates for disabled children and adults, and others who have reasoned and passionate beliefs that are at odds with one another. Keeping all of these people and the many social consequences of genetic counseling in mind, we need to be able to anticipate the various ethical issues that confront diverse populations (Parker & Gettig, 1997). We need to discuss the personal, community, and economic costs and benefits of genetic counseling. And we need to develop practice recommendations for counselors (Bennet, Pettersen, Niendorf, & Anderson, 2003). For all of these tasks, ethically informed decision-making depends on our commitment to engage in respectful dialogue, as individuals and as a society.

Prevention and Fetal Alcohol Syndrome

Fetal alcohol syndrome (FAS), one of the fetal alcohol spectrum disorders (FASD), is caused by maternal drinking during pregnancy. FAS is characterized by persistent physical, cognitive, and socio-emotional impairments, and psychopathology in infants, children, and adults (Olson, 2002; Sokol, Delaney-Black, & Nordstrom, 2003; Steinhausen, Willms, & Spohr, 1993). FAS has been identified around the world in various populations (Riley et al., 2003). Given recent U.S. Supreme Court and state court cases and legislative attempts to criminalize drug and alcohol use during pregnancy (Marshall, Menikoff, & Paltrow, 2003), and the enormous impact of FAS in personal, social, economic, and political spheres (Greenfield & Sugarman, 2001), FAS requires scientific scrutiny and thoughtful response.

Although information about FAS has become much more available in recent years (due, in part, to public awareness campaigns), much more remains to be done (Murphy-Brennan & Oei, 1999; Sokol et al., 2003). FAS is an "entirely preventable disorder" (Murphy-Brennan & Oei, 1999). Intervention efforts geared to decreasing the rates of FAS are widespread, although they achieve mixed results. Hankin (2002) describes universal, selective, and indicated prevention efforts, including education, screening, and treatment (Greenfield & Sugarman, 2001). Universal efforts include media messages about drinking while pregnant and posters and labels on alcoholic beverages. Price increases are a pragmatic attempt to reduce drinking; they appear to have an impact on heavy and binge drinkers (Abel, 1998a, 1998b).

Selective efforts include education and support directed specifically at at-risk groups, such as Native American women and adolescents (Ma, Toubbeh, Cline, & Chisholm, 1998a, 1998b, 2002), although a lack of resources hinders some of these prevention attempts (Clarren & Astley, 1997; Ma et al., 2002). Risk factors also extend beyond group status. Identifying women at risk involves understanding the ways in which at-risk women respond to messages about drinking and pregnancy (Branco & Kaskutas, 2001). What do these women understand about the nature and course of FAS? Do they believe that some drinks are safer than others? How much drinking is too much? What peer, family, and social pressures are there related to drinking or not drinking during pregnancy? (Branco & Kaskutas, 2001). And, are some prevention messages (such as failing to distinguish between alcohol use and alcohol abuse) actually counterproductive? (Abel, 1998a, 1998b). We need to think carefully about the factors that promote abstinence in at-risk women, such as higher intelligence, higher household incomes, and the availability of social support, and the ways in which these factors might be mobilized (Astley, Bailey, Talbot, & Clarren, 2000).

Targeting women who are already drinking is the most problematic of prevention and intervention efforts, with complicated ethical and legal issues. For example, the Supreme Court has ruled that nonconsensual drug screening is unlawful (*Ferguson vs. City of Charleston et al.,* 2001), and punitive policies such as incarceration or forced treatment may scare some women away from seeking help (Marshall et al., 2003). This is especially distressing given that there are data indicating that brief, focused interventions do reduce alcohol use in mothers-to-be who drink heavily (Hankin, 2002; Niccols, 1994). We will need to be cautious as we balance responsibility, blame, rehabilitation, and punishment, so that we emphasize healthy pre- and postnatal development as among the most important—and achievable—goals.

and their side effects, and poor monitoring of outcomes (Szymanski et al., 1999).

Psychological Treatment

Psychological treatments are complex and comprehensive, with research and clinical consensus that children and adolescents with MR benefit from individual, family, and group therapies. Better outcomes are associated with therapeutic practices that take into account cognitive, communication, and behav-

ior skills (Szymanski et al., 1999). Therapies include behavioral treatments (Berkson, 1993; Gardner, Graeber-Whalen, & Ford, 2001; Singh, Osborne, & Huguenin, 1996; State et al., 1997), cognitive treatments (Benson & Valenti-Hein, 2001; Repp, Favell, & Munk, 1996), and socioemotional programs (Dosen, 2001; Hollins, 2001; Hurley, Pfadt, Tomasulo, & Gardner, 1996) as well as family, educational, and vocational planning (Day & Dosen, 2001; Drotar & Sturm, 1996; Risley & Reid, 1996; Rotthaus, 2001; Thompson

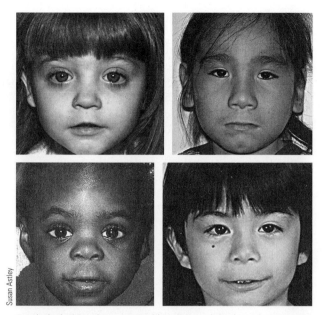

Fetal Alcohol Syndrom, caused by maternal drinking during pregnancy, often results in characteristic physical, as well as cognitive, characteristics.

et al., 2002). Educational interventions often have dramatic impact, depending on the factors underlying impaired intellectual functioning (Rutter et al., 2004; Rutter & the ERA Study Team, 1998). Increasing attention is paid to matching treatments to etiologies (Hodapp & DesJardin, 2002). As with many other treatment strategies, early intensive efforts are associated with better outcomes (Pennington, 2002; Ramey, Mulvihill, & Ramey, 1996; Ramey, Campbell, & Blair, 1998).

Following educational interventions, behavior modification therapies are among the most frequently used. The goals of behavioral strategies include enhancing adaptive skills and teaching appropriate behaviors. Given that maladaptive behaviors are a major source of difficulty at home and at school, these strategies are essential (Szymanski et al., 1999). Behavioral treatments utilizing aversive techniques such as restraint or punishment are rarely used today; alternatives such as token reinforcement strategies are almost always available (Singer, Gert, & Koegel, 1999). When aversive techniques are used, serious self-harm or aggression toward others is a concern (Szymanski et al., 1999).

Family Education and Support

Given the lifelong nature of mental retardation, the family's role in treatment is a prime concern. Parents

often serve as co-clinicians (Baker, 1996), and both direction and support are necessary. For instance, some parents are reluctant to set strict behavioral limits for their children with mental retardation. Although based in empathy or sympathy, this reluctance may also reflect a lack of understanding about the need for structure and clear expectations (Hodapp, 2004). For children and adolescents with mental retardation, eventual adjustments and outcomes depend on integrated, collaborative efforts that provide as much information, support, and optimism as is possible.

■ Key Terms

Cognitive development (pg. 103)
Intellectual development (pg. 103)
Mental retardation (pg. 104)
Intellectual functioning (pg. 104)
Adaptive behavior (pg. 104)
Mild mental retardation (pg. 104)
Moderate mental retardation (pg. 104)
Severe mental retardation (pg. 104)
Profound mental retardation (pg. 104)
Intermittent support (pg. 105)
Limited support (pg. 105)
Extensive support (pg. 105)
Pervasive support (pg. 105)
Developmental-difference debate (pg. 107)
Genotypes (pg. 107)
Behavioral phenotypes (pg. 107)
Down syndrome (pg. 107)
Williams syndrome (pg. 108)
Fragile X syndrome (pg. 108)
Organic causes (pg. 109)
Nonorganic causes (pg. 109)
Genetic counseling (pg. 116)

■ Chapter Summary

- Individual patterns of intellectual development are relatively stable by 4 or 5 years old.
- Mental retardation (MR) involves significant deficits in intellectual functioning and adaptive functioning.
- The classification levels of mild, moderate, severe, and profound mental retardation describe the degree of compromise in intellectual and adaptive functioning present in an individual diagnosed with MR.

- Adaptive behavior refers to the ability to master age-appropriate tasks of daily living.
- An alternative classification approach focuses on the relation between genetic causes (genotype) and specific behaviors and symptoms (phenotype). Examples of this approach include Down syndrome, Williams syndrome, and Fragile X syndrome.
- Both organic (physiological) and nonorganic (other risk factors such as normal range variability of intelligence and environmental challenges) causes may contribute to mental retardation. In general, poorer prognoses are associated with organic etiologies.
- In addition to careful consideration of all relevant medical and developmental background information, standardized assessment of both intellectual and adaptive functioning is critical to the valid and reliable diagnosis of mental retardation.
- In contrast to most forms of psychopathology, the focus of treatment for mental retardation is not the condition itself. Rather, the focus of intervention is the maximization of the individual's potential functioning.

CHAPTER 8

Autism Spectrum Disorders

The Case of Mark

Four-year-old Mark was referred for a psychological evaluation two years ago after his parents and pediatrician became concerned about his significantly delayed language development. Mark's parents described him as an extremely fussy baby who was hard to settle. Unlike his older sister, he was not very cuddly and, much to his parent's dismay, actually seemed to become more distressed when he was held. While Mark's motor milestones were all achieved at expected times, his language and communications skills lagged far behind. Not only did he speak much later than expected, he seemed to show little interest in any kind of communication. For example, he did not respond to his name, and did not seek his parents' attention.

Mark is very dependent on fixed and predictable routines. For instance, he plays with only a few toys and always in the same order. When playing, Mark often uses toys in unusual ways that disregard their intended purpose, such as using a doll to hammer in a peg or repeatedly spinning a horse on its side. He becomes extremely upset if these favorite toys are moved or rearranged on the shelf in his room where he keeps them. Mark also has difficulty engaging in imaginative or pretend play. Even on Halloween, he had difficulty with the idea of pretending to be a character, finding the idea confusing and upsetting.

When Mark speaks, which isn't often, his speech is atypical in rhythm and volume, and he frequently reverses his pronouns (saying, for example, "Would you like the ball?" when he wants someone to give him a ball). When his parents or evaluators attempt to speak directly to Mark, he quickly looks away, and sometimes even turns his back on them. Mark has always been extremely active and easily frustrated; at times when he is upset he bangs his head against the wall. He is described as being generally fearful and anxious in new situations and settings, and has been observed engaging in lots of hand-flapping and other self-stimulating behaviors. Mark's parents are quite worried about his starting kindergarten in a few months, knowing that he will be reluctant to be away from home and does not seem at all interested in the school setting or in meeting or playing with other children. ∎

The Case of William

William is 10 years old and having considerable difficulty at school. Although William's early motor and cognitive development were typical, he began to show both communication and social disturbances as a preschooler. For instance, William can be very affectionate and engaging, but he can also be intrusive and overwhelming when interacting with other children. Although quite talkative from an early age, William often talks at length about his own interests and is quite resistant to sharing in the interests or responding to the questions of others. By the time he entered elementary school, he had developed clear, specific, and obsessive interests. This characteristic first manifested itself in his keen interest in weather and meteorology and now includes weather radar equipment. All of his reading and nearly all conversations he initiates with others are on these topics. Although his parents, teachers, and older siblings have all explained to him that his intensity and relentlessness make others uncomfortable, he has not modified this behavior at all.

In the primary grades, the major concerns expressed by his teachers were his poor attention, impulsivity, and poor work completion. While these problems have continued, it is his poor social skills that are currently causing the most difficulties. For example, William was mostly ignored and somewhat isolated in the early school years, but now he has become the target of teasing and rejection. Recently, his classmates have goaded him into doing things that have gotten him into trouble and resulted in his being ridiculed by classmates. William is quite sensitive to the trouble he is having in regard to schoolwork and friendships, but he shows little insight into either the causes or solutions to these problems. ∎

Historical and Current Conceptualizations of Autism Spectrum Disorders

Each of the above cases presents a classic, or prototypical, presentation of child psychopathology. Mark is fairly quickly diagnosed with autism, whereas William is more likely to be diagnosed with Asperger syndrome. **Autism** and **Asperger syndrome** are identified in DSM-IV-TR (2000) as two of the five types of **pervasive developmental disorders**, along with Rett syndrome, childhood disintegrative disorder, and pervasive developmental disorder, not otherwise specified (Chakrabarti & Fombonne, 2002; Filipek et al., 1999; Fombonne, 2002; Klin & Volkmar, 1997; Tsai, 1994; Volkmar, 1994).

All of the specific pervasive developmental disorders share some common, broadly defined characteristics. As described in DSM-IV-TR, each of the disorders reflects compromised development in social interactions (both verbal and nonverbal), impaired or delayed communication, and restricted patterns of activities or interests. At the same time, of all of the categories of childhood disorders in this text, the category of pervasive developmental disorders is in the most flux. Given increasing numbers of children diagnosed with autism, Asperger syndrome, and other pervasive developmental disorders (Koenig, Rubin, Klin, & Volkmar, 2000; Lord & Volkmar, 2002; Wing & Potter, 2002), the confusion is especially disconcerting. There are complicated and unresolved issues related to the nature, identification, and classification of the various disorders in this category (Georgiades et al., 2007; Volkmar, Chawarska, & Klin, 2005). In this chapter, we provide summaries of the differing perspectives as well as a framework for thinking about the unsettled issues. But we also try to stay focused on the children themselves, who—even without definitive answers to many basic questions—still require appropriate and caring interventions.

Current conceptualizations of autism, Asperger syndrome, and related disorders are based on decades of work following clinical summaries provided by Leo Kanner (1943) and Hans Asperger (1944/1991) (Klin & Volkmar, 2003; Klinger, Dawson, & Renner, 2003; Mesibov, Adams, & Schopler, 2000; Volkmar et al., 2005; Wing, 1981, 1997, 1998; Yeung-Courchesne & Courchesne, 1997). Both Kanner, in his descriptions of children with "early infantile autism," and Asperger, in his portrayals of boys with "autistic psychopathy," emphasized the children's profound lack of social awareness. Asperger, however, described better language skills and more social interest in his small sample (Asperger, 1944). These differences underlie several current controversies covered in this chapter.

Much of the theory and research on autism in the United States, at least up until the 1990s, was based on Kanner's work. A picture of autism emerged that highlighted three areas of deviance: social isolation, impaired language and communication, and stereotypical behaviors. Some children, of course, did not fit the classic presentation; these children usually had better cognitive and language skills and were thought to have "high-functioning autism". More recently, clinicians and researchers hypothesized that some of the children diagnosed with high-functioning autism might be better understood (and better treated) if their symptoms and struggles were conceptualized as a related, but distinct, disorder: Asperger syndrome.

Whether autism and Asperger syndrome are best conceptualized as clinically distinct disorders or whether they correspond to different points along a spectrum of dysfunction (i.e., more and less severe forms of autism) remains the source of much contention (Klin & Volkmar, 2003; Klin, Volkmar, & Sparrow, 2000; Mayes, Calhoun, & Crites, 2001; Mesibov, Shea, & Adams, 2002; Schopler, 1996; 1998; Tantam, 1988, 2000; Wing, 2000). One of the most influential factors related to the recent focus on Asperger syndrome is the role of parent advocacy, as parents work to get better services for their children (Klin, Volkmar, et al., 2000). Klin et al. observe: "Decades of effective parent action in autism on the one hand and learning disabilities on the other hand have resulted in a relatively rich infrastructure of services for children with these conditions and their families, including better special education resources, entitlement programs, and more generally, increased awareness in the mental health and educational communities. Children and adults with Asperger syndrome and related disabilities have problems which appear to fall in between these more generally recognized categories of disabilities" (pp. 5-6).

Other current research in this field is similar to research described in the previous chapter on mental retardation, with investigators emphasizing subtypes and "syndrome specificity" (Coleman, 1987; Georgiades et al., 2007; Klin & Volkmar, 1997; Prior et al., 1998). Work on syndrome specificity involves attempts to move from "broad and amorphous categories" of disorder to "empirically derived and more homogenous subgroups" (Klin & Volkmar, 1997, p. 208). These attempts include theoretical and statistical accounts of autism and Asperger syndrome, as well as efforts to identify meaningful patterns in the pervasive developmental disorder, not otherwise specified, category (Paul, Cohen, Klin, & Volkmar, 1999; Szatmari et al., 2002).

One last point: neither Mark nor William, in the cases presented at the beginning of this section, displays mental retardation. The rate of comorbidity between autism and mental retardation is the focus of current research, with recent estimates ranging between 30% and 70% (Edelson, 2006; La Malfa,

Lassi, Bertelli, Salvini, & Placidi, 2004). Varying estimates also depend on whether investigators begin with samples of children with autism and then look for MR, or whether they begin with children with MR and then look for autism (de Bildt et al., 2003), as well as on specific measures of intellectual functioning (Edelson, 2005; Edelson, Schubert, & Edelson, 1998).

Developmental Tasks and Challenges Related to the Coordination of Social, Emotional, and Cognitive Domains

The sections on normal development in the three previous chapters have described many of the remarkable achievements of young children, including the emergence of self-regulation and emotional regulation, attachment processes and social relationships, and intellectual functioning, in order to provide useful contrasts for specific psychopathologies. In this chapter, rather than focusing on a particular domain of functioning, we emphasize the interdependent, coordinated nature of early development.

Social Cognition

This more integrative overview begins with a focus on **social cognition,** an ability at the intersections of self and other, emotion and cognition, and language and meaning. The construct of social cognition refers to the many ways that people think about themselves and their social worlds. We are especially concerned with the ways in which young children take in and meaningfully process socially relevant information from the vast amounts of information available to them. An appreciation of social cognition in the normally developing child is key to understanding what goes wrong for children with autism.

Two of the most important features of social cognition are the distinctions between (a) what is more and less important, and (b) what is social and nonsocial. According to Landa (2000), almost all children "pay attention to what is important. This awareness of saliency is reflected in children's first words, which typically represent a salient person, place, thing, or action such as 'ball, kitty, cookie' rather than inanimate objects having little relevance in their lives such as 'wall'" (p. 133). Among salient

people, places, and things, people receive the most attention. Almost all children recognize that the caregiver is worthy of notice, and behave as if emotional and social engagement with the caregiver is special, pleasant, and informative.

Theory of Mind

In addition to recognizing the salient and social aspects of one's surroundings, Landa (2000) discusses how simple but essential behaviors also contribute to interdependent, coordinated development. In Landa's view, "communicative intentions" such as eye contact, pointing, and shared attention, smooth out the processes of social interaction and facilitate and reward participation in the social world. Investigations of these kinds of communicative intentions, or **joint attention**, provide strong evidence for its role in fostering development in several domains (Carpenter, Nagell, & Tomasello, 1998). One important developmental achievement dependent on joint attention involves the child's theory of mind. **Theory of mind** refers to an ability to attribute mental states to others (Baron-Cohen, 1989, 1995, 2001; Phillips, Baron-Cohen, & Rutter, 1998), to see others as "bodies animated by minds" (Griffin & Baron-Cohen, 2002). Theory of mind emerges over time. It involves the understanding that others are separate selves, with their own points of view and their own feelings. We see evidence of theory of mind in all sorts of social exchanges, such as when babies look first to parents for information before approaching a large puppy, and then again when they share their delight in puppy licks and kisses.

Affective Social Competence

The development of social cognition over the early years also depends on increasingly complex emotion skills. Halberstadt, Denham, and Dunsmore's (2001) construct of affective social competence provides an important example of integrated functions. **Affective social competence** involves the coordination of the capacities to experience emotion, send emotional messages to others, and read others' emotional signals. The dynamic interaction of these types of emotion abilities with emerging cognitive abilities provides yet another way that children are able to glean salient information from their social partners. Overall, then, the developmental transition from the sensorimotor experiences of infancy to the symbolic experiences of toddlerhood and later years is marked by ever-increasing coordination among various developmental domains and processes. This in turn leads to the emphasis on the idea of the child as a social being in a social world, and the recognition that this is of central importance throughout development.

Autism Spectrum Disorders

Throughout this section, our descriptive anchor (or landmark) on the spectrum of autism disorders will be the child with classic or prototypical autism. With this anchor in place, we will present similarities and differences with Asperger syndrome and other related psychopathologies. The key impairments in classic autism involve (a) social development, (b) language and communication, and (c) restricted, stereotypic, or repetitive behaviors (DSM-IV-TR, 2002; see Table 8.1). The impact of these impairments, evident early in life, is wide-ranging. Indeed, many readers may come to agree with Pennington's (2002) assertion that autism "is the most severe psychopathology, since it disrupts very basic aspects of personhood" (p. 223).

Socioemotional Deficits and Deviance

Children with autism display a heterogeneous group of social and emotional deficits; their social development is both quantitatively and qualitatively different from normally developing children and children with other disorders (Hobson, 1999; Klin, Jones, Schultz, Volkmar, & Cohen, 2002a, 2002b; Klin & Volkmar, 1997; Rutter & Schopler, 1992). One of the basic, and earliest, deficits observed in children with autism is a relative lack of differentiation between social and nonsocial stimuli. As already noted, in a world made up of social and nonsocial things, social stimuli are much more salient and much more interesting than nonsocial stimuli (Klin, 2002; Koenig, Rubin, Klin, & Volkmar, 2000). For many babies who will later be diagnosed with autism, the diminished salience of social stimuli is reflected in a variety of atypical behaviors.

These atypical behaviors, all evidence of difficulties with joint attention, include a lack of social orienting, a failure to respond to social sounds and signals, such as the parent's voice or clapping hands (Bruinsma, Koegel, & Koegel, 2004; Dawson et al., 2004; Mundy & Neal, 2001); a lack of social reciprocity, or the turn-taking of social interactions (Bailey, Phillips, & Rutter, 1996; Wimpory, Hobson, Williams, & Nash, 2000); and fewer and more deviant social behaviors (Klin & Volkmar, 1997; Lord, 1995). Ongoing work in this area is focused on identifying the specific social mechanisms that underlie complex social behaviors (Klin, 2002). One hypothesis connects social interaction and language

---

TABLE 8:1 DSM-IV-TR CRITERIA FOR AUTISM AND ASPERGER SYNDROME

Autism

A. A total of 6 or more items from (1), (2), and (3), with at least two from (1) and one each from (2) and (3).

(1) Qualitative impairment in social interaction
   a. marked impairment in the use of multiple nonverbal behaviors
   b. failure to develop peer relationships appropriate to developmental level
   c. lack of spontaneous speaking to share enjoyment, interests, or achievements with other people
   d. lack of social or emotional reciprocity

(2) Qualitative impairment in communication
   a. delay in, or total lack of, the development of spoken language
   b. marked impairment in ability to initiate or sustain a conversation (for individuals with adequate speech)
   c. stereotyped, repetitive, or idiosyncratic language
   d. lack of varied, spontaneous make-believe play or social imitative play

(3) Restricted, repetitive, and stereotyped patterns of behaviors, interests, and activities
   a. preoccupation with one or more stereotyped and restricted patterns of interest that is abnormal in intensity or focus
   b. inflexible adherence to specific, nonfunctional routines or rituals
   c. stereotyped and repetitive motor mannerisms
   d. persistent preoccupation with parts of objects

B. Delays or abnormal functioning in at least one of the following areas, with onset prior to age 3:
   (1) Social interaction
   (2) Language as used in social communication
   (3) Symbolic/imaginative play

TABLE 8:1 (CONTINUED)

Asperger Syndrome

A. Qualitative impairment in social interaction, as manifested by at least two of the following:
   (1) Marked impairment in the use of multiple nonverbal behaviors such as eye-to-eye gaze, facial expression, body postures, and gestures to regulate social interaction
   (2) Failure to develop peer relationships appropriate to developmental level
   (3) Lack of spontaneous seeking to share enjoyment, interests, or achievements with other people
   (4) Lack of social or emotional reciprocity

B. Restricted, repetitive, and stereotyped patterns of behaviors, interests, and activities as manifested by at least one of the following:
   (1) Encompassing preoccupation with one or more stereotyped and restricted patterns of interest that is abnormal in intensity or focus
   (2) Inflexible adherence to specific nonfunctional routines or rituals
   (3) Stereotyped or repetitive motor mannerisms
   (4) Persistent preoccupation with parts of objects

C. The disturbance causes clinically significant impairment in social, occupational, or other areas of functioning.

D. There is no clinically significant delay in language.

E. There is no clinically significant delay in cognitive development or in the development of self-help skills, adaptive behavior, and curiosity about one's childhood environment.

Source: DSM-IV-TR (2000) Reprinted with permission from The Diagnostic and Statistical Manual of Mental Disorders, Text Revision, Fourth Edition (Copyright 2000). American Psychiatric Association.

---

learning (Kuhl, Coffey-Corina, Padden, & Dawson, 2005). Kuhl and her colleagues investigated *motherese*, the sounds and melody of mothers' speech to very young children. In the Kuhl study, normally developing children preferred the baby talk and display specific patterns of brain activity when exposed to it. Children with autism, however, preferred computer-generated nonspeech. Other work related to joint attention summarizes data that suggest that children with autism do attend to persons and events; however, their unusual resistance to distraction, their skill at parallel perception, and their atypical display of certain actions make typical instances of joint attention unlikely (Hamilton, Brindley, & Frith, 2007; Gernsbacher, Stevenson, Khandakar, & Goldsmith, 2008; Iarocci & Burack, 2004; Sebanz, Knoblich, Stumpf, & Prinz, 2005).

In addition to these basic social dysfunctions, there are also difficulties related to the experience, perception, and processing of emotion (Hobson, 1989a, 1989b, 1991, 1993). Children with autism display deficits in recognizing body expressions of emotion (such as those conveyed by the eyes and by the voice) (Rutherford, Baron-Cohen, & Wheelwright, 2002). Taken together, these early social and emotional deficits are linked to one of the more fascinating areas of autism research: the special role of the face (see Box 8.1).

More complex forms of social and emotional functioning have also been investigated. Children with autism display deficits in pretend play and imitation (Charman et al., 1997, 2000; Filipek et al., 1999). For instance, "children with autism do not want to use their miniature snow shovel to shovel snow just like daddy or use a screwdriver to repair a toy when mommy is doing the same" (Harris, 1995, p. 306). Other children never deviate from a particular play routine. Filipek et al. (1999) provide an example of a "verbal autistic preschooler who 'plays' by repeatedly reciting a soliloquy of the old witch scene *verbatim* from *Beauty and the Beast* while manipulating dollhouse characters in sequence precisely according to *the script*. When given the same miniature figures and dollhouse, but instructed to play something other than *Beauty and the Beast*, this same child is incapable of creating any other play scenario" (p. 445).

Children with autism also display an overall lack of social "style" (Hobson & Lee, 1998, 1999), even as their general social personalities vary, from withdrawn to more odd and eccentric (Klin & Volkmar, 1997; Wing & Attwood, 1987). The difficulties are perhaps most obvious in reciprocal relationships such as peer friendships, where expectations for social and emotional skills are higher, and are observed even in the highest functioning groups of children

The Role of the Face

Researchers in the United States and Canada are using innovative eye-tracking technology to gain new insights into how individuals with autism view their socioemotional, interpersonal worlds. Data from multiple studies (Klin et al., 2002b; Ristic et al., 2005) document the distinctive patterns of focusing and shifting attention

displayed by individuals with autism. Compared to individuals without autism, who look frequently and for relatively longer periods of time at the eyes of others, individuals with autism are more likely to gaze at the mouths and bodies of others, and at extraneous objects. Not only is this pattern of face scanning

Face scanning by toddlers with autism (left column), typically-developing toddlers (middle column), and developmentally-delayed toddlers (right column).

American Medical Association

unusual, but the information gleaned from such scanning is likely to be incomplete and less meaningful. Differences between the gaze patterns of individuals with autism and individuals without autism are illustrated in the accompanying photo.

These findings are especially interesting in light of some of the hallmark symptoms of autism, such as lack of eye contact and poor recognition of faces. In related research, also conducted at Yale (Schultz, Grelotti, Klin et al., 2003), functional MRI studies showed that research participants with autism perceived faces as if they were objects. The three-year study provided evidence of reduced activity for those with autism in the

area of the cerebral cortex dedicated to face recognition. At the same time, they showed increased activity in an adjacent area of the brain that processes information regarding objects. Recent reviews of the perceptual-cognitive and motivational-affective hypotheses related to impaired facial processing include descriptions of deficits in initial stages of face processing and later stages of face recognition (Dawson, Webb, & McPartland, 2005; Ristic et al., 2005). In addition, there is evidence that some of the abnormalities in the "social brain" circuitry may be observed in first-degree relatives of children with autism (Dawson, Webb, Wijsman, et al., 2005).

with autism (Koenig et al., 2000; Lord & Volkmar, 2002). In some cases, children with autism do better when interacting with much older or younger children, where they can adopt the clearly defined role of follower or leader (Filipek et al., 1999). This is certainly true for Mark, the 4-year-old described at the beginning of the chapter, who has the most social difficulties with other children around his age. He is somewhat more comfortable when interacting with his 13-year-old sister or his parents, who understand his routines and rituals and can adjust their behaviors to what he most needs.

Compared to children with the classic clinical presentation of autism, children with Asperger syndrome display a somewhat distinctive pattern of social and emotional functioning. They appear to be more aware of others as social beings and more interested in social interactions (Klin & Volkmar, 1997). However, although the desire and motivation are present, children with Asperger syndrome are as stymied by the seemingly intuitive give-and-take of social exchange as are children with autism (Klin & Volkmar, 1997; Tantam, 1988; Volkmar & Klin, 2001). Relying on the formal rules of social behavior, children with Asperger syndrome make more overtures to other children, but often appear awkward, rigid, and insensitive in their interactions with others (Volkmar & Klin, 1997). Their general social ineffectiveness, and the ridicule of their peers, may lead later to the withdrawal and isolation more characteristic of children with autism (Filipek et al., 1999).

With respect to emotional adjustment, children with Asperger syndrome can and do talk about emotions and relationships. But the more time one spends

in such conversations with these children, the more it is apparent that the talk is concrete and intellectualized (Klin, Volkmar et al., 2000). That is, these children appear to lack the actual sense or feeling of the word *emotion*. One of the authors works with a young adolescent who is preoccupied with violent slasher movies. In therapy, it has become clear that he responds to the highly exaggerated (and more easily perceived) emotional states of the characters. Similarly, William, the 10-year-old presented at the beginning of the chapter, is fascinated by comic books. William can talk endlessly about the clearly outlined conflicts, resolutions, and emotional states of the characters, although he never even comes close to expressing these feelings himself.

Delays and Deficits in Language and Communication

Although the structure of intelligence appears to be similar in children with and without autism, children with classic autism (without mental retardation) exhibit a number of difficulties (Goldstein et al., 2008). These include a variety of specific problems with verbal learning; there appear to be fewer difficulties with nonverbal skills, rote and rule-based learning, and memory tasks (Joseph, Tager-Flusberg, & Lord, 2002; Klinger & Dawson, 2001; Koenig et al., 2000); increasingly complex tasks reveal greater impairment (Williams, Goldstein, & Minshew, 2006a, 2006b). More global deficits are noted in executive functioning such as planning and organizational abilities (Bailey et al., 1996; Dawson, Munson, et al., 2002; Luna, Doll, Hegedus, Minshew, & Sweeney, 2007; Ozonoff & Griffith, 2000).

The intersection of cognitive and social tasks presents definite challenges. Given difficulties with emotional reciprocity, imitation, and play, it is not surprising that children with autism do poorly on cognitive tasks that depend on social understanding (Bailey et al., 1996; Charman et al., 2001; Dawson, Meltzoff, Osterling, Rinaldi, & Brown, 1998; Sigman, Yirmiya, & Capps, 1995). Impairments are also evident on tasks involving imagination and creativity, such as storytelling (Craig & Baron-Cohen, 1999, 2000).

Investigators have attempted to identify an essential cognitive deficit that would explain children's struggles. One of the best-researched possibilities involves theory-of-mind deficits. As previously defined, theory of mind (TofM) refers to an ability to attribute mental states to others (Baron-Cohen, 1989, 1995, 2001; Flavell, 2004; Phillips et al., 1998). Children and adults with autism may be described as having "**mindblindness**" (Baron-Cohen, 1989, 1995, 2001), and the vast majority of them fail even simple theory-of-mind tests (Heavey, Phillips, Baron-Cohen, & Rutter, 2000; see Figure 8.1). Those children and adolescents who understand very basic TofM tasks often do poorly on more sophisticated ones (Baron-Cohen, O'Riordan, Stone, Jones, & Plaisted, 1999).

Another possibility has to do with the **central coherence hypothesis** (Frith & Happe, 1994). The central coherence hypothesis is based on the idea that most individuals attempt to perceive and construct meaning from information that is part of an environmental whole. Information makes sense, or is coherent, because it is part of something larger than itself. Children and adolescents with autism are at a disadvantage because they process information piecemeal, in a more fragmented fashion (Bailey et al., 1996; Frith & Happe, 1994; Jolliffe & Baron-Cohen, 2001a, 2001b). Interestingly, when cognitive tasks involve parts of images, such as identifying embedded figures in a drawing, individuals with autism do better than individuals without autism (Baron-Cohen & Hammer, 1997). Indeed, the perceptual functioning of children with autism has sometimes been described as "enhanced"; this is an example of a strength-based understanding of autism (Gernsbacher et al., 2008; Mottron, Dawson, Soulieres, Hubert, & Burack, 2006). How this particular ability may be related to the infrequent appearance of specially developed, relatively isolated skills is an unanswered question (Bailey

FIGURE 8:1 Diagram of Sally Ann theory-of-mind task: Dark-haired Sally watches Ann, the light-haired girl, place the doll in the basket and leave. Sally then moves the doll to the box. Children are asked where Ann will look for the doll when she returns. Children with theory-of-mind abilities understand that Ann does not know that Sally moved the doll and so Ann will look in the basket. Children with theory-of-mind deficits perform poorly on these types of perspective-taking tasks.
Source: Axel Scheffler. Copyright © Cengage Learning, Illustrator: Macmillan Publishing Solutions.

et al., 1996; Hermelin, 2001; Mottron et al., 2006; see Box 8.2).

We want to emphasize again that the cognitive disabilities and processes described are most obvious in children with autism who are not also mentally retarded. Indeed, when researchers compare the cognitive performances of children with autism and children with mental retardation, matched for mental age, children with mental retardation often do better than children with autism on TofM, central coherence, and social cognition tasks. That is, children with mental retardation are better at understanding the mental states of others and at perceiving the

Splinter Skills and Savant Talents

One of the most unusual attributes of certain individuals diagnosed with autism is the extraordinary development of a single skill or talent. Although most children and adolescents with autism struggle with intellectual impairments, and display uneven performances in various intellectual domains, there are some individuals who possess relatively preserved sets of skills ("splinter skills") as well as others whose exceptional abilities in language, drawing, music, or mathematics ("savant talents") capture our attention (Bailey et al., 1996; Hermelin, 2001). Dustin Hoffman, in the 1989 movie *Rain Man*, portrays an adult with autism who has an amazing facility with numbers. One of Clara Park's books about her daughter Jessy, *Exiting Nirvana*, is illustrated with Jessy's brightly colored, intricately detailed architectural drawings (see Figure 8.2). For the most part, these special skills are not used for practical or constructive ends (Bailey et al., 1996).

What explains this phenomenon? As we have discussed in this chapter, there is evidence that individuals with autism process information in fragments or segments (ignoring available holistic information). Some investigators believe that this tendency is even more developed in those who display special skills (Bailey et al., 1996; Heaton, Hermelin, & Pring, 1998; Hermelin, 2001; O'Connor & Hermelin, 1994; Pring & Hermelin, 2002), although there are also lesser roles for practice and instruction (Pring, Hermelin, Buhler, & Walker, 1997). As we try to make sense of observations that reflect multiple connections among intelligence, autism, and giftedness, we need to acknowledge—again—the essential connections between normally developing and unusually developing children.

FIGURE 8:2 *St. Paul's and St. Andrew's Methodist Church and the Migraine Type Lighting and the Elves, 10/17/98,* drawing by Jessy Park. From *Exiting Nirvana: A Daughter's Life with Autism,* by C. Claiborne Park, 2001, New York: Little, Brown.

Jessica Park, St. Paul's and St. Andrew's Methodist Church and the Migraine Type Lighting and the Elves, 10/17/98. Courtesy of Pure Vision Arts.

environment in a holistic manner (Dyck, Ferguson, & Shochet, 2001; Greenspan & Love, 1997; Leffert & Siperstein, 2002; Phillips et al., 1998; Yirmiya, Erel, Shaked, & Solomonica-Levi, 1998).

These differences are most obvious in the relatively "pure" cases of autism and mental retardation. But we must keep in mind that three-quarters of children with autism also meet the diagnostic criteria for mental retardation, with 30% in the mild to moderate range and 45% in the severe to profound range; one-half of children with autism and mental retardation are without functional speech (Bailey et al., 1996; Koenig et al., 2000; Pennington, 2002). The strong association between autism and mental retardation is undeniable. The reasons for

the association will be discussed in the upcoming section on etiology, but remain to be fully explained (Bryson & Smith, 1998; Wing, 1991).

With respect to language, children with autism display both delay and deviance. Indeed, Wing and Wing (1971) suggested that children with autism seemed to be without an "inner language." There are impairments in the forms of speech, with slowed babbling and delayed use of words, later onset (or lack of onset) of intentional communication such as pointing, lack of imitation, and abnormalities in the nonverbal components of speech such as tone and prosody (Filipek et al., 1999; Klin & Volkmar, 1997; Koenig et al., 2000; Lord & Pickles, 1996; Paul, 1987; Smith & Bryson, 1994). The content of speech is also unusual, with both immediate and delayed echolalia (inappropriate or uncommunicative repetition of words or phrases). For example, in addition to the pronoun reversals of Mark (asking "would you like the ball?" when he wants a ball), he also frequently repeats the last word spoken to him in a conversation.

As with cognition, there are even more pronounced difficulties with the social use of language, or **pragmatics** (Filipek et al., 1999; Landa, 2000). Children with autism use language for instrumental reasons such as getting a dessert, rather than for social purposes such as sharing one's pleasure in completing a puzzle (Koenig et al., 2000; Wetherby, 1986). Mark's family, for example came to realize that he never initiates a conversation unless it is about something he wants or needs. Consequently, they look for these opportunities to engage with him and broaden, by very small increments, the scope of their communication with him.

Language and communication comparisons between children with classic autism and children with Asperger syndrome have been a major research and clinical focus. The original distinction between autism and Asperger syndrome highlighted differences in this domain, with children with Asperger syndrome showing normal development of early language abilities as well as normal or nearly normal intelligence. This observed distinction led to the belief that Asperger syndrome was a mild form of autism. More recently, however, abundant data suggest that children with Asperger syndrome do show early disturbances in language and social communication. Some of these disturbances are similar to those displayed by children with autism such as problems with prosody and tone; others are different and include marked verbosity and tangential speech (Klin & Volkmar, 1997; Klin, Sparrow, Marans, Carter, & Volkmar, 2000).

Because children with Asperger syndrome are impaired in their abilities to decode the social and emotional cues of others, they often engage in pedantic, one-sided conversations. In addition, they do not self-censor their speech. One child in treatment greeted a therapist with "Hi . . . hey did you know your eyes bug out, like you have some medical problem or something?" Klin (2002) provides another example of a college student with Asperger syndrome who asked a student if he would be willing to trade his girlfriend for a watch (note here the very thin line between things and people). William, for example, was often preoccupied with issues of fairness at home, where he often complained bitterly

about his baby sister getting new clothes when he did not. Although he was able to keep track of her entire wardrobe, he was not comforted by explanations that he was treated similarly as an infant, or by the fact that babies grow more rapidly than 10-year-olds.

With regard to cognitive and intellectual profiles, children and adolescents with Asperger syndrome are often hyperlogical, as if concrete operations have run amok. This is evident in, for example, the perception of humor. Children with Asperger syndrome may display a sense of humor, but it usually involves slapstick comedy or very obvious word play (Klin, 2002). On standardized tests, there are additional intriguing differences between children with autism and children with Asperger syndrome; these include relative strengths in block design (requiring skills in spatial processing and visual-motor coordination) for children with autism and relative strengths in verbal ability for children with Asperger syndrome (Ehlers, Nyden, Gillberg, & Dahlgren Sandberg, 1997; Szatmari, Archer, Fisman, & Streiner, 1995).

Behavioral Deficits

Most children with autism exhibit repetitive and/or stereotyped body movements such as rocking, hand-flapping, and twirling. Some children with autism also display specific interests and/or strong attachments to certain objects, but their attachment is often unusual. For instance, a child may be focused only on the wheel mechanisms of toy cars rather than their ability to move across the floor. A different child may be absorbed by the smell of a toy (Koenig et al., 2000). Many young children with autism are intrigued by water (Filipek et al., 1999). These obsessions in children with autism are almost always associated with "folk physics" (an interest in how *things* work) rather than in "folk psychology" (how *people* work) (Baron-Cohen & Wheelwright, 1999). These atypical behaviors are sometimes observed in children with other disorders, but the collective pattern of behaviors is unique for those with autism.

Most children with autism also insist on sameness in their environments and routines, protesting vehemently when this sameness is disturbed (Harris, 1995; Klin & Volkmar, 1997). Filipek et al. (1999) describe instances of children needing to have furniture in exact places or clothes in a single color. According to Klin (2002), this insistence on sameness in the environment is a powerful and meaningful symptom, reflecting the individual's concern and struggle with control of his or her surroundings. Additional investigations have emphasized the role of executive dysfunction (i.e., cognitive rigidity) in children's insistence on sameness (Rinehart, Bradshaw, Tonge, Brereton, & Bellgrove, 2002; South, Ozonoff, & McMahon, 2007; Szatmari et al., 2006).

A child with Asperger syndrome, in contrast, is more likely to assert control in the verbal and language domain, through dominating conversations and continuing to discuss topics long after conversational partners have wearied. With respect to the particular interests of children, "it appears that special interests in autism are more likely to involve object manipulation, visual-spatial tasks, music, or unusual savant skills, whereas in Asperger syndrome the focus is on amassing large amounts of factual information relative to the child's topic of interest" (Klin, Sparrow et al., 2000). Tantam (2000), describing the special interests of several individuals with Asperger syndrome, emphasizes the soothing and organizational qualities of these systematic activities.

Children with autism spectrum disorders also frequently display motor impairments; hypotonia (i.e., poor muscle tone) was the most common motor symptom (Ming, Brimacombe, & Wagner, 2007). Delays in achieving motor milestones and clumsiness may also differentiate children with autism and children with Asperger syndrome. Although there are some mixed data, most of the research suggests that children with Asperger syndrome do more poorly on these behavioral indices (Ghaziuddin & Butler, 1998; Klin & Volkmar, 1997; Ozonoff & Griffith, 2000; Smith, 2000).

Prevalence and Related Information

Estimates of the prevalence of autism vary widely. The Centers for Disease Control and Prevention of the U.S. Department of Health and Human Services (Centers for Disease Control and Prevention, 2007) estimate current prevalence at 1 in 150. Three to four times as many boys are diagnosed as girls, but girls with autism have higher rates of mental retardation. Some researchers believe that "fewer females with normal IQ are diagnosed with autism because they may be more socially adept than males with similar IQ" (Filipek et al., 1999, p. 440). The diagnosis of autism has increased dramatically over the last two decades, reflecting more inclusive, expanded definitions and better identification, as well as the possibility of a true increase in prevalence (Chakrabarti & Fombonne, 2005; Croen, Grether, Hoogstrate, & Selvin, 2002; Fombonne, 2007; Holburn, 2008; Lord & Volkmar, 2002; Scott, Baron-Cohen, Bolton, & Brayne, 2002b; Wing & Potter, 2002).

Increases in the diagnosis of autism parallel increases in the diagnosis of Asperger syndrome, as well as the general category of pervasive developmental disorders (Fombonne, Simmons, Ford, Meltzer, & Goodman, 2001). The ratio of autism to Asperger syndrome is unclear, with some studies suggesting more cases of autism (Fombonne & Tidmarsh, 2003), and others suggesting higher rates of Asperger syndrome (Ehlers & Gillberg, 1993; Gillberg & Gillberg, 1989). Epidemiological uncertainty is to be expected, given that conceptualizations of these disorders are in flux. As the models and definitions of the autism spectrum become more focused, epidemiological data will become more clear (Klin & Volkmar, 2003; Woodbury-Smith, Klin, & Volkmar, 2005).

Developmental Course

For almost all diagnosed children, autism is a lifelong disorder. Many cases of autism are identified in the first year of life, although the mean age of initial evaluation in a recent population sample was 48 months, with diagnosis at 61 months (Wiggins, Baio, & Rice, 2006). Although most researchers suggest that precursors to the characteristic symptoms of autism are present from birth onward, there is evidence of a subgroup of children who develop relatively normally for the first year, and then show significant regression, with a loss of verbal and social skills (e.g., Luyster et al., 2005; Richler et al., 2006). Home videos of children provide additional information about such regression (see Box 8.3).

The characteristic symptoms of autism are in place and often at peak frequency between 2 and 4 years of age (Bryson et al., 2007; Chawarska et al., 2007; Muratori & Maestro, 2007; Werner, Dawson, Munson, & Osterling, 2005; Zwaigenbaum et al., 2005). From then on, many children display unusual patterns of growth and regression ("unevenness" across domains of development) (Klin & Volkmar, 1997). Some children exhibit a decrease in the intensity of problematic behaviors and an increase in adaptive skills (Harris, 1995). A minority of individuals with autism show a decline beginning in adolescence, usually associated with the onset of seizures (Canitano, Luchetti, & Zappella, 2005; Harris, 1995; Mesibov, 1983). The outcome for those with autism is generally poor, although most long-term studies that documented the negative course were completed when children were identified at older ages, and services were less available and less comprehensive

Early Home Videos of Children with Autism

Retrospective reporting by parents is sometimes difficult to evaluate. By the time a diagnosis of a pervasive developmental disorder is made, parents have often struggled for years to sort through medical opinions and psychological hypotheses. Understanding the history of parental concerns is important, because the rates of development and their specific pathways have predictive value that is useful for parents, clinicians, and children (Klin, 2002).

The validity of parents' early concerns is supported by several creative investigations of early home videos. Family videos of infants and toddlers provide a rich source of data about social development, language and communication, and unusual behaviors. By 1 year of age, raters can distinguish children who will later be diagnosed with autism from typically developing children (Osterling & Dawson, 1994; Osterling, Dawson, & Munson, 2002; Werner, Dawson, Osterling, & Dinno, 2000). One salient difference is that children who will later be diagnosed with autism fail to respond to their names when called (Werner et al., 2000). In fact, the social, language, and behavior patterns observed not only differentiate autistic children from normal children, but also provide information about differences between the development of autism and mental retardation (Osterling, Dawson, & Munson, 2002).

Another study focused on the early course of autism, comparing videos of children across 6-month intervals (i.e., birth–6 mos, 6–12 mos, 12–18 mos, and 18–24 mos) (Bernabei, Camaioni, & Levi, 1998). The most common pattern observed in this study was one in which babies made developmental progress during the first or second periods, and then regressed between the second and third periods or the third and fourth periods, with the most significant deterioration in the domain of social behaviors. In addition to providing compelling information about the early nature of autism, each of these investigations provides support for the often-underappreciated usefulness of parent reports and concerns about their children's development.

(Koenig et al., 2000). Even with recent advances, there is evidence that suggests that many adults with autism continue to have significant difficulties, living with their parents and experiencing ongoing social and vocational struggles (Howlin, 2000; Howlin, Mawhood, & Rutter, 2000; Moxon & Gates, 2001).

Time of onset, course, and outcome provide important opportunities for comparison of autism and Asperger syndrome. Autism has historically been seen as a disorder that is evident very early in development. In contrast, Asperger syndrome has tended to be diagnosed in children who display *relatively* normal language and cognitive development in the first 3 years; later diagnosis has presumed later onset. However, once a diagnosis of Asperger syndrome is made, many parents recall delayed and deviant language in their children's younger years (Bennett et al., 2008; Klin & Volkmar, 1997; Klin, Sparrow, et al., 2000; Ozonoff, South, & Miller, 2000).

Examining how autism and Asperger syndrome play out over time, many investigators have noted the stability of Asperger syndrome, as well as certain advantages that children with Asperger syndrome possess (such as better conversational abilities) (Gilchrist et al., 2001; Starr, Szatmari, Bryson, & Zwaigenbaum, 2003; Szatmari et al., 2000). Overall, although there are a number of developmental similarities, children and adolescents with autism and Asperger syndrome appear to follow somewhat different developmental pathways (Gillberg & Ehlers, 1998; Klin & Volkmar, 1997; Klin, Sparrow et al., 2000; Schopler, Mesibov, & Kunce, 1998; Szatmari, 2000).

Neurological Domain

Researchers have documented atypicality in brain size, weight, and structure throughout childhood (Akshoomoff, Pierce, & Courchesne, 2002; Courchesne et al., 2001; DiCicco-Bloom et al. 2006; Filipek, 1999). In addition, about one-fifth of children with autism develop epilepsy as they age (Bailey et al., 1996; Rutter, 1970); as noted, these seizures often begin in early adolescence. When seizures occur during the preschool years, the autism is associated with more severe mental retardation and worse outcomes (Bailey et al., 1996).

Social and Emotional Domains

With deficits in social orienting leading to a deviant sense of self and disturbed interactions (Mundy &

Neal, 2001), we expect that children with autism will struggle with establishing and maintaining rewarding relationships. Some parents, however, report that their children become increasingly attached to them over time (Harris, 1995; Pennington, 2002). Other reports suggest that as they get older, children with autism become less withdrawn but more odd and eccentric (Klin & Volkmar, 1997). In general, social deviance continues.

Children and adolescents with Asperger syndrome display a somewhat different pattern. Remember the idea (discussed in Chapter 6, on disorders of attachment) that we learn about ourselves during our interactions with others, and that an appreciation of self depends in part on an appreciation of others. Klin (2002) has suggested that the verbosity of some with Asperger syndrome can be understood in this context. Without a strong, core self, these individuals may monopolize conversations in order to assert their presence, and to make themselves known. Individuals with Asperger syndrome are socially interested, but inept. Klin (2002) recalls a student who asked a young woman, "Can I touch your crotch?" It is easy to see how craving social contact, combined with developing sexuality and lack of insight and self-censorship, might lead quickly to social conflict and confusion. Over time, ongoing lack of success in connecting with others, especially peers, may elicit sadness, anxiety, and withdrawal for many older children with Asperger syndrome. (Ghaziuddin, Ghaziuddin, & Greden, 2002; Kim, Szatmari, Bryson, Streiner, & Wilson, 2000). It may happen, however, that the transition to adolescence provides an opportunity for more rewarding social interactions for some (Tantam, 2000).

Communication and Language

Given that early language abilities and language competence are related to better outcomes (Bennett et al., 2008; Howlin et al., 2000; Pry, Petersen, & Baghdadli, 2005; Venter, Lord, & Schopler, 1992), it is lamentable that about half of children with autism never develop useful speech (Koenig et al., 2000). Of course, many of these non-talking children also are diagnosed with mental retardation, which complicates the clinical picture. For those individuals who do develop language, and especially for those with Asperger syndrome, the "pragmatic impairment may be the most stigmatizing and handicapping aspect of these disorders. From school age onward, individuals with Asperger syndrome report that their social

language vulnerabilities give rise to anxiety, avoidance of some social situations, and self-image challenges and are a source of great concern to them. Adults with Asperger syndrome report having difficulty at jobs and establishing friendships due to their social communication impairment, despite being professionally productive and otherwise quite capable" (Landa, 2000, p. 125). The poignancy of the situation is clear for individuals with Asperger syndrome who, at each successive stage, are further compromised in their ability to deal with new challenges. This situation also illustrates in a very real way the notion of a **developmental disorder**, with different deficits and difficulties coming to the fore at various ages (Tantam, 2000, 2003).

Behavioral Domain

We have already described the up-and-down course of behavioral symptoms during the preschool years, and the possible increase in adaptive behaviors during later childhood. The next important transition for behavior happens during adolescence, with two different paths. For some, improvement continues; for others (especially those with neurological complications), deterioration occurs (Koenig et al., 2000; Rutter, 1970).

The Role of the Family

Parenting children with autism and Asperger syndrome is an obviously difficult task. Parents report a number of major stressors, with somewhat different patterns of stress described by mothers and fathers (Phares, 1996; Sivberg, 2002). Mothers report increasing stress as their children get older. Siblings also are affected. In the book *The Siege: A Family's Journey Into the World of the Autistic Child*, Clara Clairborne Park, the mother of a child with autism, describes the adjustment required of the child's siblings: "It was hard for a little boy six and little girls nine and ten to put all their minds to choosing a Christmas present for their two-year-old sister's first real Christmas and know that in all probability she wouldn't look at it or them" (p. 105). As time went on, however, the siblings of Park's daughter accepted their sister for who she was and became an integral part of her increasing engagement with the world: "The best thing they could do for Elly, as she entered the world by slow degrees, was to be children with her, to play naturally and with enjoyment the games that came to me, at forty, with such difficulty and awkwardness. They carried her about, dressed her in clothes from the dress-up chest, rode her in the wagon, chased her on the grass."

Etiology

Early Hypotheses

Although the earliest etiological hypotheses of Kanner and Asperger suggested neurophysiological origins for autism, these were quickly displaced by psychosocial explanations more in tune with the psychoanalytic era. Most frequently associated with Bruno Bettelheim, as well as other psychoanalysts, these explanations focused on poor parenting and the cool, distant "refrigerator mothers," whose infants intuitively understood that they were being rejected and so withdrew from contact and relationships. The consequences of being blamed for a pervasively debilitating disorder in one's own child were devastating. In time, although much too late for many parents, these theories were completely discredited.

Current Causal Models

As we summarize current causal models of autism and related disorders, keep in mind that autism has been described as "probably the most heritable of the psychopathologies" observed in children (Pennington, 2002, p. 226) and the "most strongly genetic of all multifactorial psychiatric disorders" (Bailey et al., 1996, p. 93). Moreover, it is possible that Asperger syndrome is even more influenced by genetics than classic autism is (Volkmar, Klin, & Pauls, 1998). A review of genetic approaches to autism begins with the findings of twin and family studies. Comparisons of monozygotic (MZ) and dizygotic (DZ) twins document clear genetic effects, with concordance rates for MZ pairs estimated to be between 36% and 91% and for DZ pairs, between 0% and 5% (Bailey et al., 1995; Folstein & Rutter, 1977; Pennington, 2002; Steffenburg, Gillberg, Hellgren, & Andersson, 1989). Family data support this notion of genetic transmission (Folstein & Santangelo, 2000; Ghaziuddin, 2005; MacLean et al., 1999; Volkmar & Klin, 2000). The observed patterns of genetic effects provide overwhelming evidence for a complex model of genetic involvement, with interactions among several different genes (Courchesne, Yeung-Courchesne, & Pierce, 1999; Folstein & Santangelo, 2000; Mueller & Courchesne, 2000; Rutter, 2000; Szatmari, 1999).

Much current research in this area involves looking for specific genetic and other chromosomal abnormalities associated with the emergence of autism (Bartlett, Gharani, Millonig, & Brzustowicz, 2005; Ghaziuddin & Burmeister, 1999; International Molecular Genetic Study of Autism Consortium, 1998; Pennington, 2002; Schellenberg et al., 2006). These investigations are consistent with evidence that autism is sometimes associated with other genetically transmitted disorders, including fragile X syndrome and tuberous sclerosis (Filipek, 1999; Pennington, 2002); they may also provide useful information about the origins of the sex difference in prevalence rates (Koenig et al., 2000). Interactions between genetic vulnerability and environmental factors are also being examined (Croen, Grether, & Selvin, 2002; Rodier & Hyman, 1998), although neither prenatal infections nor birth complications appear to be a direct cause of the disorder (Pennington, 2002; Shi, Tu, & Patterson, 2005; Zwaigenbaum et al., 2002). Childhood vaccines and immunizations have also been repeatedly and convincingly ruled out as causes of autism (Dales, Hammer, & Smith, 2001; Madsen et al., 2002, 2003; Offit, 2008; Schreibman, 2005).

Given all of the genetic data, the neuropsychological realm can be searched for further clues about etiology. Within a neuropsychological framework, we are looking for associations among brain structure, brain physiology, and brain chemistry in order to make hypotheses about brain dysfunction and the multiple domains of impairment observed in autistic children (Gillberg, 1999; Klin & Volkmar, 1997; Rourke, 1989). In addition, genetics likely explain much of the association between autism and mental retardation. Abnormalities in brain structure, physiology, and chemistry for the autism spectrum disorders overlap with abnormalities identified in mental retardation.

Another genetic hypothesis involves the **"extreme male brain theory of autism"** (Baron-Cohen, 2002a; Baron-Cohen, Wheelwright, Lawson, Griffin, & Hill, 2002). Whereas Asperger hypothesized about the transmission of personality traits observed in Asperger syndrome (Koenig et al., 2000), Baron-Cohen and his co-investigators go further. They highlight the evolutionary role of sex-linked dimensions of brain functioning (such as the logical, systematic thinking characteristic of men and the relational empathy characteristic of women) and suggest that autism may be an extreme example of the "normal" male profile. With this model, Asperger syndrome might even be understood as a *developmental difference* rather than a *developmental disability* (Baron-Cohen, 1997, 2000, 2002b; Baron-Cohen, Wheelwright, Skinner, Martin, & Clubley, 2001).

Various physical abnormalities in brain structure have been observed (Akshoomoff et al., 2004; Courchesne, 1997; Sparks et al., 2002; Tsatsanis et al., 2003), with macrocephaly (an enlarged brain and/or head) described in a subset of children (Filipek, 1999; Folstein & Santangelo, 2000; Ghaziuddin, Zaccagnini, Tsai, & Elardo, 1999). Abnormalities have also been identified in the cerebellum, medial temporal lobe, and amygdala (Allen & Courchesne, 2003; Baron-Cohen et al., 2000; Bauman & Kemper, 2005; Dawson, Meltzoff, Osterling, & Rinaldi, 1998; Pierce & Courchesne, 2001). A current focus in brain research involves the unusual brain growth patterns documented for children with autism, what Courchesne calls "growth without guidance." The **growth dysregulation hypothesis** proposes that the normally well-controlled process of brain growth and organization goes awry, leading to the clinical symptoms of autism (Akshoomoff, Pierce, & Courchesne, 2002; Courchesne & Pierce, 2005; Courchesne, Redclay, Morgan, & Kennedy, 2005).

There are mixed data about general neurophysiological differences. EEG abnormalities and variations in metabolic processing have been observed (Dawson et al., 1995; Welsh, Ahn, & Placantonakis, 2005), but not in all children with autism (Filipek, 1999). Investigators have recently put forth new hypotheses about specific hemispheric dysfunctions (Folstein & Santangelo, 2000; Gunter, Ghaziuddin, & Ellis, 2002), and impaired connectivity between hemispheres (Minshew & Williams, 2007). With respect to more specific neurophysiological differences, particularly involving the processing of social stimuli, there are interesting results. There appear to be widespread difficulties in processing facial features, facial emotion, and the inner state of others (Baron-Cohen et al., 1999, 2000; Dawson, Webb, Wijsman et al., 2005; Dawson, Carver et al., 2002; Pierce, Mueller, Ambrose, Allen, & Courchesne, 2001; Schultz, 2005; see Box 8.1). Atypical brain activation patterns are also observed during tasks involving motor activation and spatial attention (Harris, Courchesne, Townsend, Carper, & Lord, 1999; Mueller, Pierce, Ambrose, Allen, & Courchesne, 2001; Townsend et al., 2001). Elevated levels of the neurotransmitter serotonin have been described in about one-fourth of those with autism; the consequences of this are yet unclear (Chandana et al., 2005; Pennington, 2002; Scott & Deneris, 2005; Whitaker-Azmitia, 2005).

Neuropsychological approaches to etiology also contribute to discussions about the connections between autism and Asperger syndrome. With improved research designs and techniques, comparisons of neuropsychological profiles (including brain structure, physiology, and chemistry) are increasingly suggestive of differences in children with autism and children with Asperger syndrome (Folstein & Santangelo, 2000; Lincoln, Courchesne, Allen, Hanson, & Ene, 1998; Miller & Ozonoff, 2000; Volkmar & Klin, 2000). Klin and Volkmar (1997) summarize the key issues and findings: Autism is "a constitutional inability to react differentially to social stimuli, expressed developmentally in a lack of interest in, and limited capacity to attach to, others, whereas Asperger syndrome is traced to a specific cluster of neurological deficits affecting the ability to process nonverbal stimuli, expressed developmentally in terms of an inability to interact competently with others despite a keen interest in, and motivation to interact with, other people" (Klin & Volkmar, 1997, p. 217).

Assessment and Diagnosis

As with many other diagnoses, there have been important changes in the classification and diagnosis of the autism spectrum disorders over time. These changes reflect greater differentiation of related but distinct disorders within the autism spectrum, as well as changes in theories of etiology. Not all of these changes, however, have led to greater clarity. Indeed, interpretation and application of the current DSM-IV criteria are confusing and often inconsistent. Whereas broad diagnostic decisions about the presence or absence of a pervasive developmental disorder have improved, much gray area remains in regard to specific diagnostic decisions (Mayes et al., 2001; Miller & Ozonoff, 1997). Tony Attwood (1998) provides a useful analogy involving plaid fabrics. He says that most everyone agrees that many different patterns are plaid, but acknowledges that each specific pattern is unique. Children with autism spectrum disorders may all be thought of as wearing plaid clothes, yet each child's pattern of plaid is unique. However we come to understand the tremendous variability in these disorders, we are ultimately responsible for understanding and treating *the child*, not his or her diagnostic label.

Establishing Diagnostic Criteria

Remember that people in general, and anxious parents in particular, may need a diagnostic construct to help organize, order, and manage their thoughts and concerns (Klin, 2002). Consequently, there is often considerable pressure on clinicians to expand the boundaries of the autism and Asperger syndrome diagnoses. As already noted, these primary categories function as a kind of benchmark in evaluating symptoms of pervasive developmental disorders. And, in fact, clinicians are quite reliable when diagnosing **prototypical cases** (i.e., the most typical or standard examples of a disorder, with the most representative characteristics present) of autism and Asperger syndrome; clinicians have more difficulty when presented with atypical cases (Klin, Lang, Cicchetti, & Volkmar, 2000; Klin, Sparrow, et al., 2000; Mahoney et al., 1998). It remains especially challenging to distinguish between high-functioning autism and Asperger syndrome. Thus, "as [Asperger syndrome] becomes a more well-known and perhaps fashionable label, it may be applied in an often unwarranted fashion by practitioners who intend to convey only that their client is currently experiencing difficulties in social interaction and in peer relationships. As the disorder is meant as a serious and debilitating developmental syndrome... parents should be briefed about the present unsatisfactory state of knowledge about Asperger syndrome and the common confusions of use and abuse of the diagnostic concept currently prevailing in the mental health community" (Klin, Sparrow, et al., 2000, p. 312).

Although sometimes reluctant to use the **pervasive developmental disorder, not otherwise specified (PDD-NOS)** label because of its lack of precision, the truth is that the majority of children within the broad category of pervasive developmental disorder are appropriately identified with PDD-NOS. This does not reflect a lack of diagnostic rigor, but rather illustrates the myriad ways in which disruptions to the developmental domains of relatedness and communication may be expressed (Walker et al., 2004). In addition, children who receive the diagnosis of PDD-NOS often exhibit various problem behaviors in addition to the core symptoms of autism. These include aggression, impulsivity and hyperactivity, and anxiety (Holtmann, Bolte, & Poustka, 2007; Sukhodolsky et al., 2008).

In evaluating the autism spectrum disorders, the first consideration is whether the core symptoms related to sociability, communication, and dysfunctional behaviors are present. This will determine whether a PDD disorder is the focus of assessment, or whether some other category of disorder or developmental delay is more appropriately diagnosed.

If these basic criteria are met, then more detailed information-gathering will inform the decision of which specific PDD diagnosis is most relevant. Given that complex diagnoses require complex assessments, interdisciplinary teams including medical, psychological, speech and language, and other professionals provide the most effective evaluations (Filipek et al., 1999; Klin, Sparrow, et al., 2000; Koenig et al., 2000). While there remains some reluctance to increase the anxiety of parents of very young children who exhibit some of the unusual symptoms of autism, there is no question that autism, once identified, is a stable diagnosis. The positives of early identification, and immediate initiation of treatment, outweigh the negatives (Baird et al., 2000; Filipek et al., 1999; Romanczyk et al., 2005). Brief assessment as a part of well-child visits to general practitioners and pediatricians is one way to address parent questions and concerns, and the American Academy of Pediatrics now calls for screening for autism spectrum disorders as part of well-child check ups (Johnson, Myers, & the Council on Children with Disabilities, 2007).

Parent Interviews

Parent interviews are often the source of very useful information, including information about early development, medical history, and family background. A careful history involves much reliance on parent recall of past events, and retrospective data is sometimes unreliable. However, parental concerns must be taken very seriously (Glascoe, 1997, 2000; Goin & Myers, 2004; Goin-Kochel & Myers, 2005; Howlin & Moore, 1997; Mesibov, Schroeder, & Wesson, 1993), because "parents *usually are correct* in their concerns about their child's development" (Filipek et al., 1999, p. 450). Further, "parents rarely complain of social delays or problems, so any and all such concerns should be immediately investigated" (Filipek et al., 1999, p. 452).

Physical and Psychological Examinations

In addition to parent interviews, a thorough physical examination is an important part of any autism assessment. It is essential that physical factors such as hearing loss, lead poisoning, and other medical syndromes be fully considered. Once these possibilities have been ruled out, there are both general and syndrome-specific assessments that take place. General psychological assessments include examinations of cognitive and intellectual functioning, neuropsychological performance, adaptive and socioemotional adjustment, and educational evaluations (Filipek et al., 1999; Klin, Sparrow, et al., 2000). Particular patterns of results, such as uneven cognitive profiles (with children with autism doing better on performance tasks and children with Asperger syndrome doing better on verbal tasks), may provide important information for later differential diagnosis (Klin, Sparrow, et al., 2000; Joseph et al., 2002). Keeping in mind that the key diagnostic features of all of the autism spectrum disorders are severe social difficulties and deviance, clinicians pay special attention to the social domain, including any disabilities that are present, the types of odd social interests that children display, and the social elements of language such as prosody (Klin, 2002).

Checklists and Rating Scales

Syndrome-specific assessments have also been developed to aid the often difficult diagnostic process, and the design and refinement of valid, reliable, and practical measures is the focus of much current research (Boyle et al., 1997; Lord & Risi, 1998). For example, the Modified Checklist for Autism in Toddlers (M-CHAT) is designed for early identification and consists of 23 yes/no questions; the Autism Observation Scale for Infants is also designed for early assessments (Bryson, Zwaigenbaum, McDermott, Rombough, & Brian, 2008; Dumont-Mathieu & Fein, 2005; Robins, Fein, Barton, & Green, 2001). The Autism Diagnostic Interview (Lord, Rutter, & LeCouteur, 1994) is a more extensive protocol in which the child's caregiver provides a detailed description of behaviors reflecting the diagnostic criteria for autism. Similarly, the Childhood Autism Rating Scale (Schopler, Reichler, & Renner, 1988) is a scale commonly used by clinicians to assess autism spectrum symptoms throughout childhood. The Autism Diagnostic Observational Schedule (Lord et al., 2000) is an assessment instrument in which the examiner engages the child directly in a series of semi-structured interactions designed to elicit behaviors associated with autism. For example, examiners may attempt to make eye contact or play cooperatively. Finally, there are several screening instruments for Asperger syndrome (Ehlers, Gillberg, & Wing, 1999; Scott, Baron-Cohen, Bolton, & Brayne, 2002a; Wing, Leekam, Libby, Gould, & Larcombe, 2002), including the Australian Scale for Asperger's Syndrome, a rating scale completed by either the parent or the teacher of high-functioning older children.

Differential Diagnosis

With changing conceptualizations of the autism spectrum disorders, the various ways in which children present symptoms, and the frequent revisions of diagnostic criteria, clinicians are likely to have a very difficult time with differential diagnosis. Before making decisions about the specific form of pervasive developmental disorder, clinicians must consider and set aside diagnoses of language disorders, obsessive-compulsive disorder, and schizoid personality disorder (Filipek et al., 1999; Folstein & Santangelo, 2000; Klin, Sparrow, et al., 2000; Scheeringa, 2001; Wolff, 2000). The diagnosis of mental retardation requires special attention, because some children are best diagnosed with mental retardation alone, one of the autism spectrum disorders alone, or both. In addition, clinicians must carefully work through decisions about disorders such as the newly proposed multiplex developmental disorder (Klin, Mayes, Volkmar, & Cohen, 1995; Paul et al., 1999; Scheeringa, 2001; Zalsman & Cohen, 1998) and related and possibly overlapping disorders such as nonverbal learning disability and semantic-pragmatic disorder (which may be confusing because they involve different terms used by different kinds of mental health professionals) (Bishop, 2000; Rourke & Tsatsanis, 2000; Volkmar & Klin, 2000).

Comorbid Conditions

Comorbid conditions present yet another layer of difficulty. Decisions about which of several disorders best approximates a particular child's clinical presentation are often complicated by the possibility of the child having more than one disorder. Mental retardation is perhaps the most frequent co-diagnosis. But from time to time clinicians also include Tourette's syndrome (Baron-Cohen, Scahill, Izaguirre, Hornsey, & Robertson, 1999; Folstein & Santangelo, 2000; Klin, Sparrow, et al., 2000), internalizing disorders, and externalizing disorders (Ghaziuddin, 2002; Ghaziuddin, Ghaziuddin, & Greden, 2002; Kim, Szatmari, Bryson, Streiner, & Wilson, 2000). An evaluation for depression is especially important as the child ages, and may be even more so for those children diagnosed with Asperger syndrome. As Klin and Volkmar (1997) describe, "Chronically frustrated by their repeated failures to engage others and make friends, some of these individuals develop symptoms of a mood disorder" (p. 218).

Final concerns related to assessment and diagnosis include the importance of repeating assessments and reviewing the diagnosis of autism spectrum disorders throughout development (Klin, Sparrow, et al., 2000). Work continues in several directions, with additional research on identifying a biological marker for various types of autism spectrum disorders (Bristol-Power & Spinella, 1999), and more specific investigations of the symptoms of autism in infants and toddlers (Bristol-Power & Spinella, 1999), in preschool-aged children (Lord & Risi, 2000), and in adolescents and adults (Mesibov, 1988).

Intervention

Think about how frustrating it has been to read that we do not have a precise definition of autism or the disorders related to autism. Think about how much more enlightening it would have been to read about the specific etiological factors and the predictable developmental pathways of autism and Asperger syndrome. Now consider how parents and teachers of children with autism must feel as they consider the multitude of treatment options, some offering slow and steady progress and others promising miraculous improvements. Parents in particular may have limited sources of information (Mackintosh, Myers, & Goin-Kochel, 2006); they are often desperate for help and confused about their options, leading them to embrace popular yet useless strategies such as facilitated communication, chelation (i.e., the removal of heavy metals from the bloodstream), and oxygen therapy (Mesibov, 1995; Offit, 2008; Schopler, 2001; Schreibman, 2005). With these considerations and Koenig et al.'s (2000) assertion that "In the absence of a definitive cure there are a thousand treatments" (p. 306) in mind, we will emphasize the imperative for **research-based intervention** (Schopler, Yirmiya, Shulman, & Marcus, 2001).

Pharmacological Treatment

Given the evidence for genetic involvement in the autism spectrum disorders, it is reasonable to examine psychopharmacological interventions. Those with autism are a "heavily medicated clinical population," with older individuals, individuals living in out-of-home settings, and individuals with mental retardation most likely to receive medications

(Martin, Patzer, & Volkmar, 2000, p. 217). The most frequently prescribed drugs include antidepressants, stimulants, and neuroleptics; none of these drugs is specific to autism or Asperger syndrome (Martin et al., 2000). For the most part, these psychopharmacological efforts have been ineffective (Koenig et al., 2000; Pennington, 2002); indeed, "what is striking is the *lack* of major effect on the key features of autism" (Bailey et al., 1996, p. 92). There is some interesting recent work, however, with new prescription strategies (Towbin, 2003), metabolic approaches (Page, 2000), research on serotonin receptors and dysregulation (Potenza & McDougle, 1997), and some reports that drugs may be useful for children with aggressive or self-injurious behaviors (Harris, 1995; Martin et al., 2000). As with mental retardation, there are data that support the use of medications for frequently occurring comorbid disorders (Erickson, Posey, Stigler, & McDougle, 2007; Nickels et al., 2008; Parikh, Kolevzon, & Hollander, 2008).

Psychological Treatment

The most effective treatments, based on years of clinical and empirical data, are the psychological treatments that emphasize social and behavioral techniques. Early and intensive interventions appear critical for meaningful improvements (Filipek et al., 1999; Jordan & Jones, 1999; Lord, Bristol & Schopler, 1993). Common features of these interventions include significant time commitments (often more than 20 hours per week), and highly structured efforts to facilitate the acquisition of basic language and social skills (Farran, 2000; Koenig et al., 2000). With this kind of time and effort, parents frequently serve as co-therapists, working with their children along with mental health professionals and aides (Schreibman & Koegel, 2005).

One of the most widely applied intervention strategies is **applied behavior analysis**, developed by Ivar Lovaas (Lovaas, 1987, 1993, 2003; Lovaas & Buch, 1997). This is an intensive behavioral approach, with near constant control and direction of the child and his/her environment. The approach begins as early as possible and involves more than 40 hours of intervention per week for two or more years. The focus is first on decreasing negative behaviors, and then on increasing language and peer interaction. The introduction of new behaviors must take into account the positive, enjoyable aspects of prosocial actions (Berney & Corbett, 2001; Harris, 1995). Finally, for some children, school readiness skills are included. The Lovaas approach is based on the discrete trial format, with a specific single behavior presented to the child by the therapist, then an immediate reward for response and imitation. In this way, complex behaviors are built from simple ones.

Some theorists believe that the strictly behavioral approach of Lovaas fails to demonstrate an appreciation for the unique developmental status of young children (Rogers & DiLalla, 1991; Rogers & Lewis, 1988). Rogers and his colleagues suggest that the social deficits that are at the core of autism spectrum disorders must be addressed within social relationships that the child controls. This is in contrast to the approach of Lovaas, whose strategies are based on the idea that the child with autism does not easily interact with his or her environment and so needs adults to direct learning opportunities. Other experts like Farran (2000) emphasize the importance of integrating these two perspectives. Recent work by Schreibman and her colleagues that focuses on key deficits or dysfunctions in autism, individual differences in response to treatments, and integration of multiple perspectives provides an excellent example of cutting-edge intervention (Schreibman & Anderson, 2001; Sherer & Schreibman, 2005).

One of the key difficulties that has received a lot of research and clinical focus is joint attention (JA). JA, as already discussed, is believed to underlie a number of later-emerging social-communication problems. Early JA interventions are thought to change the developmental trajectories for children with autism spectrum disorders by reducing these later-emerging problems. JA interventions using behavioral techniques have led to increases in JA, as well as improvements in positive emotion, play, and spontaneous speech (Kasari, Paparella, Freeman, & Jahromi, 2008; Kasari, Freeman, & Paparella, 2006; Whalen & Schreibman, 2003; Whalen, Schreibman, & Ingersoll, 2006). It is also the case, however, that researchers and clinicians are increasingly focused on adapting to children's competencies. Several intervention studies have documented the positive outcomes of adults' joining with the focus of attention of children with autism, rather than attempting to redirect that attention (Aldred, Green, & Adams, 2004; Gernsbacher et al., 2008; Watson, 1998).

Much of the current work on treatment of autism spectrum disorders involves broadening the behavioral approach to include the natural aspects of the child's world. With respect to language, for instance, repetition of words and skills is done in the most natural context to strengthen the pragmatic impact of learning (Harris, 1995; Landa, 2000). Social interventions might require children to focus on peers and to practice their skills in real-life settings of home and school (Krasny, Williams, Provencal, & Ozonoff, 2003; Paul, 2003). In addition, some of the specific deficits associated with autism spectrum disorders require very creative techniques. One such technique involves using "thought bubbles" (used in cartoons and comic strips to indicate a character's thinking) to teach children with autism about the mental states of others (Wellman et al., 2002). Another approach makes use of nonsocial reinforcers to increase social behaviors (Ingersoll, Schreibman, & Tran, 2003). The Treatment and Education of Autistic and related Communication-Handicapped Children (TEACCH) model is a comprehensive intervention with convincing empirical support (Mesibov, 1994, 1997; Schopler, 1998). The intervention has seven components: (1) Improved adaptation, (2) Parent collaboration, (3) Individualized assessment, (4) Teaching structure, (5) Emphasis on skills, (6) Usefulness of cognitive and behavior therapy, and (7) A generalist training model (see Box 8.4).

School-Based Programs

Educational interventions present their own difficulties. Although many children with psychological disorders may benefit from time spent in mainstream classrooms, there is little actual evidence that shows benefits of inclusion for children with autism spectrum disorders (Klin & Volkmar, 2000; Mesibov & Shea, 1996). It may be that, unlike children with mental retardation, children with autism display a range and severity of social deficits that make integration less likely to succeed (Koenig et al., 2000).

Children with Asperger syndrome may require slightly different interventions than children with more classic autism presentations. As described early in this chapter, parents must often advocate forcefully for appropriate treatments for their children both at home and at school (Klin & Volkmar, 2000, 2003). The balance between academic and behavioral goals may have to be reworked, with an increased focus on social, emotional, and communication deficits (Attwood, 2003; Krasny et al., 2003; Kunce & Mesibov, 1998; Rhea, 2003; Tsatsanis, 2003). As with other PDD disorders, a symptom-focused approach is important in the treatment of Asperger syndrome. The most troubling symptoms

> **BOX 8:4   CLINICAL PERSPECTIVES**
>
> ## The TEACCH Model of Intervention
>
> The TEACCH program, originally developed by Eric Schopler and colleagues at the University of North Carolina in the 1970s, is a broad-based treatment program for autism that has become a major intervention approach used in communities throughout the world (Schopler, Mesibov, & Hearsey, 1995). This program is distinctive in its emphasis on careful individual assessment; its structured teaching program is based on that assessment and integrated into all aspects of the autistic person's day-to-day life. The structured teaching plan includes careful organization of the physical environment and daily schedule, as well as clear expectations and rules. Additionally, this approach advocates for an increased respect for what is called the "culture of autism." Understanding this culture involves recognizing the unique ways individuals with autism view their environment and experience the physical and social world. Interventions, then, are designed to be consistent with this sensibility. Methods that emphasize the relative strengths of autism—such as strong memory, good visual processing skills, and recognition of details—are utilized and promoted wherever possible. These treatment principles are then integrated across systems and settings including home and school through comprehensive services such as social skills training, vocational training, and parent counseling and training.

must be identified and made the treatment priority. This can only be accomplished through careful assessment and the input of the child, the family, and the school. Strengths, as well as weaknesses, must be considered and built upon. Intervention efforts should be consistently applied across settings, and where possible, coordinated. A desire to live in the social world, coupled with the lack of skills required to do this comfortably, is a defining trait of Asperger syndrome. Intervention techniques, then, that focus on a variety of social and communication skills are core components of any intervention plan. For example, specific techniques to improve conversation skills, especially those related to pragmatic conversation, and well-rehearsed responses to everyday social situations might be emphasized. For those with Asperger syndrome, the motivation to relate to others means that anxiety and depression are secondary clinical issues that may need to be addressed in therapy, and possibly with medication. For these kinds of issues, therapy that promotes some degree of self-awareness and recognizes what kinds of situations may cause distress becomes important.

Increasingly, schools are dedicating resources to establish educational intervention programs for students with special learning needs related to their Asperger syndrome diagnosis. The best of these programs combine individual attention and work on relationships. This combination allows for specific skills to be addressed as well as the more complex skills required to function as part of a group. Additionally, it helps to have a skilled and caring professional who can establish and mediate a meaningful therapeutic relationship that can be the basis from which other social connections develop. Above all, we must always remember that these intervention strategies are in the service of helping a child, not fixing a disorder. As Klin and Volkmar (2000) emphasize, "Care providers should embrace the wide range of expression and complexity of the disorder, avoiding dogmatism in favor of practical, individualized, and commonsense clinical judgment" (p. 347).

Although psychological treatments for the autism spectrum disorders necessarily target the child, the needs of the family must also be addressed (Koenig et al., 2000). Because in almost all cases of child disorder, the "family is the child's best resource" (Filipek et al., 1999, p. 466), an assessment of the family's functioning and resources is important. Information and supportive services make a difference. As children with autism spectrum disorders age, intervention strategies and goals are likely to be revised, with specific treatments and supports designed for adolescents and adults (Mesibov, 1992; Van Bourgondien, Reichle, & Schopler, 2003). Residential options and vocational training are necessary components of developmentally appropriate plans that are geared toward maximizing each individual's potential and well-being (Klin & Volkmar, 2000; Mesibov, 1992; Van Bourgondien et al., 2003).

■ Key Terms

Autism (pg. 122)
Asperger syndrome (pg. 122)
Pervasive developmental disorders (pg. 122)
Social cognition (pg. 124)
Joint attention (pg. 124)
Theory of mind (pg. 124)
Affective social competence (pg. 124)
Mindblindness (pg. 129)
Central coherence hypothesis (pg. 129)
Pragmatics (pg. 131)
Developmental disorder (pg. 134)
Extreme male brain theory of autism (pg. 135)
Growth dysregulation hypothesis (pg. 136)
Prototypical cases (pg. 137)
Pervasive developmental disorder, not otherwise specified (PDD-NOS) (pg. 137)
Research-based intervention (pg. 139)
Applied behavior analysis (pg. 139)

■ Chapter Summary

- Autism spectrum disorder is a broad term, used in a variety of contexts, reflecting compromised development in social functioning and communication, as well as restricted patterns of activities or interests.
- Pervasive developmental disorder (PDD) is the DSM-IV-TR general diagnostic category that includes the autism spectrum disorders, including autistic disorder and Asperger syndrome.
- Asperger syndrome is primarily differentiated from autism by the lack of delayed language development and generally normal-range intelligence.

- Current research is focused on determining whether these disorders are best conceptualized as distinct disorders or as different points along a single autism spectrum.
- Theory of mind refers to the ability to understand that others have their own mental state or perspective, and is an example of an important psychological process compromised in the development of autism spectrum disorders.
- Although children with autism spectrum disorders are a heterogeneous group, quantitative and qualitative deficits in social and emotional development are core symptoms for almost all of them; these include difficulties in differentiating between social and nonsocial stimuli.
- Children with a diagnosis of autism often have deficits and deviations in specific cognitive and language skills independent of global cognitive delays.
- Children diagnosed with Asperger syndrome show normal-range basic language development, but significant deficits in the pragmatics of cognition and language in social context.
- The core symptoms of the autism spectrum disorders generally present lifelong challenges and compromised social functioning.
- Reflecting the myriad patterns of deficits that characterize the autism spectrum disorders, most children in the spectrum are best characterized under the PDD-NOS diagnosis.
- The broad array of symptoms and varied degree of compromised functioning necessitates multiple assessment and intervention strategies. The most successful interventions are those that are delivered early and intensively across a variety of domains of functioning.

CHAPTER 9

Attention Deficit Hyperactivity Disorder

ATTENTION DEFICIT HYPERACTIVITY DISORDER (ADHD) is a disorder that is complexly-determined, both over- and underdiagnosed, and often inadequately treated. With its prevalence and readily recognizable symptoms of impulsivity, restlessness, and inattentiveness, as well as the fact that evaluations for ADHD account for a large proportion of referrals to children's primary care and mental health clinics (Brown et al., 2001; DuPaul & Barkley, 2008), ADHD is a focus of controversy. In part, controversy results from the difficulty in distinguishing between *patterns of normally distributed childhood characteristics* including behavioral characteristics such as self-control, emotional characteristics such as temperament traits, and cognitive characteristics such as information-processing style, and a *clinically significant pattern* of behavioral, emotional, and cognitive characteristics. For individuals, families, and mental health professionals, ADHD is presumed to reside a few steps across a fuzzy boundary toward disorder and impairment. Ongoing debates related to ADHD include the nature of children (boys in particular) and of schooling, the widespread use of psychotropic medication, and the extent to which those diagnosed with ADHD are "responsible" for their disorder. Given its significant impact on the development of self, relationships, and academic/vocational success, and the social and moral overtones of some discussions, ADHD requires thoughtful investigation.

Developmental Tasks and Challenges Related to Attention and Self-Control

Because ADHD is frequently diagnosed in the early school years, it makes sense to examine the normally occurring developmental challenges that children encounter as they make the transition to more structured school environments. We would not expect, for example, any 6-year-old child to sit attentively through a 90-minute university lecture. A young child who fidgeted and was distracted in such a situation would not be showing evidence of ADHD. On the other hand, it is reasonable to expect a 10-year-old child to listen to a teacher's directions before beginning a classroom assignment. The child's consistent failure to do so might indeed be cause for concern.

Without an appropriate developmental context for understanding children's behaviors, a boy's keen curiosity and classroom boredom may be misjudged as reflecting some underlying psychopathology. Another child's academic struggles may be mischaracterized as a sign of laziness, and actual signs of disorder may not be recognized. In order to avoid diagnostic errors, we need to keep in mind the many accomplishments of school-age children. During these years, there are cognitive advances, as well as progress in personal and social maturity, although there is much individual variation in the specific timing and nature of children's capacities for learning, self-regulation, and self-reflection (Blair, 2002; Rueda, Posner, & Rothbart, 2005).

With respect to academic tasks, there are a myriad of learning-related capacities and skills, each with its own maturational and practice timeline (Barkley, 1997a, 1997b; Brocki & Bohlin, 2004). For example, both memory and attentional processes show clear evidence of age-related improvement (Chang & Burns, 2005; Nelson, 1995, 1997; Posner & Rothbart, 1998; Rueda et al., 2005). Barkley (1997b, 2004) describes the cognitive development of several **executive functions** (i.e., processes involving the conscious control of thoughts, emotions, and behavior), including working memory, internalization of speech, and self-regulation of emotion, that contribute to children's increasing control over their behavior and their interactions with others and their environments (see Figure 9.1). Increases in preschoolers' effortful or inhibitory control (Kochanska, Murray, & Coy, 1997; Kochanska, Murray, & Harlan, 2000; Kopp, 1982; Li-Grining, 2007), and declines in preschoolers' distractibility and impulsivity are well-described (Kopp, 1989; Murphy, Eisenberg, Fabes, Shepard, & Guthrie, 1999). Planning and organizational abilities also develop throughout

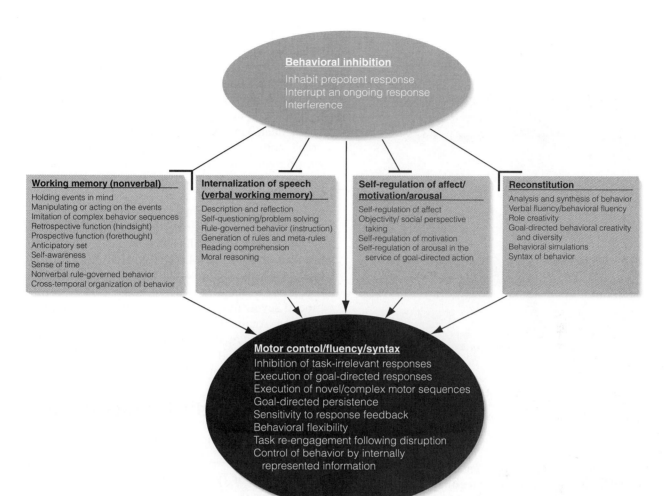

FIGURE 9:1 Four executive functions and their relations to behavioral inhibition and motor control processes.
Source: From Barkley, R.A. (1977), "Behavioral inhibition, sustained attention, and executive functions: Constructing a unifying theory of ADHD", 'Psychological Bulletin', 121 (1), 65-94. Copyright © 1977 American Psychological Association. Reprinted by permission.

the school years (Barkley, 1997a, 1997b; Hudson & Fivush, 1991; Kopp, 1997), including the identification and selection of strategies for delay of gratification (Eigsti et al., 2006; Peake, Hebl, & Mischel, 2002). In school, these abilities are reflected in young children attending to the directions for an assignment, raising a hand before calling out an answer, waiting quietly for other students to complete classwork, and following the playground rules for sharing and taking turns.

These types of cognitive abilities underlie children's expected progress and mastery of early school skills, including reading and mathematics. They also contribute to ongoing ego development related to **ego control** (i.e., the ability to modulate thoughts, feelings, and behaviors, similar to the

self-regulatory skills defined below) and **ego resiliency** (i.e., the ability to respond flexibly and adaptively to new or stressful situations) (Block & Block, 2006; Chuang, Lamb, & Hwang, 2006; Eisenberg et al., 2003; Gjerde, Block, & Block, 1986; Kochanska, Tjebkes, & Forman, 1998; Troy, 1989). In addition, there are well-documented changes in the ways in which children appraise themselves, their cognitive and academic abilities, and their progress toward goals. During the elementary school years, children view their abilities in, for example, reading and mathematics, as increasingly stable and pay more attention to performance evaluations, especially those related to competence or incompetence (Pomerantz & Altermatt, 1999; Pomerantz & Eaton, 2001).

Care must be taken to differentiate the active, often physical, play of boys from behavioral symptoms of ADHD.

Laurence Mouton/PhotoAlto/Alamy

It is clear that behavioral, cognitive, and emotional **self-regulatory skills** (i.e., a set of abilities related to control of thoughts, feelings, and behaviors) are necessary to achieve school success. More broadly, these skills also have an important impact on the development of a positive sense of self (Kopp & Wyer, 1994; Mascolo & Fischer, 1998), and on children's abilities to achieve success in relationships with parents, siblings, teachers, and peers (Karreman, van Tuijl, van Aken, & Dekovic, 2008; Kopp, 1989; Liew, Eisenberg, & Reiser, 2004; McCabe & Brooks-Gunn, 2007). Indeed, the negotiation of the ever-widening social environment is a significant developmental milestone (Barrett, 2005; Eisenberg, Spinrad, & Smith, 2004; Hartup, 1980; Sroufe, Egeland, & Carlson, 1999). As an illustration of this social achievement, Cantwell (1996) describes the "social savoir-faire" displayed by many school-age children. Again, most children are able (most of the time) to reflect on their own behaviors and emotions, read others' social signals, and modify interactions in ways that promote satisfactory relationships.

Attention Deficit Hyperactivity Disorder

With the increasingly frequent diagnosis of ADHD, there have been repeated suggestions that the very nature of children, especially boys, places them at higher risk for the misidentification of disorders such as ADHD. Young children are active, boisterous, distractible, and willful. Many young boys exhibit very strong needs for extended periods of play, including rough-and-tumble play (Panksepp, 1998). These children often require parents and teachers to creatively and patiently and repeatedly provide direction, assistance, and control. In combination with the requirements of early schooling, some adults may perceive some children's demanding characteristics as evidence of psychopathology. The accuracy or inaccuracy of these perceptions must be carefully evaluated with respect to the many varieties of developmentally *appropriate,* developmentally *meaningful,* and developmentally *necessary* challenges and struggles (Panksepp, 1998). And, while both the formal characteristics of schools and the dynamic characteristics of education change in response to social concerns, political reforms, and research on learning, the current context of schooling requires children to rein themselves in: to balance self-expression with restraint.

The Case of Tyler

Tyler is an 11-year-old boy in the fifth grade referred for a psychological evaluation by his parents following several meetings with school teachers and the assistant principal. Major concerns included Tyler's distractibility, difficulty completing tasks, verbal impulsivity, and restlessness. Tyler is a very bright, creative child who loves to read. His parents and teachers note that he loves to be busy, and "always wants to do more." Tyler has a good sense of humor. And his teachers describe his very long attention span for some subjects, such as reading, which he especially enjoys.

But most of the time Tyler does not listen or pay close attention to what is expected of him, is very easily distracted, and has difficulty organizing and following through with tasks. Tyler often forgets to bring needed items home from school and back to school from home. Tyler is also very fidgety and restless and has difficulty sitting still. As he gets up and moves about the room, sometimes making noises, he is distracting and disruptive to the other students. He sometimes carries toys with him, and plays with them at inappropriate times. Tyler needs frequent reminders to stay focused, although he is usually cooperative when teachers intervene. He is proud of his excellent reading skills, but has been discouraged by his struggles with math and his difficulty completing schoolwork in a timely way.

Tyler's behaviors with others are also troublesome. He talks "incessantly" and often socializes when he should be doing schoolwork. Tyler is verbally impulsive, frequently blurting out remarks that are hurtful. He sometimes gets into conflicts with peers because of his impulsivity and his wish to be in charge. At home, Tyler and his brother "get each other going" and can together become "wild and crazy." His 14-year-old brother has been diagnosed with ADHD and has responded well to stimulant medication. ■

The Case of Christopher

Christopher is an 8-year-old boy in the second grade who was referred for an evaluation by his parents after consultations with school staff and his pediatrician. His parents described Christopher's difficulty with schoolwork and chores, distractibility, and "spacing out." At the end of the previous school year, his report card included this teacher comment: "Christopher is easily distracted, though his off-task behaviors don't disturb others, only himself. He sometimes appears to daydream or be in his own little world. Christopher's distractions may be preventing him from working to his full potential." At the beginning of this school year, Christopher's new teacher also noticed his classroom difficulties, discussing with his parents his tendency to "drift off" and the slow pace of his work (Christopher is always the last to finish any assignment).

When asked about school, Christopher is positive, saying that he likes school, his teacher, and music class. Christopher says that he often needs extra time to complete assignments and acknowledges having difficulty listening, paying attention, and concentrating. He feels that this is particularly difficult when it is noisy in the classroom. Christopher also agrees that he frequently becomes frustrated with his own performance on school projects. At times, he may give up in disgust when he does not meet his own high standard.

His parents describe Christopher as an affectionate, sensitive child who is usually cheerful and cooperative. He is "fun to be around." Christopher enjoys art and music and loves to sing. He is a very social child who has many friends. He may hang back briefly in new

situations but warms up quickly. Christopher is occasionally fidgety but has never seemed hyperactive. His parents agree that Christopher is easily distracted and needs frequent reminders to complete everyday tasks such as picking up his room or doing his homework. He often forgets or misplaces his belongings, is critical of himself for forgetting things, and worries about doing things right. His parents believe that these behaviors are more problematic at school than at home. ■

Not all children present with identical clinical difficulties. There are differences in the particular symptoms displayed, the combination and severity of symptoms, and the range and depth of impairments. In all cases of **Attention deficit hyperactivity disorder (ADHD)**, however, the child's abilities to meet the day-to-day tasks and demands that depend on attention and impulse control—at school, at home, and during baseball or piano practice—are compromised. ADHD is characterized by a variety of specific behavioral and cognitive symptoms involving both developmental delays and developmental deficits in the areas of inattention, impulsivity, and hyperactivity (see Table 9.1). These three broad categories of problem behaviors are, in fact, usually interpreted as reflecting compromised functioning in two underlying dimensions or domains: inattention and hyperactivity/impulsivity. Consequently, the formal diagnosis of ADHD may be based on significant problems in *either one or both* of these domains.

Core Characteristics

It is important to keep in mind that much of the information about the core characteristics of ADHD is based on investigations of elementary-school-age North American boys. There are fewer data on younger children, girls, and children of different racial and ethnic backgrounds. Recent investigations have included more diverse samples of children (Abikoff et al., 2002; Gingerich, Turnock, Litfin, & Rosen, 1998; Samuel et al., 1999; Sharp et al., 1999), and have explored potential causes of variable prevalence rates across cultures. In surveys of North America, South America, Europe, Africa, Asia, Oceania, and the Middle East, the worldwide prevalence of ADHD is estimated at 5.2% (Polanczyk, de Lima, Horta, Biederman, & Rohde, 2007). Differences in prevalence were most often associated with methodological factors (e.g., combinations of diagnostic criteria); few differences in prevalence were observed in comparisons between North America and Europe (Polanczyk et al., 2007).

TABLE 9:1   SELECTED DSM-IV-TR CRITERIA FOR ATTENTION DEFICIT HYPERACTIVITY DISORDER

A. Either (1) or (2):

(1) Six or more symptoms of inattention that have persisted for at least 6 months, are maladaptive, and are inconsistent with developmental level:
   a. often fails to give close attention to details; makes careless mistakes in schoolwork or other activities
   b. often has difficulty sustaining attention in play or other activities
   c. often does not listen when spoken to directly
   d. often does not follow through on instructions and fails to finish schoolwork, chores, etc.
   e. often has difficulty organizing tasks and activities
   f. often avoids, dislikes, or is reluctant to engage in tasks that require sustained mental effort
   g. often loses things necessary for tasks or activities
   h. is often easily distracted by extraneous stimuli
   i. is often forgetful in daily activities

(2) Six or more symptoms of hyperactivity-impulsivity that have persisted for at least 6 months, are maladaptive, and are inconsistent with developmental level:
   a. often fidgets or squirms
   b. often leaves seat in classroom or in other situations
   c. often runs about or climbs excessively in situations in which it is inappropriate
   d. often has difficulty playing quietly
   e. is often "on the go" or acts as if "driven by a motor"
   f. often talks excessively
   g. often blurts out answers
   h. often has difficulty waiting turn
   i. often interrupts or intrudes on others

B. Hyperactive-impulsive or inattentive symptoms caused impairment before age 7.

C. Impairment is present in two or more settings.

SOURCE: Reprinted with permission from the Diagnostic and Statistical Manual of Mental Disorders, Text Revision, Fourth Edition, (Copyright 2000). American Psychiatric Association.

Interpretation of these data suggests that ADHD is a real disorder, not a social construct tied to permissiveness, and not a product of a profit-motivated pharmaceutical industry (Moffitt & Melchior, 2007; Rohde et al., 2005).

As described in DSM-IV-TR, there are basic delays and deficits in children's attentional processes. In Tyler's case, he meets the criterion of six symptoms of inattention, including failure to pay close attention to details, difficulty in sustaining attention, not listening, not finishing schoolwork, difficulty organizing, distraction, and forgetfulness. Christopher also meets the DSM-IV-TR criterion for problems with attention. With respect to hyperactivity-impulsivity, only Tyler meets the requirement of six symptoms. Tyler's symptoms include his need to be busy, fidgeting, leaving his seat in the classroom, excessive talking, blurting out remarks, and intrusive interactions. In addition, both Tyler and Christopher display their difficulties at school and at home. And both Tyler and Christopher have struggled since their early elementary years with these problems. That these symptoms are exhibited in multiple settings and have been apparent for several years meets the additional DSM-IV-TR criteria for pervasiveness, duration, and age of onset.

For some researchers, this set of diagnostic criteria implies that a specific number of symptoms is indicative of difficulties that are distinctively different from the difficulties experienced by typically developing children. For these individuals, ADHD is a **categorical disorder**, a disorder that is outside of the normal range of childhood behavior. In fact, the specific number of symptoms for diagnosis is somewhat arbitrary, reflecting both developmental deviance as well as the increasing likelihood that a child's functioning is compromised (Levy, Hay, McStephen, Wood, & Waldman, 1997). Even with the clinical need to make useful distinctions in terms of symptom patterns and impairment, we emphasize the probability that ADHD is best understood as a **continuous disorder**, one that lies on a continuum with normal development.

An alternative perspective on the core symptoms is provided by the work of Russell Barkley, who views ADHD as "a developmental delay in internalization and self-regulation" (Barkley, 1997b, p. 313). Barkley and others argue that the **core behavioral deficit** observed in children with ADHD is impulsivity, reflecting a basic impairment in the ability to delay responding to stimuli. In this model, the inattention and excessive motor activity are both accounted for by this impaired responding capacity. The executive functions of children with ADHD are also implicated, with differences in deficits and severity across children (Barkley, 2004; Clark, Prior, & Kinsella, 2002). According to Barkley (1997a, 1997b), the behavior of children with ADHD "will be less directed at maximizing the future and more directed at maximizing the moment. Being less internally guided and rule-governed, their behavior will seem to others as more chaotic, reactive, ill considered, and emotional, and as less organized, purposive, reflective, and objective" (p. 314). In other words, understanding the executive function deficits allows clinicians to better understand the cause and meaning of children's problematic behaviors.

Associated Difficulties

A child who struggles with the core symptoms of ADHD is also likely to struggle in a variety of other ways and in a variety of situations. Basic deficits in self-reflection and self-regulation will influence, for example, cognitive biases, communication processes, and emotional control (Saunders & Chambers, 1996). Children with ADHD may misperceive ambiguous stimuli, perhaps interpreting another child's accidental contact as intentional shoving. Children with ADHD may fail to wait their conversational turn and therefore repeatedly interrupt others. Also, children with ADHD may fail to appreciate the lingering impact of a nasty tantrum.

Some of the most common and most distressing difficulties associated with ADHD are related to **social dysfunction** (Greene et al., 2001; Hoza et al., 2005). For many, there is chronic conflict in social settings. Children with ADHD are quite unable, for example, to step back from a confusing event (such as an escalating disagreement over playground equipment), appreciate multiple perspectives, reflect on possible strategies for action, and negotiate with others. Further evidence of conflict is frequently observed at home during sibling interactions, with angry and sometimes physical exchanges over toys, seating arrangements, and television choices. This inability of children with ADHD to reflect and regulate will repeatedly interfere with the development

of easygoing, pleasant relationships at home, at school, and in neighborhoods. Indeed, Hoza et al. report that children with ADHD have fewer friends, are less well-liked, and are more often rejected by their peers.

Factor Structure and Internal Validity

The factor structure of ADHD provides basic data supporting the **internal validity** of the diagnosis. Historically, researchers and clinicians described ADHD in terms of three separate dimensions or constructs: inattention, hyperactivity, and impulsivity (DSM- III, 1980). Several years later, in DSM-III-R (1987), there was a shift to a unidimensional model of ADHD, with inattention, hyperactivity, and impulsivity all reflecting a single underlying deficit. By 1994 and DSM-IV, investigators were convinced that the clinical presentation of ADHD could not be adequately accounted for by a unidimensional model, and once again the disorder was reconceptualized, this time as bidimensional (Pillow, Pelham, Hoza, Molina, & Stultz, 1998). The current **two-factor model**, focused on inattention and hyperactivity/impulsivity, not only reflects clinical experience, but also is statistically supported by factor-analytic data of parent and teacher reports of ADHD symptoms (Bauermeister et al., 1995; Burns, Walsh, Owen, & Snell, 1997).

Another issue related to validity depends on the degree to which the particular symptoms of ADHD can be differentiated from the symptoms of other disorders, for example, oppositional-defiant disorder or conduct disorder. Again, there are data that support the notion that this particular two-factor pattern of symptoms observed in children diagnosed with ADHD is differentiated from the patterns observed in children diagnosed with other disorders of childhood (Barkley, Murphy, DuPaul, & Bush, 2002; Berlin, Bohlin, Nyberg, & Janols, 2004; Burns et al., 1997; Clark et al., 2002; Gadow & Nolan, 2002).

Diagnostic Subtypes

As seen in the DSM-IV-TR and in the case examples of Tyler and Christopher, there are several diagnostic subtypes of ADHD. Here again, the validity of the subtype classification must be considered. That is, are there meaningful differences among the patterns of symptoms and impairment in children diagnosed with ADHD-Inattentive Type, ADHD-Hyperactive/Impulsive Type, and ADHD-Combined Type? Several investigations support the validity of these classification distinctions (Faraone, Biederman, Weber, & Russell, 1998; Gaub & Carlson, 1997a; Lahey et al., 1998; Milich, Balentine, & Lynam, 2001; Power, Costigan, Eiraldi, & Leff, 2004). Gaub and Carlson, for example, reported that children diagnosed with ADHD-Inattentive Type exhibited impairment in behavioral, academic, and social domains, but more appropriate behavior and fewer externalizing problems than those children diagnosed with ADHD-Hyperactive/Impulsive Type or ADHD-Combined Type. In contrast, children with ADHD-Hyperactive/Impulsive Type had fewer additional internalizing problems than children with ADHD-Inattentive Type. As expected, children with ADHD-Combined Type exhibited the most severe and pervasive impairments.

Recent research on **sluggish cognitive tempo**, the inconsistent alertness and orientation displayed by some children (including Christopher), provides additional information about ADHD subtypes (Bauermeister et al., 2005; Hartman, Willcutt, Rhee, & Pennington, 2004; McBurnett, Pfiffner, & Frick, 2001; Todd, Rasmussen, Wood, Levy, & Hay, 2004). Children diagnosed with the inattentive subtype of ADHD who also exhibit symptoms of sluggish cognitive tempo are a relatively homogenous group with higher levels of anxiety and depression, withdrawn behavior, and social dysfunction (Carlson & Miranda , 2002).

Data related to the age of onset of ADHD also provides support for the usefulness of subtype classification. In general, the symptoms and impairments indicative of ADHD appear before the age of 7. In a clinical sample of 380 youths, ages 4 through 17, different age-of-onset patterns were observed (Applegate et al., 1997). Almost all of the children and adolescents diagnosed with the hyperactive-impulsive subtypes displayed symptoms and impairment before age 7. Most of the youths with the combined subtype (72%) also displayed symptoms and impairment before age 7. But fewer than half diagnosed with the inattentive subtype (43%) did so.

Gender, Ethnicity, and Age

One of the most replicated and controversial findings in ADHD studies is the striking gender difference in diagnosis. Boys receive diagnoses of ADHD *four to five times more often* than do girls. One explanation of the gender difference is that many more boys are diagnosed with the predominantly hyperactive subtype because parents and teachers misperceive boys' greater activity levels and impulsivity as evidence of psychopathology. Even in the case of roughly similar behaviors, boys may be the focus of

Children diagnosed with ADHD-Inattentive Type may have difficulty in the classroom, but relatively few externalizing behavior problems.

Brad Wilson/Stone/Getty Images

heightened concern, increased control, and earlier interventions.

Although there is continuing research on the clinical characteristics of ADHD in girls and children of various ethnic backgrounds, there are data that suggest that, for the most part, all children struggle in similar ways with the core symptoms of ADHD (Bauermeister et al., 2007; Biederman et al., 2005). In a review of 18 studies comparing the clinical presentations of girls and boys with ADHD, Gaub and Carlson (1997b) reported overall similarity. Some differences were observed, including more intellectual dysfunction, less hyperactivity, and fewer externalizing behaviors in girls. In another study, using mother and teacher reports, girls were more likely to be diagnosed with the inattentive subtype (Weiler, Bellinger, Marmor, Rancier, & Waber, 1999). Girls with ADHD are also more verbally aggressive (Abikoff et al., 2002). Overall, the disorder of ADHD appears to be as severe in girls as in boys (Gaub & Carlson, 1997b; Sharp et al., 1999). In studies of ADHD in African American children, preliminary evidence also suggests similarity in the clinical presentation (Samuel et al., 1998; Samuel et al., 1997).

Adolescents, like the younger boys and girls of diverse ethnic backgrounds, present a similar picture of symptoms, impairments, and comorbid disorders (Seidman et al., 2005). There are no data that support the hypothesis that those individuals diagnosed in childhood have more severe clinical difficulties than those diagnosed in adolescence (Biederman, Faraone et al., 1998). It is likely that other factors, as yet unidentified, contribute to the timing of diagnosis in certain children and adolescents. Finally, two recent patterns of diagnosis are noteworthy. First, ADHD is being identified at earlier ages, with many preschoolers meeting the diagnostic criteria (Greenhill, Posner, Vaughan, & Kratochvil, 2008). Second, ADHD is also increasingly identified at later ages, into adulthood, with adults displaying similar (although somewhat age-adjusted) patterns of symptoms (Faraone, Biederman, Mick, et al., 2000; Fayyad et al., 2007; Kessler et al., 2006; Wilens, Faraone, & Biederman, 2006).

Comorbidity

As children with ADHD get older, there are increasing rates of comorbid diagnoses, including both internalizing and externalizing disorders (Blackman, Ostrander, & Herman, 2005; Burns & Walsh,

2002; DuPaul & Barkley, 1998; Mannuzza, Klein, Abikoff, & Moulton, 2004; Murphy et al., 2002; Spencer, Wilens, Biederman, Wozniak, & Harding-Crawford, 2000; Waschbusch, 2002). Some of the most frequent psychiatric disorders seen along with ADHD, with estimated prevalence, include: oppositional defiant disorder (27–31%); conduct disorder (10–16%); mood and anxiety disorders (20–30%); learning disabilities, language disorders, and other learning problems (10–20%); and fine motor difficulties (50%) (Biederman, Faraone et al., 1998). Patterns of comorbidity appear similar for boys and girls (Biederman et al., 1999), and for children and adolescents. However, tic disorders, such as Tourette's disorder, appear to be overrepresented in boys with ADHD (Comings & Comings, 1988). The different ADHD subtypes display different patterns of risk. As expected, the ADHD-Inattentive subtype is associated with significantly greater risk for internalizing disorders such as anxiety and mood disorders, whereas the ADHD-Hyperactive/Impulsive subtype is associated with greater risk for externalizing disorders such as oppositional defiant disorder. The ADHD-Combined subtype is associated with greater risk for both internalizing and externalizing disorders. Hypotheses about the frequency of overlapping disorders include shared genetic etiologies, interactions between children with ADHD and their environments (parents, teachers, and peers), and complications from unrecognized or undertreated ADHD.

Several recent investigations have focused on the pathways between ADHD and later depression, and have emphasized the role of academic struggles, parent management strategies, and family environment in the development of depression (George, Herman, & Ostrander, 2006; Herman, Lambert, Ialongo, & Ostrander, 2007; Ostrander & Herman, 2006). A major longitudinal investigation of ADHD and mood disorders (Biederman, Faraone, et al., 1998) found that major depression occurred more frequently in their sample of 11-year-olds with ADHD (29%) compared to 11-year-olds in their comparison group (2%). Four years later, when the study participants were 15 years old, the rates of depression had risen to 45% for those with ADHD versus 6% for those without ADHD. A similar pattern was evident for the co-occurrence of anxiety disorders: 27% of the 11-year-olds with ADHD also were diagnosed with an anxiety disorder (35% at 15 years), whereas 5% of the comparison group were so diagnosed (9% at 15 years).

The comorbidity of ADHD and substance abuse has long been a research and clinical focus because of concerns that adolescents will abuse stimulants (especially if, for example, they have access to Ritalin). In fact, however, substance abuse is more common among adolescents who are not using medications (Mannuzza, Klein, & Moulton, 2003a; Wilens, Faraone, Biederman, & Gunawardene, 2003). For adolescents with diagnoses of both ADHD and substance abuse, the most frequently abused substance is marijuana (Spencer et al., 1996), although adolescents are also at risk for alcohol abuse and dependence (Biederman et al., 1997; Biederman, Wilens, et al., 1998).

More recently there has been considerable attention paid to the association between ADHD and bipolar disorder in childhood. While no clear consensus has yet emerged, there are a few early hypotheses that do seem to be supported. Children with ADHD have a small but significant risk for the development of bipolar disorder. Children with bipolar disorder have a high risk for ADHD. Children diagnosed with both ADHD and bipolar disorder are more frequently hospitalized than children with ADHD alone, have an earlier onset of bipolar disorder than children with bipolar disorder alone, and have family histories in which bipolar disorder is common (Biederman et al., 1996; Kim & Miklowitz, 2002; Spencer, Wilens et al., 2000).

Developmental Course

Although there is a great deal of individual variability in clinical presentation and patterns of chronicity, a diagnosis of ADHD demonstrates significant stability over time both in clinical samples (75–85%) and in large school samples (70%) (August, Braswell, & Thuras, 1998; Faraone, Biederman, & Mick, 2006; Mannuzza, Klein, & Moulton, 2003b). Cantwell (1985, 1996) describes three kinds of long-term outcomes: (1) **developmental delay**, with gradual improvement in symptoms, and with no significant impairment in functioning by late adolescence or adulthood (30%); (2) **continual display**, with ongoing impairment throughout adolescence and adulthood (40%); and (3) **developmental decay**, with ongoing impairment plus the development of other serious psychopathology (30%). As Cantwell summarizes, most individuals do not outgrow ADHD, but many do learn to manage the disorder

and adapt to varying levels of impairment. It is also important to keep in mind that some of the apparent age-related decline in the number of ADHD diagnoses may be due, in part, to "outgrowing the DSM item set" rather than more meaningful improvement. That is, we need to consider whether the current diagnostic criteria are appropriately sensitive to ADHD symptoms across the lifespan. In any case, even with the most optimistic forecasts, the wide-ranging impact of ADHD (particularly untreated ADHD) on children, families, and society is something that must be fully appreciated and addressed.

Early Childhood Precursors

Babies with difficult temperaments who exhibit excessive activity, poor sleeping and eating, and more emotional negativity are at greater risk for development of ADHD (Barkley, 1990). Deficits in the development of self-regulation are fairly stable in the early years, with the majority of children who will later be diagnosed with ADHD displaying poor inhibition in their preschool years (Berlin, Bohlin, & Rydell, 2003). These preschoolers are also described as "on-the-go, "into everything," very curious, and disobedient. Tantrums, aggression, and fearless behaviors are particularly noteworthy (Cantwell, 1996; Jester et al., 2005). Although only a subset of children with early attention and activity difficulties continues to struggle throughout childhood, there is clear evidence of stability between the preschool and the early school years for those children with the most severe symptoms (Campbell, 1990; Cantwell, 1996).

Childhood Outcomes

There are multiple consequences related to ADHD, including academic struggles, family disturbances, and problems with peers. Academic struggles include reading problems, difficulties with homework, and overall lack of achievement (Biederman et al., 2004; McGee, Prior, Williams, Smart, & Sanson, 2002). For many children, multiple classes with multiple teachers overwhelm limited coping skills (Cantwell, 1996). "Difficulties are especially conspicuous upon entry into the fourth and seventh grades, when classroom demands and academic assignments become increasingly more complex, take longer to complete, and rely heavily on one's ability to work independently" (Rapport,

1995, p. 357). These types of difficulties influence self-evaluations, persistence in school tasks, and attributions about success and failure (Hoza, Waschbusch, Owens, Pelham, & Kipp, 2001). For teachers as well, students with ADHD pose many challenges, with stressors related to student achievement, student behavior, and various forms of treatment for ADHD (Greene, 1996; Greene, Beszterczey, Katzenstein, Park, & Goring, 2002).

Family disturbances are also frequent complications. As noted in a National Institutes of Health [NIH] (1994) report: "It's especially hard being the parent of a child who is full of uncontrolled activity, leaves messes, throws tantrums, and doesn't listen or follow instructions" (p. 27). Children's impulsive, oppositional, and sometimes destructive behaviors may require near constant supervision, and tax many parents' abilities and sympathies. Given the on-again, off-again self-control displayed by children with ADHD, common parenting practices such as reasoning and scolding do not usually help, resulting in many instances and various intensities of parent-child conflict (DuPaul & Barkley, 2008; Rapport, 1995). The costs of medical care for children with ADHD, often not covered by insurance plans, are an additional burden for many families (NIH, 1998). These many stresses and frustrations are associated with increased marital discord and divorce (NIH, 1998).

Both core deficits and associated sequelae contribute to problems with peers. Inattention, restlessness, and impulsivity make it difficult for children with ADHD to establish rapport with other children, to pay heed to other children's emotional and behavioral messages, and to negotiate disagreements in thoughtful ways. The most significant social skills deficits appear in three areas: communication, poor emotional regulation, and cognitive biases (i.e., routinely interpreting ambiguous information as negative) (Saunders & Chambers, 1996). For some children, these deficits lead to conflictual and ineffective peer relationships (Pelham & Bender, 1982); for others, social withdrawal and/or ostracism occurs (Paulson, Buermeyer, & Nelson-Gray, 2005; Rapport, 1995). In addition to the negative impact on the child's place in the culture of playgrounds, birthday parties, and friendships, there is also a negative impact on collaborative learning situations, where academic success depends on smooth working relationships (Saunders & Chambers, 1996).

Adolescent Outcomes

For many adolescents, struggles continue with the core symptoms of ADHD, with estimates ranging between 30% and 80% (Biederman, Faraone et al., 1998; DuPaul & Barkley, 2008). There are conflicting data about the relative expression of specific symptoms. In some reports, inattention and impulsivity remain problematic, while overactivity diminishes (August et al., 1998; Hart et al., 1995; Olson, Schilling, & Bates, 1999; Rapport, 1995). In other reports, both hyperactivity and impulsivity decline at a higher rate than inattention (Biederman, Mick, & Faraone, 2000). Even when excessive activity declines, an "internal sense of restlessness" may remain (Cantwell, 1996). In school, poor performance often continues with below-normal test scores and higher rates of suspension, expulsion, and failure (Murphy et al., 2002; Rapport, 1995; Weiss & Hechtman, 1993). In family settings, noncompliant and negative behaviors occur more frequently, particularly related to issues of responsibility (e.g., chores), rights and privileges (e.g., driving), and social activities (DuPaul & Barkley, 2008). Risky behaviors are also more prevalent, with a variety of problematic outcomes including driving accidents, substance abuse, and teen pregnancy (Barkley, DuPaul, et al., 2002; DuPaul & Barkley, 2008; Spencer, Wilens, et al., 2000).

Adult Outcomes

Approximately one-half to two-thirds of adults continue to experience difficulties related to the core symptoms of ADHD and related disorganization, poor concentration, procrastination, and negative mood (Cantwell, 1996; Rapport, 1995). The additional deficits associated with ADHD, including poorly developed academic/vocational and social skills also contribute to a variety of negative experiences (Murphy et al., 2002; Weiss & Hechtman, 1999). In one longitudinal study, Mannuzza, Klein, Bessler, Malloy, and LaPadula (1998) followed over 100 boys diagnosed with ADHD. When the boys were 24-year-old men, investigators observed higher rates of antisocial personality disorder and substance abuse, but no differences in rates of anxiety or mood disorders. In another study of individuals first diagnosed with ADHD as adults, somewhat higher rates of anxiety and mood disorders were noted, but most adults had made reasonable adjustments. Even though many adults continue to experience the negative impact of ADHD, it is also important to understand that "many people with ADHD ... feel that their patterns of behavior give them unique, often unrecognized, advantages. People with ADHD tend to be outgoing and ready for action. Because of their drive for excitement and stimulation, many become successful in business, sports, construction, and public speaking. Because of their ability to think about several things at once, many have won acclaim as artists and inventors. Many choose work that gives them freedom to move around and release excess energy" (NIH, 1994, p. 33). In fact, Brooks (2002) suggests that "changing the mindset" of children, adolescents, and adults with ADHD may go a long way toward supporting more positive outcomes across the lifespan.

In general, as with all instances of childhood disorder, the more aspects of disturbance and the more complex the clinical picture, the poorer the prognosis. Lower IQ scores, severity of ADHD presentation, difficult family and peer relationships, aggressive and destructive behavior, emotional dysregulation, and parental psychopathology all contribute to continued maladjustment (Barkley, 1990; Biederman et al., 1996; DuPaul & Barkley, 1998; Hart et al., 1995; Rapport, 1995).

Etiology

There are multiple etiological factors leading to ADHD, with the disorder as the "**final common pathway**" of combinations of different types of predisposing conditions and events (Cantwell, 1996; DuPaul & Barkley, 1998). Before we review these conditions and events, some historical perspective might provide useful information. For many years, clinicians and researchers believed that the pattern of symptoms observed in children was consistent with the experience of minor head or brain injuries, from birth complications or later trauma. When actual examples of such events were not reported, the hypothesis that "minimal brain damage" explained the disorder was called into question. In fact, although head and brain injuries can produce symptoms like ADHD, very few children diagnosed with ADHD have significant structural brain damage (Rutter, 1977). But we will revisit the notion that subtle differences in brain morphology may play a role in the development of ADHD.

For a while, the presence of toxins and allergens was suggested to induce symptoms characteristic of ADHD, with a particular focus on sugar and food additives. However, there is little empirical support that these factors contribute to the development of the disorder (Cantwell, 1996; Rapport, 1995), and restricted diets improve the clinical picture for only a very few children (DuPaul & Barkley, 1998; NIH, 1994). More recent and more fruitful attempts to explain the causes of ADHD have utilized a variety of technological advances to highlight the complex interplay of genetic vulnerability, brain processes, and maintenance factors.

Genes and Heredity

Family studies, twin studies, and adoption studies provide data that support the hypothesis that some individuals are more likely to develop ADHD because of genetic factors. In family studies, there is an increased rate of ADHD in the first-degree relatives of both boys and girls diagnosed with ADHD, as well as in African American families (Ehringer, Rhee, Young, Corley, & Hewitt, 2006; Faraone, Biederman, Mick, et al., 2000; Samuel et al., 1999). Additional evidence suggests that "when ADHD persists into adolescence, it is associated with a greater risk to relatives. ... It is also consistent with data suggesting that adult ADHD is more familial than childhood ADHD" (Biederman et al., 1998). In general, estimates of heritability are high, and range between .55 and .92 (Cantwell, 1996, Hudziak, 2000).

In one of the earlier well-designed twin studies, the concordance rate for MZ twins was approximately 51%, while the concordance rate for DZ twins was approximately 33% (Goodman & Stevenson, 1989a, 1989b). The Australian Twin ADHD Project also reported an "exceptionally high heritability component" (Levy, Hay, McStephen, Wood, & Waldman, 1997; Rhee, Waldman, Hay, & Levy, 1999). A comparison of mothers' and teachers' reports of MZ and DZ twins provides additional support for a genetic contribution (Sherman, McGue, & Iacono, 1997). In large-scale studies described by Lahey and colleagues and Levy and colleagues, the mostly inattentive, mostly hyperactive, and combined subtypes tended to "breed true," with MZ twins having greater subtype matches than DZ twins did. There are other data, however, that suggest that the mostly hyperactive subtype breeds true, whereas the other subtypes do not, allowing for a more prominent role for nongenetic (i.e., environmental) factors

(Faraone, Biederman & Friedman, 2000). Finally, adoption studies also support genetic, rather than environmental, transmission (Cantwell, 1996).

Genetic analyses usually focus on a set of pertinent characteristics that is believed to be normally distributed (i.e., the dimensional approach to disorder) (DuPaul & Barkley, 1998, Hudziak, 2000; Levy et al., 1997). Specifically, data from the Australian Twin Study supports an additive, polygenic multiple threshold model (Rhee et al., 1999). According to this model, "an individual is affected with ADHD if he or she exceeds a certain threshold of liability. Girls are less likely to be affected with ADHD because they require a greater degree of liability (i.e., have to surpass a higher liability threshold) to manifest ADHD than do boys" (Rhee et al., 1999, p. 38). In other words, children who are diagnosed with ADHD are expected to score higher on a range of genetic indices; taken together, the set of extreme scores underlies the development of ADHD. Gender differences in the degree of penetrance of genetic factors are also a possibility (Faraone et al., 1992; Rhee et al., 1999). Genetic heterogeneity, in terms of evidence supporting both additive and dominance models of transmission, as well as girls and boys displaying somewhat different patterns of genetic, shared environmental, and nonshared environmental causality, requires additional investigation (Rhee et al., 1999).

Variations in the expression of ADHD during childhood, adolescence, and adulthood may be explained by the possibility that "the same genotype can manifest itself in different ways at different ages and the extent of genetic involvement can change significantly at different ages" (Levy et al., 1997, p. 743). Molecular genetic analyses also provide information related to the frequent comorbidity observed in children and adolescents with ADHD (Asherson, Kuntsi, & Taylor, 2005; Doyle et al., 2005; Faraone et al., 2005). Given numerous associations between ADHD and other internalizing and/or externalizing psychopathology, contemporary approaches emphasize the likelihood of shared genetic influences and a common physiological risk factor (Coolidge, Thede, & Young, 2000; Dick, Viken, Kaprio, Pulkkinen, & Rose, 2005; Hudziak, 2000).

Neurophysiological Factors

The characteristic deficits in inhibition, planning, and persistence point to neurological causes. With increasingly sophisticated neuroimaging techniques,

including magnetic resonance imaging (MRI), positron emission tomography (PET), and single photon emission computed tomography (SPECT), areas and processes of the brain that are implicated in ADHD can be identified (Castellanos, 1997; Hooper & Tramontana, 1997; Semrud-Clikeman et al., 2000; Shaywitz, Fletcher, Pugh, Klorman, & Shaywitz, 1999). Areas of the brain that have been examined include the corpus callosum, the temporal lobes, the frontal lobes, and the striatal regions. Although the data are inconsistent and based on small numbers of children, ADHD appears to be associated with smaller sizes of various brain regions (Barkley, 1997b; Casey et al., 1997; see Figure 9.2). This pathophysiological evidence provides extremely valuable information about possible etiologies, developmental trajectories, and interventions (Taylor, 1999).

Several investigations have noted reduced cerebral blood flow in the frontal areas of the brain (Zametkin, Nordahl, Gross, & King, 1990), particularly during periods of "intellectual stress" (Amen & Carmichael, 1997); other areas have been associated with increased flow (Lou, 1990). These areas have to do with the regulation of attention, activity, and information processing (Satterfield, Schell, Nicholas, & Satterfield, 1990; Shaywitz et al., 1999; Zametkin et al., 1990). Development itself may also be associated with changing patterns of dysfunction. For example, Oades (1998) proposes that some children "may experience an early negative neurodevelopmental influence that only appears as the brain region matures" (p. 83). There is no consistent evidence of global autonomic underreactivity, but some specific patterns of underreactivity have been proposed, including the possibility that evoked response patterns (related to performance on vigilance tests) may reflect underresponsiveness in those areas of the brain that are smaller (Barkley, 1997b; Casey et al., 1997; again, refer to Figure 9.2).

There is also evidence about the etiological role of neurotransmitter abnormalities. The current focus is on the monoamines, with speculation that there is a selective deficiency in the availability and turnover of dopamine and/or norepinephrine (Cantwell, 1996; Tannock, 1998). The processing of dopamine is associated with the brain's reward centers and attentional processes. The processing of norepinephrine is associated with behavioral inhibition and complex learning. These functions are clearly compromised in children with ADHD, with some differences in

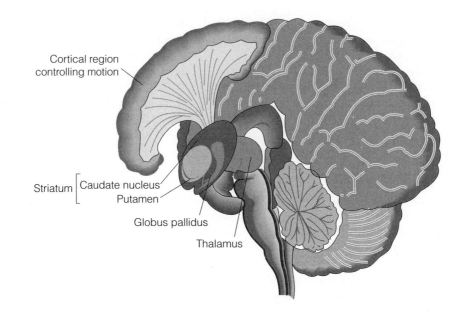

Cortical region
controlling motion

Striatum [Caudate nucleus
Putamen

Globus pallidus

Thalamus

FIGURE 9:2 Diagram of the regions of the brain's right hemisphere that are reduced in size in individuals with ADHD.

Source: From Casey, B.J., Castellanos, F.X., Giedd, J.N., & Marsh, W.L., (1997), "Implications of right frontostriatal circuitry in response inhibition and attention-deficit-hyperactivity disorder", 'Journal of the American Academy of Child & Adolescent Psychiatry', 36, 374-383. Used by permission.

clinical presentation possibly related to more or less dysfunction with one or the other neurotransmitter. With increasing dysfunction, a worse clinical presentation is expected (Rapport, 1995).

Overall, genetic, neuropsychological, and psychopharmacological research provides strong converging evidence that a central nervous system dysfunction may underlie the development of ADHD. Current and future studies will pay particular attention to the prefrontal cortex, the striatum, and the limbic regions (Casey et al. 1997; Castellanos, 1997; Oades, 1998; Shaywitz et al., 1999), the specific role of neurotransmitters (Hudziak, 2000), and the self-regulatory processes and executive functions of the brain (Barkley, 1997b; Castellanos, 1997; Taylor, 1999).

Psychosocial Factors

There is almost no empirical evidence supporting the hypothesis that psychosocial factors contribute to the *development* of ADHD; however, numerous studies have described ways in which psychosocial factors have a role in the *maintenance and exacerbation* of the disorder (DuPaul & Barkley, 1998; van den Oord & Rowe, 1997). Johnston and Freeman (1997) compared the attitudes of parents of children with ADHD and parents of children without behavior disorders. In general, most parents tended to rate children's behaviors as internally caused and controllable. How-

ever, parents of children with ADHD accepted less responsibility for child behaviors, and rated impulsivity and oppositional behaviors as more internally caused and controllable than parents of children without behavior disorders did. Parents of children with ADHD viewed impulsivity as more persistent across time, and prosocial behaviors as less consistent than parents of children without ADHD. All parents responded negatively to oppositional behaviors, but parents of children with ADHD responded even more negatively. These results suggest that parental beliefs about ADHD and about their children may contribute to an increasingly destructive cycle of negative interpretations and blame, making it difficult to intervene effectively. These types of family factors may, in fact, tell us more about the risk for the development of comorbid disorders (such as ODD or CD) than about the ADHD (Barkley, 1997b; Patterson, DeGarmo, & Knutson, 2000).

Another perspective on psychosocial factors brings us back to the model of genetic influence. Although there appears to be little support for a model of ADHD transmission that includes shared environmental factors (e.g., childrearing practices that are similar for all children in the same family), there may be a role for *nonshared* environmental influence (childrearing practices that are different for children in the same family) (Sherman et al., 1997).

Also, it is possible to reinterpret some of the evidence, suggesting a role for psychosocial factors: "the potential presence of ADHD in the parent and its association with that parent's child management ability" must be taken into account (Barkley, 1997b, p. 30).

Assessment and Diagnosis

We know that ADHD is a disorder that is often mistaken for a child's lack of ability or effort, stubborn willfulness, or the result of lackadaisical parenting. In addition, perhaps more so than any other childhood disorder, ADHD is a disorder that frequently co-occurs with other disorders. Given these circumstances, and the fact that *there is no specific psychological or neurological test for ADHD,* we must pay careful attention to the particular criteria that lead to an accurate diagnosis of ADHD. As already emphasized, ADHD reflects deficits and/or delays in key behavioral, cognitive, and emotional abilities. Assessment of children, adolescents, and adults depends, first and foremost, on appropriate knowledge of development. Thus, a clinician may observe a child who exhibits distractibility, excessive activity, and less-than-optimal decision making, but these behaviors are observed in all kinds of children for all kinds of reasons. In the case of ADHD, the clinician must look for *more frequent behaviors, more intense behaviors,* and *more impairment.*

Diagnostic Interviews

Interviews are often conducted with children, parents, and teachers. Parents and teachers usually provide more useful data, as children (and even adolescents) are not always aware of or able to describe their difficult behaviors (Smith, Pelham, Gnagy, Molina, & Evans, 2000). And although the information provided by parent and teacher reports is almost never exactly the same, research suggests that clinical diagnoses of ADHD that are based on parent reports are likely to be confirmed by teacher reports (Biederman, Faraone, Milberger, & Doyle, 1993). That said, it is essential to appreciate the factors that may influence parent and teacher descriptions of problem behaviors. For instance, parents of preschoolers may perceive certain problem behaviors as normal and put off seeking help (Maniadaki, Sonuga-Burke, Kakouros, & Karaba, 2007). Teachers may respond differently to similar behaviors in boys versus girls, and refer boys for evaluation more often than girls (Sciutto, Nolfi, & Bluhm, 2004).

Comprehensive interviews, in addition to providing baseline data, may reveal information about a family history of ADHD or the presence of additional disorders. In addition, careful review of the relations between the particular patterns of deficits and the demands of particular settings is important. In addition, for some disorders there is a question about the emergence of symptoms. For example, clinicians pay attention to the timing of clinical difficulties in response to specific events, such as parental divorce. With ADHD, the assumption is that the core difficulties are present from early childhood, and are *not* the result of a specific stressor. Diagnosis of adult ADHD remains clinically problematic, given that there is no consensus on the criteria for adult ADHD. According to McGough and Barkley (2004), "the DSM criteria have never been validated in adults, do not include developmentally appropriate symptoms and thresholds for adults, and fail to identify some significantly impaired adults who are likely to benefit from treatment" (p. 1948). Additional work in this area is essential.

Another consideration in judging the presence of ADHD and making differential diagnoses is whether or not the identified symptoms are better accounted for by another disorder. Many disorders, such as depression, generalized anxiety disorder, or schizophrenia, can disrupt the basic cognitive and behavioral processes that are the core features of ADHD. In the case of these other disorders, however, symptoms such as poor concentration and impulsivity are secondary problems relative to the primary disorder.

Rating Scales

In addition to interview data, there are a number of available rating scales for parents and teachers, specifically designed to assess the symptoms of ADHD and provide information about the degree to which an individual deviates from well-established norms. For the most part, these scales provide reasonably accurate, and in some cases, compelling information about the likely presence of ADHD (Pappas, 2006; Stevens, Quittner, & Abikoff, 1998). The widespread use of teacher rating scales, however, has been the focus of several investigations concerning the assessment of students of various racial and ethnic backgrounds. Reid et al. (1998) reviewed comparisons of teacher rating scales between American and Thai children, mainland American and Puerto

Rican children, and Anglo-American and Mexican American children. In all cases, children of minority backgrounds were rated as more symptomatic. In another study, conducted in Britain, even when the objectively measured behaviors of children were identical, teachers' ratings of Asian children reflected more ADHD symptomatology than their ratings of non-Asian children (Sonuga-Barke, Minocha, Taylor, & Sandberg, 1993). In several studies, consistent differences have been observed in comparisons between teacher ratings of African American and European American children, with African American children receiving more negative ratings (DuPaul et al., 1998). Given these data, the increased presence and expanding role of school psychologists provides valuable perspective on school-based referrals and treatments (Demaray, Schaefer, & Delong, 2003).

Observations

Given possible bias, it becomes even more important to balance parents' and teachers' reports and ratings with actual observations. Most observations are done in the school, because some children's abilities to exhibit self-control and maintain attention in the structured office setting may not reflect typical behavior (Dulcan et al., 1997). Ideally, observations

Continuous Performance Tests such as this one make use of computers to assess selective attention and impulse control.

should be made in a variety of settings, with different environmental demands, with the expectation that symptoms will be more pronounced in circumstances that are not interesting or stimulating (Rapport, 1995).

Other Sources of Information

While not definitive by themselves, a variety of **continuous performance tests** are often used as part of an ADHD assessment (Nichols & Waschbusch, 2004). These tests generally involve monitoring stimuli (visual, auditory, or both) and responding selectively to instructions. For example, letters might be presented on a computer screen and the child told to respond to a certain target letter but not to others. These tests measure various attention and impulse control skills, including the ability to remain vigilant, to demonstrate consistency of attentional focus, to respond quickly, and to inhibit responding. In many cases, additional assessment related to academic achievement is often conducted, including intelligence testing and assessment of learning disabilities (Dulcan et al., 1997). Medical evaluations are also sometimes done (Dulcan et al., 1997).

Comorbid Conditions

As described earlier, an important consideration in the assessment, diagnosis, and treatment of ADHD is the comorbidity, or co-occurrence, of other clinically significant problems (Jensen, Martin, & Cantwell, 1997; Quinlan, 2000). Over 40% of children diagnosed with ADHD have at least one other psychiatric disorder. As many as 32% have at least two other diagnosable disorders, and over 10% have three or more other disorders (Barkley, 1998; Wolraich, Hannah, Baumgaertel, & Feurer, 1998). The identification and treatment of these comorbid disorders is often as important as the identification and treatment of the ADHD itself. The phenomenon of comorbidity is especially critical when we consider the fact that many of the defining symptoms of ADHD are readily recognized. This sometimes leads clinicians to overlook other clinical difficulties.

Although any disorder can co-occur with ADHD, among the most common and most disabling are those that are also characterized by disruptive behaviors, including oppositional defiant disorder and the more serious conduct disorder. These **disruptive behavior disorders** are best understood as related to, but independent of, ADHD. Recognizing the comorbidity of these disorders has important prognostic value. For example, ADHD combined with oppositional defiant disorder is usually intermediate in terms of severity between ADHD alone and ADHD combined with conduct disorder. Conduct disorder occurring with ADHD is generally more severe and chronic than conduct disorder alone. The combination of ADHD and conduct disorder is highly predictive of antisocial personality disorder later in life. Early identification of these combinations of disorders is especially important for effective interventions. It is also critical to determine if a mood disorder complicates the clinical presentation and must be addressed in treatment planning.

Intervention

DuPaul and Barkley (1998) assert that "ADHD is a developmental disorder of self-control and social conduct that is chronic and without cure. An attitude of *coping* rather than *curing* is a reasonable clinical position" (p. 135). Thinking about the possibilities for coping with the core deficits and the many additional difficulties with which children with ADHD struggle, the need for cooperation and coordination across treatment modalities, professionals, and settings is clear (Dulcan et al., 1997; DuPaul & Barkley, 1998; Waschbusch & Hill, 2003). Given the many comorbid psychopathologies associated with ADHD, it becomes essential to address *the whole child* rather than one or several clinical disorders.

A number of different interventions have been proposed for ADHD, including "psychotropic medications, psychosocial treatment, dietary management, herbal and homeopathic treatments, biofeedback, meditation, and perceptual stimulation/training" (NIH, 1998), with psychotropic medications and psychosocial treatments receiving the most empirical and clinical support. According to Hoagwood, Kelleher, Feil, and Comer (2000), however, there are three major problems with studies of ADHD intervention. First, most studies are specifically designed to examine the efficacy of *particular* treatments in *specific* settings with *well-defined* samples. Although this type of research is certainly valuable, we cannot use it to judge the usual care that most children receive. Second, even when examination of typical service delivery is the focus, investigators frequently use samples of convenience (e.g., children seen in a clinic associated with a

research university) rather than representative samples of children. Finally, most national surveys on the treatment of children with ADHD have focused on physicians and physician interventions. In order to get a comprehensive picture of care, it is important to remember that many different mental health service providers (e.g., school psychologists, special education teachers) also work with children with ADHD. To increase the clinical relevance of treatment outcome research, the National Institute of Mental Health's Collaborative Multisite Multimodal Treatment Study of Children with ADHD combined rigorous experimental protocols with more attention to individual differences, such as optimal dose and best schedule for medication and long-term monitoring of response to medication (see Box 9.1).

Pharmacological Treatment

In hundreds of studies with thousands of children, the use of **central nervous system (CNS) stimulants** to treat ADHD has received significant support. The majority of children who are treated with long-used medications such as methylphenidate (Ritalin) and newer types of stimulants (such as Adderall and Cylert) show real and substantive improvement, with improvement measured by parent-teacher ratings, direct observations, and performance in lab tasks (Faraone, Pliszka, Olvera, Skolnik, & Biederman, 2001; Spencer, Biederman, & Wilens, 2000). CNS stimulants have worked significantly better than psychological and/or social interventions. Stimulants have been shown to work for girls as well as boys, for African American youth, and for youth from a variety of SES backgrounds (Arnold et al., 2003; Rieppi et al., 2002; Samuel et al., 1997; Sharp et al., 1999). They also work for adolescents with ADHD (Smith, Pelham, Gnagy, & Yudell, 1998; Spencer et al., 1996) and adults with ADHD (Wilens, Biederman, & Spencer, 1998).

Although the effects of the CNS stimulants are short-lived, they are observed for reduced impulsivity and increased compliance, sustained attention and short-term recall, and some types of specific learning (DuPaul & Barkley, 1998; Multimodal Treatment Study of Children with ADHD Cooperative Group [MTA Cooperative Group], 1999; Pomeroy & Gadow, 1998; Schachar, Tannock, Cunningham, & Corkum, 1997). Critics of medication management hypothesized that children would attribute improvements, when they did occur, to the pills rather than

BOX 9:1 **CLINICAL PERSPECTIVES**

The MTA Cooperative Group Study

There are frequent criticisms that research in developmental psychopathology often fails to take into account the realities of actual children in complex circumstances. In ADHD outcome-oriented research, such criticism has focused on studies of the short-term impact of stimulant medications (neglecting possible long-range negative consequences) and the inadequate consideration of multi-faceted intervention strategies (neglecting the whole child to focus on problematic symptoms). The Multimodal Treatment Study of Children with Attention Deficit Hyperactivity Disorder (MTA) Cooperative Group Study is an effort to comprehensively address previous research shortcomings (Greenhill et al., 1996; Jensen et al., 2007; MTA Cooperative Group, 2004).

The MTA Cooperative Group Study included six independent research teams (in San Francisco; Los Angeles; Durham, NC; New York; and Pittsburgh, PA) working in collaboration with the National Institute of Mental Health and the U.S. Department of Education.

Comparisons of long-range efficacy (i.e., 14-month, 24-month, and 36-month outcomes) in 579 children with ADHD-Combined Type were conducted for medication management, intensive behavioral treatment, a combined approach, and community care. Numerous outcome measures were identified, including reduction in the core ADHD symptoms, personal adjustment, academic achievements, and improvements in social skills and relationships. Across multiple settings and a diverse sample of children, strong support for medication management was demonstrated at the 14-month evaluation, with some additional benefits observed for the combined medication/behavioral treatment strategy. By 36 months, many of the advantages of the combined treatment had diminished, although all treatment groups showed improvements over baseline. This type of research collaboration is expensive and difficult to coordinate. It is, however, absolutely necessary if we as researchers, clinicians, parents, teachers, and others want to be able to describe and offer optimal care to individuals with ADHD.

themselves or their efforts; this does not appear to be the case (Pelham et al., 2002; Pelham, Waschbusch, Hoza, Pilow, & Gnagy, 2001). Most researchers, clinicians, parents, and teachers believed that general academic improvements would follow these immediate effects. Contrary to hopeful hypotheses, however, it appears that the use of stimulants alone results in little improvement in long-range academic achievement. According to DuPaul and Barkley (1998), the "most prudent conclusion" is that medication is helpful in the short-term, but is not sufficient; additional interventions are necessary to address the multiple difficulties associated with core deficits.

For some children, the beneficial impact of stimulant medication extends beyond the core symptoms, with evidence of enhanced sociability (DuPaul & Barkley, 1998; MTA Cooperative Group, 1999; Spencer et al., 1997), and decreases in aggressive and destructive behaviors (MTA Cooperative Group, 1999; Pomeroy & Gadow, 1998; Schachar & Tannock, 1993). With these changes in children's behaviors, others may begin to respond differently to the child with ADHD (Pomeroy & Gadow, 1998); positive effects of stimulant treatments are observed for relationships with parents, teachers,

and peers, although parents and teachers report different patterns of benefits and side effects (Pomeroy & Gadow, 1998; Schachar et al., 1997; Whalen, Henker, & Granger, 1990). Whether improvements are evaluated with respect to a reduction in symptoms (25% or 50%) or with respect to the "normalization" of a child's cognitive and behavioral performance remains a tricky issue (Greenhill et al., 1996). However, even with a variety of improvements, there are children who will continue to display higher-than-normal levels of inattention, activity, and impulsivity (Pomeroy & Gadow, 1998). Families' varied beliefs about medication use may provide clinicians with valuable information related to communication, decision-making, and long-term responses to children's treatment (Leslie, Plemmons, Monn, & Palinkas, 2007).

Stimulant medications result in many neurochemical effects, with particular emphasis on increasing catecholamines (i.e., dopamine and norepinephrine) in the synaptic clefts (Spencer, Biederman, et al., 2000). These stimulants usually have a demonstrable effect within about 30–45 minutes, lasting approximately 4 hours. The appropriate dosage is sometimes difficult to establish, because body weight and children's self-reports of response are not effective indices. Global rating scales (often completed by teachers) are the most frequently used, cost-effective way to monitor dosage (Greenhill et al., 1996; Rapport, 1995). Overall, stimulants are generally considered safe (Pomeroy & Gadow, 1998) and do not cause jitteriness, sedation, or "zombification" (Spencer et al., 1996, p. 422). **Adverse drug effects** are usually related to dose (NIH, 1998). Side effects associated with moderate doses include decreased appetite and incidence of insomnia (DuPaul & Barkley, 1998; NIH, 1998; Schachar et al., 1997), particularly at the beginning of treatment, as well as some other somatic complaints. There may be a negative effect on growth rate, but not apparently on ultimate height (NIH, 1998; Spencer, Biederman, & Wilens, 1998). High doses are infrequently associated with compulsive behaviors, and in some vulnerable individuals, movement disorders; rarely, hallucinations occur (NIH, 1998). As noted previously, some individuals may use or abuse other psychoactive substances that may interact with prescribed medications. Adequate monitoring and follow-up is essential.

For children with multiple diagnoses, CNS stimulants appear to work well (Spencer, Biederman, et al., 2000). Positive responses to Ritalin have been observed for children diagnosed with ADHD and anxiety symptoms (Tannock, Diamond, & Schachar, 1999), with ADHD and Tourette's/tic disorders (Gadow, Sverd, Sprafkin, Nolan, & Grossman, 1999; Pomeroy & Gadow, 1998), and with ADHD and developmental disabilities (Handen, Feldman, Lurier, & Huszar Murray, 1999). Antidepressants, including tricyclics and selective serotonin reuptake inhibitors, have also been prescribed for children, adolescents, and adults with ADHD, and work significantly better than placebos (Pomeroy & Gadow, 1998; Spencer et al., 1993; Spencer, Biederman, et al., 2000). Antidepressants may be indicated for children with comorbid mood disorders, or for some children whose tics worsen with stimulant treatment (Castellanos, 1999), or who do not respond at all. Other medications such as clonidine have also been investigated (Connor, Fletcher, & Swanson, 1999; Spencer, Biederman, et al., 2000).

A relatively recent trend in ADHD treatment is **combined pharmacotherapy**, using combinations of medications to treat the disorder. Explanations for this trend include the higher rates of comorbid psychopathologies, better symptom control, and the synergy of combined medications (Spencer,

Biederman et al., 2000; Wilens, Spencer, Biederman, Wozniak, & Connor, 1995). Another highly controversial trend concerns the increasing number of prescriptions being written for very young children diagnosed with ADHD (see Box 9.2), although these children apparently respond less well to stimulant treatments (Dulcan et al., 1997; Spencer et al., 1996). As noted earlier, stimulant treatment does not appear to increase risk for later substance abuse (Mannazza et al., 2003; Wilens et al., 2003).

Psychosocial Treatment

The data suggest that psychological and social interventions, by themselves, do not alleviate the core deficits of ADHD. Still, there are many ways in which such interventions do provide important relief. Some of the associated symptomatology, including diminished self-esteem, depression, and parent-child conflicts, may be addressed with psychosocial therapies (Cantwell, 1996; Wells et al., 2000). Treatments that combine medications and behavioral techniques show superior results (Arnold et al., 2004), and parents and teachers rate the combined treatments more favorably (MTA Cooperative Group, 1999; NIH, 1998). A potential advantage to combined treatments is the possibility that lower dosages of stimulant medication would be required (Cantwell, 1996; NIH, 1998). One necessary aspect of psychological services is **parent education**, including information about pharmacological interventions; available special educational services; practical issues such as reducing accidents, preventing pregnancies, driving privileges; and access to mental health resources such as parent support groups and individual counseling, given the higher rates of parental psychopathology (DuPaul & Barkley, 1998). Providing educational information to children and teachers is also important (Dulcan et al., 1997).

Although stimulant medications are often associated with improvements, sometimes the benefits of medication are less apparent in the home (Schachar et al., 1997); therapeutic support via parent training in child management skills may result in additional relief (Cantwell, 1996; DuPaul & Barkley, 1998; MTA Cooperative Group, 1999). DuPaul and Barkley (1998) describe a successful short-term approach for parents. Topics include: (1) Overview of ADHD; (2) Understanding parent-child relations and principles of behavior management; (3) Developing and enhancing parental attention to child behavior;

BOX 9:2 CLINICAL PERSPECTIVES

Medication and Preschoolers

With rapidly rising rates of psychopharmacological interventions for very young children, we must thoughtfully address various public health and ethical concerns. Are actual disorders increasing in younger samples? Are our methods of detection and diagnosis improving, or are we confusing normal behavioral, emotional, and cognitive variations in preschoolers with deviant behavioral, emotional, and cognitive displays in older children and adolescents? What are the costs and benefits of using drugs that have not been investigated or approved for young children? And what are the societal, clinical, and personal meanings associated with the prescription of Ritalin, or any other psychotropic medication, to a very young child?

As we have repeatedly emphasized throughout this textbook, taking a developmental view of distress, dysfunction, and disorders provides us with valuable perspective. Children experience the "terrible twos," the "often still thorny threes," and the "formidable fours." Some of their worrisome behaviors fade with time, and some continue. We must acknowledge that developmental bumps in the road are inevitable and

that there are no alternatives to patient, loving, and individualized caregiving. But we also acknowledge that psychopathology does occur in the early years.

We know that, for example, troubled preschoolers often present with a mix of clinical difficulties in many psychological domains. Whether a child is appropriately understood as anxious, depressed, learning disabled, or as having ADHD is difficult to determine. That parents are often desperate to find out exactly what is "wrong" with a child, and do something to "fix" that child is understandable. It is a public policy shame that in many ways mental health professionals cannot offer the kinds of educational services, family support, and nonmedical interventions that may be exactly what many families need.

Of course we must also consider the very small number of children with well-defined ADHD that results in significant impairments, who might be suitable candidates for what is clearly an effective intervention strategy in older children. One thing is certain. The clinical and ethical issues associated with psychopharmacology in preschoolers and across the lifespan will continue to be the focus of much scientific and public attention.

(4) Attending to appropriate behavior; (5) Establishing a home token reinforcement system; (6) Using response cost and time-out from positive reinforcement (i.e., more negative consequences for problem behaviors); (7) Managing behavior in public settings; and (8) Managing future misbehavior. Hinshaw et al. (2000) further emphasize the importance of working with parents using combined treatments; they report positive school outcomes for children whose parents reduced negative and ineffective discipline practices.

For the most part, psychotherapeutic approaches designed to target the core deficits of ADHD and improve children's self-regulation and/or focus on cognitive skills training have received little empirical support (Braswell, 1998). Much of the work done directly with children instead focuses on education and supportive therapy. Behavioral interventions, which have shown modest advantages over medication alone, have included social reinforcements, modeling, social skills training, and group problem-solving (MTA Cooperative Group, 1999). Peer interventions are sometimes utilized to address what Cantwell (1996) refers to as the "in your face" behaviors exhibited by children

with ADHD. Even with improvements, however, children with ADHD often remain impaired in their peer relationships (Hoza et al., 2005). With adolescents, psychotherapy takes a somewhat different approach, given the developmental challenges related to independence and self-control, especially if there are more negative, more pronounced oppositional behaviors and conduct problems (DuPaul & Barkley, 1998).

As we consider the variety of interventions directed at children with ADHD, we must grapple with underlying concerns about personal responsibility. For many individuals, it seems that children (especially those who are already being treated with psychostimulants) have more control over their behaviors and emotions than children with other kinds of psychological difficulties. The question of how much **accountability** is appropriate to expect from children with ADHD is hard to answer, but Barkley (1997b) points out that diagnosis and intervention does not excuse children and adolescents with ADHD from personal accountability. "Consequences must be made more immediate, increased in their frequency, made more 'external' and salient, and provided more consistently than is likely to be the case for the natural consequences associated with one's conduct" (Barkley, 1997b, p. 316). Within this framework, as children and adolescents become better at self-reflection and self-regulation, we might eventually, and appropriately, expect increases in personal responsibility for their own well-being.

School Adaptations

Most children with ADHD are placed in mainstream classes, but some may require individual tutoring and specialized plans to support academic achievement (Cantwell, 1996). Both the National Rehabilitation Act and the Individuals with Disabilities Education Act (IDEA) are legislative efforts requiring appropriate educational services for children with ADHD. Special accommodations such as having children with ADHD sit in a place with fewer distractions (e.g., in the front of the class, next to the teacher's desk), receiving written as well as oral instructions, and providing visual aids and reminders are common. Many of the investigations supporting the efficacy of classroom interventions have been conducted in special education classrooms; we will need to take into account possible differences for mainstreamed children (DuPaul & Barkley, 1998).

Targeting academic performance itself, rather than focusing on specific skills or strategies, resulted in better outcomes in many studies in the 1970s and 1980s (Cantwell, 1996; Rapport, 1995). In order to improve academic performance, individualized behavioral interventions, combining positive and mildly aversive corrective feedback, have been designed to decrease disruptive behavior (Rapport, 1995). More comprehensive behavioral approaches have also been proposed. DuPaul and Barkley (1998) distinguish between antecedent-based strategies and consequent-based strategies in their multifaceted intervention. For many mental health professionals who work in school settings with children with ADHD, the key issue is the generalization of improvements across settings, time, behaviors, and deficits (Barkley & DuPaul, 1998). Participation, collaboration, and coordination among service providers, teachers, and parents are essential.

Interventions with Adults

As previously noted, CNS stimulants and antidepressant medications have both been effective in treating the symptoms of ADHD displayed by adults (Spencer et al., 1996; Wilens, Biederman,

& Spencer, 1998). Improvements in occupational and marital functioning have also been observed with psychopharmacological management (Wender, Wood, & Reimherr, 1991). With regard to ongoing relationship problems, workplace/career difficulties, and self-esteem issues, Nadeau (1998) suggests an increased therapeutic emphasis on **life management skills**. For example, Nadeau focuses on "thing management" (papers, personal objects), "time management," and "to do management" (lists of tasks), as well as money management.

Future Trends

We expect, and hope, that in the coming years children, adolescents, and adults will receive more careful evaluations of ADHD, with an increased appreciation for the developmental context of ADHD, the overlap of normal and disruptive behaviors, and the varied clinical presentations in diverse samples. We recognize that some children whose behavior is problematic but not actually disordered will be misdiagnosed with ADHD; we also recognize that some children with ADHD will fall through the cracks and will struggle without any kind of supportive services.

In recent years, for example, there has been a decrease in the number of children who receive psychotherapy for ADHD (Hoagwood, Kelleher, et al., 2000). In part, this is because more children and adolescents are receiving stimulant medications. However, only a minority of children who meet the diagnostic criteria for ADHD are receiving such interventions. Differences in medication management are related to geographic location, the race/ethnicity of the child, and possibly gender (Hoagwood, Jensen, Feil, Bhatara, & Vitiello, 2000). It is also true that only a minority of children with ADHD receive special school services (Hoagwood, Jensen et al., 2000). In many cases, the mix of services depends more on the type of provider (e.g., psychiatrist, pediatrician, family practitioner) than on the standards of care for children with ADHD. Barriers to appropriate care include lack of medical coverage, long waiting lists, and the unavailability of specialists. There is a clear need for additional physician training, accessible school-based clinics, and more specially trained clinicians (Pliszka et al., 2003). The implications for personal adjustment and public health are great; our responsibility is to rise to the challenge of addressing children's compelling and legitimate needs.

■ Key Terms

Executive functions (pg. 144)
Ego control (pg. 145)
Ego resiliency (pg. 145)
Self-regulatory skills (pg. 146)
Attention deficit hyperactivity disorder (ADHD) (pg. 147)
Categorical disorder (pg. 148)
Continuous disorder (pg. 148)
Core behavioral deficit (pg. 149)
Social dysfunction (pg. 149)
Internal validity (pg. 149)
Two-factor model (pg. 149)
Sluggish cognitive tempo (pg. 150)
Developmental delay (pg. 152)
Continual display (pg. 152)
Developmental decay (pg. 152)
Final common pathway (pg. 154)
Continuous performance tests (pg. 158)
Disruptive behavior disorders (pg. 158)
Central nervous system (CNS) stimulants (pg. 159)
Adverse drug effects (pg. 161)
Combined pharmacotherapy (pg. 161)
Parent education (pg. 162)
Accountability (pg. 162)
Life management skills (pg. 163)

■ Chapter Summary

- Attention deficit hyperactivity disorder (ADHD) is characterized by a combination of the symptoms of impulsivity, restlessness, and inattentiveness.

- The subtypes of ADHD are primarily defined by relative prominence of impulsivity and hyperactivity symptoms.

- Self-regulatory skills in the areas of behavior, cognition, and emotion are important developmental milestones that are compromised by ADHD.

- Boys receive diagnoses of ADHD four to five times more often than do girls.

- In general, ADHD is an exceptionally stable diagnosis over time.

- Genetic and neurological factors are central to the development of ADHD, while psychosocial factors play an important role in the maintenance and exacerbation of the disorder.

- Diagnoses most commonly occurring along with ADHD include oppositional defiant disorder, and mood and anxiety disorders.

- The majority of children treated with stimulant medication show significant and sustained improvement.

- While medication is especially helpful in the short-term, environmental interventions, such as classroom adaptations, are important for sustained improvement in functioning.

Oppositional Defiant Disorder

FOUR-YEAR-OLD MARISSA yells at her mother when her mother reminds her to brush her teeth. Six-year-old Jonah sits in time-out for hours because he refuses to apologize for disrespectful behavior at the dinner table. For the third time in a week, 11-year-old Luis is sent to the principal's office, this time for ignoring his teacher's repeated requests for him to sit down and complete his math assignment.

Are these children headstrong, or spoiled, or bad? Are their parents and teachers too lenient or too harsh? Is anyone to blame in these battles for control? Defiant, uncooperative behavior is the frequent focus of adult concern (Cummings, Davies, & Campbell, 2000; Reid, Patterson, & Snyder, 2003), and a major reason for referrals of preschoolers, children, and adolescents for psychological interventions

(Campbell, 1995; DeVito & Hopkins, 2001; Keenan & Wakschlag, 2002; Loeber, Burke, Lahey, Winters, & Zera, 2000).

The disruptive behavior disorders described in DSM-IV-TR include attention deficit hyperactivity disorder (see Chapter 9), oppositional defiant disorder, and conduct disorder (see Chapter 14). All of these involve externalizing behaviors that significantly impair children's current and future adjustments. Although unruly, disrespectful, and disobedient behavior may be observed throughout development, especially during the toddler and adolescent years, the focus in this chapter is on children in the early and middle school grades. The upcoming chapter on conduct disorder will pick up the developmental thread with older children and adolescents.

Developmental Tasks and Challenges Related to Self-Control and Compliance

It is essential that we appreciate the tasks and challenges associated with cooperative and compliant behavior if we want to understand the uncooperative and noncompliant problems that some children experience. In the 18–30 month period, often characterized by frustrated parents as "the terrible twos," children's growing behavioral competence and self-awareness leads them to discover their capacity to say "no." As with many new words (or skills or toys), children initially employ it to excess; acknowledgement and acceptance of parental limits on their self-determination comes gradually. Most children between the ages of 3 and 5 move beyond this freshly autonomous phase, where misbehavior can be amusing to adults and is often tolerated, to a phase where adult demands increase for less mischievous and more appropriate behavior: "it is at this point in development where two important forces—a child's capacity for compliance and adults' expectations for compliance—are thought to intersect" (Greene & Doyle, 1999, p. 137). For some children, the developmental stage is set for trouble.

The everyday direction and control of children's behavior, initially accomplished primarily by parents and other adults, is now increasingly achieved by children themselves. From the child's perspective, making one's wishes known and doing for oneself are worth the fuss. From the adults' perspective, this shift involves letting go of some of the power and some of the limit-setting. It involves watching as children make a mess of their possessions and

their surroundings. It involves understanding that increases in oppositional and disruptive behaviors are typical (Crnic, Gaze, & Hoffman, 2005; DeVito & Hopkins, 2001; Williford, Calkins, & Keane, 2007), and understanding that the child's struggle for independence and self-control is not an easy one. For both adults and children, this shift in control represents a major developmental milestone (Barkley, 2001; Williford et al., 2007).

Self-control, or self-regulation, involves behaviors, feelings, and thoughts, and "refers to people's efforts to alter their own responses, such as overriding behavioral impulses, resisting temptation, controlling their thoughts, and altering (or artificially prolonging) their emotions" (Dale & Baumeister, 1999, p. 139). One important distinction involving self-regulation is between automatic and controlled responses. "Automatic responses are efficient and require few resources but are relatively rigid and inflexible. Controlled responses are inefficient and expensive (in terms of

Jose Luis Pelaez Inc/Blend Images/Getty Images

Parents play a crucial role in helping children develop self-control and regulate their own behavior.

psychological resources) but are highly flexible" (Dale & Baumeister, 1999, p. 141). That is, there are some responses, such as putting one's hands over one's ears in a very noisy room, that are exhibited almost immediately and without much thought. Other responses, such as not touching a fragile glass bowl filled with candy, require more effort. Some responses, such as raising one's hand in class, start out as controlled but, with practice, eventually become automatic. These controlled responses are examples of children's **effortful control**, and are important for both everyday and optimal functioning (Eisenberg, Valiente, et al., 2003; Kochanska, Murray, & Harlan, 2000; Kochanska, Murray, & Coy, 1997).

Compliance is a specific kind of self-regulation. With compliance, the child's desires take a back seat to an adult's directive. Kochanska, Coy, and Murray (2001) define compliance as doing something unpleasant (or boring) or not doing something pleasurable following the request of another. For most children, doing something is more challenging than not doing something. Turning off the television in the middle of a cartoon, then, is more problematic than not taking the toys out of the toy chest. Children may display either committed compliance (i.e., eager acceptance of the task) or situational compliance (i.e., resigned acquiescence). Compliance is a complex skill, dependent on earlier abilities to regulate emotion (Stifter, Spinrad, & Braungart-Rieker, 1999), and tied to upcoming school readiness and school achievement (Blair & Peters, 2003; Greene & Doyle, 1999; McClelland et al., 2007).

There are a number of child characteristics related to the typical development of self-regulation and effortful control. Dale and Baumeister (1999) argue that, in order to self-regulate, children must understand that there are standards or goals for behavior (cf. Carver & Scheier, 1981). They must be able to monitor, inhibit, and restrain behaviors. For certain children, temperamental attributes such as high levels of negative emotion or impulsive reactivity make it more difficult to monitor and/or inhibit behavior (Rothbart, Ellis, Rueda, & Posner, 2003). Individual differences in underlying neurobiology may also influence the development of effortful control (Blair, 2002; Davis, Bruce, & Gunnar, 2002). Differences related to children's skills in recognizing and proactively responding to challenging situations are also important (Aspinwall & Taylor, 1997; Twenge & Baumeister, 2002). In addition to behavioral standards or goals, children must also be able to monitor the match between their behaviors and the standards; this is an ongoing process involving self-awareness (Carver & Scheier, 1981; Dale & Baumeister, 1999).

Even with all of these child-related factors, parents and other adults remain critically involved. The socialization of emotion regulation, for example, is an essential component and ongoing task of early development (Calkins & Hill, 2007; Eisenberg, Cumberland, & Spinrad, 1998). And the ways in which parents provide direction and guidance, exert authority, and discipline their children can support or thwart the development of effortful control (Eisenberg, Zhou, et al., 2003). By 4 years of age, effortful control appears stable across time and consistent across situations (Kochanska & Knaack, 2003; Kochanska et al., 2000; Rothbart & Putnam, 2002). In terms of temperamental style, less angry, more inhibited children develop higher levels of effortful control, display a stronger conscience, and exhibit fewer externalizing behaviors (Kochanska & Aksan, 2004). Higher levels of effortful control are also observed in girls (Kochanska et al., 2000; Kochanska et al., 1997).

Baumeister and his colleagues have compared self-regulation to a muscle (Baumeister, Muraven, & Tice, 2000; Dale & Baumeister, 1999; Twenge & Baumeister, 2002), and propose that self-regulation must be developed and strengthened. Self-regulation must also be conserved and replenished. "Like a muscle that becomes tired and loses its ability to perform, self-regulation can accomplish only a limited amount without having some time to recover" (Dale & Baumeister, 1999, p. 142). Self-regulation, or effortful control, is a limited resource, and we cannot expect that young children (or even older children) will inhibit impulses and resist temptation for very long periods of time (Muraven & Baumeister, 2000; Twenge & Baumeister, 2002). The main form of self-regulation failure involves **underregulation**, or not exerting enough control (Dale & Baumeister, 1999). Underregulation may result from a lack of behavioral standards (e.g., a parent who fails to provide guidelines about appropriate behavior may have a child who runs amok in a restaurant), a lack of self-awareness or monitoring (e.g., a child may fail to keep track of how often she gets out of her seat in the classroom), or a lack of strength in the face of overwhelming impulses (e.g., a child playing with a friend may fail to share a train set, or may push another child out of his way on the playground) (Dale & Baumeister, 1999).

So far, this discussion of the construct of self-regulation has focused on the process of internalizing previously external control during the preschool years. In the early school years, there is also another transition, from individualized control to rule-based control. Children in the primary grades are intensely aware of rules and are often quite vocal when rules are broken or changed without warning. Self-regulation in the context of the many rules related to home, classroom, friends, and activities presents an ongoing challenge for children throughout elementary school.

It is commonly assumed that regulation involves a set of coordinated processes that develop in synchrony. That is, children's abilities to control their thoughts, their emotions, and their behaviors move forward together. But because some of the factors influencing cognitive, emotional, and behavioral development differ, *dysynchrony* (being "out of sync") is also a possibility. Some children may be more skilled in emotion regulation than behavior regulation and vice versa (Gross & Munoz, 1995). Researchers continue to explore the various temperamental and experiential factors that support or inhibit the development of self-regulation in each of these domains (Underwood, 1997; Underwood & Hurley, 1999).

Oppositional Defiant Disorder

Oppositional defiant disorder (ODD) is a sustained pattern of negativistic, hostile, and defiant behavior (see Table 10.1). The disorder is differentiated from the more severe conduct disorder that involves the violation of social norms and rules as well as the rights of others. The following two cases illustrate common ODD presentations.

The Case of Brad

Brad is a 5-year-old child who exhibits non-compliance, frequent temper tantrums, and physical aggression at home and at kindergarten. These aggressive behaviors include throwing objects, biting, punching, and kicking. Brad's mother, a single parent, reported that his difficult behaviors began at age 2, and emerged during a period of multiple life changes, including moving to a new home and enrolling in a different school. Because of the disruptive behaviors, Brad had been asked to leave several day care centers before starting kindergarten. Brad's mother is also upset with herself because she has no idea how to handle Brad's increasingly loud and obnoxious interactions with her and with his siblings at home and in public. ∎

The Case of Nick

Nick is an 11-year-old referred for a diagnostic assessment by his mother and father because of his "horrible" behavior and school difficulties. Nick is in sixth grade. His parents describe him as ornery, disrespectful, and disobedient. At times they are taken aback by his loud and threatening behavior, especially when directed at his younger brother. Grounding Nick and withholding money and other privileges has had little impact, even though there are times when Nick seems distressed by his own actions. Nick has been suspended twice this school year for disruptive behavior, including yelling at a teacher. Academically, Nick is struggling to keep his grades high enough to pass, although he had little trouble in school prior to this year. ∎

Both Brad and Nick exhibit mixes of typical and atypical behaviors that require closer study. Developmentally, Brad displays disruptive behaviors that are more frequent and more intense than expected; indeed, his repeated dismissals from day care settings suggest clinically significant disturbance. Nick displays externalizing behaviors that complicate his

TABLE 10:1 DSM-IV-TR CRITERIA FOR OPPOSITIONAL DEFIANT DISORDER
A. A pattern of negativistic, hostile, and defiant behavior lasting at least 6 months, during which four or more of the following symptoms are present. These symptoms are developmentally inappropriate or excessive. (1) often loses temper (2) often argues with adults (3) often defies or refuses to comply with adult requests or rules (4) often deliberately annoys people (5) often blames others for mistakes or misbehavior (6) often touchy or easily annoyed by others (7) often angry and resentful (8) often spiteful or vindictive
B. The behaviors are associated with clinically significant impairment in social, academic, or other settings.

Creasource/Corbis

Negativistic, hostile, and defiant behavior are the core features of oppositional defiant disorder.

personal agenda and ruin family activities. For the boys, the transition to new school situations that require additional self-control also seems more problematic than for most of their peers. Both Brad and Nick meet the diagnostic criteria for oppositional defiant disorder.

Oppositional defiant disorder is a relative newcomer to the DSM, with previous descriptions of the disorder mainly focused on its role as an early or milder expression of conduct disorder. Researchers and clinicians have since come to conceptualize ODD as a distinct entity associated with significant impairments (Burns, Walsh, Owen, & Snell, 1997; Drabick, Gadow, & Loney, 2007; Greene et al., 2002; Keenan & Wakschlag, 2000; Langbehn, Cadoret, Yates, Troughton, & Stewart, 1998; Loeber, Burke, et al., 2000; Quay, 1999; Rowe, Maughan, Costello, & Angold, 2005; Webster-Stratton, 2000). The essential features of ODD include various forms of noncompliant behavior with negative, even self-destructive, consequences. Aggression may sometimes be exhibited (Loeber, Burke, et al., 2000), although it is important to distinguish between proactive and reactive forms of aggression (Dodge, 1991; Dodge & Coie, 1987). **Proactive aggression** is more deliberate and less emotional. A bully who plans to wreck another child's science project exhibits proactive aggression. **Reactive aggression** is more impulsive and more emotional. A child who is thrown out at first base displays reactive aggression by cursing at the umpire. This kind of aggression is related to poor self-regulation (Dodge, Lochman, Harnish, Bates, & Pettit, 1997).

Negative emotion is a core component of ODD, with many frequent and intense emotional experiences

(Cummings et al., 2000). Brad's emotions, in the previous case, include anger, distress, frustration, and irritability. Nick's emotions are similar, although they sometimes include experiences of shame. Understanding irritability may be especially useful, because irritability directed toward others (rather than toward oneself) is related to a host of problems, including family and peer difficulties; this kind of irritability may also identify individuals who are responsive to mood stabilizers (Donovan et al., 2003).

Impaired social cognition, with less accurate and more aggressive interpretations of everyday social information, is usually observed (Coy, Speltz, DeKlyen, & Jones, 2001; Shure & Spivack, 1980; Zahn-Waxler, Cole, Richardson, & Friedman, 1994). Given the defiant behaviors, negative emotions, and error-prone cognitions, ODD has very deleterious effects on the child's interpersonal relationships with parents and siblings, with teachers, and with peers (Greene & Doyle, 1999; Stormshak & Webster-Stratton, 1999; Webster-Stratton & Lindsay, 1999).

Oppositional defiant disorder has been documented in many different cultures and countries (Robins, 1999). Estimates of prevalence vary from 2% to 16% (Barrickman, 2003; Maughan, Rowe, Messer, Goodman, & Meltzer, 2004; Nock, Kazdin, Hiripi, & Kessler, 2007). Although usually diagnosed before age 8, ODD can be seen in preschoolers and in adolescents. Almost all investigations of ODD report that it is more common in boys, but there is increasing work on descriptions of disruptive disorders in girls (Kann & Hanna, 2000; Loeber, Burke, et al., 2000). Increased prevalence of ODD has been noted in children from low SES backgrounds and neighborhoods with high crime rates (Loeber, Burke, et al., 2000; Robins, 1999). In addition, older adults appear to be correct in their assertions that today's children are more disrespectful and disobedient than past children; there are data to support the hypothesis of generational (i.e., cohort) differences in disruptive behaviors (Loeber, Burke, et al., 2000; Robins, 1999).

Developmental Course

As the developmental course of ODD is described, it is important to keep in mind the continuous nature of oppositional and disruptive behaviors (i.e., the connections between typically and atypically developing children), and the up-and-down experience of parenting stress during the preschool years

(Crnic et al., 2005; Williford et al., 2007). Still, early patterns of disruptive difficulties are frequently and strongly associated with later patterns of difficulties (Burke, Loeber, & Birmaher, 2002; Campbell, Shaw, & Gilliom, 2000; Caspi et al., 2003; Egeland, Pianta, & Ogawa, 1996; Farmer & Bierman, 2002; Guerin, Gottfried, & Thomas, 1997). Children with clinically significant disorders do not "grow out" of their problems.

There are several predictable pathways for children with early externalizing disorders (Frick & Loney, 1999; Greene & Doyle, 1999; Loeber et al., 2000; Nagin & Tremblay, 1999; Robins, 1999; van Lier, van der Ende, Koot, & Verhulst, 2007). One developmental pathway is for oppositional defiant disorder to continue without much improvement or deterioration, resulting in years of conflict, hostility, and disappointment. Without intervention, this pathway is the most common, especially for girls (August, Realmuto, Joyce, & Hektner, 1999; Rowe, Maughan, Pickles, Costello, & Angold, 2002). For both girls and boys, the more severe the ODD symptoms, the more stable the disorder (Loeber, Burke et al., 2000). There is, however, evidence that supports the notion of a possible reorganization, with some improvement, during early adolescence (Granic, Hollenstein, Dishion, & Patterson, 2003).

One of the most problematic pathways is from oppositional defiant disorder to conduct disorder to antisocial personality disorder, with increases in aggression, violence, and substance abuse along the way (Burke et al., 2002; Burke, Loeber, & Lahey, 2003; Loeber, Burke, et al., 2000). Aggression, in particular, exhibits very stable trajectories (Bierman & Wargo, 1995; Munson, McMahon, & Spieker, 2001). Particularly worrisome with respect to negative outcomes are those children who display callous, unemotional responses along with their disruptive behaviors (Barry et al., 2000; Frick & Morris, 2004). However, it is important to emphasize that, with increasing age, fewer and fewer individuals are diagnosed with the increasingly severe and persistent disorders.

Child Outcomes

One of the factors that most strongly predicts stability of disorder is age of onset. Those with childhood-onset ODD—the early starters—display more persistent patterns of difficulty (Keenan, Shaw, Delliquadri, Giovannelli, & Walsh, 1998; Munson et al., 2001; Pierce, Ewing, & Campbell, 1999; Speltz, McClellan, DeKlyen, & Jones, 1999; Thomas & Clark, 1998).

Gender also plays an important role. Beginning in preschool, boys exhibit more disruptive behaviors with more negative impact (Munson et al., 2001). In the Great Smoky Mountains community study, boys diagnosed with ODD displayed worse outcomes involving externalizing disorders, although girls later developed more internalizing disorders (Rowe et al., 2002). Combinations of other factors, such as early temperamental difficulties, poor self-regulation, certain forms of aggression, and socioeconomic status (SES), also appear to influence gender-specific pathways (Hill, Degnan, Calkins, & Keane, 2006; Sanson & Prior, 1999; Silverthorn & Frick; 1999; Silverthorn, Frick, & Reynolds, 2001; Underwood, Galen, & Paquette, 2001). For instance, poor self-regulation and inattention predicted worse outcomes for girls, whereas low SES and inattention predicted worse outcomes for boys (Hill et al., 2006).

With respect to short- and long-term outcomes, children's comorbid psychopathologies also play a part. Attention deficit hyperactivity disorder (ADHD) is of special concern. Lahey, Loeber, and their colleagues have proposed a model of externalizing disorders in which only those children who are diagnosed with *both* ODD and ADHD go on to develop conduct disorders, with ADHD often preceding ODD as a specific risk factor (Burke, Loeber, Lahey, & Rathouz, 2005; Lahey et al., 2004; Lahey & Loeber, 1997; Lahey, McBurnett, & Loeber, 2000; Loeber, Burke, et al., 2000). In the model, there are three deviant pathways, each with its own set of developmental challenges (although these may overlap in children): (a) the **overt pathway**, with minor aggression leading to more serious aggression that tends to be unconcealed and blatant; (b) the **covert pathway**, with minor misbehaviors leading to more serious delinquent acts that tend to be more concealed or secretive; and (c) the **authority conflict pathway**, with stubborn relationship-oriented behaviors leading to more serious disobedience and hostility (Burke et al., 2002). Other research provides support for the model, with findings related to early and reliable diagnoses of ODD and ADHD, intersecting courses of psychopathology, and a worse prognosis for children with both ODD and ADHD (Burns & Walsh, 2002; Gadow & Nolan, 2002; Shaw, Owens, Giovannelli, & Winslow, 2001; van Lier et al., 2007).

In related work on comorbid psychopathologies involving anxiety and depression, ODD is identified as "a pivotal developmental disorder," especially in boys (Burke et al., 2005). Studies have documented the connection between early ODD and later internalizing disorders. With respect to depression, Capaldi and her colleagues have hypothesized that the disruptive symptoms of ODD underlie academic and interpersonal failures, which then lead to depression (Capaldi, 1991, 1992; Capaldi & Stoolmiller, 1999).

Family Outcomes

Along with children's characteristics, parent and family characteristics also influence the ways in which ODD plays out over time. Adult patience and tolerance for oppositional behavior varies widely; similar child misbehaviors may evoke very different responses in different individuals (and in mothers versus fathers) (Calzada, Eyberg, Rich, & Querido, 2004). Compared to most parents' experiences of managing extremes of oppositional and defiant behavior for discrete periods of time, for parents of children with ODD, the prospect of chronic conflict may be overwhelming (Williford et al., 2007). Parent psychopathology is associated with additional struggles (Burke et al., 2002; Cummings & Davies, 1994; Kaplan & Liu, 1999; Robins, 1999; Weissman et al., 1999), although various forms of parental problems are related to different outcomes. For instance, a child with ODD who displays high levels of fearlessness parented by a mother with depression exhibits a somewhat different course than one parented by a rejecting mother (Shaw, Gilliom, Ingoldsby, & Nagin, 2003; see also Lindahl, 1998; Morris et al., 2002).

Different patterns of family interaction, such as negative or positive parenting, are also associated with differential impacts and stability (Forehand & Jones, 2002; Loeber, Drinkwater, et al., 2000). Negative parenting, involving either hostility and harsh discipline or timid discipline, is associated with poorer outcomes (August et al., 1999; Burke, Pardini, & Loeber, 2008). Conversely, parental warmth, coupled with active monitoring of children's activities, is associated with better outcomes (Buckner, Mezzacappa, & Beardslee, 2003). Further studies of the factors that influence parenting, such as SES, ethnicity and culture, and community, will provide valuable context for interpretation of these kinds of findings (Ackerman, Brown, & Izard, 2003; Kotchick & Forehand, 2002).

The case of Brad provides many examples of the influence of parents and parenting on the course of ODD. Brad's mother recalls how many times she has felt embarrassed over the last year as Brad has misbehaved loudly in the grocery store, the discount store, and in the entrance lobby of his school. She is positive that other parents believe that she is either unfit or stupid, and these concerns have led her to withdraw from many of her regular social activities. Her parents have tried to help with babysitting and financial support, but they have also repeatedly criticized her for not being strict enough with Brad. At this point, Brad's mother is discouraged and ready to give up on Brad to focus on her other children.

Peer Outcomes

Peers can make things easier for those with ODD, and peers can make things worse. As we can imagine, children who are disagreeable, stubborn, and emotionally unpredictable have a hard time making and keeping friends. Peer conflicts and rejection by peers are frequent consequences of ODD (Burke et al., 2002; Goodman, Stormshak, & Dishion, 2001; Miller-Johnson, Coie, Maumary-Gremaud, Bierman, & Conduct Problems Prevention Research Group, 2002). Because of conflict and rejection, children and adolescents with ODD often associate with other deviant peers (Burke et al., 2002; Stormshak, Bierman, Bruschi, Dodge, & Coie, 1999). Relationships with others who also struggle with externalizing behaviors exacerbate children's already-poor functioning at home, in schools, and in the community (Lansford, Criss, Pettit, Dodge, & Bates, 2003; Ledingham, 1999; Miller-Johnson et al., 2002; Stormshak et al., 1998).

The case of Nick provides useful illustrations of these kinds of peer influences. Nick has always had many friends, both in his neighborhood and at school. Most of them are his age, but a few are older. Some of the older boys have been in trouble for cutting school, possession of marijuana, and vandalism. In fact, several times over the past weeks, Nick has come home smelling of beer; he denies drinking himself but admits that a couple of guys do take beer to the park where they all hang out. Almost all of his friends make fun of kids who study and those involved in school activities such as band and student council. Nick's parents believe that these peers are making it more difficult to get Nick back on "the right track," and they worry that he is feeling more pressure to experiment with drugs and participate in delinquent behaviors.

Etiology

Given the various emotions and behaviors that contribute to a presentation of oppositional defiant disorder, and the various developmental pathways that may be taken by children, it makes sense to consider the possibility of multiple etiologies for this heterogeneous group of disorders. Unlike many of the psychopathologies presented in this textbook, the etiology of ODD has long been discussed within a developmental framework, with attention paid to developmental theories such as social learning and attachment (Shaw & Bell, 1993).

The Coercion Model

By far the most work that has been done has focused on the **coercion model** described by Gerald Patterson and his colleagues. In this model, often referred to as the Oregon model (where much of the research was conducted), the primary focus is on patterns of parental characteristics that lead to negative parent-child interactions. Chamberlain and Patterson (1995) describe these characteristics in detail: (1) inconsistent discipline, with parents only sometimes enforcing limits and rules; (2) irritable, explosive discipline, with parents enforcing limits and rules in harsh and angry ways; (3) inflexible, rigid discipline, with parents enforcing limits and rules without regard to individual child attributes or special circumstances; and/or (4) low supervision and involvement. The basic assumption of the coercion model is that parents and children struggle for control over a number of everyday tasks and activities, and that maladaptive parenting leads to children's externalizing behavior; the coercion model specifically examines a conditioning sequence in which children are inadvertently reinforced for their problematic behaviors (Patterson, 2002; Patterson, Reid, & Eddy, 2002; Patterson, Reid, & Dishion, 1992). If parents are ineffective and negative, children's initial misbehavior and disobedience (which may be typical and not always a major concern) escalates. The child's escalating opposition is met by the parent's increasingly punitive responses, again and again and again. Data collected from families with boys as well as girls fit the

coercion model (Beauchaine, Strassberg, Kees, & Drabick, 2002; Eddy, Leve, & Fagot, 2001; Rubin, Hastings, Chen, Stewart, & McNichol, 1998).

The Transactional Model

A recent revision of the coercion model has been advocated by Greene and Doyle and their colleagues. The more inclusive **transactional model** asserts that parent-child incompatibility is multiply determined, with multiple pathways to both externalizing and internalizing disorders, multiple interventions, and multiple outcomes. The coercion model is focused mainly on the role of the parents and, according to Greene and Doyle (1999), is one possible pathway among many. The transactional model emphasizes the investigation of several domains of risk factors, including child characteristics, maladaptive parenting, gene-environment interactions, peer influences, and sociocultural context, each of which may be tied to the diagnosis of externalizing problems. As with other psychopathologies, the more risk factors an individual experiences, the more likely the emergence of ODD (Burke et al., 2002; Deater-Deckard, Dodge, Bates, & Pettit, 1998; Greenberg, Speltz, DeKlyen, & Jones, 2001).

Child Factors

Child factors that appear to have an impact on the development of ODD include gender, temperament, and attachment status. And, in fact, there are some data suggesting that the impact of child behaviors on parenting may be greater than the impact of parenting on child behaviors (Burke et al., 2008). Boys overall are at higher risk, although girls with adolescent mothers are also quite vulnerable (Eme & Kavanaugh, 1995; Munson et al., 2001). With respect to temperament, high levels of arousal and novelty-seeking, along with low levels of harm avoidance are associated with disruptive disorders (Burke et al., 2002; Sanson & Prior, 1999; Schmeck & Poustka, 2001). Lahey and his colleagues have presented the available temperament data in a straightforward model (see Figure 10.1).

Individual differences in effortful control are also important; both verbal and behavioral self-regulation appear to be compromised (Buckner, Mezzacappa, & Beardslee, 2003; Eisenberg, Cumberland, et al., 2001; Hill et al., 2006; Murray & Kochanska, 2002; Winsler, Diaz, Atencio, McCarthy, & Adams Chabay, 2000). Dysregulated children who display aggressive behaviors and initiate conflict are at higher risk (Rubin, Burgess, Dwyer, & Hastings, 2003). The impact of attachment

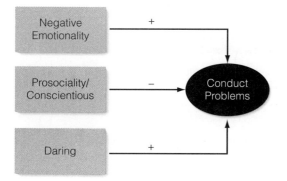

FIGURE 10:1 Temperament dimensions and disruptive behavior problems.
Source: Lahey and Waldman (2003).

remains to be fully explained (Burke et al., 2002; Gilliom, Shaw, Beck, Schonberg, & Lukon, 2002), but there is interesting evidence for the negative influence of insecure attachment, especially for boys (Munson et al. 2001; Speltz, DeKlyen, & Greenberg, 1999).

Neuropsychological factors have also been the focus of ODD research. Children with poor neonatal health are at higher risk. This risk may be related to overall cognitive functioning (Hogan, 1999; Plomin, Price, Eley, Dale, & Stevenson, 2002), with boys with ODD exhibiting lower verbal and executive function scores on neuropsychological assessments (Bellanti, Bierman, & Conduct Problems Prevention Research Group, 2000; Speltz et al., 1999). Whether low intelligence leads to increased rates of ODD remains unclear (Burke et al., 2002; Hogan, 1999). Deficits in social cognition, related to less accurate, more aggressive interpretations of others' behaviors, are hypothesized to underlie many of the negativistic patterns observed in children with ODD (Coy et al., 2001; Crick & Dodge, 1994, 1996; Webster-Stratton & Lindsay, 1999). The often comorbid diagnosis of ADHD makes executive function deficits difficult to tie specifically to ODD (Clark, Prior, & Kinsella, 2000; Crick & Dodge, 1994, 1996).

Adoption status, related to preadoption abuse/neglect, older age at adoption, prenatal drug exposure, and multiple foster placements, is associated with an increased risk for ODD (Simmel, Brooks, Barth, & Hinshaw, 2001). The trauma of sexual abuse has also been identified as a risk factor (Burke et al., 2002; Trickett & Putnam, 1998). There is no evidence that out-of-home child care in the early years increases children's vulnerability to ODD (Bacharach & Baumeister, 2003).

Parent and Family Factors

Parent factors that have an impact on the development of ODD include the types of behaviors described in the coercion model as well as a number of other maladaptive variables. Stormshak, Bierman, McMahon, Lengua, and the Conduct Problems Prevention Research Group (2000) distinguish between dimensions of positive and negative parenting behaviors, so that some parents are high on one dimension and low on the other, low on both, and so on. Positive parenting includes warmth, involvement, and monitoring (Dishion & McMahon, 1998; Jones, Forehand, Brody, & Armistead, 2003). Negative parenting includes indifference, hostility, and problems with control (i.e., both over- and undercontrol), and is repeatedly linked to problem behaviors in children (Rubin et al., 2003). These aspects of parenting may be linked to certain helpful and unhelpful thoughts of parents during struggles with their children (see Table 10.2).

As observed with children's self-regulation, both **overcontrol** and **undercontrol** by parents are associated with children's disruptive behaviors (Burke et al., 2002; DeKlyen, Speltz, & Greenberg, 1998; Stormshak et al., 2000). Permissive, timid parenting seems especially problematic (Burke et al., 2008; DeVito & Hopkins, 2001). There appears to be a nonlinear relationship between negative parenting and externalizing behaviors: Mild punishment is only weakly related to externalization, whereas severe and abusive punishment is strongly related (Deater-Deckard & Dodge, 1997). That is, parents who display relatively few harsh punishments do not end up with children with a little bit of ODD. When focusing on the impact of parenting to the exclusion of other factors, we find that only with regular and sustained negative parenting are children likely to develop clinically significant problems.

Other parent and family factors that appear to contribute to a diagnosis of ODD in a child include marital dissatisfaction (DeVito & Hopkins, 2001), maternal attachment history (Greenberg, Speltz, & DeKlyen, 1993; Speltz, DeKlyen, Greenberg, & Dryden, 1995), and domestic violence (Jaffee, Moffitt, Caspi, Taylor, & Arseneault, 2002). Interactions between child characteristics (such as gender or temperament) and certain parent characteristics may also be problematic. For example, sons and daughters who display challenging behaviors may elicit differentially effective discipline from parents

TABLE 10:2 HELPFUL AND UNHELPFUL PARENTAL BELIEFS	
UNHELPFUL BELIEFS	**HELPFUL BELIEFS**
My child acts up on purpose.	It doesn't matter whose fault it is. What matters are solutions to the problems.
My child is the cause of most of our family problems.	It is not just my child. I also play a role in the problem.
It is my fault that my child has problems.	It is not just my fault. My child also plays a role in the problems.
It is his/her (other parent) fault that my child is this way.	It doesn't help to blame him/her. We need to work together.
I give up. There is nothing more I can do for my child.	I have no choice but to parent my child. I need to think of new ways to parent my child.
I have tried everything and have no control over my child.	My belief that I have no control over my child might be contributing to the problem. Many things are in my control, and I have to figure out what I can do to solve the problem.

Adapted from Bloomquist & Schnell (2002).

(Bierman & Welsh, 1997; Burke et al., 2002; Burt, Krueger, McGue, & Iacono, 2003; Deater-Deckard et al., 2001; Fowles & Kochanska, 2000; Greene & Doyle, 1999; Keiley, Lofthouse, Bates, Dodge, & Pettit, 2003).

The specific role of fathers has received recent attention. Fathers of preschool boys diagnosed with ODD differed from fathers of boys not diagnosed in terms of increased life stress, more psychopathological symptoms, negative parenting attitudes, less positive involvement, and more harsh discipline (DeKlyen, Biernbaum, Speltz, & Greenberg, 1998). Harsh discipline in particular made a unique contribution to the child's ODD (DeKlyen et al., 1998). In fact, the father's presence was protective only if he expressed low levels of antisocial behavior (Jaffee, Moffitt, Caspi, & Taylor, 2003).

Genes and Heredity

The transactional model places the child and parent factors that contribute to ODD in genetic and environmental context. With respect to the role of genetics, the picture is complicated, with evidence for genetic, shared, and nonshared environmental influences (Burt, Krueger, McGue, & Iacono, 2001; Deater-Deckard, 2000; Deater-Deckard & Plomin, 1999; Eaves et al., 2000; Ehringer et al., 2006; Meyer et al., 2000; O'Connor, Deater-Deckard, Fulker, Rutter, & Plomin, 1998). Researchers have

repeatedly observed that disruptive disorders aggregate in families, and as just noted, are very apparent in families with fathers with externalizing problems. In addition, the early-onset form of ODD, with clear evidence for disruptive behaviors in preschoolers and poor prognosis for long-term outcome, appears to have a distinct genetic etiology (Arseneault et al., 2003). With respect to gender, partly different genes are expressed for boys and girls (Derks, Dolan, Hudziak, Neale, & Boomsma, 2007).

There are many possible mechanisms of genetic transmission that may contribute to the psychobiology of ODD (Pliszka, 1999; Simonoff, 2001). Studies of molecular genetics, chromosomal abnormalities, assortative mating (i.e., individuals choose partners who are like themselves in some important characteristic), and changes in heritability with age all provide useful data. Much of the relevant neuroscience research has targeted aggression and violence (Burke et al., 2002) which is discussed more completely in the chapter on conduct disorder (Chapter 14). Briefly, impairments and/or dysfunction have been reported in frontal lobe activation (Baying, Laucht, & Schmidt, 2000), the amygdala (Davidson, 2000), the hypothalamic-pituitary-adrenal (HPA) axis (van Goozen, Matthys, Cohen-Kettenis, Buitelaar, & van Engeland, 2000; van Goozen, van den Ban, et al., 2000), the behavioral inhibition system (Fowles, Kochanska, & Murray, 2000), and the workings of neurotransmitters (Davidson, Putnam & Larson, 2000; Pliszka, 1999; van Goozen et al., 1999) and hormones (Snoek et al., 2002; van Goozen et al., 1998).

The often-overlapping clinical presentations of ODD with ADHD and conduct disorder suggest the possibility of a shared genetic risk (Burns, Boe, Walsh, Sommers-Flanagan, & Teegarden, 2001; Burt, Krueger, McGue, & Iacono, 2001; Dick, Viken, Kaprio, Pulkkinen, & Rose, 2005; Faraone, Biederman, Jetton, & Tsuang, 1997; Nadder, Rutter, Silberg, Maes, & Eaves, 2002; Waldman, Rhee, Levy, & Hay, 2001). According to Pennington (2002): "the environment must act to differentiate individuals with a similar genetic risk into different [disruptive behavior disorders]. . . . With optimal parenting, a child with this genetic risk profile will develop ADHD only. With harsh parenting, the same child will also develop comorbid ODD or CD, whereas a child without this genetic risk profile in the same family might attract less harsh parenting and nonetheless develop different symptoms if he or she did receive similar parenting" (p. 183).

Other Environmental Factors

In the transactional model, peers play a role in the emergence of ODD as well as the developmental course of the disorder. Peer conflict, peer rejection, and associations with deviant peers all increase the likelihood of ODD (Burke et al., 2002). In addition to these peer-related factors, there are many more environmental factors that influence the emergence of disorder. We can think of these factors in terms of levels of environmental risk, from family to school to neighborhood to society (Burke et al., 2002; Caspi, Taylor, Moffitt, & Plomin, 2000; Greenberg et al., 1999; Hope & Bierman, 1998; McGee & Williams, 1999). For any specific child, these factors may include the presence of lead in the diet (Burke et al., 2002), parenting practices used by different ethnic and cultural groups, including levels of involvement, structure, and discipline (Jones, Forehand, Brody, & Armistead, 2002a, 2000b; McCoy, Frick, Loney, & Ellis, 1999), and neighborhood deprivation (Caspi et al., 2000); each additional stressor makes ODD more likely.

Assessment and Diagnosis

Assessment and diagnosis remain somewhat problematic given all of the changes in the conceptualization and the diagnostic criteria over the past decades (Angold & Costello, 1996b; Loeber et al.,

2000; Rowe et al., 2005), and are likely to remain so as investigators and clinicians continue to refine understandings of ODD. Still, children and adults are struggling now, and mental health professionals must do the best they can with currently available information. As discussed several times already, the identification of ODD often takes place against a background of developmentally expected disruptive behaviors. The differentiation of typical and atypical patterns depends on comprehensive, multimodal, and longitudinal assessments (Altepeter & Korger, 1999; Keenan & Wakschlang, 2002). Parents, teachers, and children can provide data in a variety of ways and for a variety of purposes. Correlations among these different informants are sometimes low, but each contributes information that helps to illustrate the clinical picture (Guerin et al., 1997; Hart, Lahey, Loeber, & Hanson, 1994; Owens & Hoza, 2003; Youngstrom, Loeber, & Stouthamer-Loeber, 2000). Taking note of the different settings in which symptoms are displayed—at home or school, in the clinic or the community—is also necessary (Gadow & Nolan, 2002).

Parental reports must sometimes be interpreted cautiously because of specific personality characteristics or psychopathology in the parents (Querido, Eyberg, & Boggs, 2001), but parental perspectives on functioning in the home and on especially problematic behaviors such as aggression can be very useful (Guerin et al., 1997; Halperin, McKay, & Newcorn, 2002). Teacher ratings are also important (Flanagan et al., 2003; Mattison, Gadow, Sprafkin, & Nolan, 2002; Molina, Smith, & Pelham, 2001), and are better predictors of impairment in children (Hart et al., 1994). Children themselves should also be routinely included in the assessment process (Angold & Costello, 1996a). Standardized interviews and rating scales offer children an opportunity to describe their difficulties in various settings (Friman et al., 2000; Loeber et al., 2000). Observational measures such as the Parent-Instruction-Giving Game with Youngsters may provide additional perspective (Hupp, Reitman, Forde, Shriver, & Kelley, 2008).

Good screening measures exist for preschool-age children, including the Disruptive Behavior Disorders Rating Scale and the Kiddie Disruptive Behavior Disorders Schedule (Keenan et al., 2007; Pelletier, Collet, Gimpel, & Crowley, 2006; Sprafkin, Volpe, Gadow, Nolan, & Kelly, 2002) as well as older children (August, Realmuto, Crosby, & MacDonald, 1995). Specific assessments for each kind of emotion-related dysfunction and assessments of deficits in social cognition, executive function, and problem-solving skills are essential (Bierman & Welsh, 2000; Clark, Prior, & Kinsella, 2000; Webster-Stratton & Lindsay, 1999). It is also possible that use of gender-specific norms for specific rating scales may help identify some struggling girls who are not diagnosed using the gender-neutral DSM-IV-TR criteria (Waschbusch & King, 2006).

In the two cases we have been tracking, both Brad and Nick were able to provide useful information during interviews. Brad described his frustration at not being able to control his temper, and he said that "mean words just come flying out of my mouth. I know that it's wrong, but I can't help it." He also said that his mom is always screaming at him and it makes him feel bad. He said he tries to play with his sisters but that they are annoying and babyish.

When interviewed with his mother, Nick frequently interrupted her and spoke in an aggressive and disrespectful manner. In contrast, when interviewed alone, Nick was much more cooperative. He described his interests in music and sports, but also said that he seldom feels happy, is pessimistic about the future, and does not really care about what happens.

With respect to differential diagnosis, clinicians are usually most concerned with making distinctions between the overlapping symptoms of ODD and conduct disorder (Loney & Lima, 2003) and between ODD and ADHD (Burt et al., 2003; Faraone et al., 1997; Lahey, Loeber, Burke, Rathouz, & McBurnett, 2002). The diagnosis of conduct disorder (CD) supercedes the diagnosis of ODD. So a child with a diagnosis of CD cannot also have a diagnosis of ODD. The diagnosis of ADHD does not preclude a diagnosis of ODD; ADHD may or may not explain all of a child's negativistic behaviors. So, a child may have either ODD or ADHD, or both. Finally, with the frequent ODD symptoms of irritability and mood dysregulation, it is important to rule out bipolar disorder (Spencer et al., 2001).

When considering comorbidity, relations between ODD and ADHD remain problematic (Burt et al., 2003; Faraone et al., 1997; Lahey et al., 2002). Trying to determine whether a child exhibits ADHD or ODD or both can be a confusing clinical decision. Beyond the other disruptive and externalizing disorders, clinicians also need to consider the presence of internalizing disorders such as anxiety

and depression (Loeber, Burke et al., 2000; Speltz, McClellan, DeKlyen, & Jones, 1999); these mixed symptom presentations are not uncommon (Egeland et al., 1996).

Intervention

Because oppositional defiant disorder, along with the other externalizing disorders, is so disturbing to adults and so debilitating for children, a lot of work on interventions has been done for many years (Reid, Patterson, & Snyder, 2003). There are compelling data that early and comprehensive interventions for ODD are both successful and cost effective (Altepeter & Korger, 1999; Behan & Carr, 2000; Burke et al., 2002). Comprehensive interventions such as the Incredible Years program, Fast Track model, and Early Risers program often include several components, and must take into account both child-treatment compatibility and adult-treatment compatibility (Bierman, 1996; Bierman et al., 2002; Bierman & Greenberg, 1996; Greene & Doyle, 1999; Jensen & MTA Cooperative Group, 2002; Webster-Stratton & Reid, 2007; see Box 10.1). Interventions are most likely to be useful when there is a reasonable match between the clinical presentation and various treatment components. Examples of such matches include poor parenting skills paired with parent training and support, children's social skills deficits paired with cognitive-behavioral techniques, and damaged parent-child relationships paired with family therapy.

Parent Treatments

For decades, most of the interventions focused on parent training—particularly behavioral parent training. There is overwhelming support for the role of this training in the treatment of ODD (Burke et al., 2002; Forehand & Kotchick, 2002; Forgatch & Patterson, 1998; Hartman, Stage, & Webster-Stratton, 2003; McMahon, 1999; Reid et al., 2003; Taylor & Biglan, 1998). Indeed, it appears that working with children alone is relatively ineffective unless parents are also targeted and involved (Burke et al., 2002). Recent work has provided further support for interventions at earlier stages (with parents of preschoolers) and with multiethnic families (Baydar, Reid, & Webster-Stratton, 2003; Nixon, Sweeney, Erickson, & Touyz, 2003, 2004; Reid, Webster-Stratton, & Beauchaine, 2001; Webster-Stratton & Reid, 2006).

BOX 10:1 CLINICAL PERSPECTIVES

The Early Risers Program

The Early Risers program, originally developed at the University of Minnesota and now implemented in communities across the country, is a multicomponent, high-intensity intervention program that targets aggressive elementary school children at risk for developing significant conduct problems (August, Lee, Bloomquist, Realmuto, & Hektner, 2003, 2004; Bernat, August, Hektner, & Bloomquist, 2007; August, Realmuto, Hektner, & Bloomquist, 2001). This innovative program is based on the premise that early, comprehensive intervention, sustained over time and across settings, can change the developmental pathway for at-risk children from one characterized by destructive and maladaptive behaviors to one characterized by resilience and success. The intervention includes social skills training, tutoring in reading and math, behavioral group therapy for aggressive, disruptive, and noncompliant behavior,

and parent support services, including consultation and brief intervention for acute family problems. Sessions are based in schools or community centers and emphasize communication, consistency, and coordination of the intervention approach throughout the child's environment (school, community, and home). The enhanced sense of general competence the children develop in the program has been shown to improve their self-image, decision-making, and problem-solving skills. Outcomes for individuals completing five years of continuous intervention show sustained improvement (Bernat et al., 2007). Barriers to effective treatment and positive outcomes include poor collaboration between agencies and schools, transportation difficulties, and high staff turnover; these factors must be accounted for and addressed in planning and treatment stages (August, Bloomquist, Lee, Realmuto, & Hektner, 2006).

Although there are many types of individual and group parent training (Behan & Carr, 2000), the goals of most approaches include helping parents with general parenting skills and specific responses to noncompliant or disruptive behaviors (Beauchaine, Strassberg, Kees, & Drabick, 2002). Greene and his colleagues describe Collaborative Problem Solving therapy, an especially promising approach based on the transactional model of ODD (Greene et al., 2004; Greene, Ablon, & Goring, 2003), which provides detailed feedback to parents about their behaviors. For instance, parents can respond to children's defiance by asserting their power, by removing their request or expectation, or by collaborative problem-solving. Even when parents recognize that the last option is a better choice, they may not know how to act effectively (Greene et al., 2003). Parents may need to learn how to give instructions to their children (e.g., employing a firm directive rather than a pleading question) and how to create after-school schedules to prevent nightly battles over homework. Monitoring the whereabouts and well-being of children is another specific skill that may need to be taught (Dishion & McMahon, 1998; Jones et al., 2003). And, as always, the different developmental needs of children must be taken into account: what works with difficult preschoolers is not likely to work with difficult adolescents (e.g., Barkley, Edwards, & Robin, 1999).

It is also important to keep in mind that both children and their families possess positive characteristics and strengths that can make certain interventions more effective. For example, Brad's mother is willing to try some of the behavioral techniques such as implementing clear and consistent rules, ignoring minor misbehavior, rewarding compliance with certificates for ice cream and toy cars, and avoiding escalation of conflicts that do occur. His mother is also open to connecting with other single mothers at a parenting group that meets at her church. In Nick's case, the therapist is able to capitalize on Nick's interests in music and sports to make a personal and therapeutic connection that is the basis for Nick feeling that he is a part of the solution to the family problems rather than the sole cause. Nick's parents are able to build on this by using CDs and tickets to the college basketball games as incentives for appropriate behavior and opportunities to repair the strained relationships.

In addition to treatment components that focus on parents' interactions with their children, some parents will require other types of individual support. The treatment of parent psychopathology is especially important (Altepeter & Korger, 1999). Less immediately compelling, but no less essential, are efforts to increase positive parenting characteristics such as optimism and warmth in order to promote good outcomes for both children and parents

(Biglan et al., 1997; Forehand & Kotchick, 2002; Jones et al., 2002a; Patterson, 1997; Patterson & Fisher, 2002; Sheeber, Biglan, Metzler, & Taylor, 2002).

Child and Family Treatments

Even when a main focus of intervention is parenting, children often require specific supports. Drug treatments for ODD are not common, although there is evidence that mood stabilizers may be useful at the highest levels of impairment (Burke et al., 2002; Donovan et al., 2003). When additional disorders (such as ADHD) are present, medication plus therapy improves outcomes (Burke et al., 2002). More frequent are cognitive-behavioral interventions related to deficits in the child's information-processing and problem-solving repertoires, including executive function impairments, problematic peer relationships, and difficulties at home (Marlowe, 2001; Webster-Stratton & Hammond, 1997). Greene et al.'s (2004) Collaborative Problem Solving, discussed previously, is another example of effective cognitive-behavioral treatment, this time focused on the child's role.

Increasing emotional and behavioral self-control is also an important component of ODD treatment (Muraven, Baumeister, & Tice, 1999; Speltz, McClellan, et al., 1999), and skills training is a well-documented approach (Shure & Spivack, 1980). The goal of skills training is to improve social competency skills. Although it can be done individually or in a group, the group format is preferred because it allows children to practice their skills with others in a controlled setting. Skills training focuses on solving problems, identifying and managing feelings, and coping with frustration and anger. Because children with ODD exhibit a hostile attribution bias (i.e., they perceive hostile intent in other persons' interactions with them even when no hostility is intended), skills training may support changes in the ways they think about social interactions, giving them more benign and/or positive ways of interpreting and responding to the behaviors of their peers. This in turn helps them to negotiate social situations more effectively and allows them to enjoy better relationships.

In Brad's case, helping Brad to name emotional experiences, modeling ways to appropriately express his feelings, and teaching him several methods of self-soothing were part of the comprehensive treatment plan. For Nick, special consideration was given to assisting in the development of coping strategies to deal with his school difficulties. Nick also benefited from discussions focused on better understanding of his interpersonal strengths and weaknesses. After years of arguments and name-calling, Nick needs to spend time reworking negative beliefs and feelings about himself and his mother and father.

Family interventions, including family meetings and positive family activities, are also commonly included therapeutic components (Milne, Edwards, & Murchie, 2001; Stormshak et al., 1996). Peer involvement may also be important, especially for adolescents with ODD (Milne et al., 2001); although peer involvement often results in improvements in functioning, there is also data that suggest that exposure to, and reinforcement of, new problem behaviors during group interventions may lead to deteriorating outcomes for some adolescents (Burke et al., 2002).

As noted previously, treatment that targets multiple settings in a child's life provides multiple benefits. Webster-Stratton's Incredible Years program focuses on three contexts (child-based, parent-based, teacher-based) associated with particular interaction difficulties. Psychological, social, and economic data from many studies provide support for this type of comprehensive intervention (Foster, Olchowski, & Webster-Stratton, 2007; Reid, Webster-Stratton, & Hammond, 2003, 2007; Webster-Stratton, 2005; Webster-Stratton & Reid, 2007).

School-Based Programs and Prevention Efforts

School-based programs are very important for some children, and have shown success in reducing coercive and antisocial behaviors (Barrera et al., 2002; Leff, Costigan, & Power, 2004; Leff, Power, Manz, Costigan, & Nabors, 2001; Lochman, Coie, Underwood, & Terry, 1993; Welsh, Domitrovich, Bierman, & Lang, 2003; Webster-Stratton, Reid, & Stoolmiller, 2008). Community interventions designed to promote effective discipline techniques and decrease parent-child conflicts supplement individual, family, and school plans (Bradley et al., 2003). For the most severe manifestations of disorder, residential care may be appropriate (Chamberlain, 1999).

In the hopes of minimizing future treatment needs, prevention efforts allow for the possibility of reducing the rates and/or severity of ODD, and there are universal, targeted, and individual strategies that have been pursued (Burke et al., 2002; Tremblay,

LeMarquand, & Vitaro, 1999). One example of a universal measure that has been effective in decreasing disruptive behaviors in the classroom is the school-based part of the Fast Track intervention (Conduct Problems Prevention Research Group, 1999). An example of a targeted measure involves screening high-risk children in preschool and primary grades before ODD problems have become entrenched (Jones, Dodge, Foster, Nix, & Conduct Problems Prevention Research Group, 2002; Webster-Stratton & Taylor, 2001). These types of system-wide prevention efforts continue to be developed and evaluated in order to provide vulnerable children with forms of social and curricular scaffolding that supports their self-regulation and social skills development.

■ Key Terms

Self-control (pg. 166)
Effortful control (pg. 167)
Compliance (pg. 167)
Underregulation (pg. 167)
Oppositional defiant disorder (ODD) (pg. 168)
Proactive aggression (pg. 169)
Reactive aggression (pg. 169)
Negative emotion (pg. 169)
Impaired social cognition (pg. 169)
Overt pathway (pg. 170)
Covert pathway (pg. 170)
Authority conflict pathway (pg. 170)
Coercion model (pg. 172)
Transactional model (pg. 172)
Overcontrol (pg. 173)
Undercontrol (pg. 173)

■ Chapter Summary

- The shift toward increasing self-control and self-regulation (the internalizing of previously external control) is an especially important developmental transition in early childhood.
- Compliance, a specific form of self-regulation, is of particular relevance to oppositional defiant disorder.
- Oppositional defiant disorder (ODD) is characterized by a sustained pattern of negativistic, hostile, and defiant behavior.
- Generalized negative emotion (especially irritability) and impaired social cognition are hallmark symptoms of ODD.
- Although most children diagnosed with ODD do not go on to develop more severe forms of the disorder, ODD does significantly increase the risk for later conduct disorder.
- The presence of ADHD along with ODD is associated with a more negative prognosis.
- A number of etiological risk factors may contribute to the development of ODD, including characteristics of the child, such as temperament, quality of parenting, genetics, and environmental factors.
- The etiological complexity of ODD, an evolving understanding of the disorder, frequently occurring comorbidities, and the overlap with normal range negative behavior in childhood makes assessment and diagnosis of ODD challenging.
- Intervention approaches that are comprehensive and implemented early have been shown to be especially effective.
- These intervention programs generally require the active involvement of parents as well as the child.

Anxiety Disorders

IN A WORLD THAT can be realistically frightening (with adversity, violence, and natural disasters), and unpredictably threatening (with germs, spiders, or pain), many children and adolescents are diagnosed with anxiety-based disorders. Discussion of these disorders provides a useful illustration of the distinction between childhood problems and clinically significant disorders. Many children struggle with fears and worries that have an impact on daily functioning. For some children, taking a bath is a sudsy disaster because they are afraid of the water, or of going down the drain. For other children, thunderstorms ruin a family's evening. Parents and mental health professionals need to take into account a variety of factors, including developmental context, the specific stimuli that elicit fear, and the degree of impairment, as they recognize, diagnose, and respond to children's anxiety-related problems and disorders.

Developmental Tasks and Challenges Related to Fears, Worries, and Emotional Regulation

We know that children feel, express, and control a variety of emotions, and that emotional arousal is an integral component of emotional experiences. Ideally, emotional arousal is accompanied by **emotional regulation**, or emotional control, involving the "modulation, toleration and endurance of emotions" (Denham, 1998, p. 148; see also Campos, Frankel, & Camras, 2004; Cicchetti, Ackerman, & Izard, 1995; Cole, Martin, & Dennis, 2004; Gross & Thompson, 2007). The regulation of difficult, negative, or intense emotions takes many forms, including emotion-focused strategies, cognitive strategies, and behavioral strategies (Denham, 1998). With age and experience, these strategies become more differentiated and more organized, and individual differences in children's capacity for emotion regulation become increasingly apparent (Cole, Michel, & Teti, 1994; Cole & Hall, 2008; Southam-Gerow & Kendall, 2002; Thompson, 2001). Some of these individual differences must be understood in the context of psychological variables such as control (Chorpita, 2001) and sociocultural variables such as family socialization of emotion regulation, ethnicity, and poverty (Raver, 2004; Thompson & Meyer, 2007).

The process of emotion regulation (ER) itself unfolds over time. From birth, there is an ongoing balance of independent and coordinated ER (Campos et al., 2004; Cole et al., 2004). Although we think of infants and toddlers as mostly supported in their ER efforts by their caregivers (so that a mother may pick up and soothe a frightened child), babies also initiate ER by physically turning away from overwhelming stimulation, or by cuddling with a special blanket. Preschoolers and young children are often ER partners with adults, as when a teacher and a child work together through an episode of anger.

Older children and adolescents are usually expected to manage ER independently, so that an athlete on a team having a bad day might distract himself from looming fear or sadness in order to keep playing well during an important basketball game.

It is important to keep a couple of things in mind about the development of ER. First, as new strategies emerge, earlier strategies are not lost. We accumulate and organize strategies over the years, but sometimes (like the baby with the blanket) we still crawl under the covers for comfort. And, the simple idea that we move from dependency on others to independent ER, and that independent ER reflects optimal adjustment, is somewhat inaccurate. A more complex notion includes older children's and adolescents' capacities for independent ER, but emphasizes the flexible use of a variety of ER strategies in different situations. Even well-adjusted adults sometimes seek comfort from others when afraid or anxious. Prominent child psychologists such as David Elkind (1994) suggest that ever-increasing demands for autonomy and self-reliance in youngsters are tied to changing cultural perspectives on childhood and childhood disorders. Earlier conceptions of children as innocent and in need of protection and direction have been replaced by current views of children as inherently skilled and competent. Elkind says, "While some of these demands have allowed children to demonstrate formerly unrecognized competencies, many others are age-inappropriate, overwhelming, and stressful" (p. 119), and increase risks for vulnerable youth.

Finally, with respect to normal development, it is important to emphasize the useful and adaptive nature of much of the anxiety experienced by children (Thompson, 2001). Wariness in the presence of strangers or on an unfamiliar bike path, or apprehension before an exam or a performance, provides children and adolescents with important information about the possibility of harm or the need to prepare for challenging activities. When signals are perceived and adjustments are made, anxiety usually diminishes quickly. Children who experience little or no anxiety may place themselves in risky or unsafe situations, or fail to plan for upcoming events. So, in line with the fundamentally adaptive function of emotion, we are looking for a healthy balance in the amounts of anxiety experienced, and in the situations in which anxiety is elicited and supports adaptation.

With this background information, we are able to better understand the fears and worries that are part of almost every child's life. The variety of fears and worries range from the relatively minor (such as getting poor grades, being sent to the principal, and having parents argue), to the more troubling (such as falling from high places or not being able to breathe), to the truly awful and dangerous (such as being hit by a car, getting burned in a fire, death or dead people, and being bombed or attacked) (Ollendick, Matson, & Helsel, 1985). Although discussions of anxiety do not always differentiate between fears and worries, the distinction provides added clarity. **Fears** are defined as anxieties elicited *in the presence of a specific stimulus.* **Worries** are defined as anxieties *about possible future events.*

Most children exhibit one or more fears during normal development (Bronson & Pankey, 1977; Lieberman, 1993; Muris, Merckelbach, Mayer & Prins, 2000; see Table 11.1). A predictable sequence can be observed, with initial increases in fears and worries related to the cognitive capacity to understand risk and imagine potential harm (Holaway, Rodebaugh, & Heimberg, 2006; Westenberg, Drewes, Goedhart, Siebelink, & Treffers, 2004; Muris, Merckelbach, Meesters, & van den Brand, 2002). With the growth of knowledge, self-confidence, and ER strategies, most fears decline with age (Craske, 1997; Gullone, King, & Ollendick, 2001; Muris, Merckelbach, Gadet, & Meesters, 2000). Both age-related changes and individual differences influence the number and nature of children's fears. Cognitive development is perhaps the most relevant. Children's increasing abilities to make distinctions between fantasy and reality, and to recognize, understand, and control danger are noteworthy achievements (Greenspan & Salmon, 1993; Moore & Carr, 2000; Ollendick, Yule, & Ollier, 1991; Gordon, King, Gullone, Muris, & Ollendick, 2007).

Individual differences in overall temperament, shyness, and behavioral inhibition are also key factors related to the emergence of fears (Henderson & Zimbardo, 2001; Reddy, 2001). Gender also plays a role, with girls exhibiting more fears than boys (Craske, 1997; Gordon et al., 2007). Factors such as

TABLE 11:1 FEARS IN CHILDHOOD

6-7 years
Strange, loud, or abrupt noises (e.g., animal noises, wind, and thunder)
Ghosts, witches, or other supernatural beings
Bodily injury
Separation from parents and being lost
Being alone at night
Being hurt or rejected at school

7-8 years
The dark and dark places
Real-life catastrophes (e.g, kidnapping, floods, fires, war)
Not being liked
Being left out of family or school events
Being hurt or rejected at school

8-9 years
Personal humiliation
Failure in school or play
Being caught in a lie or misbehavior
Being the victim of physical violence
Parents fighting, separating, or being hurt

9-11 years
Failure in school or sports
Becoming sick
Heights and sensations of vertigo (i.e., dizziness)
Sinister people (e.g., killers and molesters)

11-13 years
Failure in school, sports, or popularity
Looking or acting strange
Life-threatening illnesses or death
Sex (attracting others, repelling others, being attacked)
Being fooled or humiliated

Adapted from Philadelphia Child Guidance Center (1993).

race, ethnicity, religion, and ecological context influence children's fears as well (Ingman, Ollendick, & Akande, 1999; Ollendick, Yang, King, Dong, & Akande, 1996; Safren et al., 2000). Children from Africa, for instance, report higher levels of fears than children from the United States, China, or Australia; children from Christian backgrounds report higher levels than children from Muslim backgrounds (Ingman et al., 1999). Exposure to media accounts of frightening events is another variable that may need to be taken into account (Moore & Carr, 2000).

In contrast to fears, worries involve somewhat more vague concerns about possible threats. The three most common types of worries are tied to health, school, and personal harm (Silverman, La Greca, & Wasserstein, 1995). In a recent sample of normally developing children, almost 70% reported worrying "now and then" (Muris, Meesters, Merckelbach, Sermon, & Zwakhalen, 1998). Preschoolers are worried most about imaginary and supernatural events, 5- and 6-year-olds by their physical well-being, and 8- to 12-year-olds by social and behavioral competence and psychological well-being (Muris et al., 1998; Vasey & Daleiden, 1994). As with fears, age-related changes and individual differences are important. Girls, again, worry more (Craske, 1997; Muris et al., 1998; Silverman et al., 1995). African American children worry more than European American or Hispanic children (Silverman et al., 1995). Children who describe themselves as very inhibited also report more worries (Muris, Merckelbach, Wessel, & van de Ven, 1999).

In order to deal with their everyday fears and worries, children display a variety of effective and ineffective coping strategies. Emotional strategies (e.g., minimizing or maximizing facial expressions), cognitive strategies (e.g., thinking of something else, talking with others), and behavioral strategies (e.g., avoidance, asking for help) are all common (Denham, 1998; Gordon et al., 2007; Muris et al., 1998). The coordination and regulation of negative experiences also becomes more manageable over time (Zahn-Waxler, Klimes-Dougan, & Slattery, 2000). Indeed, about one-quarter of children report that worrying has a positive effect on them because it helps them to handle difficult future events (Muris et al., 1998).

For most children, specific fears and worries are distressing; now and then, they may make relationships, activities, and routines more difficult. In general, though, most anxieties are transient. Individual coping efforts, support from others, and time itself eventually lead to good adaptations. For some children, however, fears and worries are more problematic. For these children, fears and worries signal an anxiety disorder that is both painful and disabling (Bell-Dolan, Last, & Strauss, 1990; Muris, Merckelbach, Mayer & Prins, 2000). These children are the focus of the rest of the chapter.

Anxiety Disorders

Anxiety disorders are ubiquitous and are among the most frequently diagnosed psychopathologies in children, adolescents, and adults (Craske, 1997; Ollendick, Shortt, & Sander, 2005; Pine & Grun, 1999). Juxtaposed with these high rates of anxiety and impairment are relatively low rates of treatment (Chavira, Stein, Bailey, & Stein, 2004). These disorders have received considerable theoretical and

Occasional anxiety and distress are normal-range responses to novelty and new situations for most children.

empirical attention, and there are many excellent reviews available (Craske, 1997; Pine & Grun, 1999; Kovacs & Devlin, 1998; Moore & Carr, 2000; Southam-Gerow & Chorpita, 2007; Vasey & Dadds, 2001; Walkup & Ginsburg, 2002; Zahn-Waxler, Klimes-Dougan, & Slattery, 2000). Anxiety disorders are internalizing disorders in which anxiety has gone from adaptive to pathological in terms of its intensity, duration, and pervasiveness. All of the anxiety disorders are characterized by inhibition and withdrawal, exaggerated and unrealistic fears and worries, overcontrol, and somatic symptoms; each also has detection of danger and/or avoidance of danger as a key feature (Moore & Carr, 2000). Most cases involve mild to moderate impairment in daily functioning (Langley, Bergman, McCracken, & Piacentini, 2004; Pine & Grun, 1999). Although there is underlying similarity, there are distinctive perceptions, thoughts, emotions, levels of arousal, behaviors, somatic symptoms, and effects on relationships that are associated with particular types of anxiety disorders (see Table 11.2).

Various epidemiological estimates of anxiety disorders in children range from 3% to 18%; rates in adolescence approach 20% (Albano, Chorpita, & Barlow, 2003; Cartwright-Hatton, McNicol, & Doubleday, 2006; Craske, 1997; Essau, Conradt, & Petermann, 1999a, 2000a, 2000b; Southam-Gerow & Chorpita, 2007; Vasey, 1995; Velting & Albano, 2001; Weiss & Last, 2001). Prevalence increases with age, with overall rates of 7.5%, 10.7%, 19.7%, and 20.3% observed at 11, 15, 18, and 21 years of age, respectively (Costello, Egger, & Angold, 2005; Newman et al., 1996; Pennington, 2002). In both childhood

TABLE 11:2   CLINICAL COMPARISON OF ANXIETY DISORDERS

	SEPARATION ANXIETY	PHOBIAS	GENERALIZED ANXIETY DISORDER	PANIC DISORDER	PTSD	OBSESSIVE COMPULSIVE DISORDER
Perception	• Separation is perceived as threatening	• Specific objects, events or situations are perceived as threatening	• The whole environment is perceived as threatening • The child is hypervigilant, scanning the environment for threats to well-being	• The recurrence of a panic attack is seen as threatening • Attention is directed inward and benign somatic sensations are perceived but misinterpreted as threatening	• Cues that remind the person of the trauma are perceived as threatening • Hallucinations or illusions may occur where aspects of the trauma are reperceived	• Specific situations, such as those involving dirt, are perceived as threatening and elicit obsessional thoughts
Cognition	• The child believes that harm to the parent or the self will occur following separation	• The child believes that contact with the phobic object or entry into the phobic situation will lead to catastrophe	• The child catastrophizes about many minor daily events	• The youth believes that the panic attacks may lead to death or serious injury	• Recurrent memories of the trauma occur. • The child tries to distract him or herself from traumatic memories	• Obsessional thoughts, images or impulses intrude into consciousness and may involve themes of contamination, sex or aggression • The child tries to exclude these thoughts from consciousness
Affect	• Intense fear or anger occurs when separation is anticipated, during separation or following separation	• Intense fear or anger is experienced if contact with the feared object or situation is anticipated or occurs	• A continual moderately high level of fear is experienced, often called free floating anxiety	• During panic attacks intense fear occurs and between attacks a moderate level of fear of recurrence is experienced	• Periodic intrusive episodes of intense fear, horror or anger like those that occurred during the trauma are experienced • The child feels emotionally blunted and cannot experience tender emotions • Depression may occur	• The obsessions cause anxiety

TABLE 11:2 (CONTINUED)

	SEPARATION ANXIETY	PHOBIAS	GENERALIZED ANXIETY DISORDER	PANIC DISORDER	PTSD	OBSESSIVE COMPULSIVE DISORDER
Arousal	● Episodes of hyperarousal ● Sleep problems	● Episodes of hyperarousal ● Sleep problems	● Continual hyperarousal ● Sleep problems	● Episodes of extreme hyperarousal against a background of moderate hyperarousal ● Sleep problems	● Episodes of extreme hyperarousal against a background of moderate hyperarousal ● Sleep problems	● Ongoing moderate hyperarousal occurs ● Hyperarousal occurs when compulsions are resisted
Behavior	● Separation is avoided or resisted ● The child refuses to go to school ● The child refuses to sleep alone	● The phobic object or situation is avoided	● As worrying intensifies social activities become restricted	● The youth may avoid public places in case the panic attacks occur away from the safety of home. This is secondary agoraphobia	● Young children may cling to parents and refuse to sleep alone ● Teenagers may use drugs or alcohol to block the intrusive thoughts and emotions ● Suicidal attempts may occur	● Motivated by their obsessional beliefs, children engage in compulsive rituals which they believe will prevent a catastrophe from occurring or undo some potentially threatening event which has occurred ● These rituals are usually unrealistic
Interpersonal adjustment	● Peer relationships may deteriorate ● Academic performance may deteriorate	● With simple phobias interpersonal problems are confined to phobic situations ● Agoraphobia may lead to social isolation	● Peer relationships may deteriorate ● Academic performance may deteriorate	● If agoraphobia develops secondary to the panic attacks social isolation may result	● Complete social isolation may occur if the trauma was solitary ● Where the trauma was shared, the child may confine interactions to the group who shared the trauma	● Members of the child's family or social network may become involved in helping the child perform compulsive rituals and inadvertently reinforce them

Reprinted from Moore & Carr (2000).

and adolescence, girls are diagnosed with anxiety disorders more frequently than boys (Albano & Krain, 2005; Silverman & Carter, 2006). Rates and gender ratios for specific disorders will be presented in later sections of the chapter. Because of the numbers of children who struggle with anxiety, and the various clinical manifestations, classification issues are important. In DSM-IV-TR, for example, descriptions of anxiety disorders and their diagnostic criteria are roughly similar for children and adults. One important difference is that children need not understand the irrationality or excessiveness of their anxieties.

Current descriptions appear to be both internally and externally valid, although research continues in this area (Dhossche, van der Steen, & Ferdinand, 2002; Pennington, 2002; Saavedra & Silverman, 2002; Spence, 1997; Spence, Rapee, McDonald, & Ingram, 2001). Comorbidity is essential to consider, as children and adolescents with multiple disorders (e.g., anxiety and depression) experience more severe symptoms and have more psychosocial risk factors (Franco, Saavedra, & Silverman, 2007). There are also topics that are just beginning to be explored, such as the nature of anxiety in ethnic minority youths (McLaughlin, Hilt, & Nolen-Hoeksema, 2007; Pina & Silverman, 2004; Raver, 2004; Safren et al., 2000; Wren et al., 2007). Findings from these investigations include, for instance, data about higher levels of anxiety and comorbidity in Latina American girls and adolescents, and higher levels of physical symptoms of anxiety in African American boys and adolescents (McLaughlin et al., 2007).

The Case of Miranda: Generalized Anxiety Disorder

Miranda is a 9-year-old girl presenting with a high level of general distress. She was originally referred for evaluation because of concerns raised at school about some learning difficulties and problems related to extreme avoidance behavior. These problems included not talking in class, not turning things in, not going to her locker, and not interacting with other kids on the playground. For several months Miranda has refused to ride the school bus, so her mother has driven her to school. Although Miranda has always liked sports, she will only play soccer and softball with her parents or her older brother, and only in their yard. Her parents have tried several times to encourage her participation on a team, but Miranda became so anxious and upset before games that she would

become nauseated and refused to get out of the car at the playing fields. Recently, Miranda has been unable to use public restrooms because she says that they scare her. After witnessing a classmate vomit in class on a hot spring day, Miranda has become preoccupied with a fear that she will also vomit if she becomes too warm. Consequently, she has come to associate being hot with being nauseated and insists on always being in air-conditioned buildings during the summer.

Miranda has difficulty sleeping because of her tendency to ruminate. She describes this as being "unable to shut my brain off." She also worries at night that she will be kidnapped. Miranda is interested in theater and would like to participate in school plays and summer community theater programs, but says she is too nervous to try out. When asked if she could change one thing about her life, Miranda says that she would most want to be able to be in a play. Miranda's mother describes her as increasingly nervous and "afraid of her own shadow." ■

Miranda's presentation is consistent with the DSM-IV-TR criteria for **generalized anxiety disorder** (GAD), with excessive and unrealistic worries and fears about a variety of stimuli and situations (Holaway et al., 2006; Robin et al., 2006). That Miranda is a girl is also consistent with data suggesting higher rates of GAD in girls than in boys (Craske, 1997). Based on various samplings of referred and nonreferred children, GAD appears to affect between 2% and 4.6% of children (Bernstein, Borchardt, & Perwein, 1996; Costello, Angold, & Burns, 1996; Verhulst et al., 1997); GAD is observed throughout the childhood years, although it is more commonly diagnosed in older children and adolescents (Zahn-Waxler et al., 2000). There are conflicting data about whether children diagnosed with GAD report more somatic symptoms (Ginsburg, Riddle, & Davies, 2006; Hofflich, Hughes, & Kendall, 2006). Children with GAD do receive comorbid diagnoses of obsessive-compulsive disorder and mood disorders more frequently than children with other anxiety disorders (Verduin & Kendall, 2003).

The Case of Keely: Separation Anxiety Disorder

Keely is a 6-year-old girl, starting first grade. Keely enjoyed kindergarten and was in the same class as her close friend and neighbor. Early in the summer, her mother had surgery and was hospitalized for several days. Although she made a good recovery, the event was stressful for Keely. As the summer progressed, Keely became increasingly concerned about her mother's well-being, despite frequent reassurances. Keely also began to have difficulty staying with her babysitter and needed her mother to call frequently if she was away from home. The first several days of first grade were uneventful for Keely, but she was unhappy about the fact that her best friend was in a different classroom. Late in the first week of school, Keely refused to get on the school bus and her mother drove her to school. The following morning, Keely said she felt too sick to go to school. By the following week, Keely was upset about going to school every morning, often crying and pleading to stay home. On days she was allowed to stay home, she seemed quite happy and content. If forced to go to school, she was quite agitated, though she tended to calm down over the course of the day. The daily struggle, however, was extremely upsetting to her mother, and Keely's teacher was beginning to feel that it was becoming disruptive to the classroom as well. ∎

Keely's symptoms are consistent with a DSM-IV diagnosis of **separation anxiety disorder** (SAD). The symptoms include both significant distress when separated from the caregiver and clingy behaviors in the presence of the caregiver. The key developmental criterion is that the anxiety must be age-inappropriate. In younger children like Keely, anxiety is often focused on the caregiver's well-being or possible harm that may befall the caregiver. In older children and adolescents, anxiety is also frequently related to difficulties being away from home and is expressed in a reluctance or refusal to go to school (Kearney & Albano, 2004; Rabian & Silverman, 1995; Suveg, Aschenbrand, & Kendall, 2005). In fact, SAD is the most common cause of school refusal and associated impairments in academic and social domains (King et al., 1998; Moore & Carr, 2000).

Keely's struggles with somatic problems are also common (Hofflich et al., 2006); headaches and stomachaches are frequent complications of SAD. Panic symptoms may also occur with SAD (Craske, 1997). Estimates of SAD range between 3% and 4% (Bernstein et al., 1996). SAD is most common in preadolescents, although early ages of onset are sometimes noted (Last, Perrin, Hersen, & Kazdin, 1992). As with GAD, girls are more likely to be diagnosed (Craske, 1997). Compared to children with other anxiety disorders, children with SAD have the

highest number of comorbid diagnoses (Verduin & Kendall, 2003).

The Case of Danny: Obsessive-Compulsive Disorder

Danny is a 13-year-old boy referred because of concerns noted by both his parents and teachers about some of his increasingly unusual behaviors. Danny has been an excellent student throughout his school years until this term, in eighth grade, when he began to fall behind in his classes. His parents also reported that he has dropped several favorite activities and become increasingly socially isolated. During the initial assessment, Danny took an unusually long time to complete some simple questionnaires. When asked about this, Danny admitted that he felt compelled to count the words in each sentence before reading the sentence. He said that this has become a real problem because he can no longer complete his homework on time. Danny also described counting steps, and feeling that he always needed to finish climbing stairs with his right foot. In fact, he has memorized the number of steps throughout his school, church, and home so that he always knows which foot to start with. If he does finish climbing stairs with his left foot, he feels compelled to go back down the stairs and start over. Although he has never worried about germs before, he is now very concerned about them, and has begun carrying a cloth with him so that he does not have to touch things like door knobs or public telephones. He also finds himself washing and rewashing his hands as often as he can throughout the day. He also said that after he showers, he often still feels dirty and so immediately takes another shower. This has recently caused him to be late getting to school on many mornings. ∎

This description of Danny reflects the acute distress and level of impairment associated with **obsessive-compulsive disorder** (OCD). Danny's intrusive concerns about germs and contamination and his repetitive counting behaviors are among the most common symptoms. Other characteristic obsessions involve fear of harming others, death, or sex; prevalent rituals include handwashing, checking, and avoidant behaviors (Evans, Gray, & Leckman, 1999). Thomsen (1994) also describes an "almost pathological doubting" (p. 139) of oneself, with a heightened need for reassurance from others.

It is important to evaluate children's **obsessions** (i.e., persistent and intense intrusions of unwanted thoughts or images) and **compulsions** (i.e., persistent and intense impulses to perform a specific behavior) within a developmental framework, because many children display specific preferences and rituals that are not pathological (Evans, Leckman, Carter, & Reznick, 1997; Rassin, Cougle, & Muris, 2007; Thomsen, 1994). For instance, prescribed sequences of separation behaviors at day care centers or bedtime routines are common; most of these kinds of rituals fade by later childhood, when OCD is setting in (Thomsen, 1994). It is also important to consider the distinctions between the obsessions observed in OCD and the pathological worrying that is more consistent with a diagnosis of generalized anxiety disorder (Comer, Kendall, Franklin, Hudson, & Pimentel, 2004). Estimates of OCD are problematic, with many investigators arguing that the disorder is underestimated and underdiagnosed (Heyman et al., 2001). There are data that suggest that boys are at higher risk than girls, but more research remains to be done on both gender and multicultural variables (Heyman et al., 2001; Schniering, Hudson, & Rapee, 2000).

Age of onset for OCD is difficult to pin down (Heyman et al., 2001). Some researchers have subtyped children with earlier onsets (between 5 and 9 years) and those with later onsets (after 17 years) (Busatto et al., 2001; Geller et al., 1998). Early-onset children are more likely to be boys, to have family members with OCD, and to display comorbid tic disorders (Busatto et al., 2001; Diniz et al., 2004; Geller et al., 1998; Grados, Labuda, Riddle, & Walkup, 1997).

The Case of Jack: Phobic Disorder

Jack is a 7-year-old boy who has developed an intense and pervasive fear of dogs. Jack has never had a pet and has never been very comfortable around animals. Recently, while playing in the backyard, he was surprised by his neighbor's dog that had gotten out of its fenced yard. The dog barked aggressively at Jack, though it did not approach him. Jack was quite frightened and ran into his house crying. Following this incident, Jack began to refuse to play outside if the neighbor's dog was out. This progressed to refusing to play outdoors at all. Jack soon refused to visit family friends if they had dogs at their home, unless the dog was kept out of sight. If Jack is out with his parents and sees a dog, he becomes upset and agitated, and cries and clings to his mother. ∎

Phobic disorders involve excessive and exaggerated fears of particular objects or situations, intense anxiety in the presence of such objects or situations, and avoidant behaviors; the fears and anxieties are associated with significant impairment (Ollendick, King, & Muris, 2002; Rabian & Silverman, 1995; Silverman & Moreno, 2005). DSM-IV-TR lists three general types of phobias: **specific phobias** (like Jack's) (e.g., animals, injury or blood, natural phenomena); **social phobia** (e.g., fear of scrutiny or evaluation by others); and **agoraphobia** (i.e., intense anxiety in places where individuals feel insecure, trapped, or not in control). Between 2% and 9% of community samples of children meet the criteria for specific phobia; approximately 15% of children referred for anxiety disorders are diagnosed with phobias (Bernstein et al., 1996; Ollendick et al., 2002). Girls are at higher risk (Craske, 1997). As with other anxiety disorders, developmental assessment is important. Many children exhibit fears; we want to differentiate those children for whom fears are mild or moderate and short-lived from those children for whom fears are intense and long-lasting.

Social Phobia

Social phobia (in earlier editions of the DSM, this was called avoidant disorder) is not just shyness or inhibition. Shyness is a complex psychological construct, and it is sometimes difficult to distinguish between normal and abnormal social anxieties. It may be useful to think about a continuum, with groups of shy children followed by groups of socially anxious children followed by groups of socially phobic children (Albano & Hayward, 2004; Crozier & Alden, 2001; Henderson & Zimbardo, 2001; Rapee & Sweeney, 2005; V. Reddy, 2001). Shy children are those who may be slow to warm up at a friend's birthday party but who eventually join in the fun; socially anxious children are those who stay huddled next to a parent for the party's duration; and socially phobic children cannot attend a party at all.

One of the most compelling manifestations of social phobia is displayed by children and adolescents with performance anxiety. Studies of talented young musicians suggest that distress and impairment related to performance anxiety are quite common and are accompanied by a range of coping strategies (Fehm & Schmidt, 2006; Osborne & Kenny, 2005; Osborne, Kenny, & Holsomback, 2005). Other forms of social anxiety are observed in adolescents

In contrast to normal-range shyness, social phobia, anxiety often prevents children from engaging with other children in developmentally important social activities.

who cannot complete certain school projects that require oral presentations or adolescents who cannot eat with their friends in restaurants. The relation between social phobia and selective mutism has been investigated, but additional work on specific symptoms and associated psychopathology remains to be done (Yeganeh, Beidel, Turner, Pina, & Silverman; 2003). Compared to the other anxiety disorders, social phobia usually has its onset in later childhood or adolescence (Essau et al., 1999a).

The Case of Lauren: Panic Disorder

Lauren is 15 years old and in ninth grade. Lauren's parents have accompanied her for a consultation following several panic attacks that happened during the school day. Lauren's parents describe her during her early years as bright, friendly and somewhat reserved. While Lauren has always been somewhat anxious in new situations, she has a number of close friends and is a talented musician. At home, Lauren is talkative and even mildly argumentative at times; at school she is seen as quiet and serious. Lauren's parents first became concerned about her in sixth grade when she transitioned from elementary school to junior high. At the start of that school year, Lauren began to complain of stomachaches and to frequently miss school. Her symptoms gradually receded as she became more comfortable with her new environment. Lauren acknowledges that the start

of each school year has been a struggle for her, although never quite as severe as in sixth grade.

Lauren was nervous about high school but also looked forward to the new school and new experiences. Overall, Lauren's parents were pleased with her adjustment. Lauren found her classes challenging but engaging, and she was enjoying new opportunities provided by an expanded music program. Socially, she stayed close to junior high friends and said that she found it difficult to venture out and make new friends. One day while eating lunch alone in the cafeteria, Lauren began to feel ill. She felt her pulse racing and became short of breath. She was light-headed and nauseated. She made it to the first class after lunch where her teacher immediately asked her if she was alright. Lauren said she felt as if she might pass out and was sent to the nurse's office. Once there, she began to cry and told the nurse that she was afraid she would die. After lying down for a short time, Lauren began to feel better and had largely recovered by the time her mother came to pick her up. The next morning, Lauren complained of a headache and expressed anxiety about returning to school. Her mother encouraged her to go, reassuring her that she would come and get her if she became ill. After several days without incident, Lauren had a second attack during which she felt dizzy, nauseated, felt her heart pounding, and had trouble breathing. This occurred at a football game just after performing in the band's halftime program. Again Lauren reported feeling a sense of panic that she might be dying. Lauren has not been able to return to school since the second panic attack. ■

Lauren meets the DSM-IV-TR criteria for **panic disorder** (see Table 11.3). Recurrent, somewhat unpredictable panic attacks are the primary component of panic disorder. Panic attacks are extremely intense and uncomfortable episodes of anxiety. Sometimes panic occurs in normally developing children without other symptoms and with few negative consequences. Although certainly distressing, these isolated attacks are not necessarily cause for alarm. When panic attacks are associated with one of the other anxiety disorders such as SAD, OCD, or phobias, they are more likely to be understood as a complication of that specific disorder rather than as a separate disorder. Still, there are instances when it is appropriate to identify patterns of panic attacks as a panic disorder in a child or adolescent.

Panic disorder is usually diagnosed in adults, but may be observed in adolescents (Ollendick, Birmaher, & Mattis, 2004; Zahn-Waxler et al., 2000).

TABLE 11:3 DSM-IV-TR CRITERIA FOR PANIC DISORDER

A. Both (1) and (2)
  (1) recurrent unexpected panic attacks
  (2) at least one of the attacks has been followed by 1 month (or more) of one (or more) of the following:
    (a) persistent concern about having additional attacks
    (b) worry about the implications of the attack or its consequences (e.g., losing control, having a heart attack, "going crazy")
    (c) a significant change in behavior related to the attacks
 	
B. Absence of agoraphobia
 	
C. The panic attacks are not due to the direct physiological effects of a substance (e.g., a drug of abuse, a medication) or a general medical condition.
 	
D. The panic attacks are not better accounted for by another mental disorder, such as social phobia (e.g., on exposure to a specific phobic situation), specific phobia (e.g., on exposure to dirt in someone with an obsession about contamination), post-traumatic stress disorder (e.g., in response to stimuli associated with a severe stressor), or separation anxiety disorder (e.g., in response to being away from home or close relatives).

Lauren's case also illustrates the complex role of gender in the development of panic disorder. Studies of gender have yielded mixed results (Hayward, Killen, Kraemer, & Taylor, 2000). Equal rates of panic attacks have been reported for adolescent girls and boys, but girls may experience more severe attacks or respond differently to them (Hayward et al., 2000; Ollendick et al., 2004). Panic disorder is diagnosed three times as frequently in girls and women, and there is a need for additional research related to the developmental transition between panic attacks and panic disorder (Craske, 1997; Hayward et al., 2000). Comorbid disorders include other anxiety disorders, major depression, and bipolar disorder, and are observed more frequently in girls than boys with panic disorder (Diler et al., 2004; Hayward et al., 2000).

Post-Traumatic Stress Disorder

Post-traumatic stress disorder (PTSD) involves a severe and ongoing pattern of anxiety following exposure to a traumatic event. PTSD is the only anxiety disorder to specify a cause as part of the clinical presentation; that is, PTSD can only be identified in the context of a child's traumatic experience. For many years, young children were not diagnosed with PTSD; their developmental status was thought to be associated with forgetting, and "bouncing back" from terrible events. We now know that even infants and toddlers display some of the symptoms of PTSD and that these may be appropriately conceptualized as PTSD (Dyregrov & Yule, 2006; Kaufman & Henrich, 2000; Lonigan, Phillips, & Richey, 2003; Pfefferbaum, 1997; Salmon & Bryant, 2002; Scheeringa, Zeanah, Myers, & Putnam, 2003; Vernberg & Varela, 2001).

Children surviving severe trauma, such as natural disasters, are at increased risk to develop symptoms of PTSD.

WILLIAM WEST/AFP/Getty Images

PTSD has been documented in children and adolescents around the world: following hurricanes in the Carolinas and Hawaii, earthquakes in California, Athens, Taiwan, and Turkey, and tsunamis in Sri Lanka (Asarnow et al., 1999; Giannopoulou, Strouthos, Smith, Dikaiakou, Galanopoulou, & Yule, 2006; Hamada, Kameoka, Yanagida, & Chemtob, 2003; Hsu, Chong, Yang, & Yen, 2002; Neuner, Schauer, Catani, Ruf, & Elbert, 2006; Russoniello et al., 2002; Sahim, Batigun, & Yilmaz, 2007). PTSD has also been described in children and adolescents exposed to war trauma in the Middle East, in Bosnia, and in Darfur (Husain, Allwood, & Bell, 2008; Klingman, 2001; Morgos, Worden, & Gupta, 2008; Solomon & Lavi, 2005; Thabet, Tawahina, El Sarraj, & Vostanis, 2008), in child refugees from Tibet and Latin America, in children adopted from Romania (Hoksbergen et al., 2003; Kinzie, Cheng, Tsai, & Riley, 2006; Servan-Schreiber, Lin, & Birmaher, 1998), and in children and adolescents who experienced the 9/11 attacks on the World Trade Center in New York City (Brown & Goodman, 2005; Mullett-Hume, Anshel, Guevara, & Cloitre, 2008).

In addition to these types of natural disasters and manmade horrors, everyday tragedies are also associated with the emergence of PTSD. Serious car accidents, for example, are a common cause (Schafer, Barkmann, Riedesser, & Schulte-Markwort, 2006). Interpersonal trauma (such as maltreatment or exposure to family violence) is also clearly associated with high-risk status (Kaplow, Dodge, Amaya-Jackson, & Saxe, 2005; Kilpatrick et al., 2003; King et al., 2000a; Margolin & Vickerman, 2007; Scott, 2007; Stevens, Ruggiero, Kilpatrick, Resnick, & Saunders, 2005). Recent studies of children and adolescents who experience multiple and complex interpersonal trauma (e.g., recurrent or chronic physical or sexual abuse) increasingly emphasize the idea of **complex developmental trauma**, a disorder involving both exposure and adaptation to chronic trauma, with exposure often occurring in the context of a child's caregiving environment (Cook et al., 2005; Spinazzola et al., 2005; van der Kolk, 2007; van der Kolk, Roth, Pelcovitz, Sunday, & Spinazzola, 2005; see Box 11.1).

Exposure to traumatic events is not uncommon, with estimates ranging from one-fourth to two-thirds of children reporting some traumatic history by age 16 (Copeland, Keeler, Angold, & Costello, 2007; Costello, Erkanli, Fairbank, & Angold, 2002; Giaconia et al., 1995; Scheeringa & Gaensbauer, 2000). Although we usually think of trauma in terms of the direct and life-threatening experiences just described, indirect forms of exposure (such as living in dangerous environments or exposure to gun violence) are increasingly frequent (Berman, Silverman, & Kurtines, 2002; Garbarino, 2001; Garbarino, Bradshaw, & Vorrasi, 2002; Hanson et al., 2006; Lynch & Cicchetti, 1998; Pynoos, Steinberg, & Piacentini, 1999). Because increased risk is associated with additional exposure (Costello et al., 2002), the experience of both direct and indirect forms of trauma in ethnic minority children from disadvantaged backgrounds is especially troubling (Foster, Kuperminc, & Price, 2004; Neal & Brown, 1994; Richards et al., 2004; Safren et al., 2000).

PTSD is an anxiety disorder that unfolds over time. In the immediate wake of the trauma, all aspects of children's adjustment are likely to be affected (Pynoos et al., 1999; Vogel & Vernberg, 1993). During the acute stress period, emotions such as terror, helplessness, shame, and grief are common; intense physiological responses and behaviors are additional complications (Bryant & Harvey, 1999; Bryant, Harvey, Guthrie, & Moulds, 2003; Meiser-Stedman et al., 2007). Pynoos and colleagues (1999) describe a 7-year-old who reported: "My heart was beating so fast I thought it was going to break" (p. 1544). Cognitive functioning is disrupted, with confusion, uncertainty, and misunderstanding. Appraisal and misappraisal of ongoing events and their likely causes and consequences are particularly important developmental constructs to consider (Dalgleish, Meiser-Stedman, & Smith, 2005; Pynoos et al., 1999). For example, changing expectations of responsibility for personal safety, as well as individual differences in appraisal processes and stress responses, may exacerbate children's reactions to trauma (Bryant, Salmon, Sinclair, & Davidson, 2007; Ehlers, Mayou, & Bryant, 2003; Pynoos et al., 1999; Stallard & Smith, 2007).

Eventual adjustment, or lack of adjustment, is related to many internal factors, including developmental status and neurobiological maturation, temperament and attachment, and anxiety sensitivity; outcomes are also influenced by external factors related to the nature of the trauma itself, parents and families, other life events, and schools and larger social communities (Bryant et al., 2003; Harvey & Bryant, 1999; Pynoos et al., 1999; Scheeringa &

BOX 11:1 CLINICAL PERSPECTIVES

Complex Developmental Trauma

Researchers and clinicians working with children exposed to ongoing trauma are proposing a new diagnosis to better capture the unique characteristics and effects of complex trauma occurring in childhood (DeAngelis, 2007). The proposed diagnosis—developmental trauma disorder (DTD)—is being considered as a way to more accurately describe, treat, and study both the specific symptoms of this early and repeated pattern of trauma and the effect of early trauma on the children's neurological development (Spinazzola et al., 2005).

The diagnosis of post-traumatic stress disorder (PTSD) describes the pattern of pathological response that sometimes develops following acute trauma, primarily in adults. Typically, it refers to anxiety-based symptoms experienced after the trauma has occurred. In contrast, the trauma to which children tend to be exposed is often repetitive and chronic, occurring in the context of the very relationships that should provide a protective buffer to threat and stress (Spinazzola et al., 2005). Examples of this type of complex stress include physical and emotional abuse, witnessing domestic violence, and ongoing exposure to community violence. Children who struggle in the face of such stressors are given a variety of diagnoses to account for their emotional and behavioral problems. No diagnosis, however, is available to describe the core etiology and distinctive cluster of symptoms they are experiencing.

Additionally, there is increasing evidence that experiencing this kind of trauma during childhood not only leads to immediate clinical symptoms, but to more pervasive and long-term neurobiological and psychological consequences resulting from specific structural and functional changes in brain development (Gabowitz, Zucker & Cook, 2008; van der Kolk, Roth, Pelcovitz, Sunday, & Spinazzola, 2005). Long-term difficulties associated with early trauma include problems with regulation of emotions and behavioral impulses,

as well as problems with memory and attention, self-perception, and relationships.

The National Child Traumatic Stress Network is a group of over 70 child mental health centers dedicated to the study and treatment of children experiencing complex trauma. This consortium is developing an extensive database based on the over 50,000 children per year who are seen at these centers where they are studied and treated. The resulting research and clinical findings are generating a range of compelling findings that support the scientific basis for the DTD diagnosis (Cook et al., 2005; van der Kolk et al., 2005).

While work on refining the diagnostic criteria for developmental trauma disorder will continue, the current formulation includes the following criteria (van der Kolk et al., 2005):

- **Exposure:** Exposure to one or more forms of developmentally adverse interpersonal traumas, such as abandonment, betrayal, physical or sexual abuse, and emotional abuse. May also experience subjective feelings in relation to this trauma such as rage, betrayal, fear, resignation, defeat, and shame.

- **Dysregulation:** Dysregulated development in response to trauma cues, including disturbances in emotions, health, behavior, cognition, relationships, and self-attributions. Behavioral manifestations could involve self-injury; cognitive manifestations might appear as confusion or dissociation.

- **Negative attributions and expectations:** Negative beliefs in line with experience of interpersonal trauma. May stop expecting protection from others and believe that future victimization is inevitable.

- **Functional impairments:** Impairment in any or all arenas of life, including school, friendship, family relations, and the law.

Gaensbauer, 2000; Vernberg & Varela, 2001). The elements of trauma include the frequency, intensity, and duration of exposure, and the specific form of trauma (e.g., natural disaster versus parental abuse), with longer, more intense trauma and trauma involving human perpetrators associated with more severe and persistent PTSD (Vernberg & Varela, 2001). Trauma details and reminders are often upsetting; they may come from unexpected

sources such as media reports (Pfefferbaum, 1997; Saylor, Cowart, Lipovsky, Jackson, & Finch, 2003). Children's adjustments are sometimes embedded in the adjustments of others, as they witness the distress and horror of loved ones and their continuing struggles to recover; indeed, there may be "a cascade of secondary stresses" that continue to negatively impact children (Pynoos et al., 1999, p. 1546; see Figure 11.1).

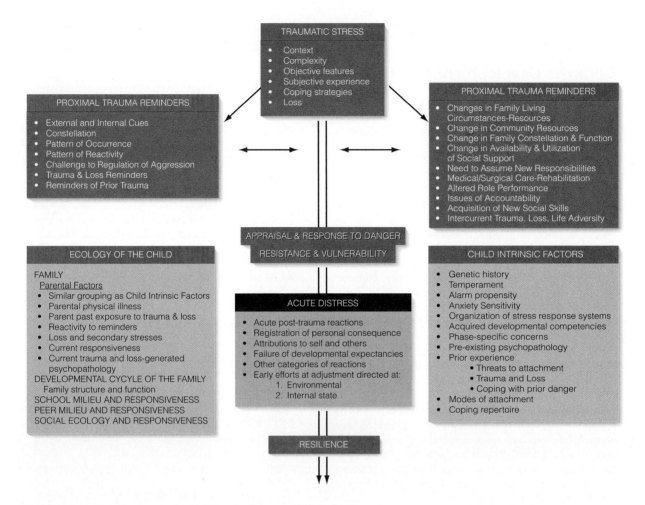

FIGURE 11:1 Developmental psychopathology model of PTSD.
Source: From Pynoos, R.S., Steinberg, A.M., & Piacentini, J.C. (1999), "A developmental psychopathology model of childhood traumatic stress and intersection with anxiety disorders", 'Biological Psychiatry', 46, 1542-1554. Reprinted by permission of Elsevier.

PTSD is diagnosed when poor adjustment lingers; differentiation between nonpathological and pathological response to trauma, however, is often very problematic (Lonigan et al., 2003). Three clusters of symptoms characterize ongoing maladjustment: intrusion and active avoidance (e.g., repetitive images or sounds, bad dreams, avoidance of trauma reminders); numbing and passive avoidance (e.g., emotional isolation or dulling, avoidance of relationships); and poorly regulated arousal (e.g., hypervigilance, sleep problems) (Anthony et al., 2005; Anthony, Lonigan, & Hecht, 1999; Pfefferbaum, 1997; Scheeringa & Gaensbauer, 2000). Both heightened and decreased levels of arousal are observed, at times overlapping with symptoms of dissociation (Kenardy et al., 2007; Pennington, 2002; Perry, Pollard, Blakley, & Vigilante, 1995). PTSD is diagnosed in

children and adolescents who display adequate adjustments prior to trauma experiences as well as children with more problematic developmental histories (Vernberg & Varela, 2001). Comorbid conditions include both internalizing disorders such as depression and externalizing disorders such as substance abuse (Vernberg & Varela, 2001).

Somatization and Somatoform Disorders

The Case of Estella

Estella is a 14-year-old girl, a good student who is well liked by her teachers. Although not rejected by peers, she is rather shy and spends most of her time with just a few friends. Estella reports feeling ill frequently and each year has missed many school days, including field trips and special events. Estella's older sister had an emergency appendectomy several years ago. Ever since this event, Estella's parents have been especially vigilant about her health. Estella's parents have extremely high expectations for their children's academic achievement; any problems with academic performance are viewed with great concern, and doing well is highly reinforced. Estella's older sister is a top student at her high school, where Estella is currently enrolled as a ninth grader. In the spring of eighth grade, Estella began to show a pattern of frequent headaches and stomachaches in the morning that sometimes led to her being late to, and occasionally missing, school.

Beginning the second week of ninth grade, Estella began complaining of severe, debilitating abdominal pain. After being called on several occasions to bring Estella home from school because of pain, Estella's parents became alarmed and brought her first to her pediatrician and then, after a particularly severe episode, to the emergency room. Preliminary assessments in each case could find no obvious cause for Estella's symptoms. Finally, the specialist the family consulted recommended hospitalization for more extensive and intrusive diagnostic procedures. After all of the findings from these tests proved negative, a psychology consult was requested. Although initially skeptical of the involvement of the psychologist, Estella and her mother were cooperative. The psychologist observed that while Estella verbalized concern about missing school, she appeared relaxed and calm. Additionally, while she reported no lessening of her pain, she showed none of the obvious symptoms generally associated with extreme discomfort. When asked if she felt stressed or anxious about starting high school, Estella denied having any worries about this other than those related to falling behind in her work since being hospitalized. ∎

Recurrent complaints of medically unexplained somatic (physical) symptoms are quite frequent among children, and under certain conditions, in adolescents. **Somatization** refers to a variety of processes in which an individual experiences physical symptoms, such as pain or loss of function, for which a physical cause cannot be found or, if present, cannot fully account for the level of impairment. Somaticizing persons generally do not differentiate between emotional and physical

experiences and have difficulty using emotion language to express anxiety. Rather, they use somatic language to describe both physical and emotional problems. Although diagnosable **somatoform disorders** are at the severe end of a continuum, occasional somatization (at least in mild and transient forms) is extremely common. Indeed, it is the rare adult who does not have a childhood memory of the early morning stomachache on the day of a big test. For some children and families, however, this process of somatization leads to clinically significant distress and impairment. Discussion of these disorders is included as part of this chapter on anxiety-based psychopathology because the somatic symptoms, like the compulsive behaviors of OCD, serve to moderate the direct experience of anxiety; this moderation comes with a very high cost.

Some of the most common somatic symptoms include headaches, fatigue, pain, sore muscles, and abdominal distress. One review of complaints reported by a pediatric clinical practice found only 5% to have a clear organic cause (Starfield, Gross, & Wood, 1980). In addition to somatic symptoms, children also exhibit **anxiety sensitivity**, involving hypervigilance and attention to bodily sensations, a tendency to focus on weak or infrequent sensations, and a disposition to react to somatic sensations with distorted cognitions (Eley, Stirling, Ehlers, Gregory, & Clark, 2004; Hayward et al., 2000). For example, a child may come to respond with alarm to any indication of a headache, believing that pain and debilitation are inevitable.

There are several types of somatoform disorders; among the most frequently diagnosed in the pediatric population are somatoform pain disorder, recurrent abdominal pain, and conversion disorder. **Somatoform pain disorder** is characterized by an onset of clinically significant pain with impairment. The disruption in everyday functioning is out of proportion to the reported pain, with clear secondary gain from the pain symptoms and exacerbations linked to increases in stress. Because there is no reliable way to differentiate "real" from "psychogenic" pain, it is important to carefully consider the role of psychological factors in somatoform pain disorder. An especially common and well-studied somatoform condition is **recurrent abdominal pain** (Dorn et al., 2003; Fritz, Fritsch, & Hagino, 1997), as seen in the case of Estella. Recurrent abdominal pain involves three or more episodes over a 3-month period of severe pain that compromises a child's functioning. Reviews of recurrent abdominal pain suggest that it tends to occur in families where illness is a central concern, and where there is both somatic and emotional distress (Fritz et al., 1997).

Conversion disorder is characterized by unexplained deficits in voluntary motor or sensory function that cannot be adequately accounted for by known pathophysiological mechanisms; psychological factors are clearly associated with the emergence of symptoms. Typical motor dysfunctions include paralysis, problems with balance, or difficulty swallowing. Typical sensory dysfunctions include loss of touch or pain sensation, double vision or vision loss, deafness, or hallucinations. Children and adolescents may display pseudoseizures (i.e., a non-epileptic seizure, one that is not associated with abnormal firing of neurons), muscle weakness, or extreme sensory sensitivity (Fritz et al., 1997). A remarkable lack of concern in regard to very serious symptoms is also present. Although less common than somatic pain symptoms, conversion disorder is a clinically-intensive and very expensive psychopathology; it is also the disorder that most clearly illustrates the mind-body interaction that is central to all the somatoform disorders.

Developmental Course

General Continuity of Anxiety Disorders

Anxiety in children and adolescents is associated with diverse outcomes, from clear improvement for some, to persistent struggles for others (Kovacs & Devlin, 1998; Pine & Grun, 1999). As Craske (1997) emphasizes, "childhood anxiety does not guarantee the development of adult anxiety, nor is it necessary for adult anxiety" (p. A13).

While keeping the diversity of outcomes in mind, it is important to emphasize that there is strong evidence for the continuity of anxiety disorders from early childhood through adulthood (Craske, 1997; Goldstein, Olfson, Wickramaratne, & Wolk, 2006; Hale, Raaijmakers, Muris, van Hoof, & Meeus, 2008; Kovacs & Devlin, 1998; Pennington, 2002; Pine & Grun, 1999). That is, anxious and internalizing preschoolers remain anxious and internalizing children, who remain anxious and internalizing adolescents. Indeed, Kovacs and Devlin (1998) describe "a developmental 'readiness' to manifest anxiety disorder" in some young children. This early vulnerability may be related to temperamental reactivity,

negative emotionality, and poor emotion regulation (Chess & Thomas, 1984; Kagan & Snidman, 1999; Pfeifer, Goldsmith, Davidson, & Rickman 2002; Shaw, Keenan, Vondra, Delliquadri, & Giovannelli, 1997), as well as complications including insecure attachments, stressful events, parental anxiety, parent-child problems, and sibling conflicts (Fox, Barrett, & Shortt, 2002; Leech, Larkby, Day, & Day, 2006; Manassis & Hood, 1998; Stein, Chavira, & Jang, 2001; Wood, McLeod, Sigman, Hwang, & Chu, 2003).

More specific outcome-related questions concern whether subsets of children with anxiety disorders can be identified who are at higher risk for continuity of psychopathology. Factors associated with these higher risks include being a girl and displaying more severe symptoms early in development (McCracken, Walkup, & Koplewicz, 2002; Pfeifer, Goldsmith, Davidson, & Rickman, 2002; Pine & Grun, 1999; Schwartz, Snidman, & Kagan, 1999). A developmental chronology of anxiety more often than not involves comorbidity. Many children with one anxiety disorder also meet the diagnostic criteria for another anxiety disorder (Craske, 1997; Hewitt et al., 1997; Schniering et al., 2000; Zahn-Waxler et al., 2000). Many others who are diagnosed with anxiety disorders later develop depression (Axelson & Birmaher, 2001; Diniz et al., 2004; Essau, Conradt, & Petermann, 2002; Goodwin et al., 2004; Kendall, Safford, Flannery-Schroeder, & Webb, 2004; Kovacs & Devlin, 1998; Muris et al., 1998; Thabet, Abed, & Vostanis, 2004; Wittchen, Beesdo, Bittner, & Goodwin, 2003). Gender, again, appears to be an important variable, with girls more likely to display two or more anxiety disorders as well as comorbid anxiety and depression (Egger, Angold, & Costello, 1998; Egger, Costello, Erkanli, & Angold, 1999; Zahn-Waxler et al., 2000). Sometimes, externalizing disorders such as substance abuse or conduct problems also emerge; this pattern is observed more often in boys (Egger et al., 1998; Egger et al., 1999; Kovacs & Devlin, 1998; Zahn-Waxler et al., 2000). For those children whose anxiety is coupled with missing school, academic achievement may also be compromised (Ialongo et al., 1995).

Specific Continuity of Various Anxiety Disorders

In addition to the general stability of anxiety over time, there are also data about the way that specific anxiety disorders play out over time. For instance, separation anxiety disorder is associated with the most improvement; obsessive-compulsive disorder, generalized anxiety disorder, and social phobia are more chronic (Cantwell & Baker, 1989; Kovacs & Devlin, 1998; Pine & Grun, 1999; Thomsen, 1994). Some phobic fears also tend to persist; those that do are often more disturbing and are more likely to be concealed, especially by boys (Lieberman, 1993; Rabian & Silverman, 1995). There have also been several investigations examining the link between separation anxiety in children and later panic disorder (or agoraphobia) in adults, with mixed results (Aschenbrand, Kendall, Webb, Safford, & Flannery-Schroeder, 2003; Black, 1995; Klein, 1995; Lewinsohn, Holm-Denoma, Small, Seely, & Joiner, 2008; Ollendick, Mattis, & King, 1994; Pine & Grun, 1999; Rabian & Silverman, 1995).

Many investigations have focused on social phobia, and there is evidence that early behavioral inhibition is a specific predictor of social phobia (and not of other anxiety disorders) (Hirshfeld-Becker et al., 2007). With respect to ongoing difficulties for children and adolescents with social phobia, developmental challenges involving relationships may be especially difficult to negotiate. The lack of self-confidence, low self-esteem, poor social skills, and negative peer interactions contribute to current and later difficulties in family and peer relationships (Albano & Detweiler, 2001; Ginsburg, La Greca, & Silverman, 1998). And the difficulties are not one-sided; there are also data that show that peers dislike children with social phobia more than children with generalized anxiety disorder or separation anxiety disorder (Verduin & Kendall, 2008).

Continuity of Post-Traumatic Stress Disorder

The developmental course of PTSD varies. For some, symptoms improve over time; for others, symptoms go from bad to worse. For most, PTSD is chronic, with ongoing difficulties tied to neurophysiological changes involving both structure and function (De Bellis & Kuchibhatla, 2006; Perkonigg et al., 2005; Perry et al., 1995; Pervanidou et al., 2007; Pfefferbaum, 1997; Pynoos et al., 1999; Shea, Walsh, MacMillan, & Steiner, 2005; van der Kolk, 2003; Vernberg & Varela, 2001). For example, trauma appears to have lasting effects on both the content and organization of memory, and on cognitive appraisal processes (Ehlers & Clark, 2000; Lynch & Cicchetti, 1998; Scheeringa &

Gaensbauer, 2000; Vernberg & Varela, 2001). To the extent that trauma reminders are present in the everyday lives of children and adolescents, these additional stressors may complicate recovery efforts (Pynoos et al., 1999).

Struggles with PTSD, as with other anxiety-based disorders, may disrupt a child's management of age-related tasks and challenges. Sleep disturbances following a trauma, for instance, can interfere with school performance (Pynoos et al., 1999). The unusual, repeated experiences of intense negative emotion can make emotion regulation more difficult; the development of certain personality characteristics, such as independence, may also be affected (Kaufman & Henrich, 2000; Pynoos et al., 1999; Scheeringa & Gaensbauer, 2000; Vernberg & Varela, 2001). Although there are several variables that appear to moderate outcomes, PTSD is associated with both internalizing and externalizing disorders (Bolton, O'Ryan, Udwin, Boyle, & Yule, 2000; Ford et al., 2000; Hubbard, Realmuto, Northwood, & Masten, 1995; Pine, 2003; Pynoos et al., 1999; Streeck-Fischer & van der Kolk, 2000). One of the most consistent outcome-related findings is that the parent's own response to trauma and his or her ability to function is linked to the child's symptom severity (Scheeringa & Gaensbauer, 2000; Scheeringa & Zeanah, 2001).

With respect to PTSD associated with complex developmental trauma, consequences include pervasive physiological and psychological dysfunction, including impaired self-regulation, impaired learning, and impaired relationships (Spinazzola et al., 2005; Streeck-Fischer & van der Kolk, 2000). Children with histories of complex developmental trauma are also at high risk for the later emergence of additional anxiety disorders (Cortes et al., 2005).

Another perspective on PTSD is provided by Bonanno (2004) and Hoge, Austin, and Pollack (2007), who suggest that resilience in the face of trauma is more common than we think. Bonanno differentiates resilience (i.e., the maintenance of pre-trauma trajectories) from recovery (i.e., a trajectory characterized by maladaptation following trauma, followed by gradual improvement) (see Figure 11.2). His research with adults suggests that hardiness, self-enhancing bias, particular types of emotion-focused coping, and the ability to experience positive emotions and laughter may provide important avenues of investigation for developmental psychopathologists.

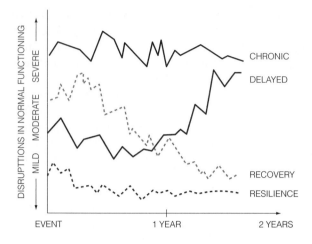

FIGURE 11:2 Developmental pathways for children with PTSD.
Source: From Bonanno, G.A. (2004), "Loss, Trauma, and human resilience: Have we underestimated the human capacity to thrive after extremely aversive events?", 'American Psychologist', 59(1), 20-28. Copyright © 2004 American Psychological Association. Reprinted by permission.

Continuity of Somatization and Somatoform Disorders

Somatoform symptoms and disorders interfere with family, peer, and school functioning. One of the factors that appears to contribute to ongoing difficulties involves the social consequences of physical symptoms. For example, when children's pain is associated with positive attention and activity restriction, symptom maintenance is more likely (Walker, Claar, & Garber, 2002). However, "children's success in their normal social roles may affect the extent to which they identify with the sick role and find it a rewarding alternative to other social roles" (Walker et al., 2002, p. 689). Once established, a somaticizing pattern is generally chronic and resistant to both psychological and medical treatment. Individuals with somatoform disorders are subject to more frequent and more invasive medical procedures, leading to increased medical costs and potential medical problems. An additional clinical concern is that there is significant overlap between the presence of somatic symptoms and both anxiety and mood disorders in adults.

Etiology

With so many types of anxiety-based psychopathology, this discussion of etiology is organized around the well-known observation that anxiety runs in families, and the multipart explanation of why

and how it does (Dadds, 2002; Manassis, Hudson, Webb, & Albano, 2004; Muris, 2006; Pennington, 2002). Before summarizing the long list of factors that influence the development and maintenance of anxiety, it is necessary to take a few steps back in order to view anxiety in evolutionary perspective. As previously discussed, much of the anxiety experienced by children and adolescents is useful and adaptive. But this understanding needs to be balanced with Pennington's (2002) more contemporary insight that "evolution has prepared us to be more anxious than we need to be, especially given the relative safety of modern life" (p. 142). With this in mind, we can appreciate the many pathways that lead to anxiety-based disorders.

Genes and Heredity

Clearly, genetics has a significant impact on the development of both normal and pathological anxiety (Boer & Lindhout, 2001; Eley, 2001; Eley et al., 2003; Elizabeth, King, & Ollendick, 2004; Goldsmith & Lemery, 2000; Hudziak et al., 2004; Kovacs & Devlin, 1998; Legrand, McGue, & Iacono, 1999). Twin and family studies have provided ample evidence that anxious parents are more likely to have anxious children, and that the fears of MZ twins are more similar than the fears of DZ twins (Craske, 1997; Dadds, 2002; Dierker, Merikangas, & Szatmari, 1999; Ehringer, Rhee, Young, Corley, & Hewitt, 2006). For the most part, the genetic role appears to involve a general vulnerability rather than a disorder-specific risk, although there may be important gender and environmental contributions (Craske, 1997; Eley, 1999; Eley & Stevenson, 1999a; Pennington, 2002; Reddy et al., 2001; Schmidt, Polak, & Spooner, 2001). Panic disorder, however, has been associated with especially high heritabilities (Merikangas, 2000). Current neuroscience research is focused on identifying gene locations associated with vulnerability (Merikangas, 2000; Pennington, 2002).

Physiological Factors

Hypotheses about genetically transmitted predispositions to anxiety-based disorders in children are numerous and likely involve multiple mechanisms. Understanding global and specific aspects of neuroanatomy, neurophysiology, and neurochemistry are important for explaining both normal and pathological anxiety. Many investigations involve the study of the brain's right hemisphere, prefrontal cortex, or cerebellum (De Bellis & Kuchibhatla,

2006; Richert, Carrion, Karchemskly, & Reiss, 2006; Zahn-Waxler et al., 2000). The limbic system is another focus of much of the research attention (Barlow, 1988; Cummins & Ninan, 2002; Davidson & Rickman, 1999; Eysenck, 1967; Pine, 1999; Pine & Grun, 1999). Amygdala abnormalities (i.e., oversensitivity) are one documented risk factor (Kagan & Snidman, 1999; Pine, 1999; Pine & Grun, 1999; Thomas et al., 2001). The autonomic nervous system and the hypothalamic-pituitary-adrenal (HPA) axis system are other contributors to risk (Dahl et al., 2000; Davidson & Rickman, 1999; Pervanidou et al., 2007; Shea et al., 2005; Stansbury & Gunnar, 1994). In addition, neurotransmitter dysfunctions have also been observed (Feder et al., 2004; Hooper & Tramontana, 1997).

Specific models of vulnerability for various anxiety disorders have been proposed (Cummins & Ninan, 2002), with links between obsessive-compulsive disorder and prefrontal cortical circuits (Rosenberg & Keshavan, 1998), OCD and the thalamus (Busatto et al., 2001), OCD and streptococcal infections (Arnold & Richter, 2001; Bessen, 2001; Leonard & Swedo, 2001; Murphy, Petitto, Voeller, & Goodman, 2001), and OCD and EEG and cardiac dysfunction (Marshall & Stevenson-Hinde, 2001). Associations between the septo-hippocampal system and generalized anxiety disorder, and between brain stem processes and separation anxiety disorder have also been examined (Pine, 1999; Pine & Grun, 1999).

Neurodevelopmental models of early abuse and post-traumatic stress that provide details about changes in brain systems associated with threat perception and threat response have also been presented. In these models, neurophysiological dysfunction is conceptualized first as an underlying vulnerability (i.e., present in some children before the experience of trauma), and second as a consequence of noxious experiences that disrupt normal functioning (i.e., resulting in additional, perhaps permanent, dysfunction) (Bremner & Vermetten, 2001; Pine, 2003; Perry et al., 1995; van der Kolk, 1997; Vermetten & Bremner, 2002a, 2002b; Vernberg & Varela, 2001). Given new technologies and data from mostly animal and adult studies, however, caution is warranted before we draw firm conclusions about children's anxiety vulnerabilities (Gunnar, 2001; Kalin, Shelton, & Davidson, 2007; Pine, Grun, & Peterson, 2001; Zahn-Waxler et al., 2000).

One conclusion that can be drawn involves the many connections between vulnerability to anxiety-based disorders and vulnerability to mood disorders. Over and over, the data suggest clear overlap between genetic influences on the development of anxiety and the development of depression (Compas & Oppedisano, 2000; Eley & Stevenson, 1999a, 1999b, 2000; Grillon et al., 2005; Pennington, 2002; Schniering et al., 2000). Children with both of these internalizing disorders exhibit negative emotion and emotion dysregulation; there are several models described by Eley and Stevenson (1999a, 1999b, 2000) that may explain the connections. First, the two types of disorders may share the same underlying etiologies. Second, there may be a temporal association, with anxiety usually preceding depression. Third, anxiety and depression may be distinct psychopathologies, each one increasing the risk that the other will develop. Other explanations involve specific environmental events that, coupled with underlying vulnerability, lead to the expression of either anxiety or depression (Eley, 1999; Eley & Stevenson, 2000; Pennington, 2002).

Child Factors

Child characteristics such as gender, attachment, and temperament, as well as more basic psychological factors including those related to emotion, cognition, and behavior, also play important roles in the emergence of anxiety-based disorders. As previously noted, being a girl places a child at risk, with increased vulnerability related to sex-linked genetic differences, physiological experiences, and socialization (Cuffe, McKeown, Addy, & Garrison, 2005; Cronk, Slutske, Madden, Bucholz, & Heath, 2004; Zahn-Waxler et al., 2000). Insecure attachments lead to both short- and long-term outcomes involving anxiety disorders (Elizabeth et al., 2004; Hayward, Killen, Kraemer, & Taylor, 2000; Muris & Meesters, 2002; Thompson, 2001; van Ijzendoorn & Bakermans-Kranenburg, 1996; Warren, Huston, Egeland, & Sroufe, 1997). The heightened risk involves not only more frequent experiences of anxiety, but difficulties engendered by the caregiver's problematic and often ineffective attempts to manage the child's distress (Thompson, 2001).

Given the many examples of heightened arousal and physiological dysregulation described in the previous section, it makes sense that temperament is one of the child variables that is associated with anxiety disorders (Kovacs & Devlin, 1998; Moehler et al., 2008; Muris et al., 2007; Zahn-Waxler et al., 2000). The temperamental trait most associated with anxiety is inhibition. Inhibition involves a unique mix of wariness, arousal, and emotional and behavioral preferences for any given child (Bernstein et al., 1996; Craske, 1997; Hirshfeld-Becker et al., 2007; Lonigan, Vasey, Phillips, & Hazan, 2004; Muris & Dietvorst, 2006). This mix is part of a developmental profile that also includes parents, peers, and cultural context (Degnan & Fox, 2007; Kagan & Fox, 2006; Neal & Edelmann, 2003; West & Newman, 2007). The many investigations by Kagan and his colleagues (Kagan, 2008; Kagan & Snidman, 1999; Kagan, Snidman, Arcus, & Reznick, 1994; Kagan, Snidman, McManis, & Woodward, 2001; Schwartz et al., 1999; Schwartz, Wright, Shin, Kagan, & Rauch, 2003) describe children at risk for later anxiety as highly inhibited and highly reactive. Pennington (2002) emphasizes a distinction between genotype and phenotype, and suggests that there are two groups of inhibited children: those who have no family history of anxiety disorders and are not themselves at increased risk for disorders; and those who do have a family history of anxiety and are at risk.

Perhaps the most important emotion variable in terms of etiology has to do with individual differences in positive and negative affectivity, with negative affectivity (or emotionality) related to the emergence of internalizing disorders (Anthony, Lonigan, Hooe, & Phillips, 2002; Chorpita, Plummer, & Moffitt, 2000; Lahey et al., 2004; Lonigan et al., 2004; Lonigan, Phillips, & Hooe, 2003; Ollendick, Seligman, Goza, Byrd, & Singh, 2003; Phillips, Lonigan, Driscoll, & Hooe, 2002). The complex psychological construct of affectivity is the basis of the **tripartite model** of anxiety and depression (see Box 11.2). The model's three core concepts are: (1) anxiety and depression share a common causal factor of negative affectivity; (2) along with negative affectivity, low levels of positive affectivity are associated with depression; and (3) along with negative affectivity, high levels of physiological arousal are associated with anxiety. Emotion regulation or dysregulation is another key component in the development of anxiety disorders. Children who experience frequent or intense negative emotions, *and who lack the skills to regulate these emotions or the confidence that their efforts will have meaningful effects*, are most vulnerable (Suveg & Zeman, 2004; Thompson, 2001).

The influence of cognitive variables on the development of anxiety disorders is also salient. Cognitive and attentional biases to perceive and attend more closely to threatening stimuli, cognitive appraisals of ambiguous situations as negative and threatening, and specific cognitive distortions related to the self and others all contribute to increased risk for anxiety disorders (Alfano, Beidel, & Turner, 2002; Barrett & Healy, 2003; Barrett, Rapee, Dadds, & Ryan, 1996; Chorpita, Albano, & Barlow, 1996; Field, 2006; Kendall & MacDonald, 1993; Leary, 2001a, 2001b; Meesters, Muris, & van Rooijen, 2007; Muris, Meesters, & Rompelberg, 2007; Muris & van der Heiden, 2006; Prins, 2001; Puliafico & Kendall, 2006; Richards, French, Nash, Hadwin, & Donnelly, 2007; Thompson, 2001; Vasey & MacLeod, 2001; Waters, Lipp, & Spence, 2004). Level of cognitive development and the ability to correctly identify problematic physical symptoms may be especially important to consider for certain anxiety and somaticizing disorders (Muris, Hoeve, Meester, & Mayer, 2004; Muris, Mayer, Vermeulen, & Hiemstra, 2007). And metacognitive variables may be equally important for disorders involving worry and obsessive thinking (de Bruin, Muris, & Rassin, 2007).

Anxiety sensitivity, "the tendency to respond fearfully to anxiety symptoms" (Hayward et al., 2000, p. 208), may further complicate cognitive processing as well as interfere with effective emotion regulation (Eley, Gregory, Clark, & Ehlers, 2007; Eley, Stirling, Ehlers, Gregory, & Clark, 2004; Lambert et al., 2004; Leen-Feldner, Feldner, Bernstein, McCormick, & Zvolensky, 2005; Muris & Meesters, 2004; and Silverman, Goedhart, Barrett, & Turner, 2003; van Beek, Perna, Schruers, Muris, & Griez, 2005). To the extent that children and adolescents are predisposed to immediately focus on and overreact to uncomfortable body sensations, high levels of anxiety sensitivity may be conceptualized as a diathesis; coupling this diathesis with significant or multiple stressors may explain the development of panic disorder in some youth (Eley et al., 2004; Hayward et al., 2000; Leen-Feldner, Zvolensky, & Feldner, 2006; Muris, Schmidt, Merckelbach, & Schouten, 2001; Pollock et al., 2002).

Early experiences with control, and lack of control, may contribute to a lack of security and a cognitive predisposition to assume that one does not control events or outcomes; this predisposition underlies a sense of helplessness and increases a child's

Tripartite Model of Anxiety and Depression

The study of the relationship between anxiety and depression has a long and interesting history. Anxiety and depression frequently occur together, though not always. Although the categorical structure of the DSM diagnostic system defines each domain of disorder independently, anxiety and depression are often difficult to differentiate empirically. Most people recognize intuitively the ways in which both types of disorders are expressions of a negative emotional state, while at the same time seeming distinct from one another. These were among the observations and questions addressed by David Watson, LeAnn Clark, and others over 20 years ago in innovative research into the underlying structure of anxiety and depression. The model they developed—the tripartite model of emotion—continues to guide research efforts today.

The tripartite model (Watson & Clark, 1991) identifies three groups of symptoms that combine to define disorders of anxiety and depression. According to this model, anxiety and depression share a common core symptom of *general emotional distress (i.e., negative affect)*. Anxiety disorders are differentiated by the additional prominence of *physiological hyperarousal,* whereas depression is characterized by a *low positive emotional state (i.e, low positive affect)*. This conceptual model led to research efforts to develop valid and reliable assessment measures of the common factor (negative affect), as well as specific symptoms of anxiety and specific symptoms of depression (Watson et al., 1995a, 1995b).

Although originally derived from research with adults, the tripartite model of emotion has been investigated in adolescents and children as well (Chorpita, Plummer et al., 2000; Lambert et al., 2004; Ollendick et al., 2003). As the model began to be considered from a developmental perspective, it was suggested that anxiety and depression may be part of a single, more global factor of psychopathology that becomes more differentiated over time. However, this does not appear to be the case. Instead, the basic three-factor structure of the tripartite model can be measured early in life and is relatively stable over time (Turner & Barrett, 2003). The preponderance of research of children with anxiety and depressive disorders generally supports the tripartite model among youth populations (Anderson & Hope, 2008; Cannon & Weems, 2006; Jacques & Mash, 2004), though anxiety and mood disorders show greater co-occurrence earlier in life, somewhat obscuring the underlying three-factor structure.

A broader developmental perspective may help further clarify the clinical and research findings that have made some of these developmental questions difficult to answer. Research integrating the broad underlying structure of emotion, emerging neuroscience, cognitive development, and psychopathology may provide especially useful insights (Posner, Russell & Peterson, 2005). Research integrating findings from several areas has shown that while the neurophysiology underlying the tripartite model may be in place early in development, the cognitive ability to label a variety of subjective emotional states takes time to emerge. In other words, perhaps what develops over time is not the differentiated core symptom domains, but the individual's ability to conceptualize and describe his or her symptoms.

In addition to considering the tripartite model across the developmental continuum, studies have also validated the model across diverse cultural groups. For example, validating studies have been conducted with an urban youth sample (Lambert, Joiner, McCreary, Schmidt, & Ialongo, 2004), European youth (de Beurs, den Hollander-Gijsman, Helmich, & Zitman, 2006; Kiernan, Laurent, Joiner, Catanzaro, & MacLachlan, 2001), and children and adolescents in South Korea (Yang, Hong, Joung & Kim, 2006). Even though some differences and inconsistencies exist, anxiety and depression are both consistently characterized by negative affect, with anxiety also associated with physiological hyperarousal and depression also associated with low positive affect.

general vulnerability (Barlow, 1988; Burhans & Dweck, 1995; Chorpita, 2001; Chorpita & Barlow, 1998; Mineka, Gunnar, and Champoux, 1986; Thompson, 2001; Weems, Silverman, Rapee, & Pina, 2003), and may be particularly relevant as a predictor of psychosomatic problems (Hagekull & Bohlin, 2004). In the integrative model proposed by Weems and Silverman (2006), understanding the relations between control and anxiety disorders involves clearly describing the kinds of control that children and adolescents actually have, as well as their perceptions of control. That these kinds of experiences occur in certain developmental periods is important. According to Pynoos et al. (1999), "the peak incidences (and surprisingly high prevalence) of serious near-drownings, burns, and dog bites are between infancy and five years of age" (p. 1550), and underlie a number of neurobiologically based cognitive changes in children.

Intolerance of uncertainty has been documented to increase levels of adolescent worry; given the unsettled nature of adolescence, this may be particularly problematic (Lugesen, Dugas, & Bukowski, 2003). Additional risks are certain personality patterns (Huey & Weisz, 1997; Robins, John, Caspi, Moffitt, & Stouthamer-Loeber, 1996; see Figure 11.3) and unsatisfactory peer relationships. Adolescents who are ignored or rejected by their peers experience, as one might expect, more social anxiety (Inderbitzen, Walters, & Bukowski, 1997).

Behavioral models of risk and psychopathology emphasize that children's learning is at the root of anxiety. Rachman's (1977) theory of fear acquisition presented three pathways to disorder: direct conditioning, modeling, and/or instruction or information. There are data to support both direct and indirect pathways (Field, Argyris, & Knowles, 2001; Field & Lawson, 2003; King, Eleonora, & Ollendick,

1998; Ollendick & King, 1991; Ollendick, Vasey & King, 2001). Contemporary explanations of behavioral risk also include aspects of neuropsychology and temperament (Mineka & Zinbarg, 2006; Pennington, 2002).

The life events experienced by children also influence risk and vulnerability, perhaps especially so for children with OCD and PTSD (Deblinger, Mannarino, Cohen, & Steer, 2006; Gothelf, Aharonovsky, Horesh, Carty, & Apter, 2004; Perry et al, 1995; Vernberg & Varela, 2001; Williamson, Birmaher, Dahl, & Ryan, 2005). Particular types of events, such as threat or loss, are differentially associated with the development of anxiety or depression (Eley & Stevenson, 2000), but other types of events may be linked to specific anxiety subtypes (Stein, Chavira, & Jang, 2001). Trauma that threatens family integrity, such as being physically abused or witnessing violence, is especially harmful (Silva et al., 2000). Chronic stressors such as discrimination, schoolwork, family problems, and friendship problems have also been identified as both syndrome-specific (tied to either anxiety or depression) and child-specific (related to nonshared environmental

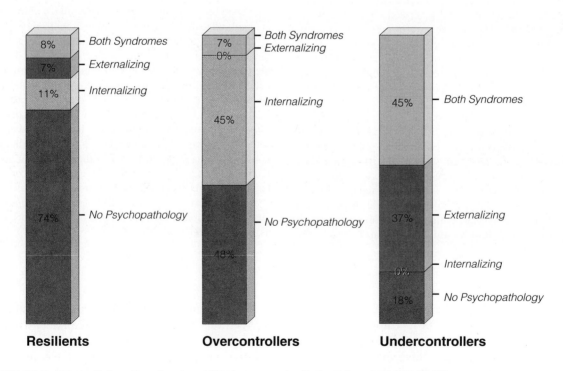

FIGURE 11:3 Internalizing disorders in resilient, overcontrolled, and undercontrolled boys.
Source: From Robins, R.W., John, O.P., Caspi A., Moffitt, T.E., & Stouthamer-Loeber, M. (1996), "Resilient, overcontrolled and undercontrolled boys: Three replicable personality types", 'Journal of Personality and Social Psychology', 70(1), p. 167. Copyright © 1996 American Psychological Association. Reprinted by permission.

causes) (Asbury, Dunn, Pike, & Plomin, 2003; Eley & Stevenson, 2000; Pike & Plomin, 1996; Szalacha et al., 2003). Certain factors moderate children's responses to negative or traumatic events, including physical proximity, emotional proximity, gender, and age (Pfefferbaum, 1997).

Parent Factors

The family context in which children's genetic inheritance and psychological makeup is embedded is key to the development of anxiety-based disorders. The transactional approach to psychopathology, discussed in many other chapters, emphasizes the connections among child variables, parent and relationship variables, and larger ethnic and cultural variables (Boer & Lindhout, 2001; Burgess, Rubin, Chea, & Nelson, 2001; Craske, 1997; Dadds, 2002; Hughes, Hedtke, & Kendall, 2008; Spence, Najman, Bor, O'Callaghan, & Williams, 2002; Suarez-Morales & Bell, 2006; Vendlinski, Silk, Shaw, & Lane, 2006). Parent fears and worries, modeling of avoidant behavior, acceptance of children's anxiety and avoidance, as well as overinvolvement and overprotection, are all potentially related to both the development and the maintenance of anxiety disorders (Barrett, Shortt, & Healy, 2002; Berg-Nielsen, Vikan, & Dahl, 2002; Bogels, van Dongen, & Muris, 2003; Burgess et al., 2001; Hastings et al., 2008; Muris, Bodden, Merckelbach, Ollendick, & King, 2003; Stein et al., 2001; Von Salisch, 2001; Waters & Barrett, 2000; Wood, McLeod, Sigman, Hwang, & Chu, 2003). These kinds of parental characteristics and parenting behaviors, understood in the broad context of emotion socialization, may contribute to a child's sense of fragility and incompetence in a scary world (Siqueland, Kendall, & Steinberg, 1996; Suveg, Zeman, Flannery-Schroeder, & Cassano, 2005).

Parents can influence the development of PTSD, for example, via the "shotgun effect," the "lack of protective shield effect," and/or a "toxic family effect" (Scheeringa & Gaensbauer, 2000, p. 375; Ostrowski, Chrisopher, & Delahanty, 2007; Punamaki, Qouta, El Sarraj, & Montgomery, 2006; Scheeringa & Zeanah, 2001). The "shotgun effect" involves trauma that is so overwhelming that it produces anxiety symptoms in all family members. In other words, parents as well as children struggle to deal with the aftermaths of awful experiences such as the loss of a home in a fire or flood. The "lack of protective shield effect" involves parents who, for varied reasons, cannot provide the comfort, support,

and security necessary for recovery. In these cases, parents may not recognize or they may minimize the impact of a particular trauma on children, believing that children are less affected by stress or that ignoring distress and dysfunction will help a child move on. And the "toxic family effect" has to do with the ways in which parent responses to trauma actually elicit and maintain anxiety symptoms in their children. In some cases, for instance, parents may exacerbate their children's distress by having their children repeatedly recall the traumatic experience or consider the possibility of new or repeat trauma.

Assessment and Diagnosis

There are two main tasks of assessment: (1) to determine whether children's anxiety reflects normal or pathological adjustment, and (2) to discriminate among anxiety disorders (Schniering, Hudson, & Rapee, 2000; Tracey, Chorpita, Douban, & Barlow, 1997). Clinicians need to make these decisions using a developmental framework and paying attention to categorical versus dimensional approaches (Dierker et al., 2001; Muris et al., 2003; Muris, Meesters, & Spinder, 2003; Zahn-Waxler et al., 2000). In pediatric settings, high rates of medically unexplained symptoms should prompt physicians to explore internalizing psychopathologies (Dhossche et al., 2002). Comprehensive assessment includes interviews, self-reports, rating scales, physiological assessments and clinical observations, and evidence-based assessment is increasingly emphasized (Hunsley & Mash, 2007; King, Muris, & Ollendick, 2005; McClure, Kubiszyn, & Kaslow, 2002; Rapee & Sweeney, 2005; Silverman & Ollendick, 2005; Southam-Gerow & Chorpita, 2007).

There are many self-report questionnaires for children and adolescents, for many different types of anxiety disorders. Among the most common are the Anxiety Disorders Interview Schedule for DSM-IV (Grisham, Brown, & Campbell, 2004; Silverman & Albano, 1996a, 1996b; Wood, Piacentini, Bergman, McCracken, & Barrious, 2002); the Multidimensional Anxiety Scale for Children ([MASC]; March, Parker, Sullivan, Stallings, & Conners, 1997), the Screen for Child Anxiety Related Emotional Disorders ([SCARED]; Birmaher, Khetarpal, Cully, Brent, & McKenzie, 2003; Mayer, Bartelds, Tierney, & Bogie, 2001), the School Refusal Assessment Scale (Kearney & Silverman, 1993), the

Trauma Symptom Checklist for Young Children (Briere et al., 2001) and the Yale-Brown Obsessive-Compulsive Scale ([Y-BOCS]; Goodman et al., 1989; Scahill et al., 1997). Many of these questionnaires demonstrate some evidence of specificity, in terms of differentiating between anxiety and mood disorders as well as among anxiety subtypes (Brotman, Kamboukos, & Theise, 2008; Chorpita, Yim, Moffitt, Umemoto, & Francis, 2000; Greenhill et al., 1998; Lerner et al., 1999; Muris, Merckelbach, Ollendick, King, & Bogie, 2002; Schniering, Hudson, & Rapee, 2000). For younger children, narrative stories may be used to elicit anxiety themes (Warren, Emde, & Sroufe, 2000). Parent and teacher forms of anxiety rating scales, such as the Child Behavior Check List and the SCARED (parent form), are also used frequently (Aschenbrand, Angelosante, & Kendall, 2005; Kendall et al., 2007; Nauta et al., 2004). Parent attitudes and expectancies can also be assessed (Eisen, Spasaro, Brien, Kearney, & Albano, 2004). A developmental systems framework focused on child-family transactions may also be useful (Mash & Hunsley, 2007).

Even with abundant data, interpretation is often difficult (Muris & Merckelbach, 2000). That's because agreement between children's reports and parents' reports of anxiety symptoms and avoidant behavior is usually poor (Choudhury, Pimentel, & Kendall, 2003; Comer & Kendall, 2004; Grills & Ollendick, 2003; Kendall & Pimentel, 2003; Klein, 1991; Meiser-Stedman, Smith, Glucksman, Yule, & Dalgleish, 2007; Safford, Kendall, Flannery-Schroeder, Webb, & Sommer, 2005; Schniering et al., 2000). Discrepancies among parent, teacher, and clinician ratings of adolescent disorders have also been reported, and these discrepancies are associated with poor outcomes (Ferdinand, van der Ende, & Verhulst, 2004). Reasons for lack of agreement include children's abilities (or inabilities) to describe their anxiety, children's willingness (or lack of willingness) to disclose their anxiety, parental awareness (or lack of awareness), parental distress, and parental motivations; these reasons underscore the need to gather data from both children and parents (Klein, 1991; Pfefferbaum, 1997; Wren, Bridge, & Birmaher, 2004; Youngstrom, Findling, & Calabrese, 2003, 2004; Youngstrom et al., 2004). Especially when making decisions about internalizing disorders, clinicians also need to take into account the cultural backgrounds of children and their families (Varela et al., 2004).

Special clinical skills are very important when assessing children who have been traumatized. Depending on the type of trauma, various accommodations related to developmental and physical status, or legal requirements, may be necessary (Foa, Johnson, Feeny, & Treadwell, 2001; Stover & Berkowitz, 2005; Strand, Sarmiento, & Pasquale, 2005). Age- and gender-sensitive techniques and multiple informants for sexually abused children and children who have witnessed family violence have received clinical and research study (Kaufman & Henrich, 2000; King et al., 2003). Children and adolescents who have suffered because of natural disasters such as earthquakes and hurricanes (Goenjian et al., 2001; Shaw, Applegate, & Schorr, 1996) and terror attacks such as the 1995 Oklahoma City bombing (Pfefferbaum, 1998, 2003; Pfefferbaum et al., 1999), or who live in war zones amid widespread violence (Parson, 1996) also benefit from knowledgeable and compassionate assessments.

Perhaps more than any other physical or psychiatric diagnosis, the somatoform disorders require an integrated approach involving combined medical and psychological perspectives. The critical starting point is to rule out known physical causes. This can then be followed by a consideration of how well symptoms meet the criteria for a somatoform disorder (Meesters, Muris, Ghys, Reumerman, & Rooijmans, 2003), although it is again important to understand symptoms in the context of culture (Varela et al., 2004). Because the child, and often the family as well, has a considerable psychological investment in the physical symptoms, both are likely to respond with frustration and even distrust when confronted by an inadequate medical explanation. Also, these patients are, by definition, resistant to an attribution focused on emotional functioning. Consequently, they are unlikely to accept a referral for psychological intervention. At least for the more severe somatization cases, then, collaboration between the psychologist and pediatrician is crucial.

Intervention

As with all psychopathologies, the prevention or reduction of anxiety disorders is the goal of mental health professionals. A number of prevention programs have demonstrated success, and new ideas related to prevention are also promising (Bernstein et al., 1996; Dadds & Roth, 2008; Lock & Barrett,

2003; Lowry-Webster, Barrett, & Lock, 2003; Rapee, 2002; Spence, 2001); some of these studies (as we would predict in the field of developmental psychopathology) have also enhanced our understanding of normal development (Hudson, Kendall, Coles, Robin, & Webb, 2002). When prevention is not possible, early interventions become very important, not only for the immediate relief of symptoms, but also for the reduction of later disorders such as substance abuse (Compton, Burns, & Egger, 2002; Kendall et al., 2004).

Psychological Treatment

Given the nature of internalizing disorders, many children and adolescents become the focus of intervention efforts only after an anxiety disorder is firmly rooted; many others who struggle remain undiscovered and untreated (Kendall, 1994). Effective treatments for the wide range of anxiety disorders are available (Silverman & Ollendick, 2005). These include psychodynamic and play-oriented approaches (Barnett, 1984; Bernstein et al., 1996; King et al., 2005; Leonard & Rapaport, 1991), but the treatment of choice is clearly cognitive-behavioral therapy. **Cognitive-behavioral therapy (CBT)** is based, in large part, on the work of Kendall and his colleagues (e.g., Albano & Kendall, 2002; Kendall, 1994; Kendall, Brady, & Verduin, 2001; Kendall et al., 1997) and is associated with both immediate and long-term improvements (Barrett, Duffy, Dadds, & Rapee, 2001; Beidel, Turner, Young, & Paulsen, 2005; Chorpita et al., 2002; Christophersen & Mortweet, 2001; Compton, Burns, Egger, & Robertson, 2002; Craske, 1997; Garcia-Lopez et al., 2006; Kendall, Hudson, Gosch, Flannery-Schroeder, & Suveg, 2008; Kendall & Southam-Gerow, 2001; King & Ollendick, 1997; Labellarte, Ginsburg, Walkup, & Riddle, 1999; Masia-Warner et al., 2005; Moore & Carr, 2000; Ollendick & King, 1998; Prins & Ollendick, 2003; Sweeney & Rapee, 2005). Both individual and group formats do very well (Barrett, Healy-Farrell, & March, 2004; Dadds & Barrett, 2001; Shortt, Barrett, & Fox, 2001; Silverman, Pina, & Viswesvaran, 2008); CBT is also helpful for children who have been diagnosed with anxiety and additional internalizing or externalizing disorders (Flannery-Schroeder, Suveg, Safford, Kendall, & Webb, 2004; Tsao, Mystkowski, Zucker, & Craske, 2002). Relaxation training is often a key component of CBT (Dobson, Bray, Kehle, Theodore, &

Peck, 2005; Gosch, Flannery-Schroeder, Mauro, & Compton, 2006; Klein-Hebling & Lohaus, 2002). Internet-based treatments, with various educational and experiential components presented in interactive formats, have also been effective and are well-received by both children and parents (Spence, Holmes, March, & Lipp, 2006). School-based interventions are another promising option; relaxation exercises, for example, have had positive impacts when taught to groups of children with asthma as well as entire classrooms (Dobson et al., 2005; Bernstein, Layne, Egan, & Tennison, 2005; Klein-Hebling & Lohaus, 2002).

Summarizing dozens of investigations, Velting, Setzer, and Albano (2004) have identified the six main components of effective CBT: psychoeducation, somatic management, cognitive restructuring, problem-solving, exposure, and relapse prevention (see Table 11.4). **Psychoeducation** involves providing children and their families with information about normal anxiety and the emergence and maintenance of pathological anxiety, and about theoretical and practical aspects of CBT. **Somatic management** involves targeting the distressing physiological symptoms, and is usually focused on relaxation and breathing techniques. In addition, children and adolescents learn how to predict and tolerate the anxiety that accompanies challenging and stressful events. **Cognitive restructuring** has to do with the identification and modification of negative thoughts that elicit and prolong anxiety. Thinking about emotions and emotional biases may also be important, and is in some instances the focus of treatment efforts (Southam-Gerow & Kendall, 2000; Suveg, Kendall, Comer, & Robin, 2006; Suveg, Southam-Gerow, Goodman, & Kendall, 2007; Zahn-Waxler et al., 2000). **Problem-solving** is a step-by-step, active, behaviorally oriented approach for coping. **Exposure** to the stimuli and situations that are associated with anxiety is systematic and controlled, with in vivo (real-life) practice preferred. **Relapse prevention** involves laying the groundwork for the maintenance and generalization of improvements. With all CBT treatments, the therapeutic alliance and developmental considerations in the design and implementation of all aspects of individual interventions must be emphasized (Chu et al., 2004; Creed & Kendall, 2005; Hughes & Kendall, 2007; Kendall & Ollendick, 2004; Kingery et al., 2006; Vernberg & Johnston, 2001; Weisz & Hawley, 2002).

Cognitive-behavioral therapy approaches, such as the Coping Cat program, have been adapted for use in treating childhood anxiety disorders.

Given the salient role of the parents in etiology and maintenance, it makes sense to work within a treatment framework that includes parents and recognizes the impact of culture on parents (Barmish & Kendall, 2005; Barrett & Shortt, 2003; Kendall et al., 2008; Pina, Silverman, Fuentes, Kurtines, & Weems, 2003; Pina, Silverman, Weems, Kurtines, & Goldman, 2003; Suveg et al., 2006). Family approaches to anxiety disorders are often used and are often very effective (Barrett, Dadds, & Rapee, 1996; Crawford & Manassis, 2001; Freeman et al., 2003; Ginsburg & Schlossberg, 2002; Weisz, 2004; Wood, Piacentini, Southam-Gerow, Chu, & Sigman, 2006). The involvement of parents appears especially helpful for younger children between the ages of 7 and 10, and for girls (Barrett et al., 1996; Christophersen & Mortweet, 2001).

TABLE 11:4 MAIN COMPONENTS OF COGNITIVE-BEHAVIORAL THERAPY

COMPONENTS	FOCUS/GOALS	ASSOCIATED TECHNIQUES
Psychoeducation	Provide corrective information about the nature of anxiety and feared stimuli	Didactic instruction; self-monitoring (diaries); assigned reading
Somatic management	Target autonomic arousal and related physiological symptoms; focus attention away from anxiety-arousing physical sensations; break the association between physiological arousal and anxiety	Breathing retraining (deep and slow diaphragmatic breathing); relaxation training (progressive muscle/cue controlled/applied relaxation); meditation; exercise
Cognitive restructuring	Identify maladaptive (unhelpful) thoughts, beliefs, and images and teach realistic, coping-focused thinking	Monitoring of thought processes (diaries); identification of automatic thoughts (ATs); teaching rational disputation of ATs; use of behavioral experiments to gather evidence to refute ATs; age-appropriate methods for younger children (e.g., Kendall's FEAR steps)
Problem solving	Develop a variety of active methods for coping with specific problem situations and a system for testing the potential solutions	Identify the specific problem; generate multiple alternative actions for improving the situation; explore costs and benefits of each potential solution; determine and implement the preferred or most feasible alternative; evaluate outcomes
Exposure	Graduated, systematic, and controlled exposure to feared situation(s) to provide experience with using anxiety management skills and consolidation of psychoeducation material	Behavioral exposure to feared situations; interoceptive exposure to feared bodily sensations (such as in panic disorder); exposure should be direct (in vivo) but may begin with imaginal or symbolic exposure (e.g., use of photos of feared object instesd of actual stimulus)
Relapse prevention	Focus on consolidating anxiety management skills and generalizing treatment gains over time; decrease reliance on therapist and others (e.g., parents) for managing anxiety	Fading of sessions (from weekly to biweekly); role reversal (child acts as therapist for a session); videotape commercial of therapy program; planned booster sessions

Source: From Vetting et al., (2004).

Designing various treatments for the children presented earlier in the chapter provides examples of these psychosocial clinical practices. Miranda, the girl diagnosed with generalized anxiety disorder, needed to spend several sessions becoming accustomed to, and comfortable with, the therapeutic setting, the therapist and the therapeutic relationship. Miranda and her parents discussed the age-related expectations and tasks that were important to her, and the ways that it would be advantageous (and even fun) to meet them. Miranda spent many of the sessions engaged in role playing, and in practicing self-talk strategies that would help her manage her base levels of anxiety and her specific anxiety symptoms.

In helping Keely with separation anxiety disorder and school refusal, it was important to first clarify for her parents and family that it was not school that was upsetting Keely. Rather, it was anxiety about separating from her mother that was interfering with her entry into first grade. Consequently, intervention efforts were aimed at restoring Keely's confidence in her relationship with her mother as well as her own self-confidence (see also Heyne et al., 2002). To help with the transition to a calmer start to the school day, a picture of her mother was taped to the inside of her desk as a reminder that her mother was fine and would be waiting for her at home at the end of the day. For several days, Keely was also allowed to call her mother after lunch if she wished. By the end of four weeks of these efforts, Keely was again looking forward to her school day and separated from her mother easily in the morning.

For Jack's dog phobia, any of four classic treatments for fears (or combinations of these treatments) might be used, including modeling, systematic desensitization, reinforced exposure, and self-talk (Weisz, 2004), with attention paid to the individual response pattern and developmental status (Davis & Ollendick, 2005; King et al., 2005; Muris, 2005). **Modeling** treatments are based on the impact of observational learning. With this approach, Jack might participate in symbolic modeling (using videos of children displaying non-fearful behavior) or live modeling (using in-person observation of non-fearful children) or participant modeling (pairing Jack with a non-fearful child). Depending on the child, modeling treatments may achieve good outcomes quite quickly (Weisz, 2004). **Systematic desensitization** involves teaching an anxious child how to relax and how to maintain relaxation when exposed to the feared stimulus. Exposure is done gradually

(i.e., systematically, from stuffed dogs to videos of dogs to real dogs), building on the child's successes over time. **Reinforced exposure** involves rewarding a child for desired behavior. In Jack's case, he might receive tokens for more functional dog-related behaviors. **Self-talk** is a cognitive technique focused on providing positive self-statements such as "I am brave," to enhance appropriate behaviors. All of these treatment approaches depend on establishing a trusting relationship with a therapist, because children need to believe (and feel deep down) that this adult will keep them safe.

Danny, who struggled with OCD, received an intervention that first involved education for Danny and his parents about the disorder. During these discussions, Danny's father also revealed that he had experienced a variety of significant anxiety symptoms, including some marginal obsessive-compulsive behaviors, as well. A cognitive-behavioral treatment plan was developed and a referral for a medication consultation was made (see King, Ollendick, & Mongomery, 1995; Kutcher, Reiter, Gardner, & Klein, 1992). Cognitive techniques were used to identify patterns of thoughts and behaviors that had become maladaptive and new, more effective strategies for dealing with anxiety were developed. Behavioral plans to limit compulsive behaviors were also created. These included techniques that exposed Danny to triggering stimuli while preventing the compulsive response. In this way, Danny became desensitized to anxiety-provoking stimuli and no longer felt the urgent need to engage in the compulsive behaviors.

After several meetings with Estella and her parents, the hospital team working with her diagnosed a somatoform pain disorder. In discussing this with Estella and her parents, it was emphasized that no one thought Estella was "faking." Rather, the facts that Estella very much wanted to do well in high school and also please her parents were noted, and the suggestion made that although Estella was not feeling directly anxious about this, the pressure to perform had begun to interfere with her ability to manage her daily demands. As part of this suggestion, the therapist mentioned that there were many ways in which bodies and minds work together, in both positive and negative ways. A plan was developed with input from the family, physician, and psychologist, in which medical monitoring would be combined with help from the psychologist in returning to school. It was emphasized that while they would continue to investigate physiological factors, most truly dangerous possibilities had already been ruled out and it was medically safe for Estella to return to school. Gradually, the psychologist helping Estella became more involved in coaching her to develop more adaptive and effective ways of managing stress in her life. Mind-body pain management strategies were an important component of ongoing treatment (Kuttner, 1997).

With respect to the treatment of post-traumatic stress disorder, there is clear need for both acute, crisis-oriented interventions and ongoing support (La Greca, Silverman, Vernberg, & Roberts, 2002; Pfefferbaum, 1997; Pine & Cohen, 2002; Vernberg & Vogel, 1993). Crisis management often includes the debriefing of traumatized children and facilitated discussions about the traumatic event; whether these techniques are effective, ineffective, or possibly harmful requires additional investigation (Pfefferbaum, 1997). The central components of PTSD treatment involve re-establishing a sense of safety for the child, processing and eventually reducing the intensity of emotional experiences, helping the child to understand the impact of the traumatic event on him- or herself, addressing secondary stresses, and providing support and guidance to the child's caregivers (Scheeringa & Gaensbauer, 2000).

As with other anxiety disorders, cognitive and cognitive-behavioral approaches for PTSD are associated with improved functioning (Cohen, Deblinger, Mannarino, & Steer, 2004; Compton et al., 2002; Feeny, Foa, Treadwell, & March, 2004; Goenjian, Karayan, Pynoos, & Minassian, 1997; Pfefferbaum, 1997). Individual, group, and family formats all appear to be successful; group treatment may be especially useful in situations in which social and economic resources are limited (Amaya-Jackson et al., 2003; Giannopoulou, Dikaiakou, & Yule, 2006; Pfefferbaum, 1997; Scheeringa & Gaensbauer, 2000; Silverman et al., 2008; Smith et al., 2007). Pharmacological additions to psychotherapy may also be useful (Cohen, Mannarino, Perel, & Staron, 2007). For PTSD that follows abuse, there are a number of comprehensive, structured interventions that are efficacious (Cicchetti & Toth, 2003; Cohen et al., 2004; King et al., 2000b; Osofsky, 2003; Putnam, 2003); these interventions target the many domains of development that have been adversely affected by ongoing trauma (Deblinger, Mannarino, Cohen, & Steer, 2006; Kinniburgh, Blaustein, Spinazzola, & van der Kolk, 2005; Spinazzola et al., 2005; Vickerman & Margolin, 2007).

Pharmacological Treatment

Many effective treatments combine psychological and pharmacological techniques, with anxiety medications prescribed most frequently for children and adolescents with obsessive-compulsive disorder (Allen, Leonard, & Swedo, 1996; Compton et al., 2002; Liebowitz & Ginsberg, 2005; Mancini, van Ameringen, Bennett, Patterson, & Watson, 2005; March & Ollendick, 2004; Pine et al., 2001; Riddle et al., 2001; Stein & Seedat, 2004; Walkup et al., 2003) and more recently, for those with social anxiety (March, Entusah, Rynn, Alvano, & Tourian, 2007; Van Ameringen & Mancini, 2001; Wagner et al., 2004). Fluoxetine has also been shown to be helpful (Birmaher et al., 2003; Clark et al., 2005). Although much more research work remains to be done, these combined therapies seem especially appropriate for older children and those with more severe symptoms, and for complex cases that involve comorbidity (Beidel, Ferrell, Alfano, & Yeganeh, 2001; Bernstein et al., 1996; Craske, 1997; Geller et al., 2003; Greenhill et al., 1998; Kearney & Silverman, 1998; Labellarte et al., 1999; March, 2002; Seedat et al., 2002; Walkup, Labellarte, & Ginsburg, 2002).

In the future, it is likely that the recent growth in the pharmacological treatment of anxiety disorders in young people will become more refined as a result of ongoing clinical trials of medications that include children and adolescents. Advances in imaging research, such as fMRI techniques, will also likely provide a more precise understanding of the brain mechanisms and brain activity that are implicated in the development of anxiety disorders. These kinds of advances will also improve the precision with which medications are prescribed for children. But even with such improvements, it is important to keep in mind that cognitive-behavioral psychotherapies will continue to play a central role in providing the most effective treatment strategies for helping children cope with anxiety.

■ Key Terms

Emotional regulation (pg. 182)
Fears (pg. 183)
Worries (pg. 183)
Anxiety disorders (pg. 184)
Generalized anxiety disorder (pg. 187)
Separation anxiety disorder (pg. 188)
Obsessive-compulsive disorder (pg. 188)
Obsessions (pg. 188)

■ Chapter Summary

- While some fears and worries are a normal and expected part of childhood, when they consistently interfere with healthy development an anxiety disorder may be present.
- Emotional regulation, the ability to modulate and organize emotions, follows a developmental course that must be considered when determining whether or not normal-range anxiety crosses over to pathological anxiety.
- Anxiety disorders represent the maladaptive experience of anxiety in terms of intensity, duration, and pervasiveness.
- Anxiety disorders are also characterized by inhibition and withdrawal, exaggerated and unrealistic fears and worries, and overcontrol.

- Anxiety disorders are among the most frequently diagnosed disorders in children, adolescents, and adults.
- Some of these disorders, such as generalized anxiety disorder, represent an anxious reaction to a wide array of stimuli, while others, for example separation anxiety disorder and specific phobias, are rooted in more specific anxiety-producing situations.
- In some anxiety disorders, including obsessive-compulsive disorder and conversion disorder, the behaviors used to block the direct experience of anxiety (i.e., avoidance) are the primary symptoms.
- Post-traumatic stress disorder is the only anxiety disorder to specify a cause (traumatic experience) as part of the clinical description.
- Somatization and somatoform disorders involve the experience of physical symptoms that appear related to the moderation of emotions, especially anxiety. Anxiety sensitivity is often exhibited.
- Genetic and other physiological risk factors are clearly linked to the development of anxiety disorders. Research suggests that anxiety and mood disorders result from closely related risk factors.
- Parenting behaviors that may potentially contribute to the development of anxiety disorders include an anxious style of parenting, such as overinvolvement and overprotection, as well as the modeling of anxious and avoidant behavior.
- One of the assessment challenges in regard to the anxiety disorders is the fact that agreement between parents' and children's reports of anxiety symptoms is relatively low.
- Comprehensive assessment, including clinical interview, self-report measures, and clinical observations, are used to differentiate normal from pathological levels of anxiety and discriminate among anxiety disorders.
- A variety of psychological interventions (cognitive-behavioral therapy in particular), often in combination with pharmacological approaches, have proven effective in the treatment of anxiety disorders.

CHAPTER 12

Mood Disorders and Suicidality

■ **CHAPTER OUTLINE**

THERE ARE MANY MYTHS about depression in children. Some people believe that children cannot experience depression. But children can. Some people believe that, even if children can be clinically depressed, few are. But depression is not rare. Others believe that childhood depression is short-lived, or a normal developmental phenomenon. It is neither. Depression is a common and serious psychopathology with lasting negative consequences; it is underrecognized and undertreated in both children and in adolescents (Cicchetti & Toth, 1998; Coyle et al., 2003). In the last 10 years, issues related to the diagnosis and treatment of mood disorders in children and adolescents are receiving increased attention from mental health professionals, from researchers, and from special interest groups, including pharmaceutical companies and parent advocacy organizations. Much of the focus has been on the use (and overuse) of antidepressant medications, and the impact of medication on youth suicidality (Bridge & Axelson, 2008). Suicidality refers to the risk of suicidal ideation (thinking about suicide) as well as the risk for suicidal behavior (attempted or completed suicide); these topics are discussed in a later section of this chapter. Another focus has been on the ever-increasing numbers of both children and adolescents diagnosed with bipolar disorder (Blader & Carlson, 2007; Moreno et al., 2007). In this chapter, we attempt to provide a scholarly overview and a compassionate analysis of the many forms of mood disorders in children and adolescents.

Developmental Tasks and Challenges Related to the Construction of Self and Identity

Given the myriad physiological, psychological, and social changes associated with the transition from late childhood to adolescence, the development of a coherent **sense of self** (i.e., "the set of attributes, abilities, attitudes, and values that an individual believes defines who he or she is," Berk, 2009, p. 451) and a **positive identity** (i.e, an individual's understanding, acceptance, and prizing of his or her self, roles, relationships, and responsibilities) become critical for ongoing healthy adjustment (Call & Mortimer, 2001; Simon, 1997; Thoits, 1999); well-differentiated and integrated experiences of self and identity underlie all of the various types of autonomy and achievement that adolescents seek (Blasi & Milton, 1991; Burke, Owens, Serpe, & Thoits, 2003; Cicchetti & Rogosch, 2002; Collins, Gleason, & Sesma, 1997; Harter, 1999, 2003; Robins & Trzesniewski, 2005). Taking into account the "torturous self-consciousness" of adolescence (Crystal, Watanabe, Weinfurt, & Wu, 1998, p. 715), the hoped-for outcome is a "balanced, stable, and accurate view of self" (Jacobs, Bleeker, & Constantino, 2003, p. 43). Indeed, according to the pioneering lifespan developmental psychologist Erik

Erikson (1968), developing a mature psychological identity is *the primary achievement* of adolescence.

The construction of self is a process that begins in infancy and stretches across a lifetime. As just described, this construction is an individual achievement, but one that is accomplished within a particular family, in a particular culture, and in a particular era (Crystal et al., 1998; Mascolo & Bhatia, 2002; Roberts et al., 1999). The convergence of such late-childhood challenges as puberty, academic demands, romantic involvements, and vocational interests means that the constructs of self and identity become increasingly important in adolescence (Graber & Brooks-Gunn, 1996). One of the most important factors that contributes to competent rather than incompetent adjustments involves adolescents' abilities to cope with increases in both daily hassles (e.g., homework difficulties, disagreements with siblings) and larger stressors (e.g., economic uncertainty, domestic violence). In the absence of psychopathology, normal age-related increases in sadness, frustration, and anger are situationally determined and transient. For most children and adolescents, the experience of these negative emotions supports the acquisition of various and flexible coping strategies (e.g., talking over problems, changing behaviors, avoiding conflict) that are more likely to result in positive outcomes (Compas, 1987; Compas, Malcarne, & Fondacaro,

1988). But for some, as a result of biological predisposition and/or traumatic experience, such negative emotions can become predominant, diminishing self-esteem and contributing to a negative self-identity and the emergence of mood disorders.

In earlier chapters we have discussed **domains of competence** as areas of challenge and resolution that have an impact on the ways in which children perceive themselves. Researchers have described domain categories—including academics, behavior and conduct, and friendships—that have an impact on younger children's developing sense of self. Others have identified domains related to sports and appearance (Cole et al., 2001; Roisman, Masten, Coatsworth, & Tellegen, 2004). In adolescence, additional domains such as romantic relationships and the world of work emerge (Roisman et al., 2004). We do not expect that children and adolescents exhibit similar achievements in each and every domain at the same time. Some kids excel in sports early, and display academic accomplishments later. Other kids become more physically or interpersonally attractive and socially comfortable as they age. Domains involve multiple tasks with their own patterns of "emergence, ascendancy and decline" (Roisman et al., 2004, p. 123). Adolescents can be characterized as more or less comfortable in each important domain

of development, and during adolescence, domains related to academics, friendships and relationships, and appearance all become increasingly salient (Cole et al., 2001; Crystal et al., 1998; Roisman et al., 2004).

Arenas of comfort are the domains in which adolescents express relative satisfaction with themselves and their accomplishments (Call & Mortimer, 2001; Simmons, 2001). For instance, some adolescents who value relationships may spend time and effort developing multiple connections with others; success is tied to a sense of one's worth. Other adolescents focus on academic achievement and school activities, and successful experiences enhance well-being (Call & Mortimer, 2001). Typically developing adolescents experience comfort in at least one arena, and two-thirds report feeling comfortable in two or more arenas (see Table 12.1). Comfort appears to increase slightly over the course of adolescence (Call & Mortimer, 2001), and varies by gender, ethnicity, and SES background (Call & Mortimer, 2001; Eccles, Barber, Jozefowicz, Malenchuk, & Vida, 1999).

There are important connections between arenas of comfort and the adolescent's sense of self and identity. First, participation in multiple arenas is associated with an adolescent having more chances to experiment with identities and skills, and these chances are tied to increased opportunities for success and enhanced

TABLE 12:1 ARENAS OF COMFORT IN ADOLESCENCE

Arena	9th GRADE Percent	n	10th GRADE Percent	n	11th GRADE Percent	n
Family Comfort						
Comfort with mother	57.9	921	59.0	918	59.5	881
Comfort with father	35.4	856	34.8	865	33.9	844
Peer Comfort						
Peer support	57.5	921	60.7	853	65.7	944
School Comfort						
Teacher support	57.9	993	56.2	949	57.8	892
Low time pressures	68.2	996	65.8	949	61.2	891
Work Comfort						
Supervisor support	41.3	269	34.1	337	35.6	491
Support from coworker	40.3	447	46.0	337	39.1	476
Work satisfaction	84.7	503	85.4	446	87.9	554
Low work stress	89.6	491	86.6	440	83.9	547
Work is interesting	73.8	504	71.0	451	69.3	554

From Call and Mortimer (2001).

esteem (Barber, Stone, Hunt, & Eccles, 2005; Call & Mortimer, 2001; Thoits, 1999). It is important, however, to balance changes in various arenas, because some adolescents may be overwhelmed if change occurs in every domain simultaneously (Costa et al., 2005; Simmons, 2001). Another connection involves the degree of commitment to a particular identity or arena (Barber, Eccles, & Stone, 2001). An adolescent who plans a career in theater may feel especially proud of a leading role in a school play; another adolescent whose parents were immigrants may seek an internship focused on immigration reform or international economics.

For both domains of competence and arenas of comfort, evidence of individual achievement and the accompanying respect and/or liking of peers contribute to a sense of competence, development of self-esteem, and the creation of social relationships that serve as protective factors. In contrast, lack of success in valued domains, lack of confidence in one's abilities, and feelings of social isolation may predispose a child or adolescent to a preponderance

of negative emotions and negative moods; these are risk factors for current and later maladjustment.

Over the years of adolescence, most typically developing individuals come to construct a coherent autobiography. Habermas and Bluck (2000) refer to this emergence of one's story as "getting a life," and emphasize that it depends on certain cognitive and social advances. Weaving together personal events (e.g., idiosyncratic family relationships) with normative cultural events (e.g., religious milestones or graduation from high school), and making sense of both continuity and discontinuity in personality are complicated tasks. The development of a life story may have particular significance for those who have struggled with psychopathology as children and for those who struggle during adolescence. As we move into a discussion of mood disorders, we will need to think carefully about the many meanings of psychopathology and how they fit (or do not fit) into developing life stories.

Mood Disorders

There are many excellent reviews of **mood disorders** in children and adolescents that provide historical perspectives (Cicchetti, Rogosch, & Toth, 1997; Fristad, Shaver, & Holderle, 2002; Garber & Smith, 2006; Harrington, Rutter, & Fombonne, 1996; Luby, 2000; Waslick, Kandel, & Kakouros, 2002; Zahn-Waxler, Klimes-Dougan, & Slattery, 2000). These reviews refute earlier theoretical models that proposed that children lacked the necessary psychological structures and processes to experience adult-like depression, and later beliefs that children's depression was often "masked" by irritability and aggression. The reviews also recall the poignant observations of Rene Spitz (1946), who described long-hospitalized infants displaying sadness, withdrawal, developmental delays, and deviance. These reviews also describe contemporary conceptualizations of children's mood disorders. Against the background of children's rapid developmental growth and change, researchers and clinicians agree that it is useful to think about a **mood-related continuum** (i.e., a range of distress and impairment) (Hankin, Fraley, Lahey, & Waldman, 2005), and to distinguish among children and adolescents who exhibit periods of sadness and/or irritability, those who struggle with longer episodes of depression and dysfunction, and those who are appropriately diagnosed with clinically significant mood disorders (Cicchetti & Toth, 1998; Garber & Smith, 2006).

As with adults, sad mood and loss of pleasure are primary characteristics of childhood depression.

Nacivet/Getty Images

The Case of Rebecca

Rebecca is an 11-year-old girl referred by her parents and pediatrician. Although Rebecca has always been somewhat shy, neither her parents nor the school had any serious concerns until she started sixth grade. Rebecca began to complain about difficulty falling asleep, and her teachers noted that she appeared tired in class. She began to have problems completing homework. Rebecca had been on the volleyball team for two years; she loved the sport and was an excellent player and popular teammate. This year, however, she said she did not want to play because she felt she wasn't very good and that volleyball was "boring."

Always a cooperative child at home, Rebecca's parents are distressed by the fact that she has recently become argumentative and irritable. She is easily frustrated and cries often. Recently, Rebecca's mother was looking through Rebecca's schoolwork and found several notes written by Rebecca saying that she wished she were dead. When confronted with this, Rebecca refused to talk about it and sobbed at her parents that they didn't understand her at all. ■

The Case of Jacob

Jacob is an 8-year-old boy in the third grade referred because of concerns raised by his parents and teachers. Specifically, they describe him as irritable, hypersensitive, and sullen. Standardized testing suggests above-average intellectual ability, but Jacob struggles in class. He is easily discouraged and gives up quickly when he does not immediately understand a lesson. In these situations, he sometimes describes the assignments as "stupid," while at other times he says he cannot do them because he is "dumb." Jacob tends to play on his own on the playground and generally avoids group activities unless they are organized and supervised by an adult.

At home, Jacob's moodiness, negativity, and quick temper are upsetting to his parents. They described him as being a bright and active boy with a good sense of humor through the early elementary grades, but said he has also always seemed more serious and guarded than his peers. While they have difficulty pinpointing when his difficult moods began to worsen and linger, they say the current problems have been present for at least two years. They report that he generally seems to expect the worst in himself and others, fights frequently with his younger brother, and spends as much time as possible playing video games by himself. Jacob's parents have tried to talk to Jacob about their concerns, but he rejects the idea that he is having any real difficulties. Jacob does say that he is frustrated with what he believes is near constant nagging by his parents and the annoying behavior of his brother. ■

The Case of Zoey

Zoey is 16 years old and in eleventh grade. She has been a good student, though her grades have recently slipped from mostly Bs to mostly Cs. Zoey's guidance counselor met with her after noticing the drop in her grades, and hearing that she had quit the school's speech team. Zoey had been an enthusiastic and successful member of the team for her first two years of high school. Her closest friends were on the speech team; after quitting, she has become increasingly withdrawn. After confiding to the counselor that she was crying for no apparent reason and had lost interest in activities she used to enjoy, her counselor spoke to Zoey's parents and suggested they schedule an appointment with a psychologist.

The psychologist met with Zoey and her parents, both individually and as a family. Zoey's parents described her as an active, social, and fun-loving teenager who enjoyed everything about high school. In addition to speech, she was a member of a number of clubs and community service organizations. While she liked the activities themselves, it was the opportunity to be with the other kids that seemed to give her the most pleasure. Zoey's parents reported that she was not an especially gifted student, but she was conscientious and worked very hard. Teachers recognized and appreciated this, and Zoey was proud of her B average. Looking back, her parents noted that things began to change the summer before eleventh grade. They recalled that she began to sleep more and more and was much less active during the day. Although she had planned on finding a job at the local mall, she never actually applied anywhere. She seemed to prefer to stay home and watch TV in the evening, and she began to gain weight. At first her friends called her often, but after Zoey repeatedly declined their invitations, they began to make plans without her. She appeared to regain some energy and enthusiasm when school started, but soon did poorly on some quizzes and tests and fell behind in her schoolwork. For the first time, she began to complain that the work was too hard and often fell asleep when trying to do homework. When her parents asked if she was using drugs, Zoey became extremely angry and agitated. She accused her parents of never trusting her and always being critical.

When informed that her parents had spoken about how well her first two years of high school had gone, Zoey seemed surprised and annoyed, saying that she had never liked school or most of the people there. She said she had participated in activities to make her parents happy, but that nothing she did was good enough so she quit. She talked at length about a group of friends that she felt had turned against her, and also that she felt "different" from the other students. She said that she last remembered being happy "maybe when I was a kid in grade school." Zoey told the psychologist that she had decided to ask for help because she had begun to experience repeated and intrusive thoughts about dying. She said that she did not have a plan for killing herself, but was finding it increasingly difficult to manage these feelings of dread. She also said that she felt her guidance counselor was the only person she could really trust. She worried, however, that referring her to a psychologist was the counselor's way of getting rid of her. ■

There are several kinds of child and adolescent mood disorders, with different causes, courses, and outcomes. **Major depression** in children and adolescents is characterized by sadness and a loss of pleasure, and is accompanied by cognitive, behavioral, and somatic symptoms (see Table 12.2). The case of Rebecca illustrates major depression in a child, while the case of Zoey illustrates major depression in an adolescent. Single or repeat episodes of depression in a child can be contrasted with his or her more usual, more adaptive functioning. The average length of episodes of major depression is between 7 and 9 months, and these episodes are often recurrent. **Dysthymia** involves a longstanding disturbance of mood, with ongoing sadness, irritability, and lack of motivation; other symptoms involving emotion, cognition, and behavior may also be observed. The case of Jacob is an example of dysthymia. Jacob is diagnosed with dysthymia rather than major depression because Jacob's mood is somewhat less extreme than either Rebecca or Zoey's, and although he is less severely impaired by his disorder, he has struggled for over a year. Childhood dysthymia lasts an average of 4 years, and about 70% of children with dysthymia eventually develop major depression (Birmaher, Ryan, Williamson, Brent, Kaufman, Dahl, et al., 1996; Cicchetti & Toth, 1998). Compared to major depression, dysthymia is

underresearched and requires additional child- and adolescent-specific investigation (Masi, Millepiedi, et al., 2003). The mood disorder variant, **seasonal affective disorder** (i.e., a mood disorder that recurs, generally in the late fall and winter months), usually begins in adolescence (Birmaher, Ryan, Williamson, Brent, & Kaufman, 1996).

Although there is much similarity in the clinical presentation of mood disorders in children and adolescents, it is still important to consider the impact of age and development on the expression of major depression (Garber, 2000; Weiss & Garber, 2003). Younger children like Rebecca often have a more depressed appearance, display more somatic difficulties and anxiety symptoms, and struggle with externalizing behaviors; adolescents are more likely to exhibit hopelessness, substance abuse, psychotic symptoms, and suicidality (Birmaher et al.,1996b; Zahn-Waxler et al., 2000). Of course, for both children and adolescents, we need to keep in mind the possibility of atypical presentations of depression (Williamson et al., 2000). Both children and adolescents struggle with rest-activity cycles, and many of them display sleep disturbances (Armitage et al., 2004; Dahl & Lewin, 2002); sleep disturbances are especially worrisome because they have been associated with worse outcomes (Armitage et al., 2004).

With respect to mood disorders in adolescence, we need to emphasize that even typically developing adolescents experience more extreme moods (especially negative ones) and more mood fluctuations than they did in childhood (Arnett, 1999); therefore, it is important to be very careful about identifying a pattern of symptoms that reflects clinically significant dysfunction or impairment. We also need to consider distinctions between an episode of major depression emerging for the first time in adolescence (that is, as initial psychopathology), and depression that emerges in adolescence following another disorder (that is, as a complicating comorbid disorder). This distinction may have even more relevance given earlier discussion of the development of self and identity during adolescence. Adolescents diagnosed with depression may have difficulties reconciling joyful and successful childhoods with their current struggles, and may have a much more difficult time constructing a sense of self characterized by self-worth and self-efficacy.

Given that only a small percentage of children and adolescents with mood disorders are seen at

---

TABLE 12:2 SUMMARY OF DSM-IV-TR CRITERIA FOR MAJOR DEPRESSIVE EPISODE AND DYSTHYMIA

Major Depressive Episode

A. Five or more of the following symptoms during a 2-week period:

   (1) Depressed mood most of the day, nearly every day. In children and adolescents, can be irritable mood

   (2) Diminished interest or pleasure in all (or almost all) activities

   (3) Significant weight loss or weight gain. In children, a failure to meet expected weight gains

   (4) Insomnia or hypersomnia nearly every day

   (5) Psychomotor agitation or retardation nearly every day

   (6) Fatigue or loss of energy nearly every day

   (7) Feelings of worthlessness or excessive or inappropriate guilt nearly every day

   (8) Diminished ability to think or concentrate, or indecisiveness, nearly every day

   (9) Recurrent thoughts of death, recurrent suicidal ideation, a suicide plan or attempt

B. Symptoms cause clinically significant distress or impairment in important areas of functioning

Dysthymia

A. Depressed mood for most of the day, for more days than not, for at least 1 year in children; mood may be irritable

B. Presence while depressed of two or more of the following symptoms:

   (1) poor appetite or overeating

   (2) insomnia or hypersomnia

   (3) low energy or fatigue

   (4) low self-esteem

   (5) poor concentration or difficulty making decisions

   (6) feelings of hopelessness

C. During the period of the disturbance (1 year for children), the person has never been without the symptoms in A or B for more than 2 months at a time.

D. No major depressive episode has been present during the first year of the disturbance.

E. Symptoms cause clinically significant distress or impairment in important areas of functioning.

---

mental health facilities, it is important to make use of population studies that calculate the prevalence of depressive disorders (Angold & Costello, 2001; Avenevoli, Knight, Kessler, & Merikangas, 2008). Several investigations have estimated that these disorders are relatively uncommon in preschoolers, and increase in following years, from 2–3% in 6-to-12 year-olds, to 10–20% in adolescents (Essau, Conradt, & Petermann, 2000b; Essau & Dobson, 1999; Hammen & Rudolph, 1996; Kessler, Avenevoli, & Merikangas, 2001); the majority of these cases involve major depression, with lower estimates for dysthymia across the developmental span. Gender differences in rates of disorder are notable, with gender ratios approximately equal before adolescence; girls' levels of depression increase rapidly in early adolescence (Cole et al., 2002; Garber, Keiley, & Martin, 2002; Hankin, Wetter, & Cheely, 2008;

Nolen-Hoeksema, 2002; Pennington, 2002; Twenge & Nolen-Hoeksema, 2002; see Box 12.1). There also appear to be group cohort differences in rates of disorder, with successive increases in diagnosis in recent years (Pennington, 2002; Twenge & Nolen-Hoeksema, 2002), although there are also data suggesting relative stability (Costello, Erkanli, & Angold, 2006). With respect to ethnic differences, rates are lower for youth of Chinese background and higher for youth of Mexican background (Roberts, Roberts, & Chen, 1997); adolescents in Hong Kong display rates similar to European American adolescents (Stewart, Lewinsohn et al., 2002). Other differences related to ethnicity and socioeconomic status require additional investigation, particularly as they relate to larger groups of Hispanic-American children and immigrant youth (Roberts et al., 1997; Yearwood, Crawford, Kelly, & Moreno, 2007).

BOX 12:1 RISK AND RESILIENCE

Gender Differences in Adolescent Depression

One of the most striking examples of developmental psychopathology can be found in the relations among depression, age, and gender. Depression occurs in childhood at relatively equal rates in boys and girls. However, as children move through puberty and into adolescence, girls develop depression at an accelerated rate until they are twice as likely to develop depression as boys. This finding is so striking and so well-replicated that it is sometimes referred to as "the big fact" (Galambos, Leadbetter, & Barker, 2004; Hankin & Abramson, 2001). While this developmental pattern is clear, the reasons for the shift in the prevalence of depression are more elusive.

A number of factors have been proposed and researched. Some researchers have examined differences in risk factors prior to adolescence that may make depression more likely within the context of the challenges of adolescence. One such risk factor is the sexual abuse of preadolescent children. A history of sexual abuse is known to predispose an individual to later depression, and girls are far more likely than boys to have been sexually abused (Weiss, Longhurst, & Mazure, 1999). We also know that genetic factors influence the onset of depression. It may be that genetic risk is unevenly distributed in girls and boys, and is not fully expressed until adolescence and in combination with environmental stressors (Silberg et al., 1999). Gender differences in cognitive variables have also been considered. For example, research has shown that boys tend to judge the physical changes they experience in puberty more positively than girls view the physical changes they undergo (Rierdan & Koff, 1997). Also, during early adolescence girls tend to show a greater need for approval and success, lower levels of positive thinking, and more self-focused negative cognitions; all of these are associated with depressive symptomatology (Calvete & Cardenoso, 2005; Papadakis, Prince, Jones, & Strauman, 2006). Other researchers have investigated the roles of biological factors interacting with social development. It may be that both hormonal and social factors promote affiliative needs during puberty for girls, and that these drives create certain vulnerabilities that lead to greater risk for depression (Hazler & Mellin, 2004).

The link between risk-taking behaviors and adolescent depression has been a recent focus of study. In an extensive National Institutes of Health–sponsored study, the development and correlates of depressive symptoms in nearly 19,000 teens were examined (Waller et al., 2006). Risky behaviors such as the use of tobacco, alcohol, and other drugs, and sexual activity, as well as level and severity of risk taking were considered. Boys and girls who abstained from these risky behaviors showed no differences in the development of depressive symptoms. The same was true (i.e., equivalent rates of depression) for teens who engaged in very high-risk behaviors such as intravenous drug use. However, the clinical picture was much different for those teens in the low and moderate risk categories. Girls who engaged in low to moderate levels of risky behaviors were significantly more likely than boys to develop depressive symptoms. The specific mechanisms leading to this correlation are not known, but researchers' hypotheses will guide further studies. It may be, for instance, that behaviors such as substance abuse and sexual activity alter girls' social contexts more than boys' and are so associated with greater risk. Or it may be that the use of drugs and alcohol affects the developing brains of adolescent boys and girls differently, which then affects cognitive and emotional development in ways that link to later depression. Of course, it is also possible that these risk behaviors are actually the result, rather than the cause, of developing depression. It is important to remember that there is no reason to assume that there is a single explanation for these findings. As with many interesting and challenging aspects of developmental psychopathology, new data on gender and the course of depression lead to new questions that, in turn, lead to innovative new research designs capable of addressing complex interactions.

The Case of Kareem

Kareem is 17 years old and in twelfth grade. He is a gifted runner and was recently voted captain of the track team. Throughout high school, Kareem has been active and popular. In addition to being on the track and cross country teams, he is also vice-president of the student council, plays trumpet in the jazz band, and has been in several school plays. Kareem experienced some difficulties in elementary and middle school where he struggled academically and got in trouble for being impulsive and somewhat oppositional. In sixth grade, a school counselor suggested that he might have ADHD. At his parents' urging, Kareem's pediatrician started him on a trial of medication typically used to treat ADHD. The trial was discontinued, however, when the medication seemed to exacerbate rather than help the problem. Despite these challenges, a combination of classroom modifications and some individual counseling allowed Kareem to finish middle school on a more positive note. Kareem appeared to thrive in high school, where his energy, extraversion, and enthusiasm found many positive outlets.

The first signs that Kareem would not end his high school career as well as he had started came early in his senior year. Kareem became preoccupied with a new girl in his English class. Although he had never spoken with her before, he came to class one day with flowers and a necklace he had bought for her. While flattered, the girl felt uncomfortable with the attention and let Kareem know this. Kareem's reaction was to profess his undying love for her and assure her that he was certain she was secretly in love with him. At first, other students found this odd but funny, and said it was just "Kareem being Kareem." This perception began to change when the girl and her parents went to the principal with a stack of sexually explicit notes that Kareem had sent by e-mail. Kareem was suspended briefly and moved to a different English class.

Kareem's behavior became more erratic and bizarre. He would get up and pace during classes, and he became increasingly impatient with other students, teachers, coaches, and his family. He often responded belligerently to questions, and also pushed a coach following a difficult track practice. Two days after the track incident, Kareem took a history exam, ignoring all questions but one. His essay was an elaborate and difficult-to-follow argument that all of human history was culminating in the emergence of a superior individual with psychic powers, and that the time was right to reveal the fact that he was that person. Later that same day, Kareem walked into the staff lounge, where he propositioned a teacher. Kareem became angry when told to leave, overturned furniture, and threatened those who tried to intervene. Eventually the police were called and he was taken to a local hospital. Along the way, Kareem began to weep. By the time he arrived at the emergency room, Kareem was exhausted and despondent. After an initial interview revealed that he was suicidal, Kareem was admitted to the adolescent psychiatric unit. ∎

Bipolar Disorder

Bipolar disorder is an especially severe form of mood disorder. It has been extensively researched in the adult population and its presentation, etiology, and treatment are fairly well understood. Bipolar disorder in adults usually involves periods of depression alternating with periods of severe or moderate **mania**. These **manic episodes** are characterized by unusual and persistent mood elevation, including decreased need for sleep, increased irritability, extremely impulsive behaviors, and sometimes even psychotic thinking (see Table 12.3). Manic symptoms in adolescents, as described in the case of Kareem, may also include grandiose delusions (related to current and later success, or great wealth), increased nighttime activity (such as rearranging furniture in bedrooms or leaving the house to be with friends), pressured speech, hypersexuality, and risk-taking behaviors (Geller & Luby, 1997; Geller, Zimerman, et al., 2002). Hypomania involves problematic emotions, thoughts, and behaviors similar to mania, although there are no psychotic symptoms and the degree of impairment is less severe. For some adolescents, it may be difficult to identify discrete episodes of disorder, as there may be a gradual worsening of distressing and dysfunctional behavior. Rapid cycling of symptoms, with periods of mania alternating with periods of depression, may occur over several days or even during a single day. Suicidality is a critical concern. There are also some reports of "model" adolescents with an abrupt onset (Geller, Zimerman, et al., 2002; Lewinsohn, 2003). One of the difficulties related to the idea of bipolar disorder in children and adolescents is that those at risk can "appear to be the happiest of patients because of their infectious, amusing, elated affect"; it is "more difficult to acknowledge conceptually that happy children have serious psychopathology" (Geller & Luby, 1997, p. 1169). In general, these clinical symptoms and diagnostic criteria are very similar for both adolescents and adults.

The picture is more complicated, however, when the issue is bipolar disorder in children. Like earlier debates over whether children actually experience major depression, the question of whether (and how often) bipolar disorder is accurately diagnosed in children remains controversial. The current consensus is that bipolar disorder can emerge in childhood, but that it is difficult to diagnose and complicated to treat (Brotman et al., 2006; Geller, Tillman, Craney, & Bolhofner, 2004; NIMH, 2000). In contrast to adults'

TABLE 12:3   DSM-IV-TR CRITERIA FOR BIPOLAR I AND II, AND CYCLOTHYMIA

Bipolar I Disorder

A. Presence of only one manic episode and no past major depressive episodes; or the presence of a hypomanic episode with previous episodes of mania

B. The manic episode is not better accounted for by another mental disorder.

C. Mood symptoms cause clinically significant distress or impairment in important domains of functioning.

Bipolar II Disorder

A. Presence or history of one or more major depressive episodes

B. Presence or history of at least one hypomanic episode

C. There has never been a manic or mixed episode.

D. Symptoms are not better accounted for by another mental disorder.

E. Mood symptoms cause clinically significant distress or impairment in important domains of functioning.

Cyclothymia

A. For at least one year in children and adolescents, the presence of numerous periods with hypomanic symptoms and numerous periods with depressive symptoms that do not meet the criteria for major depressive episode

B. During the above period, the individual has not been without symptoms for more than 2 months at a time.

C. Symptoms cause clinically significant distress or impairment in important domains of functioning.

---

longer-lasting, well-defined cycles of depression and mania, children with bipolar disorder often exhibit severe mood dysregulation, involving chronic irritability and hyperarousal, as well as more rapid cycling between depressed and elevated moods, with three or more of these cycles per day sometimes observed (Brotman et al., 2006; Geller, Zimerman, et al., 2002). These periods of intense volatility are often referred to as "**affective storms.**" When they occur, these poorly modulated states are very difficult to differentiate from oppositional defiant disorder, parent-child conflicts, or the most severe forms of ADHD (Geller, Zimerman, et al., 2002; Leibenluft, Charney, Towbin, Bhangoo, & Pine, 2003; Staton, Odden, & Volness, 2004).

Indeed, there is evidence that children who meet the diagnostic criteria for ADHD, but have a parent with bipolar disorder, may actually be displaying early symptoms of bipolar disorder. For these children, as seen with Kareem, the stimulant medications that are typically effective in treating ADHD can precipitate the onset of manic symptoms. Taken together, the clinical and research data strongly support recognizing the fact that bipolar disorder does occur in prepubertal children. However, a well-articulated developmental framework is needed to better understand how the core symptoms of bipolar disorder are expressed in children (Geller et al., 2006; Geller, Tillman, & Bolhofner, 2007), to guide better treatments (Biederman et al., 2003; Carlson, 2002; Coyle et al., 2003; Nottelmann et al., 2001), and to identify and examine relations between ADHD and bipolar disorder (Galanter & Leibenluft, 2008).

Because bipolar disorder is a relatively new diagnosis for children and adolescents, rates of disorder are difficult to estimate. Rates in adolescence are assumed to be similar to rates observed in adult populations (Geller & Luby, 1997; Lewinsohn, Seeley, & Klein, 2003); rates of admission to adolescent inpatient units for bipolar disorder more than doubled between 1995 and 2000, and continued to increase until 2004 (Blader & Carlson, 2007; Harpaz-Rotem, Leslie, Martin, & Rosenheck, 2005). Although the clinical picture appears similar for both boys and girls, more boys are diagnosed in adolescence (Biederman et al., 2003). At this point in time, there are some data that suggest that early-onset (i.e. child-onset) bipolar disorder may involve different etiologies and different courses than later-onset (i.e., adolescent-onset) bipolar disorder (Leboyer, Henry, Paillere-Martinot, & Bellivier, 2005).

Developmental Course

Developmental Continuity of Major Depression

As with all types of child psychopathology, **developmental continuity** is often observed for youngsters with major depression; that is, struggles in childhood are associated with struggles in adolescence, and struggles in adolescence are associated with struggles in adulthood (Birmaher, Arbelaez, & Brent, 2002; Craske, 1997; Fombonne, Wostear, Cooper, Harrington, & Rutter, 2001a, 2001b; Pine, Cohen, Gurley, Brook, & Ma, 1998). Retrospective reports by adults suggest that 50% of those who experienced depression as an adolescent continue to struggle as adults; 90% of adolescents who experienced mania continue to exhibit symptoms into adulthood (Kessler et al., 2001). It is also important to note that between 20% and 40% of adolescents initially diagnosed with major depression eventually receive a diagnosis of bipolar disorder (Birmaher et al., 1996a; Geller & Luby, 1997; Weller, Weller, & Fristad, 1995). Although developmental continuity is common, other pathways are also possible, including the emergence of difficulties in adolescence without previous symptomatology (Garber et al., 2002; Harrington et al., 1996; Luby, Todd, & Geller, 1996). According to Cole et al. (2002), there are several "destabilizing factors" that influence developmental continuity versus discontinuity during late childhood and early adolescence. Some of the destabilizing factors that may be coupled with either significant improvement or deterioration include changes in emotional lability, improving/deteriorating relationships, and educational transitions. By late adolescence, individual patterns are more stable.

Individual Differences in Outcomes

Individual differences in developmental trajectories and outcomes depend on a variety of factors. Repeat episodes and worse outcomes are linked to gender, early diagnosis, severity of depression, history of sexual abuse, parent psychopathology, and poor peer relationships (Barbe, Bridge, Birmaher, Kolko, & Brent, 2004; Birmaher et al., 2004; Cole et al., 2002; Essau, Conradt, & Petermann, 1999; Kovacs, Obrosky, & Sherrill, 2003). Thinking back to the case of Rebecca earlier in the chapter, there are several risk factors that portend long-term difficulties. First, she is a girl. Whereas gender ratios for depression are relatively equal in early and middle childhood, being a girl may further complicate the clinical presentation as she transitions into adolescence. Rebecca's depression is also identified before puberty. And her depression is severe, accompanied by suicidal ideation. But there are also protective factors that may balance or moderate the developmental course of the disorder. Rebecca's parents are aware and involved, and she has a history of good friendships (Brendgen, Wanner, Morin, & Vitaro, 2005). With this mixed clinical picture, either better or worse outcomes for Rebecca are possible.

Most children and adolescents who experience depression deal with multiple episodes. In addition to the chronic struggling with depressive psychopathology itself, it is also necessary to understand how repeat episodes of depression interfere with everyday challenges. For example, major depression has a negative impact on school achievement, especially for boys. To the extent that children take pride in academic success and value themselves less when they do poorly, additional cycles of depression, failure, and despair may exacerbate the initial psychopathology and contribute to a poor self-image that lasts years longer than treated, time-limited episodes of depression (Ialongo, Edelsohn, & Kellam, 2001; Patterson & Stoolmiller, 1991; Rapport, Denney, Chung, & Hustace, 2001; Street et al., 2004).

With respect to the ongoing impact of children's mood disorders on parents and families, there are many studies, a lot of data, and various conclusions. Children's depression is often accompanied by difficult communication, conflict, disturbed relationships, and decreases in nurturant parenting (Brody, 1998; Brody, Stoneman, Smith, & Gibson, 1998; Kim et al., 2003; Phares, 1996; Slesnick & Waldron, 1997). Intact, better functioning families are predictive of more rapid rates of recovery (Geller, Craney et al., 2002).

A number of professionals have noted that mood disorders in children and adolescents may also be linked with *special strengths*. For example, some children "may learn to be especially attuned to others' feelings and sensitivities, which in some contexts may be especially adaptive and valuable" (Cummings, Davies, & Campbell, 2000, p. 335). These children may focus their talents on animal care, or artistic endeavors, or volunteering and community involvement.

Comorbidity Over Time

Comorbidity is another influential factor. Major depression combined with other psychopathologies is associated with increased impairment, substance use and abuse, and suicidality (Fombonne et al., 2001a, 2001b; Rao et al., 1999). Depressed adolescents with substance abuse disorders are more likely to be later diagnosed with personality disorders (i.e., inflexible, maladaptive personality patterns together with serious personal and social distress and impairment), such as borderline personality disorder (Grilo, Walker, Becker, Edell, & McGlashan, 1997). Clinicians have hypothesized that some adolescents may attempt to "self-medicate" with either drugs or alcohol. Given that depression usually precedes substance abuse by several years, Cicchetti and Toth (1998) have described a window of opportunity (between the onset of the major depression and the later onset of substance abuse) where mental health professionals might focus specific prevention efforts.

Bipolar Disorder

With respect to bipolar disorder, a chronic pattern has been observed for children and adolescents (see Table 12.4). Relapse rates are high, and often occur during prophylactic treatment (Geller, Craney, et al., 2002; Jairam, Srinath, Girimaji, & Seshadri, 2004). There are also variations in some of the associated difficulties of mania, depending on whether the manic symptoms are more intermittent or chronic (e.g., depression and suicidality for episodic subtype versus violent behavior for chronic subtype) (Bhangoo et al., 2003). Again, early diagnosis, more severe symptoms, and comorbid conditions are associated with poor outcomes (Carlson, Bromet, & Sievers, 2000; Craney & Geller, 2003a; DelBello, Hanseman, Adler, Fleck, & Strakowski, 2007; Geller et al., 2004). Some data

also suggest that cultural factors have an impact on outcome, with adolescents from Taiwan faring better than adolescents in the United States (Strakowski et al., 2007). Better outcomes for adolescents in Taiwan were explained, in part, by lower levels of depression and substance abuse, earlier help-seeking, and longer hospitalizations (Strakowski et al., 2007).

Etiology

Depression

There are many causes, many pathways, and many outcomes for children and adolescents with depression. As with other types of psychopathology, it is necessary to construct a **multifactorial risk model** that includes multiple factors, in various combinations, that lead to disorder. One such model is provided by Goodman and Gotlib (1999, 2002), who describe several major causal mechanisms, including (1) the heritability of depression, (2) innate dysfunctional neuroregulatory mechanisms, (3) exposure to negative parental personality and parenting, and (4) the general stressful context of children's lives. Many of these factors have been identified in other investigations as well.

Genes and Heredity

Estimates of heritability for mood disorders for children and adolescents are moderate, and are similar to those observed for adults; there is some evidence for higher heritabilities in boys (Birmaher et al., 2004; Ehringer et al., 2006; Eley, 1999; Elizabeth, King, & Ollendick, 2004; Pennington, 2002). The genetic impact on depressive symptoms appears to increase as children age (Scourfield et al., 2003). Current research is focused on specifying gene locations and genetic influences that underlie these increased risks (Pennington, 2002).

TABLE 12:4	HYPOTHESIZED CLINICAL COURSE OF BIPOLAR DISORDER BY AGE OF ONSET	
	PUBERTAL AND YOUNG ADOLESCENT	**OLDER ADOLESCENT AND ADULT**
Initial episode	Major depressive disorder	Mania
Episode type	Rapid cycling, mixed	Discrete, with sudden onset
Duration	Chronic, continuous cycling	Weeks
Inter-episode functioning	Nonepisodic	Improved functioning

Physiological Factors

Neurophysiological investigations have identified a number of structural and biochemical differences that contribute to the emergence of mood disorders (Kaufman & Charney, 2003). Abnormalities have been observed in mood-regulating areas of the brain, such as the amygdala (Davidson, Pizzagalli, Nitschke, & Putnam, 2002; DelBello, Zimmerman, Mills, Getz, & Strakowski, 2004; Leibenluft, Charney, & Pine, 2003; Pine et al., 2000). There are also data depicting decreased blood flow and reduced activation patterns in the left frontal regions of the brain (Dawson et al., 2003; Kentgen et al., 2000; Rao et al., 2002), and these EEG asymmetries continue into adulthood (Miller et al., 2002). Pennington (2002) brings these sets of findings together and describes an "imbalance between top-down (prefrontal) and bottom-up (amygdala) components of the affect regulation system" (p. 117).

Additional research highlights the dysregulation of neurotransmitters, norepinephrine and serotonin in particular (Pennington, 2002). This dysregulation may, in turn, lead to chronic overactivity of the hypothalamic-pituitary-adrenal (HPA) axis (Ashman, Dawson, Panagiotides, Yamada, & Wilkinson, 2002; Gunnar, 2000). Abnormalities in the secretion of growth hormones are also consistently observed in children and adolescents at risk for major depression (Birmaher & Heydl, 2001; Dahl et al., 2000). Individual differences in heart rates and vagal tone are other factors to take into account (Luby, 2000). The physiological bases of temperament also likely play an etiological part. Infants and children with difficult temperaments, who show decreases in flexibility and increases in negative moods, are at higher risk for the development of mood disorders (Austin & Chorpita, 2004; Chang, Blasey, Ketter, & Steiner, 2003; Hirshfeld-Becker et al., 2003; Lonigan, Phillips, & Hooe, 2003).

Pennington (2002), investigating the neural consequences of social stress, emphasizes the roles of "behavioral sensitization and electrophysiological kindling" (p. 117), and states that "social stress causes a permanent vulnerability in the HPA axis" (p. 116). He suggests that over time the increasingly sensitive neurological response system requires lower thresholds of stimulation to trigger a new episode. This **kindling model** explains, in part, why later episodes of depression occur in the context of less severe stress. The kindling model may be further understood in the **social context of brain development and functioning**. That is, changes in the microstructures of the brain take place in continuous transaction with the environment. With the rapid production of neurons in early life, followed by neuronal pruning, stabilization, and sensitization, the experience of social distress and dysfunction has both immediate and long-term negative impacts (Bhangoo & Leibenluft, 2002; Dawson & Ashman, 2000). Earlier discussions about PTSD and complex developmental trauma (in Chapter 11) are extended in this chapter with a focus on a neurodevelopmental model that explores connections between **maltreatment** and children's vulnerability to depression (Kaufman et al., 2006; see Box 12.2).

Finally, given the dramatic increases in rates of mood disorders in adolescence, puberty changes and the timing of puberty are the frequent focus of study (Angold, Worthman, & Costello, 2003; Ge et al., 2003; Twenge & Nolen-Hoeksema, 2002). Early pubertal transitions are associated with greater stress, particularly for girls (Dorn et al., 2003; Graber, Lewinsohn, Seely, & Brooks-Gunn, 1997; Hayward, Gotlib, Schraedley, & Litt, 1999). Physiological challenges include changes in hormone levels and endocrine functioning; the worrisome notion of "raging hormones," is now understood to be somewhat exaggerated (Weisz & Hawley, 2002). For some girls, physical development outpaces cognitive and emotional development. Social pressures may also increase, as peers and adults expect more adult-like behavior from those whose appearance suggests greater maturity. For boys, early maturity has a mix of positive and negative impacts, with higher levels of self-esteem balanced by engaging in more frequent risk behaviors.

Psychological Factors

Cicchetti and others (Cicchetti et al., 1997; Cicchetti & Toth, 1998) have described four individual characteristics of infants and young children, problems with which increase risk for depression: (1) physiological regulation, (2) emotion differentiation and regulation, (3) the attachment relationship, and (4) the emergence of self and self-awareness. These investigators suggest that deficiencies or problems with these four characteristics influence children's lack of success in negotiating early age-related challenges, and this lack of success leads to poor outcomes. Zahn-Waxler (2000) suggests that emotion dysregulation is key. According to Zahn-Waxler, intense, prolonged, and poorly controlled experiences with

Maltreatment and Mood Disorders

As researchers in the field of childhood psychopathology come to take a developmental perspective, they are increasingly interested in the links between early risk and protective factors and later disorder. One of the most consistently demonstrated findings from these efforts is the relation between maltreatment in childhood and the development of depressive disorders (Cicchetti, 2004; Ethier, Lemelin, & Lacharite, 2004; Manly, Kim, Rogosch, & Cicchetti, 2001; Toth & Cicchetti, 1996). Child maltreatment, including all forms of abuse and neglect compromises development in many domains. For example, we have previously discussed the importance of the early attachment relationship that develops between the infant and the primary caregiver in the first year of life. If that relationship is characterized by either consistent abuse or an unpredictable pattern that includes abuse, important aspects of children's expectations of themselves, of others, and of their ability to effectively manage their environment may be disrupted or disturbed. The significant relations among abuse, attachment, and depression are especially strong in the case of sexual abuse (Toth & Cicchetti, 1996).

There is much emphasis in developmental psychopathology on the integration of different levels of analysis. A number of researchers have asserted the necessity of specifying how the effects of early adverse experiences may cascade across levels and lead to the development of psychopathology (Gunnar, 2003). For example, in addition to considering how the relation between abuse and depression is mediated by the attachment relationship, recent research has also focused on how genes, the brain, the family, and the larger social context all provide links between early maltreatment and later depression.

One such link, or pathway, being studied involves the effects of abuse on critical neuroendocrine systems. For

some time now, we have understood that stressful life events can affect certain neurocircuits and that these changes in neurocircuitry can be reliably measured. Further, there is extensive evidence linking specific neurological and endocrine pathways to the development of depressive and anxiety disorders (Heim et al., 2000; Gunnar, 2003). More recent research has demonstrated that the neurobiological alterations resulting from early abuse may, in many cases, be permanent and significantly increase the risk for depression in childhood, adolescence, and adulthood (Carpenter et al., 2004; Nemeroff, 2004; Nemeroff & Vale, 2005).

Specifically, stress early in development is associated with poor regulation of the hypothalamic-pituitary axis. This complex neuroendocrine system helps the body to mobilize in the presence of stress and helps to re-establish equilibrium after the threat has passed. Prolonged, or repeated and unpredictable stress, as is the case with many instances of child maltreatment, may lead to later emotional and behavioral problems. The pathway from maltreatment to disorder may be especially relevant for those at genetic risk for disorders like depression.

It is important to note that not all children who are maltreated develop depression. And by no means does a diagnosis of depression necessarily imply a history of abuse. However, by better understanding the relation that does exist between maltreatment and depression, more targeted and effective approaches to prevention and treatment can be designed to help many children, adolescents, and adults. Also, the models developed to understand the pathways across physiological, psychological, and social levels that may lead from maltreatment to depression will inform other investigations of developmental psychopathology.

emotion lead to the development of an affective bias. The bias or tendency to feel sad is usually most prominent, but there may also be biases related to anxiety, guilt, and shame. Garber and her colleagues (Garber, Braafladt, & Weiss, 1995) emphasize that having fewer emotion-regulation strategies, or believing that these strategies are ineffective, contributes to the development of mood disorders.

Attachment status has far-reaching impact, with an emphasis on the association between insecure attachment patterns and the emergence of

internalizing disorders such as depression (Duggal, Carlson, Sroufe, & Egeland, 2001; Herring & Kaslow, 2002; Lyons-Ruth, Easterbrooks, & Cibelli, 1997; Lyons-Ruth, Lyubchik, Wolfe, & Bronfman, 2002). Feelings of emotional security are the primary concern. According to Cummings et al. (2000), **emotional security** is central to the regulation of many kinds of behavior and is tied to three underlying processes: the child's emotional reactivity; representations of family relationships (i.e., the internalized working models); and regulation of exposure to family emotion. In addition, attachment security appears to moderate the child's response to later stress (Nachmias, Gunnar, Mangelsdorf, Parritz, & Buss, 1996).

Lack of emotional support in early development may also lead to cognitive consequences, including negative self-concept and negative beliefs about the self. Dysfunctional cognitions that develop early may become entrenched because of ongoing or additional negative events (Garber et al., 2002; Haines, Metalsky, Cardamone, & Joiner, 1999; Jordan & Cole, 1996; Nolen-Hoeksema, 1998; Pennington, 2002; Tram & Cole, 2000). Cognitive theories that emphasize self-efficacy, including Aaron Beck's (1987) information processing theory of depression, Bandura's work on self-efficacy (e.g., Bandura, Pastorelli, Barbaranelli, & Caprara, 1999), and Seligman's (1975) theory of learned helplessness, provide additional details about how cognitive factors influence developmental pathways to depression. For adolescents, low self-efficacy in more than one domain of competence (e.g, academic, social, athletic, romantic) may have cumulative effects; higher levels of self-efficacy in any domain may have protective effects (Seroczynski, Cole, & Maxwell, 1997). These efficacy hypotheses have received support in studies of adolescents in both the United States and in Hong Kong (Stewart et al., 2004).

Psychological characteristics that *decrease the likelihood of externalizing disorders* may ironically *increase the likelihood of other disorders*. Particular personality types, such as being overcontrolled, illustrate this paradoxical situation (Robins, John, Caspi, Moffitt, & Stouthamer-Loeber, 1996; Zahn-Waxler et al., 2000; see Figure 12.1). Individual differences in coping must also be considered, because short-term strategies for dealing with stress and pain often become either more positive or more negative long-term traits; "avoidance takes the form of moving out of the house. Escapes become enduring dedications, such as "working like a lion" in school, excelling in sports, [or] becoming "spiritual" (Radke-Yarrow & Klimes-Dougan, 1997, p. 386).

Parent and Family Factors

There have been numerous investigations of children of depressed parents. Longitudinal data provides clear evidence that depressed parents, *in addition to their genetic and neuropsychological impact*, have

Along with other risk factors, having depressed parents significantly increases the likelihood that a child will develop depression or other forms of psychopathology.

children who struggle with a variety of internalizing and externalizing disorders (Cummings, Davies, & Campbell, 2000; Dawson & Ashman, 2000; Diego et al., 2004; Hammen, Shih, & Brennan, 2004; Stein et al., 2000; Weissman, Warner, Wickramarabe, Moreau, & Olfson, 1997). According to Radke-Yarrow and Klimes-Dougan (1997), "being born to and reared by a depressed parent carries the expectation of problems" (p. 374). But not all children with depressed parents are depressed themselves. If they do have problems, not all of them are similar. Most research on depressed parents focuses on mothers. Results of research with fathers are mixed (Phares, 1996). There are data that document the negative impact of depressed fathers, and other data suggesting that a father's depression is less strongly related to child depression than a mother's depression (Field, 1999; Kane & Garber, 2004; Jacob & Johnson, 1997).

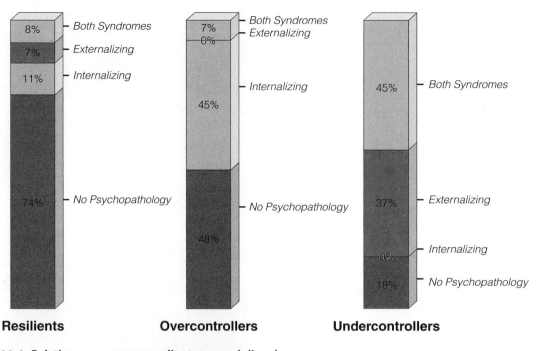

FIGURE 12:1 Relations among personality types and disorders.
SOURCE: Robins, John, Caspi, Moffitt, and Stouthamer-Loeber (1996, p. 167).

Three **pathways of parental impact** have been described (Rutter & Quinton, 1984; Cummings et al., 2000):

1. Parent depression affects parent-child relationships and interactions, and leads to child psychopathology.
2. Parent depression affects family relationships and interactions, and causes family disruptions, which lead to child psychopathology.
3. Parent depression affects marital satisfaction and this leads to child psychopathology.

With respect to the parent-child relationship, Cicchetti et al. (1997) note that depressed mothers are "affectively asynchronous" with their infants. That is, the sadness, social withdrawal, and reduced activity that are hallmarks of adult depression interfere with the typical positive emotional and behavioral exchanges that characterize mother-infant interactions (Tronick & Gianino, 1986). Some depressed parents express irritability or hostility or hold negative beliefs about their children (Cummings et al., 2000; Dawson & Ashman, 2000). The timing, severity, and chronicity of parent depression may moderate or intensify these patterns. The emotional unavailability and insensitivity sometimes seen in depressed parents hinder the development of secure attachment relationships (Cicchetti, Rogosch & Toth, 1998; Cum-

mings et al., 2000). Depressed mothers with comorbid psychopathology (such as personality disorders) have even more negative impact (Ellenbogen & Hodgins, 2004; Radke-Yarrow & Klimes-Dougan, 1997).

Parenting practices of depressed parents are also frequently inconsistent and ineffective (Cummings et al., 2000; Davis, Sheeber, & Hops, 2002; Koenig, Ialongo, Wagner, Poduska, & Kellam, 2002; Sagrestano, Paikoff, Holmbeck, & Fendrich, 2003). Family conflict is another risk factor (Duggal, Calso, Sroufe, & Egeland, 2001; Katz, 1998; Sheeber & Sorensen, 1998). But specific family factors may have differential impact, depending on ethnicity. High levels of family conflict appear to be particularly problematic for European American adolescents, whereas lack of family cohesion appears to be especially problematic for African American adolescents (Herman, Ostrander, & Tucker, 2007). Overall, many of these risk factors are consistent with a **reinforcement model** of depression (Pennington, 2002), in which parents offer fewer rewards and more punishments to their children. This reinforcement model is sometimes viewed as more consistent with the maintenance of depression in children, rather than the emergence of depression. Mental health services that support effective parenting for mothers and fathers with depression are essential (Lyons-Ruth, Wolfe, & Lyubchik, 2000).

Even as we discuss the caregiving difficulties experienced by depressed parents, we need to remember that many depressed parents exhibit average or even excellent parenting. "For example, a girl's father, despite being alcoholic and depressed, may remain very loving and caring toward her. While she may experience the negative sequelae of the father's problems, she may also firmly understand that she is loved and may treasure and benefit from those experiences that are supportive and special" (Cummings et al., 2000, p. 301). It is also the case that there is specificity observed in children's interactions with a depressed parent, so a child's relationships with non-depressed adults may serve as important protective factors (Luby, 2000).

Certain child factors moderate or exacerbate the impact of parent depression. The age and developmental stage of a child may interact with various symptoms of parental depression (Radke-Yarrow & Klimes-Dougan, 1997). Or, for instance, "a child may have an easy temperament, with a high capacity to adapt, or even profit, from adversity" (Cummings et al., 2000, p. 301). Gender again plays a role, with boys more vulnerable during childhood to depressive family environments, and girls more vulnerable during adolescence (Cummings et al., 2000; Essex, Klein, Cho, & Kraemer, 2003; Forehand, Jones, Brody, & Armistead, 2002).

With respect to family relationships and family atmosphere, parental psychopathology has varied consequences (Duggal et al., 2001; Zahn-Waxler et al., 2000). It helps to keep in mind that all families experience stress and conflict. But families with a depressed adult often experience more atypical stressors and less competent coping. According to Radke-Yarrow and Klimes-Dougan (1997), in well-functioning families, "severe stress is generally severe in ways that are 'normal' (e.g., illness, death, loss of job, husband-wife incompatibility). In the depressed families, there is a compounding of stress, not only of the 'normal' sort but also of a less normal nature (e.g., husband throws the family out of the house; the depressed mother disappears and neighbors and church members take over the running of the family; the children are abused by a live-in uncle; mother cannot manage the daily routines, so the 8-year-old takes over)" (p. 383).

Finally, parent psychopathology influences child psychopathology via mechanisms related to marital conflict (see Figure 12.2). Depressed parents are negative and critical toward their spouses as well as their children. Warmth and emotional support from the well spouse is critical in helping the struggling spouse both with the disorder and with parenting. However, "the tiresome, chronic reassurance seeking and frustrating inconsistency . . . may lead to eventual rejection by significant others" (Cummings et al., 2000, p. 313). At times, marital violence may aggravate an already tense situation (Fainsilber Katz & Low, 2004).

Environmental Factors

Even with the myriad factors related to genes, individual characteristics, and family functioning, we should not overlook the impact that larger events (such as trauma) and larger environments (such as culture and socioeconomic background) play in the development of mood disorders (Cicchetti & Toth, 1998; Rutter, 1998). However, we should also be thinking about the emergence of psychopathology in more complex ways. For example, children at high genetic risk may be more sensitive to the effects of adverse environments (Birmaher et al., 1996a). Also, individual children, even those in the same family, may respond differently to a stressor; distinctions need to be made between shared risk factors (affecting all siblings) and nonshared risk factors (affecting only one sibling, or affecting one or more siblings disproportionately) (Eley, 1999; Pennington, 2002; Pike & Plomin, 1996).

Both specific **negative life events** (such as a parent losing a job or a serious illness in the family) and **chronic hassles** have been associated with depression in children, especially in the early years (Birmaher et al., 1996a; Nolen-Hoeksema et al., 1992). With increasing age, interactions between negative events and the child's cognitive abilities and tendencies (such as pessimistic explanatory styles) become more important (Nolen-Hoeksema et al., 1992; Weisz, Sweeney, Proffitt, & Carr, 1993), as well as interactions between environmental factors (negative events and social support) (Petti et al., 2004).

Environmental factors in adolescence have received much scrutiny and are key components in the **cognitive vulnerability-stress model of depression**. In this model, an adolescent's negative attributional style coupled with negative life events leads to depression, and may contribute to feelings of hopelessness (Abela & D'Alessandro, 2001;

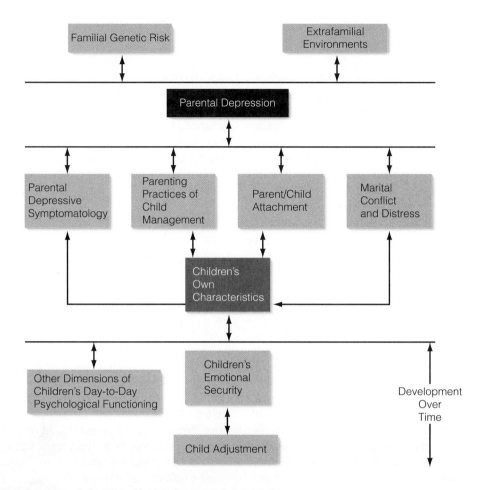

FIGURE 12:2 A framework for the effects of parental depression.
Source: Cummings, Davies, and Campbell (2000, p. 308).

Environmental factors, such as poverty, may interact with other risk factors in the development of depression.

Abela & Hankin, 2008; Abramson et al., 2002; Garber, 2001; Hankin, Abramson, Miller, & Haeffel, 2004; Nolen-Hoeksema & Corte, 2004; Waschbusch, Sellers, LeBlanc, & Kelley, 2003). There is evidence that these types of life events increase in early adolescence and peak around age 14 (Graber & Brooks-Gunn, 1996).

In addition to major life events, everyday struggles can also contribute to high levels of stress (Garber & Little, 1999). Problematic peer relationships, and romantic difficulties in particular, may also be extremely stressful for adolescents (Furman & Shaffer, 2003; Hecht, Inderbitzen, & Bukowski, 1998; Monroe, Rohde, Seeley, & Lewinsohn, 1999; Nolan, Flynn, & Garber, 2003). Evidence suggesting that girls are exposed to more episodic stressors, and more total stressors, may provide additional perspective on observed gender differences in rates of depression (Hankin, Mermelstein, & Roesch, 2007; Shih, Eberhart, Hammen, & Brennan, 2006).

Maltreatment, including physical abuse, sexual abuse, emotional abuse, and neglect, long understood to be precursors of insecure attachment, are also predictably related to later mood disorders in children and adolescents (Brown, Cohen, Johnson, & Smailes, 1999; Cicchetti & Toth, 1995, 2003; Putnam, 2003). Individual and developmental factors, the specific form, severity, and chronicity of abuse, and other environmental factors all influence children's outcomes (Barbe, Bridge, Birmaher, Kolko, & Brent, 2004; Nolen-Hoeksema, 2002; Weiss, Longhurst, & Mazure, 1999; refer to Box 12.2).

Bipolar Disorder

As with major depression, genes are important determinants of risk for bipolar disorder (Faraone, Glatt, & Tsuang, 2003; Geller & Luby, 1997; Potash et al., 2007; Rende et al., 2007); in fact, bipolar disorder is second only to autism in terms of familiality and heritability (Pennington, 2002). Genes also appear to have an impact on age of onset (Faraone, Glatt, Su, & Tsuang, 2004; Faraone, Lasky-Su, Glatt, Van Eerdewegh, & Tsuang, 2006). There are also data that suggest partial overlap between bipolar disorder and major depression (Pennington, 2002).

Neuroimaging studies reveal multiple anatomical and functional abnormalities related to the amygdala and emotion processsing and regulation (Chang et al., 2005; Chen et al., 2004; DelBello, Zimmerman, Mills, Getz, & Strakowski, 2004;

Frazier et al., 2005; Sanches et al., 2005; Singh, DelBello, Adler, Stanford, & Strakowski, 2008), as well as some unique patterns of abnormality in children and adolescents relative to adults (Del-Bello, Adler, & Strakowski, 2006). Neurophysiological and neuropsychological patterns of both overlap and distinction between bipolar disorder and ADHD have also been identified (Henin et al., 2007; Moore et al., 2006). Neurodegeneration is increasingly likely with successive episodes of disorder (Pennington, 2002).

Physiologically based explanations of bipolar disorder must not only account for episodes of both depression and mania, but for the mechanisms linked to cycling; the brain systems involving goals and rewards provide a promising focus for research (Pennington, 2002). Early, severe temperamental difficulties have also been identified as a marker for emerging bipolar disorder (Akiskal, 1998; Chang et al., 2003; Kochman et al., 2005). Sleep dysregulation may also contribute to symptoms of bipolar disorder (Rao et al., 2002). Psychological predispositions include neurocognitive problems such as impaired executive functioning (Dickstein et al., 2004; Meyer et al., 2004). For those at genetic risk, stressful life events also contribute to the development and recurrence of bipolar disorder (Hillegers et al., 2004; Tillman et al., 2003).

Assessment and Diagnosis

Assessment and Diagnosis In Children

With children, assessment of mood disorders is complex, because agreement between parents and children about the presence of depression is often low (Cole, Hoffman, Tram, & Maxwell, 2000), and many of the symptoms of depression are also observed in children with other psychopathologies. Irritability, for example, is a common complaint of parents and teachers, and may be characteristic of many internalizing and externalizing disorders (Craney & Geller, 2003a; Weller, Calvert, & Weller, 2003). Comprehensive assessments, then, must include multiple measures such as self-report, parent report, medical exams, and observations (Birmaher et al., 1996a; Essau, Hakim-Larson, Crocker, & Petermann, 1999). There are many standardized interviews and checklists; among the most frequently used is the Children's Depression Inventory (Kovacs, 1985, 1992). Consistent with the recent emphasis on early signs of developing disorder, there is also a preschooler checklist

(Luby, Heffelfinger, Koenig-McNaught, Brown, & Spitznagel, 2004). For children at risk for bipolar disorder, well-known inventories of child and adolescent symptoms may provide useful information (Faraone, Althoff, Hudziak, Monuteaux, & Biederman, 2005; Holtmann et al., 2007); brain imaging and other lab measures may also provide important data (Davanzo et al., 2003; Garber & Kaminski, 2000).

There continues to be considerable diagnostic confusion when trying to differentiate mania (and bipolar disorder) from ADHD in children. Impulsivity and hyperactivity are certainly part of the clinical presentation of both disorders. However, the same core symptoms that define adult mania can be applied, in general, to children if appropriate developmental considerations are taken into account, such as age of onset (Tillman et al., 2003). Early-onset bipolar disorder can be differentiated from ADHD by the presence of typically manic symptoms such as elated mood, flight of ideas, and grandiosity (Geller, Zimerman et al., 2002), and children themselves are often accurate reporters of such symptoms (Tillman et al., 2004). A child with *elated mood* might laugh hysterically in inappropriate situations with no obvious reason. *Flight of ideas* may be evident in rapid and continuous jumping from one topic to another, often with loud, pressured speech. Children presenting with *grandiosity* often believe that they have superior knowledge and abilities and behave as if rules do not apply to them. In extreme instances, they may state that they have supernatural powers.

Comorbid psychopathology is a critical aspect of assessment and diagnosis, because 40–70% of children with major depression also have other psychopathologies. The most frequent are dysthymia and anxiety disorders, with anxiety disorders usually preceding the mood disorder. Externalizing disorders are also common (Birmaher et al., 1996a; Zahn-Waxler et al., 2000). For children with bipolar disorder, anxiety disorders (in particular, obsessive-compulsive disorder) and externalizing disorders are frequently observed (Masi, 2001; Masi et al., 2004; Masi et al., 2003).

Assessment and Diagnosis in Adolescents

With adolescents, assessment of mood disorders is even more complicated. Parents and clinicians, and adolescents themselves, need to consider possible symptoms in the context of a developmental period characterized by emotional and personal challenges. In addition, with increases in child and adolescent suicide attempts and completions over recent years, it is imperative to screen for suicidality (Birmaher et al., 1996a). The selection of evidence-based instruments is absolutely critical, given that there is often little agreement among adolescents, parents, teachers, and clinicians about the presence of psychopathology (McClure, Kubiszyn, & Kaslow, 2002; Silverman & Ollendick, 2005); these discrepancies are associated with poorer outcomes (Ferdinand, van der Ende, & Verhulst, 2004). There are data that suggest that adolescents underreport their own symptoms, and that parent judgments are more accurate (Youngstrom, Findling, & Calabrese, 2003, 2004; Youngstrom et al., 2004). However, as noted, adolescents seem better able to identify symptoms that differentiate bipolar disorder from ADHD (Tillman et al., 2004), though progress has been reported related to increased validity of parent-report screening (Tillman & Geller, 2005). Multiple informants may provide valuable perspective (Thuppal, Carlson, Sprafkin, & Gadow, 2002).

Bipolar disorder is more frequently misdiagnosed than anxiety or major depression (Weller et al., 1995). There are many reasons for confusion. Parents with their own histories of bipolar disorder may not recognize symptoms in their children, whereas parents without psychopathology may tolerate early episodes of mania because they believe they are adolescent phases and expect their children to improve (Geller & Luby, 1997). Mental health professionals may struggle with accurate diagnosis because the clinical picture of bipolar disorder is especially complex. Irritability and belligerence are more common than euphoria, and the pattern may be more erratic than persistent; with the addition of dramatic mood swings, marked deterioration, the possibility of psychotic symptoms, and many atypical presentations, accurate diagnosis is even more problematic (McClellan et al., 1997).

Diagnostic accuracy must also take into account differential diagnosis and comorbidity; clinicians want to find the best explanation of the presenting symptoms while still recognizing that some adolescents will be appropriately diagnosed with more than one disorder. As already noted, many of the symptoms of bipolar disorder overlap with both internalizing and externalizing disorders such as anxiety, ADHD, substance abuse, and personality disorders (Geller & Luby, 1997; Tillman & Geller,

2005). Early-onset schizophrenia must also be considered and ruled out; adolescents from minority backgrounds must be evaluated carefully because there is evidence that they are more frequently misdiagnosed with schizophrenia (McClellan et al., 1997; Pavuluri, Janicak, Naylor, & Sweeney, 2003).

Comorbidity, especially involving externalizing disorders, is a common complication (Masi, Toni et al., 2003; Wozniak et al., 2004). Conduct disorder needs to be separately assessed and addressed (Biederman et al., 2003). Eating disorders, with their accompanying dysregulation of moods and eating, impulsivity, and cravings for activity, require careful consideration (McElroy, Kotwal, Keck, & Akiskal, 2005). And substance abuse is even more common and more problematic for adolescent-onset bipolar disorder than earlier emerging bipolar disorder (Wilens et al., 2004).

Intervention

As we think about the variety of efforts mobilized to treat and prevent mood disorders, and the fact that many of those treated and targeted are adolescents, it is essential to take into account the developmental context of intervention (Holmbeck & Kendall, 2002). Weisz and Hawley (2002) have argued that treatments for adolescents must address their distinctive physiological, psychological, and social functioning. For instance, motivation is a key contributor to treatment success. Most struggling adolescents do not refer themselves to therapy; once there, many remain reluctant to participate. So immediately addressing motivational issues is important to help adolescents develop a strong therapeutic alliance and engage with specific therapy techniques. Adolescents also appear to prefer active, psychological interventions; selecting such interventions (or including components of these in pharmacological treatments) may increase commitment and follow-through (Jaycox et al., 2006). Finally, Hinshaw (2002) has emphasized the need to convey an understanding of the adolescent's integrity and agency throughout the course of treatment.

The treatment of both major depression and bipolar disorder involves a number of goals, implemented over time. First, acute symptoms need to be managed. Then, attention must be paid to the maintenance of improvements (Kowatch et al., 2005). The reduction of long-term complications (such as suicidality), and

the promotion of non-disorder-related growth and development also contribute to treatment success. With these concerns in mind, it will be as important to design an integrative plan of intervention as it was to think about development of mood disorders in the context of an integrative model of risk factors (Goodman & Gotlib, 2002). This task is complicated by the fact that there are fewer well-controlled treatment studies for childhood and adolescent depression than, for example, for anxiety disorders (Compton, Burns, Egger, & Robertson, 2002; Coyle et al., 2003; Kaslow & Thompson, 1998; Olfson, Gameroff, Marcus, & Waslick, 2003). Even so, meta-analytic studies reveal the immediate positive impact of treatment for mood disorders, with possible long-term benefits (Clarke et al., 2005; Compton et al., 2002).

Pharmacological Treatment

As stated, we know that many, many children and adolescents are presenting for treatment of mood disorders at outpatient clinics (Moreno et al., 2007). We also know that these individuals are prescribed medications *more frequently* and are provided psychotherapy *less frequently* than youth with other disorders (Ma, Ky-Van, & Stafford, 2005). These data are both cause for optimism and cause for concern. Many researchers and clinicians are appropriately optimistic that previously underserved groups are receiving mental health services and responding well to pharmacological treatments (Brent, 2005; Lock, Walker, Rickert, & Katzman, 2005; Sewitch, Blais, Rahme, Bexton, & Galarneau, 2005). Others are more cautious about the use of medication in children and adolescents whose brains and nervous systems continue to develop (El-Mallakh, Peters, & Waltrip, 2000), and call for additional research into commonly used drugs and the factors that influence their prescription (Bridge & Axelson, 2008; Sewitch et al., 2005; Weller, Calvert, & Weller, 2003). Research also continues on the multiple physiological, psychological, and clinical factors that influence a child's response to drug intervention (Birmaher et al., 2007; Emslie, Mayes, Laptook, & Batt, 2003; Emslie et al., 1997; Kowatch & DelBello, 2005; Luby, 2000). In addition to thinking about what kinds of medications are effective for children of different ages (Emslie et al., 1997; Emslie et al., 2008), there are also important ethical issues involved (see Box 12.3). Preferences for particular forms of treatment, informed consent, and issues related to confidentiality are especially important when working with adolescents (Jaycox et al., 2006; McClellan et al., 1997).

The goals of pharmacological treatments include ameliorating the distress and dysfunction of children and preventing or limiting relapse (Birmaher &

BOX 12:3 CLINICAL PERSPECTIVES

Developmental and Ethical Issues Related to the Use of Antidepressant Medication in Children and Adolescents

By any measure, depression occurring during childhood and adolescence is a major clinical concern and the cause of considerable distress for youth and families. For very good reasons, parents of children and adolescents with depression, along with medical and mental health professionals working with these populations, are eager for efficacious and efficient ways to treat these disorders. It is not surprising, then, that the most recently developed and most common pharmacological approaches used for treating adults with depression have been applied to treating children and adolescents (Jureidini et al., 2004).

Indeed, for a number of years, clinicians have recognized that medications used to treat adult depression were often similarly effective with adolescents and even children. This was especially true of the newer class of antidepressants known as the SSRIs (selective serotonin reuptake inhibitors). These medications have also been shown to be helpful in treating other disorders, including obsessive-compulsive disorder and other anxiety-based disorders.

For a time, the relatively manageable side-effect profile and good clinical effect obscured the fact that careful trials on the use of these medications in children had not been done. Consequently, clinicians were caught off guard when anecdotal and case reports began to suggest that the use of SSRIs with youth might be associated with an increase in suicidality. In 2004, the Food and Drug Administration (FDA) conducted a summary review of a number of smaller studies considering these reports. The FDA review study indicated that antidepressants did, indeed, increase the risk—slightly but significantly—of suicidal thinking and behavior. In contrast to placebo samples with a 2% risk of suicidality, the use of antidepressants was associated with a 4% risk of suicidality during the first few months of treatment (USFDA, 2004). It is important to note that no completed suicides occurred during the trials.

These findings stimulated considerable controversy. Initially, a rash of media reports focused on the potential dangers of medication and the lack of standardized trials with children. However, a more balanced discussion soon took place, in which the small but real risks associated with the use of medications for depressed children was

weighed against the well-documented risks associated with untreated depression. The primary risks of using SSRIs with children include the fact that such medications have an as yet unknown effect on the developing nervous system. Additionally, there is some evidence that, in children predisposed to the development of bipolar disorder, the use of the wrong medications may actually induce the onset of mania. There is also evidence that, at least temporarily, children may exhibit greater disinhibition and impulsivity while on antidepressant medication. On the other hand, there are real risks in not treating depression in youth with all of the available tools, including medications. If left untreated or inadequately treated, depression in children and adolescents may lead to poor family and peer relationships, poor academic performance, compromised health, increased risk of substance abuse, and significant rates of suicidality.

In response to these competing concerns, the U.S. Food and Drug Administration issued guidelines that require prescribing physicians to more closely monitor patients during the first four months of medication use. Clinically, many mental health providers suggest a trial of psychotherapy for mild to moderate levels of depression and anxiety disorders before starting medication. The combination of psychotherapy and medication is generally emphasized, along with more aggressive assessment of suicide risk throughout treatment for those patients on medication (March et al., 2004).

More generally, the issues surrounding the use of antidepressant medications with youth illustrate two important trends. First, as our understanding of the interplay among genetics, developmental neurobiology, and experience grows, so does the complexity of intervention strategies and the demand for more nuanced and integrated research into the safety and effectiveness of those interventions. Second, the role of pharmaceuticals in the treatment of mental health problems continues to expand. Indeed, it was the relatively good side-effect profile of the SSRIs that contributed to the explosion of prescriptions for children and teens with psychiatric diagnoses. While medications are likely to continue to be an important tool in the treatment of psychopathology, they are not a panacea and must be used carefully after consideration of all available data.

Brent, 2002; Hughes et al., 2007; Pine, 2002). The most common medications used with children are the selective serotonin reuptake inhibitors (SSRIs); tricyclic antidepressants and MAO inhibitors have not shown much efficacy in children (Pennington, 2002). Symptom improvement usually takes about 8–12 weeks, longer than the 3–4 weeks observed in adults (Pennington, 2002), but complete remission is rare (Emslie et al., 1997). In a meta-analytic review of treatment outcome studies, the benefits of anti-depressant treatment appeared to be much greater than the risks from increased suicidality (Bridge et al., 2007). With increasing empirical data on the efficacy and long-term outcomes of antidepressant treatment for children and adolescents, informed and well-monitored use of antidepressants is often a key component of comprehensive interventions (Emslie et al., 2008; Hughes et al., 2007).

For both children and adolescents with bipolar disorder, mood stabilizers such as lithium appear to be the most effective intervention, with combinations of drugs for children who do not respond to a single mood stabilizer (Geller & Luby, 1997; Kowatch, Sethuraman, Hume, Kromelis, & Weinberg, 2003; McClellan et al., 1997; Patel et al., 2006; Weller, Danielyan, & Weller, 2002). Using lithium requires multiple appointments to check kidney, thyroid, and heart functioning; children and adolescents from "chaotic" families are likely to present special challenges with this type of treatment regimen (Geller & Luby, 1997; McClellan et al., 1997). Because the diagnosis of bipolar disorder in children is relatively recent, there are fewer long-term data available; consensus related to clinical trials and medication management of bipolar disorder is necessary (Carlson et al., 2003; Craney & Geller, 2003b; Kowatch et al., 2005). Hospitalization for those in crisis is an important clinical option, although many children and adolescents experience a range of difficulties following discharge. Only 35% of those in outpatient treatment following hospitalization displayed full medication adherence; complicating factors include comorbidity, lower SES, and lack of a psychotherapy component (DelBello et al., 2007).

Child Treatment

Psychosocial interventions for children with mood disorders are effective (Birmaher et al., 1996a; Kaslow & Thompson, 1998; Sheffield et al., 2006), with **cognitive-behavioral therapies** and **interpersonal**

therapies (i.e., relationship focused approaches) appearing equally useful (Kolko, Brent, Baugher, Bridge, & Birmaher, 2000; Kaufman, Rohde, Seeley, Clarke, & Stice, 2005; Klomek & Mufson, 2006; Mufson et al., 2004; Sherrill & Kovacs, 2002). Individual and group approaches are both associated with good outcomes (Goldberg-Arnold & Fristad, 2003; Sherrill & Kovacs, 2002). With respect to cognitively oriented therapies, we need to remember that adolescents "span a broad range of cognitive ability and cognitive sophistication" and to take these differences into account as we design individual interventions or use available treatment manuals (Weisz & Hawley, 2002, p. 29). Even with attention appropriately focused on cognitive variables, the impact of therapist empathy and the therapeutic alliance must also be appreciated (Kolko et al., 2000; Kaufman et al., 2005). Psychosocial therapies that are combined with pharmacological approaches are also effective for depression and bipolar disorder (Ginsburg, Albano, Findling, Kratochvil, & Walkup, 2005; Lofthouse & Fristad, 2004; Pavuluri et al., 2004). A recent large-scale review of treatment outcome studies affirmed the efficacy of psychotherapy in the treatment of major depression, but noted that the gains made by children and adolescents were more modest compared to children with other disorders (Weisz, McCarty, & Valeri, 2006). Another large-scale, multi-site project examining the relative strengths and weaknesses of medication, cognitive-behavior therapy (CBT), combined medication-CBT, and placebo, called the Treatment for Adolescents with Depression Study (TADS), is ongoing (Curry et al., 2006; Kennard et al., 2006; Kratochvil et al., 2005). Early results suggests the combination of medication and CBT is superior to either single therapy (March, Silva, & Vitiello, 2006).

A specific example of cognitive and cognitive-behavioral interventions for children is the program Kevin Stark and his colleagues have designed. The empirically supported treatment addresses many of the factors presumed to contribute to both development and maintenance of the disorder (Stark, Ballatore, Hamff, Valdez, & Selvig, 2001; Stark et al., 2005; Weisz, 2004). Among the treatment components are emotion education focused on children learning to identify basic emotions and depression symptoms, the scheduling of pleasant activities, personal and interpersonal problem-solving, and altering negative cognitions. Therapists work with both children and families over time to develop and strengthen new cognitive and behavioral coping skills.

Examples of cognitive and cognitive-behavioral interventions for adolescents include Weisz and colleagues' primary and seconday control enhancement training (Weisz, Southam-Gerow, Gordis, & Connor-Smith, 2003), Lewinsohn's Adolescent Coping with Depression Course (Rohde, Lewinsohn, Clarke, Hops, & Seeley, 2005), and the Adolescent Depression Empowerment Project (ADEPT), focused on helping African-American girls with depression (McClure, Connell, Zucker, Griffith, & Kaslow, 2005). For adolescents in psychosocial treatments, ongoing assessment of suicidality is imperative (Bridge, Barbe, Birmaher, Kolko, & Brent, 2005).

Interpersonal therapies (IPT) for both children and adolescents address the salient age-related personal, social, and developmental issues in the context of topics such as loss, grief, and relationship difficulties (Mufson et al., 2004), and work well in both individual and group settings (Mufson, Gallagher, Dorta, & Young, 2004). Interpersonal approaches have also paid particular attention to cultural differences (Rossello & Bernal, 2005). Both CBT and IPT treatments must include mechanisms designed to maintain improved functioning; in several studies initial gains were not maintained at 6-month follow-up (Horowitz, Garber, Ciesla, Young, & Mufson, 2007; Young, Mufson, & Davies, 2006).

Family Treatment

Both mothers and fathers may be especially powerful agents of change (Schock, Gavazzi, Fristad, & Goldberg-Arnold, 2002; Sherrill & Kovacs, 2002), with parent advocacy a key factor in new research and treatment (Hellander, 2003). Parents may be somewhat more helpful for depressed children than for depressed adolescents (Cottrell, 2003). Parent involvement in CBT treatment is one aspect of the successful protocol of the previously described TADS (Wells & Albano, 2005). Psychoeducational support and family-specific techniques are associated with decreases in children's distress and dysfunction (Fristad, Goldberg-Arnold, & Gavazzi, 2002, 2003). Psychoeducation may be especially critical for parents of children and adolescents with bipolar disorder (Miklowitz et al., 2004). The role of the family is also emphasized as we consider the ongoing need for maintenance treatment after

initial improvements (Birmaher, Ryan, Williamson, Brent, & Kaufman, 1996; Danielson, Feeny, Findling, & Youngstrom, 2004; Morris, Miklowitz, & Waxmonsky, 2007; West, Henry, & Pavuluri, 2007). In addition, given the impact of poor marital relations on children's adjustment, marital therapy may be a useful adjunct intervention (Cummings et al., 2000). Finally, recognizing that parents of children with mood disorders also struggle to remain optimistic and effective, caregiver support is critical. There are many ways to provide that support, from individual counseling to internet groups (Hellander, Sisson, & Fristad, 2003).

Prevention Efforts

Prevention efforts have included studies targeting children of depressed parents as well as samples of children with more general high-risk profiles (e.g., children of low-income families). The Penn Resiliency Program (PRP) focusing on the cultivation of optimism and coping skills in middle schoolers has shown benefits (Gillham & Reivich, 1999, 2004). Other types of prevention emphasize the timing of therapeutic techniques to coincide with developmental milestones; the hypothesis is that children and their families may be more accepting of change-related opportunities when a transition period is underway (Beardslee & Gladstone, 2001; Gladstone & Beardslee, 2002). Another type involves going where at-risk children and adolescents gather, and providing resources in community centers (Weersing & Weisz, 2002). In some prevention research, ethnicity and culture appear to moderate effects, with data from a recent study suggesting that low-income Latino fifth and sixth graders exhibited more improvements than African-American children; these findings highlight a need for more culturally specific therapy and strategies (Cardemil, Reivich, & Seligman, 2002).

Suicidality

"The young boy scrawled a note and pinned it to his shirt. Then he walked to the far side of the family Christmas tree and hanged himself from a ceiling beam. The note was short—"Merry Christmas"— and his parents never forgot or understood it" (Redfield Jamison, 1999, p. 73).

One of the saddest developmental trajectories ends with suicide. For most of us, the idea that death is preferable to even the most difficult of life's struggles is hard to understand. It is even more awful when the individual who thinks about, or attempts, or completes suicide is a child or adolescent. Although suicide in adolescence is relatively rare, with estimates ranging from .04% to .2% (Diekstra, 1995), suicide attempts and completions have quadrupled since 1950 (Birmaher et al., 1996b); these higher rates are most dramatically observed in adolescent males (Rutz & Wasserman, 2004), and in some developing countries (Aaron et al., 2004). National suicide statistics provide much of the information, although these are somewhat complicated by sociocultural factors such as religiosity (Diekstra, 1995). Adolescents attempt suicide ten times as often as they complete suicide; that is, one in ten adolescent suicide attempts results in death (Apter & Wasserman, 2003). Rising rates have leveled off in the past decade, plausibly connected to increases in prescribing antidepressant medication to adolescents (Gould, Greenberg, Velting, & Shaffer, 2003).

In order to understand some of the factors that predispose an adolescent to consider suicide, it is important to be clear about definitions related to suicidality. **Suicidal ideation** involves a variety of cognitions from "fleeting thoughts that life is not worth living" to "very concrete, well-thought out plans for killing oneself" (Diekstra, 1995, p. 214). Depending on the specific research definition, estimates of suicidal ideation in adolescence range from 3.5% when narrowly defined to 53% when broadly defined; throughout adolescence, more girls report suicidal thoughts than boys (Diekstra, 1995). **Parasuicide** includes many behaviors, from less dangerous gestures to serious but unsuccessful suicide attempts. The term *parasuicide* is increasingly preferred over *attempted suicide* because the motives and intentions of individuals are often difficult to identify: "Since parasuicide, particularly during adolescence and young adulthood, is usually carried out at the height of an interpersonal crisis by an individual feeling desperate and confused, such obscurity of intent is not at all surprising" (Diekstra, 1995, p. 215). Estimates of parasuicide range between 2.4% and 20%; again, more girls than boys exhibit this behavior (Diekstra, 1995). **Self-injurious behavior**, or **self-harm**, overlaps with many kinds of parasuicide, but can also be considered a distinct phenomenon (Joiner, Conwell, et al., 2005). Compared to adolescents who exhibit parasuicidal behavior, adolescents who display self-harm report different attitudes toward life and death and use different means of

injury (e.g., cutting versus overdosing) (Hjelmeland & Groholt; 2005; Muehlenkamp & Gutierrez, 2004; Rodham, Hawton, & Evans, 2004; see Box 12.4).

Suicide is "any death that is the direct or indirect result of a positive or negative act accomplished by the victim" (Diekstra, 1995, p. 215). In contrast to the impact of gender on suicidal ideation and parasuicide (with girls outnumbering boys), boys far outnumber girls when the focus is on actual death (Conner & Goldston, 2007). Many suicide experts believe that rates of suicide are underestimated and point, for example, to single car accidents with young male drivers as possible, unreported, instances of suicide (Diekstra, 1995). **Suicidality** is the construct that includes suicidal ideation, parasuicide, and suicide.

Many different variables increase the risk for suicidality in adolescents (Bridge, Goldstein, & Brent, 2006; Van Orden, Witte, Selby, Bender, & Joiner, 2008). Genetic effects on persistent suicidal thinking, suicide attempts. and completed suicides are observed, with concordance rates for monozygotic twins higher than rates for dizygotic twins, even after the impact of genetics on adolescent psychopathology is taken into account (Brent et al., 2004; Joiner, Brown, & Wingate, 2005). The heritability of neurobehavioral disinhibition and impulsive aggression is the focus of current research, with investigations of abnormalities in the serotonin system and the HPA-axis (Apter, 2003; Joiner, Brown, et al., 2005; Tarter, Kirisci, Reynolds, & Mezzich, 2004). Entering puberty at younger ages has also been associated with increased risk. Possible explanations for the increase in risk are the "disjunction of biological development on the one hand and psychological and social development on the other" (Diekstra, 1995, p. 231), and the connections between early puberty and risk taking.

Psychological factors are among the most frequently investigated factors. One factor that has received a great deal of clinical and research attention is child or adolescent psychopathology. Psychopathologies linked to suicide include the mood disorders (especially when they are severe or comorbid with personality disorders), anxiety disorders, and externalizing disorders such as conduct disorder (Barbe et al., 2005; Conner & Goldston, 2007; Joiner, Brown, et al., 2005; Merikangas & Angst, 1995; Rudd, Joiner, & Rumzek, 2004). Substance abuse disorders may present a special risk, with most parasuicidal behavior preceded by alcohol

Self-Harm in Adolescence

Self-injurious behavior (SIB), also called self-harm or self-mutilation, is the deliberate, self-inflicted destruction of body tissue, outside of cultural norms, and without suicidal intent (Gratz, Dukes, & Roemer, 2002; Yates, 2004). Self-injurious behaviors include cutting, scratching, and burning. Broadly conceived, SIB is thought to be a compensatory strategy for regulating emotional states and a maladaptive coping skill displayed in response to stress. SIB likely serves a variety of psychological functions, such as reducing or blocking anxiety, as well as communicating with and engaging others (Brown, Comtois, & Linehan, 2002). Although incidence rates vary considerably, it is clear that SIB is a surprisingly common clinical problem, with lifetime prevalence for repeated SIB estimated to be between 5% and 10% (Yates, 2004). These self-destructive behaviors peak in late adolescence and early adulthood, especially in psychiatric samples of individuals; as many as 21% of teens with a psychiatric diagnosis have been found to display SIB (Cleary, 2000). Generally SIB is observed in connection with borderline personality disorder, eating disorders, and dissociative disorders, although there has been recent discussion of the possibility that SIB is better understood as a distinct diagnostic category (Muehlenkamp, 2005).

As noted in Yates' (2004) comprehensive review, strong associations have been established among early trauma, dissociative processes, and later SIB. While not the only pathway to SIB, considerable research has demonstrated that child sexual abuse is a powerful risk factor. Yates notes that sexual abuse readily evokes dissociative defenses, involves specific trauma to the body, and is generally accompanied by a lack of competent parenting.

One of the most compelling aspects of SIB is that is usually occurs in absence of physical pain (Nock & Prinstein, 2005). It is thought that SIB may release neurochemicals (endorphins) that block pain and promote reinforcing feelings. This, along with the impulsive nature of the act, makes SIB especially challenging to treat. Careful research (Nock & Prinstein, 2004, 2005) into the functions of SIB indicates that it most often acts as an automatic negative reinforcer (stops unwanted feelings) but sometimes as an automatic positive reinforcer (relieves feelings of numbness by eliciting other feelings).

There may be important group differences between individuals who tend to engage in mild SIB and do so in the context of social groups, and whose who engage in more severe SIB and for whom it is a more solitary behavior. Although a history of child abuse is strongly associated with all forms of SIB, child abuse and neglect are even more likely to lead to more severe forms of disturbance (Yates, 2004). In recognition of how widespread and varied the clinical presentation of SIB is, therapeutic approaches are becoming more targeted and differentiated. For example, if SIB is primarily serving a regulatory function, then alternative methods of managing the awareness and experience of emotions may be a focus of intervention. If the self-harming behavior is primarily maintained by social reinforcement, then therapeutic efforts focused on more appropriate and effective interpersonal communication may be utilized (Nock & Prinstein, 2005). Also, as the neurophysiology of SIB is better understood, the potential role for pharmacological treatments is being more aggressively explored (Villalba & Harrington, 2003).

---

use (Conner & Goldston, 2007; Rossow, Groholt, & Wichstrom, 2005; Sher & Zalsman, 2005). Adjustment disorders (i.e., disorders associated with a specific traumatic event from which an adolescent doesn't recover) are also critical risk factors (Oquendo et al., 2005; Pelkonen, Marttunen, Henriksson, & Lonnqvist, 2005). Gender-specific patterns of risk have also been identified (Fennig et al., 2005; Rudd et al., 2004). Overall, three diagnostic clusters predict most of the adolescents who attempt suicide: adjustment disorders, major mood disorders, and externalizing behavior disorders combined with a mood disorder (Spirito, Kurkjian, & Donaldson, 2003).

There are mixed data on the impact of risk-taking behaviors. Some investigators argue that general indices of risk taking are not related to suicidality (Stanton, Spirito, Donaldson, & Boergers, 2003). Others suggest that drinking, smoking, and sexual activity do increase adolescent vulnerability (Bae, Ye, Chen, Rivers, & Singh, 2005; Cerel, Roberts, & Nilsen, 2005; Hallfors et al., 2004). Impulsivity, then, becomes an important variable to track (Conner, Meldrum, Wieczorek, Duberstein, & Welte, 2004).

Variables related to identity, self-image, and self-esteem are also noteworthy contributors to increased risk, particularly with respect to lack of self-efficacy and hopelessness (Rutter & Behrendt, 2004; Wilburn & Smith, 2005; Wild, Flisher, & Lombard, 2004). Hopelessness is significant both for the development and maintenance of suicidality; shame and guilt, as well as a sense of being a burden to others, often exacerbate hopelessness (Barbe et al., 2005; Joiner, Conwell, et al., 2005; Stewart et al., 2005). According to Habermas and Bluck (2000), "the drastic increase in suicide rates during adolescence may be a sign that adolescents start thinking about their whole life and its quality" (p. 754). To the extent that adolescents cannot envision their own continuity through time, or that they believe that their continued existence will involve unremitting psychological pain, extreme decisions may occur (Ball & Chandler, 1989; Habermas & Bluck, 2000). Adolescents' inability to communicate their ongoing struggles and their deeply felt pain, combined with hesitation about seeking help from others, further complicates difficult situations (Gould et al., 2004; Horesh, Zalsman, & Apter, 2004). Adolescents who do turn to peers may not always receive appropriate help. Peers may misperceive intent or misjudge lethality (Dunham, 2004). Even when a friend is clearly struggling, peers do not always try to connect with parents or mental health professionals; peer support and assistance may be compromised by their own history of psychopathology (Dunham, 2004).

Previous suicidal behavior is a strong predictor of future suicidality (D'Eramo, Prinstein, Freeman, Grapentine, & Spirito, 2004; Joiner, Conwell, et al., 2005; Van Orden et al., 2008). Past behavior appears to habituate individuals to the fear and pain of self-injury (Joiner et al., 2005) and underlies Joiner's (2002, 2005) **interpersonal-psychological theory of suicidality**. The theory proposes two general categories of risk: dysregulated impulse control and intense psychological pain. The idea is that adolescents "gradually acquire the ability to enact lethal self-injury through prior experience with self-injury (which in turn is encouraged by impulsive behavior underlain by serotonergic dysregulation) . . . ability not acted upon unless the desire for death is instantiated by a strong sense of perceived burdensomeness coupled with a sense of failed belongingness. . ." (Joiner, Brown, et al., 2005, p. 305). In other words, in the context of adolescent impulsivity and psychological anguish, self-destructive behavior may escalate over time, culminating in suicide.

Environmental, familial, and sociocultural contexts of suicidal behavior are also noteworthy variables (Melhem et al., 2007; Smalley, Scourfield, & Greenland, 2005; Wagner, Silverman, & Martin, 2003). Negative life events, such as loss, physical or sexual abuse, or failing academic performance, may necessitate immediate attention (Evans, Hawton, & Rodham, 2005; Horesh, Sever, & Apter, 2003; Richardson, Bergen, Martin, Roeger, & Allison, 2005). The historically relatively lower rates for African Americans and Latinos have been increasing in recent years (O'Donnell, O'Donnell, Wardlaw, & Stueve, 2004; Zayas, Lester, Cabassa, & Fortuna, 2005). Latina girls are an especially high-risk group (O'Donnell et al., 2004). Another high-risk group that has received significant amounts of research and clinical attention is American Indian adolescents. We see differences in suicidality for those living in urban areas versus those living on reservations (Freedenthal & Stiffman, 2004).

The presence of suicidal "models" must also be considered. Models of parasuicidal behavior may include close relatives, a peer, or a celebrity. The role of the media in presenting information on suicide, particularly when news reports include details about specific individuals and/or methods, requires scrutiny (Shoval et al., 2005; Stack, 2005). Internet chat rooms are a more recent phenomenon that also requires careful study (Becker & Schmidt, 2004).

Reducing adolescent suicidality involves multiple, coordinated efforts designed to identify at-risk individuals so that (1) suicide attempts and completions decline in frequency, and (2) adolescents who do attempt suicide receive immediate and ongoing treatment. With respect to prevention, general school-based education programs and staff training are viewed as more acceptable than school-wide screening (Scherff, Eckert, & Miller, 2005). Whereas universal screening may be interpreted as intrusive, there are also legal issues related to consent, confidentiality, and malpractice that must be taken into account (Judge & Billick, 2004). For adolescents contemplating suicide, telephone counseling has been shown to have an immediate positive impact (King, Nurcombe, Bickman, Hides, & Reid, 2003); publicizing such help lines in high schools, shopping malls, community centers, and on billboards may alert suicidal youth to easily accessible (and anonymous) support services. Informational campaigns that raise adult awareness are also essential, and may include lists of behaviors that increase adolescent risk

TABLE 12:5 WARNING SIGNS OF SUICIDALITY
• Change in eating and sleeping habits
• Withdrawal from friends, family, and regular activities
• Violent actions, rebellious behavior, or running away
• Drug and alcohol use
• Unusual neglect of personal appearance
• Marked personality change
• Persistent boredom, difficulty concentrating, decline in schoolwork
• Frequent complaints about physical symptoms
• Loss of interest in pleasurable activities
• Not tolerating praise or rewards

From the American Academy of Child and Adolescent Psychiatry (2000).

(see Table 12.5). Programs designed to address the individual, family, and social factors that limit access to mental health services are critical components of any prevention plan, and might usefully target the young men who are less likely to seek help and more likely to employ lethal means (Spirito, Boergers, Donaldson, Bishop, & Lewander, 2002; Suominen, Isometsa, Martunnen, Ostamo, & Lonnqvist, 2004). These types of resources are absolutely necessary, given that many studies report rates of up to 50% for suicide completions on a first attempt (Joiner, Conwell et al., 2005).

Emergency management plans for adolescents who do attempt suicide are a priority (Stewart, Manion, & Davidson, 2002). Inpatient admission is an option that should be considered. Successful outpatient treatments that bridge the crisis and recovery stages have been documented for both physiological and psychosocial therapies (Donaldson, Spirito, & Esposito-Smythers, 2005; Donaldson, Spirito, & Overholser, 2003; Fristad & Shaver, 2001; Macgowan, 2004), although the kinds of meta-analyses that have demonstrated the efficacy of cognitive-behavioral approaches for adults in preventing suicide have yet to be conducted for adolescents (Tarrier, Taylor, & Gooding, 2008). Lack of long-term treatment plans and noncompliance with treatment plans are problems that seriously hinder positive outcomes (Stewart et al., 2002). Adolescents who repeatedly attempt suicide require even more aggressive care. Compared to those who attempt suicide only once,

repeat attempters experience more anger, depression, and emotional dysregulation; these symptoms must be specifically targeted in treatment plans (Esposito, Spirito, Boergers, & Donaldson, 2003; Spirito, Valeri, Boergers, & Donaldson, 2003). Connections between programs that seek to prevent both youth suicide and youth violence also require additional support and resources (Lubell & Vetter, 2006). What we do for the desperately troubled adolescents who are in every community is a reflection of our basic humanity. Providing school-based coping skills training, better screening, and the restriction of lethal means are first steps to lowering suicide rates.

■ Key Terms

Sense of self (pg. 212)
Positive identity (pg. 212)
Domains of competence (pg. 213)
Arenas of comfort (pg. 213)
Mood disorders (pg. 214)
Mood-related continuum (pg. 214)
Major depression (pg. 216)
Dysthymia (pg. 216)
Seasonal affective disorder (pg. 216)
Bipolar disorder (pg. 219)
Mania (pg. 219)
Manic episodes (pg. 219)
Affective storms (pg. 220)
Developmental continuity (pg. 221)
Multifactorial risk model (pg. 222)
Kindling model (pg. 223)
Social context of brain development and functioning (pg. 223)
Maltreatment (pg. 223)
Emotional security (pg. 224)
Pathways of parental impact (pg. 226)
Reinforcement model (pg. 226)
Negative life events (pg. 227)
Chronic hassles (pg. 227)
Cognitive-vulnerability stress model of depression (pg. 227)
Cognitive-behavioral therapies (pg. 233)
Interpersonal therapies (pg. 233)
Suicidal ideation (pg. 235)
Parasuicide (pg. 235)
Self-injurious behavior/self-harm (pg. 235)
Suicide (pg. 235)
Suicidality (pg. 235)
Interpersonal-psychological theory of suicidality (pg. 237)

■ Chapter Summary

- Depression in childhood is frequent, can have long-term consequences, and is generally under-recognized and undertreated.
- The transition from childhood to adolescence is marked by the development of a coherent psychological identity that includes a sense of competence and self-esteem. These are among the core domains adversely affected by child and adolescent depression.
- Major depression occurring in childhood and adolescence is characterized by sadness and loss of pleasure, and is accompanied by cognitive, behavioral, and somatic symptoms.
- Dysthymia is a longstanding disturbance of mood and places the child or teen at significantly greater risk for developing major depression.
- In younger children, depression often manifests itself in depressed appearance, somatic complaints, anxiety symptoms, and externalizing behaviors. In teens, hopelessness, substance abuse, suicidality, and other serious symptoms are more common.
- Before adolescence, the rate of mood disorders is generally the same for boys and girls. However, beginning in adolescence the rate of depression is much greater for girls.
- Bipolar disorder is a severe form of mood disorder involving alternating periods of depression and mania. In adolescence, the bipolar disorder generally presents as it does in adulthood.

- Bipolar disorder in childhood is most distinctly characterized by severe mood dysregulation, irritability, hyperarousal, and more rapid cycling between depressed and elevated moods.
- There is significant developmental continuity of depression occurring in childhood, through adolescence, and into adulthood.
- Researchers are considering a range of genetic, neurological, life stress, and parenting risk factors in the development of depression.
- Parent depression is an especially important and researched risk factor for the development of depression in childhood.
- Many children and adolescents with major depression have other psychopathologies as well, especially dysthymia and anxiety disorders.
- Recent research suggests the combination of cognitive-behavioral therapy and medication is generally the most effective intervention approach in the treatment of more severe mood disorders in childhood and adolescence.
- Although still rare, adolescent suicide attempts and completions have steadily increased in recent decades.
- While adolescent girls are more likely to experience suicidal ideation and to attempt suicide, boys far outnumber girls in terms of completed suicides.
- In additional to mood disorders, substance abuse is a significant risk factor for suicide among youth.

CHAPTER 13

Conduct Disorders in Adolescence

HOW DO CHILDREN who are argumentative and disobedient go from being diagnosed with oppositional defiant disorder to adolescents who lie, cheat, and steal? How do we explain adolescents who flout rules and exploit others? How can we comprehend the heartbreaking episodes of adolescent rage and violence that destroy families, schools, and communities? Understanding conduct disorder involves thinking carefully and critically about "bad" behavior throughout history and the apparent increases in externalizing behaviors in recent decades (Collishaw, Maughan, Goodman, & Pickles, 2004; Costello & Angold, 2001; Robins, 1999; see Box 13.1). Conduct disorder is expensive, with high costs for children and adolescents and for society (Foster & Jones, 2005; Jones, Dodge, Foster, Nix, & Conduct Problems Prevention Research Group, 2002). Thinking about the varied pathways toward and away from conduct disorders in general, and aggression and violence in particular, it is essential that we continue to make use of a developmental framework (Hartup, 2005; Koops & de Castro, 2004); with such a framework, bridges between research, treatment, and public policy may be built (Coie & Dodge, 1998; Pettit & Dodge, 2003).

Developmental Tasks and Challenges Related to Relationships with Parents and Peers

Much of Chapter 12's discussion of the construction of self and identity emphasized what adolescents know about themselves and how they feel about themselves, with self-understanding and self-esteem usually conceptualized as achievements of the individual. But we need to remember that children and adolescents are embedded in social contexts that powerfully influence development. Relationships with parents and peers provide such social contexts, and they undergo significant change during adolescence (see Figure 13.1). Understanding the nature of these relationships in typically developing adolescents will help us to understand important aspects of the clinical presentation of conduct disorder.

Every relationship depends on the characteristics of the individuals involved, their personalities, their

---

BOX 13:1 THE CHILD IN CONTEXT

Historical Perspectives on Bad Behavior

Over the centuries, adults have sought to teach, control, and socialize children, and to respond appropriately to children's bad behaviors. Costello and Angold (2001) summarize multiple historical approaches to dealing with deviant behaviors and deviant children. Each of these perspectives has something to say about the nature of children (see also Hwang, Lamb, & Sigel, 1996), and about the emergence of responsibility for one's own behaviors, the relations between the family and the larger social group with respect to control of children, and institutions for out-of-control individuals.

With respect to the nature of children, Costello and Angold describe approaches that focus on the children's behavior as the result of disease (e.g., genetic and hereditary explanations), disposition, motivation, lack of knowledge (e.g., malice-related or ignorance-related explanations), or problematic environments (e.g., distressed families or dysfunctional neighborhoods). Hostile, oppositional, defiant, and aggressive behavior is at times the sole responsibility of the child, sometimes the responsibility of the parents, and sometimes the responsibility of society. Blame and recriminations are pervasive.

In various eras, adults have alternately viewed children as similar to adults (judging them accordingly), and as different from adults (responding with leniency and mercy). And societies have struggled to balance their obligations to children themselves and to communities. Many societies have developed separate legal and physical systems for dealing with difficult children. The consequences of unacceptable behaviors have ranged from education and rehabilitation through punishment, ostracism, and isolation.

Other, more recent discussions of children's behavior have held out the possibility that some types of bad behavior may in fact be adaptive for some children (Cummings et al., 2000; Underwood, 2003a, 2003b). The benefits of bad behavior may be understood within an evolutionary context (Costello & Angold, 2001; Pinker, 2002), or within more circumscribed settings including SES, ethnic background, and family environments (Underwood, 2003a, 2003b). The role of developmental level and the impact of specific developmental challenges remain to be fully explored (Underwood, 2003a). And whether we are concerned about girls or boys also influences our definitions of bad behavior, our expectations, and our responses to such behavior (Underwood, 2003a, 2003b; Underwood, Galen, & Paquette, 2001). As we grapple with our concerns, we need to remind ourselves that the questions we frame about children will need to be as complex, difficult, and genuine as they are.

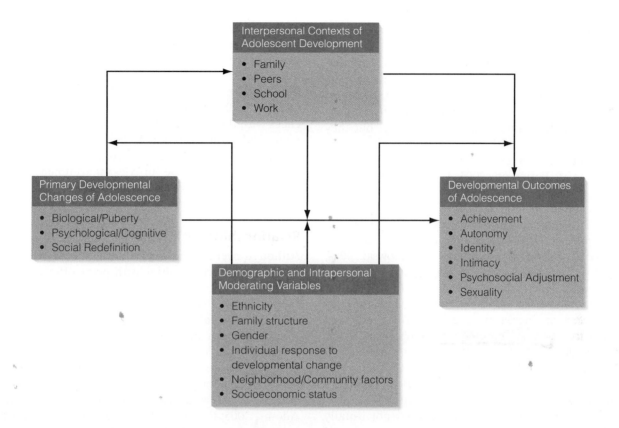

FIGURE 13:1 Adolescent development in interpersonal context.
Source: From "Handbook of Research Methods in Clinical Psychology", 2nd Edition, by Phillip C. Kendall, James N. Butcher and Grayson N. Holmbeck, p. 638. Copyright © 1999 John Wiley & Sons, Inc. Reproduced by permission of John Wiley & Sons, Inc.

ages, their skills and talents, and their relationship goals (Laursen & Bukowski, 1997). Some relationships are **instrumental**, focused on getting something useful from the other participant (e.g., information from a teacher or lunch money from an acquaintance). Other relationships are **affiliative**, focused on liking one another or sharing interests. Many relationships combine features of both instrumental and affiliative interactions. Sullivan (1953) described the strong social needs that are fulfilled by relationships, such as tenderness, participation in play, acceptance by others, intimacy, and sexual contact, with various relationships addressing different needs. Sullivan also described the alternative to a fulfilling social life—loneliness—and how absolutely critical it is to understand the impact that loneliness has on individuals and their development (Asher & Paquette, 2003).

Relationships in general, and close relationships in particular, are characterized by dimensions of permanence, power, and gender (Laursen & Bukowski, 1997). Permanence has to do with the stability of the relationship; parent-child and sibling relationships are among the most enduring, although there are certainly individual differences in the degree of closeness in these family relationships. Power has to do with control and responsibility. Parents and children provide a good example of a *vertical* relationship, where parents are typically invested with most of the power. Sibling and peer relationships tend to be *horizontal*, characterized by more egalitarian roles, and shared control and responsibility. Gender plays an important role in almost all adolescent relationships; understanding the differential impact of mothers and fathers, and same-sex and opposite-sex peers, on adolescent boys' and girls' experiences is essential. Although cultural factors (such as those influencing the interactions of adolescent boys and girls) must always be taken into account, important similarities in relationships across various ethnicities and nationalities (e.g., between Dutch and Japanese adolescents, and between Chinese and American adolescents) have also been documented (Chen, Greenberger, Lester, Dong, & Guo, 1998; Claes, 1998; Dekovic, Engels, Shirai, De Kort, & Anker, 2002).

Relationships with Parents

In all of the chapters in this textbook, we have highlighted the critical role of parents in children's adjustments. With the advent of adolescence, we need to rethink the role of parents and parenting. Relationships with parents and other family members do not disappear during adolescence, of course, but they are transformed, with new meanings created and new interactions exhibited (Granic, Hollenstein, Dishion, & Patterson, 2003; Laursen & Bukowski, 1997; Steinberg, 2001). Much of the impetus for change is driven by the adolescent, moving from "... a state of being dependent, passive, and relatively asexual to a state of being responsible, assertive, and capable of sexuality" (Laursen & Bukowski, 1997, p. 763). Expectations and demands for change can be overt or subtle, and they are often the source of conflict.

Many investigators, along with the general public, focus on increases in conflict frequency and intensity; more frequent conflicts are observed in early adolescence, and more intense conflicts in mid adolescence (Laursen, Coy, & Collins, 1998; McGue, Elkins, Walden, & Iacono, 2005). Although there is some evidence of a decrease in relationship warmth, the increase in conflict does not usually reflect a serious problem, and most adolescents and parents report continuing positive relationships (Arnett, 1999; McGue et al., 2005). Conflicts often focus on the pattern and pace of increasing independence and autonomy, and involve disagreements over matters such as school performance, appearance, dating, and curfews (Silk, Morris, Kanaya, & Steinberg, 2003; Smetana & Gettman, 2006); experiences with these conflicts appear similar across ethnicity and culture (Daddis & Smetana, 2005; Yau & Smetana, 2003). Some of these conflicts seem superficial, but in fact may be "proxies for arguments over more serious issues such as substance use, automobile driving safety, and sex" (Arnett, 1999, p. 320).

Relationships with Peers

Although overlapping somewhat with relationships with parents, relationships with peers offer unique experiences. Citing Piaget's and Kohlberg's theories, Parker, Rubin, Price, and DeRosier (1995) provide the example of **moral development** as a domain wherein what you learn from peers can be very different from what you learn from parents and other adults. Positive peer relationships, then, reflect a critical developmental achievement, with both individual and social consequences (Blos, 1979; Bukowski & Adams, 2005; Parker et al., 1995). Some of the most important aspects of adolescent life involve the density and diversity of social networks. Over the years

Peer group relationships become an increasingly important influence on moral and behavioral development during adolescence.

Peter Cade/Riser/Getty Images

of childhood and early adolescence, the availability of peers increases, with, for instance, entrance into larger schools and involvement in sports, clubs, extracurricular lessons, and community activities. Even as we note the widening circle of peers, we cannot overlook the ongoing influence of parents. In elementary school, parents design and control the peer experiences of their children; they "actively steer children toward certain friends and away from others" (Collins, Maccoby, Steinberg, Hetherington, & Bornstein, 2000, p. 227). While such direct control begins to decline in adolescence, parents' indirect influence over the emergence of their children's personalities and values continues to play a role.

Over the school years, even in a milieu of horizontal relationships, "the peer group also becomes increasingly segregated by sex, and to a lesser extent, race, and organized into more discernable hierarchies of power and popularity" (Parker et al., 1995, p. 101). Across adolescence, we see some loosening of cliques and clique behavior, and a shift to **peer subcultures**. These are larger groups of "similarly stereotyped individuals," and include "jocks, brains, loners, rogues, druggies, populars, and nerds" (Parker et al., 1995, p. 104). Other investigators have examined adolescent groups and friendships using different methods, measures, and classifications. Hawley, Little, and Pasupathi (2002), for instance, outlined the origins and outcomes of prosocial and coercive control in peer relationships. In other research, Coie, Dodge, and Coppotelli (1982) described four extreme status groups of children, based on peer nominations. The *popular* children were those who received lots of positive responses and few negative ones. The *rejected* children received many negative responses and few positives. The *neglected* children received few positive or negative responses. And the *controversial* children had both positive and negative responses. Although 60-65% of children were classified as average (i.e., not in any of the extreme groups), the results from many studies suggest that the extreme classifications of 35-40% of the children are relatively stable (Parker et al., 1995). Keep in mind, however, that there are important differences between acceptance, popularity, and friendships, as well as differences between objective and subjective indices of peer relationships (Parker et al., 1995). The "reality" observed by others does not always match the "reality" felt by an adolescent.

In addition to understanding the availability and initiation of peer relationships, the nature and continuity of relationships must also be addressed. School transitions from elementary to middle school or middle school to high school, can disrupt longstanding friendships (Parker et al., 1995). Indeed, "different environments present different challenges to individuals. For example, the maintenance of friendships may be less difficult in the well-structured environments of elementary school than in the expansive environments of secondary schools" (Laursen & Bukowski, 1997, pp. 748–749). These changes can be almost as upsetting to parents, who may for the first time not know their children's friends, as it is to young adolescents themselves. With respect to the nature of adolescent relationships, the positive qualities (e.g., intimacy, loyalty, trust) appear more important than the quantity of friendships, especially for boys (Demir & Urberg, 2004). And positive experiences in one type of relationship, such as with friends, may buffer negative experiences in others, such as with parents (and vice versa) (Laursen & Bukowski, 1997).

Understanding the impact of gender on healthy and unhealthy peer relationships is critical (Underwood, 2004a), and the ways in which adolescent boys and girls conceptualize and manage negative emotion and various forms of aggression provide relevant developmental information (Huesmann & Guerra, 1997). Both boys and girls exhibit physical and non-physical aggression, but the frequency and intensity of aggression differ; individual differences across gender also need to be taken into account (Archer, 2004; Card, Stucky, Sawalani, & Little, 2008; Crick, Casas, & Nelson, 2002; Underwood, 2002; Zimmer-Gembeck, Geiger, & Crick, 2005). Relational (or social) aggression is thought to be more common in girls, and is focused on harm caused in relationships. Examples include exclusion, gossip, and friendship manipulation (e.g., exploiting one's friends or having friends lie to parents or teachers) (Crick & Grotpeter, 1995; Underwood, 2004b); a recent meta-analysis of nearly 150 studies, however, suggests that the gender difference may be relatively trivial (Card et al., 2008). Physical aggression is more typical of boys, and like relational aggression, needs to be understood in the broader context of emotional development (Card et al., 2008; Crick & Rose, 2000).

Relationships with Romantic Partners

Like other developmental phenomena, romantic relationships follow general age-related trajectories, from mixed groups of boys and girls to group dating to romantic pairings (Furman, 2002; Seiffge-Krenke, 2003), and from relatively informal beginnings to more committed relationships (Collins & Sroufe, 1999). Romantic relationships appear to have better outcomes when they occur later in adolescence rather than earlier (Neemann, Hubbard, & Masten, 1995). Somewhat different experiences are described for gay, lesbian, and bisexual adolescents, taking into account their own individual histories as well as social responses from families, peers, and the larger culture (Furman, 2002). The development of the capacity for intimacy has its roots in earlier experiences and achievements, and is linked with other relationships such as those with parents and friends (Collins, 2003; Furman, 2002). A history of secure attachment, for example, relates to an adolescent's self-esteem, his or her social skills and peer networks, and his or her orientation toward emotional depth (Collins & Sroufe, 1999).

Rates for dating are relatively high and similar for European-American, African-American, Hispanic-American, and Native-American adolescents; rates for Asian Americans are somewhat lower (Carver, Joyner, & Udry, 2003). For many, dating is an adolescent rite of passage; social expectations for dating are high (Collins & Sroufe, 1999), with Western adolescents "'set up' to be involved in a world of romantic relationships" (Larson, Clore, & Wood, 1999, p. 27). Many adults (who clearly have forgotten their own adolescence) downplay the meaning and intensity of adolescent romance. Larson, Clore, and Wood (1999), however, present the powerful force of adolescent feelings more accurately: "Romantic emotions can grip adolescents' lives. A 13-year-old reports feeling so in love that he can think of nothing else. A 15-year-old is distressed that 'everyone has a boyfriend but me' and broods for hours in her room. Another girl finds herself in a passionate lesbian relationship and feels elated, affirmed, and 'chosen.' And a boy reports feeling so enraged by the betrayal of his girlfriend that he is obsessed with thinking up ways to hurt her" (p. 19). These strong feelings are tied, in part, to biological changes of puberty and social expectations (of the larger culture and peer groups), and involve both positive feelings (pride, love, and joy) and negative feelings (loneliness, jealousy, disappointment, shame, anxiety, and humiliation) (Larson et al., 1999).

Romantic relationships can be assessed along several dimensions, including whether an adolescent is involved at all in such relationships, the selection of partners, relationship content, and relationship quality (Collins, 2003; Giordano, Manning, & Longmore, 2006). These relationships serve the four goals of affiliation, sexual intimacy, attachment, and caregiving, with the first two goals most salient during adolescence (Furman, 2002). In addition, these relationships allow for the learning of important emotional, cognitive, and behavioral skills (Barber & Eccles, 2003; Collins, 2003). Although they provide a primary source of support for adolescents, romantic relationships also are risk factors for abuse, depression following breakups, sexually transmitted diseases, and unplanned pregnancies (Furman, 2002; Linder, Crick, & Collins, 2002; Roberts, Auinger, & Klein, 2006; Williams, Connolly, Pepler, Craig, & Laporte, 2008).

Conduct Disorders

The Case of Lucas

Lucas is a 15-year-old referred for evaluation by his mother and school principal due to concerns about escalating behavior problems, school difficulties, and suspected substance abuse. He gets in trouble at school nearly every week: sometimes for disobeying school rules, sometimes for rude comments to teachers, and occasionally for fighting with other students. Recently Lucas was suspended for stealing CDs and money from another student's locker. He was also suspended last year, that time when he punched and kicked a younger student who accidentally ran into him in the hallway. Although Lucas is not involved in any school teams or organizations and most other students avoid him, he does have a small group of friends who have also been in considerable trouble. Some of them have been arrested for property-related offenses.

Lucas's problems at school are mirrored by defiant, reactive, and disruptive behavior at home, dating all the way back to his preschool years. When younger, Lucas was hard to manage at home and at school, and by middle school Lucas's parents felt that they had very little control over him. Now, Lucas's parents tend to steer clear of him and are grateful for the occasional periods of uneasy truces. ∎

The Case of Elena

Elena is a 16-year-old referred for evaluation at the suggestion of her pediatrician. She is in the tenth grade and currently failing most of her classes. She skips school several times a week and hangs out with a group of older teens who have dropped out of high school. Elena has been stealing money from her parents and has also been arrested twice for shoplifting. She has recently come home intoxicated and her parents have found drug paraphernalia in her room.

This is not how life has always been for Elena. Elena's parents report a relatively uneventful childhood. They began to be concerned about her, however, during eighth grade. At the time, Elena dropped out of sports and her grades fell dramatically. Eventually Elena was diagnosed with depression, participated briefly in therapy, and began an antidepressant. Although Elena's mood and behavior improved somewhat, she continued to struggle throughout the year. After a period of social isolation, she began to hang out with a group of girls who prided themselves on their alienation from mainstream school and family experiences. ■

There are four categories of **conduct disorder** (CD), differentiated by the types of externalizing behaviors displayed. These externalizing behaviors are (1) aggression, (2) nonaggressive behavior that results in property loss or damage, (3) deceitfulness or theft, or (4) serious violations of rules and laws. Frick et al. (1993) plot these types using two dimensions: an **overt/covert dimension** and a **destructive/nondestructive dimension** (see Figure 13.2). These patterns are distinguished from oppositional defiant disorder (involving negativism, defiance, disobedience, and hostility) in terms of severity and impairment (see Table 13.1). Along with the core symptoms, children and adolescents with CD also exhibit problematic personality characteristics (e.g., psychopathy), cognitive challenges (e.g., poor social-problem-solving abilities), and higher levels of impairment compared to children and adolescents with other disorders (Lambert, Wahler, Andrade, & Bickman, 2001; Salekin, Leistico, Trobst, Schrum, & Lochman, 2005; Waschbusch, Walsh, Andrade, King, & Carrey, 2007).

The validity of the CD diagnosis is well-established. Although there is symptom overlap with other disorders, including oppositional defiant disorder and attention deficit hyperactivity disorder, CD can be differentiated, and even appropriately diagnosed, in young children (Kim-Cohen, Arseneault, et al., 2005; Loeber, Burke, Lahey, Winters, & Zera, 2000). In addition, there are data that support the validity of various CD subtypes (Nock, Kazdin, Hiripi, & Kessler, 2006; Tackett, Krueger, Iacono, & McGue, 2005). Before discussing these subtypes, it makes sense to step back and consider the forms and functions of aggression apart from the construct of conduct disorder (Robins, 1995).

FIGURE 13:2 Four-quadrant diagram of conduct disorder.
SOURCE: From Frick, P.J., Lahey, B.B., Loeber, R. & Tannenbaum, L. (1993), "Oppositional defiant disorder and conduct disorder: A meta-analytic review of factor analyses and cross-validation in a clinic sample", 'Clinical Psychology Review' 13 (4), 319-340. Reprinted by permission of Elsevier.

Aggression involves behaviors that are carried out with an immediate goal of causing harm to another (Archer & Coyne, 2005; Bushman & Anderson, 2001). Many investigators have attempted to understand why aggression occurs and what it involves. The *whys* of aggression focus mainly on whether aggression is instrumental or reactive. **Instrumental aggression** is aggression that is premeditated or planned. In most cases, instrumental aggression is a means to a particular end. **Reactive aggression** is aggression that occurs in response to a provocation. It is more angry and impulsive. Although this distinction is useful in many ways, it is important to remember that aggression often has multiple motives and multiple goals; these include attempts to reestablish self-esteem or public image, attempts to express grievances, or attempts to obtain benefits such as money or information (Bushman & Anderson, 2001). The *whats* of aggression have to do with whether aggression is direct or indirect. Direct, or **overt aggression**, involves harmful physical behaviors. Indirect, or **covert aggression**, may include the externalizing behaviors observed in CD, such as property damage or theft; it may also involve alternative strategies employed when the costs of direct aggression are high. Clearly, the heterogeneity of aggression and antisocial behavior present difficulties for researchers and clinicians; multiple distinctions must be understood separately as well as together (Little, Jones, Henrich, & Hawley,

---

TABLE 13:1 DSM-IV-TR CRITERIA FOR CONDUCT DISORDER

A. A repetitive and persistent pattern of behavior in which the basic rights of others or major age-appropriate societal norms or rules are violated, with three or more of the following observed in the past 12 months and at least one criterion present in the past 6 months:

Aggression to people and animals

(1) Often bullies, threatens, or intimidates others

(2) Often initiates physical fights

(3) Has used a weapon that can cause serious physical harm to others

(4) Has been physically cruel to people

(5) Has been physically cruel to animals

(6) Has stolen while confronting a victim

(7) Has forced someone into sexual activity

Destruction of property

(8) Has deliberately engaged in fire setting with the intention of causing serious damage

(9) Has deliberately destroyed others' property

Deceitfulness or theft

(10) Has broken into someone else's house, building, or car

(11) Often lies to obtain goods or favors or to avoid obligations

(12) Has stolen items of nontrivial value without confronting the victim

Serious violation of rules

(13) Often stays out at night despite parental prohibitions, beginning before age 13

(14) Has run away from home overnight at least twice

(15) Is often truant from school beginning before age 13

B. The disturbance causes clinically significant impairment in social, academic, or occupational functioning.

Source: Reprinted with permission from the Diagnostic and Statistical Manual of Mental Disorders, Text Revision, Fourth Edition, (Copyright 2000). American Psychiatric Association.

2003; Rutter et al., 1997). Aggression is, of course, observed in normally developing children and adolescents; indeed, the reality that assertive, manipulative, and aggressive behaviors are often rewarded must also be acknowledged (Hawley & Vaughn, 2003; see Box 13.2).

There are two subtypes of conduct disorder: **childhood-onset subtype** and **adolescent-onset subtype**. With childhood onset, the individual diagnosed with conduct disorder has a long history of negative personal and interpersonal behavior, deteriorating over time. With onset in adolescence, the individual's problem behavior emerges more abruptly. Adolescent-onset conduct disorder is three times as frequent as childhood-onset (Frick, 1998). The data on prevalence by age is mixed, with some studies showing increases in conduct disorder from middle childhood to adolescence, whereas other studies do not (Loeber et al., 2000). For child-onset CD, boys outnumber girls 10 to 1; for adolescent-onset CD, boys outnumber girls 5 to 1 (Moffitt & Caspi, 2001). The diagnosis is more common in youth from lower SES backgrounds (Loeber et al., 2000). Ethnicity also appears to influence prevalence rates (Bird et al., 2001; Hishinuma et al., 2005).

Child-onset and adolescent-onset conduct disorder differ not only in their timing, but in their symptom patterns, severity, and outcomes. Moffitt's (2003) theory of CD describes a **life-course persistent (LCP) trajectory** and an **adolescence-limited (AL) trajectory**. The AL form of CD is somewhat less problematic over time than the child-onset form, although there is still evidence of significant impairment in daily functioning and risk for poor outcomes (Cicchetti & Rogosch, 2002; Moffitt, 2003). LCP individuals are more likely to have a history of ODD and a family history of antisocial behavior, and are more likely to display aggression and have worse outcomes than AL individuals (Lahey et al., 1998; Loeber

BOX 13:2 THE CHILD IN CONTEXT

"The Bright Side to Bad Behavior"

Any discussion of conduct problems among youth necessarily includes a focus on the role of aggression. Clearly, aggressive behavior can be a hallmark feature of clinically significant disruptive behavior disorders. This does not, however, mean that aggression is always associated with maladaptive functioning. Indeed, depending on the context and on what is being measured, aggression may indicate either severe dysfunction or effective adaptation (Bukowski, 2003). A series of papers entitled "Aggression and Adaptive Functioning: The Bright Side to Bad Behavior," explored this issue and the complex relation between aggression and competence (Hawley & Vaughn, 2003). While taking care not to suggest that aggressive behavior, in and of itself, was good, the complexity of the relation between aggression and competence was explored in a new light. For example, there is evidence that aggressive behavior, in balance with socially skilled behavior, may reflect social competence in some settings (Hawley, 2003).

Also, the form of aggression turns out to be especially important in predicting general adaptability. Specifically, aggression that is reactive or arbitrary is far more likely to be associated with incompetence than aggression that is measured and "planful" (Little, Brauner, Jones, Nock, & Hawley, 2003). This is not to say that instrumental or planful aggression is good for interpersonal relationships or for society, but in certain circumstances the ability to control and strategically use aggression may have high survival value for the individual. Admittedly, the association is difficult to untangle. Carefully planned, extreme aggression, for instance, as we have seen with cases of school violence or sadistic acts of abusing or killing neighborhood pets, may signal the most severe forms of psychopathology. In contrast, an adolescent in a high-risk, urban setting who is able to communicate that he cannot be easily victimized and will meet aggression with proportional aggression may

be displaying effective adaptation given his environment. Or consider the following more normative observational data of preschoolers playing together for the first time. One child, known to be aggressive and a bit of a bully, picks up a football and suggests to the other child that they play catch. He then hurls the ball with unexpected force at the other child with the clear intent of intimidating his partner. The second child jumps out of the way. He does not protest, but rather picks up the football, smiles, and throws it back with equal force. That is the end of the first child trying to intimidate the second.

Another way to consider these findings is to note that while some children occasionally use aggression as one of a variety of strategies to manage conflict, they may also "show levels of adjustment and competence that can . . . be equal to that of purely prosocial children" (Bukowski, 2003, p. 395). Anyone who has observed an elementary school classroom for any length of time will see that, at a minimum, the ability to manage an environment in which aggression is sometimes used to control resources is part of adaptive functioning. A child in such an environment may show competence in a number of ways. He or she might develop strategies for avoiding conflict, for deflecting aggression, or perhaps occasionally meeting aggression with assertiveness and controlled aggression. The observer might also note a few children who are cooperative with adults, follow most of the rules, but are dominating and coercive on the playground. The observer would also likely see children whose frustration tolerance is so poor that they are repeatedly reacting with anger and aggression and are consequently shunned by classmates. Understanding the differences among forms of aggression is key to developing intervention programs designed to match specific profiles of aggressive behavior. And ongoing investigations of the intersections between adaptive and maladaptive forms of aggression will continue to provide insights into the "bright side to bad behavior."

et al., 2000). As noted in prevalence data, there are more boys who exhibit the early-onset, more severe CD pathway. However, some researchers have hypothesized that certain girls display a "delayed-onset," with similar underlying factors; this hypothesis is based, in part, on similar poor adult outcomes for girls diagnosed later with CD compared to boys diagnosed earlier (Silverthorn &

Frick, 1999). Given recent increases in the diagnosis of girls, negative consequences such as early pregnancy and later antisocial behavior, and the fact that much of our CD data is based on samples of boys, we will need to look more carefully at girls in coming years (Keenan, Loeber, & Green, 1999; Keenan, Stouthamer-Loeber, & Loeber, 2005; Loeber et al., 2000). It may also be prudent to pay attention to the "subclinical" range of problem behaviors, given long-term individual and social consequences (Cicchetti & Rogosch, 2002).

Developmental Course

The foundation for understanding the developmental course of conduct disorder was presented in Lee Robins's (1966) classic book, *Deviant Children Grown Up*. Robins documented the potential stability of the disorder, finding that troubled children and adolescents display antisocial personalities as adults along with other types of psychopathologies. However, he also observed the possibility of positive change and better outcomes in some individuals. Robins's findings have been replicated many, many times in other longitudinal studies; the stability of conduct-disordered behavior, especially related to aggression, is abundantly clear across individuals and across generations (Cicchetti & Rogosch, 2002; Huesmann, Eron, Lefkowitz, & Walder, 1984; Loeber et al., 2001; Moffitt, Caspi, Harrington, & Milne, 2002; Schaeffer, Petras, Ialongo, Poduska, & Kellam, 2003).

Adolescent-Onset CD

As just described, some instances of conduct disorder are initially identified in adolescence (i.e., adolescence-limited trajectory). Thinking back to the developmental challenges related to identity formation, changing relationships with parents, and the increasing role of peers, it is easy to imagine that some adolescents are going to go off track, experimenting with a range of externalizing behaviors. Such exploration often reflects the normal trajectory through Erikson's (1950) period of Identity versus Role Confusion. For most, this is a time-bound, albeit difficult and upsetting, phase with impairment in most domains of functioning. For others, this is the beginning of an ongoing or deteriorating pathway involving other psychopathologies such as substance abuse.

Childhood-Onset CD

According to Lahey and Waldman (2003), "Adolescents who engage in high levels of serious adolescent conduct problems rarely come out of nowhere" (p. 78). Stable externalizing trajectories are already evident in the early school years (Shaw, Gilliom, Ingoldsby, & Nagin, 2003). Researchers have identified different patterns

of disruptive behaviors in school-age children, including **reactive-oppositional patterns**, **proactive-callous patterns**, and **impulsive-overactive patterns** (Waschbusch et al., 2004). Children who display the reactive-oppositional pattern are more likely to be defiant, have temper outbursts, and stay angry at adults. Children who display the proactive-callous pattern are more likely to be purposely mean, to encourage peers to gang up on or reject another child, and to lack remorse. Children who exhibit the impulsive-overactive pattern are more likely to be easily aroused and disruptive. Each pattern has specific implications for both current and later adjustments (Waschbusch et al., 2004). There also appear to be gender-specific profiles and gender-race interactions that require additional investigation. For instance, boys and girls exhibit different sets of problem behaviors that put them at higher risk for forms of CD associated with different estimates of stability (Broidy et al., 2003; Burke, Loeber, & Birmaher, 2002; Cote, Tremblay, Nagin, Zoccolillo, & Vitaro, 2002), and African-American girls who display high levels of physical aggression have poorer outcomes than others (Miller-Johnson, Moore, Underwood, & Coie, 2005). Overall, this form of CD is "a pathway to more extreme adult antisocial behavior and more pervasive failure in adult adjustment" (Cicchetti & Rogosch, 2002, p. 13). Again, however, it is imperative to keep in mind that change is possible and does occur in both boys and girls (Loeber & Stouthamer-Loeber, 1998).

One way to help elucidate the developmental course of conduct disorder is to contrast conduct problems that occur developmentally early with those that are developmentally late (Lahey & Waldman, 2003). Developmentally early conduct problems are somewhat normative and often observed at school entry, such as minor aggression and lying. There are individual differences in the amount and severity of developmentally early conduct problems, with some young children already struggling with a mix of negative behaviors and consequences in preschool (van Lier, Verhulst, Van Der Ende, & Crijnen, 2003). Almost half of children with early problems improve over time, with a variety of protective factors balancing early risk. Developmentally late conduct problems occur later, are less normative and more serious; these may include truancy, stealing, mugging, and forced sex. According to Lahey and Waldman, children with the highest level of early problems develop the developmentally late conduct problems earlier than others and experience more maladjustment. In addition, researchers have reported that the externalizing behaviors exhibited by boys on the life-course path do not change over time; rather, their repertoire of externalizing behaviors expands to include new overt and covert problem behaviors (Frick, 1998; Lahey, Loeber, Burke, & Applegate, 2005; Patterson, Dishion, & Yoerger, 2000; Patterson & Yoerger, 1999).

Another area that provides perspective on developmental trajectories related to conduct disorder involves the association between aggression and bullying. Aggression and **bullying** are pervasive problems in families, schools, and neighborhoods. In schools, aggression and bullying are observed at all grade levels including kindergarten (Pepler, Jiang, Craig, & Connolly, 2008; Perren & Alsaker, 2006), with the roots of some forms of bullying interactions observed even earlier in development (Georgiou, 2008; Troy & Sroufe, 1987). Data suggest that bullying is stable over time, and may be the first step on the path toward delinquency (Baldry & Farrington, 2000; Schäfer, Korn, Brodbeck, Wolke, & Schulz, 2005). Especially in schools and neighborhoods, we need to think about relations among bullies, victims, and bystanders (Batsche & Porter, 2006; Orpinas & Horne, 2006a; Veenstra et al., 2005). Bullies are a heterogeneous group of children and adolescents, with various backgrounds and aggressive behaviors that have multiple and sometimes different motives; victims too are a mixed group with different developmental histories and adjustments (Graham, Bellmore, & Mize, 2006; Hanish & Guerra, 2002, 2004; Hawker & Boulton, 2000; Kochenderfer-Ladd, 2003). And while we associate bullying most frequently with physical aggression, that is not the only form of bullying being studied. Research is expanding, for example, into areas such as internet bullying (Williams & Guerra, 2007).

As discussed in Chapter 10, three developmental pathways to conduct disorder have been described by Loeber and his colleagues: (1) An **overt pathway**, with a progression from instances of minor aggression to fighting to more violent behaviors; (2) A **covert pathway**, beginning before age 15, with progression from minor covert behaviors to property damage to serious delinquency; and (3) An **authority conflict pathway**, beginning before age 12, with stubborn behavior preceding defiance and authority conflict (see also Burke et al., 2002). Trajectories specific to delinquency have been presented: one involving

Kevin Moloney/Getty Images

The different profiles of the two teens responsible for the Columbine shootings reflect contrasting pathways leading to the same extreme act of antisocial behavior.

arrests occurring before age 13 and progressing to serious and chronic adult criminal behavior, and the other involving later arrests and less frequent adult crime (Clingempeel & Henggeler, 2003; Loeber & Farrington, 2000; Patterson & Yoerger, 2002); other detailed trajectories have also been described (Blitstein, Murray, Lytle, Birnbaum, & Perry, 2005; Raskin White, Bates, & Buyske, 2001; Wiesner & Windle, 2004). Probably some of the most difficult to understand final outcomes of these trajectories are those culminating in school shootings (see Box 13.3).

Family environment certainly contributes to the presence and stability of these early negative adjustments (Kimonis et al., 2006). The impact of parent personality and coercive parenting attitudes and behaviors on young children's problem behavior has already been summarized in several sections in the chapter on oppositional defiant disorder, so we will focus here on parent factors in late childhood and adolescence. Family instability and conflict are associated with children's worsening externalizing behaviors (Burt, McGue, Krueger, & Iacono, 2005; Milan, Pinderhughes, & Conduct Problems Prevention Research Group, 2006). Parents of deviant youth appear to become disengaged over time, with less monitoring of their children's behaviors and activities (Dishion, Nelson, & Bullock, 2004). Some parents become more tolerant of externalizing behaviors, but many still express dissatisfaction with conduct problems, school difficulties, and drug use (Donohue, DeCato, Azrin, & Teichner, 2001).

BOX 13:3 THE CHILD IN CONTEXT

School Shootings

In recent years, the tragic act of homicides occurring at schools ("school shootings") has come to be seen as the ultimate expression of adolescent antisocial behavior. While accounting for fewer than 1% of homicides among school-age youth, school shootings generate tremendous media attention and contribute to a climate of fear and worry far beyond the statistical reality of the act. This is especially true of those shootings that involve multiple victims. Prominent examples include shootings in Paducah, Kentucky, in 1997, Littleton, Colorado, in 1999, and Red Lake, Minnesota, in 2005.

High-impact, low-frequency events such as school shootings are difficult to predict. Research related to common factors is being done in order to improve recognition of warning signs and to help schools develop prevention strategies. For example, a comprehensive study of 10 school shootings showed that in every case the shooters had threatened to commit violence at school, were judged to have poor coping skills, were known to be fascinated with weapons and explosives, and had access to firearms. In nearly all cases, there was a documented history of violence, social isolation resulting from rejection and bullying by peers, and association with an antisocial peer group (Verlinden, Hersen, & Thomas, 2000).

It is also important, however, to recognize that these terrible incidents can be seen as examples of *equifinality* (i.e., different developmental pathways leading to the same outcome). Even allowing for many common elements, each set of circumstances is unique, as are the developmental, personality, and mental health characteristics of each assailant. This point is well illustrated by the infamous shooting at Columbine High School in Littleton, Colorado, in 1999. An unusual aspect of that shooting was the fact that it involved a pair of teens. Extensive analysis by the FBI and mental health experts led to the conclusion that the two teens, Eric Harris and Dylan Klebold, "were radically different individuals, with vastly different motives and opposite mental conditions" (Cullen, 2004). The FBI studies concluded that Klebold fit the familiar profile of the troubled, alienated, and depressed adolescent with the potential to strike out at others in response to his own emotional distress. Harris, on the other hand, was seen as a "cold, calculating, and homicidal" psychopath.

In this age of nearly instant and worldwide media exposure, school shootings will continue to evoke feelings of vulnerability, dismay, and horror from the general public. School, mental health, and law enforcement professionals will continue to study past shootings for insight into how best to address predicting and preventing these tragic events.

The breakdown in family management leads some adolescents to associate more frequently with deviant peers, and this leads to an escalation of CD behaviors. Groups of deviant peers experience more negative emotion and exhibit more support for rule breaking and aggression (Bagwell & Coie, 2004). Sexual activity, sexually transmitted diseases, and unplanned pregnancies are primary health concerns for adolescent girls with CD. Connections between problem behaviors and disengagement from school have also been observed; symmetrically, staying in school despite problem behaviors has a protective benefit (Henry, Caspi, Moffitt, Harrington, & Silva, 1999; Steinberg & Avenevoli, 1998).

Developmental relations between conduct disorder and other psychopathologies have also been examined, and a "dynamic comorbidity" has been noted (Lahey, Loeber, Burke, Rathouz, & McBurnett, 2002). With respect to CD and ADHD, children diagnosed with ADHD exhibit increasing levels of disruptive and antisocial behaviors as they age (Loeber et al., 2000). It remains unclear whether ADHD alone is a precursor to CD, or if CD occurs only with the earlier combination of ADHD and ODD (Loeber et al., 2000). There appears to be a reciprocal relationship between CD and substance abuse, with CD sometimes preceding and sometimes following substance abuse (Loeber et al., 2000). When CD and substance abuse are both diagnosed, the risk for the emergence of antisocial personality disorder increases for both boys and girls (Myers, Stewart, & Brown, 1998).

Describing another connection, Capaldi and Stoolmiller (1999) state: "conduct problems interfere with . . . the development of competencies, thus causing a developmental chain reaction of failures" (p. 61); this chain may lead to depression. Additional links among CD, anxiety, and depression have also been explored (Lahey & Waldman, 2003; Loeber, Farrington, Stouthamer-Loeber, Moffitt, Caspi, & Lynam, 2001). For girls, these links may be especially problematic, with ties to later substance abuse (Keenan et al., 1999).

Etiology

Just as there are multiple ways in which conduct disorder unfolds over time, there are multiple factors and multiple combinations of factors that underlie its emergence. As with all other forms of psychopathology, both genetic and environmental factors contribute to the development of conduct disorder (Arseneault et al., 2003; Button, Scourfield, Martin, Purcell, & McGuffin, 2005; Dodge & Pettit, 2003; Ehringer, Rhee, Young, Corley, & Hewitt, 2006; Moffitt, 2005), and a transactional model of cause appears most useful in explaining the disorder (Brennan, Hall, Bor, Najman, & Williams, 2003; Dodge & Pettit, 2003). Similar to other psychopathologies as well is the observation that the number and accumulation of risk factors is as critical as their type (Burke et al., 2002; Farrington, 2005). With respect to the child-onset versus adolescent-onset CD, the relative strength and specific combination of risk factors are hypothesized to lead to earlier versus later emergence of disorder (Lahey & Waldman, 2003).

Genes and Heredity

There is ample evidence for familial aggregation and familial transmission of conduct disorder (Burke et al., 2002; Eley, Lichtenstein, & Moffitt, 2003; Scourfield, Van den Bree, Martin, & McGuffin, 2004), and both additive and interactive models of genetic influence are documented (Pérusse & Gendreau, 2005). As one example, Dishion, Owen, and Bullock (2004) have shown that fathers' antisocial behaviors as children are directly linked to their 9-year-old sons' already deviant behaviors. There are data that support distinctive contributions of genes to the development of conduct disorder, as well as data that support overlapping contributions among conduct disorder, oppositional defiant disorder, and attention deficit hyperactivity disorder (Dick, Viken, Kaprio, Pulkkinen, & Rose, 2005; Lahey & Waldman, 2003). Studies of gene locations are promising, with several investigations showing links between conduct disorder and alcohol abuse (Dick et al., 2004). It is important to note that there appears to be more evidence for the impact of genetics on aggressive forms of CD, compared to nonaggressive forms; there are also differences related to gender (DiLalla, 2002; Eley, Lichtenstein, & Stevenson, 1999; Miles & Carey, 1997).

Neuroanatomy and Neurochemistry

Many studies of the structure and function of the neural system and conduct disorder reveal underarousal of the autonomic nervous system and cortisol dysregulation (Burke et al., 2002), neurocognitive impairments and executive dysfunction (Coolidge, DenBoer, & Segal, 2004; Golden & Golden, 2001; Raine et al., 2005), and links between serotonin and aggression and between testosterone and social dominance (Rowe, Maughan, Worthman, Costello, & Angold, 2004). Recent examinations of brain functioning show disinhibition, emotion dysregulation, and problems with attention (Du et al., 2006; Du, Wang, Li, Wang, & Jiang, 2005; Iacono, Malone, & McGue, 2003). Although many of these difficulties are hypothetically tied to genetics, prenatal and perinatal problems such as maternal smoking and substance abuse have also been implicated (Burke et al., 2002).

Child Characteristics

Lahey and Waldman (2003) focus on the notion of **antisocial propensity** to explain the collection of child characteristics that increase the likelihood of conduct disorder. The factors that underlie antisocial propensity in the early years include temperament styles and cognitive abilities; those that become more important during adolescence include peer relationships and other social variables. Looking more closely at temperament, researchers have focused on negative emotionality (especially proneness to anger and frustration) and inflexibility as dimensions associated with externalizing behaviors (Burke et al., 2002; Caspi et al., 2003; Frick & Morris, 2004; Goldsmith, Lemery, & Essex, 2004; Sanson & Prior, 1999).

For hard-to-manage children, the transition to elementary school may be very problematic (Hughes, Cutting, & Dunn, 2001); these children may display strongly negative responses to everyday frustrations, poor behavioral regulation, and for some, a preoccupation with violent fantasy play (Dunn & Hughes, 2001; Hughes et al., 2001; Hughes, White, Sharpen & Dunn, 2000). Thinking again about the developmental course of CD, there appear to be two developmental pathways influenced by temperamental vulnerability. The first involves difficulties with emotional regulation that "seem to best explain conduct problems and aggression that are displayed in the context of high emotional arousal" (Frick & Morris, 2004, p. 59). Another pathway leading to aggression involves behaviors that are "generally unprovoked and used for personal gain" (Frick & Morris, 2004, p. 60). This more instrumental pathway is associated with the underarousal of the central nervous system (Fung et al., 2005). Low levels of fear and anxiety lead to increased risk taking and the delayed or deviant development of the capacity for empathy and guilt; indeed much of moral socialization appears dependent on negative emotional arousal (Blair, 1997, 2005). For some children, these vulnerabilities can be offset by either the development of emotion regulation skills or emotional aspects of conscience; matching child temperament and parenting style to therapeutically exploit individual differences may be key to reducing negative outcomes (Frick & Morris, 2004; Kochanska, 1995, 1997).

Avoidant or disorganized attachment histories are also likely contributors to children's deficits related to negative emotionality and emotion regulation (Aguilar, Stroufe, Egeland, & Carlson, 2000; Lyons-Ruth, 1996; Parker et al., 1995); positive attachments promote the positive friendships that are protective factors (Weinfield, Ogawa, & Sroufe, 1997; Zimmermann, 2004). Behavioral impulsivity

and lower levels of effortful control have also been observed (Burke et al., 2002; Frick & Morris, 2004). The negative consequences of impulsivity are heightened by the presence of characteristics such as being daring (i.e., the enjoyment of exciting, risky, and possibly dangerous activities) (Farrington & West, 1993; Lahey & Waldman, 2003), or being disinhibited (Iacono et al., 2003; Kagan, Reznick, & Snidman, 1988). As illustrated in the last chapters on internalizing disorders, the temperamental categories of resilient, overcontrolled, and undercontrolled boys provide a framework for understanding adolescent externalizing psychopathology (Block, 1961; Robins, John, Caspi, Moffitt, & Stouhamer-Loeber, 1996; see Figure 13.3).

Another personality trait that contributes to antisocial propensity involves a child's or adolescent's displays of **callous or unemotional traits** (i.e., a lack of empathy, concern, or guilt) (Kimonis et al., 2006; Lahey & Waldman, 2003; Waschbusch, Walsh, Andrade, King, & Carrey, 2007). Adolescents who are described as callous and unemotional exhibit more severe and more aggressive conduct disorder (Frick et al., 2003). Patterns of stability

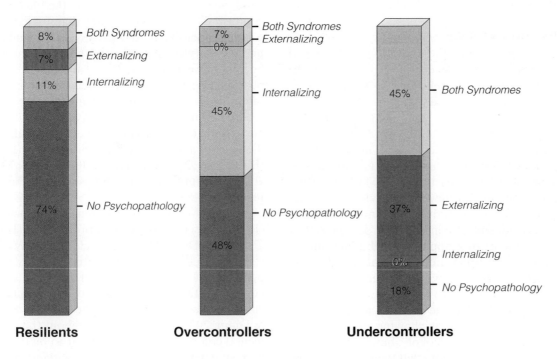

FIGURE 13:3 **Externalizing disorders in resilient, overcontrolled, and undercontrolled boys.**
Source: From Robins, R.W., John, O.P., Caspi A., Moffitt, T.E., & Stouhamer-Loeber, M. (1996), "Resilient, overcontrolled and undercontrolled boys: Three replicable personality types", 'Journal of Personality and Social Psychology', 70(1), p. 167. Original figure is titled 'three replicable personality types'. Copyright © 1996 American Psychological Association. Reprinted by permission of the American Psychological Association.

for conduct disorder also differ depending on the presence of callous and unemotional behaviors (Frick & Dantagnan, 2005). Other researchers have described the potent combination of personality factors including callousness as key elements in the emergence of full-blown conduct disorder (Lynam et al., 2005). Related to callousness is the personality construct of psychopathy (Salekin et al., 2005). Several dimensions of psychopathy have been observed in adolescents: the callous-unemotional trait, impulsivity, and narcissism (Frick, Bodin, & Barry, 2000), with different studies suggesting various relations among psychopathy, conduct disorder, and normally developing personality (Espelage, Mebane, & Adams, 2004; Lynam, 1998; Lynam et al., 2005; Lynam & Gudonis, 2005).

In addition to a hostile attributional style, deficits and delays in cognitive abilities also appear to be critical factors in the development of conduct disorders. Lower levels of verbal intelligence and slow language development predict higher rates of conduct disorders in children and adolescents (Bellmore, Witkow, Graham, & Juvonen, 2005; Brownlie et al., 2004; Dodge, 2006; Lahey & Waldman, 2003; Waschbusch, 2002). Taken together with impaired social cognition, impaired moral reasoning, and neurologically based executive dysfunction, these are youth with fewer personal coping skills and resources (Bennett, Farrington, & Huesmann, 2005; Crick, Grotpeter, & Bigbee, 2002; Raaijmakers, Engels, & Van Hoof, 2005).

The impact of gender has been repeatedly discussed in connection with conduct disorder. Boys are overrepresented in conduct-disordered populations for a variety of reasons, including higher levels of antisocial propensity and genetic influences on the timing of puberty; most of these differences are reflected in developmentally later conduct problems (Lahey & Waldman, 2003). Athletic involvement is linked to higher levels of violence in young men. Looking more carefully at the correlation, it appears that "jock" identity (rather than athletic involvement itself) is more strongly related to violence and that violence tends to be nonfamilial rather than familial (Miller, Melnick, Farrell, Sabo, & Barnes, 2006).

Other individual characteristics that are associated with CD include being a younger sibling (Brotman, Gouley, O'Neal, & Klein, 2004), having low self-esteem (Donnellan, Trzesniewski, Robins, Moffitt, & Caspi, 2005), and early puberty (Graber,

Lewinsohn, Seeley, & Brooks-Gunn, 1997; Keenan et al., 1999). Adolescents who experience early puberty in the context of harsh parenting and in an at-risk neighborhood are more likely to exhibit conduct problems (Burt, McGue, DeMarte, Krueger, & Iacono, 2006; Ge, Brody, Conger, Simons, & Murry, 2002). Maltreatment significantly increases the risk for CD (Burke et al., 2002; Hilarski, 2004; Jaffee et al., 2005; Jaffee, Caspi, Moffitt, & Taylor, 2004; Lee & Hoaken, 2007). It is hypothesized that early abuse results in alienation and dysregulation, and these lead to antisocial behavior (Egeland, Yates, Appleyard, & van Dulmen, 2002). Witnessing domestic violence and being exposed to community violence are also important risk factors for CD (Jaffee, Moffitt, Caspi, Taylor, & Arseneault, 2002; Pearce, Jones, Schwab-Stone, & Ruchkin, 2003).

Parent and Family Characteristics

The direct and indirect impact of parents on the development of most instances of conduct disorder cannot be overestimated. Keeping in mind that genetic and environmental factors exert new influences on adolescents and parent-adolescent relationships in typically developing youth (Elkins, McGue, & Iacono, 1997; Neiderhiser, Pike, Hetherington, & Reiss, 1998; Neiderhiser et al., 2004), we can begin to think carefully about the continuity of aggression and conduct problems in adolescents across multiple generations (Capaldi, Pears, Patterson, & Owen, 2003; Smith & Farrington, 2004) and the double whammy of high-risk genes and high-risk environments that some adolescents experience (Jaffee, Moffitt, Caspi, & Taylor, 2003, p. 109).

With respect to parental psychopathology, we know that depression in either mothers or fathers increases the risk for conduct disorder (Kim-Cohen, Moffitt, Taylor, Pawlby, & Caspi, 2005; Ohannessian et al., 2005). Antisocial personality disorder (ASPD) and/or substance abuse in fathers are frequently cited risks (Frick & Loney, 2002; Loukas, Zucker, Fitzgerald, & Krull, 2003). Depression in mothers coupled with ASPD in fathers is another high-risk combination (Marmorstein & Iacono, 2004). Parental psychopathology has both direct (e.g., genetic) and indirect effects (e.g., marital conflict, family dysfunction and instability, and poor parenting) that impact adolescent adjustment (Aguilar et al., 2000; Becker, Stuewig, Herrera, & McCloskey, 2004; Jester et al., 2005; Parker et al., 1995). Some children and adolescents appear to be even more harmed

David Young-Wolff /Getty Images

Lack of parental monitoring is one link to adolescent conduct problems.

than others by family conflict and chaos (Button et al., 2005); being a girl and positive relationships with siblings or friends may moderate this risk (Criss, Pettit, Bates, Dodge, & Lapp, 2002; Howe, Aquan-Assee, Bukowski, Lehoux, & Rinaldi, 2001; Kaplan & Liu, 1999; Schwartz, Dodge, Pettit, Bates, & Conduct Problems Prevention Research Group, 2000; Tucker, Barber, & Eccles, 1997). However, siblings may also collude together to "promote deviance and undermine parenting" (Bullock & Dishion, 2002).

Parenting practices such as harsh and coercive punishments have also been identified as causal factors (Burke et al., 2002; Deater-Deckard & Dodge, 1997; Stormshak, Bierman, McMahon, Lengua, & Conduct Problems Prevention Research Group, 2000). Data on physical punishment suggests that the association between physical punishment and child aggression is somewhat moderated by cultural norms, but even so, more frequent, more intense physical punishments are tied to both aggression and anxiety

(Lansford et al., 2005). Neglectful or indulgent parenting has also been associated with externalizing problems (Steinberg, Blatt-Eisengart, & Cauffman, 2006). These forms of negative parenting, including lack of warmth and regard, have been observed throughout the child's early and later years, and are similar for groups of conduct-disordered European-American and African-American children (Campbell, Shaw, & Gilliom, 2000; Caspi et al., 2004; Kim et al., 2003).

Parental permissiveness and poor monitoring of adolescents and their activities has received growing theoretical and research attention (Brody, 2003; Dishion & Bullock, 2002; Jewell & Stark, 2003; Kerr & Stattin, 2003; Steinberg & Avenevoli, 1998), with links observed between lack of monitoring and conduct disorder (Dishion & McMahon, 1998; Kiesner, Dishion, & Poulin, 2001; Laird, Pettit, Dodge, & Bates, 2003). Conversely, parental involvement has been identified as a protective factor; so has religiosity (Pearce et al., 2003). In fact, "adolescents from authoritative homes are more susceptible to prosocial peer pressure (e.g., pressure to do well in school) but less susceptible to antisocial peer pressure (e.g., pressure to use illicit drugs and alcohol)" (Collins et al., 2000, p. 227). Appropriate monitoring may be especially important in problematic, high-risk neighborhoods (Beyers, Bates, Pettit, & Dodge, 2003). Differences in parenting practices related to ethnicity have also been correlated with CD (Lansford, Deater-Deckard, Dodge, Bates, & Pettit, 2004; McCoy, Frick, Loney, & Ellis, 1999). Finally, the community context of parenting is a key variable in the emergence or prevention of CD (Broidy et al., 2003; Pinderhughes, Nix, Foster, Jones, & Conduct Problems Prevention Research Group, 2001).

Peers and Peer Relationships

Peers and peer relationships have a notable impact on both the development and the later improvement or deterioration of conduct disorder (Adams, Bukowski, & Bagwell, 2005; Kupersmidt & DeRosier, 2004; Lansford, Criss, Pettit, Dodge, & Bates, 2003; Vitaro, Tremblay, & Bukowski, 2001). Various forms of peer difficulties need to be considered, including difficulty forming and keeping relationships, aggression and bullying, and peer rejection. Related to the emergence of psychopathology, some common factors underlie many types of peer difficulties. For example, deficits in social cognition are likely to negatively influence relationships; these deficits are reflected in adolescents who misinterpret others' social intentions, who display more incompetent problem solving during peer conflicts, or who are inaccurate in predicting the outcomes of their own negative behaviors (Parker et al., 1995).

Peer dislike, rejection, and victimization often begin early, and are a key predictor of later problems (Dodge et al., 2003; Ialongo, Vaden-Kiernan, & Kellam, 1998; Kupersmidt & DeRosier, 2004; Miller-Johnson, Coie, Maumary-Gremaud, Bierman, & Conduct Problems Prevention Research Group, 2002; Rose, Swenson, & Carlson, 2004). One of the most common reasons for rejection is angry or aggressive behavior. Hughes et al. (2001) describe children who "act nasty" when frustrated. "In everyday life, it is likely that below-average cognitive abilities increase the likelihood of actual failure in school tasks, games, and sports. Thus, if children with less well developed cognitive skills and early conduct problems often fail, and react emotionally when they fail, they may be children that their well-behaved peers would reject" (Lahey & Waldman, 2003). Other rejected children behave aggressively following exclusion or ridicule (Werner & Crick, 2004). Boys with histories of externalizing problems are more reactive than other boys, and appear to hold grudges longer (Waschbusch et al., 2002). And some rejected boys become even more aggressive with ongoing rejection (Guerra, Asher, & DeRosier, 2004). Hurt feelings and rejection sensitivity may be key indices of risk, with more sensitive children and adolescents behaving more aggressively following rejection (Downey, Lebolt, Rincon, & Freitas, 1998).

One of the most negative consequences of peer rejection is that rejected children and adolescents associate with other rejected children and adolescents. Deviant groups emerge, and pathways to conduct disorder evolve (Brendgen, Vitaro, & Bukowski, 2000a, 2000b; Dishion, Poulin, & Burraston, 2001; Parker et al., 1995; Snyder et al., 2008). There may be important gender differences. Both antisocial boys and girls experience rejection by peers, but boys end up associating with more deviant peers with somewhat different developmental outcomes (Van Lier, Vitaro, Wanner, Vuijk, & Crijnen, 2005). Friendships with deviant peers do not substitute for friendships with normally developing adolescents. The quality of the relationships is different (Dishion, Eddy, Haas, & Li, 1997; Poulin, Dishion, & Hass, 1999) and being part of a delinquent group exacerbates one's own delinquent tendencies (Lacourse, Nagin, Tremblay, Vitaro, &

Claes, 2003). Violent behavior and gang activity are further steps on a worsening trajectory (Lahey, Gordon, Loeber, Stouthamer-Loeber, & Farrington, 1999). Gang association and gang membership are related to aggression, conduct problems, drug-related activity, and violent crime; this is a "powerful social influence" to understand and address (Lahey & Waldman, 2003).

Other Environmental Variables

Many studies of larger environmental variables such as ethnicity, socioeconomic status, and neighborhoods, provide context to current conceptualizations of CD. For example, once SES and neighborhood factors are accounted for, there is little or no influence of race or ethnicity on the development of CD (Burke et al., 2002; Lahey & Waldman, 2003; Stouthamer-Loeber, Loeber, Wei, Farrington, & Wikstroem, 2002). SES is inversely related to CD, even though the majority of youth from financially disadvantaged backgrounds do not exhibit disorders (Lahey & Waldman, 2003). Combinations of risk factors dramatically increase the likelihood of CD. Hypotheses exploring the social learning of conduct disorder emphasize the transactions among high-crime neighborhoods, poor parenting, delinquent peer groups, and a lack of economic resources (Chung & Steinberg, 2006; Guerra, Huesmann, & Spindler, 2003; Lahey & Waldman, 2003; Lynam et al., 2000). For some adolescents, neighborhood cohesion may, in fact, buffer the effects of poor parenting (Silk, Sessa, Sheffield Morris, Steinberg, & Avenevoli, 2004). Examining gene-environment interactions provides a last source of data on the etiology of CD. According to Lahey and Waldman (2003), "genetic influences on conduct problems can be muted by favorable social learning environments." Studies of children adopted by well-adjusted parents show lower levels of CD. Also, "different individuals respond in different ways to the social factors that encourage conduct problems." Some adolescents move toward problematic behaviors, peers, and activities; others move away.

Assessment and Diagnosis

Although there have been changes in diagnostic criteria for CD, especially for girls, patterns of externalizing behavior are usually observed more quickly compared to patterns of internalizing behavior (Delligatti, Akin-Little, & Little, 2003). Given the individual impairment associated with CD, and the effects of conduct-disordered children and adolescents on their families, teachers, peers, neighborhoods, and society, it is imperative to identify early and identify correctly. Indeed, early screening in kindergarten, with ratings made by parents and teachers, can identify children at risk for CD; this makes early prevention efforts possible (Jones et al., 2002).

Before CD is diagnosed, careful distinctions need to be made between more common adolescent problems and more severe psychopathology (Willoughby, Chalmers, & Busseri, 2004). Multiple instruments and evidence-based assessments, including observations, parent and teacher ratings, self-reports, and lab tests, are essential (Collett, Ohan, & Myers, 2003; Frick & Loney, 2000; Lewinsohn, Rohde, & Farrington, 2000; Malone, 2000; McMahon & Frick, 2005). There are also data suggesting that certain instruments provide useful information about the potential for violence in early adulthood (Gretton, Hare, & Catchpole, 2004). With genetic, parental, and familial factors influencing CD, another key to accurate assessment and treatment planning for an adolescent is an assessment of his or her parents.

Self-reporting by children and adolescents about conduct problems seems an unlikely source of good data. However, young children and adolescents provide useful information (Arseneault, Kim-Cohen, Taylor, Caspi, & Moffitt, 2005; Gadow et al., 2002; Hartung, McCarthy, Milich, & Martin, 2005). Keep in mind that even though most adolescents do not refer themselves for treatment, many with difficulties, particularly peer difficulties, do want help (Asher & Paquette, 2003; Asher, Rose, & Gabriel, 2001).

Issues related to differential diagnosis focus on distinctions among CD, ODD, and ADHD, and between CD and mania. It is possible to differentiate CD from each of these other disorders, but clinicians must understand that CD and ADHD, and CD and bipolar disorder, may co-occur, with appropriately separate diagnoses (Biederman et al., 2003; Kim & Miklowitz, 2002; Loeber et al., 2000; Waschbusch, 2002). CD may also be comorbid with either anxiety or depression (Loeber et al., 2000). Questioning about depression is especially important because the combination of CD and depression involves much higher risk for substance abuse and

suicidality; girls are more likely to display this combination (Loeber et al. 2000).

Intervention

Prevention

Conduct disorder in adolescence is often resistant to treatment, so prevention of CD assumes even more importance compared to prevention of other psychopathologies (Burke et al., 2002). Prevention programs involve schools, children, and their families and communities. There is evidence of the positive impact of universal school-based programs focused on self-control, problem solving, and peer relationships (Bierman et al., 2007; Conduct Problems Prevention Research Group, 1999; Greenberg et al., 2003; Lacourse et al., 2002; Van Lier, Vuijk, & Crijnen, 2005). In many of these school-based programs, parents and families choose to participate and levels of engagement in the therapeutic process differ (Orrell-Valente, Pinderhughes, Valente, Laird, & Conduct Problems Prevention Research Group, 1999). Programs designed to prevent bullying are increasingly incorporated in school curricula in many countries and cultures (Olweus, 2005); specific components of such programs focus on social competence and a positive school environment (Orpinas & Horne, 2006a). The timing of prevention programs is important; the earlier the implementation, the better. Plans focused on at-risk toddler boys and first graders have shown positive results (Ialongo, Poduska, Werthamer, & Kellam, 2001; Shaw, Dishion, Supplee, Gardner, & Arends, 2006).

Prevention efforts focused on youth and their families must be comprehensive to achieve positive results. That is, they must address all of the factors that contribute to the emergence and the maintenance of CD, including troublesome and daring behaviors, low IQ and academic difficulties, antisocial parents, and so on (Farrington, 2000). Several prevention programs emphasize the need to promote child competence in as many ways as possible (Brody, Kim, Murry, & Brown, 2004). Youth development programs, designed to foster adolescent-adult relationships, also show long-term positive outcomes (Roth, Brooks-Gunn, Murray, & Foster, 1998). Combining these types of programs with school programs, with multiple options for maximum effect, is a further improvement (Nix, Pinderhughes, Bierman, Maples, & Conduct Problems Prevention Research Group, 2005).

One example of a community prevention program is the "Overcoming the Odds" study, comparing African-American adolescents' participation in gangs versus community organizations. One key aspect of this successful effort is connecting developmental strengths displayed by the adolescents with supports from their ecological contexts (Taylor et al., 2005). Overall, there are nine characteristics associated with effective prevention efforts: a comprehensive approach, a theory-driven model, a well-trained staff, varied methods, sufficient intervention intensity, opportunities for positive relationships, appropriate timing, sociocultural relevance, and outcome evaluation (Nation et al., 2003).

Treatment

For both typical and struggling adolescents, there are multiple opportunities for reorganization in adolescence, but many adolescents may be reluctant to become engaged in a change process (Cicchetti & Rogosch, 2002; Weisz & Hawley, 2002); indeed, adolescents with low levels of emotional awareness and competence are likely to be especially difficult in the beginning of treatment (Ciarrochi, Deane, Wilson, & Rickwood, 2002). It is essential, then, to address the motivation for change and personal responsibility for change immediately in the therapeutic relationship. For example, in designing treatments, clinicians may want to allow an adolescent some responsibility for goal setting, and decisions about discipline and rule-breaking (DeRoma, Lassiter, & Davis, 2004). These efforts may foster motivation, attendance, and treatment adherence (Nock & Kazdin, 2005). In addition, a strong therapeutic alliance must be established that usually includes both the adolescent and his or her parents; the roles and responsibilities of all participants must be clear (Kazdin, Marciano, & Whitley, 2005).

Child and Adolescent Approaches

While there is some evidence that mood stabilizers may be useful, there is not a lot of work on medication management for CD (Burke et al., 2002). Much more research has been done on forms of psychotherapy, although we need to keep in mind that the "typical conduct-disordered child in treatment is a 9-year-old Caucasian boy from a lower middle income background, whose mother may or may not be participating in his cognitive-behavioral treatment for conduct problems" (Brestan & Eyberg, 1998, p. 187). The generalization of results of psychotherapy studies across gender, age, and ethnicity remains to be further explored. Treatments with empirical support include Kazdin's (2005) problem-solving skills training and anger management programs (Brestan & Eyberg, 1998; Weisz, 2004). Problem-solving skills training involves a focus on cognitive skills such as interpreting normal peer behavior as less threatening (Thomas, 2006) and social skills such as learning scripts for how to join a group of peers already interacting (Asher, Parker, & Walker, 1998; DeRosier & Marcus, 2005). Understanding the impact of neurological dysfunction on adolescent problem-solving abilities may enhance treatment outcomes (Coolidge, DenBoer, & Segal, 2004). Anger management therapies emphasize the identification of triggers, learning how to cope with intense emotion, role playing, and stress inoculation (Weisz, 2004).

Parent and Family Treatments

Among the most effective interventions are those involving parents (Brestan & Eyberg, 1998; Weisz, 2004). Indeed, "effective parenting is the most powerful way to reduce adolescent problem behaviors" (Kumpfer & Alvarado, 2003, p. 457), although improvements do not always bring adolescents into the normal range of functioning (Burke et al., 2002; Thomas, 2006). As noted, motivation, attendance, and treatment adherence are critical issues. Both families and parents in treatment have high drop-out rates; designing one-session interventions, therefore, may be a meaningful therapeutic approach (Lim, Stormshak, & Dishion, 2005). Parent-based therapies with proven results include behavioral parent training based on Patterson's coercion model and videotape training of effective parent skills based on Webster-Stratton's work (Brestan & Eyberg, 1998; Weisz, 2004). Other examples of comprehensive approaches with good results include the Adolescent Transitions Program (Dishion & Kavanagh, 2003) and the GREAT Families Program (Smith et al., 2004).

Group and Community Interventions

Intensive, multimodal approaches work best, such as those reviewed by the Conduct Problems Prevention Research Group (Burke et al., 2002). One example of such an approach is the Fast Track program described in Chapter 10 on ODD (Bierman et al., 2004). Another is multisystemic therapy, based on Henggeler's research (Henggeler &

Lee, 2003; Weisz, 2004). The mechanisms and direction of change in multisystemic therapy include: adherence to treatment model --> improved family relationships --> decreased delinquent associations --> decreased delinquent behavior (Huey, Henggeler, Brondino, & Pickrel, 2000).

Out-of-home treatments are increasing, with family-style residential care and token economies showing good outcomes for some adolescents (Field, Nash, Handwerk, & Friman, 2004). Specialized foster care may be an option (Dodge, Dishion, & Lansford, 2006). Military-style residential programs ("boot camps") can work, but their efficacy may depend on adolescent willingness to participate (Weis, Wilson, & Whitemarsh, 2005). Both boys and girls improve in these settings, but they appear less useful to girls with a history of maltreatment and comorbid internalizing disorders (Weis, Whitemarsh, & Wilson, 2005).

One critical caveat about treatments that involve groups of conduct-disordered adolescents relates to peer contagion. **Peer contagion** involves the sharing of information about conduct problems, including drugs, weapons, targets of negative behaviors, and immediate and powerful reinforcement of deviancy (Boxer, Guerra, Huesmann, & Morales, 2005; Burke et al., 2002; Dodge et al., 2006; Gifford-Smith, Dodge, Dishion, & McCord, 2005). Thinking back to descriptions of the role of deviant peers in eliciting and maintaining conduct-disordered behavior, it is not hard to imagine the likely effects of including deviant peers in treatment settings. Although "proponents believe that deviant youth can empathize with each other, learn valuable lessons from each other, and provide real-life interactions for each other that are grist for intervention" (Dodge et al., 2006, p. 3), numerous clinical trials indicate not only a lessening of positive impact, but increases in adverse impacts, with worse outcomes compared to control groups (Dodge et al., 2006). Participants with lower initial levels of delinquent behavior are at particular risk (Dishion, Bullock, & Granic, 2002; Macgowen & Wagner, 2005; Poulin, Dishion, & Burraston, 2001).

Well-intentioned adults need to be increasingly cautious about who to include in treatment groups (which include residential interventions, group homes, and group therapies such as social skills training), because "perversely, much of what we do as public policy is to segregate deviant youth from their mainstream peers and assign them to settings with other deviant youth" (Dodge et al., 2006, p. 3). "The best empirical evidence suggests that the first solutions are to eliminate the routine practices of tracking low-performing youth into isolated classrooms, mandatory grade retention, self-contained classrooms for unruly students in special education, group in-school suspension, placement into

When adolescents with conduct disorder are grouped together, as they are in juvenile detention centers, they may share information (peer contagion), increasing the likelihood of negative behaviors in the future.

Mike Fiala/Contributor/Getty Images

alternative schools, and expulsion" (Dodge et al., 2006, p. 11). In order to support children and adolescents with conduct disorders, prevention and treatment programs must be reworked to focus on adults (parents and teachers) and nondeviant peers, and changes must be made across disciplines, in mental health clinics, educational and school settings, the juvenile justice system, and community organizations (Dodge et al., 2006).

■ Key Terms

Instrumental relationships (pg. 243)
Affiliative relationships (pg. 243)
Moral development (pg. 244)
Peer subcultures (pg. 245)
Conduct disorder (pg. 247)
Overt/covert dimension (pg. 247)
Destructive/nondestructive dimension (pg. 247)
Aggression (pg. 247)
Instrumental aggression (pg. 247)
Reactive aggression (pg. 247)
Overt aggression (pg. 247)
Covert aggression (pg. 247)
Childhood-onset subtype (pg. 248)
Adolescent-onset subtype (pg. 248)
Life-course persistent trajectory (pg. 248)
Adolescence-limited trajectory (pg. 248)
Reactive-oppositional patterns (pg. 250)
Proactive-callous patterns (pg. 250)
Impulsive-overactive patterns (pg. 250)
Bullying (pg. 251)
Overt pathway (pg. 251)
Covert pathway (pg. 251)
Authority conflict pathway (pg. 251)
Antisocial propensity (pg. 253)
Callous/unemotional traits (pg. 254)
Peer contagion (pg. 260)

■ Chapter Summary

- Much of adolescent development occurs in the social context of relationships with peers and parents.
- Peer relationships, in particular, can serve as either protective factors or risk factors in the development of a wide range of behavioral problems.
- Social aggression in adolescence can be expressed both directly through physical aggression (more typical among boys) or through relational aggression (more typical among girls).
- In contrast to oppositional defiant disorder, conduct disorder is characterized by the severity of the externalizing behaviors and the degree of impairment associated with the disorder.
- Conduct disorders are further differentiated into categories based on the characteristic types and patterns of externalizing behaviors and whether the onset of the behaviors occurs during childhood or adolescence.
- The adolescent onset of conduct disorder is significantly more common than childhood onset.
- The relative stability of conduct disorder and the negative impact on healthy development contribute to increased risk for other forms of psychopathology.
- Two pathways, one involving behavioral undercontrol in the face of high emotional arousal, and one involving the role of underarousal of the central nervous system, may lead to the development of conduct disorder.
- Because conduct disorder in adolescence is relatively resistant to treatment, particular emphasis is placed on prevention programs and intervention approaches that involve parents along with the adolescent.

CHAPTER 14

Substance Abuse Disorders in Adolescence

COMPARED TO THEIR YOUNGER SELVES, adolescents can get into trouble in a number of new and more dangerous ways. Driving recklessly, becoming sexually active, gambling, and using drugs and alcohol are common forms of risk taking that are frequently observed as adolescents explore adult behaviors and adult roles. Some of these behaviors are associated with the three leading causes of mortality in adolescents: accidental death (including car accidents), homicide, and suicide (Kelley, Schochet, & Landry, 2004; Windle & Windle, 2006). Given this increased vulnerability, it is often difficult for concerned adults to keep a developmental perspective in mind (Schulenberg, Maggs, Steinman, & Zucker, 2001). Even so, it is essential to understand that adolescent health and development are embedded in evolutionary, historical, and cultural contexts (Crockett, 1997; Spear, 2003; Williams, Holmbeck, & Greenley, 2002), and that "risk taking and novelty seeking are hallmarks of typical adolescent behavior" (Kelley et al., 2004, p. 27).

Developmental Tasks and Challenges Related to Neurodevelopment and Risk Taking

Of all the myriad events that occur during adolescence, **brain development** is one of the most significant. Advances in MRI and fMRI technologies make it clear that the brain continues to develop throughout adolescence and early adulthood, with increases in size and the thickness and number of neuronal connections (De Bellis et al., 2001; Giedd et al., 2004; Sowell et al., 2003; Walker, 2002). This development is a dynamic, nonlinear process, with frontal lobe maturation progressing in a back-to-front direction; more complex cognitive processes (e.g., difficult decision making with multiple options, each of which has mixed positive and negative consequences) mature later than more basic cognitive processes (e.g., straightforward decision making with few options and clear consequences) (Gogtay et al., 2004; Hooper, Luciana, Conklin, & Yarger, 2004; Luna & Sweeney, 2004).

A related developmental phenomenon involves transformations in adolescent sleep patterns. As a result of biologically based changes in sleep-wake cycles, many adolescents experience inadequate sleep (increased need for sleep coupled with decreased time sleeping) with cognitive, emotional, and behavioral consequences (Carskadon, Acebo, & Jenni, 2004; Dahl & Lewin, 2002). High levels of sleepiness seen in high school students are exacerbated by incompatible weekday and weekend schedules (Dahl & Lewin, 2002). As described in Chapter 5 on infant and toddler disorders, sleep is an active process that promotes early neurological development. Sleep serves similar purposes in adolescence, making adequate sleep essential.

Connections between neurophysiological development and cognitive development affect decision-making abilities and strategies, impulsivity and novelty-seeking, and motivation and emotion (Beyth-Marom & Fischhoff, 1997; Chambers, Taylor, & Potenza, 2003; Dahl, 2004; Hooper et al., 2004; Overman et al., 2004; Rosso, Young, Femia, & Yurgelun-Todd, 2004). What are the implications of all of this brain-related information? One critical implication is that we will need to think carefully about adolescents' tendencies to use and misuse alcohol and drugs because substance use may have detrimental effects on the developing brain (Spear, 2002a). Another important implication involves the biologically based disjunction between novelty-seeking and competent self-regulation; in other words, *the development of good judgment lags behind expanding opportunities for risk taking* (Masten, 2004; Steinberg, 2004).

In addition to alcohol and drug experimentation and use, other types of **risk taking** are widespread in adolescence. Given the possibility of grave threats to self and others, reckless driving is one of the most frightening examples. Such driving is often the result of lower levels of parental modeling and peer pressure from teen male passengers (Bina, Graziano, & Bonino, 2006; Hartos, Eitel, & Simons-Morton, 2002; Jessor, Turbin, & Costa, 1997; Simons-Morton, Lerner, & Singer, 2005). Increasing parental and community limits on teen drivers have positive impacts on driving safety (Simons-Morton, Hartos, & Beck, 2004; Simons-Morton, Hartos, Leaf, & Preusser, 2006).

Gambling is another risk-taking behavior that is increasingly viewed as a public health issue, with adolescents at the highest risk for pathological gambling (Chambers & Potenza, 2003; Messerlian, Derevensky, & Gupta, 2005). Early onset of gambling is associated with other problems such as substance abuse; girls display more of these symptomatic behaviors (Desai, Maciejewski, Pantalon, & Potenza, 2005). Many instances of adolescent gambling occur on the internet, and this and other types of internet addiction are observed across countries and cultures (Johansson & Gotestam, 2004; Kaltiala-Heino, Lintonen, & Rimpela, 2004; Ko, Yen, Chen, Chen, & Yen, 2005).

Sexual activity in adolescence often has serious and unintended consequences such as sexually transmitted diseases and pregnancy (Snyder, 2006). Like other risky behaviors, the timing and extent of sexual activity are related to individual, family, and social factors, with self-regulation particularly important (Meschke, Zweig, Barber, & Eccles, 2000; Raffaelli & Crockett, 2003).

Each of these high-risk behaviors, on its own, can lead to challenging circumstances. In combination, these behaviors set in motion pathways that end in very negative outcomes. According to the **problem behavior syndrome** described by Jessor (1998; Jessor et al., 2003), if adolescents are at risk for one problem behavior, they tend to be at risk for others. In fact, adolescents at risk for negative outcomes report involvement in approximately 4 out of the following 10 categories of problem behaviors: alcohol use, smoking, marijuana use, other drug use, sexual activity, minor delinquency, major delinquency, direct aggression, indirect aggression, and gambling (Willoughby, Chalmers, & Busseri, 2004). Typically developing adolescents, at relatively low risk for clinical disorders, report involvement in one or two activities; adolescents at higher risk report more frequent and persistent involvement in greater numbers of activities (Willoughby et al., 2004).

Risk taking must be evaluated in the context of adolescent identity formation, the sampling of adult behaviors coupled with freedom from adult responsibilities, and the increasing influence of peers (Arnett, 2000; Gardner & Steinberg, 2005). Protective factors with a positive impact on adolescent health behavior and risk taking include personal variables such as the adolescent's concern with health and conventionality, family variables such as modeling of healthy behaviors, and social factors such as positive peer relationships and school involvement (Jessor, Turbin, & Costa, 1998a, 1998b).

Substance Abuse Disorders

The Case of Elijah

Elijah is a 15-year-old high school sophomore in the largest town in a rural area. Elijah moved to this community as a ninth grader when his father started a new job. Elijah was an average student through junior high school, although his impulsivity and sporadic oppositional behavior created conflict with his teachers. Elijah left behind a large network of friends and family when he moved, and found himself somewhat isolated in his new school. There were fewer peers who appreciated his quirky sense of humor and fewer opportunities to share his appetite for ethnic foods and music. Toward the end of ninth grade, Elijah began working at a local movie theater and met several boys about to graduate from high school. Over the summer, Elijah hung out with these friends after work and drank beer with them. When school started in the fall, Elijah quit his job, but continued to get together with these friends for parties that included drinking and, occasionally, other drug use. While Elijah did not try these other drugs, which he viewed as dangerous, he did drink heavily. During the first semester of school, Elijah slept through several morning classes and two exams after late-night parties.

Although uncomfortable with his spending time with these older teens and concerned by his poor school performance, Elijah's parents hesitated to limit his contact since these seemed to be the only friends he had. When they first suspected that Elijah was drinking with this group, Elijah's mother was quite upset. His father saw the behavior as "normal teenage guy stuff." However, when they began to notice liquor missing from their home, they agreed that Elijah's drinking was a problem. They told Elijah that he could not get his driver's license until he agreed to see a counselor and stop drinking. ■

The Case of Nora

Nora is an 18-year-old senior attending an alternative high school for students who have struggled in traditional school environments. Nora began high school at a large, very competitive suburban high school. Both of her parents are successful professionals; her older brother was class valedictorian and currently attends a prestigious university.

Nora was a bright and engaging child but also very strong-willed and stubborn. Nora began smoking cigarettes with her friends in seventh grade and was caught drinking with these same friends several times in eighth grade. Upset by these discoveries and Nora's insistence that nothing was wrong, Nora's parents sought mental health counseling several times, but a pattern emerged in which either Nora or her parents came to view the therapists as either unhelpful or incompetent. Multiple therapies were ended without much positive change. By the time Nora started high school, she was smoking marijuana as well as drinking. By the end of ninth grade, however, many of her friends decreased their drug use as they became more involved in academics and cocurricular activities. Nora's drug use, in contrast, increased in both severity and variety. Although unaware of her escalating drug use, Nora's parents became increasingly concerned as her grades dropped and the school administrator contacted them about repeated truancy.

Nora was skipping school and driving to the apartment of friends who attended a local college. In addition to alcohol and drugs, Nora was beginning to experiment with MDMA (Ecstasy) and prescription narcotics such as Oxycontin. Midway through her junior year, Nora was failing almost all of her classes and her health was deteriorating. With the combined insistence of her parents and a therapist, Nora again began—but never completed—several outpatient drug treatments. Typically, Nora would initially cooperate, but found staying sober physically and psychologically intolerable; she would quickly fall back into a pattern of drug and alcohol use. Late one night, returning from a dance club, Nora was driving erratically and had a minor accident. Nora had been drinking before going to the club and had later taken Ecstasy. The police were called; in addition to determining that Nora was driving while intoxicated, they found other drugs in her car and filed further charges. Nora agreed to enter an inpatient drug treatment program for adolescents. She started at the alternative high school when she was discharged. Nora likes the school, attends regularly, and feels understood and supported by the staff. She is actively attempting to avoid another relapse, but acknowledges that it is extremely difficult, because she still feels that "the only time I am really happy and alive is when I'm high." ∎

The cases of Elijah and Nora illustrate just two of the many clinical presentations of adolescent substance abuse and dependency that depend on definitions of use, abuse, tolerance, dependence, and addiction (see Tables 14.1 and 14.2). **Use** is defined as ingestion of a substance. **Experimental substance use** involves trying a drug once or a few times, often related to curiosity or peer influence. **Social substance use** occurs during social events with one or more peers; parties, concerts, dances, and athletic events are common settings for this type of use (Arnett, 2007). **Abuse** is defined as excessive use of or dependence on an addictive substance. Individual differences in the progression from use to abuse are noteworthy, with some adolescents transitioning slowly, others rapidly, and still others not at all.

Tolerance occurs when the central nervous system (CNS) gradually becomes less responsive to stimulation by particular drugs. Individuals then need to ingest higher and higher doses to achieve the same CNS effects. **Physical dependence** involves susceptibility to withdrawal symptoms; it occurs only in combination with tolerance. **Withdrawal symptoms** are noxious physical and psychological effects caused by reduction or cessation of substance intake (e.g., sleep disturbances, headaches, nausea and vomiting, tremors, restlessness, anxiety, and depression); these symptoms can range from relatively mild to life-threatening. **Psychological dependence** involves a craving or compulsion to use despite significant harm, and is not always accompanied by withdrawal symptoms. Distinctions between abuse and dependence are often tied to specific substances and their CNS effects. Impairment provides another key diagnostic criterion, with the presence of immediate negative consequences and secondhand effects (such as interrupting the sleep and study of others,

TABLE 14:1 DSM-IV-TR DIAGNOSTIC CRITERIA FOR SUBSTANCE ABUSE

A. A maladaptive pattern of substance use leading to clinically significant impairment or distress, as manifested by one or more of the following, occurring within a 12-month period:

(1) recurrent substance use resulting in a failure to fulfill major role obligations at work, school, or home

(2) recurrent substance use in situations in which it is physically hazardous (e.g., driving)

(3) recurrent substance-related legal problems

(4) continued substance use despite having persistent or recurrent social or interpersonal problems caused or exacerbated by the effects of the substance

B. The symptoms have never met the criteria for Substance Dependence for this class of substance.

SOURCE: Reprinted with permission from the Diagnostic and Statistical Manual of Mental Disorders, Text Revision, Fourth Edition, (Copyright 2000). American Psychiatric Association.

TABLE 14:2 DSM-IV-TR DIAGNOSTIC CRITERIA FOR SUBSTANCE DEPENDENCE

A maladaptive pattern of substance use, leading to clinically significant impairment or distress, as manifested by three or more of the following, occurring at any time in the same 12-month period:

(1) tolerance, defined by either of the following:

    a. a need for markedly increased amounts of the substance to achieve intoxication or desired effect

    b. markedly diminished effect with continued use of the same amount of the substance

(2) withdrawal, as manifested by either of the following:

    a. the characteristic withdrawal syndrome for the substance

    b. the same or a closely related substance is taken to relieve or avoid withdrawal symptoms

(3) the substance is often taken in larger amounts or over a longer period than was intended

(4) there is a persistent desire or unsuccessful efforts to cut down or control substance use

(5) a great deal of time is spent in activities necessary to obtain the substance, use the substance, or recover from its effects

(6) important social, occupational, or recreational activities are given up or reduced because of substance use

(7) the substance use is continued despite knowledge of having a persistent or recurrent physical or psychological problem that is likely to have been caused or exacerbated by the substance

Source: Reprinted with permission from the Diagnostic and Statistical Manual of Mental Disorders, Text Revision, Fourth Edition, (Copyright 2000). American Psychiatric Association.

or damaging property) (Windle & Windle, 2006). **Addiction** is defined as a chronic disorder characterized by compulsive drug-seeking and abuse and accompanied by neurophysiological changes.

There are multiple ongoing surveys of adolescent alcohol and drug use in the United States. Some of the most recent data disseminated by the National Institute on Drug Abuse (NIDA; www .nida.nih.gov), based on the 2006 National Survey on Drug Use and Health and the 2007 Monitoring the Future study (www.monitoringthefuture.org; Johnston, O'Malley, Bachman, & Schulenberg, 2008), show that rates of substance use continue to show gradual declines from peak rates documented in 1996–1997, with current prevalence rates of 21% in eighth grade, 38% in tenth grade and 50% in twelfth grade. By twelfth grade, then, half of high school students have tried an illicit drug. Adolescent boys and girls exhibit relatively similar patterns of illicit drug use, although there are some gender differences (Isralowitz & Rawson, 2006; Young et al., 2002). Current statistics suggest that girls have surpassed boys in rates of smoking, alcohol, and marijuana use. Specific populations at very high risk for substance abuse are runaway and homeless adolescents (Johnson, Whitbeck, & Hoyt, 2005). Across countries and cultures, there is similarity in age of onset of substance use, but differences in lifetime rates of substance abuse disorders (Vega et al., 2002). Within the United

States, rates of disorder vary across states (see Figure 14.1). Between 7% and 10% of adolescents in the United States are in need of treatment; few receive it (Kaminer & Bukstein, 2005).

Alcohol Use and Abuse

Although the legal drinking age in the United States is 21, survey results reveal that the majority of adolescents have alcohol experience by age 18. African Americans and Asian Americans have lower rates, and European Americans and Latino Americans have the highest rates (Kaminer & Bukstein, 2005; O'Malley, Johnston, & Bachman, 1998); among Latino groups (Mexican Americans, Puerto Ricans, Cuban Americans, and others), differences in rates of disorder are observed and are hypothesized to have some connection to degree of acculturation (Delva et al., 2005; Guilamo-Ramos, Jaccard, Johansson, & Tunisi, 2004). Mean age of onset for alcohol use is 14 years (National Institute on Alcohol Abuse and Alcoholism [NIAAA], 2005), although there is increasing concern about access to alcohol and use in elementary school children (Donovan et al., 2004). By eighth grade, 41% of children in the USA have tried alcohol; by tenth grade, 63% have (Johnston et al., 2008). More ninth graders report regular drinking than regular smoking (Centers for Disease Control and Prevention, 2004). Mean frequencies and quantities of drinking reported for the month just past are presented

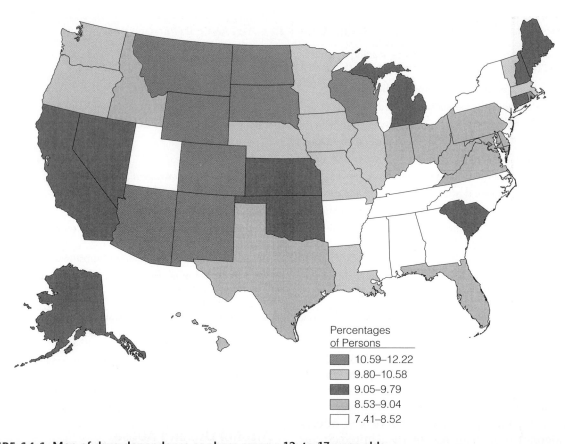

FIGURE 14:1 Map of drug dependence or abuse among 12- to 17–year-olds.
Source: Substance Abuse and Mental Health Services Administration (SAMHSA), Office of Applied Studies, *National Survey on Drug Use and Health*, 2003 and 2004.

Percentages of Persons

- 10.59–12.22
- 9.80–10.58
- 9.05–9.79
- 8.53–9.04
- 7.41–8.52

for adolescent boys and girls of various ethnic backgrounds in Figures 14.2 and 14.3. The transition to young adulthood does not signal a lessening of alcohol misuse. Drinking in college students, for instance, is widespread and often problematic (Schulenberg et al., 2001); indeed, binge drinking has been investigated as a developmental phenomenon (King, Burt, Malone, McGue, & Iacono, 2005), and is linked with poor academic performance and later alcohol dependence and abuse (Jennison, 2004; Wechsler & Wuethrich, 2002).

Several studies focus on the locations and contexts of adolescent drinking (Windle, 2003). Most adolescents report purchasing their own alcohol, suggesting that access to alcohol is not particularly difficult; girls are challenged less frequently by retailers than boys (Willner & Hart, 2001). Often-cited reasons for drinking include curiosity, the pleasurable effects of alcohol, and social drinking with friends (O'Malley, Johnston, & Bachman, 1998). Many adolescents use

alcohol and other drugs in outdoor or out-of-the-way settings that are associated with dangers such as walking home alone and driving while intoxicated (Coleman & Cater, 2005). Many adolescents are drinking to get drunk (Johnston et al., 2008). Twenty-eight percent of twelfth graders report **binge drinking** (more than five drinks) in the previous two weeks (NIAAA, 2005). Twelfth graders who drink frequently and heavily report many alcohol-related difficulties, including behaving in ways they later regret, poor decision-making, and reckless driving (O'Malley et al., 1998). For athletes with a "jock identity," binge drinking has been associated with violent behavior in young men (Miller, Melnick, Farrell, Sabo, & Barnes, 2006).

Smoking

Although less dramatic than the substance use and abuse described in the cases of Elijah and Nora, adolescent tobacco **smoking** is a major public health

Binge drinking by college students is a significant risk factor for both academic problems and later alcohol abuse.

problem (Johnston et al., 2008, NIDA, 2001b), with the long-term complications of smoking presenting a somewhat different set of clinical concerns than the immediate dysfunction and distress seen with other substance use and abuse (Chassin, Presson, & Sherman, 2005). Nicotine is one of the most frequently used drugs, and "the cigarette is a very efficient and highly engineered drug-delivery system," with nicotine reaching the brain within 10 seconds (NIDA, 2001b, p. 2; see Figure 14.4). Nicotine has both stimulant and sedative effects, with a near-immediate release of adrenalin that many individuals

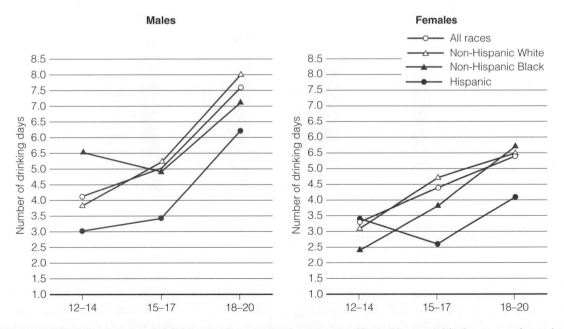

FIGURE 14:2 Mean frequency of drinking in the past 30 days among 12- to 20–year-olds, by age and race/ethnicity origin, 2003; (a) in males, (b) in females. From SAMHSA, *Results from the 2002 National Survey on Drug Use and Health: National Findings*, 2003.

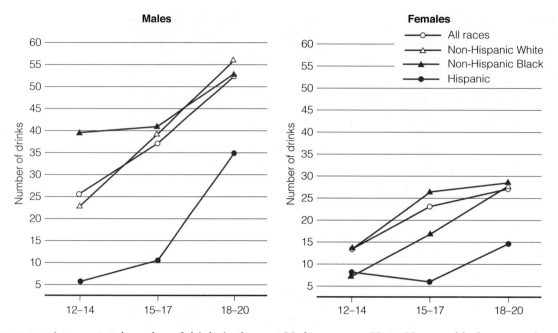

FIGURE 14:3 Average total number of drinks in the past 30 days among 12- to 20-year-olds, by age and race/ethnicity origin, 2003; (a) in males, (b) in females. From SAMHSA, *Results from the 2002 National Survey on Drug Use and Health: National Findings*, 2003.

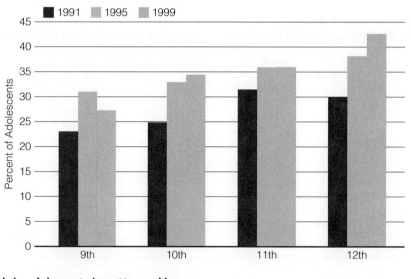

FIGURE 14:4 Trends in adolescent cigarette smoking.
Source: National Institute on Drug Abuse (NIDA, 2001b, p. 2).

perceive as pleasurable. Cigarettes and other tobacco products are highly available and sophisticatedly marketed. Nearly 25% of twelfth graders are smokers (Johnston et al., 2008), and adolescent smoking is correlated with a host of other problem behaviors, including alcohol use, early sexual activity, and delinquency (Turbin, Jessor, & Costa, 2000). With repeated use, tolerance develops. Of every five adolescent smokers, between one and three are dependent on nicotine; the withdrawal symptom described most frequently is **craving**, or "drug wanting" and a strong desire to use (Colby, Tiffany, Shiffman, & Niaura, 2000).

Marijuana

Marijuana use is leveling off, with 46% of high school seniors reporting at least one-time use and 20% reporting current use (NIDA, 2005c; see Figure 14.5). Marijuana is usually smoked. The current use of cigars ("blunts") as drug delivery devices is problematic; many users add other drugs to marijuana cigars (Soldz, Huyser, & Dorsey, 2003). The active chemical in marijuana is delata-9-tetrahydrocannabinol (THC), and the amount of THC in marijuana has risen dramatically over recent decades. THC attaches to cannabinoid receptors in many brain areas (see Table 14.3). Its use is associated with both short- and long-term physical impairments. Smoking marijuana leads to addiction in some users, who display compulsive use and impaired functioning (NIDA, 2005c). Findings related to the effects of marijuana use are mixed. Some studies show decreases in executive functioning (related to attention, memory, and learning) and brain abnormalities, and lower rates of school achievement and high school graduation; other data suggest few, if any, long-term impairments (Carlson, 2007; Lyons et al., 2004; Windle & Wiesner, 2004). Investigators have attempted to describe subtypes of marijuana users, and have found the most useful distinctions related to age of onset, difficult temperament, and whether other psychopathology is present (Babor, Webb, Burleson, & Kaminer, 2002).

Other Commonly Abused Substances

Inhalants are one of the few classes of drugs showing *increases in use* over the past several years. Inhalants are substances that produce chemical vapors that can be inhaled to produce psychoactive, or

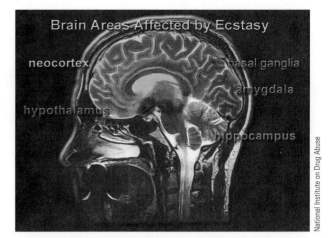

Drugs like MDMA (Ecstasy) have profound, and potentially life-threatening, effects on neurotransmitter systems.
Source: NIDA.

mind-altering, effects. These include solvents (e.g., paint thinner, gasoline, glue), aerosols (e.g., spray paint), gases (e.g., nitrous oxide), and nitrites (e.g., "poppers," "snappers"); they achieve their effects via suppression of the central nervous system. "Within seconds of inhalation, the user experiences intoxication along with other effects similar to those produced by alcohol. Alcohol-like effects may include slurred speech, an inability to coordinate movements, euphoria, and dizziness" (NIDA, 2005b, p. 4). The effects are short-lived, and "because intoxication lasts only a few minutes, abusers frequently seek to prolong the high by continuing to inhale repeatedly over the course of several hours, a very dangerous practice" (p. 4). Inhalant use peaks between seventh and ninth grades (see Figure 14.6), with sustained use more frequent in boys. Indeed, the most serious inhalant abuse is exhibited by

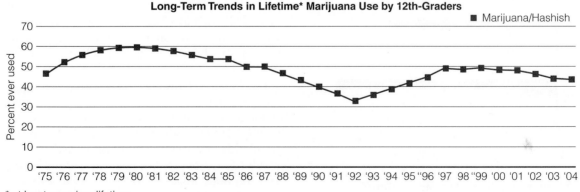

* at least once in a lifetime

FIGURE 14:5 Trends in adolescent marijuana use.
Source: NIDA (2005c).

TABLE 14:3 MARIJUANA'S EFFECTS ON THE BRAIN	
BRAIN REGION	**FUNCTIONS ASSOCIATED WITH REGION**
Brain Regions in which cannaboid receptors are abundant	
Cerebellum	Body movement coordination
Hippocampus	Learning and memory
Cerebral cortex, especially cingulate, frontal, and parietal regions	Higher cognitive functions
Nucleus accumbens	Reward
Basal ganglia Substantia nigra pars reticulata Entopeduncular nucleus Globus pallidus Putamen	Movement control
Brain regions in which cannabinoid receptors are moderately concentrated	
Hypothalamus	Body housekeeping functions (body temperature regulation, salt and water balance, reproductive function)
Amygdala	Emotional response, fear
Spinal cord	Peripheral sensation, including pain
Brain stem	Sleep and arousal, temperature regulation, motor control
Central gray	Analgesia
Nucleus of the solitary tract	Visceral sensation, nausea and vomiting

Source: NIDA (2005c).

children and adolescents who have little access to alcohol or other drugs, and is particularly awful in children from impoverished cultures who "live on the streets completely without family ties" (NIDA,

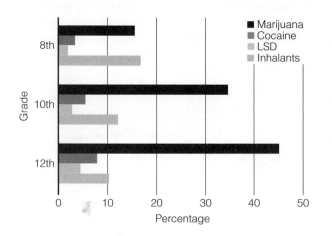

FIGURE 14:6 Eighth-, tenth-, and twelfth-grade student drug use, 2004.
Source: NIDA (2005b).

1995). Inhalant abuse has neurotoxic consequences, with immediate short-term and long-term physical and psychological complications, including progressive, permanent declines in cognitive functioning and heart arrhythmias that can lead to heart failure and death ("sudden sniffing death") (Cairney, Maruff, Burns, & Currie, 2002; NIDA, 2005b).

Cocaine has been used and abused for centuries (NIDA, 2004); following the peak in the 1980s and 1990s, cocaine use has somewhat stabilized. Cocaine has two chemical forms, hydrochloride salt and freebase (one type of which, crack, is processed for smoking), and is ingested in a variety of ways, including inhaling, smoking, and injecting. Cocaine acts on the brain's reward systems and the neurotransmitter dopamine. Cocaine is a powerfully addictive drug; tolerance and craving are frequently observed. Single or repeated use may result in cardiovascular, respiratory, and neurological complications.

Methamphetamine is a potent stimulant drug that has become increasingly widespread and extraordinarily problematic. It has a similar drug structure to amphetamines, but more dramatic and more toxic effects on the CNS (NIDA, 2002). Users often display "binge and crash" patterns; "after the initial 'rush,' there is typically a state of high agitation that in some individuals can lead to violent behavior" (NIDA, 2002, p. 2). "In contrast to cocaine, which is quickly removed and almost completely metabolized in the body, methamphetamine has a much longer duration of action and a larger percentage of the drug remains unchanged in the body" (p. 5).

Hallucinogens (such as LSD) cause hallucinations, distortions of a person's perception of reality, disrupting nerve cell interaction and the serotonin system (NIDA, 2001a), with unpredictable effects. There can be long-lasting psychological complications, including flashbacks (NIDA, 2001a). Dissociative drugs (such as PCP) affect the neurotransmitters glutamate and dopamine, also with unpredictable effects. With characteristics and effects overlapping stimulant and psychedelic drugs, MDMA (i.e., Ecstasy) is another abused substance, often used in combination with alcohol or marijuana. Originally used in nightclubs and at dance parties (McCaughan, Carlson, Falck, & Siegel, 2005), its use is associated with increases in feelings of well-being, increases in emotional and sensory perception, and decreases in anxiety. Ecstasy's effects occur via neurotransmitter systems, with immediate life-threatening consequences for some and long-term complications (such as damage to serotonin-containing neurons) (NIDA, 2006). The use of each of these classes of drugs is declining.

Heroin is another highly addictive substance; it is the most rapidly acting and most abused of the opiate class of drugs (although fewer than 2% of eighth–twelfth graders have tried heroin) (NIDA, 2005a). Heroin users exhibit high degrees of tolerance and dependence. "Once they are addicted, the heroin abuser's primary purpose in life becomes seeking and using drugs. The drugs literally change their brains and their behavior" (NIDA, 2005a, p. 3).

Prescription drugs are also increasingly abused by adolescents. The most common types are pain medications, CNS depressants (such as those prescribed for anxiety and sleep disorders), and stimulants (such as those prescribed for ADHD) (NIDA, 2005d). Four percent of 12- to 17-year-olds report prescription drug abuse.

Anabolic steroids were originally developed to treat certain medical conditions; they promote growth and strength. Their primary use and abuse are related to improvements in sports performance. Steroidal supplements such as androstenediol and other "pro-hormones," sold in many health food stores, are also widely used (see Figure 14.7). Steroids can be taken orally, injected, or rubbed on skin. Steroid abusers often take combinations of steroids ("stacking") or make use of "pyramid" doses, slowly increasing then decreasing intake. There are many adverse physical and psychological effects; these occur immediately and over the long run (see Table 14.4). Connections between steroid use and irritability and aggression have been made; however, "the most dangerous of the withdrawal symptoms is depression, because it sometimes leads to suicide attempts" and suicide completion (NIDA, 2000).

Patterns of Comorbidity

Many connections between substance abuse disorder and other psychopathologies have been documented (Kandel, Huang, & Davies, 2001; Sakai, Hall, Mikulich-Gilbertson, & Crowley, 2004; Solhkhah & Armentano, 2002). In community studies, 60% of adolescents who use or abuse substances also meet the diagnostic criteria for another psychiatric diagnosis. Disruptive, externalizing disorders, depression, and histories of abuse are common in both adolescent boys and girls; anxiety disorders and suicidality are more frequent in girls, with current research emphasizing especially vulnerable groups of adolescents at risk for multiple psychopathologies (Armstrong & Costello, 2002; Deas, St. Germaine, & Upadhyaya, 2006; Giaconia, Reinherz, Paradis, & Stashwick, 2003; O'Brien et al.,

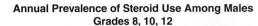
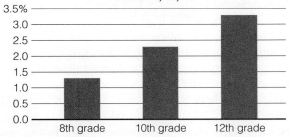

FIGURE 14:7 Eighth-, tenth-, and twelfth-grade student use of steroids.
Source: NIDA (2000).

TABLE 14:4 POSSIBLE HEALTH CONSEQUENCES OF ANABOLIC STEROID USE

Hormonal System

Men:

Infertility
Breast development
Shrinking of the testicles

Women:

Enlargement of the clitoris
Excessive growth of body hair

Both sexes:

Male-pattern baldness

Musculoskeletal System

Short stature
Tendon rupture

Cardiovascular System

Heart attacks
Enlargement of the heart's left ventricle

Liver

Cancer
Peliosis hepatis

Skin

Acne and cysts
Oily scalp

Infection

HIV/AIDS
Hepatitis

Psychiatric effects

Homicidal rage
Mania
Delusions

Source: NIDA (2000).

2004). This emphasis is consistent with work related to the problem behavior syndrome previously discussed (Jessor et al., 2003; Langhinrichsen-Rohling, Rohde, Seeley, & Rohling, 2004).

There is not much evidence for substance-specific comorbidity, except for marijuana use, which is more often observed in adolescents diagnosed with externalizing disorders and more severe psychopathology (Armstrong & Costello, 2002; Milich et al., 2000); additional investigations may provide data about the timing of marijuana use and externalizing disorders, or about the individual and environmental variables that lead to both

use and disorder. Some investigators have identified clusters of struggling adolescents, differentiating among anxious drinkers, antisocial drinkers, and depressed drug abusers (Beitchman et al., 2001); others have focused on specific patterns such as the use of alcohol by depressed adolescents or the impact of nicotine dependence on psychopathology in vulnerable individuals (Grant, Hasin, Chou, Stinson, & Dawson, 2004; Ramsey, Brown, Strong, & Sales, 2002; Ramsey, Engler, & Stein, 2004).

Developmental Course

Substance abuse disorders rarely resolve on their own (Maggs & Schulenberg, 2005; Rohde, Lewinsohn, Kahler, Seeley, & Brown, 2001). It is necessary, then, to understand the developmental context of use and abuse: *How and why do adolescents begin to use drugs and what factors underlie continued use?* There are multiple pathways, with multiple endpoints, of adolescent substance use and abuse. Over most classes of drugs, there is often a progression from exposure and opportunity to use, to experimentation, to repeat and regular use, to abuse and dependence, with different probabilities marking the transitions between stages for different drugs (Nelson & Wittchen, 1998; Tsuang et al., 1999; Turner, Mermelstein, & Flay, 2004). That is, we can describe a common sequence, but we also need to keep in mind that the likelihood that an individual moves from one stage to the next varies depending on personal and drug characteristics.

With respect to initial use, there are two periods of highest vulnerability: during early adolescence and during the transition to young adulthood. Early users are at higher risk for poor outcomes. Substance use in early adolescence often involves immediate negative consequences, including less successful resolution of developmental challenges related to self and identity (D'Amico, Ellickson, Collins, Martino, & Klein, 2005). Early substance use also predicts substance abuse in later adolescence and adulthood, and a range of negative personal and social long-term outcomes (Armstong & Costello, 2002; Merline, O'Malley, Schulenberg, Bachman, & Johnston, 2004; Myers, Stewart, & Brown, 1998; Tucker, Ellickson, Orlando, Martino, & Klein, 2005; White, Bates, & Labouvie, 1998). Substance abuse is also associated with suicidality, with increases in risk observed in both clinical and community samples of adolescents (Esposito-Smythers, 2004; Goldston, 2004).

Pathways Involving Alcohol

The general trend in alcohol use involves a gradual increase throughout adolescence, a peak in early adulthood, then a decrease (Harford, Grant, Yi, & Chen, 2005; Maggs & Schulenberg, 2004–2005). Focusing on the years of adolescence, however, provides a somewhat different perspective. Cloninger (1987) described two general types of adolescent and adult drinkers: steady drinkers and binge drinkers (i.e., those who can abstain, but who exhibit impulsivity and a lack of control when they do drink). Colder, Campbell, Ruel, Richardson, and Flay (2002) recognized five drinking patterns: occasional, light drinking; moderate escalation; infrequent but high levels of drinking; rapid escalation; and frequent and high levels of drinking.

Early drinking more often results in immediate and long-term alcohol-related complications. Age at first use is the key variable. Those who begin drinking at age 11 or 12 have higher rates of substance abuse (13.5%) and dependence (14.9%) a decade later; rates are lower for those who began drinking at 13 or 14 (13.7% and 9%, respectively), and lowest for those who began at 19 or older (2% and 1%, respectively) (DeWit, Adlaf, Offord, & Ogborne, 2000; Grant, Stinson, & Harford, 2001). Early drinking is also associated with higher rates of binge drinking, risky sexual activity, aggression and violence, and poor adult outcomes (Stueve & O'Donnell, 2005; Wells, Horwood, & Fergusson, 2004). Initiation of drinking usually precedes initiation of smoking in adolescents (Jackson, Sher, Cooper, & Wood, 2002). Early-onset alcohol abuse is also associated with suicidality; hypotheses suggest links among impulsivity, disinhibition, and comorbid psychopathology (especially mood disorders) (Kelly, Cornelius, & Clark, 2004; Nishimura, Goebert, Ramisetty-Mikler, & Caetano, 2005; Sher & Zalsman, 2005).

Important differences in alcohol use emerge in middle school and become more distinct in high school (Guo, Collins, Hill, & Hawkins, 2000). Frequent and heavy drinking that continues through adolescence is accompanied by problems including poor academic functioning, family and peer difficulties, and varied deviant behaviors (Windle, 2003; Windle, Mun, & Windle, 2005). Frequent drinking, like early drinking, is related to fighting and injuries

to self and others; this outcome is sometimes part of a wider pattern involving school misbehavior and participation in sports (Swahn & Donovan, 2005; Swahn, Simon, Hammig, & Guerrero, 2004). Transitional life events (e.g., changes in education setting or employment) may provide opportunities for some adolescents to grow out of alcohol use and abuse (Dawson, Grant, Stinson, & Chou, 2006).

Pathways Involving Smoking

Multiple trajectories and patterns of smoking in adolescence have been described (Abroms, Simons-Morton, Haynie, & Chen, 2005; Orlando, Tucker, Ellickson, & Klein, 2004; Stanton, Flay, Colder, & Mehta, 2004). These include early-onset stable smokers, late-onset stable smokers, experimenters, and quitters (Chassin, Presson, Pitts, & Sherman, 2000; White, Pandina, & Chen, 2002). Factors related to smoking in adolescence include alcohol use, peer influence, and a history of depression

Prescription drugs, relatively easy to obtain, are increasingly abused by adolescents.

(Lloyd-Richardson, Papandonatos, Kazura, Stanton, & Niaura, 2002; Windle & Windle, 2001). Young smokers are frequently young drinkers. It is relatively common to both smoke and drink, and to drink and not smoke; it is relatively rare to smoke and not drink (Hawkins, Hill, Guo, & Battin-Pearson, 2002; Orlando, Tucker, Ellickson, & Klein, 2005). Early-onset smoking and combined patterns of smoking and drinking predict later substance abuse and dependence as well as more deviance (Hanna & Grant, 1999; Grant, 1998; Orlando et al., 2005).

Pathways Involving Other Drugs

Patterns of marijuana use are varied; adolescents have been described as abstainers, experimental users, decreasers, increasers, and high chronic users (Schulenberg et al., 2005; Windle & Wiesner, 2004). Cigarette smoking often precedes marijuana use (Ellickson, Tucker, Klein, & Saner, 2004). Conduct problems in childhood predict marijuana use in adolescence; the connection is stronger for girls (Pedersen, Mastekaasa, & Wichstrom, 2001). Compared to other drugs, marijuana is associated with the highest probabilities documented for the transition between exposure and use. Heroin is associated with the highest probabilities for transitions between repeated use and regular use, and cocaine with highest probability for transitions from regular use to abuse/dependence (Tsuang et al., 1999).

The Gateway Hypothesis and Common Factors Model

The **gateway hypothesis** is an inclusive stage theory of drug involvement that proposes that the use of alcohol or marijuana acts as a "gateway" to the use of "harder" drugs such as cocaine, heroin, or methamphetamines (Kandel, 2002; Kandel & Yamaguchi, 2002). Recent data suggest that nicotine may also be a gateway drug, leading to marijuana use (Hawkins et al., 2002; Tullis, DuPont, Frost-Pineda, & Gold, 2003). Drug use trajectories of many adolescent boys and girls provide support for this model, although there are adolescent subgroups that illustrate other pathways (George & Mosehy, 2005; Miller, 1994).

There are alternatives to the gateway hypothesis. The **common factors model** assumes that there is a non-specific propensity to use drugs. This propensity is correlated with both opportunities to use various drugs and the actual use of drugs given an opportunity (Agrawal, Neale, Prescott, & Kendler,

The gateway hypothesis proposes that early use of alcohol, tobacco, or marijuana may create a pathway to the use of "harder" drugs.

2004; Morral, McCaffrey, & Paddock, 2002; Vanyukov, Tarter, et al., 2003). Shared individual and social factors, then, contribute to the use and abuse of multiple substances. More complex explanations suggest that shared factors (such as social norms) increase an adolescent's overall risk to use any drug, and personality factors influence decisions about use of particular drugs. Pharmacological effects of particular drugs (such as marijuana) may then lead an adolescent to use other drugs (Agrawal, Neale, Jacobson, Prescott, & Kendler, 2005; Hall & Lynskey, 2005; Schenk, 2002).

Substance Abuse and Other Deviant Behaviors

Previous discussion of the problem behavior syndrome emphasized how connected various forms of adolescent distress and dysfunction can be. These connections remain as we consider the more serious clinical picture observed for substance abuse disorders. For instance, there are common pathways described for alcohol, marijuana and gambling, and the earlier the onset, the greater the involvement and the more persistent the problems (Wanner, Vitaro, Ladouceur, Brendgen, & Tremblay, 2006; Winters, Stinchfield, Botzet, & Slutske, 2005). One of the most pressing problems involves associations between substance abuse, illegal activity, and violence. Correlations between substance abuse and illegal activities are complex, with offenses usually linked with serious substance abuse, impulsivity, and deviant peer relationships (Cuellar, Markowitz, & Libby, 2004; White, Tice, Loeber, & Stouthamer-Loeber, 2002). Correlations between heavy alcohol and marijuana use and violence have been documented, although most substance abusers do not display aggressive behavior (Wei, Loeber, & White, 2004; White, Loeber, Stouthamer-Loeber, & Farrington, 1999). Substance abuse has also been tied to escalations in antisocial behavior and later antisocial personality disorder (Hussong, Curran, Moffitt, Caspi, & Carrig, 2004; Malone, Taylor, Marmorstein, McGue, & Iacono, 2004). Lack of anger control appears to be the variable that accounts for the connections between drug use and violence (Weiner et al., 2004).

Etiology

Models of etiology need to explain initial experimentation and drug use, drug abuse, and drug addiction, with various factors coming into play at different points along the trajectory of use (Clark, Cornelius, Kirisci, & Tarter, 2005; Tsuang et al., 1999). For most adolescents, combinations of risk factors (such as maturational factors; emotional and cognitive development; and family, peer, and social variables) lead to disorder; for others, a single risk may be enough to set psychopathology in motion (Cicchetti & Rogosch, 1999; Clark et al., 2005; Dawes et al., 2000).

Genes and Heredity

Genetic contributions to substance abuse disorders must be understood in the context of clear environmental impact (Knopik et al., 2004; Walden, McGue, Iacono, Burt, & Elkins, 2004). That said, twin studies, family studies, and adoption studies provide overwhelming evidence of a moderate to high inherited vulnerability (Agrawal, Madden, et al., 2005; Goldman, Oroszi, & Ducci, 2005; Prescott, Maes, & Kendler, 2005). The genetic impact on drug abuse and addiction is both general (related to the use of any substance) and specific (related to the use of a particular substance), with the most unique variance observed for heroin (Tsuang et al., 1998; Vanyukov, Tarter et al., 2003). Genetic influence appears differentially related to initiation and to continued use or dependence (Sullivan & Kendler, 1999). In general, the data suggest that "the environment plays a strong role in influencing a person to try a drug and perhaps continue to use it recreationally, but genetics plays a stronger role in determining whether the person becomes addicted" (Carlson, 2007, p. 636).

The role of genetics in alcohol use and abuse has been the most intensively researched. The Stockholm Adoption study is one example of a large-scale longitudinal investigation providing valuable data (Cloninger, Bohman, & Sigvardsson, 1981; Sigvardsson, Bohman, & Cloninger, 1996). Multiple alcohol problems are genetically influenced, including motivation to drink, alcohol sensitivity, the amount of alcohol consumed, steady drinking, and eventual dependence (Heath et al., 1999; Prescott, Cross, Kuhn, Horn, & Kendler, 2004; Whitfield et al., 2004). Age of first drink is also influenced by genes, but environmental factors and gene-environment interactions are even more influential (McGue & Iacono, 2004; Rose, Dick, Viken, Pulkkinen, & Kaprio, 2001). Sibling concordance rates are higher for brothers than sisters for alcohol dependence (Bierut et al., 1998). In most of the studies of genes and alcohol, the genetic impact of fathers is most significant; some studies, however, show contributions of both fathers and mothers (Dawson & Grant, 1998; Dierker, Merikangas, & Szatmari, 1999; Grant, 1998).

Genetic explanations for combinations of substance abuse and other psychopathology have also been set forth (Krueger et al., 2002; Pickens, Svikis, McGue, & LaBuda, 1995). Specific connections between alcohol use and conduct disorder appear more likely to be influenced by environmental factors (Rose, Dick, Viken, Pulkkinen, & Kaprio, 2004), although evidence suggests genetic overlap between alcohol dependence at age 17 and antisocial personality disorder at age 20 (Malone et al., 2004). Future studies in search of more real-life validity may need to focus on more complex models of gene-environment interaction (Dick, Rose, Viken, Kaprio, & Koskenvuo, 2001).

Physiological Factors

Animal studies illustrate many of the potential mechanisms of drug use and abuse, with different brain pathways underlying drug reinforcement, tolerance, dependence, and addiction (Booze, 2004; Kelley & Rowan, 2004; Kosten, George, & Kleber, 2005; Rezvani & Levin, 2004). The adolescent brain, in and of itself, is a risk factor, with age-related changes in sensitivity to the effects of alcohol and drugs (Andersen & Navalta, 2004; Spear, 2002a, 2002b). The initial stages of drug use and drug liking are associated with the brain's reward centers, embedded in the mesolimbic system (see Figure 14.8).

FIGURE 14:8 Mesolimbic region of the brain. *Source:* NIAAA (2002).

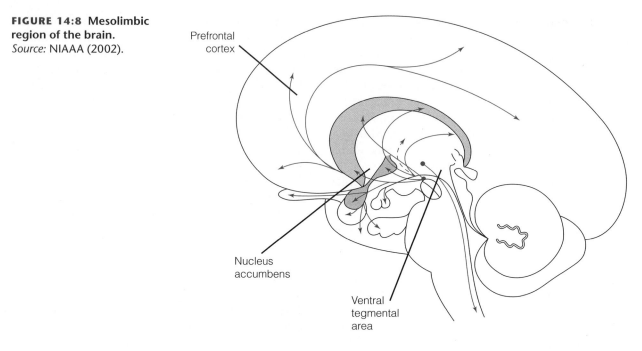

Prefrontal cortex

Nucleus accumbens

Ventral tegmental area

Activation of the mesolimbic pathway, particularly the dopamine receptors, depends on the particular substance; the most addictive drugs have the most rapid effects (Carlson, 2007; Kosten et al., 2005). Individual differences in sensitivity to these immediate effects and the ability to digest or metabolize substances (likely attributable to genetic influences) may relate to individual differences in the levels of pleasure or aversion that accompany drug experimentation (Goldman et al., 2005).

For some adolescents, the immediate pleasurable consequences of drug use "overpower the recognition of long-term aversive effects" (Carlson, 2007, p. 617). Chronic use leads to neurobiological changes that may underlie tolerance (Brown & Tapert, 2004; Kosten et al., 2005); further, "repeated exposure to escalating dosages of most drugs alters the brain, so that it functions more or less normally when the drugs are present and abnormally when they are not" (Kosten et al., 2005, p. 7). With tolerance, transitions to dependence may occur, with cravings, compulsive drug-seeking, and urgent attempts to escape withdrawal (Kosten et al., 2005).

Going beyond the hedonic view that emphasizes the pleasure associated with drug use (i.e., drug liking) and the need to avoid withdrawal symptoms, the **incentive-sensitization theory** is a multi-stage explanation of addiction (Robinson & Berridge, 2001, 2003). First, various substances alter brain organization and function. Second, these altered brain systems affect behavior in situations involving motivation and reward. The dopamine system that usually signals that certain stimuli will lead to positive reinforcement becomes hypersensitized to drugs and drug stimuli; this is referred to as **incentive salience**. At this stage, drug cues are increasingly difficult to ignore, and craving may become a more important factor in continued drug use than pleasurable effects. To understand craving as an essential aspect of drug use, researchers must address both physiological and psychological factors (Bruijnzeel, Repetto, & Gold, 2004; Koob, 2002; Robinson & Berridge, 2003; Willner, James, & Morgan, 2005).

Psychological Factors

A history of childhood psychopathology is one important influence on the development of substance abuse disorders in adolescence (Costello, Erkanli, Federman, & Angold, 1999; White, Xie, Thompson, Loeber, & Stouthamer-Loeber, 2001). Conduct problems are perhaps the most strongly linked to substance use and abuse (Cicchetti & Rogosch, 1999; Disney, Elkins, McGue, & Iacono, 1999; Putnins, 2006; Sung, Erkanli, Angold, & Costello, 2004). Depressed adolescents, especially those with additional social impairments, are also at higher risk (Cicchetti & Rogosch, 1999; Rao et al., 1999; Sung et al., 2004). Child maltreatment is another key risk factor (Agrawal et al., 2005; Bailey & McCloskey, 2005;

De Bellis, 2002; Moran, Vuchinich, & Hall, 2004). Insecure attachment, post-traumatic stress disorder, and learning disabilities are all also associated with increased vulnerability to substance use and abuse (Beitchman, Wilson, Douglas, Young, & Adlaf, 2001; Giaconia et al., 2003; Kilpatrick et al., 2003; Vungkhanching, Sher, Jackson, & Parra, 2004).

Many externalizing disorders as well as panic attacks are related to smoking in particular (Agrawal et al., 2005; Lambert, 2005; Ramsey et al., 2003). Higher rates of smoking have also been noted in adolescents prior to the emergence of schizophrenia (Weiser et al., 2004). These connections raise the issue of **self-medication**, and whether some adolescents are smoking or using other drugs to improve mood, increase cognitive function, and deal with difficulties or symptoms of other disorders. Data related to self-medication hypotheses are mixed (Bruijnzeel et al., 2004; Dinn, Aycicegi, & Harris, 2004; Putnins, 2006; Triplett & Payne, 2004; Valentiner, Mounts, & Deacon, 2004; Whalen, Jamner, Henker, Gehricke, & King, 2003).

Many of the associations between childhood disorders and adolescent substance abuse are likely mediated by individual variables such as deficits in executive function, high levels of negative emotion and emotional dysregulation, and poor self-control (Carlson, Iacono, & McGue, 2002; Fishbein et al., 2006; Habeych, Charles, Sclabassi, Kirisci, & Tarter, 2005; Iacono, Malone, & McGue, 2003; Kirisci, Tarter, Reynolds, & Vanyukov, 2006; Nigg et al., 2004; Wills, Sandy, & Yaeger, 2002). Integrating physiological and cognitive factors, the **cognitive-deficits model** of addiction is based on the idea that repeat, chronic drug use results in abnormalities in the prefrontal cortex, impairing judgment, decision-making and impulse control (Kosten et al., 2005).

Motivations, expectancies, and attitudes are cognitive variables associated with drug use. Positive attitudes and expectancies about alcohol (e.g., that recreational drug use is acceptable; that use leads to individual pleasure and social rewards) increase with age; the most dramatic increase occurs between third and fourth grades (Miller, Smith & Goldman, 1990). Positive expectancies are moderated by parent expectations (Simons-Morton, 2004). Younger children of alcoholics have more negative expectations (hypothetically related to aversive learning); in contrast, and somewhat surprisingly, adolescents with family histories of alcoholism have more

positive expectations (Wiers, Gunning, & Sergeant, 1998). Perceptions of risk related to binge drinking are highest in eighth graders, somewhat lower in tenth graders, and lower still in twelfth graders; these perceptions are associated with decreases in rates of disapproval across the upper grades (Johnston et al., 2008). There appears to be a balance between adolescent perceptions of risk and benefits, and personal experiences of drinking (Hampson, Severson, Burns, Slovic, & Fisher, 2001).

Attitudes about smoking are complex. Beginning smokers emphasize social motives (e.g., related to peer approval) and environmental factors (e.g., positive media portrayals) that influence decisions about smoking; regular and dependent smokers emphasize the automatic nature of smoking, and that smoking helps to control mood and reduce stress (Piper et al., 2004; Wetter et al., 2004). Many adolescent girls focus on the belief that smoking helps to manage weight (Austin & Gortmaker, 2001; Klesges, Elliott, & Robinson, 1997). Interactions among individual intentions and beliefs, powerful external cues, smoking escalation, and nicotine dependence require careful study (Baker, Brandon, & Chassin, 2004; Wahl, Turner, Mermelstein, & Flay, 2005; Wakefield et al., 2004). For many adolescents, continued smoking coincides with increasingly positive recall of early smoking experiences (Riedel, Blitstein, Robinson, Murray, & Klesges, 2003). Perceptions of risk related to smoking must be appreciated in the context of adolescent beliefs about overall health, the immediate impact of smoking, and future harm (Baker et al., 2004; Rubenstein, Halpern-Felsher, Thompson, & Millstein, 2003; Slovic, 2000). For instance, Baker et al. (2004) state that adolescents' "value on health as an outcome declined during the high school years and did not begin to increase until early adulthood. These data suggest that adolescence is a period of increased cognitive vulnerability to smoking, based both on decreasing perceptions of the personalized risks of smoking and decreasing values on health as an outcome."

Adolescent ideas related to marijuana reflect increases in perceived risk coupled with increases in disapproval and somewhat declining rates of use (Johnston et al., 2008). Permissive beliefs are related to marijuana use; relief-oriented beliefs are related to dependence (Chabrol, Massot, & Mullet, 2004). Marijuana attitudes are more positive in adolescents who drink than in adolescents who do not drink (Willner, 2001). Adolescents' perceptions of risk are moderately high for methamphetamines, inhalants, cocaine, ecstasy, and heroin; perceived risks of amphetamine use are lower (Johnston et al., 2008). Rates of disapproval are generally higher (over 80%) than perceptions of risk across all categories of drugs (Johnston et al., 2008).

An earlier and widely publicized study of personality and drug use suggested that experimenters were more psychologically healthy than abstainers (Shedler & Block, 1990), but these results were not always replicated. More recent data suggest that abstainers are never less psychologically healthy and are sometimes more psychologically healthy than experimenters (Milich et al., 2000). Other current research identifies two personality profiles that are linked to substance abuse: one related to a tendency toward social deviance, and the other related to an excitement- or pleasure-seeking path (Crawford, Pentz, Chou, Li, & Dwyer, 2003; Finn, Sharkansky, Brandt, & Turcotte, 2000), with similar personality profiles predicting both substance abuse and gambling problems (Slutske, Caspi, Moffitt, & Poulton, 2005). Adolescents with a "smoker" self-image that includes "toughness, sociability and precocity" are also at risk (Baker et al., 2004). Girls who both smoke and binge drink display different personality characteristics and risk profiles than girls who either smoke or drink, and girls who do neither (Pirkle & Richter, 2006). For example, girls who smoke but do not binge drink, and girls who smoke and binge drink report more symptoms of depression than do girls who only binge drink. Girls who only binge drink report greater popularity as well as a belief that drinking leads to less inhibited behavior (Pirkle & Richter, 2006).

Other adolescent factors related to drug experimentation and use include early puberty (Lanza & Collins, 2002), academic struggles (Bryant, Schulenberg, O'Malley, Bachman, & Johnston, 2003), and social impairment (Greene et al., 1999). A desire to improve self-image and obtain social approval may also lead to experimentation (Amaro, Blake, Schwartz, & Flinchbaugh, 2001). Deviance acceptance is another risk factor (Abroms et al., 2005).

Parent and Family Factors

Parents influence adolescent substance use and abuse in a variety of ways (Barnes, Welte, Hoffman, & Dintcheff, 2005; Brody & Ge, 2001; Walden et al.,

2004). The first way is through exposure. One in four children is exposed to alcohol abuse or dependence in family settings (Grant, 2000), with African-American and Latino-American children disproportionately affected (Ramisetty-Mikler & Caetano, 2004). Parental use increases adolescent use; parental non-use moderates adolescent use, even when peer use is taken into account (Li, Pentz, & Chou, 2002). Combined with genetic predispositions, heavy drinking in families leads to binge drinking in adolescents (Carlson, 2007). In some studies, fathers' alcohol abuse is more predictive of adolescent abuse than mothers' use (Ohannessian et al., 2005; Rohde et al., 2001); in other studies, fathers' alcohol problems predict drinking in daughters, whereas mothers' use predicts drinking in both daughters and sons (Coffelt et al., 2006). In addition, fathers' gambling problems predict adolescent gambling problems (Vachon, Vitaro, Wanner, & Tremblay, 2004). Marijuana use and abuse appear especially influenced by parent and family factors (Tsuang et al., 1998). Parental smoking is less consistently associated with adolescent smoking (Baker et al., 2004; Sullivan & Kendler, 1999). Parents who quit decrease their children's risk, but that risk is still higher than risk for children whose parents never smoked (Bricker et al., 2003). Siblings also have an important role to play, legitimizing, promoting, or discouraging various forms of substance use (Conger & Rueter, 1996; Pomery et al., 2005). For example, even after adjusting for parent smoking, older siblings who smoke increase rates of adolescent smoking (Rajan et al., 2003). Other types of parent and family psychopathologies likely influence all of these associations (Ohannessian et al., 2004; Yu, Stiffman, & Freedenthal, 2005).

Parenting expectations and parenting practices also influence substance use and abuse. Although parents differ in their perceptions of their ability to prevent drug use (Redmond, Spoth, Shin, & Hill, 2004), parents who convey expectations that drug use will not occur and who monitor their adolescents' activities do provide protective benefits (Bogenschneider, Wu, Raffaelli, & Tsay, 1998; Cleveland, Gibbons, Gerrard, Pomery, & Brody, 2005; Simons-Morton, 2004; Simons-Morton & Chen, 2005). African-American and Asian-American adolescents receive more antismoking messages from their parents; African-American parents report their clear impact on their adolescents' decisions to smoke (Baker et al., 2004; Mermelstein, 1999).

Although family structure, such as single-parent status, is frequently associated with increased substance abuse, family structure is better viewed as "a marker of the unequal distribution of factors" such as exposure to stress and connections with deviant peers that lead to substance abuse (Barrett & Turner, 2006). Authoritative parenting further reduces adolescent risk (Chassin, Presson, Rose, et al., 2005; Simons-Morton, Haynie, Crump, Eitel, & Saylor, 2001; Wang, Matthew, Bellamy, & James, 2005; Wills, Resko, Ainette, & Mendoza, 2004). Adolescents' perceptions of parental support are crucial (Beitchman et al., 2005). Overall, positive parent-child relationships have a "conventionalizing effect"; that is, positive relationships enable adolescents to adopt perspectives on the choices they make that are more informed, mature, and in line with what parents value (Brody, Flor, Hollett-Wright, McCoy, & Donovan, 1999).

Social and Cultural Factors

Whether friends drink, smoke, or use drugs influences adolescent beliefs and behaviors, although there are gender and cultural variations (Jaccard, Blanton, & Dodge, 2005; White et al., 2002). In mixed-sex friendships, for example, boys have influence over girls' drinking; girls do not have a similar influence over boys (Gaughan, 2006). And African-American adolescents seem less influenced by peer smoking than European-American adolescents (Mermelstein, 1999). Being a member of certain peer groups, such as sports teams or performing arts groups, increases vulnerability (Barber, Eccles, & Stone, 2001; Eccles & Barber, 1999). Relationships with deviant peers are another key risk factor (Dishion & Owen, 2002; Iervolino et al., 2002; Moss, Lynch, & Hardie, 2003; Simons-Morton et al., 2001; Walden et al., 2004). The transition to high school appears to be a turning point. At this time, peers who support deviance and rule breaking lead to increases in adolescent substance use (Dishion, Capaldi, Spracklen, & Li, 1995; Ellickson et al., 2004). Researchers describe a pattern of reciprocal influence, from peers, to substance use, to more exclusive selection of deviant peer groups, and then to more frequent and more serious substance use and abuse (Dishion & Owen, 2002).

The school setting is also extremely important. School policies that involve more monitoring of students reduce substance use (Kumar, O'Malley, & Johnston, 2005). The norms of the student and staff population, and the social image of smokers, are also influential factors (Evans, Powers, Hersey, &

Renaud, 2006; Kumar et al., 2005; Kumar, O'Malley, Johnston, Schulenberg, & Bachman, 2002).

Other environmental factors that increase or decrease risk include neighborhoods and community norms, ease of access, economic factors, and advertising and the media (Jessor et al., 2003; Johnston, O'Malley, & Terry-McElrath, 2004; Luthar & Cushing, 1999; Wagenaar, Lenk, & Toomey, 2006). Numbers of life stressors are also important (Wills, Sandy, & Yaeger, 2002b; Wills, Sandy, Yaeger, Cleary, & Shinar, 2001). Cohort effects related to **generational forgetting** of the potential harm associated with particular drugs also seem related to increases and declines in substance use (Johnston et al., 2008).

Assessment and Diagnosis

As with every other form of psychopathology, comprehensive assessment of substance abuse disorders is critical (Winters, Latimer, & Stinchfield, 2001). And given physiological complications such as tolerance or withdrawal, medical evaluations are an important component of complete assessments (Dekker, Estroff, & Hoffmann, 2001). With respect to the substance abuse itself, patterns of use (whether episodic or continuous), availability and accessibility of drugs, perceived importance of drugs, the effects of drugs, and family histories of alcohol and drug abuse are key criteria (Tarter, 2005); the heterogeneity of symptoms and limitations of the DSM-IV-TR classification schemes should be taken into account (Deas, Roberts, & Grindlinger, 2005).

The multifactorial etiology of substance abuse requires a full assessment of psychological functioning, including deficits or maladjustment related to cognition, emotion, or behavior (Tarter, 2005). Cognitive assessments include neuropsychological testing and tests of skills frequently impaired by drug use such as abstract thinking and memory. Cognitive difficulties related to attributional style, perceptions of risk, and mistaken beliefs must also be considered. The emotionality and emotional flare-ups observed in adolescents with substance abuse disorders must also be carefully assessed. Clinicians must collect information about behavioral maladjustment, in personal, family, peer, school, and employment domains. The extent to which an adolescent has access to social support from family or friends (or is connected to deviant or delinquent groups) is another important piece of data.

In addition, an adolescent's underlying personality and other comorbid psychopathologies require review and appreciation. Even though many adolescents do not see connections between substance abuse and other problems or disorders, mental health professionals need to encourage disclosure (Medeiros et al., 2005). Another critical component of assessment involves the appraisal of the adolescent's "developmental assets" or strengths (Leffert et al., 1998). Given that few adolescents seek treatment for substance abuse on their own, acknowledgement of these strengths may lay the foundation for initial rapport and allow for discussions about readiness for intervention.

Self-report inventories have demonstrated utility (Crowley, Mikulich, Ehlers, Whitmore, & Macdonald, 2001; Miller & Lazowski, 2005). And questionnaires about self-regulation have proven useful in assessment as well as treatment planning (Brown, Miller, & Lawendowski, 1999). Brief screening and preliminary interventions in primary care clinics are another source of information about substance use and abuse (Babor, Higgins-Biddle, Dauser, Higgins, & Burleson, 2005).

Intervention

Prevention

Avoidance of drugs is a developmental challenge (Simons-Morton & Haynie, 2003), with theoretical and practical issues complicating prevention research, design, program delivery, and evaluation (Nation et al., 2003; Sussman, Stacy, Johnson, Pentz, & Robertson, 2004). But even with multiple viewpoints and assorted difficulties, prevention efforts aimed at reducing substance use and abuse can be successful (Derzon, Sale, Springer, & Brounstein, 2005; Skara & Sussman, 2003; Toumbourou, Williams, Waters, & Patton, 2005). Universal prevention programs cast a very wide net and often promote healthy lifestyles and healthy choices to adolescent populations (He, Kramer, Houser, Chomitz, & Hacker, 2004; Jessor, Turbin, & Costa, 1998; Williams, Holdbeck, & Greenley, 2002). Many mental health and public health professionals point out that declines in drug use in recent years parallel the widespread use of prevention efforts in early and middle adolescence (Pentz, 2003). Even so, there is ample evidence of their ineffectiveness, in addition to data that prevention programs *increase interest* in drug use for certain adolescents (Kaminer &

Bukstein, 2005). One of the important aspects of prevention efforts, and one of the more controversial, is whether to acknowledge that most adolescents will at some time use mood-altering substances, and whether and how to include harm reduction (i.e., non-abstinence based) approaches as well as abstinence messages (MacMaster, Holleran, & Chaffin, 2005). One example of harm reduction for older adolescents involves emphasizing safe or sensible drinking with some adult supervision (Coleman & Cater, 2005). The "social norms" approach addresses the inclination of college students to believe that their peers drink much more than they actually do. It has been demonstrated to reduce levels of alcohol consumption and high-risk drinking in many campus communities (Dejong et al., 2006). Using public and institutional policies to change the environment is another prevention option (Hallfors & Van Dorn, 2002; Pentz, Mares, Schinke, & Rohrbach, 2004; Wagenaar et al., 2006). Restricting the availability of alcohol and enforcing limits on alcohol use are examples of these types of policies (Markowitz, Chatterji, & Kaestner, 2003; Wagenaar, Toomey, & Erickson, 2005).

Selective prevention efforts are more focused. Several effective programs converge on developmental transitions that are associated with increased risk (Botvin, Scheier, & Griffin, 2002; Dishion, Capaldi, & Yoerger, 1999; Furr-Holden, Ialongo, Anthony, Petras, & Kellam, 2004; Petry, 2005). For example, family-centered programs that begin in middle school can delay the initiation of substance use for both typical and at-risk adolescents (Dishion, Kavanagh, Schneiger, Nelson, & Kaufman, 2002). Parent training can also be effective (Mason, Kosterman, Hawkins, Haggerty, & Spoth, 2003). Collaborative, community-based efforts have also shown promise (Flewelling et al., 2005); community interventions require attention to variables such as rural versus urban settings and homogeneous versus diverse groups of adolescents (Komro et al., 2004).

Targeted prevention is even more specifically directed, and is based on ideas that risk and vulnerability can be reliably measured in individuals and subgroups of adolescents (Vanyukov, Kirisci, et al., 2003). Although there are many risk factors and individual differences in vulnerability to those factors (Hawkins, Catalano, & Miller, 1992), it is imperative to design programs that will reach those most in need. For example, embedding prevention programs in early, related services such as Head Start might involve fostering the personality characteristics that are associated with later drug avoidance (Kaminski, Stormshak, Good, & Goodman, 2002). Paying attention to children's gender, personalities, social challenges, and environmental contexts maximizes prevention outcomes (Amaro et al., 2001; Guthrie & Flinchbaugh, 2001; Simons-Morton & Haynie, 2003; Smith & Anderson, 2001). Prevention efforts frequently target at-risk youth, including American Indian and Alaskan Native adolescents (Hawkins, Cummins, & Marlatt, 2004). Cultural and ethnic differences related to exposure, norms, risk, and vulnerability must, of course, be taken into account. For instance, African-American adolescents are exposed to many more risk factors than European-American adolescents; prevention efforts must be tailored to the specific risks that are encountered (Wallace & Muroff, 2002). Other targeted groups include children who have already been diagnosed with other psychopathologies (Compton, Burns, Egger, & Robertson, 2002; White et al., 1999).

Treatment

The treatment of substance abuse disorders involves outpatient therapies, inpatient programs, day treatment placements, special school environments, and for some, the juvenile justice system. Treatments vary widely across settings and outcome statistics are mixed (Henggeler, Clingempeel, Brondino, & Pickrel, 2002; Stevens & Morral, 2003). Still, treatment is superior to no treatment, although the adolescents who succeed are often those with the least serious disorders (Kaminer & Bukstein, 2005). Reviews of outcome studies suggest that relapse is common and multiple therapeutic attempts are likely (Cornelius et al., 2003; Dasinger, Shane, & Martinovich, 2004; Kaminer & Bukstein, 2005).

There are many adolescent variables that cut across types of problems and therapies. Adolescent motivation for substance abuse treatment is a primary concern, because most adolescents enter treatment due to external pressure. Incentive to change in adolescents abusing substances is modest; the strongest predictors of incentive are the negative consequences attributed to drug use (Battjes, Gordon, O'Grady, Kinlock, & Carswell, 2003; Breda & Heflinger, 2004). Individual differences related to incentives to quit (such as girls who smoke to manage weight) need to be specifically addressed

(Meyers, Klesges, Winders, & Ward, 1997; Turner & Mermelstein, 2004). Adolescents who recognize that change is necessary do better in treatment than those who do not (Callaghan et al., 2005), even though some help-seeking adolescents look for help from individuals who may not be well-trained or knowledgeable (or even supportive of their efforts, in the case of troubled peers) (Stiffman, Striley, Brown, Limb, & Ostmann, 2003).

Therapeutic alliances are essential to establish. Many adolescents come into therapy with various negative beliefs: "My therapist may try to force me to do things I don't like." "This therapy may do more harm than good." "He probably thinks he knows everything." "She'll think I'm a failure if I use again." "I'm better off without therapy" (Beck, Liese, & Najavits, 2005, p. 490); these must be identified and refuted. Parents, too, may enter therapy with erroneous beliefs related to confidentiality and process. Because alliances with adolescents and their parents are both related to treatment success, ongoing attention to trust and rapport is needed (Hogue, Dauber, Stambaugh, Cecero, & Liddle, 2006; Shelef, Diamond, Diamond, & Liddle, 2005; Tetzlaff et al., 2005). Gender and ethnic matching of clients and therapists may enhance alliances for some adolescents (Shillington & Clapp, 2003; Wintersteen, Mensinger, & Diamond, 2005). Retention and premature dropout are constant concerns; addressing these concerns early and often is important (Beck et al., 2005). Adolescents who view the therapist more positively are more likely to stay in treatment; they also display less severe substance-related impairments and have fewer deviant friends (Battjes, Gordon, O'Grady, & Kinlock, 2004).

One of the first treatment decisions for adolescents involves level of care (e.g., outpatient versus inpatient). Specialty care is often needed for those who have previously failed in outpatient programs, those with comorbid psychopathologies, those experiencing suicidality, those in need of medical supervision for withdrawal, and those requiring isolation from family, friends, or communities (Kaminer & Bukstein, 2005; Vandrey, Budney, Kamon, & Stanger, 2005). Crisis situations require immediate placements (Fishman, Clemmey, & Adger, 2003). Sadly, racial and ethnic disparities exist in terms of access to specialty care and involvement in the justice system (Aarons, Brown, Garland, & Hough, 2004). For some adolescents, drug courts are more effective than family courts in reducing substance use and externalizing behavior (Belenko & Dembo, 2003; Henggeler et al., 2006).

Individual Approaches

Individual treatment is a common intervention paradigm. Variations include behavior therapy, cognitive-behavior therapy, 12-step programs, and pharmacotherapy, with modifications for particular drugs (e.g., alcohol versus heroin) (Clemmey, Payne, & Fishman, 2004). New pharmacological treatments show promise (Dawes & Johnson, 2004). Positive outcomes associated with 12-step programs are often dependent on adolescent motivation and severity of disorder (Kelly, Myers, & Brown, 2002). Among the most well-defined, well-studied, and well-supported treatments for substance abuse are the cognitive-behavioral approaches (Beck et al., 2005; Deas & Thomas, 2001; Lochman & van den Steenhoven, 2002; Waldron & Kaminer, 2004). Working with adolescent beliefs is core to the cognitive model of psychotherapy. Beliefs about self (such as negative beliefs about worth, lovability, and vulnerability), beliefs about life experiences, and substance-related beliefs are all important. Figure 14.9 provides an overall cognitive framework (Liese & Franz, 1996; Wright, Beck, Newman, & Liese, 1993). The process by which change occurs involves the identification of automatic thoughts and the eventual understanding by the adolescent that these thoughts are not completely accurate or valid.

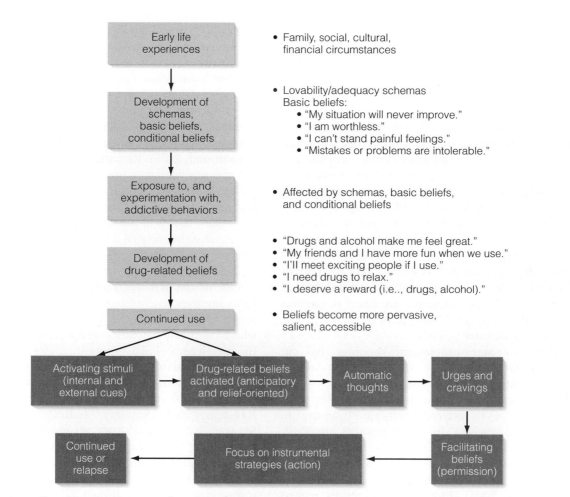

FIGURE 14:9 Cognitive developmental model of substance abuse.
Source: From Liese, B.S. & Franz, R.A. (1996), 'Treating substance use disorders with cognitive therapy: Lessons learned and implications for the future' in P.M. Salkovskis (Ed.), "Frontiers of cognitive therapy", p. 482 (New York: Guilford Press).

Modification of these thoughts must take place at both surface and deep levels for sustained improvement (Beck et al., 2005).

Motivational interviewing is another individual therapy that shows potential. Motivational interviewing is a brief intervention incorporating aspects of motivational psychology, client-centered therapy, and stages-of-change theory (Lawendowski, 1998; O'Leary Tevyaw & Monti, 2004). One unique contribution of motivational approaches is their attempt to capitalize on some of the most pertinent adolescent characteristics and control for others (Metrik, Frissell, McCarthy, D'Amico, & Brown, 2003; Neal & Carey, 2004; Weisz & Hawley, 2002).

Individual psychotherapies that account for neurocognitive and emotional deficits related to drug abuse are likely to produce better results (Fishbein et al., 2006). Psychotherapy for adolescents with substance abuse disorders must, in many cases, include treatment for additional psychopathologies (Esposito-Smythers, 2004, 2005; Funk, McDermeit, Godley, & Adams, 2003; Sakai, Mikulich-Gilbertson, & Crowley, 2006; Titus, Dennis, White, Scott, & Funk, 2003). Pharmacotherapy, and combinations of individual, family, and milieu therapies, may be beneficial for these adolescents (Kaminer & Bukstein, 2005; Randall, Henggeler, Cunningham, Rowland, & Swenson, 2001).

Family and Group Approaches

With the role of parents and families in the development and maintenance of substance abuse disorders, it makes sense that family approaches would be an important source of therapeutic impact (Brody et al., 2004; Lochman & van den Steenhoven, 2002; Thompson, Pomeroy, & Gober, 2005). For some subgroups, it appears particularly important. For instance, parents have different roles in different cultural groups (Kim, Zane, & Hong, 2002). There are differences, for example, in the degree to which families display connectedness or involvement in their adolescents' lives, as well as in the amount and type of supervision. In Latino families, with high rates of substance abuse disorders and a family-oriented culture, family therapy is effective (Sale et al., 2005); for Latina girls, family connectedness is an especially salient factor leading to delayed or reduced alcohol use. Mental health professionals working with diverse families need to account for variables such as ethnic orientation, level of acculturation, and ethnic mistrust

in order to provide culturally competent treatments (Gil, Wagner, & Tubman, 2004; Stewart-Sabin & Chaffin, 2003; Strada, Donohoe, & Lefforge, 2006).

Group approaches can also be effective, particularly those based on cognitive-behavioral principles (Waldron & Kaminer, 2004) and those focused on reducing marijuana use (Battjes et al., 2004). The role of peers is again an issue. As with treatments for conduct disorder, group treatment for substance abuse is related to both improvement and deterioration (Macgowan & Wagner, 2005; O'Leary et al., 2002), because peers often provide "deviancy training," as well as support and modeling of varieties of substance abuse (Dishion, Poulin, & Burraston, 2001; Dishion, McCord, & Poulin, 1998; Kaminer, 2005; Wagenaar et al., 2006). Managing the peer environment in group therapy is critical to treatment success (Dishion & Medici Skaggs, 2000), with "denormalization" of risk behaviors essential (Messerlian et al., 2005). School-based quitting programs are another treatment option; adolescent awareness of and access to such programs are necessary first steps (Balch et al., 2004). Students who display higher motivation to change, who have previously attempted to quit, and who experience fewer stressors are more likely to attend school programs (Turner, Mermelstein, Berbaum, & Veldhuis, 2004). Residential treatments often report the most marked improvements, but meaningful reductions in drug use must be understood in the context of the more distressed and dysfunctional adolescents who enter residential programs and who frequently relapse when discharged (Dasinger, Shane, & Martinovich, 2004).

Given that relapse is a fairly common occurrence, relapse prevention must be incorporated and emphasized in individual, family, and group treatments. Research has identified the variables most associated with relapse; these include comorbid psychopathology, negative emotion, withdrawal symptoms, and peer pressure (Cornelius et al., 2003; Kaminer & Bukstein, 2005; McCarthy, Tomlinson, Anderson, Marlatt, & Brown, 2005). The likelihood of drug exposure and renewed drug use must be addressed. It is essential to learn to manage cravings and urges, to deal with high-risk situations, and to make necessary lifestyle changes (Beck et al., 2005; Wills et al., 2001). For many adolescents leaving inpatient programs, specific and detailed aftercare plans are crucial components of ongoing success.

■ Key Terms

Brain development (pg. 264)
Risk taking (pg. 264)
Problem behavior syndrome (pg. 265)
Use (pg. 266)
Experimental substance use (pg. 266)
Social substance use (pg. 266)
Abuse (pg. 266)
Tolerance (pg. 266)
Physical dependence (pg. 266)
Withdrawal symptoms (pg. 266)
Psychological dependence (pg. 266)
Addiction (pg. 267)
Binge drinking (pg. 269)
Smoking (pg. 269)
Craving (pg. 270)
Gateway hypothesis (pg. 276)
Common factors model (pg. 276)
Incentive-sensitization theory (pg. 278)
Incentive salience (pg. 278)
Self-medication (pg. 278)
Cognitive-deficits model (pg. 279)
Generational forgetting (pg. 281)
Motivational interviewing (pg. 284)

■ Chapter Summary

- Adolescent brain development is characterized by continuing growth, heightened novelty-seeking, and evolving self-regulation.
- Substance abuse in adolescence carries particular risk for the still-developing adolescent brain.
- Substance abuse is defined as excessive use of or dependence on an addictive substance. Addiction is defined as a chronic disorder characterized by compulsive drug-seeking and abuse.
- Alcohol use and abuse by adolescents is of particular concern because of its relatively high incidence and its specific detrimental effects on adolescent brain development.

- Although less dramatic than some other forms of substance abuse, tobacco use is the source of extensive health problems and is associated with a variety of other substance abuse and behavioral problems.
- Other substances abused by adolescents include marijuana, inhalants, cocaine, methamphetamine, hallucinogens, and anabolic steroids.
- For most classes of drugs, developmental trajectories involve a progression from exposure, to experimentation, to regular use, and, potentially, abuse and dependence.
- In general, early substance abuse predicts later use and a range of negative physical and psychological outcomes.
- The gateway hypothesis is a stage theory of drug involvement that proposes that the use of drugs such as alcohol or marijuana act as a "gateway" to the use of "harder" drugs such as cocaine, heroin or methamphetamines. The common factors model assumes there is a non-specific propensity to use drugs.
- Genetic studies indicate that a strong heritable vulnerability exists for substance abuse problems.
- Conduct problems and depression occurring in childhood are both significant risk factors for the development of substance abuse during adolescence.
- Parental expectations and practices are a powerful influence on whether or not adolescents abuse substances during adolescence.
- Peer attitudes supporting substance use, especially as teens enter high school, lead to an increase in substance abuse.
- Assessment of, and treatment for, comorbid psychopathologies is particularly important when treating substance abuse in adolescence.
- Relapse prevention is an important aspect of an effective substance abuse treatment program.

IN PREVIOUS CHAPTERS, we have considered how biological and psychological processes interact and how they contribute to the challenges and achievements of normal development, as well as to the nature, progression, and treatment of disorders. This interplay between biology and psychology is particularly salient as we focus attention on relations between healthy and unhealthy eating, safe and dangerous practices for weight management, and clinically significant eating disorders. Because of the developmental status of adolescents, their increasing independence, increased autonomy in food choice, and still not fully mature cognitive abilities, they are vulnerable to an array of eating problems. It is absolutely crucial to understand the unique circumstances of adolescence and the ways in which eating disorders emerge and are maintained, because struggles with eating disorders may involve life-threatening crises.

Developmental Tasks and Challenges Related to Eating and Appearance

The physical development that occurs throughout adolescence has multiple impacts on psychological development and functioning, with the onset of puberty signaling many of the most dramatic changes. Significant growth involves proportional increases in the food intake of nutrients and energy (Stang & Story, 2005). For girls, average weight gain is approximately 38 pounds over the course of adolescence, with associated increases in body fat levels. For boys, average weight gain is about 50 pounds, with a decrease in body fat levels. There are, of course, individual and group differences related to the beginning of puberty and weight gain; African-American girls, for example, enter puberty earlier than European-American girls (Stang & Story, 2005). Keep in mind, however, that the prevalence of weight issues and dieting in ever-younger samples suggests that body-related concerns are not exclusive to a particular age or stage of development.

One of the keys to understanding eating disorders depends on understanding issues related to **body image** (i.e., a person's perception of his or her own physical appearance) and **body satisfaction** (i.e., the degree to which a person is accepting of, or pleased with, his or her physical appearance). Concerns about body image do not appear suddenly in adolescence. These concerns are present in elementary school and increase significantly from fifth to eighth grades (Lynch & Eppers-Reynolds, 2005; Pine, 2001). Body concerns have been studied mostly in girls and women; more recent studies include boys and men. Body satisfaction is relatively similar in younger girls and boys, with most children reporting satisfaction. By early adolescence, however, **body dissatisfaction** increases (Littleton & Ollendick, 2003; Ricciardelli & McCabe, 2001; Wiseman, Peltzman, Halmi, & Sunday, 2004). Girls become more preoccupied with appearance and weight (Jones, 2004; Phares, Steinberg, & Thompson, 2004); girls who are underweight are more satisfied with their bodies (Kelly, Wall, Eisenberg, Story, & Neumark-Sztainer, 2005). Dissatisfied boys are divided between wanting to lose weight and wanting to gain weight (or muscle) (Jones & Crawford, 2005; McCabe & Ricciardelli, 2004b). For both girls and boys, there is a need to explore cognitive and emotional evaluations related to negative body image and dissatisfaction (Bearman, Presnell, Martinez, & Stice, 2006; Bornholt et al., 2005).

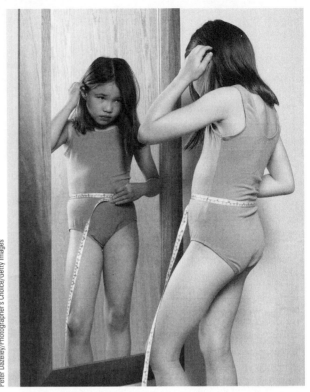

Peter Dazeley/Photographer's Choice/Getty Images

Body image and body satisfaction are important developmental issues emerging in middle childhood and early adolescence.

There are, of course, links between perception and reality. For instance, heavier body shapes and weights for girls, and both thinner and heavier shapes and weights for boys, have been associated with lower levels of popularity (indexed by peer reports of status and reputation); yet likeability (indexed by peer reports of who they want to spend time with) is not affected (Wang, Houshyar, & Prinstein, 2006). Although it is somewhat reassuring that, in the immediate context of friendships, body shape and weight do not impact how likeable one is, we must emphasize that, in the larger social context of peer relationships, shape and weight do influence perceptions of popularity. Body weight also has some impact on dating: "for each one point increase in body mass index, the probability of having a romantic relationship decreased by 6%" (Halpern, King, Oslak, & Udry, 2005). So, although girls underestimate the body size that boys find attractive, boys do regard thinness as important in rating the attractiveness of girls (Paxton, Norris, Wertheim, Durkin, & Anderson, 2005). Overall, because of various combinations of personal and social factors, negative body image is associated with poor opposite-sex relationships (Davison & McCabe, 2006).

In the United States, differences in body image and body satisfaction are related to race and ethnicity. Body satisfaction is highest (about 40%) among African-American girls (Kelly, Wall, et al., 2005; Nishina, Ammon, Bellmore, & Graham, 2006). This may be because descriptions of ideal body size are larger; this is the case for both African Americans and for Latina Americans (Perry, Rosenblatt, & Wang, 2004). Although African-American and Latina girls are aware of culturally prevalent (i.e., Western, European-American, secular) ideals that emphasize thinness, these ideals appear to be internalized less frequently compared to European-American and Asian-American girls (Hermes & Keel, 2003; Shaw, Ramirez, Trost, Randall, & Stice, 2004; White, Kohlmaier, Varnado-Sullivan, & Williamson, 2003). Ethnicity is also important for boys, with reviews of the data suggesting that boys from a range of ethnic groups (e.g., African Americans, Latino Americans, Native Americans) display more disordered eating and body change strategies than boys from European-American backgrounds (Ricciardelli, McCabe, Williams, & Thompson, 2007).

Negative body image, body dissatisfaction, and concerns related to weight and appearance are observed across many countries and cultures, including Argentina, Australia, Chile, China, Cuba, Denmark, Guatemala, India, Iran, Israel, Norway, Panama, Peru, Taiwan, Tibet, and Turkey (Canpolat, Orsel, Akdemir, & Ozbay, 2005; Latzer, 2003; Li, Hu, Ma, Wu, & Ma, 2005; McArthur, Holbert, & Pena, 2005; Nobakht & Dezhkam, 2000; Page, Lee, & Miao, 2005; Ricciardelli, McCabe, Ball, & Mellor, 2004; Shroff & Thompson, 2004; Storvoll, Strandbu, & Wichstrom, 2005; Waaddegaard & Petersen, 2002; Wang, Byrne, Kenardy, & Hills, 2005; Ying & Hong, 2005). Rapid social transformation in some countries (such as Fiji, Belize, and the countries of East Africa) has been tied to increasing concerns. It is hypothesized that among the social changes are a profusion of media images that spread Western, European-American, secular ideals of beauty and thinness (Becker, Burwell, Herzog, Hamburg, & Gilman, 2002; Eddy, Hennessey, & Thompson-Brenner, 2007). Research designed to investigate sets of risk and protective factors is taking place around the globe (Anderson-Fye, 2004; Becker, 2004).

Many investigators have examined the influence of **society and the media** on body image and body attitudes (Derenne & Beresin, 2006; Levine & Murnen,

2009; Stice, Schupak-Neuberg, Shaw, & Stein, 1994; Wiseman, Sunday, & Becker, 2005), and have described the ways in which television, movies, magazines, and internet sites glamorize specific, narrow, and often-unrealistic versions of beauty (e.g., very slender women's bodies and muscular men's bodies). Harrison and Hefner (2008) suggest that media exposure "(1) normalizes dieting and excessive thinness, and (2) encourages young people to repeatedly evaluate their bodies, to find them wanting, and to engage in extreme dieting, overexercising, and other health-compromising behaviors . . ." (p. 381).

Many investigations have distinguished between the awareness of ideas and attitudes about appearance, thinness, and beauty, and the **internalization** of such ideas and attitudes (Cafri, Yamamiya, Brannick, & Thompson, 2005; Harrison, 2001; Jones, Vigfusdottir, & Lee, 2004; Stice, Spangler, & Agras, 2001). Studies of younger (11–12 years) and older girls (15–16 years) show that both groups are aware of sociocultural images and ideals; the older girls, however, are more likely to have internalized these images and ideals (Clay, Vignoles, & Dittmar, 2005; Hermes & Keel, 2003; see Figure 15.1). According to Sherwood and Neumark-Sztainer (2001), "media exposure does not cause, but reinforces, an unhealthy body image among vulnerable women" (p. 228). In

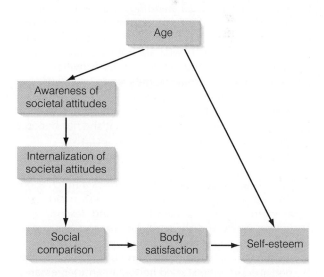

FIGURE 15:1 A conceptual model of proposed mediators of age trends in body satisfaction and self-esteem.
SOURCE: From Clay, D., Vignoles, V.L., & Dittmar, H. (2005), "Body image and self-esteem among adolescent girls: Testing the influence of sociocultural factors", 'Journal of Research on Adolescence', 15, 451-477. Reprinted by permission of Wiley-Blackwell.

other words, *internalization is more important than awareness.*

How these sociocultural factors relate to dieting (and the kinds of harmful and extreme dieting characteristic of eating disorders) is complex. This topic will be more fully explored in upcoming sections. For now, examples of some of the connections between these factors and dieting include findings that link body image, dieting, and smoking (Austin & Gortmaker, 2001; Stice & Shaw, 2003) and findings that adolescents from higher socioeconomic status backgrounds are more aware of body ideals related to thinness and have more family and friends who are trying to lose weight (Wardle et al., 2004). Dieting also appears to be related to different sets of variables (such as friends' and families' weight concerns) for adolescent girls and boys (Presnell, Bearman, & Stice, 2004; Saling, Ricciardelli, & McCabe, 2005; Thompson, Rafiroiu, & Sargent, 2003).

Eating Disorders

The Case of Elizabeth

Elizabeth is 17 years old and in eleventh grade. She is a successful student, in leadership positions on several service clubs, and student editor of her high school's literary magazine. Elizabeth's grades have been outstanding, and her teachers consider her a bright and extremely conscientious student. Elizabeth is the only child of two affluent, professional parents who are both very involved in her academic and extracurricular activities. Elizabeth reports that she gets along well with her parents, but that she would like more independence than they seem comfortable with. Elizabeth's parents have noted that she has become increasingly withdrawn and even secretive, especially toward them, in the past year.

While Elizabeth has had a very successful high school career thus far, junior high was a much more difficult time for her. Although she performed well academically, she had few friends and described feeling lonely and alienated. Her parents became concerned about her sad mood and noticeable weight gain in eighth grade and brought her to her pediatrician, who started her on an antidepressant. Within a few months of taking the medication and starting high school, Elizabeth was clearly happier, more energetic, and making more friends. Because of lingering concern over her weight, she began a very disciplined diet and program of running, resulting in the loss of 30 pounds over several

months. Elizabeth received considerable attention and praise for these efforts from her parents and friends. Elizabeth's sophomore year was successful, and her parents described her as happy and busy. The summer before her junior year, Elizabeth and her parents visited several colleges and she enrolled in a course to help her prepare for the SAT and ACT tests she would be taking in her junior year. Her parents also hired a consultant to begin working with Elizabeth in preparation for applying to colleges in the fall of her senior year. The consultant helped Elizabeth plan her upcoming schedule, including advising her on what extracurricular activities would look best to the selective colleges her parents were encouraging her to apply to.

Early in her junior year, Elizabeth's parents began to notice that her diet was increasingly restricted and that she seemed to avoid eating while out in public. Already quite thin when the school year started, Elizabeth began to lose weight at an alarming rate. She continued to run early in the morning before school and began to miss most family dinners. Her parents became increasingly worried as Elizabeth's appearance became gaunt and she admitted to them that she had not had her period in several months. Throughout this time, Elizabeth continued to excel in school and her energy level seemed especially high. At home, however, Elizabeth was isolated, seldom speaking to her parents except to argue about her refusal to eat the food her mother prepared. The only foods her parents ever saw her eat were yogurt and raw vegetables such as carrots and cauliflower. Also, despite being told by her parents and friends that she was too thin, she insisted that she was fat. Over Elizabeth's objections, her parents brought her to their physician for a checkup. There they learned that her weight had fallen to a dangerously low level and that she was experiencing clinically significant anemia and cardiac symptoms. Elizabeth was admitted directly to a medical inpatient unit for eating disorders. ■

The Case of Kayla

Kayla is 19 years old and a first-year student at a local community college. She lives in an apartment with several of her high school friends who are also students. Kayla's time in high school was characterized by considerable variability in her academic performance. She did well early in high school but, following her parents' divorce in the middle of her sophomore year, she began to disengage from school. This was a stressful time for the family as Kayla's mother made the transition to working full time while continuing to care for Kayla and her two younger siblings. Kayla began to skip classes occasionally, failed to complete homework, and began hanging out with a new group of friends who smoked and drank and did not value academic activities. After her promising start in high school, her guidance counselor became concerned about Kayla's missed classes and dropping grades, and met with Kayla and her mother toward the end of the year. That meeting led to a referral to her family physician and a mental health counselor. Kayla was treated for depression with medication and psychotherapy. She felt better, reconnected with old friends, and returned to school in the fall feeling more settled and focused. Over the next two years, Kayla did somewhat better, but continued to have intermittent academic and social problems, although never to the extent that she did in tenth grade.

Early in her senior year of high school, Kayla became concerned about her body size and shape. She was slightly overweight and a boy she was dating made some joking but rude comments about her "full and curvy" appearance. Kayla was very upset and made several unsuccessful attempts to lose weight. During this time, she also began to induce vomiting after hearing several friends talk about this as a way of controlling their weight. Soon Kayla was vomiting several times a day, generally at home but occasionally at school as well. Kayla found herself thinking about food often; this made her feel very anxious. She found that the anxiety lessened considerably when she ate, although the relief did not last. In fact, once the initial pleasure wore off, eating made her feel more anxiety and more shame. These feelings led her to induce vomiting to calm herself and keep from gaining more weight. Multiple times per day, Kayla was repeating a cycle in which she would binge on foods high in carbohydrates, such as cookies and ice cream, feel anxiety and guilt, and vomit. She began to buy food and hide it in her bedroom so that she could binge late at night when everyone else was sleeping. Although the girls at school often talked about various ways of purging (e.g., vomiting, using laxatives, exercising), Kayla kept her behavior secret. Her weight fluctuated considerably, although always returning to approximately the same weight she was when the difficulties began. Although Kayla continued to meet periodically with her therapist throughout high school to talk about her parents' divorce and to get help with symptoms of mild depression, she never mentioned her binging and purging behaviors.

Once she was living in an apartment, Kayla found it more difficult to hide her binging and purging from her roommates. While two of the women she lived with pretty much ignored the unusual behavior, one roommate expressed her concern and told Kayla that she was currently being treated for bulimia in a group program at the college. She encouraged Kayla to meet with an eating disorders specialist in the counseling department. Eventually, Kayla agreed and began both individual and group therapy. ∎

Eating disorders are psychopathologies characterized by severe disturbances in eating behaviors, disturbed perceptions of body size and shape, fear of being fat, and compensatory behaviors to lose weight or to prevent weight gain (Bulik, 2002; Reijonen, Pratt, Patel, & Greydanus, 2003; see Table 15.1). There are two main types of eating disorders: **anorexia nervosa** (illustrated in the case of Elizabeth) and **bulimia nervosa** (the case of Kayla). The DSM-IV-TR category for atypical clinical presentations is **eating disorder, not otherwise specified**.

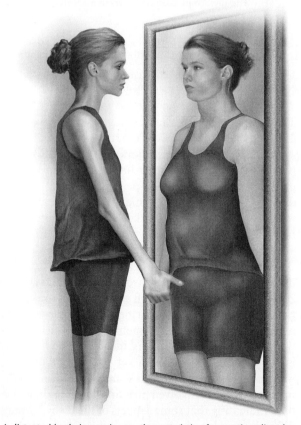

A distorted body image is one characteristic of an eating disorder.

TABLE 15:1 DSM-IV-TR CRITERIA FOR ANOREXIA NERVOSA AND BULIMIA NERVOSA

Anorexia Nervosa

A. Refusal to maintain body weight at or above a minimally normal weight for age and height

B. Intense fear of gaining weight or becoming fat, even though underweight

C. Disturbance in the way in which one's body weight or shape is experienced, undue influence of body weight or shape on self-evaluation, or denial of the seriousness of the current low body weight

D. In postmenarcheal females, amenorrhea, i.e., the absence of at least three consecutive menstrual cycles

There are two subtypes:

Restricting type: The person has not regularly engaged in binge-eating or purging behavior.
Binge-eating/Purging type: The person has regularly engaged in binge-eating or purging behavior (i.e., self-induced vomiting or the misuse of laxatives, diuretics, or enemas).

Bulimia Nervosa

A. Recurrent episodes of binge eating. An episode of binge eating is characterized by both of the following:
   (1) eating, in a discrete period of time (e.g., within any 2-hour period), an amount of food that is definitely larger than most people would eat during a similar period of time and under similar circumstances
   (2) a sense of lack of control over eating during the episode

B. Recurrent, inappropriate compensatory behavior in order to prevent weight gain, such as self-induced vomiting; misuse of laxatives, diuretics, enemas, or other medications; fasting; or excessive exercise

C. The binge eating and inappropriate compensatory behaviors both occur, on average, at least twice a week for 3 months.

D. Self-evaluation is unduly influenced by body shape and weight.

E. The disturbance does not occur exclusively during episodes of anorexia nervosa.

There are two subtypes:

Purging type: The person has regularly engaged in self-induced vomiting or the misuse of laxatives, diuretics, or enemas.
Nonpurging type: The person has used other inappropriate compensatory behaviors, such as fasting or excessive exercise.

Source: Reprinted with permission from the Diagnostic and Statistical Manual of Mental Disorders, Text Revision, Fourth Edition, (Copyright 2000). American Psychiatric Association.

The DSM-IV-TR also has a category of **binge eating disorder** that is the focus of current research.

Disturbed eating behaviors may include severe restricting of food intake or limiting food to particular types. Distorted body perceptions may involve distorted body image or denial of the seriousness of weight loss (Steiner & Lock, 1998). Compensatory behaviors include excessive exercising, vomiting, and/or laxative use (Davis et al., 1997; Reba et al., 2005; Shroff et al., 2006; Tozzi et al., 2006); laxative use is associated with increased severity (Tozzi et al., 2006). Other symptoms, such as obsessions and compulsions, are also often described. Typical obsessions include concerns with symmetry and somatic functioning; typical compulsions include rituals involving order and control (Halmi et al., 2003). Although most of the research on the clinical picture of eating disorders has involved girls and women, there are data indicating that some aspects of the disorder may differ by gender (Anderson & Bulik, 2004; Eliot & Baker, 2001; Muise, Stein, & Arbess, 2003; Robb & Dadson, 2002). For instance, the nature and function of compensatory behaviors appears to be different for adolescent boys and adolescent girls.

Research into the various subtypes of eating disorders, and whether these are best understood as continuous or discontinuous examples of disorder, continues, with important implications for assessment and treatment (Gleaves, Brown, & Warren, 2004; Grilo, 2004; Keel et al., 2004). Current explanations focus on three latent dimensions of eating disorders: (1) **binge eating;** (2) **fear of fatness, with compensatory behaviors;** and (3) **drive for thinness** (Williamson et al., 2002). Combinations of these dimensions correspond to the discrete syndromes of anorexia, bulimia, and binge eating disorder. Individuals with anorexia (like Elizabeth) score high on the second and third dimensions, not on the first. Individuals with bulimia (like Kayla) score high on the first and second dimensions, not on the third. Individuals with binge eating disorder score high on the first dimension, not on the second or third.

Anorexia nervosa can lead to dangerous levels of weight loss.

Christopher LaMarca/Redux Pictures

Additional research is focused on **partial eating disorders**, which are subclinical presentations in adolescents and adults who meet some, but not all, of the diagnostic criteria. These problems include multiple physical and psychological symptoms and reflect a range of severity. Some individuals who present with partial eating disorders will go on to develop full-blown disorders; most will display remission (Chamay-Weber, Narring, & Michaud, 2005; Stein, Meged, Bar-Hanin, & Blank, 1997).

The prevalence of eating disorders has increased over the past 50 years. Estimates of eating disorders range, for girls, from approximately 1% for anorexia nervosa (AN), 1% for bulimia nervosa (BN), 1.5–3.5% for binge eating disorder (BED), and 14% for eating disorders, not otherwise specified (ED-NOS); for boys, the corresponding percentages are .2% for AN, .4% for BN, 1–2% for BED, and 6.5% for ED-NOS (Hudson, Hiripi, Pope, & Kessler, 2007; Kjelsas, Bjornstrom, & Gotestam, 2004). Lifetime prevalence data for the United States vary widely, from 1–4% for AN and BN, to almost 3% for all eating disorders, to 7% for BED (Hoek & van Hoeken, 2003; Lewinsohn, Striegel-Moore, & Seeley, 2000; NIMH, 2008). It is generally accepted that adolescents from African-American and Latina backgrounds have lower rates of eating disorders, but recent evidence suggests that rates are increasing in these groups (Granillo,

Jones-Rodriguez, & Carvajal, 2005; Shaw, Ramirez, Trost, Randall, & Stice, 2004). Cross-cultural data is relatively similar. Across a 6-year European study, almost 9% were diagnosed with all types of eating disorders (Patton, Coffey, & Sawyer, 2003). In Spain, the rate is almost 5%, with ED-NOS the most frequent diagnosis (Lahortiga-Ramos et al., 2005). In Iran, rates are fairly comparable (Nobakht & Dezhkam, 2000).

Partial eating disorders are even more common. A recent study found that 56% of ninth-grade girls, 28% of ninth-grade boys, and 57% and 31% of twelfth-grade girls and boys report symptomatic behaviors such as skipping meals, fasting, binge eating, and compensatory behaviors such as use of diet pills and laxatives, vomiting, and smoking to control weight (Croll, Neumark-Sztainer, Story, & Ireland, 2002).

Adolescents diagnosed with eating disorders are also frequently diagnosed with other psychopathologies; depression is the most common (Lewinsohn et al., 2000; Reijonen et al., 2003). This comorbidity is reflected in Elizabeth's case. There is also considerable overlap between eating disorders and bipolar disorder, and symptom similarities in terms of eating dysregulation, mood dysregulation, impulsivity, and compulsions (McElroy, Kotwal, Keck, & Akiskal, 2005). Anxiety disorders, including obsessive-compulsive disorder and social phobia, are also frequently observed (Kaye, Bulik, Thornton, Barbarich, & Masters, 2004). Self-harm and suicidality are primary concerns. Sansone and Levitt (2002) note that between 15% and 39% of inpatients and outpatients with eating disorders report suicide attempts; 54% of those with bulimia who are also struggling with alcohol abuse report such attempts. Connections between eating disorders and substance abuse disorders are widely described; these have led some researchers to hypothesize that, for some, eating disorders are addictions, with food as a mood-altering substance, and food preoccupation, craving, and abuse despite negative consequences (Gold, Frost-Pineda, & Jacobs, 2003).

Developmental Course

As with all of the disorders discussed in this textbook, developmental pathways, courses, and outcomes of eating disorders are variable. In general, most adolescent syndromes are "brief and self-limiting" (Patton et al., 2003, p. 125) and approximately 70% have good recoveries. Other adolescents exhibit fluctuating courses of weight loss and gain, whereas still others deteriorate over time and are repeatedly hospitalized (Denda et al., 2002; Patton et al., 2003; Steinhausen, Boyadjieva, Griogoroiu-Serbanescu, & Neumarker, 2003; Steinhausen, Boyadjieva, Griogoroiu-Serbanescu, & Winkler-Metzke, 2000). There are continuities between adolescent and adult eating disorders as well. For example, bulimia in early adolescence predicts a 9-fold increase in risk for bulimia in late adolescence; bulimia in late adolescence (as illustrated in the case of Kayla) predicts a 35-fold increase in risk for bulimia in adulthood (Fairburn et al., 2003; Kotler, Cohen, Davies, Pine, & Walsh, 2001).

Age of onset peaks at two times: early adolescence and late adolescence. And these peaks represent key transition points, from childhood to adolescence, and from adolescence to adulthood (Attie & Brooks-Gunn, 1989; Keel, Leon, & Fulkerson, 2003). Younger adolescents are more likely to present with symptoms of AN, and older adolescents are more likely to present with symptoms of BN (Reijonen et al., 2003). The first transition involves puberty, and increased weight concerns may lead to compensatory and other problematic behaviors including smoking and drinking (Field et al., 2002; Stice, 2003). Both early- and late-maturing girls are more likely to engage in risky body change behaviors such as purging, laxative use, and exercise dependence (Field et al., 1999; McCabe & Ricciardelli, 2004a). Although most eating disorders emerge during adolescence, recent reports suggest that instances of middle- and late-life eating disorders are increasing; this phenomenon warrants additional attention (Zerbe, 2003b).

Although many adolescents are diagnosed with one form of eating disorder and remain so diagnosed, there is some evidence of **crossover** from AN to BN, and from BN to AN. Crossover, if it occurs, usually does so by the fifth year of the disorder; personality and family characteristics may influence the change (Tozzi et al., 2005). Alcohol abuse, for example, is associated with a trajectory from bulimia to anorexia; parental criticism is associated with a trajectory from anorexia to bulimia (Tozzi et al., 2005).

The psychological consequences of eating disorders include impairments in self-image, health, and social functioning (Graber, Tyrka, & Brooks-Gunn, 2003; Johnson, Cohen, Kasen, & Brook, 2002; Striegel-Moore, Seeley, & Lewinsohn, 2003), and as noted above, the development of major depression, dysthymia, and substance abuse (Measelle, Stice, & Hogansen, 2006; Perez, Joiner, & Lewinsohn, 2004; Steiner & Lock, 1998; Stice, Burton, & Shaw, 2004). Substance abuse may or may not be related to anxiety modulation (Bulik et al., 2004; Patton et al., 2003; Burton, Stice, Bearman, & Rohde, 2007), and is lower in adolescent women with restricting symptoms (Stock, Goldberg, Corbett, & Katzman, 2002). For those with severe and prolonged courses, suicidality is especially problematic (Stein et al., 2003).

There are, as well, immediate and long-term medical complications such as biochemical, endocrine, hematological, and bone-related difficulties (Carruth & Skinner, 2000; Reijonen et al., 2003; Rome & Ammerman, 2003; see Table 15.2). The mortality rate for eating disorders is high. For those admitted to hospitals, rates are approximately 10%. Across ages, estimates range from 5.9% to 7.4% for anorexia, and 2.4–3% for bulimia (Reijonen et al., 2003).

TABLE 15:2 MEDICAL COMPLICATIONS OF EATING DISORDERS

Medical complications of anorexia nervosa:

- Severe dehydration, possibly leading to shock
- Electrolyte imbalance (such as potassium insufficiency)
- Cardiac arrhythmias
- Severe malnutrition
- Thyroid gland deficiencies which can lead to cold intolerance and constipation
- Appearance of fine baby-like body hair (lanugo)
- Bloating or edema
- Decrease in white blood cells, which leads to increased susceptibility to infection
- Osteoporosis
- Tooth erosion and decay
- Seizures related to fluid shifts, due to excessive diarrhea or vomiting

Medical complications of bulimia nervosa:

- Type 2 diabetes
- High blood pressure
- High blood cholesterol levels
- Gallbladder disease
- Heart disease
- Certain types of cancer

Source: From MedlinePlus (2009) and National Institute of Diabetes and Digestive and Kidney Diseases (2008).

Etiology

Two of the most prominent explanations of eating disorders are related to (1) **family factors** and (2) **sociocultural factors**. Critical analyses of these explanations are necessary in order to separate fact from fiction, and to examine empirical data that support or refute these hypotheses. The idea that families create or foster eating disorders is most fully explored in psychodynamic explanations, and is often associated with the psychodynamic theorists Hilde Bruch (1973, 1982) and Salvador Minuchin. Bruch observed eating disorders in "good girls," girls who were characteristically compliant, achievement-oriented, and attuned to pleasing others. Bruch asserted that the daughters in these families with indulgent, over-involved parents lacked many basic skills of early childhood, such as the ability to distinguish among physical sensations, the ability to differentiate emotional experiences, and the ability to feel confident in one's body and oneself. Minuchin's book *Psychosomatic Families* (Minuchin, Rosman, & Baker, 1978) described families who were "enmeshed," or too closely involved and covertly controlling. These dysfunctional families allowed little opportunity for children's autonomy, a stressful situation exacerbated by an atmosphere of overt nurturing and affection. With the developmental press for independence and self-definition during early adolescence, crises were inevitable. Without a well-defined sense of self, and without the ability to appropriately identify their own needs and desires, daughters sought control over themselves in any way possible; for some, the struggle played out in the form of eating disorders.

As might be expected, parents of adolescent girls diagnosed with eating disorders were "bewildered, blamed and broken-hearted" (MacDonald, 2000) as they sought help for their children And their confusion and upset was warranted, as there is little or no empirical support in prospective studies for the causal impact of these psychodynamic family factors (Stice, 2002). Indeed, as we will review in a moment, if families of eating-disordered adolescents "tend to be perfectionistic, rigid, achievement-oriented and controlling, that may simply be a result of the fact that they have a genetic tendency toward obsessionality. The parents' controlling personalities aren't causing their daughters' anorexia; they are simply proof of the genetic disposition that they all share" (Lott, 1998). Even with this alternative framework, there remain valuable nuggets of information in the psychodynamic formulations that will be summarized below in somewhat reworked constructs that focus on the multiple meanings of the transition from childhood to adolescence, the nature of identification, and painful but unacknowledged or unexpressed emotions (Caparrotta & Ghaffari, 2006; Zerbe, 2001).

More recently, sociocultural models of eating disorders have become prominent (Markey, 2004). These explanations, briefly discussed in the opening section of this chapter on developmental challenges associated with eating and appearance, begin with the near-constant presentation of images of actresses and fashion models with impossibly thin bodies and shapes. Internalization of this thin ideal, coupled with pressure to be thin (coming from oneself, family, peers, and society) leads to body dissatisfaction, negative emotions, problematic dieting behaviors, and eating pathology. Indeed, research suggests that exposure to media images of the thin ideal and peer pressure to be thin immediately increase levels of body dissatisfaction (Groesz, Levine, & Murnen, 2002; Stice, Maxfield, & Wells, 2003), and this is especially so if girls are vulnerable in terms of already-present body dissatisfaction, perceived pressure to be thin, and lack of social support (Stice et al., 2001). According to Harrison and Hefner (2008), the "thin-ideal media exposure may coax body image disturbance and disordered eating into expression by activating related cognitions and emotions" (p. 381). Given that the vast majority of adolescent girls and young women *do not* develop clinically significant eating disorders, however, a single-factor model is unlikely to capture the real-life complexity of eating disorders.

A **biopsychosocial, multifactorial risk model** provides a more nuanced explanation of the development of eating disorders (Keel et al., 2001; Keery, van den Berg, & Thompson, 2004; Steiner et al., 2003; Stice, 2002). As we review the genetic and environmental factors, keep in mind that both the number and pattern of risk factors likely influence an individual's vulnerability (Stice, 2002). In addition, it is important to know that many of the studies summarized here do not differentiate among subtypes of eating disorders; given the distinct symptom profiles of the various subtypes, it is probable that some of the patterns of risk and maintenance factors differ (Stice, 2002).

Genetic and Physiological Factors

The first factors to examine are the genetic factors, which are investigated using family studies, twin studies, and molecular genetic analyses. Family and twin research suggests strong heritabilities for both anorexia and bulimia (Bulik et al., 2006; Kaye et al., 2004; Steiner & Lock, 1998). There are data that are consistent with both common genetic factors underlying eating symptoms, anxiety and depression, and distinct genetic factors for early symptoms of eating disorder. Evidence for shared environmental factors for eating symptoms and depression, gene-environment interactions, and gender specificity have also been described (Bulik, Reba, Siega-Riz, & Reichborn-Kjennerud, 2005; Silberg & Bulik, 2005; Wade, Bulik, Prescott, & Kendler, 2004). Current research is also examining various candidate genes for their roles in the etiology of eating disorders (Ribases et al., 2005; Slof-Op't Landt et al., 2005).

Neuroimaging and neurochemical studies provide additional perspective on the brain structures and mechanisms involved in appetite, food intake, and associated pleasure and reward (Chowdhury & Lask, 2001; Frank et al., 2006; Södersten, Bergh, & Zandian, 2006; Vanderlinden et al., 2004). Data suggest abnormal activity in various regions of the brain, including the prefrontal and temporal lobes (Chowdhury et al., 2003; Frank et al., 2004; Uher et al., 2004). Related research focuses on the role of the vagus nerve, elevated pain thresholds observed in adolescents with eating disorders, and dysregulation of the serotonin system (Faris et al., 2006; Frank et al.,

2004; Kaye et al., 2003; Papezova, Yamamotova, & Uher, 2006; Steiger, 2004). As noted previously, some of the physiological factors that appear to be implicated are similar to those observed in individuals with certain mood disorders and substance abuse disorders, including dysregulation of eating and mood, impulsivity, and craving responses after exposure to food cues (Kelley, Schiltz, & Landry, 2005; McElroy et al., 2005). These factors may be particularly salient for those adolescents and adults with more severe psychopathology (Steiner & Lock, 1998).

Individual Factors

Individual factors that influence the emergence of eating disorders have received much clinical and empirical attention. A cluster of biologically influenced personality characteristics has been identified that increases vulnerability. These include temperament (Martin et al., 2000), negative emotionality and emotion dysregulation (Stice, 2002; Vanderlinden et al., 2004), impulsivity (Favaro et al., 2005; Wunderlich, Connolly, & Stice, 2004), and reward and punishment sensitivity (Loxton & Dawe, 2006). **Perfectionism**, as part of a constellation of features of obsessionality, appears to run in families and leads to the "relentless pursuit of the thin ideal" (Bruch, 1973); this factor is central to both etiology and maintenance processes (Castro-Fornieles et al., 2007; Halmi et al., 2005; Stice, 2002; Tozzi et al., 2004; Woodside et al., 2002). The role of sexual orientation requires further exploration: gay and bisexual adolescents are at increased risk (Austin et al., 2004). Cognitive schema that overlap with those observed in adolescents who are depressed, such as the belief that one is ugly or stupid, have also been identified as risk factors (Cooper, Rose, & Turner, 2005, 2006).

Another cluster of personality characteristics is more psychodynamically informed. These include variables related to self (Bers, Blatt, & Dolinsky, 2004; Eliot, 2004; Huprich, Stepp, Graham, & Johnson, 2004). For example, with respect to levels of agency, reflectivity, differentiation, and relatedness, Bers et al. report that individuals with anorexia described lower levels of agency and relatedness, as well as a heightened and harsh self-reflectivity; these self-descriptions distinguish between psychiatric patients with anorexia and non-psychiatric patients, as well as between patients with anorexia and patients with other disorders. Other variables in the psychodynamic framework involve atypical

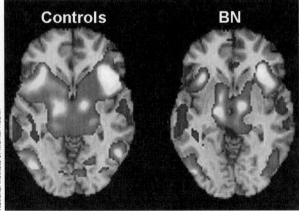

National Institute of Mental Health

Women with bulimia nervosa (BN), when compared with healthy women, showed different patterns of brain activity while doing a task that required self-regulation. This abnormality may underlie binge eating and other impulsive behaviors that occur with the eating disorder, according to an article published in the January 2009 issue of the Archives of General Psychiatry.

emotional development and functioning (such as a reluctance to express emotion or a tendency to restrict emotional experiences), with difficulties often traced back to early relationship interactions (Clinton, 2006; Panfilis, Rabbaglio, Rossi, Zita, & Maggini, 2003; Sim & Zeman, 2004). Various personality patterns also increase the risk of eating disorders (Cassin & von Ranson, 2005; Sansone, Levitt, & Sansone, 2005). Overall neuroticism, as well as combinations of a sense of incompetence, avoidant coping style, and a lack of reciprocity with parents are examples of these factors (Bulik et al., 2006; Holliday, Landau, Collier, & Treasure, 2006; Wheeler, Wintre, & Polivy, 2003).

Body-related characteristics and attitudes are another set of risk factors, with body dissatisfaction at the nexus. According to Stice and colleagues (Stice, 2002; Stice & Whitenton, 2002), body dissatisfaction results from either a history of being overweight or pressure to be thin, or both. Higher body mass index (BMI) predicts teasing from others that leads to body dissatisfaction; dissatisfaction then leads to eating pathology and impaired psychological functioning (Johnson & Wardle, 2005; Striegel-Moore et al., 2005; van den Berg, Wertheim, Thompson, & Paxton, 2002). Teasing appears to be a particularly important factor for both girls and boys (Barker & Galambos, 2003; Eisenberg, Neumark-Sztainer, Haines, & Wall, 2006). A different type of body risk factor involves participation in weight-focused sports, such as gymnastics or running (Sherwood, Neumark-Sztainer, Story, Beuhring, & Resnick, 2002). Puberty has also received research scrutiny, with current hypotheses related to gender-specific interactions of pubertal status and other variables such as social comparison (Leon, Fulkerson, Perry, & Cudeck, 1993; Morrison, Kalin, & Morrison, 2004; O'Dea & Abraham, 1999; Ricciardelli & McCabe, 2004; Stice, 2002).

Another type of risk factor involves the motivation underlying food choices and dieting. According to Lindeman and Stark (2000), low-risk dieters enjoy food more, are less depressed, and have fewer body-image issues. High-risk dieters experience less pleasure in eating, are more depressed, and have more body-image disturbances. High-risk dieters appear to use food more ideologically. For instance, those who see food as an expression of self (as do some vegetarians or vegans) are at higher risk for the development of eating disorders.

A history of negative events or psychopathology also increases an individual's risk of developing an eating disorder. Early health problems, physical and sexual abuse, date violence and rape, and both internalizing and externalizing disorders increase vulnerability (Ackard & Neumark-Sztainer, 2002; Fonseca, Ireland, & Resnick, 2002; Johnson, Cohen, Kotler, Kasen, & Brook, 2002; Moorhead et al., 2003; Perkins, Luster, & Jank, 2002). The impact of internalized racism and acculturative stress (i.e., the difficulties associated with attempts to assimilate to the majority culture) for women of color has also been emphasized (Gilbert, 2003).

Parent and Family Factors

Parent and family factors have long been implicated in the development and maintenance of eating disorders. As noted, however, we need to be very careful how we evaluate and address these factors. It may turn out that an appreciation of bidirectional influences provides the most useful information (Steinberg & Phares, 2001). It is also likely that specific family factors are more salient for already vulnerable adolescents (Stice, 2002). One basic risk variable involves general family dysfunction. For instance, families with more problematic communication, more psychopathology, and more financial difficulties have adolescents at higher risk (Moorhead et al., 2003; Steinberg & Phares, 2001). Certain patterns of dysfunction appear specific to eating disorder subtypes, with families of adolescents with anorexia more controlled and organized and families of adolescents with bulimia more chaotic and conflicted (Steiner & Lock, 1998). Perceptions of family functioning (versus actual family functioning) provide additional perspective. Daughters with eating disorders, for example, perceive more family dysfunction than their mothers, and this may be because of their feelings of inadequacy and distrust of others (Dancyger, Fornari, & Sunday, 2006).

Examining some of the specific aspects of maternal and paternal behaviors may elucidate some of these more general findings. The relationships of mothers and daughters are a frequent clinical focus. Mothers' critical comments about weight and shape and the frequency of such comments appear to be more influential than family conflict (Cooley, Toray, Wang, & Valdez, 2008; Hanna & Bond, 2006). Encouragement to diet is also related to body dissatisfaction and drive for thinness (Cooley et al., 2008; Wertheim, Martin, Prior, Sanson, & Smart, 2002). The data on mothers' own modeling of eating pathology (e.g., emotional eating or restrictive eating) and negative body image is mixed (Cooley et al., 2008; Elfhag & Linne, 2005; Stice, 2002).

Fathers who emphasize attractiveness and control food intake increase the risk of eating pathology (Dixon, Gill, & Adair, 2003). Fathers, as well as mothers and siblings, who tease daughters increase negative outcomes (Keery, Boutelle, van den Berg, & Thompson, 2005). Paternal rejection is an especially poignant risk factor (Rojo-Moreno, Livianos-Aldana, Conesa-Burquet, & Cava, 2006). There are, of course, protective family factors as well. Family connectedness, positive family communication, and parental monitoring all decrease the risk of eating disorders in adolescents (Fonseca et al., 2002).

The **tripartite influence model** of eating disorders incorporates several of the psychosocial risk factors (Keery et al., 2004; Shroff & Thompson, 2006). This model proposes that three factors (i.e., parents, peers, and media) influence the development of body dissatisfaction and eating problems through two mechanisms: the internalization of the thin ideal and appearance comparison processes. Recent work with Japanese adolescents has increased empirical support for the model (Yamamiya, Shroff, & Thompson, 2008).

Assessment and Diagnosis

Assessment and diagnosis of eating disorders can be especially problematic because most adolescents with eating disorders deny difficulties (often vehemently) and avoid contact with medical or mental health professionals (Collins & Ricciardelli, 2005; Fisher, Schneider, Burns, Symons, & Mandel, 2001). Therefore, therapeutic engagement and alliance processes, to be addressed more fully in the following section, are of the utmost priority.

There are a number of well-validated structured interview and self-report measures for screening and diagnosis, although instruments need to be designed and interpreted with regard for differences in the clinical presentation of adolescents versus adults and in ethnicity and gender (Anderson, Lundgren, Shapiro, & Paulosky, 2004; Fisher et al., 2001; Franko et al., 2004; Stice, Fisher, & Martinez, 2004). Although adolescents can be truthful and accurate in reporting their symptoms, biochemical screening may provide additional information (Turner, Batik, Palmer, Forbes, & McDermott, 2000). Because of different perspectives of adolescents and parents, particularly related to family functioning, parent reports should always be solicited (Dancyger, Fornari, Scionti, Wisotsky, & Sunday, 2005). It is, of course, absolutely necessary for a comprehensive medical examination to be part of the assessment process.

Differential diagnosis most often involves making a decision regarding the presence of body dysmorphic disorder (involving an excessive preoccupation with imagined or actual slight defects in physical appearance (Sobanski & Schmidt, 2000), obsessive compulsive disorder, and the anxiety disorders. Clinicians must also decide whether eating disorders are present by themselves or in combination with depression or other forms of psychopathology.

Intervention

Prevention

Intervention for eating disorders involves both prevention and treatment. Prevention strategies frequently target some of the more malleable risk factors, including body dissatisfaction, negative emotion, and internalization of the thin ideal, and seek to strengthen some of the protective factors such as self-esteem and social support (Durkin, Paxton, & Wertheim, 2005; Neumark-Sztainer et al., 2006; Stice, 2002; Stice, Shaw, Burton, & Wade, 2006). Key components of effective interventions include interaction, multiple sessions, and programs focused on selected groups (such as older adolescent girls) (Stice & Shaw, 2004). School-based programs in both middle schools and high schools, and across ethnic groups, can be effective. These may focus on components of healthy eating and healthy dieting, self-esteem and perfectionism, and critical analysis of media images, and may specifically address teasing and harassment related to body weight and shape (Larkin & Rice, 2005; McVey, Tweed, & Blackmore, 2007; O'Dea & Abraham, 2000; Rodriguez, Marchand, Ng, & Stice, 2008; Scime, Cook-Cottone, Kane, & Watson, 2006; Varnado-Sullivan & Zucker, 2004; Wliksch, Durbridge, & Wade, 2008). Internet-oriented school programs have also been designed (Brown, Winzelberg, Abascal, & Taylor, 2004). Peer-led prevention programs for older adolescents and college students have also received empirical support (Becker, Bull, Schaumberg, Cauble, & Franco, 2008; Becker, Smith, & Ciao, 2006). Several of these programs have more positive, immediate impacts for high-risk girls (Becker et al., 2008; McVey et al., 2007; Weiss & Wertheim, 2005).

Treatment

Treatment models range from inpatient hospitalization, partial hospitalization, intensive outpatient settings, and traditional outpatient settings (Stewart & Williamson, 2004a, 2004b). Current approaches provide multidisciplinary, comprehensive, and integrated treatments that address the medical and psychological issues of adolescents and their family and peer contexts (Haines & Neumark-Sztainer, 2006; Södersten et al., 2006). Even with excellent and effective models, there continues to be a need for more good research focused specifically on children and adolescents, related to developmental course and outcomes (Couturier & Lock, 2006; Gowers & Bryant-Waugh, 2004).

Hospitalization remains the treatment of choice for those with severe and life-threatening disorders (Steiner & Lock, 1998). In the past, hospitalization was almost always associated with emergencies; more recently, early detection has resulted in the inpatient treatment of younger adolescents with less severe symptoms (Anzai, Lindsey-Dudley, & Bidwell, 2002; Reijonen et al., 2003). Both inpatient and partial hospitalization are aggressive forms of treatment that require considerable clinical skills on the part of mental health professionals who work with therapeutically challenging adolescents. Investigations of aspects of hospital treatment are varied. They include examinations of combined adolescent-adult units and the role of exercise in reducing levels of stress for individuals being treated for eating disorders (Heinberg, Haug, Freeman, Ambrose, & Guarda, 2003; Tokumura, Tanaka, Nanri, & Watanabe, 2005).

As noted, adolescents rarely initiate or compliantly accept treatment. Even if treatment begins, dropout rates are high. Halmi et al. (2005) emphasize the need to study the personality characteristics of eating-disordered adolescents to identify those that may predict difficulty (e.g., obsessionality) or engagement (e.g., self-esteem). Readiness to recover may be key (Ametller, Castro, Serrano, Martinez, & Toro, 2005). Characteristics of the therapist, and the therapeutic alliance, also take on added significance (Constantino, Arnow, Blasey, & Agras, 2005). As with all therapists working with children and adolescents with all kinds of psychopathologies, Stewart (2004) suggests that therapists who are nonjudgmental, neutral, and accepting are more likely to engage their eating-disordered clients.

Psychopharmacological treatments are relatively unexplored with adolescents (compared to adults), but there are numerous research projects underway (Flament, Furino, & Godart, 2005; Rivas-Vazquez, Rice, & Kalman, 2003; Steiner & Lock, 1998).

Psychosocial interventions are much more prominent and include individual and family psychotherapies. The most common, empirically supported approach is cognitive-behavioral psychotherapy (Bowers, Evans, Le Grange, & Andersen, 2003; Burton et al., 2007; Carter, McIntosh, Joyce, Sullivan, & Bulik, 2003; Gowers, 2006; Williamson, White, York-Crowe, & Stewart, 2004; Wilson, 2005).

Another common treatment, for adolescents with bulimia, focuses on dieting and dietary restraint strategies. For those with bulimia, who often relapse and struggle with repeat cycles of binging and purging, dieting must be appreciated as a complex phenomenon (Stice, Martinez, Presnell, & Groesz, 2006). Although once thought to exacerbate the symptoms of bulimia, dieting actually improves the clinical picture (Stice, Presnell, Groesz, & Shaw, 2005). To the extent that early progress can be made, initial improvement often predicts eventual outcome (Fairburn, Agras, Walsh, Wilson, & Stice, 2004). Relapse prevention can be addressed by having therapists pay special attention to an adolescent's higher level of initial preoccupation with food, greater ritualization of eating, and lower motivation for change (Halmi et al., 2002).

Less prevalent, with fewer data to support them, are the psychodynamic treatments for eating disorders. These tend to center on providing a safe space to explore painful emotions, construct self and identity, and explore early and current family relationships (Bryant-Waugh, 2006; Caparrotta & Ghaffari, 2006; Ciano, Rocco, Angarano, Biasin, & Balestrieri, 2002; Zerbe, 2001, 2003a). Finally, given the reluctance of many adolescents to avail themselves of help, alternative individual resources such as telephone hotlines are essential (Latzer & Gilat, 2000).

Family therapies are often used by themselves or as adjuncts to individual therapies. Some of these are based on the most current conceptualizations of eating disorders and have been shown to be effective for adolescents with both anorexia and bulimia (Keel & Haedt, 2008; Le Grange, Lock, & Dymek, 2003; Lock, Le Grange, Forsberg, & Hewell, 2006; Tierney & Wyatt, 2005). The Maudsley model of family therapy (Le Grange, 2005), in which parents have a central role in treatment, has been the focus of much current research and has received much empirical support (Lock & Le Grange, 2005; Wallis, Rhodes, Kohn, & Madden, 2007). In addition to family-based treatments, groups of parents whose adolescents are diagnosed with eating disorders benefit from parent training programs that provide both information and support for their own struggles (Holtkamp, Herpertz-Dahlmann, Vloet, & Hagenah, 2005; Zucker, Marcus & Bulik, 2006).

Group interventions have also been widely used, with both positive and negative outcomes (Davies, 2004; Dishion & Stormshak, 2007; McGilley, 2006; Wolf & Sefferino, 2008). Groups enable children and adolescents to explore similar psychological factors underlying the emergence and maintenance of eating disorders (e.g., related to dysregulated emotion, distorted cognitions, problematic behaviors) as well as parent, peer, and media influences on eating disorders. Peers in groups also provide specific kinds of support for recovery and examples of successful treatment. However, as with other forms of psychopathology (e.g., conduct disorders, substance abuse disorders), negative influences are also observed, with peers providing information about noncompliance and strategies for treatment sabotage (Dishion & Stormshak, 2007). This kind of negative influence is especially important to counter, as it may be reinforced by numerous websites that promote eating-disordered behavior as a lifestyle choice (Lapinski, 2006; Mulveen & Hepworth, 2006). In the end, individual, family, and group treatments may each contribute to improvements in the clinical presentation and better long-term outcomes. As with all psychopathologies, the overriding goal of treatment of eating disorders is to enable children and adolescents to capitalize on their strengths, to cope with inevitable difficulties, and to move forward with confidence and hope.

■ Key Terms

Body image (pg. 288)
Body satisfaction (pg. 288)
Body dissatisfaction (pg. 288)
Society and the media (pg. 289)
Internalization (pg. 289)
Eating disorders (pg. 291)
Anorexia nervosa (pg. 291)
Bulimia nervosa (pg. 291)
Eating disorder, not otherwise specified (pg. 291)
Binge eating disorder (pg. 292)
Binge eating (pg. 292)
Fear of fatness, with compensatory behaviors (pg. 292)
Drive for thinness (pg. 292)
Partial eating disorders (pg. 293)
Crossover (pg. 294)

Family factors (pg. 295)
Sociocultural factors (pg. 295)
Biopsychosocial, multifactorial risk model (pg. 295)
Perfectionism (pg. 296)
Tripartite influence model (pg. 298)

■ Chapter Summary

- Adolescence is a time of increased risk for all types of eating disorders.
- Weight gain in adolescence is generally accompanied by an increase in body fat for girls and a decrease in body fat for boys. Attitudes of body dissatisfaction increase during adolescence for both boys and girls.
- Core eating disorder symptoms include disturbed eating behaviors, body dissatisfaction and negative body perceptions, as well as compensatory behaviors to lose weight or prevent weight gain.
- Key symptoms of anorexia nervosa include a fear of fatness and extreme behaviors leading to weight loss. Binge eating and compensatory behaviors to prevent weight loss characterize bulimia nervosa, while binge eating disorder does not include the compensatory behaviors.
- The prevalence of eating disorders has increased in recent decades.
- Depression and anxiety disorders commonly occur along with eating disorders.
- The peak onset of eating disorders is early adolescence for anorexia and late adolescence for bulimia.
- The biopsychosocial model of eating disorders emphasizes the interaction of genetic, physiological, personality, and family factors in the development and maintenance of eating disorders.
- Negative emotionality and emotional dysregulation are temperament characteristics with particular salience for eating disorders.
- Highly controlled and organized families are more commonly associated with anorexia, whereas chaotic and conflicted families more frequently associated with bulimia.
- Once established, many forms of eating disorders are relatively resistant to treatment. Severe and life-threatening forms often require hospital-based programs.
- An important component of all treatment models is a focus on healthy attitudes toward food and eating, as well as improved coping skills.

Glossary

A

Abuse Excessive use of or dependence on an addictive substance.

Accountability The idea that, even with genetic contributions to disorder and pharmacological treatments, children retain responsibility for their everyday functioning and well-being.

Adaptational failure Deviation from age-appropriate norms, exaggeration or diminishment of normal developmental expressions, interference in normal developmental progress, failure to master age-salient developmental tasks, and/or failure to develop a specific function or regulatory mechanism.

Adaptive behavior A reflection of an individual's ability to manage daily living tasks, including self-care and household tasks.

Addiction A disorder characterized by compulsive drug-seeking and abuse, accompanied by neurophysiological changes.

Adequate adaptation With respect to children's functioning, adequate adaptation refers to functioning that is okay, acceptable, or "good enough."

Adolescence-limited trajectory (AL) From Moffitt's model of conduct disorder (CD), related to adolescent-onset CD. The AL form of CD is somewhat less problematic over time than the childhood-onset form, although there is still evidence of significant impairment in daily functioning and higher risk for poor outcomes.

Adolescent-onset subtype (Conduct Disorder) With onset in adolescence, the individual's problem behavior emerges more abruptly than with childhood onset, and is more often time-limited. Adolescent-onset CD is three times as frequent as childhood-onset.

Adverse drug effects Harmful, undesired, and sometimes unpredictable effects of medications.

Affective social competence The coordination of the capacities to experience emotion, send emotional messages to others, and read others' emotional signals.

Affective storms Periods of intense volatility in children with bipolar disorder. Individuals often exhibit severe mood dysregulation, involving chronic irritability and hyperarousal, as well as more rapid cycling between depressed and elevated moods, sometimes with three or more of these cycles per day.

Affiliative relationships Relationships focused on liking one another or sharing interests.

Aggression Behaviors that are carried out with an immediate goal of causing harm to another.

Agoraphobia A type of anxiety disorder characterized by the experience of intense anxiety in places where individuals feel insecure, trapped, or not in control, most often associated with avoidance of such places.

Anorexia nervosa A type of eating disorder characterized by a refusal to maintain body weight, intense fear of gaining weight or becoming fat, disturbance in the way in which one's body weight or shape is experienced, and denial of the seriousness of the current low body weight.

Antisocial propensity The factors that increase the risk for conduct disorder, including temperament style and cognitive abilities; those that become more important during adolescence include negative peer relationships and other social variables.

Anxiety disorders Internalizing disorders in which anxiety has gone from adaptive to pathological in terms of its intensity, duration, and pervasiveness; characterized by exaggerated and unrealistic fears and worries, overcontrol, inhibition, withdrawal, avoidance, and somatic symptoms.

Anxiety sensitivity The degree to which an individual focuses on signals of anxiety; involving hypervigilance and attention to bodily sensations, a tendency to focus on weak or infrequent sensations, and a disposition to react to somatic sensations with distorted cognitions.

Applied behavior analysis One of the most widely applied intervention strategies for autism spectrum disorders; an intensive behavioral approach, with near constant control and direction of the child and his/her environment.

Arenas of comfort The domains in which children express relative satisfaction with themselves and their accomplishments.

Asperger syndrome A disorder primarily differentiated from autism by the lack of delayed language development and generally normal-range intelligence.

Assessment The systematic collection of relevant information in order to both differentiate everyday or transient difficulties from clinically significant psychopathology and classify a child's particular disorder(s).

Attachment relationship The relationship that includes caregivers and infants and reflects the degree to which infants experience safety, comfort, and affection; it is evolutionarily influenced and serves as a prototype for all later relationships. The development of an attachment relationship is the significant psychological achievement of late infancy.

Attention deficit hyperactivity disorder (ADHD) A disorder characterized by a combination of impulsivity, hyperactivity, and inattentiveness; one of the most common reasons for seeking help.

Authority conflict pathway One of three potential developmental pathways for oppositional defiant disorder and conduct disorder, with stubborn and negativistic behaviors leading to more serious disobedience and hostility.

Autism spectrum disorders A broad category of disorders, used in a variety of contexts, reflecting compromised development in social functioning and communication, as well as restricted patterns of activities or interests.

Avoidant (anxious/avoidant) attachment Form of insecure attachment that usually reflects ineffective or inappropriate caregiving.

B

Barriers to care Factors that impede access to mental health services, including structural barriers such as lack of provider availability, inconveniently located services, transportation difficulties, inability to pay and/or inadequate insurance coverage; individual barriers such as denial of problems or lack of trust in the system; and sociocultural barriers such as the stigma of psychopathology or mental illness.

Behavioral genomics The top-down process of understanding the impact of genes at the psychological level.

Behavioral models Psychological models that emphasize the individual's observable behavior within a specific environment.

Behavioral phenotypes The outwardly observable behaviors (such as physical characteristics, cognitive and linguistic profiles, perceptual skills and deficits, socioemotional patterns, and overall outcomes) associated with an underlying genetic condition. Hypotheses about links between genotypes and phenotypes must be carefully investigated.

Binge drinking Heavy consumption of alcohol in a relatively short period of time with the primary intention of becoming intoxicated.

Binge eating A dimension of some types of eating disorders; combinations of this dimension with fear of fatness and compensatory behaviors and drive for thinness correspond to the discrete syndromes of anorexia, bulimia, and binge eating disorder.

Bipolar disorder A mood disorder characterized by alternating periods of depression and mania, or hypomania.

Birth cohort Individuals born in a particular historical period who share key experiences and events.

Body image A person's perception of his or her own physical appearance.

Body satisfaction The degree to which a person is accepting of, or pleased with, his or her physical appearance.

Bulimia nervosa A type of eating disorder characterized by recurrent episodes of binge eating, a sense of lack of control over eating during the episode, and recurrent inappropriate compensatory behavior in order to prevent weight gain, such as self-induced vomiting; misuse of laxatives, diuretics, enemas, or other medications; fasting; or excessive exercise. Self-evaluation is unduly influenced by body shape and weight.

Bullying The intentional infliction of physical or emotional harm through physical aggression, harassment, intimidation, teasing, or psychological coercion.

C

Callous-unemotional traits A set of personality traits characterized by a lack of empathy, concern, guilt, or remorse.

Categorical disorder A disorder that reflects distinctive and/or qualitative differences in patterns of emotion, cognition, and behavior; a disorder that is outside of the normal range of childhood behavior.

Central coherence hypothesis A hypothesis based on the idea that most individuals attempt to perceive and construct meaning from information that is part of an environmental whole; information makes sense, or is coherent, because it is part of something larger than itself .

Central nervous system (CNS) stimulants Pharmacological treatments for ADHD, including methylphenidate (Ritalin) and newer stimulants (such as Adderall or Cylert). These treatments show real and substantive improvement, with improvement measured by parent-teacher ratings, direct observations, and performance in lab tasks.

Child maltreatment *Not* a diagnosis that is assigned to a child, but a broad category including physical abuse, sexual abuse, psychological abuse, and neglect.

Childhood-onset subtype (Conduct Disorder) With childhood onset, the individual is usually diagnosed early, and has a long history of negative personal and interpersonal behavior, deteriorating over time. With onset in adolescence, the individual's problem behavior emerges more abruptly, and is more often time-limited.

Chronic hassles Everyday, ongoing problems, such as struggles with homework or being teased at school, that are associated with depression and other disorders.

Classical conditioning A form of associative learning in which certain stimuli become paired with other stimuli resulting in the reliable elicitation of a response.

Classification A system for describing the important categories, groups, or dimensions of disorders.

Coercion model Model of ODD and CD, focused on the assumption that parents and children struggle for control over a number of everyday tasks and activities and that maladaptive parenting leads to children's externalizing behavior. The coercion model specifically examines a conditioning sequence in which children are inadvertently reinforced for their problematic behaviors.

Cognitive behavioral therapy (CBT) A psychotherapy approach that attempts to remedy dysfunctional emotions, cognitions, and behaviors through goal-oriented, systematic, empirically based treatment techniques. CBT is based on the principles and empirical findings of learning theories and cognitive psychology.

Cognitive models Psychological models that focus on the components and processes of the mind and mental development .

Cognitive restructuring A main component of *cognitive behavioral therapy.* The identification and modification of negative thoughts.

Cognitive-deficits model A model of addiction that integrates physiological and cognitive factors, the cognitive-deficits model is based on the idea that repeat, chronic drug use results in abnormalities in the prefrontal cortex, impairing judgment, decision making, and impulse control.

Cognitive-vulnerability stress model of depression A model that proposes that an individual's negative attributional style coupled with negative life events leads to depression.

Coherence From a developmental perspective, reflects the logical and meaningful links between early developmental variables and later outcomes.

Combined pharmacotherapy Use of combinations of medications; a relatively recent trend in treatments of ADHD and other disorders.

Common factors model An alternative to the *gateway hypothesis* of drug use; the model assumes that there is a non-specific propensity to use drugs.

Comorbidity The co-occurrence of two or more disorders in one individual.

Competence From a developmental perspective, reflects effective functioning in relation to relevant age-related tasks and issues; evaluations of competence are embedded in the environment within which development is occurring.

Complex developmental trauma A recently described disorder that is characterized by significant physiological, psychological, and social distress and dysfunction related to the experience of chronic trauma (most often involving child maltreatment).

Compliance A specific kind of self-regulation; doing something unpleasant (or boring), or acquiescing to a request or instruction to abstain from or stop doing something pleasurable.

Compulsions Persistent and intense impulses to perform a specific behavior.

Concurrent comorbidity When two or more disorders are experienced at the same time.

Conduct disorder (CD) A disorder characterized by a more severe pattern of negativistic, hostile, and defiant behavior that involves the violation of social norms and rules as well as the rights of others.

Consistency The degree to which an individual characteristic or pattern is similar across situations.

Continual display A developmental pathway or trajectory involving ongoing difficulties (without significant improvement or deterioration) over time.

Continuous disorder A disorder that lies on a continuum with normal development, reflecting the gradual transition from the normal range of feelings, thoughts, and behaviors to clinically significant problems.

Continuous models of psychopathology Models that emphasize the gradual transition from normal range of feelings, thoughts, and behaviors to clinically significant problems.

Continuous performance tests Tests often used as part of an ADHD assessment. These tests generally involve monitoring stimuli (visual, auditory, or both) and responding selectively to instructions; these tests measure various attention and impulse control skills, including the ability to remain vigilant, to demonstrate consistency of attentional focus, to respond quickly, and to inhibit responding.

Conversion disorder A type of anxiety disorder characterized by unexplained deficits in voluntary motor or sensory function that cannot be adequately accounted for by known pathophysiological mechanisms; psychological factors are clearly associated with the emergence of symptoms.

Core behavioral deficit The key symptom of a disorder; the feature that is most revealing of the underlying nature of the disorder.

Covert aggression Also called indirect aggression, it may include the externalizing behaviors observed in conduct disorder such as property damage or theft.

Covert pathway One of three potential developmental pathways for oppositional defiant disorder and conduct disorder, with minor misbehaviors leading to more serious delinquent acts that tend to be concealed or secretive.

Craving A symptom of addiction, described as "drug wanting," and a strong desire to use.

Crossover When individuals first diagnosed with anorexia nervosa are later diagnosed with bulimia, or when individuals first diagnosed with bulimia are later diagnosed with anorexia.

Cross-sectional research Research that collects data at a single point in time, with comparisons made among groups of participants (e.g., 4-year-olds versus 8-year-olds versus 12-year-olds).

Cross-time reliability Measure of whether a child is similarly diagnosed by the same clinician at two different points in time.

D

Deficit approach An approach to understanding cultural variation that sees the ways in which cultural differences are conceptualized as "deviation, maladaptation, or pathology."

Delay   A type of adaptational failure (e.g., the child acquires language more slowly than other children).

Destructive/nondestructive dimension   A continuum that reflects the degree to which a particular behavior or pattern of behavior results in harm or damage.

Developmental continuity   The tendency for disorders to persist over time.

Developmental decay   A developmental pathway or trajectory involving deterioration over time.

Developmental delay   A developmental pathway or trajectory involving slower-than-normal but steady growth, and relative improvement over time.

Developmental disorder   A type of disorder in which underlying impairment in brain structure and/or functioning is associated with a wide range of physical, psychological, social, and occupational outcomes; autism spectrum disorders and mental retardation are examples of developmental disorders.

Developmental pathways   Trajectories that reflect children's adjustment and/or maladjustment in the context of growth and change over a lifetime.

Developmental psychopathology   Intense, frequent, and/or persistent maladaptive patterns of emotion, cognition, and behavior considered within the context of normal development, resulting in the current and potential impairment of infants, children, and adolescents.

Developmental-difference debate   A debate on the nature of cognitive disability. Proponents of the developmental side of the debate suggest that children with mental retardation (MR) possess similar cognitive structures and slowly progress in similar cognitive sequence to children without MR. Proponents of the difference side of the debate propose that children with MR think in qualitatively distinct (and deficient) ways; an emphasis on difference is often presented along with data on genetic etiologies of MR.

Deviance   A type of adaptational failure (e.g., the child behaves strangely, unlike other children).

Diagnosis   The method of assigning children to specific classification categories.

Diagnostic and Statistical Manual (DSM)   Published by the American Psychiatric Association, the DSM, now in its fourth edition, provides a listing of forms of mental illness along with diagnostic criteria.

Diagnostic efficiency   The degree to which clinicians maximize diagnostic hits and minimize diagnostic misses.

Diathesis-stress model   A model that emphasizes the combination of underlying predispositions (risk factors related to, for example, structural abnormalities or early-occurring trauma) and additional factors (such as further physiological or environmental events) that lead to the development of psychopathology.

Difference approach   As opposed to the *deficit approach*, an approach to cultural differences where "cultural differences can be seen as legitimate, appropriate, and even desirable."

Differential diagnosis   Decisions about mutually exclusive categories of disorder.

Discontinuous models of psychopathology   Models that emphasize distinctive and/or qualitative differences between patterns of emotion, cognition, and behavior that are within the normal range, and those that exemplify clinical disorders.

Disinhibited type   A subtype of reactive attachment disorder that involves "markedly disturbed and developmentally inappropriate social relatedness," such as unrestrained overtures to strangers and impulsive behavior in high-risk situations.

Disordered attachment with inhibition   A disorder in the Zero to Three classification system that involves children who are withdrawn and clingy, hypervigilant with respect to the caregiver's whereabouts and availability, and unable to venture beyond the immediate vicinity of the attachment figure. Disordered attachment is diagnosed when a child has established emotional and behavioral preferences for a particular caregiver.

Disordered attachment with role reversal   A disorder in the Zero to Three classification system that involves children who assume, inappropriately and uncomfortably, the parental role. Disordered attachment is diagnosed when a child has established emotional and behavioral preferences for a particular caregiver.

Disordered attachment with self-endangerment   A disorder in the Zero to Three classification system that involves children who appear unconcerned with maintaining interpersonal connections, and who fail to use the attachment figure as a secure base, frequently finding themselves (or placing themselves) in situations that are likely to cause harm. Disordered attachment is diagnosed when a child has established emotional and behavioral preferences for a particular caregiver.

Disorganized attachment   Form of insecure attachment that usually reflects problematic or harmful caregiving.

Disrupted attachment   A disorder in the Zero to Three classification system that involves children who experience a breakdown in the relationship, most often related to extended separation, divorce, or death. Infants and young children display a sequence including emotional and behavioral protests related to the immediate loss of the attachment figure, followed by despair, and then emotional detachment.

Disruptive behavior disorders   A category including ADHD, oppositional defiant disorder (ODD), and conduct disorder (CD); ODD and CD are best understood as related to, but independent of, ADHD.

Domains of competence   Particular areas of skills and achievements such as academic achievement, behavioral competence, and social competence.

Down syndrome   A developmental disorder caused by an extra chromosome 21 (i.e., trisomy 21), Down syndrome is among the most widely known genetically influenced forms of mental retardation. Accompanying physical characteristics including distinctive facial features, heart problems, and poor muscle tone. Intellectual challenges almost always involve language difficulties; socioemotional functioning is often characterized by positive affect and extraversion.

Drive for thinness A dimension of some types of eating disorders; combinations of this dimension with fear of fatness and binge eating correspond to the discrete syndromes of anorexia, bulimia, and binge eating disorder.

Dynamic systems processes The idea that dysfunction involves many different individual factors at various levels of analysis (e.g., biological and psychological stressors).

Dyssomnias Disturbances in the normal rhythms or patterns of sleep (e.g., falling asleep or staying asleep).

Dysthymia A mood disorder characterized by long-standing disturbance of mood, with ongoing sadness, irritability, and lack of motivation; other symptoms involving emotion, cognition, and behavior may also be observed.

E

Eating disorder, not otherwise specified An atypical clinical presentation; may involve meeting some but not all of the diagnostic criteria for a particular subtype, or a mix of symptoms observed in both anorexia and bulimia.

Eating disorders Psychopathologies characterized by severe disturbances in eating behaviors, disturbed perceptions of body size and shape, fear of being fat, and compensatory behaviors to lose weight or prevent weight gain.

Ecological models Models that emphasize the immediate environments, or "behavior settings," in which children grow and make sense of their lives including homes, classrooms, neighborhoods, and communities.

Effortful control Attempts by infants to regulate their own stimulation and response; an individual characteristic described in current continuous, or dimensional, models of *temperament*.

Emotional regulation Emotional control, involving the "modulation, toleration and endurance of emotions."

Emotional security Related to attachment, emotional security involves the degree of safety, closeness, and comfort experienced in a relationship.

Equifinality Refers to developmental pathways in which differing beginnings and circumstances lead to similar outcomes.

Executive functions A set of processes that include working memory, internalization of speech, and self-regulation of emotion, which contribute to children's increasing control over their thoughts, feelings, and behaviors, and their interactions with others and their environments.

Experimental substance use Use that involves trying a drug once or a few times, often related to curiosity or peer influence.

Exposure A main component of cognitive behavioral therapy for anxiety disorders. Exposure to the stimuli and situations that are associated with anxiety is systematic and controlled, with in vivo (real-life) practice preferred.

Extensive support (Mental retardation) Consistent and more comprehensive assistance in most life settings to maximize an individual's well-being, usually provided over one's lifetime.

External validity In the context of classification, external validity reflects the degree to which a diagnosis provides useful information about the implications (i.e., likely outcomes, effective treatments) of a disorder.

Externalizing dimension In the empirical, dimensional classification system, the externalizing dimension involves problematic patterns that are directed outward, toward others (e.g., disruptive or aggressive behavior).

Extreme male brain theory A genetic hypothesis for autism spectrum disorders; highlights the role of evolutionary sex-linked dimensions of brain functioning (such as the logical, systematic thinking characteristic of men and the relational empathy characteristic of women) and proposes that autism spectrum disorders may be an extreme example of the "normal" male profile.

F

Familial comorbidity Whether the different disorders are understood as theoretically or clinically related to one another (such as some combinations of substance abuse, depression, and personality disorders).

Family models Models that emphasize that the best way to understand the personality and psychopathology of a particular child is to understand the dynamics of a particular family.

Fear of fatness, with compensatory behaviors A dimension of some types of eating disorders; combinations of this dimension with binge eating and drive for thinness correspond to the discrete syndromes of anorexia, bulimia, and binge eating disorder.

Fears Anxieties elicited in the presence of a specific stimulus.

Feeding disorder Clinically significant difficulties related to efficient and effective feeding—an especially salient developmental task in infancy and early childhood. May be the result of developmental delays, genetic conditions, abnormalities of oral anatomy, caregiver difficulties, or combinations of those factors.

Final common pathway There are multiple etiological factors leading to disorder, with the disorder as the result, or *final common pathway*, of combinations of different types of predisposing conditions and events.

Fixation A type of adaptational failure (e.g., the child continues to suck her thumb long after other children have stopped).

Fixation-regression model Usually emphasized by psychodynamic theorists and clinicians, this model suggests that individuals who fail to work through developmental issues become stuck in the past.

Fragile X syndrome   A developmental disorder caused by a mutation on the FMR1 gene, Fragile X syndrome is the most common type of inherited MR in boys, affecting 1 in 4,000 boys and 1 in 8,000 girls. Cognitive and language difficulties, as well as behavioral problems, are important features of the Fragile X profile.

Functional genomics   The bottom-up process of understanding, in terms of molecular biology, how individual genes work.

G

Gateway hypothesis   A stage theory of drug involvement that proposes that the use of alcohol or marijuana acts as a gateway to the use of "harder" drugs such as cocaine, heroin, or methamphetamines.

General risk factor   A risk factor associated with increased vulnerability to any, or many, possible disorders (see *nonspecific risk*).

Generalized anxiety disorder   A type of anxiety disorder characterized by excessive and unrealistic worries and fears about a variety of stimuli and situations.

Generational forgetting   A type of cohort effect, this refers to the recall of potential harm associated with substance use and abuse.

Genetic counseling   Process by which individuals at higher risk for inherited disorders are educated about the probabilities of having a child with the disorder; the medical, psychological, and family implications of the disorder; testing options; and resources for prevention, management, and/or family planning.

Genomics   The mapping, sequencing, and analysis of genes and application of this data for medical, educational, and technological benefit (term coined by Thomas Roderick in 1986).

Genotypes   The genetic make-up of a cell, an organism, or an individual.

Goodness of fit   The interplay between infant temperament and parenting.

Growth dysregulation hypothesis   A hypothesis that proposes that the normally well-controlled process of brain growth and organization goes awry, leading to the clinical symptoms of autism spectrum disorders.

H

Heterotypic comorbidity   Diagnoses from different classification groups (for instance, depression and conduct disorder).

Homotypic comorbidity   Two or more diagnoses within a classification group (for instance, generalized anxiety disorder and specific phobia).

Human Genome Project   A collaborative effort by the Department of Energy and the National Institutes of Health to identify the approximately 30,000 genes in human DNA and determine the sequences of the three billion chemical base pairs that make up human DNA.

Humanistic models   Psychological models that emphasize personally meaningful experiences, innate motivations for healthy growth, and the child's purposeful creation of a self.

Hypersensitive regulatory disorder   Clinically significant difficulties and/or impairment related to heightened or exaggerated sensitivity to auditory, visual, and tactile stimulation.

I

Impaired social cognition   Deficits and/or delays in the processing of social and emotional information and events.

Impulsive-overactive patterns   Children who exhibit these patterns of CD are more likely to be easily aroused and disruptive.

Incentive salience   When the dopamine system that usually signals that certain stimuli will lead to positive reinforcement becomes hypersensitized to drugs and drug stimuli.

Incentive-sensitization theory   A two-stage explanation of addiction: (1) various substances alter brain organization and function and (2) these altered brain systems affect behavior in situations involving motivation and reward.

Incidence   New cases of a type (or types) of disorder in a given time period.

Indicated measures   Prevention strategies for attachment disorders for groups with specific risk factors requiring more extensive help.

Indicated preventive measures   Type of preventive measure provided for groups with specific risk factors that include more extensive interventions (e.g., packages of services for families with premature infants).

Infant emotionality   The latency to respond to emotional stimuli and the average and peak intensities of emotional response; a broad concept that encompasses aspects of *surgency, negative affectivity,* and *effortful control.*

Inhibited type   A subtype of reactive attachment disorder that involves "markedly disturbed and developmentally inappropriate social relatedness," such as withdrawal, isolation, and overly dependent and clingy behavior.

Insecure attachment   Forms of attachment (including resistant, avoidant, and disorganized) that reflect inconsistent, ineffective, or harmful caregiving behavior.

Instrumental aggression   Aggression that is premeditated or planful. In most cases, instrumental aggression is a means to a particular end.

Instrumental relationships   Relationships focused on getting something useful from the other participant (e.g., information from a teacher or lunch money from an acquaintance).

Intellectual functioning   A reflection of an individual's cognitive ability, including everyday and academic problem-solving abilities.

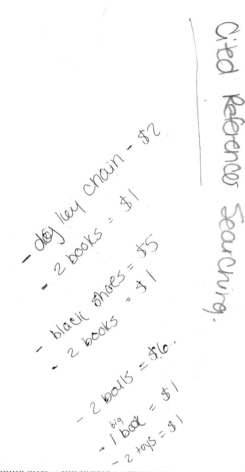

Intermittent suppor... assistance to maxi... usually provided d... ful times.

Internal validity In... validity reflects th... same diagnosis hav... current symptom p...

Internalization The... and identifies with... appearance, thinne...

Internalizing dimen... classification syste... problematic patter... self (e.g., anxiety o...

Interpersonal psycho... ity that postulates t... lated impulse cont...

Inter-rater reliabilit... clinicians, gatherin... opmental history... same decision abo...

Interviews Either s... conversations ab... allowing parents a... and more broadly,... vide opportunities... ship, an especially... cian knows that h... children and vario...

J

Joint attention "Communicative intentions such as eye contact, pointing, and shared attention, all of which smooth out the processes of social interaction and make it easier and more rewarding to participate in the social world.

K

Kindling model A hypothesis that explains why later episodes of depression often occur in the context of less severe stress: initial stress leads to vulnerability in the hypothalamic-pituitary-adrenal axis and over time, the increasingly sensitive neurological response system requires lower thresholds of stimulation to trigger a new episode.

L

Life-course persistent trajectory (LCP) From Moffitt's model of conduct disorder (CD), related to childhood-onset CD. Those with this trajectory are more likely to have a history of ODD and a family history of antisocial behavior, are more likely to display aggression, and have worse outcomes.

Limited support (Mental retardation) Consistent assistance, over longer periods of time, to maximize an individual's well-being.

... **processes** The idea that function and dys-...y out over time.

... **research** The ongoing collection of data ...ne group of participants, or the study of indi-... time.

...**sion** A mood disorder in children, adoles-...dults characterized by sadness and a loss of ...th multiple cognitive, behavioral, and somatic ...and impaired functioning.

Not a diagnosis that is assigned to a child, ...l category including physical abuse, sexual ...hological abuse, and neglect.

...ct periods characterized by unusual and per-...d elevation, high activity levels, decreased ...ep, increased irritability, extremely impulsive ...nd sometimes psychotic thinking.

...**el of psychopathology** Key assumptions ...el are that disorders are (1) categorical (i.e., ...lear distinctions between healthy and disor-...stments), (2) associated with "constitutional ..." (i.e., the idea that the child somehow fails to ...her natural function), and (3) endogenous (i.e., ...ic of the individual, rather than an individual-...t transaction).

...**definitions** Theoretical or clinically based ...istress and dysfunction.

...**ation (MR)** A developmental disability that ...gnificant deficits in intellectual functioning ...e functioning.

...**retardation** Level of intellectual and adap-...ment indicated by IQ levels between 50–55 and 70, respectively.

Mindblindness A term used to describe children and adults with autism, emphasizing their inability to attribute mental states to others (i.e., theory of mind).

Mixed category of regulatory disorder Clinically significant difficulties and/or impairment related to combinations of features of hypersensitive, underreactive, and motorically disorganized regulatory disorders.

Modeling A classic treatment for fears, based on the principles of observational learning, modeling involves watching, practicing, and imitating adaptive behavior.

Models of childhood and child development Models of childhood and child development are sets of assumptions and hypotheses about how children develop over time. They include explanations and predictions about biological, psychological, and sociocultural processes and contexts, and are embedded in particular historical and scientific eras.

Moderate mental retardation Level of intellectual and adaptive impairment indicated by IQ levels between 35–40 and 50–55.

Mood disorders A category of disorders involving distress and dysfunction related to mood (e.g., depression or mania).

Mood-related continuum A range of distress and dysfunction related to problematic emotions, from short periods of sadness with minimal impairment, to longer periods with moderate impairment, to ongoing episodes of clinically significant depression with severe impairment.

Moral development A set of ongoing psychological processes, embedded in cognitive, emotional, and social growth and change, focused on conceptions of what is right, ethical, and good.

Motivational interviewing A brief intervention for substance abuse incorporating aspects of motivational psychology, client-centered therapy, and stages-of-change theory.

Motorically disorganized, impulsive regulatory disorder Clinically significant difficulties and/or impairment related to impulsivity, frequent sensation-seeking behavior, or high-risk or destructive activity.

Multifactorial risk model A model that includes multiple factors, in various combinations, that lead to disorder.

Multifinality Refers to developmental pathways in which similar beginnings and circumstances lead to different outcomes.

N

Negative affectivity Predispositions to experience fear and frustration/anger; an individual characteristic described in current continuous, or dimensional, models of *temperament*.

Negative emotion A core component of ODD, involving anger, frustration, sadness, and fear, with many frequent and intense emotional experiences.

Negative life events Major stressful events, such as a parent losing a job or a serious illness in the family, associated with depression and other disorders.

Neglect A type of child maltreatment involving a failure to provide for physical, emotional, and/or educational needs of a child.

Neural plasticity The ability of the brain to flexibly respond to physiological and environmental challenges and insults.

Night terrors A *parasomnia* characterized by the display of extreme fright and an inability to awaken the sleeper, usually not remembered by the sleeper.

Nightmare disorder A *parasomnia* characterized by recurrent dreams associated with extreme negative emotions; frequent awakenings may keep one from getting enough sleep and then interfere with daily functioning.

Nonattachment with emotional withdrawal A disorder in the Zero to Three classification system that involves children who appear unable to make interpersonal connections with others, pulling away from contact and withholding emotional investments; nonattachment is diagnosed when a child has never exhibited an emotional or behavioral preference for a particular caregiver.

Nonattachment with indiscriminate sociability A disorder in the Zero to Three classification system that involves children who appear to easily and sometimes uncomfortably and inappropriately establish relationships with unfamiliar others; nonattachment is diagnosed when a child has never exhibited an emotional or behavioral preference for a particular caregiver.

Nonorganic causes (Mental retardation) Also referred to as familial or cultural-familial mental retardation that involve multiple factors, including variations in the normal distribution of intellectual functioning and risk variables such as poverty.

Nonshared environment The aspects of family life and function that are specific and distinct for each child.

Nonspecific risk Increased vulnerability to any, or many, kinds of disorders.

O

Observational learning A form of learning that occurs by watching, remembering, and/or imitating others.

Observations A source of valuable information involving careful watching by a clinician. Clinicians usually observe children in clinical settings such as offices, but may also observe children in naturalistic settings such as the home or school.

Obsessions Persistent and intense intrusions of unwanted thoughts or images.

Obsessive-compulsive disorder A type of anxiety disorder characterized by intrusive thoughts that lead to anxiety and ritual behaviors that are intended to reduce anxiety.

Operant conditioning A form of learning in which consequences (negative or positive) lead to changes (decreases or increases) in behavior.

Oppositional defiant disorder (ODD) A disorder characterized by a sustained pattern of negativistic, hostile, and defiant behavior.

Optimal adaptation With respect to children's functioning, optimal adaptation refers to functioning that is excellent, superior, or "the best of what is possible."

Organic causes (Mental retardation) Associated with a specific physiological or physical origin, usually associated with more severe forms of MR, and observed across all family and socioeconomic status backgrounds. Organic explanations may be either genetic or environmental.

Outcome research Studies of whether, at the end of treatment, children and adolescents have improved relative to their pre-treatment status compared to others who have not received treatment.

Overcontrol Demanding, restrictive, rule-governed parenting.

Overt aggression Also called aggression, involves harmful physical behaviors.

Overt pathway One of three potential developmental pathways for oppositional defiant disorder and conduct disorder, with minor forms and consequences of aggression leading to more serious forms and consequences of aggression.

Overt/covert dimension A continuum that reflects the degree to which a particular behavior or pattern of behavior is observable (i.e., overt) or secret (i.e., covert).

P

Panic disorder A type of anxiety disorder characterized by recurrent, somewhat unpredictable panic attacks (i.e., extremely intense and often frightening episodes of anxiety).

Parasomnias Disorders involving sleep dysfunctions, such as *night terrors*, *nightmare disorder,* or sleepwalking.

Parasuicide Includes many behaviors, from less dangerous gestures to serious but unsuccessful suicide attempts; this term is increasingly preferred over *attempted suicide* because the motives and intentions of individuals are often difficult to identify.

Parent education Intervention components designed to educate and inform parents about disorders, clinical presentations including associated distress and impairment, available treatments (and parent roles in treatment), and likely outcomes.

Partial eating disorders Subclinical presentations in individuals who meet some, but not all, of the diagnostic criteria for eating disorders; some individuals who present with partial eating disorders will go on to develop full-blown disorders but most will display remission.

Pathways of parental impact Three ways in which parents influence the development of child depression: (1) parent depression affects parent-child relationships and interactions, and leads to child psychopathology; (2) parent depression affects family relationships and interactions and family disruptions, and these lead to child psychopathology; (3) parent depression affects marital satisfaction, leading to child psychopathology.

Peer contagion A drawback of group adolescent treatments, peer contagion involves the sharing of information about conduct disorders, substance abuse disorders, as well as providing immediate and powerful reinforcement of deviancy.

Peer relationships Relationships and friendships that provide opportunities for companionship, acceptance, and intimacy. An absence of friendships, because of rejection, conflict, or withdrawal, is associated with maladjustment.

Peer subcultures Groups of children or adolescents who share interests and status; common examples include "jocks, brains, loners, rogues, druggies, populars, and nerds."

Perfectionism A personal standard or attitude that involves setting unrealistic goals and a sense of failure and/or worthlessness when those goals are not met; in individuals with eating disorders, perfectionism often accompanies

obsessionality and leads to the "relentless pursuit of the thin ideal."

Pervasive developmental disorder, not otherwise specified (PDD-NOS) A DSM category for atypical autism spectrum disorders.

Pervasive developmental disorders DSM category for disorders including autism, Asperger syndrome, Rett syndrome, and childhood disintegrative disorder.

Pervasive support (Mental retardation) The most consistent and most comprehensive assistance in all life settings to maximize an individual's well-being that is provided over one's lifetime.

Phobic disorders Types of anxiety disorders characterized by excessive and unrealistic fears of particular objects or situations, intense anxiety in the presence of such objects or situations, and avoidant behaviors.

Physical abuse A type of child maltreatment involving physical aggression that results in pain, injury, or bodily harm; this type of abuse may include hitting, beating, restraint and confinement, burning, and shaking children.

Physical dependence Susceptibility to withdrawal symptoms; occurs only in combination with tolerance.

Physiological models Models of psychopathology that emphasize biological processes, such as genes and neurological systems, as being at the core of human experience; physiological models explain the development of psychopathology, its course, and its treatment in terms of biological factors.

Pica The ingestion of non-food substances such as paint, pebbles, or dirt.

Plasticity The relatively changeable nature of the individual and the individual's environment.

Positive identity An individual's understanding, acceptance, and prizing of his or her self, roles, relationships, and responsibilities. Critical for ongoing healthy adjustment.

Positive psychology A field of psychology focusing on "positive subjective experience, positive individual traits, and positive institutions," which seeks to promote individual, family, social, and community well-being.

Post-traumatic stress disorder A type of anxiety disorder characterized by a severe and ongoing pattern of anxiety and avoidance following exposure to a traumatic event.

Pragmatics The features of language and communication that convey meaning in context.

Prevalence All current cases of a type (or types) of disorder.

Primary prevention Reducing or eliminating psychopathology-related risks, thereby reducing the incidence of disorder in children.

Primary sleep disorders Disturbance of basic functioning divided into two groups: the *dyssomnias* and the *parasomnias*.

Proactive aggression A more deliberate and less emotional form of aggression.

Proactive-callous patterns Children who display the proactive-callous pattern of CD are more likely to be purposely mean, to encourage peers to gang up on or reject another child, and to lack remorse.

Problem behavior syndrome Described by Jessor, the proposition that adolescents who are at risk for one problem behavior are likely to be at risk for others, and the observation that problem behaviors tend to cluster in adolescence.

Problem solving A main component of *cognitive behavioral therapy*. A step-by-step, active, behaviorally oriented approach for coping.

Process The idea that adaptation (or maladaptation) is an ongoing activity, with transformations of patterns of thinking, feeling, and behaving at various developmental stages.

Process research Studies of the specific mechanisms and common factors that account for therapeutic change.

Profound mental retardation Level of intellectual and adaptive impairment indicated by IQ levels below 20–25.

Projective measures Measures such as the Rorschach inkblots and the Thematic Apperception Test that are based on the assumption that, given an ambiguous stimulus, individuals' responses will reflect the projection of unconscious conflicts.

Protective factors The individual, family, and social characteristics that are associated with the positive adaptation of resiliency.

Prototypical cases The most representative or standard examples of a disorder.

Proximity maintenance A defining feature of caregivers in the attachment relationship; the degree to which an infant seeks closeness and resists separation.

Psychodynamic models Psychological models that emphasize unconscious cognitive, affective, and motivational processes; mental representations of self, others, and relationships; the subjectivity of experience; and a developmental perspective on individual adjustment and maladjustment.

Psychoeducation A main component of psychotherapy, psychoeducation provides children and their families with information about symptoms of disorders, the emergence and maintenance of disorder, and about the theoretical and practical aspects of various interventions.

Psychological abuse A type of child maltreatment (also known as emotional abuse) involving shaming, humiliating, or demeaning of a child; this type of abuse may also involve withholding affection.

Psychological dependence A craving or compulsion to use a substance despite significant harm.

Psychopathology Intense, frequent, and/or persistent maladaptive patterns of emotion, cognition, and behavior that are associated with significant distress and/or impairment in functioning.

R

Reactive aggression Aggression that occurs in response to a provocation; more angry and impulsive than *proactive aggression*.

Reactive attachment disorder A disorder in the Diagnostic and Statistical Manual that reflects insecure attachments that are associated with clinically significant distress and dysfunction.

Reactive-oppositional patterns Children who display the reactive-oppositional pattern of CD are more likely to be defiant, have temper outbursts, and stay angry at adults.

Reactivity An infant's excitability and responsiveness, including individual variations in emotions and behaviors.

Recurrent abdominal pain An especially common and well-studied somatoform condition. It involves three or more episodes over a 3-month period of severe pain that compromises a child's functioning; tends to occur in families where illness is a central concern, and where there is both somatic and emotional distress.

Regulation What an infant does to control his or her reactivity, as well as the degree to which a distressed infant accepts comfort from others.

Reinforcement The idea that positive and negative consequences lead to changes in behavior; a critical component of all learning processes.

Reinforcement model Based on the principles of operant conditioning, behavior is maintained, or changed, in response to positive or negative consequences.

Relapse prevention A main component of *cognitive behavioral therapy*. It involves laying the groundwork for the maintenance and generalization of improvements.

Reliability Measure of whether different clinicians, using the same set of criteria, classify children into the same clearly defined categories.

Research-based intervention Treatments that have received empirical support in well-designed studies.

Resiliency Adaptation (or competence) despite adversity.

Resistant (anxious/ambivalent) attachment Form of insecure attachment that usually reflects inconsistent caregiving.

Risk Increased vulnerability to disorder.

Risk factors The individual, family, and social characteristics that are associated with increased vulnerability, or risk.

Risk taking A disregard or indifference to the consequences of a behavior or situation; in less problematic terms, the disjunction between novelty-seeking and competent self-regulation.

Role of values Definitions and examples of disorder are influenced by the particular ideals and customs of individuals, groups, and mental health professionals.

Rumination The repeated chewing and regurgitation of food.

S

Safe haven A defining feature of caregivers in the attachment relationship; a person to whom the infant can turn for comfort and support.

Seasonal affective disorder A mood disorder that recurs, generally in the late fall and winter months, and usually begins in adolescence.

Secondary prevention Interventions that are implemented following the early signs of distress and dysfunction, before the disorder is clearly established in the child.

Secure attachment Form of attachment that results from consistent, sensitive responsiveness by the caregiver to the infant's physical, emotional, and social needs.

Secure base A defining feature of caregivers; a person whose presence serves as a source of security from which an infant ventures out to explore the world, and to which he or she can reliably return.

Selective measures Prevention strategies, such as home-based ones, for attachment disorders for groups at above-average risk.

Selective preventive measures Type of preventive measures; provided for at-risk groups (e.g., Head Start programs for preschoolers from disadvantaged backgrounds).

Self-control Also called self-regulation, self-control "refers to people's efforts to alter their own responses, such as overriding behavioral impulses, resisting temptation, controlling their thoughts, and altering (or artificially prolonging) their emotions."

Self-injurious behavior/self-harm Deliberate infliction of pain or injury to oneself, without suicidal intent.

Self-medication The use of drugs to improve mood, increase cognitive function, and deal with difficulties or consequences of other disorders; not specifically prescribed, directed, or supervised by a psychiatrist or physician.

Self-regulatory skills A set of abilities (related to executive functions) associated with control of thoughts, feelings, and behaviors; examples include distracting or comforting oneself, and delaying gratification.

Self-talk A cognitive technique focused on providing positive self-statements such as "I am brave" to enhance appropriate behaviors.

Sense of self The representation, understanding, and appreciation of one's identity (e.g., Who am I? Am I likeable? Am I good?); the earliest set of self-related cognitions and emotions are influenced by the attachment relationship.

Separation anxiety disorder A type of anxiety disorder characterized by intense age-inappropriate distress when separated from the caregiver, as well as clingy behaviors in the presence of the caregiver; associated with significant impairment in a child's daily functioning.

Severe mental retardation Level of intellectual and adaptive impairment indicated by IQ levels between 20–25 and 35–40.

Sexual abuse A type of child maltreatment involving adults or older adolescents using children for sexual stimulation; this type of abuse may include exposure, sexual contact, and/or sexual activities.

Shared environment The aspects of family life and function that are shared by all children in the family.

Sleep disorders Clinically significant difficulties related to falling and staying asleep, or sleep dysfunctions, associated with impairment in development and functioning.

Sluggish cognitive tempo The inconsistent, sometimes slowed alertness and orientation displayed by some children with ADHD.

Smoking One of the most common forms of recreational drug use, tobacco smoking involves the ingestion of nicotine via cigarettes.

Social cognition Psychological construct involving the processing of social and emotional information and events; this processing is observed at the intersections of self and other, emotion and cognition, and language and meaning.

Social context of brain development and functioning The understanding that changes in the microstructures of the brain take place in continuous transaction with the environment.

Social dysfunction Difficulties initiating and maintaining positive peer relationships. May include problems developing friendships and/or chronic conflict in social settings; inability to step back from a confusing event (such as an escalating disagreement over playground equipment), and failure to appreciate multiple perspectives, reflect on possible strategies for action, and negotiate with others.

Social phobia A type of anxiety disorder characterized by an intense fear of scrutiny or evaluation by others.

Social substance use Use that occurs during social events with one or more peers; parties, concerts, dances, and athletic events are common settings for this type of use.

Sociocultural models Models that emphasize the importance of the social context, including gender, race, ethnicity, and socioeconomic status, in the development, course, and treatment of psychopathology.

Sociocultural norms The beliefs and expectations of certain groups about what kinds of emotions, cognitions, and/or behaviors are undesirable or unacceptable.

Somatic management A main component of *cognitive behavioral therapy* for anxiety disorders. It involves targeting the distressing physiological symptoms and is usually focused on relaxation and breathing techniques. In addition, children and adolescents learn how to predict and tolerate the anxiety that accompanies challenging and stressful events.

Somatization A term that refers to a variety of processes in which an individual experiences physical symptoms, such as pain or loss of function, for which a physical cause cannot be found or, if present, cannot fully account for the level of impairment.

Somatoform pain disorder A type of anxiety disorder characterized by the onset of clinically significant pain with impairment; the disruption in everyday functioning is out of proportion to the reported pain, with clear secondary gain from the pain symptoms and exacerbations linked to increases in stress.

Specific phobias A type of anxiety disorder characterized by particular fear of an object, situation, or person (e.g., animals, injury or blood, natural phenomena).

Specific risk factor A risk factor associated with increased vulnerability to one particular disorder.

Specific risk Increased vulnerability to one particular disorder.

Stability The degree to which an individual characteristic or pattern is similar over time.

Standardized tests Measures such as intelligence tests and some personality tests, in which the data from a particular child can be compared to data gathered from large samples of children, including normally developing children and those with a variety of diagnoses.

Statistical deviance Compared to the distribution in a particular sample, statistical deviance refers to the relative infrequency of certain emotions, cognitions, and/or behaviors.

Stigmatization Negative attitudes (such as blaming or overconcern with dangerousness), emotions (such as shame, fear, or pity), and behaviors (such as ridicule or isolation) related to psychopathology and mental illness.

Successive comorbidity When disorders are experienced sequentially, one after the other.

Suicidal ideation Involves a variety of cognitions from "fleeting thoughts that life is not worth living" to "very concrete, well-thought out plans for killing oneself."

Suicidality A broad term that refers to the risk of suicidal ideation (thinking about suicide) as well as the risk for suicidal behavior (attempted or completed suicide).

Suicide The intentional taking of one's own life.

Surgency Extraversion; an individual characteristic described in current continuous, or dimensional, models of *temperament*.

Systematic desensitization A classic treatment for fears based on the principles of classical conditioning; involves teaching an anxious child how to relax and how to maintain relaxation when exposed to the feared stimulus. Exposure is done gradually (i.e., systematically, from stuffed dogs to videos of dogs to real dogs), building on the child's successes over time.

T

Temperament Variations in newborns' styles of reactivity (e.g., attention, activity, moods, and distress) and regulation of reactivity.

Tertiary prevention Interventions that are implemented for already present and clinically significant disorders.

Theory of mind The ability to attribute mental states to others.

Tolerance Occurs when the central nervous system (CNS) gradually becomes less responsive to stimulation by particular drugs; individuals then need to ingest higher and higher doses to achieve the same CNS effects.

Transactional model A recent revision and expansion of the coercion model that asserts that parent-child incompatibility is multiply determined, with multiple pathways to both externalizing and internalizing disorders, multiple interventions, and multiple outcomes.

Transactional processes The notion that children are embedded in environments that have an impact on dysfunction, and that children are not only influenced by these environments but influence (i.e., change, choose, create) their environments as well.

Tripartite influence model A model of eating disorders that proposes that parent, peer, and media factors influence the development of body dissatisfaction and eating problems through two mechanisms: the internalization of the thin-ideal and appearance comparison processes.

Tripartite model A model of anxiety and depression with three core concepts: (1) anxiety and depression share a common underlying factor of negative affectivity; (2) along with negative affectivity, low levels of positive affectivity are associated with depression; and (3) along with negative affectivity, high levels of physiological arousal are associated with anxiety.

Two-factor model A model of ADHD emphasizing two distinct factors that underlie impairments: inattention and hyperactivity/impulsivity.

U

Undercontrol Permissive, lax, indulgent parenting.

Underreactive regulatory disorder Clinically significant difficulties and/or impairment related to lack of interest and responsivity, limited exploration, and lagging skills in organizational processing.

Underregulation Not exerting enough self control; may result from a lack of behavioral standards, a lack of self-awareness or monitoring, or a lack of resolve or practice in the face of strong impulses.

Understanding of others and the world Early beliefs an infant has about unfamiliar persons and the new situations in which infants so often find themselves; influenced by the attachment relationship.

Universal measures Prevention strategies, such as early child education programs, for attachment disorders in the general population.

Universal preventive measures Type of preventive measure provided for entire populations (e.g. mandatory immunizations for children).

Use In the context of substance abuse, defined as ingestion of a substance.

V
Validity   Measure of whether the classification gives us true-to-life, meaningful information.

W
Williams syndrome   A developmental disorder caused by a microdeletion on chromosome 7, Williams syndrome is characterized by deficits in general cognitive function and visual-spatial skills, and relative strengths in language and music domains.

Withdrawal symptoms   Noxious physical and psychological effects caused by reduction or cessation of substance intake (e.g., sleep disturbances, headaches, nausea and vomiting, tremors and restlessness, anxiety and depression); these symptoms can range from relatively mild to life-threatening.

Worries   Anxieties about possible future events.

References

Aaron, R., Joseph, A., Abraham, S., Muliyii, J., George, K., Prasad, J., et al. (2004). Suicides in young people in rural southern India. *Lancet, 363(9415),* 1117–1118.

Aarons, G. A., Brown, S. A., Garland, A. F., & Hough, R. L. (2004). Race/ethnic disparity and correlates of substance abuse service utilization and juvenile justice involvement among adolescents with substance use disorders. *Journal of Ethnicity in Substance Abuse, 3*(1), 47–64.

Abbeduto, L., Brady, N., & Kover, S. T. (2007). Language development and fragile X syndrome: Profiles, syndrome-related specificity, and within-syndrome differences. *Mental Retardation and Developmental Disabilities Research Reviews, 13*(1), 36–46.

Abbeduto, L., Evans, J., & Dolan, T. (2001). Theoretical perspectives on language and communication problems in mental retardation and developmental disabilities. *Mental Retardation and Developmental Disabilities Research Reviews, 7*(1), 45–55.

Abbeduto, L. & Hagerman, R. J. (1997). Language and communication in fragile X syndrome. *Mental Retardation and Developmental Disabilities Research Reviews, 3*(4), 313–322.

Abbeduto, L., Warren, S. F., & Conners, F. A. (2007). Language development in Down syndrome: From the prelinguistic period to the acquisition of literacy. *Mental Retardation and Developmental Disabilities Research Reviews, 13*(3), 247–261.

Abel, E. L. (1998a). Prevention of alcohol abuse-related birth effects: I. Public education efforts. *Alcohol and Alcoholism, 33*(4), 411–416.

Abel, E. L. (1998b). Prevention of alcohol abuse-related birth effects: II. Targeting and pricing. *Alcohol and Alcoholism, 33*(4), 417–420.

Abela, J. R. Z., & D'Alessandro, D. U. (2001). An examination of the symptom component of the hopelessness theory of depression in a sample of schoolchildren. *Journal of Cognitive Psychotherapy, 15*(1), 33–48.

Abela, J. R. Z., & Hankin, B. L. (2008). Cognitive vulnerability to depression in children and adolescents: A developmental psychopathology perspective. From J. R. Z. Abela & B. L. Hankin (Eds.), *Handbook of depression in children and adolescents* (pp. 35–78). New York: Guilford Press.

Abikoff, H. B., Jensen, P. S., Arnold, L. L. E., Hoza, B., Hechtman, L., Pollack, S., et al. (2002). Observed classroom behavior of children with ADHD: Relationship to gender and comorbidity. *Journal of Abnormal Child Psychology, 30*(4), 349–359.

Abraham, H. D., & Fava, M. (1999). Order of onset of substance abuse and depression in a sample of depressed outpatients. *Comprehensive Psychiatry, 40,* 44–50.

Abrams, E. Z., & Goodman, J. F. (1998). Diagnosing developmental problems in children: Parents and professionals negotiate bad news. *Journal of Pediatric Psychology, 23*(2), 87–98.

Abramson, L. Y., Alloy, L. B., Hogan, M. E., Whitehouse, W. G., Donovan, P., Rose, D. T., et al. (2002). Cognitive vulnerability to depression: Theory and evidence. From R. L. Leahy & E. T.

Dowd (Eds.), *Clinical advances in cognitive psychotherapy: Theory and application* (pp. 75–92). New York: Springer.

Abroms, L., Simons-Morton, B., Haynie, D. L., & Chen, R. (2005). Psychosocial predictors of smoking trajectories during middle and high school. *Addiction, 100*(6), 852–861.

Achenbach, T. M. (1966). The classification of children's psychiatric symptoms: A factor-analytic study. *Psychological Monographs: General and Applied, 80(7),* 1–37.

Achenbach, T. M. (1982). *Developmental Psychopathology* (2nd ed.). New York: Wiley.

Achenbach, T. M. (1990). What is "developmental" about developmental psychopathology? In J. E. Rolf & A. S. Masten (Eds.), *Risk and protective factors in the development of psychopathology* (pp. 29–48). New York: Cambridge University Press.

Achenbach, T. M. (1991). The derivation of taxonomic constructs: A necessary stage in the development of developmental psychopathology. In D. Cicchetti & S. L. Toth (Eds.), *Rochester Symposium on Developmental Psychopathology, Vol. 3: Models and integrations* (pp. 43–74). Rochester, NY: University of Rochester Press.

Achenbach, T. M. (1993). Taxonomy and comorbidity of conduct problems: Evidence from empirically based approaches. *Development and Psychopathology, 5(1–2),* 51–64.

Achenbach, T. M. (1995). Diagnosis, assessment, and comorbidity in psychosocial treatment research. *Journal of Abnormal Child Psychology, 23(1),* 45–65.

Achenbach, T. M. (1995). Empirically based assessment and taxonomy: Applications to clinical research. *Psychological Assessment, 7(3),* 261–274.

Achenbach, T. M. (1997). What is normal? What is abnormal? Developmental perspectives on behavioral and emotional problems. In S. S. Luthar & J. A. Burack (Eds.), *Developmental psychopathology: Perspectives on adjustment, risk and disorder* (pp. 93–114). New York: Cambridge University Press.

Achenbach, T. M., & Edelbrock, C. S. (1983). Behavioral problems and competencies reported by parents of normal and disturbed children aged four through sixteen. *Monographs of the Society for Research in Child Development, 46(1),* 1–82.

Achenbach, T. M., & Howell, C. T. (1993). Are American children's problems getting worse? A 13-year comparison. *Journal of the American Academy of Child and Adolescent Psychiatry, 32(6),* 1145–1154.

Achenbach, T. M., Howell, C. T., McConaughy, S. H., & Stanger, C. (1995). Six-year predictors of problems in a national sample of children and youth: I. Cross-informant syndromes. *Journal of the American Academy of Child and Adolescent Psychiatry, 34(3),* 336–347.

Achenbach, T. M., Howell, C. T., McConaughy, S. H., & Stanger, C. (1995). Six-year predictors of problems in a national sample of children and youth: II. Signs of disturbance. *Journal of the American Academy of Child and Adolescent Psychiatry, 34(4),* 488–498.

Achenbach, T. M., Howell, C. T., McConaughy, S. H., & Stanger, C. (1995). Six-year predictors of problems in a national sample of children and youth: III. Transitions to young adult syndromes. *Journal of the American Academy of Child and Adolescent Psychiatry, 34(5),* 658–669.

Achenbach, T. M., Howell, C. T., Quay, H. C., & Conners, C. K. (1991). National survey of problems and competencies among four- to sixteen-year-olds: Parents' reports for normative and clinical samples. *Monographs of the Society for Research in Child Development, 56(3),* v-120.

Achenbach, T. M., McConaughy, S. H., & Howell, C. T. (1987). Child/adolescent behavioral and emotional problems: Implications of cross-informant correlations for situational specificity. *Psychological Bulletin, 101(2),* 213–232.

Ackard, D. M., & Neumark-Sztainer, D. (2002). Date violence and date rape among adolescents: Associations with disordered eating behaviors and psychological health. *Child Abuse and Neglect, 26,* 455–473.

Ackerman, B. P., Brown, E., & Izard, C. E. (2003). Continuity and change in levels of externalizing behavior in children from economically disadvantaged families. *Child Development, 74(3),* 694–709.

Adams, R. E., Bukowski, W. M., & Bagwell, C. (2005). Stability of aggression during early adolescence as moderated by reciprocated friendship status and friend's aggression. *International Journal of Behavioral Development, 29*(2), 139–145.

Adler, A. K., & Wahl, O. F. (1998). Children's beliefs about people labeled mentally ill. *American Journal of Orthopsychiatry, 69(2),* 321–326.

Agrawal, A., Madden, P. A. F., Heath, A. C., Andrew, C., Lynskey, M. T., Bucholz, K. K., & Martin, N. G. (2005). Correlates of regular cigarette smoking in a population-based sample of Australian twins. *Addiction, 100*(11), 1709–1719.

Agrawal, A., Neale, M. C., Jacobson, K. C., Prescott, C. A., & Kendler, K. S. (2005). Illicit drug use and abuse/dependence: Modeling of two-stage variables using the CCC approach. *Addictive Behaviors, 30*(5), 1043–1048.

Agrawal, A., Neale, M. C., Prescott, C. A., & Kendler, K. S. (2004). Cannabis and other illicit drugs: Comorbid use and abuse/dependence in males and females. *Behavior Genetics, 34*(3), 217–228.

Aguilar, B., Stroufe, L. A., Egeland, B., & Carlson, E. (2000). Distinguishing the early-onset/persistent and adolescence-onset antisocial behavior types: From birth to 16 years. *Development and Psychopathology, 12,* 109–132.

Ahrano, J. (1997). Type III: Motor processing—Impulsive, motorically disorganized. In A. Lieberman, S. Wieder, & E. Fenichel (Eds.), *DC: 0–3 Casebook* (pp. 245–266). Washington, DC: Zero to Three: National Center for Infants, Toddlers, and Families.

Ainsworth, M. D. S. (1969). Object relations, dependency, and attachment: A theoretical view of the infant-mother relationship. *Child Development, 40*(4), 969–1025.

Ainsworth, M. D. S. (1979). Infant-mother attachment. *American Psychologist, 34*(10), 932–937.

Ainsworth, M. D. S., Bell, S. M., & Stayton, D. J. (1974). Infant-mother attachment and social development: Socialisation as a product of reciprocal responsiveness to signals. In M. J. M. Richards (Ed.), *The integration of a child into a social world* (pp. 99–135). London: Cambridge University Press.

Ainsworth, M. D. S., Blehar, M. C., Waters, E., & Wall, S. (1978). *Patterns of attachment: A psychological study of the strange situation.* Oxford, England: Erlbaum.

Ainsworth, M. D. S., & Eichberg, C. G. (1991). Effects on infant-mother attachment of mothers' unresolved loss of an attachment figure, or other traumatic experience. In C. M. Parkes, J. Stevenson-Hinde, & P. Marris (Eds.), *Attachment across the life cycle* (pp. 160–183). New York: Tavistock/Routledge.

Akiskal, H. (1998). The childhood roots of bipolar disorder. *Journal of Affective Disorders, 51,* 75–76.

Aksan, N., Goldsmith, H. H., Smider, N. A., Essex, M. J., Clark, R., Hyde, J. S., et al. (1999). Derivation and prediction of temperamental types among preschoolers. *Developmental Psychology, 35*(4), 958–971.

Akshoomoff, N., Lord, C., Lincoln, A. J., Courchesne, R. Y., Carper, R. A., Townsend, J., et al. (2004). Outcome classification of preschool children with autism spectrum disorders using MRI brain measures. *Journal of the American Academy of Child and Adolescent Psychiatry, 43*(3), 349–357.

Akshoomoff, N., Pierce, K., & Courchesne, E. (2002). The neurobiological basis of autism from a developmental perspective. *Development and Psychopathology, 14,* 613–634.

Alarcon, M., Plomin, R., Fulker, D. W., Corley, R., & DeFries, J. C. (1998). Multivariate path analysis of specific cognitive abilities date at 12 years of age in the Colorado Adoption Project. *Behavior Genetics, 28*(4), 255–264.

Alarcon, M., Plomin, R., Fulker, D. W., Corley, R., & DeFries, J. C. (1999). Molarity not modularity: Multivariate genetic analysis of specific cognitive abilities in parents and their 16-year-old children in the Colorado Adoption Project. *Cognitive Development, 14*(1), 175–193.

Alarcon, R. D., Bell, C. C., Kirmayer, L. J., Lin, K., Ustun, B., & Wisner, K. L. (2002). Beyond the funhouse mirrors: Research agenda on culture and psychiatric diagnosis. In D. J. Kupfer, M. B. First, & D. A. Regier (Eds.), *A research agenda for DSM-V.* Washington, DC: American Psychiatric Association.

Albano, A. M., Chorpita, B. F., & Barlow, D. H. (2003). Childhood anxiety disorders: In E. J. Mash & R. A. Barkley (Eds.), *Child psychopathology* (2nd ed., pp. 279–329). New York: Guilford Press.

Albano, A. M., & Hayward, C. (2004). Social anxiety disorder. In T. H. Ollendick & J. S. March (Eds.), *Phobic and anxiety disorders in children and adolescents: A clinician's guide to effective psychosocial and pharmacological interventions* (pp. 198–235). New York: Oxford University Press.

Albano, A. M., & Kendall, P. C. (2002). Cognitive behavioural therapy for children and adolescents with anxiety disorders: Clinical research advances. *International Review of Psychiatry, 14*(2), 129–134.

Albano, A. M., & Krain, A. (2005). Anxiety and anxiety disorders in girls. In D. J. Bell, S. L. Foster., & E. J. Mash (Eds.), *Handbook of behavioral and emotional problems in girls* (pp. 79–116). New York: Kluwer Academic/Plenum Publishers.

Aldred, C., Green, J., & Adams, C. (2004). A new social communication intervention for children with autism: Pilot randomized controlled treatment study suggesting effectiveness. *Journal of Child Psychology and Psychiatry, 45*(8), 1420–1430.

Alfano, C. A., Beidel, D. C., & Turner, S. M. (2002). Cognition in childhood anxiety: Conceptual methodological and developmental issues. *Clinical Psychology Review, 22*(8), 1209–1238.

Allen, A. J., Leonard, H. L., & Swedo, S. E. (1996). Current knowledge of medications for the treatment of childhood anxiety disorders. *Annual Progress in Child Psychiatry and Child Development, 431–451.*

Allen, G., & Courchesne, E. (2003). Differential effects of developmental cerebellar abnormality on cognitive and motor functions in the cerebellum: An fMRI study of autism. *American Journal of Psychiatry, 160,* 262–273.

Allen, J. P., Hauser, S. T., & Borman-Spurrell, E. (1996). Attachment theory as a framework for understanding sequelae of severe adolescent psychopathology: An 11-year follow-up study. *Journal of Consulting and Clinical Psychology, 64*(2), 254–263.

Allen, J. P., Moore, C., Kupermine, G., & Bell, K. (1998). Attachment and adolescent psychosocial functioning. *Child Development, 69,* 1406–1419.

Altepeter, T. S., & Korger, J. N. (1999). Disruptive behavior: Oppositional defiant disorder and conduct disorder. In S. D. Netherton & D. Holmes (Eds.), *Child and adolescent psychological disorders: A comprehensive textbook* (pp. 118–138). London: Oxford University Press.

Amaro, H., Blake, S. M., Schwartz, P. M., & Flinchbaugh, L. J. (2001). Developing theory-based substance abuse prevention programs for young adolescent girls. *Journal of Early Adolescence, 21*(3), 256–293.

Amaya-Jackson, L., Reynolds, V., Murray, M. C., McCarthy, G., Nelson, A., Cherney, M. S., et al. (2003). Cognitive-behavioral treatment for pediatric posttraumatic stress disoders: Protocol and application in school and community settings. *Cognitive and Behavioral Practice, 10*(3), 204–213.

Amen, D. G., & Carmichael, B. D. (1997). High-resolution brain SPECT imaging in ADHD. *Annals of Clinical Psychiatry, 9,* 81–86.

American Association on Mental Retardation/American Association on Intellectual and Developmental Disabilities (2002). *Mental retardation: Definition, classification and systems of support.* Washington, DC: American Association on Intellectual and Developmental Disabilities.

American Psychiatric Association. (2000). *Diagnostic and statistical manual of mental disorders* (4th ed., text revision). Washington, DC: Author.

American Psychiatric Association Work Group on Eating Disorders (2000). Practice guidelines for the treatment of patients with eating disorders (revision). *American Journal of Psychiatry, 157,* 1–39.

Ames, E. W., & Chisholm, K. (2001). Social and emotional development in children adopted from institutions. In D. B. Bailey Jr., J. T. Bruer, F. J. Symons, & J. W. Lichtman (Eds.), *Critical thinking about critical periods* (pp. 129–148). Baltimore: Paul H. Brookes Publishing.

Ametller, L., Castro, J., Serrano, E., Martinez, E., & Toro, J. (2005). Readiness to recover in adolescent anorexia nervosa: Prediction of hospital admission. *Journal of Child Psychology and Psychiatry, 46*(4), 394–400.

Anagnostaras, S. G., Craske, M. G., & Fanselow, M. S. (1999). Anxiety: At the intersection of genes and experience. *Nature Neuroscience, 2*(9), 780–782.

Anders, T. E., & Dahl, R. (2007). Classifying sleep disorders in infants and toddlers. In W. E. Narrow, M. B. First, P. J. Sirovatka, & D. A. Regier (Eds.), *Age and gender considerations in psychiatric diagnosis: A research agenda for DSM-V* (pp. 215–226). Arlington, VA: American Psychiatric Publishing.

Anders, T. E., Goodlin-Jones, B., & Sadeh, A. (2000). Sleep disorders. In C. H. Zeanah, Jr. (Ed.), *Handbook of infant mental health* (2nd ed., pp. 326–338). New York: Guilford Press.

Andersen, S. L., & Navalta, C. P. (2004). Altering the course of neurodevelopment: A framework for understanding the enduring effects of psychotropic drugs. *International Journal of Developmental Neuroscience, 22*(5–6), 423–440.

Anderson, C. B., & Bulik, C. M. (2004). Gender differences in compensatory behaviors, weight, shape salience, and drive for thinness. *Eating Behaviors, 5,* 1–11.

Anderson, D. A., Lundgren, J. D., Shapiro, J. R., & Paulosky, C. A. (2004). Assessment of eating disorders: Review and recommendations for clinical use. *Behavior Modification, 28,* 763–782.

Anderson, G. (1998). Creating moral space in prenatal genetic services. *Qualitative Health Reasearch, 8*(2), 168–187.

Anderson, M. (1998). Mental retardation, general intelligence, and modularity. *Learning and Individual Differences, 10*(3), 159–178.

Anderson, M. (2001). Conceptions of intelligence. *Journal of Child Psychology and Psychiatry, 42*(3), 287–298.

Anderson-Fye, E. P. (2004). A "Coca-Cola" shape: Cultural change, body image, and eating disorders in San Andres, Belize. *Culture, Medicine and Psychiatry, 28,* 561–595.

Angold, A., & Costello, E. J. (1996). The relative diagnostic utility of child and parent reports of oppositional defiant behaviors. *International Journal of Methods in Psychiatric Research, 6,* 253–259.

Angold, A., & Costello, E. J. (1996). Toward establishing an empirical basis for the diagnosis of oppositional defiant disorder. *Journal of the American Academy of Child and Adolescent Psychiatry, 35,* 1205–1212.

Angold, A., & Costello, E. J. (1996a). The relative diagnostic utility of child and parent reports of oppositional defiant behaviors. *International Journal of Methods in Psychiatric Research, 6,* 253–259.

Angold, A., & Costello, J. (1996b). Toward establishing an empirical basis for the diagnosis of oppositional defiant disorder. *Journal of the American Academy of Child and Adolescent Psychiatry, 35,* 1205–1212.

Angold, A., & Costello, E. J. (2001). The epidemiology of depression in children and adolescents. In I. M. Goodyer (Ed.), *The depressed child and adolescent* (2nd ed., pp. 143–178). New York: Cambridge University Press.

Angold, A., Costello, E. J., & Erkanli, A. (1999). Comorbidity. *Journal of Child Psychology and Psychiatry and Allied Disciplines, 40(1),* 57–87.

Angold, A., Costello, E. J., Erkanli, A., & Worthman, C. M. (1999). Pubertal changes in hormone levels and depression in girls. *Psychological Medicine, 29*(5), 1043–1053.

Angold, A., Costello, E. J., & Worthman, C. M. (1998). Puberty and depression: The roles of age, pubertal status and pubertal timing. *Psychological Medicine, 28*(1), 51–61.

Angold, A., Erkanli, A., Costello, E. J., & Rutter, M. (1996). Precision, reliability and accuracy in the dating of symptom onsets in child and adolescent psychopathology. *Journal of Child Psychology and Psychiatry and Allied Disciplines, 37(6),* 657–664.

Angold, A., Erkanli, A., Farmer, E. M. Z., Fairbank, J. A., Burns, B. J., Keeler, G., et al. (2002). Psychiatric disorder, impairment, and service use in African American and White youth. *Archives of General Psychiatry, 59(10),* 893–904.

Angold, A. & Fisher, P. W. (1999). Interviewer-based interviews. In D. Shaffer & C. P. Lewis (Eds.), *Diagnostic assessment in child and adolescent psychopathology* (pp. 34–64). New York: Guilford Press.

Angold, A., Worthman, C., & Costello, E. J. (2003). Puberty and depression. In C. Hayward (Ed.), *Gender differences at puberty* (pp. 137–164). New York: Cambridge University Press.

Anisfeld, E., Casper, V., Nozyce, M., & Cunningham, N. (1990). Does infant carrying promote attachment? An experimental study of the effects of increased physical contact on the development of attachment. *Child Development, 61(5),* 1617–1627.

Anthony, E. J. (1974). The syndrome of the psychologically invulnerable child. In E. J. Anthony & C. Koupernik (Eds.), *The child in his family: Children at psychiatric risk* (pp. 529–545). New York: Wiley.

Anthony, J. L., Lonigan, C. J., Hooe, E. S., & Phillips, B. M. (2002). An affect-based, hierarchical model of temperament and its relations with internalizing symptomatology. *Journal of Clinical Child and Adolescent Psychology, 31(4),* 480–490.

Anzai, N., Lindsey-Dudley, K., & Bidwell, R. J. (2002). Inpatient and partial hospital treatment for adolescent eating disorders. *Child and Adolescent Clinics of North America, 11,* 279–309.

Apfel, N., & Seitz, V. (1997). The firstborn sons of African American teenage mothers: Perspectives on risk and resilience. In S. S. Luthar & J. A. Burack (Eds.), *Developmental psychopathology: Perspectives on adjustment risk, and disorder* (pp. 486–506). New York: Cambridge University Press.

Applegate, B., Lahey, B. B., Hart, E. L., Biederman, J., Hynd, G. W., Barkley, R. A., et al. (1997). Validity of the age-of-onset criterion for ADHD: A report from the DSM-IV field trials. *Journal of the American Academy of Child and Adolescent Psychiatry, 36,* 1211–1221.

Apter, A. (2003). Biological factors influencing suicidal behavior in adolescents. In R. A. King & A. Apter (Eds.), *Suicide in children and adolescents* (pp. 118–149). New York: Cambridge University Press.

Apter, A., & Wasserman, D. (2003). Suicide in children and adolescents. In R. A. King & A. Apter (Eds.), *Suicide in children and adolescents* (pp. 63–85). New York: Cambridge University Press.

Arbiter, E., Sato-Tanaka, R., Kolvin, I., & Leitch, I. (1999). Differences in behaviour and temperament between Japanese and British toddlers living in London: A pilot study. *Child Psychology and Psychiatry Review, 4(3),* 117–125.

Archer, J. (2004). Sex differences in aggression in real-world settings: A meta-analytic review. *Review of General Psychology, 8(4),* 291–322.

Archer, J., & Coyne, S. M. (2005). An integrated review of indirect, relational, and social aggression. *Personality and Social Psychology Review, 9(3),* 212–230.

Arend, R., Gove, F. L., & Sroufe, L. A. (1979). Continuity of individual adaptation from infancy to kindergarten: A predictive study of ego-resiliency and curiosity in preschoolers. *Child Development, 50,* 950–959.

Armitage, R., Hoffmann, R., Emslie, G., Rintelman, J., Moore, J., & Lewis, K. (2004). Rest-activity cycles in childhood and adolescent depression. *Journal of the American Academy of Child and Adolescent Psychiatry, 43(6),* 761–769.

Armitage, R., Hoffmann, R. F., Emslie, G. J., Weinberg, W. A., Mayes, T. L., & Rush, A. J. (2002). Sleep microarchitecture as a predictor of recurrence in children and adolescents with depression. *International Journal of Neuropsychopharmacology, 5(3),* 217–228.

Armstrong, T. D., & Costello, E. J. (2002). Community studies on adolescent substance use, abuse, or dependence and psychiatric comorbidity. *Journal of Consulting and Clinical Psychology, 70(6),* 1224–1239.

Arnett, J. J. (1999). Adolescent storm and stress, reconsidered. *American Psychologist, 54(5),* 317–326.

Arnett, J. J. (2000). Emerging adulthood: A theory of development from the late teens through the twenties. *American Psychologist, 55,* 469–480.

Arnett, J. J. (2007). *Adolescence and emerging adulthood: A cultural approach.* Upper Saddle River, NJ: Pearson Prentice Hall.

Arnold, L. E., Chuang, S., Davies, M., Abikoff, H. B., Conners, C. K., Elliot, G. R., et al. (2004). Nine months of multicomponent behavioral treatment for ADHD and effectiveness of MTA fading procedures. *Journal of Abnormal Child Psychology, 32(1),* 39–51.

Arnold, L. E., Elliott, M., Sachs, L., Bird, H., Kraemer, H. C., Wells, K. C., et al. (2003). Effects of ethnicity on treatment attendance, stimulant response/dose, and 14-month outcome in ADHD. *Journal of Consulting and Clinical Psychology, 71(4),* 713–727.

Arnold, P. D., & Richter, M. A. (2001). Is obsessive-compulsive disorder an autoimmune disease? *Canadian Medical Association Journal, 165(10),* 1353–1358.

Arseneault, L., Kim-Cohen, J., Taylor, A., Caspi, A., & Moffit, T. E. (2005). Psychometric evaluation of 5- and 7-year old children's self-reports of conduct problems. *Journal of Abnormal Child Psychology, 33(5),* 537–550.

Arseneault, L., Moffitt, T. E., Caspi, A., Taylor, A., Rijsdijk, F. V., Jaffee, S. R., et al. (2003). Strong genetic effects on cross-situational antisocial behaviour among 5-year-old children according to mothers, teachers, examiner-observers, and twins' self-reports. *Journal of Child Psychology and Psychiatry, 44(6),* 832–848.

Asarnow, J., Glynn, S., Pynoos, R. S., Nahum, J., Guthrie, D., Cantwell, D. P., et al. (1999). When the earth stops shaking: Earthquake sequelae among children diagnosed for pre-earthquake psychopathology. *Journal of the American Academy of Child and Adolescent Psychiatry, 38(8),* 1016–1023.

Asbury, K., Dunn, J. F., Pike, A., & Plomin, R. (2003). Nonshared environmental influences on individual differences in early behavioral development: A monozygotic twin differences study. *Child Development, 74(3),* 933–943.

Asher, S. R., & Paquette, J. A. (2003). Loneliness and peer relations in childhood. *Current Directions in Psychological Science, 12(3),* 75–78.

Asher, S. R., Parker, J. G., & Walker, D. L. (1998). Distinguishing friendship from acceptance: Implications for intervention and assessment. In W. M. Bukowski, A. F. Newcomb, & W. W. Hartup (Eds.), *The company they keep: Friendship in childhood and adolescence. Cambridge studies in social and emotional development* (pp. 366–405). New York: Cambridge University Press.

Asher, S. R., Rose, A. J., & Gabriel, S. W. (2001). Peer rejection in everyday life. In M. R. Leary (Ed.), *Interpersonal rejection* (pp. 105–142). New York: Oxford University Press.

Asherson, P., Kuntsi, J., & Taylor, E. (2005). Unravelling the complexity of attention-deficit hyperactivity disorder:

A behavioral genomic approach. *British Journal of Psychiatry, 187*(2), 103–105.

Ashman, S. B., Dawson, G., Panagiotides, H., Yamada, E., & Wilkinson, C. W. (2002). Stress hormone levels of children of depressed mothers. *Development and Psychopathology, 14*(2), 333–349.

Asperger, H. (1944/1991). Autistic psychopathy in childhood. In U. Frith (Ed.), *Asperger and his syndrome* (pp. 37–92). Cambridge: Cambridge University Press.

Aspinwall, L. G., & Taylor, S. E. (1997). A stitch in time: Self-regulation and proactive coping. *Psychological Bulletin, 121*, 417–436.

Astley, S. J., Bailey, D., Talbot, C., & Clarren, S. K. (2000). Fetal alcohol syndrome (FAS) primary prevention through FAS diagnosis: II A comprehensive profile of 80 birth mothers of children with FAS. *Alcohol and Alcoholism, 35*(5), 509–519.

Attie, I., & Brooks-Gunn, J. (1989). Development of eating problems in adolescent girls: A longitudinal study. *Developmental Psychology, 25*, 70–79.

Attwood, T. (2003). Framework for behavioral interventions. *Child and Adolescent Psychiatric Clinics of North America, 12*(1), 65–86.

Auerbach, J. G., Lerner, Y., Barasch, M., & Tepper, D. (1995). The identification in infancy of children at cognitive and behavioral risk: The Jerusalem Kindergarten Project. *Journal of Applied Developmental Psychology, 16(3)*, 319–338.

August, G. J., Bloomquist, M. L., Lee, S. S., Realmuto, G. M., & Hektner, J. M. (2006). Can evidence-based prevention programs be sustained in community practice settings? The Early Risers' advanced stage effectiveness trial. *Prevention Science, 7*(2), 151–165.

August, G. J., Braswell, L., & Thuras, P. (1998). Diagnostic stability of ADHD in a community sample of school-aged children screened for disruptive behavior. *Journal of Abnormal Child Psychology, 26*, 345.

August, G. J., Lee, S. S., Bloomquist, M. L., Realmuto, G. M., & Hektner, J. M. (2003). Maintenance effects of an evidence-based prevention innovation for aggressive children living in culturally diverse urban neighborhoods: The Early Risers effectiveness study. *Journal of Emotional and Behavioral Disorders, 12*(4), 194–205.

August, G. J., Lee, S. S., Bloomquist, M. L., Realmuto, G. M., & Hektner, J. M. (2004). Dissemination of an evidence-based prevention innovation for aggressive children living in culturally diverse, urban neighborhoods: The Early Risers effectiveness study. *Prevention Science, 4*(4), 271–286.

August, G. J., Realmuto, G. M., Crosby, R. D., & MacDonald, A. W. (1995). Community-based multiple-gate screening of children at risk for conduct disorder. *Journal of Abnormal Child Psychology, 23*, 521–544.

August, G. J., Realmuto, G. M., Joyce, T., & Hektner, J. M. (1999). Persistence and desistance of oppositional defiant disorder in a community sample of children with ADHD. *Journal of the American Academy of Child and Adolescent Psychiatry, 38*, 1262–1270.

Austin, A. A., & Chorpita, B. F. (2004). Temperament, anxiety, and depression: Comparisons across five ethnic groups of children. *Journal of Clinical Child Adolescent Psychology, 33*(2), 216–226.

Austin, S. B., & Gortmaker, S. L. (2001). Dieting and smoking initiation in early adolescent girls and boys: A prospective study. *American Journal of Public Health, 91*(3), 446–450.

Austin, S. B., Ziyadeh, N., Kahn, J. A., Camargo, C. A., Jr., Colditz, G. A., & Field, A. E. (2004). Sexual orientation, weight concerns, and eating disordered behaviors in adolescent boys and girls. *Journal of the American Academy of Child and Adolescent Psychiatry, 43*, 1115–1123.

Avenevoli, S., Knight, E., Kessler, R. C., & Merikangas, K. R. (2008). Epidemiology of depression in children and adolescents. In J. R.Z. Abela & B. L. Hankin (Eds.), *Handbook of depression in children and adolescents* (pp. 6–32). New York: Guilford Press.

Avramidis, E., Bayliss, P., & Burden, R. (2000). A survey into mainstream teachers' attitudes towards the inclusion of children with special educational needs in the ordinary school in one local education authority. *Educational Psychology, 20*(2), 191–211.

Avramidis, E., & Norwich, B. (2002). Teachers' attitudes towards integration/inclusion: A review of the literature. *European Journal of Special Needs Education, 17*(2), 129–147.

Axline, V. M. (1969). *Play Therapy.* New York: Ballantine.

Babor, T. F., Higgins-Biddle, J., Dauser, D., Higgins, P., & Burleson, J. A. (2005). Alcohol screening and brief intervention in primary care settings: Implementation models and predictors. *Journal of Studies on Alcohol, 66*(3), 361–368.

Babor, T. F., Webb, C., Burleson, J. A., & Kaminer, Y. (2002). Subtypes for classifying adolescents with marijuana use disorders: Construct validity and clinical implications. *Addiction, 97*(Suppl. 1), 58–69.

Bacharach, V. R., & Baumeister, A. A. (2003). Child care and severe externalizing behavior in kindergarten children. *Journal of Applied Developmental Psychology, 23*, 527–537.

Bae, S., Ye, R., Chen, S., Rivers, P. A., & Singh, K. P. (2005). Risky behaviors and factors associated with suicide attempt in adolescents. *Archives of Suicide Research, 9*(2), 193–202.

Bagwell, C. L., & Coie, J. D. (2004). The best friendships of aggressive boys: Relationship quality, conflict management, and rule-breaking behavior. *Journal of Experimental Child Psychology, 88*(1), 5–24.

Bailey, A., Phillips, W., & Rutter, M. (1996). Autism: Towards an integration of clinical, genetic, neuropsychological, and neurobiological perspectives. *Journal of Child Psycholology and Psychiatry, 37*, 89–126.

Bailey, D. B., Jr., Hatton, D. D., & Skinner, M. (1998). Early developmental trajectories of males with fragile X syndrome. *American Journal on Mental Retardation, 103*(1), 29–39.

Bailey, J. A., & McCloskey, L. (2005). Pathways to adolescent substance use among sexually abused girls. *Journal of Abnormal Child Psychology, 33*(1), 39–53.

Bailey, S. (1999). Young people, mental illness and stigmatization. *Psychiatric Bulletin, 23*, 107–110.

Baird, G., Charman, T., Baron-Cohen, S., Cox, A., Swettenham, J., Wheelwright, S., et al. (2000). A screening instrument for autism at 18 months of age: A 6-year follow-up study. *Journal of the American Academy of Child and Adolescent Psychiatry, 39*, 694–702.

Baker, B. L. (1996). Parent training. In J. W. Jacobson & J. A. Mulick (Eds.), *Manual of diagnosis and professional practice in mental retardation* (pp. 289–299). Washington, DC: American Psychological Association.

Baker, B. L., Balcher, J., Crnic, K. A., & Edelbrock, C. (2002). Behavior problems and parenting stress in families of three-year-old children with and without developmental delays. *American Journal on Mental Retardation, 107*(6), 433–444.

Baker, T. B., Brandon, T. H., & Chassin, L. (2004). Motivational influences on cigarette smoking. *Annual Review of Psychology, 55*, 463–491.

Bakermans-Kranenburg, M. J., Van IJzendoorn, M. H., & Juffer, F. (2003). Less is more: Meta-analysis of sensitivity and attachment interventions in early childhood. *Psychological Bulletin, 129*(2), 195–215.

Balboni, G., & Pedrabissi, L. (2000). Attitudes of Italian teachers and parents toward school inclusion of students with mental retardation: The role of experience. *Education and Training in Mental Retardation and Developmental Disabilities, 35*(2), 148–159.

Balch, G. I., Tworek, C., Barker, D. C., Sasso, B., Mermelstein, R. J., & Giovino, G. A. (2004). Opportunities for youth smoking cessation: Findings from a national focus group study. *Nicotine and Tobacco Research, 6*(1), 9–17.

Baldry, A. C., & Farrington, D. P. (2000). Bullies and delinquents: Personal characteristics and parental styles. *Journal of Community and Applied Social Psychology, 10*(1), 17–31.

Ball, L., & Chandler, M. (1989). Identity formation in suicidal and nonsuicidal youth: The role of self continuity. *Development and Psychopathology, 1*(3), 257–275.

Ballanti, C. J., Bierman, K. L., & Conduct Problems Prevention Research Group. (2000). Disentangling the impact of low cognitive ability and inattention on social behavior and peer relationships. *Journal of Clinical Child Psychology, 29*, 66–75.

Baltes, P. B., & Staudinger, U. M. (2000). Wisdom: A metaheuristic (pragmatic) to orchestrate mind and virtue toward excellence. *American Psychologist, 55(1)*, 122–136.

Bandura, A., Pastorelli, C., Barbaranelli, C., & Caprara, G. V. (1999). Self-efficacy pathways to childhood depression. *Journal of Personality and Social Psychology, 76*(2), 258–269.

Baradon, T. (2002). Psychotherapeutic work with parents and infants: Psychoanalytic and attachment perspectives. *Attachment and Human Development, 4*(1), 25–38.

Barbe, R. P., Bridge, J. A., Birmaher, B., Kolko, D. J., & Brent, D. A. (2004). Lifetime history of sexual abuse, clinical presentation, and outcome in a clinical trial for adolescent depression. *Journal of Clinical Psychiatry, 65*(1), 77–83.

Barbe, R. P., Williamson, D. E., Bridge, J. A., Birmaher, B., Dahl, R. E., Axelson, D., et al. (2005). Clinical differences between suicidal and nonsuicidal depressed children and adolescents. *Journal of Clinical Psychiatry, 66*(4), 492–498.

Barber, B. L., & Eccles, J. S. (2003). The joy of romance: Healthy adolescent relationships as an educational agenda. In P. Florsheim (Ed.), *Adolescent romantic relations and sexual behavior: Theory, research, and practical implications* (pp. 355–370). Mahwah, NJ: Erlbaum.

Barber, B. L., Eccles, J. S., & Stone, M. R. (2001). Whatever happened to the jock, the brain, and the princess? Young adult pathways linked to adolescent activity involvement and social identity. *Journal of Adolescent Research, 16*(5), 429–455.

Barber, B. L., Stone, M. R., Hunt, J. E., & Eccles, J. S. (2005). Benefits of activity participation: The roles of identity affirmation and peer group norm sharing. In J. L. Mahoney, R. W. Larson, & J. S. Eccles (Eds.), *Organized activities as contexts of development: Extracurricular activities, after-school and community programs* (pp. 185–210). Mahwah, NJ: Erlbaum.

Barker, E. T., & Galambos, N. L. (2003). Body dissatisfaction of adolescent girls and boys: Risk and resources factors. *Journal of Early Adolescence, 23,* 141–165.

Barkley, R. A. (1990). *Attention deficit hyperactivity disorder: A handbook for diagnosis and treatment.* New York: Guilford Press.

Barkley, R. A. (1997a). *ADHD and the nature of self-control.* New York: Guilford Press.

Barkley, R. A. (1997b). Behavioral inhibition, sustained attention, and executive functions: Constructing a unifying theory of ADHD. *Psychological Bulletin, 121*(1), 65–94.

Barkley, R. A. (2001). The executive functions and self-regulation: An evolutionary neuropsychological perspective. *Neuropsychology Review, 11,* 1–29.

Barkley, R. A. (2004). Attention deficit/hyperactivity disorder and self-regulation: Taking an evolutionary perspective on executive functioning. From R. F. Baumeister & K. D. Vohs (Eds.), *Handbook of self-regulation: Research, theory and applications* (pp. 301–323). New York: Guilford Press.

Barkley, R. A., Cook, E. H., Dulcan, M., Campbell, S., Prior, M., Atkins, M., et al. (2002). Consensus statement on ADHD. *European Child and Adolescent Psychiatry, 11*(2), 96–98.

Barkley, R. A., Edwards, G. H., & Robin, A L. (1999). *Defiant teens: A clinician's manual for assessment and family intervention.* New York: Guilford Press.

Barkley, R. A., Murphy, K. R., Dupaul, G. J., & Bush, T. (2002). Driving in young adults with attention deficit hyperactivity disorder: Knowledge, performance, adverse outcomes, and the role of executive functioning. *Journal of the International Neuropsychological Society, 8*(5), 655–672.

Barnard, K. E., Morisset, C. E., & Spieker, S. (1993). Preventive interventions: Enhancing parent-infant relationships. In C. H. Zeanah (Ed.), *Handbook of infant mental health* (pp. 386–401). New York: Guilford Press.

Barnes, G. M., Welte, J. W., Hoffman, J. H., & Dintcheff, B. A. (2005). Shared predictors of youthful gambling, substance use, and delinquency. *Psychology of Addictive Behaviors, 19*(2), 165–174.

Barnett, D., Hunt, K. H., Butler, C. M., McCaskill, J. W., Kaplan-Estrin, M., & Pipp-Siegel, S. (1999). Indices of attachment disorganization among toddlers with neurological and non-neurological problems. In J. Solomon & C. George (Eds.), *Attachment disorganization* (pp. 189–212). New York: Guilford Press.

Barnett, L. A. (1984). Research note: Young children's resolution of distress through play. *Journal of Child Psychology and Psychiatry and Allied Disciplines, 25*(3), 477–483.

Barnett, S. M. & Ceci, S. J. (2005). The role of transferable knowledge in intelligence. In R. J. Sternberg & J. E. Pretz (Eds.), *Cogintion and intelligence: Identifying the mechanisms of the mind* (pp. 208–224). New York: Cambridge University Press.

Barnett, W. S. (1986). Definition and classification of mental retardation: A reply to Zigler, Balla, and Hodapp. *American Journal of Mental Deficiency, 91*(2), 111–116.

Baron-Cohen, S. (1989). The autistic child's theory of mind: A case of specific developmental delay. *Journal of Child Psychology and Psychiatry, 30,* 285–297.

Baron-Cohen, S. (1995). *Mindblindness: An essay on autism and theory of mind.* Cambridge, MA: MIT Press.

Baron-Cohen, S. (1997). *The maladapted mind: Classic readings in evolutionary psychopathology.* Hove, England: Psychology Press/ Erlbaum.

Baron-Cohen, S. (2000). Is Asperger syndrome/high-functioning autism necessarily a disability? *Development and Psychopathology, 12*, 489–500.

Baron-Cohen, S. (2001). Theory of mind and autism: A review. In L. M. Glidden (Ed.), *International review of research in mental retardation: Autism* (pp. 169–184). San Diego, CA: Academic Press.

Baron-Cohen, S. (2002a). The extreme male brain theory of autism. *Trends in Cognitive Sciences, 6*, 248–254.

Baron-Cohen, S. (2002b). Is Asperger syndrome necessarily viewed as a disability? *Focus on Autism and Other Developmental Disabilities, 17*, 186–191.

Baron-Cohen, S., & Hammer, J. (1997). Parents of children with Asperger syndrome: What is the cognitive phenotype? *Journal of Cognitive Neuroscience, 9*, 548–554.

Baron-Cohen, S., Jolliffe, T., Mortimore, C., & Robertson, M. (1997). Another advanced test of theory of mind: Evidence from very high functioning adults with autism or Asperger Syndrome. *Journal of Child Psychology and Psychiatry and Allied Disciplines, 38*, 813–822.

Baron-Cohen, S., O'Riordan, M., Stone, V., Jones, R., & Plaisted, K. (1999). Recognition of faux pas by normally developing children with Asperger syndrome or high-functioning autism. *Journal of Autism and Developmental Disorders, 29*, 407–418.

Baron-Cohen, S., Ring, H. A., Bullmore, E. T., Wheelwright, S., Ashwin, C., & Williams, S. C. R. (2000). The amygdala theory of autism. *Neuroscience and Biobehavioral Reviews, 24*, 355–364.

Baron-Cohen, S., Scahill, V. L., Izaguirre, J., Hornsey, H., & Robertson, M. M. (1999). The prevalence of Gilles de la Tourette syndrome in children and adolescents with autism: A large scale study. *Psychological Medicine, 29*, 1151–1159.

Baron-Cohen, S., & Wheelwright, S. (1999). Obsessions' in children with autism or Asperger syndrome: Content analysis in terms of core domains of cognition. *British Journal of Psychiatry, 175*, 484–490.

Baron-Cohen, S., Wheelwright, S., & Jolliffe, T. (1997). Is there a "language of the eyes"? Evidence from normal adults, and adults with autism or Asperger syndrome. *Visual Cognition, 4*, 311–31.

Baron-Cohen, S., Wheelwright, S., Lawson, J., Griffin, R., & Hill, J. (2002). The exact mind: Empathizing and systemizing in autism spectrum conditions. In U. Goswami (Ed.), *Blackwell handbook of childhood cognitive development* (pp. 491–508). Malden, MA: Blackwell.

Baron-Cohen, S., Wheelwright, S., Skinner, R., Martin, J., & Clubley, E. (2001). The Autism-Spectrum Quotient (AQ): Evidence from Asperger syndrome/high-functioning autism, males and females, scientists and mathematicians. *Journal of Autism and Developmental Disorders, 31*, 5–17.

Baron-Cohen, S., Wheelwright, S., Stone, V., & Rutherford, M. (1999). A mathematician, a physicist and a computer scientist with Asperger syndrome: Performance on folk psychology and folk physics tests. *Neurocase, 5*, 475–483.

Barr, R. G., & Gunnar, M. (2000). Colic: The "transient responsivity" hypothesis. In R. G. Barr, B. Hopkins, et al. (Eds.), *Crying as a sign, a symptom, and a signal: Clinical, emotional and developmental aspects of infant and toddler crying. Clinics in Developmental Medicine, 152* (pp. 41–66). New York: Cambridge University Press.

Barr, R. G., Paterson, J. A., MacMartin, L. M., Lehtonen, L., & Young, S. N. (2005). Prolonged and unsoothable crying bouts in infants with and without colic. *Journal of Developmental and Behavioral Pediatrics, 26*(1), 14–23.

Barrera, M., Biglan, A., Taylor, T. K., Gunn, B. K., Smolkowski, K., Black, C., et al. (2002). Early elementary school intervention to reduce conduct problems: A randomized trial with Hispanic and non-Hispanic children. *Prevention Science, 3*, 83–94.

Barrett, A. E., & Turner, R. J. (2006). Family structure and substance use problems in adolescence and early adulthood: Examining explanations for the relationship. *Addiction, 101*(1), 109–120.

Barrett, K. C. (2005). The origins of social emotions and self-regulation in toddlerhood: New evidence. *Cognition and Emotion, 19*(7), 953–979.

Barrett, P. M. (2000). Treatment of childhood anxiety: Developmental aspects. *Clinical Psychology Review, 20*(4), 479–494.

Barrett, P. M., & Shortt, A. L. (2003). Parental involvement in the treatment of anxious children. In A. E. Kazdin (Ed.), *Evidence-based psychotherapies for children and adolescents* (pp. 101–119). New York: Guilford Press.

Barrett, P. M., Dadds, M. R., & Rapee, R. M. (1996). Family treatment of childhood anxiety: A controlled trial. *Journal of Consulting and Clinical Psychology, 64*(2), 333–342.

Barrett, P. M., Duffy, A. L., Dadds, M. R., & Rapee, R. M. (2001). Cognitive-behavioral treatment of anxiety disorders in children: Long-term (6-year) follow-up. *Journal of Consulting and Clinical Psychology, 69*(1), 135–141.

Barrett, P. M., & Healy, L. J. (2003). An examination of the cognitive processes involved in childhood obsessive-compulsive disorder. *Behaviour Research and Therapy, 41*(3), 285–299.

Barrett, P., Healy-Farrell, L., & March, J. S. (2004). Cognitive-behavioral family treatment of childhood obsessive-compulsive disorder: A controlled trial. *Journal of the American Academy of Child and Adolescent Psychiatry, 43*(1), 46–62.

Barrett, P., Shortt, A., & Healy, L. (2002). Do parent and child behaviours differentiate families whose children have obsessive-compulsive disorder from other clinic and non-clinic families? *Journal of Child Psychology and Psychiatry and Allied Disciplines, 43*(5), 597–607.

Barrickman, L. (2003). Disruptive behavioral disorders. *Pediatric Clinics of North America, 50*, 1005–1017.

Barrows, P. (1999). Fathers in parent-infant psychotherapy. *Infant Mental Health Journal, 20*(3), 333–345.

Barry, C. T., Frick, P. J., DeShazo, T. M., McCoy, M., Ellis, M., & Loney, B. R. (2000). The importance of callous-unemotional traits for extending the concept of psychopathy to children. *Journal of Abnormal Psychology, 109*, 335–340.

Barry, C. T., Frick, P. J., Grooms, T., McCoy, M. G., Ellis, M. L., & Loney, B. R. (2000). The importance of callous-unemotional traits for extending the concept of psychopathy to children. *Journal of Abnormal Psychology, 109*, 335–340.

Bartlett, C. W., Gharani, N., Millonig, J. H., & Brzutowicz, L. M. (2005). Three autism candidate genes: A synthesis of human genetic analysis with other disciplines. *International Journal of Developmental Neuroscience, 23*(2–3), 221–234.

Barton, M. L., & Robins, D. (2000). Regulatory disorders. In C. H. Zeanah (Ed.), *Handbook of infant mental health* (2nd ed., pp. 311–325). New York: Guilford Press.

Bateson, G., Jackson, D. D., Haley, J., & Weakland, J. (1956). Toward a theory of schizophrenia. *Behavioral Science, 1*, 251–264.

Batsche, G. M., & Porter, L. J. (2006). Bullying. In G. G. Bear & K. M. Minke (Eds.), *Children's needs III: Development, prevention, and intervention* (pp. 135–148). Washington, DC: National Association of School Psychologists.

Battjes, R. J., Gordon, M. S., O'Grady, K. E., & Kinlock, T. W. (2004). Predicting retention of adolescents in substance abuse treatment. *Addictive Behaviors, 29*(5), 1021–1027.

Battjes, R. J., Gordon, M. S., O'Grady, K. E., Kinlock, T. W., & Carswell, M. A. (2003). Factors that predict adolescent motivation for substance abuse treatment. *Journal of Substance Abuse Treatment, 24*(3), 221–232.

Battjes, R. J., Gordon, M. S., O'Grady, K. E., Kinlock, T. W., Katz, E. C., & Sears, E. A. (2004). Evaluation of a group-based substance abuse treatment program for adolescents. *Journal of Substance Abuse Treatment, 27*(2), 123–134.

Bauermeister, J. J., Bird, H. R., Canino, G., Rubio-Stipec, M., Bravo, M., & Alegria, M. (1995). Dimensions of attention deficit hyperactivity disorder: Findings from teacher and parent reports in a community sample. *Journal of Clinical Child Psychology, 24*, 264–271.

Bauermeister, J. J., Matos, M., Reina, G., Salas, C. C., Martinez, J. V., Cumba, E. et al. (2005). Comparison of the DSM-IV combined and inattentive types of ADHD in a school-based sample of Latino/Hispanic children. *Journal of Child Psychology and Psychiatry, 46*(2), 166–179.

Bauermeister, J. J., Shrout, P. E., Chavez, L., Rubio-Stipec, M., Ramirez, R., Padilla, L., et al. (2007). ADHD and gender: Are risks and sequela of ADHD the same for boys and girls? *Journal of Child Psychology and Psychiatry, 48*(8), 831–839.

Baum, S. M., & Olenchak, F. R. (2002). The alphabet children: GT, ADHD, and more. *Exceptionality, 10(2),* 77–91.

Bauman, M. L., & Kemper, T. L. (2005). Neuroanalytic observations of the brain in autism: A review and future directions. *International Journal of Developmental Neuroscience, 23*(2–3), 183–187.

Baumeister, A. A., & Baumeister, A. A. (1995). Mental retardation. In M. Hersen & R. T. Ammerman (Eds.), Advanced abnormal child psychology (pp. 283–303). Hillsdale, NJ: Erlbaum.

Baumeister, R. F., Muraven, M., & Tice, D. M. (2000). Ego depletion: A resource model of volition, self-regulation, and controlled processing. *Social Cognition, 18*, 130–150.

Baumrind, D. (1967). Child care practices anteceding three patterns of preschool behavior. *Genetic Psychology Monographs, 75(1),* 43–88.

Baumrind, D. (1971). Current patterns of parental authority. *Developmental Psychology, 4(1),* 1–103.

Baydar, N., Reid, M. J., & Webster-Stratton, C. (2003). The role of mental health factors and program engagement in the effectiveness of a preventive parenting program for Head Start mothers. *Child Development, 74*(5), 1433–1453.

Baying, L., Laucht, M., & Schmidt, M. H. (2000). Oppositional children differ from healthy children in frontal brain activation. *Journal of Abnormal Child Psychology, 28*(3), 267–275.

Beardslee, W. R., & Gladstone, T. R. G. (2001). Prevention of childhood depression: Recent findings and future prospects. *Biological Psychiatry, 49*(12), 1101–1110.

Bearman, S. K., Presnell, K., Martinez, E., & Stice, E. (2006). The skinny on body dissatisfaction: A longitudinal study of adolescent girls and boys. *Journal of Youth and Adolescence, 35,* 229–241.

Beauchaine, T. P. (2001). Vagal tone, development, and Gray's motivational theory: Toward an integrated model of autonomic nervous system functioning in psychopathology. *Development and Psychopathology, 13*(2), 183–214.

Beauchaine, T. P. (2003). Taxometrics and developmental psychopathology. *Development and Psychopathology, 15(3),* 501–527.

Beauchaine, T. P., Strassberg, Z., Kees, M. R., & Drabick, D. A. G. (2002). Cognitive response repertoires to child noncompliance by mothers of aggressive boys. *Journal of Abnormal Child Psychology, 30*, 89–101.

Beck, A. T. (1987). Cognitive models of depression. *Journal of Cognitive Psychotherapy, 1*(1), 5–37.

Beck, J. S., Liese, B. S., & Najavits, L. M. (2005). Cognitive therapy. In R. J. Frances, S. I. Miller, & A. H. Mack (Eds.), *Clinical textbook of addictive disorders* (3rd ed.). New York: Guilford Press.

Becker, A. E. (2004). Television, disordered eating, and young women in Fiji: Negotiating body image and identity during rapid social change. *Culture, Medicine and Psychiatry, 28,* 533–559.

Becker, A. E., Burwell, R. A., Herzog, D. B., Hamburg, P., & Gilman, S. E. (2002). Eating behaviours and attitudes following prolonged exposure to television among ethnic Fijian adolescent girls. *British Journal of Psychiatry, 180*(6), 509–514.

Becker, C. B., Bull, S., Schaumberg, K., Cauble, A., & Franco, A. (2008). Effectiveness of peer-led eating disorders prevention: A replication trial. *Journal of Consulting and Clinical Psychology, 76*(2), 347–354.

Becker, C. B., Smith., L. M., & Ciao, A. C. (2006). Peer-facilitated eating disorder prevention: A randomized effectiveness trial of cognitive dissonance and media advocacy. *Journal of Counseling Psychology, 53*(4), 550–555.

Becker, K. D., Stuewig, J., Herrera, V. M., & McCloskey, L. A. (2004). A study of firesetting and animal cruelty in children: Family influences and adolescent outcomes. *Journal of the American Academy of Child and Adolescent Psychiatry, 43*(7), 905–912.

Becker, K., & Schmidt, M. H. (2004). Internet chat rooms and suicide. *Journal of the American Academy of Child and Adolescent Psychiatry, 43*(3), 246–247.

Beckwith, L., Howard, J., Espinosa, M., & Tyler, R. (1999). Psychopathology, mother-child interaction, and infant development: Substance-abusing mothers and their offspring. *Development and Psychopathology, 11*, 715–725.

Behan, J., & Carr, A. (2000). Oppositional defiant disorder. In A. Carr (Ed.), *What works with children and adolescents? A critical review of psychological interventions with children, adolescents and their families* (pp. 102–130). Florence, KY: Taylor & Frances/Routledge.

Beidel, D. C., Ferrell, C., Alfano, C. A., & Yeganeh, R. (2001). The treatment of childhood social anxiety disorder. *Psychiatry Clinics of North America, 24*(4), 831–846.

Beidel, D. C., Turner, S. M., Young, B., & Paulson, A. (2005). Social effectiveness therapy for children: Three year follow-up. *Journal of Consulting and Clinical Psychology, 73*(4), 721–725.

Beitchman, J. H., Adlaf, E. M., Atkinson, L., Douglas, L., Massak, A., & Kenaszchuk, C. (2005). Psychiatric and substance use disorders in late adolescence: The role of risk and perceived social support. *American Journal on Addictions, 14*(2), 124–138.

Beitchman, J. H., Adlaf, E. M., Douglas, L., Atkinson, L., Young, A., Johnson, C. J., Escobar, M., & Wilson, B. (2001). Comorbidity of psychiatric and substance use disorders in late adolescence: A cluster analytic approach. *American Journal of Drug and Alcohol Abuse, 27*(3), 421–440.

Beitchman, J. H., Douglas, L., Wilson, B., Johnson, C., Young, A., Atkinson, L., Escobar, M., & Taback, N. (1999). Adolescent substance use disorders: Findings from a 14-year follow-up of speech/language-impaired and control children. *Journal of Clinical Child Psychology, 28*(3) , 312–321.

Beitchman, J. H., Wilson, B., Douglas, L., Young, A., & Adlaf, E. (2001). Substance use disorders in young adults with and without LD: Predictive and concurrent relationships. *Journal of Learning Disabilities, 34*(4) , 317–332.

Belenko, S., & Dembo, R. (2003). Treating adolescent substance abuse problems in the juvenile drug court. *International Journal of Law and Psychiatry. Specialty courts, 26*(1), 87–110.

Bell, K. L., & Calkins, S. D. (2000). Relationships as inputs and outputs of emotion regulation. *Psychological Inquiry, 11*(3), 160–163.

Bell, M. A., & Fox, N. A. (1996). Crawling experience is related to changes in cortical organization during infancy: Evidence from EEG coherence. *Developmental Psychobiology, 29(7),* 551–561.

Bellanti, C. J., Bierman, K. L., & Conduct Problems Prevention Research Group. (2000). Disentangling the impact of low cognitive ability and inattention on social behavior and peer relationships. *Journal of Clinical Child Psychology, 29*(1), 66–75.

Bell-Dolan, D. J., Last, C. G., & Strauss, C. C. (1990). Symptoms of anxiety disorders in normal children. *Journal of the American Academy of Child and Adolescent Psychiatry, 29*(5), 759–765.

Bellmore, A. D., Witkow, M. R., Graham, S., & Juvonen, J. (2005). From beliefs to behavior: The mediating role of hostile response selection in predicting aggression. *Aggressive Behavior, 31,* 453–472.

Bellugi, U., Lichtenberger, L., Jones, W., Lai, Z., & George, M. (2000). The neurocognitive profile of Williams syndrome: A complex pattern of strengths and weaknesses. *Journal of Cognitive Neuroscience, 12*(1), 7–29.

Belsky, J. (1980). Child maltreatment: An ecological integration. *American Psychologist, 35,* 320–335.

Belsky, J. (1993). Etiology of child maltreatment: A developmental ecological analysis. *Psychological Bulletin, 114,* 413–434.

Belsky, J. (1999). Interactional and contextual determinants of attachment security. In J. Cassidy & P. R. Shaver (Eds.), *Handbook of attachment: Theory, research, and clinical applications* (pp. 249–264). New York: Guilford Press.

Belsky, J., Campbell, S. B., Cohn, J. F., & Moore, G. (1996). Instability of infant-parent attachment security. *Developmental Psychology, 32*(5), 921–924.

Belsky, J., & Cassidy, J. (1994). Attachment and close relationships: An individual-difference perspective. *Psychological Inquiry, 5*(1), 27–30.

Belsky, J., Fish, M., & Isabella, R. A. (1991). Continuity and discontinuity in infant negative and positive emotionality: Family antecedents and attachment consequences. *Developmental Psychology, 27*(3), 421–431.

Belsky, J., & Isabella, R. A. (1988). Maternal, infant, and social-contextual determinants of attachment security. In J. Belsky & T. Nezworski (Eds.), *Clinical implications of attachment* (pp. 41–94). Hillsdale, NJ: Erlbaum.

Belsky, J., & Nezworski, T. (1988). Clinical implications of attachment. In J. Belsky & T. Nezworski (Eds.), *Clinical implications of attachment* (pp. 3–17). Hillsdale, NJ: Erlbaum.

Belsky, J., & Vondra, J. (1989). Lessons from child abuse: The determinants of parenting. In D. Cicchetti & V. Carlson (Eds.), *Child maltreatment: Theory and research on the causes and consequences of child abuse and neglect* (pp. 153–202). New York: Cambridge University Press.

Benard, B. (1999). Applications of resilience: Possibilities and promise. In M. D. Glantz & J. L. Johnson (Eds.), *Resilience and development: Positive life adaptations. Longitudinal research in the social and behavioral sciences* (pp. 269–277). Dordrecht, Netherlands: Kluwer Academic Publishers.

Benes, F. M. (1994). Developmental changes in stress adaptation in relation to psychopathology. *Development and Psychopathology, 6,* 723–739.

Benhamou, I. (2000). Sleep disorders of early childhood: A review. *Israel Journal of Psychiatry and Related Sciences, 37*(3), 190–196.

Bennett, R. L., Pettersen, B. J., Niendorf, K. B., & Anderson, R. R. (2003). Developing standard recommendations (Guidelines) for genetic counseling practice: A process of the National Society of Genetic Counselors. *Journal of Genetic Counseling, 12*(4), 287–295.

Bennett, S., Farrington, D. P., & Huesmann, L. R. (2005). Explaining gender differences in crime and violence: The importance of social cognitive skills. *Aggression and Violent Behavior, 10*(3), 263–288.

Bennett, T., Szatmari, P., Bryson, S., Volden, J., Zwaigenbaum, L., Vaccarella, L., et al. (2008). Differentiating autism and Asperger syndrome on the basis of language delay or impairment. *Journal of Autism and Developmental Disorders, 38*(4), 616–625.

Bennett-Gates, D., & Zigler, E. (1998). Resolving the developmental-difference debate: An evaluation of the triarchic and systems theory models. In J. A. Burack & R. M. Hodapp (Eds.), *Handbook of mental retardation and development* (pp. 115–131). New York: Cambridge University Press.

Benoit, D. (2000). Feeding disorders, failure to thrive, and obesity. In C. H. Zeanah (Ed.), *Handbook of infant mental health* (2nd ed., pp. 339–352). New York: Guilford Press.

Benoit, D., & Coolbear, J. (1998). Post-traumatic feeding disorders in infancy: Behaviors predicting treatment outcome. *Infant Mental Health Journal, 19*(4), 409–421.

Benson, B. A., & Valenti-Hein, D. (2001). Cognitive and social learning treatments. In A. Dosen & K. Day (Eds.), *Treating mental illness and behavior disorders in children and adults with mental retardation* (pp. 101–118). Washington, DC: American Psychiatric Publishing.

Berg-Nielsen, T. S., Vikan, A., & Dahl, A. A. (2002). Parenting related to child and parental psychopathology: A descriptive review of the literature. *Clinical Child Psychology and Psychiatry, 7*(4), 529–552.

Berk, L. E. (2009). *Child Development* (4th ed.). Boston: Pearson.

Berkson, G. (1993). *Children with handicaps: A review of behavioral research*. Hillsdale, NJ: Erlbaum.

Berlin, L. J., & Cassidy, J. (1999). Relations among relationships: Contributions from attachment theory and research. In J. Cassidy & P. R. Shaver (Eds.), *Handbook of attachment: Theory, research, and clinical applications* (pp. 688–712). New York: Guilford Press.

Berlin,, L., Bohlin, G., Nyberg, L., & Janols, L. (2004). How well do measures of inhibition and other executive functions discriminate between children with ADHD and controls? *Child Neuropsychology, 10*(1), 1–13.

Berlin, L., Bohlin, G., & Rydell, A.-M. (2003). Relations between inhibition, executive functioning, and ADHD symptoms: A longitudinal study from age 5 to 8½ years. *Child Neuropsychology, 9*(4), 255–266.

Berman, S. L., Weems, C. F., Silverman, W. K., & Kurtines, W. M. (2000). Predictors of outcome in exposure-based cognitive and behavioral treatments for phobic and anxiety disorders in children. *Behavior Therapy, 31*(4), 713–731.

Bernabei, P., Camaioni, L., & Levi, G. (1998). An evaluation of early development in children with autism and pervasive developmental disorders from home movies: Preliminary findings. *Autism, 2*(3), 243–258.

Bernat, D. H., August, G. J., Hektner, J. M., & Bloomquist, M. L. (2007). The Early Risers preventive intervention: Testing for six-year outcomes and mediational processes. *Journal of Abnormal Child Psychology, 35*(4), 605–617.

Berney, T. P., & Corbett, J. (2001). Management of pervasive developmental disorders. In A. Dosen & K. Day (Eds.), *Treating mental illness and behavior disorders in children and adults with mental retardation* (pp. 451–466). Washington, DC: American Psychiatric Publishing, Inc.

Bernstein, G. A., Borchardt, C. M., & Perwein, A. R. (1996). Anxiety disorders in children and adolescents: A review of the past 10 years. *Journal of the American Academy of Child and Adolescent Psychiatry, 35*(9), 1110–1119.

Bers, S. A., Blatt, S. J., & Dolinksy, A. (2004). The sense of self in anorexia-nervosa patients: A psychoanalytically informed method for studying self-representation. *Psychoanalytic Study of the Child, 59*, 294–315.

Berument, S. K., Rutter, M., Lord, C., Pickles, A., & Bailey, A. (1999). Autism screening questionnaire: Diagnostic validity. *British Journal of Psychiatry, 175*, 444–451.

Bessen, D. E. (2001). Genetics of childhood disorders: XXXII. Autoimmune disorders, part 5: Streptococcal infection and autoimmunity, an epidemiological perspective. *Journal of the American Academy of Child and Adolescent Psychiatry, 40*(11), 1346–1348.

Bettelheim, B. (1967). *The empty fortress: Infantile autism and the birth of the self.* New York: The Free Press.

Beyers, J. M., Bates, J. E., Pettit, G. S., & Dodge, K. A. (2003). Neighborhood structure, parenting processes, and the development of youths' externalizing behaviors: A multilevel analysis. *American Journal of Community Psychology, 31*(1–2), 35–53.

Beyth-Marom, R., & Fischoff, B. (1997). Adolescents' decisions about risks: A cognitive perspective. In J. Schulenberg, J. L. Maggs, & K. Hurrelman (Eds.), *Developmental transitions during adolescence: Health promotion implications* (pp. 110–135). New York: Cambridge University Press.

Bhangoo, R. K., Dell., M. L., Towbin, K., Myers, F. S., Lowe, C. H., Pine, D. S., et al. (2003). Clinical correlates of episodicity in juvenile mania. *Journal of Child and Adolescent Psychopharmacology, 13*(4), 507–514.

Bhangoo, R. K., & Leibenluft, E. (2002). Affective neuroscience and the study of normal and abnormal emotion regulation. *Child and Adolescent Psychiatric Clinics of North America, 11*(3), 519–532.

Biederman, J., Faraone, S. V., Keenan, K., Knee, D., & Tsuang, M. T. (1990). Family-genetic and psychosocial risk factors in DSM-III attention deficit disorder. *Journal of the American Academy of Child and Adolescent Psychiatry, 29*, 526–533.

Biederman, J., Faraone, S. V., Mick, E., & Wozniak, J. (1996). Attention-deficit hyperactivity disorder and juvenile mania: An overlooked comorbidity? *Journal of the American Academy of Child and Adolescent Psychiatry, 35*(8), 997–1008.

Biederman, J., Faraone, S. V., Mick, E., Willamson, S., Wilens, T. E., Spencer, T. J., et al. (1999). Clinical correlates of ADHD in females: findings from a large group of girls ascertained from pediatric and psychiatric referral sources. *Journal of the American Academy of Child and Adolescent Psychiatry, 38,* 966–967.

Biederman, J., Faraone, S. V., Milberger, S., & Doyle, A. (1993). Diagnoses of attention-deficit hyperactivity disorder from parent reports predict diagnoses based on teacher reports. *Journal of the American Academy of Child and Adolescent Psychiatry, 32*, 315–317.

Biederman, J., Faraone, S. V., Taylor, A., Sienna, M., Williamson, S., & Fine, C. (1998). Diagnostic continuity between child and adolescent ADHD: Findings from a longitudinal clinical sample. *Journal of the American Academy of Child and Adolescent Psychiatry, 37*, 305–313.

Biederman, J., Kwon, A., Aleardi, M., Chouinard, V., Marino, T., Cole, H., et al. (2005). Absence of gender effects on attention deficit hyperactivity disorder: Findings in nonreferred subjects. *American Journal of Psychiatry, 162*(6), 1083–1089.

Biederman, J., Mick, E., & Faraone, S. V. (2000). Age-dependent decline of symptoms of attention deficit hyperactivity disorder: Impact of remission, definition, and symptom type. *American Journal of Psychiatry, 157,* 816–818.

Biederman, J., Mick, E., Faraone, S. V., Spencer, T., Wilens, T. E., & Wozniak, J. (2003). Current concepts in the validity, diagnosis and treatment of pediatric bipolar disorder. *International Journal of Neuropsychopharmacology, 6*(3), 293–300.

Biederman, J., Mick, E., Wozniak, J., Monuteaux, M. C., Galdo, M., & Faraone, S. V. (2003). Can a subtype of conduct disorder linked to bipolar disorder be identified? Integration of findings from the Massachusetts General Hospital Pediatric Psychopharmacology Research Program. *Biological Psychiatry, 53*(11), 952–960.

Biederman, J., Monuteaux, M. C., Doyle, A. E., Seidman, L. J., Wilens, T. E., Ferrero, F., et al. (2004). Impact of executive function deficits and attention-deficit/hyperactivity disorder (ADHD) on academic outcomes in children. *Journal of Consulting and Clinical Pscyhology, 72*(5), 757–766.

Biederman, J., Wilens, T., Mick, E., Faraone, S. V., & Spencer, T. (1998). Does attention deficit hyperactivity disorder impact the developmental course of drug and alcohol abuse and dependence? *Biological Psychiatry, 44,* 269–273.

Biederman, J., Wilens, T., Mick, E., Faraone, S. V., Weber, W., Curtis, S., et al. (1997). Is ADHD a risk factor for psychoactive substance use disorders? Findings from a four-year prospective follow-up study. *Journal of the American Academy of Child and Adolescent Psychiatry, 36*(1), 21–30.

Bierman, K. L. (1996). Integrating social-skills training interventions with parent training and family-focused support to prevent conduct disorder in high-risk populations: The Fast Track multisite demonstration project. In C. F. Ferris & T. Grisso (Eds.), *Understanding aggressive behavior in children* (pp. 256–264). New York: New York Academy of Sciences.

Bierman, K. L., Coie, J. D., Dodge, K. A., Foster, E. M., Greenberg, M. T., Lochman, J. E., et al. (2004). The effects of the fast track program on serious problem outcomes at the end of elementary school. *Journal of Clinical Child and Adolescent Psychology, 33*(4), 650–651.

Bierman, K. L., Coie, J. D., Dodge, K. A., Foster, E. M., Greenberg, M. T., Lochman, J. E., et al. (2007). Fast track randomized controlled trial to prevent externalizing psychiatric disorders: Findings from grades 3 to 9. *Journal of the American Academy of Child and Adolescent Psychiatry, 46*(10), 1250–1262.

Bierman, K. L., Coie, J. D., Dodge, K. A., Greenberg, M. T., Lochman, J. E., McMahon, R. J., et al. (2002). Using the Fast Track randomized prevention trial to test the early-starter model of the development of serious conduct problems. *Development and Psychopathology, 14*, 925–943.

Bierman, K. L., & Greenberg, M. T. (1996). Social skills training in the Fast Track Program. In R. D. Peters & R. J. McMahon (Eds.), *Preventing childhood disorders, substance abuse, and delinquency* (pp. 65–89). Thousand Oaks, CA: Sage.

Bierman, K. L., & Montminy, H. P. (1993). Developmental issues in social-skills assessment and intervention with children and adolescents. *Behavior Modification, 17*, 229–254.

Bierman, K. L., & Wargo, J. B. (1995). Predicting the longitudinal course associated with aggressive-rejected, aggressive (nonrejected), and rejected (nonaggressive) status. *Development and Psychopathology, 7*(4), 669–682.

Bierman, K. L., & Welsh, J. A. (1997). Social relationship deficits. In E. J. Mash & L. G. Terdal (Eds.), *Assessment of childhood disorders* (3rd ed., pp. 328–365). New York: Guilford Press.

Bierman, K. L., & Welsh, J. A. (2000). Assessing social dysfunction: The contributions of laboratory and performance-based measures. *Journal of Clinical Child Psychology, 29*, 526–539.

Bierut, L. J., Dinwiddie, S. H., Begleiter, H., Crowe, R. R., Hesselbrock, V., Nurnberger, J. I., Jr., et al. (1998). Familial transmission of substance dependence: Alcohol, marijuana, cocaine, and habitual smoking: A report from the collaborative study on the genetics of alcoholism. *Archives of General Psychiatry, 55*(11), 982–988.

Biglan, A., Metzler, C. W., Fowler, R. C., Gunn, B., Taylor, T. K., Rusby, J., et al. (1997). Improving childrearing in America's communities. In P. A. Lamal (Ed.), *Cultural contingencies: Behavior analytic perspectives on cultural practices* (pp. 185–213). Westport, CT: Praeger Publishers/Greenwood Publishing Group.

Bina, M., Graziano, F., & Bonino, S. (2006). Risky driving and lifestyles in adolescence. *Accident Analysis and Prevention, 38*(3), 472–481.

Bird, H. R. (1996). Epidemiology of childhood disorders in a cross-cultural context. *Journal of Child Psychology and Psychiatry, 37(1)*, 35–49.

Bird, H. R., Canino, G. J., Davies, M., Zhang, H., Ramirez, R., & Lahey, B. B. (2001). Prevalence and correlates of antisocial behaviors among three ethnic groups. *Journal of Abnormal Child Psychology, 29*(6), 465–478.

Birmaher, B., Arbelaez, C., & Brent, D. (2002). Course and outcome of child and adolescent major depressive disorder. *Child and Adolescent Psychiatric Clinics of North America, 11*(3), 619–638.

Birmaher, B., & Brent, D. (2002). Pharmacotherapy for depression in children and adolescents. In D. Shaffer & B. D. Waslick (Eds.), *Review of psychiatry: Vol. 21. The many faces of depression in children and adolescents* (pp. 73–103). Washington, DC: American Psychiatric Publishing.

Birmaher, B., Brent, D., Bernet, W., Bukstein, O., Walter, H., Benson, R. S., et al. (2007). Practice parameter for the assessment and treatment of children and adolescents with depressive disorder. *Journal of the American Academy of Child and Adolescent Psychiatry, 46*(11), 1503–1526.

Birmaher, B., & Heydl, P. (2001). Biological studies in depressed children and adolescents. *International Journal of Neuropsychopharmacology, 4*(2), 149–157.

Birmaher, B., Ryan, N. D., Williamson, D. E., Brent, D. A., & Kaufman, J. (1996a). Childhood and adolescent depression: A review of the past 10 years. Part II. *Journal of the American Academy of Child and Adolescent Psychiatry, 35*(12), 1575–1583.

Birmaher, B., Ryan, N. D., Williamson, D. E., Brent, D. A., Kaufman, J., Dahl, R. E., et al. (1996b). Childhood and adolescent depression: A review of the past 10 years. Part I. *Journal of the American Academy of Child and Adolescent Psychiatry, 35*(11), 1427–1439.

Birmaher, B., Williamson, D. E., Dahl, R. E., Axelson, D. A., Kaufman, J., Dorn, L. D., et al. (2004). Clinical presentation and course of depression in youth: Does onset in childhood differ from onset in adolescence? *Journal of the American Academy of Child and Adolescent Psychiatry, 43*(1), 63–70.

Birman D., Trickett, E., & Buchanan, R. M. (2005). A tale of two cities: Replication of a study on the acculturation and adaptation of immigrant adolescents from the former Soviet Union in a different community context. *American Journal of Community Psychology, 35(1–2)*, 83–101.

Birney, D. P., & Sternberg, R. J. (2006). Intelligence and cognitive abilities as competencies in development. In E. Bialystok & F. I.M. Fergus (Eds.), *Lifespan cognition: Mechanisms of change* (pp. 315–330). New York: Oxford University Press.

Bishop, D. V. M. (2000). What's so special about Asperger syndrome? The need for further exploration of the borderlands of autism. In A. Klin, F. R. Volkmar, & S. S. Sparrow (Eds.), *Asperger syndrome* (pp. 254–277). New York: Guilford Press.

Black, B. (1995). Separation anxiety disorder and panic disorder. In J. S. March (Ed.), *Anxiety disorders in children and adolescents* (pp. 212–234). New York: Guilford Press.

Black, L. M. (1997). Type I: Hypersensitive. In A. Lieberman, S. Wieder, & E. Fenichel (Eds.), *DC: 0 –3 Casebook* (pp. 195–218). Washington, DC: Zero to Three: National Center for Infants, Toddlers, and Families.

Black, M. M., Cureton, P. L., & Berenson-Howard, J. (1999). Behavior problems in feeding: Individual, family, and cultural influences. In D. B. Kessler & P. Dawson (Eds.), *Failure to thrive and pediatric undernutrition: A transdisciplinary approach* (pp. 151–169). Baltimore: Paul H. Brookes Publishing.

Blackman, G. L., Ostrander, R., & Herman, K. C. (2005). Children with ADHD and depression: A multisource, multimethod assessment of clinical, social, and academic functioning. *Journal of Attention Disorders, 8*(4), 195–207.

Blader, J. C., & Carlson, G. A. (2007). Increased rates of bipolar disorder diagnoses among U. S. child, adolescent, and adult inpatients 1996–2004. *Biological Psychiatry, 62*(2), 107–114.

Blair, C. (2002). School readiness: Integrating cognition and emotion in a neurobiological conceptualization of children's functioning at school entry. *American Psychologist, 57*(2), 111–127.

Blair, C., & Peters, R. (2003). Physiological and neurocognitive correlates of adaptive behavior in preschool among children in Head Start. *Developmental Neuropsychology, 24*, 479–497.

Blair, R. J. R. (1997). Moral reasoning and the child with psychopathic tendencies. *Personality and Individual Differences, 22*(5), 731–739.

Blair, R. J. R. (2005). Applying a cognitive neuroscience perspective to the disorder of psychopathy. *Development and Psychopathology, 17*(3), 865–891.

Blasi, A., & Milton, K. (1991). The development of the sense of self in adolescence. *Journal of Personality, 59*(2), 217–242.

Blitstein, J. L., Murray, D. M., Lytle, L. A., Birnbaum, A. S., & Perry, C. L. (2005). Predictors of violent behavior in an early adolescent cohort: Similarities and differences across genders. *Health Education and Behavior, 32*(2), 175–194.

Block, J. & Block, J. H. (2006). Venturing a 30-year longitudinal study. *American Psychologist, 61*(4), 315–327.

Bloomquist, M. L. & Schnell, S. V. (2002). *Helping children with aggression and conduct problems: Best practices for intervention.* New York: Guilford Press.

Blos, P. (1979). Modifications in the classical psychoanalytical model of adolescence. *Adolescent Psychiatry, 7,* 6–25.

Blum, R. W., Beuhring, T., Shew, M. L., Beringer, L. H., Sieving, R. E., & Resnick, M. D. (2000). The effects of race/ethnicity, income, and family structure on adolescent risk behaviors. *American Journal of Public Health, 90,* 1879–1884.

Boer, F., & Lindhout, I. (2001). Family and genetic influences: Is anxiety "all in the family"? In W. K. Silverman & P. D. A. Treffers (Eds.), *Anxiety disorders in children and adolescents: Research, assessment and intervention* (pp. 235–254). New York: Cambridge University Press.

Bogenschneider, K., Wu, M., Raffaelli, M., & Tsay, J. C. (1998). Parent influences on adolescent peer orientation and substance use: The interface of parenting practices and values. *Child Development, 69,* 1672–1688.

Bonanno, G. A. (2004). Loss, trauma, and human resilience: Have we underestimated the human capacity to thrive after extremely aversive events? *American Psychologist, 59*(1), 20–28.

Booze, R. M. (2004). Developmental aspects of addiction. *International Journal of Developmental Neuroscience, 22*(5–6), 241–245.

Boris, N. W., Hinshaw-Fuselier, S. S., Smyke, A. T., Scheeringa, M. S., Heller, S. S., & Zeanah, C. H. (2004). Comparing criteria for attachment disorders: Establishing reliability and validity in high-risk samples. *Journal of the American Academy of Child and Adolescent Psychiatry, 43*(5), 568–577.

Boris, N. W., Zeanah, C. H., Larrieu, J. A., Scheeringa, M. S., & Heller, S. S. (1998). Attachment disorders in infancy and early childhood: A preliminary investigation of diagnostic criteria. *American Journal of Psychiatry 155*(2), 295–297.

Bornholt, L., Brake, N., Thomas, S., Russel, L., Madden, S., Anderson, G., et al. (2005). Understanding affective and cognitive self-evaluations about the body for adolescent girls. *British Journal of Health Psychology, 10,* 485–503.

Bornstein, M. H. (1998). Stability in mental development from early life: Methods, measures, models, meanings, and myths. In F. Simion & G. Butterworth (Eds.), *The development of sensory, motor and cognitive capacities in early infancy: From perception to cognition* (pp. 301–332). Hove, England: Psychology Press/Erlbaum Taylor & Francis.

Bornstein, M. H. (2002). Toward a multiculture, multiage, multimethod science. *Human Development, 45*(4), 257–263.

Bornstein, M. H., Brown, E., & Slater, A. (1996). Patterns of stability and continuity in attention across early infancy. *Journal of Reproductive and Infant Psychology, 14*(3), 195–206.

Bornstein, M. H., Davidson, L., Keyes, C. L. M., & Moore, K. A. (2003). *Well-being: Positive development across the life course.* Mahwah, NJ: Erlbaum.

Bornstein, M. H., Haynes, O. M., Azuma, H., Galper'n, C., Maital, S., Ogino, M., et al. (1998). A cross-national study of self-evaluations and attributions in parenting: Argentina, Belgium, France, Israel, Italy, Japan, and the United States. *Developmental Psychology, 34*(4), 662–676.

Bornstein, M. H., & Suess, P. E. (2000). Child and mother cardiac vagal tone: Continuity, stability, and concordance across the first 5 years. *Developmental Psychology, 36*(1), 54–65.

Bornstein, M. H. & Tamis-LeMonda, C. S. (1997). Maternal responsiveness and infant mental abilities: Specific predictive relations. *Infant Behavior and Development, 20*(3), 283–296.

Botvin, G. J., Scheier, L. M., & Griffin, K. W. (2002). Preventing the onset and developmental progression of adolescent drug use: Implications for the gateway hypothesis. In D. B. Kandel (Ed.), *Stages and pathways of drug involvement: Examining the gateway hypothesis* (pp. 115–138). New York: Cambridge University Press.

Bower, M. A., Veach, P. M., Bartels, D. M., & LeRoy, B. S. (2002). A survey of genetic counselors' strategies for addressing ethical and professional challenges in practice. *Journal of Genetic Counseling, 11*(3), 163–186.

Bowers, W. A., Evans, K., Le Grange, D. & Andersen, A. E. (2003). Treatment of adolescent eating disorders. In Reinecke, M. A. (Ed.), *Cognitive therapy with children and adolescents: A casebook for clinical practice* (pp 247–280). New York: Guilford Press.

Bowlby, J. (1953, 1982). *Attachment.* New York: Basic Books.

Bowlby, J. (1961). Separation anxiety: A critical review of the literature. *Journal of Child Psychology and Psychiatry, 1,* 251–269.

Bowlby, J. (1977). The making and breaking of affectional bonds: I. Actiology and psychopathology in the light of attachment theory. *British Journal of Psychiatry, 130,* 201–210.

Bowlby, J. (1980). *Attachment and loss.* New York: Basic Books.

Bowlby, J. (1982). Attachment and loss: Retrospect and prospect. *American Journal of Orthopsychiatry, 52*(4), 664–678.

Boxer, P., Guerra, N. G., Huesmann, L. R., & Morales, J. (2005). Proximal peer-level effects of a small-group selected prevention on aggression in elementary school children: An investigation of the peer contagion hypothesis. *Journal of Abnormal Child Psychology, 33*(3), 325–339.

Boyce, W. T., Frank, E., Jensen, P. S., Kessler, R. C., Nelson, C. A. & Steinberg, L. (1998). Social context in developmental psychopathology: Recommendations for future research from the MacArthur Network on Psychopathology and Development. *Development and Psychopathology, 10*(2), 143–164.

Boyce, W. T., Frank, E., Jensen, P. S., Kessler, R. C., Nelson, C. A., & Steinberg, L. (1998). Social context in developmental psychopathology: Recommendations for future research from the MacArthur Network on Psychopathology and Development. *Development and Psychopathology, 10*(2), 143–164.

Boyle, M. H., Offord, D. R., Racine, Y. A., Szatmari, P., Sanford, M., & Fleming, J. E. (1997). Adequacy of interviews vs. checklists for classifying childhood psychiatric disorder based on parent reports. *Archives of General Psychiatry, 54,* 793–799.

Braddock, D. (2002). Public financial support for disability at the dawn of the 21st century. *American Journal on Mental Retardation, 107*(6), 478–489.

Braddock, D., Emerson, E., Felce, D., & Stancliffe, R. J. (2001). Living circumstances of children and adults with mental retardation or developmental disabilities in the United States,

Canada, England, and Wales. *Mental Retardation and Developmental Disabilities Research Reviews, 7*(2), 115–121.

Braden, J. S. & Obrzut, J. E. (2002). Williams syndrome: Neuropsychological findings and implications for practice. *Journal of Development and Physical Disabilities, 14*(3), 203–213.

Bradley, R. H., & Corwyn, R. F. (2002). Socioeconomic status and child development. *Annual Review of Psychology, 53(1),* 371–399.

Bradley, S. J., Jadaa, D., Brody, J., Landy, S., Tallett, S. E., Watson, W., et al. (2003). Brief psychoeducational parenting program: An evaluation and 1-year follow-up. *Journal of the American Academy of Child and Adolescent Psychiatry, 42,* 1171–1178.

Branco, E. I., & Kaskutas, L. A. (2001). "If it burns going downÖ": How focus groups can shape fetal alcohol syndrome (FAS) prevention. *Substance Use and Misuse, 36*(3), 333–345.

Braswell, L. (1998). Self-regulation training for children with ADHD: Response to Harris and Schmidt. *The ADHD Report, 6,* 1–3.

Braungart, J. M., & Stifter, C. A. (1991). Regulation of negative reactivity during the strange situation: Temperament and attachment in 12-motn-old infants. *Infant Behavior and Development, 14*(3), 349–364.

Brazelton, T. B. (1994, 2006). *Touchpoints: Birth to three.* Cambridge, MA: DaCapo Press.

Brazelton, T. B., & Greenspan, S. I. (2000). *The irreducible needs of children.* Cambridge, MA: Perseus.

Breda, C., & Heflinger, C. A. (2004). Predicting incentives to change among adolescents with substance abuse disorder. *American Journal of Drug and Alcohol Abuse, 30*(2), 251–267.

Brendgen, M., Vitaro, F., & Bukowski, W. M. (2000a). Deviant friends and early adolescents' emotional and behavioral adjustment. *Journal of Research on Adolescence, 10*(2), 173–189.

Brendgen, M., Viatro, F., & Bukowski, W. M. (2000b). Stability and variability of adolescents' affiliation with delinquent friends: Predictors and consequences. *Social Development, 9*(2), 205–225.

Brendgen, M., Wanner, B., Morin, A. J.S., & Vitaro, F. (2005). Relations with parents and with peers, temperament, and trajectories of depressed mood during early adolescence. *Journal of Abnormal Psychology, 33*(15), 579.

Brennan, K. A., & Shaver, P. R. (1998). Attachment styles and personality disorders: Their connections to each other and to parental divorce, parental death, and perception of parental caregiving. *Journal of Personality, 66*(5), 835–878.

Brennan, P. A., Hall, J., Bor, W., Najman, J. M., & Williams, G. (2003). Integrating biological and social processes in relation to early-onset persistent aggression in boys and girls. *Developmental Psychology, 39*(2), 309–323.

Brent, D. A. (2005). Editorial: Is the medication bottle for pediatric and adolescent depression half-full or half-empty? *Journal of Adolescent Health, 37*(6), 431–433.

Brent, D. A., Oquendo, M., Birmaher, B., Greenhill, L., Kolko, D., Stanley, B., et al. (2004). Familial transmission of mood disorders: Convergence and divergence with transmission of suicidal behavior. *Journal of the American Academy of Child and Adolescent Psychiatry, 43*(1), 1259–1266.

Brestan, E. V., & Eyberg, S. M. (1998). Effective psychosocial treatments of conduct-disordered children and adolescents: 29

years, 82 studies, and 5,272 kids. *Journal of Clinical Child Psychology, 27*(2), 180–189.

Bretherton, I. (1990). Communication patterns, internal working models, and the intergenerational transmission of attachment relationships. *Infant Mental Health Journal, 11*(3), 237–252.

Bretherton, I. (1992). The origins of attachment theory: John Bowlby and Mary Ainsworth. *Developmental Psychology, 28*(5), 759–775.

Bretherton, I., Ridgeway, D., & Cassidy, J. (1990). Assessing internal working models of the attachment relationship: An attachment story completion task for 3-year-olds. In M. T. Greenberg, D. Cicchetti, & E. M. Cummings (Eds.), *Attachment in the preschool years: Theory, research, and intervention* (pp. 273–308). Chicago: University of Chicago Press.

Bricker, J. B., Leroux, B. G., Peterson, A. V., Kealey, K. A., Sarason, I. G., Andersen, M. R., et al. (2003). Nine-year prospective relationship between parental smoking cessation and children's daily smoking. *Addiction, 98*(5), 585–593.

Bridge, J. A., & Axelson, D. A. (2008). The contribution of pharmacoepidemiology to the antidepressant-suicidality debate in children and adolescents. *International Review of Psychiatry, 20*(2), 209–214.

Bridge, J. A., Barbe, R. P., Birmaher, B., Kolko, D. J., & Brent, D. A. (2005). Emergent suicideality in a clinical psychotherapy trial for adolescent depression. *American Journal of Psychiatry, 162*(11), 2173–2175.

Bridge, J. A., Goldstein, T. R., & Brent, D. A. (2006). Adolescent suicide and suicidal behavior. *Journal of Child Psychology and Psychiatry, 47*(3–4), 372–394.

Bridge, J. A., Iyengar, S., Salary, C. B., Barbe, R. P., Birmaher, B., Pincus, H. A., et al. (2007). Clinical response and risk for reported suicidal ideation and suicide attempts in pediatric antidepressant treatment: A meta-analysis of randomized controlled trials. *Journal of the American Medical Association, 297*(15), 1683–1696.

Bridges, L. J., & Grolnick, W. S. (1995). The development of emotional self-regulation in infancy and early childhood. In N. Eisenberg (Ed.), *Social development. Review of personality and social psychology* (Vol. 15, pp. 185–211). Thousand Oaks, CA: Sage.

Briere, J., Johnson, K., Bissada, A., Damon, L., Crouch, J., Gil, E., et al.. (2001). The Trauma Symptom Checklist for Young Children (TSCYC): reliability and association with abuse exposure in a multi-site study. *Child Abuse and Neglect, 25*(8), 1001–1014.

Bristol-Power, M. M., & Spinella, G. (1999). Research on screening and diagnosis in autism: A work in progress. *Journal of Autism and Developmental Disorders, 29,* 435–438.

Brocki, K. C., & Bohlin, G. (2004). Executive functions in children aged 6 to 13: A dimensional and developmental study. *Developmental Neuropsychology, 26*(2), 571–593.

Brody, G. H. (1998). Sibling relationship quality: Its causes and consequences. *Annual Review of Psychology, 49,* 1–24.

Brody, G. H. (2003). Parental monitoring: Action and reaction. In A. C. Crouter & A. Booth (Eds.), *Children's influence on family dynamics: The neglected side of family relationships* (pp. 163–169). Mahwah, NJ: Erlbaum.

Brody, G. H. (2004). Siblings' direct and indirect contributions to child development. *Current Directions in Psychological Science, 13(3),* 124–126.

Brody, G. H., Flor, D. L., Hollett-Wright, N., & McCoy, J. K. (1998). Children's development of alcohol use norms: Contributions fo parent and sibling norms, children's temperaments, and parent-child discussions. *Journal of Family Psychology, 12*(2), 209–219.

Brody, G. H., Flor, D. L., Hollett-Wright, N., McCoy, J. K., & Donovan, J. (1999). Parent-child relationships, child temperament profiles and children's alcohol use norms. *Journal of Studies on Alcohol, 13,* 45–51.

Brody, G. H., & Ge, X. (2001). Linking parenting processes and self-regulation to psychological functioning and alcohol use during early adolescence. *Journal of Family Psychology, 15*(1), 82–94.

Brody, G. H., Ge, X., Kim, S. Y., Murry, V. M., Simons, R. L., Gibbons, F. X., et al. (2003). Neighborhood disadvantage moderates associations of parenting and older sibling problem attitudes and behavior with conduct disorders in African American children. *Journal of Consulting and Clinical Psychology, 71*(2), 211–222.

Brody, G. H., Kim, S., Murry, V. M., & Brown, A. C. (2004). Protective longitudinal paths linking child competence to behavioral problems among African American siblings. *Child Development, 75*(2), 455–467.

Brody, G. H., Murry, V. M., Gerrard, M., Gibbons, F. X., Molgaard, V., McNair, L., et al. (2004). The Strong African American Families program: Translating research into prevention programming. *Child Development, 75*(3), 900–917.

Brody, G. H., Stoneman, Z., Smith, T., & Gibson, N. M. (1999). Sibling relationships in rural African American families. *Journal of Marriage and the Family, 61*(4), 1046–1057.

Broidy, L. M., Nagin, D. S., Tremblay, R. E., Bates, J. E., Brame, B., Dodge, K. A., et al. (2003). Developmental trajectories of childhood disruptive behaviors and adolescent delinquency: A six-site, cross-national study. *Developmental Psychology, 39*(2), 222–245.

Bronfenbrenner, U. (1986). Ecology of the family as a context for human development: Research perspectives. *Developmental Psychology, 22*(6), 723–742.

Bronfenbrenner, U., & Morris, P. A. (1998). The ecology of developmental processes. In W. Damon & R. M. Lerner (Eds.), *Handbook of child psychology: Vol. 1. Theoretical models of human development* (5th ed., pp. 993–1028). Hoboken, NJ: Wiley.

Bronson, G. W., & Pankey, W. B. (1977). On the distinction between fear and wariness. *Child Development, 48,* 1167–1183.

Bronson, M. B. (2000). *Self-regulation in early childhood: Nature and nurture.* New York: Guilford Press.

Brooks, R. B. (2002). Changing the mindset of adults with ADHD: Strategies for fostering hope, optimism, and resilience. From S. Goldstein & A. T. Ellison (Eds.), *Clinicians' guide to adult ADHD: Assessment and intervention* (pp. 127–146). San Diego, CA: Academic Press.

Brotman, L. M., Gouley, K. K., O'Neal, C., & Klein, R. G. (2004). Preschool-aged siblings of adjudicated youths: Multiple risk factors for conduct problems. *Early Education and Development, 15*(4), 387–406.

Brotman, M. A., Schmajuk, M., Rich, B. A., Dickstein, D. P., Guyer, A. E., Costello, E. J., et al. (2006). Prevalence, clinical correlates, and longitudinal course of severe mood dysregulation in children. *Biological Psychiatry, 60*(9), 991–997.

Brown, J. B., Winzelberg, A. J., Abascal, L. B., & Taylor, B. C. (2004). An evaluation of an Internet-delivered eating disorder prevention program for adolescents and their parents. *Journal of Adolescent Health, 35,* 290–296.

Brown, J. Cohen, P., Johnson, J. G., & Smailes, E. M. (1999). Childhood abuse and neglect: Specificity and effects on adolescent and young adult depression and suicidality. *Journal of the American Academy of Child and Adolescent Psychiatry, 38*(12), 1490–1496.

Brown, J. M., Miller, W. R., & Lawendowski, L. A. (1999). The self-regulation questionnaire. In L. VandeCreek & T. L. Jackson (Eds.), *Innovations in clinical practice: Vol. 17. A source book* (pp. 281–292). Sarasota, FL: Professional Resource Press/ Professional Resource Exchange.

Brown, M. Z., Comtois, K. A., & Linehan, M. M. (2002). Reasons for suicide attempts and nonsuicidal self-injury in women with borderline personality disorder. *Journal of Abnormal Psychology, 111*(1), 198–202.

Brown, R. T., Freeman, W. S., Perrin, J. M., Stein, M. T., Amler, R. W., Feldman, H. M., et al. (2001). Prevalence and assessment of attention-deficit/hyperactivity disorder in primary care settings. *Pediatrics, 107*(3), E43.

Brown, R. T., & Sammons, M. T. (2002). Pediatric psychopharmacology: A review of new developments and recent research. *Professional Psychology: Research and Practice, 33(2),* 135–147.

Brown, S. A., & Tapert, S. F. (2004). Adolescence and the trajectory of alcohol use: Basic to clinical studies. In R. E. Dahl & L. P. Spear (Eds.), *Adolescent brain development: Vulnerabilities and opportunities. Annals of the New York Academy of Sciences* Vol. 1021, pp. 234–244). New York: New York Academy of Sciences.

Brownlie, E. B., Beitchman, J. H., Escobar, M., Young, A., Atkinson, L., Johnson, C., et al. (2004). Early language impairment and young adult delinquent and aggressive behavior. *Journal of Abnormal Child Psychology, 32*(4), 453–467.

Bruch, H. (1973). *Eating disorders: Obesity, anorexia nervosa, and the person within.* New York: Basic Books.

Bruch, H. (1982). Anorexia nervosa: Therapy and theory. *American Journal of Psychiatry, 139,* 1531–1538.

Bruijnzeel, A. W., Repetto, M., & Gold, M. S. (2004). Neurobiological mechanisms in addictive and psychiatric disorders. *Psychiatric Clinics of North America, 27*(4), 661–674.

Bruinsma, Y., Koegel, R. L., & Koegel, L. K. (2004). Joint attention and children with autism: A review of the literature. *Mental Retardation and Developmental Disabilities Research Review, 10*(3), 169–173.

Bryant, A. L., Schulenberg, J. E., O'Malley, P. M., Bachman, J. G., & Johnston, L. D. (2003). How academic achievement, attitudes, and behaviors relate to the course of substance use during adolescence: A 6-year, multiwave, national longitudinal study. *Journal of Research on Adolescence, 13*(3), 361–397.

Bryant-Waugh, R. (2006). Pathways to recovery: Promoting change within a developmental-systemic framework. *Clinical Child Psychology and Psychiatry, 11,* 213–224.

Bryson, S. E., & Smith, I. M. (1998). Epidemiology of autism: Prevalence, associated characteristics, and implications for research and service delivery. *Mental Retardation and Developmental Disabilities Research Reviews, 4,* 97–103.

Bryson, S. E., Zwaigenbaum, L., Brian, J., Roberts, W., Szatmari, P., Rombough, V., et al. (2007). A prospective case series of high-risk infants who developed autism. *Journal of Autism and Developmental Disorders, 37*(1), 12–24.

Bryson, S. E., Zwaigenbaum, L., McDermott, C., Rombough, V. & Brian, J. (2008). The Autism Observation Scale for Infants: Scale development and reliability data. *Journal of Autism and Developmental Disorders, 38*(4), 731–738.

Buckner, J. C., Mezzacappa, E., & Beardslee, W. R. (2003). Characteristics of resilient youths living in poverty: The role of self-regulatory processes. *Development and Psychopathology, 15*, 139–162.

Buckner, J. C., Mezzacappa, E., & Beardslee, W. R. (2003). Characteristics of resilient youths living in poverty: The role of self-regulatory processes. *Development and Psychopathology, 15*, 139–162.

Buell, M. J., Gamel-McCormick, M., & Hallam, R. (1999). Incusion in a childcare context: Experiences and attitudes of family childcare providers. *Topics in Early Childhood Special Education, 19*(4), 217–224.

Buell, M. J., Hallam, R., Gamel-McCormick, M., & Scheer, S. (1999). A survey of general and special education teachers' perceptions and inservice needs concerning inclusion. *International Journal of Disability, Development and Education, 46*(2), 143–156.

Bukowski, W. M. (2003). What does it mean to say that aggressive children are competent or incompetent? *Merrill-Palmer Quarterly, 49*(3), 390–400.

Bukowski, W. M. & Sippola, L. K. (1998). Diversity and the social mind: Goals, constructs, culture, and development. *Developmental Psychology, 34*(4), 742–746.

Bukowski, W. M. (2002). Peer Relationships. In M. H. Bornstein, L. Davidson, C. L. M. Keyes, & K. Moore (Eds.), *Well-Being: Positive development across the life course.* Mahwah, NJ: Erlbaum.

Bukowski, W. M., & Adams, R. (2005). Peer relationships and psychopathology: Markers, moderators, mediators, mechanisms, and meanings. *Journal of Clinical Child and Adolescent Psychology, 34*(1), 3–10.

Bulik, C. M. (2002). Eating disorders in adolescents and young adults. *Child and Adolescent Psychiatric Clinics of North America, 11*, 201–218.

Bulik, C. M., Klump, K. L., Thornton, L., Kaplan, A. S., Devlin, B., Fichter, M. M., et al. (2004). Alcohol use disorder comorbidity in eating disorders: A multicenter study. *Journal of Clinical Psychiatry, 65*, 1000–1006.

Bulik, C. M., & Reba, L. (2005). Anorexia nervosa: Definition, epidemiology and cycle of risk. *International Journal of Eating Disorders, 37*, S2-S9.

Bulik, C. M., Reba, L., Siega-Riz, A., & Reichborn-Kjennerud, T. (2002). Substance use in female adolescents with eating disorders. *Journal of Adolescent Health, 31*(2), 176–182.

Bulik, C. M., Sullivan, P. F., Tozzi, F., Furberg, H., Lichtenstein, P., & Pedersen, N. L. (2006). Prevalence, heritability, and prospective risk factors for anorexia nervosa. *Archives of General Psychiatry, 63*, 305–312.

Bullock, B. M., & Dishion, T. J. (2002). Sibling collusion and problem behavior in early adolescence: Toward a process model for family mutuality. *Journal of Abnormal Child Psychology, 30*(2), 143–153.

Burack, J. A. (1997). The study of atypical and typical populations in developmental psychopathology: The quest for a common science. In S. S. Luthar, J. A. Burack, D. Cicchetti, & J. R. Weisz (Eds.), Developmental psychopathology: Perspectives on adjustment, risk, and disorder (pp. 139–165). New York: Cambridge University Press.

Burack, J. A., Evans, D. W., Klaiman, C., & Iarocci, G. (2001). The mysterious myth of attention deficits and other defect stories: Contemporary issues in the developmental approach to mental retardation. In L. M. Glidden (Ed.), *International review of research in mental retardation* (Vol. 24, pp. 299–320). San Diego, CA: Academic Press.

Burgess, K. B., Marshall, P. J., Rubin, K. H., & Fox, N. A. (2003). Infant attachment and temperament as predictors of subsequent externalizing problems and cardiac physiology. *Journal of Child Psychology and Psychiatry, 44*(6), 819–831.

Burgess, K. B., Rubin, K. H., Chea, C. S. L., & Nelson, L. J. (2001). Behavioral inhibition, social withdrawal, and parenting. In W. R. Crozier & L. E. Alden (Eds.), *International handbook of social anxiety: Concepts, research and interventions relating to the self and shyness* (pp. 137–158). New York: Wiley.

Burke, J. D., Loeber, R., & Birmaher, B. (2002). Oppositional defiant disorder and conduct disorder: A review of the past 10 years, part II. (Research Update Review). *Journal of the American Academy of Child and Adolescent Psychiatry, 41*(11), 1275–1293.

Burke, J. D., Loeber, R., & Lahey, B. B. (2003). Course and outcomes. In C. A. Essau (Ed.), *Conduct and oppositional defiant disorders: Epidemiology, risk factors, and treatment* (pp. 61–94). Mahwah, NJ: Erlbaum.

Burke, J. D., Loeber, R., Lahey, B. B., & Rathouz, P. J. (2005). Developmental transitions among affective and behavioral disorders in adolescent boys. *Journal of Child Psychology and Psychiatry, 46*(11), 1200–1210.

Burke, J. D., Pardini, D. A., & Loeber, R. (2008). Reciprocal relationships between parenting behavior and disruptive psychopathology from childhood through adolescence. *Journal of Abnormal Child Psychology, 36*(5), 679–692.

Burke, P. J., Owens, T. J., Serpe, R. T., & Thoits, P. A. (2003). *Advances in identity theory and research.* New York: Kluwer Academic/Plenum Publishers.

Burnham, M. M., Goodlin-Jones, B. L., Gaylor, E. E., & Anders, T. F. (2002). Nighttime sleep-wake patterns and self-soothing from birth to one year of age: A longitudinal intervention study. *Journal of Child Psychology and Psychiatry, 43*(6), 713–725.

Burns, B. J., & Hoagwood, K. E. (2004). Preface. Evidence-based practice, Part I: Research update. *Child and Adolescent Psychiatric Clinics of North America, 13*(4), xi-xiii.

Burns, G. L., Boe, B., Walsh, J. A., Sommers-Flanagan, R., & Teegarden, L. A. (2001). A confirmatory factor analysis on the DSM-IV ADHD and ODD symptoms: What is the best model for the organization of these symptoms? *Journal of Abnormal Child Psychology, 29*, 339–349.

Burns, G. L., & Walsh, J. A. (2002). The influence of ADHD-hyperactivity/impulsivity symptoms on the development of oppositional defiant disorder symptoms in a 2-year longitudinal study. *Journal of Abnormal Child Psychology, 30*(3), 245–256.

Burns, G. L., Walsh, J. A., Owen, S. M., & Snell, J. (1997). Internal validity of attention deficit hyperactivity disorder, oppositional defiant disorder, and overt conduct disorder symptoms in young children: Implications for teacher ratings for a dimensional approach to symptom validity. *Journal of Clinical Child Psychology, 26*, 266–275.

Burns, G. L., Walsh, J. A., Patterson, D. R., Holte, C. S., Sommers-Flanagan, R., & Parker, C. M. (1997). Internal validity of the disruptive behavior disorder symptoms: Implications from parent ratings for a dimensional approach to symptom validity. *Journal of Abnormal Child Psychology, 25*, 307–319.

Burt, A., McGue, M., DeMarte, J. A., Krueger, R. F., & Iacono, W. G. (2006). Timing of menarche and the origins of conduct disorder. *Archives of General Psychiatry, 63*(8), 890–896.

Burt, A., McGue, M., Krueger, R. F., & Iacono, W. G. (2005). How are parent-child conflict and childhood externalizing symptoms related over time? Results from a genetically informative cross-lagged study. *Development and Psychopathology, 17*(1), 145–165.

Burt, S. A., Krueger, R. F., McGue, M., & Iacono, W. G. (2001). Sources of covariation among attention-deficit/hyperactivity disorder, oppositional defiant disorder, and conduct disorder: The importance of shared environment. *Journal of Abnormal Psychology, 110*, 516–525.

Burt, S. A., Krueger, R. F., McGue, M., & Iacono, W. (2003). Parent-child conflict and the comorbidity among childhood externalizing disorders. *Archives of General Psychiatry, 60*, 505–513.

Burton, E, Stice, E., Bearman, S. K., & Rhode, P. (2007). Experimental test of the affect-regulation theory of bulimic symptoms and substance use: A randomized trial. *International Journal of Eating Disorders, 40*, 27–36.

Busatto, G. F., Buchpiguel, C. A., Zamignani, D. R., Garrido, G. E. J., Glabus, M. F., Rosario-Campos, M .C., et al. (2001). Regional cerebral blood flow abnormalities in early-onset obsessive-compulsive disorder: An exploratory SPECT study. *Journal of the American Academy of Child and Adolescent Psychiatry, 40*(3), 347–354.

Bushman, J. B., & Anderson, C. A. (2001). Is it time to pull the plug on the hostile versus instrumental aggression dichotomy? *Psychological Review, 108*, 273–279.

Buss, K. A., & Goldsmith, H. H. (1998). Fear and anger regulation in infancy: Effects on the temporal dynamics of affective expression. *Child Development, 69*(2), 359–374.

Button, T. M. M., Scourfield, J., Martin, N., Purcell, S., & McGuffin, P. (2005). Family dysfunction interacts with genes in the causation of antisocial symptoms. *Behavior Genetics, 35*(2), 115–120.

Cafri, G., Yamamiya, Y., Brannick, M., & Thompson, J. K. (2005). The influence of sociocultural factors on body image: A meta-analysis. *Clinical Psychology: Science and Practice, 12*, 421–433.

Cairney, S., Maruff, P., Burns, C., & Currie, B. (2002). The neurobehavioural consequences of petrol (gasoline) sniffing. *Neuroscience and Biobehavioral Reviews, 26*(1), 81–89.

Cairns, R. B., Cairns, B. D., Rodkin, P., & Xie, H. (1998). New directions in developmental research: Models and methods. In R. Jessor (Ed.), *New perspectives on adolescent risk behavior* (pp. 13–42). New York: Cambridge University Press.

Calkins, S. D., & Fox, N. A. (2002). Self-regulatory processes in early personality development: A multilevel approach to the study of childhood social withdrawal and aggression. *Development and Psychopathology, 14*(3), 477–498.

Calkins, S. D., & Hill, A. (2007). Caregiver influences on emerging emotion regulation: Biological and environmental transactions

in early development. In J. J. Gross (Ed.), *Handbook of emotion regulation* (pp. 229–248). New York: Guilford Press.

Calkins, S. D., Hungerford, A., & Dedmon, S. E. (2004). Mothers' interactions with temperamentally frustrated infants. *Infant Mental Health Journal, 25*(3), 219–239.

Calkins, S. D., & Johnson, M. C., (1998). Toddler regulation of distress to frustrating events: Temperamental and maternal correlates. *Infant Behavior and Development, 21*(3), 379–395.

Calkins, S. D., & Keane, S. P. (2004). Cardiac vagal regulation across the preschool period: Stability, continuity, and implications for childhood adjustment. *Developmental Psychobiology, 45*(3), 101–112.

Call, K. T., & Mortimer, J. T. (2001). *Arenas of comfort in adolescence: A study of adjustment in context.* Mahwah, NJ: Erlbaum.

Callaghan, R. C., Hathaway, A., Cunningham, J. A., Vettese, L. C., Wyatt, S., & Taylor, L. (2005). Does stage-of-change predict dropout in a culturally diverse sample of adolescents admitted to inpatient substance-abuse treatment? A test of the transtheoretical model. *Addictive Behaviors, 30*(9), 1834–1847.

Calvete, E., & Cardenoso, O. (2005). Gender differences in cognitive vulnerability to depression and behavior problems in adolescents. *Journal of Abnormal Child Psychology, 33*(2), 179–192.

Calzada, E. J., Eyberg, S. M., Rich, B., & Querido, J. G. (2004). Parenting disruptive preschoolers: Experiences of mothers and fathers. *Journal of Abnormal Child Psychology, 32*(2), 203–213.

Campbell, D. (2000). The Mozart Effect for children: Awakening your child's mind, health, and creativity with music. *Publishers Weekly, 247*(37), 83.

Campbell, S. B. (1990). *Behavior problems in preschool children: Clinical and developmental issues.* New York: Guilford Press.

Campbell, S. B. (1995). Behavior problems in preschool children: A review of recent research. *Journal of Child Psychology and Psychiatry, 36*, 113–149.

Campbell, S. B., Shaw, D. S., & Gilliom, M. (2000). Early externalizing behavior problems: Toddlers and preschoolers at risk for later maladjustment. *Development and Psychopathology, 12*(3), 467–488.

Campo, J. V., & Fritsch, S. L. (1994). Somatization in children and adolescents. *Journal of the American Academy of Child and Adolescent Psychiatry, 33*(9), 1223–1235.

Campos, J. J., Frankel, C. B., & Camras, L. (2004). On the nature of emotion regulation. *Child Development, 75*(2), 377–394.

Canino, G., Shrout, P. E., Runio-Stipec, M., Bird, H. R., Bravo, M., Ramirez, R., et al. (2004). The DSM-IV rates of child and adolescent disorders in Puerto Rico. *Archives of General Psychiatry, 61(1)*, 85–93.

Canitano, R., Luchetti, A., & Zappella, M. (2005). Epilepsy, electroencephalographic abnormalities, and regression in children with autism. *Journal of Child Neurology, 20(1)*, 27–31.

Canpolat, B. I., Orsel, S., Akdemir, A., & Ozbay, M. H. (2005). The relationship between dieting and body image, body ideal, self-perception and body mass in Turkish adolescents. *International Journal of Eating Disorders, 37*, 150–155.

Cantwell, D. P. (1985). Hyperactive children grown up. What have we learned about what happened to them? *Archives of General Psychiatry, 42*, 1026–1028.

Cantwell, D. P. (1996). Attention deficit disorder: A review of the past 10 years. *Journal of the American Academy of Child and Adolescent Psychiatry, 35*, 978–987.

Cantwell, D. P. (1996). Classification of child and adolescent psychopathology. *Journal of Child Psychology and Psychiatry, 37(1),* 3–12.

Cantwell, D. P., & Baker, L. (1991). Association between attention-deficit hyperactivity disorder and learning disorders. *Journal of Learning Disabilities, 24,* 88–95.

Capaldi, D. M. (1991). Co-occurrence of conduct problems and depressive symptoms in early adolescent boys: I. Familial factors and general adjustment at grade 6. *Development and Psychopathology, 3*(3), 277–300.

Capaldi, D. M. (1991). Co-occurrence of conduct problems and depressive symptoms in early adolescent boys: I. Familial factors and general adjustment at Grade 6. *Development and Psychopathology, 3*(3), 277–300.

Capaldi, D. M. (1992). Co-occurrence of conduct problems and depressive symptoms in early adolescent boys: II. A 2-year follow-up at Grade 8. *Development and Psychopathology, 4*(1), 125–144.

Capaldi, D. M. (1999). Co-occurrence of conduct problems and depressive symptoms in early adolescent boys: III. Prediction to young-adult adjustment. *Development and Psychopathology, 11*(1), 59–84.

Capaldi, D. M., & Stoolmiller, M. (1999). Co-occurrence of conduct problems and depressive symptoms in early adolescent boys: III. Prediction to young-adult adjustment. *Development and Psychopathology, 11*(1), 59–84.

Capaldi, D. M., Pears, K. C., Patterson, G. R., & Owen, L. D. (2003). Continuity of parenting practices across generations in an at-risk sample: A prospective comparison of direct and mediated associations. *Journal of Abnormal Child Psychology, 31*(2) , 127–142.

Caparrotta, L., & Ghaffari, K. (2006). A historical overview of the psychodynamic contributions to the understanding of eating disorders. *Psychoanalytic Psychotherapy, 20,* 175–196.

Capps, L., Sigman, M., & Mundy, P. (1994). Attachment security in children with autism. *Development and Psychopathology, 6*(2), 249–261.

Card, N. A., Stucky, B. D., Sawalani, G. M., & Little, T. D. (2008). Direct and indirect aggression during childhood and adolescence: A meta-analytic review of gender differences, intercorrelations, and relations to maladjustment. *Child Development, 79*(5), 1185–1229.

Cardemil, E. V., Reivich, K. J., & Seligman, M. E. P. (2002, May 8). The prevention of depressive symptoms in low-income minority middle school students. *Prevention and Treatment, 5.* Retrieved July 12, 2009, from http://journals.apa.org/prevention/volume5/toc-may08–02.htm

Carlson, C. L., Tamm, L., & Hogan, A. E. (1999). The child with oppositional defiant disorder and conduct disorder in the family. In H. C. Quay & A. E. Hogan (Eds.), *Handbook of disruptive behavior disorders* (pp. 337–352). Dordrecht, Netherlands: Kluwer Academic Publishers.

Carlson, C. L., & Miranda, M. (2002). Sluggish cognitive tempo predicts a different pattern of impairment in the attention deficit hyperactivity disorder, predominantly inattentive type. *Journal of Clinical Child and Adolescent Psychology, 31*(1), 123–129.

Carlson, E. A. (1998). A prospective longitudinal study of attachment disorganization/disorientation. *Child Development, 69*(4), 1107–1128.

Carlson, G. A. (1998). Mania and ADHD: Comorbidity or confusion. *Journal of Affective Disorders, 51*(2), 177–187.

Carlson, G. A. (2002). Bipolar disorder in children and adolescents: A critical review. In D. Shaffer & B. D. Waslick (Eds.), *Review of psychiatry: Vol. 21. The many faces of depression in children and adolescents* (pp. 105–128). Washington, DC: American Psychiatric Publishing.

Carlson, G. A., Bromet, E. J., & Sievers, S. (2000). Phenomenology and outcome of subjects with early- and adult-onset psychotic mania. *American Journal of Psychiatry, 157*(2), 213–219.

Carlson, G. A., Jensen, P. S., Findling, R. L., Meyer, R. E., Calabrese, J., DelBello, M. P., et al. (2003). Methodological issues and controversies in clinical trials with child and adolescent patients with bipolar disorder: Report of a consensus conference. *Journal of Child and Adolescent Psychopharmacology, 13*(1), 13–27.

Carlson, S. R., Iacono, W. G., & McGue, M. (2002). P300 amplitude in adolescent twins discordant and concordant for alcohol use disorders. *Biological Psychology, 61(1–2),* 203–227.

Carlson, V., Cicchetti, D., Barnett, D., & Braunwald, K. (1989). Disorganized/disoriented attachment relationships in maltreated infants. *Developmental Psychology, 25*(4), 525–531.

Caron, C., & Rutter, M. (1991). Comorbidity in child psychopathology: Concepts, issues and research strategies. *Journal of Child Psychology and Psychiatry and Allied Disciplines, 32(7),* 1063–1080.

Carpenter, L. L., Tyrka, A. R., McDouble, C. J., Malison, R. T., Owens, M. J., Nemeroff, C. B., et al. (2004). Cerebrospinal fluid and corticotropin-releasing factor and perceived early-life stress in depressed patients and healthy control subjects. *Neuropsychopharmacology, 29,* 777–784.

Carpenter, M., Nagell, K., & Tomasello, M. (1998). Social cognition, joint attention, and communicative competence from 9 to 15 months of age. *Monographs of the Society for Research in Child Development, 63*(4), 176.

Carrington, S., & Elkins, J. (2002). Bridging the gap between inclusive policy and inclusive culture in secondary schools. *Support for Learning, 17*(2), 51–57.

Carruth, B. R., & Skinner, J. D. (2000). Bone mineral status in adolescent girls: Effects of eating disorders and exercise. *Journal of Adolescent Health, 26,* 322–329.

Carskadon, M. A., Acebo, C., & Jenni, O. G. (2004). Regulation of adolescent sleep: Implications for behavior. In R. E. Dahl & L. P. Spear (Eds.), *Adolescent brain development: Vulnerabilities and opportunities. Annals of the New York Academy of Sciences* (Vol. 1021, pp. 276–291). New York: New York Academy of Sciences.

Carter, F. A., McIntosh, V. V. W., Joyce, P., Sullivan, P. F., & Bulik, C. M. (2003). Role of exposure with response prevention in cognitive-behavioral therapy for bulimia nervosa: Three-year follow-up results. *International Journal of Eating Disorders, 33,* 127–135.

Cartwright-Hatton, S., McNicol, K., & Doubleday, E. (2006). Anxiety in a neglected population: Prevalence of anxiety disorders in preadolescent children. *Clinical Psychology Review, 26*(7), 817–833.

Carver, C. S., & Scheier, M. S. (1981). *Attention and self-regulation: A control-theory approach to human behavior.* New York: Springer.

Carver, K., Joyner, K., & Udry, J. R. (2003). National estimates of adolescent romantic relationships. In P. Florsheim (Ed.), *Adolescent romantic relations and sexual behavior: Theory, research, and practical implications* (pp. 23–56). Mahwah, NJ: Erlbaum.

Case, R., Demetriou, A., Platsidou, M., & Kazi, S. (2001). Integrating concepts and tests of intelligence from the differential and developmental traditions. *Intelligence, 29(4)*, 307–336.

Casey, B. J., Castellanos, F. X., Giedd, J. N., & Marsh, W. L. (1997). Implication of right frontostriatal circuitry in response inhibition and attention-deficit/hyperactivity disorder. *Journal of the American Academy of Child and Adolescent Psychiatry, 36*, 374–383.

Casey, R. J., & Berman, J. S. (1985). The outcome of psychotherapy with children. *Psychological Bulletin, 98(2)*, 388–400.

Caspi, A., Harrington, H., Milne, B., Amell, J. W., Theodore, R. F., & Moffitt, T. E. (2003). Children's behavioral styles at age 3 are linked to their adult personality traits at age 26. *Journal of Personality, 71*(4), 495–513.

Caspi, A., Moffitt, T. E., Morgan, J., Rutter, M., Taylor, A., Arseneault, L., et al. (2004). Maternal expressed emotion predicts children's antisocial behavior problems: Using monozygotic-twin differences to identify environmental effects on behavioral development. *Developmental Psychology, 40*(2), 149–161.

Caspi, A., Taylor, A., Moffitt, T. E., & Plomin, R. (2000). Neighborhood deprivation affects children's mental health: Environmental risks identified in a genetic design. *Psychological Science, 11(4)*, 338–342.

Caspi, A., Taylor, A., Moffitt, T. E., & Plomin, R. (2000). Neighborhood deprivation affects children's mental health: Environmental risks identified in a genetic design. *Psychological Science, 11*, 338–342.

Cassidy, J. (1988). Child-mother attachment and the self in six-year-olds. *Child Development, 59*(1), 121–134.

Cassidy, J. (1990). Theoretical and methodological considerations in the study of attachment and the self in young children. In M. T. Greenberg, D. Cicchetti, & E. M. Cummings (Eds.), *Attachment in the preschool years: Theory, research, and intervention* (pp. 87–119). Chicago: University of Chicago Press.

Cassidy, J., & Marvin, R. S., in collaboration with the MacArthur working group on attachment. (1992). *Attachment organization in preschool children: Procedures and coding manual.* Unpublished manuscript.

Cassidy, J., & Mohr, J. J. (2001). Unsolvable fear, trauma, and psychopathology: Theory, research, and clinical considerations related to disorganized attachment across the life span. *Clinical Psychology: Science and Practice, 8*(3), 275–298.

Cassidy, J., & Shaver, P. R. (1999*). Handbook of attachment: Theory, research, and clinical applications.* New York: Guilford Press.

Cassin, S. E., & von Ranson, K. M. (2005). Personality and eating disorders: A decade in review. *Clinical Psychology Review, 25*, 895–916.

Castellanos, F. X. (1997). Toward a pathophysiology of attention-deficit/hyperactivity disorder. *Clinical Pediatrics, 36*, 381–393.

Castellanos, F. X. (1999). Stimulants and tic disorders: From dogma to data. *Archives of General Psychiatry, 56*, 337–338.

Castro-Fornieles, J., Gual, P., Lahortiga, F., Gila, A., Casula, V., Fuhrmann, C., et al. (2007). Self-oriented perfectionism in eating disorders. *International Journal of Eating Disorders, 40*(6), 562–568.

Center, Y., & Ward, J. (1987). Teachers' attitudes towards the integration of disabled children into regular schools. *Exceptional Child, 34*(1), 41–56.

Centers for Disease Control and Prevention. (2007). Autism Information Center. Retrieved July 6, 2009, from www.cdc.gov/ncbddd/autism/index.htm

Cerel, J., Roberts, T. A., & Nilsen, W. J. (2005). Peer suicidal behavior and adolescent risk behavior. *Journal of Nervous and Mental Disease, 193*(4), 237–243.

Chabris, C. F. (1999). Prelude or requiem for the ëMozart effect'? *Nature*, 826–827.

Chabrol, H., Massot, E., & Mullet, E. (2004). Factor structure of cannabis-related beliefs in adolescents. *Addictive Behaviors, 29*(5), 929–933.

Chakrabarti, S., & Fombonne, E. (2002). Pervasive developmental disorders in preschool children. *Journal of the American Academy of Child and Adolescent Psychiatry, 41*, 74.

Chakrabarti, S. & Fombonne, E. (2005). Pervasive developmental disorders in preschool children: Confirmation of high prevalence. *America Journal of Psychiatry, 162*(6), 1133–1141.

Chamay-Weber, C. Narring, F., & Michaud, P. (2005). Partial eating disorders among adolescents: A review. *Journal of Adolescent Health, 37*, 417–427.

Chamberlain, P. (1999). Residential care for children and adolescents with oppositional defiant disorder and conduct disorder. In H. C. Quay, & A. E. Hogan (Eds.), *Handbook of disruptive behavior disorders* (pp. 495–506). Dordrecht, Netherlands: Kluwer Academic Publishers.

Chamberlain, P., & Patterson, G. R. (1995). Discipline and child compliance in parenting. In M. H. Bornstein (Ed.), *Handbook of parenting: Vol. 4. Applied and practical parenting* (pp. 205–225). Mahwah, NJ: Erlbaum.

Chambers, D. A., Ringeisen, H., & Hickman, E. E. (2005). Federal, state, and foundation initiatives around evidence-based practices for child and adolescent mental health. *Child and Adolescent Psychiatric Clinics of North America, 14(2)*, 307–327.

Chambers, R. A., & Potenza, M. N. (2003). Neurodevelopment, impulsivity, and adolescent gambling. *Journal of Gambling Studies, 19*(1), 53–84.

Chambers, R. A., Taylor, J. R. & Potenza, M. N. (2003). Developmental neurocircuitry of motivation in adolescence: A critical period of addiction vulnerability. *American Journal of Psychiatry, 160*(6), 1041–1052.

Chandana, S. R., Behen, M. E., Juhasz, C., Muzik, O., Rothermel, R. D., Mangner, T. J., et al. (2005). Significance of abnormalities in developmental trajectory and asymmetry of cortical serotonin synthesis in autism. *International Journal of Developmental Neuroscience, 23*(2–3), 171–182.

Chang, F., & Burns, B. (2005). Attention in preschoolers: Associations with effortful control and motivation. *Child Development, 76*(1), 247–263.

Chang, K. D., Blasey, C. M., Ketter, T. A., & Steiner, H. (2003). Temperament characteristics of child and adolescent bipolar offspring. *Journal of Affective Disorders, 77*(1), 11–19.

Chang, K., Karchemskiy, A., Barnea-Goraly, N., Garrett, A., Simeonova, D. I., & Reiss, A. (2005). Reduced amygdalar gray matter volume in familial pediatric bipolar disorder. *Journal of the American Academy of Child and Adolescent Psychiatry, 44*(6), 565–573.

Chao, R. K. (2000). Cultural explanations for the role of parenting in the school success of Asian-American children. In R. D. Taylor & M.Wang (Eds.), *Resilience across contexts: Family, work, culture, and community* (pp. 333–363). Mahwah, NJ: Erlbaum.

Chapman, R. S., Schwartz, S. E., & Kay-Raining Bird, E. (1991). Language skills of children and adolescents with Down syndrome: I. Comprehension. *Journal of Speech and Hearing Research, 34*(5), 1106–1120.

Chapman, R. S., Seung, H., Schwartz, S. E. & Kay-Raining Bird, E. (1998). Language skills of children with Down syndrome: II. Production deficits. *Journal of Speech, Language, and Hearing Research, 41*(4), 861–873.

Charman, T., Baron-Cohen, S., Baird, G., Cox, A., Swettenham, J., Wheelwright, S., et al. (2002). Is 18 months too early for the CHAT? *Journal of the American Academy of Child and Adolescent Psychiatry, 41*, 235–236.

Charman, T., Baron-Cohen, S., Swettenham, J., Baird, G., Cox, A., & Drew, A. (2001). Testing joint attention, imitation, and play as infancy precursors to language and theory of mind. *Cognitive Development, 15*, 481–498.

Charman, T., Swettenham, J., Baron-Cohen, S., Cox, A., Baird, G., & Drew, A. (1997). Infants with autism: An investigation of empathy, pretend play, joint attention, and imitation. *Developmental Psychology, 33*, 781–789.

Charman, T., Swettenham, J., Baron-Cohen, S., Cox, A., Baird, G., & Drew, A. (2000). An experimental investigation of social-cognitive abilities in infants with autism: Clinical implications. In D. Muir & A. Slater (Eds.), *Infant development: The essential readings. Essential readings in development psychology* (pp. 343–363). Malden, MA: Blackwell.

Chassin, L., Presson, C. C., & Sherman, S. J. (1989). "Constructive" vs. "destructive" deviance in adolescent health-related behaviors. *Journal of Youth and Adolescence, 18*, 245–262.

Chassin, L., Presson, C. C., & Sherman, S. J. (2005). Adolescent cigarette smoking: A commentary and issues for pediatric psychology. *Journal of Pediatric Psychology, 30*(4), 299–303.

Chassin, L., Presson, C. C., Pitts, S. C., & Sherman, S. J. (2000). The natural history of cigarette smoking from adolescence to adulthood in a midwestern community sample: Multiple trajectories and their psychosocial correlates. *Health Psychology, 19*(3), 223–231.

Chassin, L., Presson, C. C., Rose, J., Sherman, S. J., Davis, M. J., & Gonzalez, J. L. (2005). Parenting style and smoking-specific parenting practices as predictors of adolescent smoking onset. *Journal of Pediatric Psychology, 30*(4), 334–344.

Chatoor, I. (2002). Feeding disorders in infants and toddlers: Diagnosis and treatment. *Child and Adolescent Psychiatric Clinics of North America, 11*, 163–183.

Chatoor, I., & Ammaniti, M. (2007). Classifying feeding disorders of infancy and early childhood. In W. E. Narrow, M. B. First, P. J. Sirovatka, & D. A. Regier (Eds.), *Age and gender considerations in psychiatric diagnosis: A research agenda for DSM-V* (pp. 227–242). Arlington, VA: American Psychiatric Publishing.

Chatterji, P., Dave, D., Kaestner, R., & Markowitz, S. (2004). Alcohol abuse and suicide attempts among youth. *Economics and Human Biology, 2*, 159–180.

Chavira, D. A., Stein, M. B., Bailey, K., & Stein, M. T. (2004). Child anxiety in primary care: Prevalent but untreated. *Depression and Anxiety, 20*(4), 155–164.

Chawarska, K., Paul, R., Klin, A., Hannigen, S., Dichtel, L. E. & Volkmar, F. (2007). Parental recognition of developmental problems in toddlers with autism spectrum disorders. *Journal of Autism and Developmental Disorders, 37*(1), 2007.

Chen, B. K., Sassi, R., Axelson, D., Hatch, J. P., Sanches, M., Nicoletti, M., et al. (2004). Cross-sectional study of abnormal amygdale development in adolescents and young adults with bipolar disorder. *Biological Psychiatry, 56*(6), 399–405.

Chen, C., Greenberger, E., Lester, J., Dong, Q., & Guo, M.-S. (1998). A cross-cultural study of family and peer correlates of adolescent misconduct. *Developmental Psychology, 34*(4), 770–781.

Chen, E., Matthews, K. A., & Boyce, W. T. (2002). Socioeconomic differences in children's health: How and why do these relationships change with age? *Psychological Bulletin, 128*(2), 295–329.

Cherney, S. S., Fulker, D. W., & Hewitt, J. K. (1997). Cognitive development from infancy to middle childhood. In R. J. Sternberg & E. L. Grigorenko (Eds.), *Intelligence, Heredity, and Environment* (pp. 463–482). New York: Cambridge University Press.

Chess, S., & Thomas, A. (1984). *Origins and evolution of behavior disorders: From infancy to early adult life.* New York: Brunner/Mazel Publishers.

Chi, T. C., & Hinshaw, S. P. (2002). Mother-child relationships of children with ADHD: the role of maternal depressive symptoms and depression-related distortions. *Journal of Abnormal Child Psychology, 30*(4), 387–401.

Chisholm, K., Carter, M. C., Ames, E. W., & Morison, S. J. (1995). Attachment security and indiscriminately friendly behavior in children adopted from Romanian orphanages. *Development and Psychopathology, 7*(2), 283–294.

Chorpita, B. F. (2001). Control and the development of negative emotion. In M .W. Vasey & M. R. Dadds (Eds.), *The developmental psychopathology of anxiety* (pp. 112–142). London: Oxford University Press.

Chorpita, B. F., Albano, A. M., & Barlow, D. H. (1996). Cognitive processing in children: Relation to anxiety and family influences. *Journal of Clinical Child Psychology, 25*(2), 170–176.

Chorpita, B. F. & Barlow, D. H. (1998). The development anxiety: The role of control in the early environment. *Psychological Bulletin, 124*(1), 3–21.

Chorpita, B. F., Barlow, D. H, Albano, A. M., & Daleiden, E. L. (1998). Methodological strategies in child clinical trials: Advancing the efficacy and effectiveness of psychosocial treatments. *Journal of Abnormal Child Psychology, 26*(1), 7–16.

Chorpita, B. F., Brown, T. A., & Barlow, D. H. (1998). Perceived control as a mediator of family environment in etiological models of childhood anxiety. *Behavior Therapy, 29*, 457–476.

Chorpita, B. F., Plummer, C. M., & Moffitt, C. E. (2000). Relations of tripartite dimensions of emotion to childhood anxiety and mood disorders. *Journal of Abnormal Child Psychology, 28*(3), 299–310.

Chorpita, B. F., Yim, L. M., Donkervoet, J. C., Arensdorf, A., Amundsen, M. J., McGee, C., et al. (2002). Toward large-scale implementation of empirically supported treatments for children: A review and observations by the Hawaii Empirical Basis to Services Task Force. *Clinical Psychology: Science and Practice, 9*(2), 165–190.

Chorpita, B. F., Yim, L., Moffitt, C., Umemoto, L. A., & Francis, S. E. (2000). Assessment of symptoms of DSM-IV anxiety and depression in children: A revised child anxiety and depression scale. *Behaviour Research and Therapy, 38*(8), 835–855.

Chowdhury, U., & Lask, B. (2001). Clinical implications of brain imaging in eating disorders. *Psychiatric Clinics of North America, 24*, 227–234.

Chowdhury, U., Gordon, I., Lask, B., Watkins, B., Watt, H., & Christie, D. (2003). Early-onset anorexia nervosa: Is there evidence of limbic system imbalance? *International Journal of Eating Disorders, 33,* 388–396.

Christie, K. A., Burke, J. D., Regier, D. A., Rae, D. S., Boyd, J. H., & Locke, B. Z. (1988). Epidemiologic evidence for early onset of mental disorders and higher risk of drug abuse in young adults. *American Journal of Psychiatry, 145,* 971–975.

Christophersen, E. R., & Mortweet, S. L. (2001). *Treatments that work with children: Empirically supported strategies for managing childhood problems.* Washington, DC: American Psychological Association.

Chuang, S. S., Lamb, M. E., & Hwang, C. P. (2006). Personality development from childhood to adolescence: A longitudinal study of ego-control and ego-resiliency in Sweden. *International Journal of Behavioral Development, 30*(4), 338–343.

Chugani, H. T. (1999). PET scanning studies of human brain development and plasticity. *Developmental Neuropsychology, 16(3),* 379–381.

Chung, H. L., & Steinberg, L. (2006). Relations between neighborhood factors, parenting behaviors, peer deviance, and delinquency among serious juvenile offenders. *Developmental Psychology, 42*(2), 319–331.

Ciano, R., Rocco, P. L., Angarano, A., Biasin, E., & Balestrieri, M. (2002). Group-analytic and psychoeducational therapies for binge-eating disorder: An exploratory study on efficacy and persistence of effects. *Psychotherapy Research, 12,* 231–239.

Ciarrochi, J., Deane, F. P., Wilson, C. J., & Rickwood, D. (2002). Adolescents who need help the most are the least likely to seek it: The relationship between low emotional competence and low intention to seek help. *British Journal of Guidance and Counseling, 30*(2), 173–188.

Cicchetti, D. (1984). The emergence of developmental psychopathology. *Child Development, 55,* 1–7.

Cicchetti, D. (1990a). A historical perspective on the discipline of developmental psychopathology. In J. E. Rolf, A. S. Masten, D. Cicchetti, K. H. Nuechterlein, & S. Weintraub (Eds.), *Risk and protective factors in the development of psychopathology* (pp. 2–28). New York: Cambridge University Press.

Cicchetti, D. (1990b). The organization and coherence of sociomotivational, cognitive, and representational development: Illustrations through a developmental psychopathology perspective of Down syndrome and child maltreatment. In R. A. Thompson (Ed.), *Socioemotional development. Current theory and research in motivation* (pp. 259–279). Lincoln: University of Nebraska Press.

Cicchetti, D. (1991). Fractures in the crystal: Developmental psychopathology and the emergence of self. *Developmental Review, 11,* 271–287.

Cicchetti, D. (2002). The impact of social experience on neurobiological systems: Illustration from a constructivist view of child maltreatment. *Cognitive Development, 17(3–4),* 1407–1428.

Cicchetti, D. (2004). An odyssey of discovery: Lessons learned through three decades of research on child maltreatment. *American Psychologist, 59*(8), 731–741.

Cicchetti, D. & Cannon, T. D. (1999). Neurodevelopmental processes in the ontogenesis and epigenesis of psychopathology. *Development and Psychopathology, 11,* 375–393.

Cicchetti, D., & Dawson, G. (2002). Editorial: Multiple levels of analysis. *Development and Psychopathology, 14(3),* 417–420.

Cicchetti, D., & Ganiban, J. (1990). The organization and coherence of developmental processes in infants and children with Down syndrome. In R. M. Hodapp, J. A. Burack, & E. Zigler (Eds.), *Issues in the developmental approach to mental retardation* (pp. 169–225). New York: Cambridge University Press.

Cicchetti, D., & Garmezy, N. (1993). Prospects and promises in the study of resilience. *Development and Psychopathology, 5(4),* 497–502.

Cicchetti, D., & Lynch, M. (1993). Toward an ecological/transactional model of community violence and child maltreatment: Consequences for children's development. *Psychiatry, 56,* 96–118.

Cicchetti, D., & Pogge-Hesse, P. (1982). Possible contributions of the study of organically retarded persons to developmental theory. In E. Zigler & D. Balla (Eds.), *Mental retardation: The developmental-difference controversy* (pp. 277–318). Hillsdale, NJ: Erlbaum.

Cicchetti, D., & Rogosch, F. A. (1996). Equifinality and multifinality in developmental psychopathology. *Development and Psychopathology, 8(4),* 597–600.

Cicchetti, D., & Rogosch, F. (1997). The role of self-organization in the promotion of resilience in maltreated children. *Development and Psychopathology, 9,* 797–815.

Cicchetti, D., & Rogosch, F. A. (1999). Psychopathology as risk for adolescent substance use disorders: A developmental psychopathology perspective. *Journal of Clinical Child Psychology, 28*(3), 355–365.

Cicchetti, D., & Rogosch, F. A. (2001a). Diverse patterns of neuroendocrine activity in maltreated children. *Development and Psychopathology, 13(3),* 677–693.

Cicchetti, D., & Rogosch, F. A. (2001b). The impact of child maltreatment and psychopathology on neuroendocrine functioning. *Development and Psychopathology, 13(4),* 783–804.

Cicchetti, D., & Rogosch, F. A. (2002). A developmental psychopathology perspective on adolescence. *Journal of Consulting and Clinical Psychology, 70*(1), 6–20.

Cicchetti, D., & Rogosch, F. A. (2007). Personality, adrenal steroid hormones, and resilience in maltreated children: A multilevel perspective. *Development and Pscyhopathology, 19(3),* 787–809.

Cicchetti, D., & Serafica, F. C. (1981). Interplay among behavioral systems: Illustrations from the study of attachment, affiliation, and wariness in young children with Down's syndrome. *Developmental Psychology, 17*(1), 36–49.

Cicchetti, D., & Sroufe, L. A. (2000). The past as prologue to the future: The times, they've been a-changin'. *Development and Psychopathology, 12(3),* 255–264.

Cicchetti, D., & Toth, S. L. (1987). The application of a transactional risk model to intervention with multi-risk maltreating families. *Zero to Three, 7*(5), 1–8.

Cicchetti, D., & Toth, S. L. (1995). Developmental psychopathology and disorders of affect. In D. Cicchetti & D. J. Cohen (Eds.), *Developmental psychopathology, Vol. 2 Risk, disorder, and adaptation* (pp. 369–420). Oxford, England: Wiley.

Cicchetti, D., & Toth, S. L. (1995). A developmental psychopathology perspective on child abuse and neglect. *Psychiatry, 34,* 541–565.

Cicchetti, D., & Toth, S. L. (1998). The development of depression in children and adolescents. *American Psychologist, 53*(2), 221–241.

Cicchetti, D., & Toth, S. L. (2003). Child maltreatment: Past, present, and future perspectives. In R. P. Weissberg & H. J. Walberg (Eds.), *Long-term trends in the well-being of children and youth: Issues in children's and families lives* (pp. 181–205). Washington, DC: Child Welfare League of America.

Cicchetti, D., Ackerman, B. P., & Izard, C. E. (1995). Emotions and emotion regulation in developmental psychopathology. *Development and Psychopathology, 7*, 1–10.

Cicchetti, D., Rappaport, J., Sandler, I., & Weissberg, R. P. (2000). *The promotion of wellness in children and adolescents*. Washington, DC: Child Welfare League of America.

Cicchetti, D., Rogosch, F. A., & Toth, S. L. (1997). Ontogenesis, depressotypic organization, and the depressive spectrum. In S. Luthar, J. Burack, D. Cicchetti, & J. R. Weisz (Eds.), *Developmental psychopathology: Perspectives on adjustment, risk and disorder* (pp. 273–313). New York: Cambridge University Press.

Cicchetti, D., Rogosch, F. A., & Toth, S. L. (1998). Maternal depressive disorder and contextual risk: Contributions to the development of attachment insecurity and behavior problems in toddlerhood. *Development and Psychopathology, 10*(2), 283–300.

Cicchetti, D., Rogosch, F. A., & Toth, S. L. (2006). Fostering secure attachment in infants in maltreating families through preventive interventions. *Development and Psychopathology, 18*, 623–649.

Cicchetti, D., Toth, S. L., & Lynch, M. (1995). Bowlby's dream comes full circle: The application of attachment theory to risk and psychopathology. *Advances in Clinical Child Psychology, 17*, 1–65.

Cicchetti, D., Toth, S. L., & Rogosch, F. A. (2000). The development of psychological wellness in maltreated children. In D. Cicchetti & J. Rappaport (Eds.), *The promotion of wellness in children and adolescents* (pp. 395–426). Washington, DC: Child Welfare League of America.

Cicchetti, D., Toth, S. L., & Rogosch, F. A. (2004). Toddler-parent psychotherapy for depressed mothers and their offspring: Implications for attachment theory. In L. Atkinson & S. Goldberg (Eds.), *Attachment issues in psychopathology and intervention* (pp. 229–275). Mahwah, NJ: Erlbaum.

Cicchetti, D. & Walker, E. (2003). *Neurodevelopmental mechanisms in psychopathology*. New York: Cambridge University Press.

Claes, M. (1998). Adolescents' closeness with parents, siblings, and friends in three countries: Canada, Belgium, and Italy. *Journal of Youth and Adolescence, 27*(2), 165–184.

Clahsen, H., & Temple, C. (2003). Words and rules in children with Williams syndrome. In Y. Levy & J. Schaeffer (Eds.), *Language competence across populations: Toward a definition of specific language impairment* (pp. 323–352). Mahwah, NJ: Erlbaum.

Clark, C., Prior, M., & Kinsella, G. J. (2000). Do executive function deficits differentiate between adolescents with ADHD and oppositional defiant/conduct disorder? A neuropsychological study using the Six Elements Test and Hayling Sentence Completion Test. *Journal of Abnormal Child Psychology, 28*, 403–414.

Clark, C., Prior, M., & Kinsella, G. (2002). The relationship between executive function abilities, adaptive behavior, and academic achievement in children with externalizing behavior problems. *Journal of Child Psychology and Psychiatry and Allied Disciplines, 43*(6), 785–796.

Clark, D. B., Cornelius, J. R., Kirisci, L, & Tarter, R. E. (2005). Childhood risk categories for adolescent substance involvement: A general liability typology. *Drug and Alcohol Dependence, 77*(1), 13–21.

Clark, L. A. (2005). Temperament as a unifying basis for personality and psychopathology. *Journal of Abnormal Psychology, 114*(4), 505–521.

Clark, L. A., Watson, D., & Reynolds, S. (1995). Diagnosis and classification of psychopathology: Challenges to the current system and future directions. *Annual Review of Psychology, 46*, 121–153.

Clarke, G., Debar, L., Lynch, F., Powell, J., Gale, J., O'Connor, E., et al. (2005). A randomized effectiveness trial of brief cognitive-behavioral therapy for depressed adolescents receiving antidepressant medication. *Journal of the American Academy of Child and Adolescent Psychiatry, 44*(9), 888–898.

Clarren, S., & Astley, S. (1997). Development of the FAS Diagnostic and Prevention Network in Washington State. In A. Streissguth & J. Kanter (Eds.), *The challenge of fetal alcohol syndrome: Overcoming secondary disabilities* (pp. 40–51). Seattle: University of Washington Press.

Claussen, A. H., Scott, K. G., Mundy, P. C., & Katz, L. F. (2004). Effects of three levels of early intervention services on children prenatally exposed to cocaine. *Journal of Early Intervention, 26*(3), 204–220.

Clay, D., Vignoles, V. L., & Dittmar, H. (2005). Body image and self-esteem among adolescent girls: Testing the influence of sociocultural factors. *Journal of Research on Adolescence, 15*, 451–477.

Clayton, R. R., Scutchfield, D., & Wyatt, S. W. (2000). Hutchinson Smoking Prevention Project: A new gold standard in prevention science requires new transdisciplinary thinking. *Journal of the National Cancer Institute, 92*, 1964–1965.

Cleary, C. (2000). Self-directed violence in adolescence: A psychotherapeutic perspective. In G. Boswell (Ed.), *Violent children and adolescents: Asking the question why* (pp. 91–103). Philadelphia: Whurr Publishers.

Clemmy, P., Payne, L., & Fishman, M. (2004). Clinical characteristics and treatment outcomes of adolescent heroin users. *Journal of Psychoactive Drugs, 36*(1), 85–94.

Cleveland, M. J., Gibbons, F. X., Gerrard, M., Pomery, E. A., & Brody, G. H. (2005). The impact of parenting on risk cognitions and risk behavior: A study of mediation and moderation in a panel of African American adolescents. *Child Development, 76*(4), 900–916.

Clingempeel, W. G., & Henggeler, S. W. (2003). Aggressive juvenile offenders transitioning into emerging adulthood: Factors discriminating persistors and desistors. *American Journal of Orthopsychiatry, 73*(3), 310–323.

Clinton, D. (2006). Affect regulation, object relations and the central symptoms of eating disorders. *European Eating Disorders Review, 14*, 203–211.

Cloninger, C. R. (1987). Neurogenetic adaptive mechanisms in alcoholism. *Science, 236*(4800), 410–416.

Cloninger, C. R., Bohman, M., & Sigvardsson, S. (1981). Inheritance of alcohol abuse: Cross-fostering analysis of adopted men. *Archives of General Psychiatry, 38*(8), 861–868.

Coates, D. L., & Vietze, P. M. (1996). Cultural considerations in assessment, diagnosis, and intervention. In J. W. Jacobson & J. A. Mulick (Eds.), *Manual of diagnosis and professional practice in mental retardation* (pp. 243–256). Washington, DC: American Psychological Association.

Coffelt, N. L., Forehand, R., Olson, A. L., Jones, D. J., Gaffney, C. A., & Zens, M. S. (2006). A longitudinal examination of the link between parent alcohol problems and youth drinking: The moderating roles of parent and child gender. *Addictive Behaviors, 31*(4), 593–605.

Cohen, D. J., Volkmar, F. R., Anderson, G., & Klin, A. (1993). Integrating biological and behavioral perspectives in the study and care of autistic individuals: The future ahead. *Israel Journal of Psychiatry, 30*, 15–32.

Cohen, J. A., Deblinger, E., Mannarino, A. P., & Steer, R. A. (2004). A multisite, randomized controlled trial for children with sexual abuse PTSD symptoms. *Journal of the American Academy of Child and Adolescent Psychiatry, 43*(4), 393–402.

Cohen, N. J., Lojkasek, M., Muir, E., Muir, R., & Parker, C. J. (2002). Six-month follow-up of two mother-infant psychotherapies: Convergence of therapeutic outcomes. *Infant Mental Health Journal, 23*(4), 361–380.

Cohen, N. J., Muir, E., Parker, C. J., Brown, M., Lojkasek, M., Muir, R., et al.. (1999). Watch, wait and wonder: Testing the effectiveness of a new approach to mother-infant psychotherapy. *Infant Mental Health Journal, 20*(4), 429–451.

Cohen, P., & Flory, M. (1998). Issues in the disruptive behavior disorders: Attention deficit disorder without hyperactivity and the differential validity of oppositional defiant and conduct disorders. In T. Widiger (Ed.), *DSM-IV Sourcebook, Vol. 4* (pp. 455–463). Washington, DC: American Psychiatric Press.

Cohen, P., & Kasen, S. (1999). The context of assessment: Culture, race, and socioeconomic status as influences on the assessment of children. In D. Shaffer & C. P. Lewis (Eds.), *Diagnostic assessment in child and adolescent psychopathology* (pp. 299–318). New York: Guilford Press.

Cohen, P., Cohen, J., & Brook, J. (1993). An epidemiological study of disorders in late childhood and adolescence – II. Persistence of disorders. *Journal of Child Psychology and Psychiatry, 34(6)*, 869–877.

Coie, J. D., & Dodge, K. A. (1998). Aggression and antisocial behavior. In W. Damon & N. Eisenberg (Eds.), *Handbook of child psychology* (5th ed.): *Vol. 3. Social, emotional, and personality development* (pp. 779–862). Hoboken, NJ: Wiley.

Coie, J. D., Dodge, K. A., & Coppotelli, H. (1982). Dimensions and types of social status: A cross-age perspective. *Developmental Psychology, 18*(4), 557–570.

Colby, S. M., Tiffany, S. T., Shiffman, S., & Niaura, R. S. (2000). Are adolescent smokers dependent on nicotine? A review of the evidence. *Drug and Alcohol Dependence, 59*(Suppl. 1), S83-S95.

Colder, C. R., & Chassin, L. (1999). The psychosocial characteristics of alcohol users versus problem users: Data from a study of adolescents at risk. *Development and Psychopathology, 11* , 321–348.

Colder, C. R., Campbell, R. T., Ruel, E., Richardson, J. L., & Flay, B. R. (2002). A finite mixture model of growth trajectories of adolescent alcohol use: Predictors and consequences. *Journal of Consulting and Clinical Psychology, 70*(4), 976–985.

Colder, C. R., Mehta, P., Balanda, K., Campbell, R. T., Mayhew, K. P., & Stanton, W. R. (2001). Identifying trajectories of adolescent smoking: An application of latent growth mixture model. *Health Psychology, 20*, 127–135.

Cole, D. A., Hoffman, K., Tram, J. M., & Maxwell, S. E. (2000). Structural differences in parent and child reports of children's symptoms of depression and anxiety. *Psychological Assessment, 12*(2), 174–185.

Cole, D. A., Martin, J. M., Powers, B., & Truglio, R. (1996). Modeling causal relations between academic and social competence and depression: A multitrait-multimethod longitudinal study of children. *Journal of Abnormal Psychology, 105*(2), 258–270.

Cole, D. A., Maxwell, S. E., Martin, J. M., Peeke, L. G., Seroczynski, A. D., Tram, J. M., et al. (2001). The development of multiple domains of child and adolescent self-concept: A cohort sequential longitudinal design. *Child Development, 72*(6), 1723–1746.

Cole, D. A., Tram, J. M., Martin, J. M., Hoffman, K. B., Ruiz, M. D., Jacquez, F. M., et al. (2002). Individual differences in the emergence of depressive symptoms in children and adolescents: A longitudinal investigation of parent and child reports. *Journal of Abnormal Psychology, 111*(1), 156–165.

Cole, P. (1998). Developmental versus difference approaches to mental retardation: A theoretical extension to the present debate. *American Journal on Mental Retardation, 102*(4), 379–391.

Cole, P. M., & Hall, S. E. (2008). Emotion dysregulation as a risk factor for psychopathology. In T. P. Beauchaine & S. P. Hinshaw (Eds.), *Child and adolescent psychopathology* (p. 265–298). Hoboken, NJ: Wiley.

Cole, P. M., Martin, S. E., & Dennis, T. A. (2004). Emotion regulation as a scientific construct: Methodological challenges and directions for child development research. *Child Development, 75*(2), 317–333.

Cole, P. M., Michel, M. K., & Teti, L. O. (1994). The development of emotion regulation and dysregulation: A clinical perspective. *Monographs of the Society for Research in Child Development, 59*(2–3), 73–100, 250–283.

Coleman, L., & Cater, S. (2005). Underage 'binge' drinking: A qualitative study into motivations and outcomes. *Drugs: Education, Prevention, & Policy, 12*(2), 125–136.

Coleman, M. (1987). The search for neurological subgroups in autism. In E. Schopler & G. B. Mesibov (Eds.), *Neurobiological issues in autism* (pp. 163–178). New York: Plenum Press.

Collett, B. R., Ohan, J. L., & Myers, K. M. (2003). Ten-year review of rating scales. VI: Scales assessing externalizing behaviors. *Journal of the American Academy of Child and Adolescent Psychiatry, 42*(10), 1143–1170.

Collins, R. L., & Ricciardelli, L. A. (2005). Assessment of eating disorders and obesity. In D. M. Donovan (Ed.), *Assessment of addictive behaviors* (pp. 305–333). New York: Guilford Press.

Collins, W. A. (2003). More than myth: The developmental significance of romantic relationships during adolescence. *Journal of Research on Adolescence, 13*(1), 1–24.

Collins, W. A., & Sroufe, L. A. (1999). Capacity for intimate relationships: A developmental construction. In W. Furman, B. B. Brown, & C. Feiring (Eds.), *The development of romantic relationships in adolescence* (pp. 125–147). New York: Cambridge University Press.

Collins, W. A., Gleason, T., & Sesma, A. (1997). Internalization, autonomy, and relationships: Development during adolescence. In J. E. Grusec & L. Kuczynski (Eds.). *Parenting and children's internalization of values: A handbook of contemporary theory* (pp. 78–99). Hoboken, NJ: Wiley.

Collins, W. A., Maccoby, E. E., Steinberg, L., Hetherington, M. E., & Bornstein, M. H. (2000). Contemporary research on parenting: The case for nature and nurture. *American Psychologist, 55(2)*, 218–232.

Collishaw, S., Maughan, B., Goodman, R., & Pickles, A. (2004). Time trends in adolescent mental health. *Journal of Child Psychology and Psychiatry, 45*(8), 1350–1362.

Collishaw, S., Pickles, A., Messer, J., Rutter, M., Shearer, C. & Maughan, B. (2007). Resilience to adult psychopathology following childhood maltreatment: Evidence from a community sample. *Child Abuse and Neglect, 31(3),* 211–229.

Comer, J. S., Kendall, P. C., Franklin, M. E., Hudson, J. L., & Pimentel, S. S. (2004). Obsessing/worrying about the overlap between obsessive-compulsive disorder and generalized anxiety disorder in youth. *Clinical Psychology Review, 24*(6), 663–683.

Comings, D. E., & Comings, B. G. (1988). Tourette's syndrome and attention deficit disorder. In D. J. Cohen, R. D. Bruun, & J. F. Leckman (Eds.), *Tourette's syndrome and tic disorders: Clinical understanding and treatment* (pp. 119–135). Oxford, England: Wiley.

Compas, B. E., & Oppedisano, G. (2000). Mixed anxiety/depression in childhood and adolescence. In A. J. Sameroff, M. Lewis, & S. M. Miller (Eds.), *Handbook of developmental psychopathology* (2nd ed., pp.531–548). New York: Kluwer Academic/Plenum Publishers.

Compas, B. E., Hinden, B. R., & Gerhardt, C. A. (1995). Adolescent development: Pathways and processes of risk and resilience. *Annual Review of Psychology, 46*, 265–293.

Compas, B. E., Malcarne, V. L., & Fondacaro, K. M. (1988). Coping with stressful events in older children and young adolescents. *Journal of Consulting and Clinical Psychology, 56*(3), 405–411.

Compas, B. W. (1987). Coping with stress during childhood and adolescence. *Psychological Bulletin, 101*(3), 393–403.

Compton, S. N., Burns, B. J., Egger, H. L., & Robertson, E. (2002). Review of the evidence base for treatment of childhood psychopathology: Internalizing disorders. *Journal of Consulting and Clinical Psychology, 70*(6), 1240–1266.

Conduct Problems Prevention Research Group. (1992). A developmental and clinical model for the prevention of conduct disorder: The FAST Track Program. *Development and Psychopathology, 4(4)*, 509–527.

Conduct Problems Prevention Research Group. (1999). Initial impact of the Fast Track Prevention Trial for Conduct Problems: II. Classroom effects. *Journal of Consulting and Clinical Psychology, 67*(5), 648–657.

Conduct Problems Prevention Research Group. (1999a). Initial impact of the FAST Track prevention trial for conduct problems: I. The high-risk sample. *Journal of Consulting and Clinical Psychology, 67(5),* 631–647.

Conduct Problems Prevention Research Group. (1999b). Initial impact of the FAST Track prevention trial for conduct problems: II. Classroom effects. *Journal of Consulting and Clinical Psychology, 67*(5), 648–657.

Conduct Problems Prevention Research Group. (2002). The implementation of the FAST Track Program: An example of a large-scale prevention science efficacy trial. *Journal of Abnormal Child Psychology, 30(1),* 1–17.

Conduct Problems Prevention Research Group. (2003). Initial impact of the Fast Track Prevention Trial for Conduct Problems: II. Classroom effects. In M. E. Hertzig & E. A. Farber (Eds.), *Annual progress in child psychiatry and child development: 2000–2001* (pp. 605–628). New York: Brunner-Routledge.

Conduct Problems Prevention Research Group. (2007). The Fast Track randomized controlled trial to prevent externalizing psy-chiatric disorders. *Journal of the American Academy of Child and Adolescent Psychiatry, 46,* 1250–1262.

Conger, R. D., & Rueter, M. A. (1996). Siblings, parents, and peers: A longitudinal study of social influences in adolescent risk for alcohol use and abuse. In G. H. Brody (Ed.), *Advances in applied developmental psychology: Vol. 10. Sibling relationships: Their causes and consequences* (pp. 1–30). Westport, CT: Ablex Publishing.

Connell, A. M., & Goodman, S. H. (2002). The association between psychopathology in fathers versus mothers and children's internalizing and externalizing behavior problems: A meta-analysis. *Psychological Bulletin, 128*(5), 746–773.

Conner, K. R., & Goldston, D. B. (2007). Rates of suicide among males increase steadily from age 11 to 21: Developmental framework and outline for prevention. *Aggression and Violent Behavior, 21*(2), 193–207.

Conner, K. R., Meldrum, S., Wieczorek, W. F., Duberstein, P. R., & Welte, J. W. (2004). The association of irritability and impulsivity with suicidal ideation among 15–20-year-old males. *Suicide and Life-Threatening Behavior, 34*(4), 363–373.

Connor, D. F., Fletcher, K. E., & Swanson, J. M. (1999). A meta-analysis of clonidine for symptoms of attention-deficit hyperactivity disorder. *Journal of the American Academy of Child and Adolescent Psychiatry, 38*, 1551–1559.

Consortium on the School-Based Promotion of Social Competence. (1994). The school-based promotion of social competence: Theory, research, practice and policy. In R. Haggerty, L. Sherrod, N. Garmezy, & M. Rutter (Eds.), *Stress, risk and resilience in children and adolescents: Processes, mechanisms and interventions* (pp. 268–316). New York: Cambridge University Press.

Constantino, M. J., Arnow, B. A., Blasey, C., & Agras, W. S. (2005). The association between patient characteristics and the therapeutic alliance in cognitive-behavioral and interpersonal therapy for bulimia nervosa. *Journal of Consulting and Clinical Psychology, 73,* 203–211.

Constantino, M. J., & Castonguay, L. G. (2003). Learning from the basics: Clinical implications of social, developmental, and cross-cultural study of the self. *Journal of Psychotherapy Integration, 13(1),* 3–8.

Conyers, C., Martin, T. L., Martin, G. L., & Yu, D. (2002). The 1983 AAMR manual, the 1992 AAMR manual, or the developmental disabilities act: Which do researchers use? *Education and Training in Mental Retardation and Developmental Disabilities, 37*(3), 310–316.

Cook, J. A., Heflinger, C. A., Hoven, C. W., Kelleher, K. J., Mulkern, V., Paulson, R. I., et al. (2004). A multi-site study of Medicaid-funded managed health care versus fee-for-service plans' effects on mental health service utilization of children with severe emotional disturbance. *Journal of Behavioral Health Services, 31(4),* 384–402.

Cooley, E., Toray, T., Wang, M. C., & Valdez, N. N. (2008). Maternal effects on daughters' eating pathology and body image. *Eating Behaviors, 9*(1), 52–61.

Coolidge, F. L., DenBoer, J. W., & Segal, D. L. (2004). Personality and neuropsychological correlates of bullying behavior. *Personality and Individual Differences, 36*(7), 1559–1569.

Coolidge, F. L., Thede, L. L., & Young, S. E. (2000). Heritability and the comorbidity of attention deficit hyperactivity disorder with behavioral disorders and executive function deficits: A preliminary investigation. *Developmental Neuropsychology, 17*(3), 273–287.

Cooper, M. J., Rose, K. S., & Turner, H. (2005). Core beliefs and the presence or absence of eating disorder symptoms and depressive symptoms in adolescent girls. *International Journal of Eating Disorders, 38*(1), 60–64.

Cooper, M. J., Rose, K. S., & Turner, H. (2006). The specific content of core beliefs and schema in adolescent girls high and low in eating disorder symptoms. *Eating Behaviors, 7*(1), 27–35.

Copel, J. A., & Bahado-Singh, R. O. (1999). Prenatal screening for Down's syndrome: A search for the family's values. *New England Journal of Medicine, 341*(7), 521–522.

Copeland, W. E., Keeler, G., Angold, A., & Costello, E. J. (2007). Traumatic events and posttraumatic stress in childhood. *Archives of General Psychiatry, 64*(5), 577–584.

Cornelius, J. R., Maisto, S. A., Pollock, N. K., Martin, C. S., Salloum, I. M., Lynch, K. G., et al. (2003). Rapid relapse generally follows treatment for substance use disorders among adolescents. *Addictive Behaviors, 28*(2), 381–386.

Corrigan, P. W. (2005). *On the stigma of mental illness: Practical strategies for research and social change.* Washington, DC: American Psychological Association.

Corrigan, P. W., Watson, A. C., & Barr, L. (2006). The self-stigma of mental illness: Implications for self-esteem and self-efficacy. *Journal of Social and Clinical Psychology, 25(8)*, 875–884.

Corrigan, P. W., Watson, A. C., Otey, E., Westbrook, A. L., Gardner, A. L., Lamb, T. A., et al. (2007). How do children stigmatize people with mental illness? *Journal of Applied Social Psychology, 37(7),* 1405–1417.

Costa, F. M., Jessor, R., Turbin, M. S., Dong, Q., Zhang, H., & Wang, C. (2005). The role of social contexts in adolescence: Context protection and risk in the United States and China. *Applied Developmental Science, 9*(2), 67–85.

Costello, E. J., & Angold, A. (1996). Developmental psychopathology. In R. B. Cairns, G. H. Elder., & E. J. Costello (Eds.), *Developmental science. Cambridge studies in social and emotional development* (pp. 168–189). New York: Cambridge University Press.

Costello, E. J., & Angold, A. (2000). Developmental psychology and public health: Past, present and future. *Development and Psychology, 12(4),* 599–618.

Costello, E. J., & Angold, A. (2001). Bad behaviour: An historical perspective on disorders of conduct. In J. Hill & B. Maughan (Eds.), *Conduct disorders in childhood and adolescence. Cambridge child and adolescent psychiatry* (pp. 1–31). New York: Cambridge University Press.

Costello, E. J., Angold, A., Burns, B. J., Stangl, D. K., Tweed, D. L., Erkanli, A., et al. (1996). The Great Smoky Mountains study of youth: Goals, design, methods, and the prevalence of DSM-III-R disorders. *Archives of General Psychiatry, 53(12),* 1129–1136.

Costello, E. J., Compton, S. N., Keeler, G., & Angold, A. (2003). Relationships between poverty and psychopathology: A natural experiment. *Journal of the American Medical Association, 290(15),* 2023–2029.

Costello, E. J., Egger, H. L., & Angold, A. (2005). The developmental epidemiology of anxiety disorders: Phenomenology, prevalence, and comorbidity. *Child and Adolescent Clinics of North America, 14*(4), 631–648.

Costello, E. J., Erkanli, A., & Angold, A. (2006). Is there an epidemic of child or adolescent depression? *Journal of Child Psychology and Psychiatry, 47*(12), 1263–1271.

Costello, E. J., Erkanli, A., Fairbank, J. A., & Angold, A. (2002). The prevalence of potentially traumatic events in childhood and adolescence. *Journal of Traumatic Stress, 15*(2), 99–112.

Costello, E. J., Erkanli, A., Federman, E., & Angold, A. (1999). Development of psychiatric comorbidity with substance abuse in adolescents: Effects of timing and sex. *Journal of Clinical Child Psychology, 28*(3), 298–311.

Costello, E. J., Mustillo, S., Erkanli, A., Keeler, G., & Angold, A. (2003). Prevalence and development of psychiatric disorders in childhood and adolescence. *Archives of General Psychiatry, 60(8),* 837–844.

Cote, S., Tremblay, R. E., Nagin, D. S., Zoccolillo, M., & Vitaro, F. (2002). Childhood behavioral profiles leading to adolescent conduct disorder: Risk trajectories for boys and girls. *Journal of the American Academy of Child and Adolescent Psychiatry, 41*(9), 1086–1094.

Cottrell, D. (2003). Outcome studies of family therapy in child and adolescent depression. *Journal of Family Therapy, 25*(4), 406–416.

Courchesne, E. (1997). Brainstem, cerebellar and limbic neuroanatomical abnormalities in autism. *Current Opinion in Neurobiology, 7,* 269–278.

Courchesne, E., & Pierce, K. (2005). Brain overgrowth in autism during a critical time in development: Implications for frontal pyramidal neuron and interneuron development and connectivity. *International Journal of Developmental Neuroscience, 23*(2–3), 153–170.

Courchesne, E., Karns, C. M., Davis, H. R., Ziccardi, R., Carper, R. A., Tigue, Z. D., et al. (2001). Unusual brain growth patterns in early life in patients with autistic disorder: An MRI study. *Neurology, 57*(2), 245–254.

Courchesne, E., Mueller, R-A., & Saitoh, O. (1999). Brain weight in autism: Normal in the majority of cases, megalencephalic in rare cases. *Neurology, 52,* 1057–1059.

Courchesne, E., Redclay, E., Morgan, J. T., & Kennedy, D. P. (2005). Autism at the beginning: Microstructural and growth abnormalities underlying the cognitive and affective neuroscience and developmental psychopathology. *Development and Psychopathology, 17*(3), 577–597.

Courchesne, E., Townsend, J., & Chase, C. (1995). Neurodevelopmental principles guide research on developmental psychopathologies. In D. Cicchetti & D. J. Cohen (Eds.), *Developmental psychopathology: Vol. 1. Theory and methods* (pp. 195–226). Oxford, England: Wiley.

Courchesne, E., Yeung-Courchesne, R., & Pierce, K. (1999). Biological and behavioral heterogeneity in autism: Roles of pleiotropy and epigenesis. In S. H. Broman & J. M. Fletcher (Eds.), *The changing nervous system: Neurobehavioral consequences of early brain disorders* (pp. 292–338). London: Oxford University Press.

Couturier, J. & Lock, J. (2006). What is remission in adolescent anorexia nervosa? A review of various conceptualizations and quantitative analysis. *International Journal of Eating Disorders, 39,* 175–183.

Cowan, P. A., & Cowan, C. P. (2003). Normative family transitions, normal family processes, and healthy development. In F. Walsh (Ed.), *Normal Family Processes: Growing Diversity and Complexity* (3rd ed.). New York: Guilford Press.

Cowen, E. L. (1994). The enhancement of psychological wellness: Challenges and opportunities. *American Journal of Community Psychology, 22*(2), 149–179.

Cowen, E. L. (1996). The ontogenesis of primary prevention: Lengthy strides and stubbed toes. *American Journal of Community Psychology, 24(2),* 235–249.

Cowen, E. L., & Durlak, J. A. (2000). Social policy and prevention in mental health. *Development and Psychopathology, 12(4),* 815–834.

Cowen, E. L., Work, W. C., & Wyman, P. A. (1997). The Rochester child resilience project (RCRP): Facts found, lessons learned, future directions divined. In S. S. Luthar & J. E. Burack (Eds.), *Developmental psychopathology: Perspectives on adjustment, risk, and disorder* (pp. 527–547). New York: Cambridge University Press.

Cox, A., Klein, K. Charman, T., Baird, G., Baron-Cohen, S., Swettenham, J., Drew, A., & Wheelwright, S. (1999). Autism spectrum disorders at 20 and 42 months of age: Stability of clinical and ADI-R diagnosis. *Journal of Child Psychology and Psychiatry and Allied Disciplines, 40,* 719–732.

Coy, K., Speltz, M. L., DeKlyen, M., & Jones, K. (2001). Social-cognitive processes in preschool boys with and without oppositional defiant disorder. *Journal of Abnormal Child Psychology, 29,* 107–119.

Coyle, J. T., Pine, D. S., Charney, D. S., Lewis, L., Nemeroff, C. B., Carlson, G. A., et al. (2003). Depression and bipolar support alliance consensus statement on the unmet needs in diagnosis and treatment of mood disorders in children and adolescents. *Journal of the American Academy of Child and Adolescent Psychiatry, 42*(12), 1494–1503.

Craig, J., & Baron-Cohen, S. (1999). Creativity and imagination in autism and Asperger syndrome. *Journal of Autism and Developmental Disorders, 29,* 319–326.

Craig, J., & Baron-Cohen, S. (2000). Story-telling ability in children with autism or Asperger syndrome: A window into the imagination. *Israel Journal of Psychiatry and Related Sciences, 37,* 64–70.

Craig, J., Baron-Cohen, S., & Scott, F. (2001). Drawing ability in autism: A window into the imagination. *Israel Journal of Psychiatry and Related Sciences, 38,* 242–253.

Craney, J. L., & Geller, B. (2003a). A prepubertal and early adolescent bipolar disorder-I phenotype: Review of phenomenology and longitudinal course. *Bipolar Disorders, 5*(4), 243–256.

Craney, J. L., & Geller, B. (2003b). Clinical implications of antidepressant and stimulant use on switching from depression to mania in children. *Journal of Child and Adolescent Psychopharmacology, 13*(2), 201–204.

Craske, M. G. (1997). Fear and anxiety in children and adolescents. *Bulletin of the Menninger Clinic, 61*(2, Suppl. A), A4-A36.

Craske, M. G., Poulton, R., Tsao, J. C. I., & Plotkin, D. (2001). Paths to panic disorder/agoraphobia: An exploratory analysis from age 3 to 21 in an unselected birth cohort. *Journal of the American Academy of Child and Adolescent Psychiatry, 40*(5), 556–563.

Craske, M. G., & Zucker, B. G. (2001). Prevention of anxiety disorders: A model for intervention. *Applied and Preventive Psychology, 10*(3), 155–175.

Crawford, A. M., & Manassis, K. (2001). Familial predictors of treatment outcome in childhood anxiety disorders. *Journal of the American Academy of Child and Adolescent Psychiatry, 40*(10), 1182–1189.

Crawford, A. M., Pentz, M. A., Chou, C-P., Li, C., & Dwyer, J. H. (2003). Parallel developmental trajectories of sensation seeking and regular substance use in adolescents. *Psychology of Addictive Behaviors, 17*(3), 179–192.

Crick, N. R., & Dodge, K. A. (1994). A review and reformulation of social information processing mechanisms in children's social adjustment. *Psychological Bulletin, 115,* 74–101.

Crick, N. R., & Dodge, K. A. (1996). Social information-processing mechanisms in reactive and proactive aggression. *Child Development, 67,* 993–1002.

Crick, N. R., & Grotpeter, J. K. (1995). Relational aggression, gender, and social-psychological adjustment. *Child Development, 66*(3), 710–722.

Crick, N. R., & Rose, A. J. (2000). Toward a gender-balanced approach to the study of social-emotional development: A look at relational aggression. In P. H. Miller & E. Kofsky Scholnick (Eds.), *Toward a feminist developmental psychology* (pp. 153–168). Florence, KY: Taylor and Frances/Routledge.

Crick, N. R., Casas, J. F., & Nelson, D. A. (2002). Toward a more comprehensive understanding of peer maltreatment: Studies of relational victimization. *Current Directions in Psychological Science, 11*(3), 98–101.

Crick, N. R., Grotpeter, J. K., & Bigbee, M. A. (2002). Relationally and physically aggressive children's intent attributions and feelings of distress for relational and instrumental peer provocations. *Child Development, 73(4),* 1134–1142.

Crick, N. R. & Zahn-Waxler, C. (2003). The development of psychopathology in females and males: Current progress and future challenges. *Development and Psychopathology, 15,* 719–742.

Crijen, A. A. M., Achenbach, T. M., & Verhulst, F. C. (1997). Comparisons of problems reported by parents of children in 12 cultures: Total problems, externalizing and internalizing. *Journal of the American Academy of Child and Adolescent Psychiatry, 36*(9), 1269–1277.

Crisp, A., Cowan, L., & Hart, D. (2004). The college's anti-stigma campaign, 1998–2003: A shortened version of the concluding report. *Psychiatric Bulletin, 28,* 133–136.

Criss, M. M., Pettit, G. S., Bates, J. E., Dodge, K. A., & Lapp, A. L. (2002). Family adversity, positive peer relationships, and children's externalizing behavior: A longitudinal perspective on risk and resilience. *Child Development, 73*(4), 1220–1237.

Crittenden, P. M. (1992). Children's strategies for coping with adverse home environments: An interpretation using attachment theory. *Child Abuse and Neglect, 16*(3), 329–343.

Crittenden, P. M. (1995). Attachment and psychopathology. In S. Goldberg, R. Muir, & J. Kerr (Eds.), *Attachment theory: Social, developmental, and clinical perspectives* (pp. 367–406). Hillsdale, NJ: Erlbaum.

Crnic, K. A., Gaze, C., & Hoffman, C. (2005). Cumulative parenting stress across the preschool period: Relations to maternal parenting and child behavior at age 5. Infant and *Child Development, 14*(2), 117–132.

Crnic, K. A., Greenberg, M. T., & Slough, N. M. (1986). Early stress and social support influences on mothers' and high-risk infants' functioning in late infancy. *Infant Mental Health Journal, 7*(1), 19–33.

Crnic, K. A., Friedrich, W. N., & Greenberg, M. T. (1983). Adaptation of families with mentally retarded children: A model of stress, coping, and family ecology. *American Journal of Mental Deficiency, 88*(2), 125–138.

Crockenberg, S. B. (1986). Are temperamental differences in babies associated with predictable differences in caregiving? *New Directions in Child Development, 31,* 53–73.

Crockenberg, S., & Leerkes, E. (2000). Infant social and emotional development in family context. In C. H. Zeanah (Ed.), *Handbook of infant mental health* (2nd ed., pp. 60–90). New York: Guilford Press.

Crockett, L. J. (1997). Cultural, historical, and subcultural contexts of adolescence: Implications for health and development. In J. Schulenberg, J. L. Maggs, & K. Hurrelmann (Eds.), *Health risks and developmental transitions during adolescence* (pp. 23–53). New York: Cambridge University Press.

Croen, L. A., Grether, J. K., Hoogstrate, J., & Selvin, S. (2002). The changing prevalence of autism in California. *Journal of Autism and Developmental Disorders, 32(3),* 207–215.

Croen, L. A., Grether, J. K., & Selvin, S. (2002). Descriptive epidemiology of autism in a California population: Who is at risk? *Journal of Autism and Developmental Disorders, 32*(3), 217–224.

Croll, J. K., Neumark-Sztainer, D., Story, M., & Ireland, M. (2002). Prevalence and risk and protective factors related to disordered eating behaviors among adolescents: Relationship to gender and ethnicity. *Journal of Adolescent Health, 31,* 166–175.

Crowell, J. A., Fraley, R. C., & Shaver, P. R. (1999). Measurement of individual differences in adolescent and adult attachment. In J. Cassidy & P. R. Shaver (Eds.), *Handbook of attachment: Theory, research, and clinical applications* (pp. 434–465). New York: Guilford Press.

Crowley, T. J., Mikulich, S. K., Ehlers, K. M., Whitmore, E. A., & Macdonald, M. J. (2001). Validity of structured clinical evaluations in adolescents with conduct and substance problems. *Journal of the American Academy of Child and Adolescent Psychiatry, 40*(3), 265–273.

Crozier, W. R., & Alden, L. E. (2001). The social nature of social anxiety. In W. R. Crozier & L. E. Alden (Eds.), *International handbook of social anxiety: Concepts, research and interventions relating to the self and shyness* (pp. 1–20). New York: Wiley.

Crystal, D. S., Watanabe, H., Weinfurt, K., & Wu, C. (1998). Concepts of human differences: A comparison of American, Japanese, and Chinese children and adolescents. *Developmental Psychology, 34*(4), 714–722.

Csikszentmihalyi, M., & Rathunde, K. (1998). The development of the person: An experiential perspective on the ontogenesis of psychological complexity. In W. Damon & R. M. Lerner (Eds.), *Handbook of Child Psychology: Vol. 1. Theoretical Models of Human Development* (5th ed., pp. 635–684). Hoboken, NJ: Wiley.

Cuellar, A. E., Markowitz, S., & Libby, A. M. (2004). Mental health and substance abuse treatment and juvenile crime. *Journal of Mental Health Policy and Economics, 7*(2), 59–68.

Cullen, D. (2004, April 20). The depressive and the psychopath. *Slate*, Article 2099203. Retrieved July 13, 2009, from http://www.slate.com/id/2099203

Cummings, E. M. (1999). Some considerations on integrating psychology and health from a life-span perspective. In T. L. Whitman, T. V. Merluzzi, & R. D. White (Eds.), *Life-span perspectives on health and illness* (pp. 277–294). Mahwah, NJ: Erlbaum.

Cummings, E. M., & Cicchetti, D. (1990). Toward a transactional model of relations between attachment and depression. In M. T. Greenberg, D. Cicchetti, & E. M. Cummings (Eds.), *Attachment in the preschool years: Theory, research, and intervention* (pp. 339–372). Chicago: University of Chicago Press.

Cummings, E. M., & Davies, P. (1994). *Children and marital conflict: The impact of family dispute and resolution, Guilford series on social and emotional development.* New York: Guilford Press.

Cummings, E. M., & Davies, P. T. (1994). Maternal depression and child development. *Journal of Child Psychology and Psychiatry, 35,* 73–112.

Cummings, E. M., & Davies, P. T. (1995). The impact of parents on their children: An emotional security hypothesis. *Annals of Child Development, 10,* 167–208.

Cummings, E. M., & Davies, P. T. (1996). Emotional security as a regulatory process in normal development and the development of psychopathology. *Development and Psychopathology, 8,* 123–139.

Cummings, E. M., Davies, P. T., & Campbell, S. B. (2000). *Developmental psychopathology and family process: Theory, research, and clinical implications.* New York: Guilford Press.

Cummins, T. K., & Ninan, P. T. (2002). The neurobiology of anxiety in children and adolescents. *International Review of Psychiatry, 14*(2), 114–128.

Curran, P. J., Stice, E. M., & Chassin, L. (1997). The relation between adolescent alcohol use and peer alcohol use: A longitudinal random coefficients model. *Journal of Consulting and Clinical Psychology, 65,* 130–140.

Curry, J., Rohde, P., Simons, A., Silva, S., Vitiello, B., Kratochvil, C., et al. (2006). Predictors and moderators of acute outcome in the Treatment for Adolescents with Depression Study (TADS). *Journal of the American Academy of Child and Adolescent Psychiatry, 45*(12), 1427–1439.

D'Amico, E. J., Ellickson, P. L., Collins, R. L., Martino, S., & Klein, D. J. (2005). Processes linking adolescent problems to substance-use problems in late young adulthood. *Journal of Studies on Alcohol, 66*(6), 766–775.

D'Eramo, K. S., Prinstein, M. J., Freeman, J. Grapentine, W. L., & Spirito, A. (2004). Psychiatric diagnoses and comorbidity in relation to suicidal behavior among psychiatrically hospitalized adolescents. *Child Psychiatry and Human Development, 35*(1), 21–35.

Daddis, D., & Smetana, J. (2005). Middle-class African American families' expectations for adolescents' behavioural autonomy. *International Journal of Behavioral Development, 29*(5), 371–381.

Dadds, M. R. (2002). Learning and intimacy in the families of anxious children. In R. J. McMahon & R. Peters (Eds.) *The effects of parental dysfunction on children* (pp. 87–104). New York: Kluwer Academic/Plenum Publishers.

Dadds, M. R., & Barrett, P. M. (2001). Psychological management of anxiety disorders in childhood. *Journal of Child Psychology and Psychiatry and Allied Disciplines, 42*(8), 999–1011.

Dahl, R. E. (1996). The regulation of sleep and arousal: Development and psychopathology. *Development and Psychopathology, 8,* 3–27.

Dahl, R. E. (2004). Adolescent brain development: A period of vulnerabilities and opportunities. In R. E. Dahl & L. P. Spear (Eds.), *Adolescent brain development: Vulnerabilities and opportunities. Annals of the New York Academy of Sciences* (Vol. 1021, pp. 1–22). New York: New York Academy of Sciences.

Dahl, R. E., Birmaher, B., Williamson, D. E., Dorn, L., Perel, J., Kaufman, J., et al. (2000). Low growth hormone response to growth hormone–releasing hormone in child depression. *Biological Psychiatry, 48*(10), 981–988.

Dahl, R. E., & Lewin, D. S. (2002). Pathways to adolescent health: Sleep regulation and behavior. *Journal of Adolescent Health, 31*(6), 175–184.

Dale, K. L., & Baumeister, R. F. (1999). Self-regulation and psychopathology. In Robin M. Kowalski & M. R. Leary (Eds.), *The social psychology of emotional and behavioral problems: Interfaces of social and clinical psychology* (pp. 139–166). Washington, DC: American Psychological Association.

Dales, L., Hammer, S. J., & Smith, N. J. (2001). Time trends in autism and in MMR immunization coverage in California. *JAMA, 285*, 1183–1185.

Dammann, O., & Leviton, A. (1997). The role of perinatal brain damage in developmental disabilities: An epidemiologic perspective. *Mental Retardation and Developmental Disabilities Research Reviews, 3*(1), 12–21.

Damon, W., & Lerner, R. M. (1998). *Handbook of Child Psychology: Vol. 1. Theoretical Models of Human Development* (5th ed., pp. 635–684). Hoboken, NJ: Wiley.

Dancyger, I., Fornari, V., Scionti, L., Wisotsky, W., & Sunday, S. (2005). Do daughters with eating disorders agree with their parents' perception of family functioning? *Comprehensive Psychology, 46*, 135–139.

Dancyger, I., Fornari, V., & Sunday, S. (2006). What may underlie differing perceptions of family functioning between mothers and their adolescent daughters with eating disorders? *International Journal of Adolescent Medicine and Health, 18*, 281–286.

Danielson, C. K., de Arellano, M. A., Kilpatrick, D. G., Saunders, B. E., & Resnick, H. S. (2005). Child maltreatment in depressed adolescents: Differences in symptomology based on history of abuse. *Child Maltreatment, 10*, 37–48.

Danielson, C. K., Feeny, N. C., Findling, R. L., & Youngstrom, E. A. (2004). Psychosocial treatment of bipolar disorders in adolescence: A proposed cognitive-behavioral intervention. *Cognitive and Behavioral Practice, 11*(3), 283–297.

Das, J. P. (2004). Theories of intelligence: Issues and applications. In G. Goldstein, S. Beers, & M. Hersen (Eds.), *Comprehensive handbook of psychological assessment: Vol. 1. Intellectual and neurophysical assessment* (pp. 5–23). Hoboken, NJ: Wiley.

Dasinger, L. K., Shane, P. A., & Martinovich, Z. (2004). Assessing the effectiveness of community-based substance abuse treatment for adolescents. *Journal of Psychoactive Drugs, 36*(1), 27–33.

Davanzo, P., Yue, K., Thomas, M. A., Belin, T., Mintz, J., Venkatraman, T. N., et al. (2003). Proton magnetic resonance spectroscopy of bipolar disorder versus intermittent explosive disorder in children and adolescents. *American Journal of Psychiatry, 160*(8), 1442–1452.

Davidson, R. J. (1994). Asymmetric brain function, affective style, and psychopathology: The role of early experience and plasticity. *Development and Psychopathology, 6*, 741–758.

Davidson, R. J. (1998). Affective style and affective disorders: Perspectives from affective neuroscience. *Cognition and Emotion, 12*(3), 307–330.

Davidson, R. J. (2000). Affective style, psychopathology, and resilience: Brain mechanisms and plasticity. *American Psychologist, 55*(11), 1196–1214.

Davidson, R. J. (2000). Cognitive neuroscience needs affective neuroscience (and vice versa). *Brain and Cognition, 42*, 89–92.

Davidson, R. J., Abercrombie, H., Nitschke, J. B., & Putnam, K. (1999). Regional brain function, emotion and disorder of emotion. *Current Opinion in Neurobiology, 9*(2), 228–234.

Davidson, R. J., Jackson, D. C., & Kalin, N. H. (2000). Emotion, plasticity, context, and regulation: Perspectives from affective neuroscience. *Psychological Bulletin, 126(6),* 890–909.

Davidson, R. J., Pizzagalli, D., Nitschke, J. B., & Putnam, K. (2002). Depression: Perspectives from affective neuroscience. *Annual Reviews of Psychology, 53*, 545–574.

Davidson, R. J., Putnam, K. M., & Larson, C. L. (2000). Dysfunction in the neural circuitry of emotion regulation – a possible prelude to violence. *Science, 289(5479),* 591–594.

Davidson, R. J., & Rickman, M. (1999). Behavioral inhibition and the emotional circuitry of the brain: Stability and plasticity during the early childhood years. In L. A. Schmidt & J. Schulkin (Eds.), *Extreme fear, shyness, and social phobia: Origins, biological mechanisms, and clinical outcomes* (pp. 67–87). London: Oxford University Press.

Davidson, R. J., & Sutton, S. K. (1995). Affective neuroscience: the emergence of a discipline. *Current Opinion in Nuerobiology, 5,* 217–224.

Davies, P. T., Winter, M. A., & Cicchetti, D. (2006). The implications of emotional security theory for understanding and treating childhood psychopathology. *Development and Psychopathology, 18*, 707–735.

Davies, S. (2004). A group-work approach to addressing friendship issues in the treatment of adolescents with eating disorders. *Clinical Child Psychology and Psychiatry, 9*(4), 519–531.

Davis, B., Sheeber, L., & Hops, H. (2002). Coercive family processes and adolescent depression. In J. B. Reid, G. R. Patterson, & J. Snyder (Eds.), *Antisocial behavior in children and adolescents: A developmental analysis and model for intervention* (pp. 173–192). Washington, DC: American Psychological Association.

Davis, C., Katzman, D. K., Kaptein, S., Kirsch, C., Brewer, H., Kalmbach, K., et al. (1997). The prevalence of high-level exercise in the eating disorders: Etiological implications. *Comprehensive Psychiatry, 38*, 321–326.

Davis, E. P., Bruce, J., & Gunnar, M. R. (2002). The anterior attention network: Associations with temperament and neuroendocrine activity in 6-year-old children. *Developmental Psychobiology, 40*, 43–56.

Davison, T., & McCabe, M. P. (2006). Adolescent body image and psychosocial functioning. *Journal of Social Psychology, 146,* 15–30.

Dawes, M. A., Antelman, S. M., Vanyukov, M. M., Giancola, P., Tarter, R. E., Susman, E. J., et al. (2000). Developmental sources of variation in liability to adolescent substance use disorders. *Drug and Alcohol Dependence, 61*(1), 3–14.

Dawes, M. A., & Johnson, B. A. (2004). Pharmacotherapeutic trials in adolescent alcohol use disorders: Opportunities and challenges. *Alcohol and Alcoholism, 39*(3), 166–177.

Dawson, D. A., & Grant, B. F. (1998). Family history of alcoholism and gender: Their combined effects on DSM-IV alcohol dependence and major depression. *Journal of Studies on Alcohol, 59*(1), 97–106.

Dawson, D. A., Grant, B. F., Stinson, F. S., & Chou, P. S. (2006). Maturing out of alcohol dependence: The impact of transitional life events. *Journal of Studies on Alcohol: 67*(2), 195–203.

Dawson, G., & Ashman, S. B. (2000). On the origins of a vulnerability to depression: The influence of the early social environment on the development of psychobiological systems related to the risk of affective disorder. In C. A. Nelson (Ed.), *The effects of early adversity on neurobehavioral development, The Min-*

nesota symposium on child psychology (Vol. 31, pp. 245–279). Mahwah, NJ: Erlbaum.

Dawson, G., Ashman, S. B., & Carver, L. J. (2000). The role of early experience in shaping behavioral and brain development and its implications for social policy. *Development and Psychopathology, 12*, 695–712.

Dawson, G., Ashman, S. B., Panagiotides, H., Hessl, D., Self, J., Yamada, E., et al. (2003). Preschool outcomes of children of depressed mothers: Role of maternal behavior, contextual risk, and children's brain activity. *Child Development, 74*(4), 1158–1175.

Dawson, G., Carver, L., Meltzoff, A. N., Panagiotides, H., McPartland, J. & Webb, S. J. (2002). Neural correlates of face and object recognition in young children with autism spectrum disorder, developmental delay and typical development. *Child Development, 73*(3), 700–717.

Dawson, G., Frey, K., Self, J., Panagiotides, H., Hessl, D., Yamada, E., & Rinaldi, J. (1999). Frontal brain electrical activity in infants of depressed and nondepressed mothers: Relation to variations in infant behavior. *Development and Psychopathology, 11*(3), 589–605.

Dawson, G., Klinger, L. G., Panagiotides, H., & Lewy, A. (1995). Subgroups of autistic children based on social behavior display distinct patterns of brain activity. *Journal of Abnormal Child Psychology, 23*, 569–583.

Dawson, G., Meltzoff, A. N., Osterling, J., & Rinaldi, J. (1998). Neuropsychological correlates of early symptoms of autism. *Child Development, 69*, 1276–1285.

Dawson, G., Meltzoff, A. N., Osterling, J., Rinaldi, J., & Brown, E. (1998). Children with autism fail to orient to naturally occurring social stimuli. *Journal of Autism and Developmental Disorders, 28*, 479–485.

Dawson, G., Munson, J., Estes, A., Osterling, J., McPartland, J., Toth, K., et al. (2002). Neurocognitive function and joint attention ability in young children with autism spectrum disorder versus developmental delay. *Child Development, 73*, 345–358.

Dawson, G., Toth, K., Abbott, R., Osterling, J., Munson, J., Estes, A., et al. (2004). Early social attention impairments in autism: Social orienting, joint attention, and attention to distress. *Developmental Psychology, 40*(2), 271–283.

Dawson, G., Webb, S. J., & McPartland, J. (2005). Understanding the nature of face processing impairment in autism: Insights from behavioral and electrophysiological studies. *Developmental Neuropsychology, 27*(3), 403–424.

Dawson, G., Webb, S. J., Wijsman, E., Schellenberg, G., Estes, A., Munson, J., et al. (2005) Neurocognitive and electrophysiological evidence of altered face processing in parents of children with autism: Implications for a model of abnormal development of social brain circuitry in autism. *Development and Psychopathology, 17*(3), 679–697.

Day, K., & Dosen, A. (2001). Treatment: An integrative approach. In A. Dosen & K. Day (Eds.), *Treating mental illness and behavior disorders in children and adults with mental retardation* (pp. 519–528). Washington, DC: American Psychiatric Publishing.

De Bellis, M. D. (2002). Developmental traumatology: A contributory mechanism for alcohol and substance use disorders. *Psychoneuroendocrinology, 27*, 155–170.

de Bildt, A., Sytema, S., Ketelaars, C., Kraijer, D., Volkmar, F & Mideraa, R. (2003). Measuring pervasive developmental disorders in children and adolescents with mental retardation: A comparison of two screening instruments used in a study of the total mentally retarded population from a designated area. *Journal of Autism and Developmental Disorders, 33*(6), 595–605.

De Los Reyes, A. & Kazdin, A. E. (2005). Informant discrepancies in the assessment of childhood psychopathology: A critical review, theoretical framework, and recommendations for further study. *Psychological Bulletin, 131*(4), 483–509.

De Wolff, M. S., & Van IJzendoorn, M. H. (1997). Sensitivity and attachment: A meta-analysis on parental antecedents of infant attachment. *Child Development, 68*(4), 571–591.

DeAngelis, T. (2007). A new diagnosis for childhood trauma. *Monitor on Psychology, 38*, 32–34.

Deas, D., & Thomas, S. E. (2001). An overview of controlled studies of adolescent substance abuse treatment. *American Journal on Addictions, 10*(2), 178–189.

Deas, D., Roberts, J. S., & Grindlinger, D. (2005). The utility of DSM-IV criteria in diagnosing substance abuse/dependence in adolescents. *Journal of Substance Use, 10*(1), 10–21.

Deas, D., St. Germaine, K., & Upadhyaya, H. (2006). Psychopathology in substance abusing adolescents: Gender comparisons. *Journal of Substance Use, 11*(1), 45–51.

Deas-Nesmith, D., Brady, K. T., Campbell, S. (1998). Comorbid substance use and anxiety disorders in adolescents. *Journal of Psychopathology and Behavioral Assessment, 20*, 139–148.

Deater-Deckard, K. (2000). Parenting and child behavioral adjustment in early childhood: A quantitative genetic approach to studying family processes. *Child Development, 71*, 468–484.

Deater-Deckard, K. Pike, A., Petrill, S. A., Cutting, A. L., Hughes, C., & O'Connor, T. G. (2001). Nonshared environmental processes in social-emotional development: An observational study of identical twin differences in the preschool period. *Developmental Science, 4*, F1-F6.

Deater-Deckard, K., & Dodge, K. A. (1997). Externalizing behavior problems and discipline revisited: Nonlinear effects and variation by culture, context, and gender. *Psychological Inquiry, 8*, 161–175.

Deater-Deckard, K., & Plomin, R. (1999). An adoption study of etiology of teacher and parent reports of externalizing behavior problems in middle childhood. *Child Development, 70*, 144–154.

Deater-Deckard, K., Dodge, K. A., Bates, J. E., & Pettit, G. S. (1998). Multiple risk factors in the development of externalizing behavior problems: Group and individual differences. *Development and Psychopathology, 10*, 469–493.

Deater-Deckard, K., Dunn, J., & Lussier, G. (2002). Sibling relationships and social-emotional adjustment in different family contexts. *Social Development, 11*(4), 571–590.

DeBellis, M. D. (2002). Developmental traumatology: A contributory mechanism for alcohol and substance use disorders. *Psychoneuroendocrinology, 27*(1–2), 155–170.

DeBellis, M. D., Keshavan, M. S., Beers, S. R., Hall, J., Frustaci, K., Masalehdan, A., et al. (2001). Sex differences in brain maturation during childhood and adolescence. *Cerebral Cortex, 11*(7), 552–557.

DeGangi, G. A., Breinbauer, C., Doussard Roosevelt, J., Porges, S., & Greenspan, S. (2000). Prediction of childhood problems at three years in children experiencing disorders of regulation during infancy. *Infant Mental Health Journal, 21*(3), 156–175.

DeGangi, G. A., DiPietro, J. A., Greenspan, S. I., & Porges, S. W. (1991). Psychophysiological characteristics of the regulatory disordered infant. *Infant Behavior and Development, 14*(1), 37–50.

DeGangi, G. A., Porges, S. W., Sickel, R. Z., & Greenspan, S. I. (1993). Four-year follow-up of a sample of regulatory disordered infants. *Infant Mental Health Journal, 14*(4), 330–343.

DeGangi, G., Poisson, S., Sickel, R., & Weiner, A. (1998). *Infant-Toddler Symptom Checklist.* San Antonio, TX: Psychological Corporation.

DeJong, W., Schneider, S. K., Towvim, L. G., Murphy, M. J., Doerr, E. E., Simonson, N. R., et al. (2006). A multisite randomized trial of social norms marketing campaigns to reduce college student drinking. *Journal of Studies on Alcohol, 67*(6), 868–879.

Dekker, A. H., Estroff, T. W., & Hoffmann, N. G. (2001). Medical evaluation of substance-abusing adolescents. In Estroff, T. W. (Ed.), *Manual of adolescent substance abuse treatment* (pp. 91–98). Washington, DC: American Psychiatric Publishing.

DeKlyen, M. (1996). Disruptive behavior disorder and intergenerational attachment patterns: A comparison of clinic-referred and normally functioning preschoolers and their mothers. *Journal of Consulting and Clinical Psychology, 64*(2), 357–365.

DeKlyen, M., Biernbaum, M. A., Speltz, M. L., & Greenberg, M. T. (1998). Fathers and preschool behavior problems. *Developmental Psychology, 34,* 264–275.

DeKlyen, M., Speltz, M. L., & Greenberg, M. T. (1998). Fathering and early onset conduct problems: Positive and negative parenting, father-son attachment, and the marital context. *Clinical Child and Family Psychology Review, 1,* 3–21.

Dekovic, M., Engels, R. C. M. E., Shirai, T., De Kort, G., & Anker, A. L. (2002). The role of peer relations in adolescent development in two cultures: The Netherlands and Japan. *Journal of Cross-Cultural Psychology, 33*(6), 577–595.

DelBello, M. P., Zimmerman, M. E., Mills, N. P., Getz, G. E., & Strakowski, S. M. (2004). Magnetic resonance imaging analysis of amygdala and other subcortical brain regions in adolescents with bipolar disorder. *Bipolar Disorders, 6*(1), 43–52.

DelBello, M. P., Adler, C. M., & Strakowski, S. M. (2006). The neurophysiology of childhood and adolescent bipolar disorder. *CNS Spectrums, 11*(4), 298–311.

DelBello, M. P., Hanseman, D., Adler, C. M., Fleck, D. E., & Strakowski, S. M. (2007). Twelve-month outcome of adolescents with bipolar disorder following first hospitalization for a manic or mixed episode. *American Journal of Psychiatry, 164*(4), 582–590.

Delligatti, N., Akin-Little, A., & Little, S. G. (2003). Conduct disorder in girls: Diagnostic and intervention issues. *Psychology in the Schools, 40*(2), 183–192.

Delva, J., Wallace, J. M., Jr., O'Malley, P. M., Bachman, J. G., Johnston, L. D., & Schulenberg, J. E. (2005). The epidemiology of alcohol, marijuana, and cocaine use among Mexican American, Puerto Rican, Cuban American, and other Latin American eighth-grade students in the United States: 1991–2002. *American Journal of Public Health, 95*(4), 696–702.

Demaray, M. K., Schaefer, K., & Delong, L. K. (2003). Attention-deficit/hyperactivity disorder (ADHD): A national survey of training and current assessment practices in the schools. *Psychology in the Schools, 40*(6), 583–597.

Demb, H. B. & Noskin, O. (2001). The use of the term Multiple Complex Developmental Disorder in a diagnostic clinic serving young children with developmental disabilities: A report of 15 cases. *Mental Health Aspects of Developmental Disabilities, 4,* 4960.

Demetrious, A., & Raftopoulos, A. (1999). Modeling the developmental mind: From structure to change. *Developmental Review, 19(3),* 319–368.

Demir, M., & Urberg, K. A. (2004). Friendship and adjustment among adolescents. *Journal of Experimental Child Psychology, 88*(1), 68–82.

DeMulder, E. K., & Radke-Yarrow, M. (1991). Attachment with affectively ill and well mothers: Concurrent behavioral correlates. *Development and Psychopathology, 3,* 227–242.

Denda, K., Sunami, T., Inoue, S., Sasaki, F., Sasaki, Y., Asakura, S., et al. (2002). Clinical study of early-onset eating disorders. *Japanese Journal of Child and Adolescent Psychiatry, 43,* 30–56.

Denham, S. A. (1998). *Emotional development in young children.* New York: Guilford Press.

Denham, S. A., Workman, E., Cole, P. M., Weissbrod, C., Kendziora, K. T., & Zahn-Waxler, C. (2000). Prediction of externalizing behavior problems from early to middle childhood: The role of parental socialization and emotion expression. *Development and Psychopathology, 12*(1), 23–45.

Denning, C. B., Chamberlain, J. A., & Polloway, E. A. (2000). An evaluation of state guidelines for mental retardation: Focus of definition and classification practices. *Education and Training in Mental Retardation and Developmental Disabilities, 35*(2), 226–232.

Dennis, M. (2000). Developmental plasticity in children: The role of biological risk, development, time, and reserve. *Journal of Communication Disorders, 3(4),* 321–332.

Depue, R. A., & Morrone-Strupinsky, J. V. (2005). A neurobehavioral model of affiliative bonding: Implications for conceptualizing a human trait of affiliation. *Behavioral and Brain Sciences, 28*(3), 313–395.

Depue, R. A., Collins, P. F., & Luciana, M. (1996). A model of neurobiology – Environment interaction in developmental psychopathology. *Frontiers of developmental psychopathology* (pp. 44–77). New York: Oxford University Press.

Derenne, J. L., & Beresin, E. V. (2006). Body image, media and eating disorders. *Academic Psychiatry, 30,* 257–261.

Derks, E. M., Dolan, C. V., Hudziak, J. J., Neale, M. C., & Boomsma, D. I. (2007). Assessment and etiology of attention deficit hyperactivity disorder and oppositional defiant disorder in boys and girls. *Behavior Genetics, 37*(4), 559–566.

DeRoma, V. M., Lassiter, K. S., & Davis, V. A. (2004). Adolescent involvement in discipline decision making. *Behavior Modification, 28*(3), 420–437.

DeRosier, M. E., & Marcus, S. R. (2005). Building friendships and combating bullying: Effectiveness of S. S. GRIN at one-year follow-up. *Journal of Clinical Child and Adolescent Psychology, 34*(1), 140–150.

Derryberry, D., & Rothbart, M. K. (1997). Reactive and effortful processes in the organization of temperament. *Development and Psychopathology, 9,* 633–652.

Derzon, J. H., Sale, E., Springer, J. F., & Brounstein, P. (2005). Estimating intervention effectiveness: Synthetic projection of field evaluation results. *Journal of Primary Prevention, 26*(4), 321–343.

Desai, R. A., Maciejewski, P. K., Pantalon, M. V., & Potenza, M. N. (2005). Gender differences in adolescent gambling. *Annals of Clinical Psychiatry, 17*(4), 249–258.

Desantis, A., Coster, W., Bigsby, R., & Lester, B. (2004). Colic and fussing in infancy, and sensory processing at 3 to 8 years of age. *Infant Mental Health Journal, 25*(6), 522–539.

DeVito, C., & Hopkins, J. (2001). Attachment, parenting, and marital dissatisfaction as predictors of disruptive behavior in preschoolers. *Development and Psychopathology, 13*, 215–231.

DeWit, D. J., Adlaf, E. M., Offord, D. R., & Ogborne, A. C. (2000). Age at first alcohol use: A risk factor for the development of alcohol disorders. *American Journal of Psychiatry, 157*(5), 745–750.

Dhossche, D., van der Steen, F., & Ferdinand, R. (2002). Somatoform disorders in children and adolescents: A comparison with other internalizing disorders. *Annals of Clinical Psychiatry, 14*(1), 23–31.

Diamond, A. (2002). Normal development of prefrontal cortex from birth to young adulthood: Cognitive functions, anatomy, and biochemistry. In D. T. Stuss & R. T. Knight (Eds.), *Principles of front lobe function* (pp. 466–503). New York: Oxford University Press.

DiCicco-Bloom, E., Lord, C., Zwaigenbaum, L., Courchesne, E., Dager, S. R., Schmitz, C., et al. (2006). The developmental neurobiology of autism spectrum disorder. *Journal of Neuroscience, 26*(26), 6897–6906.

Dick, D. M., Li, T.-K., Edenberg, H. J., Hesselbrock, V., Kramer, J., Kuperman, S., et al. (2004). A genome-wide screen for genes influencing conduct disorder. *Molecular Psychiatry, 9*(1), 81–86.

Dick, D. M., Rose, R. J., Viken, R. J., Kaprio, J., & Koskenvuo, M. (2001). Exploring gene-environment interactions: Socioregional moderation of alcohol use. *Journal of Abnormal Psychology, 110*(4), 625–632.

Dick, D. M., Viken, R. J., Kaprio, J., Pulkkinen, L., & Rose, R. J. (2005). Understanding the covariation among childhood externalizing symptoms: Genetic and environmental influences on conduct disorder, attention deficit hyperactivity disorder, and oppositional defiant disorder symptoms. *Journal of Abnormal Child Psychology, 33*(2), 219–229.

Dickens, W. T., & Flynn, J. R. (2001). Heritability estimates versus large environmental effects: The IQ paradox resolved. *Psychological Review, 108*(2), 346–369.

Dickstein, D. P., Treland, J. E., Snow, J., McClure, E. B., Mehta, M. S., Towbin, K. E., et al. (2004). Neuropsychological performance in pediatric bipolar disorder. *Biological Psychiatry, 55*(1), 32–39.

Dieckstra, R. F. W. (1995). Depression and suicidal behaviors in adolescence: Sociocultural and time trends. In M. Rutter (Ed.), *Psychosocial disturbances in young people: Challenges for prevention* (pp. 214–243). New York: Cambridge University Press.

Diego, M. A., Field, T., Hernandez-Reif, M., Cullen, C., Schanberg, S., Kuhn, C., et al. (2004). Prepartum, postpartum, and chronic depression effects on newborns. *Psychiatry: Interpersonal Biological Processes, 67*(1), 63–80.

Dierker, L. C., Merikangas, K. R., & Szatmari, P. (1999). Influence of parental concordance for psychiatric disorders on psychopathology in offspring. *Journal of the American Academy of Child and Adolescent Psychiatry, 38*(3), 280–288.

Dierssen, M., & Ramakers, G. J.A. (2006). Dendritic pathology in mental retardation: From molecular genetics to neurobiology. *Genes, Brain and Behavior, 5*(12), 48–60.

DiLalla, L. F. (2002). Behavior genetics of aggression in children: Review and future directions. *Developmental Review, 22*, 593–622.

DiLalla, L. F., Kagan, J., & Reznick, J. S. (1994). Genetic etiology of behavioral inhibition among 2-year-old children. *Infant Behavior and Development, 17*(4), 405–412.

Dillon, C. M., & Carr, J. E. (2007). Assessing indices of happiness and unhappiness individuals with developmental disabilities: A review. *Behavioral Interventions, 22*(3), 229–244.

Diniz, J. B., Rosario-Campos, M. D., Shavitt, R. G., Curi, M., Hounie, A. G., Brotto, S. A., et al. (2004). Impact of age at onset and duration of illness on the expression of comorbidities in obsessive-compulsive disorder. *Journal of Clinical Psychiatry, 65*(1), 22–27.

Dinn, W. M., Aycicegi, A., & Harris, C. L. (2004). Cigarette smoking in a student sample: Neurocognitive and clinical correlates. *Addictive Behaviors, 29*(1), 107–126.

Dishion, T. J., & Bullock, B. M. (2002). Parenting and adolescent problem behavior: An ecological analysis of the nurturance hypothesis. In J. G. Borkowski, & S. L. Ramey (Eds.), *Parenting and the child's world: Influences on academic, intellectual, and social-emotional development. Monographs in parenting* (pp. 231–249). Mahwah, NJ: Erlbaum.

Dishion, T. J., & Kavanagh, K. (2002). The Adolescent Transitions Program: A family-centered prevention strategy for schools. In J. B. Reid & G. R. Patterson (Eds.), *Antisocial behavior in children and adolescents: A developmental analysis and model for intervention* (pp. 257–272). Washington, DC: American Psychological Association.

Dishion, T. J., & Kavanagh, K. (2003). *Intervening in adolescent problem behavior: A family-centered approach*. New York: Guilford Press.

Dishion, T. J., & McMahon, R. J. (1998). Parental monitoring and the prevention of child and adolescent problem behavior: A conceptual and empirical formulation. *Clinical Child and Family Psychology Review, 1*, 61–75.

Dishion, T. J., & Medici Skaggs, N. (2000). An ecological analysis of monthly "bursts" in early adolescent substance use. *Applied Developmental Science, 4*(2), 89–97.

Dishion, T. J., & Owen, L. D. (2002). A longitudinal analysis of friendships and substance use: Bidirectional influence from adolescence to adulthood. *Developmental Psychology, 38*(4), 480–491.

Dishion, T. J., & Patterson, G. R. (1999). Model building in developmental psychopathology: A pragmatic approach to understanding and intervention. *Journal of Clinical Child Psychology, 28(4),* 502–512.

Dishion, T. J., & Stormshak, E. A. (2007). Child and adolescent intervention groups. In T. J. Dishion & E. A. Stormshak (Eds.), *Intervening in children's lives: An ecological, family-centered approach to mental health care* (pp. 201–215). Washington, DC: American Psychological Association.

Dishion, T. J., Bullock, B. M., & Granic, I. (2002). Pragmatism in modeling peer influence: Dynamics, outcomes and change processes. *Development and Psychopathology, 14*(4), 969–981.

Dishion, T. J., Capaldi, D., Spracklen, K. M., & Li, F. (1995). Peer ecology of male adolescent drug use. *Development and Psychopathology, 7*(4), 803–824.

Dishion, T. J., Capaldi, D. M., & Yoerger, K. (1999). Middle childhood antecedents to progressions in male adolescent substance use: An ecological analysis of risk and protection. *Journal of Adolescent Research, 14*(2), 175–205.

Dishion, T. J., Eddy, M. Haas, E., & Li, F. (1997). Friendships and violent behavior during adolescence. *Social Development,* (2), 207–223.

Dishion, T. J., Kavanagh, K., Schneiger, A., Nelson, S., & Kaufman, N. K. (2002). Preventing early adolescent substance use: A family-centered strategy for the public middle school. *Prevention Science, 3*(3), 191–201.

Dishion, T. J., McCord, J., Poulin, F. (1999). When interventions harm: Peer groups and problem behavior. *American Psychologist, 54*(9), 755–764.

Dishion, T. J., Nelson, S. E., & Bullock, B. M. (2004). Premature adolescent autonomy: Parent disengagement and deviant peer process in the amplification of problem behaviour. *Journal of Adolescence, 27*(5), 515–530.

Dishion, T. J., Owen, L. D., & Bullock, B. M. (2004). Like father, like son: Toward a developmental model for the transmission of male deviance across generations. *European Journal of Developmental Psychology, 1*(2), 105–126.

Dishion, T. J., Poulin, F., & Burraston, B. (2001). Peer group dynamics associated with iatrogenic effects in group interventions with high-risk young adolescents. In D. W. Nangle & C. A. Erdley (Eds.), *The role of friendship in psychological adjustment: New directions for child and adolescent development* (pp. 79–92). San Francisco: Jossey-Bass.

Disney, E. R., Elkins, I. J., McGue, M., & Iacono, W. G. (1999). Effects of ADHD, conduct disorder, and gender on substance use and abuse in adolescence. *American Journal of Psychiatry, 156*(10), 1515–1521.

Dixon, R. S., Gill, J. M. W., & Adair, V. A. (2003). Exploring paternal influences on the dieting behavior of adolescent girls. *Eating Disorders: The Journal of Treatment and Prevention, 11,* 39–50.

Dodge, K. A. (1991). The structure and function of reactive and proactive aggression. In D. J. Pepler & K. H. Rubin (Eds.), *The development and treatment of childhood aggression* (pp. 201–218). Hillsdale, NJ: Erlbaum.

Dodge, K. A. (2006). Translational science in action: Hostile attributional style and the development of aggressive behavior problems. *Development and Psychopathology, 18,* 791–814.

Dodge, K. A. (2007). Temperamental resistance to control increases the association between sleep problems and externalizing behavior development. *Journal of Family Psychology, 21*(1), 39–48.

Dodge, K. A., & Coie, J. D. (1987). Social-information-processing factors in reactive and proactive aggression in children's peer groups. *Journal of Personality and Social Psychology, 53*(6), 1146–1158.

Dodge, K. A., Dishion, T. J., & Lansford, J. E. (2006). The problem of deviant peer influence in public interventions. *Social Policy Report, 20*(1), 3–19.

Dodge, K. A., Lansford, J. E., Burks, V. S., Bates, J. E., Pettit, G. S., Fontaine, R., et al. (2003). Peer rejection and social information-processing factors in the development of aggressive behavior problems in children. *Child Development, 74*(2) , 374–393.

Dodge, K. A., Lochman, J. E., Harnish, J. D., Bates, J. E., & Pettit, G. S. (1997). Reactive and proactive aggression in school children and psychiatrically impaired chronically assaultive youth. *Journal of Abnormal Psychology, 106,* 37–51.

Dodge, K. A., & Pettit, G. S. (2003). A biopsychosocial model of the development of chronic conduct problems in adolescence. *Developmental Psychology, 39*(2), 349–371.

Domitrovich, C. E., & Greenberg, M. T. (2004). Preventive interventions with young children: Building on the four early intervention programs. *Early Education and Development, 15*(4), 365–370.

Donaldson, D., Spirito, A., & Esposito-Smythers, C. (2005). Treatment for adolescents following a suicide attempt: Results of a pilot trial. *Journal of the American Academy of Child and Adolescent Psychiatry, 44*(2), 113–120.

Donaldson, D., Spirito, A., & Overholser, J. (2003). Treatment of adolescent suicide attempters. In A. Spirito & J. C. Overholser (Eds.), *Evaluation and treating adolescent suicide attempters: From research to practice* (pp. 295–321). San Diego, CA: Academic Press.

Donnellan, M. B., Trzesniewski, K. H., Robins, R. W., Moffitt, T. E., & Caspi, A. (2005). Low self- esteem is related to aggression, antisocial behavior, and delinquency. *Psychological Science, 16*(4), 328–335.

Donohue, B., DeCato, L. A., Azrin, N. H., & Teichner, G. A. (2001). Satisfaction of parents with their conduct-disordered and substance-abusing youth. *Behavior Modification, 25*(1), 21–43.

Donovan, J. E., Leech, S. L., Zucker, R. A., Loveland-Cherry, C. J., Jester, J., Fitzgerald, H. E., et al. (2004). Really underage drinkers: Alcohol use among elementary students. *Alcoholism: Clinical and Experimental Research, 28*(2), 341–349.

Donovan, S. J., Nunes, E. V., Stewart, J. W., Ross, D., Quitkin, F. M., Jensen, P. S., et al. (2003). "Outer-directed irritability": A distinct mood syndrome in explosive youth with a disruptive behavior disorder? *Journal of Clinical Psychiatry, 64,* 698–701.

Dorn, L. D., Campo, J. C., Thato, S., Dahl, R. E., Lewin, D., Chandra, R., et al. (2003). Psychological comorbidity and stress reactivity in children and adolescents with recurrent abdominal pain and anxiety disorders. *Journal of the American Academy of Child and Adolescent Psychiatry, 42*(1), 66–75.

Dorn, L. D., Dahl, R. W., Williamson, D. W., Birmaher, B., Axelson, D., Perel, J., et al. (2003). Developmental markers in adolescence: Implications for studies of pubertal processes. *Journal of Youth and Adolescence, 32*(5), 315–324.

Dosen, A. (2001). Developmental-dynamic relationship therapy: An approach to more severely mentally retarded children. In A. Dosen & K. Day (Eds.), *Treating mental illness and behavior disorders in children and adults with mental retardation* (pp. 415–427). Washington, DC: American Psychiatric Publishing.

Dosen, A. (2001). Pharmacotherapy in mentally retarded children. In A. Dosen & K. Day (Eds.), *Treating mental illness and behavior disorders in children and adults with mental retardation* (pp. 429–450). Washington, DC: American Psychiatric Publishing.

Dosen, A., & Day, K. (2001). Epidemiology, etiology, and presentation of mental illness and behavior disorders in persons with mental retardation. In A. Dosen & K. Day (Eds.), *Treating mental illness and behavior disorders in children and adults with mental retardation* (pp. 3–24). Washington, DC: American Psychiatric Publishing.

Dow-Edwards, D., Mayes, L. C., Spear, L., & Hurd, Y. (1999). Cocaine and development: Clinical, behavioral and neurobiological perspectives—A symposium report. *Neurotoxicology and Teratology, 21*(5), 481–490.

Downey, G., Lebolt, A., Rincon, C., & Freitas, A. L. (1998). Rejection sensitivity and children's interpersonal difficulties. *Child Development, 69*(4), 1074–1091.

Doyle, A. E., Faraone, S. V., Seidman, L. J., Willcutt, E. G., Nigg, J. T., Waldman, I. D., et al. (2005). Are endophenotypes based on measures of executive functions useful for molecular genetic studies of ADHD? *Journal of Child Psychology and Psychiatry, 46*(7), 778–803.

Dozier, M., Stovall, K. C., & Albus, K. E. (1999). Attachment and psychopathology in adulthood. In J. Cassidy & P. R. Shaver (Eds.), *Handbook of attachment: Theory, research, and clinical applications* (pp. 497–519). New York: Guilford Press.

Drabick, D. A. G., Gadow, K. D., & Loney, J. (2007). Source-specific oppositional defiant disorder: Comorbidity and risk factors in referred elementary schoolboys. *Journal of the American Academy of Child and Adolescent Psychiatry, 46*(1), 92–101.

Drotar, D. D., & Sturm, L. A. (1996). Interdisciplinary collaboration in the practice of mental retardation. In J. W. Jacobson & J. A. Mulick (Eds.), *Manual of diagnosis and professional practice in mental retardation* (pp. 393–401). Washington, DC: American Psychological Association.

Du, J., Li, J., Wang, Y., Jiang, Q., Livesley, W. J., Jang, K. L., Wang, K., et al. (2006). Event-related potentials in adolescents with combined ADHD and CD disorder: A single stimulus paradigm. *Brain and Cognition, 60*(1), 70–75.

Du, J., Wang, W., Li, J., Wang, Y., & Jiang, Q. (2005). Passive paradigm elicited auditory event-related potentials in adolescents with aggressive hyperactivity. In J. P. Morgan (Ed.), *Psychology of aggression* (pp. 137–149). Hauppauge, NY: Nova Science Publishers.

Duggal, S., Carlson, E. A., Sroufe, L. A., & Egeland, B. (2001). Depressive symptomatology in childhood and adolescence. *Development and Psychopathology, 13*(1), 143–164.

Duhig, A. M., Renk, K., Epstein, M. K., & Phares, V. (2000). Interparental agreement on internalizing, externalizing, and total behavior problems: A meta-analysis. *Clinical Psychology: Science and Practice, 7(4)*, 435–453.

Dulcan, M., Dunne, J. E., Ayres, W., Arnold, V., Benson, R. S., Bernet, W., et al. (1997). Practice parameters for the assessment and treatment of children, adolescents, and adults with attention-deficit/hyperactivity disorder. *Journal of the American Academy of Child and Adolescent Psychiatry, 36*, 85S–121S.

Dumont-Mathieu, T. & Fein, D. (2005). Screening for autism in young children: The modified checklist for autism in toddlers (M-CHAT) and other measures. *Mental Retardation and Developmental Disabilities Research Review, 11*(3), 253–262.

Duncan, G. J., & Brooks-Gunn, J. (2000). Family poverty, welfare reform, and child development. *Child Development, 71(1)*, 188–196.

Dunham, K. (2004). Young adults' support strategies when peers disclose suicidal intent. *Suicide and Life-Threatening Behavior, 34*(1), 56–65.

Dunn, J. (2004). Understanding children's family worlds: Family transitions and children's outcomes. *Merrill-Palmer Quarterly, 50(3)*, 224–235.

Dunn, J., & Hughes, C. (2001). "I got some swords and you're dead!": Violent fantasy, antisocial behavior, friendship, and moral sensibility in young children. *Child Development, 72*(2), 491–505.

Dunn, W. (1997). The impact of sensory processing abilities on the daily lives of young children and their families: A conceptual model. *Infants and Young Children, 9*(4), 23–35.

Dunn, W., & Westman, K. (1997). The sensory profile: The performance of a national sample of children without disabilities. *American Journal of Occupational Therapy, 51*(1), 25–34.

Dunne, J. E., Arnold, V., Benson, S., Bernet, W., Bukstein, O., Kinlan, J., et al. (1997). Summary of the practice parameters for the assessment and treatment of children, adolescents, and adults with ADHD. *Journal of the American Academy of Child and Adolescent Psychiatry, 36*, 1311–1317.

Dunst, C. J., Trivette, C. M., & Deal, A. G. (Eds.). (1994). *Supporting and strengthening families: Vol. 1. Methods, strategies and practices.* Cambridge, MA: Brookline Books.

DuPaul, G. J., Anastopoulos, A. D., McGoey, K. E., Power, T. J., Reid, R., & Ikeda, M. J. (1998). Teacher ratings of attention deficit hyperactivity disorder symptoms: Factor structure and normative data. *Psychological Assessment, 9*, 436–444.

DuPaul, G. J., & Barkley, R. A. (2008). Attention deficit hyperactivity disorder. From R. J. Morris & T. R. Kratochwill (Eds.), *The practice of child therapy* (4th ed., pp. 143–186). Mahwah, NJ: Erlbaum.

Durand, V. M. (2001). Future directions for children and adolescents with mental retardation. *Behavior Therapy, 32*(4), 633–650.

Durbrow, E. H. (1999). Cultural processes in child competence: How rural Caribbean parents evaluate their children. In A. S. Masten (Ed.), *Cultural processes in child development* (pp. 97–121). Mahwah, NJ: Erlbaum.

Durbrow, E. H., Pena, L. F., Masten, A., Sesma, A., & Williamson, I. (2001). Mothers' conceptions of child competence in contexts of poverty: The Phillipines, St. Vincent, and the United States. *International Journal of Behavioral Development, 25*, 438–443.

Durkin, M. (2002). The epidemiology of developmental disabilities in low-income countries. *Mental Retardation and Developmental Disabilities Research Reviews, 8*(3), 206–211.

Durkin, S. J., Paxton, S. J., & Wertheim, E. H. (2005). How do adolescent girls evaluate body dissatisfaction prevention messages? *Journal of Adolescent Health, 37*, 381–390.

Durlak, J. A., & Wells, A. M. (1997). Primary prevention mental health programs for children and adolescents: A meta-analytic review. *American Journal of Community Psychology, 25(2)*, 115–152.

Durlak, J. A., & Wells, A. M. (1998). Evaluation of indicated preventive intervention (secondary prevention) mental health programs for children and adolescents. *American Journal of Community Psychology, 26(5)*, 775–802.

Dyck, M. J., Ferguson, K., & Schochet, I. M. (2001). Do autism spectrum disorders differ from each other and from non-spectrum disorders on emotion recognition tests? *European Child and Adolescent Psychiatry, 10*, 105–116.

Dykens, E. M. (1995). Measuring behavioral phenotypes: Provocations from the "new genetics." *American Journal on Mental Retardation, 99*(5), 522–532.

Dykens, E. M. (1997). Maladaptive behavior in children with Prader-Willi syndrome, Down syndrome, and nonspecific mental retardation. *American Journal on Mental Retardation, 102*(3), 228–237.

Dykens, E. M. (2000). Annotation: Psychopathology in children with intellectual disability. *Journal of Child Psychology and Psychiatry, 41*(4), 407–417.

Dykens, E. M. (2001). Intervention issues in persons with Williams syndrome. *Mental Health Aspects of Developmental Disabilities, 4*(4), 130–137.

Dykens, E. M. (2001). Personality and psychopathology: New insights from genetic syndromes. In H. N. Switzy (Ed.), *Personality and motivational differences in persons with mental retardation. The LEA series on special education and disability* (pp. 283–317). Mahwah, NJ: Erlbaum.

Dykens, E. M. (2003). Anxiety, fears, and phobias in persons with Williams syndrome. *Developmental Neuropsychology, 23*(1–2), 291–316.

Dykens, E. M. (2006). Toward a positive psychology of mental retardation. *American Journal of Orthopsychiatry, 76*(2), 185–193.

Dykens, E. M., & Hodapp, R. M. (1997). Treatment issues in genetic mental retardation syndromes. *Professional Psychology: Research and Practice, 28*(3), 263–270.

Dykens, E. M., & Hodapp, R. M. (1999). Behavioural phenotypes: Towards new understandings of people with developmental disabilities. In N. Bouras (Ed.), *Psychiatric and behavioural disorders in developmental disabilities and mental retardation* (pp. 96–108). New York: Cambridge University Press.

Dykens, E. M., & Hodapp, R. M. (2001). Research in mental retardation: Toward an etiologic approach. *Journal of Child Psychology and Psychiatry and Allied Disciplines, 42*(1), 49–71.

Dykens, E. M., & Kasari, C. (1997). Maladaptive behavior in children with Prader-Willi syndrome, Down syndrome, and nonspecific mental retardation. *American Journal on Mental Retardation, 102*(3), 228–237.

Dykens, E. M., Hodapp, R. M., & Evans, D. W. (1994). Profiles and development of adaptive behavior in children with Down syndrome. *American Journal on Mental Retardation, 98*(5), 580–587.

Dykens, E. M., Hodapp, R. M., & Finucane, B. M. (2000). *Genetics and mental retardation syndromes: A new look at behavior and interventions.* Baltimore: Paul H. Brookes Publishing.

Dykens, E. M., Hodapp, R. M., & Leckman, J. F. (1994). Behavior and development in fragile X syndrome. In *Developmental clinical psychology and psychiatry series*, Vol. 28. Thousand Oaks, CA: Sage.

Dykens, E. M., Hodapp, R. M., Walsh, K., & Nash, L. J. (1992). Adaptive and maladaptive behavior in Prader-Willi syndrome. *Journal of the American Academy of Child and Adolescent Psychiatry, 31*(6), 1131–1136.

Dykens, E. M., Shah, B., Sagun, J., Beck, T., & King, B. H. (2002). Maladaptive behavior in children and adolescents with Down's syndrome. *Journal of Intellectual Disability Research, 46*(6), 484–492.

Dyregrov A., & Yule, W. (2006). A review of PTSD in children. *Child and Adolescent Mental Health, 11*(4), 176–184.

Easterbrooks, M. A. (1989). Quality of attachment to mother and father: Effects of perinatal risk status. *Child Development, 60*(4), 825–830.

Eaves, L., Rutter, M., Silberg, J. L., Shillady, L., Maes, H., & Pickles, A. (2000). Genetic and environmental causes of covariation in interview assessments of disruptive behavior in child and adolescent twins. *Behavior Genetics, 30*, 321–334.

Eccles, J. S., & Barber, B. L. (1999). Student council, volunteering, basketball, or marching band: What kind of extracurricular involvement matters? *Journal of Adolescent Research, 14*(1), 10–43.

Eccles, J. Barber, B., Jozefowicz, D., Malenchuk, O., & Vida, M. (1999). Self-evaluations of competence, task values, and self-esteem. In N. G. Johnson, M. C. Roberts, & J. Worell (Eds.), *Beyond appearance: A new look at adolescent girls* (pp. 53–83). Washington, DC: American Psychological Association.

Eccles, J. S., Barber, B. L., Stone, M. R., & Templeton, J. L. (2002). Adolescence and emerging adulthood: The critical passage ways to adulthood. In M. H. Bornstein, L. Davidson, C. L. M. Keyes, & K. Moore (Eds.), *Well-Being: Positive development across the life course.* Mahwah, NJ: Erlbaum.

Eddy, J. M., Leve, L. D., & Fagot, B. I. (2001). Coercive family processes: A replication and extension of Patterson's coercion model. *Aggressive Behavior, 27*, 14–25.

Eddy, K. T., Hennessey, M., & Thompson-Brenner, H. (2007). Eating pathology in East African women: The role of media exposure and globalization. *Journal of Nervous and Mental Disease, 195*(3), 196–202.

Edelson, M. G. (2005). A car goes in the garage like a can of peas goes into the refrigerator: Do deficits in real-world knowledge affect the assessment of intelligence in individuals with autism? *Focus on Autsim and Other Developmental Disabilities, 20*(1), 2–9.

Edelson, M. G. (2006). Are the majority of children with autism mentally retarded? A systematic evaluation of the data. *Focus on Autism and other Developmental Disabilities, 21*(2), 66–83.

Edelson, M. G., Schubert, D. T., & Edelson, S. M. (1998). Factors predicting intelligence scores on the TONI in individuals with autism. *Focus on Autism and Other Developmental Disabilities, 13*(1), 17–26.

Eder, R. A., & Mangelsdorf, S. C. (1997). The emotional basis of early personality development: Implications for the emergent self-concept. In R. Hogan, J. A. Johnson, et al. (Eds.), *Handbook of personality psychology* (pp. 209–240). San Diego, CA: Academic Press.

Edwards, R. T., & Thalanany, M. (2001). Trade-offs in the conduct of economic evaluations of child mental health services. *Mental Health Services Research, 3*(2), 99–105.

Egeland, B., Carlson, E., & Sroufe, L. A. (1993). Resilience as process. *Development and Psychopathology, 5*, 517–528.

Egeland, B., Pianta, R., & Ogawa, J. (1996). Early behavior problems: Pathways to mental disorders in adolescence. *Development and Psychopathology, 8*, 735–749.

Egeland, B., & Susman-Stillman, A. (1996). Dissociation as a mediator of child abuse across generations. *Child Abuse and Neglect, 20*(11), 1123–1132.

Egeland, B., Yates, T., Appleyard, K., & van Dulmen, M. (2002). The long-term consequences of maltreatment in the early years: A developmental pathway model to antisocial behavior. *Children's Services: Social Policy, Research, and Practice, 5*(4), 249–260.

Egger, H. L., Angold, A., & Costello, E. J. (1998). Headaches and psychopathology in children and adolescents. *Journal of the American Academy of Child and Adolescent Psychiatry, 37*(9), 951–958.

Egger, H. L., Costello, E. J., Erkanli, A., & Angold, A. (1999). Somatic complaints and psychopathology in children and adolescents: Stomachaches, musculoskeletal pains, and headaches. *Journal of the American Academy of Child and Adolescent Psychiatry, 38*(7), 852–860.

Ehlers, S., & Gillberg, C. (1993). The epidemiology of Asperger syndrome: A total population study. *Journal of Child Psychology and Psychiatry, 34*(8), 1327–1350.

Ehlers, S., Gillberg, C., & Wing, L. (1999). A screening questionnaire for Asperger syndrome and other high-functioning autism spectrum disorders in school age children. *Journal of Autism and Developmental Disorders, 29*, 129–141.

Ehlers, S., Nyden, A., Gillberg, C., & Dahlgren Sandberg, A. (1997). Asperger syndrome, autism and attention disorders: A comparative study of the cognitive profiles of 120 children. *Journal of Child Psychology and Psychiatry and Allied Disciplines, 38*, 207–217.

Ehringer, M. A., Rhee, S. H., Young, S., Corley, R., & Hewitt, J. K. (2006). Genetic and environmental contributions to common psychopathologies of childhood and adolescence: A study of twins and their siblings. *Journal of Abnormal Child Psychology, 34*(1), 1–17.

Eigsti, I., Zayas, V., Mischel, W., Shoda, Y., Ayduk, O., Dadlani, M. B., et al. (2006). Predicting cognitive control from preschool to late adolescence and young adulthood. *Psychological Science, 17*(6), 478–484.

Einfield, S. L., Tonge, B. J., & Reese, V. W. (2001). Longitudinal course of behavioral and emotional problems in Williams syndrome. *American Journal on Mental Retardation, 106*(1), 73–81.

Eisenberg, M. E., Neumark-Sztainer, D., Haines, J., & Wall, M. (2006). Weight teasing and emotional well-being in adolescents: Longitudinal findings from Project EAT. *Journal of Adolescent Health, 38*, 675–683.

Eisenberg, N. (2002). Emotion-related regulation and its relation to quality of social functioning. In W. Hartup & R. A. Weinberg (Eds.), *Child psychology in retrospect and prospect. The Minnesota symposia on child psychology* (Vol. 32, pp. 133–171). Mahwah, NJ: Erlbaum.

Eisenberg, N., Cumberland, A., & Spinrad, T. L. (1998). Parental socialization of emotion. *Psychological Inquiry, 9*, 241–273.

Eisenberg, N., Cumberland, A., Spinrad, T. L., Fabes, R. A., Shepard, S. A., Reiser, M., et al. (2001). The relations of regulation and emotionality to children's externalizing and internalizing problem behavior. *Child Development, 72*, 1112–1134.

Eisenberg, N., Spinrad, T.L, & Smith, C. L. (2004). Emotion-related regulation: Its conceptualization, relations to social functioning, and socialization. In P. Philippot & R. S. Feldman (Eds.), *The regulation of emotion* (pp. 277–306). Mahwah, NJ: Erlbaum.

Eisenberg, N., Valiente, C., Fabes, R. A., Smith, C. L., Reiser, M., Shepard, S. A., et al. (2003). The relations of effortful control and ego control to children's resiliency and social functioning. *Developmental Psychology, 39*(4), 761–776.

Eisenberg, N., Zhou, Q., Losoya, S. H., Fabes, R. A., Shepard, S. A., Murphy, B. C., et al. (2003). The relations of parenting, effortful control, and ego control to children's emotional expressivity. *Child Development, 74*, 875–895.

Eleonora, E., King, N. J., & Ollendick, T. H. (2001). Self-reported anxiety in children and adolescents: A three-year follow-up study. *Journal of Genetic Psychology, 162*(1), 5–19.

Eley, T. C. (1999). Behavioral genetics as a tool for developmental psychology: Anxiety and depression in children and adolescents. *Clinical Child and Family Psychology Review, 2*(1), 21–36.

Eley, T. C. (2001). Contributions of behavioral genetics research: Quantifying genetic, shared environmental and nonshared environmental influences. In M. W. Vasey & M. R. Dadds (Eds.), *The developmental psychopathology of anxiety* (pp. 45–59). London: Oxford University Press.

Eley, T. C., Bolton, D., O'Connor, T. G., Perrin, S., Smith, P., & Plomin, R. (2003). A twin study of anxiety-related behaviours in pre-school children. *Journal of Child Psychology and Psychiatry and Allied Disciplines, 44*(7), 945–960.

Eley, T. C., Lichtenstein, P., & Moffitt, T. E. (2003). A longitudinal behavioral genetic analysis of the etiology of aggressive and nonaggressive antisocial behavior. *Development and Psychopathology, 15*(2), 383–402.

Eley, T. C., Lichtenstein, P., & Stevenson, J. (1999). Sex differences in the etiology of aggressive and nonaggressive antisocial behavior: Results from two twin studies. *Child Development, 70*(1), 155–168.

Eley, T. C., & Stevenson, J. (1999a). Exploring the covariation between anxiety and depression symptoms: A genetic analysis of the effects of age and sex. *Journal of Child Psychology and Psychiatry and Allied Disciplines, 40*(8), 1273–1282.

Eley, T. C., & Stevenson, J. (1999b). Using genetic analyses to clarify the distinction between depressive and anxious symptoms in children. *Journal of Abnormal Child Psychology, 27*(2), 105–114.

Eley, T. C., & Stevenson, J. (2000). Specific life events and chronic experiences differentially associated with depression and anxiety in young twins. *Journal of Abnormal Child Psychology, 28*(4), 383–394.

Eley, T. C., Stirling, L., Ehlers, A., Gregory, A. M., & Clark, D. M. (2004). Heart-beat perception, panic/somatic symptoms and anxiety sensitivity in children. *Behaviour Research and Therapy, 42*(4), 439–448.

Elfhag, K., & Linne, Y. (2005). Gender differences in associations of eating pathology between mothers and their adolescent offspring. *Obesity Research, 13*, 1070–1076.

Eliot, A. O. (2004). A concept of self in eating disordered adolescent girls: A consideration of genetic factors. *Annals of the American Psychotherapy Association, 7*, 14–22.

Eliot, A. O., & Baker, C. W. (2001). Eating disordered adolescent males. *Adolescence, 36*, 535–543.

Elizabeth, J., King, N., & Ollendick, T. H. (2004). Etiology of social anxiety disorder in children and youth. *Behaviour Change, 21*(3), 162–172.

Elkind, D. (1994). *Ties that stress.* Cambridge, MA: Harvard University Press.

Elkins, I. J., King, S. M., McGue, M., & Iacono, W. G. (2006). Personality traits and the development of nicotine, alcohol, and illicit drug disorders: Prospective links from adolescence to young adulthood. *Journal of Abnormal Psychology, 115*(1), 26–39.

Elkins, I. J., McGue, M., & Iacono, W. G. (1997). Genetic and environmental influences on parent-son relationships: Evidence for increasing genetic influence during adolescence. *Developmental Psychology, 33*(2), 351–363.

Ellenbogen, M. A., & Hodgins, S. (2004). The impact of high neuroticism in parents on children's psychosocial functioning in a population at high risk for major affective disorder: A family-environmental pathway of intergenerational risk. *Development and Psychopathology, 16*(1), 113–136.

Ellickson, P. L., Tucker, J. S., Klein, D. J., & Saner, H. (2004). Antecedents and outcomes of marijuana use initiation during adolescence. *Preventive Medicine: An International Journal Devoted to Practice and Theory, 39*(5), 976–984.

Ellis, C. R., Singh, N. N., & Ruane, A. L. (1999). Nutritional, dietary, and hormonal treatments for individuals with mental retardation and developmental disabilities. *Mental Retardation and Developmental Disabilities Research Reviews, 5*(4), 335–341.

El-Mallakh, R. S., Peters, C., & Waltrip, C. (2000). Antidepressant treatment and neural plasticity. *Journal of Child and Adolescent Psychopharmacology, 10*(4), 287–294.

Else-Quest, N. M., Hyde, J. S., Goldsmith, H. H., & Van Hulle, C. A. (2006). Gender differences in temperament: A meta-analysis. *Psychological Bulletin, 132*(1), 33–72.

El-Sheikh, M., Buckhalt, J. A., Cummings, E. M., & Keller, P. (2007). Sleep disruptions and emotional insecurity are pathways of risk for children. *Journal of Child Psychology and Psychiatry, 48*(1), 88–96.

Emde, R. N. (1985). The affective self: Continuities and transformations from infancy. In J. Call & E. Galenson (Eds.), *Frontiers of infant psychiatry* (Vol. 2, pp. 38–54). New York: Basic Books.

Emde, R. N. (1992). Individual meaning and increasing complexity: Contributions of Sigmund Freud and Rene Spitz to developmental psychology. *Developmental Psychology, 28(3),* 347–359.

Emde, R. N., Bingham, R. D., & Harmon, R. J. (1993). Classification and the diagnostic process in infancy. In C. H. Zeanah (Ed.), *Handbook of Infant Mental Health* (pp. 225–235). New York: Guilford Press.

Emde, R. N., & Hewitt, J. K. (Eds.). (2001). *Infancy to early childhood: Genetic and environmental influences on developmental change.* New York: Oxford University Press.

Emde, R. N. & Robinson, J. (2000). Guiding principles for a theory of early intervention: A developmental-psychoanalytic perspective. In J. P. Shonkoff & S. J. Meisels (Eds.), *Handbook of Early Childhood Intervention (2ⁿᵈ ed.) (pp. 160- 178).* Cambridge: Cambridge University Press.

Emde, R. N., & Spicer, P. (2000). Experience in the mist of variation: New horizons for development and psychopathology. *Development and Psychopathology, 12*(3), 313–331.

Eme, R. F., & Kavanaugh, L. (1995). Sex differences in conduct disorder. *Journal of Clinical Child Psychology, 24,* 406–426.

Emery, R. E., & Kitzmann, K. M. (1995). The child in the family: Disruptions in family functions. In D. Cicchetti & D. J. Cohen (Eds.), *Developmental Psychopathology: Vol. 2. Risk, disorder, and adaptation* (pp. 3–31). Oxford, England: Wiley.

Emslie, G. J., Kennard, B. D., Mayes, T. L., Nightingale-Teresi, J., Carmody, T., Hughes, C. W., et al. (2008). Fluoxetine versus placebo in preventing relapse of major depression in children and adolescents. *American Journal of Psychiatry, 165*(4), 459–467.

Emslie, G. J., Mayes, T. L., Laptook, R. S., & Batt, M. (2003). Predictors of response to treatment in children and adolescents with mood disorders. *Psychiatric Clinics of North America, 26*(2), 435–456.

Emslie, G. J., Rush, J, Weinberg, W. A., Kowatch, R. A., Hughes, C. W., Carmody, T., et al. (1997). A double-blind, randomized, placebo-controlled trial of fluoxetine in children and adolescents with depression. *Archives of General Psychiatry, 54*(11), 1031–1037.

Eppright, T. D., Bradley, S., & Sanfacon, J. A. (1998). The diagnosis of infant psychopathology: Current challenges and recent contributions. *Child Psychiatry and Human Development, 28*(4), 213–222.

Erickson, C. A., Posey, D. J., Stigler, K. A., & McDougle, C. J. (2007). Pharmacotherapy of autism and related disorders. *Psychiatric Annals, 37*(7), 490–500.

Erickson, M. F., Korfmacher, J., & Egeland, B. (1992). Attachments past and present: Implications for therapeutic interventions with mother-infant dyads. *Development and Psychopathology, 4*(4), 495–507.

Erickson, M. F., Sroufe, L. A., & Egeland, B. (1985). The relationship between quality of attachment and behavior problems in preschool in a high-risk sample. *Monographs of the Society for Research in Child Development, 50*(1–2), 147–166.

Erikson, E. H. (1968). *Identity: Youth and crisis.* Oxford, England: Norton.

Espelage, D. L., Mebane, S. E., & Adams, R. S. (2004). Empathy, caring, and bullying: Toward an understanding of complex associations. In D. L. Espelage & S. M. Swearer (Eds.), *Bullying in American schools: A social-ecological perspective on prevention and intervention* (pp. 37–61). Mahwah, NJ: Erlbaum.

Esposito, C., Spirito., A. Boergers, J., & Donaldson, D. (2003). Affective, behavioral, and cognitive functioning in adolescents with multiple suicide attempts. *Suicide and Life-Threatening Behavior, 33*(4), 389–399.

Esposito-Smythers, C. (2004). Adolescent substance use and suicidal behavior: A review with implications for treatment research. *Alcoholism: Clinical and Experimental Research, 28*(5), 77S-88S.

Esposito-Smythers, C. (2005). Adolescent substance abuse and co-morbid conditions: An integrated treatment model. *DATA: The Brown University Digest of Addiction Theory and Application, 24*(7), 8–13.

Essau, C. A., & Dobson, K. S. (1999). Epidemiology of depressive disorders. In C. A. Essau & F. Petermann (Eds.), *Depressive disorders in children and adolescents: Epidemiology, risk factors, and treatment* (pp. 69–103). Northvale, N J: Jason Aronson, Inc.

Essau, C. A., Conradt, J., & Petermann, F. (1999). Course and outcome of depressive disorders. In C. A. Essau & F. Petermann (Eds.), *Depressive disorders in children and adolescents: Epidemiology, risk factors, and treatment* (pp. 105–135). Northvale, NJ: Jason Aronson.

Essau, C., Conradt, J., Petermann, F. (1999a). Frequency and comorbidity of social phobia and social fears in adolescents. *Behaviour Research and Therapy, 37*(9), 831–843.

Essau, C., Conradt, J., & Petermann, F. (1999b). Frequency of panic attacks and panic disorder in adolescents. *Depression and Anxiety, 9,* 19–26.

Essau, C. A., Conradt, J., & Petermann, F. (2000a). Frequency, comorbidity, and psychosocial impairment of anxiety disorders in German adolescents. Journal of Anxiety Disorders, 14(3), 263–279.

Essau, C. A., Conradt, J., & Petermann, F. (2000b). Frequency, co-morbidity, and psychosocial impairment of specific phobia in adolescents. Journal of Clinical Child Psychology, 29(2), 221–231.

Essau, C. A., Conradt, J., & Petermann, F. (2002). Course and outcome of anxiety disorders in adolescents. Journal of Anxiety Disorders, 16(1), 67–81.

Essau, C. A., Hakim-Larson, J., Crocker, A., & Petermann, F. (1999). Assessment of depressive disorders in children and adolescents. In C. A. Essau & F. Petermann (Eds.), *Depressive disorders in children and adolescents: Epidemiology, risk factors, and treatment* (pp. 27–67). Northvale, NJ: Jason Aronson.

Essex, M. J., Klein, M. H., Cho, E., & Kraemer, H. C. (2003). Exposure to maternal depression and marital conflict: Gender differences in children's later mental health symptoms. *Journal of the American Academy of Child and Adolescent Psychiatry, 42*(6), 728–737.

Ethier, L. S., Lemelin, J., & Lacharite, C. (2004). A longitudinal study of the effects of chronic maltreatment on children's behavioral and emotional problems. *Child Abuse and Neglect, 28*, 1265–1278.

Evans, D. W., Gray, F. L., & Leckman, J. F. (1999). The rituals, fears, and phobias of young children: Insights from development, psychopathology, and neurobiology. *Child Psychiatry and Human Development, 29*(4), 261–276.

Evans, D. W., Leckman, J. F., Carter, A., & Reznick, J. S. (1997). Ritual, habit, and perfectionism: The prevalence and development of compulsive-like behavior in normal young children. *Child Development, 68*(1), 58–68.

Evans, E., Hawton, K., & Rodham, K. (2005). Suicidal phenomena and abuse in adolescents: A review of epidemiological studies. *Child Abuse and Neglect, 29*(1), 45–58.

Evans, W. D., Powers, A., Hersey, J., & Renaud, J. (2006). The influence of social environment and social image on adolescent smoking. *Health Psychology, 25*(1), 26–33.

Fainsilber Katz, L., & Low, S. M. (2004). Marital violence, co-parenting, and family-level processes in relation to children's adjustment. *Journal of Family Psychology, 18*(2), 372–382.

Fairburn, C. G., Agras, W. S., Walsh, B. T., Wilson, G. T., & Stice, E. (2004). Prediction of outcome in bulimia nervosa by early change in treatment. *American Journal of Psychiatry, 161*, 2322–2324.

Fairburn, C. G., Stice, E., Cooper, Z., Doll, H. A., Norman, P. A., & O'Connor, M. E. (2003). Understanding persistence in bulimia nervosa: A 5-year naturalistic study. *Journal of Consulting and Clinical Psychiatry, 71*, 103–109.

Faraone, S. V., Biederman, J., & Friedman, D. (2000). Validity of DSM-IV subtypes of attention-deficit/hyperactivity disorder: A family study perspective. *Journal of the American Academy of Child and Adolescent Psychiatry, 39*, 300.

Faraone, S. V., Biederman, J., Jetton, J. G., & Tsuang, M. T. (1997). Attention deficit disorder and conduct disorder: Longitudinal evidence for a familial subtype. *Psychological Medicine, 27*, 291–300.

Faraone, S. V., Biederman, J., Mick, E., Williamson, S., Wilens, T., Spencer, T., et al. (2000). Family study of girls with attention deficit hyperactivity disorder. *American Journal of Psychiatry, 157*, 1077–1083.

Faraone, S. V., Biederman, J., Weber, W., & Russell, R. L. (1998). Psychiatric, neuropsychological, and psychosocial features of DSM-IV subtypes of attention-deficit/hyperactivity disorder: Results from a clinically referred sample. *Journal of the American Academy of Child and Adolescent Psychiatry, 37*, 185–193.

Faraone, S. V., Glatt, S. J., & Tsuang, M. T. (2003). The genetics of pediatric-onset bipolar disorder. *Biological Psychiatry, 53*(11), 970–977.

Faraone, S. V., Althoff, R. R., Hudziak, J. J., Monuteaux, M., & Biederman, J. (2005). The CBCL predicts DSM bipolar disorder in children: A receiver operating characteristic curve analysis. *Bipolar Disorder, 7*, 518–524.

Faraone, S. V., Biederman, J., & Mick, E. (2006). The age-dependent decline of attention deficit hyperactivity disorder: A meta-analysis of follow-up studies. *Psychological Medicine, 36*(2), 159–165.

Faraone, S. V., Biederman, J., Spencer, T., Wilens, T., Larry, J., Mick, E, et al. (2000). Attention-deficit disorder in adults: an overview. *Biological Psychiatry, 48*(1), 9–20.

Faraone, S. V., Glatt, S. J., Su, J., & Tsuang, M. T. (2004). Three potential susceptibility loci shown by a genome-wide scan for regions influencing the age at onset of mania. *American Journal of Psychiatry, 161*(4), 625–630.

Faraone, S. V., Lasky-Su, J., Glatt, S. J., Van Eerdewegh, P., & Tsuang, M. T. (2006). Early onset bipolar disorder: Possible linkage to chromosome 9q34. *Bipolar Disorders, 8*(2), 144–151.

Faraone, S. V., Perlis, R. H., Doyle, A. E., Smoller, J. W., Goralnick, J. J., Holmgren, M., et al. (2005). Molecular genetics of attention-deficit/hyperactivity disorder. *Biological Psychiatry, 57*(11), 1313–1323.

Faraone, S. V., Pliszka, S. R., Olvera, R. L., Skolnik, R., & Biederman, J. (2001). Efficacy of Adderall and methylphenidate in attention deficit hyperactivity disorder: A reanalysis using drug-placebo and drug-drug response curve methodology. *Journal of Child and Adolescent Psychopharmacology, 11*(2), 171–180.

Faris, P. L,, Eckert, E. D., Kim, S. W., Meller, W. H. Pardo, J. V, Goodale, R. L., et al. (2006). Evidence for a vagal pathophysiology for bulimia nervosa and the accompanying depressive symptoms. *Journal of Affective Disorders, 92*, 79–90.

Farmer, A. D., & Bierman, K. L. (2002). Predictors and consequences of aggressive-withdrawn problem profiles in early grade school. *Journal of Clinical Child and Adolescent Psychology, 31*, 299–311.

Farmer, E. M.Z., Burns, B. J., Phillips, S. D., Angold, A., & Costello, E. J. (2003). Pathways into and through mental health services for children and adolescents. *Psychiatric Services, 54(1)*, 60–66.

Farran, D. C. (2000). Another decade of intervention for children who are low income or disabled: What do we know now? In J. P. Shonkoff & S. J. Meisels (Eds.), *Handbook of early childhood intervention* (2nd ed.) (pp. 510–548). New York: Cambridge University Press.

Farrell, P. (1997). The integration of children with severe learning difficulties: A review of the recent literature. *Journal of Applied Research in Intellectual Disabilities, 10*(1), 1–14.

Farrington, D. P. (2000). Adolescent violence: Findings and implications from the Cambridge Study. In Boswell, G. (Ed.), *Violent children and adolescents: Asking the question why* (pp. 19–35). Philadelphia: Whurr Publishers.

Farrington, D. P. (2005). Childhood origins of antisocial behavior. *Clinical Psychology and Psychotherapy, 12*(3), 177–190.

Farrington, D. P., & West, D. (1993). Criminal, penal, and life histories of chronic offenders: Risk and protective factors and early identification. *Criminal Behaviour and Mental Health, 3*(4), 492–523.

Favaro, A., Zanetti, T., Tenconi, E., Degortes, D., Ronzan, A., Veronses, A., et al. (2005). The relationship between temperament and impulsive behaviors in eating disordered subjects. *Eating Disorders: The Journal of Treatment and Prevention, 13*, 61–70.

Fayyad, J., de Graaf, R., Kessler, R., Alonso, J., Angermeyer, M., Demyttenaere, K., et al. (2007). Cross-national prevalence and correlates of adult attention-deficit hyperactivity disorder. *British Journal of Psychiatry, 190,* 402–409.

Feeney, J. A. (1999). Adult romantic attachment and couple relationships. In J. Cassidy & P. R. Shaver (Eds.), *Handbook of attachment: Theory, research, and clinical applications* (pp. 355–377). New York: Guilford Press.

Fehm, L., & Schmidt, K. (2006). Performance anxiety in gifted adolescent musicians. *Journal of Anxiety Disorders, 20*(1), 98–109.

Feinberg, M. E., & Kan, M. L. (2008). Establishing family foundations: Intervention effects on coparenting, parent/infant well-being, and parent-child relations. *Journal of Family Psychology, 22*(2), 253–263.

Feldman, R. (2007). Maternal versus child risk and the development of parent-child and family relationships in five high-risk populations. *Development and Psychopathology, 19*(2), 293–312.

Feldman, R., Keren, M., Gross-Rozval, O., & Tyano, S. (2004). Mother-child touch patterns in infant feeding disorders: Relation to maternal, child, and environmental factors. *Journal of the American Academy of Child and Adolescent Psychiatry, 43*(9), 1089–1097.

Feldman, R., Weller, A., Sirota, L., & Eidelman, A. (2002). Skin-to-skin contact (kangaroo care) promotes self-regulation in premature infants: Sleep-wake cyclicity, arousal modulation, and sustained exploration. *Developmental Psychology, 38*(2), 194–207.

Fennig, S., Geva, K., Zalsman, G., Wietzman, A., Fenning, S., & Apter, A. (2005). Effect of gender on suicide attempters versus nonattempters in an adolescent inpatient unit. *Comprehensive Psychiatry, 46*(2), 90–97.

Ferdinand, R. F., van der Ende, J., & Verhulst, F. C. (2004). Parent-adolescent disagreement regarding psychopathology in adolescents from the general population as a risk factor for adverse outcome. *Journal of Abnormal Psychology, 113(2),* 198–206.

Ferguson vs. City of Charleston et al., 532 U. S. 67 (2001).

Ferrari, M. (1986). Fears and phobias in childhood: Some clinical and developmental considerations. *Child Psychiatry and Human Development, 17*(2), 75–87.

Fidler, D. J. (2006). The emergence of a syndrome-specific personality profile in young children with Down syndrome. *Down Syndrome: Research and Practice, 10*(2), 53–60.

Fidler, D. J., Hodapp, R. M., & Dykens, E. M. (2000). Stress in families of young children with Down syndrome, Williams syndrome, and Smith-Magenis syndrome. *Early Education and Development, 11*(4), 395–406.

Fidler, D. J., Hodapp, R. M., & Dykens, E. M. (2002). Behavioral phenotypes and special education: Parent report of educational issues for children with Down syndrome, Prader-Willi syndrome and Williams syndrome. *Journal of Special Education, 36*(2), 80–88.

Fidler, D. J., Most, D. E., Booth-LaForce, C., & Kelly, J. F. (2006). Temperament and behavior problems in young children with Down syndrome at 12, 30, and 45 months. *Down Syndrome Research and Practice, 10*(1), 23–29.

Field, A. E., Austin, S. B., Frazier, A. L., Gillman, M. W., Camarog, C. A., Jr., & Colditz, G. A. (2002). Smoking, getting drunk and engaging in bulimic behaviors: In which order are the behaviors adopted? *Journal of the American Academy of Child and Psychiatry, 41,* 846–853.

Field, A. E., Camargo, C. A., Taylor, C. B., Berkey, C. S., Frazier, L. Gillman, M. W., et al. (1999). Overweight, weight concerns, and bulimic behaviors among girls and boys. *Journal of the American Academy of Child and Adolescent Psychiatry, 38,* 754–760.

Field, A. P., Argyris, N. G., & Knowles, K. A. (2001). Who's afraid of the big bad wolf: A prospective paradigm to test Rachman's indirect pathways in children. *Behaviour Research and Therapy, 39*(11), 1259–1276.

Field, A. P., & Lawson, J. (2003). Fear information and the development of fears during childhood: Effects on implicit fear responses and behavioural avoidance. *Behaviour Research and Therapy, 41*(11), 1277–1293.

Field, C. E., Nash, H. M., Handwerk, M. L., & Friman, P. C. (2004). A modification of the token economy for nonresponsive youth in family-style residential care. *Behavior Modification, 28*(3), 438–457.

Field, T. (2002). Infants' need for touch. *Human Development, 45*(2), 100–103.

Field, T. M. (1998). Touch therapy effects on development. *International Journal of Behavioral Development, 22*(4), 779–797.

Field, T. M. (2002). Prenatal effects of maternal depression. In S. H. Goodman & I. H. Gotlib (Eds.), *Children of depressed parents: Mechanisms of risk and implications for treatment* (pp. 59–88). Washington, DC: American Psychological Association.

Field, T. M., Hossain, Z., & Malphurs, J. (1999). "Depressed" fathers' interactions with their infants. *Infant Mental Health Journal, 20*(3), 322–332.

Field, T. M., & Liepack, S. (1999). Infancy. In W. K. Silverman & T. H. Ollendick (Eds.), *Developmental issues in the clinical treatment of children* (pp. 77–87). Needham Heights, MA: Allyn & Bacon.

Fiese, B. H., Tomcho, T. J., Douglas, M., Josephs, K., Poltrock, S., & Baker, T. (2002). A review of 50 years of research on naturally occurring family routines and rituals: Cause for celebration? *Journal of Family Psychology, 16(4),* 381–390.

Fiese, B. H. Winter, M. A., Sliwinski, M., & Anbar, R. D. (2007). Nighttime waking in children with asthma: An exploratory study of daily functioning in family climate. *Journal of Family Psychology, 21*(1), 95–103.

Figueroa, R. A. (1979). The system of multicultural pluralistic assessment. *School Psychology Review, 8*(1), 28–36.

Figueroa, R. A., & Sassenrath, J. M. (1989). A longitudinal study of the predictive validity of the System of Multicultural Pluralistic Assessment (SOMPA). *Psychology in the Schools, 26*(1), 5–19.

Filipek, P. A. (1999). Neuroimaging in the developmental disorders: The state of the science. *Journal of Child Psychology and Psychiatry and Allied Disciplines, 40,* 113–128.

Filipek, P. A., Accardo, P. J., Baranek, G. T., Cook, E. H., Dawson, G., Gordon, B., et al. (1999). The screening and diagnosis of autistic spectrum disorders. *Journal of Autism and Developmental Disorders, 29,* 439–484.

Finlay, W. M. L., & Lyons, E. (2001). Methodological issues in interviewing and using self-report questionnaires with people with mental retardation. *Psychological Assessment, 13*(3), 319–335.

Finn, P. R., Sharkansky, E. J., Brandt, K. M., & Turcotte, N. (2000). The effects of familial risk, personality, and expectancies on alcohol use and abuse. *Journal of Abnormal Psychology, 109*(1), 122–133.

Fischer, K. W., Ayoub, C., Singh, I., Noam, G., Maraganore, A., & Raya, P. (1997). Psychopathology as adaptive development along distinctive pathways. *Development and Psychopathology, 9,* 749–779.

Fischer, K. W., & Pare-Blagoev, J. (2000). From individual differences to dynamic pathways of development. *Child Development, 71(4),* 850–853.

Fishbein, D., Hyde, C., Coe, B., & Paschall, M. J. (2004). Neurocognitive and physiological prerequisites for prevention of adolescent drug abuse. *Journal of Primary Prevention, 24*(4), 471–495.

Fishbein, D., Hyde, C., Eldreth, D., Paschall, M. J., Hubal, R., Das, A., et al. (2006). Neurocognitive skills moderate urban male adolescents' responses to preventive intervention materials. *Drug and Alcohol Dependence, 82*(1), 47–60.

Fisher, C. B., Jackson, J. F., & Villarruel, F. A. (1998). The study of African American and Latin American children and youth. In W. Damon & R. M. Lerner (Eds.), *Handbook of child psychology: Vol. 1. Theoretical models of human development* (5th ed., pp. 1145–1207). Hoboken, NJ: Wiley.

Fisher, C. B., Hoagwood, K., Boyce, C., Duster, T., Frank, D. A., Grisso, T., et al. (2002). Research ethics for mental health science involving ethnic minority children and youths. *American Psychologist, 57,* 1024–1040.

Fisher, L., Ames, E. W., Chisholm, K., & Savoie, L. (1997). Problems reported by parents of Romanian orphans adopted to British Columbia. *International Journal of Behavioral Development, 20*(1), 67–82.

Fisher, M, Schneider, M, Burns, J., Symons, H. & Mandel, F. S. (2001). Differences between adolescents and young adults at presentation to an eating disorders program. *Journal of Adolescent Health, 28,* 222–227.

Fisher, P. A., Gunnar, M. R., Chamberlain, P., & Reid, J. B. (2000). Preventive intervention for maltreated preschool children: Impact on children's behavior, neuroendocrine activity, and foster parent functioning. *Journal of the American Academy of Child and Adolescent Psychiatry, 39(11),* 1356–1364.

Fishman, M., Clemmey, P., & Adger, H. (2003). Mountain Manor Treatment Center: Residential adolescent addictions treatment program. In S. J. Stevens & A. R. Morral (Eds.), *Adolescent substance abuse treatment in the United States: Exemplary models from a national evaluation study* (pp. 135–154). New York: Haworth Press.

Flament, M. F., Furino, C., & Godart, N. (2005). Evidence-based pharmacotherapy of eating disorders. In D. J. Stein (Ed.), *Evidence-based psychopharmacology* (pp. 204–254). New York: Cambridge University Press.

Flanagan, K. S., Bierman, K. L., Kam, C., Coie, J. D., Dodge, K. A., Foster, E. M., et al. (2003). Identifying at-risk children at school entry: The usefulness of multibehavioral problem profiles. *Journal of Clinical Child and Adolescent Psychology, 32,* 396–407.

Flannery-Schroeder, E., Suveg, C., Safford, S., Kendall, P. C., & Webb, A. (2004). Comorbid externalizing disorders and child anxiety treatment outcomes. *Behaviour Change, 21*(1), 14–25.

Flavell, J. H. (1982). On cognitive development. *Child Development, 53(1),* 1–10.

Flavell, J. H. (1982a). Structures, stages, and sequences of cognitive development. In W. A. Collins (Ed.), *The concept of development: The Minnesota symposia on child psychology* (pp. 1–27). Hillsdale, NJ: Erlbaum.

Flavell, J. H. (2004). Theory-of-mind development: Retrospect and prospect. *Merrill-Palmer Quarterly, 50*(3), 274–290.

Flewelling, R. L., Austin, D., Hale, K., LoPlante, M., Liebig, M., Piasecki, L., et al. (2005). Implementing research-based substance abuse prevention in communities: Effects of a coalition-based prevention initiative in Vermont. *Journal of Community Psychology, 33*(3), 333–353.

Flisher, A. J., Kramer, R. A., Grosser, R. C., Alegria, M., Bird, H. R., Bourdon, K. H., et al. (1997). Correlates of unmet need for mental health services by children and adolescents. *Psychological Medicine, 27(5),* 1145–1154.

Flores, E., Cicchetti, D., & Rogosch, F. (2005). Predictors of resilience in maltreated and nonmaltreated Latino children. *Developmental Psychology, 2,* 338–351.

Floyd, F. J., Singer, G. H. S., Powers, L. E. & Costigan, C. L. (1996). Families coping with mental retardation: Assessment and therapy. In J. W. Jacobson & J. A. Mulick (Eds.), *Manual of diagnosis and professional practice in mental retardation* (pp. 277–288). Washington, DC: American Psychological Association.

Flynn, J. R. (1987). Massive IQ gains in 14 nations: What IQ tests really measure. *Psychological Bulletin, 101*(2), 171–191.

Flynn, J. R. (1998). IQ gains over time: Toward finding the causes. In U. Neisser (Ed.), *The Rising Curve: Long-term gains in IQ and related measures* (pp. 25–66). Washington, DC: American Psychological Association.

Flynn, J. R. (2007). *What is intelligence? Beyond the Flynn effect.* New York: Cambridge University Press.

Folstein, S., & Rutter, M. (1977). Genetic influences and infantile autism. *Nature, 265(5596),* 726–728.

Folstein, S., & Santangelo, S. L. (2000). Does Asperger syndrome aggregate in families? In A. Klin, F. R. Volkmar, & S. S. Sparrow (Eds.), *Asperger syndrome* (pp. 159–171). New York: Guilford Press.

Fombonne, E. (2002). Prevalence of childhood disintegrative disorder. *Autism, 6,* 149–157.

Fombonne, E. (2003). The prevalence of autism. *Journal of the American Medical Association, 289,* 87–89.

Fombonne, E. (2007). Epidemiological surveys of pervasive developmental disorders. In F. R. Volkmar (Ed.), *Autism and pervasive developmental disorders* (2nd ed., pp. 33–68). New York: Cambridge University Press.

Fombonne, E., & Tidmarsh, L. (2003). Epidemiologic data on Asperger disorder. *Child and Adolescent Psychiatric Clinics of North America, 12,* 15–21.

Fombonne, E., Simmons, H., Ford, T., Meltzer, H., & Goodman, R. (2001). Prevalence of pervasive developmental disorders in the British Nationwide Survey of Child Mental Health. *Journal of the American Academy of Child and Adolescent Psychiatry, 40,* 820–827.

Fombonne, E., Wostear, G., Cooper, V., Harrington, R., & Rutter, M. (2001a). The Maudsley long-term follow-up of child and adolescent depression: Psychiatric outcomes in adulthood. *British Journal of Psychiatry, 179*(3), 210–217.

Fombonne, E., Wostear, G., Cooper, V., Harrington, R., & Rutter, M. (2001b). The Maudsley long-term follow-up of child and adolescent depression: 2. Suicidality, criminality and social dysfunction in adulthood. *British Journal of Psychiatry, 179*(3), 218–223.

Fonagy, P. (1998). Prevention, the appropriate target of infant psychotherapy. *Infant Mental Health Journal, 19(2),* 124–150.

Fonagy, P., & Target, M. (1996). Playing with reality: I. Theory of mind and the normal development of psychic reality. *International Journal of Psychoanalysis, 77*(2), 217–233.

Fonagy, P., & Target, M. (1997). Attachment and reflective function: Their role in self-organization. *Development and Psychopathology, 9*(4), 679–700.

Fonagy, P., & Target, M. (2000). The place of psychodynamic theory in developmental psychopathology. *Development and Psychopathology, 12,* 407–425.

Fonseca, H., Ireland, M., & Resnick, M. D. (2002). Familial correlates of extreme weight control behaviors among adolescents. *International Journal of Eating Disorders, 32,* 441–448.

Ford, T., Goodman, R., & Meltzer, H. (2003). The British child and adolescent mental health survey 1999: The prevalence of DSM-IV disorders. *Journal of the American Academy of Child and Adolescent Psychiatry, 42(10),* 1203–1211.

Forehand, R., & Jones, D. J. (2002). The stability of parenting: A longitudinal analysis of inner-city African-American mothers. *Journal of Child and Family Studies, 11,* 469–483.

Forehand, R., & Kotchick, B. A. (2002). Behavioral parent training: Current challenges and potential solutions. *Journal of Child and Family Studies, 11,* 377–384.

Forehand, R., Jones, D. J., Brody, G. H., & Armistead, L. (2002). African American children's adjustment: The roles of maternal and teacher depressive symptoms. *Journal of Marriage and Family, 64*(4), 1012–1023.

Forgatch, M. S., & Patterson, G. R. (1998). Behavioral family therapy. In F. M. Dattilio (Ed.), *Case studies in couple and family therapy: Systemic and cognitive perspectives* (pp. 85–107). New York: Guilford Press.

Foster, E. M., & Jones, D. E. (2005). The high costs of aggression: Public expenditures resulting from conduct disorder. *American Journal of Public Health, 95*(10), 1767–1772.

Foster, E. M., Olchowski, A. E., & Webster-Stratton, C. H. (2007). Is stacking intervention components cost-effective? An analysis of the Incredible Years program. *Journal of the American Academy of Child and Adolescent Psychiatry, 46*(11), 1414–1424.

Foster, J. D., Kuperminc, G. P., & Price, A. W. (2004). Gender differences in posttraumatic stress and related symptoms among inner-city minority youth exposed to community violence. *Journal of Youth and Adolescence, 33*(1), 59–69.

Fowles, D. C., & Kochanska, G. (2000). Temperament as a moderator of pathways to conscience in children: The contribution of electrodermal activity. *Psychophysiology, 37,* 788–795.

Fowles, D. C., Kochanska, G., & Murray, K. (2000). Electrodermal activity and temperament in preschool children. *Psychophysiology, 37,* 777–787.

Fox, N. A. (1991). If it's not left, it's right: Electroencephalograph asymmetry and the development of emotion. *American Psychologist, 46*(8), 863–872.

Fox, N. A., Calkins, S. D., & Bell, M. A. (1994). Neural plasticity and development in the first two years of life: Evidence from cognitive and socioemotional domains of research. *Development and Psychopathology, 6(4),* 677–696.

Fox, N. A., & Card, J. A. (1999). Psychophysiological measures in the study of attachment. In J. Cassidy & P. R. Shaver (Eds.), *Handbook of attachment: Theory, research, and clinical applications* (pp. 226–245). New York: Guilford Press.

Fox, N. A., & Henderson, H. A. (1999). Does infancy matter? Predicting social behavior from infant temperament. *Infant Behavior and Development, 22*(4), 445–455.

Fox, N. A., Henderson, H. A., Marshall, P. J., Nichols, K. E., & Ghera, M. M. (2005). Behavioral inhibition: Linking biology and behavior within a developmental framework. *Annual Review of Psychology, 56,* 235–262.

Fox, N. A., Henderson, H. A., Rubin, K. H., Calkins, S. D., & Schmidt, L. A. (2001). Continuity and discontinuity of behavioral inhibition and exuberance: Psychophysiological and behavioral influences across the first four years of life. *Child Development, 72*(1), 1–21.

Fox, T. L., Barrett, P. M., & Shortt, A. L. (2002). Sibling relationships of anxious children: A preliminary investigation. *Journal of Clinical Child and Adolescent Psychology, 31*(3), 375–383.

Fraiberg, S. (1980). *Clinical studies in infant mental health.* New York: Basic Books.

Fraiberg, S., Adelson, E., & Shapiro, V. (1980). *Ghosts in the nursery: A psychoanalytic approach.* New York: Basic Books.

Franco, X., Saavedra, L. M., & Silverman, W. K. (2007). External validation of comorbid patterns of anxiety disorders in children and adolescents. *Journal of Anxiety Disorders, 21*(5), 717–729.

Frank, G. K., Bailer, U. F., Henry, S., Wagner, A., & Kaye, W. H. (2004). Neuroimaging studies in eating disorders. *CNS Spectrums, 9,* 539–548.

Frank, G. K., Wagner, A., Achenbach, S., McConaha, C., Skovira, K., Aizenstein, H., et al. (2006). Altered brain activity in women recovered from bulimic-type eating disorders after a glucose challenge: A pilot study. *International Journal of Eating Disorders, 39,* 76–79.

Franko, D. L., Striegel-Moore, R. H., Barton, B. A., Schumann, B. C., Garner, D. M., Daniels, S. R., et al. (2004). Measuring eating concerns in black and white adolescent girls. *International Journal of Eating Disorders, 35,* 179–189.

Frazier, J. A., Ahn, M. S., DeJong, S., Bent, E. K., Breeze, J. L., & Giuliano, A. J. (2005). Magnetic resonance imaging studies in early-onset bipolar disorder: A critical review. *Harvard Review of Psychiatry, 13*(3), 125–140.

Freedenthal, S., & Stiffman, A. R. (2004). Suicidal behavior in urban American Indian adolescents: A comparison with reservation youth in a southwestern state. *Suicide and Life-Threatening Behavior, 34*(2), 160–171.

Freeman, J. B., Garcia, A. B., Fucci, C., Karitani, M., Miller, L., & Leonard, H. L. (2003). Family-based treatment of early-onset obsessive-compulsive disorder. *Journal of Child and Adolescent Psychopharmacology, 13*(2, Suppl), S71-S80.

Freitas, A. L., & Downey, G. (1998). Resilience: a dynamic perspective. *International Journal of Behavioral Development, 22(2),* 263–285.

Freud, A. (1946). *The Psycho-Analytical Treatment of Children.* International University Press.

Freud, A. (1966). A short history of child analysis. *Psychoanalytic Study of the Child, 21,* 7–14.

Frick, P. J. (1998). Classification of conduct disorders. In P. J. Frick (Ed.), *Conduct disorders and severe antisocial behavior* (pp. 20–39). New York: Plenum Press.

Frick, P. J. (1998). The nature of antisocial behaviors and conduct disorders. In P. J. Frick (Ed.), *Conduct disorders and severe antisocial behavior* (pp. 9–19). New York: Plenum Press.

Frick, P. J., Bodin, D., & Barry, C. T. (2000). Psychopathic traits and conduct problems in community and clinic-referred samples of children: Further development of the psychopathy screening device. *Psychological Assessment, 12*(4), 382–393.

Frick, P. J., Cornell, A. H., Bodin, S. D., Dane, H. E., Barry, C. T., & Loney, B. R. (2003). Callous-unemotional traits and developmental pathways to severe conduct problems. *Developmental Psychology, 39*(2), 246–260.

Frick, P. J., & Dantagnan, A. L. (2005). Predicting the stability of conduct problems in children with and without callous-unemotional traits. *Journal of Child and Family Studies, 14*(4), 469–485.

Frick, P. J., & Loney, B. R. (1999). Outcomes of children and adolescents with oppositional defiant disorder and conduct disorder. In H. C. Quay & A. E. Hogan (Eds.), *Handbook of disruptive behavior disorders* (pp. 507–524). Dordrecht, Netherlands: Kluwer Academic Publishers.

Frick, P. J., & Loney, B. R. (2000). The use of laboratory and performance-based measures in the assessment of children and adolescents with conduct disorders. *Journal of Clinical Child Psychology, 29*(4), 540–554.

Frick, P. J., & Loney, B. R. (2002). Understanding the association between parent and child antisocial behavior. In R. J. McMahon & R. Peters (Eds.), *The effects of parental dysfunction on children* (pp. 105–126). New York: Kluwer Academic/Plenum Publishers.

Frick, P. J., & Morris, A. S. (2004). Temperament and developmental pathways to conduct problems. *Journal of Clinical Child and Adolescent Psychology, 33*(1), 54–68.

Frick, P. J., Lahey, B. B., Loeber, R., & Tannenbaum, L. (1993). Oppositional defiant disorder and conduct disorder: A meta-analytic review of factor analyses and cross-validation in a clinic sample. *Clinical Psychology Review, 13*(4), 319–340.

Frilo, C. M. (2004). Subtyping female adolescent psychiatric inpatients with features of eating disorders along dietary restraint and negative affect dimensions. *Behavior Research and Therapy, 42,* 67–78.

Friman, P. C., Handwerk, M. L., Smith, G. L., Larzelere, R. E., Lucas, C. P., & Shaffer, D. M. (2000). External validity of conduct and oppositional defiant disorders determined by the NIMH Diagnostic Interview Schedule for Children. *Journal of Abnormal Child Psychology, 28,* 277–286.

Fristad, M. A., Goldberg-Arnold, J. S., & Gavazzi, S. M. (2002). Multifamily psychoeducation groups (MFPG) for families of children with bipolar disorder. *Bipolar Disorders, 4*(4), 254–262.

Fristad, M. A., Goldberg-Arnold, J. S., & Gavazzi, S. M. (2003). Multi-family psychoeducation groups in the treatment of children with disorders. *Journal of Marital and Family Therapy, 29*(4), 491–504.

Fristad, M. A., & Shaver, A. E. (2001). Psychosocial interventions for suicidal children and adolescents. *Depression and Anxiety, 14*(3), 192–197.

Fristad, M. A., Shaver, A. E., & Holderle, K. E. (2002). Mood disorders in childhood and adolescence. In D. T. Marsh & M. A. Fristad (Eds.), *Handbook of serious emotional disturbance in children and adolescents* (pp. 228–265). New York: Wiley.

Frith, U., & Happe, F. (1994). Autism: Beyond "theory of mind." *Cognition, 50*(1–3), 115–132.

Fritz, G. K., Fritsch, S., & Hagino, O. (1997). Somatoform disorder in children and adolescents: A review of the past 10 years. *Journal of the American Academy of Child and Adolescent Psychiatry, 36*(10), 1329–1338.

Frosch, C. A., Mangelsdorf, S. C., & McHale, J. L. (2000). Marital behavior and the security of preschooler-parent attachment relationships. *Journal of Family Psychology, 14*(1), 144–161.

Fuligni, A. J. (1997). The academic achievement of adolescents from immigrant families: The roles of family background, attitudes, and behavior. *Child Development, 68(2),* 351–363.

Fuligni, A. J. (1998a). The adjustment of children from immigrant families. *Current Directions in Psychological Science, 7(4),* 99–103.

Fuligni, A. J. (1998b). Authority, autonomy, and parent-adolescent conflict and cohesion: A study of adolescents from Mexican, Chinese, Filipino, and European backgrounds. *Developmental Psychology, 34(4),* 782–792.

Fuligni, A. J., Tseng, V., & Lam, M. (1999). Attitudes toward family obligations among American adolescents with Asian, Latin American, and European backgrounds. *Child Development, 70(4),* 1030–1044.

Fuligni, A. J., Witkow, M., & Garcia, C. (2005). Ethnic identity and the academic adjustment of adolescents from Mexican, Chinese, and European backgrounds. *Developmental Psychology, 41(5),* 799–811.

Fung, M. T., Raine, A., Loeber, R., Lynam, D. R., Steinhaur, S. R., Venables, P. H., et al. (2005). Reduced electrodermal activity in psychopathy-prone adolescents. *Journal of Abnormal Psychology, 114*(2), 187–196.

Funk, R. R., McDermeit, M., Godley, S. H., & Adams, L. (2003). Maltreatment issues by level of adolescent substance abuse treatment: The extent of the problem at intake and relationship to early outcomes. *Child Maltreatment: Journal of the American Professional Society on the Abuse of Children, 8*(1), 36–45.

Furman, W. (1999). Friends and lovers: The role of peer relationships in adolescent heterosexual relationships. In Collins, W. A., & Laursen, B. (Eds.), *The Minnesota symposia on child psychology: Vol. 29. Relationships as developmental constructs* (pp. 133–154). Hillsdale, NJ: Erlbaum.

Furman, W. (2002). The emerging field of adolescent romantic relationships. *Current Directions in Psychological Science, 11*(5), 177–180.

Furman, W., & Shaffer, L. (2003). The role of romantic relationships in adolescent development. From P. Florsheim (Ed.), *Adolescent romantic relations and sexual behavior: Theory, research, and practical implications* (pp. 3–22). Mahwah, NJ: Erlbaum.

Furr-Holden, C. D. M., Ialongo, N. S., Anthony, J. C., Petras, H., & Kellam, S. G. (2004). Developmentally inspired drug prevention: Middle school outcomes in a school-based randomized prevention trial. *Drug Alcohol Dependence, 73*(2), 149–158.

Gabowitz, D., Zucker, M., & Cook, A. (2008). Neuropsychological assessment in clinical evaluation of children and adolescents with complex trauma. *Journal of Child and Adolescent Trauma, 1,* 163–178.

Gadow, K. D., & Nolan, E. E. (2002). Differences between preschool children with ODD, ADHD, and ODD+ADHD symptoms. *Journal of Child Psychology and Psychiatry and Allied Disciplines, 43* (2), 191–201.

Gadow, K. D., Sprafkin, J., Carlson, G. A., Schneider, J., Nolan, E. E., Mattison, R. E., et al. (2002). A DSM-IV-referenced, adolescent self-report rating scale. *Journal of the American Academy of Child and Adolescent Psychiatry, 41*(6), 671–679.

Gadow, K. D., Sverd, J., Sprafkin, J., Nolan, E. E., & Grossman, S. (1999). Long-term methylphenidate therapy in children with comorbid attention-deficit hyperactivity disorder and chronic multiple tic disorder. *Archives of General Psychiatry, 56,* 330–336.

Galambos, N., Leadbetter, B., & Barker, E. (2004). Gender differences in and risk factors for depression in adolescence: A 4-year longitudinal study. *International Journal of Behavioral Development, 28*(1), 16–25.

Galanter, C. A., & Leibenluft, E. (2008). Frontiers between attention deficit hyperactivity disorder and bipolar disorder. *Child and Adolescent Psychiatry Clinics of North America, 17*(2), 325–346.

Galanter, C. A., Wasserman, G., Sloan, R. P, & Pine, D. S. (1999). Changes in autonomic regulation with age: Implications for psychopharmacologic treatments in children and adolescents. *Journal of Child and Adolescent Psychopharmacology, 9(4),* 257–265.

Gallay, L. S., & Flanagan, C. A. (2000). The well-being of children in a changing economy: Time for a new social contract in America. In R. D. Taylor & M. Wang (Eds.), *Resilience across contexts: Family, work, culture and community* (pp. 3–330). Mahwah, NJ: Erlbaum.

Galvin, M. R., Stilwell, B. M., Shekhar, A., Kipta, S. M., & Goldfarb, S. M. (1997). Maltreatment, conscience functioning and dopamine beta hydroxylase in emotionally disturbed boys. *Child Abuse and Neglect, 21,* 83–92.

Ganiban, J., Barnett, D., & Cicchetti, D. (2000). Negative reactivity and attachment: Down syndrome's contribution to the attachment-temperament debate. *Development and Psychopathology, 12*(1), 1–21.

Garb, H. N., Wood, J. M., Lilienfeld, S. O., & Nezworski, M. T. (2002). Effective use of projective techniques in clinical practice: Let the data help with selection and interpretation. *Professional Psychology: Research and Practice, 33(5),* 454–463.

Garber, J. (1984). Classification of childhood psychopathology: A developmental perspective. *Child Development, 55,* 30–48.

Garber, J. (2000). Development and depression. In A. J. Sameroff & M. Lewis et al. (Eds.), *Handbook of developmental psychopathology* (2nd ed., pp. 467–490), Dordrecht, Netherlands: Kluwer Academic Publishers.

Garber, J., Braafladt, N., & Weiss, B. (1995). Affect regulation in depressed and nondepressed children and young adolescents. *Development and Psychopathology, 7,* 93–115.

Garber, J., & Carter, J. S. (2006). Major depression. In R. T. Ammerman (Ed.), *Comprehensive handbook of personality and psychopathology* (Vol. 3, pp. 165–216). Hoboken, NJ: Wiley.

Garber, J., & Kaminski, K. M. (2000). Laboratory and performance-based measures of depression in children and adolescents. *Journal of Clinical Child Psychology, 29*(4), 509–525.

Garber, J., Keiley, M. K., & Martin, N. C. (2002). Developmental trajectories of adolescents' depressive symptoms: Predictors of change. *Journal of Consulting and Clinical Psychology, 70*(1), 79–95.

Garber, J., & Little, S. (1999). Predictors of competence among offspring of depressed mothers. *Journal of Adolescent Research, 14*(1), 44–71.

Garber, J., & Martin, N. C. (2002). Negative cognitions in offspring of depressed parents: Mechanisms of risk. In S. H. Goodman & I. H. Gotlib (Eds.), *Children of depressed parents: Mechanisms*

of risk and implications for treatment (pp. 121–153). Washington, DC: American Psychological Association.

Garcia Coll, C. (2001). Cultural influences on children's and families' well-being. In A. Thornton (Ed.), *The well-being of children and families: Research and data needs* (pp. 244–261). Ann Arbor: The University of Michigan Press.

Garcia Coll, C., Akerman, A., & Cicchetti, D. (2000). Cultural influences on developmental processes and outcomes: Implications for the study of development and psychopathology. *Development and Psychopathology, 12,* 333–356.

Garcia Coll, C., & Magnuson, K. (1999). Cultural influences on child development: Are we ready for a paradigm shift? In A. S. Masten (Ed.), *Cultural Processes in Child Development, Minnesota Symposium on Child Psychology* (Vol. 29, pp. 1–24). Mahwah, NJ: Erlbaum.

Garcia Coll, C. T., & Meyer, E. C. (1993). The sociocultural context of infant development. In C. H. Zeanah (Ed.), *Handbook of infant mental health* (pp. 56–69). New York: Guilford Press.

Garcia, J. A., & Weisz, J. R. (2002). When youth mental health care stops: Therapeutic relationships problems and other reasons for ending youth outpatient treatment. *Journal of Consulting and Clinical Psychology, 70(2),* 439–443.

Garcia-Lopez, L. J., Olivares, J., Beidel, D., Albano, A. M., Turner, S., & Rosa, A. I. (2006). Efficacy of three treatment protocols for adolescents with social anxiety disorder: A 5-year follow-up assessment. *Journal of Anxiety Disorders, 20*(2), 175–191.

Gardner, H. (1993). *Multiple intelligences.* New York: Basic Books.

Gardner, J., Carran, D. T., & Nudler, S. (2001). Measuring quality of life and quality of services through personal outcomes measures: Implication for public policy. In L. M. Glidden (Ed.), *International review of research in mental retardation* (Vol. 24, pp. 75–100). San Diego, CA: Academic Press.

Gardner, M., & Steinberg, L. (2005). Peer influence on risk taking, risk preference, and risky decision making in adolescence and adulthood: An experimental study. *Developmental Psychology, 41*(4), 625–635.

Gardner, W. I., Graeber-Whalen, J. L., & Ford, D. R. (2001). Behavioral therapies: Individualizing interventions through treatment formulations. In A. Dosen & K. Day (Eds.), *Treating mental illness and behavior disorders in children and adults with mental retardation* (pp. 69–100). Washington, DC: American Psychiatric Publishing.

Garfield, J. L., & Perry, T. (2001). Social cognition, language acquisition and the development of the theory of mind. *Mind and Language, 16*(5), 494–541.

Garland, A. F., Lau, A. S., Yeh, M., McCabe, K. M., Hough, R. L., & Landsverk, J. A. (2005). Racial and ethnic differences in utilization of mental health services among high-risk youths. *American Journal of Psychiatry, 162(7),* 1336–1343.

Garmezy, N. (1974). The study of competence in children at risk for severe psychopathology. In E. J. Anthony & C. Koupernick (Eds.), *The child in his family: Children at psychiatric risk.* New York: Wiley.

Garmezy, N. (1985). The NIMH-Israeli high-risk study: Commendation, comments, and cautions. *Schizophrenia Bulletin, 11(3),* 349–353.

Garmezy, N., Masten, A. S., & Tellegen, A. (1984). The study of stress and competence in children: A building block for developmental psychopathology. *Child Development, 55,* 97–111.

Garmezy, N., & Rutter, M. (1983). *Stress, coping and development in children*. Baltimore, MD: John Hopkins University Press.

Garrett, J. N., Thorp, E. K., Behrmann, M. M., & Denham, S. A. (1998). The impact of early intervention legislation: Local perceptions. *Topics in Early Childhood Special Education, 18(3)*, 183–190.

Gartstein, M. A., Gonzalez, C., Carranza, J. A., Ahadi, S. A., Ye, R., Rothbart, M. K., et al. (2006). Studying cross-cultural differences in the development of infant temperament: People's Republic of China, the United States of America, and Spain. *Child Psychiatry Human Development, 37*, 145–161.

Gaub, M., & Carlson, C. L. (1997a). Behavioral characteristics of DSM-IV ADHD subtypes in a school-based population. *Journal of Abnormal Child Psychology, 25*, 103–111.

Gaub, M., & Carlson, C. L. (1997b). Gender differences in ADHD: a meta-analysis and critical review. *Journal of the American Academy of Child and Adolescent Psychiatry, 36*, 1036–1045.

Gaughan, M. (2006). The gender structure of adolescent peer influence on drinking. *Journal of Health and Social Behavior, 47*(1), 47–61.

Gaylor, E. E., Burnham, M. M., Goodlin-Jones, B. L., & Anders, T. F. (2005). A longitudinal follow-up study of young children's sleep patterns using a developmental classification system. *Behavioral Sleep Medicine, 3*(1), 44–61.

Ge, X., Brody, G. H., Conger, R. D., Simons, R. L., & Murry, V. M. (2002). Contextual amplification of pubertal transition effects on deviant peer affiliation and externalizing behavior among African American children. *Developmental Psychology, 38*(1), 42–54.

Ge, X., Kim, I. J., Brody, G. H., Conger, R. D., Simons, R. L., Gibbons, F. X., et al.. (2003). It's about timing and change: Pubertal transition effects on symptoms of major depression among African American youths. *Developmental Psychology, 39*(3), 430–439.

Gelb, S. A. (1997). The problem of typological thinking in mental retardation. *Mental Retardation, 35*(6), 448–457.

Gelb, S. A. (2002). The dignity of humanity is not a scientific construct. *Mental Retardation, 40*(1), 55–56.

Gelfand, D. M. (2001). Infant mental health in a changing society. In G. Bremner & A. Fogel (Eds.), *Blackwell handbook of infant development. Handbooks of developmental psychology* (pp. 589–616). Malden, MA: Blackwell Publishing.

Gelfand, D. M., & Teti, D. M. (1990). The effects of maternal depression on children. *Clinical Psychology Review, 10*(3), 329–353.

Geller, B., & Luby, J. (1997). Child and adolescent bipolar disorder: A review of the past 10 years. *Journal of the American Academy of Child and Adolescent Psychiatry, 36*(9), 1168–1176.

Geller, B., Craney, J. L., Bolhofner, K., DelBello, M. P., Axelson, D., Luby, J. L., et al. (2003). Phenomenology and longitudinal course of children with a prepubertal and early adolescent bipolar disorder phenotype. In B. Geller & M. P. DelBello (Eds.), *Bipolar disorder in childhood and early adolescence* (pp. 25–50). New York: Guildford Press.

Geller, B., Craney, J. L., Bolhofner, K., Nickelsburg, M. J., Williams, M., & Zimerman, B. (2002). Two-year prospective follow-up of children with a prepubertal and early adolescent bipolar disorder phenotype. *American Journal of Psychiatry, 159*(6), 927–933.

Geller, B., Tillman, R., & Bolhofner, K. (2007). Proposed definitions of bipolar I disorder episodes and daily rapid cycling phenomena in preschoolers, school-aged children, adolescents, and adults. *Journal of Child and Adolescent Psychopharmacology, 17*(2), 217–222.

Geller, B., Tillman, R., Bolhofner, K., Zimmerman, B., Strauss, N. A., & Kaufmann, P. (2006). Controlled, blindly rated, direct-interview family study of a prepubertal and early-adolescent bipolar I disorder phenotype. *Archives of General Psychiatry, 63*(10), 1130–1138.

Geller, B., Tillman, R., Craney, J. L., & Bolhofner, K. (2004). Four-year prospective outcome and natural history of mania in children with a prepubertal and early adolescent bipolar disorder phenotype. *Archives of General Psychiatry, 61*(5), 459–467.

Geller, B., Zimerman, B., Williams, M., Bolhofner, K., & Craney, J. L. (2001). Adult psychosocial outcome of prepubertal major depressive disorder. *Journal of the American Academy of Child and Adolescent Psychiatry, 40*(6), 673–677.

Geller, B., Zimerman, B., Williams, M., DelBello, M. P., Bolhofner, K., Craney, J. L., Frazier, J., Beringer, L., & Nickelsburg, M. J. (1997). Bipolar disorder at prospective follow-up of adults who had prepubertal major depressive disorder. *Journal of Child and Adolescent Psychiatry, 36*(9), 1168–1176.

Geller, B., Zimerman, B., Williams, M., DelBello, M. P., Frazier, J., & Beringer, W. (2002). Phenomenology of prepubertal and early adolescent bipolar disorder: Examples of elated mood, grandiose behaviors, decreased need for racing thoughts and hypersexuality. *Journal of Child and Adolescent Psychopharmacology, 12*(1), 3–9.

Geller, D. A., Biederman, J., Stewart, S. E., Mullin, B., Farrell, C., Wagner, K. D., et al. (2003). Impact of comorbidity on treatment response to Paroxetine in pediatric obsessive-compulsive disorder: Is the use of exclusion criteria empirically supported in randomized clinical trials? *Journal of Child and Adolescent Psychopharmacology, 13*(1), 19–29.

Geller, D., Biederman, J., Jones, J., Park, K., Schwartz, S., Shapiro, S., et al. (1998). Is juvenile obsessive-compulsive disorder a developmental sub-type of the disorder? A review of the pediatric literature. *Journal of the American Academy of Child and Adolescent Psychiatry, 37*, 420–427.

George, C., & Solomon, J. (1999). Attachment and caregiving: The caregiving behavioral system. In J. Cassidy & P. R. Shaver (Eds.), *Handbook of attachment: Theory, research, and clinical applications* (pp. 649–670). New York: Guilford Press.

George, C., Herman, K., & Ostrander, R. (2006). The family environment and developmental psychopathology: The unique and interactive effects of depression, attention, and conduct problems. *Child Psychiatry and Human Development, 37*(2), 163–177.

George, C., Kaplan, N., & Main, M. (1984/1996). Adult attachment interview. Unpublished protocol, Department of Psychology, University of California, Berkeley.

George, S., & Moselhy, H. (2005). "Gateway hypothesis"—A preliminary evaluation of variables predicting non-conformity. *Addictive Disorders and Their Treatment, 4*(1), 39–40.

Georgiades, S., Szatmari, P., Zwaigenbaum, L., Duku, E., Bryson, S., Roberts, W., et al. (2007). Structure of the autism symptom phenotype: A proposed multidimensional model. *Journal of the American Academy of Child and Adolescent Psychiatry, 46*(2), 188–196.

Georgiou, S. N. (2008). Parental style and child bullying and victimization experiences in school. *Social Psychology of Education, 11*(3), 213–227.

Gernsbacher, M. A., Stevenson, J. L., Khandakar, S., & Goldsmith, H. H. (2008). Why does joint attention look atypical in autism? *Society for Research in Child Development, 2*(1), 38–45.

Ghaziuddin, M. (2002). Asperger syndrome: Associated psychiatric and medical conditions. *Focus on Autism and Other Developmental Disabilities, 17*, 138–144.

Ghaziuddin, M. (2005). A family history study of Asperger syndrome. *Journal of Autism and Developmental Disorders, 35*(2), 177–182.

Ghaziuddin, M., & Burmeister, M. (1999). Deletion of chromosome 2 q37 and autism: A distinct subtype? *Journal of Autism and Developmental Disorders, 29*, 259–263.

Ghaziuddin, M., & Butler, E. (1998). Clumsiness in autism and Asperger syndrome: A further report. *Journal of Intellectual Disability Research, 42*, 43–48.

Ghaziuddin, M., Ghaziuddin, N., & Greden, J. (2002). Depression in persons with autism: Implications for research and clinical care. *Journal of Autism and Developmental Disorders, 32*, 299–306.

Ghaziuddin, M., Zaccagnini, J., Tsai, L., & Elardo, S. (1999). Is megalencephaly specific to autism? *Journal of Intellectual Disability Research, 43*, 279–282.

Giaconia, R. M., Reinherz, H. Z., Paradis, A. D., & Stashwick, C. K. (2003). Comorbidity of substance use disorders and posttraumatic stress disorder in adolescents. In P. Ouimette & P. J. Brown (Eds.), *Trauma and substance abuse: Causes, consequences, and treatment of comorbid disorders* (pp. 227–242). Washington, DC: American Psychological Association.

Giaconia, R. M., Reinherz, H. Z., Silverman, A. B., Pakiz, B., Frost, A. K., & Cohen, E. (1995). Traumas and posttraumatic stress disorder in a community population of older adolescents. *Journal of the American Academy of Child and Adolescent Psychiatry, 34*, 1369–1380.

Giannopoulou, I., Dikaiakou, A., & Yule, W. (2006). Cognitive-behavioural group intervention for PTSD symptoms in children following the Athens 1999 earthquake: A pilot study. *Clinical Child Psychology and Psychiatry, 11*(4), 543–553.

Giannopoulou, I., Strouthos, M., Smith, P., Dikaiakou, A., Galanopoulou, V., & Yule, W. (2006). Post-traumatic stress reactions of children and adolescents exposed to the Athens 1999 earthquake. *European Psychiatry, 21*(3), 160–166.

Giedd, J. N., Rosenthal, M. A., Rose, A. B., Blumenthal, J. D., Molloy, E., Dopp, R. R., et al. (2004). Brain development in healthy children and adolescents: Magnetic imaging studies. In M. S. Keshavan, J. L. Kennedy, & R. M. Murray (Eds.), *Neurodevelopment and schizophrenia* (pp. 35–44). New York: Cambridge University Press.

Gifford-Smith, M., Dodge, K. A., Dishion, T. J., & McCord, J. (2005). Peer influence in children and adolescents: Crossing the bridge from developmental to intervention science. *Journal of Abnormal Child Psychology, 33*(3), 255–265.

Gil, A. G., Wagner, E. F., & Tubman, J. G. (2004). Culturally sensitive substance abuse intervention for Hispanic and African American adolescents: Empirical examples from the Alcohol Treatment Targeting Adolescents in Need (ATTAIN) Project. *Addiction, 99*(Suppl. 2), 140–150.

Gilbert, S. C. (2003). Eating disorders in women of color. *Clinical Psychology: Science and Practice, 10*, 444–455.

Gilchrist, A., Green, J., Cox, A., Burton, D., Rutter, M., & LeCouteur, A. (2001). Development and current functioning in adolescents with Asperger syndrome: A comparative study. *Journal of Child Psychology and Psychiatry and Allied Disciplines, 42*, 227–240.

Gildner, J., & Zionts, L. (1997). Planning for inclusion in an elementary setting. In P. Zionts (Ed.), *Inclusion strategies for students with learning and behavioral problems: Perspectives, experiences, and best practices* (pp. 101–115). Austin, TX: PRO-ED.

Gillham, J. E., & Reivich, K. (2004). Cultivating optimism in childhood and adolescence. *Annals of the American Academy of Political and Social Science, 591*, 146–163.

Gillberg, C. (1999). Neurodevelopmental processes and psychological functioning in autism. *Development and Psychopathology, 11*(3), 567–587.

Gillberg, C., & Ehlers, S. (1998). High-functioning people with autism and Asperger syndrome: A literature review. In E. Schopler & G. B. Mesibov (Eds.), *Asperger syndrome or high-functioning autism? Current issues in autism* (pp. 79–106). New York: Plenum Press.

Gillberg, I. C., & Gillberg, C. (1989). Asperger syndrome: Some epidemiological considerations: A research note. *Journal of Child Psychology and Psychiatry, 30*(4), 631–638.

Gillham, J. E., & Reivich, K. J. (1999). Prevention of depressive symptoms in school children: A research update. *Psychological Science, 10*(5), 461–462.

Gillham, J. E., Reivich, K. J., Jaycox, L. H., & Seligman, M. E. P. (1995). Prevention of depressive symptoms in schoolchildren: Two-year follow-up. *Psychological Science, 6*(6), 343–351.

Gilliom, M., Shaw, D. S., Beck, J. E., Schonberg, M. A., & Lukon, J. L. (2002). Anger regulation in disadvantaged preschool boys: Strategies, antecedents, and the development of self-control. *Developmental Psychology, 38*(2), 222–235.

Gilmore, L., Campbell, J. & Cuskelly, M. (2003). Developmental expectations, personality stereotypes, and attitudes towards inclusive education: Community and teacher views of Down syndrome. *International Journal of Disability, Development and Education, 50*(1), 65–76.

Gingerich, K. J., Turnock, P., Litfin, J. K., & Rosen, L. A. (1998). Diversity and attention deficit hyperactivity disorder. *Journal of Clinical Psychology, 54*, 415–426.

Ginsburg, G. S., Albano, A. M., Findling, R. L., Kratochvil, C., & Walkup, J. (2005). Integrating cognitive behavioral therapy and pharmacotherapy in the treatment of adolescent depression. *Cognitive and Behavioral Practice, 12*(2), 252–262.

Ginsburg, G. S., Riddle, M. A., & Davies, M. (2006). Somatic symptoms in children and adolescents with anxiety disorders. *Journal of the American Academy of Child and Adolescent Psychiatry, 45*(10), 1179–1187.

Ginsburg, G. S., & Schlossberg, M. C., (2002). Family-based treatment of childhood anxiety disorders. *International Review of Psychiatry, 14*(2), 143–154.

Giordano, P. C., Manning, W. D., & Longmore, M. A. (2006). Adolescent romantic relationships: An emerging portrait of their nature and developmental significance. In A. C. Crouter & A. Booth (Eds.), *Romance and sex in adolescence and early adulthood: Risks and opportunities. The Penn State University family issues symposia series* (pp. 127–150). Mahwah, NJ: Erlbaum.

Girouard, P. C., Baillargeon, R. H., Tremblay, R. E., Glorieux, J., Lefebvre, F., & Robaey, P. (1998). Developmental pathways leading to externalizing behaviors in 5 year olds born before 29 weeks of gestation. *Journal of Developmental and Behavioral Pediatrcs, 19*, 244–253.

Giummarra, M. J., & Haslam, N. (2005). The lay concept of childhood mental disorder. *Child Psychiatry and Human Development, 35(3),* 265–280.

Gjerde, P. F., Block, J., & Block J. H. (1986). Egocentrism and ego resiliency: Personality characteristics associated with perspective-taking from early childhood to adolescence. *Journal of Personality and Social Psychology, 51,* 423–434.

Gladstone, T. R. G., & Beardslee, W. R. (2002). Treatment, intervention, and prevention with children of depressed parents: A developmental perspective. In S. H. Goodman & I. H. Gotlib (Eds.), *Children of depressed parents: Mechanisms of risk and implications for treatment* (pp. 277–305). Washington, DC: American Psychological Association.

Glascoe, F. P. (1995). The role of parents in the detection of developmental and behavioral problems. *Pediatrics, 95(6),* 829–836.

Glascoe, F. P. (1997). Parents' concerns about children's development: Prescreening technique or screening test? *Pediatrics, 99(4),* 522–528.

Glascoe, F. P. (2000). Evidence-based approach to developmental and behavioral surveillance using parents' concerns. *Child: Care, Health and Development, 26*(2), 137–149.

Glascoe, F. P. (2001). Can teachers' global ratings identify children with academic problems? *Journal of Developmental and Behavioral Pediatrics, 22(3),* 163–168.

Gleaves, D. H., Brown, J. D., & Warren, C. S. (2004). The continuity/discontinuity models of eating disorders: A review of the literature and implications for assessment, treatment and prevention. *Behavior Modification, 28,* 739–762.

Glidden, L. M. (2002). Parenting children with developmental disabilities: A ladder of influence. In J. G. Borowski, S. Landesman, & M. Bristol-Power (Eds.), *Parenting and the child's world: Influences on academic, intellectual, and social-emotional development. Monographs in Parenting* (pp. 329–344). Mahwah, NJ: Erlbaum.

Goenjian, A. K., Karayan, I., Pynoos, R. S., & Minassian, D. (1997). Outcome of psychotherapy among early adolescents after trauma. *American Journal of Psychiatry, 154*(4), 536–542.

Goenjian, A. K., Pynoos, R. S., Steinberg, A. M., Najarian, L. M., Asarnow, J. R., & Karayan, I., (1995). Psychiatric co-morbidity in children after the 1988 earthquake in Armenia. *Journal of the American Academy of Child and Adolescent Psychiatry, 34,* 1174–1184.

Goenjian, A. K., Stilwell, B. M., Steinberg, A. M., Fairbanks, L. A., Galvin, M., Karayan, I., et al. (1999). Moral development among adolescents after trauma. *Journal of the American Academy of Child and Adolescent Psychiatry, 38,* 376–384.

Gogtay, N., Giedd, J. N., Lusk, L., Hayashi, K. M., Greenstein, D., Vaituzis, A. C., et al. (2004). Dynamic mapping of human cortical development during childhood through early adulthood. *Procedures of the National Academy of Science, 101*(21), 8174–8179.

Goin, R. & Myers, B. J. (2004). Characteristics of infantile autism: Moving toward earlier detection. *Focus on Autism and Other Developmental Disabilities, 19*(1), 5–12.

Goin-Kochel, R., & Myers, B. J. (2005). Parental report of early autistic symptoms: Differences in ages of detection and frequencies of characteristics among three autism-spectrum disorders. *Journal on Developmental Disabilities, 11*(2), 21–39.

Gold, M. S., Frost-Pineda, K., & Jacobs, W. S. (2003). Overeating, binge eating, and eating disorders as addictions. *Psychiatric Annals, 33,* 117–122.

Goldberg, S., Gotowiec, A., & Simmons, R. J. (1995). Infant-mother attachment and behavior problems in healthy and chronically ill preschoolers. *Development and Psychopathology, 7*(2), 267–282.

Goldberg-Arnold, J. S., & Fristad, M. A. (2003). Psychotherapy for children with bipolar disorder. In B. Geller & M. P. DelBello (Eds.), *Bipolar disorder in childhood and early adolescence* (pp. 272–294). New York: Guildford Press.

Golden, Z. L., & Golden, C. J. (2001). Do early onset conduct disordered adolescents perform like brain injured or normal adolescents on cognitive tests? *International Journal of Neuroscience, 111*(1–2), 109–121.

Goldman, D., Oroszi, G., & Ducci, F. (2005). The genetics of addictions: Uncovering the genes. *National Review of Genetics, 6*(7), 521–532.

Goldsmith, H. H., Buss, K. A., & Lemery, K. S. (1997). Toddler and childhood temperament: Expanded content, stronger genetic evidence, new evidence for the importance of environment. *Developmental Psychology, 33*(6), 891–905.

Goldsmith, H. H., & Lemery, K. S. (2000). Linking temperamental fearfulness and anxiety symptoms: A behavior-genetic perspective. *Biological Psychiatry, 48*(12), 1199–1209.

Goldsmith, H. H., Lemery, K. S., Aksan, N., & Buss, K. A. (2000). Temperamental substrates of personality. In V. J. Molfese & D. L. Molfese (Eds.), *Temperament and personality development across the life span* (pp. 1–32). Mahwah, NJ: Erlbaum.

Goldsmith, H. H., Lemery, K. S., Essex, M. J. (2004). Temperament as a liability factor for childhood behavioral disorders: The concept of liability. In L. F. DiLalla (Ed.), *Behavior genetics principles: Perspectives in development, personality, and psychopathology. Decade of behavior* (pp. 19–39). Washington, DC: American Psychological Association.

Goldstein, G., Allen, D. N., Minshew, N. J., Williams, D. L., Volkmar, F., Klin, A., et al. (2008). The structure of intelligence in children and adults with high functioning autism. *Neuropsychology, 22*(3), 301–312.

Goldston, D. B. (2004). Conceptual issues in understanding the relationship between suicidal behavior and substance use during adolescence. *Drug and Alcohol Dependence, 76*(Suppl. 7), S79-S91.

Goodey, C. F. (2001). What is developmental disability? The origin and nature of our conceptual models. *Journal on Developmental Disabilities, 8*(2), 1–18.

Goodlin-Jones, B. L., Burnham, M. M., & Anders, T. F. (2000). Sleep and sleep disturbances: Regulatory processes in infancy. In A. J. Sameroff & M. Lewis (Eds.), *Handbook of developmental psychopathology* (2nd ed., pp. 309–325). Dordrecht, Netherlands: Kluwer Academic Publishers.

Goodman, M. R., Stormshak, E. A., & Dishion, T. J. (2001). The significance of peer victimization at two points in development. *Journal of Applied Developmental Psychology, 22,* 507–526.

Goodman, R., & Stevenson, J. (1989a). A twin study of hyperactivity: I. An examination of hyperactivity scores and categories derived from Rutter teacher and parent questionnaires. *Journal of Child Psychology and Psychiatry, 30*(5), 671–689.

Goodman, R., & Stevenson, J. (1989b). A twin study of hyperactivity: II. The aetiological role of genes, family relationships and perinatal adversity. *Journal of Child Psychology and Psychiatry, 30*(5), 691–709.

Goodman, S. H., & Gotlib, I. H. (1999). Risk for psychopathology in the children of depressed mothers: A developmental model for understanding mechanisms of transmission. *Psychological Review, 106*(3), 458–490.

Goodman, S. H., & Gotlib, I. H. (2002). Transmission of risk to children of depressed parents: Integration and conclusions. In S. H. Goodman & I. H. Gotlib (Eds.), *Children of depressed parents: Mechanisms of risk and implications for treatment* (pp. 307–326). Washington, DC: American Psychological Association.

Goodnight, J. A., Bates, J. E., Staples, A. D., Pettit, G. S., & Dodge, K. A. (2007). Temperamental resistance to control increases the association between sleep problems and externalizing behavior development. *Journal of Family Psychology, 21(1)*, 39–48.

Goodnow, J. J. (1999). Families and development. In M. Bennett (Ed.), *Developmental psychology: Achievements and prospects* (pp. 72–88). New York: Psychology Press.

Goodwin, R. D., Lieb, R., Hoefler, M., Pfister, H., Bittner, A., Beesdo, K., et al. (2004). Panic attack as a risk factor for severe psychopathology. *American Journal of Psychiatry, 161*(12), 2207–2214.

Gordon, B., & Saklofske, D. H. (1994). New approaches to the developmental-difference debate. *Developmental Disabilities Bulletin, 22*(1), 54–72.

Gordon, J., King, N., Gullone, E., Muris, P., & Ollendick, T. H. (2007). Nighttime fears of children and adolescents: Frequency, content, severity, harm expectations, disclosure, and coping behaviours. *Behaviour Research and Therapy, 45*(10), 2464–2472.

Gordon, R. (1983). An operational classification of disease prevention. *Public Health Reports, 98*, 107–109.

Gordon, R. (1987). An operational classification of disease prevention. In J. A. Steinberg & M. M. Silverman (Eds.), *Preventing mental disorders* (pp. 20–26). Rockville, MD: Department of Health and Human Services.

Gothelf, D., Aharonovsky, O., Horesh, N., Carty, T., & Apter, A. (2004). Life events and personality factors in children and adolescents with obsessive-compulsive disorder and other anxiety disorders. *Comprehensive Psychiatry, 45*(3), 192–198.

Gotlib, I. H., & Sommerfeld, B. K. (1999). Cognitive functioning in depressed children and adolescents: A developmental perspective. In C. A. Essau & F. Petermann (Eds.), *Depressive disorders in children and adolescents: Epidemiology, risk factors, and treatment* (pp. 195–236). Northvale, NJ: Jason Aronson.

Gottlieb, G. (2003). On making behavioral genetics truly developmental. *Human Development, 46(6)*, 337–355.

Gottlieb, G., Wahlsten, D., & Lickliter, R. (1998). The significance of biology for human development: A developmental psychobiological systems view. In W. Damon & R. M. Lerner (Eds.), *Handbook of Child Psychology: Vol. 1. Theoretical Models of Human Development* (5th ed., pp. 635–684). Hoboken, NJ: Wiley.

Gould, M. S., Greenberg, T., Velting, D. M., & Shaffer, D. (2003). Youth suicide risk and preventive interventions: A review of the past 10 years. *Journal of the American Academy of Child and Adolescent Psychiatry, 42*(4), 386–405.

Gould, M. S., Velting, D., Kleinman, M., Lucas, C., Thomas, J. G., & Chung, M. (2004). Teenagers' attitudes about coping strategies and help-seeking behavior for suicidality. *Journal of the*

American Academy of Child and Adolescent Psychiatry, 43(9), 1124–1133.

Gowers, S. G. (2006). Evidence based research in CBT with adolescent eating disorders. *Child and Adolescent Mental Health, 11*, 9–12.

Gowers, S., & Bryant-Waugh, R. (2004). Management of child and adolescent eating disorders: The current evidence base and future directions. *Journal of Child Psychology and Psychiatry, 45*, 63–83.

Graber, J. A., & Brooks-Gunn, J. (1996). Transitions and turning points: Navigating the passage from childhood through adolescence. *Developmental Psychology, 32*(4), 768–776.

Graber, J. A., Lewinsohn, P. M., Seeley, J. R., & Brooks-Gunn, J. (1997). Is psychopathology associated with the timing of pubertal development? *Journal of the American Academy of Child and Adolescent Psychiatry, 36*(12), 1768–1776.

Graber, J. A., Tyrka, A. R., & Brooks-Gunn, J. (2003). How similar are correlates of different subclinical eating problems and bulimia nervosa? *Journal of Child Psychology and Psychiatry, 44*, 262–273.

Grados, M. A., Labuda, M. C., Riddle, M. A., & Walkup, J. T. (1997). Obsessive-compulsive disorder in children and adolescents. *International Review of Psychiatry, 9*(1), 83–98.

Graham, J. E., Kennard, B. D., Mayes, T. L., Nightingale-Teresi, J., Carmody, T., Hughes, C. W., et al. (2008). Fluoxene versus placebo in preventing relapse of major depression in children and adolescents. *American Journal of Psychiatry, 165*, 459–467.

Graham, S., Bellmore, A. D., & Mize, J. (2006). Peer victimization, aggression, and their co-occurrence in middle school: Pathways to adjustment problems. *Journal of Abnormal Child Psychology, 34*(3), 363–378.

Granic, I., Hollenstein, T., Dishion, T. J., & Patterson, G. R. (2003). Longitudinal analysis of flexibility and reorganization in early adolescence: Dynamic systems study of family interactions. *Developmental Psychology, 39*(3), 606–617.

Granillo, T., Jones-Rodriguez, G., & Carvajal, S. C. (2005). Prevalence of eating disorders in Latina adolescents: Associations with substance use and other correlates. *Journal of Adolescent Health, 36*, 214–220.

Grant, B. F. (1997). Prevalence and correlates of alcohol use and DSM-IV alcohol dependence in the United States: Results of the National Longitudinal Alcohol Epidemiologic Survey. *Journal of Studies on Alcohol, 58*(5), 464–473.

Grant, B. F. (1998). Age at smoking onset and its association with alcohol consumption and DSM-IV alcohol abuse and dependence: Results from the National Longitudinal Alcohol Epidemiologic Survey. *Journal of Substance Abuse, 10*(1), 59–73.

Grant, B. F. (1998). The impact of a family history of alcoholism on the relationship between age at onset of alcohol use and DSM-IV alcohol dependence: Results from the National Longitudinal Alcohol Epidemiologic Survey. *Alcohol Health and Research World, 22*(2), 144–147.

Grant, B. F. (2000). Estimates of US children exposed to alcohol abuse and dependence in the family. *American Journal of Public Health, 90*(1), 112–115.

Grant, B. F., Hasin, D. S., Chou, S. P., Stinson, F. S., & Dawson, D. A. (2004). Nicotine dependence and psychiatric disorders in the United States. *Archives of General Psychiatry, 61*(11), 1107–1115.

Grant, B. F., Stinson, F. S., & Harford, T. C. (2001). Age at onset of alcohol use and DSM-IV alcohol abuse and dependence: A 12-year follow-up. *Journal of Substance Abuse, 13*(4), 493–504.

Gratz, K. L., Conrad, S. D., & Roemer, L. (2002). Risk factors for deliberate self-harm among college students. *American Journal of Orthopsychiatry, 72*(1), 128–140.

Graziano, W. G., & Tobin, R. M. (2002). Emotional regulation from infancy through adolescence. In M H. Bornstein, L. Davidson, C. L. M. Keyes, C. L. M., & K. Moore (Eds.), *Well-Being: Positive development across the life course.* Mahwah, NJ: Erlbaum.

Graziano, W. G., Jensen-Campbell, L. A., & Sullivan-Logan, G. M. (1998). Temperament, activity, and expectations for later personality development. *Journal of Personality and Social Psychology, 74*(5), 1266–1277.

Greenberg, M. T. (1999). Attachment and psychopathology in childhood. In J. Cassidy & P. R. Shaver (Eds.), *Handbook of attachment: Theory, research, and clinical applications* (pp. 469–496). New York: Guilford Press.

Greenberg, M. T., Lengua, L. J., Coie, J. D., Pinderhughes, E. E., Bierman, K., Dodge, K. A., et al. (1999). Predicting developmental outcomes at school entry using a multiple-risk model: Four American communities. *Developmental Psychology, 35*, 403–417.

Greenberg, M. T., & Snell, J. L. (1997). Brain development and emotional development: The role of teaching in organizing the frontal lobe. In P. Salovey & D. J. Sluyter (Eds.), *Emotional development and emotional intelligence: Educational implications* (pp. 93–126). New York: Basic Books.

Greenberg, M. T., Speltz, M. L., & DeKlyen, M. (1993). The role of attachment in the early development of disruptive behavior problems. *Development and Psychopathology, 5*(1–2), 191–213.

Greenberg, M. T., Speltz, M. L., DeKlyen, M., & Jones, K. (2001). Correlates of clinic referral for early conduct problems: Variable- and person-oriented approaches. *Development and Psychopathology, 13*, 255–276.

Greenberg, M. T., Weissberg, R. P., O'Brien, M. U., Fredericks, L., Resnik, H., & Elias, M. J. (2003). Enhancing school-based prevention and youth development through coordinated social, emotional, and academic learning. *American Psychologist, 58* (6/7), 466–474.

Greene, R. S., & Doyle, A. E. (1999). Toward a transactional conceptualization of oppositional defiant disorder: Implications for assessment and treatment. *Clinical Child and Family Psychology Review, 2*, 129–148.

Greene, R. W. (1996). Students with attention-deficit hyperactivity disorder and their teachers: Implications of a goodness-of-fit perspective. From T. H. Ollendick & R. J. Prinz (Eds.), *Advances in clinical child psychology* (Vol. 18, pp. 205–230). New York: Plenum Press.

Greene, R. W., Ablon, J. S., & Goring, J. C. (2003). A transactional model of oppositional behavior: Underpinnings of the Collaborative Problem Solving approach. *Journal of Psychosomatic Research, 55*, 67–75.

Greene, R. W., Ablon, J. S., Goring, J. C., Raezer-Blakely, L., Markey, J., Monuteaux, M. C., et al., (2004). Effectiveness of collaborative problem solving in affectively dysregulated children with oppositional defiant disorder: Initial findings. *Journal of Consulting and Clinical Psychology, 72*(6), 1157–1164.

Greene, R. W., Beszterczey, S. K., Katzenstein, T., Park, K., & Goring, J. (2002). Are students with ADHD more stressful to teach? Patterns of teacher stress in an elementary school sample. *Journal of Emotional and Behavioral Disorders, 10*(2), 79–89.

Greene, R. W., Biederman, J., Faraone, S. V., Monuteaux, M. C., Mick, E., DuPre, E. P., et al. (2001). Social impairment in girls with ADHD: Patterns, gender comparisons, and correlates. *Journal of the American Academy of Child and Adolescent Psychiatry, 4*(6), 704–710.

Greene, R. W., Biederman, J., Faraone, S. V., Wilens, T. E., Mick, E., & Blier, H. K. (1999). Further validation of social impairment as a predictor of substance use disorders: Findings from a sample of siblings of boys with and without ADHD. *Journal of Clinical Child Psychology, 28*(3), 349–354.

Greene, R. W., Biederman, J., Zerwas, S., Monuteaux, M., Goring, J. C., & Faraone, S. V. (2002). Psychiatric comorbidity, family dysfunction, and social impairment in referred youth with oppositional defiant disorder. *American Journal of Psychiatry, 159*, 1214–1224.

Greenfield, S. F., & Sugarman, D. E. (2001). The treatment and consequences of alcohol abuse and dependence during pregnancy. In K. Yonkers & B. Little (Eds.), *Management of Psychiatric Disorders in Pregnancy* (pp. 213–227.) London: Oxford University Press.

Greenhill, L. L., Abikoff, H. B., Arnold, L. E., Cantwell, D. P., Conners, C. K., Elliott, G., et al. (1996). Medication treatment strategies in the MTA study: Relevance to clinicians and researchers. *Journal of the American Academy of Child and Adolescent Psychiatry, 35*, 1304–1313.

Greenhill, L. L., Jensen, P. S., Abikoff, H., Blumer, J. L., DeVeaugh-Geiss, J., Fisher, C., et al. (2003). Developing strategies for psychopharmacological studies in preschool children. *Journal of the American Academy of Child and Adolescent Psychiatry, 42*(4), 406–414.

Greenhill, L. L., Posner, K., Vaughan, B. S., & Kratochvil, C. J. (2008). Attention deficit hyperactivity disorder in preschool children. *Child and Adolescent Psychiatric Clinics of North America, 17*(2), 347–366.

Greenough, W. T., & Black, J. E. (1992). Induction of brain structure by experience: Substrates for cognitive development. In M. R. Gunnar & C. A. Nelson (Eds.), *Developmental behavioral neuroscience. Minnesota Symposium on Child Psychology* (Vol. 24, pp.155–200). Hillsdale, NJ: Erlbaum.

Greenough, W., Black, J., & Wallace, C. (1987). Experience and brain development. *Child Development, 58*, 539–559.

Greenspan, S. I., & Lieberman, A. F. (1988). A clinical approach to attachment. In J. Belsky & T. Nezworski (Eds.), *Clinical implications of attachment* (pp. 387–424). Hillsdale, NJ: Erlbaum.

Greenspan, S. I., & Salmon, J. (1993). *Playground politics: Understanding the emotional life of your school-age child.* New York: Addison-Wesley.

Greenspan, S. I., & Weider, S. (1993). *The child with special needs: Encouraging intellectual and emotional growth.* Reading, MA: Addison-Wesley.

Greenspan, S., & Love, P. F. (1997). Social intelligence and developmental disorder: Mental retardation, learning disabilities, and autism. In W. E. MacLean (Ed.), *Ellis' handbook of mental deficiency, psychological theory and research* (3rd ed., pp. 311–342). Mahwah, NJ: Erlbaum.

Gretton, H. M., Hare, R. D., & Catchpole, R. E. H. (2004). Psychopathy and offending from adolescence to adulthood: A 10-year follow-up. *Journal of Consulting and Clinical Psychology, 72*(4), 636–645.

Griffin, R., & Baron-Cohen, S. (2002). The intentional stance: Developmental and neurocognitive perspectives. In A. Brook & D. Ross (Eds.), *Daniel Dennett. Contemporary philosophy in focus* (pp. 83–116). New York: Cambridge University Press.

Grilo, C. M. (2004). Subtyping female adolescent psychiatric inpatients with features of eating disorders along dietary restraint and negative affect dimensions. *Behavior Research and Therapy, 42,* 67–78.

Grilo, C. M., Walker, M. L., Becker, D. F., Edell, W. S., & McGlashan, T. H. (1997). Personality disorders in adolescents with major depression, substance abuse disorders, and coexisting major depression and substance use disorders. *Journal of Consulting and Clinical Psychology, 65*(2), 328–332.

Grisham, J. R., Brown, T. A., & Campbell, L. A., (2004). The Anxiety Disorders Interview Schedule for DSM-IV (ADIS-IV). In M. J. Hilsenroth & D. L. Segal (Eds.), *Comprehensive handbook of psychological assessment: Vol. 2. Personality assessment* (pp. 163–177). Hoboken, NJ: Wiley.

Groesz, L. M., Levine, M. P., & Murnen, S. K. (2002). The effect of experimental presentation of thin media images on body satisfaction: A meta-analytic review. *International Journal of Eating Disorders, 31,* 1–16.

Grolnick, W. S., McMenamy, J. M., & Kurowski, C. O. (1999). Emotional self-regulation in infancy and toddlerhood. In L. Balter & C. S. Tamis-LeMonda (Eds.), *Child psychology: A handbook of contemporary issues* (pp. 3–22). Philadelphia: Psychology Press.

Gross, J. J., & Munoz, R. F. (1995). Emotion regulation and mental health. *Clinical Psychology: Science and Practice, 2*(2), 151–164.

Gross, J. J., & Thompson, R. A. (2007). Emotion regulation: Conceptual foundations. In J. J. Gross (Ed.), *Handbook of emotion regulation* (pp. 3–24). New York: Guilford Press.

Grossman, K. E., & Grossman, K. (1991). Attachment quality as an organizer of emotional and behavioral responses in a longitudinal perspective. In C. M. Parkes, J. Stevenson-Hinde, & P. Marris (Eds.), *Attachment across the life cycle* (pp. 93–114). New York: Routledge.

Grossman, K., & Grossman, K. (Eds.). (2005). *The longitudinal studies of attachment.* New York: Guilford Press.

Grossmann, K. E., Grossmann, K., & Keppler, A. (2005). Universal and culture-specific aspects of human behavior: The case of attachment. In W. Friedlmeier, P. Chakkarath, & B. Schwarz (Eds.), *Culture and human development: The importance of cross-cultural research for the social sciences* (pp. 75–97). Hove, England: Psychology Press/Erlbaum (UK) Taylor and Francis.

Guerin, D. W., Gottfried, A. W., & Thomas, C. W. (1997). Difficult temperament and behaviour problems: A longitudinal study from 1.5 to 12 years. *International Journal of Behavioral Development, 21,* 71–90.

Guerin, P. J., & Chabot, D. R. (1997). Development of family systems theory. In P. L. Wachtel & S. B. Messer (Eds.), *Theories of psychotherapy: Origins and evolution* (pp. 181–225). Washington, DC: American Psychological Association.

Guerra, N. G., Huesmann, L. R., & Spindler, A. (2003). Community violence exposure, social cognition, and aggression among urban elementary school children. *Child Development, 74*(5), 1561–1576.

Guerra, V. S., Asher, S. R., & DeRosier, M. E. (2004). Effect of children's perceived rejection on physical aggression. *Journal of Abnormal Child Psychology, 32*(5), 551–563.

Guilamo-Ramos, V., Jaccard, J., Johansson, M., & Tunisi, R. (2004). Binge drinking among Latino youth: Role of acculturation-related variables. *Psychology of Addictive Behaviors, 18*(2), 135–142.

Gullone, E., King, N. J., & Ollendick, T. H. (2001). Self-reported anxiety in children and adolescents: A three-year follow-up study. *Journal of Genetic Psychology, 162*(1), 5–19.

Gunnar, M. R. (1994). Psychoendocrine studies of temperament and stress in early childhood: Expanding current models. In J. E. Bates & T. D. Wachs (Eds.), *Temperament: Individual differences at the interface of biology and behavior. APA science volumes* (pp. 175–198). Washington, DC: American Psychological Association.

Gunnar, M. R. (1998). Quality of early care and buffering of neuroendocrine stress reactions: Potential effects on the developing human brain. *Preventive Medicine: An International Journal Devoted to Practice and Theory, 27*(2), 208–211.

Gunnar, M. R. (2000). Early adversity and the development of stress reactivity and regulation. In C. A. Nelson (Ed.), *The Minnesota symposia on child psychology: Vol. 31. The effects of early adversity on neurobehavioral development* (pp. 163–200). Mahwah, NJ: Erlbaum.

Gunnar, M. R. (2001). The role of glucocorticoids in anxiety disorders: A critical analysis. In M. W. Vasey & M. R. Dadds (Eds.), *The developmental psychopathology of anxiety* (pp. 143–159). London: Oxford University Press.

Gunnar, M. R. (2003). Integrating neurosciences and psychological approaches in the study of early experiences. In J. A. King, C. F. Ferris, & I. I. Lederhendler (Eds.), *Annals of the New York Academy of Sciences: Vol. 1008. Roots of mental illness in children* (pp. 238–247). New York: Academy of Sciences.

Gunnar, M. R., Brodersen, L., Krueger, K., & Rigatuso, J. (1996). Dampening of adrenocortical responses during infancy: Normative changes and individual differences. *Child Development, 67*(3), 877–889.

Gunnar, M. R., Bruce, J., & Donzella, B. (2001). Stress physiology, health, and behavioral development. In A. Thornton (Ed.), *The well-being of children and families: Research and data needs* (pp. 188–212). Ann Arbor: The University of Michigan Press.

Gunnar, M. R., & Donzella, B. (1999). "Looking for the Rosetta Stone": An essay on crying, soothing, and stress. In M. Lewis & D. Ramsay (Eds.), *Soothing and Stress* (pp. 39–56). Mahwah, NJ: Erlbaum.

Gunnar, M. R., & Donzella, B. (2002). Social regulation of the cortisol levels in early human development. *Psychoneuroendocrinology, 27*(1–2), 199–220.

Gunnar, M. R., & Mangelsdorf, S. (1989). The dynamics of temperament-physiology relations: A comment on biological processes in temperament. In G. A. Kohnstamm & J. E. Bates (Eds.), *Temperament in childhood* (pp. 145–152). Oxford, England: Wiley.

Gunnar, M. R., Mangelsdorf, S., Larson, M., & Hertsgaard, L. (1989). Attachment, temperament, and adrenocortical activity in infancy: A study of psychoendocrine regulation. *Developmental Psychology, 25*(3), 355–363.

Gunnar, M. R., Porter, F. L., Wolf, C. M., & Rigatuso, J. (1995). Neonatal stress reactivity: Predictions to later emotional temperament. *Child Development, 66*(1), 1–13.

Gunter, H. L., Ghaziuddin, M., & Ellis, H. D. (2002). Asperger syndrome: Tests of right hemisphere functioning and interhemispheric communication. *Journal of Autism and Developmental Disorders, 32*, 262–281.

Guo, J., Collins, L. M., Hill, K. G., & Hawkins, J. D. (2000). Developmental pathways to alcohol abuse and dependence in young adulthood. *Journal of Studies on Alcohol, 61*(6), 799–808.

Guthrie, B. J., & Flinchbaugh, L. J. (2001). Gender-specific substance prevention programming: Going beyond just focusing on girls. *Journal of Early Adolescence, 21*(3), 354–372.

Habermas, T., & Bluck, S. (2000). Getting a life: The emergence of the life story in adolescence. *Psychological Bulletin, 126*(5), 748–769.

Habeych, M. E., Charles, P. J., Sclabassi, R. J., Kirisci, L., & Tarter, R. E. (2005). Direct and mediated associations between P300 amplitude in childhood and substance use disorders outcome in young adulthood. *Biological Psychiatry, 57*(1), 76–82.

Hackett, R., & Hackett, L. (1999). Child psychiatry across cultures. *International Review of Psychiatry, 11*, 225–235.

Hadadian, A., & Merbler, J. (1995a). Fathers of young children with disabilities: How do they want to be involved? *Child and Youth Care Forum, 24*(5), 327–338.

Hadadian, A., & Merbler, J. (1995b). Parents of infants and toddlers with special needs: Sharing views of desired services. *Infant-Toddler Intervention, 5*(2), 141–152.

Hagekull, B., & Bohlin, G. (2004). Predictors of middle childhood psychosomatic problems: An emotion regulation approach. *Infant and Child Development, 13*, 389–405.

Haggerty, R. J., Sherrod, L. R., Garmezy, N., & Rutter, M. (1994). *Stress, risk, and resilience in children and adolescents: Processes, mechanisms, and interventions.* New York: Cambridge University Press.

Haines, B. A., Metalsky, G. I., Cardamone, A. L., & Joiner, T. (1999). Interpersonal and cognitive pathways into the origins of attributional style: A developmental perspective. From T. Joiner & J. C. Coyne (Eds.), *The interactional nature of depression: Advances in interpersonal approaches* (pp. 65–92). Washington, DC: American Psychological Association.

Haines, J., & Neumark-Sztainer, D. (2006). Prevention of obesity and eating disorders: A consideration of shared risk factors. *Health Education Research, 21*, 770–782.

Halberstadt, A. G., Denham, S. A., & Dunsmore, J. C. (2001). Affective social competence. *Social Development, 10*(1), 79–119.

Haley, J. (1976). *Problem-Solving therapy: New strategies for effective family therapy.* San Francisco: Jossey-Bass.

Hall, W. A., Zubrick, S. R., Silburn, S. R., Parsons, D. E., & Kurinczuk, J. J. (2007). A model for predicting behavioural sleep problems in a random sample of Australian pre-schoolers. *Infant and Child Development, 16*, 509–523.

Hall, W. D., & Lynskey, M. (2005). Is cannabis a gateway drug? Testing hypotheses about the relationship between cannabis use and the use of other illicit drugs. *Drug and Alcohol Review, 24*(1), 39–48.

Halle, T. (2002). Emotional development. In M. H. Bornstein, L. Davidson, C. L. M. Keyes, & K. Moore (Eds.), *Well-Being: Positive development across the life course.* Mahwah, NJ: Erlbaum.

Hallfors, D., & Van Dorn, R. A. (2002). Strengthening the role of two key institutions in the prevention of adolescent substance abuse. *Journal of Adolescent Health, 30*(1), 17–28.

Hallfors, D. D., Waller, M. W., Ford, C. A., Halpern, C. T., Brodish, P. H., & Iritani, B. (2004). Adolescent depression and suicide risk: Association with sex and behavior. *American Journal of Preventative Medicine, 27*(3), 224–230.

Halmi, K. A., Agras, W. S., Crow, S., Mitchell, J., Wilson, G. T., Bryson, S. W., et al. (2005). Predictors of treatment acceptance and completion in anorexia nervosa: Implications for future study designs. *Archives of General Psychiatry, 62,* 776–781.

Halmi, K. A., Agras, W. S., Mitchell, J., Wilson, G. T., Crow, S. Bryson, S. W., et al. (2002). Relapse predictors of patients with bulimia nervosa who achieved abstinence through cognitive behavioral therapy. *Archives of General Psychiatry, 59,* 1105–1109.

Halmi, K. A., Sunday, S. R., Klump, K. L., Strober, M., Leckman, J. F.-L., Fichter, M., et al. (2003). Obsessions and compulsions in anorexia nervosa subtypes. *International Journal of Eating Disorders, 33,* 308–319.

Halmi, K. A., Tozzi, F., Thornton, L. M., Crow, S., Fichter, M. M., Kaplan, A. S., et al. (2005). The relation among perfectionism, obsessive-compulsive personality disorder and obsessive-compulsive disorder in individuals with eating disorders. *International Journal of Eating Disorders, 38*, 371–374.

Halperin, J. M., McKay, K. E., Newcorn, J. H. (2002). Development, reliability and validity of the Children's Aggression Scale-Parent Version. *Journal of the American Academy of Child and Adolescent Psychiatry, 41*, 245–252.

Halpern, C. T., King, R. B., Oslak, S. G., & Udry, J. R. (2005). Body mass index, dieting, romance, and sexual activity in adolescent girls: Relationships over time. *Journal of Research on Adolescence, 15,* 535–559.

Halpern, R. (1993). Poverty and infant development. In C. H. Zeanah (Ed.), *Handbook of infant mental health* (pp. 73–86). New York: Guilford Press.

Hamada, R. S., Kameoka, V., Yanagida, E., & Chemtob, C. M. (2003). Assessment of elementary school children for disaster-related posttraumatic stress disorder symptoms: The Kauai recovery index. *Journal of Nervous and Mental Disease, 191*(4), 268–272.

Hamilton, A. F. de C., Brindley, R. M., & Frith, U. (2007). Imitation and action understanding in autistic spectrum disorders: How valid is the hypothesis of a deficit in the mirror neuron system? *Neuropsychologia, 45*(8), 1859–1868.

Hammen, C., & Rudolph, K. D. (1996). Childhood depression. In E. J. Mash & R. A. Barkley (Eds.), *Child psychopathology* (pp. 153–195). New York: Guilford Press.

Hammen, C., Shih, J. H., & Brennan, P. A. (2004). Intergenerational transmission of depression: Test of an interpersonal stress model in a community sample. *Journal of Consulting and Clinical Psychology, 72*(3), 511–522.

Hampe, E., Noble, H., Miller, L. C., & Barrett, C. L. (1973). Phobic children one and two years post treatment. *Journal of Abnormal Psychology, 82*, 446–453.

Hampson, S. E., Severson, H. H., Burns, W. J., Slovic, P., & Fisher, K. J. (2001). Risk perception, personality factors and alcohol use among adolescents. *Personality and Individual Differences, 30*(1), 167–181.

Handen, B. L., Feldman, H. M., Lurier, A., & Huszar Murray, P. J. (1999). Efficacy of methylphenidate among preschool children with developmental disabilities and ADHD. *Journal of the American Academy of Child and Adolescent Psychiatry, 38,* 805–812.

Hanish, L. D., & Guerra, N. G. (2002). A longitudinal analysis of patterns of adjustment following peer victimization. *Development and Psychopathology, 14,* 69–89.

Hanish, L. D., & Guerra, N. G. (2004). Aggressive victims, passive victims, and bullies: Developmental continuity or developmental change? *Merrill-Palmer Quarterly, 50*(1), 17–38.

Hankin, B. L., & Abramson, L. Y. (2001). Development of gender differences in depression: An elaborated cognitive vulnerability-transactional stress theory. *Psychological Bulletin, 127*(6), 773–796.

Hankin, B. L., Abramson, L. Y., Miller, N., & Haeffel, G. J. (2004). Cognitive vulnerability-stress theories of depression: Examining positive affectivity specificity in the prediction of depression versus anxiety in three prospective studies. *Cognitive Therapy and Research, 28*(3), 309–345.

Hankin, B. L., Fraley, R. C., Lahey, B. B., & Waldman, I. D. (2005). Is depression best viewed as a continuum or discrete category? A taxometric analysis of childhood and adolescent depression in a population-based sample. *Journal of Abnormal Psychology, 114*(1), 96–110.

Hankin, B. L., Mermelstein, R., Roesch, L. (2007). Sex differences in adolescent depression: Stress exposure and reactivity models. *Child Development, 78*(1), 279–295.

Hankin, B. L., Wetter, E., & Cheely, C. (2008). Sex differences in child and adolescent depression: A developmental psychopathological approach. In J. R.Z. Abela & B. L. Hankin (Eds.), *Handbook of depression in children and adolescents* (pp. 377–414). New York: Guilford Press.

Hankin, J. R. (2002). Fetal alcohol syndrome prevention research. *Alcohol Research and Health, 26*(1), 58–62.

Hanna, A. C., & Bond, M. J. (2006). Relationships between family conflict, perceived maternal verbal messages, and daughters' disturbed eating symptomology. *Appetite, 47,* 205–211.

Hanna, E. Z., & Grant, B. F. (1999). Parallels to early onset alcohol use in the relationship of early onset smoking with drug use and DSM-IV drug and depressive disorders: Findings from the National Longitudinal Epidemiologic Survey. *Alcoholism: Clinical and Experimental Research, 23*(3), 513–522.

Hardan, A., & Sahl, R. (1997). Psychopathology in children and adolescents with developmental disorders. *Research in Developmental Disabilities, 18*(5), 369–382.

Harford, T. C., Grant, B. F., Yi, H., & Chen, C. M. (2005). Patterns of DSM-IV alcohol abuse and dependence criteria among adolescents and adults: Results from the 2001 National Household Survey on Drug Abuse. *Alcoholism: Clinical and Experimental Research, 29*(5), 810–828.

Harkness, S., & Super, C. M. (2000). Culture and psychopathology. In A. J. Sameroff & M. Lewis et al. (Eds.), *Handbook of developmental psychopathology* (2nd ed., pp. 197–214). Dordrecht, Netherlands: Kluwer Academic Publishers.

Harmon, R. J. (2002). The administration of programs for infants and toddlers. *Child and Adolescent Psychiatric Clinics of North America, 11(1),* 1–21.

Harmon, R. J., & Frankel, K. A. (1997). The growth and development of an infant mental health program: An integrated perspective. *Infant Mental Health Journal, 18*(2), 126–134.

Harold, R. D. (2000). *Becoming a family: Parents' stories and their implications for practice, policy and research.* Mahwah, NJ: Erlbaum.

Harpaz-Rotem, I., Leslie, D. L., Martin, A., & Rosenheck, R. A. (2005). Changes in child and adolescent inpatient psychiatric admission diagnoses between 1995 and 2000. *Social Psychiatry and Psychiatric Epidemiology, 40*(8), 642–647.

Harrington, R., Rutter, M., & Fombonne, E. (1996). Developmental pathways in depression: Multiple meanings, antecedents, and endpoints. *Development and Psychopathology, 8*(4), 601–616.

Harris, N. S., Courchesne, E., Townsend, J., Carper, R. A., & Lord, C. (1999). Neuroanatomic contributions to slowed orienting of attention in children with autism. *Cognitive Brain Research, 8,* 61–71.

Harris, P. L. (1995). Children's awareness and lack of awareness of mind and emotion. In D. Cicchetti & S. L. Toth (Eds.), *Rochester symposium on developmental psychopathology: Emotion, cognition, and representation* (Vol. 6, pp. 35–57). Rochester: University of Rochester Press.

Harris, S. L., Glasberg, B., & Delmolino, L. (1998). Families and the developmentally disabled adolescent. In V. B. Van Hasselt & M. Hersen (Eds.) *Handbook of psychological treatment protocols for children and adolescents. The LEA series in personality and clinical psychology* (pp. 519–548). Mahwah, NJ: Erlbaum.

Harrison, K. (2001). Ourselves, our bodies: Thin-ideal media, self-discrepancies, and eating disorder symptomatology in adolescents. *Journal of Social and Clinical Psychology, 20(3),* 289–323.

Harrison, K., & Hefner, V. (2008). Media, body image, and eating disorders. In S. L. Calvert & B. J. Wilson (Eds.), *The handbook of children, media, and development* (pp. 381–406). Malden, MA: Blackwell.

Hart, E. L., & Lahey, B. B. (1999). General child behavior rating scales. In D.Shaffer & C. Lucas (Eds.), *Diagnostic assessment in child and adolescent psychopathology* (pp. 65–87). New York: Guilford Press.

Hart, E. L., Lahey, B. B., Loeber, R., & Hanson, K. S. (1994). Criterion validity of informants in the diagnosis of disruptive behavior disorders in children: A preliminary study. *Journal of Consulting and Clinical Psychology, 62,* 410–414.

Hart, E. L., Lahey, B. B., Loeber, R., Applegate, B., Green, S. M., & Frick, P. J. (1995). Developmental change in attention-deficit hyperactivity disorder in boys: A four-year longitudinal study. *Journal of Abnormal Child Psychology, 23*(6), 729–749.

Harter, S. (1993). Visions of self: Beyond the me in the mirror. In J. E. Jacobs (Ed.), *Nebraska symposium on motivation, 1992: Developmental perspectives on motivation. Current theory and research in motivation* (pp. 99–144). Lincoln: University of Nebraska Press.

Harter, S. (1999). *The construction of the self: A developmental perspective.* New York: Guilford Press.

Harter, S. (2003). The development of self-representations during childhood and adolescence. In M. R. Leary & J. P. Tangney (Eds.), *Handbook of self and identity* (pp. 610–642). New York: Guilford Press.

Harter, S., Whitesell, N. R., & Junkin, L. J. (1998). Similarities and differences in domain-specific and global self-evaluations of learning-disabled, behaviorally disordered, and normally achieving adolescents. *American Educational Research Journal, 35(4),* 653–680.

Hartman, C., Hox, J., Mellenbergh, G. J., Boyle, M. H., Offord, D. R., Racine, Y., et al. (2001). DSM-IV internal construct validity: When a taxonomy meets data. *Journal of Child Psychology and Psychiatry and Allied Disciplines, 42(6),* 817–836.

Hartman, C. A., Willcutt, E. G., Rhee, S. H., & Pennington, B. F. (2004). The relation between sluggish cognitive tempo and DSM-IV ADHD. *Journal of Abnormal Child Psychology, 32*(5), 491–503.

Hartman, R. R., Stage, S. A., & Webster-Stratton, C. (2003). A growth curve analysis of parent training outcomes: Examining the influence of child risk factors (inattention, impulsivity, and hyperactivity problems), parental and family risk factors. *Journal of Child Psychology and Psychiatry, 44*(3), 388–398.

Hartos, J., Eitel, P., & Simons-Morton, B. (2002). Parenting practices and adolescent risky driving: A three-month prospective study. *Health Education and Behavior, 29*(2), 194–206.

Hartung, C. M., McCarthy, D. M., Milich, R., & Martin, C. A. (2005). Parent-adolescent agreement on disruptive behavior symptoms: A multitrait-multimethod model. *Journal of Psychopathology and Behavioral Assessment, 27*(3), 159–168.

Hartup, W. W. (1980). Peer relations and family relations: Two social worlds. In M. Rutter (Ed.), *Developmental psychiatry.* Arlington, VA: American Psychiatric Association.

Hartup, W. W. (2005). The development of aggression: Where do we stand? In R. E. Tremblay, W. W. Hartup, & J. Archer (Eds.), *Developmental origins of aggression* (pp. 3–22). New York: Guilford Press.

Hartup, W. W., & Laursen, B. (1999). Relationships as developmental contexts: Retrospective themes and contemporary issues. In W. A. Collins & B. Laursen (Eds.), *Relationships as developmental contexts: The Minnesota Symposia on Child Psychology* (Vol. 30, pp. 13–35). Mahwah, NJ: Erlbaum.

Harum, K. H., & Johnston, M. V. (1998). Developmental neurobiology: New concepts in learning, memory, and neuronal development. *Mental Retardation and Developmental Disabilities Research Reviews, 4*(1), 20–25.

Hastings, R. P., & Oakford, S. (2003). Student teachers' attitudes towards the inclusion of children with special needs. *Educational Psychology, 23*(1), 87–94.

Hawker, D. S. J., & Boulton, M. J. (2000). Twenty years' research on peer victimization and psychosocial maladjustment: A meta-analytic review of cross-sectional studies. *Journal of Child Psychology and Psychiatry, 41*(4), 441–455.

Hawkins, E. H., Cummins, L. H., & Marlatt, G. A. (2004). Preventing substance abuse in American Indian and Alaska native youth: Promising strategies for healthier communities. *Psychological Bulletin, 130*(2), 304–323.

Hawkins, J. D., Catalano, R. F., & Miller, J. Y. (1992). Risk and protective factors for alcohol and other drug problems in adolescence and early adulthood: Implications for substance abuse prevention. *Psychological Bulletin, 112*(1), 64–105.

Hawkins, J. D., Hill, K. G., Guo, J., & Battin-Pearson, S. R. (2002). Substance use norms and transitions in substance use: Implications for the gateway hypothesis. In D. B. Kandel (Ed.), *Stages and pathways of drug involvement: Examining the gateway hypothesis* (pp. 42–64). New York: Cambridge University Press.

Hawley, K. M. & Weisz, J. R. (2003). Child, parent, and therapist (dis)agreement on target problems in outpatient therapy: The therapist's dilemma and its implications. *Journal of Consulting and Clinical Psychology, 71(1), 62–70.*

Hawley, P. (2003). Prosocial and coercive configurations of resource control in early adolescence: A case for the well-adapted Machiavellian. *Merrill-Palmer Quarterly, 49*(3), 279–309.

Hawley, P. H., Little, T. D., & Pasupathi, M. (2002). Winning friends and influencing peers: Strategies of peer influence in late childhood. *International Journal of Behavioral Development, 26*(5), 466–474.

Hawley, P., & Vaughn, B. (2003). Aggression and adaptive functioning: The bright side to bad behavior. *Merrill-Palmer Quarterly, 49*(3), 239–242.

Hay, D. F., Pawlby, S., Sharp, D., Schmücker, G., Mills, A., Allen, H., et al. (1999). Parents' judgements about young children's problems: Why mothers and fathers might disagree yet still predict later outcomes. *Journal of Child Psychology and Psychiatry and Allied Disciplines, 40(8),* 1249–1258.

Hayward, C., Gotlib, I. H., Schraedley, P. K., & Litt, I. F. (1999). Ethnic differences in the association between pubertal status and symptoms of depression in adolescent girls. *Journal of Adolescent Health, 25*(2), 143–149.

Hayward, C., Killen, J. D., Kraaemer, H. C., & Taylor, C. B. (2000). Predictors of panic attacks in adolescents. *Journal of the American Academy of Child and Adolescent Psychiatry, 39*(2), 207–214.

Hazan, C., & Shaver, P. R. (1994). Attachment as an organizational framework for research on close relationships. *Psychological Inquiry, 5*(1), 1–22.

Hazler, R., & Mellin, E. (2004). The developmental origins and treatment needs of female adolescents with depression. *Journal of Counseling and Development, 82*(1), 18–24.

He, K., Kramer, E., Houser, R. F., Chomitz, V. R., & Hacker, K. A. (2004). Defining and understanding healthy lifestyles choices for adolescents. *Journal of Adolescent Health, 35*(1), 26–33.

Heal, L. W., Borthwick-Duffy, S. A., & Saunders, R. R. (1996). Assessment of quality of life. In J. W. Jacobson & J. A. Mulick (Eds.), *Manual of diagnosis and professional practice in mental retardation* (pp. 199–209). Washington, DC: American Psychological Association.

Heath, A. C., Madden, P. A. F., Bucholz, K. K., Dinwiddie, S. H., Slutske, W. S., Bierut, L. J., et al. (1999). Genetic differences in alcohol sensitivity and the inheritance of alcoholism risk. *Psychological Medicine, 29*(5), 1069–1081.

Heaton, P., Hermelin, B., & Pring, L. (1998). Autism and pitch processing: A precursor for savant musical ability. *Music Perception, 15*(3), 291–305.

Heavey, L., Phillips, W., Baron-Cohen, S., & Rutter, M. (2000). The Awkward Moments Test: A naturalistic measure of social understanding in autism. *Journal of Autism and Developmental Disorders, 30,* 225–236.

Heflinger, C. A., Cook, V. J., & Thackrey, M. (1987). Identification of mental retardation by the System of Multicultural Pluralistic Assessment: Nondiscriminatory or nonexistent? *Journal of School Psychology, 25*(2), 177–183.

Heim, C., & Nemeroff, C. B. (2001). The role of childhood trauma in the neurobiology of mood and anxiety disorders: Preclinical and clinical studies. *Biological Psychiatry, 49,* 1023–1039.

Heim, C., Meinlschmidt, G., & Nemeroff, C. B. (2003). Neurobiology of early-life stress. *Psychiatric Annals, 33,* 18–26.

Heim, C., Newport, D. J., Heit, S, Graham, Y. P., Wilcox, M., Bonsall, R., et al. (2000). Pituitary-adrenal and autonomic responses to stress in women after sexual and physical abuse in childhood. *Journal of the American Medical Association, 284*(5), 592–597.

Heiman, T. (2000). Friendship quality among children in three educational settings. *Journal of Intellectual and Developmental Disability, 25*(1), 1–12.

Heiman, T. (2001). Inclusive schooling—Middle school teachers' perceptions. *School Psychology International, 22*(4), 451–462.

Heiman, T. (2002). Parents of children with disabilities: Resilience, coping, and future expectations. *Journal of Developmental and Physical Disabilities, 14*(2), 159–171.

Heiman, T., & Margalit, M. (1998). Loneliness, depression, and social skills among students with mild mental retardation in different educational settings. *Journal of Special Education, 32*(3), 154–163.

Heinberg, L. J., Haug, N. A., Freeman, L. M. Y., Ambrose, D., & Guarda, A. S. (2003). Clinical course and short-term outcome of hospitalized adolescents and adults on an eating disorders unit. *Eating and Weight Disorders, 8,* 326–331.

Heine, R. G., Jordan, B., Lubitz, L., Meehan, M., Catto-Smith, A. G. (2006). Clinical predictors of gastro-esophageal reflux in infants with persistent distress. *Journal of Paediatrics and Child Health, 42,* 134–139.

Heinicke, C. M., Fineman, N. R., Ruth, G., Recchia, S. L., Guthrie, D., & Rodning, C. (1999). Relationship-based intervention with at-risk mothers: Outcome in the first year of life. *Infant Mental Health Journal, 20*(4), 349–374.

Held, K. R. (1993). Ethical aspects of sexuality of persons with mental retardation. InM. Nagler (Ed.), *Perspectives on disability* (2nd ed., pp. 255–259). Palo Alto, CA: Health Markets Research.

Hellander, M. (2003). Pediatric bipolar disorder: The parent advocacy perspective. *Biological Psychiatry, 53*(11), 935–937.

Hellander, M., Sisson, D. P., & Fristad, M. A. (2003). Internet support for parents of children with early-onset bipolar disorder. In B. Geller & M. P. DelBello (Eds.), *Bipolar disorder in childhood and early adolescence* (pp.314–329). New York: Guilford Press.

Henderson, H. A., & Wachs, T. D. (2007). Temperament theory and the study of cognition-emotion interactions across development. *Developmental Review, 27,* 396–427.

Henderson, L., & Zimbardo, P. (2001). Shyness, social anxiety, and social phobia. In S. G. Hofmann & P. M. DiBartolo (Eds.), *From social anxiety to social phobia: Multiple perspectives* (pp. 46–85). Needham Heights, MA: Allyn & Bacon.

Henggeler, S. W., & Lee, T. (2003). Multisystemic treatment of serious clinical problems. In A. E. Kazdin & J. R. Weisz (Eds.), *Evidence-based psychotherapies for children and adolescents* (pp. 301–322). New York: Guilford Press.

Henggeler, S. W., Clingempeel, W. G., Brondino, M. J., & Pickrel, S. G. (2002). Four-year follow-up of multisystemic therapy with substance-abusing and substance-dependent juvenile offenders. *Journal of the American Academy of Child and Adolescent Psychiatry, 41*(7), 868–874.

Henggeler, S. W., Halliday-Boykins, C. A., Cunningham, P. B., Randall, J., Shapiro, S. B., & Chapman, J. E. (2006). Juvenile drug court: Enhancing outcomes by integrating evidence-based treatments. *Journal of Consulting and Clinical Psychology, 74*(1), 42–54.

Henin, A., Mick, E., Biederman, J., Fried, R., Wozniak, J., Faraone, S. V., et al. (2007). Can bipolar disorder-specific neuropsychological impairments in children be identified? *Journal of Consulting and Clinical Psychology, 75*(2), 210–220.

Henningfield, J. E., Michaelides, T., & Sussman, S. (2000). Developing treatment for tobacco addicted youth – Issues and challenges. *Journal of Child and Adolescent Substance Abuse, 9,* 5–26.

Henry, B., Caspi, A., Moffitt, T. E., Harrington, H., & Silva, P. A. (1999). Staying in school protects boys with poor self-regulation in childhood from later crime: A longitudinal study. *International Journal of Behavioral Development, 23*(4), 1049–1073.

Herman, K. C., Lambert, S. F., Ialongo, N. S., & Ostrander, R. (2007). Academic pathways between attention problems and depressive symptoms among urban African American children. *Journal of Abnormal Child Psychology, 35*(2), 265–274.

Herman, K. C., Ostrander, R., & Tucker, C. M. (2007). Do family environments and negative cognitions of adolescents with depressive symptoms vary by ethnic group? (2007). *Journal of Family Psychology, 21*(2), 325–330.

Hermelin, B. (2001). *Bright splinters of the mind: A personal story of research with autistic savants.* Philadelphia: Jessica Kingsley Publishers.

Hermes, S. F., & Keel, P. K. (2003). The influence of puberty and ethnicity on awareness and internalization of the thin ideal. *International Journal of Eating Disorders, 33,* 465–467.

Herring, M., & Kaslow, N. J. (2002). Depression and attachment in families: A child-focused perspective. *Family Process, 41*(3), 494–518.

Hertsgaard, L., Gunnar, M. R., Erickson, M. F., & Nachmias, M. (1995). Adrenocortical responses to the strange situation in infants with disorganized/disoriented attachment relationships. *Child Development, 66*(4), 1100–1106.

Hesse, E. (1999). The adult attachment interview: Historical and current perspectives. In J. Cassidy & P. R. Shaver (Eds.), *Handbook of attachment: Theory, research, and clinical applications* (pp. 395–433). New York: Guilford Press.

Hetherington, E. M., Bridges, M., & Insabella, G. M. (1998). What matters? What does not? Five perspectives on the association between marital transitions and children's adjustment. *American Psychologist, 53(2),* 167–184.

Hewitt, J. K., Silberg, J. L., Rutter, M., Simonoff, E., Meyer, J. M., Maes, H., et al. (1997). Genetics and developmental psychopathology: 1. Phenotypic assessment in the Virginia Twin Study of Adolescent Behavioral Development. *Journal of Child Psychology and Psychiatry and Allied Disciplines, 38*(8), 943–963.

Heyman, I., Fombonne, E., Simmons, H., Ford, T., Meltzer, H., & Goodman, R. (2001). Prevalence of obsessive-compulsive disorder in the British nationwide survey of child mental health. *British Journal of Psychiatry, 179,* 324–329.

Heyne, D., King, N. J., Tonge, B. J., Rollings, S., Young, D., Pritchard, M., et al. (2002). Evaluation of child therapy and caregiver training in the treatment of school refusal. *Journal of the American Academy of Child and Adolescent Psychiatry, 41*(6), 687–695.

Higgins, E. T., Loeb, I., & Moretti, M. (1995). Self-discrepancies and developmental shifts in vulnerability: Life transitions in the regulatory significance of others. In D. Cicchetti & S. L. Toth (Eds.), *Emotion, cognition and representation.* Rochester, NY: University of Rochester Press.

Hilarski, C. (2004). Victimization history as a risk factor for conduct disorder behaviors: Exploring connections in a national sample of youth. *Stress, Trauma and Crisis: An International Journal, 7*(1), 47–59.

Hill, A. L., Degnan, K. A., Calkins, S. D., & Keane, S. P. (2006). Profiles of externalizing behavior problems for boys and girls across preschool: The roles of emotion regulation and inattention. *Developmental Psychology, 42*(5), 913–928.

Hillegers, M. H. J., Burger, H., Wals, M., Reichart, C. G., Verhulst, F. C., Nolen, W. A., et al. (2004). Impact of stressful life events, familial loading and their interaction on the onset of mood disorders: Study in a high-risk cohort of adolescent offspring of parents with bipolar disorder. *British Journal of Psychiatry, 185*(2), 97–101.

Hinshaw, S. P. (2005). The stigmatization of mental illness in children and parents: developmental issues, family concerns, and research needs. *Journal of Child Psychology and Psychiatry, 46(7),* 714–734.

Hinshaw, S. P., & Cicchetti, D. (2000). Stigma and mental disorder: Conceptions of illness, public attitudes, personal disclosure, and social policy. *Development and Psychopathology, 12,* 555–598.

Hinshaw, S. P., Owens, E. B., Wells, K. C., Kraemer, H. C., Abikoff, H. B., Arnold, L. E., et al. (2000). Family processes and treatment outcome in the MTA: Negative/ineffective parenting practices in relation to multimodal treatment. *Journal of Abnormal Child Psychology, 28*(6), 555–568.

Hipke, K., Wolchik, S. A., Sandler, I. N., & Braver, S. L. (2002). Predictors of children's intervention-induced resilience in a parenting program for divorced mothers. *Family Relations: Interdisciplinary Journal of Applied Family Studies, 51,* 121–129.

Hirshberg, L. M. (1993). Clinical interviews with infants and their families. In C. H. Zeanah (Ed.), *Handbook of infant mental health* (pp. 173–190). New York: Guilford Press.

Hirshfeld-Becker, D. R., Biederman, J., Calltharp, S., Rosenbaum, E. D., Faraone, S. V., & Rosenbaum, J. F. (2003). Behavioral inhibition and disinhibition as hypothesized precursors to psychopathology: Implications for pediatric bipolar disorder. *Biological Psychiatry, 53*(11), 985–999.

Hirshfeld-Becker, D. R., Biederman, J., Faraone, S. V., Vioilette, H., Wrightsman, J., & Rosenbaum, J. F. (2002). Temperamental correlates of disruptive behavior disorders in young children: Preliminary findings. *Biological Psychiatry, 51*(7), 563–574.

Hishinuma, E. S., Johnson, R. C., Kim, P., Nishimura, S. T., Makini Jr., G. K., Andrade, N. N., et al. (2005). Prevalence and correlates of misconduct among ethnically diverse adolescents of native Hawaiian/part-Hawaiian and non-Hawaiian ancestry. *International Journal of Social Psychiatry, 51*(3), 242–258.

Hjelmeland, H., & Groholt, B. (2005). A comparative study of young and adult deliberate self-harm patients. *Crisis: The Journal of Crisis Intervention and Suicide Prevention, 26*(2), 64–72.

Hoagwood, K. (2000). Commentary: The dose effect in children's mental health services. *Journal of the American Academy of Child and Adolescent Psychiatry, 39(2),* 172–175.

Hoagwood, K., & Erwin, H. D. (1997). Effectiveness of school-based mental health services for children: A 10-year research review. *Journal of Child and Family Studies, 6(4),* 435–451.

Hoagwood, K., & Jensen, P. S. (1997). Developmental psychopathology and the notion of culture: Introduction to the special section on "The fusion of cultural horizons: Cultural influences on the assessment of psychopathology in children and adolescents." *Applied Developmental Science, 1(3),* 108–112.

Hoagwood, K., Jensen, P. S., Petti, T., & Burns, B. J. (1996). A comprehensive conceptual model. *Journal of the American Academy of Child and Adolescent Psychiatry, 35(8),* 1055–1063.

Hoagwood, K., Jensen, P. S., Feil, M., Bhatara, V. S., & Vitiello, B. (2000). Medication management of stimulants in pediatric practice settings: A national perspective. *Journal of Developmental and Behavioral Pediatrics, 21*(5), 322–331.

Hoagwood, K., Kelleher, K. J., Feil, M., & Comer, D. M. (2000). Treatment services for children with ADHD: A national perspective. *Journal of the American Academy of Child and Adolescent Psychiatry, 39,* 198.

Hobson, R. P. (1989a). Beyond cognition: A theory of autism. In G. Dawson (Ed.), *Autism: Nature, diagnosis, and treatment* (pp. 22–48). New York: Guilford Press.

Hobson, R. P. (1989b). On sharing experiences. *Development and Psychopathology, 1,* 197–203.

Hobson, R. P. (1990). On the origins of self and the case of autism. *Development and Psychopathology, 2,* 163–181.

Hobson, R. P. (1991). What is autism? *Psychiatric Clinics of North America, 14,* 1–17.

Hobson, R. P. (1993). *Essays in developmental psychology.* Hillsdale, NJ: Erlbaum.

Hobson, R. P. (1999). Beyond cognition: A theory of autism. In P. Lloyd & C. Fernyhough (Eds.), *Lev Vygotsky: Critical assessments: Future directions* (Vol. IV, pp. 253–281). Florence, KY: Taylor & Francis/Routledge.

Hobson, R. P. (1999). Developmental psychopathology: Revolution and reformation. In M. Bennett (Ed.), *Developmental psychology: Achievements and prospects* (pp. 126–146). Philadelphia: Psychology Press.

Hobson, R. P., & Lee, A. (1998). Hello and goodbye: A study of social engagement in autism. *Journal of Autism and Developmental Disorders, 28,* 117–127.

Hobson, R. P., & Lee, A. (1999). Imitation and identification in autism. *Journal of Child Psychology and Psychiatry and Allied Disciplines, 40,* 649–659.

Hobson, R. P., Ouston, J., & Lee, A. (1988). Emotion recognition in autism: Coordinating faces and voices. *Psychological Medicine, 18,* 911–923.

Hodapp, R. M., & Burack, J. A. (1990). What mental retardation tells us about typical development: The examples of sequences, rates, and cross-domain relations. *Development and Psychopathology, 2,* 213–226.

Hodapp, R. M., & Zigler, E. (1993). Comparison of families of children with mental retardation and families of children without mental retardation. *Mental Retardation, 31*(2), 75–77.

Hodapp, R. M., & Zigler, E. (1995). Past, present, and future issues in the developmental approach to mental retardation and developmental disabilities. In D. Cicchetti & D. J. Cohen (Eds.), *Developmental psychopathology: Vol. 2. Risk, disorder, and adaptation* (pp. 299–331). Oxford, England: Wiley.

Hodapp, R. M., & Zigler, E. (1997). New issues in the developmental approach to mental retardation. In W. E. MacLean (Ed.), *Ellis' handbook of mental deficiency, psychological theory and research* (3rd ed., pp. 115–136). Mahwah, NJ: Erlbaum.

Hodapp, R. M., & Zigler, E. (1999). Intellectual development and mental retardation – Some continuing controversies. In M. Anderson (Ed.), *The development of intelligence: Studies in developmental psychology* (pp. 295–308). Hove, England: Psychology Press/Taylor & Francis.

Hodapp, R. M., & Dykens, E. M. (2001). Strengthening behavioral research on genetic mental retardation syndromes. *American Journal on Mental Retardation, 106*(1), 4–15.

Hodapp, R. M. (2002). Parenting children with mental retardation. In M. H. Bornstein (Ed.), *Handbook of parenting: Vol. 1. Children and parenting* (2nd ed., pp. 355–381). Mahwah, NJ: Erlbaum.

Hodapp, R. M., & DesJardin, J. L. (2002). Genetic etiologies of mental retardation: Issues for interventions and interventionists. *Journal of Developmental and Physical Disabilities, 14*(4), 323–338.

Hodapp, R. M., & Dykens, E. M. (2003). Mental retardation (intellectual disabilities). In E. J. Mash & R. A. Barkley (Eds.), *Child psychopathology* (2nd ed., pp. 486–519). New York: Guilford Press.

Hodapp, R. M. (2004). A model for socialization studies in mental retardation? *Parenting: Science and Practice, 4*(4), 325–328.

Hodapp, R. M., & Dykens, E. M. (2005). Measuring behavior in genetic disorders of mental retardation. *Mental Retardation and Developmental Disabilities Research Reviews, 11,* 340–346.

Hodapp, R. M., & Burack, J. A. (2006). Developmental approaches to children with mental retardation: A second generation? In D. Cicchetti & D. J. Cohen (Eds.), *Developmental psychopathology, Vol. 3: Risk, disorder, and adaptation* (2nd ed., pp. 235–267). Hoboken, NJ: Wiley.

Hodapp, R. M. (2006). Developmental approaches to children with mental retardation: A second generation? In D. Cicchetti & D. J. Cohen (Eds.), *Developmental psychopathology: Vol. 3. Risk, disorder, and adaptation* (2nd ed., pp. 235–267). Hoboken, NJ: Wiley.

Hodapp, R. M. (2007). Families of persons with Down syndrome: New perspectives, findings, and research and service needs. *Mental Retardation and Developmental Disabilities Research Reviews, 13,* 279–287.

Hoek, H. W., & van Hoeken, D. (2003). Review of the prevalence and incidence of eating disorders. *International Journal of Eating Disorders, 34,* 383–396.

Hofacker, N. V., & Papoušek, M. (1998). Disorders of excessive crying, feeding, and sleeping: The Munich interdisciplinary research and intervention program. *Infant Mental Health Journal, 19*(2), 180–201.

Hofferth, S., Phillips, D., & Cabrera, N. (2001). Public policy and family and child well-being. In A. Thornton (Ed.), *The well-being of children and families: Research and data needs* (pp. 384–415). Ann Arbor: The University of Michigan Press.

Hofflich, S. A., Hughes, A. A., & Kendall, P. C. (2006). Somatic complaints and childhood anxiety disorders. *International Journal of Clinical and Health Psychology, 6*(2), 229–242.

Hogan, A. E. (1999). Cognitive functioning in children with oppositional defiant disorder. In H. C. Quay & A. E. Hogan (Eds.), *Handbook of disruptive behavior disorders* (pp. 317–335). Dordrecht, Netherlands: Kluwer Academic Publishers.

Hogue, A., Dauber, S., Stambaugh, L. F., Cecero, J. J., & Liddle, H. A. (2006). Early therapeutic alliance and treatment outcome in individual and family therapy for adolescent behavior problems. *Journal of Consulting and Clinical Psychology, 74*(1), 121–129.

Hoksbergen, R. A. C., ter Laak, J., van Dijkum, C., Rijk, S., Rijk, K., & Stoutjesdijk, F. (2003). Posttraumatic stress disorder in children adopted from Romania. *American Journal of Orthopsychiatry, 73*(3), 255–265.

Holaway, R. M., Rodebaugh, T. L., & Heimberg, R. G. (2006). The epidemiology of worry and generalized anxiety disorder. In G. C. L. Davey & A. Wells (Eds.), *Worry and its psychological disorders: Theory, assessment and treatment* (pp. 3–20). Hoboken, NJ: Wiley.

Holburn, C. S. (2008). Detrimental effects of overestimating the occurrence of autism. *Intellectual and Developmental Disabilities, 46*(3), 243–246.

Holliday, J., Landau, S., Collier, D., & Treasure, J. (2006). Do illness characteristics and familiar risk differ between women with anorexia nervosa grouped on the basis of personality pathology? *Psychological Medicine, 36,* 529–538.

Hollins, S. (2001). Psychotherapeutic methods. In A. Dosen & K. Day (Eds.), *Treating mental illness and behavior disorders in children and adults with mental retardation* (pp. 27–44). Washington, DC: American Psychiatric Publishing.

Holmbeck, G. N. (1997). Toward terminological, conceptual, and statistical clarity in the study of mediators and moderators: Examples from the child-clinical and pediatric psychology literatures. *Journal of Consulting and Clinical Psychology, 65,* 599–610.

Holmbeck, G. N., Colder, C., Shapera, W., Westhoven, V., Kenealy, L. & Updegrove, A. L. (2000). Working with adolescents: Guides from developmental psychology. In P. C. Kendall (Ed.), *Child and adolescent therapy: Cognitive-behavioral procedures* (2nd ed., pp. 334–385). New York: Guilford Press.

Holmbeck, G. N., & Kendall, P. C. (2002). Introduction to the special section on clinical adolescent psychology: Developmental psychopathology and treatment. *Journal of Consulting and Clinical Psychology, 70,* 3–5.

Holtkamp, K., Herpertz-Dahlmann, B., Vloet, T., & Hagenah, U. (2005). Group psychoeducation for parents of adolescents with eating disorders: The Aachen Program. *Eating Disorders, 13*(4), 381–390.

Holtmann, M., Bolte, S., Goth, K., Dopfner, M., Pluck, J., Huss, M., et al. (2007). Prevalence of the child behavior checklist-pediatric bipolar disorder phenotype in a German general population sample. *Bipolar Disorders, 9*(8), 895–900.

Holtmann, M., Bolte, S., & Poustka, F. (2007). Attention deficit hyperactivity disorder symptoms in pervasive developmental disorders: Association with autistic behavior domains and coexisting psychopathology. *Psychopathology, 40*(3), 172–177.

Hooper, C. J., Luciana, M., Conklin, H. M., & Yarger, R. S. (2004). Adolescents' performance on the Iowa Gambling Task: Implications for the development of decision making and ventromedial prefrontal cortex. *Developmental Psychology, 40*(6), 1148–1158.

Hooper, S. R., & Tramontana, M. G. (1997). Advances in the neuropsychological bases of child and adolescent psychopathology: Proposed models, findings, and ongoing issues. *Advances in Clinical Child Psychology, 19,* 133–175.

Hope, T. L., Adams, C., Reynolds, L., Powers, D., Perez, R. A., & Kelley, M. L. (1999). Parent vs. self-report: Contributions toward diagnosis of adolescent psychopathology. *Journal of Psychopathology and Behavioral Assessment, 21(4),* 349–363.

Hope, T. L., & Bierman, K. L. (1998). Patterns of home and school behavior problems in rural and urban settings. *Journal of School Psychology, 36,* 45–58.

Horesch, N., Sever, J., & Apter, A. (2003). A comparison of life events between suicidal adolescents with major depression and borderline personality disorder. *Comprehensive Psychiatry, 44*(4), 277–283.

Horesch, N. Zalsman, G., & Apter, A. (2004). Suicidal behavior and self-disclosure in adolescent psychiatric inpatients. *Journal of Nervous and Mental Disease, 192*(12), 837–842.

Horowitz, J. L., Garber, J., Ciesla, J. A., Young, J. F., & Mufson, L. (2007). Prevention of depressive symptoms in adolescents: A randomized trial of cognitive-behavioral and interpersonal prevention programs. *Journal of Consulting and Clinical Psychology, 75*(5), 693–706.

Howe, N., Aquan-Assee, J., Bukowski, W. M., Lehoux, P. M., & Rinaldi, C. (2001). Siblings as confidants: Emotional understanding, relationship warmth, and sibling self-disclosure. *Social Development, 10*(4), 439–454.

Howerton, K., Fernandez, G., Touchette, P., Gurbani, S., Sandman, C. A., Ashurst, J., et al. (2002). Psychotropic mediations in community based individuals with developmental disabilities: Observations of an interdisciplinary team. *Mental Health Aspects of Developmental Disabilities, 5*(3), 78–86.

Howes, P. W., Cicchetti, D., Toth, S. L., & Rogosch, F. A. (2000). Affective, organizational, and relational characteristics of maltreating families: A systems perspective. *Journal of Family Psychology, 14,* 95–110.

Howlin, P. (2000). Outcome in adult life for more able individuals with autism or Asperger syndrome. *Autism, 4,* 63–83.

Howlin, P., Mawhood, L., & Rutter, M. (2000). Autism and developmental receptive language disorder—A follow-up comparison in early adult life. II: Social, behavioural, and psychiatric outcomes. *Journal of Child Psychology and Psychiatry and Allied Disciplines, 41,* 561–578.

Howlin, P., & Moore, A. (1997). Diagnosis in autism: A survey of over 1200 patients in the UK. *Autism, 1,* 135–162.

Hoza, B., Gerdes, A.,C., Mrug, S., Hinshaw, S. P., Bukowski, W. M., Gold, J. A., et al. (2005). Peer-assessed outcomes in the multimodal treatment study of children with attention deficit hyperactivity disorder. *Journal of Clinical Child and Adolescent Psychology, 34*(1), 74–86.

Hoza, B., Mrug, S., Gerdes, A. C., Hinshaw, S. P., Bukowski, W. M., Gold, J. A., et al. (2005). What aspects of peer relationships are impaired in children with attention-deficit/hyperactivity disorder? *Journal of Consulting and Clinical Psychology, 73*(3), 411–423.

Hoza, B., Waschbusch, D. A., Owens, J. S., Pelham, W. E., & Kipp, H. (2001). Academic persistence of normally achieving ADHD and control boys: Self-evaluations, and attributions. *Journal of Consulting and Clinical Psychology, 69*(2), 271–283.

Hsu, C., Chong, M., Yang, P., & Yen, C. (2002). Posttraumatic stress disorder among adolescent earthquake victims in Taiwan. *Journal of the American Academy of Child and Adolescent Psychiatry, 41*(7), 875–881.

Huang, L., Sadler, L., O'Riordan, M., & Robin, N. H. (2002). Delay in diagnosis of Williams syndrome. *Clinical Pediatrics, 41*(4), 257–261.

Hudson, J. A., & Fivush, R. (1991). Planning in the preschool years: The emergence of plans from general event knowledge. *Cognitive Development, 6*(4), 393–415.

Hudson, J. I., Hiripi, E., Pope, H. G., & Kessler, R. C. (2007). The prevalence and correlates of eating disorders in the national co-morbidity survey replication. *Biological Psychology, 61,* 348–358.

Hudson, J. I., Lalonde, J. K., Berry, J. M., Pindyck, L. J., Bulik, C. M., Crow, S. J., et al. (2006). Binge-eating disorder as a distinct familial phenotype in obese individuals. *Archives of General Pscyhology, 63,* 313–319.

Hudson, J. L., Kendall, P. C., Coles, M. E., Robin, J. A., & Webb, A. (2002). The other side of the coin: Using intervention research in child anxiety disorders to inform developmental psychopathology. *Development and Psychopathology, 14*(4), 819–841.

Hudziak, J. J. (2000). Genetics of attention-deficit/hyperactivity disorder. In T. E. Brown (Ed.), *Attention deficit disorders and co-morbidities in children, adolescents, and adults* (pp. 57–78). Arlington, VA: American Psychiatric Publishing.

Huesmann, L. R., Eron, L. D., Lefkowitz, M. M., & Walder, L. O. (1984). Stability of aggression over time and generations. *Developmental Psychology, 20*(6), 1120–1134.

Huesmann, L. R., & Guerra, N. G. (1997). Children's normative beliefs about aggression and aggressive behavior. *Journal of Personality and Social Psychology, 72*(2), 408–419.

Huey, S. J. Jr., Henggeler, S. W., Brondno, M. J., & Pickrel, S. G. (2000). Mechanisms of change in multisystemic therapy: Reducing delinquent behavior through therapist adherence and improved family and peer functioning. *Journal of Consulting and Clinical Psychology, 68*(3), 451–467.

Hughes, C., Cutting, A. L., & Dunn, J. (2001). Acting nasty in the face of failure? Longitudinal observations of "hard-to-manage" children playing a rigged competitive game with a friend. *Journal of Abnormal Child Psychology, 29*(5), 403–416.

Hughes, C., White, A., Sharpen, J., & Dunn, J. (2000). Antisocial, angry, and unsympathetic: "Hard-to-manage" preschoolers' peer problems and possible cognitive influences. *Journal of Child Psychology and Psychiatry, 41*(2), 169–179.

Hughes, C. W., Emslie, G. J., Crismon, M. L., Posner, K., Birmaher, B., Neal, R., et al. (2007).Texas children's medication algorithm project: Update from Texas Consensus Conference Panel on Medication Treatment of Childhood Major Depressive Disorder. *American Academy of Child and Adolescent Psychiatry, 46*(6), 667–686.

Hupp, S. D. A., Reitman, D., Forde, D. A., Shriver, M. D., & Kelley, M. J. (2008). Advancing the assessment of parent-child interactions: Development of the parent instruction-giving game with youngsters. *Behavior Therapy, 39*(1), 91–106.

Huprich, S. K., Stepp, S. D., Graham, A., & Johnson, L. (2004). Gender differences in dependency, separation, object relations and pathological eating behavior and attitudes. *Personality and Individual Differences, 36,* 801–811.

Hurley, A. D. N. (2001). Axis IV and Axis V: Assessment of persons with mental retardation and developmental disabilities. *Mental Health Aspects of Developmental Disabilities, 4*(1), 17–20.

Hurley, A. D. N., Pfadt, A., Tomasulo, D., & Gardner, W. (1996). Counseling and psychotherapy. In J. W. Jacobson & J. A. Mulick (Eds.), *Manual of diagnosis and professional practice in mental retardation* (pp. 371–378). Washington, DC: American Psychological Association.

Hussong, A. M., Curran, P. J., Moffitt, T. E., Caspi, A., & Carrig, M. M. (2004). Substance abuse hinders desistance in young adults' antisocial behavior. *Development and Psychopathology, 16*(4), 1029–1046.

Huttenlocher, P. R. (1994). Synaptogenesis, synapse elimination, and neural plasticity in human cerebral cortex. In C. A. Nelson (Ed.), *Threats to optimal development: Integrating biological, psychological, and social risk factors. The Minnesota Symposia on Child Psychology* (Vol. 27, pp. 35–54). Hillsdale, NJ: Erlbaum.

Huttenlocher, P. R. (1999). Dendritic synaptic development in human cerebral cortex: Time course and critical periods. *Developmental Neuropsychology, 16(3),* 347–349.

Hwang, C. P., Lamb, M. E., & Sigel, I. E. (1996). *Images of childhood.* Mahwah, NJ: Erlbaum.

Iacono, W. G., Malone, S. M., & McGue, M. (2003). Substance use disorders, externalizing psychopathology, and P300 event-related potential amplitude. *International Journal of Psychophysiology, 48*(2), 147–178.

Ialongo, N. S., Edelsohn, G., & Kellam, S. G. (2001). A further look at the prognostic power of young children's reports of depressed mood. *Child Development, 72*(3), 736–747.

Ialongo, N. S., Vaden-Kiernan, N., & Kellam, S. (1998). Early peer rejection and aggression: Longitudinal relations with adolescent behavior. *Journal of Development and Physical Disabilities, 10*(2), 199–213.

Ialongo, N., Edelsohn, G., Werthamer-Larsson, L., & Crockett, L. (1995). The significance of self-reported anxious symptoms in first grade children: Prediction to anxious symptoms and adaptive functioning in fifth grade. *Journal of Child Psychology and Psychiatry and Allied Disciplines, 36*(3), 427–437.

Ialongo, N., Edelsohn, G., Werthamer-Larsson, L., Crockett, L., & Kellam, S. (1996). Social and cognitive impairment in first-grade children with anxious and depressive symptoms. *Journal of Clinical Child Psychology, 25*(1), 15–24.

Ialongo, N., Poduska, J., Werthamer, L., & Kellam, S. (2001). The distal impact of two first-grade preventive interventions on conduct problems and disorder in early adolescence. *Journal of Emotional and Behavioral Disorders, 9*(3), 146–160.

Iarocci, G., & Burack, J. A. (2004). Intact covert orienting to peripheral cues among children with autism. *Journal of Autism and Developmental Disorders, 34*(3), 257–264.

Iervolino, A. C., Pike, A., Manke, B., Reiss, D., Hetherington, E. M., & Plomin, R. (2002). Genetic and environmental influences in adolescent peer socialization: Evidence from two genetically sensitive designs. *Child Development, 73*(1), 162–174.

Ingber, S., & Dromi, E. (2002, April). *Family characteristics and mother's expectations from early intervention.* Poster presented at the Conference on Human Development, Charlotte, NC.

Ingersoll, B., Schreibman, L., & Tran. Q. H. (2003). Effect of sensory feedback on immediate object imitation in children with autism. *Journal of Autism and Developmental Disorders, 33*(6), 673–683.

Ingman, K. A., Ollendick, T. H., & Akande, A. (1999). Cross-cultural aspects of fears in African children and adolescents. *Behaviour Research and Therapy, 37*(4), 337–343.

International Molecular Genetic Study of Autism Consortium. (1998). A full genome screen for autism with evidence for linkage to a region on chromosome 7q. *Human Molecular Genetics, 7,* 571–578.

Ispa, J. M., Fine, M. A., Halgunseth, L. C., Harper, S., Robinson, J., Boyce, L., et al. (2004). Maternal intrusiveness, maternal warmth, and mother-toddler relationship outcomes: Variations across low-income ethnic and acculturation groups. *Child Development, 75*(6), 1613–1631.

Isralowitz, R., & Rawson, R. (2006). Gender differences in prevalence of drug use among high-risk adolescents in Israel. *Addictive Behaviors, 31*(2), 355–358.

Izard, C. E. (2002). Translating emotion theory and research into preventive interventions. *Psychological Bulletin, 128(5),* 796–824.

Jaccard, J., Blanton, H, & Dodge, T. (2005). Peer influences on risk behavior: An analysis of the effects of a close friend. *Developmental Psychology, 41*(1), 135–147.

Jackson, K. M., Sher, K. J., Cooper, M., L., & Wood, P. K. (2002). Adolescent alcohol and tobacco use: Onset, persistence, and trajectories of use across two samples. *Addiction, 97*(5), 517–531.

Jacob, T., & Johnson, S. L. (1997). Parent-child interaction among depressed fathers and mothers: Impact on child functioning. *Journal of Family Psychology, 11*(4), 391–409.

Jacobs, J. E., Bleeker, M. M., & Constantino, M. J. (2003). The self-system during childhood and adolescence: Development, influences, and implications. *Journal of Psychotherapy Integration, 13*(1), 33–65.

Jacobvitz, D., & Hazan, N. (1999). Developmental pathways from infant disorganization to childhood peer relationships. In J. Solomon & C. George (Eds.), *Attachment disorganization* (pp. 127–159). New York: Guilford Press.

Jaffee, S. R., Caspi, A., Moffitt, T. E., & Taylor, A. (2004). Physical maltreatment victim to antisocial child: Evidence of an environmentally mediated process. *Journal of Abnormal Psychology, 113(1),* 44–55.

Jaffee, S. R., Caspi, A., Moffitt, T. E., Dodge, K. A., Turrer, M., Taylor, A., et al. (2005). Nature x nurture: Genetic vulnerabilities interact with physical maltreatment to promote conduct problems. *Development and Psychopathology, 17*(1), 67–84.

Jaffee, S. R., Harrington, H., Cohen, P., & Moffitt, T. E. (2005). Cumulative prevalence of psychiatric disorder in youths. *Journal of the American Academy of Child and Adolescent Psychiatry, 44(5),* 406–407.

Jaffee, S. R., Moffitt, T. E., Caspi, A., & Taylor, A. (2003). Life with (or without) father: The benefits of living with two biological parents depend on the father's antisocial behavior. *Child Development, 74*(1), 109–126.

Jaffee, S. R., Moffitt, T. E., Caspi, A., Taylor, A., & Arseneault, L. (2002). Influence of adult domestic violence on children's internalizing and externalizing problems: An environmentally informative twin study. *Journal of the American Academy of Child and Adolescent Psychiatry, 41*(9), 1095–1103.

Jahromi, L. B., Putnam, S. P., & Stifter, C. A. (2004). Maternal regulation of infant reactivity from 2 to 6 months. *Developmental Psychology, 40*(4), 477–487.

Jain, A., Belsky, J., & Crnic, K. (1996). Beyond fathering behaviors: Types of dads. *Journal of Family Psychology, 10*(4), 431–442.

Jairam, R., Srinath, S., Girimaji, S. C., & Seshadri, S. P. (2004). A prospective 4–5 year follow-up of juvenile onset bipolar disorder. *Bipolar Disorders, 6*(5), 386–394.

Janney, R. E., Snell, M. E. Beers, M. K., & Raynes, M. (1995). Integrating students with moderate and severe disabilities into general education classes. *Exceptional Children, 61*(5), 425–439.

Jaycox, L. H., Asarnow, J. R., Sherbourne, C. D., Rea, M. M., LaBorde, A. P., & Wells, K. B. (2006). Adolescent primary care patients' preferences for depression treatment. *Administration and Policy in Mental Health and Mental Health Services Research, 33*(2), 198–207.

Jaycox, L. H., Reivich, K. J., Gillham, J., & Seligman, M. E. P. (1994). Prevention of depressive symptoms in school children. *Behaviour Research and Therapy, 32*(8), 801–816.

Jennison, K. M. (2004). The short-term effects and unintended long-term consequences of binge drinking in college: A 10-year follow-up study. *American Journal of Drug and Alcohol Abuse, 30*(3), 659–684.

Jensen, P. S. (1999). Links among theory, research, and practice: Cornerstones of clinical scientific progress. *Journal of Clinical Child Psychology, 28(4),* 553–557.

Jensen, P. S., Arnold, L. E., Swanson, J. M., Vitiello, B., Abikoff, H., Greenhill, L. L., et al. (2007). 3-year follow-up of the NIMH MTA study. *Journal of American Academy of Child and Adolescent Psychiatry, 46*(8), 989–1002.

Jensen, P. S., & members of the MTA Cooperative Group (2002). ADHD comorbidity findings from the MTA Study: New diagnostic subtypes and their optimal treatments. In J. E. Helzer & J. J. Hudziak (Eds.), *Defining psychopathology in the 21st century: DSM-V and beyond* (pp. 169–192). Washington, DC: American Psychiatric Publishing.

Jensen, P. S., Hoagwood, K., & Petti, T. (1996). Literature review and application of a comprehensive model. *Journal of the American Academy of Child and Adolescent Psychiatry, 35(8),* 1064–1077.

Jensen, P. S., Rubio-Stipec, M., Canino, G., Bird, H. R., Dulan, M. K., Schwab-Stone, M. E., et al. (1999). Parent and child contributions to diagnosis of mental disorder: Are both informants always necessary? *Journal of the American Academy of Child and Adolescent Psychiatry, 38(2),* 1569–1579.

Jensen, P. S., Martin, D., & Cantwell, D. P. (1997). Comorbidity in ADHD: Implications for research, practice, and DSM-V. *Journal of the American Academy of Child and Adolescent Psychiatry, 36*(8), 1065–1080.

Jessor, R. (1998). *New perspectives on adolescent risk behavior.* New York: Cambridge University Press.

Jessor, R., Turbin, M. S., & Costa, F. M. (1997). Predicting developmental change in risky driving: The transition to adulthood. *Applied Developmental Science, 1*(1), 4–16.

Jessor, R., Turbin, M. S., & Costa, F. M. (1998). Protective factors in adolescent health behavior. *Journal of Personality and Social Psychology, 75*(3), 788–800.

Jessor, R., Turbin, M. S., & Costa, F. M. (1998). Risk and protection in successful outcomes among disadvantaged adolescents. *Applied Developmental Science, 2*(4), 194–208.

Jessor, R., Turbin, M. S., Costa, F. M., Dong, Q., Zhang, H., & Wang, C. (2003). Adolescent problem behavior in China and the United States: A cross-national study of psychosocial protective factors. *Journal of Research on Adolescence, 13*(3), 329–360.

Jester, J. M., Nigg, J. T., Adams, K., Fitzgerald, H. E., Puttler, L. I., Wong, M., et al. (2005). Inattention/hyperactivity and aggression from early childhood to adolescence: Heterogeneity of trajectories and differential influences on environment characteristics. *Development and Psychopathology, 17*(1), 99–125.

Jewell, J. D., & Stark, K. D. (2003). Comparing the family environments of adolescents with conduct disorder and depression. *Journal of Child and Family Studies, 12*(1), 77–89.

Johansson, A., & Götestam, K. G. (2004). Internet addiction: Characteristics of a questionnaire and prevalence in Norwegian youth (12–18 years). *Scandinavian Journal of Psychology, 45*(3), 223–229.

Johnson, C. P., Myers, S. M., & the Council of Children with Disabilities. (2007). Identification and evaluation of children with autism spectrum disorders. *Pediatrics, 120*(5), 1183–1215.

Johnson, F., & Wardle, J. (2005). Dietary restraint, body disatisfaction, and psychological distress: A prospective analysis. *Journal of Abnormal Psychology, 114,* 119–125.

Johnson, J. G., Cohen, P., Kasen, S., & Brook, J. S. (2002). Eating disorders during adolescence and the risk for physical and mental disorders during early adulthood. *Archives of General Psychology, 59,* 545–552.

Johnson, J. G., Cohen, P., Kotler, L., Kasen, S., & Brook, J. S. (2002). Psychiatric disorders associated with risk for the development of eating disorders during adolescence and early adulthood. *Journal of Consulting and Clinical Psychology, 70,* 1119–1128.

Johnson, K. D., Whitbeck, L. B., & Hoyt, D. R. (2005). Substance abuse disorders among homeless and runaway adolescents. *Journal of Drug Issues, 35*(4), 799–816.

Johnson, M. H. (1999). Cortical plasticity in normal and abnormal cognitive development: Evidence and working hypotheses. *Development and Pscyhopathogy, 11(3),* 419–437.

Johnston, C., & Freeman, W. (1997). Attributions for child behavior in parents of children without behavior disorders and children with attention deficit hyperactivity disorder. *Journal of Consulting and Clinical Psychology, 65,* 636–645.

Johnston, L. D., O'Malley, P. M., Bachman, J. G., & Schulenberg, J. W. (2008). Monitoring the Future: National Survey Results on Drug Use, 1975–2007. Volume 1: Secondary School Students (NIH Pub. No. 08–6418A). Bethesda, MD: National Institute on Drug Abuse.

Johnston, L. D., O'Malley, P. M., & Terry-McElrath, Y. M. (2004). Methods, locations, and ease of cigarette access for American youth, 1997–2002. *American Journal of Preventive Medicine, 27*(4), 267–276.

Joiner, T. E. (2002). The trajectory of suicidal behavior over time. *Suicide and Life-Threatening Behavior, 32*(1), 33–41.

Joiner, T. E. (2005). *Why people die by suicide.* Cambridge: Harvard University Press.

Joiner, T. E., Brown, J. S., & Wingate, L. R. (2005). The psychology and neurobiology of suicidal behavior. *Annual Review of Psychology, 56,* 287–314.

Joiner, T. E., Conwell, Y., Fitzpatrick, K. K., Witte, T. K., Schmidt, N. B., Berlim, M. T., et al. (2005). Four studies on how past and current suicidality relate even when "everything but the kitchen sink" is covaried. *Journal of Abnormal Psychology, 114*(2), 291–303.

Jolliffe, T., & Baron-Cohen, S. (2001a). A test of central coherence theory: Can adults with high-functioning autism or Asperger syndrome integrate fragments of an object? *Cognitive Neuropsychiatry, 6,* 193–216.

Jolliffe, T., & Baron-Cohen, S. (2001b). A test of central coherence theory: Can adults with high-functioning autism or Asperger syndrome integrate objects in context? *Visual Cognition, 8,* 67–101.

Jones, D. C. (2004). Body image among adolescent girls and boys: A longitudinal study. *Developmental Psychology, 40,* 823–835.

Jones, D. C., & Crawford, J. K. (2005) Adolescent boys and body image: Weight and muscularity concerns as dual pathways to body dissatisfaction. *Journal of Youth and Adolescence, 34,* 629–636.

Jones, D. C., Vigfusdottir, T. H., & Lee, Y. (2004). Body image and the appearance culture among adolescent girls and boys: An examination of friend conversations, peer criticism, appearance magazines, and the internalization of appearance ideals. *Journal of Adolescent Research, 19,* 323–339.

Jones, D. J., Forehand, R., Brody, G. H., & Armistead, L. (2002a). Positive parenting and child psychosocial adjustment in inner-city single-parent African American families: The role of maternal optimism. *Behavior Modification, 26*, 464–481.

Jones, D. J., Forehand, R., Brody, G., & Armistead, L. (2002b). Psychosocial adjustment of African American children in single-mother families: A test of three risk models. *Journal of Marriage and Family, 64*, 105–115.

Jones, D. J., Forehand, R., Brody, G., & Armistead, L. (2003). Parental monitoring in African American, single mother-headed families: An ecological approach to the identification of predictors. *Behavior Modification, 27*, 435–457.

Jones, D., Dodge, K. A., Foster, E. M., Nix, R., & Conduct Problems Prevention Research Group. (2002). Early identification of children at risk for costly mental health service use. *Prevention Science, 3*(4), 247–256.

Jones, W., Bellugi, U., Lai, Z., Chiles, M., Reilly, J., Lincoln, A., et al. (2000). Hypersociability: The social and affective phenotype of Williams syndrome. *Journal of Cognitive Neuroscience, 12*(1), 30–46.

Jones, W., Hesselink, J., Courchesne, E., Duncan, T., Matsuda, K., & Bellugi, U. (2002). Cerebellar abnormalities in infants and toddlers with Williams syndrome. *Developmental Medicine and Child Neurology, 44*(10), 688–694.

Jordan, A., & Cole, D. A. (1996). Relation of depressive symptoms to the structure of self-knowledge in childhood. *Journal of Abnormal Psychology, 105*(4), 530–540.

Jordan, R., & Jones, G. (1999). Review of research into educational interventions for children with autism in the UK. *Autism, 3*, 101–110.

Jose, P. E., D'Anna, C. A., Cafasso, L. L., Bryant, F. B., Chiker, V., Gein, N., et al. (1998). Stress and coping among Russian and American early adolescents. *Developmental Psychology, 34(4)*, 757–769.

Joseph, R. M., Tager-Flusberg, H., & Lord, C. (2002). Cognitive profiles and social-communicative functioning in children with autism spectrum disorder. *Journal of Child Psychology and Psychiatry and Allied Disciplines, 43*, 807–821.

Judge, B., & Billick, S. B. (2004). Suicidality in adolescence: Review and legal considerations. *Behavioral Sciences and the Law, 22*(5), 681–695.

Jureidini, J., Doecke, C., Mansfield, P., Haby, M, Michelle, M., Menkes, D., et al. (2004). Efficacy and safety of antidepressants for children and adolescents. *British Medical Journal, 328*(7444), 879–883.

Kagan, J. (1997). Conceptualizing psychopathology: The importance of development profiles. *Development and Psychopathology, 9(2)*, 321–334.

Kagan, J., & Snidman, N. (1991). Temperamental factors in human development. *American Psychologist, 46*(8), 856–862.

Kagan, J., & Snidman, N. (1999). Early childhood predictors of adult anxiety disorders. *Biological Psychiatry, 46*, 1536–1541.

Kagan, J., Reznick, J. S., & Snidman, N. (1988). Biological bases of childhood shyness. *Science, 240*(4849), 167–171.

Kagan, J., Snidman, N., & Arcus, D. (1998). Childhood derivatives of high and low reactivity in infancy. *Child Development, 69*(6), 1483–1493.

Kagan, J., Snidman, N., Arcus, D., & Reznick, J. S. (1994). *Galen's prophecy: Temperament in human nature.* New York: Basic Books.

Kagan, J., Snidman, N., McManis, M., & Woodward, S. (2001). Temperamental contributions to the affect family of anxiety. *Psychiatric Clinics of North America, 24*(4), 677–688.

Kagan, J., Snidman, N., Zentner, M., & Peterson, E. (1999). Infant temperament and anxious symptoms in school age children. *Development and Psychopathology, 11*(2), 209–224.

Kail, R. (1992). General slowing of information-processing by persons with mental retardation. *American Journal on Mental Retardation, 97*(3), 333–341.

Kail, R. (2000). Speed of information processing: Developmental change and links to intelligence. *Journal of School Psychology, 38*(1), 51–61.

Kail, R. V. (2003). Information processing and memory. In M. H. Bornstein, L. Davidson, C. L. M. Keyes, & A. Moore (Eds.), Well-being: Positive development across the life course (pp. 269–279). Mahwah, NJ: Erlbaum.

Kalachnik, J. E. (1999). Measuring side effects of psychopharmacologic medication in individuals with mental retardation and developmental disabilities. *Mental Retardation and Developmental Disabilities Research Reviews, 5*(4), 348–359.

Kalmanson, B. (1997). Type II: Underreactive. In A. Lieberman, S. Wieder, & E. Fenichel (Eds.), *DC: 0–3 Casebook* (pp. 233–244). Washington, DC: Zero to Three: National Center for Infants, Toddlers, and Families.

Kaltiala-Heino, R., Lintonen, T., & Rimpelä, A. (2004). Internet addiction? Potentially problematic use of the Internet in a population of 12–18 year-old adolescents. *Addiction Research and Theory, 12*(1), 89–96.

Kaminer, Y. (2005). Challenges and opportunities of group therapy for adolescent substance abuse: A critical review. *Addictive Behaviors, 30*(9), 1765–1774.

Kaminer, Y., & Bukstein, O. G. (2005). Treating adolescent substance abuse. In R. J. Frances, S. I. Miller & A. H. Mack (Eds.), *Clinical textbook of addictive disorders* (3rd ed.). New York: Guilford Press.

Kaminski, R. A., Stormshak, E. A., Good, R. H., III, & Goodman, M. R. (2002). Prevention of substance abuse with rural head start children and families: Results of project STAR. *Psychology of Addictive Behaviors, 16*(4S), S11-S26.

Kanaya, T., & Ceci, S. J. (2007). Are all IQ scores created equal? The differential costs of IQ cutoff scores for at-risk children. *Child Development Perspectives, 1*(1), 52–56.

Kanaya, T., Scullin, M. H., & Ceci, S. J. (2003). The Flynn effect and U. S. policies: The impact of rising IQ scores on American society via mental retardation diagnosis. *American Psychologist, 58*(10), 778–790.

Kandel, D. B. (2002). Examining the gateway hypothesis: Stages and pathways of drug involvement. In D. B. Kandel (Ed.), *Stages and pathways of drug involvement: Examining the gateway hypothesis* (pp. 3–15). New York: Cambridge University Press.

Kandel, D. B., Huang, F-Y., & Davies, M. (2001). Comorbidity between patterns of substance use dependence and psychiatric syndromes. *Drug and Alcohol Dependence, 64*(2), 233–241.

Kandel, D. B., & Yamaguchi, K. (2002). Stages of drug involvement in the U. S. population. In D. B. Kandel (Ed.), *Stages and pathways of drug involvement: Examining the gateway hypothesis* (pp. 65–89). New York: Cambridge University Press.

Kandel, E. R. (1999). Biology and the future of psychoanalysis: A new intellectual framework for psychiatry revisited. *American Journal of Psychiatry, 156(4)*, 505–524.

Kane, P., & Garber, J. (2004). The relations among depression in fathers, children's psychopathology, and father-child conflict: A meta-analysis. *Clinical Psychology Review, 24*(3), 339–360.

Kann, R. T., & Hanna, F. J. (2000). Disruptive behavior disorders in children and adolescents: How do girls differ from boys? *Journal of Counseling and Development, 78*, 267–274.

Kanner, L. (1943). Autistic disturbances of affective contact. *Nervous Child, 2*, 217–250.

Kaplan, H. B., & Liu, X. (1999). Explaining transgenerational continuity in antisocial behavior during early adolescence. In P. Cohen, C. Slomkowski, & L. N. Robins (Eds.), *Historical and geographical influences on psychopathology* (pp. 163–191). Mahwah, NJ: Erlbaum.

Kaplow, J. B., Dodge, K. A., Amaya-Jackson, L., & Saxe, G. N. (2005). Pathways to PTSD, part II: Sexually abused children. *American Journal of Psychiatry, 162*(7), 1305–1310.

Karreman, A., van Tuijl, C., van Aken, M. A.G., & Dekovic, M. (2008). Parenting, coparenting and effortful control in preschoolers. *Journal of Family Psychology, 22*(1), 30–40.

Kasari, C., Freeman, S., & Paparella, T. (2006). Joint attention and symbolic play in young children with autism: A randomized controlled intervention study. *Journal of Child Psychology and Psychiatry, 47*(6), 611–620.

Kasari, C., Paparella, T., Freeman, S., & Jahromi, L. B. (2008). Language outcome in autism: Randomized comparison of joint attention and play interventions. *Journal of Consulting and Clinical Psychology, 76*(1), 125–137.

Kasius, M. C., Ferdinand, R. F., van den Berg, H., & Verhulst, F. C. (1997). Associations between different diagnostic approaches for child and adolescent psychopathology. *Journal of Child Psychology and Psychiatry and Allied Disciplines, 38(6)*, 625–632.

Kaslow, N. J., & Thompson, M. P. (1998). Applying the criteria for empirically supported treatments to studies of psychosocial interventions for child and adolescent depression. *Journal of Clinical Child Psychology, 27*(2), 146–155.

Katz, P. A., & Kofkin, J. A. (1997). Race, gender and young children. In S. S. Luthar & J. A. Burack (Eds.), *Developmental psychopathology: Perspectives on adjustment, risk and disorder* (pp. 51–74). New York: Cambridge University Press.

Katz, S. H. (1998). The role of family interactions in adolescent depression: A review of research findings. In A. H. Esman, L. T. Flaherty, & H. A. Horowitz (Eds.), *Adolescent psychiatry: Developmental and clinical studies* (Vol. 23, pp. 41–58). Mahwah, NJ: Erlbaum.

Kaufman, J., & Charney, D. (2003). The neurobiology of child and adolescent depression: Current knowledge and future directions. In D. Cicchetti & E. Walker (Eds.), *Neurodevelopmental mechanisms in psychopathology* (pp. 461–490). New York: Cambridge University Press.

Kaufman, J., & Henrich, C. (2000). Exposure to violence and early childhood trauma. In C. H. Zeanah (Ed.), *Handbook of infant mental health* (2nd ed., pp. 195–207). New York: Guilford Press.

Kaufman, J., Plotsky, P. M., Nemeroff, C. B., & Charney, D. S. (2000). Effects of early adverse experiences on brain structure and function: Clinical implications. *Biological Psychiatry, 48,* 778–790.

Kaufman, J., Yang, B., Douglas-Palumberi, H., Grasso, D., Lipschitz, D., Houshyar, S., et al. (2006). Brain-derived neurotrophic factor-5-HTTLPR gene interactions and environmental modifiers of depression in children. *Biological Psychiatry, 59*(8), 673–680.

Kaufman, N. K., Rohde, P., Seeley, J. R., Clarke, G. N., & Stice, E. (2005). Potential mediators of cognitive-behavioral therapy for adolescents with comorbid major depression and conduct disorder. *Journal of Consulting and Clinical Psychology, 73*(1), 38–46.

Kavale, K. A. (2002). Mainstreaming to full inclusion: From orthogenesis to pathogenesis of an idea. *International Journal of Disability, Development and Education, 49*(2), 201–214.

Kavale, K. A., & Forness, S. R. (2000). History, rhetoric, and reality: Analysis of the inclusion debate. *Remedial and Special Education, 21*(5), 279–296.

Kaye, W. H., Barbarich, N. C., Putnam, K., Gendall, K. A., Fernstrom, J., Fernstrom, M., et al. (2003). Anxiolytic effects of acute tryptophan depletion in anorexia nervosa. *International Journal of Eating Disorders, 33*, 257–267.

Kaye, W. H., Bulik, C. M., Thornton, L., Barbarich, N., & Masters, K. (2004). Comorbidity of anxiety disorders with anorexia and bulimia nervosa. *American Journal of Psychiatry, 161*, 2215–2221.

Kaye, W. H., Devlin, B., Barbarich, B., Bulik, C. M., Thornton, L., Bacanu. S. A., et al. (2004). Genetic analysis of bulimia nervosa: Methods and sample description. *International Journal of Eating Disorders, 35,* 556–570.

Kazdin, A. (2005). *Parent management training: Treatment for oppositional, aggressive, and antisocial behavior in children and adolescents.* New York: Oxford University Press.

Kazdin, A. E. (2000). Understanding change: From description to explanation in child and adolescent psychotherapy research. *Journal of School Psychology, 337*–347.

Kazdin, A. E. (2003). Psychotherapy for children and adolescents. *Annual Review of Psychology, 54*, 253–276.

Kazdin, A. E., Holland, L., & Crowley, M. (1997). Family experience of barriers to treatment and premature termination from child therapy. *Journal of Consulting and Clinical Psychology, 65(3),* 453–463.

Kazdin, A. E., Marciano, P. L., & Whitley, M. K. (2005). The therapeutic alliance in cognitive-behavioral treatment of children referred for oppositional, aggressive, and antisocial behavior. *Journal of Consulting and Clinical Psychology, 73*(4), 726–70.

Kazdin, A. E., & Nock, M. K. (2003). Delineating mechanisms of change in child and adolescent therapy: Methodological issues and research recommendations. *Journal of Child Psychology and Psychiatry, 44(8),* 1116–1129.

Kearney, C. A., & Albano, A. M. (2004). The functional profiles of school refusal behavior: Diagnostic aspects. *Behavior Modification, 28*(1), 147–161.

Kearney, C. A., & Silverman, W. K. (1993). Measuring the function of school refusal behavior: The school refusal assessment scale. *Journal of Clinical Child Psychology, 22*(1), 85–96.

Kearney, C. A., & Silverman, W. K. (1998). A critical review of pharmacotherapy for youth with anxiety disorders: Things are not as they seem. *Journal of Anxiety Disorders, 12*(2), 83–102.

Keel, P. K., & Haedt, A. (2008). Evidence-based psychosocial treatments for eating problems and eating disorders. *Journal of Clinical Child and Adolescent Psychology, 37*(1), 39–61.

Keel, P. K., Fichter, M., Quadfleig, N., Bulik, C. M., Baxter, M. G., Thornton, L., et al. (2004). Application of a latent class analysis to empirically define eating disorder phenotypes. *Archives of General Psychology, 61,* 192–200.

Keel, P. K., Leon, G. R., & Fulkerson, J. A. (2001). Vulnerability to eating disorders in childhood and adolescence. In Ingram, R. E. (Ed.), *Vulnerability to psychopathology: Risk across the lifespan* (pp. 389–411). New York: Guilford Press.

Keenan, K. (2000). Emotion dysregulation as a risk factor for child psychopathology. *Clinical Psychology: Science and Practice, 7*(4), 418–434.

Keenan, K., Loeber, R., & Green, S. (1999). Conduct disorder in girls: A review of the literature. *Clinical Child and Family Psychology Review, 2*(1), 3–19.

Keenan, K., Shaw, D., Delliquadri, E., Giovannelli, J., & Walsh, B. (1998). Evidence for the continuity of early problem behaviors: Application of a developmental model. *Journal of Abnormal Child Psychology, 26,* 441–452.

Keenan, K., Stouthamer-Loeber M., & Loeber, R. (2005). Developmental approaches to studying conduct problems in girls. In D. J. Pepler, K. C. Madsen, C. Webster, & K. S. Levene (Eds.), *The development and treatment of girlhood aggression* (pp. 29–46). Mahwah, NJ: Erlbaum.

Keenan, K., & Wakschlag, L. S. (2000). More than the terrible twos: The nature and severity of behavior problems in clinic-referred preschool children. *Journal of Abnormal Child Psychology, 28,* 33–46.

Keenan, K., & Wakschlag, L. S. (2002). Can a valid diagnosis of disruptive behavior disorder be made in preschool children? *American Journal of Psychiatry, 159,* 351–358.

Keenan, K., Wakschlag, L. S., Danis, B., Hill, C., Humphries, M., Duax, J., et al. (2007). Further evidence of the reliability and validity of DSM-IV ODD and CD in preschool children. *Journal of the American Academy of Child and Adolescent Psychiatry, 46*(4), 457–468.

Keener, M. A., Zeanah, C. H., & Anders, T. F. (1989). Infant temperament, sleep organization, and nighttime parental interventions. *Annual Progress in Child Psychiatry and Child Development,* 257–274.

Keery, H., Boutelle, K., van den Berg, P., & Thompson, J. K. (2005). The impact of appearance-related teasing by family members. *Journal of Adolescent Health, 37,* 120–127.

Keery, H., van den Berg, P., & Thompson, J. K. (2004). An evaluation of the Tripartite Influence Model of body dissatisfaction and eating disturbance with adolescent girls. *Body Image, 1*(3), 237–251.

Keil, F. C. (1999). Cognition, content and development. In M. Bennet (Ed.), *Developmental psychology: Achievements and prospects* (pp. 165–184). Philadelphia: Psychology Press.

Keiley, M. K., Lofthouse, N., Bates, J. E., Dodge, K. A., & Pettit, G. S. (2003). Differential risks of covarying and pure components in mother and teacher reports of externalizing and internalizing behavior across ages 5 to 14. *Journal of Abnormal Child Psychology, 31,* 267–283.

Keith, K. D., Heal, L. W., Schalock, R. L. (1996). Cross-cultural measurement of critical quality of life concepts. *Journal of Intellectual and Developmental Disability, 21*(4), 273–293.

Kelley, A. E., Schochet, T., & Landry, C. F. (2004). Risk taking and novelty seeking in adolescence: Introduction to part I. In R. E. Dahl & L. P. Spear (Eds.), *Adolescent brain development: Vulnerabilities and opportunities. Annals of the New York Academy of Sciences* (Vol. 1021, pp. 27–32). New York: New York Academy of Sciences.

Kelly, A. E., Schiltz, C. A., & Landry, C. F. (2005). Neural systems recruited by drug-and food-related cues: Studies of gene activation in corticolimbic regions. *Physiology and Behavior, 86,* 11–14.

Kelly, A. M., Wall, M., Eisenberg, M. E., Story, M., & Neumark-Sztainer, D. (2005). Adolescent girls with high body image satisfaction: Who are they and what can they teach us? *Journal of Adolescent Health, 37,* 391–396.

Kelley, B. M., & Rowan, J. D. (2004). Long-term, low-level adolescent nicotine exposure produces dose-dependent changes in cocaine sensitivity and reward in adult mice. *International Journal of Developmental Neuroscience, 22*(5–6), 339–348.

Kelly, J. F., Myers, M. G., & Brown, S. A. (2002). Do adolescents affiliate with 12-step groups? A multivariate process model of effects. *Journal of Studies on Alcohol, 63*(3), 293–304.

Kelly, T. M., Cornelius, J. R., & Clark, D. B. (2004). Psychiatric disorders and attempted suicide among adolescents with substance use disorders. *Drug and Alcohol Dependence, 73*(1), 87–97.

Kempton, W., & Kahn, E. (1991). Sexuality and people with intellectual disabilities: A historical perspective. *Sexuality and Disability, 9*(2), 93–111.

Kendall, P. C., Brady, E. U., & Verduin, T. L. (2001). Comorbidity in childhood anxiety disorders and treatment outcome. *Journal of the American Academy of Child and Adolescent Psychiatry, 40*(7), 787–794.

Kendall, P. C., & Dobson, K. S. (1993). On the nature of cognition and its role in psychopathology. In K. S. Dobson & P. C. Kendall (Eds.), *Psychopathology and cognition. Personality, psychopathology, and psychotherapy series.* San Diego, CA: Academic Press.

Kendall, P. C., Flannery-Schroeder, E., Panichelli-Mindel, S. M., Southam-Gerow, M., Henin, A., & Warman, M. (1997). Therapy for youths with anxiety disorders: A second randomized clinical trial. *Journal of Consulting and Clinical Psychology, 65*(3), 366–380.

Kendall, P. C., & MacDonald, J. P. (1993). Cognition in the psychopathology of youth and implications for treatment. In K. S. Dobson & P. C. Kendall (Eds.), *Psychopathology and cognition. Personality, psychopathology, and psychotherapy series* (pp. 387–427). San Diego, CA: Academic Press.

Kendall, P. C., Safford, S., Flannery-Schroeder, E., & Webb, A. (2004). Child anxiety treatment: Outcomes in adolescence and impact on substance use and depression at 7.4-year follow-up. *Journal of Consulting and Clinical Psychology, 72*(2), 276–287.

Kendall, P. C., & Southam-Gerow, M. A. (1996). Long-term follow-up of a cognitive-behavioral therapy for anxiety-disordered youth. *Journal of Consulting and Clinical Psychology, 64*(4), 724–730.

Kendler, K. S. (2005). "A gene for Ö": The nature of gene action in psychiatric disorders. *American Journal of Psychiatry, 162*(7), 1243–1252.

Kennard, B., Silva, S., Vitiello, B., Curry, J., Kratochvil, C., Simons, A., et al. (2006). Remission and residual symptoms after short-term treatment in the Treatment of Adolescents with Depression Study (TADS). *Journal of the American Academy of Child and Adolescent Psychiatry, 45*(12), 1404–1411.

Kentgen, L. M., Tenke, C. E., Pine, D. S., Fong, R., Klein, R. G., & Bruder, G. E. (2000). Electroencephalographic asymmetries in adolescents with major depression: Influence of comorbidity with anxiety disorders. *Journal of Abnormal Psychology,* *109*(4), 797–802.

Keren, M., Feldman, R., & Tyano, S. (2001). Diagnoses and interactive patterns of infants referred to a community-based infant mental health clinic. *Journal of the American Academy of Child and Adolescent Psychiatry, 40*(1), 27–35.

Kerkorian, D., McKay, M., & Bannon, W. M., Jr. (2006). Seeking help a second time: Parents'/caregivers' characterizations of previous experiences with mental health services for their children and perceptions of barriers to future use. *American Journal of Orthopsychiatry, 76(2),* 161–166.

Kerr, M. (2001). Culture as a context for temperament: Suggestions from the life courses of shy Swedes and Americans. In T. D. Wachs & G. A. Kohnstamm (Eds.), *Temperament in context* (pp. 139–152). Mahwah, NJ: Erlbaum.

Kerr, M., & Stattin, H. (2003). Parenting of adolescents: Action or reaction? In A. C. Crouter & A. Booth (Eds.), *Children's influence on family dynamics: The neglected side of family relationships* (pp. 121–151). Mahwah, NJ: Erlbaum.

Kerwin, M. E. (1999). Empirically supported treatments in pediatric psychology: Severe feeding problems. *Journal of Pediatric Psychology, 24*(3), 193–214.

Kessler, R. C., Adler, L., Barkley, R., Biederman, J., Conners, C. K., Demler, O., et al. (2006). The prevalence and correlates of adult ADHD in the United States: Results from the National Comorbidity Survey replication. *American Journal of Psychiatry, 163*(4), 716–723.

Kessler, R. C., Avenevoli, S., & Merikangas, K. R. (2001). Mood disorders in children and adolescents: An epidemiologic perspective. *Biological Psychiatry, 49*(12), 1002–1014.

Keyes, C. L. M., & Lopez, S. J. (2002). Toward a science of mental health: Positive directions in diagnosis and interventions. In C. R. Snyder & S. J. Lopez (Eds.), *Handbook of Positive Psychology* (pp. 45–59). New York: Oxford University Press.

Kichler, J., Luyster, R., Risi, S., Hsu, W., Dawson, G., Bernier, R., et al. (2006). Is there a ëregressive phenotype' of autism spectrum disorder associated with the measles-mumps-rubella vaccine? A CPEA study. *Journal of Autism and Developmental Disorders, 36*(3), 299–316.

Kiesner, J., Dishion, T. J., & Poulin, F. (2001). A reinforcement model of conduct problems in children and adolescents: Advances in theory and intervention. In J. Hill & B. Maughan (Eds.), *Conduct disorders in childhood and adolescence: Cambridge child and adolescent psychiatry* (pp. 264–291). New York: Cambridge University Press.

Kilmer, R. P., Cowen, E. L., & Wyman, P. A. (2001). A microlevel analysis of developmental, parenting, and family milieu variables that differentiate stress-resilient and stress-affected children. *Journal of Community Psychology, 29(4),* 391–416.

Kilmer, R. P., Cowen, E. L., Wyman, P. A., Work, W. C., & Magnus, K. B. (1998). Differences in stressors experienced by urban African American, White, and Hispanic children. *Journal of Community Psychology, 26*(5), 415–428.

Kilpatrick, D. G., Ruggiero, K. J., Acierno, R., Saunders, B. E., Resnick, H. S., & Best, C. L. (2003). Violence and risk of PTDS, major depression, substance abuse/dependence, and comorbidity: Results from the National Survey of Adolescents. *Journal of Consulting and Clinical Psychology, 71*(4), 692–700.

Kim, E. Y., & Miklowitz, D. J. (2002). Childhood mania, attention deficit hyperactivity disorder, and conduct disorder: A critical review of diagnostic dilemmas. *Bipolar Disorders, 4*(4), 215–225.

Kim, I. J., Ge, X., Brody, G. H., Conger, R. D., Gibbons, F. X., & Simons, R. L. (2003). Parenting behaviors and the occurrence and co-occurrence of depressive symptoms and conduct problems among African American children. *Journal of Family Psychology, 17*(4), 571–583.

Kim, I. J., Zane, N. W. S., & Hong, S. (2002). Protective factors against substance use among Asian American youth: A test of the peer cluster theory. *Journal of Community Psychology, 30*(5), 565–584.

Kim, J. A., Szatmari, P., Bryson, S. E., Streiner, D. L., & Wilson, F. J. (2000). The prevalence of anxiety and mood problems among children with autism and Asperger syndrome. *Autism, 4,* 117–132.

Kim, S., Larson, S. A., & Lakin, K. C. (2001). Behavioural outcomes of deinstitutionalisation for people with intellectual disability: A review of US studies conducted between 1980 and 1999. *Journal of Intellectual and Developmental Disability, 26*(1), 35–50.

Kim-Cohen, J., Arseneault, L., Caspi, A., Tomás, M. P., Taylor, A., & Moffitt, T. E. (2005). Validity of DSM-IV conduct disorder in 4 ½–5-year-old children: A longitudinal epidemiological study. *American Journal of Psychiatry, 162*(6), 1108–1117.

Kim-Cohen, J., Moffitt, T. E., Taylor, A., Pawlby, S. J., & Caspi, A. (2005). Maternal depression and children's antisocial behavior: Nature and nurture effects. *Archives of General Psychiatry, 62*(2), 173–181.

Kim-Cohen, J., Moffitt, T. E., Caspi, A., & Taylor, A. (2004). Genetic and environmental processes in young children's resilience and vulnerability to socioeconomic deprivation. *Child Development, 75,* 651–668.

Kimonis, E. R., Frick, P. J., Boris, N. W., Smyke, A. T., Cornell, A. H., Farrell, J. M., et al. (2006). Callous-unemotional features, behavioral inhibition, and parenting: Independent predictors of aggression in a high-risk preschool sample. *Journal of Child and Family Studies, 15*(6), 745–756.

King, B. H., State, M. W., Shah, B., Davanzo, P., & Dykens, E. (1997). A review of the past 10 years. *Journal of the American Academy of Child and Adolescent, 36*(12), 1656–1663.

King, N. A., Eleonora, G., Tonge, B. J., & Ollendick, T. H. (1993). Self-reports of panic attacks and manifest anxiety in adolescents. *Behaviour Research and Therapy, 31,* 111–116.

King, N. J., & Ollendick, T. H. (1997). Treatment of childhood phobias. *Journal of Child Psychology and Psychiatry and Allied Disciplines, 38*(4), 389–400.

King, N. J., Eleonora, E., & Ollendick, T. H. (1998). Etiology of childhood phobias: Current status of Rachman's three pathways theory. *Behaviour Research and Therapy, 36*(3), 297–309.

King, N. J., Heyne, D., Tonge, B. J., Mullen, P., Myerson, N., Rollings, S., et al. (2003). Sexually abused children suffering from post-traumatic stress disorder: Assessment and treatment strategies. *Cognitive Behaviour Therapy, 32*(1), 2–12.

King, N. J., Muris, P., & Ollendick, T. H. (2005). Childhood fears and phobias: assessment and treatment. *Child and Adolescent Mental Health, 10*(2), 50–56.

King, N. J., Ollendick, T. H., Mattis, S. G., Yang, B., & Tonge, B. (1996). Nonclinical panic attacks in adolescents: Prevalece, symptomatology, and associated features. *Behaviour Change, 13,* 171–183.

King, N. J., Ollendick, T., & Montgomery, I. A. (1995). Obsessive-compulsive disorder in children and adolescents. *Behaviour Change, 12*(1), 51–58.

King, N. J., Tonge, B. J., Mullen, P., Myerson, N., Heyne, D., Rollings, S., et al. (2000b). Treating sexually abused children with posttraumatic stress symptoms: A randomized clinical trial. *Journal of the American Academy of Child and Adolescent Psychiatry, 39*(11), 1347–1355.

King, N. J., Ollendick, T. H., & Murphy, G. C. (1997). Assessment of childhood phobias. *Clinical Psychology Review, 17*(7), 667–687.

King, N., Ollendick, T. H., Tonge, B. J., Heyne, D., Pritchard, M., Rollings, S., et al. (1998). School refusal: An overview. *Behaviour Change, 15*(1), 5–15.

King, N., Tonge, B. J., Heyne, D., Turner, S., Pritchard, M., Young, D., et al. (2001). Cognitive-behavioural treatment of school-refusing children: Maintenance of improvement at 3- to 5-year follow-up. *Scandinavian Journal of Behaviour Therapy, 30*(2), 85–89.

King, N., Tonge, B. J., Mullen, P., Myerson, N., Heyne, D., Rollings, S., et al. (2000a). Sexually abused children and post-traumatic stress disorder. *Counseling Psychology Quarterly, 13*(4), 365–375.

King, R., Nurcombe, B., Bickman, L., Hides, L., & Reid, W. (2003). Telephone counseling for adolescent suicide prevention: Changes in suicidality and mental state from beginning to end of a counseling session. *Suicide and Life-Threatening Behavior, 33*(4), 400–411.

King, S. M., Burt, A., Malone, S. M., McGue, M., & Iacono, W. G. (2005). Etiological contributions to heavy drinking from late adolescence to young adulthood. *Journal of Abnormal Psychology, 114*(4), 587–598.

King, S. M., Iacono, W. G., & McGue, M. (2004). Childhood externalizing and internalizing psychopathology in the prediction of early substance use. *Addiction, 99*(12), 1548–1559.

Kinzie, J. D., Cheng, K., Tsai, J., & Riley, C. (2006). Traumatized refugee children: The case for individualized diagnosis and treatment. *Journal of Nervous and Mental Disease, 194*(7), 534–537.

Kirisci, L., Tarter, R. E., Reynolds, M., & Vanyukov, M. (2006). Individual differences in childhood neurobehavior disinhibition predict decision to desist substance use during adolescence and substance use disorder in young adulthood: A prospective study. *Addictive Behaviors, 31*(4), 686–696.

Kjelsas, E., Bjornstrom, C., & Gotestam, K. G. (2004). Prevalence of eating disorders in female and male adolescents (14–15). *Eating Behaviors, 5*, 13–25.

Klasen, H. (2000). A name, what's in a name? The medicalization of hyperactivity, revisited. *Harvard Review of Psychology, 7(6)*, 334–344.

Klein, M. (1955). The psychoanalytic play technique. *American Journal of Orthopsychiatry, 25*, 223–237.

Klein, R. G. (1991). Parent-child agreement in clinical assessment of anxiety and other psychopathology: A review. *Journal of Anxiety Disorders, 5*(2), 187–198.

Klein, R. G. (1995). Is panic disorder associated with childhood separation anxiety disorder? *Clinical Neuropharmacology,18*(Suppl 2), S7-S14.

Klesges, R., Elliott, V., & Robinson, L. (1997). Chronic dieting and the belief that smoking controls body weight in a biracial population-based adolescent sample. *Tobacco Control, 6*, 89–94.

Klin, A. (1994). Asperger syndrome. *Child and Adolescent Psychiatry Clinics of North America, 3*, 131–148.

Klin, A. (2002). *Asperger syndrome: Clinical features, assessment, and intervention.* Clinical presentation to Minnesota Association of Child Psychologists, Minneapolis, MN.

Klin, A., & Volkmar, F. R. (1994). The development of individuals with autism: Implications for the theory of mind hypothesis. In S. Baron-Cohen & H. Tager-Flusberg (Eds.), *Understanding other minds: Perspectives from autism* (pp. 317–331). London: Oxford University Press.

Klin, A., & Volkmar, F. R. (1997). Asperger's syndrome. In D. J. Cohen & F. R. Volkmar (Eds.), *Handbook of autism and pervasive developmental disorders* (2nd ed.). (pp. 94–122). New York: Wiley.

Klin, A., & Volkmar, F. R. (2000). Treatment and intervention guidelines for individuals with Asperger syndrome. In A. Klin, F. R. Volkmar, & S. S. Sparrow (Eds.), *Asperger syndrome* (pp. 340–366). New York: Guilford Press.

Klin, A., & Volkmar, F. R. (2003). Asperger syndrome: Diagnosis and external validity. *Child and Adolescent Psychiatric Clinics of North America, 12*, 1–13.

Klin, A., Jones, W., Schultz, R., Volkmar, F., & Cohen, D. (2002a). Defining and quantifying the social phenotype in autism. *American Journal of Psychiatry, 159*, 909–916.

Klin, A., Jones, W., Schultz, R., Volkmar, F., & Cohen, D. (2002b). Visual fixation patterns during viewing of naturalistic social situations as predictors of social competence in individuals with autism. *Archives of General Psychiatry, 59*, 809–816.

Klin, A., Lang, J., Cicchetti, D. V., & Volkmar, F. R. (2000). Brief report: Interrater reliability of clinical diagnosis and DSM-IV criteria for autistic disorder: Results of the DSM-IV Autism Field Trial. *Journal of Autism and Developmental Disorders, 30*, 163–167.

Klin, A., Mayes, L. C., Volkmar, F. R., & Cohen, D. J. (1995). Multiplex developmental disorder. *Journal of Developmental and Behavioral Pediatrics, 16*, S7-S11.

Klin, A., Sparrow, S. S., Marans, W. D., Carter, A., & Volkmar, F. R. (2000). Assessment issues in Asperger syndrome. In A. Klin, F. R. Volkmar, & S. S. Sparrow (Eds.), *Asperger syndrome* (pp. 309–339). New York: Guilford Press.

Klin, A., Sparrow, S. S., Volkmar, F. R., Cicchetti, D. V., & Rourke, B. . (1995). Asperger syndrome. In B. P. Rourke (Ed.), *Syndrome of nonverbal learning disabilities: Manifestations in neurological disease, disorder, and dysfunction* (pp. 93–118). New York: Guilford Press.

Klin, A., Volkmar, F. R., & Sparrow, S. S. (2000). *Asperger syndrome.* New York: Guilford Press.

Klin, A., Volkmar, F. R., Sparrow, S. S., & Cicchetti, D. V. (1995). Validity and neuropsychological characterization of Asperger syndrome: Convergence with nonverbal learning disabilities syndrome. *Journal of Child Psychology and Psychiatry and Allied Disciplines, 36*, 1127–1140.

Klinger, L. G., & Dawson, G. (2001). Prototype formation in autism. *Development and Psychopathology, 13*, 111–124.

Klinger, L. G., Dawson, G., & Renner, P. (2003). Autistic disorder. In E. J. Mash & R. A. Barkley (Eds.), *Child psychopathology* (2nd ed., pp. 409–454). New York: Guilford Press.

Klomek, A. B., & Mufson, L. (2006). Interpersonal psychotherapy for depressed adolescents. *Child and Adolescent Psychiatric Clinics of North America, 15*(4), 959–975.

Knopik, V. S., Heath, A. C., Madden, P. A. F., Bucholz, K. K., Slutske, W. S., Nelson, E. C., et al. (2004). Genetic effects on alcohol dependence risk: Re-evaluating the importance of psychiatric and other heritable risk factors. *Psychological Medicine, 34*(8), 1519–1530.

Ko, C-H., Yen, J-Y, Chen, C-C., Chen, S-H., & Yen, C-F. (2005). Gender differences and elated factors affecting online gaming addiction among Taiwanese adolescents. *Journal of Nervous and Mental Disease, 193*(4), 273–277.

Kochanska, G. (1995). Children's temperament, mother's discipline, and security of attachment: Multiple pathways to emerging internalization. *Child Development, 66*(3), 597–615.

Kochanska, G. (1997). Multiple pathways to conscience for children with different temperaments: From toddlerhood to age 5. *Developmental Psychology, 33*(2), 228–240.

Kochanska, G., & Aksan, N. (2004). Conscience in childhood: Past, present, and future. *Merrill-Palmer Quarterly, 50*(3), 299–310.

Kochanska, G., Coy, K. C., & Murray, K. T. (2001). The development of self-regulation in the first four years of life. *Child Development, 72*(4), 1091–1111.

Kochanska, G., Coy, K. C., Tjebkes, T. L., & Husarek, S. J. (1998). Individual differences in emotionality in infancy. *Child Development, 69*(2), 375–390.

Kochanska, G., & Knaack, A. (2003). Effortful control as a personality characteristic of young children: Antecedents, correlates, and consequences. *Journal of Personality, 71*, 1087–1112.

Kochanska, G., Murray, K. T., & Harlan, E. T. (2000). Effortful control in early childhood: Continuity and change, antecedents, and implications for social development. *Developmental Psychology, 36*(2), 220–232.

Kochanska, G., Murray, K., & Coy, K. C. (1997). Inhibitory control as a contributor to conscience in childhood: From toddler to early school age. *Child Development, 68*(2), 263–277.

Kochanska, G., Tjebkes, T. L., & Forman, D. R. (1998). Children's emerging regulation of conduct: Restraint, compliance, and internalization from infancy to the second year. *Child Development, 69*, 1378–1389.

Kochenderfer-Ladd, B. (2003). Identification of aggressive and asocial victims and the stability of their peer victimization. *Merrill-Palmer Quarterly, 49*(4), 401–425.

Kochman, F. J., Hantouche, E. G., Ferrari, P., Lancrenon, S., Bayart, D., & Akiskal, H. S. (2005). Cyclothymia temperament as a prospective predictor of bipolarity and suicidality in children and adolescents with major depressive disorder. *Journal of Affective Disorders, 85*(1–2), 181–189.

Kodjo, C. M., Auinger, P., & Ryan, S. A. (2004). Prevalence of, and factors associated with, adolescent physical fighting while under the influence of alcohol and drugs. *Journal of Adolescent Health, 35*(4),11–16.

Koenig, A. L., Ialongo, N., Wagner, B. M., Poduska, J., & Kellam, S. (2002). Negative caregiver strategies and psychopathology in urban, African-American young adults. *Child Abuse and Neglect, 26*(12), 1211–1233.

Koenig, K., Rubin, E., Klin, A., & Volkmar, F. R. (2000). Autism and the pervasive developmental disorders. In C. H. Zeanah (Ed.), *Handbook of infant mental health* (2nd ed., pp. 298–310). New York: Guilford Press.

Kohen, D. E., Leventhal, T., Dahinten, V. S., & McIntosh, C. N. (2008). Neighborhood disadvantage: Pathways of effects for young children. *Child Development, 79,* 156–169.

Kolko, D, J., Brent, D. A., Baugher, M., Bridge, J., & Birmaher, B. (2000). Cognitive and family therapies for adolescent depression: Treatment specificity, mediation, and moderation. *Journal of Consulting and Clinical Psychology, 68*(4), 603–614.

Komro, K. A., Perry, C. L., Veblen-Mortenson, S., Bosma, L. M., Dudovitz, B. S., Williams, C., et al. (2004). Brief report: The adaptation of Project Northland for urban youth. *Journal of Pediatric Psychology, 29*(6), 457–466.

Komro, K. A., & Toomey, T. L. (2002). Strategies to prevent underage drinking. *Alcohol Research and Health, 26*(1), 5–14.

Koob, G. F. (2002). Neurobiology of drug addiction. In D. B. Kandel (Ed.), *Stages and pathways of drug involvement: Examining the gateway hypothesis* (pp. 337–361). New York: Cambridge University Press.

Koops, W., & de Castro, B. O. (2004). The development of aggression and its linkages with violence and youth delinquency. *European Journal of Developmental Psychology, 1*(3), 241–269.

Kopp, C. B. (1982). Antecedents of self-regulation: A developmental perspective. *Developmental Psychology, 18*(2), 199–214.

Kopp, C. B. (1989). Regulation of distress and negative emotions: A developmental view. *Developmental Psychology, 25*(3), 343–354.

Kopp, C. B. (1997). Young children: Emotion management, instrumental control, and plans. In S. L. Friedman & E. K. Scholnick (Eds.), *The developmental psychology of planning: Why, how, and when do we plan?* (pp. 103–124). Mahwah, NJ: Erlbaum.

Kopp, C. B., & Wyer, N. (1994). Self-regulation in normal and atypical development. In *Disorders and dysfunctions of the self* (pp. 31–56). Rochester, NY: University of Rochester Press.

Korkman, M., Kemp, S. L., & Kirk, U. (2001). Effects of age on neurocognitive measures of children ages 5 to 12: A cross-sectional study on 800 children from the United States. *Developmental Neuropsychology, 20(1),* 331–354.

Kosten, T. R., George, T. P., & Kleber, H. D. (2005). The neurobiology of substance dependence: Implications for treatment. In R. J. Frances, S. I. Miller, & A. H. Mack (Eds.), *Clinical textbook of addictive disorders* (3rd ed.). New York: Guilford Press.

Kotchick, B. A., & Forehand, R. (2002). Putting parenting in perspective: A discussion of the contextual factors that shape parenting practices. *Journal of Child and Family Studies, 11,* 255–269.

Kotler, L. A., Cohen, P., Davies, M., Pine, D. S., & Walsh, B. T. (2001). Longitudinal relationships between childhood, adolescent and adult eating disorders. *Journal of the American Academy of Child and Adolescent Psychiatry, 40,* 1434–1440.

Koukoui, S. D., & Chaudhuri, A. (2007). Neuroanatomical, molecular genetic, and behavioral correlates of fragile X syndrome. *Brain Research Reviews, 53*(1), 27–38.

Kovacs, M. (1985). The Children's Depression Inventory (CDI). *Psychopharmacology Bulletin, 21,* 995–998.

Kovacs, M. (1992). *Manual for the Children's Depression Inventory.* North Tonawanda, NJ: Multi-Health Systems.

Kovacs, M., & Devlin, B. (1998). Internalizing disorders in childhood. *Journal of Child Psychology and Psychiatry, 39*(1), 47–63.

Kovacs, M., Obrosky, D. S., & Sherrill, J. (2003). Developmental changes in the phenomenology of depression in girls compared to boys from childhood onward. *Journal of Affective Disorders, 74*(1), 33–48.

Kowatch, R. A., Sethuraman, G., Hume, J. H., Kromelis, M., & Weinberg, W. A. (2003). Combination pharmacotherapy in children and adolescents with bipolar disorder. *Biological Psychiatry, 53*(11), 978–984.

Kowatch, R. A., Fristad, M., Birmaher, B., Wagner, K. D., Findling, R., Hellander, M., et al. (2005). Treatment guidelines for children and adolescents with bipolar disorder. *American Academy of Child and Adolescent Psychiatry, 44*(3), 213–235.

Krajewski, J. J., Hyde, M. S., & O'Keefe, M. K. (2002) Teen attitudes toward individuals with mental retardation from 1987 to 1998: Impact of respondent gender and school variables. *Education and Training in Mental Retardation and Developmental Disabilities, 37*(1), 27–39.

Krasny, L., Williams, B. J., Provencal, S., & Ozonoff, S. (2003). Social skills interventions for the autism spectrum: Essential ingredients and a model curriculum. *Child and Adolescent Psychiatric Clinics of North America, 12*, 107–122.

Kratochvil, C. J., Simons, A., Vitiello, B., Walkup, J., Emslie, G., Rosenberg, D., et al. (2005). A multisite psychotherapy and medication trial for depressed adolescents: Background and benefits. *Cognitive and Behavioral Practice, 12*(2), 159–165.

Kratochwill, T. R., & Stoiber, K. C. (2000). Diversifying theory and science: Expanding the boundaries of empirically supported interventions in school psychology. *Journal of School Psychology, 38(4),* 349–358.

Krauss, M. W., Simeonsson, R., & Ramey, S. L. (Eds.). (1989). Research on families [Special issue]. *American Journal on Mental Retardation, 94* (3).

Kris, E. (1950). Notes on the development and on some current problems of psychoanalytic child psychology. *The Psychoanalytic Study of the Child, 5*, 24–46. New York: International Universities Press.

Kroes, M., Kalff, A. C., Kessels, A. G. H., Setaert, J., Feron, F. J. M., van Someren, A. J. W. G. M., et al. (2001). Child psychiatric diagnoses in a population of Dutch schoolchildren aged 6 to 8 years. *Journal of the American Academy of Child and Adolescent Psychiatry, 40(12),* 1401–1409.

Krueger, R. F., Hicks, B. M., Patrick, C. J., Carlson, S. R., Iacono, W. G., & McGue, M. (2002). Etiologic connections among substance dependence, antisocial behavior, and personality: modeling the externalizing spectrum. *Journal of Abnormal Psychology, 111*(3), 411–424.

Krueger, R. F., Silva, P. A., Avshalom, C., & Moffitt, T. E. (1998). The structure and stability of common mental disorders (DSM-III-R): A longitudinal-epidemiological study. *Journal of Abnormal Psychology, 107(2),* 216–227.

Kuhl, P. K., Coffey-Corina, S., Padden, D., & Dawson, G. (2005). Links between social and linguistic processing of speech in preschool children with autism: Behavioral and electrophysiological measures. *Developmental Science, 8*(1), F1-F12.

Kumar, R., O'Malley, P. M., & Johnston, L. D. (2005). School tobacco control policies related to students' smoking and attitudes toward smoking: National survey results, 1999–2000. *Health Education and Behavior, 32*(6), 780–794.

Kumar, R., O'Malley, P. M., Johnston, L. D., Schulenberg, J. E., & Bachman, J. G. (2002). Effects of school-level norms on student substance use. *Prevention Science, 3*(2), 105–124.

Kumpfer, K. L., & Alvarado, R. (2003). Family-strengthening approaches for the prevention of youth problem behaviors. *American Psychologist, 58(6/7),* 457–465.

Kunce, L., & Mesibov, G. B. (1998). Educational approaches to high-functioning autism and Asperger syndrome. In E. Schopler & G. B. Mesibov (Eds.), *Asperger syndrome or high-functioning autism? Current issues in autism* (pp. 227–261). New York: Plenum Press.

Kupersmidt, J. B., & DeRosier, M. E. (2004). How peer problems lead to negative outcomes: An integrative mediational model. In J. B. Kupersmidt & K. A. Dodge (Eds.), *Children's peer relations: From development to intervention. Decade of behavior* (pp. 119–138). Washington, DC: American Psychological Association.

Kutcher, S. P., Reiter, S., Gardner, D. M., & Klein, R. G. (1992). The pharmacotherapy of anxiety disorders in children and adolescents. *Psychiatric Clinics of North America, 15*(1), 41–67.

Kuttner, L. (1997). Mind-body methods of pain management. *Child and Adolescent Psychiatric Clinics of North America, 6*(4), 783–796.

La Greca, A. M., Silverman, W. K., Vernberg, E. M., & Roberts, M. C. (2002). *Helping children cope with disasters and terrorism.* Washington, DC: American Psychological Association.

La Malfa, G., Lassi, S., Bertelli, M., Salvini, R., & Placidi, G. F. (2004). Autism and intellectual disability: A study of prevalence on a sample of the Italian population. *Journal of Intellectual Disability Research, 48*(3), 262–267.

Labellarte, M. J., Ginsburg, G. S., Walkup, J. T., & Riddle, M. A. (1999). The treatment of anxiety disorders in children and adolescents. *Biological Psychiatry, 46*(11), 1567–1578.

Lacourse, E., Cote, S., Nagin, D. S., Vitaro, F., Brendgen, M., & Tremblay, R. E. (2002). A longitudinal-experimental approach to testing theories of antisocial behavior development. *Development and Psychopathology, 14*(4), 909–924.

Lacourse, E., Nagin, D., Tremblay, R. E., Vitaro, F., & Claes, M. (2003). Developmental trajectories of boys' delinquent group membership and facilitation of violent behaviors during adolescence. *Development and Psychopathology, 15*(1), 183–197.

Lahey, B. B., Appelgate, B., Barkley, R. A., & Garfinkel, B. (1994). DSM-IV field trials for oppositional defiant disorder and conduct disorder in children and adolescents. *American Journal of Psychiatry, 151(8),* 1163–1171.

Lahey, B. B., Applegate, B., McBurnett, K., & Biederman, J. (1994). DSM-IV field trials for attention deficit hyperactivity disorder in children and adolescents. *American Journal of Psychiatry, 151*(11), 1673–1685.

Lahey, B. B., Applegate, B., Waldman, I. D., Loft, J. D., Hankin, B. L., & Frick, J. (2004). The structure of child and adolescent psychopathology: Generating new hypotheses. *Journal of Abnormal Psychology, 113*(3), 358–385.

Lahey, B. B., Flagg, E. W., Bird, H. R., Schwab-Stone, M. E., Canino, G., Dulcan, M. K., et al. (1996). The NIMH methods for the epidemiology of child and adolescent mental disorders (MECA) study: Background and methodology. *Journal of the American Academy of Child and Adolescent Psychiatry, 35(7),* 855–865.

Lahey, B. B., Gordon, R. A., Loeber, R., Stouthamer-Loeber, M., & Farrington, D. P. (1999). Boys who join gangs: A prospective study of predictors of first gang entry. *Journal of Abnormal Child Psychology, 27*(4), 261–276.

Lahey, B. B., & Loeber, R. (1997). Attention-deficit/hyperactivity disorder, oppositional defiant disorder, conduct disorder, and adult antisocial behavior: A life span perspective. In D. M. Stoff & J. Breiling (Eds.), *Handbook of antisocial behavior* (pp. 51–59). New York: Wiley.

Lahey, B. B., Loeber, R., Burke, J. D., & Applegate, B. (2005). Predicting future antisocial personality disorder in males from a clinical assessment in childhood. *Journal of Consulting and Clinical Psychology, 73*(3), 389–399.

Lahey, B. B., Loeber, R., Burke, J., Rathouz, P. J., & McBurnett, K. (2002). Waxing and waning in concert: Dynamic comorbidity of conduct disorder with other disruptive and emotional problems over 17 years among clinic-referred boys. *Journal of Abnormal Psychology, 111*(4), 556–567.

Lahey, B. B., Loeber, R., Quay, H. C., Applegate, B., Shaffer, D., Waldman, I., et al. (1998). Validity of DSM-IV subtypes of conduct disorder based on age of onset. *Journal of the American Academy of Child and Adolescent Psychiatry, 37*(4), 435–442.

Lahey, B. B., McBurnett, K., & Loeber, R. (2000). Are attention-deficit/hyperactivity disorder and oppositional defiant disorder developmental precursors to conduct disorder? In A. J. Sameroff & M. Lewis (Eds.), *Handbook of developmental psychopathology* (2nd ed., pp. 431–446). Dordrecht, Netherlands: Kluwer Academic Publishers.

Lahey, B. B., Pelham, W. E., Stein, M. A., Loney, J., Trapani, C., Nugent, K., et al. (1998). Validity of DSM-IV attention-deficit/hyperactivity disorder for younger children. *Journal of the American Academy of Child and Adolescent Psychiatry, 37*(7), 695–702.

Lahey, B. B., & Waldman, I. D. (2003). A developmental propensity model of the origins of conduct problems during childhood and adolescence. In B. B. Lahey, T. E. Moffitt, & A. Caspi (Eds.), *Causes of conduct disorder and juvenile delinquency* (pp. 76–117). New York: Guilford Press.

Lahortiga-Ramos, F., De Irala-Estevez, J, Cano-Prous, A., Gual-Garcia, P., Martinez-Gonzalez, M. A., & Cervera-Enguix, S. (2005). Incidence of eating disorders in Navarra (Spain). *European Psychology, 20,* 179–185.

Laible, D. J., & Thompson, R. A. (1998). Attachment and emotional understanding in preschool children. *Developmental Psychology, 34*(5), 1038–1045.

Laing, E. (2002). Investigating reading development in atypical populations: The case of Williams syndrome. *Reading and Writing, 15*(5–6), 575–587.

Laird, R. D., Pettit, G. S., Dodge, K. A., & Bates, J. E. (2003). Change in parents' monitoring knowledge: Links with parenting, relationship quality, adolescent beliefs, and antisocial behavior. *Social Development, 12*(3), 401–419.

Lambert, E. W., Wahler, R. G., Andrade, A. R., & Bickman, L. (2001). Looking for the disorder in conduct disorder. *Journal of Abnormal Psychology, 110*(1), 110–123.

Lambert, M. C., Weisz, J. R., Knight, F., Desrosiers, M-F., Overly, K., & Thesiger, C. (1992). Jamaican and American adult perspectives on child psychopathology: Further exploration of the threshold model. *Journal of Consulting and Clinical Psychology, 60(1),* 146–149.

Lambert, N. (2005). The contribution of childhood ADHD, conduct problems, and stimulant treatment to adolescent and adult tobacco and psychoactive substance abuse. *Ethical Human Psychology and Psychiatry, 7*(3), 197–221.

Lambert, S. F., McCreary, B. T., Preston, J. L., Schmidt, N. B., Joiner, T., & Ialongo, N. S. (2004). Anxiety sensitivity in African-American adolescents: Evidence of symptom specificity of anxiety sensitivity components. *Journal of the American Academy of Child and Adolescent Psychiatry, 43*(7), 887–895.

Landa, R. (2000). Social language use in Asperger syndrome and high-functioning autism. In A. Klin, F. R. Volkmar, & S. S. Sparrow (Eds.), *Asperger syndrome* (pp. 125–155). New York: Guilford Press.

Langbehn, D. R., Cadoret, R. J., Yates, W. R., Troughton, E. P., & Stewart, M. A. (1998). Distinct contributions of conduct and oppositional defiant symptoms to adult antisocial behav-

ior: Evidence from an adoption study. *Archives of General Psychiatry, 55,* 821–829.

Langhinrichsen-Rohling, J., Rohde, P., Seeley, J. R., & Rohling, M. L. (2004). Individual, family, and peer correlates of adolescent gambling. *Journal of Gambling Studies, 20*(1), 23–46.

Langley, A. K., Bergman, R. L., McCracken, J., & Piacentini, J. C. (2004). Impairment in childhood anxiety disorders: Preliminary examination of the Child Anxiety Impact Scale – Parent Version. *Journal of Child and Adolescent Psychopharmacology, 14*(1), 105–114.

Lansford, J. E., Chang, L., Dodge, K. A., Malone, P. S., Oburu, P., Palmérus, K., et al. (2005). Physical discipline and children's adjustment: Cultural normativeness as a moderator. *Child Development, 76*(6), 1234–1246.

Lansford, J. E., Criss, M. M., Pettit, G. S., Dodge, K. A., & Bates, J. E. (2003). Friendship quality, peer group affiliation, and peer antisocial behavior as moderators of the link between negative parenting and adolescent externalizing behavior. *Journal of Research on Adolescence, 13,* 161–184.

Lansford, J. E., Deater-Deckard, K., Dodge, K. A., Bates, J. E., & Pettit, G. S. (2004). Ethnic differences in the link between physical discipline and later adolescent externalizing behaviors. *Journal of Child Psychology and Psychiatry, 45*(4), 801–812.

Lanza, S. T., & Collins, L. M. (2002). Pubertal timing and the onset of substance use in females during early adolescence. *Prevention Science, 3*(1), 69–82.

Lapinski, M. K. (2006). StarvingforPerfect.com: A theoretically based content analysis of pro-eating disorder web sites. *Health Communication, 20*(3), 243–253.

Larkin, J., & Rice, C. (2005). Beyond "healthy eating" and "healthy weights": Harassment and the health curriculum in middle schools. *Body Image, 2,* 219–232.

Larkin, M. (1999). "Mozart effect" comes under strong fire. *The Lancet, 354(9180),* 749.

Larson, R. W. (2000). Toward a psychology of positive youth development. *American Psychologist, 55(1),* 170–183.

Larson, R. W., Clore, G. L., & Wood, G. A. (1999). The emotions of romantic relationships: Do they wreak havoc on adolescents? In W. Furman, B. B. Brown, & C. Feiring (Eds.), *The development of romantic relationships in adolescence* (pp. 19–49). New York: Cambridge University Press.

Larson, S. A., Lakin, K. C., Anderson, L., Kwak, N., Lee, J. H., & Anderson, D. (2001). Prevalence of mental retardation and developmental disabilities: Estimates from the 1995/1995 National Health Interview Survey Disability Supplements. *American Journal on Mental Retardation, 106*(3), 231–252.

Last, C. G., Perrin, S., Hersen, M., & Kazdin, A. E. (1996). A prospective study of childhood anxiety disorders. *Journal of the American Academy of Child and Adolescent Psychiatry, 35*(11), 1502–1510.

Latzer, Y. (2003). Disordered eating behaviors and attitudes in diverse groups in Israel. In G. M. Ruggeiro (Ed.), *Eating disorders in the Mediterranean area: An exploration in transcultural psychology* (pp. 159–181). Hauppauge, NY: Nova Science Publishers.

Latzer, Y., & Gilat, I. (2000). Calls to the Israeli hotline from individuals who suffer from eating disorders: An epidemiological study. *Eating Disorders: The Journal of Treatment and Prevention, 8,* 31–42.

Laursen, B., & Bukowski, W. M. (1997). A developmental guide to the organization of close relationships. *International Journal of Behavioral Development, 21*(4), 747–770.

Laursen, B., Coy, K. C., & Collins, W. A. (1998). Reconsidering changes in parent-child conflict across adolescence: A meta-analysis. *Child Development, 69*(3), 817–832.

Lawendowski, L. A. (1998). A motivational intervention for adolescent smokers. *Preventive Medicine: An International Journal Devoted to Practice and Theory, 27*(5, Pt. 3), A39-A46.

Lawlor, D. A., Batty, G. D., Morton, S. M. B., Deary, I. J., Macintyre, S., Ronalds, G., et al. (2005). Early life predictors of childhood intelligence: Evidence from the Aberdeen children of the 1950s study. *Journal of Epidemiology and Community Health, 59*(8), 656–663.

Lazarus, R. S., & Folkman, S. (1984). *Coping and adaptation.* New York: Guilford Press.

Le Grange, D. (2004). Family-based treatment for adolescent anorexia nervosa: A promising approach? *Clinical Psychologist, 8*(2), 56–63.

Le Grange, D., Lock, J., & Dymek, M. (2003). Family-based therapy for adolescents with bulimia nervosa. *American Journal of Psychotherapy, 57,* 237–251.

Leaf, P. J., Alegria, M., Cohen, P., Goodman, S. H., Horwitz, S. M. and Hoven, C. W., et al. (1996).Mental health service use in the community and schools: Results from the four-community MECA study. *Journal of the American Academy of Child and Adolescent Psychiatry, 35*(7), 889–897.

Leary, M. R. (2001a). Shyness and the self: Attentional, motivational, and cognitive self-processes in social anxiety and inhibition. In W. R. Crozier & L. E. Alden (Eds.), *International handbook of social anxiety: Concepts, research and interventions relating to the self and shyness* (pp. 217–234). New York: Wiley.

Leary, M. R. (2001b). Social anxiety as an early warning system: A refinement and extension of the self-presentation theory of social anxiety. In S. G. Hofmann & P. M. DiBartolo (Eds.), *From social anxiety to social phobia: Multiple perspectives* (pp. 321–334). Needham Heights, MA: Allyn & Bacon.

Leary, M. R., & Springer, C. A. (2001). Hurt feelings: The neglected emotion. In R. M. Kowalski (Ed.), *Behaving badly: Aversive behaviors in interpersonal relationships* (pp. 151–175). Washington, DC: American Psychological Association.

Leboyer, M., Henry, C., Paillere-Martinot, M., & Bellivier, F. (2005). Age at onset in bipolar affective disorders: A review. *Bipolar Disorders, 7*(2), 111–118.

Ledingham, J. E. (1999). Children and adolescents with oppositional defiant disorder and conduct disorder in the community: Experiences at school and with peers. In H. C. Quay & A. E. Hogan (Eds.), *Handbook of disruptive behavior disorders* (pp. 353–370). Dordrecht, Netherlands: Kluwer Academic Publishers.

LeDoux, J. E. (1995). Emotion: Clues from the brain. *Annual Review of Psychology, 46,* 209–235.

Lee, V., & Hoaken, P. N. (2007). Cognition, emotion, and neurobiological development: Mediating the relation between maltreatment and aggression. *Child Maltreatment, 12*(3), 281–298.

Leff, S. S., Costigan, T., & Power, T. J. (2004). Using participatory research to develop a playground-based prevention program. *Journal of School Psychology, 42*(1), 3–21.

Leff, S. S., Power, T. J., Manz, P. H., Costigan, T. E., & Nabors, L. A. (2001). School-based aggression prevention programs for young children: Current status and implications for violence prevention. *School Psychology Review, 30*(3), 344–362.

Leffert, J. S., & Siperstein, G. N. (2002). Social cognition: A key to understanding adaptive behavior in individuals with mild mental retardation. In L. M. Glidden (Ed.), *International review of research in mental retardation* (Vol. 25, pp. 135–181). San Diego, CA: Academic Press.

Leffert, N., Benson, P. L., Scales, P. C., Sharma, A. R., Drake, D. R., & Blyth, D. (1998). Developmental assets: Measurement and prediction of risk behavior in adolescents. *Applied Developmental Science, 2*(4), 209–230.

Legrand, L. N., McGue, M., & Iacono, W. G. (1999). A twin study of state and trait anxiety in childhood and adolescence. *Journal of Child Psychology and Psychiatry, 40*(6), 953–958.

Leibenluft, E., Charney, D. S., & Pine, D. S. (2003). Resesarching the pathophysiology of pediatric bipolar disorder. *Biological Psychiatry, 53*(11), 1009–1020.

Leibenluft, E., Charney, D. S., Towbin, K. E., Bhangoo, R. K., & Pine, D. S. (2003). Defining clinical phenotypes of juvenile mania. *American Journal of Psychiatry, 160*(3), 430–437.

Leon, G. R., Fulkerson, J. A., Perry, C. L., & Cudeck, R. (1993). Personality and behavioral vulnerabilities associated with risk status for eating disorders in adolescent girls. *Journal of Abnormal Psychology, 102,* 438–444.

Leonard, H. L., & Swedo, S. E. (2001). Paediatric autoimmune neuropsychiatric disorders associated with streptococcal infection (PANDAS). *International Journal of Neuropsychopharmacology, 4*(2), 191–198.

Leonard, H., & Wen, X. (2002). The epidemiology of mental retardation: Challenges and opportunities in the new millennium. *Mental Retardation and Developmental Disabilities Research Reviews, 8*(3), 117–134.

Lépine, J-P., & Pélissolo, A. (2000). Why take social anxiety disorder seriously? *Depression and Anxiety, 11,* 87–92.

Lerner, J., Safren, S. A., Henin, A., Warman, M., Heimberg, R. G., & Kendall, P. C. (1999). Differentiating anxious and depressive self-statements in youth: Factor structure of the Negative Affect Self-Statement Questionnaire among youth referred to an anxiety disorders clinic. *Journal of Clinical Child Psychology, 28*(1), 82–93.

Lerner, R. M. (1998). Theories of human development: Contemporary perspectives. In W. Damon & R. M. Lerner (Eds.), *Handbook of child psychology: Vol. 1. Theoretical models of human development* (5th ed., pp. 1–24). Hoboken, NJ: Wiley.

Lerner, R. M. (2001). Toward a democratic ethnotheory of parenting for families and policymakers: A developmental systems perspective. *Parenting: Science and Practice, 1(4),* 339–351.

Lerner, R. M. (2003). What are SES effects effects of? A developmental systems perspective. In M. H. Bornstein & R. H. Bradley (Eds.), *Socioeconomic status, parenting, and child development. Monographs in parenting series* (pp. 231–255). Mahwah, NJ: Erlbaum.

Lerner, R. M., Ostrom, C. W., & Freel, M. A. (1997). Preventing health-compromising behaviors among youth and promoting their positive development: A developmental contextual perspective. In J. Schulenberg, J. L. Maggs, & K. Hurrelmann (Eds.), *Health risks and developmental transitions during adolescence* (pp. 498–521). New York: Cambridge University Press.

Lerner, R. M., Villarruel, F. A., & Castellino, D. R. (1999). Adolescence. In W. K. Silverman & T. H. Ollendick (Eds.), *Developmental issues in the clinical treatment of children* (pp. 125–136). Boston: Allyn and Bacon.

Leslie, L. K., Plemmons, D., Monn, A. R., & Palinkas, L. A. (2007). Investigating ADHD treatment trajectories: Listening to families' stories about medication use. *Journal of Developmental and Behavioral Pediatrics, 28*(3), 179–188.

Lester, B. M., & Tronick, E. Z. (1994). The effects of prenatal cocaine exposure and child outcome. *Infant Mental Health Journal, 15*(2), 107–120.

Lester, B. M., Boukydis, C. F. Z., & Twomey, J. E. (2000). Maternal substance abuse and child outcome. In C. H. Zeanah (Ed.), *Handbook of infant mental health* (2nd ed., pp. 161–175). New York: Guilford Press.

Levant, R. F., Tolan, P., & Dodge, D. (2002) New directions in children's mental health policy: Psychology's role. *Professional Psychology: Research and Practice, 33(2),* 115–124.

Levine, K. & Wharton, R. (2000). Williams syndrome and happiness. *American Journal on Mental Retardation, 105*(5), 363–371.

Levine, M. P., & Murnen, S. K. (2009). "Everybody knows that mass media are/are not (pick one) a cause of eating disorders": A critical review of evidence for a causal link between media, negative body image, and disordered eating in females. *Journal of Social and Clinical Psychology, 28*(1), 9–42.

Levitas, A. S., & Gilson, S. F. (2001). Predictable crises in the lives of people with mental retardation. *Mental Health Aspects of Developmental Disabilities, 4*(3), 89–100.

Levitas, A. S., Hurley, A. D., & Pary, R. (2001). The mental status examination in patients with mental retardation and developmental disabilities. *Mental Health Aspects of Developmental Disabilities, 4*(1), 2–16.

Levitas, A. S., & Silka, V. R. (2001). Mental health clinical assessment of persons with mental retardation and developmental disabilities: History. *Mental Health Aspects of Developmental Disabilities, 4*(1), 31–42.

Levy, F. (1999). DSM-IV subtypes: A genetic perspective. *The ADHD Report, 7,* 8–9.

Levy, F., Hay, D. A., McStephen, M., Wood, C., & Waldman, I. (1997). Attention-deficit hyperactivity disorder: A category or a continuum? Genetic analysis of a large-scale twin study. *Journal of the American Academy of Child and Adolescent Psychiatry, 36,* 737–744.

Lewinsohn, P. M., Rohde, P., & Farrington, D. P. (2000). The OADP-CDS: A brief screener for adolescent conduct disorder. *Journal of the American Academy of Child and Adolescent Psychiatry, 39*(7), 888–895.

Lewinsohn, P. M., Rohde, P., & Seeley, J. R. (1995). Adolescent psychopathology: III. The clinical consequences of comorbidity. *Journal of the American Academy of Child and Adolescent Psychiatry, 34,* 510–519.

Lewinsohn, P. M., Seeley, J. R., & Klein, D. N. (2003). Bipolar disorder in adolescents: Epidemiology and suicidal behavior. In B. Geller & M. P. DelBello (Eds.), *Bipolar disorder in childhood and early adolescence* (pp. 7–24). New York: Guilford Press.

Lewinsohn, P. M., Striegel-Moore, R. H., & Seeley, J. H. (2000). Epidemiology and natural course of eating disorders in young women from adolescence to adulthood. *Journal of the American Academy of Child and Adolescent Psychiatry, 39,* 1284–1292.

Lewinsohn, P. M., Zinbarg, R., Seeley, J. R., Lewinsohn, M., & Sack, W. H. (1997). Lifetime comorbidity among anxiety disorders and between anxiety disorders and other mental disorders in adolescents. *Journal of Anxiety Disorders, 11,* 377–394.

Lewis, M. W., Misra, S., Johnson, H. L., & Rosen, T. S. (2004). Neurological and developmental outcomes of prenatally cocaine-exposed offspring from 12 to 36 months. *American Journal of Drug and Alcohol Abuse, 30*(2), 299–320.

Li, C., Pentz, M. A., & Chou, C-P. (2002). Parental substance use as a modifier of adolescent substance use risk. *Addiction, 97*(12), 1537–1550.

Li, Y., Hu. X., Ma, W., Wu, J., & Ma, G. (2005). Body image perceptions among Chinese children and adolescents. *Body Image, 2,* 91–103.

Lieberman, A. F. (1993). *The emotional life of the toddler.* New York: Free Press.

Lieberman, A. F., & Pawl, J. H. (1988). Clinical applications of attachment theory. In J. Belsky & T. Nezworski (Eds.), *Clinical implications of attachment* (pp. 327–351). Hillsdale, NJ: Erlbaum.

Lieberman, A. F., & Pawl, J. H. (1990). Disorders of attachment and secure base behavior in the second year of life: Conceptual issues and clinical intervention. In M. T. Greenberg, D. Cicchetti., & E. M. Cummings (Eds.), *Attachment in the preschool years: Theory, research, and intervention.* Chicago: University of Chicago Press.

Lieberman, A. F., and Pawl, J. H. (1993). Infant-parent psychotherapy. In C. H. Zeanah (Ed.), *Handbook of infant mental health* (pp. 427–442). New York: Guilford Press.

Lieberman, A. F., Van Horn, P., Grandison, C. M.. & Pekarsky, J. H. (1997). Mental health assessment of infants, toddlers, and preschoolers in a service program and a treatment outcome research program. *Infant Mental Health Journal, 18*(2), 158–170.

Lieberman, A. F., Weston, D. R., & Pawl, J. H. (1991). Preventive intervention and outcome with anxiously attached dyads. *Child Development, 62*(1), 199–209.

Lieberman, A. F., Wieder, S., & Fenichel, E. (1997). *The DC: 0–3 casebook: A guide to the use of 0 to 3's diagnostic classification of mental health and developmental disorders of infancy and early childhood in assessment and treatment planning.* Washington, DC: National Center for Infants, Toddlers and Families.

Lieberman, A. F., & Zeanah, C. H. (1999). Contributions of attachment theory to infant-parent psychotherapy and other interventions with infants and young children. In J. Cassidy & P. R. Shaver (Eds.), *Handbook of attachment: Theory, research, and clinical applications* (pp. 555–574). New York: Guilford Press.

Liebowitz, M. R., & Ginsberg, D. L. (2005). Integrating neurobiology and psychopathology into evidence-based treatment of social anxiety disorder. *CNS Spectrums, 10*(10), 1–5.

Liese, B. S., & Franz, R. A. (1996). Treating substance use disorders with cognitive therapy: Lessons learned and implications for the future. In P. M. Salkovskis (Ed.), *Frontiers of cognitive therapy* (pp. 470–508). New York: Guilford Press.

Liew, J., Eisenberg, N., & Reiser, M. (2004). Preschoolers' effortful control and negative emotionality, immediate reactions to disappointment, and quality of social functioning. *Journal of Experimental Child Psychology, 89*(4), 298–313.

Li-Grining, C. P. (2007). Effortful control among low-income preschoolers in three cities: Stability, change, and individual differences. *Developmental Psychology, 43*(1), 208–221.

Lilienfeld, S. O., Waldman, I. D., & Israel, A. C. (1994). A critical examination of the use of the term and concept of comorbidity in psychopathology research. *Clinical Psychology: Science and Practice, 1(1),* 71–83.

Lim, M., Stormshak, E. A., & Dishion, T. J. (2005). A one-session intervention for parents of young adolescents: Videotape modeling and motivational group discussion. *Journal of Emotional and Behavioral Disorders, 13*(4), 194–199.

Lincoln, A., Courchesne, E., Allen, M., Hanson, E., & Ene, M. (1998). Neurobiology of Asperger syndrome: Seven case studies and quantitative magnetic resonance imaging findings. In E. Schopler & G. B. Mesibov (Eds.), *Asperger syndrome or high-functioning autism? Current issues in autism* (pp. 145–163). New York: Plenum Press.

Lindahl, K. M. (1998). Family process variables and children's disruptive behavior problems. *Journal of Family Psychology, 12*, 420–436.

Lindeman, M., & Stark, K. (2000). Loss of pleasure, ideological food choice reasons and eating pathology. *Appetite, 35,* 263–268.

Linder, J. R., Crick, N. R., & Collins, W. A. (2002). Relational aggression and victimization in young adults' romantic relationships: Associations with perceptions of parent, peer, and romantic relationship quality. *Social Development, 11*(1), 69–86.

Linscheid, T. R., Iwata, B. A., & Foxx, R. M. (1996). Behavioral assessment. In J. W. Jacobson & J. A. Mulick (Eds.), *Manual of diagnosis and professional practice in mental retardation* (pp. 191–198). Washington, DC: American Psychological Association.

Liotti, G. (1992). Disorganized/disoriented attachment in the etiology of the dissociative disorders. *Dissociation: Progress in the Dissociative Disorders, 5*(4), 196–204.

Little, T. D., Brauner, J., Jones, S. M., Nock, M. K., & Hawley, P. H. (2003). Rethinking aggression: A typological examination of the functions of aggression. *Merrill-Palmer Quarterly, 49*(3), 343–369.

Little, T. D., Jones, S. M., Henrich, C. C., & Hawley, P. H. (2003). Disentangling the "whys" from the "whats" of aggressive behaviour. *International Journal of Behavioral Development, 27*(2), 122–133.

Littleton, H. L. & Ollendick, T. (2003). Negative body image and disordered eating behavior in children and adolescents: What places youth at risk and how can these problems be prevented? *Clinical Child and Family Psychology Review, 6,* 51–66.

Lloyd-Richardson, E. E., Papandonatos, G., Kazura, A., Stanton, C., & Niaura, R. (2002). Differentiating stages of smoking intensity among adolescents: Stage-specific psychological and social influences. *Journal of Consulting and Clinical Psychology, 70*(4), 998–1009.

Lochman, J. E. (2004). Contextual factors in risk and prevention research. *Merrill-Palmer Quarterly, 50(3)*, 311–325.

Lochman, J. E., Coie, J. D., Underwood, M. K., & Terry, R. (1993). Effectiveness of a social relations intervention program for aggressive and nonaggressive, rejected children. *Journal of Consulting and Clinical Psychology, 61*(6), 1053–1058.

Lochman, J. E., & van den Steenhoven, A. (2002). Family-based approaches to substance abuse prevention. *Journal of Primary Prevention, 23*(1), 49–114.

Lock, J., & Le Grange, D. (2005). Family-based treatment of eating disorders. *International Journal of Eating Disorders, 37*, S64-S67.

Lock, J., Le Grange, D., Forsberg, S., & Hewell, K. (2006). Is family therapy useful for treating children with anorexia nervosa? *Journal of the American Academy of Child and Adolescent Psychiatry, 45,* 1323–1328.

Lock, J., Walker, L. R., Rickert, V. I., & Katzman, D. K. (2005). Suicidality in adolescents being treated with antidepressant medications and the black box label: Position paper of the Society for Adolescent Medicine. *Journal of Adolescent Health, 36*(1), 92–93.

Lock, S., & Barrett, P. M. (2003). A longitudinal study of developmental differences in universal preventive intervention for child anxiety. *Behaviour Change, 20*(4), 183–199.

Loeber, R. (1991). Antisocial behavior: More enduring than changeable? *Journal of the Academy of Child and Adolescent Psychiatry, 30(3),* 393–397.

Loeber, R., Burke, J. D., Lahey, B. B., Winters, A., & Zera, M. (2000). Oppositional defiant and conduct disorder: A review of the past 10 years, Part I. *Journal of the American Academy of Child and Adolescent Psychiatry, 39*(12), 1468–1484.

Loeber, R., Drinkwater, M., Yin, Y., Anderson, S. J., Schmidt, L. C., & Crawford, A. (2000). Stability of family interaction from ages 6 to 18. *Journal of Abnormal Child Psychology, 28*, 353–369.

Loeber, R., & Farrington, D. P. (Eds.). (1998). *Serious and violent juvenile offenders: Risk factors and successful interventions.* Thousand Oaks, CA: Sage.

Loeber, R., & Stouthamer-Loeber, M. (1998). Development of juvenile aggression and violence: Some common misconceptions and controversies. *American Psychologist, 53*(2), 242–259.

Loeber, R., Farrington, D. P., Stouthamer-Loeber, M., Moffitt, T. E., Caspi, A., & Lynam, D. (2001). Male mental health problems, psychopathy, and personality traits: Key finding from the first 14 years of the Pittsburgh Youth Study. *Clinical Child and Family Psychology Review, 4*, 273–297.

Loeber, R., & Farrington, D. P. (2000). Young children who commit crime: Epidemiology, developmental origins, risk factors, early interventions, and policy implications. *Development and Psychopathology, 12*(4), 737–762.

Lofthouse, N., & Fristad, M. A. (2004). Psychosocial interventions for children with early-onset bipolar spectrum disorder. *Clinical Child Family Psychology Review, 7*(2), 71–88.

Loney, B. R., & Lima, E. N. (2003). Classification and assessment. In C. A. Essau (Ed.), *Conduct and oppositional defiant disorders: Epidemiology, risk factors, and treatment* (pp. 3–31). Mahwah, NJ: Erlbaum.

Lonigan, C. J., Phillips, B. M., & Hooe, E. S. (2003). Relations of positive and negative affectivity to anxiety and depression in children: Evidence from a latent variable longitudinal study. *Journal of Consulting and Clinical Psychology, 71*(3), 465–481.

Lonigan, C. J., Phillips, B. M., & Richey, J. A. (2003). Posttraumatic stress disorder in children: Diagnosis, assessment, and associated features. *Child and Adolescent Psychiatric Clinics of North America, 12*(2), 171–194.

Lonigan, C. J., Vasey, M. W., Phillips, B. M., & Hazen, R. A. (2004). Temperament, anxiety, and the processing of threat-relevant stimuli. *Journal of Clinical Child Adolescent Psychology, 33*(1), 8–20.

Lopez, S. R., & Guarnaccia, P. J. J. (2000). Cultural psychopathology: Uncovering the social world of mental illness. *Annual Review of Psychology, 51,* 571–598.

Lord, C. (1994). The complexity of social behaviour in autism. In S. Baron-Cohen & H. Tager-Glusberg (Eds.), *Understanding other minds: Perspectives from autism* (pp. 292316). London: Oxford University Press.

Lord, C. (1995). Follow-up of two-year-olds referred for possible autism. *Journal of Child Psychology and Psychiatry and Allied Disciplines, 36*, 1365–1382.

Lord, C., Bristol, M. M., & Schopler, E. (1993). Early intervention for children with autism and related developmental disorders. In E. Schopler & M. E. Van Bourgondien (Eds.), *Preschool issues in autism. Current issues in autism* (pp. 199–221). New York: Plenum Press.

Lord, C., & Magill-Evans, J. (1995). Peer interactions of autistic children and adolescents. *Development and Psychopathology, 7*, 611–626.

Lord, C., & Paul, R. (1997). Language and communication in autism. In D. Cohen & F. Volkmar (Eds.), *Handbook of autism and pervasive developmental disorders* (2nd ed., pp. 707–729). New York: Wiley.

Lord, C., & Pickles, A. (1996). Language level and nonverbal social-communicative behaviors in autistic and language-delayed children. *Journal of the American Academy of Child and Adolescent Psychiatry, 35*, 1542–1550.

Lord, C., & Risi, S. (1998). Frameworks and methods in diagnosing autism spectrum disorders. *Mental Retardation and Developmental Disabilities Research Reviews, 4*, 90–96.

Lord, C., & Risi, S. (2000). Diagnosis of autism spectrum disorders in young children. In A. M. Wetherby & B. M. Prizant (Eds.), *Communication and language intervention series: Vol. 9. Autism spectrum disorders: A transactional developmental perspective* (pp. 11–30). Baltimore: Paul H. Brookes Publishing.

Lord, C., & Volkmar, F. (2002). Genetics of childhood disorders: XLII. Autism, Part 1: Diagnosis and assessment in autistic spectrum disorders. (Development and Neurobiology). *Journal of the American Academy of Child and Adolescent Psychiatry, 41*, 1134–1136.

Lord, C., Pickles, A., McLennan, J., Rutter, M., Bregman, J., Folstein, S., et al. (1997). Diagnosing autism: Analyses of data from the Autism Diagnostic Interview. *Journal of Autism and Developmental Disorders, 27*, 501–517.

Lord, C., Risi, S., Lambrecht, L., Cook, E. H., Levethal, B. L., DiLavore, P. C., et al. (2000). The autism diagnostic observation schedule—generic: A standard measure of social and communication deficits associated with the spectrum of autism. *Journal of Autism and Developmental Disorders, 30*(3), 205–223.

Lord, C., Rutter, M., & LeCouteur, A. (1994). Autism diagnostic interview—revised: A revised version of a diagnostic interview for caregivers of individuals with possible pervasive developmental disorders. *Journal of Autism and Developmental Disorders, 24*(5), 659–685.

Lott, D. A. (1998). Eating disorders and the family: controversies and questions. *Psychiatric Times, 15*(9). Retrieved July 27 from www.psychiatrictimes.com/p980952.html

Loukas, A., Zucker, R. A., Fitzgerald, H. E., & Krull, J. L. (2003). Developmental trajectories of disruptive behavior problems among sons of alcoholics: Effects of parent psychopathology, family conflict, and child undercontrol. *Journal of Abnormal Psychology, 112*(1), 119–131.

Lovaas, O. I. (1987). Behavioral treatment and normal educational and intellectual functioning in young autistic children. *Journal of Consulting and Clinical Psychology, 55*, 3–9.

Lovaas, O. I. (1993). The development of a treatment-research project for developmentally disabled and autistic children. *Journal of Applied Behavior Analysis, 26*, 617–630.

Lovaas, O. I. (2003). *Teaching individuals with developmental delays: Basic intervention techniques.* Austin, TX: PRO-ED.

Lovaas, O. I., & Buch, G. (1997). Intensive behavioral intervention with young children with autism. In N. N. Singh (Ed.), *Prevention and treatment of severe behavior problems: Models and methods in developmental disabilities* (pp. 61–86). Belmont, CA: Thomson.

Lowenthal, B. (1999). Early childhood inclusion in the United States. *Early Child Development and Care, 150*, 17–32.

Lowry-Webster, H. M., Barrett, P. M., & Lock, S. (2003). A universal prevention trial of anxiety symptomology during childhood: Results at 1-year follow-up. *Behaviour Change, 20*(1), 25–43.

Loxton, N. J., & Dawe, S. (2006). Reward and punishment sensitivity in dysfunctional eating and hazardous drinking women: Associations with family risk. *Appetite, 47*, 361–371.

Lubell, K. M., & Vetter, J. B. (2006). Suicide and youth violence prevention: The promise of an integrated approach. *Aggression and Violent Behavior, 11*(2), 167–175.

Luby, J. L. (2000). Depression. In C. H. Zeanah (Ed.), *Handbook of infant mental health* (2nd ed., pp. 382–396). New York: Guilford Press.

Luby, J. L., Heffelfinger, A., Koenig-McNaught, A. L., Brown, K., & Spitznagel, E. (2004). The preschool feelings checklist: A brief and sensitive screening measure for depression in young children. *Journal of the American Academy of Child Adolescent Psychiatry, 43*(6), 708–717.

Luby, J., Todd, R. D., & Geller, B. (1996). Outcome of depressive syndromes: Infancy to adolescence. In K. I. Shulman & M. Tohen et al. (Eds.), *Mood disorders across the life span* (pp. 83–100). New York: Wiley-Liss.

Luckasson, R., & Reeve, A. (2001). Naming, defining, and classifying in mental retardation. *Mental Retardation, 39*(1), 47–52.

Luckasson, R., Schalock, R. L., Snell, M. E. & Spitalnik, D. M. (1996). The 1992 AAMR definition and preschool children: Response from the Committee on Terminology and Classification. *Mental Retardation, 34*(4), 247–253.

Luecken, L. J., & Lemery, K. S. (2004). Early caregiving and physiological stress responses. *Clinical Psychology Review, 24*, 171–191.

Lumley, V. A., & Scotti, J. R. (2001). Supporting the sexuality of adults with mental retardation: Current status and future directions. *Journal of Positive Behavior Interventions, 3*(2), 109–119.

Luna, B., Doll, S. K., Hegedus, S. J., Minshew, N. J., & Sweeney, J. A. (2007). Maturation of executive function in autism. *Biological Psychiatry, 61*(4), 474–481.

Luna, B., & Sweeney, J. A. (2004). Cognitive development: Functional magnetic resonance imaging studies. In M. S. Keshavan, J. L. Kennedy, & R. M. Murray (Eds.), *Neurodevelopment and schizophrenia* (pp. 45–68). New York: Cambridge University Press.

Lunsky, Y., & Konstantareas, M. M. (1998). The attitudes of individuals with autism and mental retardation towards sexuality. *Education and Training in Mental Retardation and Developmental Disabilities, 33*(1), 24–33.

Lustig, D. C. (2002). Family coping in families with a child with a disability. *Education and Training in Mental Retardation and Developmental Disabilities, 27*(1), 14–22.

Lustig, D. C., & Strauser, D. R. (2002). An empirical typology of career thoughts of individuals with disabilities. *Rehabilitation Counseling Bulletin, 46*(2), 98–107.

Luthar, S. S. (1997). Sociodemographic disadvantage and psychosocial adjustment: Perspectives form developmental psychopathology. In S. S. Luthar & J. A. Burack (Eds.), *Perspectives on adjustment, risk, and disorder* (pp. 459–485). New York: Cambridge University Press.

Luthar, S. S. (2000). *Resilience and vulnerability: Adaptation in the context of childhood adversities.* New York: Cambridge University Press.

Luthar, S. S., Cicchetti, D., & Becker, B. (2000a). The construct of resilience: A critical evaluation and guidelines for future work. *Child Development, 71(3),* 543–562.

Luthar, S. S., & Cushing, G. (1999). Neighborhood influences and child development: A prospective study of substance abusers' offspring. *Development and Psychopathology, 11*(4), 763–784.

Luthar, S. S., Cicchetti, D., & Becker, B. (2000b). Research on resilience: Response to commentaries. *Child Development, 71(3),* 573–575.

Luyster, R., Richler, J., Risi, S., Hsu, W., Dawson, G., Bernier, R., et al. (2005). Early regression in social communication in autism spectrum disorders: A CPA study. *Developmental Neuropsychology, 27*(3), 311–336.

Lynam, D. R. (1998). Early identification of the fledgling psychopath: Locating the psychopathic child in the current nomenclature. *Journal of Abnormal Psychology, 107*(4), 566–575.

Lynam, D. R., & Gudonis, L. (2005). The development of psychopathy. *Annual Review of Clinical Psychology, 1*(1), 381–407.

Lynam, D. R., Caspi, A., Moffitt, T. E., Raine, A., Loeber, R., & Stouthamer-Loeber, M. (2005). Adolescent psychopathy and the Big Five: Results from two samples. *Journal of Abnormal Child Psychology, 33*(4), 431–443.

Lynam, D. R., Caspi, A., Moffitt, T. E., Wikstroem, P., Loeber, R., & Novak, S. (2000). The interaction between impulsivity and neighborhood context on offending: The effects of impulsivity are stronger in poorer neighborhoods. *Journal of Abnormal Psychology, 109*(4), 563–574.

Lynch, M., & Ciccetti, D. (1998). Trauma, mental representation, and the organization of memory for mother-referent material. *Development and Psychopathology, 10*(4), 739–759.

Lynch, M., & Cicchetti, D. (1998). An ecological-transactional analysis of children and contents: The longitudinal interplay among child maltreatment, community violence, and children's symptomatology. *Development and Psychopathology, 10*(2), 235–257.

Lynch, W. C., & Eppers-Reynolds, K. (2005) Children's Eating Attitudes Test: Revised factor structure for adolescent girls. *Eating and Weight Disorders, 10,* 222–235.

Lyons, M. J., Bar, J. L., Panizzon, M. S., Toomey, R., Eisen, S., Xian, H., et al. (2004). Neuropsychological consequences of regular marijuana use: A twin study. *Psychological Medicine, 34*(7), 1239–1250.

Lyons-Ruth, K. (1996). Attachment relationships among children with aggressive behavior problems: The role of disorganized early attachment patterns. *Journal of Consulting and Clinical Psychology, 64*(1), 64–73.

Lyons-Ruth, K., Alpern, L., & Repacholi, B. (1993). Disorganized infant attachment classification and maternal psychosocial problems as predictors of hostile-aggressive behavior in the preschool classroom. *Child Development, 64*(2), 572–585.

Lyons-Ruth, K. (1995). Broadening our conceptual frameworks: Can we reintroduce relational strategies and implicit represen-

tational systems to the study of psychopathology? *Developmental Psychology, 31*(3), 432–436.

Lyons-Ruth, K., Bronfman, E., & Atwood, G. (1999). A relational diathesis model of hostile-helpless states of mind: Expressions in mother-infant interaction. In J. Solomon & C. George (Eds.), *Attachment disorganization* (pp. 33–70). New York: Guilford Press.

Lyons-Ruth, K., Connell, D. B., Gruenbaum, H. U., & Botein, S. (1990). Infants at social risk: Maternal depression and family support services as mediators of infant development and security of attachment. *Child Development, 61*(1), 85–98.

Lyons-Ruth, K., Easterbrooks, M. A., & Cibelli, C. D. (1997). Infant attachment strategies, infant mental lag, and maternal depressive symptoms: Predictors of internalizing and externalizing problems at age 7. *Developmental Psychology, 33*(4), 681–692.

Lyons-Ruth, K., & Jacobvitz, D. (1999). Attachment disorganization: Unresolved loss, relational violence, and lapses in behavioral and attentional strategies. In J. Cassidy & P. R. Shaver (Eds.), *Handbook of attachment: Theory, research, and clinical applications* (pp. 520–554). New York: Guilford Press.

Lyons-Ruth, K., Lyubchik, A., Wolfe, R., & Bronfman, E. (2002). Parental depression and child attachment: Hostile and helpless profiles of parent and child behavior among families at risk. In S. H. Goodman & I. H. Gotlib (Eds.), *Children of depressed parents: Mechanisms of risk and implications for treatment* (pp. 89–120). Washington, DC: American Psychological Association.

Lyons-Ruth, K., Melnick, S., Bronfman, E., Sherry, S., & Llanas, L. (2004). Hostile-helpless relational models and disorganized attachment patterns between parents and their young children: Review of research and implications for clinical work. In L. Atkinson & S. Goldberg (Eds.), *Attachment issues in psychopathology and intervention* (pp. 65–94). Mahwah, NJ: Erlbaum.

Lyons-Ruth, K., Repacholi, B., McLeod, S., & Silva, E. (1991). Disorganized attachment behavior in infancy: Short-term stability, maternal and infant correlates, and risk-related subtypes. *Development and Psychopathology, 3*(4), 377–396.

Lyons-Ruth, K., Wolfe, R., & Lyubchik, A. (2000). Depression and the parenting of young children: Making the case for early preventive mental health services. *Harvard Review of Psychiatry, 8*(3), 148–153.

Lyons-Ruth, K., & Zeanah, C. H. (1993). The family context of infant mental health: I. Affective development in the primary caregiving relationship. In C. H. Zeanah, Jr. (Ed.), *Handbook of infant mental health* (pp. 14–37). New York: Guilford Press.

Ma, G. X., Toubbeh, J., Cline, J., & Chisholm, A. (1998a). Fetal alcohol syndrome among Native American adolescents: A model prevention program. *Journal of Primary Prevention, 19*(1), 43–55.

Ma, G. X., Toubbeh, J., Cline, J., & Chisholm, A. (1998b). The use of a qualitative approach in fetal alcohol syndrome prevention among American Indian youth. *Journal of Alcohol and Drug Education, 43*(3), 53–65.

Ma, G. X., Toubbeh, J., Cline, J, & Chisholm, A. (2002). A model for fetal alcohol syndrome prevention in Native American population. In G. Xuequin Ma & G. Henderson (Eds.), *Ethnicity and substance abuse: Prevention and intervention* (pp. 284–295). Springfield, IL: Charles C. Thomas.

Maccoby, E. E. (2000). Parenting and its effects on children: On reading and misreading behavior genetics. *Annual Review of Psychology, 51,* 1–27.

MacDonald, M. (2000). Bewildered, blamed and broken-hearted: Parents' views of anorexia nervosa. In B. Lask (Ed.), *Anorexia nervosa and related eating disorders in childhood and adolescence* (pp. 11–24). Hove, England: Psychology Press/Taylor & Francis.

MacDonald, V. M., Tsiantis, J., Achenbach, T. M., Motti-Stefanidi, F., & Richardson, S. C. (1995). Competencies and problems reported by parents of Greek and American children, ages 6–11. *European Child and Adolescent Psychiatry, 4,* 1–13.

Macgowan, M. J. (2004). Psychosocial treatment of youth suicide: A systematic review of the research. *Research on Social Work Practice, 14*(3), 147–162.

Macgowen, M. J., & Wagner, E. F. (2005). Iatrogenic effects of group treatment on adolescents with conduct and substance use problems: A review of the literature and a presentation of a model. In C. Hilarski (Ed.), *Addiction, assessment, and treatment with adolescents, adults, and families* (pp. 79–90). Binghamton, NY: Haworth Social Work Practice Press.

Mackintosh, V. H., Myers, B. J., & Goin-Kochel, R. P. (2006). Sources of information and support used by parents of children with autism spectrum disorders. *Journal on Developmental Disabilities, 12*(1), 41–52.

MacLean, J. E., Szatmari, P., Jones, M. B., Bryson, S. E., Mahoney, W. J., Bartolucci, G., et al. (1999). Familial factors influence level of functioning in pervasive developmental disorder. *Journal of the American Academy of Child and Adolescent Psychiatry, 38,* 746–753.

MacLean, K. (2003). The impact of institutionalization on child development. *Development and Psychopathology, 15*(4), 853–884.

MacMaster, S. A., Holleran, L. K., & Chaffin, K. (2005). Empirical and theoretical support for the inclusion of non-abstinence-based perspectives in prevention services for substance using adolescents. In C. Hilarski (Ed.), *Addiction, assessment, and treatment with adolescents, adults, and families* (pp. 91–111). Binghamton, NY: Haworth Social Work Practice Press.

Madsen, K. M., Hviid, A., Vestergaard, M., Schendel, D., Wohlfahrt, J., Thorsen, P., et al. (2002). A population-based study of measles, mumps, and rubella vaccination and autism. *New England Journal of Medicine, 347,* 1477–1482.

Madsen, K. M., Lauritsen, M. B., Pedersen, C. B., Thorsen, P., Plesner, A. M., Andersen, P. H., et al. (2003). Thimerosal and the occurrence of autism: Negative ecological evidence from Danish population-based data. *Pediatrics, 112,* 604–606.

Magai, C. (1999). Affect, imagery, and attachment: Working models of interpersonal affect and the socialization of emotion. In J. Cassidy & P. R. Shaver (Eds.), *Handbook of attachment: Theory, research, and clinical applications* (pp. 787–802). New York: Guilford Press.

Maggs, J. L., & Schulenberg, J. E. (2004–2005). Trajectories of alcohol use during the transition to adulthood. *Alcohol Research and Health, 28*(4), 195–201.

Maggs, J. L., & Schulenberg, J. E. (2005). Initiation and course of alcohol consumption among adolescents and young adults. In M. Galanter (Ed.), *Recent developments in alcoholism: Volume 17. Alcohol problems in adolescents and young adults. Epidemiology neurobiology prevention treatment* (pp. 29–47). New York: Kluwer Academic/Plenum Publishers.

Magnus, K. B., Cowen, E. L., Wyman, P. A., Fagen, D. B., & Work, W. C. (1999). Correlates of resilient outcomes among highly stressed African-American and White urban children. *Journal of Community Psychology, 27(4),* 473–488.

Maguire, J., & Philadelphia Child Guidance Center. (1993). *Your child's emotional health: The middle years.* New York: Macmillan.

Mahoney, W. J., Szatmari, P., MacLean, J. E., Bryson, S. E., Bartolucci, G., Wlater, S. D., et al. (1998). Reliability and accuracy of differentiating pervasive developmental disorder subtypes. *Journal of the American Academy of Child and Adolescent Psychiatry, 37,* 278–285.

Main, M. (1996). Introduction to the special section on attachment and psychopathology: 2. Overview of the field of attachment. *Journal of Consulting and Clinical Psychology, 64*(2), 237–243.

Main, M. (2000). The organized categories of infant, child, and adult attachment: Flexible vs. inflexible attention under attachment-related stress. *Journal of the American Psychoanalytic Association, 48,* 1055–1096.

Main, M., & Hesse, E. (1990). Parents' unresolved traumatic experiences are related to infant disorganized attachment status: Is frightened and/or frightening parental behavior the linking mechanism? In M. T. Greenberg, D. Cicchetti, & E. M. Cummings (Eds.), *Attachment in the preschool years: Theory, research, and intervention* (pp. 161–182). Chicago: University of Chicago Press.

Main, M., & Solomon, J. (1990). Procedures for identifying infants as disorganized/disoriented during the Ainsworth strange situation. In M. T. Greenberg, D. Cicchetti, & E. M. Cummings (Eds.), *Attachment in the preschool years: Theory, research, and intervention* (pp. 121–160). Chicago, IL: University of Chicago Press.

Main, M., Hesse, E., & Kaplan, N. (2005). Predictability of attachment behavior and representational processes at 1, 6, and 19 years of age: The Berkeley Longitudinal Study. In K. E. Grossman, K. Grossman, & E. Waters (Eds.), *Attachment from infancy to adulthood: The major longitudinal studies* (pp. 245–304). New York: Guilford Press.

Main, M., Kaplan, N., & Cassidy, J. (1985). Security in infancy, childhood, and adulthood: A move to the level of representation. *Monographs of the Society for Research in Child Development, 50*(1–2), 66–104.

Mainemer, H., Gilman, L. C., & Ames, E. W. (1998). Parenting stress in families adopting children from Romanian orphanages. *Journal of Family Issues, 19*(2), 164–180.

Maldonado-Duran, M., & Sauceda-Garcia, J-M. (1996). Excessive crying in infants with regulatory disorders. *Bulletin of the Menninger Clinic, 60*(1), 62–78.

Malone, R. P. (2000). Assessment and treatment of abnormal aggression in children and adolescents. In M. L. Crowner (Ed.), *Understanding and treating violent psychiatric patients. Progress in psychiatry, 60* (pp. 21–47). Washington, DC: American Psychiatric Association.

Malone, S. M., Iacono, W. G., & McGue, M. (2002). Drinks of the father: Father's maximum number of drinks consumed predicts externalizing disorders, substance use, and substance use disorders in preadolescent and adolescent offspring. *Alcoholism: Clinical and Experimental Research, 26*(12), 1823–1832.

Malone, S. M., Taylor, J., Marmorstein, N. R., McGue, M., & Iacono, W. G. (2004). Genetic and environmental influences on antisocial behavior and alcohol dependence from adolescence to early adulthood. *Development and Psychopathology, 16*(4), 943–966.

Manassis, K., Bradley, S., Goldberg, S., Hood, J., & Price Swinson, R. (1994). Attachment in mothers with anxiety disorders and their children. *Journal of American Academy of Child and Adolescent Psychiatry, 33,* 1106–1113.

Manassis, K., & Hood, J. (1998). Individual and familial predictors of impairment in childhood anxiety disorders. *Journal of the American Academy of Child and Adolescent Psychiatry, 37*(4), 428–434.

Mancini, C., Van Ameringen, M., Bennett, M., Patterson, B., & Watson, C. (2005). Emerging treatments for child and adolescent social phobia: A review. *Journal of Child and Adolescent Psychopharmacology, 15*(4), 589–607.

Mangelsdorf, S., C. Gunnar, M., Kestenbaum, R., & Lang, S. (1990). Infant proneness-to-distress temperament, maternal personality, and mother-infant attachment: Associations and goodness of fit. *Child Development, 61*(3), 820–831.

Mangelsdorf, S. C., Schoppe, S. J., & Buur, H. (2000). The meaning of parental reports: A contextual approach to the study of temperament and behavior problems in childhood. In V. J. Molfese & D. L. Molfese (Eds.), *Temperament and personality development across the life span* (pp. 121–140). Mahwah, NJ: Erlbaum.

Mangelsdorf, S. C., Shapiro, J. R., & Marzolf, D. (1995). Developmental and temperamental differences in emotional regulation in infancy. *Child Development, 66*(6), 1817–1828.

Mangione, P. L., & Speth, T. (1998). The transition to elementary school: A framework for creating early childhood continuity through home, school, and community partnerships. *The Elementary School Journal, 98,* 381–397.

Maniadaki, K, Sonuga-Barke, E., Kakouros, E., & Karaba, R. (2007). Parental beliefs about the nature of ADHD behaviors and their relationship to referral intentions in preschool children. *Child: Care, Health and Development, 33*(2), 188–195.

Manly, J. T., Kim, J. E., Rogosch, F. A., & Cicchetti, D. (2001). Dimensions of child maltreatment and children's adjustment: Contributions of developmental timing and subtype. *Development and Psychopathology, 13*(4), 759–782.

Mannuzza, S., Klein, R. G., Bessler, A., Malloy, P., & LaPadula, M. (1998). Adult psychiatric status of hyperactive boys grown up. *American Journal of Psychiatry, 155,* 493–498.

Mannuzza, S., Klein, R. G., & Moulton, J. L. (2003a). Does stimulant treatment place children at risk for adult substance abuse? A controlled, prospective follow-up study. *Journal of Child and Adolescent Psychpharmacology, 13*(3), 273–282.

Mannuzza, S., Klein, R. G., & Moulton, J. L. (2003b). Persistence of attention-deficit/hyperactivity disorder into adulthood: What have we learned from the prospective follow-up studies? *Journal of Attention Disorders, 7*(2), 93–100.

Mannuzza, S., Klein, R. G., Abikoff, H., & Moulton, J. L. (2004). Significance of childhood conduct problems to later development of conduct disorder among children with ADHD: A prospective follow-up study. *Journal of Abnormal Child Psychology, 32*(5), 565–573.

Marcell, M. M., & Falls, A. L. (2001). Online data collection with special populations over the World Wide Web. *Down Syndrome: Research and Practice, 7,* 106–123.

Marcell, M. M., & Jett, D. A. (1985). Identification of vocally expressed emotions by mentally retarded and nonretarded individuals. *American Journal of Mental Deficiency, 89*(5), 537–545.

March, J. S. (2002). Combining medication and psychosocial treatments: An evidence-based medicine approach. *International Review of Psychiatrys, 14*(2), 155–163.

March, J., Silva, S., & Vitiello, B. (2006). The Treatment for Adolescents with Depression Study (TADS): Methods and message

at 12 weeks. *Journal of the American Academy of Child and Adolescent Psychiatry, 45*(12), 1393–1403.

March, J., Silva, S., Petrycki, S., Curry, J., Wells, K., Fairanks, J., et al. (2004). Fluoxine, cognitive, behavioral therapy, and their combination for adolescents with depression: Treatment for Adolescents with Depression Study (TADS) randomized controlled trial. *Journal of the American Medical Association, 292*(7), 807–820.

Margolin, G., & Vickerman, K. A. (2007). Posttraumatic stress in children and adolescents exposed to family violence: I. Overview and issues. *Professional Psychology: Research and Practice, 38*(6), 613–619.

Markey, C. N. (2004). Culture and the development of eating disorders: A tripartite model. *Eating Disorders: The Journal of Treatment and Prevention, 12,* 139–156.

Markowitz, S., Chatterji, P., & Kaestner, R. (2003). Estimating the impact of alcohol policies on youth suicides. *Journal of Mental Health Policy and Economics, 6*(1), 37–46.

Marlowe, W. B. (2001). An intervention for children with disorders of executive functions. *Developmental Neuropsychology, 18,* 445–454.

Marmorstein, N. R., & Iacono, W. G. (2004). Major depression and conduct disorder in youth: Associations with parental psychopathology and parent-child conflict. *Journal of Child Psychology and Psychiatry, 45*(2), 377.

Mars, A. E., Mauk, J. E., & Dowrick, P. (1998). Symptoms of pervasive developmental disorders as observed in prediagnostic home videos of infants and toddlers. *Journal of Pediatrics, 132,* 500–504.

Marshall, M. F., Menikoff, J., & Paltrow, L. M. (2003). Perinatal substance abuse and human subjects research: Are privacy protections adequate? *Mental Retardation and Developmental Disabilities Research Reviews, 9*(2), 54–59.

Marshall, P. J., & Stevenson-Hinde, J. (2001). Behavioral inhibition: Physiological correlates. In W. R. Crozier & L. E. Alden (Eds.), *International handbook of social anxiety: Concepts, research and interventions relating to the self and shyness* (pp. 53–76). New York: Wiley.

Martin, A., Patzer, D. K., & Volkmar, F. R. (2000). Psychopharmacological treatment of higher-functioning pervasive developmental disorders. In A. Klin, F. R. Volkmar, & S. S. Sparrow (Eds.), *Asperger syndrome* (pp. 210–228). New York: Guilford Press.

Martin, G. C., Wertheim, E. H,, Prior, M., Smart, D., Sanson, A. & Oberklaid, F. (2000). A longitudinal study of the role of childhood temperament in the later development of eating concerns. *International Journal of Eating Disorders, 27,* 150–162.

Martin, J. K., Pescosolido, B. A., Olafsdottir, S., & Mcleod, J. D. (2007). The construction of fear: Americans' preferences for social distance from children and adolescents with mental health problems. *Journal of Health and Social Behavior, 48,* 50–67.

Marvin, R. S., & Pianta, R. C. (1996). Mothers' reactions to their child's diagnosis: Relations with security of attachment. *Journal of Clinical Child Psychology, 25*(4), 436–445.

Mascolo, M. F., & Fischer, K. W. (1998). The development of self through the coordination of component systems. In *Self-awareness: Its nature and development* (pp. 332–384). New York: Guilford Press.

Mascolo, M. F., & Bhatia, S. (2002). The dynamic construction of culture, self and social relations. *Psychology and Developing Societies, 14*(1), 55–90.

Mash, E. J., & Dozois, D. J. A. (1996). Child psychopathology: A developmental-systems perspective. In E. J. Mash & R. A. Barkley (Eds.), *Child psychopathology* (pp. 3–60). New York: Guilford Press.

Mash, E. J., & Hunsley, J. (2005). Evidence-based assessment of child and adolescent disorders: Issues and challenges. *Journal of Clinical Child and Adolescent Psychology, 34(3),* 362–379.

Masi, G., Millepiedi, S., Mucci, M., Pascale, R. R., Perugi, G., & Akiskal, H. S. (2003). Phenomenology and comorbidity of dysthmic disorder in 100 consecutively referred chidren and adolescents: Beyond DSM-IV. *Canadian Journal of Psychiatry, 48*(2), 99–105.

Masi, G., Perugi, G., Toni, C., Millepiedi, S., Mucci, M., Bertini, N., & Akiskal, H. S. (2004). Obsessive-compulsive bipolar comorbidity: Focus on children and adolescents. *Journal of Affective Disorders, 78*(3), 175–183.

Masi, G., Toni, C., Perugi, G., Mucci, M., Millepiedi, S., & et al. (2001). Anxiety disorders in children and adolescents with bipolar disorder: A neglected comorbidity. *Canadian Journal of Psychiatry, 46*(9), 795–796.

Masi, G., Toni, C., Perugi, G., Travierso, M. C., Millepiedi, S., Mucci, M., et al. (2003). Externalizing disorders in consecutively referred children and adolescents with bipolar disorder. *Comprehensive Psychiatry, 44*(3), 184–189.

Masia-Warner, C., Klein, R. G., Dent, H. C., Fisher, P. H., Alvir, J., Albano, A. M., et al. (2005). School-based intervention for adolescents with social anxiety disorder: Results of a controlled study. *Journal of Abnormal Child Psychology, 33*(6), 707–722.

Mason, W. A., Kosterman, R., Hawkins, J. D., Haggerty, K. P., & Spoth, R. L. (2003). Reducing adolescents' growth in substance use and delinquency: Randomized trial effects of a parent-training prevention intervention. *Prevention Science, 4*(3), 203–212.

Masten, A. S. (2001). Ordinary magic: Resilience processes in development. *American Psychologist, 56(3),* 227–238.

Masten, A. S. (2004). Regulatory processes, risk, and resilience in adolescent development. In R. E. Dahl & L. P. Spear (Eds.), *Adolescent brain development: Vulnerabilities and opportunities. Annals of the New York Academy of Sciences* (Vol. 1021, pp. 310–319). New York: New York Academy of Sciences.

Masten, A. S., Best, K. M., & Garmezy, N. (1990). Resilience and development: Contributions from the study of children who overcome adversity. *Development and Psychopathology, 2,* 425–444.

Masten, A. S., & Braswell, L. (1991). Developmental psychopathology: An integrative framework. In P. R. Martin (Ed.), *Handbook of behavior therapy and psychological science: An integrative approach* (pp. 35–56). Elmsford, NY: Pergamon Press.

Masten, A. S., Coatsworth, J. D., Neemann, J., Gest, S. D., Tellegen, A., & Garmezy, N. (1995). The structure and coherence of competence from childhood through adolescence. *Child Development, 66,* 1635–1659.

Masten, A. S., & Coatsworth, J. D. (1995). Competence, resilience, and psychopathology. In D. Cicchetti & D. J. Cohen (Eds.), *Developmental psychopathology: Vol. 2. Risk, disorder, and adaptation* (pp. 715–752). Oxford, England: Wiley.

Masten, A. S., & Coatsworth, J. D. (1998). The development of competence in favorable and unfavorable environments. *American Psychologist, 53(2),* 205–220.

Masten, A. S., Hubbard, J. J., Gest, S. D., Tellegen, A., Garmezy, M., & Ramirez, M. (1999). Competence in the context of adversity: Pathways to resilience and maladaptation from childhood to late adolescence. *Development and Psychopathology, 11(1),* 143–169.

Masten, A. S., Morison, P., Pellegrini, D., & Tellegen, A. (1990). Competence under stress: Risk and protective factors. In J. E. Rolf & A. S. Masten (Eds.), *Risk and protective factors in the development of psychopathology* (pp. 236–256). New York: Cambridge University Press.

Masten, A. S. & Reed, M-G. J. (2002). Resilience in development. In C. R. Snyder & S. J. Lopez (Eds.), *Handbook of Positive Psychology* (pp. 74–88). New York: Oxford University Press.

Matson, J. L., Bamburg, J. W., Mayville, E. A., Pinkston, J., Bielecki, J., Kuhn, D., et al. (2000). Psychopharmacology and mental retardation: A 10 year review. *Research in Developmental Disabilities, 21*(4), 263–296.

Matson, J. L., & Hammer, D. (1996). Assessment of social functioning. In J. W. Jacobson & J. A. Mulick (Eds.), *Manual of diagnosis and professional practice in mental retardation* (pp. 157–163). Washington, DC: American Psychological Association.

Matson, J. L., & Smiroldo, B. B. (1999). Intellectual disorders. In W. K. Silverman & T. H. Ollendick (Eds.), *Developmental issues in the clinical treatment of children* (pp. 295–306). Needham Heights, MA: Allyn & Bacon.

Mattison, R. E., Gadow, K. D., Sprafkin, J., & Nolan, E. E. (2002). Discriminant validity of a DSM-IV-based teacher checklist: Comparison of regular and special education students. *Behavioral Disorders, 27,* 304–316.

Matts, L., & Zionts, P. (1997). Implementing inclusion in a middle school setting. In P. Zionts (Ed.), *Inclusion strategies for students with learning and Behavioral Problems: Perspectives, experiences, and best practices,* (pp. 83–100). Austin, TX: PRO-ED.

Maughan, B., Iervolino, A. C., & Collishaw, S. Time trends in child and adolescent mental disorders. *Current Opinion in Psychiatry, 18(4),* 381–385.

Maughan, B., Rowe, R., Messer, J.. Goodman, R., & Meltzer, H. (2004). Conduct disorder and oppositional defiant disorder in a national sample: Developmental epidemiology. *Journal of Child Psychology and Psychiatry, 45*(3), 609–621.

Mawhood, L., Howlin, P. & Rutter, M. (2000). Autism and developmental receptive language disorder – A comparative follow-up in early adult life. I: Cognitive and language outcomes. *Journal of Child Psychology and Psychiatry and Allied Disciplines, 41,* 547–559.

Mayes, L. C. (2002). A behavioral teratogenic model of the impact of prenatal cocaine exposure on arousal regulatory systems. *Neurotoxicology and Teratology, 24*(3), 385–395.

Mayes, L. C., & Bornstein, M. H. (1996). The context of development for young children from cocaine-abusing families. In P. M. Kato & T. Mann (Eds.), *Handbook of diversity issues in health psychology. The Plenum series in culture and health* (pp. 69–95). New York: Plenum Press.

Mayes, L. C., & Bornstein, M. H. (1997a). Attention regulation in infants born at risk: Prematurity and prenatal cocaine exposure. In J. A. Burack, & J. T. Enns (Eds.), *Attention, development, and psychopathology* (pp. 97–122). New York: Guilford Press.

Mayes, L. C., & Bornstein, M. H. (1997b). The development of children exposed to cocaine. In S. S. Luthar, J. A. Burack, D. Cicchetti, J. R. Weisz (Eds.), *Developmental psychopathology: Perspectives on adjustment, risk, and disorder* (pp. 166–188). New York: Cambridge University Press.

Mayes, L. C., Grillon, C., Granger, R., & Schottenfeld, R. (1998). Regulation of arousal and attention in preschool children exposed to cocaine prenatally. In J. A. Harvey & B. E. Kosofsky (Eds.), *Cocaine: Effects on the developing brain, Annals of the New York Academy of Sciences* (Vol. 846, pp. 126–143). New York: New York Academy of Sciences.

Mayes, S. D., Calhoun, S. L., & Crites, D. L. (2001). Does DSM-IV Asperger's disorder exist? *Journal of Abnormal Child Psychology, 29,* 263–271.

McArdle, J. J., Ferrer-Caja, E., Hamagami, F., & Woodcock, R. W. (2002). Comparative longitudinal structural analysis of the growth and decline of multiple intellectual abilities over the life span. *Developmental Psychology, 38*(1), 115–142.

McArthur, L. H., Holbert, D., & Pena, M. An exploration of the attitudinal and perceptual dimensions of body image among male and female adolescents from six Latin American cities. *Adolescence, 40,* 801–813.

McBurnett, K., Pfiffner, L. J., & Frick, P. J. (2001). Symptom properties as a function of ADHD type: An argument for continued study of sluggish cognitive tempo. *Journal of Abnormal Child Psychology, 29*(3), 207–213.

McCabe, L. A., & Brooks-Gunn, J. (2007). With a little help from my friends? Self-regulation in groups of young children. *Infant Mental Health, 28(*6), 584–605.

McCabe, M. P., & Ricciardelli, L. A. (2004a). A longitudinal study of pubertal timing and extreme body change behaviors among adolescent boys and girls. *Adolescence, 39,* 145–166.

McCabe, M. P., & Ricciardelli, L. A. (2004b). Body image dissatisfaction among males across the lifespan: A review of past literature. *Journal of Psychosomatic Research, 56,* 675–685.

McCall, J. N. (1999). Research on the psychological effects of orphanage care: A critical review. In R. B. McKenzie (Ed.), *Rethinking orphanages for the 21st century* (pp. 127–150). Thousand Oaks, CA: Sage.

McCarthy, D. M., Tomlinson, K. L., Anderson, K. G., Marlatt, G. A., & Brown, S. A. (2005). Relapse in alcohol- and drug-disordered adolescents with comorbid psychopathology: Changes in psychiatric symptoms. *Psychology of Addictive Behaviors, 19*(1), 28–34.

McCarty, C. A., Weisz, J. R., Wanitromanee, K., Eastman, K. L., Suwanlert, S., Chaiyasit, W., et al. (1999). Culture, coping, and context: Primary and secondary control among Thai and American youth. *Journal of Child Psychology and Psychiatry and Allied Disciplines, 40(5),* 809–818.

McCaughan, J. A., Carlson, R. G., Falck, R. S., & Siegel, H. A. (2005). From "candy kids" to "chemi-kids": A typology of young adults who attend raves in the midwestern United States. *Substance Use and Misuse, 40*(9–10), 1503–1523.

McCauley, E., Pavidis, K., & Kendall, K. (2001). Developmental precursors of depression. In I. Goodyer (Ed.), *The depressed child and adolescent: Developmental and clinical perspectives* (pp. 46–78). New York: Cambridge University Press.

McClellan, J. M., & Werry, J. S. (2000). Research psychiatric diagnostic interviews for children and adolescents. *Journal of the American Academy of Child and Adolescent Psychiatry, 39,* 19–99.

McClellan, J., McCurry, C., Ronnei, M., & Adams, J. (1997). Relationship between sexual abuse, gender, and sexually inappropriate behaviors in seriously mentally ill youths. *Journal of the American Academy of Child and Adolescent Psychiatry, 36*(7), 959–965.

McClelland, M. M., Cameron, C. E., Connor, C. M., Farris, C. L., Jewkes, A. M., & Morrison, F. J. (2007). Links between behavioral regulation and preschoolers' literacy, vocabulary, and math skills. *Developmental Psychology, 43*(4), 947–959.

McClure, E. B., Kubiszyn, T., & Kaslow, N. J. (2002). Advances in the diagnosis and treatment of childhood disorders. *Professional Psychology: Research and Practice, 33*(2), 125–134.

McClure, E. G., Connell, A. M., Zucker, M., Griffith, J. R., & Kaslow, N. J. (2005). The Adolescent Depression Empowerment Project (ADEPT): A culturally sensitive family treatment for African American girls. In E. D. Hibbs & P. S. Jensen (Eds.), *Psychosocial treatments for child and adolescent disorders: Empirically based strategies for clinical practice* (2nd ed., pp. 149–164). Washington, DC: American Psychological Association.

McConatha, J. T., & Huba, H. M. (1999). Primary, secondary, and emotional control across adulthood. *Current Psychology, 18*(2), 164–170.

McConaughy, S. H., & Achenbach, T. M. (1994). Comorbidity of empirically based syndromes in matched general population and clinical samples. *Journal of Child Psychology and Psychiatry and Allied Disciplines, 35*(6), 1141–1157.

McConkey, R., & Ryan, D. (2001). Experiences of staff in dealing with client sexuality in services for teenagers and adults with intellectual disability. *Journal of Intellectual Disability Research, 45*(1), 83–87.

McCoy, M. G., Frick, P. J., Loney, B. R., & Ellis, M. L. (1999). The potential mediating role of parenting practices in the development of conduct problems in a clinic-referred sample. *Journal of Child and Family Studies, 8*(4), 477–494.

McCracken, J. T., Walkup, J. T., & Koplewicz, H. S. (2002). Childhood and early-onset anxiety: Treatment and biomarker studies. *Journal of Clinical Psychiatry, 63*(Suppl 6), 8–11.

McCrae, R. R., Costa, P. T., Ostendorf, F., Angleitner, A., Hrebickova, M., Avia, M. D., et al. (2000). Nature over nurture: Temperament, personality, and life span development. *Journal of Personality and Social Psychology, 78*(1), 173–186.

McDonough, S. C. (1993). Interaction guidance: Understanding and treating early infant-caregiver relationship disturbances. In C. H. Zeanah (Ed.), *Handbook of infant mental health* (pp. 414–426). New York: Guilford Press.

McDougle, C. J. (1997). Psychopharmacology. In D. J. Cohen & F. R. Volkmar (Eds.), *Handbook of autism and pervasive developmental disorders* (2nd ed., pp. 707–729). New York: Wiley.

McElroy, S. L., Kotwal, R., Keck, P. E., & Akiskal, H. S. (2005). Comorbidity of bipolar and eating disorders: Distinct or related disorders with shared dysregulations? *Journal of Affective Disorders, 86*(2–3), 107–127.

McGee, R., Prior, M., Williams, S., Smart, D., & Sanson, A. (2002). The long-term significance of teacher-rated hyperactivity and reading ability in childhood: Findings from two longitudinal studies. *Journal of Child Psychology and Psychiatry and Applied Disciplines, 43*(8), 1004–1016.

McGee, R., & Williams, S. (1999). Environmental risk factors in oppositional-defiant disorder and conduct disorder. In H. C. Quay & A. E. Hogan (Eds.), *Handbook of disruptive behavior disorders* (pp. 419–440). Dordrecht, Netherlands: Kluwer Academic Publishers.

McGilley, B. H. (2006). Group therapy for adolescents with eating disorders. *Group, 30*(4), 321–336.

McGough, J. J., & Barkley, R. A. (2004). Diagnostic controversies in adult attention deficit hyperactivity disorder. *American Journal of Psychiatry, 161*(11), 1948–1956.

McGue, M., Elkins, I., Walden, B., & Iacono, W. G. (2005). Perceptions of the parent-adolescent relationship: A longitudinal investigation. *Developmental Psychology, 41*(6), 971–984.

McGue, M., & Iacono, W. G. (2004). The initiation of substance use in adolescence: A behavioral genetics perspective. In L. F. DiLalla (Ed.), *Behavior genetics principles: Perspectives in development, personality, and psychopathology. Decade of behavior* (pp. 41–57). Washington, DC: American Psychological Association.

McGuffin, P. (2004). Behavioral genomics: Where molecular genetics is taking psychiatry and psychology. In L. F. DiLalla (Ed.), *Behavior genetics principles: Perspectives in development, personality, and psychopathology. Decade of behavior* (pp. 191–204). Washington, DC: American Psychological Association.

McGuffin, P., Riley, B., & Plomin, R. (2001). Toward behavioral genomics. *Science, 291*(5507), 1232–1249.

McIntosh, V. V.W., Jordan, J., Carter, F. A., Luty, S. E., McKenzie, J. M., Bulik, C. M., et al. (2005). Three psychotherapies for anorexia nervosa: A randomized, controlled trial. *American Journal of Psychology, 162,* 741–747.

McLaughlin, K. A., Hilt, L. M., & Nolen-Hoeksema, S. (2007). Racial/ethnic differences in internalizing and externalizing symptoms in adolescents. *Journal of Abnormal Child Psychology, 35*(5), 801–816.

McLoyd, V. C. (1999). Culture and development in our postcultural age. In A. Masten (Ed.), *Cultural processes in child development. The Minnesota symposia on child psychology* (pp. 123–135). Mahwah, NJ: Erlbaum.

McMahon, R. J. (1999). Parent training. In S. W. Russ & T. H. Ollendick (Eds.), *Handbook of psychotherapies with children and families: Issues in clinical child psychology* (pp. 153–180). Dordrecht, Netherlands: Kluwer Academic Publishers.

McMahon, R. J., & Frick, P. J. (2005). Evidence-based assessment of conduct problems in children and adolescents. *Journal of Clinical Child and Adolescent Psychology, 34*(3), 477–505.

McManis, M. H., Kagan, J., Snidman, N. C., & Woodward, S. A. (2002). EEG asymmetry, power, and temperament in children. *Developmental Psychobiology, 41*(2), 169–177.

McVey, G., Tweed, S., & Blackmore, E. (2007). Healthy Schools-Healthy Kids: A controlled evaluation of a comprehensive universal eating disorder prevention program. *Body Image, 4*(2), 115–136.

Measelle, J. R., Stice, E., & Hogansen, J. M. (2006). Developmental trajectories of co-occurring depressive, eating, antisocial, and substance abuse problems in female adolescents. *Journal of Abnormal Psychology, 115,* 524–538.

Medeiros, D., Carlson, E., Surko, M., Munoz, N., Castillo, M., & Epstein, I. (2005). Adolescents' self-reported substance risks and need to talk about them in mental health counseling. In K. Peake, I. Epstein, & D. Medeiros (Eds.), *Clinical and research uses of an adolescent mental health intake questionnaire: What kids need to talk about* (pp. 171–189). Binghamton, NY: Haworth Social Work Practice Press.

MedlinePlus Medical Encyclopedia. (2009, January 20). Anorexia nervosa. Retrieved July 20, 2009, from http://www.nlm.nih.gov/medlineplus/ency/article/000362.htm

Mednick, S. A., & Schulsinger, F. (1968). Some premorbid characteristics related to breakdown in children with schizophrenic mothers. *Journal of Psychiatric Research, 11*(Supplement 1), 267–291.

Meesters, C., Muris, P. Ghys, A., Reumerman, T., & Rooijmans, M. (2003). The Children's Somatization Inventory: Further evidence for its reliability and validity in a pediatric sample and a community sample of Dutch children and adolescents. *Journal of Pediatric Psychology, 28*(6), 413–422.

Meichenbaum, D. (1977). *Cognitive-behavior modification: An integrative approach.* New York: Springer.

Meijer, A. M., & van den Wittenboer, G. L. H. (2007). Contribution of infants' sleep and crying to marital relationship of first-time parent couples in the first year after childbirth. *Journal of Family Psychology, 21*(1), 49–57.

Meisels, S. J., & Atkins-Burnett, S. (2000). The elements of early childhood assessment. In J. P. Shonkoff & S. J. Meisels (Eds.), *Handbook of early childhood intervention* (2nd ed., pp. 231–257). New York: Cambridge University Press.

Meisels, S. J., Dichtelmiller, M., & Liaw, F-R. (1993). A multidimensional analysis of early childhood intervention programs. In C. H. Zeanah (Ed.), *Handbook of infant mental health* (pp. 361–442). New York: Guilford Press.

Melhem, N. M., Brent, D. A., Ziegler, M., Iyengar, S., Kolko, D., Oquendo, M., et al. (2007). Familial pathways to early-onset suicidal behavior: Familiar and individual antecedents of suicidal behavior. *American Journal of Psychiatry, 164*(9), 1364–1370.

Meltzer, L. J., & Mindell, J. A. (2006). Sleep and sleep disorders in children and adolescents. *Psychiatric Clinics of North America, 29,* 1059–1076.

Meltzer, L. J., & Mindell, J. A. (2007). Relationship between child sleep disturbances and maternal sleep, mood, and parenting stress: A pilot study. *Journal of Family Psychology, 21*(1), 67–73.

Mendola, P., Selevan, S. G., Gutter, S., & Rice, D. (2002). Environmental factors associated with a spectrum of neurodevelopmental deficits. *Mental Retardation and Developmental Disabilities Research Reviews, 8*(3), 188–197.

Merikangas, K. R. (2000). Familial and genetic factors and psychopathology. In C. Nelson (Ed.), *The effects of early adversity on neurobehavioral development. The Minnesota symposia on child psychology* (pp. 281–315). Mahwah, NJ: Erlbaum.

Merikangas, K. R., & Angst, J. (1995). The challenge of depressive disorders in adolescence. In M. Rutter (Ed.), *Psychosocial disturbances in young people: Challenges for prevention* (pp. 131–165). New York: Cambridge University Press.

Merline, A. C., O'Malley, P. M., Schulenberg, J. E., Bachman, J. G., & Johnston, L. D. (2004). Substance use among adults 35 years of age: Prevalence, adulthood predictors, and impact of adolescent substance use. *American Journal of Public Health, 94*(1), 96–102.

Mermelstein, R. (1999). Ethnicity, gender, and risk factors for smoking initiation: An overview. *Nicotine and Tobacco Research, 1,* 45–51.

Mermelstein, R. (1999). Explanations of ethnic and gender differences in youth smoking: A multi-site, qualitative investigation. *Nicotine and Tobacco Research, 1* (Suppl. 1), S91-S98.

Mervis, C. B., Robinson, B. F., Bertrand, J., Morris, C. A., Klein-Tasman, B. P., & Armstrong, S. C. (2000). The Williams syndrome cognitive profile. *Brain and Cognition, 44*(3), 604–628.

Meschke, L. L., Zweig, J. M., Barber, B. L., & Eccles, J. S. (2000). Demographic, biological, psychological, and social predictors of the timing of first intercourse. *Journal of Research on Adolescence, 10*(3), 315–338.

Mesibov, G. B. (1976). Mentally retarded people: 200 years in America. *Journal of Clinical Child Psychology, Winter,* 25–29.

Mesibov, G. B. (1983). Current perspectives and issues in autism and adolescence. In E. Schopler & G. B. Mesibov (Eds.), *Autism in adolescents and adults* (pp. 37–53). New York: Plenum Press.

Mesibov, G. B. (1986). A cognitive program for teaching social behaviors to verbal autistic adolescents and adults. In E. Schopler & G. B. Mesibov (Eds.), *High-functioning individuals with autism* (pp. 143–156). New York: Plenum Press.

Mesibov, G. B. (1992). Treatment issues with high-functioning adolescents and adults with autism. In E. Schopler & G. B. Mesibov (Eds.), *High-functioning individuals with autism: Current issues in autism* (pp. 143–155). New York: Plenum Press.

Mesibov, G. B. (1994). A comprehensive program for serving people with autism and their families: The TEACCH model. In J. L. Matson (Ed.), *Autism in children and adults: Etiology, assessment, and intervention* (pp. 85–97). Belmont, CA: Brooks/Cole Publishing.

Mesibov, G. B. (1995). Facilitated communication: A warning for pediatric psychologists. *Journal of Pediatric Psychology, 20,* 127–130.

Mesibov, G. B. (1997). Formal and informal measures on the effectiveness of the TEACCH programme. *Autism, 1,* 25–35.

Mesibov, G. B. (1998). Diagnosis and assessment of autistic adolescents and adults. In E. Schopler & G. B. Mesibov (Eds.), *Diagnosis and assessment in autism: Current issues in autism* (pp. 227–238). New York: Plenum Press.

Mesibov, G. B., Adams, L. W., & Schopler, E. (2000). Autism: A brief history. *Psychoanalytic Inquiry, 20,* 637–647.

Mesibov, G. B., Schroeder, C. S., & Wesson, L. (1993). Parental concerns about their children. In M. C. Roberts & G. P. Koocher (Eds.), *Readings in pediatric psychology* (pp. 307–316). New York: Plenum Press.

Mesibov, G. B., & Shea, V. (1996). Full inclusion and students with autism. *Journal of Autism and Developmental Disorders, 26,* 337–346.

Mesibov, G. B., Shea, V., & Adams, L. W. (2002). Understanding Asperger syndrome and high functioning autism. *Journal of the American Academy of Child and Adolescent Psychiatry, 41,* 1137.

Messerlian, C., Derevensky, J., & Gupta, R. (2005). Youth gambling problems: A public health perspective. *Health Promotion International, 20*(1), 69–79.

Metrik, J., Frissell, K. C., McCarthy, D. M., D'Amico, E. J., & Brown, S. A. (2003). Strategies for reduction and cessation of alcohol use: Adolescent preferences. *Alcoholism: Clinical and Experimental Research, 27*(1), 74–80.

Meyer, J. M., Rutter, M., Silberg, J. L., Maes, H. H., Simonoff, E., Shillady, L. L., et al. (2000). Familial aggregation for conduct disorder symptomatology: The role of genes, marital discord and family adaptability. *Psychological Medicine, 30,* 759–774.

Meyer, S. E., Carlson, G. A., Wiggs, E. A., Martinez, P. E., Ronsaville, D. S., Klimes-Dougan, B., et al. (2004). A prospective study of the association among impaired executive functioning, childhood attentional problems, and the development of bipolar disorder. *Development and Psychopathology, 16*(2), 461–476.

Meyers, A. W., Klesges, R. C., Winders, S. E., & Ward, K. D. (1997). Are weight concerns predictive of smoking cessation? A prospective analysis. *Journal of Consulting and Clinical Psychology, 65*(3), 448–452.

Micklowitz, D. J., George, E. L., Axelson, D. A., Kim, E. Y., Birmaher, B., Schneck, C., et al. (2004). Family-focused treatment for adolescents with bipolar disorder. *Journal of Affective Disorders, 82*(1), S113-S128.

Milan, S., Pinderhughes, E. E., & Conduct Problems Prevention Research Group (2006). Family instability and child maladjustment trajectories during elementary school. *Journal of Abnormal Child Psychology, 34,* 43–56.

Milan, S., Snow, S., & Belay, S. (2007). The context of preschool children's sleep: Racial/ethnic differences in sleep locations, routines, and concerns. *Journal of Family Psychology, 21*(1), 20–28.

Miles, D. R., & Carey, G. (1997). Genetic and environmental architecture of human aggression. *Journal of Personality and Social Psychology, 72*(1), 207–217.

Milich, R., Balentine, A. C., & Lynam, D. R. (2001). ADHD combined type and ADHD predominantly inattentive type are distinct and unrelated disorders. *Clinical Psychology: Science and Practice, 8*(4), 463–488.

Milich, R., Lynam, D., Zimmerman, R., Logan, T. K., Martin, C., Leukefeld, C., et al. (2000). Differences in young adult psychopathology among drug abstainers, experimenters, and frequent users. *Journal of Substance Abuse, 11*(1), 69–88.

Miller, A., Fox, N. A., Cohn, J. F., Forbes, E. E., Sherrill, J. T., & Kovacs, M. (2002). Regional patterns of brain activity in adults with a history of childhood depression: Gender differences and clinical variability. *American Journal of Psychiatry, 159*(6), 934–940.

Miller, F. G., & Lazowski, L. E. (2005). Substance Abuse Subtle Screening Inventory for Adolescents – second version. In T. Grisso, G. Vincent, & D. Seagrave (Eds.), *Mental health screening and assessment in juvenile justice* (pp. 139–151). New York: Guilford Press.

Miller, J. N., & Ozonoff, S., (1997). Did Asperger's cases have Asperger disorder? A research note. *Journal of Child Psychology and Psychiatry and Allied Disciplines, 38,* 247–251.

Miller, J. N., & Ozonoff, S. (2000). The external validity of Asperger disorder: Lack of evidence from the domain of neuropsychology. *Journal of Abnormal Psychology, 109,* 227–238.

Miller, K. E., Melnick, M. J., Farrell, M. P., Sabo, D. F., & Barnes, G. M. (2006). Jocks, gender, binge drinking, and adolescent violence. *Journal of Interpersonal Violence, 21*(1), 105–120.

Miller, K. J., Fullmer, S. L., & Walls, R. T. (1996). Reflections on "A dozen years of mainstreaming literature: A content analysis." *Exceptionality, 6*(12)*,* 129–131.

Miller, P. M., Smith, G. T., & Goldman, M. S. (1990). Emergence of alcohol expectancies in childhood: A possible critical period. *Journal of Studies on Alcohol, 51*(4), 343–349.

Miller, S. M., & Green, M. L. (1985) Coping with stress and frustration: Origins, nature, and development. In M. Lewis & C. Saarni (Eds.), *The socialization of emotions* (pp. 263–314). New York: Plenum Press.

Miller, T. Q. (1994). A test of alternative explanations for the stage-like progression of adolescent substance use in four national samples. *Addictive Behaviors, 19*(3), 287–293.

Miller-Johnson, S., Coie, J. D., Maumary-Gremaud, A., Bierman, K., & Conduct Problems Prevention Research Group. (2002). Peer rejection and aggression and early starter models of conduct disorder. *Journal of Abnormal Child Psychology, 30*(3), 217–230.

Miller-Johnson, S., Moore, B. L., Underwood, M. K., & Coie, J. D. (2005). African-American girls and physical aggression: Does stability of childhood aggression predict later negative outcomes? In D. J. Pepler, K. C. Madsen, C. Webster, & K. S. Leven (Eds.), *The development and treatment of girlhood aggression* (pp. 75–95). Mahwah, NJ: Erlbaum.

Milne, J. M., Edwards, J. K., & Murchie, J. C. (2001). Family treatment of oppositional defiant disorder: Changing views and strength-based approaches. *Family Journal-Counseling and Therapy for Couples and Families, 9*, 17–28.

Minde, K. (2002). Sleep disorders in infants and young children. In J. M. Maldonado-Duran (Ed.), *Infant and toddler mental health: Models of clinical intervention with infants and their families* (pp. 269–307). Arlington, VA: American Psychiatric Publishing.

Mindell, J. A., Kuhn, B., Lewin, D. S., Meltzer, L. J., & Sadeh, A. (2006). Behavioral treatment of bedtime problems and night wakings in infants and young children. *American Academy of Sleep Medicine, 29*(10), 1263–1276.

Ming, X., Brimacombe, M., & Wagner, G. C., (2007). Prevalence of motor impairment in autism spectrum disorders. *Brain and Development, 29*(9), 565–570.

Minke, K. M., Bear, G. G., Deemer, S. A., & Griffin, S. M. (1996). Teachers' experiences with inclusive classrooms: Implications for special education reform. *Journal of Special Education, 30*(2), 152–186.

Minnes, P. M. (1988). Family stress associated with a developmentally handicapped child. In N. W. Bray (Ed.), *International review of research in mental retardation* (pp. 195–226). San Diego, CA: Academic Press.

Minnes, S., Singer, L. T., Arendt, R., & Satayathum, S. (2005). Effects of prenatal cocaine/polydrug use on maternal-infant feeding interactions during the first year of life. *Journal of Developmental and Behavioral Pediatrics, 26*(3), 194–200.

Minshew, N. J., & Williams, D. L. (2007). The new neurobiology of autism: Cortex, connectivity, and neuronal organization. *Archives of Neurology, 64*(7), 945–950.

Mintz, S. (2006). *Huck's raft: A history of American childhood.* Cambridge, MA: Belknap Press.

Minuchin, S. (1974). *Families and family therapy.* Oxford, England: Harvard University Press.

Minuchin, S., Rosman, S., & Baker, L. (1978). *Psychosomatic families.* Cambridge, MA: Harvard University Press.

Mirmiran, M., & Lunshof, S. (1996). Perinatal development of human circadian rhythms. Progress in Brain Research, 111, 217–226.

Mirsky, J. (1997). Psychological distress among immigrant adolescents: Culture-specific factors in the case of immigrants from the former Soviet Union. *International Journal of Psychology, 32(4),* 221–230.

Modell, J., & Elder, G. H. (2002). Children develop in history: So what's new? In W. Hartup & R. A. Weinberg (Eds.), *Child psychology in retrospect and prospect: In celebration of the 75th anniversary of the Institute of Child Development. The Minnesota symposia on child psychology (Vol 32, pp. 173–205).* Mahwah, NJ: Erlbaum.

Moffitt, T. E. (2003). Life-course-persistent and adolescence-limited antisocial behavior: A 10-year research review and a research agenda. In B. B. Lahey, T. E. Moffitt, & A. Caspi (Eds.), *Causes of conduct disorder and juvenile delinquency* (pp. 49–75). New York: Guilford Press.

Moffitt, T. E. (2005). The new look of behavioral genetics in developmental psychopathology: Gene-environment interplay in antisocial behaviors. *Psychological Bulletin, 131*(4), 533–554.

Moffitt, T. E., & Caspi, A. (2001). Childhood predictors differentiate life-course persistent and adolescence-limited antisocial pathways among males and females. *Development and Psychopathology, 13*(2), 355–375.

Moffitt, T. E., Caspi, A., Harrington, H., & Milne, B. J. (2002). Males on the life-course-persistent and adolescence-limited antisocial pathways: Follow-up at age 26 years. *Development and Psychopathology, 14*(1), 179–207.

Moffitt, T. E., & Melchior, M. (2007). Why does worldwide prevalence of childhood attention deficit hyperactivity disorder matter? *American Journal of Psychiatry, 164*(6), 856–858.

Molina, B. S. G., Smith, B. H., & Pelham, W. E. (2001). Factor structure and criterion validity of secondary school teacher ratings of ADHD and ODD. *Journal of Abnormal Child Psychology, 29*, 71–82.

Monroe, S. M., Rohde, P., Seeley, J. R., & Lewinsohn, P. M. (1999). Life events and depression in adolescence: Relationship loss as a prospective risk factor for first onset of major depressive disorder. *Journal of Abnormal Psychology, 108*(4), 606–614.

Moore, C. M., Biederman, J., Wozniak, J., Mick, E., Aleardi, M., Wardrop, M., et al. (2006). Differences in brain chemistry in children and adolescents with attention deficit hyperactivity disorder with and without comorbid bipolar disorder: A proton magnetic resonance spectroscopy study. *American Journal of Psychiatry, 163*, 316–318.

Moore, D. G. (2001). Reassessing emotion recognition performance in people with mental retardation: A review. *American Journal on Mental Retardation, 106*(6), 481–502.

Moore, K. A., & Keyes, C. L. M. (2002). A brief history of well-being: In children and adults. In M. H. Bornstein, L. Davidson, C. L. M. Keyes, & K. Moore (Eds.), *Well-Being: Positive development across the life course.* Mahwah, NJ: Erlbaum.

Moore, M., & Carr, A. (2000). Anxiety disorders. In Carr, A. (Ed.), *What works for children and adolescents? A critical review of psychological interventions with children, adolescents and their families* (pp. 178–202). New York: Routledge.

Moorhead, D. J., Stashwick, C. K., Reinhertz, H. Z., Gianconia, R. M., Striegel-Moore, R. M., & Paradis, A. D. (2003). Child and adolescent predictors for eating disorders in a community population of young adult women. *International Journal of Eating Disorders, 33,* 1–9.

Morales, J. R., & Guerra, N. G. (2006). Effects of multiple context and cumulative stress on urban children's adjustment in elementary school. *Child Development, 77,* 907–923.

Moran, P. B., Vuchinich, S., & Hall, N. K. (2004). Associations between types of maltreatment and substance use during adolescence. *Child Abuse and Neglect, 28*(5), 565–574.

Moreno, C., Laje, G., Blanco, C., Jiang, H., Schmidt, A. B., & Olfson, M. (2007). National trends in the outpatient diagnosis and treatment of bipolar disorder in youth. *Archive of General Psychology, 64*(9), 1032–1039.

Morison, S. J., Ames, E. W., & Chisholm, K. (1995). The development of children adopted from Romanian orphanages. *Merrill-Palmer Quarterly, 41*(4), 411–430.

Morison, S. J., & Ellwood, A. L. (2000). Resiliency in the aftermath of deprivation: A second look at the development of Romanian orphanage children. *Merrill-Palmer Quarterly, 46*(4), 717–737.

Morral, A. R., McCaffrey, D. F., & Paddock, S. M (2002). Reassessing the marijuana gateway effect. *Addiction, 97*(12), 1493–1504.

Morrell, J., & Steele, H. (2003). The role of attachment security, temperament, maternal perception, and care-giving behavior in persistent infant sleeping problems. *Infant Mental Health Journal, 24*(5), 447–468.

Morris, A. S., Silk, J. S., Steinberg, L., Sessa, F. M., Avenevoli, S., & Essex, M. J. (2002). Temperamental vulnerability and negative parenting as interacting of child adjustment. *Journal of Marriage and Family, 64*, 461–471.

Morris, C. D., Miklowitz, D. J., & Waxmonsky, J. A. (2007). Family-focused treatment for bipolar disorder in adults and youth. *Journal of Clinical Psychology, 63*(5), 433–445.

Morris, R. J., & Kratochwill, T. R. (1998). *The practice of child therapy.* Needham Heights, MA: Allyn & Bacon.

Morrison, F. J., & Ornstein, P. A. (1996). Cognitive development. In R. B. Cairns & G. H. Elder (Eds.), *Developmental science. Cambridge studies in social and emotional development* (121–134). New York: Cambridge University Press.

Morrison, T. G., Kalin, R., & Morrison, M. A. (2004). Body-image evaluation and body-image investment among adolescents: A test of sociocultural and social comparison theories. *Adolescence, 39*, 571–592.

Moss, E., St-Laurent, D., & Parent, S. (1999). Disorganized attachment and developmental risk at school age. In J. Solomon & C. George (Eds.), *Attachment disorganization* (pp. 160–186). New York: Guilford Press.

Moss, H. B., Lynch, K. G., & Hardie, T. L. (2003). Affiliation with deviant peers among children of substance-dependent fathers from pre-adolescence into adolescence: Associations with problem behaviors. *Drug and Alcohol Dependence, 71*(2), 117–125.

Motti, F., Cicchetti, D., & Sroufe, L. A. (1983). From infant affect expression to symbolic play: The coherence of development in Down syndrome children. *Child Development, 54*(5), 1168–1175.

Mottron, L., Dawson, M., Soulieres, I., Hubert, B., & Burack, J. (2006). Enhanced perceptual functioning in autism: An update, and eight principles of autistic perception. *Journal of Autism and Developmental Disorders, 36*(1), 27–43.

Moxon, L., & Gates, D. (2001). Children with autism: Supporting the transition to adulthood. *Educational and Child Psychology, 18*, 28–40.

Muehlenkamp, J. J. (2005). Self-injurious behavior as a separate clinical syndrome. *American Journal of Orthopsychiatry, 75*(2), 324–333.

Muehlenkamp, J. J., & Gutierrez, P. M. (2004). An investigation of differences between self-injurious behavior and suicide attempts in a sample of adolescents. *Suicide and Life-Threatening Behavior, 34*(1), 12–23.

Mueller, R-A., & Courchesne, E. (2000). Autism's home in the brain: Reply. *Neurology, 54*, 270.

Mueller, R-A., Pierce, K., Ambrose, J. B., Allen, G., & Courchesne, E. (2001). Atypical patterns of cerebral motor activation in autism: A functional magnetic resonance study. *Biological Psychiatry, 49*, 665–676.

Mufson, L., Dorta, K. P., Wickramaratne, P., Nomura, Y., Olfson, M., & Myrna, M. W. (2004). A randomized effectiveness trial of interpersonal therapy for depressed adolescents. *Archives of General Psychiatry, 61*(6), 577–584.

Mufson, L., Gallagher, T., Dorta, K. P., & Young, J. F. (2004). A group adaptation of interpersonal therapy for depressed adolescents. *American Journal of Psychotherapy, 58*(2), 220–237.

Muise, A. M., Stein, D. G., & Arbess, G. (2003). Eating disorders in adolescent boys: A review of the adolescent and young adult literature. *Journal of Adolescent Health, 33*, 427–435.

Multimodal Treatment Study of Children with ADHD Cooperative Group, US. (1999). A 14-month randomized clinical trial of treatment strategies for attention-deficit/hyperactivity disorder. *Archives of General Psychiatry, 56*(12), 1073–1086.

Multimodal Treatment Study of Children with ADHD Cooperative Group (2004). National Institute of Mental Health multimodal treatment study of ADHD follow-up: 24-month outcomes of treatment strategies for attention-deficit/hyperactivity disorder. *Pediatrics, 113*(4), 754–761.

Mulveen, R., & Hepworth, J. (2006). An interpretive phenomenological analysis of participation in a pro-anorexia Internet site and its relationship with disordered eating. *Journal of Health Psychology, 11(2)*, 283–296.

Mundy, P., & Neal, A. R. (2001). Neural plasticity, joint attention, and a transactional social-orienting model of autism. In L. M. Glidden (Ed.), *International review of research in mental retardation: Autism* (Vol. 23, pp. 139–168). San Diego, CA: Academic Press.

Munson, J. A., McMahon, R. J., & Spieker , S. J. (2001). Structure and variability in the developmental trajectory of children's externalizing problems: Impact of infant attachment, maternal depressive symptomatology, and child sex. *Development and Psychopathology, 13*, 277–296.

Muratori, F., & Maestro, S. (2007). Early signs of autism in the first year of life. In S. Acquarone (Ed.), *Signs of autism in infants: Recognition and early intervention* (pp. 46–62). London: Karnac Books.

Muraven, M., & Baumeister, R. F. (2000). Self-regulation and depletion of limited resources: Does self-control resemble a muscle? *Psychological Bulletin, 126*, 247–259.

Muraven, M., Baumeister, R. F., & Tice, D. M. (1999). Longitudinal improvement of self-regulation through practice: Building self-control strength through repeated exercise. *Journal of Social Psychology, 139*, 446–457.

Muris, P., Bodden, D., Merckelbach, H., Ollendick, T. H., & King, N. (2003). Fear of the beast: A prospective study on the effects of negative information on childhood fear. *Behaviour Research and Therapy, 41*(2), 195–208.

Muris, P., & Ollendick, T. H. (2005). The role of temperament in the etiology of child psychopathology. *Clinical Child and Family Psychology Review, 8*(4), 271–289.

Muris, P., Mayer, B., Bartelds, E., Tierney, S., & Bogie, N. (2001). The revised version of the Screen for Child Anxiety Related Emotional Disorders (SCARED-R): Treatment sensitivity in an early intervention trial for childhood anxiety disorders. *British Journal of Clinical Psychology, 40*(Pt. 3), 323–336.

Muris, P., Meesters, C., Merckelbach, H., Sermon, A., & Zwakhalen, S. (1998). Worry in normal children. *Journal of the American Academy of Child and Adolescent Psychiatry, 37*(7), 703–710.

Muris P., & Meesters, C. (2002). Symptoms of anxiety disorders and teacher-reported school functioning of normal children. *Psychological Reports, 91*(2), 588–590.

Muris, P., & Meesters, C. (2004). Children's somatization symptoms: Correlations with trait anxiety, anxiety sensitivity, and learning experiences. *Psychological Reports, 94*(3), 1269–1275.

Muris, P., Merckelbach, H., & Collaris, R. (1997). Common childhood fears and their origins. *Behaviour Research and Therapy, 35*, 929–937.

Muris, P., Merckelbach, H., Gadet, B., & Meesters, C. (2000). Monitoring and anxiety disorders in children. *Personality and Individual Differences, 29*(4), 775–781.

Muris, P., & Merckelbach, H. (2000). The parent's point of view. *Behaviour Research and Therapy, 38*(8), 813–818.

Muris, P., Merckelbach, H., Mayer, B., & Prins, E. (2000). How serious are common childhood fears? *Behaviour Research and Therapy, 38*(3), 217–228.

Muris, P., Merckelbach, H., Meesters, C., & van den Brand, K. (2002). Cognitive development and worry in normal children. *Cognitive Therapy and Research, 26*(6), 775–785.

Muris, P., Merckelbach, H., Ollendick, T., King, N., & Bogie, N. (2002). Three traditional and three new childhood anxiety questionnaires: Their reliability and validity in a normal adolescent sample. *Behaviour Research and Therapy, 40*(7), 753–772.

Muris, P., Merckelbach, H., Wessel, I., & van de Ven, M. (1999). Psychopathological correlates of self-reported behavioural inhibition in normal children. *Behaviour Research and Therapy, 37*(6), 575–576.

Murphy, B. C., Eisenberg, N., Fabes, R. A., Shepard, S., & Guthrie, I. K. (1999). Consistency and change in children's emotionality and regulation: A longitudinal study. *Merrill-Palmer Quarterly, 45*, 413–444.

Murphy, K. R., Barkley, R. A., & Bush, T. (2002). Young adults with attention deficit hyperactivity disorder: Subtype differences in comorbidity, educational and clinical history. *Journal of Nervous and Mental Disease, 190*(3), 147–157.

Murphy, L. B. (1962). *The widening world of childhood.* New York: Basic Books.

Murphy, L. B. (1974). *Growing up in Garden Court.* Oxford, England: Child Welfare League of America.

Murphy, L. B., & Moriarty, A. E. (1976). *Vulnerability, coping and growth from infancy to adolescence.* Oxford, England: Yale University Press.

Murphy, T. K., Petitto, J. M., Voeller, K. K., & Goodman, W. K. (2001). Obsessive compulsive disorder: Is there an association with childhood streptococcal infections and altered immune function? *Seminars in Clinical Neuropsychiatry, 6*(4), 266–276.

Murphy-Brennan, M. G., & Oei, T. P.S. (1999). Is there evidence to show that fetal alcohol syndrome can be prevented? *Journal of Drug Education, 29*(1), 5–24.

Murray, K. T., & Kochanska, G. (2002). Effortful control: Factor structure and relation to externalizing and internalizing behaviors. *Journal of Abnormal Child Psychology, 30*(5), 503–514.

Myers, M. G., Stewart, D. G., & Brown, S. A. (1998). Progression from conduct disorder to antisocial personality disorder following treatment for adolescent substance abuse. *American Journal of Psychiatry, 155*, 479–485.

Nachmias, M., Gunnar, M. R., Mangelsdorf, S., Parritz, R. H., & Buss, K. (1996). Behavioral inhibition and stress reactivity: The moderating role of attachment security. *Child Development, 67*(2), 508–522.

Nadder, T. S., Rutter, M., Silberg, J. L., Maes, H. H., & Eaves, L. J. (2002). Genetic effects on the variation and covariation of attention deficit-hyperactivity disorder (ADHD) and oppositional-defiant disorder/conduct disorder (ODD/CD) symptomalogies across informant and occasion of measurement. *Psychological Medicine, 32*, 39–53.

Nadeau, K. G. (1998). Psychotherapy for adults with ADHD: A call to training. *The ADHD Report, 6*, 9–11.

Nadel, L. (1999). Down syndrome in cognitive neuroscience perspective. In H. Tager-Flusberg (Ed.), *Neurodevelopmental disorders: Developmental cognitive neuroscience* (pp. 197–221). Cambridge, MA: The MIT Press.

Nagin, D., & Tremblay, R. E. (1999). Trajectories of boys' physical aggression, opposition, and hyperactivity on the path to physically violent and nonviolent juvenile delinquency. *Child Development, 70*, 1181–1196.

Nanson, J. L., & Gordon, B. (1999). Psychosocial correlates of mental retardation. In V. L. Schwean & D. H. Saklofske (Eds.), *Handbook of psychosocial characteristics of exceptional children. Plenum series on human exceptionality* (pp. 377–400). Dordrecht, Netherlands: Kluwer Academic Publishers.

Nation, M., Crusto, C., Wandersman, A., Kumpfer, K. L., Seybolt, D., Morrissey-Kane, E., et al. (2003). What works in prevention: Principles of effective prevention programs. *American Psychologist, 58(6/7)*, 449–456.

National Institute of Diabetes and Digestive and Kidney Diseases. (2008, June). Binge eating disorders (NIH Publication No. 04–3589). Retrieved July 20, 2009, from http://win.niddk.nih.gov/publications/binge.htm

National Institute of Mental Health. Child and Adolescent Bipolar Disorder: An Update from the National Institute of Mental Health. Bethesda (MD): National Institute of Mental Health, National Institutes of Health, US Department of Health and Human Services; 2000. (NIH Publication No. 00–4778).

National Institute of Mental Health. (2004). *Preventing child and adolescent mental disorders: Research roundtable on economic burden and cost effectiveness.* Rockville, MD: Author.

National Institute of Mental Health. (2008). The numbers count: Mental disorders in America. Retrieved July 20, 2009, from http://nimh.nih.gov/health/publications/the-numbers-count-mental-disorders-in-america/index.shtml#Eating

National Institute on Alcohol Abuse and Alcoholism (NIAAA). (2005). Underage drinking and related risk behaviors among youth. http://www.niaaa.nih.gov/Resources/DatabaseResources/QuickFacts/Youth/default.htm

National Institute on Drug Abuse (NIDA) (1995). *Epidemiology of inhalant abuse: An international perspective* (Research Monograph #148). Bethesda, MD.

National Institute on Druge Abuse (NIDA). (2000). Anabolic steroid abuse. (Research Report Series, NIH Pub. No. 00–3721). Bethesda, MD.

National Institute on Drug Abuse (NIDA). (2001a). *Hallucinogens and dissociative drugs: Including LSD, PCP, ketamine, dextromethorphan* (Research Report Series, NIH Pub. No. 01–4209). Bethesda, MD.

National Institute on Drug Abuse (NIDA). (2001b). Nicotine addiction. (Research Report Series, NIH Pub. No. 01–4342). Bethesda, MD.

National Institute on Drug Abuse (NIDA). (2002). *Methamphetamine: Abuse and addiction* (Research Report Series, NIH Pub. No. 02–4210). Bethesda, MD.

National Institute on Drug Abuse (NIDA). (2004). *Cocaine: Abuse and addiction* (Research Report Series, NIH Pub. No. 99–4342). Bethesda, MD.

National Institute on Drug Abuse (NIDA). (2005a). *Heroin: Abuse and addiction* (Research Report Series, NIH Pub. No. 05–4165). Bethesda, MD.

National Institute on Drug Abuse (NIDA). (2005b). Inhalant abuse. (Research Report Series, NIH Pub. No. 05–3818). Bethesda, MD.

National Institute on Drug Abuse (NIDA). (2005c). Marijuana abuse. (Research Report Series, NIH Pub. No. 05–3859). Bethesda, MD.

National Institute on Drug Abuse (NIDA). (2005d). *Prescription drugs: Abuse and addiction* (Research Report Series, NIH Pub. No. 05–4881). Bethesda, MD.

National Institute on Drug Abuse (NIDA). (2006). *MDMA (ecstasy) abuse* (Research Report Series, NIH Pub. No. 06–4728). Bethesda, MD.

National Institutes of Health (1994). Attention deficit hyperactivity disorder. NIH Publication No. 96–3572.

National Institutes of Health. (1998). Diagnosis and treatment of attention deficit hyperactivity disorder [Electronic version]. *NIH Consensus Statement Online, 16*(2): 1–37. Available at: consensus.nih.gov/1998/1998AttentionDeficitHyperactivityDisorder110PDF.pdf

Neal, A. M., & Brown, B. J. W. (1994). Fears and anxiety disorders in African American children. In S. Friedman (Ed.), *Symposium on anxiety disorders in African Americans* (pp. 65–75). New York: Springer.

Neal, D. J., & Carey, K. B. (2004). Developing discrepancy within self-regulation theory: Use of personalized normative feedback and personal strivings with heavy-drinking college students. *Addictive Behaviors, 29*(2), 281–297.

Neal, J. A., & Edelmann, R. J. (2003). The etiology of social phobia: Toward a developmental profile. *Clinical Psychology Review, 23*(6), 761–786.

Neemann, J., Hubbard, J., & Masten, A. S. (1995). The changing importance of romantic relationship involvement to competence from late childhood to late adolescence. *Development and Psychopathology, 7*(4), 727–750.

Neiderhiser, J. M., Pike, A., Hetherington, E. M., & Reiss, D. (1998). Adolescent perceptions as mediators of parenting: Genetic and environmental contributions. *Developmental Psychology, 34*(6), 1459–1469.

Neiderhiser, J. M., Reiss, D., Hetherington, E. M., & Plomin, R. (1999). Relationships between parenting and adolescent adjustment over time: Genetic and environmental contributions. *Developmental Psychology, 35*, 680–692.

Neiderhiser, J. M., Reiss, D., Pedersen, N. L., Lichtenstein, P., Spotts, E. L., Hansson, K., et al. (2004). Genetic and environmental influences on mothering of adolescents: A comparison of two samples. *Developmental Psychology, 40*(3), 335–351.

Nelson, C. A. (1995). The ontogeny of human memory: A cognitive neuroscience perspective. *Developmental Psychology, 31*, 723–738.

Nelson, C. A. (1997). The neurobiological basis of early memory development. In *The development of memory in childhood* (pp. 41–82). Hove, England: Psychology Press/Erlbaum.

Nelson, C. A. (1999). How important are the first 3 years of life? *Applied Developmental Science, 3*(4), 235–238.

Nelson, C. A. (2000). Neural plasticity and human development: The role of early experience in sculpting memory systems. *Developmental Science, 3(2)*, 115–136.

Nelson, C. A. (2007). A neurobiological perspective on early human deprivation. *Child Development Perspectives, 1*, 13–18.

Nelson, C. A., & Bloom, F. E. (1997). Child development and neuroscience. *Child Development, 68(5)*, 970–987.

Nelson, C. A., Bloom, F. E., Cameron, J. L., Amaral, D., Dahl, R. E., & Pine, D. (2002). An integrative, multidisciplinary approach to the study of brain-behavior relations in the context of typical and atypical development. *Development and Psychopathology, 14(3)*, 499–520.

Nelson, C. A., & Bosquet, M. (2000). Neurobiology of fetal and infant development: Implications for infant mental health. In C. H. Zeanah (Ed.), *Handbook of infant mental health* (pp. 37–59). New York: Guilford Press.

Nelson, C. A., Zeanah, C. H., & Fox, N. A. (2007). The effects of early deprivation on brain-behavioral development: The Bucharest early intervention project. In D. Romner & E. F. Walker (Eds.), *Adolescent psychopathology and the developing brain: Integrating brain and prevention science* (pp. 197–215). New York: Oxford University Press.

Nelson, C. A., Zeanah, C. H., Fox, N. A., Marshall, P. J., Smyke, A. T., & Guthne, D. (2007). Cognitive recovery in socially deprived young children: The Bucharest early intervention project. *Science, 318*, 1937–1940.

Nelson, C. B., & Wittchen, H-U. (1998). DSM-IV alcohol disorders in a general population sample of adolescents and young adults. *Addiction, 93*(7), 1065–1077.

Nelson-LeGall, S. (1981). Help-seeking: An understudied problem-solving skill in children. *Developmental Review, 1*, 224–246.

Nemeroff, C. B. (2004). Neurobiological consequences of childhood trauma. *Journal of Clinical Psychiatry, 65*, 18–28.

Nemeroff, C. B., & Vale, W. W. (2005). The neurobiology of depression: Inroads to treatment and new drug discovery. *Journal of Clinical Psychiatry, 66*(Suppl. 7), 5–13.

Neumark-Sztainer, D, Levine, M. P., Paxton, S. J., Smolak, L., Piran, N., & Wertheim, E. H. (2006). Prevention of body dissatisfaction and disordered eating: What next? *Eating Disorders: The Journal of Treatment and Prevention, 14*, 265–285.

Neuner, F., Schauer, E., Catani, C., Ruf, M., & Elbert, T. (2006). Post-tsunami stress: A study of posttraumatic stress disorder in children living in three severely affected regions in Sri Lanka. *Journal of Traumatic Stress, 19*(3), 339–347.

Nevo, B., & Bin Khader, A. M. (1995). Cross-cultural, gender, and age differences in Singaporean mothers' conceptions of children's intelligence. *The Journal of Social Psychology, 135*(4), 509–517.

Newcombe, N. S. (2002). The nativist-empiricist controversy in the context of recent research on spatial and quantitative development. *Psychological Science, 13(5)*, 395–401.

Newes-Adeyi, G., Chen, C. M., Williams, G. D., & Faden, V. B. (2005). *Surveillance Report #74: Trends in underage drinking in the United States, 1991–2003*. Bethesda, MD: National Institute on Alcohol Abuse and Alcoholism.

Newman, D. L., Moffitt, T. E., Caspi, A., Magdol, L., Silva, P. A., & Stanton, W. R. (1996). Psychiatric disorder in a birth cohort young adults: Prevalence, comorbidity, clinical significance, and new case incidence from ages 11 to 21. *Journal of Consulting and Clinical Psychology, 64(3)*, 552–562.

Niccols, G. A. (1994). Fetal alcohol syndrome: Implications for psychologists. *Clinical Psychology Review, 14*(2), 91–111.

Nichols, S. L., & Waschbusch, D. A. (2004). A review of the validity of laboratory cognitive tasks used to assess symptoms of ADHD. *Child Psychiatry and Human Development, 34*(4), 297–315.

Nickels, K. C., Katusic, S. K., Colligan, R. C., Weaver, A. L., Voight, R. G., & Barbaresi, W. J. (2008). Stimulant medication treatment of target behaviors in children with autism: A population-based study. *Journal of Developmental and Behavioral Pediatrics, 29*(2), 75–81.

Nigg, J. T. (2006). Temperament and developmental psychopathology. *Journal of Child Psychology and Psychiatry, 47*(3/4), 395–422.

Nigg, J. T., Glass, J. M., Wong, M. M., Poon, E., Jester, J. M., Fitzgerald, H., et al. (2004). Neuropsychological executive functioning in children at elevated risk for alcoholism: Findings in early adolescence. *Journal of Abnormal Psychology, 113*(2), 302–314.

Nishimura, S. T., Goebert, D. A., Ramisetty-Mikler, S., & Caetano, R. (2005). Adolescent alcohol use and suicide indicators among adolescents in Hawaii. *Cultural Diversity and Ethnic Minority Psychology, 11*(4), 309–320.

Nishina, A., Ammon, N. Y., Bellmore, A. D., & Graham, S. (2006). Body disatisfaction and physical development among ethnic minority adolescents. *Journal of Youth and Adolescence, 35,* 189–201.

Nix, R. L., Pinderhughes, E. E., Bierman, K. L., Maples, J. J., & Conduct Problems Prevention Research Group. (2005). Decoupling the relation between risk factors for conduct problems and the receipt of intervention services: Participation across multiple components of a prevention program. *American Journal of Community Psychology, 36*(3–4), 307–325.

Nixon, R. D. V., Sweeney, L., Erickson, D. B., & Touyz, S. W. (2003). Parent-child interaction therapy: One- and two-year follow-up of standard and abbreviated treatments for oppositional preschoolers. *Journal of Abnormal Child Psychology, 32*(3), 263–271.

Nixon, R. D. V., Sweeney, L., Erickson, D. B., & Touyz, S. W. (2004). Parent-child interaction therapy: A comparison of standard and abbreviated treatments for oppositional defiant preschoolers. *Journal of Consulting and Clinical Psychology, 71*(2), 251–260.

Nobakht, M., & Dezhkam, M. (2000). An epidemiological study of eating disorders in Iran. *International Journal of Eating Disorders, 28,* 265–271.

Nock, M. K., & Kazdin, A. E. (2005). Randomized controlled trial of a brief intervention for increasing participation in parent management training. *Journal of Consulting and Clinical Psychology, 73*(5), 872–879.

Nock, M. K., Kazdin, A. E., Hiripi, E., & Kessler, R. C. (2006). Prevalence, subtypes, and correlates of DSM-IV conduct disorder in the National Comorbidity Survey Replication. *Psychological Medicine, 36,* 699–710.

Nock, M. K., Kazdin, A. E., Hiripi, E., & Kessler, R. C. (2007). Lifetime prevalence, correlates, and persistence of oppositional defiant disorder: Results from the National Comorbidity Study replication. Journal of Child Psychology and Psychiatry, 48(7), 703–713.

Nock, M. K., & Prinstein, M. J. (2004). A functional approach to the assessment of self-mutilative behavior. *Journal of Consulting and Clinical Psychology, 72*(5), 885–890.

Nock, M. K., & Prinstein, M. J. (2005). Contextual features and behavioral functions of self-mutilation among adolescents. *Journal of Abnormal Psychology, 114*(1), 140–146.

Nolan, S. A., Flynn, C., & Garber, J. (2003). Prospective relations between rejection and depression in young adolescents. *Journal of Personality and Social Psychology, 85*(4), 745–755.

Nolen-Hoeksema, S. (1998). Ruminative coping with depression. In J. Heckhausen & C. S. Dweck (Eds.), *Motivation and self-regulation across the life span* (pp. 237–256). New York: Cambridge University Press.

Nolen-Hoeksema, S. (1998). The other end of the continuum: The costs of rumination. *Psychological Inquiry, 9*(3), 216–219.

Nolen-Hoeksema, S. (2002). Gender differences in depression. In I. H. Gotlib & C. L. Hammen (Eds.), *Handbook of depression* (pp. 492–509). New York: Guilford Press.

Nolen-Hoeksema, S., & Corte, C. (2004). Gender and self-regulation. From R. F. Baumeister & K. D. Vohs (Eds.), *Handbook of self-regulation: Research theory and applications* (pp. 411–421). New York: Guilford Press.

Nolen-Hoeksema, S., & Girgus, J. S. (1994). The emergence of gender differences in depression during adolescence. *Psychological Bulletin, 115*(3), 424–443.

Nolen-Hoeksema, S., Girgus, J. S., & Seligman, M. E. (1992). Predictors and consequences of childhood depressive symptoms: A 5-year longitudinal study. *Journal of Abnormal Psychology, 101*(3), 405–422.

Nottelmann, E. D., & Jensen, P. S. (1995). Comorbidity of disorders in children and adolescents: Developmental perspectives. In T. H. Ollendick & R. J. Prinz (Eds.), *Advances in Clinical Child Psychology* (Vol. 17, pp. 109–155). New York: Plenum Press.

Nottelmann, E., Biederman, J., Birmaher, B., Carlson, G. A., Chang, K. D., Fenton, W. S., et al. (2001). National Institute of Mental Health research roundtable on prepubertal bipolar disorder. *Journal of the American Academy of Child and Adolescent Psychiatry, 40*(8), 871–878.

Nowicki, E. A., & Sandieson, R. (2002). A meta-analysis of school-age children's attitudes towards persons with physical or intellectual disabilities. *International Journal of Disability, Development and Education, 49*(3), 243–265.

O'Brien, C. P., Charney, D. S., Lewis, L., Cornish, J., Post, R., Woody, G. et al. (2004). Priority actions to improve the care of persons with co-occurring substance abuse and other mental disorders: A call to action. *Biological Psychiatry, 56*(10), 703–713.

O'Brien, G. V. (1999). Protecting the social body: Use of the organism metaphor in fighting the "menace of the feebleminded." *Mental Retardation, 37*(3), 188–200.

O'Connor, N. & Hermelin, B. (1994). Two autistic savant readers. *Journal of Autism and Developmental Disorders, 24*(4), 501–515.

O'Connor, T. G., Deater-Deckard, K., Fulker, D., Rutter, M., & Plomin, R. (1998). Genotype-environment correlations in late childhood and early adolescence: Antisocial behavioral problems and coercive parenting. *Developmental Psychology, 34,* 970–981.

O'Connor, T. G., McGuire, S., Reiss, D., & Hetherington, E. M. (1998). Co-occurrence of depressive symptoms and antisocial behavior in adolescence: A common genetic liability. *Journal of Abnormal Pscyhology, 107,* 27–37.

O'Connor, T. G., & Zeanah, C. H. (2003). Attachment disorders: Assessment strategies and treatment approaches. *Attachment and Human Development, 5*(3), 223–244.

O'Dea, J. A., & Abraham, S. (1999). Onset of disordered eating attitudes and behaviors in early adolescence: Interplay of pubertal status, gender, weight, and age. *Adolescence, 34,* 671–679.

O'Dea, J. A., & Abraham, S. (2000). Improving the body image, eating attitudes, and behaviors of young male and female adolescents: A new educational approach that focuses on self-esteem. *International Journal of Eating Disorders, 28,* 43–57.

O'Donnell, L., O'Donnell, C., Wardlaw, D. M., & Stueve, A. (2004). Risk and resiliency factors influencing suicidality among urban African American and Latino youth. *American Journal of Community Psychology, 33*(1–2), 37–49.

O'Leary Tevyaw, T., & Monti, P. M. (2004). Motivational enhancement and other brief interventions for adolescent substance abuse: Foundations, applications and evaluations. *Addiction, 99*(Suppl. 2), 63–75.

O'Leary, T. A., Brown, S. A., Colby, S. M., Cronce, J. M., D'Amico, E. J., Fader, J. S., et al. (2002). Treating adolescents together or individually? Issues in adolescent substance abuse interventions. *Alcoholism: Clinical and Experimental Research, 26*(6), 890–899.

O'Malley, P. M., & Johnston, L. D. (2003). Unsafe driving by high school seniors: National trends from 1976 to 2001 in ticket and accidents after use of alcohol, marijuana and other illegal drugs. *Journal of Studies on Alcohol, 64*(3), 305–312.

O'Malley, P. M., Johnston, L. D., & Bachman, J. G. (1998). Alcohol use among adolescents. *Alcohol Health and Research World, 22*(2), 85–93.

Oades, R. D. (1998). Frontal, temporal and lateralized brain function in children with attention-deficit hyperactivity disorder: A psychophysiological and neuropsychological viewpoint on development. *Behavioural Brain Research, 94,* 83–95.

Oberklaid, F., Prior, M., Nolan, T., & Smith, P. (1986). Temperament in infants born prematurely. *Annual Progress in Child Psychiatry and Child Development,* 386–396.

Offer, D. (1999). Normality and the boundaries of psychiatry. In S. Weissman & M. Sabshin (Eds.), *Psychiatry in the new millennium* (pp. 67–77). Washington, DC: American Psychiatric Association.

Offit, P. A. (2008). *Autism's false prophets.* New York: Columbia University Press.

Offord, D. R., Boyle, M. H., Racine, Y., Szatmari, P., Fleming, J. E., Sanford, M., et al. (1996). Integrating assessment data from multiple informants. *Journal of the American Academy of Child and Adolescent Psychiatry, 35*(8), 1078–1085.

Ogawa, J. R., Sroufe, L. A., Weinfield, N. S., Carlson, E. A., & Egeland, B. (1997). Development and the fragmented self: Longitudinal study of dissociative symptomatology in a nonclinical sample. *Development and Psychopathology, 9,* 855–879.

Ohannessian, C. M., Hesselbrock, V. M., Kramer, J., Kuperman, S., Bucholz, K. K., Schuckit, M. A., et al. (2004). The relationship between parental alcoholism and adolescent psychopathology: A systematic examination of parental comorbid psychopathology. *Journal of Abnormal Child Psychology, 32*(5), 519–533.

Ohannessian, C. M., Hesselbrock, V. M., Kramer, J., Kuperman, S., Bucholz, K. K., Schuckit, M. A., et al. (2005). The relationship between parental psychopathology and adolescent psychopathology: An examination of gender patterns. *Journal of Emotional and Behavioral Disorders, 13*(2), 67–76.

Okasha, A. (2002). The new ethical context of psychiatry. In N. Sartorius & W. Gaebel (Eds.), *Psychiatry in society* (pp. 101–130). New York: Wiley.

Oldehinkel, A. J., Hartman, C. A., Ferdinand, R. F., Verhulst, F. C., & Ormel, J. (2007). Effortful control as modifier of the association between negative emotionality and adolescents'

mental health problems. *Development and Psychopathology, 19,* 523–539.

Olfson, M., Gameroff, M. H., Marcus, S. C., & Waslick, B. D. (2003). Outpatient treatment of child and adolescent depression in the United States. *Archives of General Psychiatry, 60*(12), 1236–1242.

Ollendick, T. H., Birmaher, B., & Mattis, S. G. (2004). Panic disorder. In T. L. Morris & J. S. March (Eds.), *Anxiety disorders in children and adolescents* (2nd ed., pp. 189–211). New York: Guilford Press.

Ollendick, T. H., King, N. J., & Muris, P. (2002). Fears and phobias in children: Phenomenology, epidemiology, and aetiology. *Child and Adolescent Mental Health, 7*(3), 98–106.

Ollendick, T. H., & King, N. J. (1991). Origins of childhood fears: An evaluation of Rachman's theory of fear acquisition. *Behaviour Research and Therapy, 29*(2), 117–123.

Ollendick, T. H, & King, N. J. (1998). Empirically supported treatments for children with phobic and anxiety disorders: Current status. *Journal of Clinical Child Psychology, 27*(2), 156–167.

Ollendick, T. H., Matson, J. L., & Helsel, W. J. (1985). Fears in children and adolescents: Normative data. *Behaviour Research and Therapy, 23*(4), 465–467.

Ollendick, T. H., Mattis, S. G., & King, N. J. (1994). Panic in children and adolescents: A review. *Journal of Child Psychology and Psychiatry and Allied Disciplines, 35*(1), 113–134.

Ollendick, T. H., Shortt, A. L., & Sander, J. B. (2005). Internalizing disorders of childhood and adolescence. In J. E. Maddux & B. A. Winstead (Eds.), *Psychopathology: Foundations for a contemporary understanding* (pp. 353–376). Mahwah, NJ: Erlbaum.

Ollendick, T. H., & Vasey, M. W. (1999). Developmental theory and the practice of clinical child psychology. *Journal of Clinical Child Psychology, 28*(4), 457–466.

Ollendick, T. H., Vasey, M. W., & King, N. J. (2001). Operant conditioning influences in childhood anxiety. In M. W. Vasey & M. R. Dadds (Eds.), *The developmental psychopathology of anxiety* (pp. 231–252). London: Oxford University Press.

Ollendick, T. H., Yang, B., King, N. J., Dong, Q., & Akande, A. (1996). Fears in American, Australian, Chinese, and Nigerian children and adolescents: A cross-cultural study. *Journal of Child Psychology and Psychiatry and Allied Disciplines, 37*(2), 213–220.

Ollendick, T. H., Yule, W., & Ollier, K. (1991). Fears in British children and their relationship to manifest anxiety and depression. *Journal of Child Psychology and Psychiatry, 32*(2), 321–331.

Olson, H. C. (2002). Helping children with fetal alcohol syndrome and related conditions: A clinician's overview. In R. J. McMahon & R. D. Peters (Eds.), *The effects of parental dysfunction on children* (pp. 147–177). New York: Kluwer Academic/Plenum Press.

Olson, S. L., Schilling, E. M., & Bates, J. E. (1999). Measurement of impulsivity: Construct coherence, longitudinal stability, and relationship with externalizing problems in middle childhood and adolescence. *Journal of Abnormal Child Psychology, 27,* 151–165.

Olweus, D. (2005). A useful evaluation design, and effects of the Olweus Bullying Prevention Program. *Psychology, Crime and Law, 11*(4), 389–402.

Oquendo, M., Brent, D. A., Birmaher, B., Greenhill, L., Kolko, D., Stanley, B., et al. (2005). Posttraumatic stress disorder comorbid with major depression: Factors mediating the association with suicidal behavior. *American Journal of Psychiatry, 162*(3), 560–566.

Orenstein, S., Izadnia, F., & Kahn, S. (1999). Gastroesophageal reflux in children. *Gastroenterology Clinics of North America, 28*(4), 947–969.

Orlando, M., Tucker, J. S., Ellickson, P. L., & Klein, D. J. (2004). Developmental trajectories of cigarette smoking and their correlates from early adolescence to young adulthood. *Journal of Consulting and Clinical Psychology, 72*(3), 400–410.

Orlando, M., Tucker, J. S., Ellickson, P. L., & Klein, D. J. (2005). Concurrent use of alcohol and cigarettes from adolescence to young adulthood: An examination of developmental trajectories and outcomes. *Substance Use and Misuse, 40*(8), 1051–1069.

Ornoy, A. (2002). The effects of alcohol and illicit drugs on the human embryo and fetus. *Israel Journal of Psychiatry and Related Sciences, 39*(2), 120–132.

Orpinas, P., & Horne, A. M. (2006a). Bullies: The problem and its impact. In P. Orpinas & A. M. Horne (Eds.), *Bullying prevention: Creating a positive school climate and developing social competence* (pp. 11–31). Washington, DC: American Psychological Association.

Orpinas, P., & Horne, A. M. (2006b). *Bullying prevention: Creating a positive school climate and developing social competence.* Washington, DC: American Psychological Association.

Orrell-Valente, J. K., Pinderhughes, E. E., Valente, E. Jr., Laird, R. D., & Conduct Problems Prevention Research Group. (1999). If it's offered, will they come? Influences on parents' participation in a community-based conduct problems prevention program. *American Journal of Community Psychology, 27*(6), 753–783.

Osborne, L. & Pober, B. (2001). Genetics of childhood disorders: XXVII. Genes and cognition in Williams syndrome. *Journal of the American Academy of Child and Adolscent Psychiatry, 40*(6), 732–735.

Osborne, M. S., & Kenny, D. T. (2005). Development and validation of a music performance anxiety inventory for gifted adolescent musicians. *Journal of Anxiety Disorders, 19*(7), 725–751.

Osborne, M. S., Kenny, D. T., & Holsomback, R. (2005). Assessment of music performance anxiety in late childhood: A validation study of the Music Performance Anxiety Inventory for Adolescents (MPAI-A). *International Journal of Stress Management, 12*(4), 312–330.

Osofsky, J. D. (2003). Prevalence of children's exposure to domestic violence and child maltreatment: Implications for prevention and intervention. *Clinical Child and Family Psychology Review, 6*(3), 161–170.

Osterling, J. A., & Dawson, G. (1994). Early recognition of children with autism: A study of first birthday home videotapes. *Journal of Autism and Developmental Disorders, 24*, 247–257.

Osterling, J. A., Dawson, G., & Munson, J. A. (2002). Early recognition of 1-year-old infants with autism spectrum disorder versus mental retardation. *Development and Psychopathology, 14*, 239–251.

Ostrander, R., & Herman, K. C. (2006). Potential cognitive, parenting, and developmental mediators of the relationship between ADHD and depression. *Journal of Consulting and Clinical Psychology, 74*(1), 89–98.

Overman, W. H., Frassrand, K., Ansel, S., Trawalter, S., Bies, B., & Redmond, A. (2004). Performance on the IOWA card task by adolescents and adults. *Neuropsychologia, 42*(13), 1838–1851.

Owens, E. B., Shaw, D. S., & Vondra, J. I. (1998). Relations between infant irritability and maternal responsiveness in low-income families. *Infant Behavior and Development, 21*(4), 761–777.

Owens J. S., & Hoza, B. (2003). Diagnostic utility of DSM-IV-TR symptoms in the prediction of DSM-IV-TR ADHD subtypes and ODD. *Journal of Attention Disorders, 7*(1), 11–27.

Owens, P. L., Hoagwood, K., Horwitz, S. M., Leaf, P. J., Poduska, J. M., Kellam, S. G., et al. (2002). Barriers to children's mental health services. *Journal of the American Academy of Child and Adolescent Psychiatry, 41*(6), 731–738.

Ozonoff, S. (1997). Components of executive function in autism and other disorders. In J. Russell (Ed.), *Autism as an executive disorder* (pp. 179–211). New York: Oxford University Press.

Ozonoff, S. (1998). Assessment and remediation of executive dysfunction in autism and Asperger syndrome. In E. Schopler, G. Mesibov & L. J. Kunce (Eds.), *Asperger syndrome or high functioning autism?* (pp. 263–289). New York: Plenum Press.

Ozonoff, S., & Griffith, E. M. (2000). Neuropsychological function and the external validity of Asperger syndrome. In A. Klin, F. R. Volkmar, & S. S. Sparrow (Eds.), *Asperger syndrome* (pp. 72–96). New York: Guilford Press.

Ozonoff, S., South, M., & Miller, J. N. (2000). DSM-IV-defined Asperger syndrome: Cognitive, behavioral and early history differentiation from high-functioning autism. *Autism, 4*, 29–46.

Page, R. M., Lee, C., & Miao, N. (2005). Self-perception of body weight among high school students in Taipei, Taiwan. *International Journal of Adolescent Medicine and Health, 17*, 123–136.

Page, T. (2000). Metabolic approaches to the treatment of autism spectrum disorders. *Journal of Autism and Developmental Disorders, 30*, 463–469.

Palmer, D. S., Borthwick-Duffy, S. A., Widman, K., & Best, S. J. (1998). Influences on parent perceptions of inclusive practices for their children with mental retardation. *American Journal on Mental Retardation, 103*(3), 272–287.

Panfilis, C. de, Rabbaglio, P., Rossi, C., Zita G., & Maggini, C. (2003). Body image disturbance, parental bonding and alexithymia in patients with eating disorders. *Psychopathology, 36*, 239–246.

Panksepp, J. (1998). Attention deficit hyperactivity disorders, psychostimulants, and intolerance of childhood playfulness: A tragedy in the making. *American Psychological Society, 7*(3), 91–98.

Papadakis, A. A., Prince, R. P., Jones, N. P., & Strauman, T. J. (2006). Self-regulation, rumination, and vulnerability to depression in adolescent girls. *Development and Psychopathology, 18*, 815–829.

Papezova, H, Yamamotova, A., & Uher, R. (2005). Elevated pain threshold in eating disorders: Physiological and psychological factors. *Journal of Psychiatric Research, 39*, 431–438.

Pappas, D. (2006). Review of ADHD rating scale-IV: Checklists, norms, and clinical interpretation. *Journal of Psychoeducational Assessment, 24*(2), 172–178.

Parent, S., Normandeua, S., & Larivée, S. (2000). A quest for the holy grail in the new millennium: In search of a unified theory of cognitive development. *Child Development, 71*(4), 860–861.

Parikh, M. S., Kolevzon, A., & Hollander, E. (2008). Psychopharmacology of aggression in children and adolescents with autism: A critical review of efficacy and tolerability. *Journal of Child and Adolescent Psychopharmacology, 18*(2), 157–178.

Parke, R. D. (2001). Introduction to the special section on families and religion: A call for a recommitment by researchers, practitioners, and policymakers. *Journal of Family Psychology, 15*(4), 555–558.

Parke, R. D. (2004a). Development in the family. *Annual Review of Psychology, 55,* 365–399.

Parke, R. D. (2004b). Fathers, families, and the future: A plethora of plausible predictions. *Merrill-Palmer Quarterly, 50(4),* 456–470.

Parke, R. D., Dennis, J., Flyr, M. L., Morris, K. L., Leidy, M. S., & Schofield, T. J. (2005). Fathers: Cultural and ecological perspectives. In T. Luster & L. Okagaki (Eds.), *Parenting: An ecological perspective* (2nd ed., pp. 103–144). Mahwah, NJ: Erlbaum.

Parker, J. G., Rubin, K. H., Price, J. M., & DeRosier, M. E. (1995). Peer relationships, child development, and adjustment: A developmental psychopathology perspective. In D. Cicchetti & D. J. Cohen (Eds.), *Developmental psychopathology: Vol. 2. Risk, disorder, and adaptation* (pp. 96–161). New York: Wiley.

Parker, L. S., & Gettig, E. (1997). Ethical issues in genetic screening and testing, gene therapy, and scientific conduct. In K. Blum & E. P. Noble (Eds.), *Handbook of Psychiatric Genetics,* (pp. 469–478). Boca Raton, FL: CRC Press.

Parmelee, A. H. (1986). Children's illnesses: Their beneficial effects on behavioral development. *Child Development, 57,* 1–10.

Patel, N. C., DelBello, M. P., Cecil, K. M., Adler, C. M., Bryan, H. S., Stanford, K. E., et al. (2006). Lithium treatment effects on myo-inositol in adolescents with bipolar depression. *Biological Psychiatry, 60*(9), 998–1004.

Patterson, G. R. (1997). Performance models for parenting: A social interactional perspective. In J. E. Grusec & L. Kuczynski (Eds.), *Parenting and children's internalization of values: A handbook of contemporary theory* (pp. 193–226). New York: Wiley.

Patterson, G. R. (2002). The early development of coercive family process. In J. B. Reid & G. R. Patterson (Eds.), *Antisocial behavior in children and adolescents: A developmental analysis and model for intervention* (pp. 25–44). Washington, DC: American Psychological Association.

Patterson, G. R., DeGarmo, D. S., & Knutson, N. (2000). Hyperactivity and antisocial behaviors: Comorbid or two points in the same process? *Development and Psychopathology, 12*(1), 91–106.

Patterson, G. R., Dishion, T. J., & Yoerger, K. (2000). Adolescent growth in new forms of problem behavior: Macro- and micro-peer dynamics. *Prevention Science, 1*(1), 3–13.

Patterson, G. R., & Fisher, P. A. (2002). Recent developments in our understanding of parenting: Bidirectional effects, causal models, and the search for parsimony. In M. H. Bornstein (Ed.), *Handbook of parenting: Vol. 5. Practical issues in parenting* (2nd ed., pp. 59–88). Mahwah, NJ: Erlbaum.

Patterson, G. R., & Yoerger, K. (2002). A developmental model for early- and late-onset delinquency. In J. B. Reid & G. R. Patterson (Eds.) *Antisocial behavior in children and adolescents: A developmental analysis and model for intervention* (pp. 147–172). Washington, DC: American Psychological Association.

Patterson, G. R., Reid, J. B., & Dishion, T. J. (1992). *Antisocial boys.* Eugene, OR: Castalia.

Patterson, G. R., Reid, J. B., & Eddy, J. M. (2002). A brief history of the Oregon model. In J. B. Reid & G. R. Patterson (Eds.), *Antisocial behavior in children and adolescents: A developmental analysis and model for intervention* (pp. 3–20). Washington, DC: American Psychological Association.

Patterson, G. R., & Stoolmiller, M. (1991). Replications of a dual failure model for boys' depressed mood. *Journal of Consulting and Clinical Psychology, 59*(4), 491–498.

Patterson, G. R., & Yoerger, K. (1999). Intraindividual growth in covert antisocial behavior: A necessary precursor to chronic juvenile and adult arrests? *Criminal Behaviour and Mental Health, 9*(1), 24–38.

Patton, G. C., Coffey, C., & Sawyer, S. M. (2003). The outcome of adolescent eating disorders: Findings from the Victorian adolescent health cohort study. *European Child and Adolescent Psychiatry, 12,* 125–129.

Paul, R. (1987). Communication. In D. J. Cohen & A. M. Donnellan (Eds.), *Handbook of autism and pervasive developmental disorders* (pp. 61–84). New York: Wiley.

Paul, R. (2003). Promoting social communication in high functioning individuals with autistic spectrum disorders. *Child and Adolescent Psychiatric Clinics of North America, 12,* 87–106.

Paul, R., Cohen, D., Klin, A., & Volmar, F. (1999). Multiplex developmental disorders: The role of communication in the construction of a self. *Child and Adolescent Psychiatric Clinics of North America, 8,* 189–202.

Paulson, J. F., Buermeyer, C., & Nelson-Gray, R. O. (2005). Social rejection and ADHD in young adults: An analogue experiment. *Journal of Attention Disorders, 8*(3), 127–135.

Pavuluri, M. N., Graczyk, P. A., Henry, D. B., Carbray, J. A., Heidenreich, J., & Miklowitz, D. J. (2004). Child- and family-focused cognitive-behavioral therapy for pediatric bipolar disorder: Development and preliminary results. *Journal of the American Academy of Child Adolescent Psychiatry, 43*(5), 528–537.

Pavuluri, M. N., Janicak, P. G., Naylor, M. W., & Sweeney, J. A. (2003). Early recognition and differentiation of pediatric schizophrenia and bipolar disorder. In L. T. Flaherty (Ed.), *Adolescent psychiatry: Developmental and clinical studies* (pp. 117–134). New York: Analytic Press/Taylor & Francis Group.

Paxton, S. J., Norris, M., Wertheim, E. H., Durkin, S. J., & Anderson, J. (2005). Body dissatisfaction, dating, and the importance of thinness to attractiveness in adolescent girls. *Sex Roles, 53,* 663–675.

Peake, P. K., Hebl, M., & Mischel, W. (2002). Strategic attention deployment for the delay of gratification in working and waiting situations. *Developmental Psychology, 38*(2), 313–326.

Pearce, M. J., Jones, S. M., Schwab-Stone, M .E., & Ruchkin, V. (2003). The protective effects of religiousness and parent involvement on the development of conduct problems among youth exposed to violence. *Child Development, 74*(6), 1682–1696.

Pearlman-Avnion, S., & Eviatar, Z. (2002). Narrative analysis in developmental social and linguistic pathologies: Dissociation between emotional and informational language use. *Brain and Cognition, 49(2–3),* 494–499.

Pedersen, W., Mastekaasa, A., & Wichstrom, L. (2001). Conduct problems and early cannabis initiation: A longitudinal study of gender differences. *Addiction, 96*(3), 415–431.

Pelham, W. E., & Bender, M. E. (1982). Peer relationships in hyperactive children: Description and treatment. In K. Gadow & E. Bialer (Eds.), *Advances in learning and behavioral disabilities* (pp. 365–436). Greenwich, CT: JAI Press.

Pelham, W. E., Hoza, B., Pillow, D. R., Gnagy, E. M., Kipp, H. L., Greiner, A. R., et al. (2002). Effects of methyphenidate and expectancy on children with ADHD: Behavior, academic performance, and attributions in a summer treatment program and regular classroom settings. *Journal of Consulting and Clinical Psychology, 70*(2), 320–335.

Pelham, W. E., Waschbusch, D. A., Hoza, B., Pillow, D. R., & Gnagy, E. (2001). Effects of methylphenidate and expectancy on performance, self-evaluation, persistence, and attributions on a social task in boys with ADHD. *Experimental and Clinical Psychopharmacology, 9*(4), 425–437.

Pelkonen, M., Marttunen, M., Henriksson, M., & Lonnqvist, J. (2005). Suicidality in adjustment disorder: Clinical characteristics of adolescent outpatients. *European Child and Adolescent Psychiatry, 14*(3), 174–180.

Pelletier, J., Collett, B., Gimpel, G., & Crowley, S. (2006). Assessment of disruptive behaviors in preschoolers: Psychometric properties of the Disruptive Behavior Disorders Rating Scale and School Situations Questionnaire. *Journal of Psychoeducational Assessment, 24*(1), 3–18.

Pelletier, S., & Dorval, M. (2004). Predictive genetic testing raises new professional challenges of psychologists. *Canadian Psychology, 45*(1), 16–30.

Pennington, B. F. (2002). *The development of psychopathology: Nature and nurture.* New York: Guilford Press.

Pennington, B. F., Moon, J., Edgin, J., Stedron, J., & Nadel, L. (2003). The neuropsychology of Down syndrome: Evidence for hippocampal dysfunction. *Child Development, 74*(1), 75–93.

Pentz, M. A. (2003). Evidence-based prevention: Characteristics, impact, and future. *Journal of Psychoactive Drugs, 35*(Suppl. 1), 143–152.

Pentz, M. A., Mares, D., Schinke, S., & Rohrbach, L. A. (2004). Political science, public policy, and drug use prevention. *Substance Use and Misuse, 39*(10–12), 1821–1865.

Pepler, D., Jiang, D., Craig, W., & Connolly, J. (2008). Developmental trajectories of bullying and associated factors. *Child Development, 79*(2), 325–338.

Perez, M, Joiner, T. E., & Lewinsohn, P. M. (2004). Is major depressive disorder or dysthymia more strongly associated with bulimia nervosa? *International Journal of Eating Disorders, 36,* 55–61.

Perkins, D. F., & Jones, K. R. (2004). Risk behaviors and resiliency within physically abused adolescents. *Child Abuse and Neglect, 28,* 547–563.

Perkins, D. F., Luster, T., & Jank, W. (2002). Protective factors, physical abuse, and purging from community-wide surveys of female adolescents. *Journal of Adolescent Research, 17,* 377–400.

Perkonigg, A., Pfister, H., Stein, M. B., Höfler, M., Lieb, R., Maercker, A., et al. (2005). Longitudinal course of posttraumatic stress disorder and posttraumatic stress disorder symptoms in a community sample of adolescents and young adults. *American Journal of Psychiatry, 162*(7), 1320–1327.

Perren, S., & Alsaker, F. D. (2006). Social behavior and peer relationship of victims, bully-victims, and bullies in kindergarten. *Journal of Child Psychology and Psychiatry, 47*(1), 45–57.

Perry, A. C., Rosenblatt, E. B., & Wang, X. (2004). Physical, behavioral, and body image characteristics in a tri-racial group of adolescent girls. *Obesity Research, 12,* 1670–1679.

Perry, B. D., Pollard, R. A., Blakley, T. L., Baker, W. L., & Vigilante, D. (1995). Childhood trauma, the neurobiology of adaptation, and use-dependent development of the brain: How states become traits. *Infant Mental Health Journal, 16,* 271–291.

Pérusse, D., & Gendreau, P. L. (2005). Genetics and the development of aggression. In R. E. Tremblay, W. W. Hartup, & J. Archer (Eds.), *Developmental origins of aggression* (pp. 220–241). New York: Guilford Press.

Pescosolido, B. A. (2007). Culture, children, and mental health treatment: Special section on the National Stigma Study—Children. *Psychiatric Services, 58*(5), 611–612.

Pescosolido, B. A., Fettes, D. L., Martin, J. K., Monahan, J. & McLeod, J. D. (2007). Perceived dangerousness of children with mental health problems and support for coerced treatment. *Psychiatric Services, 58*(5), 619–625.

Peterson, A. V., Kealey, K. A., Mann, S. L., Marek, P. M., & Sarason, I. G. (2000). Hutchinson Smoking Prevention Project: Long-term randomized trial in school-based tobacco use prevention – Results on smoking. *Journal of the National Cancer Institute, 92,* 1979–1991.

Petrill, S. A., Lipton, P. A., Hewitt, J. K., Plomin, R., Cherny, S. A., Corley, R., et al. (2004). Genetic and environmental contributions to general cognitive ability through the first 16 years of life. *Developmental Psychology, 40*(5), 805–812.

Petry, N. M. (2005). Prevention: Focus on gambling in youth and young adults. In Petry, N. M. *Pathological gambling: Etiology, comorbidity, and treatment* (pp. 269–278). Washington, DC: American Psychological Association.

Petti, T., Reich, W., Todd, R. D., Joshi, P., Galvin, M., Reich, T., et al. (2004). Psychosocial variables in children and teens of extended families identified through bipolar affective disorder probands. *Bipolar Disorders, 6*(2), 106–114.

Pettit, G. S., & Dodge, K. A. (2003). Violent children: Bridging development, intervention, and public policy. *Developmental Psychology, 39*(2), 187–188.

Pfefferbaum, B. (1997). Posttraumatic stress disorder in children: A review of the past 10 years. *Journal of the American Academy of Child and Adolescent Psychiatry, 36*(11), 1503–1511.

Pfeifer, M., Goldsmith, H. H., Davidson, R. J., & Rickman, M. (2002). Continuity and change in inhibited and uninhibited children. *Child Development, 73*(5), 1474–1485.

Phares, V. (1996). *Fathers and developmental psychopathology.* New York: Wiley.

Phares, V., Steinberg, A. R., & Thompson, J. K. (2004). Gender differences in peer and parental influences: Body image disturbance, self-worth, and psychological functioning in preadolescent children. *Journal of Youth and Adolescence, 33,* 421–429.

Philadelphia Child Guidance Center. (1993). *Your child's emotional health: The middle years.*

Phillips, B. M., Lonigan, C. J., Driscoll, K., & Hooe, E. S. (2002). Positive and negative affectivity in children: A multitrait-multimethod investigation. *Journal of Clinical Child and Adolescent Psychology, 31*(4), 465–479.

Phillips, W., Baron-Cohen, S., & Rutter, M. (1998). Understanding intention in normal development and in autism. *British Journal of Developmental Psychology, 16,* 337–348.

Pickens, R. W., Svikis, D. S., McGue, M., & LaBuda, M. C. (1995). Common genetic mechanisms in alcohol, drug, and mental disorder comorbidity. *Drug and Alcohol Dependence, 39*(2), 129–138.

Pierce, E. W., Ewing, L. J., & Campbell, S. B. (1999). Diagnostic status and symptomatic behavior of hard-to-manage preschool children in middle childhood and early adolescence. *Journal of Clinical Child Psychology, 28,* 44–57.

Pierce, K., & Courchesne, E. (2001). Evidence for a cerebellar role in reduced exploration and stereotyped behavior in autism. *Biological Psychiatry, 49,* 655–664.

Pierce, K., Muller, R., Ambrose, J., Allen, G., & Courchesne, E. (2001). Face processing occurs outside the fusiform "face area" in autism: Evidence from functional MRI. *Brain: A Journal of Neurology, 124(10),* 2059–2073.

Pike, A., & Plomin, R. (1996). Importance of nonshared environmental factors for childhood adolescent psychopathology. *Journal of the American Academy of Child and Adolescent Psychiatry, 35(5),* 560–570.

Pike, A., Reiss, D., Hetherington, E. M., & Plomin, R. (1996). Using MZ differences in the search for nonshared environmental effects. *Journal of Psychology and Psychiatry and Allied Disciplines, 37(6),* 695–704.

Pillow, D. R., Pelham, W. E., Hoza, B., Molina, B. S. G., & Stultz, C. H. (1998). Confirmatory factor analyses examining attention deficit hyperactivity disorder symptoms and other childhood disruptive behaviors. *Journal of Abnormal Child Psychology, 26,* 293–309.

Pina, A. A., & Silverman, W. K. (2004). Clinical phenomenology, somatic symptoms, and distress in Hispanic/Latino and European American youths with anxiety disorders. *Journal of Clinical Child and Adolescent Psychology, 33(2),* 227–236.

Pina, A. A., Silverman, W. K., Fuentes, R. M., Kurtines, W. M. & Weems, C. F. (2003). Exposure-based cognitive-behavioral treatment for phobic and anxiety disorders: Treatment effects and maintenance for Hispanic/Latino relative to European-American youths. *Journal of the American Academy of Child and Adolescent Psychiatry, 42(10),* 1179–1187.

Pina, A. A., Silverman, W. K., Weems, C. F., Kurtines, W. M., & Goldman, M. L. (2003). A comparison of completers and noncompleters of exposure-based cognitive and behavioral treatment for phobic and anxiety disorders in youth. *Journal of Consulting and Clinical Psychology, 71(4),* 701–705.

Pinderhughes, E. E., Nix, R., Foster, E. M., Jones, D., & Conduct Problems Prevention Research Group. (2001). Parenting in context: Impact of neighborhood poverty, residential stability, public services, social networks, and danger on parental behaviors. *Journal of Marriage and the Family, 63(4),* 941–953.

Pine, D. S. (1999). Pathophysiology of childhood anxiety disorders. *Biological Psychiatry, 46,* 1555–1566.

Pine, D. S. (2002). Treating children and adolescents with selective serotonin reuptake inhibitors: How long is appropriate? *Journal of Child and Adolescent Psychopharmacology, 12(3),* 189–203.

Pine, D. S. (2003). Developmental psychobiology and response to threats: Relevance to trauma in children and adolescents. *Biological Psychiatry, 53(9),* 796–808.

Pine, D. S., Alegria, M., Cook, E. H., Costello, E. J., Dahl, R. E., Koretz, D., et al. (2002). Advances in developmental sciences andDSM-V. In D. J. Kupfer, M. B. First, & D. A. Regier (Eds.), *A research agenda for DSM-V.* Washington, DC: American Psychiatric Association.

Pine, D. S., & Cohen, J. A. (2002). Trauma in children and adolescents: Risk and treatment of psychiatric sequelae. *Biological Psychiatry, 51(7),* 519–531.

Pine, D. S., Cohen, P. Gurley, D., Brook, J., & Ma, Y. (1998). The risk for early-adulthood anxiety and depressive disorders in adolescents with anxiety and depressive disorders. *Archives of General Psychiatry, 55(1),* 56–64.

Pine, D. S., & Grun, J. (1999). Childhood anxiety: Integrating developmental psychopathology and affective neuroscience. *Journal of Child and Adolescent Psychopharmacology, 9(1),* 1–12.

Pine, D. S., Grun, J., & Peterson, B. S. (2001). Use of magnetic resonance imaging to visualize circuits implicated in developmental disorders: The examples of attention-deficit/hyperactivity disorder and anxiety. In D. D. Dougherty & S. L. Rauch (Eds.), *Psychiatric neuroimaging research: Contemporary strategies* (pp. 335–365). Washington, DC: American Psychiatric Publishing.

Pine, D. S., Walkup, J. T., Labellarte, M. J., Riddle, M. A., Greenhill, L., Klein, R., et al. (2001). Fluvoxamine for the treatment of anxiety disorders in children and adolescents. *New England Journal of Medicine, 344(17),* 1279–1285.

Pine, K. J. (2001). Children's perceptions of body shape: A thinness bias in preadolescent girls and associations with femininity. *Clinical Child Psychology and Psychiatry, 6,* 519–536.

Pinker, S. (2002). *The blank slate: The modern denial of human nature.* New York: Viking.

Piper, M. E., Piasecki, T. M., Federman, E. B., Bolt, D. M., Smith, S. S., Fiore, M. C., et al. (2004). A multiple motives approach to tobacco dependence: The Wisconsin Inventory of Smoking Dependence Motives (WISDM-68). *Journal of Consulting and Clinical Psychology, 72(2),* 139–154.

Pipp-Siegel, S., Siegel, C. H., & Dean, J. (1999). Neurological aspects of the disorganized/disoriented attachment classification system: Differentiating quality of the attachment relationship from neurological impairment. *Monographs of the Society for Research in Child Development, 64(3),* 25–44.

Pirkle, E. C., & Richter, L. (2006). Personality, attitudinal and behavioral risk profiles of young female binge drinkers and smokers. *Journal of Adolescent Health, 38(1),* 44–54.

Pitre, N., Stewart, S., Adams, S., Bedard, T., & Landry, S. (2007). The use of puppets with elementary school children in reducing stigmatizing attitudes towards mental illness. *Journal of Mental Health, 16(3),* 415–429.

Pliszka, S. R. (1999). The psychobiology of oppositional defiant disorder and conduct disorder. In H. C. Quay & A. E. Hogan (Eds.), *Handbook of disruptive behavior disorders* (pp. 371–395). New York: Kluwer Academic/Plenum Publishers.

Pliszka, S. R., Lopez, M., Crismon, M. L., Toprac, M. G., Hughes, C. W., Emslie, G. J., et al. (2003). A feasibility study of the Children's Medication Algorithm Project (CMAP) algorithm for the treatment of ADHD. *Journal of the American Academy of Child and Adolescent Psychiatry, 42(3),* 279–287.

Plomin, R. (2002). Individual differences in a postgenomic era. *Personality and Individual Differences, 33(6),* 909–920.

Plomin, R. (2004). Genetics and developmental psychology. *Merrill-Palmer Quarterly, 50(3),* 341–352.

Plomin, R., DeFries, J. C., Craig, I. W., & McGuffin, P. (2003). Behavioral genomics. In R. Plomin & J. DeFries (Eds.), *Behavioral genetics in the postgenomic era* (pp. 531–540). Washington, DC: American Psychological Association.

Plomin, R., & Kovas, Y. (2005). Generalist genes and learning disabilities. *Psychological Bulletin, 131(4),* 592–617.

Plomin, R., & McGuffin, P. (2003). Psychopathology in the postgenomic era. *Annual Review of Psychology, 54,* 205–228.

Plomin, R., Price, T. S., Eley, T. C., Dale, P. S., & Stevenson, J. (2002). Associations between behaviour problems and verbal and nonverbal cognitive abilities and disabilities in early childhood. *Journal of Child Psychology and Psychiatry, 43*(5), 619–633.

Plunkett,, J. W., Meisels, S. J., Steifel, G. S., & Pasik, P. L. (1986). Patterns of attachment among preterm infants of varying biological risk. *Journal of the American Academy of Child Psychiatry, 25*(6), 794–800.

Polak-Toste, C. P., & Gunnar, M. R. (2006). Temperamental exuberance: Correlates and consequences. In P. J. Marshall & N. A. Fox (Eds.), *The development of social engagement: Neurobiological perspectives* (pp. 19–45). New York: Oxford University Press.

Polanczyk, G., de Lima, M. S., Horta, B. L., Biederman, J., & Rohde, L. A. (2007). The worldwide prevalence of ADHD: A systematic review and metaregression analysis. *American Journal of Psychiatry, 164*(6), 942–948.

Pollak, S. D., Klorman, R., Thatcher, J. E., & Cicchetti, D. (2001). P3b reflects maltreated children's reactions to facial displays of emotion. *Psychophysiology, 38(2),* 267–274.

Pollard, E. L., & Rosenberg, M. L. (2002). The strength-based approach to child well-being: Let's begin with the end in mind. In M. H. Bornstein, L. Davidson, C. L. M. Keyes, & K. Moore (Eds.), *Well-Being: Positive development across the life course.* Mahwah, NJ: Erlbaum.

Pomerantz, E. M., & Altermatt, E. R. (1999). Considering the role of development in self-regulation. In R. S. Wyer (Ed.), *Perspectives on behavioral self-regulation* (pp. 175–192). Mahweh, NJ: Erlbaum.

Pomerantz, E. M., & Eaton, M. M. (2001). Maternal intrusive support in the academic context: Transactional socialization processes. *Developmental Psychology, 37,* 174–186.

Pomerleau, A., Sabatier, C., & Malcuit, G. (1998). Québécois, Haitian, and Vietnamese mothers' report of infant temperament. *International Journal of Psychology, 33*(5), 337–344.

Pomeroy, J. C., & Gadow, K. D. (1998). An overview of psychopharmacology for children and adolescents. In R. J. Morris & T. R. Kratochwill (Eds.), *The practice of child therapy* (3rd ed., pp. 419–470). Needham Heights, MA: Allyn & Bacon.

Pomery, E. A., Gibbons, F. X., Gerrard, M., Cleveland, M. J., Brody, G. H., & Wills, T. A. (2005). Families and risk: Prospective analyses of familial and social influences on adolescent substance use. *Journal of Family Psychology, 19*(4), 560–570.

Porges, S. W. (2003). The polyvagal theory: Phylogenetic contributions to social behavior. *Physiology and Behavior, 79*(3), 503–513.

Porges, S. W., & Doussard-Roosevelt, J. A. (1994). Vagal tone and the physiological regulation of emotion. *Monographs of the Society for Research in Child Development, 59*(2/3), 167–186.

Porter, F. L. (2001). Vagal tone. In L. T. Singer & P. S. Zeskind (Eds.), *Biobehavioral assessment of the infant* (pp. 109–124). New York: Guilford Press.

Posada, G., & Jacobs, A. (2001). Child-mother attachment relationships and culture. *American Psychologist, 56*(10), 821–822.

Posada, G., Carbonell, O. A., Alzate, G., & Plata, S. J. (2004). Through Colombian lenses: Ethnographic and conventional analyses of maternal care and their associations with secure base behavior. *Developmental Psychology, 40*(4), 508–518.

Posner, M. I., & Rothbart, M. K. (1980). The development of attentional mechanisms. *Nebraska Symposium on Motivation* (Vol. 28, pp. 1–52). Lincoln: University of Nebraska Press.

Posner, M. I., & Rothbart, M. K. (1998). Summary and commentary: Developing attentional skills. In *Cognitive neuroscience of attention: A developmental perspective* (pp. 317–323). Mahwah, NJ: Erlbaum.

Posner, M. I., Rothbart, M. K., Sheese, B. E., & Tang, Y. (2007). The anterior cingulate gyrus and the mechanism of self-regulation. *Cognitive, Affective, and Behavioral Neuroscience, 7*(4), 391–395.

Potash, J. B., Toolan, J., Steele, J., Miller, E. B., Pearl, J., Zandi, P. P., et al. (2007). The bipolar disorder phenome database: A resource for genetic studies. *American Journal of Psychiatry, 164,* 1229–1237.

Potenza, M. N., & McDougle, C. T. (1997). The role of serotonin in autistic-spectrum disorders. *CNS Spectrum, 2,* 25–42.

Poulin, F., Dishion, T. J., & Burraston, B. (2001). 3-year iatrogenic effects associated with aggregating high-risk adolescents in cognitive-behavioral preventive interventions. *Applied Developmental Science, 5*(4), 214–224.

Poulin, F., Dishion, T. J., & Haas, E. (1999). The peer influence paradox: Friendship quality and deviancy training within male adolescent friendships. *Merrill-Palmer Quarterly, 45*(1), 42–61.

Poulton, R., Milne, B. J., Craske, M. G., & Menzies, R. G. (2001). A longitudinal study of the etiology of separation anxiety. *Behaviour Research and Therapy, 39*(12), 1395–1410.

Power, T. J., Costigan, T. E., Eiraldi, R. B., & Leff, S. S. (2004). Variations in anxiety and depression as a function of ADHD subtypes defined by DSM-IV: Do subtype differences exist or not? *Journal of Abnormal Child Psychology, 32*(1), 27–37.

Power, T. J., Eiraldi, R. B., Clarke, A. T., Mazzuca, L. B., & Krain, A. L. (2005). Improving mental health service utilization for children and adolescents. *School Psychology Quarterly, 20(2),* 187–205.

Power, T. J., Shapiro, E. D., & DuPaul, G. J. (2003). Preparing psychologists to link systems of care in managing and preventing children's health problems. *Journal of Pediatric Psychology, 28(2),* 147–155.

Prescott, C. A., Cross, R. J., Kuhn, J. W., Horn, J. L., & Kendler, K. S. (2004). Is risk for alcoholism mediated by individual differences in drinking motivations? *Alcoholism: Clinical and Experimental Research, 28*(1), 29–39.

Prescott, C. A., Maes, H. H., & Kendler, K. S. (2005). Genetics of substance use disorders. In K. S. Kendler & L. J. Eaves (Eds.), *Review of psychiatry series: Vol. 24, no. 1. Psychiatric genetics* (pp. 167–196). Washington, DC: American Psychiatric Publishing,.

Presnell, K, Bearman, S. K., & Stice, E. (2004). Risk factors for body dissatisfaction in adolescent boys and girls. *International Journal of Eating Disorders, 36,* 389–401.

Pring, L., & Hermelin, B. (2002). Numbers and letters: Exploring an autistic savant's unpractised ability. *Neurocase, 8*(4), 330–337.

Pring, L., Hermelin, B., Buhler, M., & Walker, I. (1997). Native savant talent and acquired skill. *Autism, 1*(2), 199–214.

Prins, P. J. M. (2001). Affective and cognitive processes and the development and maintenance of anxiety and its disorders. In W. K. Silverman & P. D. A. Treffers (Eds.), *Anxiety disorders in children and adolescents: Research, assessment and intervention* (pp. 23–44). New York: Cambridge University Press.

Prins, P. J. M., & Ollendick, T. H. (2003). Cognitive change and enhanced coping: Missing mediational links in cognitive behavior therapy with anxiety-disordered children. *Clinical Child and Family Psychology Review, 6*(2)*,* 87–105.

Prior, M., Eisenmajer, R., Leekam, S., Wing, L., Gould, J., Ong, B., et al. (1998). Are there subgroups within the autistic spectrum? A cluster analysis of a group of children with autistic spectrum disorders. *Journal of Child Psychology and Psychiatry and Allied Disciplines, 39*, 893–902.

Prior, M., Smart, D., Sanson, A., & Oberklaid, F. (2000). Does shy-inhibited temperament in childhood lead to anxiety problems in adolescence? *Journal of the American Academy of Child and Adolescent Psychiatry, 39*(4), 461–468.

Prosser, J., & McArdle, P. (1996). The changing mental health of children and adolescents: Evidence for a deterioration? *Psychological Medicine, 26(4),* 715–725.

Prudhomme White, B., Gunnar, M. R., Larson, M. C., Donzella, B., & Barr, R. G. (2000). Behavioral and physiological responsivity, sleep, and patterns of daily cortisol production in infants with and without colic. *Child Development, 71*(4), 862–877.

Pry, R., Petersen, A., & Baghdadli, A. (2005). The relationship between expressive language level and psychological development in children with autism 5 years of age. *Autism, 9*(2), 179–189.

Putnam, F. W. (2003). Ten-year research update review: Child sexual abuse. *Journal of the American Academy of Child and Adolescent Psychiatry, 42*(3), 269–278.

Putnam, S. P., Sanson, A. V., & Rothbart, M. K. (2002). Child temperament and parenting. In M. H. Bornstein (Ed.), *Handbook of parenting: Vol. 1. Children and parenting* (2nd ed., pp. 255–277). Mahwah, NJ: Erlbaum.

Putnins, A. L. (2006). Substance use among young offenders: Thrills, bad feelings, or bad behavior? *Substance Use and Abuse, 41*(3), 415–422.

Pynoos, R. S., Steinberg, A. M., & Piacentini, J. C. (1999). A developmental psychopathology model of childhood traumatic stress and intersection with anxiety disorders. *Biological Psychiatry, 46*, 1542–1554.

Quay, H. C. (1999). Classification of the disruptive behavior disorders. In H. C. Quay & A. E. Hogan (Eds.) *Handbook of disruptive behavior disorders* (pp. 3–21). New York: Kluwer Academic/Plenum Publishers.

Querido, J. G., Eyberg, S. M., & Boggs, S. R. (2001). Revisiting the accuracy hypothesis in families of young children with conduct problems. *Journal of Clinical Child Psychology, 30*, 253–261.

Quinlan, D. M. (2000). Assessment of attention-deficit/hyperactivity disorder and comorbidities. In T. E. Brown (Ed.), *Attention-deficit disorders and comorbidities in children, adolescents, and adults* (pp. 455–507). Arlington, VA: American Psychiatric Publishing.

Raaijmakers, Q., Engels, R., & Van Hoof, A. (2005). Delinquency and moral reasoning in adolescence and young adulthood. *International Journal of Behavioral Development, 29*(3), 247–258.

Rabian B., & Silverman, W. K. (1995). Anxiety disorders. In M. Hersen & R. T. Ammerman (Eds.), *Advanced abnormal child psychology* (pp. 235–252). Hillsdale, NJ: Erlbaum.

Rachman, S. (1977). The conditioning theory of fear-acquisition: A critical examination. *Behaviour Research and Therapy, 15*(5), 375–387.

Radke-Yarrow, M., & Klimes-Dougan, B. (1997). Children of depressed mothers: A developmental and interactional perspective. In S. Luthar, J. Burack, D. Cicchetti, & J. R. Weisz (Eds.), *Developmental psychopathology: Perspectives on ad-*

justment, risk and disorder. New York: Cambridge University Press.

Raffaelli, M., & Crockett, L. J. (2003). Sexual risk taking in adolescence: The role of self-regulation and attraction to risk. *Developmental Psychology, 39*(6), 1036–1046.

Raine, A., Moffitt, T. E., Caspi, A., Loeber, R., Stouthamer-Loeber, M., & Lynam, D. (2005). Neurocognitive impairments in boys on the life-course persistent antisocial path. *Journal of Abnormal Psychology, 114*(1), 38–49.

Rajan, K. B., Leroux, B. G., Peterson, A. V., Jr., Bricker, J. B., Andersen, M. R., Kealey, K. A., & Sarason, I. G. (2003). Nine-year prospective association between older siblings' smoking and children's daily smoking. *Journal of Adolescent Health, 33*(1), 25–30.

Ramey, C. T., Mulvihill, B. A., & Ramey, S. L. (1996). Prevention: Social and educational factors and early intervention. In J. W. Jacobson & J. A. Mulick (Eds.), *Manual of diagnosis and professional practice in mental retardation* (pp. 215–227). Washington, DC: American Psychological Association.

Ramey, C. T., Campbell, F. A., & Blair, C. (1998). Enhancing the life course for high risk children: Results from the Abecedarian Project. In J. Crane (Ed.), *Social programs that work* (pp. 163–183). New York: Russell Sage Foundation.

Ramisetty-Mikler, S., & Caetano, R. (2004). Ethnic differences in the estimates of children exposed to alcohol problems and alcohol dependence in the United States. *Journal of Studies on Alcohol, 65*(5), 593–599.

Ramisetty-Mikler, S., Caetano, R., Goebert, D., & Nishimura, S. (2004). Ethnic variation in drinking, drug use, and sexual behavior among adolescents in Hawaii. *Journal of School Health, 74*(1), 16–22.

Ramsey, S. E., Brown, R. A., Strong, D. R., & Sales, S. D. (2002). Cigarette smoking among adolescent psychiatric inpatients: Prevalence and correlates. *Annals of Clinical Psychiatry, 14*(3), 149–153.

Ramsey, S. E., Engler, P. A., & Stein, M. D. (2004). The negative impact of alcohol use among depressed patients. *DATA: The Brown University Digest of Addiction Theory and Application, 23*(11), 8–12.

Ramsey, S. E., Strong, D. R., Stuart, G. L., Weinstock, M. C., Williams, L. A., Tarnoff, G., et al. (2003). Substance use and diagnostic characteristics that differentiate smoking and nonsmoking adolescents in a psychiatric setting. *Journal of Nervous and Mental Disease, 191*(11), 759–762.

Randall, J., Henggeler, S. W., Cunningham, P. B., Rowland, M. D., & Swenson, C. C. (2001). Adapting multisystemic therapy to treat adolescent substance abuse more effectively. *Cognitive and Behavioral Practice, 8*(4), 359–366.

Rao, R., & Georgieff, M. K. (2000). Early nutrition and brain development. In C. A. Nelson (Ed.), *The effects of early adversity on neurobehavioral development. The Minnesota symposium on child psychology* (Vol. 30, pp. 1–30). Mahwah, NJ: Erlbaum.

Rao, U., Ryan, N. D., Dahl, R. E., Birmaher, B., Rao, R., Williamson, D. E., et al. (1999). Factors associated with the development of substance abuse disorder in depressed adolescents. *Journal of the American Academy of Child and Adolescent Psychiatry, 38*(9), 1109–1117.

Rapaport, J. L., & Ismond, D. R. (1996). *DSM-IV training guide for diagnosis of childhood disorders.* New York: Brunner/Mazel.

Rapee, R. M. (2002). The development and modification of temperamental risk for anxiety disorders: Prevention of a lifetime of anxiety? *Biological Psychiatry, 52*(10), 947–957.

Rapee, R. M., & Sweeney, L. (2005). Social phobia in children and adolescents: Nature and assessment. In W. R. Crozier & L. E. Alden (Eds.), *The essential handbook of social anxiety for clinicians* (pp. 133–151). New York: Wiley.

Rapport, M. (1995). Attention deficit hyperactivity disorder. In M. Hersen & R. T. Ammerman (Eds.), *Advanced abnormal child psychology* (pp. 353–373). Hillsdale, NJ: Erlbaum.

Rapport, M. D., Denney, C. B., Chung, K.-M., & Hustace, K. (2001). Internalizing behavior problems and scholastic achievement in children: Cognitive and behavioral pathways as mediators of outcome. *Journal of Clinical Child Psychology, 30*(4), 536–551.

Raskin White, H., Bates, M. E., & Buyske, S. (2001). Adolescence-limited versus persistent delinquency: Extending Moffitt's hypothesis into adulthood. *Journal of Abnormal Psychology, 110*(4), 600–609.

Rassin, E., Cougle, J. R., & Muris, P. (2007). Content difference between normal and abnormal obsessions. *Behaviour Research and Therapy, 45*(11), 2800–2803.

Rauscher, F. H., Shaw, G. L., & Ky, C. N. 1993. Music and spatial task performance. *Nature, 365,* 611.

Raver, C. C. (2004). Placing emotional self-regulation in sociocultural and socioeconomic contexts. *Child Development, 75*(2), 346–353.

Reba, L., Thornton, L., Tozzi, F., Klump, K., Brandt, H., Crawford, S., et al. (2005). Relationships between features associated with vomiting in purging-type disorders. *International Journal of Eating Disorders, 38,* 287–294.

Reddy, P. S., Reddy, Y. C. J., Srinath, S., Khanna, S., Sheshadri, S. P., & Girimaji, S. R. (2001). A family study of juvenile obsessive-compulsive disorder. *Canadian Journal of Psychiatry, 46*(4), 346–351.

Reddy, V. (2001). Positively shy! Developmental continuities in the expression of shyness, coyness, and embarrassment. In W. R. Crozier & L. E. Alden (Eds.), *International handbook of social anxiety: Concepts, research and interventions relating to the self and shyness* (pp. 77–99). New York: Wiley.

Reddy, V., Williams, E., & Vaughan, A. (2001). Sharing laughter: The humor of pre-school children with Down syndrome. *Down Syndrome: Research and Practice, 7*(3)*,* 125–128.

Redfield Jamison, K. (1999). *Night falls fast: Understanding suicide.* New York: Knopf.

Redmond, C., Spoth, R., Shin, C., & Hill, G. J. (2004). Engaging rural parents in family-focused programs to prevent youth substance abuse. *Journal of Primary Prevention, 24*(3), 223–242.

Reese, L., Kroesen, K., & Gallimore, R. (2000). Agency and school performance among urban Latino youth. In R. D. Taylor & M. Wang (Eds.), *Resilience across contexts: Family, work, culture, and community* (pp. 295–332). Mahwah, NJ: Erlbaum.

Reid, J. B., Patterson, G. R., & Snyder, J. J. (Eds.). (2003). Antisocial behavior in children and adolescents: A developmental analysis and model for intervention. *American Journal of Psychiatry, 160,* 805.

Reid, M. J., Webster-Stratton, C., & Beauchaine, T. P. (2001). Parent training in Head Start: A comparison of program response among African-American, Asian American, Caucasian, and Hispanic mothers. *Prevention Science, 2*(4), 209–227.

Reid, M. J., Webster-Stratton, C., & Hammond, M. (2003). Follow-up of children who received the Incredible Years intervention for oppositional-defiant disorder: Maintenance and prediction of 2-year outcome. *Behavior Therapy, 34*(4), 471–491.

Reid, M. J., Webster-Stratton, C., & Hammond, M. (2007). Enhancing a classroom social competence and problem-solving curriculum by offering parent training to families of moderate- to high-risk elementary school children. *Journal of Clinical Child and Adolescent Psychology, 36*(4), 605–620.

Reid, M., Landesman, S., Treder, R., & Jaccard, J. (1989). "My family and friends": Six-to twelve-year-old children's perceptions of social support. *Child Development, 60,* 896–910.

Reid, R., DuPaul, G. J., Power, T. J., Anastopoulos, A. D., Rogers-Adkinson, D., Noll, M., et al. (1998). Assessing culturally different students for attention deficit hyperactivity disorder using behavior rating scales. *Journal of Abnormal Child Psychology, 26,* 187–198.

Reijonen, J. H., Pratt, H. D., Patel, D. R., & Greydanus, D. E. (2003). Eating disorders in the adolescent population: An overview. *Journal of Adolescent Research, 18,* 209–222.

Reiss, S., & Valenti-Hein, D. (1994). Development of a psychopathology rating scale for children with mental retardation. *Journal of Consulting and Clinical Psychology, 62*(1), 28–33.

Rende, R., Birmaher, B., Axelson, D., Strober, M., Gill, M. K., Valeri, S., et al. (2007). Childhood-onset bipolar disorder: Evidence for increased familial loading of psychiatric illness. *Journal of the American Academy of Child and Adolescent Psychiatry, 46*(2), 197–204.

Renouf, A. G., Kovacs, M., & Mukerji, P. (1997). Relationship of depressive, conduct, and comorbid disorders and social functioning in childhood. *Journal of the American Academy of Child and Adolescent Psychiatry, 36*(7), 998–1004.

Repetti, R. L., Taylor, S. E., & Seeman, T. E. (2002). Risky families: Family social environments and the mental and physical health of offspring. *Psychological Bulletin, 128(2),* 330–366.

Repp, A. C., Favell, J., & Munk, D. (1996). Cognitive and vocational interventions for school-age children and adolescents with mental retardation. In J. W. Jacobson & J. A. Mulick (Eds.), *Manual of diagnosis and professional practice in mental retardation* (pp. 265–276). Washington, DC: American Psychological Association.

Reschly, D. J. (1981). Evaluation of the effects of SOMPA measures on classification of students as mildly mentally retarded. *American Journal of Mental Deficiency, 86*(1), 16–20.

Rezvani, A. H., & Levin, E. D. (2004). Adolescent and adult rats respond differently to nicotine and alcohol: Motor activity and body temperature. *International Journal of Developmental Neuroscience, 22*(5–6), 349–354.

Rhee, S. H., Waldman, I. D., Hay, D. A., & Levy, F. (1999). Sex differences in genetic and environmental influences on DSM-III-R attention-deficit/hyperactivity disorder. *Journal of Abnormal Psychology, 108,* 24–41.

Rhodes, R. (1993). Mental retardation and sexual expression: An historical perspective. *Journal of Social Work and Human Sexuality, 8*(2), 1–27.

Ribases, M., Gratacos, M., Badia, A., Badia, A., Jeminez, L., Solano, R., et al. (2005). Contribution of NTRK2 to the genetic susceptibility to anorexia nervosa, harm avoidance and minimum body mass index. *Molecular Psychiatry,10,* 851–860.

Ricciardelli, L. A., & McCabe, M. P. (2001). Children's body image concerns and eating disturbance: A review of the literature. *Clinical Psychology Review, 21,* 325–344.

Ricciardelli, L. A., & McCabe, M. P. (2004). A biopsychosocial model of disordered eating and the pursuit of muscularity in adolescent boys. *Psychological Bulletin, 130,* 179–205.

Ricciarelli, L. A., McCabe, M. P., Ball, K., & Mellor, D. (2004). Sociocultural influences on body image concerns and body change strategies among indigenous and non-indigenous Australian adolescent girls and boys. *Sex Roles, 51,* 731–741.

Ricciarelli, L. A., McCabe, M. P., Williams, R. J., & Thompson, J. K. (2007). The role of ethnicity and culture in body image and disordered eating among males. *Clinical Psychology Review, 27*(5), 582–606.

Rice, C. (2001). Making moral decisions: Comparing two theories. *Mental Retardation, 39*(2), 155–157.

Richards, J. M., & Gross, J. (1999). Composure at any cost? The cognitive consequences of emotion suppression. *Personality and Social Psychology Bulletin, 25,* 1033–1044.

Richards, M. H., Larson, R., Miller, B. V., Luo, Z., Sims, B., Parrella, D. P., et al. (2004). Risky and protective contexts and exposure to violence in urban African American young adolescents. *Journal of Clinical Child and Adolescent Psychology, 33*(1), 138–148.

Richardson, A. S., Bergen, H. A., Martin, G., Roeger, L., & Allison, S. (2005). Perceived academic performance as an indicator of risk of attempted suicide in young adolescents. *Archives of Suicide Research, 9*(2), 163–167.

Richler, J., Luyster, R., Risi, S., Hsu, W., Dawson, G., Bernier, R., et al., (2006). Is there a "regressive phenotype" of autism spectrum disorder associated with the measles-mumps-rubella vaccine? A CPEA study. *Journal of Autism and Developmental Disorders, 36*(3), 299–316.

Rickel, A. U., & Becker, E. (1997). Risk factors in infancy and early childhood. In A. U. Rickel & E. Becker (Eds.), *Keeping children from harm's way: How national policy affects psychological development* (pp. 27–57). Washington, DC: American Psychological Association.

Riddle, M. A., Reeve, E. A., Yaryura-Tobias, J. A., Yang, H. M., Claghorn, J. L., Gaffney, G., et al. (2001). Fluvoxamine for children and adolescents with obsessive-compulsive disorder: A randomized, controlled, multicenter trial. *Journal of the American Academy of Child and Adolescent Psychiatry, 40*(2), 222–229.

Riedel, B. W., Blitstein, J. L., Robinson, L. A., Murray, D. M., & Klesges, R. C. (2003). The reliability and predictive value of adolescents' reports of initial reactions to smoking. *Nicotine and Tobacco Research, 5*(4), 553–559.

Rieppi, R., Greenhill, L. L., Ford, R. E., Chuang, S., Wu, M., Davies, M., et al. (2002). Socioeconomic status as a moderator of ADHD treatment outcomes. *Journal of the American Academy of Child and Adolescent Psychiatry, 41*(3), 269–277.

Rierdan, J., & Koff, E. (1997). Weight, weight-related aspects of body image, and depression in early adolescent girls. *Adolescence, 32(127),* 615–624.

Riley, E. P., Guerri, C., Calhoun, F., Charness, M. E., Foroud, T. M., Li, T., et al. (2003). Prenatal alcohol exposure: Advancing knowledge through international collaborations. *Alcoholism: Clinical and Experimental Research, 27*(1), 118–135.

Rind, B., Tromovitch, P., & Bauserman, R. (1998). A meta-analytic examination of assumed properties of child sexual abuse using college samples. *Psychological Bulletin, 124,* 22–53.

Rinehart, N. J., Bradshaw, J. L., Tonge, B. J., Brereton, A. V., & Bellgrove, M. A. (2002). A neurobehavioral examination of individuals with high-functioning autism and Asperger disorder using a fronto-striatal model of dysfunction. *Behavioral and Cognitive Neuroscience Reviews, 1*(2), 164–177.

Ringeisen, H., Henderson, K., & Hoagwood, K. (2003). Context matters: Schools and the "research to practice gap" in children's mental health. *School Psychology Review, 32(2),* 153–168.

Ripple, C. H., & Zigler, E. (2003). Research, policy, and the federal role in prevention initiatives for children. *American Psychologist, 58(6–7),* 482–490.

Risley, T. R., & Reid, D. H. (1996). Management and organizational issues in the delivery of psychological services for people with mental retardation. In J. W. Jacobson & J. A. Mulick (Eds.), *Manual of diagnosis and professional practice in mental retardation* (pp. 383–391). Washington, DC: American Psychological Association.

Ristic, J., Mottron, L., Friesen, C. K., Iarocci, G., Burack, J. A., & Kingstone, A. (2005). Eyes are special but not for everyone: The case of autism. *Cognitive Brain Research, 24*(3), 715–718.

Rivas-Vazquez, R. A., Rice, J., & Kalman, D. (2003). Pharmacotherapy of obesity and eating disorders. *Professional Psychology Research and Practice, 34,* 562–566.

Robb, A. S., & Dadson, M. J. (2002). Eating disorders in males. *Child and Adolescent Psychiatric Clinics of North America, 11,* 399–418.

Roberts, C., Kane, R., Thomson, H., Bishop, B., & Hart, B. (2003). The prevention of depressive symptoms in rural school children: A randomized controlled trial. *Journal of Consulting and Clinical Psychology, 71*(3), 622–628.

Roberts, E., Bornstein, M. H., Slater, A. M., & Barrett, J. (1999). Early cognitive development and parental education. *Infant and Child Development, 8*(1), 49–62.

Roberts, J. E., Boccia, M. L., Hatton, D. D., Skinner, M. L., & Sideris, J. (2006). Temperament and vagal tone in boys with fragile X syndrome. *Journal of Developmental and Behavioral Pediatrics, 27*(3), 193–201.

Roberts, R. E., Attkisson, C. C., & Rosenblatt, A. (1998). Prevalence of psychopathology among children and adolescents. *American Journal of Psychiatry, 155(6),* 715–725.

Roberts, R. E., Phinney, J. S., Masse, L. C., Chen, Y. R., Roberts, C. R., & Romero, A. (1999). The structure of ethnic identity of young adolescents from diverse ethnocultural groups. *Journal of Early Adolescence, 19*(3), 301–322.

Roberts, R. E., Roberts, C. R., & Chen, Y. (1997). Ethnocultural differences in prevalence of adolescent depression. *American Journal of Community Psychology, 25,* 95–110.

Roberts, T. A., Auinger, P., & Klein, J. D. (2006). Predictors of partner abuse in a nationally representative sample of adolescents involved in heterosexual dating relationships. *Violence and Victims, 21*(1), 81–89.

Roberts, T. A., Auinger, P., & Ryan, S. A. (2004). Body piercing and high-risk behavior in adolescents. *Journal of Adolescent Health, 34*(3), 224–229.

Robert-Tissot C., Cramer, B., Stern, D. N., & Serpa, S. R. (1996). Outcome evaluation in brief infant-mother psychotherapies: Report on 75 cases. *Infant Mental Health Journal, 17*(2), 97–114.

Robin, J. A., Puliafico, A. C., Creed, T. A., Comer, J. S., Hofflich, S. A., Barmish, A. J., et al. (2006). Generalized anxiety disorder. In R. T. Ammerman (Ed.), *Comprehensive handbook of* personality and psychopathology (Vol. 3, pp. 117–134). Hoboken, NJ: Wiley.

Robins, D. L., Fein, D., Barton, M. L., & Green, J. A. (2001). The Modified Checklist for Autism in Toddlers: An initial study investigating the early detection of autism and pervasive developmental disorders. *Journal of Autism and Developmental Disorders, 31*(2), 131–144.

Robins, L. (1966). *Deviant children grown up.* Philadelphia: Williams & Wilkins.

Robins, L. (1999). A 70-year history of conduct disorder: Variations in definition, prevalence, and correlates. In P. Cohen & C. Slomkowski (Eds.), *Historical and geographical influences on psychopathology* (pp. 37–56). Mahwah, NJ: Erlbaum.

Robins, L. N. (1995). The epidemiology of aggression. In E. Hollander & D. J. Stein (Eds.), *Impulsivity and aggression* (pp. 43–55). Oxford, England: Wiley.

Robins, L. N. (1999). A 70-year history of conduct disorder: Variations in definition, prevalence and correlates. In P. Cohen, C. Slomkowski, & L. N. Robins (Eds.), *Historical and geographical influences on psychopathology* (pp. 37–56). Mahwah, NJ: Erlbaum.

Robins, R. W., John, O. P., Caspi, A., Moffitt, T. E., & Stouthamer-Loeber, M. (1996). Resilient, overcontrolled, and undercontrolled boys: Three replicable personality types. *Journal of Personality and Social Psychology, 70*(1), 157–171.

Robins, R. W., & Trzesniewski, K. H. (2005). Self-esteem development across the lifespan. *Current Directions in Psychological Science, 14*(3), 158–162.

Robinson, T. E., & Berridge, K. C. (2001). Incentive-sensitization and addiction. *Addiction, 96*(1), 103–114.

Robinson, T. E., & Berridge, K. C. (2003). Addiction. *Annual Review of Psychology, 54*, 25–53.

Rodham, K., Hawton, K., & Evans, E. (2004). Reasons for self-harm: Comparison of self-poisoners and self-cutters in a community sample of adolescents. *Journal of the American Academy of Child and Adolescent Psychiatry, 43*(1), 80–87.

Rodier, P. M., & Hyman, S. L. (1998). Early environmental factors in autism. *Mental Retardation and Developmental Disabilities Research Reviews, 4*, 121–128.

Rodriguez, R., Marchand, E., Ng, J., & Stice, E. (2008). Effects of a cognitive dissonance-based eating disorder prevention program are similar for Asian American, Hispanic, and White participants. *International Journal of Eating Disorders, 41*(7), 618–625.

Roeleveld, N., Zielhuis, G. A., & Gabreels, F. (1997). The prevalence of mental retardation: A critical review of recent literature. *Developmental Medicine and Child Neurology, 39*(2), 125–132.

Rogers, S., & DiLalla, D. (1991). A comparative study of the effects of a developmentally based instructional model on young children with autism and young children with other disorders of behavior and development. *Topics in Early Childhood Special Education, 11*, 29–47.

Rogers, S., & Lewis, H. (1988). An effective day treatment model for young children with pervasive developmental disorders. *Journal of the American Academy of Child and Adolescent Psychiatry, 28*, 207–214.

Rogoff, B., & Morelli, G. (1989). Perspectives on children's development from cultural psychology. *American Psychologist 44(2),* 343–348.

Rohde, L. A., Szobot, C., Polanczyk, G., Schmitz, M., Martins, S., & Tramontina, S. (2005). Attention-deficit/hyperactivity disorder in a diverse culture: Do research and clinical findings support the notion of a cultural construct for the disorder? *Biological Psychiatry, 57*(11), 1436–1441.

Rohde, P., Lewinsohn, P. M., Clarke, G. N., Hops, H., & Seeley, J. R. (2005). The Adolescent Coping with Depression Course: A cognitive-behavioral approach to the treatment of adolescent depression. In E. D. Hibbs & P. S. Jensen (Eds.), *Psychosocial treatments for child and adolescent disorders: Empirically based strategies for clinical practice* (2nd ed., pp. 219–237). Washington, DC: American Psychological Association.

Rohde, P., Lewinsohn, P. M., Kahler, C. W., Seeley, J. R., & Brown, R. A. (2001). Natural course of alcohol use disorders from adolescence to young adulthood. *Journal of the American Academy of Child and Adolescent Psychiatry, 40*(1), 83–90.

Roid, G. H. (2003). *Stanford-Binet Intelligence Scale* (5th ed.). Itasca, IL: Riverside.

Roisman, G. I., Masten, A. S., Coatsworth, J. D., & Tellegen, A. (2004). Salient and emerging developmental tasks in the transition to adulthood. *Child Development, 75*(1), 123–133.

Roisman, G. I., Padron, E., Sroufe, L. A., & Egeland, B. (2002). Earned-secure attachment status in retrospect and prospect. *Child Development, 73*(4), 1204–1219.

Rojahn, J., & Tasse, M. J. (1996). Psychopathology in mental retardation. In J. W. Jacobson & J. A. Mulick (Eds.), *Manual of diagnosis and professional practice in mental retardation* (pp. 147–156). Washington, DC: American Psychological Association.

Rojo-Moreno, L., Livianos-Aldana, L., Conesa-Burguet, L., & Cava, G. Dysfunctional rearing in community and clinic based populations with eating problems: Prevalence and mediating role of psychiatric morbidity. *European Eating Disorders Review, 14*, 32–42.

Romanczyk, R. G., Gillis, J. M., Noyes-Grosser, D. M., Holland, J. P., Holland, C. L., & Lyons, D. (2005). Clinical clues, developmental milestones, and early identification/assessment of children with disabilities: Practical applications and conceptual considerations. *Infants and Young Children, 18*(3), 212–221.

Rome, E. S., & Ammerman, S. (2003). Medical complications of eating disorders: An update. *Journal of Adolescent Health, 33,* 418–426.

Rose, A. J., Swenson, L. P., & Carlson, W. (2004). Friendships of aggressive youth: Considering the influences of being disliked and of being perceived as popular. *Journal of Experimental Child Psychology, 88*(1), 24–45.

Rose, R. J., & Ditto, W. B. (1983). A developmental-genetic analysis of common fears from early adolescence to early adulthood. *Child Development, 54*, 361–368.

Rose, R. J., Dick, D. M., Viken, R. J., Pulkkinen, L., & Kaprio, J. (2001). Drinking or abstaining at age 14? A genetic epidemiological study. *Alcoholism: Clinical and Experimental Research, 25*(11), 1594–1604.

Rose, R. J., Dick, D. M., Viken, R. J., Pulkkinen, L., & Kaprio, J. (2004). Genetic and environmental effects on conduct disorder and alcohol dependence symptoms and their covariation at age 14. *Alcoholism: Clinical and Experimental Research, 28*(10), 1541–1548.

Rose, R. J., Viken, R. J., Dick, D. M., Bates, J. E., Pulkkinen, L., & Kaprio, J. (2003) It does take a village: Nonfamilial environments and children's behavior. *Psychological Science, 14(3),* 273–277.

Rosenberg, D. R., & Keshavan, M. S. (1998). Toward a neurodevelopmental model of obsessive-compulsive disorder. *Biological Psychiatry, 43,* 623–640.

Rosenfield, S., Lennon, M. C., & White, H. R. (2005). The self and mental health: Self-salience and the emergence of internalizing and externalizing problems. *Journal of Health and Social Behavior, 46(4),* 323–340.

Rosenzweig, M. R., & Bennett, E. L. (1996). Psychobiology of plasticity: Effects of training and experience on brain and behavior. *Behavioural Brain Research, 78(1),* 57–65.

Rosner, B. A., Hodapp, R. M., Fidler, D. J., Sagun, J. N., & Dykens, E. M. (2004). Social competence in persons with Prader-Willi, Williams, and Down's syndromes. *Journal of Applied Research in Intellectual Disabilities, 17*(3), 209–217.

Rossello, J., & Bernal, G. (2005). New developments in cognitive-behavioral and interpersonal treatments for depressed Puerto Rican adolescents. In E. D. Hibbs & P. S. Jensen (Eds.), *Psychosocial treatments for child and adolescent disorders: Empirically based strategies for clinical practice* (2nd ed., pp. 187–217). Washington, DC: American Psychological Association.

Rosso, I. M., Young, A. D., Femia, L. A., & Yurgelun-Todd, D. A. (2004). Cognitive and emotional components of frontal lobe functioning in childhood and adolescence. In R. E. Dahl & L. P. Spear (Eds.), *Adolescent brain development: Vulnerabilities and opportunities. Annals of the New York Academy of Sciences* (Vol. 1021, pp. 355–362). New York: New York Academy of Sciences.

Rossow, I., Groholt, B., & Wichstrom, L. (2005). Intoxicants and suicidal behavior among adolescents: Changes in levels and associations from 1992–2002. *Addiction, 100*(1), 79–88.

Roth, J., Brooks-Gunn, J., Murray, L., & Foster, W. (1998). Promoting healthy adolescents: Synthesis of youth development program evaluations. *Journal of Research on Adolescence, 8*(4), 423–459.

Rothbart, M. K. (1991). Temperament: A developmental framework. In J. Strelau & A. Angleitner (Eds.), *Explorations in temperament: International perspectives on theory and measurement* (pp. 61–74). New York: Plenum Press.

Rothbart, M. K. (2007). Temperament, development, and personality. *Current Directions in Psychological Science, 16*(4), 207–212.

Rothbart, M. K., Ellis, L. K., Rueda, M. R., & Posner, M. (2003). Developing mechanisms of temperamental effortful control. *Journal of Personality, 71,* 1113–1143.

Rothbart, M. K., & Hwang, J. (2002). Measuring infant temperament. *Infant Behavior and Development, 25*(1), 113–116.

Rothbart, M. K. & Jones, L. B. (1999). Temperament: Developmental perspectives. In R. Gallimore, L. P. Bernheimer, D. L. MacMillan, D. L. Speece, & S. Vaughn (Eds.), *Developmental perspectives on children with high-incidence disabilities* (pp. 33–53). Mahwah, NJ: Erlbaum.

Rothbart, M. K., Posner, M. I., & Hershey, K. L. (1995). Temperament, attention, and developmental psychopathology. In *Developmental Psychopathology: Vol. 1. Theory and methods* (pp. 315–340). New York: Wiley.

Rothbart, M. K., & Putnam, S. P. (2002). Temperament and socialization. In L. Pulkkinen, & A. Caspi, (Eds.), *Paths to successful development: Personality in the life course* (pp. 19–45). New York: Cambridge University Press.

Rothbaum, F., Kakinuma, M., Nagaoka, R., & Azuma, H. (2007). Attachment and AMAE: Parent-child closeness in the United States and Japan. *Journal of Cross-Cultural Psychology, 38*(4), 465–486.

Rothbaum, F., & Morelli, G. (2005). Attachment and culture: Bridging relativism and universalism. In W. Friedlmeier, P. Chakkarath, & B. Schwarz (Eds.), *Culture and human development: The importance of cross-cultural research for the social sciences* (pp. 99–123). Hove, England: Psychology Press/Erlbaum (UK) Taylor and Francis.

Rothbaum, F., Weisz, J., Pott, M., Miyake, K., & Morelli, G. (2000). Attachment and culture: Security in the United States and Japan. *American Psychologist, 55*(10), 1093–1104.

Rothbaum, F., Weisz, J. R., & Snyder, S. S. (1982). Changing the world and changing the self: A two-process model of perceived control. *Journal of Personality and Social Psychology, 42(1),* 5–37.

Rotthaus, W. (2001). Systemic therapy. In A. Dosen & K. Day (Eds.), *Treating mental illness and behavior disorders in children and adults with mental retardation* (pp. 167–180). Washington, DC: American Psychiatric Publishing.

Rourke, B. P. (1989). *Nonverbal learning disabilities: The syndrome and the model.* New York: Guilford Press.

Rourke, B. P., & Tsatsanis, K. D. (2000). Nonverbal learning disabilities and Asperger syndrome. In A. Klin, F. R. Volkmar, & S. S. Sparrow (Eds.), *Asperger syndrome* (pp. 231–253). New York: Guilford Press.

Rowe, R., Maughan, B., Costello, E. J., & Angold, A. (2005). Defining oppositional defiant disorder. *Journal of Child Psychology and Psychiatry, 46*(12), 1309–1316.

Rowe, R., Maughan, B., Pickles, A., Costello, E. J., & Angold, A. (2002). The relationship between DSM-IV oppositional defiant disorder and conduct disorder: Findings from the Great Smoky Mountains Study. *Journal of Child Psychology and Psychiatry and Allied Disciplines, 43,* 365–373.

Rowe, R., Maughan, B., Worthman, C. M., Costello, E. J., & Angold, A. (2004). Testosterone, antisocial behavior, and social dominance in boys: Pubertal development and biosocial interaction. *Biological Psychiatry, 55*(5), 546–552.

Roy, P., Rutter, M., & Pickles, A. (2004). Institutional care: Associations between overactivity and lack of selectivity in social relationships. *Journal of Child Psychology and Psychiatry, 45*(4), 866–873.

Rubin, K. H. (1998). Social and emotional development from a cultural perspective. *Developmental Psychology, 34(4),* 611–615.

Rubin, K. H., Burgess, K. B., Dwyer, K. M., & Hastings, P. D. (2003). Predicting preschoolers' externalizing behaviors from toddler temperament, conflict, and maternal negativity. *Developmental Psychology, 39*(1), 164–176.

Rubin, K. H., Hastings, P. D., Stewart, S. L., & Henderson, H. A. (1997). The consistency and concomitants of inhibition: Some of the children, all of the time. *Child Development, 68*(3), 467–483.

Rubin, K. H., Hastings, P., Chen, X., Stewart, S., & McNichol, K. (1998). Intrapersonal and maternal correlates of aggression, conflict, and externalizing problems in toddlers. *Child Development, 69*(6), 1614–1629.

Rubinstein, M. L., Halpern-Felsher, B. L., Thompson, P. J., & Millstein, S. G. (2003). Adolescents discriminate between types of smokers and related risks: Evidence from nonsmokers. *Journal of Adolescent Research, 18*(6), 651–663.

Rudd, M. D., Joiner, T. E., & Rumzek, H. (2004). Childhood diagnoses and later risk for multiple suicide attempts. *Suicide and Life-Threatening Behavior, 34*(2), 113–125.

Rudolph, K. D., & Asher, S. R. (2000). Adaptation and maladaptation in the peer system: Developmentall processes and outcomes. In A. J. Sameroff, M. Lewis, & S. M. Miller (Eds.), *Handbook of developmental psychopathology* (2nd ed.) (pp. 157–175). Dordrecht, Netherlands: Kluwer Academic Publishers.

Rueda, M. R., Posner, M. I., & Rothbart, M. K. (2005). The development of executive attention: Contributions to the emergences of self-regulation. *Developmental Neuropsychology, 28*(2), 573–594.

Russell, R. L., & Shirk, S. R. (1998). Child psychotherapy process research. *Advances in Child Psychology, 20,* 93–124.

Russo, M. F., & Beidel, D. C. (1994). Comorbidity of childhood anxiety and externalizing disorders: Prevalence, associated characteristics, and validation issues. *Clinical Psychology Review, 14*(3), 199–221.

Russoniello, C. V., Skalko, T. K., O'Brien, K., McGhee, S. A., Bingham-Alexander, D., & Beatley, J. (2002). Childhood posttraumatic stress disorder and efforts to cope after Hurricane Floyd. *Behavioral Medicine, 28*(2), 61–70.

Rutherford, M. D., Baron-Cohen, S., & Wheelwright, S. (2002). Reading the mind in the voice: A study with normal adults and adults with Asperger syndrome and high functioning autism. *Journal of Autism and Developmental Disorders, 32,* 189–194.

Rutter, M. (1970). Autistic children: Infancy to adulthood. *Seminars in Psychiatry, 2,* 435–450.

Rutter, M. (1977). Brain damage syndromes in childhood: Concepts and findings. *Journal of Child Psychology and Psychiatry, 18*(1), 1–21.

Rutter, M. (1979). Maternal deprivation, 1972–1978: New findings, new concepts, new approaches. *Child Development, 50(2),* 283–305.

Rutter, M. (1980). Attachment and the development of social relationship In M. Rutter (Ed.), *Scientific Foundations of Developmental Psychiatry* (pp. 267–279). London: Heinemann.

Rutter, M. (1987). Psychosocial resilience and protective mechanisms. *American Journal of Orthopsychiatry, 57(3),* 316–331.

Rutter, M. (1990). Psychosocial resilience and protective mechanisms. In J. E. Rolf & A. S. Masten (Eds.), *Risk and protective factors in the development of psychopathology* (pp. 181–214). New York: Cambridge University Press.

Rutter, M. (1995). Clinical implications of attachment concepts: Retrospect and prospect. *Journal of Child Psychology and Psychiatry, 86*(4), 549–571.

Rutter, M. (1996). Transitions and turning points in developmental psychopathology: As applied to the age span between childhood and mid-adulthood. *International Journal of Behavioral Development, 19(3),* 603–626.

Rutter, M., (1999). Psychosocial adversity and child psychopathology. *British Journal of Psychiatry, 174,* 480–493.

Rutter, M. (2000). Genetic studies of autism: From the 1970s into the millennium. *Journal of Abnormal Child Psychology, 28,* 3–14.

Rutter, M. and the English and Romanian Adoptees (ERA) Study Team (1998). Developmental catch-up and deficit, following adoption after severe global early privation. *Journal of Child Psychology and Psychiatry, 39*(4), 465–476.

Rutter, M., & Quinton, D. (1984). Parental psychiatric disorder: Effects on children. *Psychological Medicine, 14*(4), 853–880.

Rutter, M., & Schopler, E. (1992). Classification of pervasive developmental disorders: Some concepts and practical considerations. *Journal of Autism and Developmental Disorders, 22*(4), 459–482.

Rutter, M., & Silberg, J. (2002). Gene-environment interplay in relation to emotional and behavioral disturbance. *Annual Review of Psychology, 53(1),* 463–490.

Rutter, M., & Smith, D. J. (1995). *Psychological disorders in young people: Time trends and their causes.* Chichester, UK: Wiley.

Rutter, M., & Sroufe, L. A. (2000). Developmental psychopathology: Concepts and challenges. *Development and Psychopathology, 12,* 265–296.

Rutter, M., Maughan, B., Meyer, J., Pickles, A., Silberg, J., Simonoff, E., et al. (1997). Heterogeneity of antisocial behavior: Causes, continuities, and consequences. In D. W. Osgood (Ed.), *Motivation and delinquency. Nebraska symposium on motivation, vol. 44* (pp. 45–118). Lincoln: University of Nebraska Press.

Rutter, M., O'Connor, T. G., & English and Romanian Adoptees (ERA) Study Team (2004). Are there biological programming effects for psychological development? Findings from a study of Romanian adoptees. *Developmental Psychology, 40*(1), 81–94.

Rutter, P. A., & Behrendt, A. E. (2004). Adolescent suicide risk: Four psychosocial factors. *Adolescence, 39*(154), 295–302.

Rutz, E. M., & Wasserman, D. (2004). Trends in adolescent suicide mortailty in the WHO European region. *European Child and Adolescent Psychiatry, 13*(5), 321–331.

Ryan, N. D., Puig-Antich, J., Ambrosini, P., Rabinovich, H., et al. (1987). The clinical picture of major depression in children and adolescents. *Archives of General Psychiatry, 44(10),* 854–861.

Saarni, C. (1998). Issues of cultural meaningfulness in emotional development. *Developmental Psychology, 34(4),* 647–652.

Saarni, C. (1999). *The development of emotional competence.* New York: Guilford Press.

Saavedra, L. M., & Silverman, W. K. (2002). Classification of anxiety disorders in children: What a difference two decades make. *International Review of Psychiatry, 14*(2), 87–101.

Sachs, H. T., & Barrett, R. P. (2000). Psychopathology in individuals with mental retardation. In A. J. Sameroff & M. Lewis (Eds.), *Handbook of developmental psychopathology* (2nd ed., pp. 657–670). Dordrecht, Netherlands: Kluwer Academic Publishers.

Sadeh, A., Flint-Ofir, E., Tirosh, T., & Tidotzky, L. (2007). Infant sleep and parental sleep-related cognitions. *Journal of Family Psychology, 21*(1), 74–87.

Safford, S. M., Kendall, P. C., Flannery-Shroeder, E., Webb, A., & Sommer, H. (2005). A longitudinal look at parent-child diagnostic agreement in youth treated for anxiety disorders. *Journal of Clinical Child and Adolescent Psychology, 34*(4), 747–757.

Safren, S. A., Gonzalez, R. E., Horner, K. J., Leung, A. W., Heimberg, R. G. & Juster, H. R. (2000). Anxiety in ethnic minority youth: Methodological and conceptual issues and review of the literature. *Behavior Modification, 24*(2), 147–183.

Sagrestano, L. M., Paikoff, R. L., Holmbeck, G. N., & Fendrich, M. (2003). A longitudinal examination of familial risk factors for depression among inner-city African American adolescents. *Journal of Family Psychology, 17*(1), 108–120.

Sahin, N. H., Batigun, A. D., & Yilmaz, B. (2007). Psychological symptoms of Turkish children and adolescents after the 1999 earthquake: Exposure, gender, location, and time duration. *Journal of Traumatic Stress, 20*(3), 335–345.

Sakai, J. R., Hall, S. K., Mikulich-Gilberson, S. K., & Crowley, T. J. (2004). Inhalant use, abuse, and dependence among adolescent patients: Commonly comorbid problems. *Journal of the American Academy of Child and Adolescent Psychiatry, 43*(9), 1080–1088.

Sakai, J. T., Mikulich-Gilbertson, S. K., & Crowley, T. J. (2006). Adolescent inhalant use among male patients in treatment for substance and behavior problems: Two-year outcome. *American Journal of Drug and Alcohol Abuse, 32*(1), 29–40.

Sale, E., Sambrano, S., Springer, J. F., Pena, C., Pan, W., & Kasim, R. (2005). Family protection and prevention of alcohol use among Hispanic youth at high risk. *American Journal of Community Psychology, 36(3–4)*, 195–205.

Salekin, R. T., Leistico, A. R., Trobst, K. K., Schrum, C. L., & Lochman, J. E. (2005). Adolescent psychopathology and personality theory—the Interpersonal Circumplex: Expanding evidence of a nomological net. *Journal of Abnormal Child Psychology, 33*(4), 445–460.

Saling, M., Ricciardelli, L. A., & McCabe, M. P. (2005). A prospective study of individual factors in the development of weight and muscle concerns among preadolescent children. *Journal of Youth and Adolescence, 34,* 651–661.

Salmon, K., & Bryant, R. A. (2002). Posttraumatic stress disorder in children: The influence of developmental factors. *Clinical Psychology Review, 22*(2), 163–188.

Sameroff, A. J. (1993). Models of development and developmental risk. In C. H. Zeanah (Ed.), *Handbook of infant mental health* (pp. 3–13). New York: Guilford Press.

Sameroff, A. J. (2000). Developmental systems and psychopathology. *Development and Psychopathology, 12(3),* 297–312.

Sameroff, A. J., Seifer, R., & Bartko, W. T. (1997). Environmental perspectives on adaptation during childhood and adolescence. In. S. S. Luthar & J. Burack (Eds.), *Developmental psychopathology: Perspectives on adjustment, risk, and disorder* (pp. 507–526). New York: Cambridge University Press.

Sameroff, A. J., Seifer, R., Baldwin, A., & Baldwin, C. (1993). Stability of intelligence from preschool to adolescence: The influence of social and family risk factors. *Child Development, 64,* 80–97.

Samuel, V. J., Biederman, J., Faraone, S. V., George, P., Mick, E., Thornell, A., et al. (1998). Clinical characteristics of attention deficit hyperactivity disorder in African American children. *American Journal of Psychiatry, 155,* 696–698.

Samuel, V. J., Curtis, S., Thornell, A., George, P., Taylor, A., Brome, D. R., et al. (1997). The unexplored void of ADHD and African-American research: A review of the literature. *Journal of Attention Disorders, 1*(4), 197–207.

Samuel, V. J., George, P., Thornell, A., Curtis, S., Taylor, A., Brome, D., et al. (1999). A pilot controlled family study of DSM-III-R and DSM-IV ADHD in African American children. *Journal of the American Academy of Child and Adolescent Psychiatry, 38*(1), 34–39.

Sanches, M., Roberts, R. L., Sassi, R. B., Axelson, D., Nicoletti, M., Brambilla, P. ,et al. (2005). Developmental abnormalities in striatum in young bipolar patients: A preliminary study. *Bipolar Disorders, 7*(2), 153–158.

Sanson, A., & Prior, M. (1999). Temperament and behavioral precursors to oppositional defiant disorder and conduct disorder. In H. C. Quay & A. E. Hogan (Eds.), *Handbook of disruptive behavior disorders* (pp. 397–417). New York: Kluwer Academic/Plenum Publishers.

Sansone, R. A., & Levitt, J. L. (2002). Self-harm behaviors among those with eating disorders: An overview. *Eating Disorders: The Journal of Treatment and Prevention, 10,* 205–213.

Sansone, R. A., Levitt, J. L., & Sansone, L. A. (2005). The prevalence of personality disorders among those with eating disorders. *Eating Disorders: The Journal of Treatment and Prevention, 13*(1), 7–21.

Santalahti, P., Hemminki, E., Latikka, A. & Ryynaenen, M. (1998). Womens' decision-making in prenatal screening. *Social Science and Medicine, 46*(8), 1067–1076.

Satterfield, J. H., Schell, A. M., Nicholas, T. W., & Satterfield, B. T. (1990). Ontogeny of selective attention effects on event-related potentials in attention-deficit hyperactivity disorder and normal boys. *Biological Psychiatry, 28*(1), 879–903.

Saunders, B., & Chambers, S. M. (1996). A review of the literature on attention-deficit hyperactivity disorder children: Peer interactions and collaborative learning. *Psychology in the Schools, 33,* 333–340.

Sawyer, M. G., Arney, F. M., Baghurst, P. A., Clark, J. J., Graetz, B. W., Kosky, R. J., et al. (2001). The mental health of young people in Australia: Key findings from the child and adolescent component of the national survey of mental health and well-being. *Australian and New Zealand Journal of Psychiatry, 35(6),* 806–814.

Sbarra, D. A., & Pianta, R. C. (2001). Teacher ratings of behavior among African American and Caucasian children during the first two years of school. *Psychology in the Schools, 38(3),* 229–238.

Scarr, S. (1997). The development of individual differences in intelligence and personality. In H. W. Reese & M. D. Franzen (Eds.), *Biological and neuropsychological mechanisms: Life-span developmental psychology* (pp. 1–22). Hillsdale, NJ: Erlbaum.

Scarr, S. (1998). How do families affect intelligence? Social environmental and behavior genetic predictions. In J. J. McArdle & R. W. Woodcock (Eds.), *Human cognitive abilities in theory and practice* (pp. 113–136). Mahwah, NJ: Erlbaum.

Schachar, R. J., Tannock, R., Cunningham, C., & Corkum, P. V. (1997). Behavioral, situational, and temporal effects of treatment of ADHD with methylphenidate. *Journal of the American Academy of Child and Adolescent Psychiatry, 36,* 754–763.

Schachar, R., & Tannock, R. (1993). Childhood hyperactivity and psychostimulants: A review of extended treatment studies. *Journal of Child and Adolescent Psychopharmacology, 3*(2), 81–97.

Schaeffer, C. M., Petras, H., Ialongo, N., Poduska, J., & Kellam, S. (2003). Modeling growth in boys' aggressive behavior across elementary school: Links to later criminal involvement, conduct disorder, and antisocial personality disorder. *Developmental Psychology, 39*(6), 1020–1035.

Schafer, I., Barkmann, C., Riedesser, P., & Schulte-Markwort, M. (2006). Posttraumatic syndromes in children after road traffic accidents: A prospective cohort study. *Psychopathology, 39*(4), 159–164.

Schäfer, M., Korn, S., Brodbeck, F. C., Wolke, D., & Schulz, H. (2005). Bullying roles in changing contexts: The stability of victim and bully roles from primary to secondary school. *International Journal of Behavioral Development, 29*(4), 323–335.

Schalock, R. L. (1996). The quality of children's lives. In A. H. Fine & N. M. Fine (Eds.), *Therapeutic recreation for exceptional children: Let me in, I want to play,* (2nd ed., pp. 83–94). Springfield, IL: Charles C. Thomas.

Schalock, R. L. (1997). The conceptualization and measurement of quality of life: Current status and future considerations. *Journal on Developmental Disabilities, 5*(2), 1–21.

Schalock, R. L. (2000). Three decades of quality of life. *Focus on Autism and Other Developmental Disabilities, 15*(2), 116–127.

Schalock, R. L., Stark, J. A., Snell, M. E., & Coulter, D. L. (1994). The changing conception of mental retardation: Implications for the field. *Mental Retardation, 32*(3), 181–193.

Scheeringa, M. S. (2001). The differential diagnosis of impaired reciprocal social interaction in children: A review of disorders. *Child Psychiatry and Human Development, 32*, 71–89.

Scheeringa, M. S., & Gaensbauer, T. J. (2000). Posttraumatic stress disorder. In C. H. Zeanah (Ed.), *Handbook of infant mental health* (2nd ed., pp. 369–381). New York: Guilford Press.

Scheeringa, M. S., & Zeanah, C. H. (2001). A relational perspective on PTSD in early childhood. *Journal of Traumatic Stress, 14*(4), 799–815.

Scheeringa, M. S., Zeanah, C. H., Myers, L., & Putnam, F. W. (2003). New findings on alternative criteria for PTSD in preschool children. *Journal of the American Academy of Child and Adolescent Psychiatry, 42*(5), 561–570.

Schellenberg, G. D., Dawson, G., Sung, Y. G., Estes, A., Muson, J., Rosenthal, E., et al. (2006). Evidence for genetic linkage of autism to chromosomes 7 and 4. *Molecular Psychiatry, 11*(11), 979.

Schenk, S. (2002). Sensitization as a process underlying the progression of drug use via gateway drugs. In D. B. Kandel (Ed.), *Stages and pathways of drug involvement: Examining the gateway hypothesis* (pp. 318–336). New York: Cambridge University Press.

Scherff, A. R., Eckert, T. L., & Miller, D. N. (2005). Youth suicide prevention: A survey of public school superintendents' acceptability of school-based programs. *Suicide and Life-Threatening Behavior, 35*(2), 154–169.

Schmeck, K., & Poustka, F. (2001). Temperament and disruptive behavior disorders. *Psychopathology, 34*, 159–163.

Schmidt, L. A., & Fox, N. A. (2002). Molecular genetics of temperamental differences in children. In J. Benjamin & R. P. Ebstein (Eds.), *Molecular genetics and the human personality* (pp. 245–255). Washington, DC: American Psychiatric Publishing.

Schmidt, L. A., Polak, C. P., & Spooner, A. I. (2001). Biological and environmental contributions to childhood shyness: A diathesis-stress model. In W. R. Crozier & L. E. Alden (Eds.), *International handbook of social anxiety: Concepts, research and interventions relating to the self and shyness* (pp. 29–51). New York: Wiley.

Schneider, B. H. (1998). Cross-cultural comparison as doorkeeper in research on the social and emotional adjustment of children and adolescents. *Developmental Psychology, 34*(4), 793–797.

Schneider, B. H., Attili, G., Vermigli, P., & Younger, A. (1997). A comparison of middle class English-Canadian and Italian mothers' beliefs about children's peer-directed aggression and social withdrawal. *International Journal of Behavioral Development, 21*(1), 133–154.

Schneider-Rosen, K. (1993). The developmental reorganization of attachment relationships. In M. T. Greenberg, D. Cicchetti, & E. M. Cummings (Eds.), *Attachment in the preschool years: Theory, research, and intervention* (pp. 185–220). Chicago: University of Chicago Press.

Schneider-Rosen, K., & Cicchetti, D. (1984). The relationship between affect and cognition in maltreated infants: Quality of attachment and the development of visual self-recognition. *Child Development, 55*(2), 648–658.

Schniering, C. A., Hudson, J. L., & Rapee, R. M. (2000). Issues in the diagnosis and assessment of anxiety disorders in children and adolescents. *Clinical Psychology Review, 20*(4), 453–478.

Schock, A. M., Gavazzi, S. M., Fristad, M. A., & Goldberg-Arnold, J. S. (2002). The role of father participation in the treatment of childhood mood disorders. *Family Relations: Interdisciplinary Journal of Applied Family Studies, 51*(3), 230–237.

Schopler, E. (1996). Are autism and Asperger syndrome (AS) different labels or different disabilities? *Journal of Autism and Developmental Disorders, 26*, 109–110.

Schopler, E. (1998). Premature popularization of Asperger syndrome. In E. Schopler, G. B. Mesibov, & L. J. Kunce (Eds.), *Asperger syndrome or high-functioning autism?* (pp. 385–399). New York: Plenum Press.

Schopler, E. (1998). Prevention and management of behavior problems: The TEACCH approach. In E. Sanavio (Ed.), *Behavior and cognitive therapy today: Essays in honor of Hans J. Eysenck* (pp. 249–259). Oxford, England: Elsevier Science.

Schopler, E. (2001). Treatment for autism: From science to pseudoscience or anti-science. In E. Schopler, N. Yirmiya, C. Shulman & L. M. Marcus (Eds.), *The research basis for autism intervention* (pp. 9–24). New York: Kluwer Academic/Plenum Publishers.

Schopler, E., & Mesibov, G. B. (2000). Cross-cultural priorities in developing autism services. *International Journal of Mental Health, 1, 29*, 3–21.

Schopler, E., Mesibov, G. B., & Hearsey, K. (1995). Structured teaching in the TEACCH system. In E. Schopler & G. B. Mesibov (Eds.), *Learning and cognition in autism* (pp.243–268). New York: Plenum Press.

Schopler, E., Mesibov, G. B., & Kunce, L. J. (Eds.). (1998). *Asperger syndrome or high-functioning autism?* New York: Plenum Press.

Schopler, E., Reichler, R. J., & Renner, B. R. (1988). The Childhood Autism Rating Scale. Los Angeles: Western Psychological Services.

Schopler, E., Yirmiya, N., Shulman, C., & Marcus, L. M. (Eds.). (2001). *The research basis for autism intervention.* New York: Kluwer Academic/Plenum Publishers.

Schore, A. N. (1994). *Affect regulation and the origin of the self: The neurobiology of emotional development.* Hillsdale, NJ: Erlbaum.

Schore, A. N. (1996). The experience-dependent maturation of a regulatory system in the orbital prefrontal cortex and the origin of developmental psychopathology. *Development and Psychopathology, 8*(1), 59–87.

Schore, A. N. (1997). Early organization of the nonlinear right brain and development of a predisposition to psychiatric disorders. *Development and Psychopathology, 9*(4), 595–631.

Schore, A. N. (2000). The self-organization of the right brain and the neurobiology of emotional development. In M. D. Lewis & I. Granic (Eds.), *Emotion, development, and self-organization: Dynamic systems approaches to emotional development. Cambridge studies in social and emotional development* (pp. 155–185). New York: Cambridge University Press.

Schore, A. N. (2001). Effects of a secure attachment relationship on right brain development, affect regulation and infant mental health. *Infant Mental Health Journal, 22*(1–2), 7–66.

Schreibman, L. (2005). *The science and fiction of autism.* Cambridge, MA: Harvard University Press.

Schreibman, L. & Anderson, A. (2001). Focus on integration: The future of the behavioral treatment of autism. *Behavior Therapy, 32*(4), 619–632.

Schreibman, L. & Koegel, R. L. (2005). Training for parents of children with autism: Pivotal responses, generalization, and individualization of interventions. In E. Hibbs & P. Jensen (Eds.), *Psychological treatments for child and adolescent disorders: Empirically based strategies for clinical practice* (2nd ed., pp. 605–631). Washington, DC: American Psychological Association.

Schulenberg, J. E., Merline, A. C., Johnston, L. D., O'Malley, P. M., Bachman, J. G., & Laetz, V. B. (2005). Trajectories of marijuana use during the transition to adulthood: The big picture based on national panel data. *Journal of Drug Issues, 35*(2), 255–280.

Schulenberg, J., & Maggs, J. L. (2001). Moving targets: Modeling developmental trajectories of adolescent alcohol misuse, individual and peer risk factors, and intervention effects. *Applied Developmental Science, 5(4),* 237–253.

Schulenberg, J., Maggs, J. L., Long, S. W., Sher, K. J., Gotham, H. J., Baer, J. S., et al. (2001). The problem of college drinking: Insights from a developmental perspective. *Alcoholism: Clinical and Experimental Research, 25*(3), 473–477.

Schulenberg, J., Maggs, J. L., Steinman, K. J., & Zucker, R. A. (2001). Developmental matters: Taking the long view on substance abuse etiology and intervention during adolescence. In P. M. Monti & S. M. Colby (Eds.), *Adolescents, alcohol, and substance abuse: Reaching teens through brief interventions* (pp. 19–57). New York: Guilford Press.

Schuler, M. E., Nair, P., & Black, M. M. (2002). Ongoing maternal drug use, parenting attitudes, and a home intervention: Effects on mother-child interaction at 18 months. *Journal of Developmental and Behavioral Pediatrics, 23*(2), 87–94.

Schultz, R. T. (2005). Developmental deficits in social perception in autism: The role of the amygdale and fusiform face area. *International Journal of Developmental Neuroscience, 23*(2–3), 125–141.

Schultz, R. T., Grelotti, D. J., Klin, A., Kleinman, J., Van der Gaag, C., Marois, R., et al. (2003). The role of the fusiform face area in social cognition: Implications for the pathobiology of autism. In U. Frith & E. Hill (Eds.), *Autism: Mind and brain* (pp.267–293). New York: Oxford University Press.

Schumann, C. M., Buonocore, M. H., & Amaral, D. G. (2001). Magnetic resonance imaging of the post-mortem autistic brain. *Journal of Autism and Developmental Disorders, 31*, 561–568.

Schwab-Stone, M., Ruchkin, V., Vermeiren, R., & Leckman, P. (2001). Cultural considerations in the treatment of children and adolescents: Operationalizing the importance of culture in treatment. *Child and Adolescent Psychiatric Clinics of North America, 10(4),* 729–743.

Schwarte, A. R. (2008). Fragile X syndrome. *School Psychology Quarterly, 23*(2), 290–300.

Schwartz, C. E., Snidman, N., & Kagan, J. (1996). Early childhood temperament as a determinant of externalizing behavior in adolescence. *Development and Psychopathology, 8*(3), 527–537.

Schwartz, C. E., Snidman, N., & Kagan, J. (1999). Adolescent social anxiety as an outcome of inhibited temperament in childhood. *Journal of the American Academy of Child and Adolescent Psychiatry, 38*(8), 1008–1015.

Schwartz, D., Dodge, K. A., Pettit, G. S., Bates, J. E., & Conduct Problems Prevention Research Group. (2000). Friendship as a moderating factor in the pathway between early harsh home environment and later victimization in the peer group. *Developmental Psychology, 36*(5), 646–662.

Scime, M., Cook-Cottone, C., Kane, L., & Watson, T. (2006). Group prevention of eating disorders with fifth-grade females: Impact on body dissatisfaction, drive for thinness, and media influence. *Eating Disorders: The Journal of Treatment and Prevention 14*(2), 143–155.

Sciutto, M. J., Nolfi, C. J., & Bluhm, C. (2004). Effects of gender and symptom type on referrals for ADHD by elementary school teachers. *Journal of Emotional and Behavioral Disorders, 12*(4), 247–253.

Scorgie, K., & Sobsey, D. (2000). Transformational outcomes associated with parenting children who have disabilities. *Mental Retardation, 38*(3), 195–206.

Scorgie, K., Wilgosh, L., & McDonald, L. (1996). A qualitative study of managing life when a child has a disability. *Developmental Disabilities Bulletin, 24*(2), 68–90.

Scorgie, K., Wilgosh, L., & McDonald, L. (1998). Stress and coping in families of children with disabilities: An examination of recent literature. *Developmental Disabilities Bulletin, 26*(1), 22–42.

Scott, F. J., Baron-Cohen, S., Bolton, P., & Brayne, C. (2002a). The CAST (Childhood Asperger Syndrome Test): Preliminary development of a UK screen for mainstream primary-school-age children. *Autism, 6*, 9–31.

Scott, F. J., Baron-Cohen, S., Bolton, P., & Brayne, C. (2002b). Brief report: Prevalence of autism spectrum conditions in children aged 5–11 years in Cambridgeshire, UK. *Autism, 6*, 231–237.

Scott, M. M., & Deneris, E. S. (2005). Making and breaking serotonin neurons and autism. *International Journal of Developmental Neuroscience, 23*(2–3), 277–285.

Scotti, J. R., Morris, T. L., McNeil, C. B., & Hawkins, R. P. (1996). DSM-IV and disorders of childhood and adolescence: Can structural criteria be functional? *Journal of Consulting and Clinical Psychology, 64*(6), 1177–1191.

Scourfield, J., Rice, F., Thapar, A., Gordon, T., Martin, N., & McGuffin, P. (2003). Depressive symptoms in children and adolescents: Changing aetiological influences with development. *Journal of Child Psychology and Psychiatry, 44*(7), 968–976.

Scourfield, J., Van den Bree, M., Martin, N., & McGuffin, P. (2004). Conduct problems in children and adolescents: A twin study. *Archives of General Psychiatry, 61*(5), 489–496.

Sebanz, N., Knoblich, G., Stumpf, L., & Prinz, W. (2005). Far from action-blind: Representation of others' actions in individuals with autism. *Cognitive Neuropsychology, 22*(3–4), 433–454.

Seidman, L. J., Biederman, J., Monuteaux, M. C., Valera, E., Doyle, A. E., & Faraone, S. V. (2005). Impact of gender and age on executive functioning: Do girls and boys with and without attention deficit hyperactivity disorder differ neuropsychologically in preteen and teenage years? *Developmental Neuropsychology, 27*(1), 79–105.

Seifer, R. (1995). Perils and pitfalls of high-risk research. *Developmental Psychology, 31(3),* 420–424.

Seifer, R. (2000). Temperament and goodness of fit: Implications for developmental psychopathology. In A. J. Sameroff & M. Lewis (Eds.), *Handbook of developmental psychopathology* (2nd ed., pp. 257–276). Dordrecht, Netherlands: Kluwer Academic Publishers.

Seifer, R. (2001). Conceptual and methodological basis for understanding development and risk in infants. In L. T. Singer & P.

S. Zeskind (Eds.), *Biobehavioral assessment of the infant* (pp. 18–39). New York: Guilford Press.

Seifer, R., & Dickstein, S. (2000). Parental mental illness and infant development. In C. H. Zeanah (Ed.), *Handbook of infant mental health* (2nd ed., pp. 145–160). New York: Guilford Press.

Seiffge-Krenke, I. (1998). Chronic disease and perceived developmental progression in adolescence. *Developmental Psychology, 34*, 1073–1084.

Seiffge-Krenke, I. (2003). Testing theories of romantic development from adolescence to young adulthood: Evidence of a developmental sequence. *International Journal of Behavioral Development, 27*(6), 519–531.

Seligman, M .E. (1975). *Helplessness: On depression, development, and death.* Oxford, England: W. H. Freeman.

Seligman, M. E. P. & Csikszentmihalyi, M. (2000). Positive psychology: An introduction. *American Psychologist, 55(1),* 5–14.

Seligman, S. (2000). Clinical interviews with families of infants. In C. H. Zeanah (Ed.), *Handbook of infant mental health* (2nd ed., pp. 211–221). New York: Guilford Press.

Sellinger, M. H., Hodapp, R. M., & Dykens, E. M. (2006). Leisure activities of individuals with Prader-Willi, Williams, and Down syndromes. *Journal of Developmental and Physical Disabilities, 18*(1), 59–71.

Semel, E., & Rosner, S. R. (2003). *Understanding Williams syndrome: Behavioral patterns and interventions.* Mahwah, NJ: Erlbaum.

Semrud-Clikeman, M., Steingard, R. J., Filipek, P., Biederman, J., Bekken, K., & Renshaw, P. F. (2000). Using MRI to examine brain-behavior relationships in males with attention deficit disorder with hyperactivity. *Journal of the American Academy of Child and Adolescent Psychiatry, 39*(4), 477–484

Serafucam F. C., & Cicchetti, D. (1976). Down's syndrome children in a strange situation: Attachment and exploration behaviors. *Merrill-Palmer Quarterly, 22*(2), 137–150.

Seroczynski, A. D., Cole, D. A., & Maxwell, S. E. (1997). Cumulative and compensatory effects of competence and incompetence on depressive symptoms in children. *Journal of Abnormal Psychology, 106*(4), 586–597.

Servan-Schreiber, D., Lin, B. L., & Birmaher, B. (1998). Prevalence of posttraumatic stress disorder and major depressive disorder in Tibetan refugee children. *Journal of the American Academy of Child and Adolescent Psychiatry, 37*(8), 874–879.

Sessa, F. M., Avenevoli, S., Steinberg, L., & Morris, A. S. (2001). Correspondence among informants on parenting: Preschool children, mothers, and observers. *Journal of Family Psychology, 25(1),* 53–68.

Sewitch, M. J., Blais, R., Rahme, E., Bexton, B., & Galarneau, S. (2005). Pharmacologic response to depressive disorders among adolescents. *Psychiatric Services, 56*(9), 1089–1097.

Sharp, W. S., Walter, J. M., Marsh, W. L., Ritchie, G. F., Hamburger, S. D., & Castellanos, F. X. (1999). ADHD in girls: Clinical comparability of a research sample. *Journal of the American Academy of Child and Adolescent Psychiatry, 38*(1), 40–47.

Shaw, D. S., & Bell, R. Q. (1993). Developmental theories of parental contributors to antisocial behavior. *Journal of Abnormal Child Psychology, 21*, 493–518.

Shaw, D. S., Dishion, T. J., Supplee, L., Gardner, F., & Arends, K. (2006). Randomized trial of a family-centered approach to the prevention of early conduct problems: 2-Year effects of the family check-up in early childhood. *Journal of Consulting and Clinical Psychology, 74*(1), 1–9.

Shaw, D. S., Gilliom, M., Ingoldsby, E. M., & Nagin, D. S. (2003). Trajectories leading to school-age conduct problems. *Developmental Psychology, 39*(2), 189–200.

Shaw, D. S., Keenan, K., Vondra, J. I., Delliquadri, E., & Giovannelli, J. (1997). Antecedents of preschool children's internalizing problems: A longitudinal study of low-income families. *Journal of the American Academy of Child and Adolescent Psychiatry, 36*(12), 1760–1767.

Shaw, D. S., Owens, E. B., Giovannelli, J., & Winslow, E. B. (2001). Infant and toddler pathways leading to early externalizing disorders. *Journal of the American Academy of Child and Adolescent Psychiatry, 40*, 36–43.

Shaw, H., Ramirez, L., Trost, A., Randall, P., & Stice, E. (2004). Body image and eating disturbances across ethnic groups: More similarities than differences. *Psychology of Addictive Behaviors, 18*, 12–18.

Shaywitz, B. A., Fletcher, J. M., Pugh, K. R., Klorman, R., & Shaywitz, S. E. (1999). Progress in imaging attention deficit hyperactivity disorder. *Mental Retardation and Developmental Disabilities Research Reviews, 5*, 185–190.

Shedler, J., & Block, J. (1990). Adolescent drug use and psychological health: A longitudinal inquiry. *American Psychologist, 45*(5), 612–630.

Sheeber, L., Biglan, A., Metzler, C. W., & Taylor, T. K. (2002). Promoting effective parenting practices. In L. A. Jason & D. S. Glenwick (Eds.), *Innovative strategies for promoting health and mental health across the life span* (pp. 63–84). New York: Springer.

Sheeber, L., & Sorensen, E. (1998). Family relationships of depressed adolescents: A multimethod assessment. *Journal of Clinical Child Psychology, 27*(3), 268–277.

Sheffield, J. K., Spence, S. H., Rapee, R. M., Kowalenko, N., Wignall, A., Davis, A., et al. (2006). Evaluation of universal, indicated, and combined cognitive-behavioral approaches to the prevention of depression among adolescents. *Journal of Consulting and Clinical Psychology, 74*(1), 66–79.

Sheinkopf, S. J., Lester, B. M., LaGasse, L. L., Seifer, R., Bauer, C. R., Shankaran, S., et al. (2006). Interactions between maternal characteristics and neonatal behavior in the prediction of parenting stress and perception of infant temperament. *Journal of Pediatric Psychology, 31*(1), 27–40.

Shelef, K., Diamond, G. M., Diamond, G. S., & Liddle, H. A. (2005). Adolescent and parent alliance and treatment outcome in multidimensional family therapy. *Journal of Consulting and Clinical Psychology, 73*(4), 689–698.

Sher, L., & Zalsman, G. (2005). Alcohol and adolescent suicide. *International Journal of Adolescent Medicine and Helath 17*(3), 197–203.

Sherer, M. R., & Schreibman, L. (2005). Individual behavioral profiles and predictors of treatment effectiveness for children with autism. *Journal of Consulting and Clinical Psychology, 73*(3), 525–538.

Sherman, D. K., McGue, M. K., & Iacono, W. G. (1997). Twin concordance for attention deficit hyperactivity disorder: A comparison of teachers' and mothers' reports. *American Journal of Psychiatry, 154*, 532–535.

Sherrill, J. T., & Kovacs, M. (2002). Nonsomatic treatment of depression. *Child and Adolescent Psychiatric Clinics of North America, 11*(3), 579–594.

Sherwood, N. E., & Neumark-Sztainer, D. (2001). Internalization of the sociocultural ideal: Weight-related attitudes and dieting behaviors among young adolescent girls. *American Journal of Health Promotion, 15,* 228–231.

Sherwood, N. E., Neumark-Sztainer, D, Story, M. Beuhring, T., & Resnick, M. D. (2002). Weight-related sports involvement in girls: Who is at risk for disordered eating? *American Journal of Health Promotion, 16,* 341–344.

Shi, L., Tu, N., & Patterson, P. H. (2005). Maternal influenza is likely to alter fetal brain development indirectly: The virus is not detected in the fetus. *International Journal of Developmental Neuroscience, 23*(2–3), 299–305.

Shields, A., Dickstein, S., Seifer, R., Giusti, L. Magee, K. D., & Spritz, B. (2001). Emotional competence and early school adjustment: A study of preschoolers at risk. *Early Education and Development, 12*(1), 73–96.

Shih, J. H., Eberhart, N. K., Hammen, C. L., & Brennan, P. A. (2006). Differential exposure and reactivity to interpersonal stress predict sex differences in adolescent depression. *Journal of Clinical Child and Adolescent Psychology, 35*(1), 103–115.

Shillington, A. M., & Clapp, J. D. (2003). Adolescents in public substance abuse treatment programs: The impacts of sex and race on referrals and outcomes. *Journal of Child and Adolescent Substance Abuse, 12*(4), 69–91.

Shin, J. Y. (2002). Social support for families of children with mental retardation: Comparison between Korea and the United States. *Mental Retardation, 40*(2), 103–118.

Shirk, S. R. (2001). The road to effective child psychological services: Treatment processes and outcome research. In J. N. Hughes, A. M. La Greca, et al. (Eds.), *Handbook of psychological services for children and adolescents* (pp. 43–59). London: Oxford University Press.

Shirk, S. R., & Saiz, C. C. (1992). Clinical, empirical, and developmental perspectives on the therapeutic relationship in child psychotherapy. *Development and Psychopathology, 4,* 713–728.

Shirk, S., Talmi, A., & Olds, D. (2000). A developmental psychopathology perspective on child and adolescent treatment policy. *Development and Psychopathology, 12,* 835–855.

Shonkoff, J. P., & Marshall, P. C. (2000). The biology of developmental vulnerability. In J. P. Shonkoff & S. J. Meisels (Eds.), *Handbook of early childhood intervention* (pp. 31–53). New York: Cambridge University Press.

Shonkoff, J. P., & Meisels, S. J. (2000). *Handbook of early childhood intervention.* New York: Cambridge University Press.

Shonkoff, J. P., & Phillips, D. A. (Eds.). (2000). *From neurons to neighborhoods: The science of early childhood development.* Washington, DC: National Academy Press.

Shortt, A. L., Barrett, P. M., & Fox, T. L. (2001). Evaluating the FRIENDS program: A cognitive-behavioral group treatment for anxious children and their parents. *Journal of Clinical Child Psychology, 30*(4), 525–535.

Shoval, G., Zalsman, G., Polakevitch, J., Shtein, N., Sommerfeld, E., & Apter, A. (2005). Effect of the broadcast of a television documentary about a teenage suicide in Israel on suicidal behavior and methods. *Crisis: The Journal of Crisis Intervention and Suicide Prevention, 26*(1), 20–24.

Shroff, H., Reba, L., Thornton, L. M.., Tozzi, F., Klump, K. L., Berrettini, W. H., et al. (2006). Features associated with excessive exercise in women with eating disorders. *International Journal of Eating Disorders, 39,* 454–461.

Shroff, H., & Thompson, J. K. (2004). Body image and eating disturbance in India: Media and interpersonal influences. *International Journal of Eating Disorders, 35,* 198–203.

Shroff, H., & Thompson, J. K. (2006). The Tripartite Influence Model of body image and eating disturbance: A replication with adolescent girls. *Body Image, 3*(1), 17–23.

Shumow, L., Vandell, D. L., & Posner, J. (1999). Risk and resilience in the urban neighborhood: Predictors of academic performance among low-income elementary school children. *Merrill-Palmer Quarterly, 45(2),* 309–331.

Shure, M. B., & Spivack, G. (1980). Interpersonal problem solving as a mediator of behavioral adjustment in preschool and kindergarten children. *Journal of Applied Developmental Psychology, 1*(1), 29–44.

Shweder, R. A., Goodnow, J., Hatano, G., LeVine, R. A., Markus, H., & Miller, P. (1988). The cultural psychology of development: One mind, many mentalities. In W. Damon & R. M. Lerner (Eds.), *Handbook of child psychology: Vol. 1. Theoretical models of human development* (5th ed., pp. 635–684). Hoboken, NJ: Wiley.

Siegler, R. S. (2003). Thinking and intelligence. In M. H. Bornstein, L. Davidson, C. L. M. Keyes, & A. Moore (Eds.), *Well-being: Positive development across the life course* (pp. 311–320). Mahwah, NJ: Erlbaum.

Sigman, M. D., Yirmiya, N., & Capps, L. (1995). Social and cognitive understanding in high-functioning children with autism. In E. Schopler & G. B. Mesibov (Eds.), Learning and cognition in autism (pp. 159–176). New York: Plenum Press.

Sigman, M., & Ruskin, E. (1999). Continuity and change in the social competence of children with autism, Down syndrome, and developmental delays. *Monographs of the Society for Research in Child Development, 64*(1), v-114.

Sigvardsson, S., Bohman, M., & Clonginger, C. R. (1996). Replication of the Stockholm Adoption Study of alcoholism: Confirmatory cross-fostering analysis. *Archives of General Psychiatry, 53*(8), 681–687.

Silberg, J. L., & Bulik, C. M. (2005). The developmental association between eating disorders symptoms and symptoms of depression and anxiety in juvenile twin girls. *Journal of Child Psychology and Psychiatry, 46,* 1317–1326.

Silberg, J., Pickles, A., Rutter, M., Hewitt, J., Simonoff, E., Maes, J., et al. (1999). The influence of genetic favors and life stress on depression among adolescent girls. *Archives of General Psychology, 56*(3), 225–232.

Silk, J. S., Morris, A. S., Kanaya, T., & Steinberg, L. (2003). Psychological control and autonomy granting: Opposite ends of a continuum or distinct constructs? *Journal of Research on Adolescence, 13*(1), 113–128.

Silk, J. S., Sessa, F. M., Sheffield Morris, A., Steinberg, L., & Avenevoli, S. (2004). Neighborhood cohesion as a buffer against hostile maternal parenting. *Journal of Family Psychology, 18*(1), 135–146.

Silverman, W. K., & Carter, R. (2006). Anxiety disturbance in girls and women. In J. Worell & C. D. Goodheart (Eds.), *Handbook of girls' and women's psychological health: Gender and well-being across the lifespan* (pp. 60–68). New York: Oxford University Press.

Silverman, W. K., & Moreno, J. (2005). Specific phobia. *Child and Adolescent Psychiatric Clinics of North America, 14*(4), 819–843.

Silverman, W. K., & Ollendick, T. H. (2005). Evidence-based assessment of anxiety and its disorders in children and adolescents. *Journal of Clinical Child and Adolescent Psychology, 34*(3), 380–411.

Silverman, W. K., Kurtines, W. M., Ginsburg, G. S., Weems, C. F., Lumpkin, P. W., & Carmichael, D. H. (1999). Treating anxiety disorders in children with group cognitive-behavioral therapy: A randomized clinical trial. *Journal of Consulting and Clinical Psychology, 67*(6)*,* 995–1003.

Silverman, W. K., La Greca, A. M., & Wasserstein, S. (1995). What do children worry about? Worries and their relation to anxiety. *Child Development, 66*(3), 671–686.

Silverthorn, P., & Frick, P. J. (1999). Developmental pathways to antisocial behavior: The delayed-onset pathway in girls. *Development and Psychopathology, 11,* 101–126.

Silverthorn, P., Frick, P. J., & Reynolds, R. (2001). Timing of onset and correlates of severe conduct problems in adjudicated girls and boys. *Journal of Psychopathology and Behavioral Assessment, 23,* 171–181.

Sim, L., & Zeman, J. (2004). Emotion awareness and identification skills in adolescent girls with bulimia nervosa. *Journal of Clinical Child and Adolescent Psychology, 33,* 760–771.

Simeonsson, R. J., & Short, R. J. (1996). Adaptive development, survival roles, and quality of life. In J. W. Jacobson & J. A. Mulick (Eds.), *Manual of diagnosis and professional practice in mental retardation* (pp. 137–146). Washington, DC: American Psychological Association.

Simmel, C., Brooks, D., Barth, R. P., & Hinshaw, S. P. (2001). Externalizing symptomatology among adoptive youth: Prevalence and preadoption risk factors. *Journal of Abnormal Child Psychology, 29,* 57–69.

Simmerman, S., & Baker, B. L. (2001). Fathers' and mothers' perceptions of father involvement in families with young children with a disability. *Journal of Intellectual and Developmental Disability, 26*(4), 325–338.

Simmons, R. G. (2001). Comfort with the self. In T. J. Owens, S. Stryker, & N. Goodman (Eds.), *Extending self-esteem theory and research: Sociological and psychological currents* (pp. 198–222). New York: Cambridge University Press.

Simmons, R. G., & Blyth, D. A. (1987). *Moving into adolescence: The impact of pubertal change and school context.* Hawthorne, NY: Aldine de Gruyter.

Simon, R. W. (1997). The meanings individuals attach to role identities and their implications for mental health. *Journal of Health and Social Behavior, 38,* 256–274.

Simonoff, E. (2001). Gene-environment interplay in oppositional defiant and conduct disorder. *Child and Adolescent Psychiatric Clinics of North America, 10,* 351–374.

Simonoff, E., Bolton, P., & Rutter, M. (1996). Mental retardation: Genetic findings, clinical implications and research agenda. *Journal of Child Psychology and Psychiatry, 37*(3), 259–280.

Simons-Morton, B. (2004). Prospective association of peer influence, school engagement, drinking expectancies, and parent expectations with drinking initiation among sixth graders. *Addictive Behaviors, 29*(2), 299–309.

Simons-Morton, B. G. (2004). The protective effect of parental expectations against early adolescent smoking initiation. *Health Education Research, 19*(5), 561–569.

Simons-Morton, B., & Chen, R. (2005). Latent growth curve analyses of parent influences on drinking progression among early adolescents. *Journal of Studies on Alcohol, 66*(1), 5–13.

Simons-Morton, B. G., Hartos, J. L., & Beck, K. H. (2004). Increased parent limits on teen driving: Positive effects from a brief intervention administered at the Motor Vehicle Administration. *Prevention Science, 5*(2), 101–111.

Simons-Morton, B. G., Hartos, J. L., Leaf, W. A., & Preusser, D. F. (2006). Increasing parent limits on novice young drivers: Cognitive mediation of the effect of persuasive messages. *Journal of Adolescent Research, 21*(1), 83–105.

Simons-Morton, B. G., & Haynie, D. L. (2003). Growing up drug free: A developmental challenge. In M. H. Bornstein & L. Davidson (Eds.), *Well-being: Positive development across the life course* (pp. 109–122). Mahwah, NJ: Erlbaum.

Simons-Morton, B. G., Haynie, D. L., Crump, A. D., Eitel, P., & Saylor, K. E. (2001). Peer and parent influences on smoking and drinking among early adolescents. *Health Education and Behavior, 28*(1), 95–107.

Simons-Morton, B. G., Lerner, N., & Singer, J. (2005). The observed effects of teenage passengers on the risky driving behavior of teenage drivers. *Accident Analysis & Prevention, 37*(6), 973–982.

Simpson, R. L., Myles, B. S., & Simpson, J. D. (1997). Inclusion of students with disabilities in general education settings: Structuring for successful management. In P. Zionts (Ed.), *Inclusion strategies for students with learning and behavioral problems: Perspectives, experiences, and best practices* (pp. 171–196). Austin, TX: PRO-ED.

Singer, G. H.S., Gert, B., & Koegel, R. L. (1999). A moral framework for analyzing the controversy over aversive behavioral interventions for people with severe mental retardation. *Journal of Positive Behavior Interventions, 1*(2)*,* 88–100.

Singer, L. T., Minnes, S., Short, E., Arendt, R., Farkas, K., Lewis, B., et al. (2004). Cognitive outcomes of preschool children with prenatal cocaine exposure. *Journal of the American Medical Association, 291*(20), 2448–2456.

Singh, M. K., DelBello, M. P., Adler, C. M., Stanford, K. E., & Strakowski, S. M. (2008). Neuroanatomical characterization of child offspring of bipolar patients. *Journal of the American Academy of Child and Adolescent Psychiatry, 47*(5), 526–531.

Singh, N. N., Osborne, J. G., & Huguenin, N. H. (1996). Applied behavioral interventions. In J. W. Jacobson & J. A. Mulick (Eds.), *Manual of diagnosis and professional practice in mental retardation* (pp. 341–353). Washington, DC: American Psychological Association.

Sivberg, B. (2002). Family system and coping behaviors: A comparison between parents of children with autistic spectrum disorders and parents with non-autistic children. *Autism, 6,* 397–409.

Skara, S., & Sussman, S. (2003). A review of 25 long-term adolescent tobacco and other drug use prevention program evaluations. *Preventive Medicine: An International Journal Devoted to Practice and Theory, 37*(5), 451–474.

Slesnick, N., & Waldron, H. B. (1997). Interpersonal problem-solving interactions of depressed adolescents and their parents. *Journal of Family Psychology, 11*(2), 234–245.

Slof-Op't, Landt, M. C. T., van Furth, E. F., Meulenbelt, I., Slagboom, P. E., Bartels, M., Boomsma, D. I., et al. (2005). Eating disorders: From twin studies to candidate genes and beyond. *Twin Research and Human Genetics, 8,* 467–482.

Slonim-Nevo, V., Sharaga, Y., Mirsky, J., Petrovsky, V., & Borodenko, M. (2006). Ethnicity versus migration: Two hypotheses about the psychosocial adjustment of immigrant adolescents. *International Journal of Social Psychiatry, 52(1),* 41–53.

Slovic, P. (2000). What does it mean to know a cumulative risk? Adolescents' perceptions of short-term and long-term consequences of smoking. *Journal of Behavioral Decision Making, 13*(2), 259–266.

Slutske, W. S., Caspi, A., Moffitt, T. E., & Poulton, R. (2005). Personality and problem gambling: A prospective study of a birth cohort of young adults. *Archives of General Psychiatry, 62*(7), 769–775.

Smalley, N., Scourfield, J., & Greenland, K. (2005). Young people, gender, and suicide: A review of research on the social context. *Journal of Social Work, 5*(2), 133–154.

Smetana, J. G., & Gettman, D. C. (2006). Autonomy and relatedness with parents and romantic development in African American adolescents. *Developmental Psychology, 42*(6), 1347–1351.

Smith, B. H., Pelham, W. E., Gnagy, E., & Yudell, R. S. (1998). Equivalent effects of stimulant treatment for attention-deficit hyperactivity disorder during childhood and adolescence. *Journal of the American Academy of Child and Adolescent Psychiatry, 37*, 314–321.

Smith, B. H., Pelham, W. E., Gnagy, E., Molina, B., & Evans, S. (2000). The reliability, validity, and unique contributions of self-report by adolescents receiving treatment for attention-deficit/hyperactivity disorder. *Journal of Consulting and Clinical Psychology, 68*(3), 489–499.

Smith, C. A., & Farrington, D. P. (2004). Continuities in antisocial behavior and parenting across three generations. *Journal of Child Psychology and Psychiatry, 45*(2), 230–247.

Smith, E. P., Gorman-Smith, D., Quinn, W. H., Rabiner, D. L., Tolan, P. H., & Winn, D. (2004). Community-based multiple family groups to prevent and reduce violent and aggressive behavior: The GREAT families program. *American Journal of Preventative Medicine, 26*(suppl), 39–47.

Smith, G. T., & Anderson, K. G. (2001). Personality and learning factors combine to create risk for adolescent problem drinking: A model and suggestions for intervention. In P. M. Monti, S. M. Colby, & T. A. O'Leary (Eds.), *Adolescents, alcohol, and substance abuse: Reaching teens through brief interventions* (pp. 109–141). New York: Guilford Press.

Smith, I. M. (2000). Motor functioning in Asperger syndrome. In A. Klin, F. R. Volkmar, & S. S. Sparrow (Eds.), *Asperger syndrome* (pp. 97–124). New York: Guilford Press.

Smith, I. M., & Bryson, S. E. (1994). Imitation and action in autism: A critical review. *Psychological Bulletin, 116*, 259–273.

Smith, J. D. (2002). The myth of mental retardation: Paradigm shifts, dissaggregation, and developmental disabilities. *Mental Retardation, 40*(1), 62–64.

Smith, J., & Prior, M. (1995). Temperament and stress resilience in school-age children: A within-families study. *Journal of the American Academy of Child and Adolescent Psychiatry, 34(2)*, 168–179.

Snell, M. E., & Janney, R. E. (2000). Teachers' problem-solving about children with moderate and severe disabilities in elementary classrooms. *Exceptional Children, 66*(4), 472–490.

Snidman, N., Kagan, J., Riordan, L., & Shannon, D. C. (1995). Cardiac function and behavioral reactivity during infancy. *Psychophysiology, 32*(3), 199–207.

Snoek, H., van Goozen, S. H. M., Matthys, W., Sigling, H. O., Koppeschaar, H. P. F., Westenberg, H. G. M., et al. (2002). Serotinergic functioning in children with oppositional defiant disorder: A sumatriptan challenge study. *Biological Psychiatry, 51*, 319–325.

Snyder, A. R. (2006). Risky and casual sexual relationships among teens. In A. C. Crouter & A. Booth (Eds.), *Romance and sex in adolescence and emerging adulthood: Risks and opportunities. The Penn State University family issues symposia series* (pp. 161–169). Mahwah, NJ: Erlbaum.

Snyder, J., Schrepferman, L., McEachern, A., Barner, S., Johnson, K., & Provines, J. (2008). Peer deviancy training and peer coercion: Dual processes associated with early-onset conduct problems. *Child Development, 79*(2), 252–268.

Sobanski, E., & Schmidt, M. H. (2000). Body dysmorphic disorder: A review of the current knowledge. *Child Psychology and Psychiatry Review, 5,* 17–24.

Södersten, P., Bergh, C., & Zandian, M. (2006). Understanding eating disorders. *Hormones and Behavior, 50*, 572–578.

Sokol, R. J., Delaney-Black, V., & Nordstrom, B. (2003). Fetal alcohol spectrum disorder. *Journal of the American Medical Association, 290*(22), 2996–2999.

Soldz, S., Huyser, D. J., & Dorsey, E. (2003). The cigar as a drug delivery device: Youth use of blunts. *Addiction, 98*(10), 1379–1386.

Solhkhah, R., & Armentano, M. (2002). Adolescent substance abuse and psychiatric comorbidity. In D. R. Marsh & M. A. Fristad (Eds.), *Handbook of serious emotional disturbance in children and adolescents* (pp. 304–319). Hoboken, NJ: Wiley.

Solomon, J., & George, C. (1999a). The measurement of attachment security in infancy and childhood. In J. Cassidy & P. R. Shaver (Eds.), *Handbook of attachment: Theory, research, and clinical applications* (pp. 287–316). New York: Guilford Press.

Solomon, J., & George, C. (1999b). The place of disorganization in attachment theory: Linking classic observations with contemporary findings. In J. Solomon & C. George (Eds.), *Attachment disorganization* (pp. 3–32). New York: Guilford Press.

Solomon, J., George, C., & DeJong, A. (1995). Children as controlling at age six: Evidence of disorganized representational strategies and aggression at home and at school. *Development and Psychopathology, 7*(3), 447–463.

Sonuga-Barke, E. J. S. (1998). Categorical models of childhood disorder: A conceptual and empirical analysis. *Journal of Child Psychology and Psychiatry, 39(1)*, 115–133.

Sonuga-Barke, E. J. S., Minocha, K., Taylor, E. A., & Sandberg, S. (1993). Inter-ethnic bias in teacher's ratings of childhood hyperactivity. *British Journal of Developmental Psychology, 11*, 187–200.

Soodak, L. C., Podell, D. M., & Lehman, L. R. (1998). Teacher, student, and school attributes as predictors of teachers' responses to inclusion. *Journal of Special Education, 31*(4), 480–497.

South, M., Ozonoff, S., & McMahon, W. M. (2007). The relationship between executive functioning, central coherence, and repetitive behaviors in the high-functioning autism spectrum. *Autism, 11*(5), 437–451.

Southam-Gerow, M. A., & Kendall, P. C. (2000). A preliminary study of the emotion understanding of youths referred for treatment of anxiety disorders. *Journal of Clinical Child Psychology, 29*(3), 319–327.

Southam-Gerow, M.. A., & Kendall, P. C. (2002). Emotion regulation and understanding: Implications for child psychopathology and therapy. *Clinical Psychology Review, 22*(2), 189–222.

Sowell, E. R., Peterson, B. S., Thompson, P. M., Welcome, S. E., Henkenius, A. L., & Toga, A. W. (2003). Mapping cortical change across the human life span. *Nature Neuroscience, 6*(3), 309–315.

Spangler, G., & Grossman, K. E. (1993). Biobehavioral organization in securely and insecurely attached infants. *Child Development, 64*(5), 1439–1450.

Spangler, G., & Grossmann, K. (1999). Individual and physiological correlates of attachment disorganization in infancy. In J. Solomon & C. George (Eds.), *Attachment Disorganization* (pp. 95–124). New York: Guilford Press.

Sparks, B. F., Friedman, S. D., Shaw, D. W., Aylward, E. H., Echelard, D., Artru, A. A., et al. (2002). Brain structural abnormalities in young children with autism spectrum disorder. *Neurology, 59*(2), 184–192.

Sparrow, S. S., Cicchetti, D. V., & Balla, D. A. (2005). *Vineland-II: Vineland adaptive behavior scales* (2nd ed). Circle Pines, MN: AGS Publishing.

Spear, L. P. (2002a). Alcohol's effects on adolescents. *Alcohol Research and Health, 26*(4), 287–291.

Spear, L. P. (2002b). The adolescent brain and the college drinker: Biological basis of propensity to use and misuse alcohol. *Journal of Studies on Alcohol, 14*, 71–81.

Spear, L. P. (2003). Neurodevelopment during adolescence. In D. Cicchetti & E. Walker (Eds.), *Neurodevelopmental mechanisms in psychopathology* (pp. 62–83). New York: Cambridge University Press.

Spelke, E. (2002). Developmental neuroimaging: A developmental psychologist looks ahead. *Developmental Science, 5(3)*, 392–396.

Speltz, M. L., DeKlyen, M., Calderon, R., Greenberg, M. T., & Fisher, P. A. (1999). Neuropsychological characteristics and test behaviors of boys with early onset conduct problems. *Journal of Abnormal Psychology, 108*, 315–325.

Speltz, M. L., DeKlyen, M., & Greenberg, M. T. (1999). Attachment in boys with early onset conduct problems. *Development and Psychopathology, 11*, 269–285.

Speltz, M. L., DeKlyen, M., Greenberg, M. T., & Dryden, M. (1995). Clinic referral for oppositional defiant disorder: Relative significance of attachment and behavioral variables. *Journal of Abnormal Child Psychology, 23*, 487–507.

Speltz, M. L., McClellan, J., DeKlyen, M., & Jones, K. (1999). Preschool boys with oppositional defiant disorder: Clinical presentation and diagnostic change. *Journal of the American Academy of Child and Adolescent Psychiatry, 38*, 838–845.

Spence, S. H. (1997). Structure of anxiety symptoms among children: A confirmatory factor-analytic study. *Journal of Abnormal Psychology, 106*(2), 280–297.

Spence, S. H., Rapee, R., McDonald, C., & Ingram, M. (2001). The structure of anxiety symptoms among preschoolers. *Behaviour Research and Therapy, 39*(11), 1293–1316.

Spencer, M. B. (1990). Development of minority children: An introduction. *Child Development, 61*, 267–269.

Spencer, M. B., Cole, S. P., DuPree, D., Glymph, A., & Pierre, P. (1993). Self-efficacy among urban African American early adolescents: Exploring issues of risk, vulnerability, and resilience. *Development and Psychopathology, 5*, 719–739.

Spencer, T., Biederman, J., Kerman, K., & Steingard, R. (1993). Desipramine treatment of children with attention-deficit hyperactivity disorder and tic disorder or Tourette's syndrome. *Journal of the American Academy of Child and Adolescent Psychiatry, 32*, 354–360.

Spencer, T., Biederman, J., & Wilens, T. (1998). Growth deficits in children with attention deficit hyperactivity disorder. *Pediatrics, 102*, 501–506.

Spencer, T., Biederman, J., & Wilens, T. (2000). Pharmacotherapy of attention deficit hyperactivity disorder. *Child and Adolescent Psychiatric Clinics of North America, 9*(1), 77–97.

Spencer, T., Biederman, J., Wilens, T., Harding, M., O'Donnell, D., & Griffin, S. (1996). Pharmacotherapy of attention-deficit hyperactivity disorder across the life cycle. *Journal of the American Academy of Child and Adolescent Psychiatry, 35*, 409–432.

Spencer, T. J., Biederman, J., Wozniak, J., Faraone, S. V., Wilens, T. E., & Mick, E. (2001). Parsing pediatric bipolar disorder from its associated comorbidity with the disruptive behavior disorders. *Biological Psychiatry, 49*, 1062–1070.

Spencer, T., Wilens, T., Biederman, J., Wozniak, J. & Harding-Crawford, M. (2000). Attention-deficit/hyperactivity disorder with mood disorders. From T. E. Brown (Ed.), *Attention-deficit disorders and comorbidities in children, adolescents, and adults* (pp. 79–124). Washington, DC: American Psychiatric Publishing.

Spiker, D., Boyce, G. C., & Boyce, L. K. (2002). Parent-child interactions when young children have disabilities. In L. M. Glidden (Ed.), *International review of research in mental retardation*, Vol. 25 (pp. 35–70). San Diego, CA: Academic Press.

Spirito, A., Boergers, J., Donaldson, D., Bishop, D., & Lewander, W. (2002). An intervention trial to improve adherence to community treatment by adolescents after a suicide attempt. *Journal of the American Academy of Child and Adolescent Psychiatry, 41*(4), 435–442.

Spirito, A., Kurkjian, J., & Donaldson, D. (2003). Case examples. In A. Spirito & J. C. Overholser (Eds.), *Evaluating and treating adolescent suicide attempters: From research to practice* (pp. 277–294). San Diego, CA: Academic Press.

Spirito, A., Valeri, S., Boergers, J., & Donaldson, D. (2003). Predictors of continued suicidal behavior in adolescents following a suicide attempt. *Journal of Clinical Child and Adolescent Psychology, 32*(2), 284–289.

Spitz, R. (1946). Anaclitic depression: An inquiry into the genesis of psychiatric conditions in early childhood. *The Psychoanalytic Study of the Child, I*, 47–53.

Spitz, R. A. (1945). Hospitalism: An inquiry into the genesis of psychiatric conditions. *Psychoanalytic Study of the Child, 1*, 53–74.

Spitz, R. A., & Wolf, K. M. (1946). Anaclitic depression: An inquiry into the genesis of psychiatric conditions in early childhood. *Psychoanalytic Study of the Child, 2*, 313–342.

Sprafkin, J., Volpe, R. J., Gadow, K. D., Nolan, E. E., & Kelly, K. (2002). A DSM-IV-referenced screening instrument for preschool children: The Early Childhood Inventory. *Journal of the American Academy of Child and Adolescent Psychiatry, 41*, 604–612.

Sroufe, L. A. (1977). Attachment as an organizational construct. *Child Development, 48*, 1184–1199.

Sroufe, L. A. (1986). Appraisal: Bowlby's contribution to psychoanalytic theory and developmental psychology. *Journal of Child Psychology and Psychiatry, 27*(6), 841–849.

Sroufe, L. A., Carlson, E. A., Levy, A. K., & Egeland, B. (1999). Implications of attachment theory for developmental psychopathology. *Development and Psychopathology, 11*, 1–13.

Sroufe, L. A., Egeland, B., & Carlson, E. A. (1999). One social world: the integrated development of parent-child and peer relationships. In W. A. Collins & B. Laursen (Eds.), *Relationships as developmental contexts: The Minnesota symposia on child psychology* (Vol. 30, pp. 241–261). Mahwah, NJ: Erlbaum.

Sroufe, L. A. (1995). *Emotional development: The organization of emotional life in the early years.* Cambridge: Cambridge University Press.

Sroufe, L. A., & Fleeson, J. (1986). Attachment and the construction of relationships. In W. W. Hartup & Z. Rubin (Eds.), *Relationships and development* (pp. 51–71). Mahwah, NJ: Erlbaum.

Sroufe, L. A. (1983). Infant-caregiver attachment and patterns of adaptation in preschool: The roots of maladaptation and competence. In M. Perlmutter (Ed.), *Minnesota symposium on child psychology* (Vol. 16, pp. 41–81). Minneapolis: University of Minnesota Press.

Sroufe, L. A. (1997). Psychopathology as an outcome of development. *Development and Psychopathology, 9,* 251–268.

Sroufe, L. A., & Rutter, M. (1984). The domain of developmental psychopathology. *Child Development, 55,* 17–29.

Sroufe, L. A., Schork, E., Motti, F., Lawroski, N., & LaFreniere, P. (1984). The role of affect in social competence. In C. E. Izard, J. Kagan, & R. B. Zajonc (Eds.), *Emotions, cognition and behavior* (pp. 289–319). Cambridge: Cambridge University Press.

Sroufe, L. A. (1979). Socioemotional development. In *Handbook of Infant Development* (pp. 462–516). New York: Wiley.

Sroufe, L. A. (1979). The coherence of individual development: Early care, attachment, and subsequent developmental issues. *American Psychologist, 34*(10), 834–841.

Sroufe, L. A. (1982). The organization of emotional development. *Psychoanalytic Inquiry, 1*(4), 575–599.

Sroufe, L. A. (1988). The role of infant-caregiver attachment in development. In J. Belsky & T. Nezworski (Eds.), *Clinical implications of attachment* (pp. 18–38). Hillsdale, NJ: Erlbaum.

Sroufe, L. A., & Waters, E. (1977). Attachment as an organizational construct. *Child Development, 48*(4), 1184–1199.

Stack, S. (2005). Suicide in the media: A quantitative review of the studies based on nonfictional stories. *Suicide and Life-Threatening Behavior, 35*(2), 121–133.

Stainton, T. (2003). Identity, difference and the ethical politics of parental testing. *Journal of Intellectual Disability Research, 47*(7), 533–539.

Stainton, T., & Besser, H. (1998). The positive impact of children with an intellectual disability on the family. *Journal of Intellectual and Developmental Disabilities, 23*(1), 57–70.

Stainton, T. & McDonagh, P. (2001). Chasing shadows: The historical construction of developmental disability. *Journal on Developmental Disabilities, 8*(2), ix-xvi.

Stang, J., & Story, M. (2005). Adolescent growth and development. In J. Stang & M. Story (Eds.), *Guidelines for Adolescent Nutrition Services.* Retrieved July 17, 2009, from http://www.epi.umn.edu/let/pubs/adol_book.shtm

Stansbury, K., & Gunnar, M. R. (1994). Adrenocortical activity and emotion regulation. *Monographs of the Society for Research in Child Development, 59*(2–3), 108–134, 250–283.

Stanton, C., Spirito, A., Donaldson, D., & Boergers, J. (2003). Risk-taking behavior and adolescent suicide attempts. *Suicide and Life-Threatening Behavior, 33*(1), 74–79.

Stanton, W. R., Flay, B. R., Colder, C. R., & Mehta, P. (2004). Identifying and predicting adolescent smokers' developmental trajectories. *Nicotine and Tobacco Research, 6*(5), 843–852.

Starfield, B., Gross, E., & Wood, M. (1980). Psychosocial and psychosomatic diagnoses in primary care of children. *Pediatrics, 66,* 159–167.

Stark, K. D., Ballatore, M., Hamff, A., Valdez, C., & Selvig, L. (2001). Childhood depression. In H. Orvaschel, J. Faust, & M. Hersen (Eds.), *Handbook of conceptualization and treatment of child psychopathology* (pp.107–132). Amsterdam: Pergamon/Elsevier Science.

Stark, K. D., Hoke, J., Ballatore, M., Valdez, C., Scammaca, N., & Griffin, J. (2005). Treatment of child and adolescent depressive disorders. In E. D. Hibbs, & P. S. Jensen (Eds.), *Psychosocial treatments for child and adolescent disorders: Empirically based strategies for clinical practice* (2nd ed., pp. 239–265). Washington, DC: American Psychological Association.

Starr, E., Szatmari, P., Bryson, S. S., & Zwaigenbaum, L. (2003). Stability and change among high-functioning children with pervasive developmental disorders: A 2-year outcome study. *Journal of Autism and Developmental Disorders, 33,* 15–22.

State, M. W., King, B. H., & Dykens, E. (1997). A review of the past 10 years. *Journal of the American Academy of Child and Adolescent Psychiatry, 36*(12), 1664–1671.

Staton, D., Odden, R. L., & Volness, L. J. (2004). Defining subtypes of childhood bipolar illness. *Journal of the American Academy of Child and Adolescent Psychiatry, 43*(1), 2–3.

Staudinger, U. M., Marsiske, M., & Baltes, P. B. (1993). Resilience and levels of reserve capacity in later adulthood: Perspectives from life-span theory. *Development and Psychopathology, 5,* 541–566.

Steele, H., Steele, M., & Fonagy, P. (1996). Associations among attachment classifications of mothers, fathers, and their infants. *Child Development, 67*(2), 541–555.

Steele, K. M., Bass, K. E., & Crook, M. D. (1999). The mystery of the Mozart effect: Failure to replicate. *Psychological Science, 10*(4), 366–369.

Steffenburg, S., Gillberg, C., Hellgren, L., & Andersson, L. (1989). A twin study of autism in Denmark, Finland, Iceland, Norway and Sweden. *Journal of Child Psychology and Psychiatry, 30*(3), 405–416.

Steiger, H. (2004). Eating disorders and the serotonin connection: State, trait and developmental effects. *Journal of Psychiatry and Neuroscience, 29,* 20–29.

Stein, D., Meged, S., Bar-Hanin, T. & Blank, S. (1997). Partial eating disorders in a community sample of female adolescents. *Journal of the American Academy of Child and Adolescent Psychiatry, 36,* 1116–1123.

Stein, D., Orbach, I., Shani-Sela, M., Har-Even, D., Yaruslasky, A., Roth, D., et al. (2003). Suicidal tendencies and body image and experience in anorexia nervosa and suicidal female adolescent inpatients. *Psychotherapy and Psychosomatics, 72,* 16–25.

Stein, D., Williamson, D. E., Birmaher, B., Brent, D. A., Kaufman, J., Dahl, R. E., et al. (2000). Parent-child bonding and family functioning in depressed children and children at high risk and low risk for future depression. *Journal of the American Academy of Child and Adolescent Psychiatry, 39*(10), 1387–1395.

Stein, M. B., Chavira, D. A., & Jang, K. L. (2001). Bringing up bashful baby: Developmental pathways to social phobia. *Psychiatric Clinics of North America, 24*(4), 661–675.

Steinberg, A. B., & Phares, V. (2001). Family functioning, body image, and eating disturbances. In J. K. Thompson (Ed.), *Body image, eating disorders, and obesity in youth: Assessment, prevention, and treatment* (pp. 127–141). Washington, DC: American Psychological Association.

Steinberg, L. (2001). We know some things: Parent-adolescent relationships in retrospect and prospect. *Journal of Research on Adolescence, 11*(1), 1–19.

Steinberg, L. (2004). Risk taking in adolescence: What changes, and why? In R. E. Dahl & L. P. Spear (Eds.), *Adolescent brain development: Vulnerabilities and opportunities. Annals of the New York Academy of Sciences* (Vol. 1021, pp. 51–58). New York: New York Academy of Sciences.

Steinberg, L., & Avenevoli, S. (1998). Disengagement from school and problem behavior in adolescence: Developmental-contextual analysis of the influences of family and part-time work. In R. Jessor (Ed.), *New perspectives on adolescent risk behavior* (pp. 392–424). New York: Cambridge University Press.

Steinberg, L., Blatt-Eisengart, I., & Cauffman, E. (2006). Patterns of competence and adjustment among adolescents from authoritative, authoritarian, indulgent, and neglectful homes: A replication in a sample of serious juvenile offenders. *Journal of Research on Adolescence, 16*(1), 47–58.

Steiner, H., & Lock, J. (1998). Anorexia nervosa and bulimia nervosa in children and adolescents: A review of the past 10 years. *Journal of the American Academy of Child and Adolescent Psychiatry, 37,* 352–372.

Steiner, H., Kwan, W., Shaffer, T. G., Walker, S., Miller, S., Sagar, A., et al. (2003) Risk and protective factors for juvenile eating disorders. *European Child and Adolescent Psychiatry, 12,* 138–146.

Steinhausen, H. C., Boyadjieva, S, Griogoroiu-Serbanescu, M., & Neumarker, K. J. (2003). The outcome of adolescent eating disorders: Finds from an international collaborative study. *European Child and Adolescent Pyschiatry, 12,* 191–198.

Steinhausen, H. C., Boyadjieva, S., Griogoroiu-Serbanescu, M., Seidel, R., & Winkler-Metzke, C. (2000). A transcultural outcome study of adolescent eating disorders. *Acta Psychiatrica Scandinavica, 101,* 60–66.

Steinhausen, H. C., Willms, J., & Spohr, H. L. (1993). Long-term psychopathological and cognitive outcome of children with fetal alcohol syndrome. *Journal of the American Academy of Child and Adolescent Psychiatry, 32*(5), 990–994.

Stern, D. N. (1985). *The interpersonal world of the infant.* New York: Basic Books.

Stern, D. N. (1995). *The motherhood constellation: A unified view of parent-infant psychotherapy.* New York: Basic Books.

Sternberg, R. J., & Grigorenko, E. L. (2004). Why we need to explore development in its cultural context. *Merrill-Palmer Quarterly, Vol. 50(3)*, 369–386.

Stevens, J., Quittner, A. L., & Abikoff, H. (1998). Factors influencing elementary school teachers' ratings of ADHD and ODD behaviors. *Journal of Clinical Child Psychology, 27,* 406–414.

Stevens, S. J., & Morral, A. R. (Eds.). (2003). *Adolescent substance abuse treatment in the United States: Exemplary models from a national evaluation study.* New York: Haworth Press.

Stewart, S. E., Manion, I. G., & Davidson, S. (2002). Emergency management of the adolescent suicide attemptor: A review of the literature. *Journal of Adolescent Health, 30*(5), 312–325.

Stewart, S. M., Kennard, B. D., Lee, P. W. H., Hughes, C. W., Mayes, T. L., Emslie, G. J., et al. (2004). A cross-cultural investigation of cognitions and depressive symptoms in adolescents. *Journal of Abnormal Psychology, 113*(2), 248–257.

Stewart, S. M., Kennard, B. D., Lee, P. W.H., Mayes, T., Hughes, C., & Emslie, G. (2005). Hopelessness and suicidal ideation among adolescents in two cultures. *Journal of Child Psychology and Psychiatry, 46*(4), 364–372.

Stewart, S. M., Lewinsohn, P. M., Lee, P. W.H., Ho, L. M., Kennard, B., Hughes, C., et al. (2002). Symptom patterns in depression and "subthreshold" depression among adolescents in Hong Kong and the United States. *Journal of Cross-Cultural Psychology, 33*(6), 559–576.

Stewart, T. M. (2004). Light on body image treatment: Acceptance through mindfulness. *Behavior Modification, 28,* 783–811.

Stewart, T. M. & Williamson, D. A. (2004). Multidisciplinary treatment of eating disorders—part I: Structure and costs of treatment. *Behavior Modification, 28,* 812–830.

Stewart, T. M. & Williamson, D. A. (2004). Multidisciplinary treatment of eating disorders—part II: Primary goals and content of treatment. *Behavior Modification, 28,* 831–853.

Stewart-Sabin, C., & Chaffin, M. (2003). Culturally competent substance abuse treatment for American Indian and Alaska native youths. In S. J. Stevens & A. R. Morral (Eds.), *Adolescent substance abuse treatment in the United States: Exemplary models from a national evaluation study* (pp. 155–182). New York: Haworth Press.

Stice, E., Burton, E. M., & Shaw, H. (2004). Prospective relations between bulimic pathology, depression, and substance abuse: Unpacking comorbidity in adolescent girls. *Journal of Consulting and Clinical Psychology, 72,* 62–71

Stice, E., Fisher, M., & Martinez, E. (2004). Eating disorder diagnostic scale: Additional evidence of reliability and validity. *Psychological Assessment, 16,* 60–71.

Stice, E., Martinez, E. E., Presnell, K., & Groesz, L. M. (2006). A prospective study of adolescent girls. *Health Psychology, 25,* 274–281.

Stice, E., Maxfield, J., & Wells, T. (2003). Adverse effects of social pressure to be thin on young women: An experimental investigation of "fat talk." *International Journal of Eating Disorders, 34,* 108–117.

Stice, E., Presnell, K., Groesz, L., & Shaw, H. (2005). Effects of a weight maintenance diet on bulimic symptoms in adolescent girls: An experimental test of the dietary restraint theory. *Health Psychology, 24,* 402–412.

Stice, E. (2003). Puberty and body image. In C. Hayward (Ed.), *Gender differences at puberty* (pp. 61–76). New York: Cambridge University Press.

Stice, E. (2002). Risk and maintenance factors for eating pathology: A meta-analytic review. *Psychology Bulletin, 128,* 825–848.

Stice, E., Schupak-Neuberg, E., Shaw, H. E., & Stein, R. I. (1994). Relation of media exposure to eating disorder symptomatology: An examination of mediating mechanisms. *Journal of Abnormal Psychology, 103*(4), 836–840.

Stice, E., Shaw, H., Burton, E., & Wade, E. (2006). Dissonance and healthy weight eating disorder prevention programs: A randomized efficiency trial. *Journal of Consulting and Clinical Psychology, 74,* 263–275.

Stice, E., & Shaw, H. (2004). Eating disorder prevention programs: A meta-analytic review. *Psychological Bulletin, 130,* 206–227.

Stice, E., & Shaw, H. (2003). Prospective relations of body image, eating, and affective disturbances to smoking onset in adolescent girls: How Virginia slims. *Journal of Consulting and Clinical Psychology, 71,* 129–135.

Stice, E., Spangler, D., & Agras, W. S. (2001). Exposure to media-portrayed thin-ideal images adversely affects vulnerable girls:

A longitudinal experiment. *Journal of Social and Clinical Psychology, 20(3)*, 270–288.

Stice, E., & Whitenton, K. (2002). Risk factors for body dissatisfaction in adolescent girls: A longitudinal investigation. *Developmental Psychology, 38,* 339–378.

Stiffman, A., Striley, C., Brown, E., Limb, G., & Ostmann, E. (2003). American Indian youth: Who southwestern urban and reservation youth turn to for help with mental health or addictions. *Journal of Child and Family Studies, 12*(3), 319–333.

Stifter, C. A. (2002). Individual differences in emotion regulation in infancy: A thematic collection. *Infancy, 3*(2), 129–132.

Stifter, C. A., & Spinrad, T. L. (2002). The effect of excessive crying on the development of emotion regulation. *Infancy, 3*(2), 133–152.

Stifter, C. A., Spinrad, T. L., & Braungart-Rieker, J. M. (1999). Toward a developmental model of child compliance: The role of emotion regulation in infancy. *Child Development, 70,* 21–32.

Stock, S. L., Goldberg, E., Corbett, S., & Katzman, D. K. (2002). Substance use in female adolescents with eating disorders. *Journal of Adolescent Health, 31,* 176–182.

Stormshak, E. A., Bierman, K. L., Bruschi, C., Dodge, K. A., & Coie, J. D. (1999). The relation between behavior problems and peer preference in different classroom contexts. *Child Development, 70,* 169–182.

Stormshak, E. A., Bierman, K. L., Coie, J. D., Dodge, K. A., Greenberg, M. T., Lochman, J. E., et al. (1998). The implications of different developmental patterns of disruptive behavior problems for school adjustment. *Development and Psychopathology, 10,* 451–467.

Stormshak, E. A., Bierman, K. L., McMahon, R. J., Lengua, L. J., & Conduct Problems Prevention Research Group. (2000). Parenting practices and child disruptive behavior problems in early elementary school. *Journal of Clinical Child Psychology, 29*(1), 17–29.

Stormshak, E. A., & Webster-Stratton, C. (1999). The qualitative interactions of children with conduct problems and their peers: Differential correlates with self-report measures, home behavior, and school behavior problems. *Journal of Applied Developmental Psychology, 20*(2), 295–317.

Storvoll, E. E., Strandbu, A., & Wichstrom, L. (2005). A cross-sectional study of changes in Norwegian adolescents' body image from 1992–2002. *Body Image, 2,* 5–18.

Story, T. J., Zucker, B. G., & Craske, M. G. (2004). Secondary prevention of anxiety disorders. In D. J. A. Dozois & K. S. Dobson (Eds.), *The prevention of anxiety and depression: Theory, research, and practice* (pp. 131–160). Washington, DC: American Psychological Association.

Stouthamer-Loeber, M., Loeber, R., Wei, E., Farrington, D. P., & Wikstroem, P-O. H. (2002). Risk and promotive effects in the explanation of persistent serious delinquency in boys. *Journal of Consulting and Clinical Psychology, 70*(1), 111–123.

Stovall, K. C., & Dozier, M. (2000). The development of attachment in new relationships: Single subject analyses for 10 foster infants. *Development and Psychopathology, 12,* 133–156.

Strada, M. J., Donohue, B., & Lefforge, N. L. (2006). Examination of ethnicity in controlled treatment outcome studies involving adolescent substance abusers: A comprehensive literature review. *Psychology of Addictive Behaviors, 20*(1), 11–27.

Strakowski, S. M., Shang-Ying, T., DelBello, M. P., Chiao-Chicy, C., Fleck, D. E., Adler, C. M., et al. (2007) Outcome following a first manic episode: Cross-national US and Taiwan comparison. *Bipolar Disorders, 9*(8), 820–827.

Street., H., Nathan, P., Durkin, K., Morling, J., Dzahari, M. A., Carson, J., et al. (2004). Understanding the relationships between well-being, goal-setting and depression in children. *Australian and New Zealand Journal of Psychiatry, 38*(3), 155–161.

Striegel-Moore, R. H., Fairburn, C. G., Wilfley, D. E., Pike, K. M., Dohm, F., & Kraemer, H. C. (2005). Toward an understanding of risk factors for binge-eating disorder in black and white women: A community-based case-control study. *Psychological Medicine, 35,* 907–917.

Striegel-Moore, R. H., Seeley, J. R., & Lewinsohn, P. M. (2003). Psychosocial adjustment in young adulthood of women who experienced an eating disorder during adolescence. *Journal of the American Academy of Child and Adolescent Psychiatry, 42,* 587–593.

Stromme, P., Bjornstad, P. G., & Ramstad, K. (2002). Prevalence estimation of Williams syndrome. *Journal of Child Neurology, 17*(4), 269–271.

Stueve, A., & O'Donnell, L. N. (2005). Early alcohol initiation and subsequent sexual and alcohol risk behaviors among urban youths. *American Journal of Public Health, 95*(5), 887–893.

Sturmey, P. (1998). Classification and diagnosis of psychiatric disorders in persons with developmental disabilities. *Journal of Developmental and Physical Disabilities, 10*(4), 317–330.

Suizzo, M-A. (2000). The social-emotional and cultural contexts of cognitive development: Neo-Piagetian perspectives. *Child Development, 71*(4), 846–849.

Sukhodolsky, D. G., Scahill, L., Gadow, K.d., Arnold, LE., Aman, M. G., McDougle, C. J., et al. (2008). Parent-rated anxiety symptoms in children with pervasive developmental disorders: Frequency and association with core autism symptoms and cognitive functioning. *Journal of Abnormal Child Psychology, 36*(1), 117–128.

Sullivan, H. S. (1953). *The interpersonal theory of psychiatry.* New York: Norton.

Sullivan, M. L. (1998). Integrating qualitative and quantitative methods in the study of developmental psychopathology in context. *Development and Psychopathology, 10*(2), 377–393.

Sullivan, P. F., & Kendler, K. S. (1999). The genetic epidemiology of smoking. *Nicotine and Tobacco Research, 1*(Suppl. 2), S51-S57.

Sundram, C. J., & Stavis, P. F. (1994). Sexuality and mental retardation: Unmet challenges. *Mental Retardation, 32*(4), 255–264.

Sung, M., Erkanli, A., Angold, A., & Costello, E. J. (2004). Effects of age at first substance use and psychiatric comorbidity on the development of substance use disorders. *Drug and Alcohol Dependence, 75*(3), 287–299.

Suominen, K., Isometsa, E., Martunnen, M., Ostamo, A., & Lonnqvist, J. (2004). Health care contacts before and after attempted suicide among adolescent and young adult versus older suicide attempters. *Psychological Medicine, 34*(2), 313–321.

Sussman, S., Stacy, A. W., Johnson, C. A., Pentz, M. A., & Robertson, E. (2004). A transdisciplinary focus on drug abuse prevention: An introduction. *Substance Use and Misuse, 39*(10–12), 1441–1456.

Suveg, C., Aschenbrand, S. G., & Kendall, P. C. (2005). Separation anxiety disorder, panic disorder, and school refusal. *Child and Adolescent Psychiatric Clinics of North America, 14*(4), 773–795.

Suveg, C., & Zeman, J. (2004). Emotion regulation in children with anxiety disorders. *Journal of Clinical Child and Adolescent Psychology, 33*(4), 750–759.

Svanberg, P. O. G. (1998). Attachment, resilience and prevention. *Journal of Mental Health, 7(6),* 543–578.

Swahn, M. H., & Donovan, J. E. (2005). Predictors of fighting attributed to alcohol use among adolescent drinkers. *Addictive Behaviors, 30*(7), 1317–1334.

Swahn, M. H., Simon, T. R., Hammig, B. J., & Guerrero, J. L. (2004). Alcohol-consumption behaviors and risk for physical fighting and injuries among adolescent drinkers. *Addictive Behaviors, 29*(5), 959–963.

Swain, J. E., Lorberbaum, J. P., Kose, S., & Strathearn, L. (2007). Brain basis of early parent-infant interactions: Psychology, physiology, and in vivo functional neuroimaging studies. *Journal of Child Psychology and Psychiatry, 48*(3–4), 262–287.

Sweeney, L., & Rapee, R. M. (2005). Social phobia in children and adolescents: Psychological treatments. In W. R. Crozier & L. E. Alden (Eds.), *The essential handbook of social anxiety for clinicians* (pp. 153–165). New York: Wiley.

Szatmari, P. (1999). Heterogeneity and the genetics of autism. *Journal of Psychiatry and Neuroscience, 24,* 159–165.

Szatmari, P. (2000). The classification of autism, Asperger's syndrome, and pervasive developmental disorder. *Canadian Jounal of Psychiatry, 45(8),* 731–738.

Szatmari, P., Archer, L., Fisman, S., & Streiner, D. L. (1995). Asperger's syndrome and autism: Differences in behavior, cognition, and adaptive functioning. *Journal of the American Academy of Child and Adolescent Psychiatry, 34,* 1662–1671.

Szatmari, P., Bryson, S. E., Streiner, D. L., Wilson, F., Archer, L., & Ryerse, C. (2000). Two-year outcome of preschool children with autism or Asperger's syndrome. *American Journal of Psychiatry, 157,* 1980–1987.

Szatmari, P., Georgiades, S., Bryson, S., Zwaigenbaum, L., Roberts, W., Mahoney, W., Goldberg, J., & Tuff, L. (2006). Investigating the structure of the restricted, repetitive behaviors and interests domain of autism. *Journal of Child Psychology and Psychiatry, 47*(6), 582–590.

Szatmari, P., Jones, M. B., Zwaigenbaum, L., & MacLean, J. E. (1998). Genetics of autism: Overview and new directions. *Journal of Autism and Developmental Disorders, 28,* 351–368.

Szatmari, P., Merette, C., Bryson, S. E., Thivierge, J., Roy, M-A., Cayer, M., et al. (2002). Quantifying dimensions in autism: A factor-analytic study. *Journal of the American Academy of Child and Adolescent Psychiatry, 41,* 467–474.

Szymanski, L., King, B. H., Bernet, W., Dunne, J. E., Adair, M., Arnold, V., et al. (1999). Practice parameters for the assessment and treatment of children, adolescents, and adults with mental retardation and comorbid mental disorders. *Journal of the American Academy of Child and Adolescent Psychiatry, 38*(12), 5S-31S.

Tackett, J. L., Krueger, R. G., Iacono, W. G., & McGue, M. (2005). Symptom-based subfactors of DSM-defined conduct disorder: Evidence for etiologic distinctions. *Journal of Abnormal Psychology, 114*(3), 483–487.

Tager-Flusberg, H., Boshart, J., & Baron-Cohen, S. (1998). Reading the windows to the soul: Evidence of domain-specific sparing in Williams syndrome. *Journal of Cognitive Neuroscience, 10*(5), 631–639.

Tangri, S. S., & Kahn, J. R. (1993). Ethical issues in the new reproductive technologies: Perspectives from feminism and the psychology profession. *Professional Psychology: Research and Practice, 24*(3), 271–280.

Tanguay, P. E., Robertson, J., & Derrick, A. (1998). A dimensional classification of autism spectrum disorder by social communication domains. *Journal of the American Academy of Child and Adolescent Psychiatry, 37,* 271–277.

Tannock, R. (1998). Attention deficit hyperactivity disorder: Advances in cognitive, neurobiological, and genetic research. *Journal of Child Psychology and Psychiatry and Allied Disciplines, 39,* 65–99.

Tannock, R., Diamond, I. R., & Schachar, R. J. (1999). Response to methylphenidate in children with ADHD and comorbid anxiety. *Journal of the American Academy of Child and Adolescent Psychiatry, 38,* 402–409.

Tantam, D. (1988). Asperger's syndrome. *Journal of Child Psychology and Psychiatry and Allied Disciplines, 29,* 245–255.

Tantam, D. (2000). Psychological disorder in adolescents and adults with Asperger syndrome. *Autism, 4*(1), 47–62.

Tantam, D. (2003). The challenge of adolescents and adults with Asperger syndrome. *Child and Adolescent Psychiatric Clinics of North America, 12,* 143–163.

Tarrier, N., Taylor, K., & Gooding, P. (2008). Cognitive-behavioral interventions to reduce suicide behavior: A systematic review and meta-analysis. *Behavior Modification, 32*(1), 77–108.

Tarter, R. E. (2005). Psychological evaluation of substance use disorders in adolescents and adults. In R. J. Frances, S. I. Miller, & A. H. Mack (Eds.), *Clinical textbook of addictive disorders* (3rd ed.). New York: Guilford Press.

Tarter, R. E., Kirisci, L., Reynolds, M., & Mezzich, A. (2004). Neurobehavior disinhibition in childhood predicts suicide potential and substance use disorder by young adulthood. *Drug and Alcohol Dependence, 76*(17), S45-S52.

Tarter, R. E., Vanyukov, M., Giancola, P., Dawes, M., Blackson, T., Mezzich, A., et al. (1999). Etiology of early age onset substance use disorder: A maturational perspective. *Development and Psychopathology, 11*(4), 657–683.

Tasi, L. Y. (1994). Rett syndrome. *Child and Adolescent Psychiatric Clinics of North America, 3,* 105–118.

Taylor, C. S., Smith, P. R., Taylor, V. A., von Eye, A., Lerner, R. M., Balsano, A. B., et al. (2005). Individual and ecological assets and thriving among African American adolescent male gang and community-based organization members: A report from Wave 3 of the "Overcoming the Odds" study. *Journal of Early Adolescence, 25*(1), 72–93.

Taylor, E. (1999). Developmental neuropsychopathology of attention deficit and impulsiveness. *Development and Psychopathology, 11,* 607–628.

Taylor, H. G., & Alden, J. (1997). Age-related differences in outcomes following childhood brain insults: An introduction and overview. *Journal of the International Neuropsychological Society, 3(6),* 555–567.

Taylor, R. D., Jacobson, L., Rodriguez, A., Dominguez, A., Cantic, R., Doney, J., et al. (2000). Stressful experiences and the psychological functioning of African-American and Puerto Rican families and adolescents. In R. D. Taylor & M. C. Wang (Eds.), *Resilience across contexts: Family, work, culture, and community* (pp. 35–53). Mahwah, NJ: Erlbaum.

Taylor, S. E., Repetti, R. L., & Seeman, T. (1997). Health psychology: What is an unhealthy environment and how does it get under the skin? *Annual Review of Psychology, 48,* 411–447.

Taylor, T. K., & Biglan, A. (1998). Behavioral family interventions for improving child-rearing: A review of the literature for clinicians and policy makers. *Clinical Child and Family Psychology Review, 1,* 41–60.

Teicher, M., Ito, Y., Glod, C. A., Andersen, S. L., Dumont, N., & Ackerman, E. (1997). Preliminary evidence for abnormal cortical development in physically and sexually abused children using EEG coherence and MRI. *Annual New York Academy of Science, 821,* 160–175.

Temple, C. M., Almazan, M., & Sherwood, S. (2002). Lexical skills in Williams syndrome: A cognitive neuropsychological analysis. *Journal of Neurolinguistics, 15*(6), 463–495.

Teti, D. M. (1999). Conceptualizations of disorganization in the preschool years: An integration. In J. Solomon & C. George (Eds.), *Attachment disorganization* (pp. 213–242). New York: Guilford Press.

Teti, D. M., Gelfand, D. M., Messinger, D. S., & Isabella, R. (1995). Maternal depression and the quality of early attachment: An examination of infants, preschoolers, and their mothers. *Developmental Psychology, 31,* 364–376.

Tetzlaff, B. T., Kahn, J. H., Godley, S. H., Godley, M .D., Diamond, G. S., & Funk, R. R. (2005). Working alliance, treatment satisfaction, and patterns of posttreatment use among adolescent substance users. *Psychology of Addictive Behaviors, 19*(2), 199–207.

Thabet, A. A. M., Abed, Y., & Vostanis, P. (2004). Comorbidity of PTSD and depression among refugee children during war conflict. *Journal of Child Psychology and Psychiatry, 45(3),* 533–542.

Thakker, J., & Ward, T. (1998). Culture and classification: The cross-cultural application of the DSM-IV. *Clinical Psychology Review, 18(5),* 501–529.

Thoits, P. A. (1999). Self, identity, stress, and mental health. In C. S. Aneshensel & J. C. Phelan (Eds.), *Handbook of sociology of mental health* (pp. 345–368). Dordrecht, Netherlands: Kluwer Academic Publishers.

Thomas, A., & Chess, S. (1977). *Temperament and development.* New York: Brunner/Mazel.

Thomas, C. R. (2006). Evidence-based practice for conduct disorder symptoms. *Journal of the American Academy of Child and Adolescent Psychiatry, 45*(1), 109–114.

Thomas, J. M., & Clark, R. (1998). Disruptive behavior in the very young child: Diagnostic classification: 0–3 guides to identification of risk factors and relational interventions. *Infant Mental Health Journal, 19*(2), 229–244.

Thomas, K. M., Drevets, W. C., Dahl, R. E., Ryan, N. D., Birmaher, B., Eccard, C. H., et al. (2001). Amygdala response to fearful faces in anxious and depressed children. *Archives of General Psychiatry, 58*(11), 1057–1063.

Thomas, R. M. (2001). *Recent theories of human development.* Thousand Oaks, CA: Sage.

Thompson, J. R., Hughes, C., Schalock, R. L., Silverman, W., Tasse, M. J., Bryant, B., et al. (2002). Integrating supports in assessment and planning. *Mental Retardation, 40*(5), 390–405.

Thompson, R. A. (1997). Sensitivity and security: New questions to ponder. *Child Development, 68*(4), 595–597.

Thompson, R. A. (1998). Early sociopersonality development. In W. Damon & N. Eisenberg (Eds.), *Handbook of child psychology (5th ed.): Vol. 3. Social, emotional, and personality development* (pp. 25–104). Hoboken, NJ: Wiley.

Thompson, R. A. (1999). Early attachment and later development. In J. Cassidy & P. R. Shaver (Eds.), *Handbook of attachment: Theory, research, and clinical applications* (pp. 265–286). New York: Guilford Press.

Thompson, R. A. (2001). Childhood anxiety disorders from the perspective of emotion regulation and attachment. In M. W. Vasey & M. R. Dadds (Eds.), *The developmental psychopathology of anxiety* (pp. 160–182). New York: Oxford University Press.

Thompson, R. A., Flood, M. F., & Lundquist, L. (1995). Emotional regulation: Its relations to attachment and developmental psychopathology. In D. Cicchetti & S. L. Toth (Eds.), *Emotion, cognition, and representation* (pp. 261–299). Rochester, NY: University of Rochester Press.

Thompson, R. A., & Lamb, M. E. (1983). Security of attachment and stranger sociability in infancy. *Developmental Psychology, 19*(2), 184–191.

Thompson, R. A., & May, M. A. (2006). Caregivers' perceptions of child mental health needs and service utilization: An urban 8-year old sample. *The Journal of Behavioral Health Services and Research, 33(4),* 474–482.

Thompson, R. A., & Meyer, S. (2007). Socialization of emotion regulation in the family. In J. J. Gross (Ed.), *Handbook of emotion regulation* (pp. 249–268). New York: Guilford Press.

Thompson, R. A., & Nelson, C. A. (2001). Developmental science and the media: Early brain development. *American Psychologist, 56(1),* 5–15.

Thompson, S. H., Rafiroiu, A. C., & Sargent, R. G. (2003). Examining gender, racial, and age differences in weight concern among third, fifth, eighth, and eleventh graders. *Eating Behaviors, 3,* 307–323.

Thompson, S. J., Pomeroy, E. C., & Gober, K. (2005). Family-based treatment models targeting substance use and high-risk behaviors among adolescents: A review. In Hilarski, C. (Ed.), *Addiction, assessment, and treatment with adolescents, adults, and families* (pp. 207–233). Binghamton, NY: Haworth Social Work Practice Press.

Thompson, W. F., Schellenberg, E. G., & Husain, G. (2001). Arousal, mood, and the Mozart Effect. *Psychological Science, 12(3),* 248.

Thomsen, P. H. (1994). Obsessive-compulsive disorder in children and adolescents: A review of the literature. *European Child and Adolescent Psychiatry, 3*(3), 138–158.

Thuppal, M., Carlson, G. A., Sprafkin, J., & Gadow, K. D. (2002). Correspondence between adolescent report, parent report and teacher report of manic symptoms. *Journal of Child and Adolescent Psychopharmacology, 12*(1), 27–35.

Tierney, S, & Wyatt, K. (2005). What works for adolescents with AN: A systematic review of psychosocial interventions. *Eating and Weight Disorders, 10,* 66–75.

Tiet, Q. Q., Bird, H. R., Hoven, C. W, Moore, R., Wu, P., Wicks, J., et al. (2001). Relationship between specific adverse life events and psychiatric disorders. *Journal of Abnormal Child Psychology, 29(2),* 153–164.

Tiet, Q. Q., Bird, H. R., Hoven, C. W., Wu, P., Moore, R., & Davies, M. (2001). Resilience in the face of maternal psychopathology and adverse life events. *Journal of Child and Family Studies, 10(3),* 347–363.

Tillman, R., & Geller, B. (2005). A brief screening tool for a prepubertal and early adolescent bipolar disorder phenotype. *American Journal of Psychiatry, 162*(6), 1214–1216.

Tillman, R., Geller, B., Bolhofner, K., Craney, J. L., Williams, M., & Zimerman, B. (2003). Ages of onset and rates of syndromal and subsyndromal cormobid DSM-IV diagnoses in a prepubertal and early adolescent bipolar disorder phenotype. *Journal of the American Academy of Child and Adolescent Psychiatry, 42*(12), 1486–1493.

Tillman, R., Geller, B., Craney, J. L., Bolhofner, K., Williams, M., & Zimerman, B. (2004). Relationship of parent and child informants to prevalence of mania symptoms in children with a prepubertal and early adolescent bipolar disorder phenotype. *American Journal of Psychiatry, 161*(7), 1278–1284.

Tirosh, E., Bendrian, S. B., Golan, G., Tamir, A., & Dar, M. C. (2003). Regulatory disorders in Israeli infants: Epidemiologic perspective. *Journal of Child Neurology, 18,* 748–754.

Titus, J. C., Dennis, M. L., White, W. L., Scott, C. K., & Funk, R. R. (2003). Gender differences in victimization severity and outcomes among adolescents treated for substance abuse. *Child Maltreatment, 8*(1), 19–35.

Tizard, B., & Hodges, J. (1978). The effect of early institutional rearing on the development of eight year old children. *Journal of Child Psychology and Psychiatry, 19*(2), 99–118.

Tizard, B., & Rees, J. (1975). The effect of early institutional rearing on the behaviour problems and affectional relationships of four-year-old children. *Journal of Child Psychology and Psychiatry, 16*(1), 61–73.

Todd, R. D., Rasmussen, E. R., Wood, C., Levy, F., & Hay, D. A. (2004). Should sluggish cognitive tempo symptoms be included in the diagnosis of attention-deficit/ hyperactivity disorder? *Journal of the American Academy of Child and Adolescent Psychiatry, 43*(5), 588–597.

Tokumura, M., Tanaka, T., Nanri, S., & Watanabe, H. (2005). Prescribed exercise training for convalescent children and adolescents with anorexia nervosa: Reduced heart rate response to exercise is an important parameter for early recurrence diagnosis of anorexia nervosa. In P. I. Swain (Ed.), *Adolescent eating disorders* (pp. 69–83). Hauppauge, NY: Nova Biomedical Books.

Tolan, P. H., & Dodge, K. A. (2005). Children's mental health as a primary care and concern: A system for comprehensive support and service. *American Psychologist, 60*(6), 601–614.

Tomoe, K. & Ceci, S. J. (2007). Are all IQ scores created equal? The differential costs of IQ cutoff scores for at-risk children. *Child Development Perspectives, 1*(1), 52–56.

Toth, S. L., & Cicchetti, D. (1996). Patterns of relatedness, depressive symptomology, and perceived competence in maltreated children. *Journal of Consulting and Clinical Psychology, 64*(1), 32–41.

Toumbourou, J. W., Williams, J., Waters, E., & Patton, G. (2005). What do we know about preventing drug-related harm through social developmental intervention with children and young people? In T. Stockwell, P. J. Gruenewald, J. W. Toumbourou, & W. Loxley (Eds.), *Preventing harmful substance use: The evidence base for policy and practice* (pp. 87–100). New York: Wiley.

Towbin, K. E. (2003). Strategies for pharmacologic treatment of high functioning autism and Asperger syndrome. *Child and Adolescent Psychiatric Clinics of North America, 12*(1), 23–45.

Towers, H., Spotts, E. L., & Neiderhiser, J. M. (2001). Genetic and environmental influences on parenting and marital relationships: Current findings and future directions. *Marriage and Family Review, 33,* 11–29.

Townsend, J., Westerfield, M., Leaver, E., Makeig, S., Jung, T-P., Pierce, K., et al. (2001). Event-related brain response abnormalities in autism: Evidence for impaired cerebello-frontal spatial attention networks. *Cognitive Brain Research, 11,* 127–145.

Tozzi, F., Aggen, S. H., Neale, B. M., Anderson, C. B., Mazzeo, S. E., Neale, M. C., et al. (2004). The structure of perfectionism: A twin study. *Behavior Genetics, 34,* 483–494.

Tozzi, F., Thornton, L. M., Klump, K. L., Fichter, M. M., Halmi, K. A., Kaplan, A. S., et al. (2005). Symptom fluctuation in eating disorders: Correlates of diagnostic crossover. *American Journal of Psychology, 162,* 732–740.

Tozzi, F., Throngon, L. M., Mitchell, J., Fichter, M. M., Klump, K. L., Lilenfeld, L. R., et al. (2006). Features associated with laxative abuse in individuals with eating disorders. *Psychosomatic Medicine, 68,* 470–477.

Tracey, S. A., Chorpita, B. F., Douban, J., & Barlow, D. H. (1997). Empirical evaluation of DSM-IV generalized anxiety disorder criteria in children and adolescents. *Journal of Clinical Child Psychology, 26*(4), 404–414.

Tram, J. M., & Cole, D. M. (2000). Self-perceived competence and the relation between life events and depressive symptoms in adolescence: Mediator or moderator? *Journal of Abnormal Psychology, 109*(4), 753–760.

Tremblay, R. E., LeMarquand, D., & Vitaro, F. (1999). The prevention of oppositional defiant disorder and conduct disorder. In H. C. Quay & A. E. Hogan (Eds.), *Handbook of disruptive behavior disorders* (pp. 525–555). Dordrecht, Netherlands: Kluwer Academic Publishers.

Trickett, P. K., & Putnam, F. W. (1998). Developmental consequences of child sexual abuse. In P. K. Trickett & C. J. Schellenbach (Eds.), *Violence against children in the family and the community* (p. 39–56). Washington, DC: American Psychological Association.

Triplett, R., & Payne, B. (2004). Problem solving as reinforcement in adolescent drug use: Implications for theory and policy. *Journal of Criminal Justice, 32*(6), 617–630.

Tronick, E. Z., & Gianino, A. F. (1986). The transmission of maternal disturbance to the infant. *New Directions for Child Development, 34,* 5–11.

Tronick, E. Z., Messinger, D. S., Weinberg, M. K., Lester, B. M., LaGasse, L., Seifer, R., et al. (2005). Cocaine exposure is associated with subtle compromises of infants' and mothers' social-emotional behavior and dyadic features of their interaction in the face-to-face paradigm. *Developmental Psychology, 41*(5), 711–722.

Troy, M. F. (1989). Antecedents, correlates, and continuity of ego-control and ego-resiliency in a high-risk sample of preschool children. *Dissertation Abstracts International, 49 (9-B),* 4028.

Troy, M. (2003). Structure of psychopathology: Childhood conduct problems. Presentation on June 20, 2003 for Children's Hospitals and Clinics, Psychological Services, St. Paul, MN.

Troy, M., & Sroufe, L. A. (1987). Victimization among preschoolers: Role of attachment relationship history. *Journal of the American Academy of Child and Adolescent Psychiatry, 26*(2), 166–172.

Troy, M., & Walker, J. (2003). Identifying and treating childhood conduct problems. Presentation on June 17 and 19, 2003 for

Children's Hospitals and Clinics, Psychological Services, St. Paul, MN.

Tsatsanis, K. D. (2003). Outcome research in Asperger syndrome and autism. *Child and Adolescent Psychiatric Clinics of North America, 12*(1), 47–63.

Tsatsanis, K. D., Rourke, B. P., Klin, A., Volkmar, F. R., Cicchetti, D., & Schultz, R. T. (2003). Reduced thalamic volume in high-functioning individuals with autism. *Biological Psychiatry, 53,* 121–129.

Tsuang, M. T., Lyons, M. J., Harley, R. M., Xian, H., Eisen, S., Goldberg, J., et al. (1999). Genetic and environmental influences on transitions in drug use. *Behavior Genetics, 29*(6), 473–479.

Tsuang, M. T., Lyons, M. J., Meyer, J. M., Doyle, T., Eisen, S. A., Goldberg, J., et al. (1998). Co-occurrence of abuse of different drugs in men: The role of drug-specific and shared vulnerabilities. *Archives of General Psychiatry, 55*(11), 967–972.

Tucker, C. J., Barber, B. L., & Eccles, J. S. (1997). Advice about life plans and personal problems in late adolescent sibling relationships. *Journal of Youth and Adolescence, 26*(1), 63–76.

Tucker, J. S., Ellickson, P. L., Orlando, M., Martino, S. C., & Klein, D. J. (2005). Substance use trajectories from early adolescence to emerging adulthood: A comparison of smoking, binge drinking, and marijuana use. *Journal of Drug Issues, 35*(2), 307–332.

Tullis, L. M., DuPont, R., Frost-Pineda, K., & Gold, M. S. (2003). Marijuana and tobacco: A major connection? *Journal of Addictive Diseases, 22*(3), 51–62.

Turbin, M. S., Jessor, R., & Costa, F. M. (2000). Adolescent cigarette smoking: Health-related behavior or normative transgression? *Prevention Science, 1*(3), 115–124.

Turkheimer, E., & Waldron, M. (2000). Nonshared environment: A theoretical, methodological, and quantitative review. *Psychological Bulletin, 126*(1), 78–108.

Turner, C. M. & Barrett, P. M. (2003). Does age play a role in structure of anxiety and depression in children and youths? An investigation of the tripartite model in three age cohorts. *Journal of Consulting and Clinical Psychology, 71*(4), 826–833.

Turner, J., Batik, M., Palmer, L. J., Forbes, D., & McDermott, B. M. (2000). Detection and importance of laxative use in adolescents with anorexia nervosa. *Journal of the American Academy of Child and Adolescent Psychiatry, 39,* 378–385.

Turner, L. R., & Mermelstein, R. (2004). Motivation and reasons to quit: Predictive validity among adolescent smokers. *American Journal of Health Behavior, 28*(6), 542–550.

Turner, L. R., Mermelstein, R., Berbaum, M. L., & Veldhuis, C. B. (2004). School-based smoking cessation programs for adolescents: What predicts attendance? *Nicotine and Tobacco Research, 6*(3), 559–568.

Turner, L., Mermelstein, R., & Flay, B. (2004). Individual and contextual influences on adolescent smoking. In R. E. Dahl & L. P. Spear (Eds.), *Adolescent brain development: Vulnerabilities and opportunities. Annals of the New York Academy of Sciences* (Vol. 1021, pp. 175–197). New York: New York Academy of Sciences.

Twenge, J. M., & Baumeister, R. F. (2002). Self-control: A limited yet renewable resource. In Y. Kashima & M. Foddy (Eds.), *Self and identity: Personal, social, and symbolic* (pp. 57–70). Mahwah, NJ: Erlbaum.

Twenge, J. M., & Nolen-Hoeksema, S. (2002). Age, gender, race, socioeconomic status, and birth cohort differences on the children's depression inventory: A meta-analysis. *Journal of Abnormal Psychology, 111*(4), 578–588.

Tyrer, S., & Hill, S. (2001). Psychopharmacological approaches. In A. Dosen & K. Day (Eds.), *Treating mental illness and behavior disorders in children and adults with mental retardation* (pp. 45–67). Washington, DC: American Psychiatric Publishing.

U.S. Census Bureau. (2000). Percent of people in poverty by definition of income and selected characteristics: 1998. Available: http://www.census.gov/hhes/poverty/poverty98/table5.html

U.S. Department of Health and Human Services. (1999). *Mental health: A report of the Surgeon General.* Rockville, MD: Author.

U.S. Department of Health and Human Services. (2002). *Closing the gap: A national blueprint to improve the health of persons with mental retardation.* Report of the Surgeon General's Conference on Health Disparities and Mental Retardation, Rockville, MD.

U.S. Department of Health and Human Services. (2007). Administration on Children, Youth and Families. *Child Maltreatment 2005.* Washington, DC: U. S. Government Printing Office.

U.S. Food and Drug Administration: Antidepressant Use in Children, Adolescents, and Adults, 2004. http://www.fda.gov/cder/drug/antidepressants/default.htm

Uher, R., Murphy, T, Brammer, M. J., Brammer, M. J., Dalgleish, T., Phillips, M. L., et al. (2004). Medial prefrontal cortex activity associate with symptom provocation in eating disorders. *American Journal of Psychiatry, 161,* 1238–1246.

Underwood, M. K. (1997). Top ten pressing questions about the development of emotion regulation. *Motivation and Emotion, 21,* 127–146.

Underwood, M. K. (2002). Sticks and stones and social exclusion: Aggression among girls and boys. In P. K. Smith & C. H. Hart (Eds.), *Blackwell handbook of childhood social development* (pp. 533–548). Malden, MA: Blackwell.

Underwood, M. K. (2003a). The comity of modest manipulation, the importance of distinguishing among bad behaviors. *Merrill-Palmer Quarterly, 49*(3), 373–389.

Underwood, M. K. (2003b). *Social aggression among girls.* New York: Guilford Press.

Underwood, M. K. (2004a). Gender and peer relations: Are the two gender cultures really all that different? In J. B. Kupersmidt & K. A. Dodge (Eds.), *Children's peer relations: From development to intervention. Decade of behavior* (pp. 21–36). Washington, DC: American Psychological Association.

Underwood, M. K. (2004b). III. Glares of contempt, eye rolls of disgust and turning away to exclude: Non-verbal forms of social aggression among girls. *Feminism and Psychology, 14*(3), 371–375.

Underwood, M. K., Galen, B. R., & Paquette, J. A. (2001). Top ten challenges for understanding gender and aggression in children: Why can't we all just get along? *Social Development, 10*(2), 248–266.

Underwood, M. K., & Hurley, J. C. (1999). Emotion regulation in peer relationships during middle childhood. In L. Balter & C. S. Tamis-LeMonda (Eds.), *Child psychology: A handbook of contemporary issues* (pp. 237–258). New York: Psychology Press.

Vachon, J., Vitaro, F., Wanner, B., & Tremblay, R. E. (2004). Adolescent gambling: Relationships with parent gambling and parenting practices. *Psychology of Addictive Behaviors, 18*(4), 398–401.

Valenti-Hein, D., & Dura, J. R. (1996). Sexuality and sexual development. In J. W. Jacobson & J. A. Mulick (Eds.), *Manual of diagnosis and professional practice in mental retardation* (pp. 301–310). Washington, DC: American Psychological Association.

Valentiner, D. P., Mounts, N. S., & Deacon, B. J. (2004). Panic attacks, depression and anxiety symptoms, and substance use behaviors during late adolescence. *Journal of Anxiety Disorders, 18*(5), 573–585.

Van Ameringen, M., & Mancini, C. (2001). Pharmacotherapy of social anxiety disorder at the turn of the millennium. *Psychiatry Clinics of North America, 24*(4), 783–803.

Van Bourgondien, M. E., Reichle, N. C., & Schopler, E. (2003). Effects of a model treatment approach on adults with autism. *Journal of Autism and Developmental Disorders, 33*, 131–140.

van den Berg, P., Wertheim, E. H., Thompson, J. K., & Paxton, S. J. (2002). Development of body image, eating disturbance, and general psychological functioning in adolescent females: A replication using covariance structure modeling in an Australian sample. *International Journal of Eating Disorders, 32*, 46–51.

van den Oord, E. J. C. G., & Rowe, D. C. (1997). Continuity and change in children's social maladjustment: A developmental behavior genetic study. *Developmental Psychology, 33*(2), 319–332.

van der Kolk, B. A., Roth, S., Pelcovitz, D., Sunday, S., & Spinazzola, J. (2005). Disorders of extreme stress: The empirical foundation of a complex adaptation to trauma. *Journal of Traumatic Stress, 18*(5), 389–399.

van Furth, E. F., van Strein, D. C., Martin, L. M. L., van Son, M. J. M, Hendrickx, J. P., & van Engeland, H. (1996). Expressed emotion and the prediction of outcome in adolescent eating disorders. *International Journal of Eating Disorders, 20*, 19–31.

van Goozen, S. H. M., Matthys, W., Cohen-Kettenis, P. T., Buitelaar, J. K., & van Engeland, H. (2000). Hypothalamic-pituitary-adrenal axis and autonomic nervous system activity in disruptive children and matched controls. *Journal of the American Academy of Child and Adolescent Psychiatry, 39*, 1438–1445.

van Goozen, S. H. M., Matthys, W., Cohen-Kettenis, P. T., Gispen-de Wied, C., Wiegant, V. M., & Engeland, H. (1998). Salivary cortisol and cardiovascular activity during stress in oppositional-defiant disorder boys and normal controls. *Biological Psychiatry, 43*, 531–539.

van Goozen, S. H. M., Matthys, W., Cohen-Kettenis, P. T., Westenberg, H., & van Engeland, H. (1999). Plasma monoamine metabolites and aggression: Two studies of normal and oppositional defiant disorder children. *European Neuropsychopharmacology, 9*, 141–147.

van Goozen, S. H. M., van den Ban, E., Matthys, W., Cohen-Kettenis, P. T., Thijssen, J. H. H., & van Engeland, H. (2000). Increased adrenal androgen functioning in children with oppositional defiant disorder: A comparison with psychiatric and normal controls. *Journal of the American Academy of Child and Adolescent Psychiatry, 39*, 1446–1451.

Van IJzendoorn, M. (1995). Adult attachment representations, parental responsiveness, and infant attachment: A meta-analysis on the predictive validity of the Adult Attachment Interview. *Psychological Bulletin, 117*(3), 387–403.

Van IJzendoorn, M. H., & De Wolff, M. S. (1997). In search of the absent father—meta-analysis of infant-father attachment: A rejoinder to our discussants. *Child Development, 68*(4), 604–609.

Van IJzendoorn, M. H., Goldberg, S., Kroonenberg, P. M., & Frenkel, O. J. (1992). The relative effects of maternal and child problems on the quality of attachment: A meta-analysis in clinical samples. *Child Development, 63*(4), 840–858.

Van IJzendoorn, M. H., Juffer, F., & Duyvesteyn, M. G. C. (1995). Breaking the intergenerational cycle of insecure attachment: A review of the effects of attachment-based interventions on maternal sensitivity and infant security. *Journal of Child Psychology and Psychiatry, 36*(2), 225–248.

Van IJzendoorn, M. H., & Sagi, A. (1999). Cross-cultural patterns of attachment: Universal and contextual dimensions. In J. Cassidy & P. R. Shaver (Eds.), *Handbook of attachment: Theory, research, and clinical applications* (pp. 713–734). New York: Guilford Press.

Van IJzendoorn, M. H., Schuengel, C., & Bakermans-Kranenburg, M. J. (1999). Disorganized attachment in early childhood: Meta-analysis of precursors, concomitants, and sequelae. *Development and Psychopathology, 11*, 225–249.

Van Lier, P. A. C., van der Ende, J., Koot, H. M., & Verhulst, F. C. (2007). Which better predicts conduct problems? The relationships of trajectories of conduct problems with ODD and ADHD symptoms from childhood into adolescence. *Journal of Child Psychology and Psychiatry, 48*(6), 601–608.

Van Lier, P. A. C., Verhulst, F. C., Van Der Ende, J., & Crijnen, A. A. M (2003). Classes of disruptive behavior in a sample of young elementary school children. *Journal of Child Psychology and Psychiatry, 44*(3), 377–387.

Van Lier, P. A. C., Vitaro, F., Wanner, B., Vuijk, P., & Crijnen, A. A. M. (2005). Gender differences in developmental links among antisocial behavior, friends' antisocial behavior, and peer rejection in childhood: Results from two cultures. *Child Development, 76*(4), 841–855.

Van Lier, P. A. C., Vuijk, P., & Crijnen, A. A. M. (2005). Understanding mechanisms of change in the development of antisocial behavior: The impact of a universal intervention. *Journal of Abnormal Child Psychology, 33*(5), 521–535.

van Lieshout, C. F. M., De Meyer, R. E., Curfs, L. M.G., & Fryns, J. (1998). Family contexts, parental behavior, and personality profiles of children and adolescents with Prader-Willi, fragile X, or Williams syndrome. *Journal of Child Psychology and Psychiatry, 39*(5), 699–710.

Van Orden, K. A., Witte, T. K., Selby, E. A., Bender, T. W., & Joiner, T. E. (2008). Suicidal behavior in youth. In J. R.Z. Abela & B. L. Hankin (Eds.), *Handbook of depression in children and adolescents (*pp. 441–461). New York: Guilford Press.

Vanderlinden, J, Grave, R. D., Fernandez, F, Vandereycken, W., Pieters, G., & Noorduin, C. (2004). Which factors do provoke binge eating? An exploratory study in eating disorder patients. *Eating and Weight Disorders, 9*, 300–305.

Vandrey, R., Budney, A. J., Kamon, J. L., & Stanger, C. (2005). Cannabis withdrawal in adolescent treatment seekers. *Drug and Alcohol Dependence, 78*(2), 205–210.

VanFleet, R. (2000). Understanding and overcoming parent resistance to play therapy. *International Journal of Play Therapy, 9*(1), 35–46.

VanFleet, R., Ryan, S. D., & Smith, S. K. (2005). Filial therapy: A critical review. In L. A. Reddy, T. M. Files-Hall, & C. E. Schaefer (Eds.), *Empirically based play interventions for chil-dren* (pp. 241–264). Washington, DC: American Psychological Association.

Vanyukov, M. M., Kirisci, L., Tarter, R. E., Simkevitz, H. F., Kirillova, G. P., Maher, B. S., et al. (2003). Liability to substance use disorders: 2. A measurement approach. *Neuroscience and Biobehavioral Reviews, 27*(6), 517–526.

Vanyukov, M. M., Tarter, R. E., Kirisci, L., Kirillova, G. P., Maher, B. S., & Clark, D. B. (2003). Liability to substance use disorders: 1. Common mechanisms and manifestations. *Neuroscience and Biobehavioral Reviews, 27*(6), 507–515.

Varnado-Sullivan, P. J., & Zucker, N. (2004). The Body Logic Program for Adolescents: A treatment manual for the prevention of eating disorders. *Behavior Modification, 28,* 854–875.

Vasey, M. W. (1995). Social anxiety disorders. In A. R. Eisen, C. A. Kearney, & C. E. Schaefer (Eds.), *Clinical handbook of anxiety disorders in children and adolescents* (pp. 131–168). Lanham, MA: Jason Aronson.

Vasey, M. W., & Daleiden, E. L. (1994). Worry in children. In *Worrying: Perspectives on theory, assessment and treatment* (pp. 185–207). Chichester, England: Wiley.

Vasey, M. W. & Dadds, M. R. (Eds.) (2001). *The developmental psychopathology of anxiety.* London: Oxford University Press.

Vaughn, B. E., & Bost, K. K. (1999). Attachment and temperament: Redundant, independent, or interacting influences on interpersonal adaptation and personality development? In J. Cassidy & P. R. Shaver (Eds.), *Handbook of attachment: Theory, research, and clinical applications* (pp. 198–225). New York: Guilford Press.

Vaughn, B. E., Egeland, B. R., Sroufe, L. A., & Waters, E. (1979). Individual differences in infant-mother attachment at twelve and eighteen months: Stability and change in families under stress. *Child Development, 50*(4), 971–975.

Vaughn, B. E., Goldberg, S., Atkinson, L., & Marcovitch, S. (1994). Quality of toddler-mother attachment in children with Down syndrome: Limits to interpretation of strange situation behavior. *Child Development, 65*(1), 95–108).

Veach, P. M., Bartels, D.M, & LeRoy, B. S. (2001). Ethical and professional challenges posed by patients with genetic concerns: A report of focus group discussions with genetic counselors, physicians and nurses. *Journal of Genetic Counseling, 10*(2), 97–119.

Veach, P. M., Bartels, D. M., & LeRoy, B. S. (2002). Commentary on genetic counseling—A profession in search of itself. *Journal of Genetic Counseling, 11*(3), 187–191.

Vedder, P., & Virta, E. (2005). Language, ethnic identity, and the adaptation of Turkish immigrant youth in the Netherlands and Sweden. *International Journal of Intercultural Relations, 29(3),* 317–337.

Veenstra, R., Lindenberg, S., Oldehinkel, A. J., De Winter, A. F., Verhulst, F. C., & Ormel, J. (2005). Bullying and victimization in elementary schools: A comparison of bullies, victims, bully/victims, and uninvolved preadolescents. *Developmental Psychology, 41*(4), 672–682.

Vega, W. A., Aguilar-Gaxiola, S., Andrade, L., Bijl, R., Borges, G., Caraveo-Anduaga, J. J., et al. (2002). Prevalence and ages of onset for drug use in seven international sites: Results from the International Consortium of Psychiatric Epidemiology. *Drug and Alcohol Dependence, 68*(3), 285–297.

Velting, O. N., & Albano, A. M. (2001). Current trends in the understanding and treatment of social phobia in youth. *Journal of Child Psychology and Psychiatry and Allied Disciplines, 42*(1), 127–140.

Velting, O. N., Setzer, N. J., & Albano, A. M. (2004). Update on and advances in assessment and cognitive-behavioral treatment of anxiety disorders in children and adolescents. *Professional Psychology: Research and Practice, 35*(1), 42–54.

Venter, A., Lord, C., & Schopler, E. (1992). A follow-up study of high-functioning autistic children. *Journal of Child Psychology and Psychiatry and Allied Disciplines, 33,* 489–507.

Verduin, T. L., & Kendall, P. C. (2003). Differential occurrence of comorbidity within childhood anxiety disorders. *Journal of Clinical Child and Adolescent Psychology, 32*(2), 290–295.

Verhulst, F. C., & Achenbach, T. M. (1995). Empirically based assessment and taxonomy of psychopathology: Cross-cultural applications: A review. *European Child and Adolescent Psychiatry, 4(2),* 61–76.

Verhulst, F. C., Dekker, M. C., & van der Ende, J. (1997). Parent, teacher and self-reports as predictors of signs of disturbance in adolescents: Whose information carries the most weight? *Acta Psychiatrica Scandinavica, 96(1),* 75–81.

Verhulst, F. C., & van der Ende, J. (1997). Factors associated with child mental health service use in the community. *Journal of the American Academy of Child and Adolescent Psychiatry, 36(7),* 901–909.

Verhulst, F. C., Van der Ende, J., Ferdinand, R. F., & Kasius, M. C. (1997). The prevalence of DSM-III-R diagnoses in a national sample of Dutch adolescents. *Archives of General Psychiatry, 54,* 329–336.

Verlinden, S., Hersen, M., & Thomas, J. (2000). Risk factors in school shootings. *Clinical Psychology Review, 20*(1), 3–56.

Vernberg, E. M., Routh, D. K., & Koocher, G. P. (1992). The future of psychotherapy with children: Developmental psychotherapy. *Psychotherapy, 29(1),* 72–80.

Vernberg, E. M., & Varela, R. E. (2001). Posttraumatic stress disorder: A developmental perspective. In M. W. Vasey & M. R. Dadds (Eds.), *The developmental psychopathology of anxiety* (pp. 386–406). New York: Oxford University Press.

Vernberg, E. M., & Vogel, J. M. (1993). Psychological responses of children to natural and human-made disasters: II. Interventions with children after disasters. *Journal of Child Clinical Psychology, 22*(4), 485–498.

Vicari, S., Caselli, M. C., Gagliardi, C., Tonucci, F., & Volterra, V. (2002). Language acquisition in special populations: A comparison between Down and Williams syndrome. *Neuropsychologia, 40*(13), 2461–2470.

Vickerman, K. A., & Margolin, G. (2007). Posttraumatic stress in children and adolescents exposed to family violence: II. Treatment. *Professional Psychology: Research and Practice, 38*(6), 620–628.

Villa, R. A., Thousand, J. S., Meyers, H., & Nevin, A. (1996). Teacher and administrator perceptions of heterogeneous education. *Exceptional Children, 63*(1), 29–45.

Villalba, R., & Harrington, C. (2003). Repetitive self-injurious behavior: The emerging potential of psychotropic intervention. *Psychiatric Times, 20*(2), 66–70.

Vitaro, F., Tremblay, R. E., & Bukowski, W. M. (2001). Friends, friendships and conduct disorders. In J. Hill & B. Maughan (Eds.), *Conduct disorders in childhood and adolescence* (pp. 346–378). New York: Cambridge University Press.

Vogel, J. M., & Vernberg, E. M. (1993). Psychological responses of children to natural and human-made disasters: I. Children's psychological responses to disasters. *Journal of Clinical Child Psychology, 22*(4), 464–484.

Volkmar, F. R. (1994). Childhood disintegrative disorder. *Child and Adolescent Psychiatric Clinics of North America, 3,* 119–130.

Volkmar, F. R., Chawarska, K., & Klin, A. (2005). Autism in infancy and early childhood. *Annual Review of Psychology, 56,* 315–336.

Volkmar, F. R., & Lord, C. (1998). Diagnosis and definition of autism and other pervasive developmental disorders. In F. R. Volkmar (Ed.), *Autism and pervasive developmental disorders: Cambridge monographs in child and adolescent psychiatry* (pp. 1–31). New York: Cambridge University Press.

Volkmar, F. R., & Klin, A. (1994). Social development in autism: Historical and clinical perspectives. In S. Baron-Cohen & H. Tager-Flusberg (Eds.), *Understanding other minds: Perspectives from autism* (pp. 40–55). London: Oxford University Press.

Volkmar, F. R., & Klin, A. (2000). Diagnostic issues in Asperger syndrome. In A. Klin, F. R. Volkmar, & S. S. Sparrow (Eds.), *Asperger syndrome* (pp. 25–71). New York: Guilford Press.

Volkmar, F. R., & Klin, A. (2001). Asperger's disorder and higher functioning autism: Same or different? In L. M. Glidden (Ed.), *International review of research in mental retardation: Autism* (Vol. 23, pp. 83–110). San Diego, CA: Academic Press.

Volkmar, F. R., Klin, A., & Pauls, D. (1998). Nosological and genetic aspects of Asperger syndrome. *Journal of Autism and Developmental Disorders, 28,* 457–463.

Volkmar, F. R., Klin, A., Marans, W., & Cohen, D. J. (1996). The pervasive developmental disorders: Diagnosis and assessment. *Child and Adolescent Psychiatric Clinics of North America, 5,* 963–977.

Volkmar, F. R., Klin, A., Siegel, B., & Szatmari, P. (1994). Field trial for autistic disorder in DSM-IV. *American Journal of Psychiatry, 151(9),* 1361–1367.

Volterra, V., Capirci, O., & Caselli, M. C. (2001). What atypical populations can reveal about language development: The contrast between deafness and Williams syndrome. *Language and Cognitive Processes, 16*(2), 219–239.

Von Korff, M. R., Eaton, W. W., & Keyl, P. M. (1985). The epidemiology of panic attacks and panic disorder. *American Journal of Epidemiology, 122,* 970–981.

Von Salisch, M. (2001). Children's emotional development: Challenges in their relationships to parents, peers, and friends. *International Journal of Behavioral Development, 25*(4), 310–319.

Von Salisch, M., & Saarni, C. (2001). Introduction to the Special Section: Emotional development in interpersonal relationships. *International Journal of Behavioral Development, 25*(4), 289.

Vungkhanching, M., Sher, K. J., Jackson, K. M., & Parra, G. R. (2004). Relation of attachment style to family history of alcoholism and alcohol use disorders in early adulthood. *Drug and Alcohol Dependence, 75*(1), 47–53.

Vythilingam, M., Heim, C., Newport, J., Miller, A. H., Anderson, E., Bronen, R., et al. (2002). Childhood trauma associated with smaller hippocampal volume in women with major depression. *The American Journal of Psychiatry, 159,* 2072–2080.

Waaddegaard, M., & Petersen, T. (2002). Dieting and desire for weight loss among adolescents in Denmark: A questionnaire survey. *European Eating Disorders Review, 10,* 329–346.

Wachs, T. D., & Kohnstamm, G. A. (2001). The bidirectional nature of temperament-context links. In T. D. Wachs & G. A. Kohnstamm (Eds.), *Temperament in context* (pp. 201–222). Mahwah, NJ: Erlbaum.

Wade, T. D., Bulik, C. M., Prescott, C. A., & Kendler, K. S. (2004). Sex influences on shared risk factors for bulimia nervosa and other psychiatric disorders. *Archives of General Pyschiatry, 61,* 251–256.

Wagenaar, A. C., Lenk, K. M., & Toomey, T. L. (2006). Policies to reduce underage drinking. In M. Galanter (Ed.), *Alcohol problems in adolescents and young adults: Epidemiology, neurobiology, prevention, and treatment* (pp. 275–297). New York: Springer Science and Business Media.

Wagenaar, A. C., Toomey, T. L., & Erickson, D. J. (2005). Preventing youth access to alcohol: Outcomes from a multi-community time-series trial. *Addiction, 100*(3), 335–345.

Wagner, B. M., Silverman, M. A.C., & Martin, C. E. (2003). Family factors in youth suicidal behaviors. *American Behavioral Scientist, 46*(9), 1171–1191.

Wagner, E. F., Brown, S. A., Monti, P. M., Myers, M. G., & Waldron, H. B. (1998). Innovations in adolescent substance abuse intervention. *Alcoholism: Clinical and Experimental Research, 23,* 236–249.

Wahl, O. F. (1999). Mental health consumers' experience of stigma. *Schizophrenia Bulletin, 25(3),* 467–478.

Wahl, O. F. (2002). Children's views of mental illness: A review of the literature. *Psychiatric Rehabilitation Skills, 6(2),* 134–158.

Wahl, S. K., Turner, L. R., Mermelstein, R. J., & Flay, B. R. (2005). Adolescents' smoking expectancies: Psychometric properties and prediction of behavior change. *Nicotine and Tobacco Research, 7*(4), 613–623.

Wakefield, J. C. (1992). The concept of mental disorder: On the boundary between biological facts and social values. *American Psychologist, 47(3),* 373–388.

Wakefield, J. C. (1997). When is development disordered? Developmental psychopathology and the harmful dysfunction analysis of mental disorder. *Development and Psychopathology, 9(2),* 269–290.

Wakefield, J. C. (2002). Values and the validity of diagnostic criteria: Disvalued versus disordered conditions of childhood and adolescence. In J. Z. Sadler (Ed.), *Descriptions and prescriptions: Values, mental disorders and the DSMs* (pp. 148–164). Baltimore, MD: Johns Hopkins University Press.

Wakefield, M., Kloska, D. D., O'Malley, P. M., Johnston, L. D., Chaloupka, F., Pierce, J., et al. (2004). The role of smoking intentions in predicting future smoking among youth: Findings from Monitoring the Future data. *Addiction, 99*(7), 914–922.

Walden, B., McGue, M., Iacono, W. G., Burt, S. A., & Elkins, I. (2004). Identifying shared environmental contributions to early substance use: The respective roles of peers and parents. *Journal of Abnormal Psychology, 113*(3) , 440–450.

Waldman, I. D., & Lilienfeld, S. O. (2001). Applications of taxometric methods to problems of comorbidity: Perspectives and challenges. *Clinical Psychology: Science and Practice, 8(4),* 520–527.

Waldman, I. D., Rhee, S. H., Levy, F., & Hay, D. A. (2001). In F. Levy & D. A. Hay (Eds.), *Attention, genes, and ADHD* (pp. 115–138). New York: Brunner-Routledge.

Waldron, H. B., & Kaminer, Y. (2004). On the learning curve: The emerging evidence supporting cognitive-behavioral therapies for adolescent substance abuse. *Addiction, 99*(Suppl. 2), 93–105.

Walker, D. R., Thompson, A., Zwaigenbaum, L., Goldberg, J., Bryson, S. E., Mahoney, W. J., et al. (2004). Specifying PDD-NOS: A comparison of PDD-NOS, Asperger syndrome, and autism.

Journal of the American Academy of Child and Adolescent Psychiatry, 43(2), 172–780.

Walker, E. F. (2002). Adolescent neurodevelopment and psychopathology. *Current Directions in Psychological Science, 11*(1), 24–28.

Walker, L. S., Claar, R. L., & Garber, J. (2002). Social consequences of children's pain: When do they encourage symptom maintenance? *Journal of Pediatric Psychology, 27*(8), 680–698.

Walkup, J. T., & Ginsburg, G. S. (2002). Anxiety disorders in children and adolescents. *International Review of Psychiatry, 14*(2), 85–86.

Walkup, J. T., Labellarte, M. J., & Ginsburg, G. S. (2002). The pharmacological treatment of childhood anxiety disorders. *International Review of Psychiatry, 14*(2), 135–142.

Walkup, J. T., Labellarte, M. J., Riddle, M. A., Pine, D., Greenhill, L., Klein, R., et al. (2003). Searching for moderators and mediators of pharmacological treatment effects in children and adolescents with anxiety disorders. *Journal of the American Academy of Child and Adolescent Psychiatry, 42*(1), 13–21.

Wallace, J. M., Jr., & Muroff, J. R. (2002). Preventing substance abuse among African American children and youth: Race differences in risk factor exposure and vulnerability. *Journal of Primary Prevention, 22*(3), 235–261.

Waller, M., Hallfors, D., Halpern, C., Iritani, B., Ford, C., & Cuo, G. (2006). Depressive symptoms and patterns of substance use and risky sexual behavior among nationally representative samples of U. S. adolescents, *Archives of Women's Mental Health, 9*(3), 139–150.

Wallis, A., Rhodes, P., Kohn, M., & Madden, S. (2007). Five years of family based treatment for anorexia nervosa: The Maudsley model at the Children's Hospital at Westmead. *International Journal of Adolescent Medicine and Health, 19*(3), 277–283.

Wang, M. Q., Matthew, R. F., Bellamy, N., & James, S. (2005). A structural model of the substance use pathways among minority youth. *American Journal of Health Behavior, 29*(6), 531–541.

Wang, S. S., Houshyar, S., & Prinstein, M. J. (2006). Adolescent girls' and boys' weight-related health behaviors and cognitions: Associations with reputation- and preference-based peer status. *Health Psychology, 25,* 358–663.

Wang, Z., Byrne, N. M., Kenardy, J. A., & Hills, A. P. (2005). Influences of ethnicity and socioeconomic status on the body dissatisfaction and eating behavior of Australian children and adolescents. *Eating Behaviors, 6,* 23–33.

Wanner, B., Vitaro, F., Ladouceur, R., Brendgen, M., & Tremblay, R. E. (2006). Joint trajectories of gambling, alcohol and marijuana use during adolescence: A person- and variable-centered developmental approach. *Addictive Behaviors, 31*(4), 566–580.

Wardle, K. A., Robb, F. J., Griffith, J., Brunner, E., Power, C., & Tovee, M. (2004). Socioeconomic variation in attitudes to eating and weight in female adolescents. *Health Psychology, 23,* 275–282.

Warren, S. L., Emde, R., & Sroufe, L. A. (2000). Internal representations: Predicting anxiety from children's play narratives. *Journal of the American Academy of Child and Adolescent Psychiatry, 39*(1), 100–107.

Warren, S. L., Huston, L., Egeland, B., & Sroufe, L. A. (1997). Child and adolescent anxiety disorders and early attachment. *Journal of the American Academy of Child and Adolescent Psychiatry, 36*(5), 637–644.

Warren, Z. E., Malik, N. M., Lindahl, K. M., & Claussen, A. H. (2006). Behavioral control dynamics and developmental outcomes in infants prenatally exposed to cocaine. *Infant Mental Health Journal, 27*(2), 121–140.

Waschbusch, D. A. (2002). A meta-analytic examination of co-morbid hyperactive-impulsive-attention problems and conduct problems. *Psychological Bulletin, 128*(1), 118–150.

Waschbusch, D. A., & Hill, G. P. (2003). Empirically supported, promising, and unsupported treatments for children with attention-deficit/hyperactivity disorder. From S. O. Lilienfeld & S. J. Lynn (Eds.), *Science and pseudoscience in clinical psychology* (pp. 333–362). New York: Guilford Press.

Waschbusch, D. A., & King, S. (2006). Should sex-specific norms be used to assess attention-deficit/hyperactivity disorder or oppositional defiant disorder? Journal of Consulting and Clinical Psychology, 74(1), 179–185.

Waschbusch, D. A., Pelham, W. E. Jr., Jennings, J. R., Greiner, A. R., Tarter, R. E., & Moss, H. B. (2002). Reactive aggression in boys with disruptive behavior disorders: Behavior physiology, and affect. *Journal of Abnormal Child Psychology, 30*(6), 641–656.

Waschbusch, D. A., Porter, S., Carrey, N., Kazmi, S. O., Roach, K. A., & D'Amico, D. A. (2004). Investigation of the heterogeneity of disruptive behaviour in elementary-age children. *Canadian Journal of Behavioural Science, 36*(2), 97–112.

Waschbusch, D. A., Sellers, D. P., LeBlanc, M., & Kelley, M. L. (2003). Helpless attributions and depression in adolescents: The roles of anxiety, event valence and demographics. *Journal of Adolescence, 26*(2), 169–183.

Waschbusch, D. A., Walsh, T. M., Andrade, B. F., King, S., & Carrey, N. J. (2007). Social problem solving, conduct problems, and callous-unemotional traits in children. *Child Psychiatry and Human Development, 37,* 293–305.

Waslick, B. D., Kandel, R., & Kakouros, A. (2002). Depression in children and adolescents: An overview. In D. Shaffer & B. D. Waslick (Eds.), *Review of psychiatry: Vol. 21. The many faces of depression in children and adolescents* (pp. 1–36). Washington, DC: American Psychiatric Publishing.

Waters, E. (1995). Attachment Q-Set (Appendix A). *Monographs of the Society for Research in Child Development, 60*(2–3), 234–346.

Waters, E., & Sroufe, L. A. (1983). Social competence as a developmental construct. *Developmental Review, 3,* 79–97.

Waters, E., Merrick, S., Treboux, D., Crowell, J., & Albersheim, L. (2000). Attachment security in infancy and early adulthood: A twenty-year longitudinal study. *Child Development, 71,* 684–689.

Waters, T. L., & Barrett, P. M. (2000). The role of the family in childhood obsessive-compulsive disorder. *Clinical Child and Family Psychology Review, 3*(3), 173–184.

Watson, A. C., Miller, F. E., & Lyons, J. S. (2005). Adolescent attitudes toward serious mental illness. *Journal of Nervous and Mental Disease, 193(11),* 769–772.

Watson, A. C., Otey, E., Westbrook, A. L., Gardner, A. L., Lamb, T. A., Corrigan, P. W., et al. (2004). Changing middle schoolers' attitudes about mental illness through education. *Schizophrenia Bulletin, 30(3),* 563–572.

Watson, A. C., Painter, K. M., & Bornstein, M. H. (2001). Longitudinal relations between 2-year-olds' language and 4-year-olds' theory of mind. *Journal of Cognition and Development, 2,* 449–457.

Watson, D., & Clark, L. A. (1984). Negative affectivity: The disposition to experience aversive emotional states. *Psychological Bulletin, 96,* 465–490.

Watson, D., Kotov, R., & Gamez, W. (2006). Basic dimensions of temperament in relation to personality and psychopathology. In R. F. Krueger & J. L. Tackett (Eds.), *Personality and Psychopathology* (pp. 7–38). New York: Guilford Press.

Watson, L. R. (1998). Following the child's lead: Mothers' interactions with children with autism. *Journal of Autism and Developmental Disorders, 28*(1), 51–59.

Webster-Stratton, C. (2000). Oppositional-defiant and conduct-disordered children. In M. Hersen & R. T. Ammerman (Eds.), *Advanced abnormal child psychology* (2nd ed.) (pp. 387–412). Mahwah, NJ: Erlbaum.

Webster-Stratton, C. (2005). The Incredible Years: A training program for the prevention and treatment of conduct problems in young children. In E. D. Hibbs & P. S. Jensen (Eds.), *Psychosocial treatments for child and adolescent disorders: Empirically based strategies for clinical practice* (2nd ed., pp. 507–555). Washington, DC: American Psychological Association.

Webster-Stratton, C., & Reid, M. J. (2006). Treatment and prevention of conduct problems: Parent training interventions for young children (2–7 years old). In K. McCartney & D. Phillips (Eds.), *Blackwell handbook of early childhood development* (pp. 616–641). Malden, MA: Blackwell.

Webster-Stratton, C., & Reid, M. J. (2007). Incredible Years parents and teachers training series: A Head Start partnership to promote social competence and prevent conduct problems. In P. Tolan, J. Szapocznik, & S. Sambrano (Eds.), *Preventing youth substance abuse: Science-based programs for children and adolescents* (pp. 67–88). Washington, DC: American Psychological Association.

Webster-Stratton, C., Reid, M. J., & Stoolmiller, M. (2008). Preventing conduct problems and improving school readiness: Evaluation of the Incredible Years teacher and child training programs in high-risk schools. *Journal of Child Psychology and Psychiatry, 49*(5), 251–263.

Webster-Stratton, C. & Taylor, T. (2001). Nipping early risk factors in the bud: Preventing substance abuse, delinquency, and violence in adolescence through interventions targeted at young children (0 to 8 years). *Prevention Science, 2*, 165–192.

Webster-Stratton, C. & Lindsay, D. W. (1999). Social competence and conduct problems in young children: Issues in assessment. *Journal of Clinical Child Psychology, 28*, 25–43.

Webster-Stratton, C., & Hammond, M. (1997). Treating children with early-onset conduct problems: A comparison of child and parent training interventions. *Journal of Consulting and Clinical Psychology, 65*(1), 93–109.

Wechsler, D. (2003). *Wechsler Intelligence Scale for Children, 4th ed. (WISC-IV)*. San Antonio, TX: The Psychological Corporation.

Wechsler, H., & Wuethrich, B. (2002*). Dying to drink: Confronting binge drinking on college campuses.* Emmaus, PA: Rodale Press.

Weersing, V. R., & Weisz, J. R. (2002). Community clinic treatment of depressed youth: Benchmarking usual care against CBT clinical trials. *Journal of Consulting and Clinical Psychology, 70*(2), 299–310.

Wei, E. H., Loeber, R., & White, H. R. (2004). Teasing apart the developmental associations between alcohol and marijuana use and violence. *Journal of Contemporary Criminal Justice, 20*(2), 166–183.

Weil, J. (2003). Psychosocial genetic counseling in the post-nondirective era: A point of view. *Journal of Genetic Counseling, 12*(3), 199–211.

Weiler, M. D., Bellinger, D., Marmor, J., Rancier, S., & Waber, D. (1999). Mother and teacher reports of ADHD symptoms: DSM-IV questionnaire data. *Journal of the American Academy of Child and Adolescent Psychiatry, 38*, 1139–1147.

Weine, A. M., Phillips, J. S., & Achenbach, T. M. (1995). Behavioral and emotional problems among Chinese and American children: Parent and teacher reports for ages 6 to 13. *Journal of Abnormal Child Psychology, 23*(5), 619–639.

Weiner, M. D., Pentz, M. A., Skara, S. N., Li, C., Chou, C-P., & Dwyer, J. H. (2004). Relationship of substance use and associated predictors of violence in early, middle, and late adolescence. *Journal of Child and Adolescent Substance Abuse, 13*(4), 97–117.

Weinfield, N. S., Ogawa, J. R., & Sroufe, L. A. (1997). Early attachment as a pathway to adolescent peer competence. *Journal of Research on Adolescence, 7*(3), 241–265.

Weinfield, N. S., Sroufe, L. A., Egeland, B., & Carlson, E. A. (1999). The nature of individual differences in infant-caregiver attachment. In J. Cassidy & P. R. Shaver (Eds.), *Handbook of attachment: Theory, research, and clinical applications* (pp. 68–88). New York: Guilford Press.

Weis, R., Whitemarsh, S. M., & Wilson, N. L. (2005). Military-style residential treatment for disruptive adolescents: Effective for some girls, all girls, when, and why? *Psychological Services, 2*(2), 105–122.

Weis, R., Wilson, N. L., & Whitemarsh, S. M. (2005). Evaluation of a voluntary, military-style residential treatment program for adolescents with academic and conduct problems. *Journal of Clinical Child and Adolescent Psychology, 34*(4), 692–705.

Weiser, M., Reichenberg, A., Grotto, I., Yasvitzky, R., Rabinowitz, J., Lubin, G., et al. (2004). Higher rates of cigarette smoking in male adolescents before the onset of schizophrenia: A historical-prospective cohort study. *American Journal of Psychiatry, 161*(7), 1219–1223.

Weisner, T. S. (2005). Attachment as a cultural and ecological problem with pluralistic solution. *Human Development, 48*(1–2), 89–94.

Weiss, B., & Garber, J. (2003). Developmental differences in the phenomenology of depression. *Development and Psychopathology, 15*(2), 403–430.

Weiss, B., Susser, K., & Catron, T. (1998). Common and specific features of childhood psychopathology. *Journal of Abnormal Psychology, 107(1),* 118–127.

Weiss, D. D., & Last, C. G. (2001). Developmental variations in the prevalence and manifestations of anxiety disorders. In M. W. Vasey & M. R. Dadds (Eds.), *The developmental psychopathology of anxiety* (pp. 27–42). London: Oxford University Press.

Weiss, E. L., Longhurst, J. G., & Mazure, C. M. (1999). Childhood sexual abuse as a risk factor for depression in women: Psychosocial and neurobiological correlates. *American Journal of Psychiatry, 156*(6), 816–828.

Weiss, G., & Hechtman, L. (1993). *Hyperactive children grown up: ADHD in children, adolescents, and adults* (2nd ed.). New York: Guilford Press.

Weiss, G., & Hechtman, L. T. (1999). *ADHD in adulthood: A guide to current theory, diagnosis and treatment.* Baltimore: Johns Hopkins University.

Weiss, K., & Wertheim, E. H. (2005). An evaluation of a prevention program for disordered eating in adolescent girls: Examining responses of high- and low-risk girls. *Eating Disorders: The Journal of Prevention and Treatment, 13*(2), 143–156.

Weissberg, R. P., Kumpfer, K. L., & Seligman, M. E. (2003). Prevention that works for children and youth. *American Psychologist, 58 (6–7),* 425–432.

Weissman, M. M., McAvay, G., Goldstein, R. B., Nunes, E. V., Verdeli, H., & Wickramaratne, P. J. (1999). Risk/protective factors among addicted mothers' offspring: A replication study. *American Journal of Drug and Alcohol Abuse, 25,* 661–679.

Weissman, M. M., Warner, V., Wickramaratne, P., Moreau, D., & Olfson, M. (1997). Offspring of depressed parents: 10 years later. *Archives of General Psychiatry, 54*(10), 932–940.

Weisz, J. R. (2004). *Psychotherapy for children and adolescents: Evidence-Based treatments and case examples.* New York: Cambridge University Press.

Weisz, J. R., Chaiyasit, W., Weiss, B., Eastman, K. L., & Jackson, E. W. (1995). A multimethod study of problem behavior among Thai and American children in school: Teacher reports versus direct observations. *Child Development, 66*(2), 402–415.

Weisz, J. R., & Eastman, K. L. (1995). Cross-national research on child and adolescent psychopathology. In F. C. Verhulst (Ed.), *The epidemiology of child and adolescent psychopathology* (pp. 42–65). London: Oxford University Press.

Weisz, J. R., & Hawley, K. M. (2002). Developmental factors in the treatment of adolescents. *Journal of Consulting and Clinical Psychology, 70*(1), 21–43.

Weisz, J. R., & Hawley, K. M. (2002). Developmental factors in the treatment of adolescents. *Journal of Consulting and Clinical Psychology, 70*(1), 21–43.

Weisz, J. R., & McCarty, C. A. (1999). Can we trust parent reports in research on cultural and ethnic differences in child psychopathology? Using the bicultural family design to test parental culture effects. *Journal of Abnormal Psychology, 108*(4), 598–603.

Weisz, J. R., Doss, A. J., & Hawley, K. M. (2005). Youth psychotherapy outcome research: A review and critique of the evidence base. *Annual Review of Psychology, 56,* 337–363.

Weisz, J. R., McCarty, C. A., Eastman, K. L., Chaiyasit, W., & Suwanlert, S. (1997). Developmental psychopathology and culture: Ten lessons from Thailand. In S. Luthar, J. A. Burack, D. Cicchetti, & J. R. Weisz (Eds.), *Developmental psychopathology: Perspectives on adjustment, risk, and disorder* (pp. 568–592). New York: Cambridge University Press.

Weisz, J. R., McCarty, C. A., & Valeri, S. M. (2006). Effects of psychotherapy for depression in children and adolescents: A meta-analysis. *Psychological Bulletin, 132*(1), 132–149.

Weisz, J. R., Sandler, I. N., Durlak, J. A., & Anton, B. S. (2005). Promoting and protecting youth mental health through evidence-based prevention and treatment. *American Psychologist, 60*(6), 628–648.

Weisz, J. R., Sigman, M., Weiss, B., & Mosk, J. (1993). Parent reports of behavioral and emotional problems among children in Kenya, Thailand, and the United States. *Child Development, 64*(1), 98–109.

Weisz, J. R., Southam-Gerow, M. A., Gordis, E. B., & Connor-Smith, J. (2003). Primary and secondary control enhancement training for youth depression: Applying the deployment-focused model of treatment development and testing. From A. E. Kazdin & J. R. Weisz (Eds.), *Evidence-based psychotherapies for children and adolescents* (pp. 165–182). New York: Guilford Press.

Weisz, J. R., Suwanlert, S., Chaiyasit, W., Weiss, B., Walter, B. R., & Anderson, W. W. (1988). Thai and American perspectives on over- and undercontrolled child behavior problems: Exploring the threshold model among parents, teachers, and psychologists. *Journal of Consulting and Clinical Psychology, 56*(4), 601–609.

Weisz, J. R., Suwanlert, S., Chaiyasit, W., Weiss, B., Walter, B. R. & Anderson, W. W. (1991). Adult attitudes toward over- and undercontrolled child problems: Urban and rural parents and teachers from Thailand and the United States. *Journal of Child Psychology and Psychiatry and Allied Disciplines, 32*(4), 645–654.

Weisz, J. R., Sweeney, L., Proffitt, V., & Carr, T. (1993). Control-related beliefs and self-reported depressive symptoms in late childhood. *Journal of Abnormal Psychology, 102*(3), 411–418.

Weisz, J. R., Weiss, B., Alicke, M. D., & Klotz, M. L. (1987). Effectiveness of psychotherapy with children and adolescents: A meta-analysis for clinicians. *Journal of Consulting and Clinical Psychology, 55*(4), 542–549.

Weisz, J. R., Weiss, B., & Donenberg, G. R. (1992). The lab versus the clinic: Effects of child and adolescent psychotherapy. *American Psychologist, 47,* 1578–1585.

Weller, E. B., Calvert, S. M., & Weller, R. A. (2003). Bipolar disorder in children and adolescents: Diagnosis and treatment. *Current Opinion in Psychiatry, 16*(4), 383–388.

Weller, E. B., Danielyan, A. K., & Weller, R. A. (2002). Somatic treatment of bipolar disorder in children and adolescents. *Child and Adolescent Psychiatric Clinics of North America, 11*(3), 595–618.

Weller, E. B., Weller, R. A., & Fristad, M. A. (1995). Bipolar disorder in children: Misdiagnosis, underdiagnosis, and future directions. *Journal of the American Academy of Child and Adolescent Psychiatry, 34*(6), 709–714.

Wellman, H. M., Baron-Cohen, S., Caswell, R., Gomez, J. C., Swettenham, J., Toye, E. et al. (2002). Thought bubbles help children with autism acquire an alternative to a theory of mind. *Autism, 6*(4), 343–363.

Wells, J. E., Horwood, L. J., & Fergusson, D. M. (2004). Drinking patterns in mid-adolescence and psychosocial outcomes in late adolescence and early adulthood. *Addiction, 99*(12), 1529–1541.

Wells, K. C., & Albano, A. M. (2005). Parent involvement in CBT treatment of adolescent depression: Experiences in the Treatment for Adolescents with Depression Study (TADS). *Cognitive and Behavioral Practice, 12*(2), 209–220.

Wells, K. C., Pelham, W. E., Kotkin, R. A., Hoza, B., Abikoff, H. B., Abramowitz, A., et al. (2000). Psychosocial treatment strategies in the MTA study: Rationale, methods, and critical issues in design and implementation. *Journal of Abnormal Child Psychology, 28*(6), 483–505.

Welsh, J., Domitrovich, C. E., Bierman, K., & Lang, J. (2003). Promoting safe schools and healthy students in rural Pennsylvania. *Psychology in the Schools, 40,* 457–472.

Welsh, J. P., Ahn, E. S., & Placantonakis, D. G. (2005). Is autism due to brain desynchronization? *International Journal of Developmental Neuroscience, 23*(2–3), 253–263.

Wender, P. H., Wood, D. R., & Reimherr, F. W. (1991). *Pharmacological treatment of attention deficit disorder, residual type (ADD-RT) in adults.* New York: Mary Ann Liebert Publishers.

Wentworth, N., & Witryol, S. L. (2003). Curiosity, exploration, and novelty seeking. In M. H. Bornstein, L. Davidson, C. L. M. Keyes, & A. Moore (Eds.), Well-being: Positive development across the life course (pp. 281–294). Mahwah, NJ: Erlbaum.

Werner, E., Dawson, G., Muson, J., & Osterling, J. (2005). Variation in early developmental course in autism and its relation with behavioral outcome at 3–4 years of age. *Journal of Autism and Developmental Disorders, 35*(3), 337–350.

Werner, E., Dawson, G., Osterling, J., & Dinno, N. (2000). Recognition of autism spectrum disorder before one year of age: A retrospective study based on home videotapes. *Journal of Autism and Developmental Disorders, 30*(2), 157–162.

Werner, E. E. (1993). Risk, resilience and recovery: Perspectives from the Kauai longitudinal study. *Development and Psychology, 5*, 503–515.

Werner, E. E., & Smith, R. S. (1977). *Kauai's Children Come of Age*. Honolulu: University of Hawaii Press.

Werner, E. E., & Smith, R. S. (1982, 1989). Vulnerable but invincible: A study of resilient children. New York: McGraw-Hill.

Werner, N. E., & Crick, N. R. (2004). Maladaptive peer relationships and the development of relational and physical aggression during middle childhood. *Social Development, 13*(4), 495–514.

Wertheim, E. H., Martin, G., Prior, M., Sanson, A., & Smart, D. (2002). Parent influences in the transmission of eating- and weight-related values and behaviors. *Eating Disorders: The Journal of Treatment and Prevention, 10*, 321–334.

West, A., Henry, D. B., & Pavuluri, M. (2007). Maintenance model of integrated psychosocial treatment in pediatric bipolar disorder: A pilot feasibility study. *Journal of the American Academy of Child and Adolescent Psychiatry, 46*(2), 205–212.

Westen, D. (1998). The scientific legacy of Sigmund Freud: Toward a psychodynamically informed psychological science. *Psychological Bulletin, 124(3)*, 333–371.

Westenberg, P. M., Drewes, M. J., Goedhart, A. W., Siebelink, B. M., & Treffers, P. D. (2004). A developmental analysis of self-reported fears in late childhood through mid-adolescence: Social-evaluative fears on the rise? *Journal of Child Psychology and Psychiatry, 45*(3), 481–495.

Wetherby, A. M. (1986). Ontogeny of communicative functions in autism. *Journal of Autism and Developmental Disorders, 16*(3), 157–162.

Wetter, D. W., Kenford, S. L., Welsch, S. K., Smith, S. S., Fouladi, R. T., Fiore, M. C., et al. (2004). Prevalence and predictors of transitions in smoking behavior among college students. *Health Psychology, 23*(2), 168–177.

Whalen, C. K., Henker, B., & Granger, D. A. (1990). Social judgment processed in hyperactive boys: Effects of methylphenidate and comparisons with normal peers. *Journal of Abnormal Child Psychology, 18*(3), 297–316.

Whalen, C. K., Jamner, L. D., Henker, B., Gehricke, J-G., & King, P. S. (2003). Is there a link between adolescent cigarette smoking and pharmacotherapy for ADHD? *Psychology of Addictive Behaviors, 17*(4), 332–335.

Whalen, C. & Schreibman, L. (2003). Joint attention training for children with autism using behavior modification procedures. *Journal of Child Psychology and Psychiatry, 44*(3), 456–468.

Whalen, C., Schreibman, L., & Ingersoll, B. (2006). The collateral effects of joint attention training on social initiations, positive affect, imitation, and spontaneous speech for young children with autism. *Journal of Autism and Developmental Disorders, 36*(5), 655–664.

Wheeler, H. A., Wintre, M. G., & Polivy, J. (2003). The association of low parent-adolescent reciprocity, a sense of incompetence, and identity confusion with disordered eating. *Journal of Adolescent Research, 18,* 405–429.

Whitaker-Azmitia, PM. (2005). Behavioral and cellular consequences of increasing serotonergic activity during brain development: A role in autism? *International Journal of Developmental Neuroscience, 23*(2–3), 75–83.

White, H. R., Bates, M. E., & Labouvie, E. (1998). Adult outcomes of adolescent drug use: A comparison of process-oriented and incremental analyses. In R. Jessor (Ed.), *New perspectives on adolescent risk behavior* (pp. 150–181). New York: Cambridge University Press.

White, H. R., Loeber, R., Stouthamer-Loeber, M., & Farrington, D. P. (1999). Developmental associations between substance use and violence. *Development and Psychopathology, 11*(4), 785–803.

White, H. R., Pandina, R. J., & Chen, P-H. (2002). Developmental trajectories of cigarette use from early adolescence into young adulthood. *Drug and Alcohol Dependence, 65*(2), 167–178.

White, H. R., Tice, P. C., Loeber, R., & Stouthamer-Loeber, M. (2002). Illegal acts committed by adolescents under the influence of alcohol and drugs. *Journal of Research in Crime and Delinquency, 39*(2), 131–152.

White, H. R., Xie, M., Thompson, W., Loeber, R., & Stouthamer-Loeber, M. (2001). Psychopathology as a predictor of adolescent drug use trajectories. *Psychology of Addictive Behaviors, 15*(3), 210–218.

White, M. A., Kohlmaier, J. R., Varnado-Sullivan, P., & Williamson, D. A. (2003). Racial/ethnic differences in weight concerns: Protective and risk factors for the development of eating disorders and obesity among adolescent females. *Eating and Weight Disorders, 8,* 20–25.

White, S. H. (1996). Developmental psychopathology: From attribution toward information. In S. Matthysse & D. L. Levy (Eds.), *Psychopathology: The evolving science of mental disorder* (pp. 161–197). New York: Cambridge University Press.

Whitfield, J. B., Zhu, G., Madden, P. A., Neale, M. C., Heath, A. C., & Martin, N. G. (2004). The genetics of alcohol intake and of alcohol dependence. *Alcoholism: Clinical and Experimental Research, 28*(8), 1153–1160.

Whitman, T. L., O'Callaghan, M., & Sommer, K. (1997). Emotion and mental retardation. In W. E. MacLean (Ed.), *Ellis' handbook of mental deficiency, psychological theory and research* (3rd ed., pp. 77–98).

Wicker, A. W. (1992). Making sense of environments. In W. B. Walsh & K. H. Craik (Eds.), *Person-environment psychology: Models and perspectives* (pp. 157–192). Hillsdale, NJ: Erlbaum.

Widaman, K. F., & McGrew, K. S. (1996). The structure of adaptive behavior. In J. W. Jacobson & J. A. Mulick (Eds.), *Manual of diagnosis and professional practice in mental retardation* (pp. 97–110). Washington, DC: American Psychological Association.

Wiers, R. W., Gunning, W. B., & Sergeant, J. A. (1998). Do young children of alcoholics hold more positive or negative alcohol-related expectancies than controls? *Alcoholism: Clinical and Experimental Research, 22*(8), 1855–1863.

Wiesner, M., & Windle, M. (2004). Assessing covariates of adolescent delinquency trajectories: A latent growth mixture modeling approach. *Journal of Youth and Adolescence, 33*(5), 431–442.

Wiggins, L. D., Baio, J., & Rice, C. (2006). Examination of the time between first evaluation and first autism spectrum diagnosis in a population-based sample. *Journal of Developmental and Behavioral Pediatrics, 27*(12), S79-S87.

Wikler, L. M. (1986). Periodic stresses of families of older mentally retarded children: An exploratory study. *American Journal of Mental Deficiency, 90*(6), 703–706.

Wilburn, V. R., & Smith, D. E. (2005). Stress, self-esteem, and suicidal ideation in late adolescents. *Adolescence, 40*(157), 33–45.

Wild, L. G., Flisher, A. J., & Lombard, C. (2004). Suicidal ideation and attempts in adolescents: Association with depression and six domains of self-esteem. *Journal of Adolescence, 27*(6), 611–624.

Wilens, T. E., Biederman, J., & Spencer, T. J. (1998). Pharmacotherapy of attention deficit hyperactivity disorder in adults. *CNS Drugs, 9*, 347–356.

Wilens, T. E., Biederman, J., Kwon, A., Ditterline, J., Forkner, P., Moore, H., et al. (2004). Risk of substance use disorders in adolescents with bipolar disorder. *Journal of the American Academy of Child and Adolescent Psychiatry, 43*(11), 1380–1386.

Wilens, T. E., Faraone, S. V., & Biederman, J. (2006). Attention-deficit/hyperacticity disorder in adults. *Journal of the American Medical Association, 292*(5), 619–623.

Wilens, T. E., Faraone, S. V., Biederman, J. & Gunawardene, S. (2003). Does stimulant therapy of attention-deficit/hyperactivity disorder beget later substance abuse? A meta-analytic review of the literature. *Pediatrics, 111*(1), 179–185.

Wilens, T. E., Spencer, T., Biederman, J., Wozniak, J., & Connor, D. (1995). Combined pharmacotherapy: An emerging trend in pediatric psychopharmacology. *Journal of the American Academy of Child and Adolescent Psychiatry, 34*, 110–112.

Wille, D. E. (1991). Relation of preterm birth with quality of infant-mother attachment at one year. *Infant Behavior and Development, 14*(2), 227–240.

Williams, C., Alderson, P. & Farsides, B. (2002). 'Drawing the line' in prenatal screening and testing: Health practitioners' discussions. *Health, Risk and Society, 4*(1), 61–75.

Williams, D. L., Goldstein, G., & Minshew, N. J. (2006a). Neuropsychologic functioning in children with autism: Further evidence for disordered complex information-processing. *Child Neuropsychology, 12*(4–5), 279–298.

Williams, D. L., Goldstein, G., Minshew, N. J. (2006b). The profile of memory function in children with autism. *Neuropsychology, 20*(1), 21–29.

Williams, K. R., & Guerra, N. G. (2007). Prevalence and predictors of internet bullying. *Journal of Adolescent Health, 41*(6, Suppl.), S14-S21.

Williams, P. G., Holmbeck, G. N., & Greenley, R. N. (2002). Adolescent health psychology. *Journal of Consulting and Clinical Psychology, 70*(3), 828–842.

Williams, T. S., Connolly, J., Pepler, D., Craig, W., & Laporte, L. (2008). Risk models of dating aggression across different adolescent relationships: A developmental psychopathology approach. *Journal of Consulting and Clinical Psychology, 76*(4), 622–632.

Williamson, D. A., Marney, A, York-Crowe, E. & Stewart, T. M. (2004). Cognitive-behavior theories of eating disorders. *Behavior Modification, 28,* 711–738.

Williamson, D. A., Womble, L. G., Smeets, M. A. M., Thaw, J. M., Kutlesic, V., & Gleaves, D. H. (2002). Latent structure of eating disorder symptoms: A factor analytic and taxometric investigation. *American Journal of Psychiatry, 159,* 412–418.

Williamson, D. E., Birmaher, B., Brent, D. A., Balach, L., Dahl, R. E., & Ryan, N. D. (2000). Atypical symptoms of depression in a sample of depressed child and adolescent outpatients. *Journal of the American Academy of Child and Adolescent Psychiatry, 39*(1), 1253–1259.

Williford, A. P., Calkins, S. D., & Keane, S. P. (2007). Predicting change in parenting stress across early childhood: Child and maternal factors. *Journal of Abnormal Child Psychology, 35*(2), 251–263.

Willner, P. (2001). A view through the gateway: Expectancies as a possible pathway from alcohol to cannabis. *Addiction, 96*(5), 691–703.

Willner, P., & Hart, K. (2001). Adolescents' reports of their illicit alcohol purchases. *Drugs: Education, Prevention and Policy, 8*(3), 233–242.

Willner, P., James, D., & Morgan, M. (2005). Excessive alcohol consumption and dependence on amphetamine are associated with parallel increases in subjective ratings of both 'wanting' and 'liking'. *Addiction, 100*(10), 1487–1495.

Willoughby, T., Chalmers, H., & Busseri, M. A. (2004). Where is the syndrome? Examining co-occurrence among multiple problem behaviors in adolescence. *Journal of Consulting and Clinical Psychology, 72*(6), 1022–1037.

Wills, T. A., & Cleary, S. D. (1999). Peer and adolescent substance use among 6th-9th graders: Latent growth analyses of influence versus selection mechanisms. *Health Psychology, 18*, 453–463.

Wills, T. A., Resko, J. A., Ainette, M. G., & Mendoza, D. (2004). Role of parent support and peer support in adolescent substance use: A test of mediated effects. *Psychology of Addictive Behaviors, 18*(2), 122–134.

Wills, T. A., Sandy, J. M., & Yaeger, A. (2000). Temperament and adolescent substance use: An epigenetic approach to risk and protection. *Journal of Personality, 68*, 1127–1151.

Wills, T. A., Sandy, J. M., & Yaeger, A. M. (2002a). Moderators of the relation between substance use level and problems: Test of a self-regulation model in middle adolescence. *Journal of Abnormal Psychology, 111*(1), 3–21.

Wills, T. A., Sandy, J. M., & Yaeger, A. M. (2002b). Stress and smoking in adolescence: A test of directional hypotheses. *Health Psychology, 21*(2), 122–130.

Wills, T. A., Sandy, J. M., Yaeger, A., & Shinar, O. (2001). Family risk factors and adolescent substance use: Moderation effects for temperament dimensions. *Developmental Psychology, 37*, 283–297.

Wills, T. A., Sandy, J. M., Yeager, A. M., Cleary, S. D., & Shinar, O. (2001). Coping dimensions, life stress, and adolescent substance use: A latent growth analysis. *Journal of Abnormal Psychology, 110*(2), 309–323.

Wilson, G. T. (2005). Psychological treatment of eating disorders. *Annual Review of Clinical Psychology, 1*(1), 439–465.

Wimpory, D. C., Hobson, R. P., Williams, J. M. G., & Nash, S. (2000). Are infants with autism socially engaged? A study of recent retrospective parental reports. *Journal of Autism and Developmental Disorders, 30*, 525–536.

Windle, M. (2003). Alcohol use among adolescents and young adults. *Alcohol Research and Health, 27*(1), 79–85.

Windle, M., & Wiesner, M. (2004). Trajectories of marijuana use from adolescence to young adulthood: Predictors and outcomes. *Development and Psychopathology, 16*(4), 1007–1027.

Windle, M., & Windle, R. C. (2001). Depressive symptoms and cigarette smoking among middle adolescents: Prospective associations and intrapersonal and interpersonal influences. *Journal of Consulting and Clinical Psychology, 69*(2), 215–226.

Windle, M., & Windle, R. C. (2006). Alcohol consumption and its consequences among adolescents and young adults. In M. Galanter (Ed.), *Alcohol problems in adolescents and young adults: Epidemiology, neurobiology, prevention, and treatment* (pp. 67–83). New York: Springer.

Windle, M., Mun, E. Y., & Windle, R. C. (2005). Adolescent-to-young adulthood heavy drinking trajectories and their prospective predictors. *Journal of Studies on Alcohol, 66*(3), 313–322.

Wing, L. (1981). Asperger's syndrome: A clinical account. *Psychological Medicine, 11*, 115–130.

Wing, L. (1991). Mental retardation and the autistic continuum. In P. E. Bebbington (Ed.), *Social psychiatry: Theory, methodology, and practice* (pp. 113–138). New Brunswick, NJ: Transaction Publishers.

Wing, L. (1991). The relationship between Asperger's syndrome and Kanner's autism. In U. Firth (Ed.), *Autism and Asperger syndrome* (pp. 93–121). New York: Cambridge University Press.

Wing, L. (1993). The definition and prevalence of autism: A review. *European Child and Adolescent Psychiatry, 2*, 61–74.

Wing, L. (1997). The history of ideas on autism. *Autism, 1*, 13–23.

Wing, L. (1998). The history of Asperger syndrome. In E. Schopler & G. B. Mesibov (Eds.), *Asperger syndrome or high-functioning autism? Current issues in autism* (pp. 11–28). New York: Plenum Press.

Wing, L. (2000). Past and future of research on Asperger syndrome. In A. Klin & F. R. Volkmar (Eds.), *Asperger syndrome* (pp. 418–432). New York: Guilford Press.

Wing, L., & Attwood, A. (1987). Syndromes of autism and atypical development. In D. J. Cohen & A. M. Donnellan (Eds.), *Handbook of autism and pervasive developmental disorders* (pp. 3–19). New York: Wiley.

Wing, L., Leekam, S. R., Libby, S. J., Gould, J., & Larcombe, M. (2002). The Diagnostic Interview for Social and Communication Disorders: Background, inter-rater reliability and clinical use. *Journal of Child Psychology and Psychiatry and Allied Disciplines, 43*, 307–325.

Wing, L., & Potter, D. (2002). The epidemiology of autistic spectrum disorders: Is prevalence rising? *Mental Retardation and Developmental Disabilities Research Reviews, 8*, 151–161.

Wing, L., & Wing. J. K. (1971). Multiple impairments in early childhood autism. *Journal of Autism and Childhood Schizophrenia, 1*, 256–266.

Winnepenninckx, B., Rooms, L., & Kooy, R. F. (2003). Mental retardation: A review of the genetic causes. *British Journal of Developmental Disabilities, 49*, 29–44.

Winsler, A., Diaz, R. M., Atencio, D. J., McCarthy, E. M., & Adams Chabay, L. (2000). Verbal self-regulation over time in preschool children at risk for attention and behavior problems. *Journal of Child Psychology and Psychiatry and Allied Disciplines, 41*, 875–886.

Winters, K. C., Latimer, W. W., & Stinchfield, R. (2001). Assessing adolescent substance use. In E. F. Wagner & H. B. Waldron (Eds.), *Innovations in adolescent substance abuse interventions* (pp. 1–29). Amsterdam: Pergamon/Elsevier Science.

Winters, K. C., Stinchfield, R. D., Botzet, A., & Slutske, W. S. (2005). Pathways of youth gambling problem severity. *Psychology of Addictive Behaviors, 19*(1), 104–107.

Winters, N. C., Myers, K., & Proud, L. (2002). Ten-year review of rating scales. III: Scales assessing suicidality, cognitive style, and self esteem. *Journal of the American Academy of Child and Adolescent Pyschiatry, 41*(10), 1150–1181.

Wintersteen, M. B., Mensinger, J. L., & Diamond, G. S. (2005). Do gender and racial differences between patient and therapist affect therapeutic alliance and treatment retention in adolescents? *Professional Psychology: Research and Practice, 36*(4), 400–408.

Wiseman, C. V., Peltzman, B., Halmi, K., A., & Sunday, S. R. (2004). Risk factors for eating disorders: Surprising similarities between middle school boys and girls. *Eating Disorders: The Journal of Treatment and Prevention, 12*, 315–320.

Wiseman, C. V., Sunday, S. R., & Becker, A. E. (2005). Impact of the media on adolescent body image. *Child and Adolescent Psychiatric Clinics of North America, 14*, 453–471.

Wliksch, S. M., Durbridge, M. R., & Wade, T. D. (2008). A preliminary controlled comparison of programs designed to reduce risk of eating disorders targeting perfectionism and media literacy. *Journal of the American Academy of Child and Adolescent Psychiatry, 47*(8), 939–947.

Wolf, E. M., & Sefferino, M. R. (2008). Group treatments of eating disorders with children and adolescents. In L. VandeCreek & J. B. Allen (Eds.), *Innovations in clinical practice: Focus on group, couples, and family therapy* (pp. 29–45). Sarasota, FL: Professional Resource Press/Professional Resource Exchange.

Wolff, S. (2000). Schizoid personality disorder in childhood and Asperger syndrome. In A. Klin, F. R. Volkmar, & S. S. Sparrow (Eds.), *Asperger syndrome* (pp. 278–305). New York: Guilford Press.

Wolraich, M. L., Hannah, J. N., Baumgaertel, A., & Feurer, I. D. (1998). Examination of DSM-IV criteria in a county-wide sample. *Journal of Developmental and Behavioral Pediatrics, 19*(3), 162–268.

Wood, J. J., McLeod, B. D., Sigman, M., Hwang, W-C., & Chu, B. C. (2003). Parenting and childhood anxiety: Theory, empirical findings, and future directions. *Journal of Child Psychology and Psychiatry, 44*(1), 134–151.

Woodbury-Smith, M., Klin, A., & Volkmar, F. (2005). Asperger's syndrome: A comparison of clinical diagnoses and those made according to the ICD-10 and DSM-IV. *Journal of Autism and Developmental Disorders, 35*(2), 235–240.

Woodhead, M. (1988). When psychology informs public policy: The case of early childhood intervention. *American Psychologist, 43(6)*, 443–454.

Woodside, D. B., Bulik, C. M., Halmi, K. A., Fichter, M. M., Kaplan, A. S., Berrettini, W. H., et al. (2002). Personality, perfectionism, and attitudes towards eating in parents of individuals with eating disorders. *International Journal of Eating Disorders, 31*, 290–299.

Woodward, S. A., Lenzenweger, M. F., Kagan, J., Snidman, N., & Arcus, D. (2000). Taxonic structure of infant reactivity: Evidence from a taxometric perspective. *Psychological Science, 11*(4), 296–301.

Woolfolk, R. L. (2001). The concept of mental illness: An analysis of four pivotal issues. *The Journal of Mind and Behavior, 22(2)*, 161–178.

Wozniak, J. Spencer, T., Biederman, J., Kwon, A., Monuteaux, M., Rettew, J., et al. (2004). The clinical characteristics of unipolar versus bipolar major depression in ADHD youth. *Journal of Affective Disorders, 82*(1), S59-S69.

Wren, F. J. Berg, E. A., Heiden, L. A., Kinnamon, C. J., Ohlson, L. A., Bridge, J. A., et al. (2007). Childhood anxiety in a diverse primary care population: Parent-child reports, ethnicity and SCARED factor structure. *Journal of the American Academy of Child and Adolescent Psychiatry, 46*(3), 332–340.

Wright, F. D., Beck, A. T., Newman, C. F., & Liese, B. S. (1993). Cognitive therapy of substance abuse: Theoretical rationale. *NIDA Research Monograph, 137,* 123–146.

Wunderlich, S. A., Connolly, K. M., & Stice, E. (2004). Impulsivity as a risk factor for eating disorder behavior: Assessment implications with adolescents. *International Journal of Eating Disorders, 36,* 172–182.

Yamamiya, Y., Shroff, H., & Thompson, J. K. (2008). The Tripartite Influence Model of body image and eating disturbance: A replication with a Japanese sample. *Eating Behaviors, 41*(1), 88–91.

Yan, Z., & Fischer, K. (2002). Always under construction: Dynamic variations in adult cognitive microdevelopment. *Human Development, 45(3),* 141–160.

Yates, T. M. (2004). The developmental psychopathology of self-injurious behavior: Compensatory regulation in posttraumatic adaptation. *Clinical Psychology Review, 24*(1), 35–74.

Yates, T. M., Egeland, B., & Sroufe, L. A. (2003). Rethinking resilience: A developmental process perspective. In S. S. Luthar (Ed.), *Resilience and vulnerability: Adapatation in the context of childhood adversities* (pp. 243–266). New York: Cambridge University Press.

Yates, T. M., & Masten, A. S. (2004). Fostering the future: Resilience theory and the practice of positive psychology. In P. A. Linsley & S. Joseph (Eds.), *Positive Psychology in practice* (pp. 521–539). Hoboken, NJ: Wiley.

Yau, J., & Smetana, J. (2003). Adolescent-parent conflict in Hong Kong and Shenzen: A comparison of youth in two cultural contexts. *International Journal of Behavioral Development, 27*(3), 201–211.

Yearwood, E. L., Crawford, S., Kelly, M., & Moreno, N. (2007). Immigrant youth at risk for disorders of mood: Recognizing complex dynamics. *Archives of Psychiatric Nursing, 21*(3), 162–171.

Yeganeh, R., Beidel, D. C., Turner, S. M., Pina, A. A., & Silverman, W.. K. (2003). Clinical distinctions between selective mutism and social phobia: An investigation of childhood psychopathology. *Journal of the American Academy of Child and Adolescent Psychiatry, 42*(9), 1069–1075.

Yeh, M., & Weisz, J. R. (2001). Why are we here at the clinic? Parent-child (dis)agreement on referral problems at outpatient treatment entry. *Journal of Consulting and Clinical Psychology, 69(6),* 1018–1025.

Yeung-Courchesne, R., & Courchesne, E. (1997). From impasse to insight in autism research: From behavioral symptoms to biological explanations. *Development and Psychopathology, 9,* 389–419.

Ying, Z., & Hong, C. (2005). Physical self-satisfaction of adolescents from Han, Tibet and Yi nationalities. *Chinese Mental Health Journal, 19,* 796–797.

Yirmiya, N., Erel, O., Shaked, M., & Solomonica-Levi, D. (1998). Meta-analyses comparing theory of mind abilities of individuals with autism, individuals with mental retardation, and normally developing individuals. *Psychological Bulletin, 124,* 283–307.

Young, J. F., Mufson, L., & Davies, M. (2006). Efficacy of interpersonal psychotherapy-adolescent skills training: An indicated preventive intervention for depression. *Journal of Child Psychology and Psychiatry, 47*(12), 1254–1262.

Young, S. E., Corley, R. P., Stallings, M. C., Rhee, S. H., Crowley, T. J., & Hewitt, J. K. (2002). Substance use, abuse, and dependence in adolescence: Prevalence, symptom profiles, and correlates. *Drug and Alcohol Dependence, 68*(3), 309–322.

Youngstrom, E., Findling, R. L., & Calabrese, J. R. (2003). Who are the comorbid adolescents? Agreement between psychiatric diagnosis, youth, parent, and teacher report. *Journal of Abnormal Psychology, 31(3),* 231–246.

Youngstrom, E. A., Findling, R. L., & Calabrese, J. R. (2004). Effects of adolescent manic symptoms on agreement between youth, parent, and teacher ratings of behavior problems. *Journal of Affective Disorders, 82*(1), S5-S16.

Youngstrom, E. A., Findling, R. L., Calabrese, J. R., Gracious, B. L., Demeter, C., Bedoya, D. D., et al. (2004). Comparing the diagnostic accuracy of six potential screening instruments for bipolar disorder in youths aged 5 to 17 years. *Journal of the American Academy of Child and Adolescent Psychiatry, 43*(7), 847–858.

Youngstrom, E., Loeber, R., & Stouthamer-Loeber, M. (2000). Patterns and correlates of agreement between parent, teacher, and male adolescent ratings of externalizing and internalizing problems. *Journal of Consulting and Clinical Psychology, 68(6),* 1038–1050.

Yu, M., Stiffman, A. R., Freedenthal, S. (2005). Factors affecting American Indian adolescent tobacco use. *Addictive Behaviors, 30*(5), 889–904.

Zahn-Waxler, C. (2000). The development of empathy, guilt, and internalization of distress. In R. Davidson (Ed.), *Wisconsin Symposium on Emotion: Vol. 1. Anxiety, depression and emotion* (pp. 222–265). New York: Oxford University Press.

Zahn-Waxler, C., Cole, P. M., Richardson, D. T., & Friedman, R. J. (1994). Social problem solving in disruptive preschool children: Reactions to hypothetical situations of conflict and distress. *Merrill-Palmer Quarterly, 40*(1), 98–119.

Zahn-Waxler, C., Cole, P., Welsh, J., & Fox, N. (1995). Psychophysiological correlates of empathy and prosocial behavior in preschool children with behavior problems. *Development and Psychopathology, 7,* 27–48.

Zahn-Waxler, C., Klimes-Dougan, B., & Slattery, M. J. (2000). Internalizing problems of childhood and adolescence: Prospects, pitfalls, and progress in understanding the development of anxiety and depression. *Development and Psychopathology, 12,* 443–466.

Zalsman, G., & Cohen, D. J. (1998). Multiplex developmental disorder. *Israel Journal of Psychiatry and Related Sciences, 35,* 300–306.

Zametkin, A. J., Nordahl, T. E., Gross, M., & King, A. C. (1990). Cerebral glucose metabolism in adults with hyperactivity of childhood onset. *New England Journal of Medicine, 323*(20), 1361–1366.

Zayas, L. H., Lester, R. J., Cabassa, L. J., & Fortuna, L. R. (2005). Why do so many Latina teens attempt suicide? A conceptual model of research. *American Journal of Orthopsychiatry, 75*(2), 275–287.

Zeanah, C. H., Anders, T. F., Seifer, R., & Stern, D. N. (1989). Implications of research on infant development for psychodynamic theory and practice. *Journal of the American Academy of Child and Adolescent Psychiatry, 28*(5), 657–668.

Zeanah, C. H. (1996). Beyond insecurity: A reconceptualization of attachment disorders of infancy. *Journal of Consulting and Clinical Psychology, 64*(1), 42–52.

Zeanah, C. H., Boris, N. W., & Larrieu, J. A. (1997). Infant development and developmental risk: A review of the past 10 years. *Journal of the American Academy of Child and Adolescent Psychiatry, 36*(2), 165–178.

Zeanah, C. H., Boris, N. W., & Scheeringa, M. S. (1997). Psychopathology in infancy. *Journal of Child Psychology and Psychiatry, 38*(1), 81–99.

Zeanah, C. H., & Boris, N. W. (2000). Disturbances and disorders of attachment in early childhood. In C. H. Zeanah, Jr. (Ed.), *Handbook of infant mental health* (pp. 353–368). New York: Guilford Press.

Zeanah, C. H., & Emde, R. N. (1994). Attachment disorders in infancy. In M. Rutter, L. Hersov & E. Taylor (Eds), *Child and adolescent psychiatry: Modern approaches* (pp. 490–504). Oxford, England: Blackwell.

Zeanah, C. H. (2000). *Handbook of infant mental health.* New York: Guilford Press.

Zeanah, C. H., Mammen, O. K., & Lieberman, A. F. (1993). Disorders of attachment. In C. H. Zeanah (Ed.), *Handbook of infant mental health* (pp. 332–349). New York: Guilford Press.

Zeanah, C. H., Scheeringa, M., Boris, N. W., Heller, S. S., Smyke, A. T., & Trapani, J. (2004). Reactive attachment disorder in maltreated toddlers. *Child Abuse and Neglect, 28*, 877–888.

Zeanah, C. H., Smyke, A. T., Koga, S. F., & Carlson, E. (2005). Attachment in institutionalized and community children in Romania. *Child Development, 76*(5), 1015–1028.

Zeanah, C. H., & Zeanah, P. D., (1989). Intergenerational transmission of maltreatment: Insights from attachment theory and research. *Psychiatry: Journal for the Study of Interpersonal Processes, 52*(2), 177–196.

Zerbe, K. J. (2001). The crucial role of psychodynamic understanding in the treatment of eating disorders. *Psychiatric Clinics of North America, 24*, 305–313.

Zerbe, K. J. (2003a). Eating disorders in middle and late life: A neglected problem. *Primary Psychiatry, 10*, 80–82.

Zerbe, K. J. (2003b). Eating disorders over the life cycle: Diagnosis and treatment. *Primary Psychiatry, 10*, 28–29.

Zero to Three Association. (1994, 2005). *Diagnostic classification of mental health and developmental disorders of infancy and early childhood.* Washington, DC: Zero to Three: National Center for Infants, Toddlers, and Families.

Zigler, E. (1969). Developmental versus difference theories of mental retardation and the problem of motivation. American Journal of Mental Deficiency, 73(4), 536–556.

Zigler, E. (1971). The retarded child as a whole person. In H. E. Adams & W. K. Boardman III (Eds.), Advances in experimental clinical psychology (Vol. 1, pp. 47–121). New York: Pergamon Press.

Zigler, E. (1999). The individual with mental retardation as a whole person. In E. Zigler & D. Bennett-Gates (Eds.), *Personality development in individuals with mental retardation* (pp. 1–16). New York: Cambridge University Press.

Zigler, E., Balla, D., & Hodapp, R. (1984). On the definition and classification of mental retardation. *American Journal of Mental Deficiency, 89*(3), 215–230.

Zigler, E., & Bennett-Gates, D. (Eds.), (1999). *Personality development in individuals with mental retardation.* New York: Cambridge University Press.

Zigler, E., Bennett-Gates, D., Hodapp, R., & Henrich, C. C. (2002). Assessing personality traits of individuals with mental retardation. *American Journal on Mental Retardation, 107*(3), 181–193.

Zigler, E. F., & Finn-Stevenson, M. (1992). Applied developmental psychology. In M. H. Bornstein & M. E. Lamb (Eds.), *Developmental psychology: An advanced textbook* (3rd ed., pp. 677–729). Hillsdale, NJ: Erlbaum.

Zigler, E., & Glick, M. (1986). *A developmental approach to adult psychopathology.* New York: Wiley.

Zigler, E., & Valentine, J. (1979). *Head Start: The legacy of the war on poverty.* New York: Free Press.

Zigman, W. B., Schupf, N., Devenny, D. A., Miezejeski, C., Ryan, R., Urv, T. K., et al. (2004). Incidence and prevalence of dementia in elderly adults with mental retardation without Down syndrome. *American Journal on Mental Retardation, 109*(2), 126–141.

Zill, N., Morrison, D. R., & Coiro, M. J. (1993). Long-term effects of parental divorce on parent child relationships, adjustment, and achievement in young adulthood. *Journal of Family Psychology, 71(1),* 91–103.

Zimmer-Gembeck, M. J., Geiger, T. C., & Crick, N. R. (2005). Relational and physical aggression, prosocial behavior, and peer relations: Gender moderation and bidirectional associations. *Journal of Early Adolescence, 25*(4), 421–452.

Zimmermann, P. (2004). Attachment representations and characteristics of friendship relations during adolescence. *Journal of Experimental Child Psychology, 88*(1), 83–101.

Zucker, N. L., Marcus, M., & Bulik, C. A group parent-training program: A novel approach for eating disorder management. *Eating and Weight Disorders, 11*(2), 78–82.

Zuker-Weiss, R. (1994). Sex, mental retardation and ethics. *International Journal of Adolescent Medicine and Health, 7*(3), 193–197.

Zwaigenbaum, L., Bryson, S., Rogers, T., Roberts, W., Brian, J., & Szatmari, P. (2005). Behavioral manifestations of autism in the first year of life. *International Journal of Developmental Neuroscience, 23*(2–3), 143–152.

Zwaigenbaum, L., Szatmari, P., Jones, M. B., Bryson, S. E., MacLean, J. E., Mahoney, W. J., et al. (2002). Pregnancy and birth complications in autism and liability to the broader autism phenotype. *Journal of the American Academy of Child and Adolescent Psychiatry, 41*, 572–579.

Name Index

Subject Index

A

AAIDD Adaptive Behavior Scale, 116
abuse, in substance abuse diagnosis, 266
accessibility of care, psychopathology and, 6–7
accountability, attention deficit hyperactivity disorder therapy, 162–163
adaptational failure, psychopathology defined as, 28
adaptive behavior and functioning
  aggression and, 249b
  assessment of, 116
  mental retardation and, 104–108
addiction, defined, 267
adequate adaptation, defined, 3–5
adolescence
  antidepressants in, developmental and ethical issues, 232b
  arenas of comfort in, 213–214, 213t
  attachment disorders in, 92, 96
  attention deficit hyperactivity disorder in, 151, 153
  bipolar disorder in, 219–220, 220t
  conduct disorders in
    development of, 250, 254f
    intervention and treatment, 259–261
    parent-child relationships and, 242–244, 242b, 243f
    peer relationships, 242–244
    treatment, 259
  depression in, 218b, 230–231
  eating disorders in, 293–294
  interpersonal development and, 243f
  mood disorders in, 213–218, 214f, 222–223, 230–231
  parent relationships in, 244
  psychopathic disorders of, 2
  romantic relationships in, 245–246
  self-harm in, 237b
  self-identity in, 212–214
  substance abuse in
    alcohol use and abuse, 267–268, 269f–270f, 275
    anabolic steroid use, 273, 274t
    assessment and diagnosis, 281–282
    cocaine, 272
    comorbidity with, 273–274
    developmental pathways, 274–277
    deviant behaviors and, 277–278
    diagnostic criteria, 266t–267t
    disorders of, 266–274
    drug and narcotic abuse trends, 272f
    drug dependency map, 268f
    etiology, 277–281, 278f

gateway hypothesis and common factors model, 277
  hallucinogens, 273
  heroin, 273
  inhalants, 271–272, 271f
  intervention, 282–286, 284f
  marijuana, 271, 271f, 272t, 276f
  methamphetamine, 272–273
  neurodevelopment and risk taking, 264–265
  prescription drugs, 273, 275f
  smoking, 268–270, 270f, 275–276, 276f
  suicidality in, 235–238, 238t
adolescence-limited (AL) trajectory, 248
adolescent-onset type conduct disorder, 248, 250
adopted infants, attachment disorder and, 82
Adult Attachment Interview (AAI), attachment disorder assessment, 95–96
adult outcomes
  attention deficit hyperactivity disorder, 153–154, 163
  mental retardation and, 114
adults, attachment disorders in, 92–93
adverse drug effects, attention deficit hyperactivity disorder treatments, 161
affective social competence, autism spectrum disorders, 124–125
affective storms, 220
affiliative relationships, conduct disorders and, 243
age factors
  attention deficit hyperactivity disorder, 150–151
  oppositional defiant disorder, 170–171
aggression
  conduct disorders, 247–248
  oppositional defiant disorder, 169
  positive aspects of, 249b
agoraphobia, 189–194
alcohol use and abuse, in adolescence, 267–268, 269f–270f, 275
"alphabet children," diagnostic labeling and, 53–54
American Association onf Intellectual and Developmental Disabilities (AAIDD), 104–105, 105f, 105t, 115–116
American Association on Mental Retardation (AAMR), 104

anabolic steroids, adolescent abuse of, 273, 273f, 274t
animal studies, of neural plasticity, 16
anorexia nervosa, 291–292, 293f
antidepressants, developmental and ethical issues for children and adolescents and, 232b
antisocial personality disorder, 251–252, 255–256
antisocial propensity, conduct disorders in children, 253–255
anxiety disorders
  assessment and diagnosis, 203–204
  in childhood, 199–203, 202f
  clinical comparisons, 184–194, 185t–186t, 190f–191f, 191t, 193b, 194f
  developmental pathways, 196–198
  etiology, 198–203
  fears, worries, and emotional regulation, 182–184, 183t, 184f
  genetics and heredity, 198
  intervention, 204–208
  parent factors in, 203
  pharmacological treatment, 208
  physiological factors, 198–199
  psychological treatment, 205–208, 206f, 206t
  somatization and somatoform disorders, 194–196
  tripartite model, 200, 201b
anxious/ambivalent attachment, 85, 85f
anxious/avoidant attachment, 85, 85f
applied behavior analysis, autism spectrum disorders, 139–140
arenas of comfort, developmental psychopathology and, 33–34
art, psychopathology and role of, 17–18
Asperger syndrome, 77
  affective social competence, 124–125
  assessment and diagnosis, 136–139
  behavioral deficits, 131–132, 134
  developmental pathways, 132–134
  diagnostic criteria, 125–126, 125t–126t, 127b–128b, 128–132, 130b
  early home videos, 133b
  etiology, 135–136
  facial role in, 127b–128b
  family role in, 134
  historical and current conceptualizations, 122–124
  intervention, 139–141
  language and communication delays and deficits, 128–131, 134

foster parenting, attachment disorders
and, 98
Fragile X syndrome, 108–109
friendships, psychopathology and, 22–23
functional genomics, developmental
psychopathology and, 15b
functional magnetic resonance imaging
(fMRI), neuroimaging and, 14t

G
gambling, by adolescents, 264
gateway hypothesis, substance abuse in
adolescents and, 276
gender
adolescent depression and, 218b
anxiety disorders and, 183–184, 199–203
attention deficit hyperactivity disorder,
150–151
eating disorders and, 295–297
oppositional defiant disorder, 170–171
temperament and, 67
generalized anxiety disorder (GAD),
187–194
general risk factor, temperament and
psychopathology, 70–71
genetics
anxiety disorders, 198
attention deficit hyperactivity disorder,
154–155
conduct disorders, 253
eating disorders and, 296
mental retardation etiology and,
109–110, 109f–110f, 109t
mood disorders, 222–223
neurobehavioral dysfunction in infants
of drug-addicted parents, 68b
oppositional defiant disorder and,
174–175
psychopathology and, 14–15, 15t
substance abuse in adolescence and, 277
genetic screening, in mental retardation,
116–118, 117b
genomics, developmental psychopathology
and, 15b
genotypes, mental retardation, 107–108
goodness of fit, infant temperament and
parenting and, 69, 69f
Great Smoky Mountains Study, 6
group interventions
conduct disorders, 259–261
eating disorders treatment, 300
substance abuse in adolescence and, 285
growth dysregulation hypothesis, autism
spectrum disorder etiology, 136

H
hallucinogens, adolescent abuse of, 273
heredity
anxiety disorders, 198
attention deficit hyperactivity disorder,
154–155

conduct disorders, 253
environment and, 104
mood disorders, 222–223
oppositional defiant disorder and,
174–175
substance abuse in adolescence
and, 277
heroin, adolescent abuse of, 273
heterotypic comorbidity, 52
history taking, attachment disorder
assessment, 95–96
home-based strategies, attachment
disorder prevention, 97
homotypic comorbidity, 51–52
hospitalization, eating disorders treatment,
298–299
Human Genome Project, genomics and,
14–15, 15b
humanistic models, psychopathology,
19–20
hyperactive/impulsive subtype,
attention deficit hyperactivity
disorder, 149–150
hypersensitive regulatory disorder, 77
hypersensitivity, early development
disorders, 71
hypotheses, developmental
psychopathology research, 43

I
identity, mood disorders and, 212–214
impaired social cognition, oppositional
defiant disorder, 169
inattentive subtype, attention deficit
hyperactivity disorder, 149–150
incentive salience, 278
incentive-sensitization theory, substance
abuse in adolescence and, 278
incidence of disorders, 6
incompetence, developmental
psychopathology and, 32–34, 32b
indicated preventive measures, 61
attachment disorders, 97
indirect developmental pathways, 30–32,
31f
Individualized Education Plan (IEP), 62
individual risk factors, developmental
psychopathology and, 34–35
individual therapy, substance abuse in adolescence, 284–285
infancy, psychopathic disorders of, 2
infant emotionality, temperament and, 67
"infant in context" observations,
attachment assessment using, 96
infant-parent psychotherapy, 98
inhalants, adolescent abuse of, 271–272,
271f
inhibited reactive attachment disorder,
87–88
inhibition, disordered attachment with, 89
insecure attachment, 84

institutionalized infants, attachment
disorder and, 82b
instrumental aggression, 247
instrumental relationships, conduct
disorders and, 243
Integrated Visual and Auditory
Continuous Performance Test,
58–59
intellectual development and functioning,
103–104
assessment of, 115–116
mental retardation and, 104–108,
111–112
poverty and, 104
intelligence
components and mechanisms, 102–104
developmental tasks and challenges,
102–104
intelligence quotient (IQ), 102
bimodal distribution of scores, 104–105,
105f, 105t
mental retardation and, 104–108
"interaction guidance" therapy,
attachment disorders prevention,
97–98
internalizing dimension, 48
internal validity
attention deficity hyperactivity disorder
diagnosis, 149
of classification systems, 47–48
interpersonal-psychological theory of
suicidality, 237
interpersonal relationships
adolescent development and, 242–243,
243f
attachment disorders in children and, 92
interpersonal therapies, for mood
disorders, 233–234
inter-rater reliability, of classification
systems, 47
intervention
anxiety disorders, 204–208
in attachment disorders, 96–97
attention deficit hyperactivity disorder,
159–161
autism spectrum disorders, 139–141,
141b
in children, 61–62
conduct disorders, 258–261
developmental psychopathology and,
59–62, 60f
early intervention programs, 43–44
eating disorders, 298–300
feeding disorders, 73–74
in mental retardation, 116–117
in mood disorders, 231–234
neurobehavioral dysfunction in
infants of drug-addicted parents
and, 68b
oppositional defiant disorder, 176–177
parents and families involvement in, 62

risk-taking behavior
  adolescent depression and, 218b
  substance abuse in adolescents and, 264–265
role reversal, disordered attachment with, 89–90
romantic partners, in adolescence, 245–246
Rorschach inkblot test, 57, 59
rumination, defined, 71

S
safe haven, attachment and, 83
savant talents, autism spectrum disorder, 130b
school-age children
  attachment disorders in, 92, 96
  attention deficit hyperactivity disorder therapy in, 163
school-based programs
  autism spectrum disorders, 140–141
  oppositional defiant disorder, 178–179
  therapeutic intervention and, 62
school shootings, 252b
science, media images of, 8b
seasonal affective disorder, 216
secondary prevention, 61
secure attachment, 84–85, 85f
secure base, attachment and, 83
selective preventive measures, 61
  attachment disorders, 97
  substance abuse in adolescence, 282–283
selective serotonin reuptake inhibitors (SSRIs), 231–233, 232b
self, sense of, 83
  mood disorders and, 212–214
self-control, oppositional defiant disorder and, 166–168, 167f
self-endangerment, disordered attachment with, 89
self-injurious behavior (SIB), 237b
self-medication, substance abuse in adolescence and, 279
self-regulatory skills
  attention deficit hyperactivity disorder, 146
  oppositional defiant disorder and, 166–168, 167f, 171–172
self-report questionnaires, 58–59, 58b
  anxiety disorder assessment, 203–204
  eating disorders diagnosis, 298
self-talk, anxiety disorder intervention, 207
separation anxiety disorder (SAD), 187–194
sexual abuse, developmental psychopathology and, 36–37
sexuality
  adolescent sexual activity and, 265
  mental retardation and, 114–115

sexually transmitted diseases, adolescent sexual activity and, 265
shared environment, family model of psychopathology, 21–22
siblings, autism spectrum disorder and, 134
sleep disorders, 74–76, 74t, 76t
sleep patterns, adolescent changes in, 264
sleepwalking, 74–76, 74t, 76t
sluggish cognitive tempo, attention deficit hyperactivity disorder, 150
smoking, in adolescence, 268–271, 270f, 275–276, 276f
social cognition
  autism spectrum disorders, 124
  oppositional defiant disorder and impairment of, 169
social context of brain development and functioning, mood disorders and, 223
social development
  autism spectrum disorders, 124–125, 133–134
  mental retardation and, 112–113
social dysfunction, attention deficiency hyperactivity disorder, 149
social phobias, 189–194
social protective factors, 39
  attachment disorders and, 94
social risk factors, developmental psychopathology and, 34–35, 35f
social substance use, 266
sociocultural factors
  eating disorders and, 289–290, 295–297
  in psychopathology, 22–25, 24f
  substance abuse in adolescence and, 281
sociocultural norms
  developmental expectations and, 5f
  normality and psychopathology and, 3
socioeconomic status, conduct disorders and, 257
socioemotional deficits and deviance, 125–128
somatic management, anxiety disorder intervention, 205, 206t
somatization/somatiform disorders, 194–196
  continuity of, 198
specific risk
  developmental psychopathology and, 34–35
  temperament and psychopathology, 70–71
splinter skills, autism spectrum disorder, 130b
stability
  attachment and, 86
  developmental pathways and, 29–32, 30f–31f
  in temperament development, 70

standardized testing, as assessment tool, 57–59, 57f, 58b
Stanford-Binet test, 57
statistical analysis, structural model of psychopathology and, 50–51
statistical deviance, normality and psychopathology and, 3
Steps Toward Effective, Enjoyable Parenting (STEEP) model, attachment disorder prevention, 97
stigmatization of psychopathology, 8, 9b, 106b
Strange Situation Procedure, attachment assessment, 84b, 96
stress and coping mechanisms
  anxiety disorders and, 202–203
  mental retardation and, 114–115
  mood disorders, 222–223
structural model of psychopathology, 50–51, 51f
structured tasks, attachment disorder assessment, 96
subcultures, peer relationships and, 245
substance abuse
  in adolescence
    alcohol use and abuse, 267–268, 269f–270f, 275
    anabolic steroid use, 273, 273f, 274t
    assessment and diagnosis, 281–282
    cocaine, 272
    comorbidity with, 273–274
    developmental pathways, 274–277
    deviant behaviors and, 277–278
    diagnostic criteria, 266t–267t
    disorders of, 266–274
    drug and narcotic abuse trends, 272f
    drug dependency map, 268f
    etiology, 277–281, 278f
    gateway hypothesis and common factors model, 277
    hallucinogens, 273
    heroin, 273
    inhalants, 271–272, 271f
    intervention, 282–286, 284f
    marijuana, 271, 271f, 272t, 276f
    methamphetamine, 272–273
    neurodevelopment and risk taking, 264–265
    prescription drugs, 273, 275f
    smoking, 268–270, 270f, 275–276, 276f
  conduct disorders and, 251–252, 255–256
  eating disorders and, 293
successive comorbidity, 52–53
suicidal ideation, 235
suicidality, 234–238
  warning signs of, 238t